CRIMINAL PROCEDURE
CASES, PROBLEMS & EXERCISES
Third Edition

By

Russell L. Weaver
Professor of Law & Distinguished University Scholar
University of Louisville, Louis D. Brandeis School of Law

Leslie W. Abramson
Frost, Brown, Todd Professor of Law
University of Louisville, Louis D. Brandeis School of Law

Ronald Bacigal
Professor of Law
University of Richmond, T.C. Williams School of Law

John M. Burkoff
Professor of Law
University of Pittsburgh School of Law

Catherine Hancock
Professor of Law
Tulane University School of Law

Donald E. Lively
Vice President for Program Development, Infilaw

Janet C. Hoeffel
Associate Professor of Law
Tulane University School of Law

AMERICAN CASEBOOK SERIES®

Mat # 40440867

American Casebook Series and West Group are trademarks registered in the U.S. Patent and Trademark Office.

© West, a Thomson business, 2001, 2004
© 2007 Thomson/West
    610 Opperman Drive
    P.O. Box 64526
    St. Paul, MN 55164–0526
    1–800–328–9352
Printed in the United States of America

ISBN–13: 978–0–314–16697–5
ISBN–10: 0–314–16697–1

 *TEXT IS PRINTED ON 10% POST CONSUMER RECYCLED PAPER*

To Ben, Kate, and Laurence with love, RLW

For Lisa, Sam, Shel & Will, LWA

To Grant and Peyton, RJB

Dedicated, with love, to Nancy, Amy, David,
Sean, Emmy, Emma & Molly, JMB

For Elizabeth, Caitlin & Margaret, CH

To Pam, Rico & Rica, DEL

To Steve, Ben & Sam, JCH

*

Preface to Third Edition

In creating the third edition of this book, our primary goal was the same as it was when we created the first edition: to create a "teacher's book"—a book that is easy to use and that produces rewarding and insightful classroom discussion. This third edition includes many more problems and exercises all designed to stimulate and encourage thought and discussion.

A subsidiary objective was to help students understand and evaluate the competing policy considerations that underlie the law. Over the last thirty years, so many criminal procedure cases have been decided that it is impossible to thoroughly discuss and do justice to all of them. In this book, we include modern cases that reflect the current state of the law. In addition, we include older cases (*e.g., Spinelli v. United States*) because they help students understand and evaluate the modern approach, and in any event should lead to interesting classroom discussions.

A second subsidiary objective was to create a book that helps students develop skills that they will need in practice. While we recognize that the MacCrate Report was focused on clinics and other more active forms of skills training, substantive classes can be an effective forum for skills development. As a result, we frequently put students in real-life situations, and ask them how they would argue a case for a client (*e.g.*, what facts might they use to make a particular type of argument).

Of course, in any book, space limitations make tradeoffs necessary. One choice that we made was to limit the scope and extent of notes. Rather than deal with criminal procedure in an encyclopedic way, we wanted to include more problems and exercises.

We give thanks to the many people who assisted us in the creation and revision of this book, including our research assistants and secretaries. We are particularly grateful to students who helped us find and correct errors. Finally, we are thankful to our spouses, significant others, and children who supported us through the various stages of this project.

RLW, LWA, RJB, JMB, CH, DEL, JCH

*

Acknowledgments

Excerpts from the following books and articles appear with the kind permission of the copyright holders.

Bandes, Susan A., Repression and Denial in Criminal Lawyering, 9 Buff. Crim. L. Rev. 339 (2006). Reprinted by permission.

Freedman, Monroe H., Lawyers(Ethics in an Adversary System (Bobbs-Merrill Co. 1975). Reprinted by permission.

Hodes, W. William., Seeking the Truth Versus Telling the Truth at the Boundaries of the Law: Misdirection, Lying and (Lying With an Explanation,(44 S. Tex. L. Rev. 53 (2002). Reprinted by permission.

Rhode, Deborah L., The Future of the Legal Profession: Institutionalizing Ethics, 44 Case W. Res. L. Rev. 665 (1994). Reprinted by permission.

Richman, Daniel C., Prosecutors and Their Agents, Agents and Their Prosecutors, 103 Colum. L. Rev. 749 (2003). Reprinted by permission.

Simon, William H., The Ethics of Criminal Defense, 91 Mich. L. Rev. 1703 (1993). Reprinted by permission.

Van Kessle, Gordon, The Adversary Excesses in the American Criminal Trial, Vol. 67 Notre Dame L. Rev. 403, 405-06, 407-09, 410, 413-15, 415-20, 548-51 (1992). Reprinted with permission © by Notre Dame Law Review, University of Notre Dame.

Zacharias, Fred C., Structuring the Ethics of Prosecutorial Trial Practice: Can Prosecutors Do Justice?, 44 Vand. L. Rev. 45 (Jan. 1991). © 1991 by the Vanderbilt Law Review. Reprinted by permission.

*

Summary of Contents

APPENDIX

Table of Contents

*

Table of Cases

The principal cases are in bold type. Cases cited or discussed in the text are roman type. References are to pages. Cases cited in principal cases and within other quoted materials are not included.

CRIMINAL PROCEDURE
CASES, PROBLEMS & EXERCISES
Third Edition

*

Part I

INTRODUCTION

Chapter 1

INTRODUCTION TO THE CRIMINAL JUSTICE PROCESS

Lawyers who work in the criminal justice system rely on many sources of law, including the constitutional case law of the United States Supreme Court. These famous federal precedents are part of the bedrock knowledge of defense counsel and prosecutors who practice in municipal, state and federal courts, and roughly a dozen precedents are produced by the Court every year. This case law is the primary source for most criminal procedure casebooks, but the significance of the Court's rulings can be difficult to understand in context because of the narrow doctrinal focus exhibited in a single case. The Court's opinions rarely describe the procedures and lawyering activities that occurred before a case is briefed and argued in the rarified forum of the Court's chambers. Each opinion usually gives the reader only a tiny glimpse of the large backdrop of law, custom, and practice that surrounds each case. This chapter provides a brief overview of that backdrop, which practicing lawyers take for granted as a frame of reference for understanding the Court's precedents.

A. SOURCES OF LAW THAT CREATE LEGAL RIGHTS FOR CRIMINAL DEFENDANTS AND REGULATE THE PROCEDURES OF THE CRIMINAL JUSTICE SYSTEM

Certain federal constitutional rights are available to all defendants who are charged with crimes. These rights are established in particular provisions of the Bill of Rights, such as the Fourth, Fifth, Sixth, and Eighth Amendments, and by the Due Process and Equal Protection Clauses of the Fourteenth Amendment. A defendant in a federal prosecution is also entitled to rights that are provided by federal statutes, such as the Federal Code of Criminal Procedure. A defendant in a state prosecution is entitled to invoke not only federal constitutional rights, but also rights provided by state statutes, such as state codes of criminal procedure.

Most importantly, state defendants also have state constitutional rights that may provide greater protections than federal constitutional rights. Most state constitutions have provisions that are similar to the Bill of Rights, and each state supreme court is the final authority on the meaning of these provisions. From a state supreme court's point of view, federal Supreme Court interpretations of a particular right provide a model for interpretation of the state constitutional version of that right. However, the federal model may be rejected by state courts that choose to provide greater protections for state court defendants. While many rulings by the United States Supreme Court are borrowed by state supreme courts as interpretations of parallel state constitutional provisions, some rulings are rejected by state courts that choose to take an independent course. In effect, the federal constitution creates a "floor" that establishes the minimum rights that must be recognized in all criminal prosecutions, but the state courts are free to establish their own "ceilings" that establish the maximum rights that will be enforced in state prosecutions. These ceilings may be expressed in state constitutional case law, in rulings based on interpretations of state statutes, or in rulings based on other legal sources. From a defense counsel's perspective, representation of a client in a particular state court requires a bedrock knowledge of that state's constitutional and statutory law, in order to raise all relevant state-law claims in tandem with arguments based on the federal constitution. State prosecutors also possess the same bedrock knowledge, which enables them to respond to all these claims.

In addition to constitutional and statutory law, there are other sources of law that create rights for criminal defendants or regulate the criminal justice process in important ways. One case-law source is the body of judge-made rules that derive from a court's "supervisory" authority over the criminal court system and its evidentiary rules. One statutory source is the rules of court adopted by judges to govern procedure in particular courts. These sources exist in both federal and state jurisdictions. There are also "local" sources of law that create rights and regulate criminal procedure, such as city ordinances and municipal court rules.

Occasionally, it may be unclear whether a person is charged with a "crime," or only with a "civil" offense that does not entitle her to state and federal constitutional and statutory rights reserved for criminal defendants. When the Congress or a state legislature labels a sanction as criminal, courts recognize this as sufficient to allow a defendant to invoke such rights. However, if the legislature labels a sanction as civil, this does not end the inquiry. The Supreme Court has ruled that it is theoretically possible for a defendant to persuade a court to treat a proceeding as criminal despite its legislative classification as civil. However, it is usually very difficult for defense counsel to win such an argument, without strong evidence that the statutory scheme is punitive in purpose or effect.

While the Supreme Court's federal constitutional precedents have been likened to a "code" of criminal procedure, they are neither as systematic nor as comprehensive as a legislative code. Instead, they reveal the Court's historical preoccupations with particular issues that raise fundamental questions about fairness in the treatment of people who are charged with crime, and about the needs of law enforcement officers to prosecute crimes effectively. For example, the Prohibition era provided the setting for the Court's early development of Fourth Amendment law defining police powers to perform searches and seizures, and the focus on the prosecution of drug crimes in recent decades has provoked the Court to establish many new Fourth Amendment precedents. Moreover, the Court's precedents are concentrated in particular fields of criminal procedure, so that some fields are heavily influenced by them and other fields are not. Even in fields where many precedents exist, the Court's decisions often provide sketchy guidance for lower courts that must attempt to interpret and enforce these holdings. Thus, in most fields of criminal procedure, the Court's decisions provide a starting point for analyzing some issues, and create a limited degree of legal uniformity in the decisions produced by state and federal courts.

When state legislatures and courts consider the need to define or interpret statutory codes governing criminal procedure, they are often influenced by the Federal Rules of Criminal Procedure and other federal statutes, and by the American Bar Association Standards for Criminal Justice. They also may be influenced by the American Law Institute's Model Code of Pre–Arraignment Procedure. However, there is little pressure for the "nationalization" of criminal procedure doctrine and practice, in part because of the long history of state and local autonomy and diversity in this field. In fact, the politicization of "law and order" issues in recent decades has created the opposite kind of pressure for constant local experimentation with criminal procedure rules. Public criticism of the weaknesses of the criminal justice system is a permanent feature of the modern legal landscape, and political calls for reform of the system have affected many aspects of criminal procedure, ranging from the election of state supreme court justices based on their doctrinal views to legislative attempts to repeal or restrict various criminal procedure rules that benefit defendants, such as the writ of habeas corpus and exclusionary rules of evidence.

B. PROSECUTION SYSTEMS

1. *Multiple Jurisdictions, Major and Minor Crimes*

When a person does a criminal act, he may violate simultaneously the criminal law of multiple jurisdictions, such as federal and state laws, or state laws and municipal ordinances. According to the Court's Double Jeopardy doctrine, multiple prosecutions for the same act by different "sovereign" governments are not prohibited by the constitution. Therefore, if an act violates state and federal law, for example, it is up to the prosecutors in each jurisdiction to decide how to coordinate the two potential prosecutions. It is possible that a statute of limitations may bar prosecution in one jurisdiction, or that prosecution in one jurisdiction is particularly advantageous because of the penalty, the procedural rules, or some other reason. Or, some prosecutors may lack resources that other prosecutors possess, and this difference may influence the timing and outcome of decisions to prosecute in only one or both jurisdictions.

In federal and state jurisdictions, most prosecutions are for minor crimes. While the definition of a "minor" crime is not uniform among the states, in most states a misdemeanor cannot be punished for more than one year in prison. Fewer than one tenth of state prosecutions are for felonies. By contrast, about one third of federal prosecutions are for felonies. Not surprisingly states have established different procedures to deal with the almost 12 million minor-crime prosecutions that occur every year. For example, a defendant who is charged with a misdemeanor may not be entitled to a preliminary hearing, grand jury review, pretrial discovery, or a jury trial. Also, prosecutions for minor crimes may be tried in municipal court before a magistrate who may not be a lawyer.

2.   *The Gap Between Law and Practice*

When lawyers practice criminal law, they find that the criminal procedure rules "on the books" may not be reflected in reality, and that a defendant's rights may be rarely invoked or enforced. This may be the result of defense counsel's advice to waive these rights, as when a defendant pleads guilty and thereby waives the right to trial by jury and the privilege against self-incrimination, among others. Or, it may be that a defense counsel lacks the resources to pursue all potential legal arguments available to an indigent defendant, or that such counsel is incompetent under A.B.A. standards but not provably "ineffective" under federal constitutional standards. It may be that a defense counsel lacks evidence that will persuade a judge or prosecutor to accept a defendant's claim, as when a judge credits a police officer's testimony concerning an event and rejects the defendant's testimony. Even when a defendant has a good claim, it may be that she has no right to the assistance of appointed counsel to pursue such a claim. According to Supreme Court precedents, the Sixth Amendment guarantees trial counsel for indigent federal defendants in all criminal prosecutions, but guarantees trial counsel for an indigent state defendant only when she will receive a jail sentence. For appeals, the Fourteenth Amendment guarantees indigent defendants a right to counsel only for the first appeal. Defendants who seek to pursue claims in other circumstances have no federal constitutional right to counsel, although they may have such rights based on state constitutional or statutory law.

The gap between law and practice also is created by the decentralized nature of prosecution systems. The federal system is the most centralized institution, because police and prosecutors both answer to a single prosecutorial authority, the Department of Justice (DOJ). The DOJ attempts to create some uniformity among its agents through the promulgation of policy positions to be followed by all United States Attorneys and, for example, all Drug Enforcement Administration officers. By contrast, in state prosecution systems, police and prosecutors work for different authorities, so that police actions may not be authorized by prosecutors, but only by the police department. Typically, state prosecutors have "territorial" jurisdiction over a particular county (which often overlaps with the jurisdiction of certain local prosecutors or city attorneys), and a variety of police departments also have overlapping jurisdictions within the same territory. This collection of autonomous groups in the prosecution system makes it difficult for uniform policies or practices to be implemented without the cooperation of all the agents in the system.

Finally, both police and prosecutors are vested with considerable discretion, which further widens the gap between law and practice. For example, the police have some discretion to ignore criminal acts, or to arrest one person for certain crimes but not others. Prosecutors have discretion in their charging decisions, and in plea bargaining. When there are no legal consequences for particular actions by these prosecuting agents, their discretion allows for discriminatory law enforcement. Some of the Supreme Court's remedies for constitutional violations by police and prosecutors are assumed to be necessary in order to create incentives for these prosecuting agents to adhere to constitutional requirements. Yet even the existence of incentives cannot guarantee the enforcement of constitutional rights on the streets or in court.

C. THE ROLES OF PROSECUTORS AND DEFENSE COUNSEL IN VARIOUS STAGES OF A CRIMINAL PROSECUTION

1. *The Pre–Arrest Investigation Stage*

One goal of most pre-arrest investigations, whether conducted by police or by prosecutors working together with police, is to obtain evidence that will satisfy the "probable cause" standard required both for arrest and for judicial validation of any decision to charge a person with a crime. This standard does not require as much evidence as the "preponderance" (more likely than not) standard for proving liability in a typical civil case. But the probable cause standard requires more proof than the lower "reasonable suspicion" standard that allows police to stop, question, frisk, and briefly detain people during pre-arrest investigations. A second goal of most pre-arrest investigations is to obtain sufficient evidence to satisfy the "beyond a reasonable doubt" standard required for conviction at trial or for a guilty plea. If this kind of evidence cannot be obtained before an arrest is made, then police and prosecutors will attempt to obtain it by using a variety of investigatory techniques after the arrest.

A prosecutor's first contact with a case usually occurs after police have engaged in some investigative procedures following the report of a crime, or after police have arrested a person following such a report and investigation. Police may not be able to make a crime-scene arrest, but they usually will interview the victim and any witnesses and collect evidence, in order to effectively preserve a record for later prosecution. Unlike the police activities portrayed in television dramas, investigations for most crimes do not go beyond these simple activities.

When further investigation is called for, prosecutors sometimes may be asked to participate in police efforts to obtain a warrant for searches and seizures of a person's home, or in interviews of witnesses or interrogations of a person who is a possible suspect but not in custody. Occasionally, a prosecutor must participate in investigations of unreported crimes. They may help to supervise "sting" operations, for example, or to advise the police concerning the use of undercover police agents or informants, or the use of police surveillance techniques such as electronic monitoring. Prosecutors may also investigate crimes through the use of grand jury proceedings, and rely on subpoenas to compel witnesses to testify and provide evidence to grand juries.

A defense counsel usually will not play a role in most pre-arrest investigative activities by prosecutors and police, unless called upon to do so by a client. For example, a person with retained counsel may ask for advice concerning the advisability of agreeing to a police interview, and may decide to agree to the interview only in the presence of counsel. A witness who is required to appear before a grand jury may consult retained counsel during breaks in the course of the grand jury proceedings. A person who believes he may be the "target" of the grand jury investigation may also employ retained counsel to communicate with prosecutors concerning the case, in order to protect his interests or to attempt to influence the ultimate charging decision.

2. *The Arrest Stage*

There are two different kinds of arrests: the non-custodial "citation" arrest and the "full-custody" arrest. Both require probable cause, but the citation arrest is used typically only for minor offenses such as traffic crimes. Many states and municipalities authorize police to issue an arrest citation for such crimes, in their discretion, and to release the arrested person after giving them the citation. The arrestee has the obligation to respond to the citation, either by pleading guilty and paying a fine, or by appearing in court to contest guilt. Even for minor offenses, however, police may retain the discretion to perform a full-custody arrest, and usually they will follow this practice when arresting a person for a serious crime. After forcibly detaining the arrestee, the police will take him to the police station for "booking," and then the arrestee will be jailed or possibly released to await the outcome of the prosecutor's review and decision to charge.

Most arrests are made without warrants, as authorized by the Supreme Court's precedents establishing a variety of exceptions to the Fourth Amendment's warrant requirement. Thus, police will seek an arrest warrant from a magistrate only when this is required by law, or when there is some practical reason to do so. Prosecutors may work together with police in preparing the documents to present to a magistrate. The request for a warrant must be supported by sworn affidavits describing the investigation that led the police to believe there is probable cause that a crime has been committed by a particular person. The magistrate's hearing on the police request for an arrest warrant is *ex parte*, so that defense counsel usually have no role to play in this procedure.

The power to make a full-custody arrest carries with it other powers. It entitles police to perform a full search of the arrestee's person at the scene of arrest, and to search the compartment of a car when arresting a driver. Once a person is in custody, more intrusive searches may be allowed for arrestees who are going to be jailed. Even though these searches may be made without probable cause, a warrantless arrest must be based upon probable cause that will be reviewed by a magistrate at a hearing after the arrest. The Supreme Court's precedents establish 48 hours as the normal deadline for such a hearing, but some states have a 24–hour deadline.

3. *The Booking and Jailing Stage*

People who have undergone a full-custody arrest will also undergo the booking process, which usually occurs at the police station or jail. The purpose of booking is to allow the police to keep a record of arrests, and to obtain photographs and fingerprints of arrestees. There is no connection between booking and the formal "charging" process, which occurs sometime later. During booking, the arrestee is asked to supply biographical information, such as name and address, but may not be asked questions about the crime. After booking, police may allow people who are arrested for minor crimes to post "bail" immediately, and to be released on their own recognizance, pending the outcome of later decisions to bring a formal charge against them. However, people who lack the money to pay such bail will be jailed, as will people who are charged with serious crimes. Someone who is jailed may be subjected to a thorough search of his person, and a complete inventory of his possessions may be performed. State or local law, or police custom or practice may allow him to telephone a lawyer or a friend at this stage, but if no such calls may be allowed, an arrested person who is indigent may not have any contact with defense counsel until the arraignment stage.

4. *The Post–Arrest Investigation Stage*

After an arrest, a prosecutor may participate in the same kinds of investigative activity that precedes an arrest, such as witness interviews or interrogations, and the procuring of search warrants. Additionally, a prosecutor may participate in activities that usually occur after arrest, such as a "lineup." An indigent arrestee has no per se right to have appointed counsel present during the lineup, where police require the arrestee to stand with a group of people who roughly resemble her, and ask a witness to attempt to identify the person who committed the crime. Not until the initiation of formal "adversarial judicial proceedings" does such a right to counsel exist. Nor does the arrestee have a right to have appointed counsel present at a photographic "showup," where police show a witness an "array" of photographs which includes a picture of the defendant, and ask the witness to attempt to identify the guilty party. A prosecutor also may participate in the interrogation of an arrested person, who is now entitled to *Miranda* rights because of the existence of "custodial" interrogation. While the arrestee has no right to the presence of defense counsel at this interrogation, the arrestee may invoke the right to counsel by asking for a lawyer, and thereby preclude further interrogation in the absence of counsel.

5. *The Decision to Bring a Formal Charge by Filing a Complaint*

When a person is arrested, the police have, in a sense, "charged" that person with committing a crime. But the prosecution does not begin until a "complaint" is filed, either by the prosecutor or by the police. Many arrests do not result in the filing of complaint. In some cases, a supervising police officer will decide that the charge should not be pursued. In many jurisdictions, a prosecutor will make this decision, although it is possible that the decision to drop a case may not be made until after the defendant's "first appearance," or even later, after the filing of an information or issuance of an indictment. When a prosecutor decides to drop a charge, it is most often because of insufficient evidence, or because of the unavailability of witnesses whose testimony is believed to be necessary for conviction. In making charging decisions, a prosecutor also may decide to change the original charge, or to add additional charges. It is common for a prosecutor to review all felony arrests before deciding which charges to pursue by filing a complaint, and to allow police to file a complaint for most misdemeanor charges without a prosecutor's review.

When a complaint is filed either by a prosecutor or by police, it is filed in a magistrate's court. At this point, the arrestee is now a "defendant." The complaint usually sets forth a description of the crime and a citation to the criminal code concerning the offense being charged. Either the police or the victim will sign the complaint, and swear to the truth of its allegations. The act of filing the complaint is not necessarily accompanied by other immediate formal judicial proceedings. However, this filing sets other procedures in motion under state or local law, such as the requirement that a defendant must make a "first appearance" in court within a certain time period. If the defendant is not in jail, there may be a time lapse of several days before this hearing, but any defendant in jail must be brought "promptly" before a magistrate. Further, if a defendant was arrested without a warrant, the validity of probable cause for the arrest must also be determined promptly by a magistrate.

If the crime is a misdemeanor, the complaint will remain the "charging instrument" for the prosecutor, and the case usually will be tried in the magistrate's court. However, if the crime is a felony, the complaint will be replaced with a different instrument after proceedings in the magistrate's court are finished, and the case proceeds to the court where the trial will occur. In cases where the grand jury is involved, that instrument will be the indictment, and in other cases, that instrument will be a document called the "information." Defense counsel usually do not play a role at the charging stage, unless they have been retained by a client to communicate with the prosecutor and to attempt to negotiate the disposition of the charge.

6. The Defendant's First Appearance in Court

The defendant's first appearance occurs after the complaint is filed. This initial hearing before the magistrate may occur as early as a few hours after arrest, or as late as several days after the arrest, depending on the defendant's custodial status and the nature of the arrest. Usually, the hearing has three purposes. First, the magistrate informs the defendant of the charges set forth in the complaint, and typically describes the defendant's various rights, such as the right to remain silent and the right to counsel. Second, the magistrate must determine whether the defendant is indigent, and ask an indigent defendant whether he wishes to be represented by appointed counsel. Most defendants are indigent. Most often, these defendants will be represented by attorneys who are employed by a state or local public defender agency. However, some jurisdictions continue to use a system of appointing attorneys from the private bar. A few jurisdictions allow a private law firm or other group to have a contract for representation of indigents. The magistrate is supposed to take whatever steps are necessary to begin the process of having counsel appointed in a particular jurisdiction. Finally, the magistrate sets bail for the defendant at this hearing, assuming that this is necessary because the defendant is in custody. The magistrate may require the defendant to post cash or a bond that is secured from a professional bonding agency. In the alternative, the magistrate may decide to release a defendant, but impose conditions on that release. Some states allow the magistrate to perform a fourth function at this hearing, which is to review the grounds for probable cause for a warrantless arrest. For misdemeanor cases triable in the magistrate's court, a fifth function of the first appearance is to ask for the defendant's plea on the record. It is possible for a misdemeanor defendant to plead guilty, assuming that any right to counsel and other rights are properly waived. The magistrate's acceptance of a guilty plea is regulated by standards set forth in constitutional precedents as well as statutory law. In felony cases, the defendant's plea on the record will occur at the arraignment. While indigent defendants will not be represented by appointed counsel at the first appearance, retained defense counsel may participate in the hearing.

7. The Preliminary Hearing or Grand Jury Stage

The preliminary hearing usually will be the first stage where an indigent defendant will have representation by appointed counsel, and thus for most defendants, it will be the first proceeding where the prosecutor and the defense counsel meet formally as adversaries. However, a preliminary hearing may not occur for a variety of reasons. A prosecutor may decide not to pursue the charge and file a *nolle prosequi* motion in order to have the complaint dismissed. A defense counsel may advise a client to plead guilty, and to waive the preliminary hearing in anticipation of the plea. Or, a prosecutor may decide to avoid the disadvantages of a preliminary hearing by seeking an indictment from a grand jury.

The primary disadvantage of a hearing, from a prosecutor's point of view, is that it provides advantages to defense counsel. Specifically, it allows defense counsel to cross-examine the "probable cause" witnesses who will testify at the hearing, and thereby to obtain a record that may be used for impeachment of these witnesses at trial. Defense counsel may also discover a prosecutor's evidence or strategy that would otherwise be difficult to learn about before trial. Typically, the defense does not present evidence at a preliminary hearing, in order to avoid the very disadvantages that may provoke a prosecutor to avoid such a hearing. By taking the same witnesses to a secret grand jury proceeding where defense counsel is absent, the prosecutor may obtain a finding of probable cause, and avoid the need for a magistrate to make this determination at a preliminary hearing.

In any event, even if the prosecutor does decide to go forward with a preliminary hearing, and to minimize the exposure of witnesses by presenting a small amount of evidence, it is the rare case where a magistrate rejects a complaint for lack of probable cause. After all, another magistrate has determined that probable cause existed for the arrest, and unless other evidence casts doubt upon that determination, the result of this second probable cause determination will be the same. Once this decision is made, there are two possible routes that the prosecution will take, depending on the requirements of state law. In a majority of states, the defendant must be bound over to the trial court, where the prosecutor will file an "information" which will supplant the complaint. In the other states, and in federal prosecutions, the defendant must be "bound over" to the grand jury, so that an indictment may issue from that body, and supplant the complaint. In states where a prosecutor has the options of using the grand jury or filing an information, the latter procedure is typically used. If the grand jury option must be used, this group is required to make an independent determination of probable cause, based on a prosecutor's marshalling of the evidence. Defense counsel do not have access to these secret proceedings. It is the rare case where a grand jury refuses to indict a defendant, whether or not the grand jury's proceeding was preceded by a preliminary hearing.

Once an indictment is issued or an information is filed, Supreme Court precedents create some limitations for a prosecutor's investigative activities. For example, if secret police agents deliberately elicit incriminating statements from a defendant at this stage, such statements are not admissible at trial on the charged offense. If a prosecutor wishes to conduct a lineup, and does so in the absence of counsel, any identification obtained at the lineup is likewise inadmissible.

8.   *The Arraignment Stage*

The arraignment has two functions. It is a hearing in the trial court where the judge will inform the defendant of the felony charges in the indictment or information, and where the defendant will be asked to enter a plea to the charges on the record. Most defendants will enter a plea of not guilty, and the judge will then set the case for trial. An indigent defendant is entitled to representation by appointed counsel at arraignment. If counsel has not been appointed and a defendant asks for counsel, this will operate as a bar to further police interrogation about the charged crime, but not necessarily other crimes.

Once the arraignment occurs, plea negotiations will begin, although in some cases they may occur earlier. A defense counsel may advise a defendant to plead guilty because of the benefits offered by a prosecutor in exchange for a plea, whether in the form of an agreement to reduce charges or to recommend a lower sentence. However, a prosecutor may refuse to offer such benefits, especially for serous charges. Most cases are resolved by guilty plea, but the rate of pleas varies among jurisdictions and among crimes. If no guilty plea occurs, a prosecutor may either dismiss the charges as in earlier stages, or continue to investigate the case and prepare for trial. The prosecutor will seek discovery material from the defense as permitted by statutory law, such as a list of trial witnesses. In some jurisdictions, the defense must give the prosecution notice of the intent to raise certain defenses at trial, such as insanity. The prosecutor may also rely on expert witnesses to assist with forensic evidence, or with preparation for rebuttal of certain defenses.

Ideally, if a defense counsel has the resources and time to investigate a case thoroughly, she will hire a private investigator to assist in interviewing witnesses and collecting evidence. She will interview the defendant, examine the police report, and seek discovery of exculpatory material from the prosecutor, as well as other discovery material allowed by state or federal law, such as a list of trial witnesses. She may seek to have an expert appointed for an indigent defendant to assist in trial preparation of crucial issues. She will attempt to follow the A.B.A. Standards concerning the proper representation of the defendant. There are especially complex duties of preparation required by the A.B.A. Standards for capital cases. However, appointed defense counsel are sometimes burdened with large case loads and have few or no resources for investigating a case thoroughly. In some jurisdictions, there are caps on the maximum fees that appointed counsel may receive, such as $1,000 for all the work involved in preparing and trying a capital case. In a few jurisdictions, these caps have been challenged on constitutional grounds, and legislative and judicial responses to these challenges have created some changes in the kinds of resources available to defense counsel.

9.   The Pre–Trial Motions Stage

As part of a defense counsel's investigation of a case, certain pre-trial motions may be filed, such as a motion to compel disclosure of evidence, or for the appointment of expert witnesses to testify at trial concerning a mental state defense. Other motions will be made in order to pursue a defendant's claims that the police or prosecutor violated the constitution or statutory law. These motions include a motion to exclude inadmissible evidence at trial, usually referred to as a "motion to suppress" evidence. Other standard motions include a motion to quash the indictment because of particular defects, a motion for reduction of bail, and a motion *in limine* to limit the prosecutor's examination of witnesses in some way.

Most motions to suppress are filed in order to exclude materials seized in illegal searches, or incriminating statements by the defendants obtained in illegal interrogations, or pre-trial identifications by witnesses obtained in an illegal manner. In the small percentage of cases where a motion to suppress is granted, this ruling may result in a prosecutor's filing a *nolle prosequi* motion to dismiss, because the prosecutor now believes there is insufficient evidence of proof of guilt "beyond a reasonable doubt" to obtain a conviction at trial. However, the prosecutor may obtain more evidence later and proceed with the same charge against the same defendant again, because the protection of the Double Jeopardy Clause does not attach until the jury is sworn at trial.

10.   The Trial Stage

Defendants are guaranteed the right to a speedy trial, and some defendants will receive a trial within the time limits set by federal or state statutes, which often require that the trial occur within six months of the indictment. However, a defense counsel may advise a defendant to waive the right to a speedy trial, and if not, a case may fall within a statutory exemption to the required deadline.

A defense counsel and a prosecutor will conduct *voir dire* of the jury in most states, although in some state courts and the federal courts the judge conducts *voir dire*. Based on the information obtained from juror questionnaires and the answers obtained from jurors during *voir dire* questioning, the prosecutor and defense counsel will challenge jurors "for cause" and with "peremptory challenges." This process is regulated by Supreme Court precedents governing jury selection, as well as by statutory laws that define the grounds for challenges and limit each side to a certain number of peremptory challenges.

Most cases are tried to a jury, although a defense counsel will advise the defendant to waive the right to a jury trial in some cases. Only a small percentage of trials end in a mistrial because the jury cannot agree on a verdict. Supreme Court precedents limit the right to jury trial to cases where the maximum sentence is more than six months in prison, but some states provide for this right in other cases. Most states require that the jury verdict be unanimous, although Supreme Court precedents allow for non-unanimous verdicts. Most states also require a jury of twelve for serious felonies and capital cases, and some states use six-person juries for misdemeanors or less serious felonies. The Court's precedents hold that a unanimous jury of six is the smallest size that can be used for a criminal trial. Most trials end in conviction, and the conviction rates vary significantly for different crimes.

11. The Sentencing Stage

In most states, a convicted defendant in a non-capital case will be sentenced by the trial judge, but in a small number of states the jury will sentence the defendant. In a capital case, the jury has the responsibility of choosing between life and death. Some states have adopted complex sentencing guidelines for non-capital cases, modeled on the federal sentencing guidelines. These guidelines, or the existence of statutory "mandatory minimum" sentences, may influence or limit the discretion of a sentencing judge.

An indigent defendant is entitled to representation by appointed counsel at the sentencing hearing, which is usually held some weeks after the trial so that the probation department may prepare a presentence report for the judge. This report will contain information about the defendant's history that the probation officer believes is relevant to sentencing. At the hearing, the defense counsel may try to challenge information in the report, and may produce new information for the judge's consideration. Usually, however, the role of a defense counsel and prosecutor is confined to argument concerning the appropriate exercise of judicial discretion, based on the facts in the presentence report. Most defendants convicted of misdemeanors receive a fine or community service, or both, instead of a jail sentence, but most defendants convicted of serious felonies receive a substantial prison sentence. Once a sentence is imposed, the state corrections system takes on the responsibility for administering it. The availability of parole and "good time" may mean that a defendant will not serve the same time as the sentence that is imposed by the judge.

12. The Appeal Stage

When a defendant appeals a conviction, Supreme Court precedents hold that this action constitutes a waiver of Double Jeopardy rights, so the defendant may be tried again in the event that the conviction is reversed. The Court's precedents also hold that an indigent defendant is entitled to appointed counsel to pursue the first appeal "of right." While there is no federal constitutional right to such an appeal, all states have a long tradition of providing this right. For a state defendant, this appeal usually lies in the intermediate appellate court, or in the state supreme court of a state that has no such courts. For a federal defendant, the appeal lies in the federal circuit court. In most states with intermediate appellate courts, once the defendant loses the first appeal of right, a further appeal to the state supreme court will be heard only if that court exercises its discretion and decides to hear the case. Supreme Court precedents do not establish a right to appointed counsel for indigent defendants for this second discretionary appeal, or for the later stages, such as the pursuit of a writ of certiorari from the Supreme Court, or of subsequent avenues of judicial review. Only after the appeal process is exhausted will the conviction be termed "final," and then an indigent defendant must pursue the inaptly named "post-conviction remedies" that are available in state and federal court.

13.   *The Post–Appeal Stage of "Post–Conviction" Remedies*

Once a conviction is final, a state defendant usually must pursue his claims by filing a petition in the state trial court, seeking state "habeas" or *"coram nobis"* relief. A defendant may seek an evidentiary hearing on such claims, and some states provide that indigents have a right to appointed counsel at this stage. Even in states that do not provide counsel automatically at this stage, a trial court may decide to appoint counsel in a particular case, in order to have the merits of the case briefed and argued, or in order to provide representation at the evidentiary hearing. Most requests for evidentiary hearings are not granted. If the hearing is granted, it will be conducted as a civil proceeding. The losing party may appeal to the intermediate appellate court, and then to the state supreme court. At this point, a losing defendant usually will have "exhausted" his available post-conviction remedies in state court, and may file a petition for a writ of habeas corpus in federal district court, in order to pursue federal constitutional claims. A federal defendant begins the post-conviction process by filing that petition at the outset in federal district court. In non-capital cases, post-conviction relief is granted in a small percentage of cases. In capital cases, however, there is a higher percentage of cases where relief is granted, especially in some federal circuits.

Chapter 2

FOURTEENTH AMENDMENT DUE PROCESS: INCORPORATION AND RETROACTIVITY

A. INCORPORATION OF THE BILL OF RIGHTS

Federal criminal procedure, like other exercises in national governance, are subject to the United States Constitution. Notwithstanding the Bill of Rights' comprehensive and uncontroverted pertinence to federal investigative, prosecutorial and adjudicative processes, its applicability to the states is a more recent and debated phenomenon. The impact of federal constitutional guarantees upon state practice owes to the union's reconstruction pursuant to the Fourteenth Amendment.[1]

Adoption of the Fourteenth Amendment represented a fundamental redistribution of power from state to national government. Although the provision heightened federal interest in and responsibility over civil rights, debate has persisted over whether the amendment enhanced the significance of the Bill of Rights so as to make it applicable to the states. United States Supreme Court opinions have advanced several analytical methods for applying the Bill of Rights to the states.

In the first half of the twentieth century, the leading method for determining how and whether the Bill of Rights was applicable to the states through the Fourteenth Amendment was the "fundamental rights" approach. The Bill of Rights indicate what rights are fundamental, and provide a reference point for measuring which state practices are so shocking to the conscience that they are inconsistent with the concept of "ordered liberty." *Palko v. Connecticut*, 302 U.S. 319 (1937). The court evaluated each case under a totality of circumstances approach. For example, long before the Court held in *Gideon v. Wainwright* that the Sixth Amendment required appointment of counsel for state felony defendants, it had held that the Sixth Amendment right to counsel was

---

1. U.S. Const., amend. XIX. The history of Reconstruction is discussed comprehensively in CHARLES FAIRMAN, VII HISTORY OF THE SUPREME COURT OF THE UNITED STATES, RECONSTRUCTION AND REUNION (1987).

not a "fundamental right" which the states had to follow. In other words, it did not "shock the conscience" for a state to refuse appointment of counsel for indigent defendant accused of felonies. *Betts v. Brady*, 316 U.S. 455 (1942). Decisions like *Betts* produced criticism that the rights of a state defendant were substantially limited in comparison with a federal defendant.

The second method used to evaluate the applicability of the Bill of Rights to the states through the Fourteenth Amendment was the "total incorporation" approach. All the protections of the Bill of Rights applied to the states. Critics of this approach relied on the lack of legislative history of the Bill of Rights to support any legislative intent that all the protections applied to the states. Although Justice Hugo Black was unable to convince a majority of his colleagues that the total incorporation approach was the proper course, his advocacy nevertheless influenced the "selective incorporation" approach used by the current Court.

Selective incorporation represents a hybrid or compromise between the earlier analytical methods. Its advocates believe that Fourteenth Amendment Due Process includes rights which are essential to "ordered liberty," and that the protections in the Bill of Rights are the only fundamental protections. They also find that the fundamental rights approach is too subjective and unstructured.

In *Duncan v. Louisiana*, 391 U.S. 145 (1968), Justice White described the difference in the approaches.

In one sense recent cases applying provisions of the first eight Amendments to the States represent a new approach to the "incorporation" debate. Earlier the Court can be seen as having asked, when inquiring into whether some particular procedural safeguard was required of a State, if a civilized system could be imagined that would not accord the particular protection. For example, *Palko v. State of Connecticut* stated: "The right to trial by jury and the immunity from prosecution except as the result of an indictment may have value and importance. Even so, they are not of the very essence of a scheme of ordered liberty. * * * Few would be so narrow or provincial as to maintain that a fair and enlightened system of justice would be impossible without them." The recent cases, on the other hand, have proceeded upon the valid assumption that state criminal processes are not imaginary and theoretical schemes but actual systems bearing virtually every characteristic of the common-law system that has been developing contemporaneously in England and in this country. The question thus is whether given this kind of system a particular procedure is fundamental— whether, that is, a procedure is necessary to an Anglo–American regime of ordered liberty. It is this sort of inquiry that can justify the conclusions that state courts must exclude evidence seized in violation of the Fourth Amendment, *Mapp v. State of Ohio;* and that state prosecutors may not comment on a defendant's failure to testify, *Griffin v. State of California.* * * * Of each of these determinations that a constitutional provision originally written to bind the Federal Government should bind the States as well it might be said that the limitation in question is not necessarily fundamental to fairness in every criminal system that might be imagined but is fundamental in the context of the criminal processes maintained by the American States. When the inquiry is approached in this way the question whether the States can impose criminal punishment without granting a jury trial appears quite different from the way it appeared in the older cases opining that States might abolish jury trial. A criminal process which was fair and equitable but used no juries is easy to imagine. It would make use of alternative guarantees and protections which would serve the purposes that the jury serves in the English and American systems. Yet no American State has undertaken to construct such a system. Instead, every American State, including Louisiana, uses the jury extensively, and imposes very serious punishments only after a trial at which the defendant has a right to a jury's verdict. In every State, including Louisiana, the structure and style of the criminal process—the supporting framework and the subsidiary procedures—are of the sort that naturally complement jury trial, and have developed in connection with and in reliance upon jury trial.

To determine whether a protection from the Bill of Rights applies to the states under the selective incorporation approach, it is necessary to look at 1) the entirety of the right, not just as it applies to a particular set of facts (as with the fundamental rights approach), and 2) whether the provision is fundamental to Anglo–American jurisprudence. In *Malloy v. Hogan*, 378 U.S. 1 (1964), Justice Brennan observed that if the right applies to the states, all aspects of the right will apply to every state case as it applies to every federal case.

> We hold that the Fourteenth Amendment guaranteed the petitioner the protection of the Fifth Amendment's privilege against self-incrimination, and that under the applicable federal standard, the [state court] erred in holding that the privilege was not properly invoked. [The state urges] that the availability of the federal privilege to a witness in a state inquiry is to be determined according to a less stringent safeguard than is applicable in a federal proceeding. We disagree. We have held that the guarantees [aspects of the Bill of Rights] are all to be enforced against the States under the Fourteenth Amendment according to the same standards that protect those personal rights against federal encroachment. [The] Court thus has rejected the notion that the Fourteenth Amendment applies to the States only a "watered-down, subjective version of the individual guarantees of the Bill of Rights."

Despite criticism that the selective incorporation approach is arbitrary and prevents local experimentation, it was the basis for applying most of the Bill of Rights protections to the states in the second half of the twentieth century. Of the Bill of Rights provisions related to criminal procedure, the Court has refused to find that only two portions are expressly applicable to the states through the Fourteenth Amendment. The Eighth Amendment prohibition on excessive bail, although it may be regarded by the Court as fundamental, is not applicable to the states. As recently as the 1990's, the Court has noted that the Fifth Amendment requirement for a grand jury indictment in felony cases is inapplicable to the states. *Albright v. Oliver*, 510 U.S. 266 (1994).

B. RETROACTIVITY

Constitutional interpretation that generates a new rule of law presents an issue with respect to scope of application. Traditionally, the Court has allowed a prevailing litigant to be the beneficiary of a new rule. Initial determinations that illegally seized evidence must be excluded from trial,[2] or that persons in custodial interrogation must be informed of certain rights they possess,[3] thus redounded to the benefit of the individuals who first prevailed. Application at least to the prevailing litigant is justified for purposes of satisfying the case or controversy requirement and providing inducement for challenges that may improve the law.

Beyond a party whose case engendered a constitutional rule change, the scope of a new principle's operation has been widely debated especially over the past few decades. During the 1960s, as federal case law became increasingly protective of defendant's rights, the Court asserted that the benefit of a new rule would not extend to persons whose convictions became final prior to its adoption.[4] In *Linkletter v. Walker*, 381 U.S. 618, 637–38 (1965), the Court thus applied the exclusionary rule in a forward-looking fashion except to the extent the litigant and persons who had not played out the full string of appeals. Reluctance to allow greater retroactivity reflected the sense that such a distribution of benefits would subvert the interest of finality, generate numerous retrials and undermine good-faith reliance by police and courts on the existing state of constitutional law.

Pursuant to the *Linkletter* doctrine, the benefits of a new rule did not extend to habeas corpus petitioners but could be claimed by persons whose cases still were on direct review. Further tightening of the retroactivity principles occurred thereafter. In *Stovall v. Denno*, the Court determined that a newly imposed requirement of counsel at lineups[5] governed only police activity that post-dated the new rule.[6] Like claims would not be heard, therefore, even if asserted in cases for which a final judgment had not been rendered. Nonretroactivity (except for the litigant) reflected the work of a Court that, in expanding the ambit of defendants' rights, locked onto prospectivity as a device for minimizing

2. *Mapp v. Ohio*, 367 U.S. 643 (1961).

3. *Miranda v. Arizona*, 384 U.S. 436 (1966).

4. *Linkletter v. Walker*, 381 U.S. 618 (1965).

5. *Gilbert v. California*, 388 U.S. 263 (1967); *United States v. Wade*, 388 U.S. 218 (1967).

6. *Stovall v. Denno*, 388 U.S. 293, 299–301 (1967).

disruption of and costs to the criminal justice system.[7] Whatever virtues the Court attached to such a premise, however, were not consensually acknowledged. In *Desist v. United States*, Justice Harlan argued that prospectivity was a handmaiden of arbitrariness and judicial over-reaching. Responding to a majority decision refusing to apply retroactively a rule requiring counsel at certain line-ups, Harlan concluded that he could

> no longer accept the rule first announced two years ago in *Stovall v. Denno*, and reaffirmed today, which permits this Court to apply a "new" constitutional rule entirely prospectively, while making an exception only for the particular litigant whose case was chosen as the vehicle for establishing that rule. Indeed, I have concluded that Linkletter was right in insisting that all "new" rules of constitutional law must, at a minimum, be applied to all those cases which are still subject to direct review by this Court at the time the "new" decision is handed down.

> Matters of basic principle are at stake. In the classical view of constitutional adjudication, which I share, criminal defendants cannot come before this Court simply to request largesse. This Court is entitled to decide constitutional issues only when the facts of a particular case require their resolution for a just adjudication on the merits. We do not release a criminal from jail because we like to do so, or because we think it wise to do so, but only because the government has offended constitutional principle in the conduct of his case. And when another similarly situated defendant comes before us, we must grant the same relief or give a principled reason for acting differently. We depart from this basic judicial tradition when we simply pick and choose from among similarly situated defendants those who alone will receive the benefit of a "new" rule of constitutional law.

> The unsound character of the rule reaffirmed today is perhaps best exposed by considering the following hypothetical. Imagine that the Second Circuit in the present case had anticipated the line of reasoning this Court subsequently pursued in *Katz v. United States*, concluding—as this Court there did—that "the underpinnings of *Olmstead* and *Goldman* have been so eroded by our subsequent decisions that the 'trespass' doctrine there enunciated can no longer be regarded as controlling." Would we have reversed the case on the ground that the principles the Second Circuit had announced—though identical with those in *Katz*—should not control because *Katz* is not retroactive? To the contrary, I venture to say that we would have taken satisfaction that the lower court had reached the same conclusion we subsequently did in *Katz*. If a "new" constitutional doctrine is truly right, we should not reverse lower courts which have accepted it; nor should we affirm those which have rejected the very arguments we have embraced. Anything else would

---

7. *See, e.g., Jenkins v. Delaware*, 395 U.S. 213, 219–22 (1969).

belie the truism that it is the task of this Court, like that of any other, to do justice to each litigant on the merits of his own case. It is only if our decisions can be justified in terms of this fundamental premise that they may properly be considered the legitimate products of a court of law, rather than the commands of a superlegislature.

Re-examination of prior developments in the field of retroactivity leads me irresistibly to the conclusion that the only solid disposition of this case lies in vacating the judgment of the Court of Appeals and in remanding this case to that court for further consideration in light of *Katz*.[8]

Harlan's reasoning had long-term significance. In *Griffith v. Kentucky*, the Court determined that a new rule should be applied to all cases pending on direct review. It observed that

in Justice Harlan's view, and now in ours, failure to apply a newly declared constitutional rule to criminal cases pending on direct review violates basic norms of constitutional adjudication. First, it is a settled principle that this Court adjudicates only "cases" and "controversies." Unlike a legislature, we do not promulgate new rules of constitutional criminal procedure on a broad basis. Rather, the nature of judicial review requires that we adjudicate specific cases, and each case usually becomes the vehicle for announcement of a new rule. But after we have decided a new rule in the case selected, the integrity of judicial review requires that we apply that rule to all similar cases pending on direct review. Justice Harlan observed:

"If we do not resolve all cases before us on direct review in light of our best understanding of governing constitutional principles, it is difficult to see why we should so adjudicate any case at all.... In truth, the Court's assertion of power to disregard current law in adjudicating cases before us that have not already run the full course of appellate review, is quite simply an assertion that our constitutional function is not one of adjudication but in effect of legislation."

As a practical matter, of course, we cannot hear each case pending on direct review and apply the new rule. But we fulfill our judicial responsibility by instructing the lower courts to apply the new rule retroactively to cases not yet final. Thus, it is the nature of judicial review that precludes us from "simply fishing one case from the stream of appellate review, using it as a vehicle for pronouncing new constitutional standards, and then permitting a stream of similar cases subsequently to flow by unaffected by that new rule."

Second, selective application of new rules violates the principle of treating similarly situated defendants the same. As we pointed out in *United States v. Johnson*, the problem with not applying new

---

8. *Desist v. United States*, 394 U.S. 244, 258–59 (1969).

rules to cases pending on direct review is "the actual inequity that results when the Court chooses which of many similarly situated defendants should be the chance beneficiary" of a new rule. Although the Court had tolerated this inequity for a time by not applying new rules retroactively to cases on direct review, we noted: "The time for toleration has come to an end."[9]

Although arguing for retroactivity to cases in which convictions had not been finalized, Justice Harlan also distinguished collateral from direct review. Given the unique purpose of the writ of habeas corpus, to ensure that states comply with federal principles at the time they were in force, he identified no logic for retroactivity in collateral proceedings except when punished conduct was beyond a state's law-making power or so fundamental as to be an implication of "ordered liberty." In *Teague v. Lane*, 489 U.S. 288 (1989), a plurality subscribed to Harlan's argument that retroactivity generally should not extend to habeas actions. The determination was notable not only for its investment in Harlan's thesis but for further narrowing the possibility of retroactivity in habeas proceedings.

The Court noted two limited exceptions suggested by Justice Harlan to the general prohibition on announcing or applying new rules in collateral proceedings. First, a new rule should be applied retroactively if it places "certain kinds of primary, private individual conduct beyond the power of the criminal law-making authority to proscribe." The second exception was that a new rule should be applied retroactively if it requires the observance of "watershed rules of criminal procedure." Although *Teague* did not generate a majority opinion, the reasoning of the O'Connor plurality was adopted soon thereafter in *Penry v. Lynaugh*, 492 U.S. 302, 314 (1989).

A critical determinant of retroactivity is whether a principle is driven by precedent or establishes a new rule. The *Linkletter* doctrine reflected Blackstonian theory that regarded new rulings as a discovery of the law as it actually existed. The *Teague* decision and its progeny reject the notion that the law is decoded and accept prior legal condition as a reality. In *Yates v. Aiken*, 484 U.S. 211, 216 (1988), the Court distinguished between a result generated by a rule that breaks new ground and an outcome that is dictated by precedent. It referenced Harlan's understanding "that most collateral attacks on final judgments should be resolved by reference to the state of the law at the time of the petitioner's conviction, [and his sense] that many "new" holdings are merely applications of principles that were well settled at the time of conviction."

Justice Harlan in *Desist* had distinguished between rules that were genuinely new and holdings that applied established principles to different factual settings. In *Teague*, the plurality stressed that a new rule is announced "if the result was not *dictated* by precedent existing at the time the defendant's conviction became final." 489 U.S. at 301. Whatev-

---

9. *Griffith v. Kentucky*, 479 U.S. 314, 322–23 (1987).

er room the *Teague* and *Penry* decisions left, for results ordained by existing precedent, was compressed further in *Butler v. McKellar*, 494 U.S. 407 (1990). The *McKellar* Court determined that a rule was new "if the outcome [was] susceptible to debate among reasonable minds." The depiction of a new rule elicited criticism by dissenting justices and commentators to the effect that the majority had gutted the writ of habeas corpus and thus "infring[ed] upon legislative prerogatives."[10] Supporting that perspective is the fact that the Court typically does not grant review unless reasonable minds differ over the applicability of existing law.

BUTLER v. McKELLAR

494 U.S. 407 (1990).

CHIEF JUSTICE REHNQUIST delivered the opinion of the Court.

Petitioner Horace Butler was convicted and sentenced to death for the murder of Pamela Lane. After his conviction became final on direct appeal, Butler collaterally attacked his conviction by way of a petition for federal habeas corpus. Butler relied on our decision in *Arizona v. Roberson,* decided after his conviction became final on direct appeal. We have held, however, that a new decision generally is not applicable in cases on collateral review unless the decision was dictated by precedent existing at the time the petitioner's conviction became final. *Penry v. Lynaugh*; *Teague v. Lane.* We hold that our ruling in *Roberson* was not so dictated and that Butler's claim is not within either of two narrow exceptions to the general rule. * * *

[Butler was indicted and convicted of murder, after the trial court denied his motion to suppress statements he had given to police. In a separate proceeding, the jury sentenced him to death. Butler lost his direct appeal and his petition for state collateral relief. His federal petition for habeas corpus relief was rejected by the trial court and Fourth Circuit. On the same day the Fourth Circuit denied his rehearing petitions, the Supreme Court issued its decision in *Roberson*.]

We held in *Roberson* that the Fifth Amendment bars police-initiated interrogation following a suspect's request for counsel in the context of a separate investigation. On Butler's motion for reconsideration, the original Fourth Circuit panel considered Butler's new contention that *Roberson* requires suppression of his statements taken in the separate investigation of Lane's murder. Although the panel conceded that the substance of its prior conclusion "was cast into immediate and serious doubt" by our subsequent decision in *Roberson*, it nevertheless determined that Butler was not entitled to the retroactive benefit of *Roberson*. According to the panel, the *Edwards-Roberson* limitations on police interrogation are only tangentially related to the truth-finding function. They are viewed most accurately as part of the prophylactic protection of the Fifth Amendment right to counsel created to be "guidelines" for

---

10. 494 U.S. at 432 (Brennan, J., dissenting).

the law enforcement profession. The interrogation of Butler, while unquestionably contrary to present "guidelines," was conducted in strict accordance with established law at the time. The panel, therefore, denied Butler's petition for rehearing. A majority of the Circuit Judges denied, over a dissent, Butler's petition for a rehearing en banc. We granted certiorari, and now affirm.

The "new rule" principle [validates] reasonable, good-faith interpretations of existing precedents made by state courts even though they are shown to be contrary to later decisions....

Butler contends that *Roberson* did not establish a new rule and is, therefore, available to support his habeas petition. Butler argues that *Roberson* was merely an application of *Edwards* to a slightly different set of facts. In support of his position, Butler points out that the majority had said that *Roberson's* case was directly controlled by *Edwards*.

But the fact that a court says that its decision is within the "logical compass" of an earlier decision, or indeed that it is "controlled" by a prior decision, is not conclusive for purposes of deciding whether the current decision is a "new rule" under *Teague*. Courts frequently view their decisions as being "controlled" or "governed" by prior opinions even when aware of reasonable contrary conclusions reached by other courts. In *Roberson*, for instance, the Court found *Edwards* controlling but acknowledged a significant difference of opinion on the part of several lower courts that had considered the question previously. That the outcome in *Roberson* was susceptible to debate among reasonable minds is evidenced further by the differing positions taken by the judges of the Courts of Appeals for the Fourth and Seventh Circuits noted previously. It would not have been an illogical or even a grudging application of *Edwards* to decide that it did not extend to the facts of *Roberson*. We hold, therefore, that *Roberson* announced a "new rule."

The question remains whether the new rule in *Roberson* nevertheless comes within one of the two recognized exceptions under which a new rule is available on collateral review.

Under the first exception, "a new rule should be applied retroactively if it places 'certain kinds of primary, private individual conduct beyond the power of the criminal law-making authority to proscribe.'" This exception is clearly inapplicable. The proscribed conduct in the instant case is capital murder, the prosecution of which is, to put it mildly, not prohibited by the rule in *Roberson*. Nor did *Roberson* address any "categorical guarantees accorded by the Constitution" such as a prohibition on the imposition of a particular punishment on a certain class of offenders.

Under the second exception, a new rule may be applied on collateral review "if it requires the observance of 'those procedures that [are] "implicit in the concept of ordered liberty." '" *Teague*, it should be noted, however, discerned a latent danger in relying solely on this famous language from *Palko*: "Were we to employ the *Palko* test without more, we would be doing little more than importing into a very different context the terms of the debate over incorporation.... Reviving the *Palko* test now, in this area of law, would be unnecessarily anachronistic." [W]e believe that Justice Harlan's concerns about the difficulty in identifying both the existence and the value of accuracy-enhancing procedural rules can be addressed by limiting the scope of the second exception to those new procedures without which the likelihood of an accurate conviction is seriously diminished. "Because we operate from the premise that such procedures would be so central to an accurate determination of innocence or guilt, we believe it unlikely that many such components of basic due process have yet to emerge."

Because a violation of *Roberson's* added restrictions on police investigatory procedures would not seriously diminish the likelihood of obtaining an accurate determination—indeed, it may increase that likelihood—we conclude that *Roberson* did not establish any principle that would come within the second exception.

The judgment of the Court of Appeals is therefore Affirmed.

[Justice Brennan dissented, joined by Justices Marshall, Blackmun and Stevens. He argued that the Court had narrowed the window for identifying a new rule in habeas proceedings. *Arizona v. Roberson* was not a "new rule,"was dictated by prior precedent, and therefore, should be retroactively applicable to cases on collateral review.]

Chapter 3

THE RIGHT TO COUNSEL

A. GENERALLY

In 1938, the United States Supreme Court held that *federal* defendants who could not afford an attorney had a constitutional right to appointed counsel under the Sixth Amendment. *Johnson v. Zerbst*, 304 U.S. 458 (1938). Justice Black, writing for the majority, emphasized that "[t]he Sixth Amendment stands as a constant admonition that if the constitutional safeguards it provides be lost, justice will not 'still be done.' It embodies a realistic recognition of the obvious truth that the average defendant does not have the professional legal skills to protect himself when brought before a tribunal with power to take his life or liberty, wherein the prosecution is presented by experienced and learned counsel. [The] Sixth Amendment withholds from federal courts, in all criminal proceedings, the power and authority to deprive an accused of his life or liberty unless he has or waives the assistance of counsel." *Id.* at 463.

BETTS v. BRADY

316 U.S. 455 (1942).

MR. JUSTICE ROBERTS delivered the opinion of the Court.

[Smith Betts] was indicted for robbery in the Circuit Court of Carroll County, Maryland. Due to lack of funds he was unable to employ counsel, and so informed the judge at his arraignment. He requested that counsel be appointed for him. The judge advised him that this could not be done as it was not the practice in Carroll County to appoint counsel for indigent defendants save in prosecutions for murder and rape.

Without waiving his asserted right to counsel the petitioner pleaded not guilty and elected to be tried without a jury. At his request witnesses were summoned in his behalf. He cross-examined the State's witnesses and examined his own. The latter gave testimony tending to establish an alibi. Although afforded the opportunity, he did not take the witness stand. The judge found him guilty and imposed a sentence of eight years. [Betts' petition for a writ of *habeas corpus* was denied.]

Was the petitioner's conviction and sentence a deprivation of his liberty without due process of law, in violation of the Fourteenth Amendment, because of the court's refusal to appoint counsel at his request?

The Sixth Amendment of the national Constitution applies only to trials in federal courts. The due process clause of the Fourteenth Amendment does not incorporate, as such, the specific guarantees found in the Sixth Amendment although a denial by a State of rights or privileges specifically embodied in that and others of the first eight amendments may, in certain circumstances, or in connection with other elements, operate, in a given case, to deprive a litigant of due process of law in violation of the Fourteenth. [The] phrase [due process of law] formulates a concept less rigid and more fluid than those envisaged in other specific and particular provisions of the Bill of Rights. Its application is less a matter of rule. Asserted denial is to be tested by an appraisal of the totality of facts in a given case. That which may, in one setting, constitute a denial of fundamental fairness, shocking to the universal sense of justice, may, in other circumstances, and in the light of other considerations, fall short of such denial. In the application of such a concept there is always the danger of falling into the habit of formulating the guarantee into a set of hard and fast rules the application of which in a given case may be to ignore the qualifying factors therein disclosed.

[The] question we are now to decide is whether due process of law demands that in every criminal case, whatever the circumstances, a State must furnish counsel to an indigent defendant. Is the furnishing of counsel in all cases whatever dictated by natural, inherent, and fundamental principles of fairness? The answer to the question may be found in the common understanding of those who have lived under the Anglo–American system of law. By the Sixth Amendment the people ordained that, in all criminal prosecutions, the accused should "enjoy the right [to] have the Assistance of Counsel for his defence." We have construed the provision to require appointment of counsel in all cases where a defendant is unable to procure the services of an attorney, and where the right has not been intentionally and competently waived. Though, as we have noted, the Amendment lays down no rule for the conduct of the States, the question recurs whether the constraint laid by the Amendment upon the national courts expresses a rule so fundamental and essential to a fair trial, and so, to due process of law, that it is made obligatory upon the states by the Fourteenth Amendment. Relevant data on the subject are afforded by constitutional and statutory provisions subsisting in the colonies and the states prior to the inclusion of the Bill of Rights in the national Constitution, and in the constitutional, legislative, and judicial history of the States to the present date.

[The] Constitutions of the thirteen original States, as they were at the time of federal union, exhibit great diversity in respect of the right to have counsel in criminal cases. [It] is evident that the constitutional provisions to the effect that a defendant should be "allowed" counsel or should have a right "to be heard by himself and his counsel," or that he might be heard by "either or both," at his election, were intended to do away with the rules which denied representation, in whole or in part, by counsel in criminal prosecutions, but were not aimed to compel the State to provide counsel for a defendant.

[The] constitutions of all the States, presently in force, save that of Virginia, contain provisions with respect to the assistance of counsel in criminal trials. Those of nine States may be said to embody a guarantee textually the same as that of the Sixth Amendment, or of like import. In the fundamental law of most States, however, the language used indicates only that a defendant is not to be denied the privilege of representation by counsel of his choice.

[This] demonstrates that, in the great majority of the States, it has been the considered judgment of the people, their representatives and their courts that appointment of counsel is not a fundamental right, essential to a fair trial. On the contrary, the matter has generally been deemed one of legislative policy. In the light of this evidence, we are unable to say that the concept of due process incorporated in the Fourteenth Amendment obligates the States, whatever may be their own views, to furnish counsel in every such case. Every court has power, if it deems proper, to appoint counsel where that course seems to be required in the interest of fairness.

[In] this case there was no question of the commission of a robbery. The State's case consisted of evidence identifying the petitioner as the perpetrator. The defense was an alibi. Petitioner called and examined witnesses to prove that he was at another place at the time of the commission of the offense. The simple issue was the veracity of the testimony for the State and that for the defendant. As Judge Bond says, the accused was not helpless, but was a man forty-three years old, of ordinary intelligence, and ability to take care of his own interests on the trial of that narrow issue. He had once before been in a criminal court, pleaded guilty to larceny and served a sentence and was not wholly unfamiliar with criminal procedure. It is quite clear that in Maryland, if the situation had been otherwise and it had appeared that the petitioner was, for any reason, at a serious disadvantage by reason of the lack of counsel, a refusal to appoint would have resulted in the reversal of a judgment of conviction.

[To] deduce from the due process clause a rule binding upon the states in this matter would be to impose upon them [a] requirement without distinction between criminal charges of different magnitude or in respect of courts of varying jurisdiction. [" 'Presumably] it would be argued that trials in the Traffic Court would require it.[']" And indeed it was said by petitioner's counsel both below and in this court, that as the

Fourteenth Amendment extends the protection of due process to property as well as to life and liberty, if we hold with the petitioner, logic would require the furnishing of counsel in civil cases involving property.

As we have said, the Fourteenth Amendment prohibits the conviction and incarceration of one whose trial is offensive to the common and fundamental ideas of fairness and right, and while want of counsel in a particular case may result in a conviction lacking in such fundamental fairness, we cannot say that the Amendment embodies an inexorable command that no trial for any offense, or in any court, can be fairly conducted and justice accorded a defendant who is not represented by counsel.

The judgment is *Affirmed*.

MR. JUSTICE BLACK, dissenting, with whom MR. JUSTICE DOUGLAS and MR. JUSTICE MURPHY concur.

[The] petitioner, a farm hand, out of a job and on relief, was indicted in a Maryland state court on a charge of robbery. He was too poor to hire a lawyer. He so informed the court and requested that counsel be appointed to defend him. His request was denied. Put to trial without a lawyer, he conducted his own defense, was found guilty, and was sentenced to eight years' imprisonment. The court below found that the petitioner had "at least an ordinary amount of intelligence." It is clear from his examination of witnesses that he was a man of little education.

If this case had come to us from a federal court, it is clear we should have to reverse it, because the Sixth Amendment makes the right to counsel in criminal cases inviolable by the Federal Government. I believe that the Fourteenth Amendment made the Sixth applicable to the states. But this view, although often urged in dissents, has never been accepted by a majority of this Court and is not accepted today.

[This] Court has [declared] that due process of law is denied if a trial is conducted in such manner that it is "shocking to the universal sense of justice" or "offensive to the common and fundamental ideas of fairness and right." On another occasion, this Court has recognized that whatever is "implicit in the concept of ordered liberty" and "essential to the substance of a hearing" is within the procedural protection afforded by the constitutional guaranty of due process. [The] right to counsel in a criminal proceeding is "fundamental."

[An] historical evaluation of the right to a full hearing in criminal cases, and the dangers of denying it, were set out in the *Powell* [*v. Alabama*, 287 U.S. 45 (1932)] case, where this Court said: "What [does] a hearing include? Historically and in practice, in our own country at least, it has always included the right to the aid of counsel when desired and provided by the party asserting the right. [Even] the intelligent and educated layman [lacks] both the skill and knowledge adequately to prepare his defense, even though he have a perfect one. He requires the guiding hand of counsel in every step in the proceedings against him.

Without it, though he be not guilty, he faces the danger of conviction because he does not know how to establish his innocence."

A practice cannot be reconciled with "common and fundamental ideas of fairness and right," which subjects innocent men to increased dangers of conviction merely because of their poverty. Whether a man is innocent cannot be determined from a trial in which, as here, denial of counsel has made it impossible to conclude, with any satisfactory degree of certainty, that the defendant's case was adequately presented.* * *

GIDEON v. WAINWRIGHT

372 U.S. 335 (1963).

MR. JUSTICE BLACK delivered the opinion of the Court.

Petitioner was charged in a Florida state court with having broken and entered a poolroom with intent to commit a misdemeanor. This offense is a felony under Florida law. Appearing in court without funds and without a lawyer, petitioner asked the court to appoint counsel for him, whereupon the following colloquy took place:

"The COURT: Mr. Gideon, I am sorry, but I cannot appoint Counsel to represent you in this case. Under the laws of the State of Florida, the only time the Court can appoint Counsel to represent a Defendant is when that person is charged with a capital offense. I am sorry, but I will have to deny your request to appoint Counsel to defend you in this case.

"The DEFENDANT: The United States Supreme Court says I am entitled to be represented by Counsel."

Put to trial before a jury, Gideon conducted his defense about as well as could be expected from a layman. He made an opening statement to the jury, cross-examined the State's witnesses, presented witnesses in his own defense, declined to testify himself, and made a short argument "emphasizing his innocence to the charge contained in the Information filed in this case." The jury returned a verdict of guilty, and petitioner was sentenced to serve five years in the state prison. [Gideon subsequently filed a habeas corpus petition attacking his conviction on the ground that the trial court's refusal to appoint counsel for him was unconstitutional. The Florida Supreme Court denied him any relief without opinion.] Since 1942, when *Betts v. Brady* was decided by a divided Court, the problem of a defendant's federal constitutional right to counsel in a state court has been a continuing source of controversy and litigation in both state and federal courts.

[The] Sixth Amendment provides, "In all criminal prosecutions, the accused shall enjoy the right [to] have the Assistance of Counsel for his defence." We have construed this to mean that in federal courts counsel must be provided for defendants unable to employ counsel unless the right is competently and intelligently waived. Betts argued that this right is extended to indigent defendants in state courts by the Fourteenth Amendment. In response the Court stated that, while the Sixth Amendment laid down "no rule for the conduct of the States, the question recurs whether the constraint laid by the Amendment upon the national courts expresses a rule so fundamental and essential to a fair trial, and so, to due process of law, that it is made obligatory upon the States by the Fourteenth Amendment." In order to decide whether the Sixth Amendment's guarantee of counsel is of this fundamental nature, the Court in *Betts* set out and considered "[r]elevant data on the subject [afforded] by constitutional and statutory provisions subsisting in the colonies and the states prior to the inclusion of the Bill of Rights in the national Constitution, and in the constitutional, legislative, and judicial history of the States to the present date." On the basis of this historical data the Court concluded that "appointment of counsel is not a fundamental right, essential to a fair trial." It was for this reason the *Betts* Court refused to accept the contention that the Sixth Amendment's guarantee of counsel for indigent federal defendants was extended to or, in the words of that Court, "made obligatory upon the states by the Fourteenth Amendment." Plainly, had the Court concluded that appointment of counsel for an indigent criminal defendant was "a fundamental right, essential to a fair trial," it would have held that the Fourteenth Amendment requires appointment of counsel in a state court, just as the Sixth Amendment requires in a federal court.

[We] accept *Betts v. Brady*'s assumption, based as it was on our prior cases, that a provision of the Bill of Rights which is "fundamental and essential to a fair trial" is made obligatory upon the States by the Fourteenth Amendment. We think the Court in *Betts* was wrong, however, in concluding that the Sixth Amendment's guarantee of counsel is not one of these fundamental rights.

[The] fact is that in deciding as it did—that "appointment of counsel is not a fundamental right, essential to a fair trial"—the Court in *Betts v. Brady* made an abrupt break with its own well-considered precedents. In returning to these old precedents, sounder we believe than the new, we but restore constitutional principles established to achieve a fair system of justice. Not only these precedents but also reason and reflection require us to recognize that in our adversary system of criminal justice, any person haled into court, who is too poor to hire a lawyer, cannot be assured a fair trial unless counsel is provided for him. This seems to us to be an obvious truth. Governments, both state and federal, quite properly spend vast sums of money to establish machinery to try defendants accused of crime. Lawyers to prosecute are everywhere deemed essential to protect the public's interest in an orderly society. Similarly, there are few defendants charged with crime, few indeed, who fail to hire the best lawyers they can get to prepare and present their defenses. That government hires lawyers to prosecute and defendants who have the money hire lawyers to defend are the strongest indications of the wide-spread belief that lawyers in criminal courts are necessities, not luxuries. The right of one charged with crime to counsel may not be deemed fundamental and essential to fair trials in some countries, but it is in ours. From the very beginning, our state and national constitutions and laws have laid great emphasis on procedural and substantive safeguards designed to assure fair trials before impartial tribunals in which every defendant stands equal before the law. This noble ideal cannot be realized if the poor man charged with crime has to face his accusers without a lawyer to assist him. A defendant's need for a lawyer is nowhere better stated than in the moving words of Mr. Justice Sutherland in *Powell v. Alabama*[, 287 U.S. 45 (1932)]:

> "The right to be heard would be, in many cases, of little avail if it did not comprehend the right to be heard by counsel. Even the intelligent and educated layman has small and sometimes no skill in the science of law. If charged with crime, he is incapable, generally, of determining for himself whether the indictment is good or bad. He is unfamiliar with the rules of evidence. Left without the aid of counsel he may be put on trial without a proper charge, and convicted upon incompetent evidence, or evidence irrelevant to the issue or otherwise inadmissible. He lacks both the skill and knowledge adequately to prepare his defense, even though he have a perfect one. He requires the guiding hand of counsel at every step in the proceedings against him. Without it, though he be not guilty, he faces the danger of conviction because he does not know how to establish his innocence."

The Court in *Betts v. Brady* departed from the sound wisdom upon which the Court's holding in *Powell v. Alabama* rested. Florida, supported by two other States, has asked that *Betts v. Brady* be left intact. Twenty-two States, as friends of the Court, argue that *Betts* was "an anachronism when handed down" and that it should now be overruled. We agree.

Reversed.

MR. JUSTICE HARLAN, concurring.

[When] we hold a right or immunity [to] be "implicit in the concept of ordered liberty" and thus valid against the States, [we do not] automatically carry over an entire body of federal law and apply it in full sweep to the States. Any such concept would disregard the frequently wide disparity between the legitimate interests of the States and of the Federal Government, the divergent problems that they face, and the significantly different consequences of their actions. * * *

Notes

1. Representation for the literally millions of indigent criminal defendants charged in state and federal court each year is provided through a public-defender or contract-attorney system, or simply by an appropriate judge or judicial officer assigning the indigent's defense to a private attorney by order of appointment. An estimated $1.2 billion was spent on indigent criminal defense in the 100 largest counties in the United States in 1999, with about 73% spent by public defender programs, 21% by assigned counsel

programs, and about 6% on awarded contracts. Public defenders handled about 82% of the 4.2 million criminal cases in these counties, assigned counsel attorneys handled 15%, and contract attorneys about 3%. U.S. Dept. of Justice, Bur. of Justice Statistics, Indigent Defense Services in Large Counties, 1999 (rev. December 6 2000). Court-appointed counsel represented 66% of federal felony defendants in 1998. U.S. Dept. of Justice, Bur. of Justice Statistics, Defense Counsel in Criminal Cases (November 2000). Convicted defendants represented by assigned counsel were more likely than those who hired a private attorney to be sentenced to a term of incarceration. About 7 in 10 with appointed counsel and 5 in 10 with a private attorney were sentenced to a prison or jail term.

Unfortunately, skyrocketing caseloads and inadequate funding for such programs has led to what some commentators deem "a crisis of extraordinary proportions in many states throughout the country." Richard Klein & Robert Spangenberg, *The Indigent Defense Crisis* 25 (ABA Section of Criminal Justice 1993). *See also id.* ("Justice often does not reach impoverished urban centers or poor rural counties where limited funding for indigent defense cannot provide effective representation to those accused of crime."); Stephen B. Bright, *Turning Celebrated Principles Into Reality*, Champion 6 (January/February 2003):

> No constitutional right is celebrated so much in the abstract and observed so little in reality as the right to counsel. While leaders of the judiciary, legal profession and government give speeches every Law Day about the essential role of lawyers in protecting the individual rights of people accused of crimes, many states have yet to create and fund adequately independent programs for providing legal representation. As a result, some people—even people accused of felonies—enter guilty pleas and are sentenced to imprisonment without any representation. Others languish in jail for weeks or months—often for longer than any sentence they would receive—before being assigned a lawyer. Many receive only perfunctory representation—sometimes nothing more than hurried conversations with a court-appointed lawyer outside the courtroom or even in open court—before entering a guilty plea or going to trial. The poor person who is wrongfully convicted may face years in prison, or even execution, without any legal assistance to pursue avenues of post-conviction review.

2.   The Supreme Court has never defined "indigency" for purposes of an indigent criminal defendant's right to the appointment of counsel. States use varying formulae and income levels to define indigency for these purposes. The American Bar Association, in *ABA Standards for Criminal Justice, Providing Defense Services* Standard 5–7.1 (3d ed. 1992), has recommended the following standard be applied: "Counsel should be provided to persons who are financially unable to obtain adequate representation without substantial hardship. Counsel should not be denied because of a person's ability to pay part of the cost of representation, because friends or relatives have resources to obtain counsel, or because bond has been or can be posted."

ARGERSINGER v. HAMLIN

407 U.S. 25 (1972).

M R. J USTICE D OUGLAS delivered the opinion of the Court.

Petitioner, an indigent, was charged in Florida with carrying a concealed weapon, an offense punishable by imprisonment up to six months, a $1,000 fine, or both. [The] Florida Supreme Court [followed] the line we marked out in *Duncan v. Louisiana*, 391 U.S. 145, 159, as respects the right to trial by jury and held that the right to court-appointed counsel extends only to trials "for non-petty offenses punishable by more than six months imprisonment." [We] reverse.

[The] right to trial by jury, also guaranteed by the Sixth Amendment by reason of the Fourteenth, was limited by *Duncan* to trials where the potential punishment was imprisonment for six months or more. But [the] right to trial by jury has a different genealogy and is brigaded with a system of trial to a judge alone. [While] there is historical support for limiting the "deep commitment" to trial by jury to "serious criminal cases," there is no such support for a similar limitation on the right to assistance of counsel[.]

The Sixth Amendment [extended] the right to counsel beyond its common-law dimensions. But there is nothing in the language of the Amendment, its history, or in the decisions of this Court, to indicate that it was intended to embody a retraction of the right in petty offenses wherein the common law previously did require that counsel be provided.

[The] assistance of counsel is often a requisite to the very existence of a fair trial. [The] requirement of counsel may well be necessary for a fair trial even in a petty-offense prosecution. We are by no means convinced that legal and constitutional questions involved in a case that actually leads to imprisonment even for a brief period are any less complex than when a person can be sent off for six months or more.

Beyond the problem of trials and appeals is that of the guilty plea, a problem which looms large in misdemeanor as well as in felony cases. Counsel is needed so that the accused may know precisely what he is doing, so that he is fully aware of the prospect of going to jail or prison, and so that he is treated fairly by the prosecution.

In addition, the volume of misdemeanor cases, far greater in number than felony prosecutions, may create an obsession for speedy dispositions, regardless of the fairness of the result. [We] must conclude, therefore, that the problems associated with misdemeanor and petty offenses often require the presence of counsel to insure the accused a fair trial. Mr. Justice Powell suggests that these problems are raised even in situations where there is no prospect of imprisonment. We need not consider the requirements of the Sixth Amendment as regards the right to counsel where loss of liberty is not involved, however, for here petitioner was in fact sentenced to jail. And, as we said in *Baldwin*, "the prospect of imprisonment for however short a time will seldom be viewed by the accused as a trivial or 'petty' matter and may well result in quite serious repercussions affecting his career and his reputation."

We hold, therefore, that absent a knowing and intelligent waiver, no person may be imprisoned for any offense, whether classified as petty, misdemeanor, or felony, unless he was represented by counsel at his trial.

[We] do not sit as an ombudsman to direct state courts how to manage their affairs but only to make clear the federal constitutional requirement. How crimes should be classified is largely a state matter. The fact that traffic charges technically fall within the category of "criminal prosecutions" does not necessarily mean that many of them will be brought into the class where imprisonment actually occurs.

[Under] the rule we announce today, every judge will know when the trial of a misdemeanor starts that no imprisonment may be imposed, even though local law permits it, unless the accused is represented by counsel. He will have a measure of the seriousness and gravity of the offense and therefore know when to name a lawyer to represent the accused before the trial starts.

The run of misdemeanors will not be affected by today's ruling. But in those that end up in the actual deprivation of a person's liberty, the accused will receive the benefit of "the guiding hand of counsel" so necessary when one's liberty is in jeopardy.

Reversed.

Mr. Chief Justice Burger, concurred in the result. Mr. Justice Brennan, with whom Mr. Justice Douglas and Mr. Justice Stewart joined, concurred, adding:

[Law] students [may] provide an important source of legal representation for the indigent. [More] than 125 of the country's 147 accredited law schools have established clinical programs in which faculty supervised students aid clients in a variety of civil and criminal matters. These programs supplement practice rules enacted in 38 States authorizing students to practice law under prescribed conditions. [Most] of these regulations permit students to make supervised court appearances as defense counsel in criminal cases. Given the huge increase in law school enrollments over the past few years, [law] students can be expected to make a significant contribution, quantitatively and qualitatively, to the representation of the poor in many [areas].

Mr. Justice Powell, with whom Mr. Justice Rehnquist joins, concurring in the result.

[The] flat six-month rule of the Florida court and the equally inflexible rule of the majority opinion apply to all cases within their defined areas regardless of circumstances. It is precisely because of this mechanistic application that I find these alternatives unsatisfactory. Due process [embodies] principles of fairness rather than immutable line drawing as to every aspect of a criminal trial. While counsel is often essential to a fair trial, this is by no means a universal fact. Some petty offense cases are complex; others are exceedingly simple. [Where] the possibility of a jail sentence is remote and the probable fine seems small, or where the evidence of guilt is overwhelming, the costs of assistance of counsel may exceed the benefits. It is anomalous that the Court's opinion today will extend the right of appointed counsel to indigent defendants in cases where the right to counsel would rarely be exercised by nonindigent defendants.

[It] would be illogical—and without discernible support in the Constitution—to hold that no discretion may ever be exercised where a nominal jail sentence is contemplated and at the same time endorse the legitimacy of discretion in "non-jail" petty-offense cases which may result in far more serious consequences than a few hours or days of incarceration. [I] would hold that the right to counsel in petty-offense cases is not absolute but is one to be determined by the trial courts exercising a judicial discretion on a case-by-case basis. * * *

Notes

1.   In *Scott v. Illinois*, 440 U.S. 367 (1979), Scott was convicted of theft and fined $50 after a bench trial in which he was unrepresented. The applicable Illinois statute set the maximum penalty for theft at a $500 fine and/or one year in jail. Scott challenged his conviction on the basis that *Argersinger* requires state provision of counsel whenever imprisonment is an authorized penalty. The Court rejected this challenge: "[T]he central premise of *Argersinger*—that actual imprisonment is a penalty different in kind from fines or the mere threat of imprisonment—is eminently sound and warrants adoption of actual imprisonment as the line defining the constitutional right to appointment of counsel." Justice Brennan dissented: "The offense of 'theft' [is] certainly not a 'petty' one. It is punishable by a sentence of up to one year in jail. [I]t carries the moral stigma associated with common-law crimes traditionally recognized as indicative of moral depravity. [Scott's] right to the assistance of appointed counsel is thus plainly mandated by the logic of the Court's prior cases, including *Argersinger* [itself]."

2.   In *Alabama v. Shelton*, 535 U.S. 654 (2002), the Supreme Court ruled 5–to–4 that the *Argersinger* and *Scott* day-in-jail rule applies to defendants who receive suspended sentences rather than actual incarceration. Shelton was convicted of third-degree assault and sentenced to 30 days in jail, but the trial court immediately suspended the sentence, placing him on probation for two years. The majority held that "the Sixth Amendment right to appointed counsel, as delineated in *Argersinger* and *Scott*, applies to a defendant in Shelton's situation. We hold that a suspended sentence that may 'end up in the actual deprivation of a person's liberty' may not be imposed unless the defendant was accorded 'the guiding hand of counsel' in the prosecution for the crime charged." The Court added that "[a] suspended sentence is a prison term imposed for the offense of conviction. Once the prison term is triggered, the defendant is incarcerated not for the probation

violation, but for the underlying offense. The uncounseled conviction at that point 'result[s] in imprisonment'; it 'end[s] up in the actual deprivation of a person's liberty.' This is precisely what the Sixth Amendment, as interpreted in *Argersinger* and *Scott*, does not allow."

3. In *Baldasar v. Illinois*, 446 U.S. 222 (1980), the Supreme Court held that an uncounseled misdemeanor conviction, although lawful under *Scott*, could not be used to enhance a defendant's sentence for a subsequent misdemeanor conviction into a felony conviction under a sentencing enhancement statute. Subsequently, however, the Court reversed itself, overruling *Baldasar*, and holding that "an uncounseled misdemeanor conviction, valid under *Scott* because no prison term was imposed, is also valid when used to enhance punishment at a subsequent conviction." *Nichols v. United States*, 511 U.S. 738, 749 (1994).

4. *Gideon* and *Scott* focus upon the right to counsel at trial. The text of the Sixth Amendment embraces, however, "all criminal *prosecutions*," not just criminal *trials*. The Supreme Court has ruled, accordingly, that the right to counsel attaches prior to trial, at any "critical stage of the criminal prosecution" after the "initiation of adversary judicial criminal proceedings—whether by way of formal charge, preliminary hearing, indictment, information, or arraignment." *Kirby v. Illinois*, 406 U.S. 682, 683, 689 (1972). A proceeding is a critical stage of the prosecution when "potential substantial prejudice to the defendant's rights inheres in the particular confrontation," and "the ability of counsel [can] help avoid that prejudice." *United States v. Wade*, 388 U.S. 218, 227 (1967). The right to counsel applies, for example, when a defendant appears at a sentencing proceeding, *Mempa v. Rhay*, 389 U.S. 128 (1967), and when a defendant appears at a preliminary hearing, *Coleman v. Alabama*, 399 U.S. 1 (1970).

5. A criminal defendant with adequate resources has the right to retain counsel of his or her choice. *United States v. Gonzalez–Lopez*, 126 S.Ct. 2557 (2006); *Chandler v. Fretag*, 348 U.S. 3 (1954). However, such retained counsel must be admitted to practice in the jurisdiction in which the trial is being held, unless the trial court exercises its discretion to grant counsel special admission to the Bar for purposes of that trial only ("*pro hac vice* admission"). *Leis v. Flynt*, 439 U.S. 438 (1979).

6. Unlike criminal defendants who have adequate resources to employ their own counsel, indigent defendants do not have a right to "choose" their counsel. As the Court explained in *Wheat v. United States*, 486 U.S. 153, 159 (1988), "the essential aim of the [Sixth] Amendment is to guarantee an effective advocate for each criminal defendant rather than to insure that a defendant will inexorably be represented by the lawyer whom he prefers. [A] defendant may not insist on representation by an attorney he cannot afford or who for other reasons declines to represent the defendant." A judge may, however, as a discretionary matter, appoint an attorney that an indigent defendant desires, assuming that such attorney is available and agrees to accept the (minimal) compensation that is typically provided for such appointed services.

Problems

1.   Herbert Deets owns and operates a large manufacturing facility near Louisville, Kentucky and has been charged criminally with violations of various state environmental statutes. The case is a complicated one involving complex environmental statutes and expert witnesses. Although these violations are punishable by both fines and imprisonment, the prosecutor has indicated that he intends to seek only fines. Nevertheless, Deets (whose company is insolvent and who is now indigent) requests the appointment of counsel to represent him. Under the *Gideon–Argersinger–Scott* line of cases, is he entitled to appointed counsel? What arguments can be made on his behalf? How might the prosecutor respond to this request?

2.   Does a respondent in a driver's license revocation proceeding have a right to appointed counsel? Would your answer be any different if the judge made it clear in advance that no jail time would be imposed?

3.   *Should a defendant's choice of counsel control when the accused has a special relationship with a particular attorney who wants to undertake the representation?* Defendants Emily and William Harris, members of the so-called "Symbionese Liberation Army," were charged with kidnapping, robbery, assault with a deadly weapon and false imprisonment. Defendants asked the trial judge to appoint attorneys Susan Johnson and Leonard Weinberg to represent them. Both attorneys were willing to undertake the representation, had represented defendants in a prior related proceeding, and purported to have a special relationship with defendants. Many of the witnesses in the prior proceeding were likely to be witnesses in this proceeding. The defendants also asserted that these attorneys shared their political and social beliefs so that there was a sense of mutual trust and confidence between them. Defendants had come to regard the attorneys as true champions of their cause. In their view, to appoint "strangers" in whom they had no such confidence and trust would be to deprive them of a true representation of their interests. *Should* the judge grant defendants' motion to appoint these attorneys? How would you argue this case for the State? How might defendants respond? How would you rule? Suppose that the judge felt that it would be better to appoint other attorneys based on their reputation among the local bench and bar, their experience in the trial of capital cases, and the fact that the other attorneys were certified as criminal law specialists by the State Bar? *See Harris v. Superior Court*, 19 Cal.3d 786, 567 P.2d 750, 140 Cal.Rptr. 318 (In Banc, 1977).

B.   WAIVER OF THE RIGHT TO COUNSEL

IOWA v. TOVAR

541 U.S. 77 (2004).

JUSTICE GINSBURG delivered the opinion of the Court.

The Sixth Amendment safeguards to an accused who faces incarceration the right to counsel at all critical stages of the criminal process. The entry of a guilty plea, whether to a misdemeanor or a felony charge, ranks as a "critical stage" at which the right to counsel adheres. Waiver of the right to counsel, as of constitutional rights in the criminal process generally, must be a "knowing, intelligent ac[t] done with sufficient awareness of the relevant circumstances." This case concerns the extent to which a trial judge, before accepting a guilty plea from an uncounseled defendant, must elaborate on the right to representation.

Beyond affording the defendant the opportunity to consult with counsel prior to entry of a plea and to be assisted by counsel at the plea hearing, must the court, specifically: (1) advise the defendant that "waiving the assistance of counsel in deciding whether to plead guilty [entails] the risk that a viable defense will be overlooked"; and (2) "admonis[h]" the defendant "that by waiving his right to an attorney he will lose the opportunity to obtain an independent opinion on whether, under the facts and applicable law, it is wise to plead guilty"? The Iowa Supreme Court held both warnings essential to the "knowing and intelligent" waiver of the Sixth Amendment right to the assistance of counsel.

We hold that neither warning is mandated by the Sixth Amendment. The constitutional requirement is satisfied when the trial court informs the accused of the nature of the charges against him, of his right to be counseled regarding his plea, and of the range of allowable punishments attendant upon the entry of a guilty plea.

On November 2, 1996, respondent Felipe Edgardo Tovar, then a 21–year-old college student, was arrested in Ames, Iowa, for operating a motor vehicle while under the influence of alcohol (OWI). [At] arraignment, the court's inquiries of Tovar began: "Mr. Tovar appears without counsel and I see, Mr. Tovar, that you waived application for a court appointed attorney. Did you want to represent yourself at today's hearing?" Tovar replied: "Yes, sir." The court soon after asked: "[H]ow did you wish to plead?" Tovar answered: "Guilty." Tovar affirmed that he had not been promised anything or threatened in any way to induce him to plead guilty.

Conducting the guilty plea colloquy required by the Iowa Rules of Criminal Procedure, the court explained that, if Tovar pleaded not guilty, he would be entitled to a speedy and public trial by jury, and would have the right to be represented at that trial by an attorney, who "could help [Tovar] select a jury, question and cross-examine the State's witnesses, present evidence, if any, in [his] behalf, and make arguments to the judge and jury on [his] behalf." By pleading guilty, the court cautioned, "not only [would Tovar] give up [his] right to a trial [of any kind on the charge against him], [he would] give up [his] right to be represented by an attorney at that trial." The court further advised Tovar that, if he entered a guilty plea, he would relinquish the right to remain silent at trial, the right to the presumption of innocence, and the right to subpoena witnesses and compel their testimony.

Turning to the particular offense with which Tovar had been charged, the court informed him that an OWI conviction carried a maximum penalty of a year in jail and a $1,000 fine, and a minimum penalty of two days in jail and a $500 fine. Tovar affirmed that he understood his exposure to those penalties. The court next explained that, before accepting a guilty plea, the court had to assure itself that Tovar was in fact guilty of the charged offense. To that end, the court informed Tovar that the OWI charge had only two elements: first, on the date in question, Tovar was operating a motor vehicle in the State of Iowa; second, when he did so, he was intoxicated. Tovar confirmed that he had been driving [on] the night he was apprehended and that he did not dispute the results of the intoxilyzer test administered by the police that night, which showed that his blood alcohol level exceeded the legal limit nearly twice over.

After the plea colloquy, the court asked Tovar if he still wished to plead guilty, and Tovar affirmed that he did. The court then accepted Tovar's plea, observing that there was "a factual basis" for it, and that Tovar had made the plea "voluntarily, with a full understanding of [his] rights, [and] of the consequences of [pleading guilty]."

On December 30, 1996, Tovar appeared for sentencing on the OWI charge[.] Noting that Tovar was again in attendance without counsel, the court inquired: "Mr. Tovar, did you want to represent yourself at today's hearing or did you want to take some time to hire an attorney to represent you?" Tovar replied that he would represent himself. The court then engaged in essentially the same plea colloquy on the suspension charge as it had on the OWI charge the previous month. After accepting Tovar's guilty plea[,] the court imposed the minimum sentence of two days in jail and a $500 fine, plus a surcharge and costs[.]

On March 16, 1998, Tovar was convicted of OWI for a second time. He was represented by counsel in that proceeding, in which he pleaded guilty. [On] December 14, 2000, Tovar was again charged with OWI, this time as a third offense[. Represented] by an attorney, Tovar pleaded not guilty[.]

In March 2001, through counsel, Tovar filed a [motion arguing that] Tovar's first OWI conviction, in 1996, could not be used to enhance the December 2000 OWI charge from a second-offense aggravated misdemeanor to a third-offense felony. [Tovar] did not allege that he was unaware at the November 1996 arraignment of his right to counsel prior to pleading guilty and at the plea hearing. Instead, he maintained that his 1996 waiver of counsel was invalid—not "full knowing, intelligent, and voluntary"—because he "was never made aware by the court [of] the dangers and disadvantages of self-representation."

The court denied Tovar's motion. [Tovar] then waived his right to a jury trial and was found guilty[. On] the OWI third-offense charge, he received a 180–day jail term, with all but 30 days suspended, three years of probation, and a $2,500 fine plus surcharges and costs. [The] Iowa Court of Appeals affirmed, but the Supreme Court of Iowa [reversed, holding] that the colloquy preceding acceptance of Tovar's 1996 guilty plea had been constitutionally inadequate[. We] granted certiorari [and] we now reverse[.]

The Sixth Amendment secures to a defendant who faces incarceration the right to counsel at all "critical stages" of the criminal process. A plea hearing qualifies as a "critical stage." Because Tovar received a two-day prison term for his 1996 OWI conviction, he had a right to counsel both at the plea stage and at trial had he elected to contest the charge.

A person accused of crime, however, may choose to forgo representation. While the Constitution "does not force a lawyer upon a defendant," it does require that any waiver of the right to counsel be knowing, voluntary, and intelligent. Tovar contends that his waiver of counsel [at] his first OWI plea hearing, was insufficiently informed, and therefore constitutionally invalid. In particular, he asserts that the trial judge did not elaborate on the value, at that stage of the case, of an attorney's advice and the dangers of self-representation in entering a plea.

We have described a waiver of counsel as intelligent when the defendant "knows what he is doing and his choice is made with eyes open." We have not, however, prescribed any formula or script to be read to a defendant who states that he elects to proceed without counsel. The information a defendant must possess in order to make an intelligent election [will] depend on a range of case-specific factors, including the defendant's education or sophistication, the complex or easily grasped nature of the charge, and the stage of the proceeding.

[B]efore a defendant may be allowed to proceed *pro se,* he must be warned specifically of the hazards ahead. [In] *Faretta v. California*[,] we cautioned: "Although a defendant need not himself have the skill and experience of a lawyer in order competently and intelligently to choose self-representation, he should be made aware of the dangers and disadvantages of self-representation, so that the record will establish that he knows what he is doing. . . ."

[In] Tovar's case, [he] first indicated that he waived counsel at his Initial Appearance, affirmed that he wanted to represent himself at the plea hearing, and declined the court's offer of "time to hire an attorney" at sentencing, when it was still open to him to request withdrawal of his plea. . . . "Does the Sixth Amendment require a court to give a rigid and detailed admonishment to a *pro se* defendant pleading guilty of the usefulness of an attorney, that an attorney may provide an independent opinion whether it is wise to plead guilty and that without an attorney the defendant risks overlooking a defense?" [This] Court recently explained, in reversing a lower court determination that a guilty plea was not voluntary: "[T]he law ordinarily considers a waiver knowing, intelligent, and sufficiently aware if the defendant fully understands the nature of the right and how it would likely apply *in general* in the circumstances—even though the defendant may not know the *specific detailed* consequences of invoking it." We [have] similarly observed[:] "If [the defendant] . . . lacked a full and complete appreciation of all of the consequences flowing from his waiver, it does not defeat the State's showing that the information it provided to him satisfied the constitutional minimum."

[In] a collateral attack on an uncounseled conviction, it is the defendant's burden to prove that he did not competently and intelligently waive his right to the assistance of counsel. [Tovar] has never claimed that he did not fully understand the charge or the range of punishment for the crime prior to pleading guilty. Further, he has never "articulate[d] with precision" the additional information counsel could have provided, given the simplicity of the charge. Nor does he assert that he *was* unaware of his right to be counseled prior to and at his arraignment. [H]e suggests only that he "*may have been* under the mistaken belief that he had a right to counsel at trial, but not if he was merely going to plead guilty."

[We] note, finally, that States are free to adopt by statute, rule, or decision any guides to the acceptance of an uncounseled plea they deem useful. We hold only that the two admonitions the Iowa Supreme Court ordered are not required by the Federal Constitution.

[For] the reasons stated, the judgment of the Supreme Court of Iowa is reversed[.]

FARETTA v. CALIFORNIA

422 U.S. 806 (1975).

MR. JUSTICE STEWART delivered the opinion of the Court.

The Sixth and Fourteenth Amendments of our Constitution guarantee that a person brought to trial in any state or federal court must be afforded the right to the assistance of counsel before he can be validly convicted and punished by imprisonment. This clear constitutional rule has emerged from a series of cases decided here over the last 50 years. The question before us now is whether a defendant in a state criminal trial has a constitutional right to proceed *without* counsel when he voluntarily and intelligently elects to do so. Stated another way, the question is whether a State may constitutionally hale a person into its criminal courts and there force a lawyer upon him, even when he insists that he wants to conduct his own defense. It is not an easy question, but we have concluded that a State may not constitutionally do so.

Anthony Faretta was charged with grand theft in an information filed in the Superior Court of Los Angeles County, Cal. At the arraignment, the Superior Court Judge assigned to preside at the trial appointed the public defender to represent Faretta. Well before the date of trial, however, Faretta requested that he be permitted to represent himself. Questioning by the judge revealed that Faretta had once represented himself in a criminal prosecution, that he had a high school education, and that he did not want to be represented by the public defender because he believed that office was "very loaded down with [a] heavy case load." The judge responded that he believed Faretta was "making a mistake" and emphasized that in further proceedings Faretta would receive no special favors. Nevertheless, after establishing that Faretta wanted to represent himself and did not want a lawyer, the judge, in a "preliminary ruling," accepted Faretta's waiver of the assistance of counsel. The judge indicated, however, that he might reverse this ruling if it later appeared that Faretta was unable adequately to represent himself.

Several weeks thereafter, but still prior to trial, the judge *sua sponte* held a hearing to inquire into Faretta's ability to conduct his own defense, and questioned him specifically about both the hearsay rule and the state law governing the challenge of potential jurors. After consideration of Faretta's answers, and observation of his demeanor, the judge ruled that Faretta had not made an intelligent and knowing waiver of his right to the assistance of counsel, and also ruled that Faretta had no constitutional right to conduct his own defense. The judge, accordingly, reversed his earlier ruling permitting self-representation and again appointed the public defender to represent Faretta. Faretta's subsequent request for leave to act as co-counsel was rejected, as were his efforts to make certain motions on his own behalf. Throughout the subsequent trial, the judge required that Faretta's defense be conducted only through the appointed lawyer from the public defender's office. At the conclusion of the trial, the jury found Faretta guilty as charged, and the judge sentenced him to prison. [The] California Court of Appeal [affirmed] the trial judge's ruling that Faretta had no federal or state constitutional right to represent himself.

[In] the federal courts, the right of self-representation has been protected by statute since the beginnings of our Nation. [In] *Adams v. United States ex rel. McCann*, 317 U.S. 269, 279 [(1942)], the Court recognized that the Sixth Amendment right to the assistance of counsel implicitly embodies a "correlative right to dispense with a lawyer's help." The defendant in that case, indicted for federal mail fraud violations, insisted on conducting his own defense without benefit of counsel. He also requested a bench trial and signed a waiver of his right to trial by jury. The prosecution consented to the waiver of a jury, and the waiver was accepted by the court. The defendant was convicted, but the Court of Appeals reversed the conviction on the ground that a person accused of a felony could not competently waive his right to trial by jury except upon the advice of a lawyer. This Court reversed and reinstated the conviction, holding that "an accused, in the exercise of a free and intelligent choice, and with the considered approval of the court, may waive trial by jury, and so likewise may he competently and intelligently waive his Constitutional right to assistance of counsel."

The *Adams* case does not, of course, necessarily resolve the issue before us. It held only that "the Constitution does not force a lawyer upon a defendant." Whether the Constitution forbids a State from forcing a lawyer upon a defendant is a different question. But the Court in *Adams* did recognize, albeit in dictum, an affirmative right of self-representation:

"The right to assistance of counsel and the *correlative right to dispense with a lawyer's help* are not legal formalisms. They rest on considerations that go to the substance of an accused's position before the law . . .

"[What] were contrived as protections for the accused should not be turned into fetters. [To] deny an accused a choice of procedure in circumstances in which he, though a layman, is as capable as any lawyer of making an intelligent choice, is to impair the worth of great Constitutional safeguards by treating them as empty verbalisms.

"[When] the administration of the criminal law [is] hedged about as it is by the Constitutional safeguards for the protection of an accused, to deny him in the exercise of his free choice the right to dispense with some of these safeguards [is] to imprison a man in his privileges and call it the Constitution."

[This] Court's past recognition of the right of self-representation, the federal-court authority holding the right to be of constitutional dimension, and the state constitutions pointing to the right's fundamental nature form a consensus not easily ignored. [We] confront here a nearly universal conviction, on the part of our people as well as our courts, that forcing a lawyer upon an unwilling defendant is contrary to his basic right to defend himself if he truly wants to do so.

This consensus is soundly premised. The right of self-representation finds support in the structure of the Sixth Amendment, as well as in the English and colonial jurisprudence from which the Amendment emerged. [Because Sixth Amendment] rights are basic to our adversary system of criminal justice, they are part of the "due process of law" that is guaranteed by the Fourteenth Amendment to defendants in the criminal courts of the States. [The] Sixth Amendment does not provide merely that a defense shall be made for the accused; it grants to the accused personally the right to make his defense. It is the accused, not counsel, who must be "informed of the nature and cause of the accusation," who must be "confronted with the witnesses against him," and who must be accorded "compulsory process for obtaining witnesses in his favor." Although not stated in the Amendment in so many words, the right to self-representation—to make one's own defense personally—is thus necessarily implied by the structure of the Amendment. The right to defend is given directly to the accused; for it is he who suffers the consequences if the defense fails.

The counsel provision supplements this design. It speaks of the "assistance" of counsel, and an assistant, however expert, is still an assistant. The language and spirit of the Sixth Amendment contemplate that counsel, like the other defense tools guaranteed by the Amendment, shall be an aid to a willing defendant—not an organ of the State interposed between an unwilling defendant and his right to defend himself personally. To thrust counsel upon the accused, against his considered wish, thus violates the logic of the Amendment. In such a case, counsel is not an assistant, but a master; and the right to make a defense is stripped of the personal character upon which the Amendment insists. It is true that when a defendant chooses to have a lawyer manage and present his case, law and tradition may allocate to the counsel the power to make binding decisions of trial strategy in many areas. This allocation can only be justified, however, by the defendant's consent, at the outset, to accept counsel as his representative. An unwanted counsel "represents" the defendant only through a tenuous and unacceptable legal fiction. Unless the accused has acquiesced in such representation, the defense presented is not the defense guaranteed him by the Constitution, for, in a very real sense, it is not *his* defense.

[There] can be no blinking the fact that the right of an accused to conduct his own defense seems to cut against the grain of this Court's decisions holding that the Constitution requires that no accused can be convicted and imprisoned unless he has been accorded the right to the assistance of counsel. For it is surely true that the basic thesis of those decisions is that the help of a lawyer is essential to assure the defendant a fair trial. And a strong argument can surely be made that the whole thrust of those decisions most inevitably lead to the conclusion that a State may constitutionally impose a lawyer upon even an unwilling defendant.

But it is one thing to hold that every defendant, rich or poor, has the right to the assistance of counsel, and quite another to say that a State may compel a defendant to accept a lawyer he does not want. The value of state-appointed counsel was not unappreciated by the Founders, yet the notion of compulsory counsel was utterly foreign to them. And whatever else may be said of those who wrote the Bill of Rights, surely there can be no doubt that they understood the inestimable worth of free choice.

It is undeniable that in most criminal prosecutions defendants could better defend with counsel's guidance than by their own unskilled efforts. But where the defendant will not voluntarily accept representation by counsel, the potential advantage of a lawyer's training and experience can be realized, if at all, only imperfectly. To force a lawyer on a defendant can only lead him to believe that the law contrives against him. Moreover, it is not inconceivable that in some rare instances, the defendant might in fact present his case more effectively by conducting his own defense. Personal liberties are not rooted in the law of averages. The right to defend is personal. The defendant, and not his lawyer or the State, will bear the personal consequences of a conviction. It is the defendant, therefore, who must be free personally to decide whether in his particular case counsel is to his advantage. And although he may conduct his own defense ultimately to his own detriment, his choice must be honored out of "that respect for the individual which is the lifeblood of the law."[1]

---

1. We are told that many criminal defendants representing themselves may use the courtroom for deliberate disruption of their trials. But the right of self-representa-

When an accused manages his own defense, he relinquishes, as a purely factual matter, many of the traditional benefits associated with the right to counsel. For this reason, in order to represent himself, the accused must "knowingly and intelligently" forgo those relinquished benefits. Although a defendant need not himself have the skill and experience of a lawyer in order competently and intelligently to choose self-representation, he should be made aware of the dangers and disadvantages of self-representation, so that the record will establish that "he knows what he is doing and his choice is made with eyes open."

Here, weeks before trial, Faretta clearly and unequivocally declared to the trial judge that he wanted to represent himself and did not want counsel. The record affirmatively shows that Faretta was literate, competent, and understanding, and that he was voluntarily exercising his informed free will. The trial judge had warned Faretta that he thought it was a mistake not to accept the assistance of counsel, and that Faretta would be required to follow all the "ground rules" of trial procedure. We need make no assessment of how well or poorly Faretta had mastered the intricacies of the hearsay rule and the California code provisions that govern challenges of potential jurors on *voir dire*. For his technical legal knowledge, as such, was not relevant to an assessment of his knowing exercise of the right to defend himself.

In forcing Faretta, under these circumstances, to accept against his will a state-appointed public defender, the California courts deprived him of his constitutional right to conduct his own defense. Accordingly, the judgment before us is vacated[.]

MR. CHIEF JUSTICE BURGER, with whom MR. JUSTICE BLACKMUN and MR. JUSTICE REHNQUIST join, dissenting.

This case [is] another example of the judicial tendency to constitutionalize what is thought "good." That effort fails on its own terms here, because there is nothing desirable or useful in permitting every accused person, even the most uneducated and inexperienced, to insist upon conducting his own defense to criminal charges. [If] we were to assume that there will be widespread exercise of the newly discovered constitutional right to self-representation, it would almost certainly follow that there will be added congestion in the courts and that the quality of justice will suffer.* * *

MR. JUSTICE BLACKMUN, with whom THE CHIEF JUSTICE and MR. JUSTICE REHNQUIST join, dissenting.

tion has been recognized from our beginnings by federal law and by most of the States, and no such result has thereby occurred. Moreover, the trial judge may terminate self-representation by a defendant who deliberately engages in serious and obstructionist misconduct. Of course, a State may—even over objection by the accused—appoint a "standby counsel" to aid the accused if and when the accused requests help, and to be available to represent the accused in the event that termination of the defendant's self-representation is necessary.

[Whatever] else may or may not be open to him on appeal, a defendant who elects to represent himself cannot thereafter complain that the quality of his own defense amounted to a denial of "effective assistance of counsel."

[I] fear that the right to self-representation constitutionalized today frequently will cause procedural confusion without advancing any significant strategic interest of the defendant. I therefore dissent. [Although] the Court indicates that a *pro se* defendant necessarily waives any claim he might otherwise make of ineffective assistance of counsel, the opinion leaves open a host of other procedural questions. Must every defendant be advised of his right to proceed *pro se*? If so, when must that notice be given? [If] a defendant has elected to exercise his right to proceed *pro se*, does he still have a constitutional right to assistance of standby counsel? How soon [must] a defendant decide between proceeding by counsel or *pro se*? Must he be allowed to switch in midtrial? [If] there is any truth to the old proverb that "one who is his own lawyer has a fool for a client," the Court by its opinion today now bestows a *constitutional* right on one to make a fool of himself.

Note

Not only must a waiver of Sixth Amendment rights be "knowing and intelligent," defendant must also be "competent." In *Godinez v. Moran*, 509 U.S. 389 (1993), the Supreme Court held that the standard of proof on the issue of whether a defendant is competent to waive his or her right to counsel (or to plead guilty), is precisely the same as required to demonstrate competency to stand trial. The Court explained the application of this test to waiver of counsel as follows: "The focus of a competency inquiry is the defendant's mental capacity; the question is whether he has the *ability* to understand the proceedings. The purpose of the 'knowing and voluntary' inquiry, by contrast, is to determine whether the defendant actually *does* understand the significance and consequences of a particular decision and whether the decision is uncoerced."

Problems

1. *Can the right to counsel be waived by silence?* Suppose that you are a federal district court judge. A defendant fails to assert her right to counsel, and fails to ask for appointment of counsel. Can you assume from these failures that she has waived her right to counsel?

2. The *Faretta* Court talks about a "knowing and intelligent" waiver of counsel and the *Tovar* Court similarly speaks of a waiver made by a defendant who "knows what he is doing." In most instances, criminal defendants do not know the rules of evidence, and have studied neither criminal law nor criminal procedure. Under these circumstances, how can there ever be a *truly* "knowing" and "intelligent" waiver of the right to counsel?

3. Assuming that defendants can make a less than intelligent choice, how do they do so? Again, you are a judge. A robbery defendant has stated that he is aware of his right to counsel, but that he prefers to proceed *pro se*. In light of *Faretta's* requirement that a waiver be "knowing and intelligent," how should you proceed? Should you accept his request at face value? Should you interrogate him about his knowledge of the rules of evidence and the

criminal law? Should it matter if he did not know, or was not able to recall, most of the exceptions to the hearsay rule?

4. A judge is required to inform a defendant of his or her right to counsel. As Justice Blackmun queried in his dissent in *Faretta*, must the judge also inform defendant of the right to proceed *pro se*?

5. If a *pro se* defendant has a valid objection to inadmissible evidence introduced by the prosecutor but fails to make the objection (because he or she doesn't know the applicable law), should the trial judge act *sua sponte* to keep the evidence out? Should the judge inform the *pro se* defendant of the law? Or should the judge say nothing and simply permit the prosecution to introduce otherwise inadmissible evidence?

6. You are the federal judge assigned to hear the Unabomber case. The defendant, Theodore Kaczysnki, is the individual who was charged with having murdered a number of people with mail bombs. Defendant wants to conduct his own defense, but his own attorneys question his competency. The reality is that Kaczysnki is very bright, but his sanity is questionable (to put it mildly). How do you decide whether Kaczynski is competent to represent himself? How much weight should you give to the fact that Kaczynski may not be insane, but is, any event, clearly not in sound mental health?

7. Should states be allowed to require a greater showing of competency before permitting a waiver of the right to counsel than for standing trial? Wisconsin has done so and its position has been upheld by the Seventh Circuit Court of Appeals. *See Brooks v. McCaughtry*, 380 F.3d 1009 (7th Cir.2004), *cert. denied*, 543 U.S. 1054 (2005) ("Because being competent to stand trial and having waived the right to counsel do not require the same information, and because the former competence does not imply an effective waiver in all cases, we do not think that Wisconsin's approach violates the rule of *Godinez*.") Do you agree? If a criminal defendant is competent to stand trial, isn't he or she competent to proceed pro se?

Exercise

You are the law clerk to a trial judge. Defendant Jane Jones has been charged with arson in your court and has demanded to proceed *pro se* at trial. She was examined by a clinical psychologist one year ago who found that Jones suffered from "an active psychotic disorder of a paranoid type" and has "auditory hallucinations, delusions of a bizarre and persecutory nature, and is intent on using the legal process as a vehicle for acting out many of her paranoid psychotic preoccupations." After interrogating Jones at length, your judge has told you that she believes that Jones understands the seriousness of the charge filed against her and comprehends the disadvantages of proceeding *pro se*, and that Jones told her that although she heard voices in the past, she no longer does. The file also discloses that Jones has extensive familiarity with the courts in that she has previously filed seventeen motions in state court, eleven in federal court, and has instituted two Court of Claims actions, one for damages for false arrest and the other for an assault allegedly committed on her at a state mental institution. Your judge has asked you to provide her with a bench memo (of no longer than 5 double-spaced pages) that summarizes the applicable federal law on this subject and recommends to her whether or not she should permit Jones to proceed *pro se*.

* * *

The *Faretta* Court indicated in a footnote that trial judges could appoint "standby counsel" to assist *pro se* defendants in presenting their cases, or simply to be available when and if the *pro se* defendant decides that he or she would rather be represented by counsel. As the following decision illustrates, however, standby counsel's appropriate role is still controversial.

McKASKLE v. WIGGINS

465 U.S. 168 (1984).

JUSTICE O'CONNOR delivered the opinion of the Court.

In *Faretta v. California*, this Court recognized a defendant's Sixth Amendment right to conduct his own defense. The Court also held that a trial court may appoint "standby counsel" to assist the *pro se* defendant in his defense. Today we must decide what role standby counsel who is present at trial over the defendant's objection may play consistent with the protection of the defendant's *Faretta* rights.

Carl Edwin Wiggins was convicted of robbery and sentenced to life imprisonment as a recidivist. [In his petition for federal habeas corpus relief, Wiggins argued that] standby counsel's conduct deprived him of his right to present his own defense, as guaranteed by *Faretta*. [The] Court of Appeals held that Wiggins' Sixth Amendment right of self-representation was violated by the unsolicited participation of overzealous standby counsel: "[T]he rule that we establish today is that court-appointed standby counsel is 'to be seen, but not heard.' By this we mean that he is not to compete with the defendant or supersede his defense. Rather, his presence is there for advisory purposes only, to be used or not used as the defendant sees fit." We do not accept the Court of Appeals' rule, and reverse its judgment.

[A] defendant's right to self-representation plainly encompasses certain specific rights to have his voice heard. The *pro se* defendant must be allowed to control the organization and content of his own defense, to make motions, to argue points of law, to participate in *voir dire*, to question witnesses, and to address the court and the jury at appropriate points in the trial. The record reveals that Wiggins was in fact accorded all of these rights.

Before trial Wiggins moved the trial court to order preparation of a transcript of the first trial. He, not standby counsel, then waived receipt of the transcript and announced ready for trial. He filed and argued at least 12 *pro se* motions in pretrial proceedings. Wiggins alone conducted the defense's *voir dire* of prospective jurors and made the opening statement for the defense to the jury.

Wiggins filed numerous *pro se* motions in the course of the trial. He cross-examined the prosecution's witnesses freely, and registered his own objections. Throughout the trial Wiggins selected the witnesses for the defense, examined them, decided that certain questions would *not* be asked by the defense, and decided which witnesses would not be called. Against counsel's advice, Wiggins announced that the defense rested. Wiggins filed his own requested charges to the jury, and made his own objections to the court's suggested charge. He obtained the removal of one of the court's proposed charges over counsel's express objection, approved the verdict form supplied to the jury, and gave a closing argument to the jury. Wiggins elected to go to the jury at the punishment phase of his trial, and he argued his case to the jury at that stage as well.

[Wiggins'] complaint is directed not at limits placed on *his* participation in the trial, for there clearly were none. [Wiggins] contends [that his right] to present his defense *pro se* was impaired by the distracting, intrusive, and unsolicited participation of counsel throughout the trial.

[*Faretta's*] logic [indicates] that no absolute bar on standby counsel's unsolicited participation is appropriate or was intended. The right to appear *pro se* exists to affirm the dignity and autonomy of the accused and to allow the presentation of what may, at least occasionally, be the accused's best possible defense. Both of these objectives can be achieved without categorically silencing standby counsel.

In determining whether a defendant's *Faretta* rights have been respected, the primary focus must be on whether the defendant had a fair chance to present his case in his own way. *Faretta* itself dealt with the defendant's affirmative right to participate, not with the limits on standby counsel's additional involvement. The specific rights to make his voice heard that Wiggins was plainly accorded form the core of a defendant's right of self-representation.

We recognize, nonetheless, that the right to speak for oneself entails more than the opportunity to add one's voice to a cacophony of others. As Wiggins contends, the objectives underlying the right to proceed *pro se* may be undermined by unsolicited and excessively intrusive participation by standby counsel. In proceedings before a jury the defendant may legitimately be concerned that multiple voices "for the defense" will confuse the message the defendant wishes to convey, thus defeating *Faretta's* objectives. Accordingly, the *Faretta* right must impose some limits on the extent of standby counsel's unsolicited participation.

First, the *pro se* defendant is entitled to preserve actual control over the case he chooses to present to the jury. This is the core of the *Faretta* right. If standby counsel's participation over the defendant's objection effectively allows counsel to make or substantially interfere with any significant tactical decisions, or to control the questioning of witnesses, or to speak *instead* of the defendant on any matter of importance, the *Faretta* right is eroded.

Second, participation by standby counsel without the defendant's consent should not be allowed to destroy the jury's perception that the defendant is representing himself. The defendant's appearance in the status of one conducting his own defense is important in a criminal trial, since the right to appear *pro se* exists to affirm the accused's individual dignity and autonomy. In related contexts the courts have recognized that a defendant has a right to be present at all important stages of trial, that he may not normally be forced to appear in court in shackles or prison garb, and that he has a right to present testimony in his own behalf. Appearing before the jury in the status of one who is defending himself may be equally important to the *pro se* defendant. From the jury's perspective, the message conveyed by the defense may depend as much on the messenger as on the message itself. From the defendant's own point of view, the right to appear *pro se* can lose much of its importance if only the lawyers in the courtroom know that the right is being exercised.

Participation by standby counsel outside the presence of the jury engages only the first of these two limitations. A trial judge, who in any event receives a defendant's original *Faretta* request and supervises the protection of the right throughout the trial, must be considered capable of differentiating the claims presented by a *pro se* defendant from those presented by standby counsel. Accordingly, the appearance of a *pro se* defendant's self-representation will not be unacceptably undermined by counsel's participation outside the presence of the jury.

Thus, *Faretta* rights are adequately vindicated in proceedings outside the presence of the jury if the *pro se* defendant is allowed to address the court freely on his own behalf and if disagreements between counsel and the *pro se* defendant are resolved in the defendant's favor whenever the matter is one that would normally be left to the discretion of counsel.

Most of the incidents of which Wiggins complains occurred when the jury was not in the courtroom. In the jury's absence Wiggins' two standby counsel frequently explained to the trial judge their views and points of disagreement with Wiggins. Counsel made motions, dictated proposed strategies into the record, registered objections to the prosecution's testimony, urged the summoning of additional witnesses, and suggested questions that the defendant should have asked of witnesses. [On] several occasions Wiggins expressly adopted standby counsel's initiatives.

[On] several other occasions Wiggins strongly opposed the initiatives of counsel. He resisted counsel's suggestion that the trial be postponed so that the transcript of his prior trial could be prepared, and he waived counsel's right to a 10–day preparation period, which counsel wished to invoke. In the course of a pretrial discussion concerning a discovery request Wiggins indignantly demanded that counsel not participate further without invitation. Later, Wiggins successfully opposed the inclusion in the jury instructions of a charge that counsel felt should be included.

The most acrimonious exchange between [standby counsel] Graham and Wiggins occurred in the course of questioning a witness on *voir dire*. Wiggins suggests this exchange was typical of counsel's overbearing conduct, but he fails to place the incident in context. Wiggins had expressly agreed to have Graham conduct the *voir dire*, but Wiggins attempted to take over the questioning in midstream. Plainly exasperated, Graham used profanity and curtly directed Wiggins to "[s]it down."

Though several of these incidents are regrettable, we are satisfied that counsel's participation outside the presence of the jury fully satisfied the first standard we have outlined. Wiggins was given ample opportunity to present his own position to the court on every matter discussed. He was given time to think matters over, to explain his problems and concerns informally, and to speak to the judge off the record. Standby counsel participated actively, but for the most part in an orderly manner. [Equally] important, all conflicts between Wiggins and counsel were resolved in Wiggins' favor. The trial judge repeatedly explained to all concerned that Wiggins' strategic choices, not counsel's, would prevail. Not every motion made by Wiggins was granted, but in no instance was counsel's position adopted over Wiggins' on a matter that would normally be left to the defense's discretion.

Participation by standby counsel in the presence of the jury is more problematic. It is here that the defendant may legitimately claim that excessive involvement by counsel will destroy the appearance that the defendant is acting *pro se*. This, in turn, may erode the dignitary values that the right to self-representation is intended to promote and may undercut the defendant's presentation to the jury of his own most effective defense. Nonetheless, we believe that a categorical bar on participation by standby counsel in the presence of the jury is unnecessary.

[In] measuring standby counsel's involvement against the standards we have described, it is important not to lose sight of the defendant's own conduct. A defendant can waive his *Faretta* rights. Participation by counsel with a *pro se* defendant's express approval is, of course, constitutionally unobjectionable. A defendant's invitation to counsel to participate in the trial obliterates any claim that the participation in question deprived the defendant of control over his own defense. Such participation also diminishes any general claim that counsel unreasonably interfered with the defendant's right to appear in the status of one defending himself.

Although this is self evident, it is also easily overlooked. A defendant like Wiggins, who vehemently objects at the beginning of trial to standby counsel's very presence in the courtroom, may express quite different views as the trial progresses. Even when he insists that he is not waiving his *Faretta* rights, a *pro se* defendant's solicitation of or acquiescence in certain types of participation by counsel substantially undermines later protestations that counsel interfered unacceptably.

[The] record in this case reveals that Wiggins' *pro se* efforts were undermined primarily by his own, frequent changes of mind regarding counsel's role. Early in the trial Wiggins insisted he wished to proceed entirely without assistance, but shortly thereafter he expressly agreed that counsel should question a witness on *voir dire*. Wiggins objected vehemently to some of counsel's motions, but warmly embraced others. Initially Wiggins objected to standby counsel's presence; later he refused to allow the trial to proceed in their absence; in the end he agreed that counsel would make a closing statement for the defense. The only two long appearances by counsel at Wiggins' trial, one before the jury and one outside its presence, were both initiated with Wiggins' express approval. In these circumstances it is very difficult to determine how much of counsel's participation was in fact contrary to Wiggins' desires of the moment.

Faretta does not require a trial judge to permit "hybrid" representation of the type Wiggins was actually allowed. But if a defendant is given the opportunity and elects to have counsel appear before the court or jury, his complaints concerning counsel's subsequent unsolicited participation lose much of their force. A defendant does not have a constitutional right to choreograph special appearances by counsel. Once a *pro se* defendant invites or agrees to any substantial participation by counsel, subsequent appearances by counsel must be presumed to be with the defendant's acquiescence, at least until the defendant expressly and unambiguously renews his request that standby counsel be silenced.

[*Faretta*] rights are also not infringed when standby counsel assists the *pro se* defendant in overcoming routine procedural or evidentiary obstacles to the completion of some specific task, such as introducing evidence or objecting to testimony, that the defendant has clearly shown he wishes to complete. Nor are they infringed when counsel merely helps to ensure the defendant's compliance with basic rules of courtroom protocol and procedure. In neither case is there any significant interference with the defendant's actual control over the presentation of his defense. The likelihood that the defendant's appearance in the status of one defending himself will be eroded is also slight, and in any event it is tolerable. A defendant does not have a constitutional right to receive personal instruction from the trial judge on courtroom procedure. Nor does the Constitution require judges to take over chores for a *pro se* defendant that would normally be attended to by trained counsel as a matter of course.

[Accordingly,] we make explicit today what is already implicit in *Faretta*: A defendant's Sixth Amendment rights are not violated when a trial judge appoints standby counsel—even over the defendant's objection—to relieve the judge of the need to explain and enforce basic rules of courtroom protocol or to assist the defendant in overcoming routine obstacles that stand in the way of the defendant's achievement of his own clearly indicated goals. Participation by counsel to steer a defendant through the basic procedures of trial is permissible even in the unlikely event that it somewhat undermines the *pro se* defendant's appearance of control over his own defense.

At Wiggins' trial a significant part of standby counsel's participation both in and out of the jury's presence involved basic mechanics of the type we have described—informing the court of the whereabouts of witnesses, supplying Wiggins with a form needed to elect to go to the jury at the punishment phase of trial, explaining to Wiggins that he should not argue his case while questioning a witness, and so on. When Wiggins attempted to introduce a document into evidence, but failed to mark it for identification or to lay a predicate for its introduction, counsel, at the trial court's suggestion, questioned the witness to lay an appropriate predicate, and Wiggins then resumed his examination. Similarly, the trial judge repeatedly instructed Wiggins to consult with counsel, not with the court, regarding the appropriate procedure for summoning witnesses.

Notwithstanding Wiggins' several general objections to the presence and participation of counsel, we find these aspects of counsel's involvement irreproachable. None interfered with Wiggins' actual control over his defense; none can reasonably be thought to have undermined Wiggins' appearance before the jury in the status of a *pro se* defendant.

[Putting] aside participation that was either approved by Wiggins or attendant to routine clerical or procedural matters, counsel's unsolicited comments in front of the jury were infrequent and for the most part innocuous. On two occasions Graham interrupted a witness' answer to a question put by Wiggins. The first interruption was trivial. When the second was made the jury was briefly excused and subsequently given a cautionary instruction as requested by Graham. Wiggins made no objection. Standby counsel also moved for a mistrial three times in the presence of the jury. Each motion was in response to allegedly prejudicial questions or comments by the prosecutor. Wiggins did not comment on the first motion, but he opposed the following two. All three motions were immediately denied by the trial court. Regrettably, counsel used profanity to express his exasperation on the second occasion. Finally, counsel played an active role at the punishment phase of the trial. The record supplies no explanation for the sudden change in this regard. Wiggins made no objection to counsel's participation in this phase of the trial. We can only surmise that by then Wiggins had concluded that appearing *pro se* was not in his best interests.

The statements made by counsel during the guilt phase of the trial, in the presence of the jury and without Wiggins' express consent, occupy only a small portion of the transcript. Most were of an unobjectionable, mechanical sort. While standby counsel's participation at Wiggins' trial should not serve as a model for future trials, we believe that counsel's involvement fell short of infringing on Wiggins' *Faretta* rights. Wiggins unquestionably maintained actual control over the presentation of his own defense at all times.

We are also persuaded that Wiggins was allowed to appear before the jury in the status of one defending himself. At the outset the trial judge carefully explained to the jury that Wiggins would be appearing *pro se*. Wiggins, not counsel, examined prospective jurors on *voir dire*, cross-examined the prosecution's witnesses, examined his own witnesses, and made an opening statement for the defense. Wiggins objected to the prosecutor's case at least as often as did counsel. If Wiggins closing statement to the jury had to compete with one made by counsel, it was only because Wiggins agreed in advance to that arrangement.

By contrast, counsel's interruptions of Wiggins or witnesses being questioned by Wiggins in the presence of the jury were few and perfunctory. Most of counsel's uninvited comments were directed at the prosecutor. Such interruptions present little threat to a defendant's *Faretta* rights, at least when the defendant's view regarding those objections has not been clearly articulated. On the rare occasions that disagreements between counsel and Wiggins were aired in the presence of the jury the trial judge consistently ruled in Wiggins' favor. This was a pattern more likely to reinforce than to detract from the appearance that Wiggins was controlling his own defense. The intrusions by counsel at Wiggins' trial were simply not substantial or frequent enough to have seriously undermined Wiggins' appearance before the jury in the status of one representing himself.

Faretta affirmed the defendant's constitutional right to appear on stage at his trial. We recognize that a *pro se* defendant may wish to dance a solo, not a *pas de deux*. Standby counsel must generally respect that preference. But counsel need not be excluded altogether, especially when the participation is outside the presence of the jury or is with the defendant's express or tacit consent. The defendant in this case was allowed to make his own appearances as he saw fit. In our judgment counsel's unsolicited involvement was held within reasonable limits.

The judgment of the Court of Appeals is therefore

Reversed.

Justice White, with whom Justice Brennan and Justice Marshall join, dissenting.

[T]he trial court designated [two] appointed attorneys as standby counsel and made it clear that they served in a purely advisory capacity. One of the attorneys soon began to assume a more active role in the proceedings, and Wiggins protested that counsel's unsolicited participation was frustrating the conduct of his defense. The trial court informed Wiggins that he would receive counsel's aid whether he wanted it or not, and it refused to instruct standby counsel not to volunteer their assistance without a request from Wiggins.

[T]he trial did not go smoothly, for standby counsel "continuously participated in the proceedings, both in and outside the presence of the jury." In addition to making objections and motions too numerous to cite, counsel argued with Wiggins, moved for a mistrial against his wishes at several points during the trial, and twice cursed, once in the presence of the jury.

Although petitioner characterizes counsel's participation as "limited" and "intermittent," nothing could be farther from the truth. Standby counsel intervened in a substantial manner without Wiggins' permission well over 50 times during the course of the 3–day trial; many of these interruptions precipitated direct conflicts between Wiggins and counsel, often in the presence of the jury. Although the trial court appears to have resolved the conflicts calling for a ruling in Wiggins' favor, their mere existence disrupted the proceedings and turned the trial into an ordeal through which the jury was required to suffer. At several points during the trial, moreover, counsel blatantly interfered with Wiggins' attempt to present his defense in a manner not calling for a ruling from the bench, and we of course have no way of knowing the extent to which Wiggins' defense was subtly undermined or adversely affected by counsel's extensive unsolicited participation. [The] continuous and substantial intervention of standby counsel, despite Wiggins' repeated demands that he play a passive role, could not have had "anything but a negative impact on the jury. It also destroyed Wiggins' own perception that he was conducting *his* defense."

[Under] the Court's new test, it is necessary to determine whether the *pro se* defendant retained "actual control over the case he [chose] to present to the jury," and whether standby counsel's participation "destroy[ed] the jury's perception that the defendant [was] representing himself." Although this test purports to protect all of the values underlying our holding in *Faretta*, it is unclear whether it can achieve this result.

As long as the *pro se* defendant is allowed his say, the first prong of the Court's test accords standby counsel at a bench trial or any proceeding outside the presence of a jury virtually untrammeled discretion to present any factual or legal argument to which the defendant does not object.

[Although] the Court is more solicitous of a *pro se* defendant's interests when standby counsel intervenes before a jury, the test's second prong suffers from similar shortcomings. To the extent that trial and appellate courts can discern the point at which counsel's unsolicited participation substantially undermines a *pro se* defendant's appearance before the jury, a matter about which I harbor substantial doubts, their decisions will, to a certain extent, "affirm the accused's individual dignity and autonomy." But they will do so incompletely, for in focusing on how the jury views the defendant, the majority opinion ignores *Faretta's* emphasis on the defendant's own perception of the criminal justice system, and implies that the Court actually adheres to the result-oriented harmless error standard it purports to reject.

As a guide for standby counsel and lower courts, moreover, the Court's two-part test is clearly deficient. Instead of encouraging counsel to accept a limited role, the Court plainly invites them to participate despite their clients' contrary instructions until the clients renew their objections and trial courts draw the line. Trial courts required to rule on *pro se* defendants' objections to counsel's intervention also are left at sea. They clearly must prevent standby counsel from overtly muzzling their *pro se* clients and resolve certain conflicts in defendants' favor. But the Court's opinion places few, if any, other clear limits on counsel's uninvited participation; instead it requires trial courts to make numerous subjective judgments concerning the effect of counsel's actions on defendants' *Faretta* rights. [In] short, I believe that the Court's test is unworkable and insufficiently protective of the fundamental interests we recognized in *Faretta*.

Problems

1. *Would standby counsel's conduct have been tolerated had defendant been an attorney?* Suppose that you graduated from law school, passed the bar, and were assigned to represent a defendant in a criminal case. Your criminal procedure professor, interested to see how much you learned in law school, comes to observe. Unhappy with your performance, the professor offers interjections and suggestions while you are trying the case. Is a court likely to tolerate the professor's conduct? If not, should the court be any more willing to tolerate such conduct when a *pro se* defendant is involved? Given a defendant's constitutional right to proceed *pro se*, why doesn't the *pro se* defendant have the right to represent himself in the manner he deems most appropriate—free from *any* intrusions by standby counsel?

2. Suppose that you are a judge in a criminal case involving a *pro se* defendant and standby counsel. Prior to trial, would you give counsel any special instructions regarding his or her role? What instructions? Suppose that counsel subsequently intrudes in the case inappropriately. How should you (the trial judge) respond?

C. INEFFECTIVE ASSISTANCE OF COUNSEL

In *Powell v. Alabama*, 287 U.S. 45 (1932), the United States Supreme Court made it clear that a criminal defendant's constitutional right to counsel includes the right to the "effective" assistance of counsel. However, the Court did not establish a test to determine when defense counsel violates the Sixth Amendment due to ineffective assistance of counsel until 1984.

STRICKLAND v. WASHINGTON
466 U.S. 668 (1984).

JUSTICE O'CONNOR delivered the opinion of the Court.

This case requires us to consider the proper standards for judging a criminal defendant's contention that the Constitution requires a conviction or death sentence to be set aside because counsel's assistance at the trial or sentencing was ineffective.

[During] a 10–day period in September 1976, respondent planned and committed three groups of crimes, which included three brutal stabbing murders, torture, kidnaping, severe assaults, attempted murders, attempted extortion, and theft. After his two accomplices were arrested, respondent surrendered to police and voluntarily gave a lengthy statement confessing to the third of the criminal episodes. The State of Florida indicted respondent for kidnaping and murder and appointed an experienced criminal lawyer to represent him.

Counsel actively pursued pretrial motions and discovery. He cut his efforts short, however, and he experienced a sense of hopelessness about the case, when he learned that, against his specific advice, respondent had also confessed to the first two murders. By the date set for trial, respondent was subject to indictment for three counts of first-degree murder and multiple counts of robbery, kidnaping for ransom, breaking and entering and assault, attempted murder, and conspiracy to commit robbery. Respondent waived his right to a jury trial, again acting against counsel's advice, and pleaded guilty to all charges, including the three capital murder charges.

In the plea colloquy, respondent told the trial judge that, although he had committed a string of burglaries, he had no significant prior criminal record and that at the time of his criminal spree he was under extreme stress caused by his inability to support his family. He also stated, however, that he accepted responsibility for the crimes. The trial judge told respondent that he had "a great deal of respect for people who are willing to step forward and admit their responsibility" but that he was making no statement at all about his likely sentencing decision.

Counsel advised respondent to invoke his right under Florida law to an advisory jury at his capital sentencing hearing. Respondent rejected the advice and waived the right. He chose instead to be sentenced by the trial judge without a jury recommendation.

In preparing for the sentencing hearing, counsel spoke with respondent about his background. He also spoke on the telephone with respondent's wife and mother, though he did not follow up on the one unsuccessful effort to meet with them. He did not otherwise seek out character witnesses for respondent. Nor did he request a psychiatric examination, since his conversations with his client gave no indication that respondent had psychological problems.

Counsel decided not to present and hence not to look further for evidence concerning respondent's character and emotional state. That decision reflected trial counsel's sense of hopelessness about overcoming the evidentiary effect of respondent's confessions to the gruesome crimes. It also reflected the judgment that it was advisable to rely on the plea colloquy for evidence about respondent's background and about his claim of emotional stress: the plea colloquy communicated sufficient information about these subjects, and by forgoing the opportunity to present new evidence on these subjects, counsel prevented the State from cross-examining respondent on his claim and from putting on psychiatric evidence of its own.

Counsel also excluded from the sentencing hearing other evidence he thought was potentially damaging. He successfully moved to exclude respondent's "rap sheet." Because he judged that a presentence report might prove more detrimental than helpful, as it would have included respondent's criminal history and thereby would have undermined the claim of no significant history of criminal activity, he did not request that one be prepared.

At the sentencing hearing, counsel's strategy was based primarily on the trial judge's remarks at the plea colloquy as well as on his reputation as a sentencing judge who thought it important for a convicted defendant to own up to his crime. Counsel argued that respondent's remorse and acceptance of responsibility justified sparing him from the death penalty. Counsel also argued that respondent had no history of criminal activity and that respondent committed the crimes under extreme mental or emotional disturbance, thus coming within the statutory list of mitigating circumstances. He further argued that respondent should be spared death because he had surrendered, confessed, and offered to testify against a codefendant and because respondent was fundamentally a good person who had briefly gone badly wrong in extremely stressful circumstances. The State put on evidence and witnesses largely for the purpose of describing the details of the crimes. Counsel did not cross-examine the medical experts who testified about the manner of death of respondent's victims.

The trial judge found several aggravating circumstances with respect to each of the three murders. He found that all three murders were especially heinous, atrocious, and cruel, all involving repeated stabbings. All three murders were committed in the course of at least one other dangerous and violent felony, and since all involved robbery, the murders were for pecuniary gain. All three murders were committed to avoid arrest for the accompanying crimes and to hinder law enforcement. In the course of one of the murders, respondent knowingly subjected numerous persons to a grave risk of death by deliberately stabbing and shooting the murder victim's sisters-in-law, who sustained severe—in one case, ultimately fatal—injuries.

With respect to mitigating circumstances, the trial judge made the same findings for all three capital murders. First, although there was no admitted evidence of prior convictions, respondent had stated that he had engaged in a course of stealing. In any case, even if respondent had no significant history of criminal activity, the aggravating circumstances "would still clearly far outweigh" that mitigating factor. Second, the judge found that, during all three crimes, respondent was not suffering from extreme mental or emotional disturbance and could appreciate the criminality of his acts. Third, none of the victims was a participant in, or consented to, respondent's conduct. Fourth, respondent's participation in the crimes was neither minor nor the result of duress or domination by an accomplice. Finally, respondent's age (26) could not be considered a factor in mitigation, especially when viewed in light of respondent's planning of the crimes and disposition of the proceeds of the various accompanying thefts.

In short, the trial judge found numerous aggravating circumstances and no (or a single comparatively insignificant) mitigating circumstance. [He] therefore sentenced respondent to death on each of the three counts of murder and to prison terms for the other crimes. The Florida Supreme Court upheld the convictions and [sentences. In subsequent postconviction proceedings, a federal district court denied Strickland's petition for habeas corpus, but the court of appeals reversed.]

In a long line of cases that includes *Powell v. Alabama*, 287 U.S. 45 (1932), *Johnson v. Zerbst*, 304 U.S. 458 (1938), and *Gideon v. Wainwright*, 372 U.S. 335 (1963), this Court has recognized that the Sixth Amendment right to counsel exists, and is needed, in order to protect the fundamental right to a fair trial. [A] fair trial is one in which evidence subject to adversarial testing is presented to an impartial tribunal for resolution of issues defined in advance of the proceeding. The right to counsel plays a crucial role in the adversarial system embodied in the Sixth Amendment, since access to counsel's skill and knowledge is necessary to accord defendants the "ample opportunity to meet the case of the prosecution" to which they are entitled.

[T]he Court has recognized that "the right to counsel is the right to the effective assistance of counsel." Government violates the right to effective assistance when it interferes in certain ways with the ability of counsel to make independent decisions about how to conduct the defense. Counsel, however, can also deprive a defendant of the right to effective assistance, simply by failing to render "adequate legal assistance."

The Court has not elaborated on the meaning of the constitutional requirement of effective assistance in [cases] presenting claims of "actual ineffectiveness." In giving meaning to the requirement, however, we must take its purpose—to ensure a fair trial—as the guide. The benchmark for judging any claim of ineffectiveness must be whether counsel's conduct so undermined the proper functioning of the adversarial process that the trial cannot be relied on as having produced a just result.

The same principle applies to a capital sentencing proceeding such as that provided by Florida law. We need not consider the role of counsel in an ordinary sentencing, which may involve informal proceedings and standardless discretion in the sentencer, and hence may require a different approach to the definition of constitutionally effective assistance. A capital sentencing proceeding like the one involved in this case, however, is sufficiently like a trial in its adversarial format and in the existence of standards for decision, that counsel's role in the proceeding is comparable to counsel's role at trial—to ensure that the adversarial testing process works to produce a just result under the standards governing decision. For purposes of describing counsel's duties, therefore, Florida's capital sentencing proceeding need not be distinguished from an ordinary trial.

A convicted defendant's claim that counsel's assistance was so defective as to require reversal of a conviction or death sentence has two components. First, the defendant must show that counsel's performance was deficient. This requires showing that counsel made errors so serious that counsel was not functioning as the "counsel" guaranteed the defendant by the Sixth Amendment. Second, the defendant must show that the deficient performance prejudiced the defense. This requires showing that counsel's errors were so serious as to deprive the defendant of a fair trial, a trial whose result is reliable. Unless a defendant makes both showings, it cannot be said that the conviction or death sentence resulted from a breakdown in the adversary process that renders the result unreliable.

[T]he proper standard for attorney performance is that of reasonably effective assistance. [When] a convicted defendant complains of the ineffectiveness of counsel's assistance, the defendant must show that counsel's representation fell below an objective standard of reasonableness. More specific guidelines are not appropriate. The Sixth Amendment refers simply to "counsel," not specifying particular requirements of effective assistance. It relies instead on the legal profession's maintenance of standards sufficient to justify the law's presumption that counsel will fulfill the role in the adversary process that the Amendment envisions. The proper measure of attorney performance remains simply reasonableness under prevailing professional norms.

Representation of a criminal defendant entails certain basic duties. Counsel's function is to assist the defendant, and hence counsel owes the client a duty of loyalty, a duty to avoid conflicts of interest. From counsel's function as assistant to the defendant derive the overarching duty to advocate the defendant's cause and the more particular duties to consult with the defendant on important decisions and to keep the defendant informed of important developments in the course of the prosecution. Counsel also has a duty to bring to bear such skill and knowledge as will render the trial a reliable adversarial testing process.

These basic duties neither exhaustively define the obligations of counsel nor form a checklist for judicial evaluation of attorney performance. In any case presenting an ineffectiveness claim, the performance inquiry must be whether counsel's assistance was reasonable considering all the circumstances. Prevailing norms of practice as reflected in American Bar Association standards and the like, *e.g.*, ABA Standards for Criminal Justice 4–1.1 to 4–8.6 (2d ed. 1980) ("The Defense Function"), are guides to determining what is reasonable, but they are only guides. No particular set of detailed rules for counsel's conduct can satisfactorily take account of the variety of circumstances faced by defense counsel or the range of legitimate decisions regarding how best to represent a criminal defendant. Any such set of rules would interfere with the constitutionally protected independence of counsel and restrict the wide latitude counsel must have in making tactical decisions. Indeed, the existence of detailed guidelines for representation could distract counsel from the overriding mission of vigorous advocacy of the defendant's cause. Moreover, the purpose of the effective assistance guarantee of the Sixth Amendment is not to improve the quality of legal representation, although that is a goal of considerable importance to the legal system. The purpose is simply to ensure that criminal defendants receive a fair trial.

Judicial scrutiny of counsel's performance must be highly deferential. It is all too tempting for a defendant to second-guess counsel's assistance after conviction or adverse sentence, and it is all too easy for a court, examining counsel's defense after it has proved unsuccessful, to conclude that a particular act or omission of counsel was unreasonable. A fair assessment of attorney performance requires that every effort be made to eliminate the distorting effects of hindsight, to reconstruct the circumstances of counsel's challenged conduct, and to evaluate the conduct from counsel's perspective at the time. Because of the difficulties inherent in making the evaluation, a court must indulge a strong presumption that counsel's conduct falls within the wide range of reasonable professional assistance; that is, the defendant must overcome the presumption that, under the circumstances, the challenged action "might be considered sound trial strategy." There are countless ways to provide effective assistance in any given case. Even the best criminal defense attorneys would not defend a particular client in the same way.

The availability of intrusive post-trial inquiry into attorney performance or of detailed guidelines for its evaluation would encourage the proliferation of ineffectiveness challenges. Criminal trials resolved unfavorably to the defendant would increasingly come to be followed by a second trial, this one of counsel's unsuccessful defense. Counsel's performance and even willingness to serve could be adversely affected. Intensive scrutiny of counsel and rigid requirements for acceptable assistance could dampen the ardor and impair the independence of defense counsel, discourage the acceptance of assigned cases, and undermine the trust between attorney and client.

Thus, a court deciding an actual ineffectiveness claim must judge the reasonableness of counsel's challenged conduct on the facts of the particular case, viewed as of the time of counsel's conduct. A convicted defendant making a claim of ineffective assistance must identify the acts or omissions of counsel that are alleged not to have been the result of reasonable professional judgment. The court must then determine whether, in light of all the circumstances, the identified acts or omissions were outside the wide range of professionally competent assistance. In making that determination, the court should keep in mind that counsel's function, as elaborated in prevailing professional norms, is to make the adversarial testing process work in the particular case. At the same time, the court should recognize that counsel is strongly presumed to have rendered adequate assistance and made all significant decisions in the exercise of reasonable professional judgment.

These standards require no special amplification in order to define counsel's duty to investigate, the duty at issue in this case. As the Court of Appeals concluded, strategic choices made after thorough investigation of law and facts relevant to plausible options are virtually unchallengeable; and strategic choices made after less than complete investigation are reasonable precisely to the extent that reasonable professional judgments support the limitations on investigation. In other words, counsel has a duty to make reasonable investigations or to make a reasonable decision that makes particular investigations unnecessary. In any ineffectiveness case, a particular decision not to investigate must be directly assessed for reasonableness in all the circumstances, applying a heavy measure of deference to counsel's judgments.

The reasonableness of counsel's actions may be determined or substantially influenced by the defendant's own statements or actions. Counsel's actions are usually based, quite properly, on informed strategic choices made by the defendant and on information supplied by the defendant. In particular, what investigation decisions are reasonable depends critically on such information. For example, when the facts that support a certain potential line of defense are generally known to counsel because of what the defendant has said, the need for further investigation may be considerably diminished or eliminated altogether. And when a defendant has given counsel reason to believe that pursuing certain investigations would be fruitless or even harmful, counsel's failure to pursue those investigations may not later be challenged as unreasonable. In short, inquiry into counsel's conversations with the defendant may be critical to a proper assessment of counsel's investigation decisions, just as it may be critical to a proper assessment of counsel's other litigation decisions.

An error by counsel, even if professionally unreasonable, does not warrant setting aside the judgment of a criminal proceeding if the error had no effect on the judgment. The purpose of the Sixth Amendment guarantee of counsel is to ensure that a defendant has the assistance necessary to justify reliance on the outcome of the proceeding. Accordingly, any deficiencies in counsel's performance must be prejudicial to the defense in order to constitute ineffective assistance under the Constitution.

[Conflict] of interest claims aside, actual ineffectiveness claims alleging a deficiency in attorney performance are subject to a general requirement that the defendant affirmatively prove prejudice. The government is not responsible for, and hence not able to prevent, attorney errors that will result in reversal of a conviction or sentence. Attorney errors come in an infinite variety and are as likely to be utterly harmless in a particular case as they are to be prejudicial. They cannot be classified according to likelihood of causing prejudice. Nor can they be defined with sufficient precision to inform defense attorneys correctly just what conduct to avoid. Representation is an art, and an act or omission that is unprofessional in one case may be sound or even brilliant in another. Even if a defendant shows that particular errors of counsel were unreasonable, therefore, the defendant must show that they actually had an adverse effect on the defense.

It is not enough for the defendant to show that the errors had some conceivable effect on the outcome of the proceeding. Virtually every act or omission of counsel would meet that test, and not every error that conceivably could have influenced the outcome undermines the reliability of the result of the proceeding. Respondent suggests requiring a showing that the errors "impaired the presentation of the defense." That standard, however, provides no workable principle. Since any [error] "impairs" the presentation of the defense, the proposed standard is inadequate because it provides no way of deciding what impairments are sufficiently serious to warrant setting aside the outcome of the proceeding.

On the other hand, we believe that a defendant need not show that counsel's deficient conduct more likely than not altered the outcome in the case. This outcome-determinative standard has several strengths. It defines the relevant inquiry in a way familiar to courts, though the inquiry, as is inevitable, is anything but precise. The standard also reflects the profound importance of finality in criminal proceedings. Moreover, it comports with the widely used standard for assessing motions for new trial based on newly discovered evidence. Nevertheless, the standard is not quite appropriate.

Even when the specified attorney error results in the omission of certain evidence, the newly discovered evidence standard is not an apt source from which to draw a prejudice standard for ineffectiveness claims. The high standard for newly discovered evidence claims presupposes that all the essential elements of a presumptively accurate and fair proceeding were present in the proceeding whose result is challenged. An ineffective assistance claim asserts the absence of one of the crucial assurances that the result of the proceeding is reliable, so finality concerns are somewhat weaker and the appropriate standard of prejudice should be somewhat lower. The result of a proceeding can be rendered unreliable, and hence the proceeding itself unfair, even if the errors of counsel cannot be shown by a preponderance of the evidence to have determined the outcome.

Accordingly, the appropriate test for prejudice finds its roots in the test for materiality of exculpatory information not disclosed to the defense by the prosecution, and in the test for materiality of testimony made unavailable to the defense by Government deportation of a witness. The defendant must show that there is a reasonable probability that, but for counsel's unprofessional errors, the result of the proceeding would have been different. A reasonable probability is a probability sufficient to undermine confidence in the outcome.

In making the determination whether the specified errors resulted in the required prejudice, a court should presume, absent challenge to the judgment on grounds of evidentiary insufficiency, that the judge or jury acted according to law. An assessment of the likelihood of a result more favorable to the defendant must exclude the possibility of arbitrariness, whimsy, caprice, "nullification," and the like. A defendant has no entitlement to the luck of a lawless decisionmaker, even if a lawless decision cannot be reviewed. The assessment of prejudice should proceed on the assumption that the decisionmaker is reasonably, conscientiously, and impartially applying the standards that govern the decision. It should not depend on the idiosyncracies of the particular decisionmaker, such as unusual propensities toward harshness or leniency. Although these factors may actually have entered into counsel's selection of strategies and, to that limited extent, may thus affect the performance inquiry, they are irrelevant to the prejudice inquiry. Thus, evidence about the actual process of decision, if not part of the record of the proceeding under review, and evidence about, for example, a particular judge's sentencing practices, should not be considered in the prejudice determination.

The governing legal standard plays a critical role in defining the question to be asked in assessing the prejudice from counsel's errors. When a defendant challenges a conviction, the question is whether there is a reasonable probability that, absent the errors, the factfinder would have had a reasonable doubt respecting guilt. When a defendant challenges a death sentence such as the one at issue in this case, the question is whether there is a reasonable probability that, absent the errors, the sentencer—including an appellate court, to the extent it independently reweighs the evidence—would have concluded that the balance of aggravating and mitigating circumstances did not warrant death.

In making this determination, a court hearing an ineffectiveness claim must consider the totality of the evidence before the judge or jury. [A] verdict or conclusion only weakly supported by the record is more likely to have been affected by errors than one with overwhelming record support. Taking the unaffected findings as a given, and taking due account of the effect of the errors on the remaining findings, a court making the prejudice inquiry must ask if the defendant has met the burden of showing that the decision reached would reasonably likely have been different absent the errors.

A number of practical considerations are important for the application of the standards we have outlined. Most important, in adjudicating a claim of actual ineffectiveness of counsel, a court should keep in mind that the principles we have stated do not establish mechanical rules. Although those principles should guide the process of decision, the ultimate focus of inquiry must be on the fundamental fairness of the proceeding whose result is being challenged. In every case the court should be concerned with whether, despite the strong presumption of reliability, the result of the particular proceeding is unreliable because of a breakdown in the adversarial process that our system counts on to produce just results.

To the extent that this has already been the guiding inquiry in the lower courts, the standards articulated today do not require reconsideration of ineffectiveness claims rejected under different standards. [With] regard to the prejudice inquiry, only the strict outcome-determinative test, among the standards articulated in the lower courts, imposes a heavier burden on defendants than the tests laid down today. The difference, however, should alter the merit of an ineffectiveness claim only in the rarest case.

Although we have discussed the performance component of an ineffectiveness claim prior to the prejudice component, there is no reason for a court deciding an ineffective assistance claim to approach the inquiry in the same order or even to address both components of the inquiry if the defendant makes an insufficient showing on one. [If] it is easier to dispose of an ineffectiveness claim on the ground of lack of sufficient prejudice, which we expect will often be so, that course should be followed. Courts should strive to ensure that ineffectiveness claims not become so burdensome to defense counsel that the entire criminal justice system suffers as a result.

[Application] of the governing principles is not difficult in this case. The facts as described above make clear that the conduct of respondent's counsel at and before respondent's sentencing proceeding cannot be found unreasonable. They also make clear that, even assuming the challenged conduct of counsel was unreasonable, respondent suffered insufficient prejudice to warrant setting aside his death sentence.

With respect to the performance component, the record shows that respondent's counsel made a strategic choice to argue for the extreme emotional distress mitigating circumstance and to rely as fully as possible on respondent's acceptance of responsibility for his crimes. Although counsel understandably felt hopeless about respondent's prospects, nothing in the record indicates [that] counsel's sense of hopelessness distorted his professional judgment. Counsel's strategy choice was well within the range of professionally reasonable judgments, and the decision not to seek more character or psychological evidence than was already in hand was likewise reasonable.

The trial judge's views on the importance of owning up to one's crimes were well known to counsel. The aggravating circumstances were utterly overwhelming. Trial counsel could reasonably surmise from his conversations with respondent that character and psychological evidence would be of little help. Respondent had already been able to mention at the plea colloquy the substance of what there was to know about his financial and emotional troubles. Restricting testimony on respondent's character to what had come in at the plea colloquy ensured that contrary character and psychological evidence and respondent's criminal history, which counsel had successfully moved to exclude, would not come in. On these facts, there can be little question, even without application of the presumption of adequate performance, that trial counsel's defense, though unsuccessful, was the result of reasonable professional judgment.

With respect to the prejudice component, the lack of merit of respondent's claim is even more stark. The evidence that respondent says his trial counsel should have offered at the sentencing hearing would barely have altered the sentencing profile presented to the sentencing judge. [At] most this evidence shows that numerous people who knew respondent thought he was generally a good person and that a psychiatrist and a psychologist believed he was under considerable emotional stress that did not rise to the level of extreme disturbance. Given the overwhelming aggravating factors, there is no reasonable probability that the omitted evidence would have changed the conclusion that the aggravating circumstances outweighed the mitigating circumstances and, hence, the sentence imposed. Indeed, admission of the evidence respondent now offers might even have been harmful to his case: his "rap sheet" would probably have been admitted into evidence, and the psychological reports would have directly contradicted respondent's claim that the mitigating circumstance of extreme emotional disturbance applied to his case.

[Failure] to make the required showing of either deficient performance or sufficient prejudice defeats the ineffectiveness claim. Here there is a double failure. More generally, respondent has made no showing that the justice of his sentence was rendered unreliable by a breakdown in the adversary process caused by deficiencies in counsel's assistance. Respondent's sentencing proceeding was not fundamentally unfair.

We conclude, therefore, that the District Court properly declined to issue a writ of habeas corpus. The judgment of the Court of Appeals is accordingly

Reversed.

JUSTICE MARSHALL, dissenting.

[My] objection to the performance standard adopted by the Court is that it is so malleable that, in practice, it will either have no grip at all or will yield excessive variation in the manner in which the Sixth Amendment is interpreted and applied by different courts.

[I] object to the prejudice standard adopted by the Court for two independent reasons. First, it is often very difficult to tell whether a defendant convicted after a trial in which he was ineffectively represented would have fared better if his lawyer had been competent. Seemingly impregnable cases can sometimes be dismantled by good defense counsel. On the basis of a cold record, it may be impossible for a reviewing court confidently to ascertain how the government's evidence and arguments would have stood up against rebuttal and cross-examination by a shrewd, well-prepared lawyer. The difficulties of estimating prejudice after the fact are exacerbated by the possibility that evidence of injury to the defendant may be missing from the record precisely because of the incompetence of defense counsel. In view of all these impediments to a fair evaluation of the probability that the outcome of a trial was affected by ineffectiveness of counsel, it seems to me senseless to impose on a defendant whose lawyer has been shown to have been incompetent the burden of demonstrating prejudice.

Second and more fundamentally, the assumption on which the Court's holding rests is that the only purpose of the constitutional guarantee of effective assistance of counsel is to reduce the chance that innocent persons will be convicted. In my view, the guarantee also functions to ensure that convictions are obtained only through fundamentally fair procedures. The majority contends that the Sixth Amendment is not violated when a manifestly guilty defendant is convicted after a trial in which he was represented by a manifestly ineffective attorney. I cannot agree. Every defendant is entitled to a trial in which his interests are vigorously and conscientiously advocated by an able lawyer.

[In] defining the standard of attorney performance required by the Constitution, the majority appropriately notes that many problems confronting criminal defense attorneys admit of "a range of legitimate" responses. And the majority properly cautions courts, when reviewing a lawyer's selection amongst a set of options, to avoid the hubris of hindsight. The majority goes on, however, to suggest that reviewing courts should "indulge a strong presumption that counsel's conduct" was constitutionally acceptable and should "appl[y] a heavy measure of deference to counsel's judgments."

I am not sure what these phrases mean, and I doubt that they will be self-explanatory to lower courts. If they denote nothing more than that a defendant claiming he was denied effective assistance of counsel has the burden of proof, I would agree. But the adjectives "strong" and "heavy" might be read as imposing upon defendants an unusually weighty burden of persuasion. If that is the majority's intent, I must respectfully dissent. The range of acceptable behavior defined by "prevailing professional norms" seems to me sufficiently broad to allow defense counsel the flexibility they need in responding to novel problems of trial strategy. To afford attorneys more latitude, by "strongly presuming" that their behavior will fall within the zone of reasonableness, is covertly to legitimate convictions and sentences obtained on the basis of incompetent conduct by defense counsel.

The only justification the majority itself provides for its proposed presumption is that undue receptivity to claims of ineffective assistance of counsel would encourage too many defendants to raise such claims and thereby would clog the courts with frivolous suits and "dampen the ardor" of defense counsel. I have more confidence than the majority in the ability of state and federal courts expeditiously to dispose of meritless arguments and to ensure that responsible, innovative lawyering is not inhibited. [L]ittle will be gained and much may be lost by instructing the lower courts to proceed on the assumption that a defendant's challenge to his lawyer's performance will be insubstantial.

Curiously, though, the Court discounts the significance of its rulings, suggesting that its choice of standards matters little and that few if any cases would have been decided differently if the lower courts had always applied the tests announced today. Surely the judges in the state and lower federal courts will be surprised to learn that the distinctions they have so fiercely debated for many years are in fact unimportant. * * *

[The] majority suggests that, "[f]or purposes of describing counsel's duties," a capital sentencing proceeding "need not be distinguished from an ordinary trial." I cannot agree. [The] performance of defense counsel is a crucial component of the system of protections designed to ensure that capital punishment is administered with some degree of rationality. "Reliability" in the imposition of the death sentence can be approximated only if the sentencer is fully informed of "all possible relevant information about the individual defendant whose fate it must determine." The job of amassing that information and presenting it in an organized and persuasive manner to the sentencer is entrusted principally to the defendant's lawyer. [If] counsel had investigated the availability of mitigating evidence, he might well have decided to present some such material at the hearing. If he had done so, there is a significant chance that respondent would have been given a life sentence. In my view, those possibilities, conjoined with the unreasonableness of counsel's failure to investigate, are more than sufficient to establish a violation of the Sixth Amendment and to entitle respondent to a new sentencing proceeding.

Notes

1. In a companion case to *Strickland*, *United States v. Cronic*, 466 U.S. 648 (1984), the Supreme Court rejected defendant's "extrinsic" claims of defense counsel's ineffectiveness in all but the rarest of cases. "Extrinsic" claims are those that focus upon alleged general problems with counsel or the case (*e.g.* counsel was too young and/or inexperienced, the case was too complex for this attorney and/or there was too little time to prepare) without accompanying claims of "actual" incidents of ineffectiveness. Cronic was indicted on mail fraud charges involving the transfer of over $9,400,000 in checks between banks in Florida and Oklahoma during a 4–month period. Shortly before the scheduled trial date, retained counsel withdrew. The court then appointed a young lawyer with a real estate practice to represent Cronic, but allowed counsel only 25 days for pretrial preparation even though it had taken the Government over four and one-half years to investigate the case and it had reviewed thousands of documents during that time. Cronic was subsequently convicted on 11 of the 13 counts in the indictment and received a 25–year sentence. The court of appeals overturned Cronic's conviction based on five extrinsic factors: " '(1) [T]he time afforded for investigation and preparation; (2) the experience of counsel; (3) the gravity of the charge; (4) the complexity of possible defenses; and (5) the accessibility of witnesses to counsel.' " The Supreme Court reversed, however, holding that a criminal defendant can "make out a claim of ineffective assistance only by pointing to specific errors made by trial counsel."

2. In *Kimmelman v. Morrison*, 477 U.S. 365 (1986), the Court refused to extend *Stone v. Powell*, 428 U.S. 465 (1976) to Sixth Amendment claims of ineffectiveness. In *Stone*, the Court held that exclusionary rule arguments relating to Fourth Amendment violations could not be asserted on collateral

review in federal habeas corpus proceedings if the defendant had a full and fair opportunity to raise the issues in state court. In *Kimmelman*, the Court held that this rule did not apply to claims of ineffective assistance where the principal allegation and manifestation of inadequate representation was counsel's failure to file a timely motion to suppress evidence allegedly obtained in violation of the Fourth Amendment.

3. In *Nix v. Whiteside*, 475 U.S. 157 (1986), Whiteside was convicted of second degree murder. At trial, Whiteside claimed self-defense and wanted to testify that he had seen something metallic (presumably, a gun) in the victim's hand. However, Whiteside's attorney concluded that the testimony would be perjury and "advised him that if he did do that it would be my duty to advise the Court of what he was doing and that I felt he was committing perjury." Counsel also stated that he would attempt to withdraw from representing Whiteside if he insisted on committing perjury. Following his conviction, Whiteside sought habeas corpus, claiming that the attorney's conduct deprived him of effective assistance of counsel. The Court rejected this argument: "[A]n attorney's ethical duty to advance the interests of his client is limited by an equally solemn duty to comply with the law and standards of professional conduct; it specifically ensures that the client may not use false evidence.... Whether [counsel's] conduct is seen as a success-ful attempt to dissuade his client from committing the crime of perjury, or whether seen as a 'threat' to withdraw from representation and disclose the illegal scheme, [his] representation of Whiteside falls well within accepted standards of professional conduct and the range of reasonable professional conduct acceptable under *Strickland*."

Problems

1. *Does the Cronic presumption of effective assistance make sense?* Where defense counsel is inexperienced and is given insufficient time and resources to prepare his case, does it really make sense to simply *presume* that counsel functioned effectively? Does the *Strickland* standard make sense in light of public defender systems that are often dramatically under-staffed and overworked? In fiscal year 2003, Kentucky's Department of Public Advocacy (DPA) handled 117,132 cases or 484 cases per lawyer. As a proportion of its budget, DPA was spending an average of $238 per case. In light of these statistics, what would happen if the Court overruled *Strickland* and simply required "quality" representation for indigent defendants?

2. *Should ineffective assistance be presumed sometimes?* Should the *Strickland* rule require automatic reversal if defendant's counsel showed up for trial drunk, and occasionally went to sleep during the trial. In such a situation, would and/or should defendant have to show that counsel commit-ted specific errors to gain reversal?

* * *

Since the reasonableness of defense counsel's conduct is a very fact-specific inquiry under *Strickland*, sometimes it may be perfectly reasonable for counsel to engage in counter-intuitive conduct for good reasons, e.g. actually conceding the defendant's guilt. Then again, defense counsel's strategic decisions are not immune from some second guessing. In this regard, consider the following two Supreme Court decisions:

FLORIDA v. NIXON

543 U.S. 175 (2004).

JUSTICE GINSBURG delivered the opinion of the Court.

This capital case concerns defense counsel's strategic decision to concede, at the guilt phase of the trial, the defendant's commission of murder, and to concentrate the defense on establishing, at the penalty phase, cause for sparing the defendant's life. Any concession of that order, the Florida Supreme Court held, made without the defendant's express consent—however gruesome the crime and despite the strength of the evidence of guilt—automatically ranks as prejudicial ineffective assistance of counsel necessitating a new trial. We reverse the Florida Supreme Court's judgment.

Defense counsel undoubtedly has a duty to discuss potential strategies with the defendant. *See Strickland v. Washington*, 466 U.S. 668 (1984). But when a defendant, informed by counsel, neither consents nor objects to the course counsel describes as the most promising means to avert a sentence of death, counsel is not automatically barred from pursuing that course. The reasonableness of counsel's performance, after consultation with the defendant yields no response, must be judged in accord with the inquiry generally applicable to ineffective-assistance-of-counsel claims: Did counsel's representation "f[a]ll below an objective standard of reasonableness"? The Florida Supreme Court erred in applying, instead, a presumption of deficient performance, as well as a presumption of prejudice; that latter presumption, we have instructed, is reserved for cases in which counsel fails meaningfully to oppose the prosecution's case. A presumption of prejudice is not in order based solely on a defendant's failure to provide express consent to a tenable strategy counsel has adequately disclosed to and discussed with the defendant.

On Monday, August 13, 1984, near a dirt road in the environs of Tallahassee, Florida, a passing motorist discovered Jeanne Bickner's charred body. Bickner had been tied to a tree and set on fire while still alive. Her left leg and arm, and most of her hair and skin, had been burned away. The next day, police found Bickner's car, abandoned on a Tallahassee street corner, on fire. Police arrested 23–year-old Joe Elton Nixon later that morning, after Nixon's brother informed the sheriff's office that Nixon had confessed to the murder.

Questioned by the police, Nixon described in graphic detail how he had kidnaped Bickner, then killed her. He recounted that he had approached Bickner, a stranger, in a mall, and asked her to help him jump-start his car. Bickner offered Nixon a ride home in her 1973 MG sports car. Once on the road, Nixon directed Bickner to drive to a remote place; en route, he overpowered her and stopped the car. Nixon next put

Bickner in the MG's trunk, drove into a wooded area, removed Bickner from the car, and tied her to a tree with jumper cables. Bickner pleaded with Nixon to release her, offering him money in exchange. Concerned that Bickner might identify him, Nixon decided to kill her. He set fire to Bickner's personal belongings and ignited her with burning objects. Nixon drove away in the MG, and later told his brother and girlfriend what he had done. He burned the MG on Tuesday, August 14, after reading in the newspaper that Bickner's body had been discovered.

The State gathered overwhelming evidence establishing that Nixon had committed the murder in the manner he described. A witness saw Nixon approach Bickner in the mall's parking lot on August 12, and observed Bickner taking jumper cables out of the trunk of her car and giving them to Nixon. Several witnesses told police they saw Nixon driving around in the MG in the hours and days following Bickner's death. Nixon's palm print was found on the trunk of the car. Nixon's girlfriend, Wanda Robinson, and his brother, John Nixon, both stated that Nixon told them he had killed someone and showed them two rings later identified as Bickner's. According to Nixon's brother, Nixon pawned the rings and attempted to sell the car. At a local pawnshop, police recovered the rings and a receipt for them bearing Nixon's driver's license number; the pawnshop owner identified Nixon as the person who sold the rings to him.

In late August 1984, Nixon was indicted in Leon County, Florida, for first-degree murder, kidnaping, robbery, and arson. Assistant public defender Michael Corin, assigned to represent Nixon, filed a plea of not guilty and deposed all of the State's potential witnesses. Corin concluded, given the strength of the evidence, that Nixon's guilt was not "subject to any reasonable dispute." Corin thereupon commenced plea negotiations, hoping to persuade the prosecution to drop the death penalty in exchange for Nixon's guilty pleas to all charges. Negotiations broke down when the prosecutors indicated their unwillingness to recommend a sentence other than death.

Faced with the inevitability of going to trial on a capital charge, Corin turned his attention to the penalty phase, believing that the only way to save Nixon's life would be to present extensive mitigation evidence centering on Nixon's mental instability. Experienced in capital defense, Corin feared that denying Nixon's commission of the kidnaping and murder during the guilt phase would compromise Corin's ability to persuade the jury, during the penalty phase, that Nixon's conduct was the product of his mental illness. Corin concluded that the best strategy would be to concede guilt, thereby preserving his credibility in urging leniency during the penalty phase.

Corin attempted to explain this strategy to Nixon at least three times. Although Corin had represented Nixon previously on unrelated charges and the two had a good relationship in Corin's estimation, Nixon was generally unresponsive during their discussions. He never verbally approved or protested Corin's proposed strategy. [Corin] eventually exercised his professional judgment to pursue the concession strategy. As he explained: "There are many times lawyers make decisions because they have to make them because the client does nothing."

When Nixon's trial began on July 15, 1985, his unresponsiveness deepened into disruptive and violent behavior. On the second day of jury selection, Nixon pulled off his clothing, demanded a black judge and lawyer, refused to be escorted into the courtroom, and threatened to force the guards to shoot him. An extended on-the-record colloquy followed Nixon's bizarre behavior, during which Corin urged the trial judge to explain Nixon's rights to him and ascertain whether Nixon understood the significance of absenting himself from the trial. Corin also argued that restraining Nixon and compelling him to be present would prejudice him in the eyes of the jury. When the judge examined Nixon on the record in a holding cell, Nixon stated he had no interest in the trial and threatened to misbehave if forced to attend. The judge ruled that Nixon had intelligently and voluntarily waived his right to be present at trial.

The guilt phase of the trial thus began in Nixon's absence. In his opening statement, Corin acknowledged Nixon's guilt and urged the jury to focus on the penalty phase:

> "In this case, there won't be any question, none whatsoever, that my client, Joe Elton Nixon, caused Jeannie Bickner's death.... [T]hat fact will be proved to your satisfaction beyond any doubt.

> "This case is about the death of Joe Elton Nixon and whether it should occur within the next few years by electrocution or maybe its natural expiration after a lifetime of confinement. ...

> "Now, in arriving at your verdict, in your penalty recommendation, for we will get that far, you are going to learn many facts ... about Joe Elton Nixon. Some of those facts are going to be good. That may not seem clear to you at this time. But, and sadly, most of the things you learn of Joe Elton Nixon are not going to be good. But, I'm suggesting to you that when you have seen all the testimony, heard all the testimony and the evidence that has been shown, there are going to be reasons why you should recommend that his life be spared."

During its case in chief, the State introduced the tape of Nixon's confession, expert testimony on the manner in which Bickner died, and witness testimony regarding Nixon's confessions to his relatives and his possession of Bickner's car and personal effects. Corin cross-examined these witnesses only when he felt their statements needed clarification and he did not present a defense case. Corin did object to the introduction of crime scene photographs as unduly prejudicial and actively contested several aspects of the jury instructions during the charge conference. In his closing argument, Corin again conceded Nixon's guilt and reminded the jury of the importance of the penalty phase: "I will hope to ... argue to you and give you reasons not that Mr. Nixon's life be spared one final and terminal confinement forever, but that he not be sentenced to die." The jury found Nixon guilty on all counts.

At the start of the penalty phase, Corin argued to the jury that "Joe Elton Nixon is not normal organically, intellectually, emotionally or educationally or in any other way." Corin presented the testimony of eight witnesses. Relatives and friends described Nixon's childhood emotional troubles and his erratic behavior in the days preceding the murder. A psychiatrist and a psychologist addressed Nixon's antisocial personality, his history of emotional instability and psychiatric care, his low IQ, and the possibility that at some point he suffered brain damage. The State presented little evidence during the penalty phase, simply incorporating its guilt-phase evidence by reference, and introducing testimony, over Corin's objection, that Nixon had removed Bickner's underwear in order to terrorize her.

In his closing argument, Corin emphasized Nixon's youth, the psychiatric evidence, and the jury's discretion to consider any mitigating circumstances; Corin urged that, if not sentenced to death, "Joe Elton Nixon would [n]ever be released from confinement." The death penalty, Corin maintained, was appropriate only for "intact human being[s]," and "Joe Elton Nixon is not one of those. He's never been one of those. He never will be one of those." Corin concluded: "You know, we're not around here all that long. And it's rare when we have the opportunity to give or take life. And you have that opportunity to give life. And I'm going to ask you to do that. Thank you." After deliberating for approximately three hours, the jury recommended that Nixon be sentenced to death.

In accord with the jury's recommendation, the trial court imposed the death penalty. Notably, at the close of the penalty phase, the court commended Corin's performance during the trial, stating that "the tactic employed by trial counsel . . . was an excellent analysis of [the] reality of his case." The evidence of guilt "would have persuaded any jury . . . beyond all doubt," and "[f]or trial counsel to have inferred that Mr. Nixon was not guilty . . . would have deprived [counsel] of any credibility during the penalty phase." [The Florida Supreme Court subsequently reversed, finding ineffective assistance of counsel.]

[We] granted certiorari to resolve an important question of constitutional law, i.e., whether counsel's failure to obtain the defendant's express consent to a strategy of conceding guilt in a capital trial automatically renders counsel's performance deficient, and whether counsel's effectiveness should be evaluated under *Cronic* or *Strickland*. We now reverse the judgment of the Florida Supreme Court.

An attorney undoubtedly has a duty to consult with the client regarding "important decisions," including questions of overarching defense strategy. That obligation, however, does not require counsel to obtain the defendant's consent to "every tactical decision." But certain decisions regarding the exercise or waiver of basic trial rights are of such moment that they cannot be made for the defendant by a surrogate. A defendant, this Court affirmed, has "the ultimate authority" to determine "whether to plead guilty, waive a jury, testify in his or her own behalf, or take an appeal." Concerning those decisions, an attorney must both consult with the defendant and obtain consent to the recommended course of action.

[The] Florida Supreme Court [required] Nixon's "affirmative, explicit acceptance" of Corin's strategy because it deemed Corin's statements to the jury "the functional equivalent of a guilty plea." We disagree with that assessment.

[Corin] was obliged to, and in fact several times did, explain his proposed trial strategy to Nixon. Given Nixon's constant resistance to answering inquiries put to him by counsel and court, Corin was not additionally required to gain express consent before conceding Nixon's guilt. The two evidentiary hearings conducted by the Florida trial court demonstrate beyond doubt that Corin fulfilled his duty of consultation by informing Nixon of counsel's proposed strategy and its potential benefits. Nixon's characteristic silence each time information was conveyed to him, in sum, did not suffice to render unreasonable Corin's decision to concede guilt and to home in, instead, on the life or death penalty issue.

The Florida Supreme Court's erroneous equation of Corin's concession strategy to a guilty plea led it to apply the wrong standard in determining whether counsel's performance ranked as ineffective assistance. The court first presumed deficient performance, then applied the presumption of prejudice that *United States v. Cronic* [reserved] for situations in which counsel has entirely failed to function as the client's advocate. The Florida court therefore did not hold Nixon to the standard prescribed in *Strickland* [which] would have required Nixon to show that counsel's concession strategy was unreasonable.

[Corin's] concession of Nixon's guilt does not rank as a "fail[ure] to function in any meaningful sense as the Government's adversary." Although such a concession in a run-of-the-mine trial might present a closer question, the gravity of the potential sentence in a capital trial and the proceeding's two-phase structure vitally affect counsel's strategic calculus. Attorneys representing capital defendants face daunting challenges in developing trial strategies, not least because the defendant's guilt is often clear. Prosecutors are more likely to seek the death penalty, and to refuse to accept a plea to a life sentence, when the evidence is overwhelming and the crime heinous. In such cases, "avoiding execution [may be] the best and only realistic result possible."

Counsel therefore may reasonably decide to focus on the trial's penalty phase, at which time counsel's mission is to persuade the trier that his client's life should be spared. Unable to negotiate a guilty plea in exchange for a life sentence, defense counsel must strive at the guilt phase to avoid a counterproductive course. In this light, counsel cannot be deemed ineffective for attempting to impress the jury with his candor and his unwillingness to engage in "a useless charade." Renowned advocate Clarence Darrow, we note, famously employed a similar strategy as counsel for the youthful, cold-blooded killers Richard Loeb and Nathan Leopold. Imploring the judge to spare the boys' lives, Darrow declared: "I do not know how much salvage there is in these two boys. ...I will be honest with this court as I have tried to be from the beginning. I know that these boys are not fit to be at large."

To summarize, in a capital case, counsel must consider in conjunction both the guilt and penalty phases in determining how best to proceed. When counsel informs the defendant of the strategy counsel believes to be in the defendant's best interest and the defendant is unresponsive, counsel's strategic choice is not impeded by any blanket rule demanding the defendant's explicit consent. Instead, if counsel's strategy, given the evidence bearing on the defendant's guilt, satisfies the *Strickland* standard, that is the end of the matter; no tenable claim of ineffective assistance would remain.

For the reasons stated, the judgment of the Florida Supreme Court is reversed, and the case is remanded for further proceedings not inconsistent with this opinion.

ROMPILLA v. BEARD

545 U.S. 374 (2005).

JUSTICE SOUTER delivered the opinion of the Court.

This case calls for specific application of the standard of reasonable competence required on the part of defense counsel by the Sixth Amendment. We hold that even when a capital defendant's family members and the defendant himself have suggested that no mitigating evidence is available, his lawyer is bound to make reasonable efforts to obtain and review material that counsel knows the prosecution will probably rely on as evidence of aggravation at the sentencing phase of trial.

[On] the morning of January 14, 1988, James Scanlon was discovered dead in a bar he ran in Allentown, Pennsylvania, his body having been stabbed repeatedly and set on fire. Rompilla was indicted for the murder and related offenses, and the Commonwealth gave notice of intent to ask for the death penalty. Two public defenders were assigned to the case.

The jury at the guilt phase of trial found Rompilla guilty on all counts, and during the ensuing penalty phase, the prosecutor sought to prove three aggravating factors to justify a death sentence: that the murder was committed in the course of another felony; that the murder was committed by torture; and that Rompilla had a significant history of felony convictions indicating the use or threat of violence. The Commonwealth presented evidence on all three aggravators, and the jury found all proven. Rompilla's evidence in mitigation consisted of relatively brief testimony: five of his family members argued in effect for residual doubt, and beseeched the jury for mercy, saying that they believed Rompilla was innocent and a good man. Rompilla's 14–year-old son testified that he loved his father and would visit him in prison. The jury acknowledged this evidence to the point of finding, as two factors in mitigation, that Rompilla's son had testified on his behalf and that rehabilitation was possible. But the jurors assigned the greater weight to the aggravating factors, and sentenced Rompilla to death. The Supreme Court of Pennsylvania affirmed both conviction and sentence. [Subsequently, a federal District Court granted Rompilla's habeas corpus petition on ineffectiveness grounds, but the Third Circuit Court of Appeals reversed. We] granted certiorari, and now reverse.

[Ineffective] assistance under *Strickland* is deficient performance by counsel resulting in prejudice, with performance being measured against an "objective standard of reasonableness," "under prevailing professional norms." This case, like some others recently, looks to norms of adequate investigation in preparing for the sentencing phase of a capital trial, when defense counsel's job is to counter the State's evidence of aggravated culpability with evidence in mitigation. In judging the defense's investigation, as in applying *Strickland* generally, hindsight is discounted by pegging adequacy to "counsel's perspective at the time" investigative decisions are made, and by giving a "heavy measure of deference to counsel's judgments."

[A] standard of reasonableness applied as if one stood in counsel's shoes spawns few hard-edged rules, and the merits of a number of counsel's choices in this case are subject to fair debate. This is not a case in which defense counsel simply ignored their obligation to find mitigating evidence, and their workload as busy public defenders did not keep them from making a number of efforts, including interviews with Rompilla and some members of his family, and examinations of reports by three mental health experts who gave opinions at the guilt phase. None of the sources proved particularly helpful.

Rompilla's own contributions to any mitigation case were minimal. Counsel found him uninterested in helping, as on their visit to his prison to go over a proposed mitigation strategy, when Rompilla told them he was "bored being here listening" and returned to his cell. To questions about childhood and schooling, his answers indicated they had been normal, save for quitting school in the ninth grade. There were times when Rompilla was even actively obstructive by sending counsel off on false leads.

The lawyers also spoke with five members of Rompilla's family (his former wife, two brothers, a sister-in-law, and his son), and counsel testified that they developed a good relationship with the family in the course of their representation. [The] third and final source tapped for mitigating material was the cadre of three mental health witnesses who were asked to look into Rompilla's mental state as of the time of the offense and his competency to stand trial[,] but their reports revealed "nothing useful" to Rompilla's case, and the lawyers consequently did not go to any other historical source that might have cast light on Rompilla's mental condition.

When new counsel entered the case to raise Rompilla's postconviction claims, however, they identified a number of likely avenues the trial lawyers could fruitfully have followed in building a mitigation case. School records are one example, which trial counsel never examined in spite of the professed unfamiliarity of the several family members with Rompilla's childhood, and despite counsel's knowledge that Rompilla left school after the ninth grade. Others examples are records of Rompilla's juvenile and adult incarcerations, which counsel did not consult, although they were aware of their client's criminal record. And while counsel knew from police reports provided in pretrial discovery that Rompilla had been drinking heavily at the time of his offense, and although one of the mental health experts reported that Rompilla's troubles with alcohol merited further investigation, counsel did not look for evidence of a history of dependence on alcohol that might have extenuating significance.

Before us, trial counsel and the Commonwealth respond to these unexplored possibilities by emphasizing this Court's recognition that the duty to investigate does not force defense lawyers to scour the globe on the off-chance something will turn up; reasonably diligent counsel may draw a line when they have good reason to think further investigation would be a waste. The Commonwealth argues that the information trial counsel gathered from Rompilla and the other sources gave them sound reason to think it would have been pointless to spend time and money on the additional investigation espoused by postconviction counsel, and we can say that there is room for debate about trial counsel's obligation to follow at least some of those potential lines of enquiry. There is no need to say more, however, for a further point is clear and dispositive: the lawyers were deficient in failing to examine the court file on Rompilla's prior conviction.

There is an obvious reason that the failure to examine Rompilla's prior conviction file fell below the level of reasonable performance. Counsel knew that the Commonwealth intended to seek the death penalty by proving Rompilla had a significant history of felony convictions indicating the use or threat of violence, an aggravator under state law. Counsel further knew that the Commonwealth would attempt to establish this history by proving Rompilla's prior conviction for rape and assault, and would emphasize his violent character by introducing a transcript of the rape victim's testimony given in that earlier trial. There is no question that defense counsel were on notice, since they acknowledge that a "plea letter," written by one of them four days prior to trial, mentioned the prosecutor's plans. It is also undisputed that the prior conviction file was a public document, readily available for the asking at the very courthouse where Rompilla was to be tried.

It is clear, however, that defense counsel did not look at any part of that file, including the transcript, until warned by the prosecution a second time. In a colloquy the day before the evidentiary sentencing phase began, the prosecutor again said he would present the transcript of the victim's testimony to establish the prior conviction.

[At] the postconviction evidentiary hearing, Rompilla's lawyer confirmed that she had not seen the transcript before the hearing in which this exchange took place, and crucially, even after obtaining the transcript of the victim's testimony on the eve of the sentencing hearing, counsel apparently examined none of the other material in the file.

With every effort to view the facts as a defense lawyer would have done at the time, it is difficult to see how counsel could have failed to realize that without examining the readily available file they were seriously compromising their opportunity to respond to a case for aggravation. The prosecution was going to use the dramatic facts of a similar prior offense, and Rompilla's counsel had a duty to make all reasonable efforts to learn what they could about the offense. Reasonable efforts certainly included obtaining the Commonwealth's own readily available file on the prior conviction to learn what the Commonwealth knew about the crime, to discover any mitigating evidence the Commonwealth would downplay and to anticipate the details of the aggravating evidence the Commonwealth would emphasize. Without making reasonable efforts to review the file, defense counsel could have had no hope of knowing whether the prosecution was quoting selectively from the transcript, or whether there were circumstances extenuating the behavior described by the victim. The obligation to get the file was particularly pressing here owing to the similarity of the violent prior offense to the crime charged and Rompilla's sentencing strategy stressing residual doubt. Without making efforts to learn the details and rebut the relevance of the earlier crime, a convincing argument for residual doubt was certainly beyond any hope.

The notion that defense counsel must obtain information that the State has and will use against the defendant is not simply a matter of common sense. As the District Court points out, the American Bar Association Standards for Criminal Justice in circulation at the time of Rompilla's trial describes the obligation in terms no one could misunderstand in the circumstances of a case like this one:

> "It is the duty of the lawyer to conduct a prompt investigation of the circumstances of the case and to explore all avenues leading to facts relevant to the merits of the case and the penalty in the event of conviction. The investigation should always include efforts to secure information in the possession of the prosecution and law enforcement authorities. The duty to investigate exists regardless of the accused's admissions or statements to the lawyer of facts constituting guilt or the accused's stated desire to plead guilty."

[At] argument the most that Pennsylvania (and the United States as amicus) could say was that defense counsel's efforts to find mitigating evidence by other means excused them from looking at the prior conviction file. And that, of course, is the position taken by the state postconviction courts. Without specifically discussing the prior case file, they too found that defense counsel's efforts were enough to free them from any obligation to enquire further.

We think this conclusion of the state court fails to answer the considerations we have set out, to the point of being an objectively unreasonable conclusion. It flouts prudence to deny that a defense lawyer should try to look at a file he knows the prosecution will cull for aggravating evidence, let alone when the file is sitting in the trial courthouse, open for the asking. No reasonable lawyer would forgo examination of the file thinking he could do as well by asking the defendant or family relations whether they recalled anything helpful or damaging in the prior victim's testimony. Nor would a reasonable lawyer compare possible searches for school reports, juvenile records, and evidence of drinking habits to the opportunity to take a look at a file disclosing what the prosecutor knows and even plans to read from in his case. Questioning a few more family members and searching for old records can promise less than looking for a needle in a haystack, when a lawyer truly has reason to doubt there is any needle there. But looking at a file the prosecution says it will use is a sure bet: whatever may be in that file is going to tell defense counsel something about what the prosecution can produce.

The dissent thinks this analysis creates a "rigid, per se" rule that requires defense counsel to do a complete review of the file on any prior conviction introduced, but that is a mistake. Counsel fell short here because they failed to make reasonable efforts to review the prior conviction file, despite knowing that the prosecution intended to introduce Rompilla's prior conviction not merely by entering a notice of conviction into evidence but by quoting damaging testimony of the rape victim in that case. The unreasonableness of attempting no more than they did was heightened by the easy availability of the file at the trial courthouse, and the great risk that testimony about a similar violent crime would hamstring counsel's chosen defense of residual doubt.

[Since] counsel's failure to look at the file fell below the line of reasonable practice, there is a further question about prejudice, that is, whether "there is a reasonable probability that, but for counsel's unprofessional errors, the result of the proceeding would have been different." [We] think Rompilla has shown beyond any doubt that counsel's lapse was prejudicial; Pennsylvania, indeed, does not even contest the claim of prejudice.

If the defense lawyers had looked in the file on Rompilla's prior conviction, it is uncontested they would have found a range of mitigation leads that no other source had opened up. In the same file with the transcript of the prior trial were the records of Rompilla's imprisonment on the earlier conviction, which defense counsel testified she had never seen. The prison files pictured Rompilla's childhood and mental health very differently from anything defense counsel had seen or heard. An evaluation by a corrections counselor states that Rompilla was "reared in the slum environment of Allentown, Pa. vicinity. He early came to the attention of juvenile authorities, quit school at 16, [and] started a series of incarcerations in and out Penna. often of assaultive nature and commonly related to over-indulgence in alcoholic beverages." The same file discloses test results that the defense's mental health experts would have viewed as pointing to schizophrenia and other disorders, and test scores showing a third grade level of cognition after nine years of schooling.

The accumulated entries would have destroyed the benign conception of Rompilla's upbringing and mental capacity defense counsel had formed from talking with Rompilla himself and some of his family members, and from the reports of the mental health experts. With this information, counsel would have become skeptical of the impression given by the five family members and would unquestionably have gone further to build a mitigation case. Further effort would presumably have unearthed much of the material postconviction counsel found, including testimony from several members of Rompilla's family, whom trial counsel did not interview. Judge Sloviter [dissenting in the Third Circuit] summarized this evidence:

> "Rompilla's parents were both severe alcoholics who drank constantly. His mother drank during her pregnancy with Rompilla, and he and his brothers eventually developed serious drinking problems. His father, who had a vicious temper, frequently beat Rompilla's mother, leaving her bruised and black-eyed, and bragged about his cheating on her. His parents fought violently, and on at least one occasion his mother stabbed his father. He was abused by his father who beat him when he was young with his hands, fists, leather straps, belts and sticks. All of the children lived in terror. There were no expressions of parental love, affection or approval. Instead, he was subjected to yelling and verbal abuse. His father locked Rompilla and his brother Richard in a small wire mesh dog pen that was filthy and excrement filled. He had an isolated background, and was not allowed to visit other children or to speak to anyone on the phone. They had no indoor plumbing in the house, he slept in the attic with no heat, and the children were not given clothes and attended school in rags."

The jury never heard any of this and neither did the mental health experts who examined Rompilla before trial. While they found "nothing helpful to [Rompilla's] case," their postconviction counterparts, alerted by information from school, medical, and prison records that trial counsel never saw, found plenty of " 'red flags' " pointing up a need to test further. When they tested, they found that Rompilla "suffers from organic brain damage, an extreme mental disturbance significantly impairing several of his cognitive functions." They also said that "Rompilla's problems relate back to his childhood, and were likely caused by fetal alcohol syndrome [and that] Rompilla's capacity to appreciate the criminality of his conduct or to conform his conduct to the law was substantially impaired at the time of the offense."

These findings in turn would probably have prompted a look at school and juvenile records, all of them easy to get, showing, for example, that when Rompilla was 16 his mother "was missing from home frequently for a period of one or several weeks at a time.'' The same report noted that his mother ''has been reported … frequently under the influence of alcoholic beverages, with the result that the children have always been poorly kept and on the filthy side which was also the condition of the home at all times.'' School records showed Rompilla's IQ was in the mentally retarded range.

This evidence adds up to a mitigation case that bears no relation to the few naked pleas for mercy actually put before the jury, and although we suppose it is possible that a jury could have heard it all and still have decided on the death penalty, that is not the test. It goes without saying that the undiscovered ''mitigating evidence, taken as a whole, 'might well have influenced the jury's appraisal' of [Rompilla's] culpability,'' and the likelihood of a different result if the evidence had gone in is ''sufficient to undermine confidence in the outcome'' actually reached at sentencing, *Strickland*.

The judgment of the Third Circuit is reversed, and Pennsylvania must either retry the case on penalty or stipulate to a life sentence. * * *

JUSTICE O'CONNOR, concurring.

I write separately to put to rest one concern. The dissent worries that the Court's opinion ''imposes on defense counsel a rigid requirement to review all documents in what it calls the 'case file' of any prior conviction that the prosecution might rely on at trial.'' But the Court's opinion imposes no such rule. Rather, today's decision simply applies our longstanding case-by-case approach to determining whether an attorney's performance was unconstitutionally deficient under *Strickland*. Trial counsel's performance in Rompilla's case falls short under that standard, because the attorneys' behavior was not ''reasonable considering all the circumstances.'' In particular, there were three circumstances which made the attorneys' failure to examine Rompilla's prior conviction file unreasonable.

First, Rompilla's attorneys knew that their client's prior conviction would be at the very heart of the prosecution's case. The prior conviction went not to a collateral matter, but rather to one of the aggravating circumstances making Rompilla eligible for the death penalty. The prosecutors intended not merely to mention the fact of prior conviction, but to read testimony about the details of the crime. That crime, besides being quite violent in its own right, was very similar to the murder for which Rompilla was on trial, and Rompilla had committed the murder at issue a mere three months after his release from prison on the earlier conviction. In other words, the prosecutor clearly planned to use details of the prior crime as powerful evidence that Rompilla was a dangerous man for whom the death penalty would be both appropriate punishment and a necessary means of incapacitation. This was evidence the defense should have been prepared to meet: A reasonable defense lawyer would have attached a high importance to obtaining the record of the prior trial, in order to anticipate and find ways of deflecting the prosecutor's aggravation argument.

Second, the prosecutor's planned use of the prior conviction threatened to eviscerate one of the defense's primary mitigation arguments. Rompilla was convicted on the basis of strong circumstantial evidence. His lawyers structured the entire mitigation argument around the hope of convincing the jury that residual doubt about Rompilla's guilt made it inappropriate to impose the death penalty. In announcing an intention to introduce testimony about Rompilla's similar prior offense, the prosecutor put Rompilla's attorneys on notice that the prospective defense on mitigation likely would be ineffective and counterproductive. The similarities between the two crimes, combined with the timing and the already strong circumstantial evidence, raised a strong likelihood that the jury would reject Rompilla's residual doubt argument. Rompilla's attorneys' reliance on this transparently weak argument risked damaging their credibility. Such a scenario called for further investigation, to determine whether circumstances of the prior case gave any hope of saving the residual doubt argument, or whether the best strategy instead would be to jettison that argument so as to focus on other, more promising issues.

Third, the attorneys' decision not to obtain Rompilla's prior conviction file was not the result of an informed tactical decision about how the lawyers' time would best be spent. Although Rompilla's attorneys had ample warning that the details of Rompilla's prior conviction would be critical to their case, their failure to obtain that file would not necessarily have been deficient if it had resulted from the lawyers' careful exercise of judgment about how best to marshal their time and serve their client. But Rompilla's attorneys did not ignore the prior case file in order to spend their time on other crucial leads. They did not determine that the file was so inaccessible or so large that examining it would necessarily divert them from other trial-preparation tasks they thought more promising. They did not learn at the 11th hour about the prosecution's intent to use the prior conviction, when it was too late for them to change plans. Rather, their failure to obtain the crucial file "was the result of inattention, not reasoned strategic judgment." As a result, their conduct fell below constitutionally required standards. * * *

JUSTICE KENNEDY, with whom THE CHIEF JUSTICE, JUSTICE SCALIA, and JUSTICE THOMAS join, dissenting.

Today the Court brands two committed criminal defense attorneys as ineffective–"outside the wide range of professionally competent counsel"—because they did not look in an old case file and stumble upon something they had not set out to find. [To] reach this result, the majority imposes on defense counsel a rigid requirement to review all documents in what it calls the "case file" of any prior conviction that the prosecution might rely on at trial.

[The] majority's holding has no place in our Sixth Amendment jurisprudence and, if followed, often will result in less effective counsel by diverting limited defense resources from other important tasks in order to satisfy the Court's new per se rule. [The] majority's analysis contains barely a mention of *Strickland* and makes little effort to square today's holding with our traditional reluctance to impose rigid requirements on defense counsel. While the Court disclaims any intention to create a bright-line rule, this affords little comfort. The Court's opinion makes clear it has imposed on counsel a broad obligation to review prior conviction case files where those priors are used in aggravation—and to review every document in those files if not every single page of every document, regardless of the prosecution's proposed use for the prior conviction.

[The] majority also disregards the sound strategic calculation supporting the decisions made by Rompilla's attorneys. Charles and Dantos were "aware of [Rompilla's] priors" and "aware of the circumstances" surrounding these convictions. [They] reasonably could conclude that reviewing the full prior conviction case file was not the best allocation of resources. The majority concludes otherwise only by ignoring *Strickland's* command that "[j]udicial scrutiny of counsel's performance must be highly deferential." [Rompilla's] attorneys * * * devoted their limited time and resources to developing a mitigation case. That those efforts turned up little useful evidence does not make the ex ante strategic calculation of Rompilla's attorneys constitutionally deficient.

One of the primary reasons this Court has rejected a checklist approach to effective assistance of counsel is that each new requirement risks distracting attorneys from the real objective of providing vigorous advocacy as dictated by the facts and circumstances in the particular case. The Court's rigid requirement that counsel always review the case files of convictions the prosecution seeks to use at trial will be just such a distraction. [The] net effect of today's holding in many cases—instances where trial counsel reasonably can conclude that reviewing old case files is not an effective use of time—will be to diminish the quality of representation. We have "consistently declined to impose mechanical rules on counsel—even when those rules might lead to better representation"; I see no occasion to depart from this approach in order to impose a requirement that might well lead to worse representation. * * *

Notes & Questions

1. A 5–to–4 majority of the Supreme Court ruled in *Williams v. Taylor*, 529 U.S. 362, 412 (2000), that The Antiterrorism & Effective Death Penalty Act of 1996 ("AEDPA"), 28 U. S. C. § 2254, "places a new constraint on the power of a federal habeas court to grant a state prisoner's application for a writ of habeas corpus with respect to claims adjudicated on the merits in state court." More particularly, the Court held, under this new provision,

> the writ may issue only if one of the following two conditions is satisfied—the state-court adjudication resulted in a decision that (1) "was contrary to . . . clearly established Federal law, as determined by the Supreme Court of the United States," or (2) "involved an unreason-

able application of ... clearly established Federal law, as determined by the Supreme Court of the United States." Under the "contrary to" clause, a federal habeas court may grant the writ if the state court arrives at a conclusion opposite to that reached by this Court on a question of law or if the state court decides a case differently than this Court has on a set of materially indistinguishable facts. Under the "unreasonable application" clause, a federal habeas court may grant the writ if the state court identifies the correct governing legal principle from this Court's decisions but unreasonably applies that principle to the facts of the prisoner's case.

Id. at 412–13. Accordingly, the fact that a state court may have made an incorrect constitutional ruling on an ineffectiveness inquiry no longer suffices—under this AEDPA provision—to entitle a defendant to habeas corpus relief. *Woodford v. Visciotti*, 537 U.S. 19 (2002) ("[u]nder [the] 'unreasonable application' clause, a federal habeas court may not issue the writ simply because that court concludes in its independent judgment that the state-court decision applied *Strickland* incorrectly[.] Rather, it is the habeas applicant's burden to show that the state court applied *Strickland* to the facts of his case in an objectively unreasonable manner."); *Bell v. Cone*, 535 U.S. 685 (2002).

In *Rompilla*, the dissenters argued that "the Pennsylvania Supreme Court gave careful consideration to Rompilla's Sixth Amendment claim and concluded that 'counsel reasonably relied upon their discussions with [Rompilla] and upon their experts to determine the records needed to evaluate his mental health and other potential mitigating circumstances.' This decision was far from unreasonable [under the AEDPA]." The 5–justice majority concluded, however, not only that defense counsel were ineffective, but that the state court decision finding them not to have been ineffective "was contrary to, or involved an unreasonable application of, clearly established Federal law, as determined by the Supreme Court of the United States," pursuant to the AEDPA. Do you agree?

2. Why was defense counsels' decision to focus on mitigation in the penalty phase of a capital case held in *Nixon* to be reasonable and the same decision held to be unreasonable in *Rompilla*? Does this difference in result make sense?

3. Justice Kennedy, in his dissent in *Rompilla*, accuses the majority of creating a "rigid requirement to review all documents [in] the 'case file' of any prior conviction that the prosecution might rely on at trial." The majority and Justice O'Connor, concurring, vigorously dispute that accusation. Who is right? Isn't it true after decision in *Rompilla* that defense counsel in a capital case *must* always look at the file documents relating to a prior offense if the prosecution indicates that it intends to rely on that conviction for purposes of sentence enhancement? If it is true, is that an inappropriate result?

* * *

What exactly constitutes "prejudice" under *Strickland*? Consider the following decision:

GLOVER v. UNITED STATES

531 U.S. 198 (2001).

JUSTICE KENNEDY delivered the opinion of the Court.

[Petitioner contends that] the trial court erred in a Sentencing Guidelines determination[.] The legal error, petitioner alleges, increased his prison sentence by at least 6 months and perhaps by 21 months. We must decide whether this would be "prejudice" under *Strickland v. Washington*, 466 U.S. 668 (1984). [W]e reverse and remand for further proceedings.

[Petitioner] Paul Glover was the Vice President and General Counsel of the Chicago Truck Drivers, Helpers, and Warehouse Workers Union (Independent). [Glover] used his control over the union's investments to enrich himself and his co-conspirators through kickbacks. [The] presentence investigation report [recommended] that the convictions for labor racketeering, money laundering, and tax evasion be grouped together under United States Sentencing Commission, Guidelines Manual § 3D1.2 (Nov.1994), which allows the grouping of "counts involving substantially the same harm." [The] District Court [ruled that the] money laundering counts [should] not be grouped with Glover's other offenses. [Glover's] attorneys did not submit papers or offer extensive oral arguments contesting the no-grouping argument [and, accordingly,] Glover's offense level was increased by two levels, yielding a concomitant increase in the sentencing range. Glover was sentenced to 84 months in prison, which was in the middle of the Guidelines range of 78 to 97 months. [On appeal], Glover's counsel (the same attorneys who represented him in District Court) did not raise the grouping issue[.] A short time after argument on Glover's appeal, a different panel of the Seventh Circuit held that, under some circumstances, grouping of money laundering offenses with other counts was proper under § 3D1.2. *United States v. Wilson*, 98 F.3d 281 (1996). [A month later], the Seventh Circuit * * * affirmed his conviction and sentence.

Glover filed a pro se motion to correct his sentence[.] The failure of his counsel to press the grouping issue, he argued, was ineffective assistance, a position confirmed, in his view, by the Court of Appeals' decision in *Wilson*. The performance of counsel, he contended, fell below a reasonable standard both at sentencing, when his attorneys did not with any clarity or force contest the Government's argument, and on appeal, when they did not present the issue in their briefs or call the *Wilson* decision to the panel's attention following the oral argument. He further argued that absent the ineffective assistance, his offense level would have been two levels lower, yielding a Guidelines sentencing range of 63 to 78 months. Under this theory, the 84-month sentence he received was an unlawful increase of anywhere between 6 and 21 months.

The District Court denied Glover's motion [and the] Court of Appeals affirmed. We granted certiorari. [It] appears the Seventh Circuit [relied on] *Lockhart v. Fretwell*, 506 U.S. 364 (1993). *Lockhart* holds that in some circumstances a mere difference in outcome will not suffice to establish prejudice. The Seventh Circuit extracted from this holding the rule at issue here, which denies relief when the increase in sentence is said to be not so significant as to render the outcome of sentencing unreliable or fundamentally unfair. The Court explained last Term that our holding in *Lockhart* does not supplant the *Strickland* analysis. The Seventh Circuit was incorrect to rely on *Lockhart* to deny relief. [Our] jurisprudence suggests that any amount of actual jail time has Sixth Amendment significance. *Argersinger v. Hamlin*, 407 U.S. 25 (1972).

[The] Seventh Circuit's rule is not well considered in any event, because there is no obvious dividing line by which to measure how much longer a sentence must be for the increase to constitute substantial prejudice. [Although] the amount by which a defendant's sentence is increased by a particular decision may be a factor to consider in determining whether counsel's performance in failing to argue the point constitutes ineffective assistance, under a determinate system of constrained discretion such as the Sentencing Guidelines it cannot serve as a bar to a showing of prejudice. We hold that the Seventh Circuit erred in engrafting this additional requirement onto the prejudice branch of the *Strickland* test. This is not a case where trial strategies, in retrospect, might be criticized for leading to a harsher sentence. Here we consider the sentencing calculation itself, a calculation resulting from a ruling which, if it had been error, would have been correctable on appeal. We express no opinion on the ultimate merits of Glover's claim because the question of deficient performance is not before us, but it is clear that prejudice flowed from the asserted error in sentencing.

[The] judgment of the Seventh Circuit is reversed. * * *

Problems

1. On July 1, 1997, the Commonwealth of Kentucky executed convicted murderer Harold McQueen, Jr. The evidence revealed that McQueen had an I.Q. of 82. When he was tried and sentenced to death in 1981, McQueen was represented by state-appointed counsel. The evidence suggests that the average death penalty trial (through the guilt and penalty phases) requires 500 hours of work. McQueen's counsel was paid a total of $1,000 (the state hired defense counsel on a set fee per case). Is it really reasonable to assume that counsel, paid so poorly, nonetheless provided effective representation in terms of investigating the law and the facts, drawing reasonable legal inferences, and in providing effective representation?

2. Defendant is on trial for possession of narcotics. The prosecution has overwhelming evidence of guilt in the form of cocaine found in defendant's home. However, the evidence was obtained as a result of an illegal search. Defense counsel fails to file a suppression motion and defendant is convicted. Was counsel ineffective under either *Strickland* or *Cronic*?

3. Should ineffectiveness be presumed where counsel referred to his client with a racist epithet and told him that he "hoped he gets life"?

Counsel also stated that, if defendant "insists on going to trial," he would be "very ineffective." *See Frazer v. U. S.*, 18 F.3d 778 (9th Cir.1994).

4. Do you think that criminal defense counsel should be deemed to be *automatically* ineffective when he failed to show up for most of the direct and cross-examination of an important prosecution witness—a victim—without any excuse for his absence? What if counsel failed to show up for any of the cross-examination? Would it make any difference in your analysis if counsel was prepared to finish the cross-examination, but asked for a recess to review what he had missed before proceeding? *See McKnight v. State*, 320 S.C. 356, 465 S.E.2d 352 (1995).

5. Defendant is convicted of armed robbery. He had been convicted of this crime twice before. During voir dire, defense counsel asked the members of the venire whether they could judge defendant fairly and with an open mind if they learned he had been convicted of armed robbery twice previously. At no other point in the trial was the subject of defendant's prior convictions mentioned. Was counsel ineffective because he mentioned them during voir dire?

6. In 1997, Richard Dieter, Executive Director of the Death Penalty Information Center, issued a report finding that, since 1963, 69 death row inmates have been found innocent and released from prison. These individuals represent approximately 1% of all death penalty cases. *See* Terry Carter, *Numbers Tell the Story: Timing Was Right for Report on Death Row Reprieves*, 83 A.B.A.J. 20 (1997). Do these findings suggest that the Court's approach to ineffective assistance is too strict, too lax, or about right?

7. Massachusetts suffered from a shortage of lawyers willing to accept indigent appointments. The trial court concluded that the unavailability of lawyers was directly related to inadequate levels of compensation. Suppose that you are a trial court judge, and you have a number of indigent defendants who are entitled to counsel but who remain unrepresented. What remedies are available to you? Should you: order attorneys to accept indigent cases at prevailing compensation rates; order the state to pay attorneys more for indigent representation; order that defendants be released and their cases be dismissed without prejudice? *See Lavallee v. Justices in the Hampden Superior Court*, 442 Mass. 228, 812 N.E.2d 895 (2004).

Exercise

Defendant Larry Hall was convicted at trial along with a codefendant, G, of the rape and murder of a young woman. The crime was one of a series of similar, seemingly-random abductions, rapes, and grisly murders of young women which took place during 1981 and 1982. Hall's defense at trial—which was apparently not credited by the jury—was strictly one of factual innocence. Hall was sentenced to death. His conviction and death sentence were affirmed on direct appeal.

Hall has now sought postconviction relief in state court, arguing that he is entitled to a new trial because of the ineffective assistance of his trial counsel, Karen LaBomba (which he did not raise in his direct appeal since LaBomba was also his appellate counsel and failed to question her own ineffectiveness). The postconviction court denied Hall the opportunity for an evidentiary hearing on his claim of LaBomba's ineffectiveness, concluding that he did not make a sufficient showing of arguable ineffectiveness to justify such a hearing. Hall has appealed this decision to a state appellate court, arguing that he is entitled to a hearing. Attached to his appeal papers are affidavits from a number of psychiatrists which claim that defendant was psychotic and "psychologically adrift" at the time of the rape and murder for which he was sentenced to death and, further, that he was under the influence of the co-defendant, Linda Sanders, wh initiated all of the crimes and "possessed a Charles Manson-like persona, subjugating Hall to her will."

Hall argues that LaBomba was ineffective in that she failed to raise any psychiatric defenses at trial. More important, Hall argues in his appeal papers, LaBomba failed even to obtain any psychiatric evaluation of Hall to assess whether or not such a defense might be tenable. It is Hall's argument that he is at least entitled to an evidentiary hearing wherein he should be given an opportunity to show that LaBomba was constitutionally ineffective in failing to investigate and raise psychiatric defenses to these charges.

Half of you will be assigned to the defense, half to the prosecution. Prepare a brief (1 to 2 page) outline of the arguments which support your side of the issue on appeal whether Hall should be entitled to such an evidentiary hearing on LaBomba's ineffectiveness.

D.   CONFLICTS OF INTEREST

In *Strickland*, the Court stated that, when an attorney represents clients with conflicting interests, a limited presumption of incompetence can arise. *Cuyler* squarely presents that issue.

CUYLER v. SULLIVAN

446 U.S. 335 (1980).

MR. JUSTICE POWELL delivered the opinion of the Court.

The question presented is whether a state prisoner may obtain a federal writ of habeas corpus by showing that his retained defense counsel represented potentially conflicting interests.

[Respondent] John Sullivan was indicted with Gregory Carchidi and Anthony DiPasquale for the first-degree murders of John Gorey and Rita Janda. The victims, a labor official and his companion, were shot to death in Gorey's second-story office at the Philadelphia headquarters of Teamsters' Local 107. Francis McGrath, a janitor, saw the three defendants in the building just before the shooting. They appeared to be awaiting someone, and they encouraged McGrath to do his work on another day. McGrath ignored their suggestions. Shortly afterward, Gorey arrived and went to his office. McGrath then heard what sounded like firecrackers exploding in rapid succession. Carchidi, who was in the room where McGrath was working, abruptly directed McGrath to leave the building and to say nothing. McGrath hastily complied. When he returned to the building about 15 minutes later, the defendants were gone. The victims' bodies were discovered the next morning.

Two privately retained lawyers, G. Fred DiBona and A. Charles Peruto, represented all three defendants throughout the state proceedings that followed the indictment. Sullivan had different counsel at the medical examiner's inquest, but he thereafter accepted representation from the two lawyers retained by his codefendants because he could not afford to pay his own lawyer. At no time did Sullivan or his lawyers object to the multiple representation. Sullivan was the first defendant to come to trial. The evidence against him was entirely circumstantial, consisting primarily of McGrath's testimony. At the close of the Commonwealth's case, the defense rested without presenting any evidence. The jury found Sullivan guilty and fixed his penalty at life imprisonment. [The] Pennsylvania Supreme Court affirmed his conviction by an equally divided vote. Sullivan's codefendants, Carchidi and DiPasquale, were acquitted at separate trials. [In subsequent postconviction proceedings, a federal district court denied Sullivan's request for habeas corpus relief, but the Third Circuit Court of Appeals reversed, finding a conflict of interest sufficient to raise Sixth Amendment concerns.]

We come [to] Sullivan's claim that he was denied the effective assistance of counsel guaranteed by the Sixth Amendment because his lawyers had a conflict of interest. [In] *Holloway*, a single public defender represented three defendants at the same trial. The trial court refused to consider the appointment of separate counsel despite the defense lawyer's timely and repeated assertions that the interests of his clients conflicted. This Court recognized that a lawyer forced to represent codefendants whose interests conflict cannot provide the adequate legal assistance required by the Sixth Amendment. Given the trial court's failure to respond to timely objections, however, the Court did not consider whether the alleged conflict actually existed. It simply held that the trial court's error unconstitutionally endangered the right to counsel.

Holloway requires state trial courts to investigate timely objections to multiple representation. But nothing in our precedents suggests that the Sixth Amendment requires state courts themselves to initiate inquiries into the propriety of multiple representation in every case. Defense counsel have an ethical obligation to avoid conflicting representations and to advise the court promptly when a conflict of interest arises during the course of trial. Absent special circumstances, therefore, trial courts may assume either that multiple representation entails no conflict or that the lawyer and his clients knowingly accept such risk of conflict as may exist. [Unless] the trial court knows or reasonably should know that a particular conflict exists, the court need not initiate an inquiry.

[*Holloway*] reaffirmed that multiple representation does not violate the Sixth Amendment unless it gives rise to a conflict of interest. Since a possible conflict inheres in almost every instance of multiple representation, a defendant who objects to multiple representation must have the opportunity to show that potential conflicts impermissibly imperil his right to a fair trial. But unless the trial court fails to afford such an opportunity, a reviewing court cannot presume that the possibility for conflict has resulted in ineffective assistance of counsel. Such a presumption would preclude multiple representation even in cases where " '[a] common defense [gives] strength against a common attack.' "

In order to establish a violation of the Sixth Amendment, a defendant who raised no objection at trial must demonstrate that an actual conflict of interest adversely affected his lawyer's performance. In *Glasser v. United States*, for example, the record showed that defense counsel failed to cross-examine a prosecution witness whose testimony linked Glasser with the crime and failed to resist the presentation of arguably inadmissible evidence. The Court found that both omissions resulted from counsel's desire to diminish the jury's perception of a codefendant's guilt. Indeed, the evidence of counsel's "struggle to serve two masters [could not] seriously be doubted." Since this actual conflict of interest impaired Glasser's defense, the Court reversed his conviction.

[*Glasser*] established that unconstitutional multiple representation is never harmless error. Once the Court concluded that Glasser's lawyer had an actual conflict of interest, it refused "to indulge in nice calculations as to the amount of prejudice" attributable to the conflict. The conflict itself demonstrated a denial of the "right to have the effective assistance of counsel." Thus, a defendant who shows that a conflict of interest actually affected the adequacy of his representation need not demonstrate prejudice in order to obtain relief. But until a defendant shows that his counsel actively represented conflicting interests, he has not established the constitutional predicate for his claim of ineffective assistance.

[The] Court of Appeals granted Sullivan relief because he had shown that the multiple representation in this case involved a possible conflict of interest. We hold that the possibility of conflict is insufficient to impugn a criminal conviction. In order to demonstrate a violation of his Sixth Amendment rights, a defendant must establish that an actual conflict of interest adversely affected his lawyer's performance. Sullivan believes he should prevail even under this standard. He emphasizes Peruto's admission that the decision to rest Sullivan's defense reflected a reluctance to expose witnesses who later might have testified for the other defendants. The petitioner, on the other hand, points to DiBona's contrary testimony and to evidence that Sullivan himself wished to avoid taking the stand. Since the Court of Appeals did not weigh these conflicting contentions under the proper legal standard, its judgment is vacated and the case is remanded for further proceedings consistent with this opinion.

MR. JUSTICE BRENNAN, concurring * * * in the result.

["A] possible conflict inheres in almost every instance of multiple representation." Therefore, upon discovery of joint representation, the duty of the trial court is to ensure that the defendants have not unwittingly given up their constitutional right to effective counsel. This is necessary since it is usually the case that defendants will not know what their rights are or how to raise them. [Had] the trial record in the present case shown that respondent made a knowing and intelligent choice of joint representation, I could accept the Court's standard for a post conviction determination as to whether respondent in fact was denied effective assistance. [Here,] however, where there is no evidence that the court advised respondent about the potential for conflict or that respondent made a knowing and intelligent choice to forgo his right to separate counsel, I believe that respondent, who has shown a significant possibility of conflict, is entitled to a presumption that his representation in fact suffered. * * *

MR. JUSTICE MARSHALL, concurring in part and dissenting in part.

[If] "[t]he possibility of the inconsistent interests of [the clients] was brought home to the court" by means of an objection at trial, the court may not require joint representation. But if no objection was made at trial, the appropriate inquiry is whether a conflict actually existed during the course of the representation. [Because] it is the simultaneous representation of conflicting interests against which the Sixth Amendment protects a defendant, he need go no further than to show the existence of an actual conflict. An actual conflict of interests negates the unimpaired loyalty a defendant is constitutionally entitled to expect and receive from his attorney. [In] the present case Peruto's testimony, if credited by the court, would be sufficient to make out a case of ineffective assistance by reason of a conflict of interests under even a restrictive reading of the Court's standard. * * *

Notes

1. It has become increasingly common for prosecutors to file pretrial motions to disqualify defense counsel. Such motions may be aimed at preventing counsel from engaging in the simultaneous representation of all or any one or more of multiple codefendants. Trial courts hearing such motions have the inherent judicial authority to oversee the conduct of the Bar, including the power to grant or deny such motions to disqualify. Typically, trial courts considering such motions in criminal cases look for guidance both to Sixth Amendment law and to applicable lawyer ethics code provisions relating to impermissible conflicts of interests.

2. American Bar Association Standards for Criminal Justice Defense Function Standard 4–3.5(c)(3rd ed. 1993) provides as follows:

> Except for preliminary matters such as initial hearings or applications for bail, defense counsel who are associated in practice should not undertake to defend more than one defendant in the same criminal case if the duty to one of the defendants may conflict with the duty to another. The potential for conflict of interest in representing multiple defendants is so grave that ordinarily defense counsel should decline to act for more than one of several codefendants except in unusual situations when, after careful investigation, it is clear that no conflict is likely to develop at trial, sentencing, or at any other time in the proceeding or

that common representation will be advantageous to each of the code-fendants represented and, in either case, that:

(i) the several defendants give an informed consent to such multiple representation; and

(ii) the consent of the defendants is made a matter of judicial record. In determining the presence of consent by the defendants, the trial judge should make appropriate inquiries respecting actual or potential conflicts of interest of counsel and whether the defendants fully comprehend the difficulties that defense counsel sometimes encounters in defending multiple clients.

3. In *Burger v. Kemp*, 483 U.S. 776 (1987), petitioner was convicted of capital murder and sentenced to death. Petitioner claimed that his lawyer labored under a conflict of interest because the lawyer's law partner represented petitioner's co-indictee. Although the Supreme Court assumed that "two law partners are considered as one attorney," the court refused to presume ineffective assistance. "[W]e presume prejudice only if the defendant demonstrates that counsel 'actively represented conflicting interests' and that 'an actual conflict of interest adversely affected his lawyer's performance.'" The Court found that petitioner was unable to satisfy this standard:

[Petitioner] argues that the joint representation adversely affected the quality of the counsel he received in two ways: Leaphart did not negotiate a plea agreement resulting in a life sentence, and he failed to take advantage of petitioner's lesser culpability when compared with his coindictee Stevens. We find that neither argument provides a basis for relief.

The notion that the prosecutor would have been receptive to a plea bargain is completely unsupported in the record. The evidence of both defendants' guilt, including their confessions, and eyewitness and tangible evidence, was overwhelming and uncontradicted; the prosecutor had no need for petitioner's eyewitness testimony to persuade the jury to convict Stevens and to sentence him to [death]. Mr. Burger tried to negotiate a plea with the district attorney for a life sentence. [He] flatly refused to even discuss it in any terms[.]

The argument that his partner's representation of Stevens inhibited Leaphart from arguing petitioner's lesser culpability because such reliance would be prejudicial to Stevens is also [unsupported]. [Because] the trials were separate, Leaphart would have had no particular reason for concern about the possible impact of the tactics in petitioner's trial on the outcome of Stevens' [trial].

Justice Blackmun dissented:

[The] right to conflict-free assistance of counsel [is] so fundamental in our adversarial system of criminal justice that public defender offices in many jurisdictions have rules precluding representation of more than one of the criminal defendants involved in the same [offense].

[There] can be no doubt that petitioner's court-appointed attorney actively represented conflicting interests through his role in the defenses of petitioner and his coindictee. [The] separate trials in this case [did] absolutely nothing to reduce the potential for divergence of interests at the two critical stages that petitioner argues were adversely affected by the conflict of interest, that is, pretrial plea negotiations and post-trial appeal. [Counsel's] joint representation [precluded] him, as a matter of professional responsibility, from pursuing the lesser culpability argument in petitioner's appellate brief. It would have been inconsistent with his duty of loyalty to Stevens to argue that the [court] should reduce petitioner's sentence to life imprisonment because Stevens was the more culpable defendant who deserved the death sentence for this heinous murder. [It] is difficult to imagine a more direct conflict than existed here, where counsel was preparing the appellate brief for petitioner at the same time that he was preparing the appellate brief for [Stevens].

Although it is easy to assume that the prosecutor would not have indulged in plea bargaining in this case because of the significant evidence of guilt, that approach ignores the reality of bargaining in capital cases. The evidence of guilt is not the only factor prosecutors consider. Rather, the relevant factors include the aggravating and mitigating circumstances surrounding the case as well as practical considerations such as the cost of pursuing the death penalty. Such practical considerations might weigh even more heavily prior to a second capital-sentencing trial on remand from the state appellate court's reversal of the first death [sentence]. * * *

4. The *Holloway* Court established that where counsel has brought the issue of potential conflict to a trial court's attention and the trial court failed properly to respond to the motion, e.g. by failing to either grant it or to ascertain the potentiality of a conflict at an appropriate hearing, in contrast to ordinary ineffectiveness inquiries, reversal of a defendant's conviction is "automatic," *even in the absence of a demonstration of prejudice*. As the Supreme Court has more recently reiterated this rule: "*Holloway* [creates] an automatic reversal rule [where] defense counsel is forced to represent codefendants over his timely objection, unless the trial court has determined that there is no conflict." *Mickens v. Taylor*, 535 U.S. 162, 168 (2002).

But, as Justice Scalia added for a majority of the *Mickens* Court in a 5–to–4 decision, involving defense counsel who was representing his client's victim at the time of the victim's death, reversal need not be automatic *every time* a trial court fails to inquire into a potential conflict of interest about which it knew or reasonably should have known:

Petitioner argues that [we have] established an "unambiguous rule" that where the trial judge neglects a duty to inquire into a potential conflict, the defendant, to obtain reversal of the judgment, need only show that his lawyer was subject to a conflict of interest, and need not show that the conflict adversely affected counsel's performance. [Petitioner's] proposed rule [makes] little policy sense. [T]he rule applied when the trial judge is not aware of the conflict (and thus not obligated to inquire) is that prejudice will be presumed only if the conflict has significantly affected counsel's performance—thereby rendering the verdict unreliable, even though *Strickland* prejudice cannot be shown. The trial court's awareness of a potential conflict neither renders it more likely that counsel's performance was significantly affected nor in any other way renders the verdict unreliable.

[Nor] is automatic reversal simply an appropriate means of enforcing *Sullivan's* mandate of inquiry. [We] do not presume that judges are as careless or as partial as those police officers who need the incentive of the exclusionary rule. And in any event, the *Sullivan* standard, which requires proof of effect upon representation but (once such effect is shown) presumes prejudice, already creates an "incentive" to inquire into a potential conflict. In those cases where the potential conflict is in fact an actual one, only inquiry will enable the judge to avoid all possibility of reversal by either seeking waiver or replacing a conflicted attorney. We doubt that the deterrence of "judicial dereliction" that would be achieved by an automatic reversal rule is significantly greater.

Since this was not a case in which (as in *Holloway*) counsel protested his inability simultaneously to represent multiple defendants; and since the trial court's failure to make the *Sullivan*-mandated inquiry does not reduce the petitioner's burden of proof; it was at least necessary, to void the conviction, for petitioner to establish that the conflict of interest adversely affected his counsel's performance. The Court of Appeals having found no such effect, the denial of habeas relief must be affirmed.

Justice Kennedy, joined by Justice O'Connor, concurred. Justice Stevens and Souter dissented in separate opinions. Justice Breyer, joined by Justice Ginsburg argued in dissent:

The Commonwealth of Virginia seeks to put the petitioner, Walter Mickens, Jr., to death after having appointed to represent him as his counsel a lawyer who, at the time of the murder, was representing the very person Mickens was accused of killing. [A] categorical approach is warranted and automatic reversal is required. [By] appointing this lawyer to represent Mickens, the Commonwealth created a "structural defect affecting the framework within which the trial [and sentencing] proceeds, rather than simply an error in the trial process itself."

[This] kind of breakdown in the criminal justice system creates, at a minimum, the appearance that the proceeding will not " 'reliably serve its function as a vehicle for determination of guilt or innocence,' " and the resulting " 'criminal punishment' " will not " 'be regarded as fundamentally fair.' " This appearance, together with the likelihood of prejudice in the typical case, are serious enough to warrant a categorical rule—a rule that does not require proof of prejudice in the individual case.

[The] Commonwealth seeks to execute a defendant, having provided that defendant with a lawyer who, only yesterday, represented the victim. In my view, to carry out a death sentence so obtained would invariably "diminis[h] faith" in the fairness and integrity of our criminal justice system. * * *

5. *Can Defendant Waive a Conflict of Interest?* In *Wheat v. United States*, 486 U.S. 153 (1988), Wheat was charged with participating in a drug distribution conspiracy. Also charged were Gomez–Barajas and Bravo, who

were represented by attorney Iredale. Gomez–Barajas was tried and acquitted on drug charges overlapping with those against Wheat. To avoid a trial on other charges, Gomez–Barajas offered to plead guilty to tax evasion and illegal importation of merchandise. At the commencement of Wheat's trial, the plea had not been accepted and could have been withdrawn. Bravo decided to plead guilty to one count of transporting marijuana. After the plea was accepted, Iredale notified the court that he had been asked to defend Wheat. When the Government objected because of a possible conflict of interest, the trial court refused to allow the representation. Wheat's conviction was upheld on appeal:

> [Nor] may a defendant insist [on retaining an] attorney who has a previous or ongoing relationship with an opposing party, even when the opposing party is the Government. [Where] a court justifiably finds an actual conflict of interest, [it] may decline a proffer of waiver, and insist that defendants be separately represented. [The] court must be allowed substantial latitude in refusing waivers of conflicts of interest not only in those rare cases where an actual conflict may be demonstrated before trial, but in the more common cases where a potential for conflict exists which may or may not burgeon into an actual conflict as the trial progresses.

Problems

1. Suppose that, in *Mickens*, the attorney had informed the trial judge of his prior representation of Hall, stated that he was conflicted, asked to be replaced, and the trial judge dismissed the request without further inquiry. Would automatic reversal be required?

2. A codefendant in a Baltimore heroin distribution prosecution, Jones, was represented by Denholm. Another codefendant, Wise, was represented by Salkin, Denholm's law partner. Just prior to trial, Wise agreed to plead guilty and to testify against her codefendants in exchange for a suspended sentence. The trial judge then issued a "gag order," ordering Salkin not to talk to his partner, Denholm, about the case as Salkin's client's interests now differed from the interests of Denholm's client. Dehholm objected to the issuance of the order, noting that if Salkin weren't his partner, he could talk to him about his client's testimony. His objections were overruled. At trial, Wise did testify against Jones. Her testimony about Jones' involvement in the heroin distribution scheme differed from the story she had told Denholm when she was a codefendant (that Jones was not involved), however Denholm did not try to impeach her on the basis of prior inconsistent statements. Jones was convicted and argued on appeal that his Sixth Amendment rights were violated, that Denholm had an impermissible conflict of interest due to the participation of his law partner in the proceedings, and that Jones was, accordingly, entitled to a new trial. Do you agree? What arguments can appellate counsel make to support this argument? In any event, how could or should the trial court have handled this matter better to avoid any potential conflict of interest? *See Austin v. State*, 327 Md. 375, 609 A.2d 728 (Md.Ct. App.1992).

3. Should a non-indigent defendant be able to complain that his or her counsel was "ineffective?" As a general rule, non-indigent defendants have

the right to choose the counsel they prefer (subject, of course, to their ability to pay the attorney's fees and the attorney's willingness to take the case). If the non-indigent chooses poorly, and counsel commits prejudicial error, should the conviction be reversed for ineffectiveness?

E. THE GRIFFIN–DOUGLAS DOCTRINE

In *Griffin v. Illinois*, 351 U.S. 12 (1956), the Supreme Court concluded that an indigent prisoner appealing from his conviction in state court had a Fourteenth Amendment right (under both the due process and equal protection clauses) to a free transcript of his trial where such transcripts were often a practical necessity for securing an appeal. In a plurality opinion, writing for four justices, Justice Black concluded that "[t]here can be no equal justice where the kind of trial a man gets depends on the amount of money he has. Destitute defendants must be afforded as adequate appellate review as defendants who have money enough to buy transcripts." *Id.* at 19.

Thereafter, the Court held in *Douglas v. California*, 372 U.S. 353 (1963), a companion case to *Gideon*, that indigent convicted defendants have a Fourteenth Amendment right (under both the due process and equal protection clauses) to the assistance of counsel on a first appeal where the state has granted them the right to appeal (as opposed to those instances where entitlement to appeal is only discretionary). Justice Douglas opined that "where the merits of the one and only appeal an indigent has as of right are decided without benefit of counsel, we think an unconstitutional line has been drawn between rich and poor." *Id.* at 357.

Subsequently, the Court declined to extend this so-called "Griffin–Douglas Doctrine" so as to require a Fourteenth Amendment entitlement to counsel by indigents in discretionary state appeals and applications for review to the Supreme Court, holding that "[t]he duty of the State under our cases is not to duplicate the legal arsenal that may be privately retained by a criminal defendant in a continuing effort to reverse his conviction, but only to assure the indigent defendant an adequate opportunity to present his claims fairly in the context of the State's appellate process." *Ross v. Moffitt*, 417 U.S. 600, 616 (1974).

The Supreme Court's 2005 decision in *Halbert v. Michigan* made it clear, however, that *Ross* did not supplant the Court's *Griffin-Douglas* commitment to equal justice for rich and poor:

HALBERT v. MICHIGAN

545 U.S. 605 (2005).

JUSTICE GINSBURG delivered the opinion of the Court.

In 1994, Michigan voters approved a proposal amending the State Constitution to provide that "an appeal by an accused who pleads guilty or nolo contendere shall be by leave of the court." Mich. Const., Art. 1, § 20. Thereafter, "several Michigan state judges began to deny appointed appellate counsel to indigents" convicted by plea. Rejecting challenges based on the Equal Protection and Due Process Clauses of the Fourteenth Amendment to the Federal Constitution, the Michigan Supreme Court upheld this practice[.]

Petitioner Antonio Dwayne Halbert, convicted on his plea of nolo contendere, sought the appointment of counsel to assist him in applying for leave to appeal to the Michigan Court of Appeals. The state trial court and the Court of Appeals denied Halbert's requests for appointed counsel, and the Michigan Supreme Court declined review.

Michigan Court of Appeals review of an application for leave to appeal, Halbert contends, ranks as a first-tier appellate proceeding requiring appointment of counsel under *Douglas v. California*, 372 U.S. 353 (1963). Michigan urges that appeal to the State Court of Appeals is discretionary and, for an appeal of that order, *Ross v. Moffitt*, 417 U.S. 600 (1974), holds counsel need not be appointed. [Today, we] conclude that Halbert's case is properly ranked with *Douglas* rather than *Ross*. Accordingly, we hold that the Due Process and Equal Protection Clauses require the appointment of counsel for defendants, convicted on their pleas, who seek access to first-tier review in the Michigan Court of Appeals.

The Federal Constitution imposes on the States no obligation to provide appellate review of criminal convictions. Having provided such an avenue, however, a State may not "bolt the door to equal justice" to indigent defendants. [*Griffin*] held that, when a State conditions an appeal from a conviction on the provision of a trial transcript, the State must furnish free transcripts to indigent defendants who seek to appeal. *Douglas* relied on *Griffin 's* reasoning to hold that, in first appeals as of right, States must appoint counsel to represent indigent defendants. *Ross* held, however, that a State need not appoint counsel to aid a poor person in discretionary appeals to the State's highest court, or in petitioning for review in this Court.

Cases on appeal barriers encountered by persons unable to pay their own way, we have observed, "cannot be resolved by resort to easy slogans or pigeonhole analysis." Our decisions in point reflect "both equal protection and due process concerns." "The equal protection concern relates to the legitimacy of fencing out would-be appellants based solely on their inability to pay core costs," while "[t]he due process concern homes in on the essential fairness of the state-ordered proceedings."

Two considerations were key to our decision in *Douglas* that a State is required to appoint counsel for an indigent defendant's first-tier appeal as of right. First, such an appeal entails an adjudication on the "merits." Second, first-tier review differs from subsequent appellate stages "at which the claims have once been presented by [appellate counsel] and passed upon by an appellate court."

[In] *Ross*, we explained why the rationale of *Douglas* did not extend to the appointment of counsel for an indigent seeking to pursue a second-tier discretionary appeal to the North Carolina Supreme Court or, thereafter, certiorari review in this Court. The North Carolina Supreme Court, in common with this Court we perceived, does not sit as an error-correction instance. Principal criteria for state high court review, we noted, included "whether the subject matter of the appeal has significant public interest, whether the cause involves legal principles of major significance to the jurisprudence of the State, [and] whether the decision below is in probable conflict" with the court's precedent. Further, we pointed out, a defendant who had already benefited from counsel's aid in a first-tier appeal as of right would have, "at the very least, a transcript or other record of trial proceedings, a brief on his behalf in the Court of Appeals setting forth his claims of error, and in many cases an opinion by the Court of Appeals disposing of his case."

[Petitioner] Halbert's case is framed by [these] two prior decisions of this Court concerning state-funded appellate counsel, *Douglas* and *Ross*. The question before us is essentially one of classification: With which of those decisions should the instant case be aligned? We hold that *Douglas* provides the controlling instruction. Two aspects of the Michigan Court of Appeals' process following plea-based convictions lead us to that conclusion. First, in determining how to dispose of an application for leave to appeal, Michigan's intermediate appellate court looks to the merits of the claims made in the application. Second, indigent defendants pursuing first-tier review in the Court of Appeals are generally ill equipped to represent themselves.

A defendant who pleads guilty or nolo contendere in a Michigan court does not thereby forfeit all opportunity for appellate review. Although he relinquishes access to an appeal as of right, he is entitled to apply for leave to appeal, and that entitlement is officially conveyed to him. Of critical importance, the tribunal to which he addresses his application, the Michigan Court of Appeals, unlike the Michigan Supreme Court, sits as an error-correction instance.

[Whether] formally categorized as the decision of an appeal or the disposal of a leave application, the Court of Appeals' ruling on a plea-convicted defendant's claims provides the first, and likely the only, direct review the defendant's conviction and sentence will receive. Parties like Halbert, however, are disarmed in their endeavor to gain first-tier review. As the Court in *Ross* emphasized, a defendant seeking State Supreme Court review following a first-tier appeal as of right earlier had the assistance of appellate counsel. The attorney appointed to serve at the intermediate appellate court level will have reviewed the trial court record, researched the legal issues, and prepared a brief reflecting that review and research. The defendant seeking second-tier review may also be armed with an opinion of the intermediate appellate court addressing the issues counsel raised. A first-tier review applicant, forced to act pro se, will face a record unreviewed by appellate counsel, and will be equipped with no attorney's brief prepared for, or reasoned opinion by, a court of review.

[Persons] in Halbert's situation are particularly handicapped as self-representatives. As recounted earlier this Term, "[a]pproximately 70% of indigent defendants represented by appointed counsel plead guilty, and 70% of those convicted are incarcerated." "[Sixty-eight percent] of the state prison populatio[n] did not complete high school, and many lack the most basic literacy skills." "[S]even out of ten inmates fall in the lowest two out of five levels of literacy—marked by an inability to do such basic tasks as write a brief letter to explain an error on a credit card bill, use a bus schedule, or state in writing an argument made in a lengthy newspaper article." Many, Halbert among them, have learning disabilities and mental impairments.

Navigating the appellate process without a lawyer's assistance is a perilous endeavor for a layperson, and well beyond the competence of individuals, like Halbert, who have little education, learning disabilities, and mental impairments. Appeals by defendants convicted on their pleas may involve "myriad and often complicated" substantive issues, and may be "no less complex than other appeals." One who pleads guilty or nolo contendere may still raise on appeal "constitutional defects that are irrelevant to his factual guilt, double jeopardy claims requiring no further factual record, jurisdictional defects, challenges to the sufficiency of the evidence at the preliminary examination, preserved entrapment claims, mental competency claims, factual basis claims, claims that the state had no right to proceed in the first place, including claims that a defendant was charged under an inapplicable statute, and claims of ineffective assistance of counsel."

[While] the State has a legitimate interest in reducing the workload of its judiciary, providing indigents with appellate counsel will yield applications easier to comprehend. Michigan's Court of Appeals would still have recourse to summary denials of leave applications in cases not warranting further review. And when a defendant's case presents no genuinely arguable issue, appointed counsel may so inform the court.

[For] the reasons stated, we vacate the judgment of the Michigan Court of Appeals and remand the case for further proceedings not inconsistent with this opinion. * * *

JUSTICE THOMAS, with whom JUSTICE SCALIA joins, and with whom the CHIEF JUSTICE joins [in part], dissenting.

[The] majority [holds] that Michigan's system is constitutionally inadequate. It finds that all plea-convicted indigent defendants have the right to appellate counsel when seeking leave to appeal. [*Douglas*,] however, does not support extending the right to counsel to any form of discretionary review, as *Ross v. Moffitt*, and later cases make clear. Moreover, Michigan has not engaged in the sort of invidious discrimination against indigent defendants that *Douglas* condemns. Michigan has done no more than recognize the undeniable difference between defendants who plead guilty and those who maintain their innocence, in an attempt to divert resources from largely frivolous appeals to more meritorious ones. The majority substitutes its own policy preference for that of Michigan voters, and it does so based on an untenable reading of *Douglas*.

[The] rationale of *Douglas* does not support extending the right to counsel to this particular form of discretionary review. Admittedly, the precise rationale for the *Griffin/Douglas* line of cases has never been made explicit. Those cases, however, have a common theme. States may not impose financial barriers that preclude indigent defendants from securing appellate review altogether. Nor may States create " 'unreasoned distinctions' " among defendants that "arbitrarily cut off appeal rights for indigents while leaving open avenues of appeals for more affluent persons." [Far] from being an "arbitrary" or "unreasoned" distinction, Michigan's differentiation between defendants convicted at trial and defendants convicted by plea is sensible.

[Today] the Court confers on defendants convicted by plea a right nowhere to be found in the Constitution or this Court's cases. It does so at the expense of defendants whose claims are, on average, likely more meritorious. [I] respectfully dissent.

* * *

One of the most significant applications of the *Griffin-Douglas* Doctrine in the criminal justice system involves the question of what assistance–other than defense counsel–the government must provide to indigent defendants.

AKE v. OKLAHOMA

470 U.S. 68 (1985).

JUSTICE MARSHALL delivered the opinion of the Court.

The issue in this case is whether the Constitution requires that an indigent defendant have access to the psychiatric examination and assistance necessary to prepare an effective defense based on his mental condition, when his sanity at the time of the offense is seriously in question.

Late in 1979, Glen Burton Ake was arrested and charged with murdering a couple and wounding their two children. [His] behavior at arraignment, and in other prearraignment incidents at the jail, was so bizarre that the trial judge, *sua sponte*, ordered him to be examined by a psychiatrist "for the purpose of advising with the Court as to his impressions of whether the Defendant may need an extended period of mental observation." The examining psychiatrist reported: "At times [Ake] appears to be frankly delusional.... He claims to be the 'sword of vengeance' of the Lord and that he will sit at the left hand of God in heaven." He diagnosed Ake as a probable paranoid schizophrenic and recommended a prolonged psychiatric evaluation to determine whether Ake was competent to stand trial.

In March, Ake was committed to a state hospital to be examined with respect to his "present sanity," *i.e.*, his competency to stand trial.

On April 10, less than six months after the incidents for which Ake was indicted, the chief forensic psychiatrist at the state hospital informed the court that Ake was not competent to stand trial. The court then held a competency hearing, at which a psychiatrist testified:

> "[Ake] is a psychotic ... his psychiatric diagnosis was that of paranoid schizophrenia—chronic, with exacerbation, that is with current upset, and that in addition ... he is dangerous.... [B]ecause of the severity of his mental illness and because of the intensities of his rage, his poor control, his delusions, he requires a maximum security facility within—I believe—the State Psychiatric Hospital system."

The court found Ake to be a "mentally ill person in need of care and treatment" and incompetent to stand trial, and ordered him committed to the state mental hospital.

Six weeks later, the chief forensic psychiatrist informed the court that Ake had become competent to stand trial. At the time, Ake was receiving 200 milligrams of Thorazine, an antipsychotic drug, three times daily, and the psychiatrist indicated that, if Ake continued to receive that dosage, his condition would remain stable. The State then resumed proceedings against Ake.

At a pretrial conference in June, Ake's attorney informed the court that his client would raise an insanity defense. To enable him to prepare and present such a defense adequately, the attorney stated, a psychiatrist would have to examine Ake with respect to his mental condition at the time of the offense. During Ake's 3–month stay at the state hospital, no inquiry had been made into his sanity at the time of the offense, and, as an indigent, Ake could not afford to pay for a psychiatrist. Counsel asked the court either to arrange to have a psychiatrist perform the examination, or to provide funds to allow the defense to arrange one. The trial judge rejected counsel's argument that the Federal Constitution requires that an indigent defendant receive the assistance of a psychiatrist when that assistance is necessary to the defense, and he denied the motion for a psychiatric evaluation at state expense[.]

Ake was tried for two counts of murder in the first degree, a crime punishable by death in Oklahoma, and for two counts of shooting with intent to kill. At the guilt phase of trial, his sole defense was insanity. Although defense counsel called to the stand and questioned each of the psychiatrists who had examined Ake at the state hospital, none testified about his mental state at the time of the offense because none had examined him on that point. The prosecution, in turn, asked each of these psychiatrists whether he had performed or seen the results of any examination diagnosing Ake's mental state at the time of the offense, and each doctor replied that he had not. *As a result, there was no expert testimony for either side on Ake's sanity at the time of the offense.* The jurors were then instructed that Ake could be found not guilty by reason of insanity if he did not have the ability to distinguish right from wrong at the time of the alleged offense. They were further told that Ake was to be presumed sane at the time of the crime unless *he* presented evidence sufficient to raise a reasonable doubt about his sanity at that time. If he raised such a doubt in their minds, the jurors were informed, the burden of proof shifted to the State to prove sanity beyond a reasonable doubt. The jury rejected Ake's insanity defense and returned a verdict of guilty on all counts.

At the sentencing proceeding, the State asked for the death penalty. No new evidence was presented. The prosecutor relied significantly on the testimony of the state psychiatrists who had examined Ake, and who had testified at the guilt phase that Ake was dangerous to society, to establish the likelihood of his future dangerous behavior. Ake had no expert witness to rebut this testimony or to introduce on his behalf evidence in mitigation of his punishment. The jury sentenced Ake to death on each of the two murder counts, and to 500 years' imprisonment on each of the two counts of shooting with intent to kill.

[The Oklahoma Court of Criminal Appeals upheld Ake's conviction on appeal.] We hold that when a defendant has made a preliminary showing that his sanity at the time of the offense is likely to be a significant factor at trial, the Constitution requires that a State provide access to a psychiatrist's assistance on this issue if the defendant cannot otherwise afford one.

[This] Court has long recognized that when a State brings its judicial power to bear on an indigent defendant in a criminal proceeding, it must take steps to assure that the defendant has a fair opportunity to present his defense. This elementary principle, grounded in significant part on the Fourteenth Amendment's due process guarantee of fundamental fairness, derives from the belief that justice cannot be equal where, simply as a result of his poverty, a defendant is denied the opportunity to participate meaningfully in a judicial proceeding in which his liberty is at stake. In recognition of this right, this Court held almost 30 years ago that once a State offers to criminal defendants the opportunity to appeal their cases, it must provide a trial transcript to an indigent defendant if the transcript is necessary to a decision on the merits of the appeal. *Griffin v. Illinois*, 351 U.S. 12 (1956). Since then, this Court has held that an indigent defendant may not be required to pay a fee before filing a notice of appeal of his conviction, that an indigent defendant is entitled to the assistance of counsel at trial, and on his first direct appeal as of right, and that such assistance must be effective.

[Meaningful] access to justice has been the consistent theme of these cases. We recognized long ago that mere access to the courthouse doors does not by itself assure a proper functioning of the adversary process, and that a criminal trial is fundamentally unfair if the State proceeds against an indigent defendant without making certain that he has access to the raw materials integral to the building of an effective defense. Thus, while the Court has not held that a State must purchase for the indigent defendant all the assistance that his wealthier counterpart might buy, it has often reaffirmed that fundamental fairness entitles indigent defendants to "an adequate opportunity to present their claims fairly within the adversary system." To implement this principle, we have focused on identifying the "basic tools of an adequate defense or appeal," and we have required that such tools be provided to those defendants who cannot afford to pay for them.

To say that these basic tools must be provided is, of course, merely to begin our inquiry. In this case we must decide whether, and under what conditions, the participation of a psychiatrist is important enough to preparation of a defense to require the State to provide an indigent defendant with access to competent psychiatric assistance in preparing the defense. Three factors are relevant to this determination. The first is the private interest that will be affected by the action of the State. The second is the governmental interest that will be affected if the safeguard is to be provided. The third is the probable value of the additional or substitute procedural safeguards that are sought, and the risk of an erroneous deprivation of the affected interest if those safeguards are not provided.

[The] private interest in the accuracy of a criminal proceeding that places an individual's life or liberty at risk is almost uniquely compelling. Indeed, the host of safeguards fashioned by this Court over the years to diminish the risk of erroneous conviction stands as a testament to that concern. The interest of the individual in the outcome of the State's effort to overcome the presumption of innocence is obvious and weighs heavily in our analysis.

We consider, next, the interest of the State. Oklahoma asserts that to provide Ake with psychiatric assistance on the record before us would result in a staggering burden to the State. We are unpersuaded by this assertion. Many States, as well as the Federal Government, currently make psychiatric assistance available to indigent defendants, and they have not found the financial burden so great as to preclude this assistance. This is especially so when the obligation of the State is limited to provision of one competent psychiatrist, as it is in many States, and as we limit the right we recognize today. At the same time, it is difficult to identify any interest of the State, other than that in its economy, that weighs against recognition of this right. The State's interest in prevailing at trial—unlike that of a private litigant—is necessarily tempered by its interest in the fair and accurate adjudication of criminal cases. Thus, also unlike a private litigant, a State may not legitimately assert an interest in maintenance of a strategic advantage over the defense, if the result of that advantage is to cast a pall on the accuracy of the verdict obtained. We therefore conclude that the governmental interest in denying Ake the assistance of a psychiatrist is not substantial, in light of the compelling interest of both the State and the individual in accurate dispositions.

Last, we inquire into the probable value of the psychiatric assistance sought, and the risk of error in the proceeding if such assistance is not offered. We begin by considering the pivotal role that psychiatry has come to play in criminal proceedings. More than 40 States, as well as the Federal Government, have decided either through legislation or judicial decision that indigent defendants are entitled, under certain circumstances, to the assistance of a psychiatrist's expertise. [These] statutes and court decisions reflect a reality that we recognize today, namely, that when the State has made the defendant's mental condition relevant to his criminal culpability and to the punishment he might suffer, the assistance of a psychiatrist may well be crucial to the defendant's ability to marshal his defense. In this role, psychiatrists gather facts, through professional examination, interviews, and elsewhere, that they will share with the judge or jury; they analyze the information gathered and from it draw plausible conclusions about the defendant's mental condition, and about the effects of any disorder on behavior; and they offer opinions about how the defendant's mental condition might have affected his behavior at the time in question.

[Psychiatry] is not [an] exact science, and psychiatrists disagree widely and frequently on what constitutes mental illness, on the appropriate diagnosis to be attached to given behavior and symptoms, on cure and treatment, and on likelihood of future dangerousness. Perhaps because there often is no single, accurate psychiatric conclusion on legal insanity in a given case, juries remain the primary factfinders on this issue, and they must resolve differences in opinion within the psychiatric profession on the basis of the evidence offered by each party. When jurors make this determination about issues that inevitably are complex and foreign, the testimony of psychiatrists can be crucial and "a virtual necessity if an insanity plea is to have any chance of success." [In] so saying, we neither approve nor disapprove the widespread reliance on psychiatrists but instead recognize the unfairness of a contrary holding in light of the evolving practice.

The foregoing leads inexorably to the conclusion that, without the assistance of a psychiatrist to conduct a professional examination on issues relevant to the defense, to help determine whether the insanity defense is viable, to present testimony, and to assist in preparing the cross-examination of a State's psychiatric witnesses, the risk of an inaccurate resolution of sanity issues is extremely high. With such assistance, the defendant is fairly able to present at least enough information to the jury, in a meaningful manner, as to permit it to make a sensible determination.

A defendant's mental condition is not necessarily at issue in every criminal proceeding, however, and it is unlikely that psychiatric assistance of the kind we have described would be of probable value in cases where it is not. The risk of error from denial of such assistance, as well as its probable value, is most predictably at its height when the defendant's mental condition is seriously in question. When the defendant is able to make an *ex parte* threshold showing to the trial court that his sanity is likely to be a significant factor in his defense, the need for the assistance of a psychiatrist is readily apparent. It is in such cases that a defense may be devastated by the absence of a psychiatric examination and testimony; with such assistance, the defendant might have a reasonable chance of success. In such a circumstance, where the potential accuracy of the jury's determination is so dramatically enhanced, and where the interests of the individual and the State in an accurate proceeding are substantial, the State's interest in its fisc must yield.

We therefore hold that when a defendant demonstrates to the trial judge that his sanity at the time of the offense is to be a significant factor at trial, the State must, at a minimum, assure the defendant access to a competent psychiatrist who will conduct an appropriate examination and assist in evaluation, preparation, and presentation of the defense. This is not to say, of course, that the indigent defendant has a constitutional right to choose a psychiatrist of his personal liking or to receive funds to hire his own. Our concern is that the indigent defendant have access to a competent psychiatrist for the purpose we have discussed, and as in the case of the provision of counsel we leave to the States the decision on how to implement this right.

Ake also was denied the means of presenting evidence to rebut the State's evidence of his future dangerousness. The foregoing discussion compels a similar conclusion in the context of a capital sentencing proceeding, when the State presents psychiatric evidence of the defendant's future dangerousness. We have repeatedly recognized the defendant's compelling interest in fair adjudication at the sentencing phase of a capital case. The State, too, has a profound interest in assuring that its ultimate sanction is not erroneously imposed, and we do not see why monetary considerations should be more persuasive in this context than at trial.

[We] turn now to apply these standards to the facts of this case. On the record before us, it is clear that Ake's mental state at the time of the offense was a substantial factor in his defense, and that the trial court was on notice of that fact when the request for a court-appointed psychiatrist was made. [In] addition, Ake's future dangerousness was a significant factor at the sentencing phase. The state psychiatrist who treated Ake at the state mental hospital testified at the guilt phase that, because of his mental illness, Ake posed a threat of continuing criminal violence. This testimony raised the issue of Ake's future dangerousness, which is an aggravating factor under Oklahoma's capital sentencing scheme, and on which the prosecutor relied at sentencing. We therefore conclude that Ake also was entitled to the assistance of a psychiatrist on this issue and that the denial of that assistance deprived him of due process.

Accordingly, we reverse and remand for a new trial. * * *

CHIEF JUSTICE BURGER concurred in the judgment. JUSTICE REHNQUIST dissented.

Problem

Defendant James Kelly was convicted of the robbery, rape and murder of a college student who was working as a pizza delivery person and who had delivered a pizza to Kelly's girlfriend's apartment. He was sentenced to death. On appeal, Kelly contended that the trial judge erred by denying his pretrial request for state funds to hire a private investigator and other experts. The trial judge had concluded that the *Ake* decision does not give a defendant a constitutional right to any expert other than a psychiatrist. Kelly argued that, although he had consensual sex with the victim, he did not kill her, and that a private investigator would have enabled him to find key (unnamed) witnesses who would have helped to confirm his story. Moreover, he argued that he should have been provided with: (1) a forensic expert to assess the truthfulness of the prosecution's forensic experts (who "matched" his DNA with DNA in sperm found in the victim's vagina and on the victim's underwear and jeans); and (2) a medical expert to "go over" the medical examiner's report. Do you think that the trial court's ruling was correct? Do you think that Kelly is entitled to a new trial? *See Rogers v. Oklahoma*, 890 P.2d 959 (Okla.Cr.App.1995).

*

Part II

POLICE PRACTICES

Chapter 4

ARREST, SEARCH & SEIZURE

A. SEARCH WARRANTS

1. The Warrant Preference

The Supreme Court has instructed law enforcement officers and lower courts that it has a strong "preference" that warrants should be used even where a warrantless search would otherwise be constitutional. As the Court explained in a key 1984 decision:

> Because a search warrant "provides the detached scrutiny of a neutral magistrate, which is a more reliable safeguard against improper searches than the hurried judgment of a law enforcement officer 'engaged in the often competitive enterprise of ferreting out crime,' "[we] have expressed a strong preference for warrants and declared that "in a doubtful or marginal case a search under a warrant may be sustainable where one without it may fail."

United States v. Leon, 468 U.S. 897, 913–14 (1984), *quoting United States v. Chadwick*, 433 U.S. 1, 9 (1977) (*Chadwick quoting Johnson v. United States*, 333 U.S. 10, 14 (1948)), and *United States v. Ventresca*, 380 U.S. 102, 106 (1965).

2. The Warrant Requirement

The Supreme Court has also long established that a warrant "requirement" is—at least as a matter of theory—one of the first principles of its Fourth Amendment jurisprudence. As the Court explained in *Thompson v. Louisiana*, 469 U.S. 17, 19–20 (1984), *quoting Katz v. United States*, 389 U.S. 347, 357 (1967):

> In a long line of cases, this Court has stressed that "searches conducted outside the judicial process, without prior approval by judge or magistrate, are *per se* unreasonable under the Fourth Amendment—subject only to a few specifically established and well delineated exceptions." [I]n all cases outside the exceptions to the warrant requirement the Fourth Amendment requires the interposi-

tion of a neutral and detached magistrate between the police and the "persons, houses, papers and effects" of the citizen.

Why are warrants required? The Court answered this question in *Skinner v. Railway Labor Executives' Ass'n*, 489 U.S. 602, 621–22 (1989) as follows:

> An essential purpose of a warrant requirement is to protect privacy interests by assuring citizens subject to a search or seizure that such intrusions are not the random or arbitrary acts of government agents. A warrant assures the citizen that the intrusion is authorized by law, and that it is narrowly limited in its objectives and [scope]. A warrant also provides the detached and neutral scrutiny of a neutral magistrate, and thus ensures an objective determination whether an intrusion is justified in any given case.

Despite the fact that the warrant requirement is such a firm theoretical fixture of Fourth Amendment law, the truth of the matter is that, in actual practice, the number of searches justified under one of the "few specifically established and well delineated exceptions" to the warrant requirement far outnumber the number of searches actually undertaken with a warrant. In short, while only a relatively few exceptions to the warrant requirement exist, *most* searches fall within these exceptional categories. As a result, a more useful and practical way to view this rule of law is to use the following rule of practice, even if it puts the cart before the horse: *If a search is not justified by one of the warrant requirement "exceptions," then a search warrant must be obtained.*

3. *Obtaining Warrants*

In most jurisdictions, any law enforcement or prosecuting officer is authorized to apply for a search warrant simply by taking an application for a search warrant to a magistrate authorized by law to issue warrants. Typically, the application must include an attachment of one or more written affidavits. In such affidavits, the affiant must have sworn under oath to facts sufficient to establish probable cause to believe *both* that the items to be listed for seizure in the warrant are in fact evidence of specified criminal activity, *and* that these items are presently located at the premises for which the search warrant is being sought. In addition, under F.R.Cr.P. 41(d)(3)(A) (as amended, eff. December 1, 2006), "[a] magistrate judge may issue a warrant based on information communicated by telephone or other reliable electronic means." Many states have similar court rule provisions.

Exercise #1

You are an FBI Special Agent working in New York City. You have recently been contacted by e-mail by a confidential informant (CI), who has not revealed his or her identity to you, but who sent you information by e-mail six months ago identifying by name and address a person the CI said was selling sexually explicit images of children over the internet. (Assume that this is a federal crime.). A subsequent investigation of that individual by your office revealed that he was indeed engaged in such criminal activity and criminal charges have been filed against him. In the message you have just received, the CI has stated as follows:

> I've got another scoop for you guys. In the past week, I've downloaded 67 GIF [image] files from a guy calling himself Nick9795 who is operating on USOL[, the "United States OnLine" computer service]. I paid Nick9795 $19.95 twice to gain access to these files. All of the pictures were of young children (boys and girls) engaged in gross sex acts with grown women. I hacked around in the USOL files and I think that Nick9795 is a guy named Gary Durham who lives in Oswego. GO GET HIM!!!

You have located four people named Gary Durham who live in Oswego, New York, and have placed a "dialed number recorder" ("DNR") (a device which records outgoing phone numbers) on each of their home telephone lines. The DNR on one of the phone lines, a line belonging to Gary Durham of 234 Ash Street in Oswego, indicates numerous phone calls have been placed in the last three months to telephone numbers associated with USOL. Accordingly, you have decided to obtain a search warrant to search 234 Ash Street for child pornography.

You have also tried to find out both the identity of "Nick9795" and the frequency of his or her usage of USOL services. However, you have contacted USOL and they refuse to give you that information, citing customer privacy concerns. You have decided, accordingly, that you also need to obtain a search warrant to search USOL's files in order to seize the file of "Nick9795."

Your class will be divided in half. The first group should prepare an affidavit based on the information set forth above which will support the issuance of a search warrant for the Gary Durham residence in Oswego. The second group should prepare an affidavit based on the information set forth above which will support the issuance of a search warrant for the "Nick9795" file at the offices of USOL.

(If, in preparing your affidavit, you decide that you do not possess sufficient information to support the issuance of a search warrant, you should include all the relevant information that you do possess in your affidavit, but add a separate page at the end of this assignment discussing what additional investigative techniques you would use in order to turn up additional information which would be sufficient to support the issuance of such a search warrant.)

4. *Challenging Warrants*

After a search has been made pursuant to a warrant, defense counsel can subsequently challenge the lawfulness of the search based upon the insufficiency of the supporting affidavit in two different ways. First, defense counsel can argue that the supporting affidavit *on its face* did not establish sufficient probable cause to support issuance of the warrant (and, hence, that the evidence seized pursuant to execution of the warrant must be suppressed as the fruits of an unconstitutional search). Second, defense counsel can try to challenge the accuracy or veracity of the statements in the affidavit which on their face establish probable cause. However, it is very difficult for counsel to win such a challenge, to *"go behind"* the warrant.

FRANKS v. DELAWARE

438 U.S. 154 (1978).

MR. JUSTICE BLACKMUN delivered the opinion of the Court.

This case presents an important and longstanding issue of Fourth Amendment law. Does a defendant in a criminal proceeding ever have the right, under the Fourth and Fourteenth Amendments, subsequent to the *ex parte* issuance of a search warrant, to challenge the truthfulness of factual statements made in an affidavit supporting the warrant?

In the present case the Supreme Court of Delaware held, as a matter of first impression for it, that a defendant under *no* circumstances may so challenge the veracity of a sworn statement used by police to procure a search warrant. We reverse, and we hold that, where the defendant makes a substantial preliminary showing that a false statement knowingly and intentionally, or with reckless disregard for the truth, was included by the affiant in the warrant affidavit, and if the allegedly false statement is necessary to the finding of probable cause, the Fourth Amondmont roquiroo that a hoaring bo hold at tho dcfondant'o requeѕt. In the event that at that hearing the allegation of perjury or reckless disregard is established by the defendant by a preponderance of the evidence, and, with the affidavit's false material set to one side, the affidavit's remaining content is insufficient to establish probable cause, the search warrant must be voided and the fruits of the search excluded to the same extent as if probable cause was lacking on the face of the affidavit.

[Whether] the Fourth and Fourteenth Amendments, and the derivative exclusionary rule made applicable to the States under *Mapp v. Ohio*, 367 U.S. 643 (1961), ever mandate that a defendant be permitted to attack the veracity of a warrant affidavit after the warrant has been issued and executed, is a question that encounters conflicting values. The bulwark of Fourth Amendment protection, of course, is the Warrant Clause, requiring that, absent certain exceptions, police obtain a warrant from a neutral and disinterested magistrate before embarking upon a search. In deciding today that, in certain circumstances, a challenge to a warrant's veracity must be permitted, we derive our ground from language of the Warrant Clause itself, which surely takes the affiant's good faith as its premise: "[N]o Warrants shall issue, but upon probable cause, supported by Oath or [affirmation]." Judge Frankel, in *United States v. Halsey*, 257 F. Supp. 1002, 1005 (S.D.N.Y.1966), aff'd, Docket No. 31369 (CA2, June 12, 1967) (unreported), put the matter simply: "[W]hen the Fourth Amendment demands a factual showing sufficient to comprise 'probable cause,' the obvious assumption is that there will be a *truthful* showing" (emphasis in original). This does not mean "truthful" in the sense that every fact recited in the warrant affidavit is necessarily correct, for probable cause may be founded upon hearsay and upon information received from informants, as well as upon information within the affiant's own knowledge that sometimes must be garnered hastily. But surely it is to be "truthful" in the sense that the information put forth is believed or appropriately accepted by the affiant as true. It is established law that a warrant affidavit must set forth particular facts and circumstances underlying the existence of probable cause, so as to allow the magistrate to make an independent evaluation of the matter. [Because] it is the magistrate who must determine independently whether there is probable cause, it would be an unthinkable imposition upon his authority if a warrant affidavit, revealed after the fact to contain a deliberately or recklessly false statement, were to stand beyond impeachment.

In saying this, however, one must give cognizance to competing values that lead us to impose limitations. They perhaps can be best addressed by noting the arguments of respondent and others against allowing veracity challenges. [First,] respondent argues that the exclusionary rule [is] not a personal constitutional right, but only a judicially created remedy extended where its benefit as a deterrent promises to outweigh the societal cost of its use; that the Court has declined to apply the exclusionary rule when illegally seized evidence is used to impeach the credibility of a defendant's testimony, is used in a grand jury proceeding, or is used in a civil trial; and that the Court similarly has restricted application of the Fourth Amendment exclusionary rule in federal habeas corpus review of a state conviction. Respondent argues that applying the exclusionary rule to another situation—the deterrence of deliberate or reckless untruthfulness in a warrant affidavit—is not justified for many of the same reasons that led to the above restrictions; interfering with a criminal conviction in order to deter official misconduct is a burden too great to impose on society.

Second, respondent argues that a citizen's privacy interests are adequately protected by a requirement that applicants for a warrant submit a sworn affidavit and by the magistrate's independent determination of sufficiency based on the face of the affidavit.

[Third,] it is argued that the magistrate already is equipped to conduct a fairly vigorous inquiry into the accuracy of the factual affidavit supporting a warrant application. He may question the affiant, or summon other persons to give testimony at the warrant proceeding. The incremental gain from a post-search adversary proceeding, it is said, would not be great.

Fourth, it is argued that it would unwisely diminish the solemnity and moment of the magistrate's proceeding to make his inquiry into probable cause reviewable in regard to veracity. The less final, and less deference paid to, the magistrate's determination of veracity, the less initiative will he use in that task.

[Fifth,] it is argued that permitting a post-search evidentiary hearing on issues of veracity would confuse the pressing issue of guilt or innocence with the collateral question as to whether there had been official misconduct in the drafting of the affidavit.

[Sixth] and finally, it is argued that a post-search veracity challenge is inappropriate because the accuracy of an affidavit in large part is beyond the control of the affiant. An affidavit may properly be based on hearsay, on fleeting observations, and on tips received from unnamed informants whose identity often will be properly protected from revelation under *McCray v. Illinois*, 386 U.S. 300 (1967).

None of these considerations is trivial. Indeed, because of them, the rule announced today has a limited scope, both in regard to when exclusion of the seized evidence is mandated, and when a hearing on allegations of misstatements must be accorded. But neither do the considerations cited by respondent and others have a fully controlling weight; we conclude that they are insufficient to justify an *absolute* ban on post-search impeachment of veracity. On this side of the balance, also, there are pressing considerations:

First, a flat ban on impeachment of veracity could denude the probable-cause requirement of all real meaning. The requirement that a warrant not issue "but upon probable cause, supported by Oath or affirmation," would be reduced to a nullity if a police officer was able to use deliberately falsified allegations to demonstrate probable cause, and, having misled the magistrate, then was able to remain confident that the ploy was worthwhile.

[Second,] the hearing before the magistrate not always will suffice to discourage lawless or reckless misconduct. The pre-search proceeding is necessarily *ex parte*, since the subject of the search cannot be tipped off to the application for a warrant lest he destroy or remove evidence. The usual reliance of our legal system on adversary proceedings itself should be an indication that an *ex parte* inquiry is likely to be less vigorous.

[Third,] the alternative sanctions of a perjury prosecution, administrative discipline, contempt, or a civil suit are not likely to fill the gap. *Mapp v. Ohio* implicitly rejected the adequacy of those alternatives.

[Fourth,] allowing an evidentiary hearing, after a suitable preliminary proffer of material falsity, would not diminish the importance and solemnity of the warrant-issuing process. [Our] reluctance today to extend the rule of exclusion beyond instances of deliberate misstatements, and those of reckless disregard, leaves a broad field where the magistrate is the sole protection of a citizen's Fourth Amendment rights, namely, in instances where police have been merely negligent in checking or recording the facts relevant to a probable-cause determination.

Fifth, the claim that a post-search hearing will confuse the issue of the defendant's guilt with the issue of the State's possible misbehavior is footless. The hearing will not be in the presence of the jury. An issue extraneous to guilt already is examined in any probable-cause determination or review of probable cause.

[Sixth] and finally, as to the argument that the exclusionary rule should not be extended to a "new" area, we cannot regard any such extension really to be at issue here. Despite the deep skepticism of Members of this Court as to the wisdom of extending the exclusionary rule to collateral areas, such as civil or grand jury proceedings, the Court has not questioned, in the absence of a more efficacious sanction, the continued application of the rule to suppress evidence from the State's case where a Fourth Amendment violation has been substantial and deliberate. We see no principled basis for distinguishing between the question of the sufficiency of an affidavit, which also is subject to a post-search reexamination, and the question of its integrity.

In sum, and to repeat with some embellishment what we stated at the beginning of this opinion: There is, of course, a presumption of validity with respect to the affidavit supporting the search warrant. To mandate an evidentiary hearing, the challenger's attack must be more than conclusory and must be supported by more than a mere desire to cross-examine. There must be allegations of deliberate falsehood or of reckless disregard for the truth, and those allegations must be accompanied by an offer of proof. They should point out specifically the portion of the warrant affidavit that is claimed to be false; and they should be accompanied by a statement of supporting reasons. [Allegations] of negligence or innocent mistake are insufficient. The deliberate falsity or reckless disregard whose impeachment is permitted today is only that of the affiant, not of any nongovernmental informant. Finally, if these requirements are met, and if, when material that is the subject of the alleged falsity or reckless disregard is set to one side, there remains sufficient content in the warrant affidavit to support a finding of probable cause, no hearing is required. On the other hand, if the remaining content is insufficient, the defendant is entitled, under the Fourth and Fourteenth Amendments, to his hearing. Whether he will prevail at that hearing is, of course, another issue.

Because of Delaware's absolute rule, its courts did not have occasion to consider the proffer put forward by petitioner Franks. [The] judgment of the Supreme Court of Delaware is reversed * * *

MR. JUSTICE REHNQUIST, with whom THE CHIEF JUSTICE joins, dissenting.

[If] the function of the warrant requirement is to obtain the determination of a neutral magistrate as to whether sufficient grounds have been urged to support the issuance of a warrant, that function is fulfilled at the time the magistrate concludes that the requirement has been met. Like any other determination of a magistrate, of a court, or of countless other fact-finding tribunals, the decision may be incorrect as a matter of law. Even if correct, some inaccurate or falsified information may have gone into the making of the determination. But unless we are to exalt as the *ne plus ultra* of our system of criminal justice the absolute correctness of every factual determination made along the tortuous route from the filing of the complaint or the issuance of an indictment to the final determination that a judgment of conviction was properly obtained, we shall lose perspective as to the purposes of the system as well as of the warrant requirement of the Fourth and Fourteenth Amendments. * * *

Note

The *Franks* test for determining when defense counsel may successfully "go behind" statements in a warrant affidavit also applies to an affiant's reckless or intentional *omission* of material information from an affidavit. If the affiant knows—and withholds—relevant information from an affidavit which would have cast doubt upon the existence of probable cause had it been considered by the issuing magistrate, the search warrant is defective and the fruits of its execution may be suppressed.

Problem

On June 15, 1990, officers from the Chester, Pennsylvania Police Department obtained a search warrant for defendant, George Clark's, home based upon an affidavit reporting that a confidential informant (CI) had witnessed Clark take orders for cocaine within the past 48 hours, drive to his home in his 1977 Pontiac Ventura, and retrieve cocaine. The search pursuant to the warrant turned up cocaine in small plastic baggies in Clark's bedroom. Defense counsel for Clark has produced a receipt from an auto service station establishing that Clark's Ventura was in the shop having work done on it from June 12 to June 16, 1990. Other witnesses testify to the fact that Clark did not drive his car at all during the first two weeks of June, 1990. Counsel argues that the CI has lied about the information contained in the affidavit and that, as a result, the cocaine seized in Clark's bedroom should be suppressed. How can the district attorney respond to this argument? What do you think the suppression court's ruling will (and should) be? *See Commonwealth v. Clark*, 412 Pa.Super. 92, 602 A.2d 1323 (1992), *cert. denied*, 507 U.S. 1030 (1993).

Exercise #2

Take home and review one of the affidavits prepared previously in Exercise #1. You are now defense counsel representing Durham after the search pursuant to a search warrant based upon this affidavit has taken place (and has produced evidence that the U.S. Attorney's Office seeks to use against Durham in a federal criminal prosecution). Assuming that the warrant issued based solely upon this affidavit (and ignoring any standing issues that might be present), prepare a Brief in Support of Defendant Durham's Motion to Suppress (of no more than 5 pages in length) contending that the affidavit was either insufficient to support the warrant on its face and/or that it was recklessly or intentionally misleading within the meaning of *Franks*.

5. *The Particularity Requirement*

The Fourth Amendment expressly requires that "no Warrants shall issue, but upon probable cause, *and particularly describing the place to be searched, and the persons or things to be seized.*" The Supreme Court has made clear that "[t]he uniformly applied rule is that a search conducted pursuant to a warrant that fails to conform to the particularity requirement of the Fourth Amendment is unconstitutional." *Massachusetts v. Sheppard*, 468 U.S. 981, 988 n. 5 (1984). To answer the question *how particular* a description of the place to be searched must be to satisfy the particularity requirement, the Supreme Court has adopted the following test: "It is enough if the description is such that the officer with a search warrant can with reasonable effort ascertain and identify the place intended." *Steele v. United States No. 1*, 267 U.S. 498, 503 (1925). As to the things to be seized, the Supreme Court has stated that if the language in a search warrant description is so imprecise as to have an "indiscriminate sweep," the search warrant is, accordingly, "constitutionally intolerable." *Stanford v. Texas*, 379 U.S. 476, 486 (1965).

UNITED STATES v. GRUBBS

547 U.S. ___, 126 S.Ct. 1494 (2006).

JUSTICE SCALIA delivered the opinion of the Court.

Federal law enforcement officers obtained a search warrant for respondent's house on the basis of an affidavit explaining that the warrant would be executed only after a controlled delivery of contraband to that location. We address two challenges to the constitutionality of this anticipatory warrant.

Respondent Jeffrey Grubbs purchased a videotape containing child pornography from a Web site operated by an undercover postal inspector. Officers from the Postal Inspection Service arranged a controlled delivery of a package containing the videotape to Grubbs' residence. A postal inspector submitted a search warrant application to a Magistrate Judge for the Eastern District of California, accompanied by an affidavit describing the proposed operation in detail. The affidavit stated:

> "Execution of this search warrant will not occur unless and until the parcel has been received by a person(s) and has been physically taken into the residence.... At that time, and not before, this search warrant will be executed by me and other United States Postal inspectors, with appropriate assistance from other law enforcement officers in accordance with this warrant's command."

In addition to describing this triggering condition, the affidavit referred to two attachments, which described Grubbs' residence and the items officers would seize. These attachments, but not the body of the affidavit, were incorporated into the requested warrant. The affidavit concluded: "Based upon the foregoing facts, I respectfully submit there exists probable cause to believe that the items set forth in Attachment B to this affidavit and the search warrant, will be found [at Grubbs' residence], which residence is further described at Attachment A."

The Magistrate Judge issued the warrant as requested. Two days later, an undercover postal inspector delivered the package. Grubbs' wife signed for it and took the unopened package inside. The inspectors detained Grubbs as he left his home a few minutes later, then entered the house and commenced the search. Roughly 30 minutes into the search, Grubbs was provided with a copy of the warrant, which included both attachments but not the supporting affidavit that explained when the warrant would be executed. Grubbs consented to interrogation by the postal inspectors and admitted ordering the videotape. He was placed under arrest, and various items were seized, including the videotape. [After moving unsuccessfully to suppress evidence seized during the search of his residence, Grubbs pleaded guilty to one count of receiving a visual depiction of a minor engaged in sexually explicit conduct, but reserved his right to appeal the denial of his motion to suppress. The Court of Appeals for the Ninth Circuit reversed.]

[An] anticipatory warrant is "a warrant based upon an affidavit showing probable cause that at some future time (but not presently) certain evidence of crime will be located at a specified place." Most anticipatory warrants subject their execution to some condition precedent other than the mere passage of time-a so-called "triggering condition." The affidavit at issue here, for instance, explained that "[e]xecution of th[e] search warrant will not occur unless and until the parcel [containing child pornography] has been received by a person(s) and has been physically taken into the residence." If the government were to execute an anticipatory warrant before the triggering condition occurred, there would be no reason to believe the item described in the warrant could be found at the searched location; by definition, the triggering condition which establishes probable cause has not yet been satisfied when the warrant is issued. Grubbs argues that for this reason anticipatory warrants contravene the Fourth Amendment's provision that "no Warrants shall issue, but upon probable cause."

We reject this view, as has every Court of Appeals to confront the issue[.] Probable cause exists when "there is a fair probability that contraband or evidence of a crime will be found in a particular place." Because the probable-cause requirement looks to whether evidence will be found when the search is conducted, all warrants are, in a sense, "anticipatory." In the typical case where the police seek permission to search a house for an item they believe is already located there, the magistrate's determination that there is probable cause for the search amounts to a prediction that the item will still be there when the warrant is executed. The anticipatory nature of warrants is even clearer in the context of electronic surveillance. When police request approval to tap a telephone line, they do so based on the probability that, during the course of the surveillance, the subject will use the phone to engage in crime-related conversations.

[Anticipatory] warrants are, therefore, no different in principle from ordinary warrants. They require the magistrate to determine (1) that it is now probable that (2) contraband, evidence of a crime, or a fugitive will be on the described premises (3) when the warrant is executed. It should be noted, however, that where the anticipatory warrant places a condition (other than the mere passage of time) upon its execution, the first of these determinations goes not merely to what will probably be found if the condition is met. (If that were the extent of the probability determination, an anticipatory warrant could be issued for every house in the country, authorizing search and seizure if contraband should be delivered-though for any single location there is no likelihood that contraband will be delivered.) Rather, the probability determination for a conditioned anticipatory warrant looks also to the likelihood that the condition will occur, and thus that a proper object of seizure will be on the described premises. In other words, for a conditioned anticipatory warrant to comply with the Fourth Amendment's requirement of probable cause, two prerequisites of probability must be satisfied. It must be true not only that if the triggering condition occurs "there is a fair probability that contraband or evidence of a crime will be found in a particular place," but also that there is probable cause to believe the triggering condition will occur. The supporting affidavit must provide the magistrate with sufficient information to evaluate both aspects of the probable-cause determination.

In this case, the occurrence of the triggering condition-successful delivery of the videotape to Grubbs' residence-would plainly establish probable cause for the search. In addition, the affidavit established probable cause to believe the triggering condition would be satisfied. Although it is possible that Grubbs could have refused delivery of the videotape he had ordered, that was unlikely. The Magistrate therefore "had a 'substantial basis for ... conclud[ing]' that probable cause existed."

The Ninth Circuit invalidated the anticipatory search warrant at issue here because the warrant failed to specify the triggering condition. The Fourth Amendment's particularity requirement, it held, "applies with full force to the conditions precedent to an anticipatory search warrant."

The Fourth Amendment, however, does not set forth some general "particularity requirement." It specifies only two matters that must be "particularly describ[ed]" in the warrant: "the place to be searched" and "the persons or things to be seized." We have previously rejected efforts to expand the scope of this provision to embrace unenumerated matters.

Respondent, drawing upon the Ninth Circuit's analysis below, relies primarily on two related policy rationales. First, he argues, setting forth the triggering condition in the warrant itself is necessary "to delineate the limits of the executing officer's power." [That] principle is not to be found in the Constitution. The Fourth Amendment does not require that the warrant set forth the magistrate's basis for finding probable cause, even though probable cause is the quintessential "precondition to the valid exercise of executive power." Much less does it require description of a triggering condition.

Second, respondent argues that listing the triggering condition in the warrant is necessary to " 'assur[e] the individual whose property is searched or seized of the lawful authority of the executing officer, his need to search, and the limits of his power to search.' " [This] argument assumes that the executing officer must present the property owner with a copy of the warrant before conducting his search. In fact, however, neither the Fourth Amendment nor Rule 41 of the Federal Rules of Criminal Procedure imposes such a requirement.

[Because] the Fourth Amendment does not require that the triggering condition for an anticipatory search warrant be set forth in the warrant itself, the Court of Appeals erred in invalidating the warrant at issue here. The judgment of the Court of Appeals is reversed, and the case is remanded for further proceedings consistent with this opinion.

JUSTICE ALITO took no part in the consideration or decision of this case. JUSTICE SOUTER, with whom Justice STEVENS and Justice GINSBURG join, concurring in part and concurring in the judgment.

[The] Court notes that a warrant's failure to specify the place to be searched and the objects sought violates an express textual requirement of the Fourth Amendment, whereas the text says nothing about a condition placed by the issuing magistrate on the authorization to search (here, delivery of the package of contraband). That textual difference is, however, no authority for neglecting to specify the point or contingency intended by the magistrate to trigger authorization, and the government should beware of banking on the terms of a warrant without such specification. The notation of a starting date was an established feature even of the objectionable 18th-century writs of assistance. And it is fair to say that the very word "warrant" in the Fourth Amendment means a statement of authority that sets out the time at which (or, in the case of anticipatory warrants, the condition on which) the authorization begins.

An issuing magistrate's failure to mention that condition can lead to several untoward consequences with constitutional significance. To begin with, a warrant that fails to tell the truth about what a magistrate authorized cannot inform the police officer's responsibility to respect the limits of authorization, a failing assuming real significance when the warrant is not executed by the official who applied for it and happens to know the unstated condition. The peril is that if an officer simply takes such a warrant on its face and makes the ostensibly authorized search before the unstated condition has been met, the search will be held unreasonable. * * *

* * *

If executing officers mistakenly search the wrong search premises, *i.e.* a place *not* particularly described in the search warrant, that does not necessarily mean that the search is unconstitutional (or that the fruits of the search must be suppressed).

MARYLAND v. GARRISON

480 U.S. 79 (1987).

JUSTICE STEVENS delivered the opinion of the Court.

Baltimore police officers obtained and executed a warrant to search the person of Lawrence McWebb and "the premises known as 2036 Park Avenue third floor apartment." When the police applied for the warrant and when they conducted the search pursuant to the warrant, they reasonably believed that there was only one apartment on the premises described in the warrant. In fact, the third floor was divided into two apartments, one occupied by McWebb and one by respondent Garrison. Before the officers executing the warrant became aware that they were in a separate apartment occupied by respondent, they had discovered the contraband that provided the basis for respondent's conviction for violating Maryland's Controlled Substances Act. The question presented is whether the seizure of that contraband was prohibited by the Fourth Amendment.

[There] is no question that the warrant was valid and was supported by probable cause. The trial court found, and the two appellate courts did not dispute, that after making a reasonable investigation, including a verification of information obtained from a reliable informant, an exterior examination of the three-story building at 2036 Park Avenue, and an inquiry of the utility company, the officer who obtained the warrant reasonably concluded that there was only one apartment on the third floor and that it was occupied by McWebb. [Only] after respondent's apartment had been entered and heroin, cash, and drug paraphernalia had been found did any of the officers realize that the third floor contained two apartments. As soon as they became aware of that fact, the search was discontinued. All of the officers reasonably believed that they were searching McWebb's apartment. No further search of respondent's apartment was made.

[The] manifest purpose of th[e] particularity requirement was to prevent general searches. By limiting the authorization to search to the specific areas and things for which there is probable cause to search, the requirement ensures that the search will be carefully tailored to its justifications, and will not take on the character of the wide-ranging exploratory searches the Framers intended to prohibit. Thus, the scope of a lawful search is "defined by the object of the search and the places in which there is probable cause to believe that it may be found. Just as probable cause to believe that a stolen lawnmower may be found in a garage will not support a warrant to search an upstairs bedroom, probable cause to believe that undocumented aliens are being transported in a van will not justify a warrantless search of a suitcase."

In this case there is no claim that the "persons or things to be seized" were inadequately described or that there was no probable cause to believe that those things might be found in "the place to be searched" as it was described in the warrant. With the benefit of hindsight, however, we now know that the description of that place was broader than appropriate because it was based on the mistaken belief that there was only one apartment on the third floor of the building at 2036 Park Avenue. The question is whether that factual mistake invalidated a warrant that undoubtedly would have been valid if it had reflected a completely accurate understanding of the building's floor plan.

Plainly, if the officers had known, or even if they should have known, that there were two separate dwelling units on the third floor of 2036 Park Avenue, they would have been obligated to exclude respondent's apartment from the scope of the requested warrant. But we must judge the constitutionality of their conduct in light of the information available to them at the time they acted. Those items of evidence that emerge after the warrant is issued have no bearing on whether or not a warrant was validly issued. Just as the discovery of contraband cannot validate a warrant invalid when issued, so is it equally clear that the discovery of facts demonstrating that a valid warrant was unnecessarily broad does not retroactively invalidate the warrant. The validity of the warrant must be assessed on the basis of the information that the officers disclosed, or had a duty to discover and to disclose, to the issuing Magistrate. On the basis of that information, we agree with the conclusion of all three Maryland courts that the warrant, insofar as it authorized a search that turned out to be ambiguous in scope, was valid when it issued.

[The] question whether the execution of the warrant violated respondent's constitutional right to be secure in his home is somewhat less clear. [If] the officers had known, or should have known, that the third floor contained two apartments before they entered the living quarters on the third floor, and thus had been aware of the error in the warrant, they would have been obligated to limit their search to McWebb's apartment. Moreover, as the officers recognized, they were required to discontinue the search of respondent's apartment as soon as they discovered that there were two separate units on the third floor and therefore were put on notice of the risk that they might be in a unit erroneously included within the terms of the warrant. The officers' conduct and the limits of the search were based on the information available as the search proceeded. While the purposes justifying a police search strictly limit the permissible extent of the search, the Court has also recognized the need to allow some latitude for honest mistakes that are made by officers in the dangerous and difficult process of making arrests and executing search warrants. [The] objective facts available to the officers at the time suggested no distinction between McWebb's apartment and the third-floor premises.

For that reason, the officers properly responded to the command contained in a valid warrant even if the warrant is interpreted as authorizing a search limited to McWebb's apartment rather than the entire third floor. Prior to the officers' discovery of the factual mistake, they perceived McWebb's apartment and the third-floor premises as one and the same; therefore their execution of the warrant reasonably included the entire third floor.[1] * * *

The judgment of the Court of Appeals is reversed[.]

JUSTICE BLACKMUN, with whom JUSTICE BRENNAN and JUSTICE MARSHALL join, dissenting.

[Even] if one accepts the majority's view that there is no Fourth Amendment violation where the officers' mistake is reasonable, it is questionable whether that standard was met in this case. [The] place at issue here is a small multiple-occupancy building. Such forms of habitation are now common in this country, particularly in neighborhoods with changing populations and of declining affluence. Accordingly, any analysis of the "reasonableness" of the officers' behavior here must be done with this context in mind. [In] the Court's view, the "objective facts" did not put the officers on notice that they were dealing with two separate apartments on the third floor until the moment, considerably into the search after they had rummaged through a dresser and a closet in respondent's apartment and had discovered evidence incriminating him, when they realized their "mistake." The Court appears to base its conclusion that the officers' error here was reasonable on the fact that neither McWebb nor respondent ever told the officers during the search that they lived in separate apartments.

In my view, however, the "objective facts" should have made the officers aware that there were two different apartments on the third floor well before they discovered the incriminating evidence in respondent's apartment. Before McWebb happened to drive up while the search party was preparing to execute the warrant, one of the officers, Detective Shea, somewhat disguised as a construction worker, was already on the porch of the row house and was seeking to gain access to the locked first-floor door that permitted entrance into the building. From this vantage point he had time to observe the seven mailboxes and bells; indeed, he rang *all* seven bells, apparently in an effort to summon some resident to open the front door to the search party. A reasonable officer in Detective Shea's position, already aware that this was a multiunit building and now armed with further knowledge of the number of units in the structure, would have conducted *at that time* more investigation to specify the exact location of McWebb's apartment before proceeding further. For example, he might have questioned another resident of the building.

---

1. We expressly distinguish the facts of this case from a situation in which the police know there are two apartments on a certain floor of a building, and have probable cause to believe that drugs are being sold out of that floor, but do not know in which of the two apartments the illegal transactions are taking place. A search pursuant to a warrant authorizing a search of the entire floor under those circumstances would present quite different issues from the ones before us in this case.

[A] reasonable officer would have realized the mistake in the warrant during the moments following the officers' entrance to the third floor. [In] the open doorway to his apartment, they encountered respondent, clad in pajamas and wearing a half-body cast as a result of a recent spinal operation. [It] appears that respondent, together with McWebb and the passenger from McWebb's car, were shepherded into McWebb's apartment across the vestibule from his own. Once again, the officers were curiously silent. The informant had not led the officers to believe that anyone other than McWebb lived in the third-floor apartment; the search party had McWebb, the person targeted by the search warrant, in custody when it gained access to the vestibule; yet when they met respondent on the third floor, they simply asked him who he was but never where he lived. Had they done so, it is likely that they would have discovered the mistake in the warrant before they began their search.

Finally and most importantly, even if the officers had learned nothing from respondent, they should have realized the error in the warrant from their initial security sweep. Once on the third floor, the officers first fanned out through the rooms to conduct a preliminary check for other occupants who might pose a danger to them. As the map of the third floor demonstrates, the two apartments were almost a mirror image of each other—each had a bathroom, a kitchen, a living room, and a bedroom. Given the somewhat symmetrical layout of the apartments, it is difficult to imagine that, in the initial security sweep, a reasonable officer would not have discerned that two apartments were on the third floor, realized his mistake, and then confined the ensuing search to McWebb's residence. * * *

Notes

1. When faced with a challenge at a suppression hearing to the particularity of the description contained in a search warrant, courts generally look both to the actual descriptive language in the warrant itself and to the description contained in any accompanying affidavits, if such affidavits are physically attached to the warrant (and thus available to the executing officers for their consultation) and incorporated by suitable words of reference. Where there has been no such incorporation by reference, however, a warrant that does not otherwise satisfy the particularity requirement is unconstitutional. See *Groh v. Ramirez*, 540 U.S. 551 (2004).

2. An error in the description of the place to be searched or the things to be seized in a search warrant does not render the warrant defective provided that other descriptive information in the warrant establishes with reasonable certainty the place to be searched or the things to be seized. *See, e.g., United States v. Hang Le–Thy Tran*, 433 F.3d 472, 479–81 (6th Cir. 2006) ("937 28th Street S.W." instead of "931 28th Street S.W." error OK where executing officers knew correct address and mistake was typographic error); *People v. Amador*, 24 Cal.4th 387, 100 Cal.Rptr.2d 617, 621–25, 9 P.3d 993 (2000) ("two story single family residence located at 10817 Leland, Santa Fe Springs, County of Los Angeles" instead of correct one-story residence at 10811 Leland held not to constitute defective warrant where the

executing officer knew the correct house and it had been shown to him by the informant).

3. Where an item to be seized has not been particularly described, a search warrant which has otherwise been lawfully obtained and executed remains constitutional with respect to any remaining items to be seized that have been properly described in the warrant. *See, e.g., State v. Tucker,* 133 N.H. 204, 575 A.2d 810, 813–15 (1990) (Opinion of now-Justice Souter) ("it is not apparent why the public interest in prosecuting crime should be taxed by suppressing any evidence beyond that obtained under the ostensible authority of the warrant's unduly general element"). In addition, those items "particularly described" may be seizable under the plain view doctrine.

6. *Warrant Execution*

WILSON v. ARKANSAS
514 U.S. 927 (1995).

Justice Thomas delivered the opinion of the Court.

At the time of the framing, the common law of search and seizure recognized a law enforcement officer's authority to break open the doors of a dwelling, but generally indicated that he first ought to announce his presence and authority. In this case, we hold that this common-law "knock and announce" principle forms a part of the reasonableness inquiry under the Fourth Amendment.

[During] November and December 1992, petitioner Sharlene Wilson made a series of narcotics sales to an informant acting at the direction of the Arkansas State Police. In late November, the informant purchased marijuana and methamphetamine at the home that petitioner shared with Bryson Jacobs. On December 30, the informant telephoned petitioner at her home and arranged to meet her at a local store to buy some marijuana. According to testimony presented below, petitioner produced a semiautomatic pistol at this meeting and waved it in the informant's face, threatening to kill her if she turned out to be working for the police. Petitioner then sold the informant a bag of marijuana.

The next day, police officers applied for and obtained warrants to search petitioner's home and to arrest both petitioner and Jacobs. Affidavits filed in support of the warrants set forth the details of the narcotics transactions and stated that Jacobs had previously been convicted of arson and firebombing. The search was conducted later that afternoon. Police officers found the main door to petitioner's home open. While opening an unlocked screen door and entering the residence, they identified themselves as police officers and stated that they had a warrant. Once inside the home, the officers seized marijuana, methamphetamine, valium, narcotics paraphernalia, a gun, and ammunition. They also found petitioner in the bathroom, flushing marijuana down the toilet. Petitioner and Jacobs were arrested and charged with delivery of marijuana, delivery of methamphetamine, possession of drug paraphernalia, and possession of marijuana.

Before trial, petitioner filed a motion to suppress the evidence seized during the search. Petitioner asserted that the search was invalid on various grounds, including that the officers had failed to "knock and announce" before entering her home. The trial court summarily denied the suppression motion. After a jury trial, petitioner was convicted of all charges and sentenced to 32 years in prison. [The Arkansas Supreme Court affirmed, finding "no authority for [petitioner's] theory that the knock and announce principle is required by the Fourth Amendment."] We granted certiorari to resolve the conflict among the lower courts as to whether the common-law knock-and-announce principle forms a part of the Fourth Amendment reasonableness inquiry. We hold that it does, and accordingly reverse and remand.

The Fourth Amendment to the Constitution protects "[t]he right of the people to be secure in their persons, houses, papers, and effects, against unreasonable searches and seizures." In evaluating the scope of this right, we have looked to the traditional protections against unreasonable searches and seizures afforded by the common law at the time of the framing. [An] examination of the common law of search and seizure leaves no doubt that the reasonableness of a search of a dwelling may depend in part on whether law enforcement officers announced their presence and authority prior to entering.

Although the common law generally protected a man's house as "his castle of defense and asylum," common-law courts long have held that "when the King is party, the sheriff (if the doors be not open) may break the party's house, either to arrest him, or to do other execution of the K[ing]'s process, if otherwise he cannot enter." To this rule, however, common-law courts appended an important qualification:

> "But before he breaks it, he ought to signify the cause of his coming, and to make request to open doors ... , for the law without a default in the owner abhors the destruction or breaking of any house (which is for the habitation and safety of man) by which great damage and inconvenience might ensue to the party, when no default is in him; for perhaps he did not know of the process, of which, if he had notice, it is to be presumed that he would obey it...."

Several prominent founding-era commentators agreed on this basic principle. According to Sir Matthew Hale, the "constant practice" at common law was that "the officer may break open the door, if he be sure the offender is there, if after acquainting them of the business, and demanding the prisoner, he refuses to open the door." William Hawkins propounded a similar principle: "the law doth never allow" an officer to break open the door of a dwelling "but in cases of necessity," that is, unless he "first signify to those in the house the cause of his coming, and request them to give him admittance." Sir William Blackstone stated simply that the sheriff may "justify breaking open doors, if the possession be not quietly delivered."

The common-law knock-and-announce principle was woven quickly into the fabric of early American law. Most of the States that ratified the Fourth Amendment had enacted constitutional provisions or statutes generally incorporating English common law, and a few States had enacted statutes specifically embracing the common-law view that the breaking of the door of a dwelling was permitted once admittance was refused.

Our own cases have acknowledged that the commonlaw principle of announcement is "embedded in Anglo–American law," but we have never squarely held that this principle is an element of the reasonableness inquiry under the Fourth Amendment. We now so hold. Given the longstanding common-law endorsement of the practice of announcement, we have little doubt that the Framers of the Fourth Amendment thought that the method of an officer's entry into a dwelling was among the factors to be considered in assessing the reasonableness of a search or seizure. Contrary to the decision below, we hold that in some circumstances an officer's unannounced entry into a home might be unreasonable under the Fourth Amendment.

This is not to say, of course, that every entry must be preceded by an announcement. The Fourth Amendment's flexible requirement of reasonableness should not be read to mandate a rigid rule of announcement that ignores countervailing law enforcement interests. As even petitioner concedes, the common-law principle of announcement was never stated as an inflexible rule requiring announcement under all circumstances.

[Because] the common-law rule was justified in part by the belief that announcement generally would avoid "the destruction or breaking of any house ... by which great damage and inconvenience might ensue," courts acknowledged that the presumption in favor of announcement would yield under circumstances presenting a threat of physical violence. [And] courts have indicated that unannounced entry may be justified where police officers have reason to believe that evidence would likely be destroyed if advance notice were given.

We need not attempt a comprehensive catalog of the relevant countervailing factors here. For now, we leave to the lower courts the task of determining the circumstances under which an unannounced entry is reasonable under the Fourth Amendment. We simply hold that although a search or seizure of a dwelling might be constitutionally defective if police officers enter without prior announcement, law enforcement interests may also establish the reasonableness of an unannounced entry.

Respondent contends that the judgment below should be affirmed because the unannounced entry in this case was justified for two reasons. First, respondent argues that police officers reasonably believed that a prior announcement would have placed them in peril, given their knowledge that petitioner had threatened a government informant with a semiautomatic weapon and that Mr. Jacobs had previously been convicted of arson and firebombing. Second, respondent suggests that prior announcement would have produced an unreasonable risk that petitioner would destroy easily disposable narcotics evidence.

These considerations may well provide the necessary justification for the unannounced entry in this case. Because the Arkansas Supreme Court did not address their sufficiency, however, we remand to allow the state courts to make any necessary findings of fact and to make the determination of reasonableness in the first instance. The judgment of the Arkansas Supreme Court is reversed, and the case is remanded for further proceedings not inconsistent with this opinion.[2]

RICHARDS v. WISCONSIN

520 U.S. 385 (1997).

JUSTICE STEVENS delivered the opinion of the Court.

In *Wilson v. Arkansas*, 514 U.S. 927 (1995), we held that the Fourth Amendment incorporates the commonlaw requirement that police officers entering a dwelling must knock on the door and announce their identity and purpose before attempting forcible entry. At the same time, we recognized that the "flexible requirement of reasonableness should not be read to mandate a rigid rule of announcement that ignores countervailing law enforcement interests" and left "to the lower courts the task of determining the circumstances under which an unannounced entry is reasonable under the Fourth Amendment."

In this case, the Wisconsin Supreme Court concluded that police officers are never required to knock and announce their presence when executing a search warrant in a felony drug investigation. [We] disagree with the court's conclusion that the Fourth Amendment permits a blanket exception to the knock-and-announce requirement for this entire category of criminal activity.

[On] December 31, 1991, police officers in Madison, Wisconsin obtained a warrant to search Steiney Richards' hotel room for drugs and related paraphernalia. The search warrant was the culmination of an investigation that had uncovered substantial evidence that Richards was one of several individuals dealing drugs out of hotel rooms in Madison. The police requested a warrant that would have given advance authori-

---

2. Respondent and its amici also ask us to affirm the denial of petitioner's suppression motion on an alternative ground: that exclusion is not a constitutionally compelled remedy where the unreasonableness of a search stems from the failure of announcement. Analogizing to the "independent source" doctrine [and] the "inevitable discovery" rule[,] respondent and its amici argue that any evidence seized after an un- reasonable, unannounced entry is causally disconnected from the constitutional violation and that exclusion goes beyond the goal of precluding any benefit to the government flowing from the constitutional violation. Because this remedial issue was not addressed by the court below and is not within the narrow question on which we granted certiorari, we decline to address these arguments.

zation for a "no-knock" entry into the hotel room, but the magistrate explicitly deleted those portions of the warrant.

The officers arrived at the hotel room at 3:40 a.m. Officer Pharo, dressed as a maintenance man, led the team. With him were several plainclothes officers and at least one man in uniform. Officer Pharo knocked on Richards' door and, responding to the query from inside the room, stated that he was a maintenance man. With the chain still on the door, Richards cracked it open. Although there is some dispute as to what occurred next, Richards acknowledges that when he opened the door he saw the man in uniform standing behind Officer Pharo. He quickly slammed the door closed and, after waiting two or three seconds, the officers began kicking and ramming the door to gain entry to the locked room. At trial, the officers testified that they identified themselves as police while they were kicking the door in. When they finally did break into the room, the officers caught Richards trying to escape through the window. They also found cash and cocaine hidden in plastic bags above the bathroom ceiling tiles.

Richards sought to have the evidence from his hotel room suppressed on the ground that the officers had failed to knock and announce their presence prior to forcing entry into the room. The trial court denied the motion[. The] Wisconsin Supreme Court [affirmed], conclud[ing] that exigent circumstances justifying a no-knock entry are always present in felony drug cases.

[We] recognized in *Wilson* that the knock-and-announce requirement could give way "under circumstances presenting a threat of physical violence," or "where police officers have reason to believe that evidence would likely be destroyed if advance notice were given." It is indisputable that felony drug investigations may frequently involve both of these circumstances. The question we must resolve is whether this fact justifies dispensing with case-by-case evaluation of the manner in which a search was executed.

The Wisconsin court explained its blanket exception as necessitated by the special circumstances of today's drug culture, and the State asserted at oral argument that the blanket exception was reasonable in "felony drug cases because of the convergence in a violent and dangerous form of commerce of weapons and the destruction of drugs." But creating exceptions to the knock-and-announce rule based on the "culture" surrounding a general category of criminal behavior presents at least two serious concerns.[3]

First, the exception contains considerable overgeneralization. For example, while drug investigation frequently does pose special risks to

3. It is always somewhat dangerous to ground exceptions to constitutional protections in the social norms of a given historical moment. The purpose of the Fourth Amendment's requirement of reasonableness "is to preserve that degree of respect for the privacy of persons and the inviola-bility of their property that existed when the provision was adopted—even if a later, less virtuous age should become accustomed to considering all sorts of intrusion 'reasonable.' " *Minnesota v. Dickerson*, 508 U.S. 366, 380 (1993) (SCALIA, J., concurring).

officer safety and the preservation of evidence, not every drug investigation will pose these risks to a substantial degree.

[A] second difficulty with permitting a criminal-category exception to the knock-and-announce requirement is that the reasons for creating an exception in one category can, relatively easily, be applied to others. Armed bank robbers, for example, are, by definition, likely to have weapons, and the fruits of their crime may be destroyed without too much difficulty. If a per se exception were allowed for each category of criminal investigation that included a considerable—albeit hypothetical—risk of danger to officers or destruction of evidence, the knock-and-announce element of the Fourth Amendment's reasonableness requirement would be meaningless.

Thus, the fact that felony drug investigations may frequently present circumstances warranting a no-knock entry cannot remove from the neutral scrutiny of a reviewing court the reasonableness of the police decision not to knock and announce in a particular case. Instead, in each case, it is the duty of a court confronted with the question to determine whether the facts and circumstances of the particular entry justified dispensing with the knock-and-announce requirement.

In order to justify a "no-knock" entry, the police must have a reasonable suspicion that knocking and announcing their presence, under the particular circumstances, would be dangerous or futile, or that it would inhibit the effective investigation of the crime by, for example, allowing the destruction of evidence. This standard—as opposed to a probable cause requirement—strikes the appropriate balance between the legitimate law enforcement concerns at issue in the execution of search warrants and the individual privacy interests affected by no-knock entries. This showing is not high, but the police should be required to make it whenever the reasonableness of a no-knock entry is challenged.

[Although] we reject the Wisconsin court's blanket exception to the knock-and-announce requirement, we conclude that the officers' no-knock entry into Richards' hotel room did not violate the Fourth Amendment. [The] circumstances in this case show that the officers had a reasonable suspicion that Richards might destroy evidence if given further opportunity to do so.

The judge who heard testimony at Richards' suppression hearing concluded that it was reasonable for the officers executing the warrant to believe that Richards knew, after opening the door to his hotel room the first time, that the men seeking entry to his room were the police. Once the officers reasonably believed that Richards knew who they were, the court concluded, it was reasonable for them to force entry immediately given the disposable nature of the drugs.

In arguing that the officers' entry was unreasonable, Richards places great emphasis on the fact that the magistrate who signed the search warrant for his hotel room deleted the portions of the proposed warrant that would have given the officers permission to execute a no-knock entry. But this fact does not alter the reasonableness of the officers' decision, which must be evaluated as of the time they entered the hotel room. At the time the officers obtained the warrant, they did not have evidence sufficient, in the judgment of the magistrate, to justify a no-knock warrant. Of course, the magistrate could not have anticipated in every particular the circumstances that would confront the officers when they arrived at Richards' hotel room.[4] These actual circumstances—petitioner's apparent recognition of the officers combined with the easily disposable nature of the drugs—justified the officers' ultimate decision to enter without first announcing their presence and authority.

Accordingly, although we reject the blanket exception to the knock-and-announce requirement for felony drug investigations, the judgment of the Wisconsin Supreme Court is affirmed. * * *

Problems

1. Police officers receive an anonymous uncorroborated tip that a house contains a methamphetamine lab and firearms. Based on the tip, they obtain a warrant to search the house. Must the police knock and announce themselves before entering the residence? *See Doran v. Eckold*, 409 F.3d 958 (8th Cir.2005).

2. Would your answer to the prior problem be affected by the fact that, before conducting the search, the police staked out the house and obtained additional evidence suggesting:

   A. A certainty that a methamphetamine lab existed on the premises?

   B. A certainty that firearms were present on the premises?

   C. The presence of individuals with criminal records evidencing their prior commission of violent felonies?

Notes

1. In *Ybarra v. Illinois*, 444 U.S. 85 (1979), the Court struck down an Illinois statute that authorized law enforcement officers to detain and search any person found on premises being searched pursuant to a search warrant. "The 'narrow scope' of the Terry exception does not permit a frisk for weapons on less than reasonable belief or suspicion directed at the person to be frisked, even though that person happens to be on premises where an authorized narcotics search is taking place." Nevertheless, in *Michigan v. Summers*, 452 U.S. 692 (1981), the Court upheld police detention of the occupant of a house while a search warrant for the house was being

---

4. A number of States give magistrate judges the authority to issue "no-knock" warrants if the officers demonstrate ahead of time a reasonable suspicion that entry without prior announcement will be appropriate in a particular context. [The] practice of allowing magistrates to issue no-knock warrants seems entirely reasonable when sufficient cause to do so can be demonstrated ahead of time. But, as the facts of this case demonstrate, a magistrate's decision not to authorize a no-knock entry should not be interpreted to remove the officers' authority to exercise independent judgment concerning the wisdom of a no-knock entry at the time the warrant is being executed.

executed. The Court held that the "limited intrusion on the personal security" of the person detained was justified "by such substantial law enforcement interests" that the seizure could be made on articulable suspicion not amounting to probable cause. And, more recently, the Court in *Muehler v. Mena*, 544 U.S. 93 (2005), ruled that–in the proper circumstances–an individual detained while a search warrant is being executed may be held for a period of 2 to 3 hours, and also may be handcuffed during that period. As Chief Justice Rehnquist explained for a majority of the Court:

> [T]his was no ordinary search. The governmental interests in not only detaining, but using handcuffs, are at their maximum when, as here, a warrant authorizes a search for weapons and a wanted gang member resides on the premises. In such inherently dangerous situations, the use of handcuffs minimizes the risk of harm to both officers and occupants. Though this safety risk inherent in executing a search warrant for weapons was sufficient to justify the use of handcuffs, the need to detain multiple occupants made the use of handcuffs all the more reasonable.

544 U.S. at 100.

2. A search warrant must be executed within the time period prescribed by the issuing magistrate, not to exceed the period established for execution of a search warrant in the applicable jurisdiction. This time limit, established by statute or court rule, is most commonly 10 days, although states have set limits as various as 2 to 60 days. See, e.g., Fed. R. Crim. P. 41(e)(2)(A)(federal time period not to exceed 10 days).

3. Most jurisdictions require law enforcement officers applying for a search warrant to be executed during the nighttime to make a special showing of necessity to search at that time. In about half of these jurisdictions, however, law enforcement failures to follow nighttime search requirements have been held not to constitute error of a constitutional dimension. Although three justices of the Supreme Court held in 1974 that this requirement *is* a constitutional requirement (and, hence, the exclusionary rule applies), *Gooding v. United States*, 416 U.S. 430 (1974), this proposition has never been expressly adopted by a majority of the Court.

UNITED STATES v. BANKS

540 U.S. 31 (2003).

JUSTICE SOUTER delivered the opinion of the Court.

Officers executing a warrant to search for cocaine in respondent Banks's apartment knocked and announced their authority. The question is whether their 15–to–20–second wait before a forcible entry satisfied the Fourth Amendment[.] We hold that it did.

[With] information that Banks was selling cocaine at home, North Las Vegas Police Department officers and Federal Bureau of Investigation agents got a warrant to search his two-bedroom apartment. As soon as they arrived there, about 2 o'clock on a Wednesday afternoon, officers posted in front called out 'police search warrant' and rapped hard enough on the door to be heard by officers at the back door. There was no indication whether anyone was home, and after waiting for 15 to 20 seconds with no answer, the officers broke open the front door with a battering ram. Banks was in the shower and testified that he heard nothing until the crash of the door, which brought him out dripping to confront the police. The search produced weapons, crack cocaine, and other evidence of drug dealing.

In response to drug and firearms charges, Banks moved to suppress evidence, arguing that the officers executing the search warrant waited an unreasonably short time before forcing entry, and so violated [the] Fourth Amendment[.] The District Court denied the motion, and Banks pleaded guilty, reserving his right to challenge the search on appeal. [The Ninth Circuit Court of Appeals reversed in a 2–to–1 panel opinion.]

We granted certiorari to consider how to go about applying the standard of reasonableness to the length of time police with a warrant must wait before entering without permission after knocking and announcing their intent in a felony case. We now reverse.

There has never been a dispute that these officers were obliged to knock and announce their intentions when executing the search warrant, an obligation they concededly honored. [The] Fourth Amendment says nothing specific about formalities in exercising a warrant's authorization, speaking to the manner of searching as well as to the legitimacy of searching at all simply in terms of the right to be 'secure ... against unreasonable searches and seizures.' Although the notion of reasonable execution must therefore be fleshed out, we have done that case by case, largely avoiding categories and protocols for searches. Instead, we have treated reasonableness as a function of the facts of cases so various that no template is likely to produce sounder results than examining the totality of circumstances in a given case; it is too hard to invent categories without giving short shrift to details that turn out to be important in a given instance, and without inflating marginal ones. We have, however, pointed out factual considerations of unusual, albeit not dispositive, significance.

[Since] most people keep their doors locked, entering without knocking will normally do some damage, a circumstance too common to require a heightened justification when a reasonable suspicion of exigency already justifies an unwarned entry. We have accordingly held that police in exigent circumstances may damage premises so far as necessary for a no-knock entrance without demonstrating the suspected risk in any more detail than the law demands for an unannounced intrusion simply by lifting the latch. Either way, it is enough that the officers had a reasonable suspicion of exigent circumstances.

[This] case turns on the significance of exigency revealed by circumstances known to the officers[. Here] the Government claims that a risk of losing evidence arose shortly after knocking and announcing. Although the police concededly arrived at Banks's door without reasonable suspicion of facts justifying a no-knock entry, they argue that announcing their presence started the clock running toward the moment of apprehension that Banks would flush away the easily disposable cocaine, prompted by knowing the police would soon be coming in.

[Banks] does not, of course, deny that exigency may develop in the period beginning when officers with a warrant knock to be admitted, and the issue comes down to whether it was reasonable to suspect imminent loss of evidence after the 15 to 20 seconds the officers waited prior to forcing their way. Though we agree with [the] dissenting opinion [below] that this call is a close one, we think that after 15 or 20 seconds without a response, police could fairly suspect that cocaine would be gone if they were reticent any longer. Courts of Appeals have, indeed, routinely held similar wait times to be reasonable in drug cases with similar facts including easily disposable evidence (and some courts have found even shorter ones to be reasonable enough).

A look at Banks's counterarguments shows why these courts reached sensible results, for each of his reasons for saying that 15 to 20 seconds was too brief rests on a mistake about the relevant enquiry: the fact that he was actually in the shower and did not hear the officers is not to the point, and the same is true of the claim that it might have taken him longer than 20 seconds if he had heard the knock and headed straight for the door. As for the shower, it is enough to say that the facts known to the police are what count in judging reasonable waiting time, and there is no indication that the police knew that Banks was in the shower and thus unaware of an impending search that he would otherwise have tried to frustrate.

And the argument that 15 to 20 seconds was too short for Banks to have come to the door ignores the very risk that justified prompt entry. True, if the officers were to justify their timing here by claiming that Banks's failure to admit them fairly suggested a refusal to let them in, Banks could at least argue that no such suspicion can arise until an occupant has had time to get to the door, a time that will vary with the size of the establishment, perhaps five seconds to open a motel room door, or several minutes to move through a townhouse. In this case, however, the police claim exigent need to enter, and the crucial fact in examining their actions is not time to reach the door but the particular exigency claimed. On the record here, what matters is the opportunity to get rid of cocaine, which a prudent dealer will keep near a commode or kitchen sink. The significant circumstances include the arrival of the police during the day, when anyone inside would probably have been up and around, and the sufficiency of 15 to 20 seconds for getting to the bathroom or the kitchen to start flushing cocaine down the drain. That is, when circumstances are exigent because a pusher may be near the point of putting his drugs beyond reach, it is imminent disposal, not travel time to the entrance, that governs when the police may reasonably enter; since the bathroom and kitchen are usually in the interior of a dwelling, not the front hall, there is no reason generally to peg the travel time to the location of the door, and no reliable basis for giving the proprietor of a mansion a longer wait than the resident of a bungalow, or an apartment like Banks's. And 15 to 20 seconds does not seem an unrealistic guess about the time someone would need to get in a position to rid his quarters of cocaine.

Once the exigency had matured, of course, the officers were not bound to learn anything more or wait any longer before going in, even though their entry entailed some harm to the building. [The] exigent need of law enforcement trumps a resident's interest in avoiding all property damage[. One] point in making an officer knock and announce, then, is to give a person inside the chance to save his door. That is why, in the case with no reason to suspect an immediate risk of frustration or futility in waiting at all, the reasonable wait time may well be longer when police make a forced entry, since they ought to be more certain the occupant has had time to answer the door. It is hard to be more definite than that[.] Suffice it to say that the need to damage property in the course of getting in is a good reason to require more patience than it would be reasonable to expect if the door were open. Police seeking a stolen piano may be able to spend more time to make sure they really need the battering ram.

[The] judgment of the Court of Appeals is reversed.

Problem

On May 16, 1989, FBI agents, armed with a lawfully-obtained search warrant, approached the door to premises to be searched for evidence of an extensive cocaine distribution operation, knocked on the door and stated, "[O]pen the door. FBI." The agents heard "shuffling" noises inside the apartment both before and after they knocked. The agents also testified that they waited 15–20 seconds after knocking and then, when they did not observe any effort being made to open the door, they broke it down with a sledgehammer. Once inside the premises, the officers observed and seized numerous items (including cocaine) sought to be introduced at trial. Defense counsel argues that the items must be suppressed as the fruits of an unconstitutional execution of a search warrant. What response can you make to these arguments as the prosecutor in this case? Is the defense likely to win this suppression motion? Why or why not? *See United States v. Anderson*, 39 F.3d 331 (D.C.Cir.1994).

Notes & Questions

1. *More on "Knock and Announce."* In *Hudson v. Michigan*, 126 S.Ct. 2159 (2006), police waited only three to five seconds after knocking on a suspect's door before entering pursuant to a warrant. Although the Court held that the police violated the "knock and announce" requirement a majority of the Court nonetheless refused to hold that the evidence should be excluded, holding that the federal exclusionary rule does not apply to knock and announce violations.

2. *When is destructive behavior on the part of the executing officers excessive or unnecessary?* In *United States v. Ramirez*, 523 U.S. 65, 71

(1998), the Supreme Court held that "[e]xcessive or unnecessary destruction of property in the course of a search may violate the Fourth Amendment, even though the entry itself is lawful and the fruits of the search are not subject to suppression." *See also, e.g., Ginter v. Stallcup*, 869 F.2d 384, 389 (8th Cir.1989) (there is a "Fourth Amendment right to be free from an unnecessarily destructive search and seizure.... Thus, any destruction caused by law enforcement officers in the execution of a search or an arrest warrant must be necessary to effectively execute that warrant."); *Gurski v. New Jersey State Police Dept.*, 242 N.J.Super. 148, 576 A.2d 292, 299 (1990) ("No police officer in the course of executing a warrant can or should, without justification or sufficient reason, destroy private property, take or use any personal property of another without permission, or use abusive language.").

3. *When can executing officers kill animals living on the search premises?* The Ninth Circuit Court of Appeals has held that the intentional killing of three dogs, two of them "guard dogs," on search premises, one of them a Rottweiler, during the execution of a search warrants on a Hells Angels clubhouse and residences was not justified under the Fourth Amendment:

> Reasonableness is the touchstone of any seizure under the Fourth Amendment. Thus, to comply with the Fourth Amendment, the seizure—in this case, shooting and death—of the [dogs] must have been reasonable under the circumstances. We look to the totality of the circumstances to determine whether the destruction of property was reasonably necessary to effectuate the performance of the law enforcement officer's duties. To determine whether the shooting of the dogs was reasonable, we balance "the nature and quality of the intrusion on the individual's Fourth Amendment interests against the countervailing governmental interests at stake."

> Here, the intrusion was severe. [We] have recognized that dogs are more than just a personal effect. The emotional attachment to a family's dog is not comparable to a possessory interest in furniture. [The] seizures were unreasonable, in violation of the Fourth Amendment. Most important, both entry teams had a week to plan the execution of the entry. [Despite] advance knowledge of the presence of two guard dogs, the full extent of the plan to protect the entry team from the dogs was to either "isolate" or shoot the dogs. The officers had no specific plan for isolating the dogs.

> The [contention] that shooting the dogs was necessary to preserve stealth is [unpersuasive]. It was the officers' own method of entry that compromised their ability to effectuate a quiet entry. At [one] residence, the [executing officers] used a ram to break down the front door before they even dealt with the dogs; at [a second] residence, the residents were awakened not by the barking of their dogs, but rather by the four shotgun blasts discharged at the dogs. If [officers] truly feared that continued barking would "alert the residents and possibly jeopardize the mission," it was an unreasonable response—indeed, an utterly irrational one—to fire four shotgun blasts to "engage" the dogs. All of the above considerations support the conclusion that the officers violated the plaintiffs' Fourth Amendment rights by unnecessarily shooting the dogs.

San Jose Chapter of Hells Angels Motorcycle Club v. City of San Jose, 402 F.3d 962 (9th Cir.2005). Do you think that the Ninth Circuit was correct? Did these dogs pose a danger to the executing officers and/or to the successful completion of the search that justified the officers' actions? This case was a civil rights action brought against the city of San Jose for damages occasioned by the shooting of the dogs and other property damage that occurred during the raids. San Jose ultimately settled the case by paying $990,000, $530,000 of which was payment of the plaintiffs' attorneys' fees. CNN, *"Hells Angels get $990 K for dead dogs,"* http://www.cnn.com/2006/LAW/02/07/hells.angels.ap/intex.html (February 7, 2006).

B. PROTECTED FOURTH AMENDMENT INTERESTS

In order for the Fourth Amendment to apply, a government official (or someone whose acts are chargeable to the government) must first conduct a "search" or a "seizure." In this section, we examine the meaning of terms.

KATZ v. UNITED STATES

389 U.S. 347 (1967).

MR. JUSTICE STEWART delivered the opinion of the Court.

[Katz was convicted of transmitting wagering information by telephone.] At trial the Government was permitted [to] introduce evidence of the petitioner's end of telephone conversations, overheard by FBI agents who had attached an electronic listening and recording device to the outside of the public telephone booth from which he had placed his calls. [The agents obtained six recordings, averaging about three minutes each, and preserved only his end of conversations concerning the placing of bets.]

[P]etitioner [argued] that the booth was a "constitutionally protected area." The Government has maintained with equal vigor that it was not. But this effort to decide whether or not a given "area," viewed in the abstract, is "constitutionally protected" deflects attention from the problem presented by this case. For the Fourth Amendment protects people, not places. What a person knowingly exposes to the public, even in his own home or office, is not a subject of Fourth Amendment protection. But what he seeks to preserve as private, even in an area accessible to the public, may be constitutionally protected.

The Government stresses [that] the telephone booth from which the petitioner made his calls was constructed partly of glass, so that he was as visible after he entered it as he would have been if he had remained outside. But what he sought to exclude when he entered the booth was not the intruding eye—it was the uninvited ear. He did not shed his right to do so simply because he made his calls from a place where he might be seen. No less than an individual in a business office, in a friend's apartment, or in a taxicab, a person in a telephone booth may rely upon the protection of the Fourth Amendment. One who occupies it, shuts the door behind him, and pays the toll that permits him to place a call is surely entitled to assume that the words he utters into the mouthpiece will not be broadcast to the world. To read the Constitution more narrowly is to ignore the vital role that the public telephone has come to play in private communication.

The Government contends [that] the activities of its agents in this case should not be tested by Fourth Amendment requirements, for the surveillance technique they employed involved no physical penetration of the telephone booth from which the petitioner placed his calls. It is true that the absence of such penetration was at one time thought to foreclose further Fourth Amendment inquiry, for that Amendment was thought to limit only searches and seizures of tangible property. But "[t]he premise that property interests control the right of the Government to search and seize has been discredited." *Warden v. Hayden*, 387 U.S. 294, 304 [(19)]. Indeed, we have expressly held that the Fourth Amendment governs not only the seizure of tangible items, but extends as well to the recording of oral statements overheard without any "technical trespass under [local] property law." *Silverman v. United States*, 365 U.S. 505. [O]nce it is recognized that the Fourth Amendment protects people—and not simply "areas"—against unreasonable searches and seizures it becomes clear that the reach of that Amendment cannot turn upon the presence or absence of a physical intrusion into any given enclosure.

We conclude that [the] "trespass" doctrine [can] no longer be regarded as controlling. The Government's activities in electronically listening to and recording the petitioner's words violated the privacy upon which he justifiably relied while using the telephone booth and thus constituted a "search and seizure" within the meaning of the Fourth Amendment. The fact that the electronic device employed to achieve that end did not happen to penetrate the wall of the booth can have no constitutional significance.

The question remaining [is] whether the search and seizure conducted in this case complied with constitutional standards. [T]he Government's position is that its agents acted in an entirely defensible manner: They did not begin their electronic surveillance until investigation of the petitioner's activities had established a strong probability that he was using the telephone in question to transmit gambling information to persons in other States, in violation of federal law. Moreover, the surveillance was limited, both in scope and in duration, to the specific purpose of establishing the contents of the petitioner's unlawful telephonic communications. The agents confined their surveillance to the brief periods during which he used the telephone booth, and they took great care to overhear only the conversations of the petitioner himself.

[I]t is clear that this surveillance was so narrowly circumscribed that a duly authorized magistrate, properly notified of the need for such investigation, specifically informed of the basis on which it was to proceed, and clearly apprised of the precise intrusion it would entail, could constitutionally have authorized, with appropriate safeguards, the

very limited search and seizure that the Government asserts in fact took place. [The] Government urges that [we] should retroactively validate their conduct. That we cannot do. [Searches] conducted without warrants have been held unlawful "notwithstanding facts unquestionably showing probable cause," for the Constitution requires "that the deliberate, impartial judgment of a judicial officer [be] interposed between the citizen and the [police]." *Wong Sun v. United States*, 371 U.S. 471, 481.
* * *

MR. JUSTICE HARLAN, concurring.

As the Court's opinion states, "the Fourth Amendment protects people, not places." [My] understanding of the rule that has emerged from prior decisions is that there is a twofold requirement, first that a person have exhibited an actual (subjective) expectation of privacy and, second, that the expectation be one that society is prepared to recognize as "reasonable." Thus a man's home is, for most purposes, a place where he expects privacy, but objects, activities, or statements that he exposes to the "plain view" of outsiders are not "protected" because no intention to keep them to himself has been exhibited. On the other hand, conversations in the open would not be protected against being overheard, for the expectation of privacy under the circumstances would be unreasonable.

The critical fact in this case is that "[o]ne who occupies it, (a telephone booth) shuts the door behind him, and pays the toll that permits him to place a call is surely entitled to assume" that his conversation is not being intercepted. The point is not that the booth is "accessible to the public" at other times, but that it is a temporarily private place whose momentary occupants' expectations of freedom from intrusion are recognized as reasonable.

[I] do not read the Court's opinion to declare that no interception of a conversation one-half of which occurs in a public telephone booth can be reasonable in the absence of a warrant. As elsewhere under the Fourth Amendment, warrants are the general rule, to which the legitimate needs of law enforcement may demand specific exceptions. It will be time enough to consider any such exceptions when an appropriate occasion presents itself, and I agree with the Court that this is not one.

Notes

1. *The State Action Requirement. Katz's* "reasonable expectation of privacy" test helps define the term "search" for purposes of the Fourth Amendment. Since the Fourth Amendment does not regulate the actions of private individuals, in addition to the requirement of a "search," it must also be shown that there is "state action" in that the intrusion must be the result of official government conduct (*i.e.*, a search by a police officer or other governmental official) or by a private individual acting in concert with, or at the behest of, governmental officials. *See United States v. Jacobsen*, 466 U.S. 109 (1984).

2. Most post-*Katz* cases address the second *Katz* question: Was a person's expectation of privacy "reasonable"? Usually, the Court's rulings are narrowly grounded and rooted in the facts. However, the Court's reasoning may sometimes be broadly stated so that the impact of a privacy holding may be broad as well.

When the Court determines that an expectation of privacy is "unreasonable," the police conduct does not constitute a search within the meaning of the Fourth Amendment, and the Fourth Amendment's procedural protections do not apply.

In later sections of this chapter, the Fourth Amendment's requirements will be studied in detail. To summarize briefly, the Fourth Amendment does not prohibit all searches, but rather prohibits only "unreasonable" ones. Although the Fourth Amendment does not require police to obtain a warrant, the Court has imposed a warrant preference. In other words, when the police fail to obtain a warrant, the Court presumes that the search is unreasonable. However, there are numerous exceptions to the warrant requirement. These exceptions are based on strong policy reasons favoring a Fourth Amendment exemption for police investigative action, and on doubts about the practicability of applying the warrant and probable cause requirements in a particular setting,

3. *Communications to Third Parties.* In *United States v. White*, 401 U.S. 745 (1971), defendant was convicted of narcotics violations based on conversations between himself and a government informant which were overheard by government agents over a radio transmitter concealed on the informant's person. The Court rejected White's challenge to the admissibility of the evidence: "[T]he Fourth Amendment [affords] no protection to 'a wrongdoer's misplaced belief that a person to whom he voluntarily confides his wrongdoing will not reveal it.' [If] the law gives no protection to the wrongdoer whose trusted accomplice is or becomes a police agent, neither should it protect him when that same agent has recorded or transmitted the conversations which are later offered in evidence to prove the State's case." *See also United States v. Jacobsen*, 466 U.S. 109 (1984) (upholding police examination of a damaged package turned over to police by the employees of a private freight carrier who observed a white powdery substance originally concealed within eight layers of wrappings.); *United States v. Miller*, 425 U.S. 435 (1976) (upholding conviction based on checks and records obtained by subpoena from defendant's bank because "[t]he depositor takes the risk, in revealing his affairs to another, that the information will be conveyed by that person to the Government.").

4. *Open Fields.* In *Oliver v. United States*, 466 U.S. 170 (1984), the Court held that the "open fields" doctrine, which permits officers to enter and search an open field without a warrant, survives *Katz*. In *Oliver*, two narcotics agents entered Oliver's field by going around a locked gate posted with a "no trespassing" sign. In the field, they found marijuana. The Court upheld the search:

> [There is an "overriding respect for the sanctity of the home that has been embedded in our traditions since the origins of the Republic."] In contrast, open fields do not provide the setting for those intimate activities that the Amendment is intended to shelter from government

interference or surveillance. There is no societal interest in protecting the privacy of those activities, such as the cultivation of crops, that occur in open fields. Moreover, as a practical matter these lands usually are accessible to the public and the police in ways that a home, an office, or commercial structure would not be. [T]he public and police lawfully may survey lands from the air. For these reasons, the asserted expectation of privacy in open fields is not an expectation that "society recognizes as reasonable."

[T]he common law distinguished "open fields" from the "curtilage," the land immediately surrounding and associated with the home. [At] common law, the curtilage is the area to which extends the intimate activity associated with the "sanctity of a man's home and the privacies of life," and therefore has been considered part of home itself for Fourth Amendment [purposes].

The Court rejected the argument that the fact that governmental officials trespassed on defendant's property, in violation of posted "no trespassing" signs, altered the analysis or created an expectation of privacy in an open field: "The existence of a property right is but one element in determining whether expectations of privacy are [legitimate]. [T]he general rights of property protected by the common law of trespass have little or no relevance to the applicability of the Fourth Amendment."

5. *Curtilage*. In *United States v. Dunn*, 480 U.S. 294 (1987), the Court held that "[C]urtilage questions should be resolved with particular reference to four factors: the proximity of the area claimed to be curtilage to the home, whether the area is included within an enclosure surrounding the home, the nature of the uses to which the area is put, and the steps taken by the resident to protect the area from observation by people passing by."

6. *More on Open Fields*. Sometimes the first *Katz* inquiry may pose a difficult problem for a person who wishes to assert a Fourth Amendment privacy interest. In *Dunn*, *supra*, defendant's barn was in the "open field" outside his "curtilage," and therefore vulnerable to police surveillance under *Oliver*. The following steps were held to be insufficient to satisfy the *Katz* requirement that a person manifest a subjective expectation of privacy: "[The barn] was enclosed by a wooden fence and had an open overhang. Locked, waist-high gates barred entry into the barn proper, and netting material stretched from the ceiling to the top of the wooden gates. [The DEA agents smelled phenylacetic acid, and crossed a barbed wire fence before crossing the wooden fence around the barn.] The officers walked under the barn's overhang to the locked wooden gates and, shining a flashlight through the netting on top of the gates, peered into the barn. They observed what the DEA agent thought to be a phenylacetone laboratory." However, the defendant's drug lab in *Dunn* was visible to police without entry into the barn. Where objects are not visible except by entry into a building outside the curtilage, *Dunn* has been distinguished, and a defendant's privacy interest upheld as sufficiently manifested and reasonable. See *People v. Pitman*, 211 Ill.2d 502, 813 N.E.2d 93 (2004) (police violated privacy interest by entering barn (located fifty feet from house) outside the curtilage, when no incriminating object was visible from outside barn).

7. *Privacy interest in dwellings. Oliver* suggests that after *Katz*, the Fourth Amendment protects people *and* places, when those places are associated, like a dwelling, with the "intimate activities" of a person's daily life. Even after *Katz*, property law analysis may play a role, as in *Oliver*, in defining the "traditions" that shape "societal" support for reasonable expectations of privacy. The Court has recognized that overnight guests have such expectations in a home based on "longstanding social custom," as well as a guest's "measure of control over the premises." See *Minnesota v. Olson*, 495 U.S. 91 (1990). But a first-time transient visitor without connection to the householder, except being "permitted on the premises" to perform a commercial transaction, has no reasonable privacy interest in a home. See *Minnesota v. Carter*, 525 U.S. 83 (1983) (where "visitor" is bagging cocaine). Compare *Stoner v. California*, 376 U.S. 483 (1964) (reasonable expectation of privacy of temporary hotel guest staying in hotel room); *Whiting v. State*, 389 Md. 334, 885 A.2d 785 (2005) (person living with other "squatters" without permission in unrented house owned by city agency has no privacy interest).

8. *Privacy interest in cars.* The Court often notes that people have a "lesser" privacy expectation in an automobile. See *California v. Carney*, 471 U.S. 386 (1985) (motor home analogous to car for purposes of privacy interests). Compare *Rakas v. Illinois*, 439 U.S. 128 (1978)(passengers have no privacy interest when asserting "neither a property nor a possessory interest" in a car or in the property within it); *Parker v. State*, 182 S.W.3d 923 (Tex.Crim.App. 2006) (recognizing privacy interest of non-renting driver in rental car, when such driver has permission of renting-driver to use car, despite lease provision that no one may drive the car except the renting-driver).

Problems

1. *Reconsidering Katz.* In *Katz*, how could Katz have a "reasonable expectation of privacy" in the contents of his conversation? After all, Katz made the call from a public phone booth and was talking to someone else through an intermediary (the phone company). Under the circumstances, how can it be said that his call was private?

2. *Modern Phone Booths.* In *Katz*, the Court placed particular emphasis on the fact that Katz entered the phone booth and closed the door before making his phone call. Today, few public phones are in booths with doors. Most are hung on walls or posts, sometimes in clusters of phones, with only slight coverings that do not provide much privacy. When someone makes a phone call from such a phone, does he have the same expectation of privacy that Katz had (that the call will not be bugged)?

3. *Backpacks and Safety Deposit Boxes.* A safety deposit box is one of the most secure and private ways to protect property against the police or others. But few individuals keep all of their valuables in safety deposit boxes. Suppose that a student brings a backpack to class. If the backpack remains zipped, does the student have a reasonable expectation of privacy in the contents of the backpack? Does the reasonable expectation of privacy apply even if the student leaves the class to go to the bathroom and leaves the backpack lying in the classroom?

4. *The Student Party.* Larry Hall, a law student, decides to hold a party for all students in the law school, their spouses, significant others and friends. A total of 200 actually attend the party. During the course of the evening, there is a constant flow of people in and out of Larry's home. People are lounging around in the house, as well as in the front and back yards. Larry leaves rolled marijuana cigarettes on his coffee table for his guest's enjoyment. He also has other illegal "recreational" drugs lying about the house. Under the circumstances, does Larry have a reasonable expectation of privacy regarding the cigarettes on his coffee table?

5. *The Undercover Agent.* Defendant invites a "friend" to his home to discuss possible drug dealings. Unknown to the suspect, the "friend" is actually an undercover police officer who is carrying a hidden video camera. The officer uses the camera to take pictures of the inside of defendant's house, including contraband drugs in plain view. Did the officer's entry and use of the video camera constitute an invasion of the suspect's reasonable expectation of privacy? *See United States v. Davis*, 326 F.3d 361 (2d Cir. 2003).

6. *More on Curtilage.* Mabel McCown, a police officer, suspects that a college student is selling drugs. Lacking probable cause, Mabel goes to his house looking for evidence which will justify a warrant. The house is in an ordinary city neighborhood of single-family dwellings. Mabel enters the yard and notices that the side yard is littered with obstructions. No defined pathway leads to this yard, which is obstructed by stacked wood, a rusting truck, a wheelbarrow, and garden tools. The side yard is filled with large and thick foliage. Mabel scrambles over all the obstructions, and walks through the side yard into the back yard. She looks up at a window, and sees some plants on the inside window sill that appear to be marijuana. Mabel then returns to the police station and obtains a search warrant based on what she has seen. When the student is charged with possession of drugs, he argues that Mabel violated his reasonable expectation of privacy before she obtained the warrant, and therefore that the evidence should be suppressed. You are the prosecutor. What arguments will you make to defend Mabel's actions? What counter-arguments do you expect defense counsel to make?

7. *Guest Expectations.* A guest attends a party at a friend's home. During the party, the police decide to search the home. Does a party-attending guest have a "reasonable expectation of privacy" in the premises? Suppose that the guest is in the bathroom? Is there a reasonable expectation of privacy in the bathroom? *See State v. Smith*, 322 Mont. 466, 97 P.3d 567 (Mont. 2004).

8. *Unexpected police audience.* Mark is a drug dealer who employs Phoebe as a "salesperson." He calls Phoebe's cell phone and doesn't realize that it is being answered by Juliana, a police officer who lawfully seized Phoebe's cell phone and is questioning her. Mark arranges to deliver drugs to Phoebe and he is arrested by Juliana when he arrives at the appointed

location with the drugs. Did Juliana violated Mark's expectation of privacy by answering Phoebe's cell phone? *State v. Gonzalez*, 898 A.2d 149 (Conn. 2006).

CALIFORNIA v. GREENWOOD

486 U.S. 35 (1988).

JUSTICE WHITE delivered the opinion of the Court.

The issue here is whether the Fourth Amendment prohibits the warrantless search and seizure of garbage left for collection outside the curtilage of a home. We conclude, in accordance with the vast majority of lower courts, [that] it does not.

In early 1984, Investigator Jenny Stracner of the Laguna Beach Police Department received information indicating that respondent Greenwood might be engaged in narcotics trafficking. Stracner learned that a criminal suspect had informed a federal drug enforcement agent in February 1984 that a truck filled with illegal drugs was en route to the Laguna Beach address at which Greenwood resided. In addition, a neighbor complained of heavy vehicular traffic late at night in front of Greenwood's single-family home. The neighbor reported that the vehicles remained at Greenwood's house for only a few minutes. * * *

[Stracner] asked the neighborhood's regular trash collector to pick up the plastic garbage bags that Greenwood had left on the curb in front of his house and to turn the bags over to her without mixing their contents with garbage from other houses. The trash collector cleaned his truck bin of other refuse, collected the garbage bags from the street in front of Greenwood's house, and turned the bags over to Stracner. The officer searched through the rubbish and found items indicative of narcotics use. She recited the information that she had gleaned from the trash search in an affidavit in support of a warrant to search Greenwood's home.

[The police executed the warrant, and found drugs during the search of the house. Greenwood and others were arrested. The next month, the police obtained the garbage again in the same manner, obtained another search warrant based on the evidence of narcotics use in the garbage, and executed another search of the house, which yielded more evidence of drugs and led to another arrest of Greenwood and others.]

The warrantless search and seizure of the garbage bags left at the curb outside the Greenwood house would violate the Fourth Amendment only if [Greenwood] manifested a subjective expectation of privacy in [his] garbage that society accepts as objectively reasonable. [Greenwood asserts] that [he] had, and exhibited, an expectation of privacy with respect to the trash that was searched by the police. The trash, which was placed on the street for collection at a fixed time, was contained in opaque plastic bags, which the garbage collector was expected to pick up, mingle with the trash of others, and deposit at the garbage dump. The trash was only temporarily on the street, and there was little likelihood that it would be inspected by anyone.

[W]e conclude that [Greenwood] exposed [his] garbage to the public sufficiently to defeat [his] claim to Fourth Amendment protection. It is common knowledge that plastic garbage bags left on or at the side of a public street are readily accessible to animals, children, scavengers, snoops, and other members of the public. Moreover, [Greenwood] placed [his] refuse at the curb for the express purpose of conveying it to a third party, the trash collector, who might himself have sorted through respondents' trash or permitted others, such as the police, to do so. Accordingly, having deposited [his] garbage "in an area particularly suited for public inspection and, in a manner of speaking, public consumption, for the express purpose of having strangers take it," [Greenwood] could have had no reasonable expectation of privacy in the inculpatory items that [he] discarded.

[T]he police cannot reasonably be expected to avert their eyes from evidence of criminal activity that could have been observed by any member of the public. Hence, "[w]hat a person knowingly exposes to the public, even in his own home or office, is not a subject of Fourth Amendment protection." *Katz v. United States, supra.* We held in *Smith v. Maryland,* 442 U.S. 735 (1979), for example, that the police did not violate the Fourth Amendment by causing a pen register to be installed at the telephone company's offices to record the telephone numbers dialed by a criminal suspect. An individual has no legitimate expectation of privacy in the numbers dialed on his telephone, we reasoned, because he voluntarily conveys those numbers to the telephone company when he uses the telephone. Again, we observed that "a person has no legitimate expectation of privacy in information he voluntarily turns over to third parties."

JUSTICE BRENNAN, with whom JUSTICE MARSHALL joins, dissenting.

[Scrutiny] of another's trash is contrary to commonly accepted notions of civilized behavior. I suspect [that] members of our society will be shocked to learn that the Court, the ultimate guarantor of liberty, deems unreasonable our expectation that the aspects of our private lives that are concealed safely in a trash bag will not become public. * * *

[H]ad [Greenwood] been carrying [his] personal effects in opaque, sealed plastic bags—identical to the ones [he] placed on the curb—[his] privacy would have been protected from warrantless police intrusion. [Greenwood deserves] no less protection just because Greenwood used the bags to discard rather than to transport his personal effects. Their contents are not inherently any less private, and Greenwood's decision to discard them, at least in the manner in which he did, does not diminish his expectation of privacy.

A trash bag, like any of the above-mentioned containers, "is a common repository for one's personal effects" and, even more than many of them, is "therefore [inevitably] associated with the expectation of privacy." [A] single bag of trash testifies eloquently to the eating, reading, and recreational habits of the person who produced it. A search of trash, like a search of the bedroom, can relate intimate details about sexual practices, health, and personal hygiene. Like rifling through desk drawers or intercepting phone calls, rummaging through trash can divulge the target's financial and professional status, political affiliations and inclinations, private thoughts, personal relationships, and romantic interests. It cannot be doubted that a sealed trash bag harbors telling evidence of the "intimate activity associated with the 'sanctity of a man's home and the privacies of life,' " which the Fourth Amendment is designed to protect.

The Court properly rejects the State's attempt to distinguish trash searches from other searches on the theory that trash is abandoned and therefore not entitled to an expectation of privacy. [In] evaluating the reasonableness of Greenwood's expectation that his sealed trash bags would not be invaded, the Court has held that we must look to "understandings that are recognized and permitted by society." Most of us, I believe, would be incensed to discover a meddler—whether a neighbor, a reporter, or a detective—scrutinizing our sealed trash containers to discover some detail of our personal lives. * * *

The mere possibility that unwelcome meddlers might open and rummage through the containers does not negate the expectation of privacy in their contents any more than the possibility of a burglary negates an expectation of privacy in the home; or the possibility of a private intrusion negates an expectation of privacy in an unopened package; or the possibility that an operator will listen in on a telephone conversation negates an expectation of privacy in the words spoken on the telephone. "What a person [seeks] to preserve as private, even in an area accessible to the public, may be constitutionally protected."

Nor is it dispositive that "[Greenwood] placed [his] refuse at the curb for the express purpose of conveying it to a third party, [who] might himself have sorted through respondents' trash or permitted others, such as the police, to do so." In the first place, Greenwood can hardly be faulted for leaving trash on his curb when a county ordinance commanded him to do so, and prohibited him from disposing of it in any other way. Unlike in other circumstances where privacy is compromised, Greenwood could not "avoid exposing personal belongings [by] simply leaving them at home." More importantly, even the voluntary relinquishment of possession or control over an effect does not necessarily amount to a relinquishment of a privacy expectation in it. Were it otherwise, a letter or package would lose all Fourth Amendment protection when placed in a mailbox or other depository with the "express purpose" of entrusting it to the postal officer or a private carrier; those bailees are just as likely as trash collectors (and certainly have greater incentive) to "sor[t] through" the personal effects entrusted to them, "or permi[t] others, such as police to do so." Yet, it has been clear for at least 110 years that the possibility of such an intrusion does not justify a warrantless search by police in the first instance. * * *

Notes

1. *Abandonment.* Although the *Greenwood* Court rejected the "abandonment" rationale as a grounds for upholding the police action, it is possible for a court to find that the first *Katz* inquiry is not satisfied because a person has abandoned her privacy interest, and therefore no longer "manifests" the interest under *Katz. Compare People v. Mims*, 205 A.D.2d 78, 617 N.Y.S.2d 316 (1994) (no abandonment where defendant hid a bag in a pile of trash but remained close to the pile) with *United States v. Stallings*, 28 F.3d 58 (8th Cir. 1994) (abandonment where defendant left a bag in the tall grass in a field behind his house, later retrieved it, and was arrested).

2. *More on the "Reasonable Expectation of Privacy" Test.* In *New York v. Class*, 475 U.S. 106 (1986), the Court held that a police officer could reach into the passenger compartment of a vehicle and move papers in order to observe the Vehicle Identification Number (VIN). "[B]ecause of the important role played by the VIN in the pervasive governmental regulation of the automobile and the efforts by the Federal Government to ensure that the VIN is placed in plain view, we hold that there was no reasonable expectation of privacy in the VIN." In *Cardwell v. Lewis*, 417 U.S. 583 (1974), the police had probable cause to believe that defendant's car was used in the commission of a murder. After arresting defendant, police towed his car to an impoundment lot where a police technician examined the tire tread and took paint scrapings. The Court concluded that defendant's "expectation of privacy was [not] infringed."

Problems

1. *Variations on Greenwood.* Suppose that a person places garbage in opaque bags and leaves them in garbage cans with closed lids. The cans are kept behind the person's house, and are collected at that location by the garbage service. Police officers enter the property and retrieve the garbage the night before the garbage service is due to pick up. In doing so, the officers hid behind trees and bushes as they approached. The cans were located on a driveway 50 feet from the house, and 20 feet from the unattached garage. In addition, the cans were 25 to 30 feet from the street, and 18 feet from the public sidewalk. What arguments can defense counsel make to distinguish *Greenwood*, and to claim that his expectation of privacy was reasonable on these facts, and what counter-arguments will the prosecutor make in response? *See United States v. Hedrick*, 922 F.2d 396 (7th Cir. 1991).

2. *State Courts and Garbage.* Some state supreme courts, applying their state constitutions, have rejected *Greenwood's* reasoning. For example, in *State v. Hempele*, 120 N.J. 182, 576 A.2d 793 (1990), the police believed that Hempele was distributing illicit drugs, and seized his garbage bags from trash cans left on the curb for collection. In the bags, the police found traces of "marijuana, cocaine, and methamphetamine in the trash." The Court concluded that the seizure violated the New Jersey Constitution:

> [A] single bag of trash testifies eloquently to the eating, reading, and recreational habits of the person who produced it. A search of trash,

like a search of the bedroom, can relate intimate details about sexual practices, health, and personal hygiene. Like rifling through desk drawers or intercepting phone calls, rummaging through trash can divulge the target's financial and professional status, political affiliations and inclinations, private thoughts, personal relationships, and romantic interests.

Most people seem to have an interest in keeping such matters private; few publicize them voluntarily. Undoubtedly many would be upset to see a neighbor or stranger sifting through their garbage, perusing their discarded mail, reading their bank statements, looking at their empty pharmaceutical bottles, and checking receipts to see what videotapes they rent. * * *

Leaving a garbage bag alongside the street near one's home is similar in some respects to leaving a letter in one's curbside mailbox for the carrier to pick up. Like a trash bag, that letter is "readily accessible" to snoops and others. Nevertheless, an expectation of privacy in that letter is reasonable. [J]ust as federal law prohibits tampering with letters left in mailboxes, local ordinances prohibit garbage-picking. [We] expect officers of the State to be more knowledgeable and respectful of people's privacy than are dogs and curious children.

[Conveying] information to another is different from conveying an opaque bag containing information. [Entrusting] the disposal of a trash bag to the garbage collector does not negate a reasonable expectation of privacy in the contents. It should be reasonable to expect that those who are authorized to remove trash will do so in the manner provided by ordinance or private contract.

[T]he regulation of garbage in New Jersey strengthens the presumption that the protections of [our Constitution] apply. Many local ordinances prohibit garbage-picking. Others prohibit scavenging without a license. We doubt that such ordinances are enacted to protect the privacy of people's garbage. However, [s]uch regulations are likely to increase people's expectation that the contents of their garbage set out on the curb will remain private. * * *

Because we find no special state interest that makes the warrant requirement impracticable, we hold that the State must secure a warrant based on probable cause in order to search garbage bags left on the curb for collection. * * *

Is the *Hempele* approach preferable to the *Greenwood* approach? *See also State v. Goss*, 150 N.H. 46, 834 A.2d 316 (2003) (relying on state constitution and rejecting *Greenwood*); *State v. Galloway*, 198 Or.App. 585, 109 P.3d 383 (2005) (same).

3. *Reasonable suspicion for garbage "dive."* Assume that a court is considering the option of requiring reasonable suspicion, as a matter of state constitutional law, that evidence is located in the garbage bags that police wish to search, before police may perform a *"Greenwood*-style" garbage "dive." Explain the pros and cons of this solution, compared to the *Greenwood* solution. See *State v. A Blue in Color, 1993 Chevrolet Pickup*, 328 Mont. 10, 116 P.3d 800 (2005).

4. *Failure to claim car.* Sara drives her car into a ditch during a snowstorm. She contacts a towing company to get the car out of the ditch and promises to meet the tow driver there. After Sara fails to appear, a police officer appears on the scene and learns that the car has been in the ditch, unclaimed by Sara, for three hours. Does the police officer violate Sara's expectation of privacy when he performs an inventory search in preparing to impound the car as a traffic hazard? See *United States v. Le*, 402 F.Supp.2d 1068 (D. N. D. 2005).

———

Advancing Technology. As technology improves, it becomes easier for the police to spy on citizens. One can imagine, as George Orwell did in his book 1984, a situation where government is capable of monitoring closely the actions of individuals. How does such technology affect a citizen's "reasonable expectation of privacy" under *Katz*? Consider the following cases in which "canine sniffs" and beepers are used.

UNITED STATES v. PLACE

462 U.S. 696 (1983).

JUSTICE O'CONNOR delivered the opinion of the Court.

[DEA agents, suspicious of Place's behavior, seized his luggage and subjected it to a canine sniff. In deciding whether the seizure was permissible, the Court was called on to decide whether the sniff constituted a search within the meaning of the Fourth Amendment.]

The Fourth Amendment "protects people from unreasonable government intrusions into their legitimate expectations of privacy." We have affirmed that a person possesses a privacy interest in the contents of personal luggage that is protected by the Fourth Amendment. A "canine sniff" by a well-trained narcotics detection dog, however, does not require opening the luggage. It does not expose noncontraband items that otherwise would remain hidden from public view, as does, for example, an officer's rummaging through the contents of the luggage. Thus, the manner in which information is obtained through this investigative technique is much less intrusive than a typical search. Moreover, the sniff discloses only the presence or absence of narcotics, a contraband item. Thus, despite the fact that the sniff tells the authorities something about the contents of the luggage, the information obtained is limited. This limited disclosure also ensures that the owner of the property is not subjected to the embarrassment and inconvenience entailed in less discriminate and more intrusive investigative methods.

In these respects, the canine sniff is *sui generis*. We are aware of no other investigative procedure that is so limited both in the manner in which the information is obtained and in the content of the information revealed by the procedure. Therefore, we conclude that the particular course of investigation that the agents intended to pursue here—exposure of respondent's luggage, which was located in a public place, to a trained canine—did not constitute a "search" within the meaning of the Fourth Amendment.

Note: Squeezing Luggage

In *Bond v. United States*, 529 U.S. 334 (2000), the Court held that a police officer may not squeeze a bus passenger's carry-on luggage in order to ascertain the contents: "[When] a bus passenger places a bag in an overhead bin, he expects that other passengers or bus employees may move it for one reason or another. Thus, a bus passenger clearly expects that his bag may be handled. He does not expect that other passengers or bus employees will, as a matter of course, feel the bag in an exploratory manner." The government argued that by exposing his bag to the public, the defendant lost his expectation that it would not be physically manipulated by either members of the public or by police on the bus. Justices Souter and Scalia dissented in *Bond*, and saw no distinction between the access of the public to squeezing luggage on a bus, and the access of the public to sifting through garbage bags on a public street in *Greenwood*. By contrast the *Bond* majority emphasized that the luggage-squeeze intrusion was a "tactile" one, rather than a "visual" one, and that privacy precedents such as *Place* did not authorize such intrusions.

ILLINOIS v. CABALLES

543 U.S. 405 (2005).

Justice Stevens delivered the opinion of the Court.

[When a state trooper stopped Caballes for speeding on the interstate, a police dispatcher reported the stop; another trooper overheard the transmission and went to the scene of the traffic stop with his narcotics-detection dog. This trooper was a member of the Illinois State Police Drug Interdiction Team. He walked his dog around Caballes's car, which was parked on the shoulder of the road, while the first trooper wrote out a speeding ticket. The dog alerted at the trunk, and when the troopers searched the trunk, they found marijuana and arrested Caballes after a stop that took less than 10 minutes.]

[A] seizure that is justified solely by the interest in issuing a warning ticket to the driver can become unlawful if it is prolonged beyond the time reasonably required to complete that mission. [W]e accept the state court's conclusion that the duration of the stop in this case was entirely justified by the traffic offense and the ordinary inquiries incident to such a stop. [In] our view, conducting a dog sniff would not change the character of a traffic stop that is lawful at its inception and otherwise executed in a reasonable manner, unless the dog sniff itself infringed [Caballes's] constitutionally protected interest in privacy. [It] does not.

Official conduct that does not "compromise any legitimate interest in privacy" is not a search subject to the Fourth Amendment. We have held that any interest in possessing contraband cannot be deemed "legitimate," and thus, governmental conduct that *only* reveals the possession of contraband "compromises no legitimate privacy interest." [In] *United States v. Place,* 462 U. S. 696 (1983), we treated a canine sniff by a well-trained narcotics-detection dog as *"sui generis"* because it "discloses only the presence or absence of narcotics, a contraband item." [Although] [Caballes] argues that the error rates, particularly the existence of false positives, call into question the premise that drug-detection dogs alert only to contraband, the record contains no evidence or findings that support his argument. Accordingly, the use of a well-trained narcotics-detection dog—one that "does not expose noncontraband items that otherwise would remain hidden from public view"— during a lawful traffic stop, generally does not implicate legitimate privacy interests. * * *

This conclusion is entirely consistent with our recent decision that the use of a thermal-imaging device to detect the growth of marijuana in a home constituted an unlawful search. *Kyllo v. United States,* 533 U. S. 27 (2001). Critical to that decision was the fact that the device was capable of detecting lawful activity—in that case, intimate details in a home, such as "at what hour each night the lady of the house takes her daily sauna and bath." The legitimate expectation that information about perfectly lawful activity will remain private is categorically distinguishable from [Caballes's] hopes or expectations concerning the nondetection of contraband in the trunk of his car. A dog sniff conducted during a concededly lawful traffic stop that reveals no information other than the location of a substance that no individual has any right to possess does not violate the Fourth Amendment.

The judgment of the Illinois Supreme Court is vacated, and the case is remanded for further proceedings not inconsistent with this opinion.

It is so ordered.

JUSTICE SOUTER, dissenting.

[What] we have learned about the fallibility of dogs in the years since *Place* was decided would itself be reason to call for reconsidering *Place*'s decision against treating the intentional use of a trained dog as a search. [An] uncritical adherence to *Place* would render the Fourth Amendment indifferent to suspicionless and indiscriminate sweeps of cars in parking garages and pedestrians on sidewalks; if a sniff is not preceded by a seizure subject to Fourth Amendment notice, it escapes Fourth Amendment review entirely unless it is treated as a search. * * *

At the heart both of *Place* and the Court's opinion today is the proposition that sniffs by a trained dog are *sui generis* because a reaction by the dog in going alert is a response to nothing but the presence of contraband. [The] infallible dog, however, is a creature of legal fiction. [T]he evidence is clear that the dog that alerts hundreds of times will be wrong dozens of times. [Once] the dog's fallibility is recognized, however, that ends the justification claimed in *Place* for treating the sniff as *sui generis* under the Fourth Amendment[.] [And] when that aura of uniqueness disappears, there is no basis in *Place*'s reasoning [to] ignore the actual function that dog sniffs [perform]. [G]iven the fallibility of the dog, the sniff is the first step in a process that may disclose "intimate details" without revealing contraband, just as a thermal-imaging device might do, as described in *Kyllo v. United States,* 533 U. S. 27 (2001).

[This] sniff search must stand or fall on its being ancillary to the traffic stop that led up to it. [As] a consequence, the reasonableness of the search must be assessed in relation to the actual delay the police chose to impose. [In] *Berkemer v. McCarty,* 468 U. S. 420 (1984), [we] held that the analogue of the common traffic stop was the limited detention for investigation authorized by *Terry v. Ohio,* 392 U. S. 1 (1968). [In] *Terry*[,] the Court took care to keep a *Terry* stop from automatically becoming a foot in the door for all investigatory purposes; the permissible intrusion was bounded by the justification for the detention. [Unless] facts disclosed by enquiry within this limit [give police] grounds to go further, the government could not otherwise take advantage of a suspect's immobility to search for evidence unrelated to the reason for the detention. [T]hat rule requires holding that the police do not have reasonable grounds to conduct sniff searches for drugs simply because they have stopped someone to receive a ticket for a highway offense. Since the police had no indication of illegal activity beyond the speed of the car in this case, the sniff search should be held unreasonable under the Fourth Amendment and its fruits should be suppressed . . . * * *

JUSTICE GINSBURG, with whom JUSTICE SOUTER joins, dissenting.

[A] drug-detection dog is an intimidating animal. Injecting such an animal into a routine traffic stop changes the character of the encounter between the police and the motorist. The stop becomes broader, more adversarial, and (in at least some cases) longer. Caballes—who, as far as Troopers Gillette and Graham knew, was guilty solely of driving six miles per hour over the speed limit—was exposed to the embarrassment and intimidation of being investigated, on a public thoroughfare, for drugs. Even if the drug sniff is not characterized as a Fourth Amendment "search," the sniff surely broadened [improperly] the scope of the traffic-violation-related seizure [and therefore the evidence should be suppressed].

Problems

1. *Longer Automobile Stops.* The *Caballes* Court and the dissenters assume that the dog sniff did not lengthen the traffic stop. Suppose that the evidence suggested, to the contrary, that the sniff actually did lengthen the stop (for example, by ten minutes). Would that fact necessarily cause the dog sniff to become a "search or seizure"? Explain.

2. *Canine Sniffs in Parking Lots.* Consider the suggestion by Justice Souter that the *Caballes* rationale could justify police use of drug-sniffing dogs on people and cars on public streets and public parking lots. Does the

decision necessarily lead to that conclusion? See *Myers v. State*, 839 N.E.2d 1146 (Ind. 2005).

3. *Canine Sniffs of Non–Movable Property or Residence.* Could a drug sniffing dog be used to sniff around the outside of self-storage units? *See State v. Carter*, 697 N.W.2d 199 (Minn. 2005). Could the police walk drug-sniffing dogs through the common hallways of apartment buildings, and have the dogs sniff near the doorways of individual apartments, in the absence of reasonable suspicion or probable cause? *Compare State v. Davis*, 711 N.W.2d 841 (Minn.App. 2006); *Fitzgerald v. State*, 384 Md. 484, 864 A.2d 1006 (2004). Assume that in each of these cases, the state court considers the option of requiring reasonable suspicion, as a matter of state constitutional law, that drugs or other "sniffable" evidence is present. What are the pros and cons of endorsing that requirement instead of labeling the canine sniff as "not a Fourth Amendment search or seizure"?

4. *Weapons-Sniffing Dog.* Does the level of public need affect the outcome? Suppose that, in each of the examples in problem 3 above, instead of using a drug sniffing dog, the police sought to use a dog that could detect nuclear, chemical or biological weapons. Under what circumstances should the use of a dog for such purposes be treated differently from a dog used for drug interdiction?

UNITED STATES v. KNOTTS
460 U.S. 276 (1983).

REHNQUIST, JUSTICE.

[Suspicion] attached to [Knotts and three co-defendants] when the 3M Company, * * * notified a narcotics investigator for the Minnesota Bureau of Criminal Apprehension that Armstrong, a former 3M employee, had been stealing chemicals which could be used in manufacturing illicit drugs. Visual surveillance of Armstrong revealed [that he was] purchasing similar chemicals from the Hawkins Chemical Company in Minneapolis. * * *

With the consent of the Hawkins Chemical Company, officers installed a beeper inside a five gallon container of chloroform, one of the so-called "precursor" chemicals used to manufacture illicit drugs. * * * When Armstrong made the purchase, officers followed the car in which the chloroform had been placed, maintaining contact by using both visual surveillance and a monitor which received the signals sent from the beeper.

Armstrong proceeded to Petschen's house, where the container was transferred to Petschen's automobile. Officers then followed that vehicle eastward [into] Wisconsin. [When] Petschen began making evasive maneuvers, [the] pursuing agents ended their visual surveillance. At about the same time officers lost the signal from the beeper, but with the assistance of a monitoring device located in a helicopter the approximate location of the signal was picked up again about one hour later. The signal now was stationary and the location identified was a cabin occupied by [Knotts] [in] Wisconsin. [The] beeper was [not] used after [the cabin's location] had been initially determined.

Relying on the location of the chloroform derived through the use of the beeper and additional information obtained during three days of intermittent visual surveillance of [the Knotts] cabin, officers secured a search warrant. During execution of the warrant, officers discovered a fully operable, clandestine drug laboratory in the cabin. In the laboratory area officers found formulas for amphetamine and methamphetamine, over $10,000 worth of laboratory equipment, and chemicals in quantities sufficient to produce 14 pounds of pure amphetamine. Under a barrel outside the cabin, officers located the five gallon container of chloroform.

After his motion to suppress evidence based on the warrantless monitoring of the beeper was denied, [Knotts] was convicted for conspiring to manufacture controlled substances in violation of 21 U.S.C. § 846 (1976). He was sentenced to five years imprisonment. A divided panel of the United States Court of Appeals for the Eighth Circuit reversed. We granted certiorari and we now reverse the judgment of the Court of Appeals.

[The] governmental surveillance conducted by means of the beeper in this case amounted principally to the following of an automobile on public streets and [highways]. "One has a lesser expectation of privacy in a motor vehicle because its function is transportation and it seldom serves as one's residence or as the repository of personal effects. A car has little capacity for escaping public scrutiny. It travels public thoroughfares where both its occupants and its contents are in plain view." *Cardwell v. Lewis*, 417 U.S. 583, 590 (1974) (plurality).

A person traveling in an automobile on public thoroughfares has no reasonable expectation of privacy in his movements from one place to another. When Petschen traveled over the public streets he voluntarily conveyed to anyone who wanted to look the fact that he was traveling over particular roads in a particular direction, the fact of whatever stops he made, and the fact of his final destination when he exited from public roads onto private property.

[Knotts,] [A]s the owner of the cabin and surrounding premises to which Petschen drove, [Knotts] undoubtedly had the traditional expectation of privacy within a dwelling place insofar as the cabin was concerned. [But] no such expectation of privacy extended to the visual observation of Petschen's automobile arriving on his premises after leaving a public highway, nor to movements of objects such as the drum of chloroform outside the cabin in the "open fields." *Hester v. United States*, 265 U.S. 57 (1924).

Visual surveillance from public places along Petschen's route or adjoining Knotts' premises would have sufficed to reveal all of these facts to the police. The fact that the officers in this case relied not only on visual surveillance, but on the use of the beeper to signal the presence of Petschen's automobile to the police receiver, does not alter the situation. Nothing in the Fourth Amendment prohibited the police from augmenting the sensory faculties bestowed upon them at birth with such enhancement as science and technology afforded them in this case. In *United States v. Lee*, 274 U.S. 559 (1927) [(upholding the use of a search light by a police boat on the high seas)].

[Knotts expresses] the generalized view that the result of the holding sought by the government would be that "twenty-four hour surveillance of any citizen of this country will be possible, without judicial knowledge or supervision." [But] if such dragnet type law enforcement practices as [Knotts] envisions should eventually occur, there will be time enough then to determine whether different constitutional principles may be applicable. Insofar as [his] complaint appears to be simply that scientific devices such as the beeper enabled the police to be more effective in detecting crime, it simply has no constitutional foundation. We have never equated police efficiency with unconstitutionality, and we decline to do so now.

[Knotts] specifically attacks the use of the beeper insofar as it was used to determine that the can of chloroform had come to rest on his property. [H]e states that "[t]he government thus overlooks the fact that this case involves the sanctity of Respondent's residence, which is accorded the greatest protection available under the Fourth Amendment." * * * We think that [Knotts'] contentions * * * lose sight of the limited use which the government made of the signals from this particular beeper. [N]othing in this record indicates that the beeper signal was received or relied upon after it had indicated that the drum containing the chloroform had ended its automotive journey at rest on [Knotts'] premises. [Admittedly], because of the failure of the visual surveillance, the beeper enabled the law enforcement officials [to] ascertain the ultimate resting place of the chloroform when they would not have been able to do so had they relied solely on their naked eyes. But scientific enhancement of this sort raises no constitutional issues which visual surveillance would not also raise. A police car following Petschen at a distance throughout his journey could have observed him leaving the public highway and arriving at the cabin. [This] fact, along with others, was used by the government in obtaining a search warrant which led to the discovery of the clandestine drug laboratory. But there is no indication that the beeper was used in any way to reveal information as to the movement of the drum within the cabin, or in any way that would not have been visible to the naked eye from outside the cabin. Just as notions of physical trespass based on the law of real property were not dispositive in *Katz,* neither were they dispositive in *Hester.*

We thus return to the question posed at the beginning of our inquiry[:] did monitoring the beeper signals complained of by [Knotts] invade any legitimate expectation of privacy on his part? [W]e hold they did not. Since they did not, there was neither a "search" nor a "seizure" within the contemplation of the Fourth Amendment. The judgment of the Court of Appeals is therefore

Reversed.

Justice Stevens, with whom Justice Brennan, and Justice Marshall join, concurring in the judgment.

[T]he Court suggests that the Fourth Amendment does not inhibit "the police from augmenting the sensory facilities bestowed upon them at birth with such enhancement as science and technology afforded them." But the Court held to the contrary in *Katz*. Although the augmentation in this case was unobjectionable, it by no means follows that the use of electronic detection techniques does not implicate especially sensitive [concerns].

Notes

1. *More on Beepers*. In *United States v. Karo*, 468 U.S. 705 (1984), the Court held that police monitoring of an electronic tracking device (beeper) violates a person's reasonable expectation of privacy when it reveals information that could not have been obtained through visual surveillance. *Karo* was like *Knotts* in that the police placed a beeper in a can of chloroform. Using both visual and beeper surveillance, agents tracked the truck to Rhodes' residence. Agents then observed Rhodes and a woman loading boxes and other items into the trunk of the automobile. The car was followed by physical and electronic surveillance to a house where there was no surveillance for fear of detection. When the vehicle left, the agents determined that the can was inside the house. They used this information to obtain a warrant to search the house, and discovered an illegal drug laboratory. The Court justified its decision as follows:

> [P]rivate residences are places in which the individual normally expects privacy free of governmental intrusion[,] and that expectation is plainly one that society is prepared to recognize as justifiable. * * * In this case, had a DEA agent thought it useful to enter [the] residence to verify that the ether was actually in the house and had he done so surreptitiously and without a warrant, there is little doubt that he would have engaged in an unreasonable search within the meaning of the Fourth [Amendment]. The monitoring of an electronic device such as a beeper is, of course, less intrusive than a full-scale search, but it does reveal a critical fact about the interior of the premises [that] could not have otherwise obtained without a warrant. The case is thus not like *Knotts*, for there the beeper told the authorities nothing about the interior of *Knotts'* cabin. [Here], the monitoring indicated that the beeper was inside the house, a fact that could not have been visually verified. [Indiscriminate] monitoring of property that has been withdrawn from public view would present far too serious a threat to privacy interests in the home to escape entirely some sort of Fourth Amendment oversight.

2. *Aerial Surveillance*. In several cases the Court has considered privacy issues in the context of aerial surveillance. In its first case, *California v. Ciraolo*, 476 U.S. 207 (1986), the Court held that the police could perform "naked-eye" aerial surveillance from a fixed-wing aircraft at an altitude of 1,000 feet, and use the evidence of drug cultivation that they observed in a back yard within the curtilage of a home. In two subsequent cases, the Court

approved the use of an aerial mapping camera during such surveillance, and approved naked-eye aerial surveillance by helicopter at 400 feet.

In *Florida v. Riley*, 488 U.S. 445 (1989), a four-justice plurality approved helicopter surveillance of a mobile home and greenhouse located on five acres of property. Two sides of the greenhouse were enclosed, and the other two sides were surrounded by trees, shrubs and the mobile home. The greenhouse was covered by corrugated roofing panels, some translucent and some opaque, two of which were missing. An investigating officer, who could not see the contents of the greenhouse from the road, circled twice over respondent's property in a helicopter at the height of 400 feet. With his naked eye, he was able to see through the openings in the greenhouse roof and to identify what he thought were marijuana plants. The officer obtained a warrant based on his observations, and the search revealed marijuana growing in the greenhouse. The Court held that the officer's helicopter observations did not constitute a search:

> [Because] the sides and roof of his greenhouse were left partially open[,] what was growing in the greenhouse was subject to viewing from the air. [T]he inspection was made from a helicopter, but as is the case with fixed-wing planes, "private and commercial flight [by helicopter] in the public airways is routine" in this country, and there is no indication that such flights are unheard of in Pasco County, Florida. Riley could not reasonably have expected that his greenhouse was protected from public or official observation from a helicopter had it been flying within the navigable airspace for fixed-wing aircraft.

> [We] would have a different case if flying at that altitude had been contrary to law or regulation. But helicopters are not bound by the lower limits of the navigable airspace allowed to other aircraft. Any member of the public could legally have been flying over Riley's property in a helicopter at the altitude of 400 feet and could have observed Riley's greenhouse. The police officer did no more. This is not to say that an inspection of the curtilage of a house from an aircraft will always pass muster under the Fourth Amendment simply because the plane is within the navigable airspace specified by law. [Neither] is there any intimation here that the helicopter interfered with respondent's normal use of the greenhouse or of other parts of the curtilage. [N]o intimate details connected with the use of the home or curtilage were observed, and there was no undue noise, and no wind, dust, or threat of injury. In these circumstances, there was no violation of the Fourth Amendment. * * *

Justice Brennan, joined by two other justices, dissented: "Suppose the police employed this miraculous tool to discover not only what crops people were growing in their greenhouses, but also what books they were reading and who their dinner guests were. [Would] today's plurality continue to assert that "[t]he right of the people to be secure in their persons, houses, papers, and effects, against unreasonable searches and seizures" was not infringed by such surveillance? Yet that is the logical consequence of the plurality's rule that, so long as the police are where they have a right to be under air traffic regulations, the Fourth Amendment is offended only if the aerial surveillance interferes with the use of the backyard as a garden spot.…"

3. *Aerial Photography.* Consider the reasoning in *Dow Chemical v. United States*, 476 U.S. 227 (1986), where the Court upheld the use of an aerial mapping camera to take photographs of Dow's 2,000 acre facility from 1200 feet above. Dow's elaborate security barred ground-level views of its buildings, most of which were covered, although some equipment was exposed to visual observation from the air. Dow sought to enjoin the EPA from further photography. While the Court recognized that Dow has "a reasonable, legitimate, and objective expectation of privacy within the interior of its covered buildings," one that society is prepared to recognize, it held that the EPA's use of the camera was not a "search":

> [S]urveillance of private property by using highly sophisticated surveillance equipment not generally available to the public, such as satellite technology, might be constitutionally proscribed absent a warrant. But the photographs here are not so revealing of intimate details as to raise constitutional concerns. Although they undoubtedly give EPA more detailed information than naked-eye views, they remain limited to an outline of the facility's buildings and equipment. The mere fact that human vision is enhanced somewhat [does] not give rise to constitutional problems. An electronic device to penetrate walls or windows so as to hear and record confidential discussions of chemical formulae or other trade secrets would raise very different and far more serious questions.

Problems

1. *Challenging the Installation.* Could Knotts have challenged the initial installation of the beeper in the chloroform container? Consider Justice Brennan's concurrence in *Knotts*: "[I] think this would have been a much more difficult case if [Knotts] had challenged [the initial installation of the beeper in the chloroform container.]" Do you agree? Explain.

2. *Technology in a Digital Age.* As we move into a "digital age," keeping information on computers and transmitting data to friends all over the world, how does the *Katz* test apply? For example, suppose that defendant enters into a "chat room" where he exchanges information with other chat participants. Do the police conduct a "search" if they monitor the chat room and pay particular attention to troublesome communications (e.g., discussions of child sexuality)?

3. *The GPS tracking device.* The police in New Orleans suspect that Sally is a drug dealer because one police informant has heard rumors that she is, but the police have no evidence that is sufficient to obtain a search warrant for Sally's house or an arrest warrant for Sally. So the police manage surreptitiously to attach a tracking device to the 12–volt electrical system of Sally's car. It is a "global positioning system" (GPS) device which uses a more advanced technology than a "beeper" because it allows the car's positions to be tracked precisely when data from the device is downloaded on a computer. This data shows precisely what Sally's route of travel is whenever the car is in motion, the precise locations where the car stops, and

the number of minutes used in travel and during each stop. The police rely on the GPS device to compile tracking information about Sally's vehicular travels and stops for a ten day period, 24 hours a day. The data shows that during this period Sally traveled to a dentist's office, a bank, a tanning salon, a church, a lot of small grocery stores, the local headquarters of a political party, a lot of small restaurants, a baseball game and a peace vigil at local universities, a health club, a family planning clinic, the zoo, and several libraries. Late one night, Sally drives her car across the lake to a remote location 30 miles away, and down a dirt road that is virtually impassible, until she comes to a small run-down cottage. Based on the information about the location of the cabin provided by the GPS, the police perform a helicopter flyover and discover marijuana plants under cultivation near the cabin. Sally is charged with possession of marijuana and her defense counsel's pre-trial motion to suppress the evidence of the marijuana plants is denied. The plants are admitted as evidence in her trial and she is convicted. On appeal, Sally argues that the government's use of the GPS violated her reasonable expectation of privacy. What arguments will be made on both sides?

KYLLO v. UNITED STATES

533 U.S. 27 (2001).

JUSTICE SCALIA delivered the opinion of the Court.

This case presents the question whether the use of a thermal-imaging device aimed at a private home from a public street to detect relative amounts of heat within the home constitutes a "search" within the meaning of the Fourth Amendment.

I

[Agent] William Elliott [suspected] that marijuana was being grown in [a] home belonging to petitioner Danny Kyllo.... Indoor marijuana growth typically requires high-intensity lamps. In order to determine whether [heat] was emanating from petitioner's home[, Agent Elliott used] an Agema Thermovision 210 thermal imager to scan the triplex. Thermal imagers detect infrared radiation, which virtually all objects emit but which is not visible to the naked eye. The imager converts radiation into images based on relative warmth—black is cool, white is hot, shades of gray connote relative differences; in that respect, it operates somewhat like a video camera showing heat images. [T]he Agema 210 "is a non-intrusive device which emits no rays or beams and shows a crude visual image of the heat being radiated from the outside of the house, [t]he device [cannot] penetrate walls or windows to reveal conversations or human activities, and "[n]o intimate details of the home were observed." The scan of Kyllo's home took only a few minutes and was performed [across] the street [in] back of the house. The scan showed that the roof over the garage and a side wall of [the] home were relatively hot compared to the rest of the home and substantially warmer than neighboring homes. [Agent] Elliott concluded that [Kyllo] was using halide lights to grow marijuana in his house, which indeed he was. Based on tips from informants, utility bills, and the thermal imaging, [a magistrate] issued a warrant authorizing a search of [Kyllo's] home, and the agents found an indoor growing operation involving more than 100 plants. [Kyllo] was indicted on one count of manufacturing marijuana. * * * He unsuccessfully moved to suppress the evidence seized from his home and then entered a conditional guilty plea. [T]he District Court upheld the validity of the warrant [and the Court of Appeals affirmed]. We granted certiorari.

"At the very core" of the Fourth Amendment "stands the right of a man to retreat into his own home and there be free from unreasonable governmental intrusion." *Silverman v. United States*, 365 U.S. 505 (1961). With few exceptions, the question whether a warrantless search of a home is reasonable and hence constitutional must be answered no. [T]he antecedent question of whether or not a Fourth Amendment "search" has occurred is not so simple under our precedent. The permissibility of ordinary visual surveillance of a home used to be clear because, well into the 20th century, our Fourth Amendment jurisprudence was tied to common-law trespass. Visual surveillance was unquestionably lawful because " 'the eye cannot by the laws of England be guilty of a trespass.' " *Boyd v. United States*, 116 U.S. 616, 628 (1886) *(quoting Entick v. Carrington*, 19 How. St. Tr. 1029, 95 Eng. Rep. 807 (K.B.1765)). We have since decoupled violation of a person's Fourth Amendment rights from trespassory violation of his property, but the lawfulness of warrantless visual surveillance of a home has still been preserved. * * *

One might think [that] examining the portion of a house that is in plain public view, while it is a "search" despite the absence of trespass, is not an "unreasonable" one under the Fourth Amendment. [I]n fact we have held that visual observation is no "search" at all. *See Dow Chemical Co. v. United States*, 476 U.S. 227 (1986). [Under] *Katz v. United States*, 389 U.S. 347 (1967)[,a] Fourth Amendment search does not occur—even when the explicitly protected location of a house is concerned—unless "the individual manifested a subjective expectation of privacy in the object of the challenged search," and "society [is] willing to recognize that expectation as reasonable." * * *

The present case involves officers on a public street engaged in more than naked-eye surveillance of a home. We have previously reserved judgment as to how much technological enhancement of ordinary perception from such a vantage point, if any, is too much. While we upheld enhanced aerial photography of an industrial complex in *Dow Chemical*, [we] found "it important that this is not an area immediately adjacent to a private home, where privacy expectations are most heightened."

It would be foolish to contend that the degree of privacy secured to citizens by the Fourth Amendment has been entirely unaffected by the advance of technology. [The] technology enabling human flight has exposed to public view (and hence [to] official observation) uncovered portions of the house and its curtilage that once were private. The question we confront today is what limits there are upon this power of technology to shrink the realm of guaranteed privacy.

[While] it may be difficult to refine *Katz* when the search of areas such as telephone booths, automobiles, or even the curtilage and uncovered portions of residences are at issue, in the case of the search of the interior of homes—the prototypical and hence most commonly litigated area of protected privacy—there is a ready criterion, with roots deep in the common law, of the minimal expectation of privacy that exists, and that is acknowledged to be reasonable. To withdraw protection of this minimum expectation would be to permit police technology to erode the privacy guaranteed by the Fourth Amendment. We think that obtaining by sense-enhancing technology any information regarding the interior of the home that could not otherwise have been obtained without physical "intrusion into a constitutionally protected area" constitutes a search—at least where (as here) the technology in question is not in general public use. This assures preservation of that degree of privacy against government that existed when the Fourth Amendment was adopted. On the basis of this criterion, the information obtained by the thermal imager in this case was the product of a search.[2]

The Government maintains [that] the thermal imaging must be upheld because it detected "only heat radiating from the external surface of the house." The dissent [contends] that there is a fundamental difference between what it calls "off-the-wall" observations and "through-the-wall surveillance." But just as a thermal imager captures only heat emanating from a house, so also a powerful directional microphone picks up only sound emanating from a house-and a satellite capable of scanning from many miles away would pick up only visible light emanating from a house. We rejected such a mechanical interpretation of the Fourth Amendment in *Katz*, where the eavesdropping device picked up only sound waves that reached the exterior of the phone booth. Reversing that approach would leave the homeowner at the mercy of advancing technology—including imaging technology that could discern all human activity in the home. While the technology used in the present case was relatively crude, the rule we adopt must take account of more sophisticated systems that are already in use or in development.[3] The dissent's reliance on the distinction between "off-the-wall" and

---

2. [The] dissent's comparison of the thermal imaging to various circumstances in which outside observers might be able to perceive, without technology, the heat of the home—for example, by observing snowmelt on the roof—[is] irrelevant. [O]n the night of January 16, 1992, no outside observer could have discerned the relative heat of Kyllo's home without thermal imaging.

3. The ability to "see" through walls and other opaque barriers is a clear, and scientifically feasible, goal of law enforcement research and development. The Na-

tional Law Enforcement and Corrections Technology Center, a program within the United States Department of Justice, features [projects] that include a "Radar–Based Through-the-Wall Surveillance System," "Handheld Ultrasound Through the Wall Surveillance," and a "Radar Flashlight" that "will enable law officers to detect individuals through interior building walls." Some devices may emit low levels of radiation that travel "through-the-wall," but others, such as more sophisticated thermal imaging devices, are entirely passive, or "off-the-wall" as the dissent puts it.

"through-the-wall" observation is entirely incompatible with the dissent's belief [that] thermal-imaging observations of the intimate details of a home are impermissible. The most sophisticated thermal imaging devices continue to measure heat "off-the-wall" rather than "through-the-wall"; the dissent's disapproval of those more sophisticated thermal-imaging devices is an acknowledgement that there is no substance to this distinction. As for the dissent's extraordinary assertion that anything learned through "an inference" cannot be a search that would validate even the "through-the-wall" technologies that the dissent purports to disapprove. Surely the dissent does not believe that the through-the-wall radar or ultrasound technology produces an 8–by–10 Kodak glossy that needs no analysis. And [the] novel proposition that inference insulates a search is blatantly contrary to *United States v. Karo*, 468 U.S. 705 (1984), where the police "inferred" from the activation of a beeper that a certain can of ether was in the home. * * *

The Government also contends that the thermal imaging was constitutional because it did not "detect private activities occurring in private areas." [the] Fourth Amendment's protection of the home has never been tied to measurement of the quality or quantity of information obtained. In *Silverman*, for example, we made clear that any physical invasion of the structure of the home, "by even a fraction of an inch," was too much, and there is certainly no exception to the warrant requirement for the officer who barely cracks open the front door and sees nothing but the nonintimate rug on the vestibule floor. In the home, all details are intimate details, because the entire area is held safe from prying government eyes[,] just as was the detail of how warm—or even how relatively warm—Kyllo was heating his residence.

Limiting the prohibition of thermal imaging to "intimate details" would not only be wrong in principle; it would [fail] to provide "a workable accommodation between the needs of law enforcement and the interests protected by the Fourth Amendment." [T]here is no necessary connection between the sophistication of the surveillance equipment and the "intimacy" of the details that it observes—which means that one cannot say (and the police cannot be assured) that use of the relatively crude equipment at issue here will always be lawful. The Agema Thermovision 210 might disclose, for example, at what hour each night the lady of the house takes her daily sauna and bath—a detail that many would consider "intimate"; and a much more sophisticated system might detect nothing more intimate than the fact that someone left a closet light on. We could [not] develop a rule approving only that through-the-wall surveillance which identifies objects no smaller than 36 by 36 inches, but would have to develop a jurisprudence specifying which home activities are "intimate" and which are not. And [no] police officer would be able to know in advance whether his through-the-wall surveillance picks up "intimate" details—and thus * * * whether it is constitutional.

The dissent's proposed standard—whether the technology offers the "functional equivalent of actual presence in the area being searched"—would seem quite similar to our own at first blush. The dissent concludes that *Katz* was such a case, but then inexplicably asserts that if the same listening device only revealed the volume of the conversation, the surveillance would be permissible. Yet if, without technology, the police could not discern volume without being actually present in the phone booth, [the dissent] should conclude a search has occurred. The same should hold for the interior heat of the home if only a person present in the home could discern the heat. Thus the driving force of the dissent [appears] to be a distinction among different types of information—whether the "homeowner would even care if anybody noticed." The dissent offers no practical guidance for the application of this standard. [The] people in their houses, as well as the police, deserve more precision.

[The] Fourth Amendment draws "a firm line at the entrance to the house." That line [must] be not only firm but also bright—which requires clear specification of those methods of surveillance that require a warrant. While it is certainly possible to conclude from the videotape of the thermal imaging that occurred in this case that no "significant" compromise of the homeowner's privacy has occurred, we must take the long view, from the original meaning of the Fourth Amendment forward. "The Fourth Amendment is to be construed in the light of what was deemed an unreasonable search and seizure when it was adopted, and in a manner which will conserve public interests as well as the interests and rights of individual citizens." Where, as here, the Government uses a device that is not in general public use, to explore details of the home that would previously have been unknowable without physical intrusion, the surveillance is a "search" and is presumptively unreasonable without a warrant.

[I]t will remain for the District Court to determine whether, without the evidence it provided, the search warrant [was] supported by probable cause—and if not, whether there is any other basis for supporting admission of the evidence that the search [produced]. [The] judgment of the Court of Appeals is reversed; the case is remanded for further proceedings consistent with this opinion.

It is so ordered.

JUSTICE STEVENS, with whom THE CHIEF JUSTICE, JUSTICE O'CONNOR, and JUSTICE KENNEDY join, dissenting.

There is [a] distinction of constitutional magnitude between "through-the-wall surveillance" that gives the observer or listener direct access to information in a private area, on the one hand, and the thought processes used to draw inferences from information in the public domain, on the other hand. [T]he case before us merely involves indirect deductions from "off-the-wall" surveillance, that is, observations of the exterior of the home. [T]his case [is] controlled by established principles from our Fourth Amendment jurisprudence. One of those core principles [is] that "searches and seizures inside a home without a warrant are presumptively unreasonable." But it is equally well settled that searches and seizures of property in plain view are presumptively reasonable.

" 'What a person knowingly exposes to the public, even in his own home or office, is not a subject of Fourth Amendment protection.' " That is the principle implicated here.

While the Court "take[s] the long view" and decides this case based largely on the potential of yet-to-be-developed technology that might allow "through-the-wall surveillance," this case involves nothing more than off-the-wall surveillance by law enforcement officers to gather information exposed to the general public from the outside of [Kyllo's] home. All that the infrared camera did in this case was passively measure heat emitted from the exterior surfaces of [his] home; all that those measurements showed were relative differences in emission levels, vaguely indicating that some areas of the roof and outside walls were warmer than others. [N]o details regarding the interior of petitioner's home were revealed. Unlike an x-ray scan, or other possible "through-the-wall" techniques, the detection of infrared radiation emanating from the home did not accomplish "an unauthorized physical penetration into the premises," nor did it "obtain information that it could not have obtained by observation from outside the curtilage of the house."

[T]he ordinary use of the senses might enable a neighbor or passer-by to notice the heat emanating from a building, particularly if it is vented, as was the case here. [A]ny member of the public might notice that one part of a house is warmer than another part or a nearby building if, for example, rainwater evaporates or snow melts at different rates across its surfaces. Such use of the senses would not convert into an unreasonable search if, instead, an adjoining neighbor allowed an officer onto her property to verify her perceptions with a sensitive thermometer. [Nor] does such observation become an unreasonable search if made from a distance with the aid of a device that merely discloses that the exterior of one house, or one area of the house, is much warmer than another. Nothing more occurred in this case.

[T]he notion that heat emissions from the outside of a dwelling is a private matter implicating the protections of the Fourth Amendment is not only unprecedented but also quite difficult to take seriously. Heat waves, like aromas that are generated in a kitchen, or in a laboratory or opium den, enter the public domain if and when they leave a building. [T]he homeowner has a reasonable expectation of privacy concerning what takes place within the home, and the Fourth Amendment's protection against physical invasions of the home should apply to their functional equivalent. But the equipment in this case did not penetrate the walls of [Kyllo's] home, and while it did pick up "details of the home" that were exposed to the public, it did not obtain "any information regarding the interior of the home." [B]ased on what the thermal imager "showed" regarding the outside of [Kyllo's] home, the officers "concluded" that [he] was engaging in illegal activity inside the home. It would be quite absurd to characterize their thought processes as "searches," regardless of whether they inferred (rightly) that [Kyllo] was growing marijuana in his house, or (wrongly) that "the lady of the house [was taking] her daily sauna and bath." In either case, the only conclusions the officers reached concerning the interior of the home were at least as indirect as those that might have been inferred from the contents of discarded garbage, or pen register data, or, as in this case, subpoenaed utility records. For the first time in its history, the Court assumes that an inference can amount to a Fourth Amendment violation.

[Just] as "the police cannot reasonably be expected to avert their eyes from evidence of criminal activity that could have been observed by any member of the public," so too public officials should not have to avert their senses or their equipment from detecting emissions in the public domain such as excessive heat, traces of smoke, suspicious odors, odorless gases, airborne particulates, or radioactive emissions, any of which could identify hazards to the community. [M]onitoring such emissions with "sense-enhancing technology," and drawing useful conclusions from such monitoring, is an entirely reasonable public service.

[T]he countervailing privacy interest is at best trivial. [H]omes generally are insulated to keep heat in, rather than to prevent the detection of heat going out, [and] society will [not] suffer from a rule requiring the rare homeowner who both intends to engage in uncommon activities that produce extraordinary amounts of heat, and wishes to conceal that production from outsiders, to make sure that the surrounding area is well insulated. The interest in concealing the heat escaping from one's house pales in significance to the "the chief evil against which the wording of the Fourth Amendment is directed," the "physical entry of the home," and it is hard to believe that it is an interest the Framers sought to protect in our Constitution.

[T]he Court has fashioned a rule that is intended to provide essential guidance for the day when "more sophisticated systems" gain the "ability to 'see' through walls and other opaque barriers." [I] would not erect a constitutional impediment to the use of sense-enhancing technology unless it provides its user with the functional equivalent of actual presence in the area being searched.

Despite the Court's attempt to draw a line that is "not only firm but also bright," the contours of its new rule are uncertain because its protection apparently dissipates as soon as the relevant technology is "in general public use." Yet how much use is general public use is not even hinted at by the Court's opinion.... [5] [T]he threat to privacy will grow, rather than recede, as the use of intrusive equipment becomes more readily available.

It is clear, however, that the category of "sense-enhancing technology" covered by the new rule is far too broad. It would, for example,

---

5. The record describes a device that numbers close to a thousand manufactured units; that has a predecessor numbering in the neighborhood of 4,000 to 5,000 units; that competes with a similar product numbering from 5,000 to 6,000 units; and that is "readily available to the public" for commercial, personal, or law enforcement purposes, and is just an 800–number away from being rented ... by anyone who wants one....

embrace potential mechanical substitutes for dogs trained to react when they sniff narcotics. But in *United States v. Place*, 462 U.S. 696 (1983), we held that a dog sniff that "discloses only the presence or absence of narcotics" does "not constitute a 'search' within the meaning of the Fourth Amendment," and it must follow that sense-enhancing equipment that identifies nothing but illegal activity is not a search either. Nevertheless, the use of such a device would be unconstitutional under the Court's rule, as would the use of other new devices that might detect the odor of deadly bacteria or chemicals for making a new type of high explosive, even if the devices (like the dog sniffs) are "so limited in both the manner in which" they obtain information and "in the content of the information" they reveal.

The application of the Court's new rule to "any information regarding the interior of the home," is also unnecessarily broad. If it takes sensitive equipment to detect an odor that identifies criminal conduct and nothing else, the fact that the odor emanates from the interior of a home should not provide it with constitutional protection. The criterion, moreover, is too sweeping in that information "regarding" the interior of a home apparently is not just information obtained through its walls, but also information concerning the outside of the building that could lead to inferences "regarding" what might be inside. [A]n officer using an infrared camera to observe a man silently entering the side door of a house at night carrying a pizza might conclude that its interior is now occupied by someone who likes pizza, and by doing so the officer would be guilty of conducting an unconstitutional "search" of the home.

Because the new rule applies to information regarding the "interior" of the home, it is too narrow as well as too broad. Clearly, a rule that is designed to protect individuals from the overly intrusive use of sense-enhancing equipment should not be limited to a home. If such equipment did provide its user with the functional equivalent of access to a private place—such as [the] telephone booth involved in *Katz*, or an office building—then the rule should apply to such an area as well as to a home.

The final requirement of the Court's new rule, that the information "could not otherwise have been obtained without physical intrusion into a constitutionally protected area," also extends too far. [T]he Court effectively treats the mental process of analyzing data obtained from external sources as the equivalent of a physical intrusion into the home. [T]he process of drawing inferences from data in the public domain should not be characterized as a search. [I] respectfully dissent.

Problems

1. *Other Observations*. After *Kyllo*, are the police free to observe the outsides of houses with their naked eyes? Consider an example raised in the *Kyllo* opinion: Suppose that the police have reason to believe that defendant is growing marijuana in his attic using Halide lights. The police wait until a big snowfall and observe defendant's roof to see how fast the snow melts vis-

a-vis nearby houses. After *Kyllo*, does this sort of observation violate Kyllo's reasonable expectation of privacy?

2. *Technology & Open fields.* In *Riley,* the Court held that the police could conduct aerial surveillance at relatively low altitudes. Are the police free to use high-powered satellite technology as well? Suppose that the police decide to use existing technology which enables satellites to take very precise pictures of small things from great distance (e.g., by taking pictures from outer space and beaming them back to earth, the police can examine an area as small as 12 inches across). Can the police use this technology to examine open fields for marijuana? Can they use the technology to peer into greenhouses as in *Riley*?

3. *Peering Into Windows.* Would you reach a different result if the police used high-powered satellite technology to peer into an open window in a home (a window that was open with the curtains parted)? Would it matter whether or not an individual with binoculars on a nearby street could also see through the window? What if the individual on the street could see in with the naked eye?

4. *Audio Surveillance.* The police believe that Melissa Johnson is selling marijuana, and they begin "audio surveillance" of her home using equipment that enables them to monitor transmissions from her cordless phone to a base station. The police locate their monitoring equipment in an apartment complex across the street from Johnson's apartment, approximately seventy-five yards away, and conduct intermittent monitoring every evening for 7 days. Johnson is unaware of the existence of devices that could monitor cordless telephone conversations. However, unknown to her, the handset on her cordless phone, and the literature accompanying the equipment, explain that one's privacy cannot be assured on a cordless telephone. The information gained by the "audio surveillance" is used to obtain a warrant, and the police find marijuana in Johnson's house. What arguments will defense counsel use for the proposition that the police monitoring constituted a search? How might the prosecutor respond? *See State v. Pendergrass,* 1995 WL 108248 (Tenn.Crim.App.1995).

5. *"Reasonable Expectations" and the Availability of Technology.* In recent years, various types of technology have become much more common and are readily available to the general citizenry. In addition to portable and cellular phones, citizens can use "scanners" to monitor the conversations on others on these phones. Is it possible to have a "reasonable expectation of privacy" in the contents of a cellular phone call given the existence of monitoring technology? If not, are the police free to monitor cellular calls for evidence of criminal activity? How do wiretapping laws affect the expectation of privacy? For example, Title III of the Omnibus Crime and Control and Safe Streets Act of 1968 which prohibits non-consensual interception of "wire," "oral," and "electronic" communications without prior judicial approval and precludes the use of such communications and derivative information as evidence in court.

6. *More on the Availability of Technology.* Suppose that devices are developed which allow the police to stand well away from a house (across the street), but to hear normal conversations inside the house. Suppose that other devices allow police to ''see'' through walls and ascertain what people are doing on the other side. Does the concept of a ''reasonable expectation of privacy'' disappear in light of such devices? Does it matter whether these devices are readily available (purchasable at any store for $19.95), or whether they are extremely expensive ($50,000) so that only law enforcement agencies and wealthy individuals can afford them?

7. *May Government Manipulate the Citizenry's ''Expectation of Privacy?''* Suppose that listening devices (like the one referred to in the prior problem) are not readily available, but the government has purchased them and announces that it will place such monitoring devices on public property outside each home and monitor all conversations in every house twenty-four hours a day. *See* Anthony G. Amsterdam, *Perspectives on the Fourth Amendment,* 58 Minn. L. Rev. 349 (1974). Is it possible for citizens to have a ''reasonable expectation of privacy'' in their conversations? Would it be permissible to take the less intrusive step of monitoring all public streets with video surveillance cameras?

8. *Grave Side Eavesdropping.* The police were investigating the murder of a five year-old boy, but were unable to conclusively determine the identity of the murderer. Suspecting that a family murder was the culprit, the police bugged the grave in hopes of obtaining a grave side confession. Several weeks later, the mother made incriminating statements while she was alone at the grave site. The police want to use a tape of the statements against the mother. In obtaining the statements, did the police engage in a ''search'' under the Fourth Amendment?

9. *Katz Reconsidered.* In light of recent decisions, would you expect *Katz* to be decided the same way if it arose today? Is it still impermissible for the police to use a listening device in the way that they used it in that case?

10. *Kyllo and Canine Sniffs of a Dwelling.* Suppose that the police decide to use drug-sniffing dogs to sniff at the doors of private residences in apartment buildings. At all times, the police remain outside the apartments. Under *Kyllo,* may the police employ such tactics? How might defense counsel argue that such sniffs are not permitted? How may a prosecutor respond to such arguments? See *State v. Rabb,* 920 So.2d 1175 (Fla. App. 2006).

C. PROBABLE CAUSE

Probable cause is an integral part of the Fourth Amendment's prohibition against unreasonable searches and seizures: ''no Warrants shall issue, but upon probable cause, supported by Oath or [affirmation].'' When the police obtain a warrant, the warrant must be based on probable cause. In addition, some exceptions to the warrant requirement also require probable cause (i.e., the automobile exception).

Why was the probable cause requirement included in the Fourth Amendment? Dissenting in *Marshall v. Barlow's, Inc.*, 436 U.S. 307 (1978), Mr. Justice Stevens explained: "Since the general warrant, not the warrantless search, was the immediate evil at which the Fourth Amendment was directed, it is not surprising that the Framers placed precise limits on its issuance. The requirement that a warrant only issue on a showing of particularized probable cause was the means adopted to circumscribe the warrant power." *See also United States v. Leon*, 468 U.S. 897 (1984) (Stevens, J., concurring) ("[I]n the Framers['] minds the paradigm of an abusive search was the execution of a warrant not based on probable cause."). So, not only must a warrant particularly describe the place to be searched and the things to be seized, but it must be based on probable cause to believe that the searched for items can be found in the place to be searched.

What must be "probable?" When the police want to conduct a search, probable cause requires proof of two things: that the fruits, instrumentalities or evidence of crime exist, and that they can be found at the place to be searched. When the police want to arrest, probable cause requires proof that a crime was committed and that the person to be arrested committed it.

Applied literally, "probable cause" requires that something be "more probable than not." However, the courts have not applied the probable cause requirement literally. In *Draper v. United States, supra*, the Court defined probable cause in the following way:

In dealing with probable cause, [as] the very name implies, we deal with probabilities. These are not technical; they are the factual and practical considerations of everyday life on which reasonable and prudent men, not legal technicians, "act." *Bringar v. United States, supra*, 338 U.S. at page 175. Probable cause exists where "the facts and circumstances within their [the arresting officers'] knowledge and of which they had reasonably trustworthy information [are] sufficient in themselves to warrant a man of reasonable caution in the belief that 'an offense has been or is being committed.'" *Carroll v. United States*, 267 U.S. 132, 162.

CARROLL v. UNITED STATES

267 U.S. 132 (1925).

Mr. Chief Justice Taft, [delivered] the opinion of the Court.

Section 25, title 2, of the National Prohibition Act, passed to enforce the Eighteenth Amendment, makes it unlawful to have or possess any liquor intended for use in violating the act. * * *

[Grand] Rapids is about 152 miles from Detroit. [Detroit] and its neighborhood along the Detroit river, which is the international boundary, is one of the most active centers for introducing illegally into this country spirituous liquors for distribution into the interior. [T]he prohibition agents were engaged in a regular patrol along the important highways from Detroit to Grand Rapids to stop and seize liquor carried in automobiles. They knew or had convincing evidence to make them believe that the Carroll boys, as they called them, were so-called "bootleggers" in Grand Rapids; i.e., that they were engaged in plying the unlawful trade of selling such liquor in that city. The officers had soon after noted their going from Grand Rapids half way to Detroit, and attempted to follow them to that city to see where they went, but they escaped observation. Two months later these officers suddenly met the same men on their way westward presumably from Detroit. The partners in the original combination to sell liquor in Grand Rapids were together in the same automobile they had been in the night when they tried to furnish the whisky to the officers, which was thus identified as part of the firm equipment. They were coming from the direction of the great source of supply for their stock to Grand Rapids, where they plied their trade. That the officers, when they saw the defendants, believed that they were carrying liquor, we can have no doubt, and we think it is equally clear that they had reasonable cause for thinking so. Emphasis is put by defendants' counsel on the statement made by one of the officers that they were not looking for defendants at the particular time when they appeared. [As] soon as they appeared, the officers were entitled to use their reasoning faculties upon all the facts of which they had previous knowledge in respect to the defendants.

In the light of these authorities, and what is shown by this record, it is clear the officers here had justification for the search and seizure. This is to say that the facts and circumstances within their knowledge and of which they had reasonably trustworthy information were sufficient in themselves to warrant a man of reasonable caution in the belief that intoxicating liquor was being transported in the automobile which they stopped and searched.

The judgment is affirmed.

The separate opinion of MR. JUSTICE MCREYNOLDS.

While quietly driving an ordinary automobile along a much frequented public road, plaintiffs in error were arrested by federal officers without a warrant and upon mere [suspicion]. [The] facts known by the officers who arrested plaintiffs in error were wholly insufficient to create a reasonable belief that they were transporting liquor contrary to law. [The] negotiation concerning three cases of whisky on September 29th was the only circumstance which could have subjected plaintiffs in error to any reasonable suspicion. No whisky was delivered, and it is not certain that they ever intended to deliver any. The arrest came 2 ½ months after the negotiation. Every act in the meantime is consistent with complete innocence. Has it come about that merely because a man once agreed to deliver whisky, but did not, he may be arrested whenever thereafter he ventures to drive an automobile on the road to Detroit!

Notes on Probable Cause

In *Maryland v. Pringle*, 540 U.S. 366 (2003), a police officer stopped a vehicle for a speeding violation and found rolled-up case and cocaine between the back seat and the arm rest. When all three passengers denied ownership, the officer arrested all three. The Court held that the officer had probable cause to arrest all three despite the denials. Later, after being given a *Miranda* warning, Pringle admitted that the cocaine belonged to him and that he planned to sell it at a party. When the admission was used against him at trial, Pringle appealed claiming that the admission was the illegal fruit of an unlawful arrest. The Court concluded that, when the officer found the five plastic glassine baggies containing suspected cocaine, he had probable cause to believe a felony had been committed. The Court held that the officer had probable cause to arrest all three passengers. "We think it an entirely reasonable inference from these facts that any or all three of the occupants had knowledge of, and exercised dominion and control over, the cocaine. Thus a reasonable officer could conclude that there was probable cause to believe Pringle committed the crime of possession of cocaine, either solely or jointly."

Problems

1. *Applying the Probable Cause Requirement.* Suppose that there is a street in your city where a large number of drug transactions occur. A significant percentage (in excess of 50%) of people on that street are drug pushers, or are drug users there to purchase drugs. Given these facts, do the police have "probable cause" to believe that everyone they find on the street is in possession of drugs? As a result, would the police have probable cause as to those suspiciously "hanging-out" on the street corner? What about a little old lady walking down the street pulling a shopping cart? If the police do not have probable cause as to everyone, how does the character of the street affect the probable cause determination in an individual case—*i.e.*, a case involving the person suspiciously hanging out on the street corner or the little old lady?

2. *Refusing Consent.* Suppose that a police officer validly stops a motorist for a traffic violation (a burnt out headlight). After issuing the motorist a citation, the officer asks the motorist for permission to search the motorist's trunk, but the motorist refuses. The officer, who honestly believes that any law-abiding citizen would graciously consent to a search request, believes that the motorist has "something to hide." "Otherwise, he would have given consent." Does the motorist's refusal give the officer probable cause to believe that the car contains contraband?

3. *The Stolen Record Player.* A police officer, assigned to a special "shop-lifting" detail, was in his parked automobile on a street in a commercial area about 6:30 p.m. in December (when it was presumably dark). The officer observed two men, both of whom he recognized as having prior

convictions for theft, walking with a console-type record player. When the men went into a liquor store, the officer followed them and observes the record player was new and bore the store tags of the Western Auto Supply Company. When the officer questioned the men about the machine, defendant stated that it belonged to his mother and that he was taking it in for repairs. When the officer pointed out that the machine had store tags on it, and was obviously new, defendant changed his story and stated that the machine was given to him by an unknown person nearby. When asked for a description of the person, defendant was unable to do so. At this point, the officer placed defendant under arrest. The Western Auto store's manager later identified the machine as store property, stated that it was not sold, and stated that the machine was on the floor 30 minutes earlier. Did the officer have probable cause to arrest the men? What weight is to be given to the store manager's statement? *See Brooks v. United States*, 159 A.2d 876 (D.C.Mun.App., 1960).

4. *Retracting Consent.* Defendant is stopped at a roadblock set up to check driver's licenses. After checking defendant's driver's license and registration, the officer requests permission to search the car. In making this request, the officer is acting on his "hunch" that the odor of a deodorizing agent emanating from the car might indicate the presence of narcotics. When defendant opens a garment bag in the trunk, the officer sees a "heavily taped" cardboard box. When the officer presses on the box, defendant zips the garment bag, puts a briefcase on top of the bag, closed the trunk, and states that he desires for the search to stop. Based upon the odor, the taped box, and defendant's conduct, the officer believes that he has probable cause to believe that defendant is in possession of narcotics. Did the police have probable cause to arrest defendant? Did they have probable cause to search the bag? What might the police argue? How might defendant respond? *See State v. Zelinske*, 108 N.M. 784, 779 P.2d 971 (App. 1989).

SPINELLI v. UNITED STATES

393 U.S. 410 (1969).

Mr. Justice Harlan delivered the opinion of the Court.

William Spinelli was convicted [of] traveling to St. Louis, Missouri, from a nearby Illinois suburb with the intention of conducting gambling activities proscribed by Missouri law. [Believing] it desirable that the principles of *Aguilar* [*v. Texas*, 378 U.S. 108 (1964)] should be further explicated, we granted certiorari * * *.

In *Aguilar*, a search warrant had issued upon an affidavit of police officers who swore only that they had "received reliable information from a credible person and do believe" that narcotics were being illegally stored on the described premises. [R]ecognizing that the constitutional requirement of probable cause can be satisfied by hearsay information, this Court held the affidavit inadequate for two reasons. First, the application failed to set forth any of the "underlying circumstances" necessary to enable the magistrate independently to judge of the validity of the informant's conclusion that the narcotics were where he said they were. Second, the affiant-officers did not attempt to support their claim that their informant was "credible" or his information "reliable." The Government is, however, quite right in saying that the FBI affidavit in the present case is more ample than that in *Aguilar*. Not only does it contain a report from an anonymous informant, but it also contains a report of an independent FBI investigation which is said to corroborate the informant's tip. We are then, required to delineate the manner in which *Aguilar's* two-pronged test should be applied in these circumstances.

In essence, the affidavit [contained] the following allegations:

1. The FBI had kept track of Spinelli's movements on five days during the month of August 1965. On four of these occasions, Spinelli was seen crossing one of two bridges leading from Illinois into St. Louis, Missouri, between 11 a.m. and 12:15 p.m. On four of the five days, Spinelli was also seen parking his car in a lot used by residents of an apartment house at 1108 Indian Circle Drive in St. Louis, between 3:30 p.m. and 4:45 p.m.[6] On one day, Spinelli was followed further and seen to enter a particular apartment in the building.

2. An FBI check with the telephone company revealed that this apartment contained two telephones listed under the name of Grace P. Hagen, and carrying the numbers WYdown 4–0029 and WYdown 4–0136.

3. The application stated that "William Spinelli is known to this affiant and to federal law enforcement agents and local law enforcement agents as a bookmaker, an associate of bookmakers, a gambler, and an associate of gamblers."

4. Finally it was stated that the FBI "has been informed by a confidential reliable informant that William Spinelli is operating a handbook and accepting wagers and disseminating wagering information by means of the telephones which have been assigned the numbers WYdown 4–0029 and WYdown 4–0136."

There can be no question that the last item mentioned, detailing the informant's tip, has a fundamental place in this warrant application. Without it, probable cause could not be established. The first two items reflect only innocent-seeming activity and data. Spinelli's travels to and from the apartment building and his entry into a particular apartment on one occasion could hardly be taken as bespeaking gambling activity; and there is surely nothing unusual about an apartment containing two separate telephones. Many a householder indulges himself in this petty luxury. Finally, the allegation that Spinelli was "known" to the affiant and to other federal and local law enforcement officers as a gambler and

---

6. No report was made as to Spinelli's movements during the period between his arrival in St. Louis at noon and his arrival at the parking lot in the late afternoon. [E]vidence at trial indicated that Spinelli frequented the offices of his stockbroker during this period.

an associate of gamblers is but a bald and unilluminating assertion of suspicion that is entitled to no weight in appraising the magistrate's decision.

So much indeed the Government does not deny. Rather, [the] Government claims that the informant's tip gives a suspicious color to the FBI's reports detailing Spinelli's innocent-seeming conduct and that, conversely, the FBI's surveillance corroborates the informant's tip, thereby entitling it to more weight. It is true, of course, that the magistrate is obligated to render a judgment based upon a common-sense reading of the entire affidavit. We believe, however, that the "totality of circumstances" approach taken by the Court of Appeals paints with too broad a brush. Where, as here, the informer's tip is a necessary element in a finding of probable cause, its proper weight must be determined by a more precise analysis.

The informer's report must first be measured against *Aguilar's* standards so that its probative value can be assessed. If the tip is found inadequate under *Aguilar*, the other allegations which corroborate the information contained in the hearsay report should then be considered. At this stage as well, however, the standards enunciated in *Aguilar* must inform the magistrate's decision. He must ask: Can it fairly be said that the tip, even when certain parts of it have been corroborated by independent sources, is as trustworthy as a tip which would pass *Aguilar's* tests without independent corroboration? *Aguilar* is relevant at this stage of the inquiry as well because the tests it establishes were designed to implement the long-standing principle that probable cause must be determined by a "neutral and detached magistrate," and not by "the officer engaged in the often competitive enterprise of ferreting out crime." A magistrate cannot be said to have properly discharged his constitutional duty if he relies on an informer's tip which—even when partially corroborated—is not as reliable as one which passes *Aguilar's* requirements when standing alone.

Applying these principles to the present case, we first consider the weight to be given the informer's tip when it is considered apart from the rest of the affidavit. It is clear that a Commissioner could not credit it without abdicating his constitutional function. Though the affiant swore that his confidant was "reliable," he offered the magistrate no reason in support of this conclusion. Perhaps even more important is the fact that *Aguilar's* other test has not been satisfied. The tip does not contain a sufficient statement of the underlying circumstances from which the informer concluded that Spinelli was running a bookmaking operation. We are not told how the FBI's source received his information—it is not alleged that the informant personally observed Spinelli at work or that he had ever placed a bet with him. Moreover, if the informant came by the information indirectly, he did not explain why his sources were reliable. In the absence of a statement detailing the manner in which the information was gathered, it is especially important that the tip describe the accused's criminal activity in sufficient detail that the magistrate may know that he is relying on something more substantial than a casual rumor circulating in the underworld or an accusation based merely on an individual's general reputation.

The detail provided by the informant in *Draper v. United States*, 358 U.S. 307 (1959), provides a suitable benchmark. While Hereford, the Government's informer in that case did not state the way in which he had obtained his information, he reported that Draper had gone to Chicago the day before by train and that he would return to Denver by train with three ounces of heroin on one of two specified mornings. Moreover, Hereford went on to describe, with minute particularity, the clothes that Draper would be wearing upon his arrival at the Denver station. A magistrate, when confronted with such detail, could reasonably infer that the informant had gained his information in a reliable way.[7] Such an inference cannot be made in the present case. Here, the only facts supplied were that Spinelli was using two specified telephones and that these phones were being used in gambling operations. This meager report could easily have been obtained from an offhand remark heard at a neighborhood bar.

Nor do we believe that the patent doubts *Aguilar* raises as to the report's reliability are adequately resolved by a consideration of the allegations detailing the FBI's independent investigative efforts. At most, these allegations indicated that Spinelli could have used the telephones specified by the informant for some purpose. This cannot by itself be said to support both the inference that the informer was generally trustworthy and that he had made his charge against Spinelli on the basis of information obtained in a reliable way. Once again, *Draper* provides a relevant comparison. Independent police work in that case corroborated much more than one small detail that had been provided by the informant. There, the police, upon meeting the inbound Denver train on the second morning specified by informer Hereford, saw a man whose dress corresponded precisely to Hereford's detailed description. It was then apparent that the informant had not been fabricating his report out of whole cloth; since the report was of the sort which in common experience may be recognized as having been obtained in a reliable way, it was perfectly clear that probable cause had been established.

We conclude, then, that in the present case the informant's tip— even when corroborated to the extent indicated—was not sufficient to provide the basis for a finding of probable cause. This is not to say that the tip was so insubstantial that it could not properly have counted in the magistrate's determination. Rather, it needed some further support. When we look to the other parts of the application, however, we find nothing alleged which would permit the suspicions engendered by the informant's report to ripen into a judgment that a crime was probably being [committed].

---

7. While *Draper* involved the question whether the police had probable cause for an arrest without a warrant, the analysis required for [this] question is basically similar to that demanded [when] a magistrate [considers] whether a search warrant should issue.

The judgment of the Court of Appeals is [*reversed*].

Mr. Justice White, concurring.

[The] tension between *Draper* and the *Nathanson-Aguilar* line of cases is evident from the course followed by the majority opinion. First, it is held that the report from a reliable informant that Spinelli is using two telephones with specified numbers to conduct a gambling business plus Spinelli's reputation in police circles as a gambler does not add up to probable cause. This is wholly consistent with *Aguilar* and *Nathanson*: the informant did not reveal whether he had personally observed the facts or heard them from another and, if the latter, no basis for crediting the hearsay was presented. Nor were the facts, as Mr. Justice HARLAN says, of such a nature that they normally would be obtainable only by the personal observation of the informant himself. The police, however, did not stop with the informant's report. Independently, they established the existence of two phones having the given numbers and located them in an apartment house which Spinelli was regularly frequenting away from his home. There remained little question but that Spinelli was using the phones, and it was a fair inference that the use was not for domestic but for business purposes. The informant had claimed the business involved gambling. Since his specific information about Spinelli using two phones with particular numbers had been verified, did not his allegation about gambling thereby become sufficiently more believable if the *Draper* principle is to be given any scope at all? I would think so, particularly since information from the informant which was verified was not neutral, irrelevant information but was material to proving the gambling allegation: two phones with different numbers in an apartment used away from home indicates a business use in an operation, like bookmaking, where multiple phones are needed. The *Draper* approach would reasonably justify the issuance of a warrant in this case, particularly since the police had some awareness of Spinelli's past activities. The majority, however, while seemingly embracing *Draper*, confines that case to its own facts. [I] join the opinion of the Court and the judgment of reversal. * * *

Mr. Justice Black, dissenting.

[T]he affidavit given the magistrate was more than ample to show probable cause of the petitioner's guilt. The affidavit meticulously set out facts sufficient to show the following:

1.   The petitioner had been shown going to and coming from a room in an apartment which contained two telephones listed under the name of another person. Nothing in the record indicates that the apartment was of that large and luxurious type which could only be occupied by a person to whom it would be a "petty luxury" to have two separate telephones, with different numbers, both listed under the name of a person who did not live there.

2.   The petitioner's car had been observed parked in the apartment's parking lot. This fact [was] highly relevant in showing that the

petitioner was extremely interested in some enterprise which was located in the apartment.

3.   The FBI had been informed by a reliable informant that the petitioner was accepting wagering information by telephones—the particular telephones located in the apartment the defendant had been repeatedly visiting. Unless the Court, going beyond the requirements of the Fourth Amendment, wishes to require magistrates to hold trials before issuing warrants, it is not necessary—as the Court holds—to have the affiant explain "the underlying circumstances from which the informer concluded that Spinelli was running a bookmaking operation."

4.   The petitioner was known by federal and local law enforcement agents as a bookmaker and an associate of gamblers. I cannot agree [that] this knowledge was only a "bald and unilluminating assertion of suspicion that is entitled to no weight in appraising the magistrate's decision." Although the statement is hearsay that might not be admissible in a regular trial, everyone knows, unless he shuts his eyes to the realities of life, that this is a relevant fact which, together with other circumstances, might indicate a factual probability that gambling is taking place.

The foregoing facts should be enough to constitute probable cause for anyone who does not believe that the only way to obtain a search warrant is to prove beyond a reasonable doubt that a defendant is guilty. Even *Aguilar*, on which the Court relies, cannot support the contrary result * * *.

Mr. Justice Fortas, dissenting.

[A] policeman's affidavit should not be judged as an entry in an essay contest. [A] policeman's affidavit is entitled to common-sense evaluation. So viewed, I conclude that the judgment of the Court of Appeals for the Eighth Circuit should be affirmed.

Note: Informants and Hearsay

Ordinarily, when the police seek a warrant, they do so based on the testimony or affidavits of police officers. However, informants are an integral part of the investigative process, and are often relied on by police in their affidavits and testimony. The difficulty is that the testimony of informants is often used in a "hearsay" way (hearsay being defined as an out-of-court statement offered to prove the truth of the matter asserted in the statement). In criminal and civil trials, the use of hearsay is usually prohibited except when the prosecution can fit the testimony into one of the many exceptions to the hearsay rule. However, hearsay is usually admissible in a probable cause hearing. In *Draper v. United States*, 358 U.S. 307 (1959), the Court rejected petitioner's contention that "because hearsay is not legally competent evidence in a criminal trial, [it] could not legally have been considered, but should have been put out of mind" in deciding whether probable cause existed to arrest petitioner. The Court justified its holding by stating that there "is a large difference between the two things to be proved [guilt and probable cause], as well as between the tribunals which determine them, and therefore a like difference in the quanta and modes of proof required to establish them." Although *Spinelli* made clear that the police could use hearsay testimony in a probable cause hearing, the Court placed limits on the use of such testimony by imposing the *Aguilar-Spinelli* test.

Problem: The Eyewitness Report

A woman was sweeping the front porch of her home when she saw a man walk onto a neighbor's porch and peer in the front door. The man then walked in a northerly direction, stopped at another house, and then disappeared out of sight. The woman later saw the man standing at a nearby bus stop where he had taken off his shirt and was using it to cover a television set. He was pacing nervously and was trying to hitchhike while waiting for the bus to arrive. The woman called the police, told them about the man's activities and location, and reported her suspicions of burglary. Officer Freeman, a twenty year veteran, arrived five minutes after the call. He asked the man for identification which he could not produce. When asked about the television set, the man stated that he had bought the television set from someone in the neighborhood for $100. A "pat down" search for weapons revealed that the man (who was wearing only an undershirt) had brown wool gloves in his back pocket. While he was being questioned, the woman made herself known to the officers as the woman who had called the police. The man was then arrested and searched. Did the officer have probable cause to arrest the man? Would it matter that, after the arrest, the owners of a house one block south of the woman's house reported that their house had been burglarized and that a television set (the one found in the man's possession) had been stolen? *See People v. Quintero*, 657 P.2d 948 (Colo., En Banc, 1983).

ILLINOIS v. GATES

462 U.S. 213 (1983).

Justice Rehnquist delivered the opinion of the Court.

[Bloomingdale, Ill.], is a suburb of Chicago located in DuPage County. On May 3, 1978, the Bloomingdale Police Department received by mail an anonymous handwritten letter which read as follows:

> "This letter is to inform you that you have a couple in your town who strictly make their living on selling drugs. They are Sue and Lance Gates, they live on Greenway, off Bloomingdale Rd. in the condominiums. Most of their buys are done in Florida. Sue his wife drives their car to Florida, where she leaves it to be loaded up with drugs, then Lance flies down and drives it back. Sue flies back after she drops the car off in Florida. May 3 she is driving down there again and Lance will be flying down in a few days to drive it back. At the time Lance drives the car back he has the trunk loaded with over $100,000.00 in drugs. Presently they have over $100,000.00 worth of drugs in their basement.

They brag about the fact they never have to work, and make their entire living on pushers. I guarantee if you watch them carefully you will make a big catch. They are friends with some big drugs dealers, who visit their house often.

Lance & Susan Gates

Greenway

in Condominiums"

The letter was referred by the Chief of Police of the Bloomingdale Police Department to Detective Mader, who decided to pursue the tip. Mader learned, from the office of the Illinois Secretary of State, that an Illinois driver's license had been issued to one Lance Gates, residing at a stated address in Bloomingdale. He contacted a confidential informant, whose examination of certain financial records revealed a more recent address for the Gates, and he also learned from a police officer assigned to O'Hare Airport that "L. Gates" had made a reservation on Eastern Airlines flight 245 to West Palm Beach, Fla., scheduled to depart from Chicago on May 5 at 4:15 p.m.

Mader then made arrangements with an agent of the Drug Enforcement Administration for surveillance of the May 5 Eastern Airlines flight. The agent later reported to Mader that Gates had boarded the flight, and that federal agents in Florida had observed him arrive in West Palm Beach and take a taxi to the nearby Holiday Inn. They also reported that Gates went to a room registered to one Susan Gates and that, at 7:00 a.m. the next morning, Gates and an unidentified woman left the motel in a Mercury bearing Illinois license plates and drove northbound on an interstate frequently used by travelers to the Chicago area. In addition, the DEA agent informed Mader that the license plate number on the Mercury registered to a Hornet station wagon owned by Gates. The agent also advised Mader that the driving time between West Palm Beach and Bloomingdale was approximately 22 to 24 hours.

Mader signed an affidavit setting forth the foregoing facts, and submitted it to a judge of the Circuit Court of DuPage County, together with a copy of the anonymous letter. The judge [thereupon] issued a search warrant for the Gates' residence and for their automobile. The judge, in deciding to issue the warrant, could have determined that the modus operandi of the Gates had been substantially corroborated. As the anonymous letter predicted, Lance Gates had flown from Chicago to West Palm Beach late in the afternoon of May 5th, had checked into a hotel room registered in the name of his wife, and, at 7:00 a.m. the following morning, had headed north, accompanied by an unidentified woman, out of West Palm Beach on an interstate highway used by travelers from South Florida to Chicago in an automobile bearing a license plate issued to him.

At 5:15 a.m. on May 7th, only 36 hours after he had flown out of Chicago, Lance Gates, and his wife, returned to their home in Bloomingdale, driving the car in which they had left West Palm Beach some 22 hours earlier. The Bloomingdale police were awaiting them, searched the trunk of the Mercury, and uncovered approximately 350 pounds of marijuana. A search of the Gates' home revealed marijuana, weapons, and other contraband. The Illinois Circuit Court ordered suppression of all these items, on the ground that the affidavit submitted to the Circuit Judge failed to support the necessary determination of probable cause to believe that the Gates' automobile and home contained the contraband in question. [T]he Illinois Appellate Court and [the] Supreme Court of Illinois [affirmed].

The Illinois Supreme Court concluded—and we are inclined to agree—that, standing alone, the anonymous letter sent to the Bloomingdale Police Department would not provide the basis for a magistrate's determination that there was probable cause to believe contraband would be found in the Gates' car and home. The letter provides virtually nothing from which one might conclude that its author is either honest or his information reliable; likewise, the letter gives absolutely no indication of the basis for the writer's predictions regarding the Gates' criminal activities. Something more was required, then, before a magistrate could conclude that there was probable cause to believe that contraband would be found in the Gates' home and car.

The Illinois Supreme Court also properly recognized that Detective Mader's affidavit might be capable of supplementing the anonymous letter with information sufficient to permit a determination of probable cause. In holding that the affidavit in fact did not contain sufficient additional information to sustain a determination of probable cause, the Illinois court applied a "two-pronged test," derived from our decision in *Spinelli v. United States*. The Illinois Supreme Court, like some others, apparently understood *Spinelli* as requiring that the anonymous letter satisfy each of two independent requirements before it could be relied on. According to this view, the letter, as supplemented by Mader's affidavit, first had to adequately reveal the "basis of knowledge" of the letter writer—the particular means by which he came by the information given in his report. Second, it had to provide facts sufficiently establishing either the "veracity" of the affiant's informant, or, alternatively, the "reliability" of the informant's report in this particular case.

The Illinois court, alluding to an elaborate set of legal rules that have developed among various lower courts to enforce the "two-pronged test,"[8] found that the test had not been satisfied. First, the "veracity" prong was not satisfied because, "there was simply no basis [for] conclud[ing] that the anonymous person [who wrote the letter to the

---

8. [T]he "veracity" prong of the *Spinelli* test has two "spurs"—the informant's "credibility" and the "reliability" of his information. [Both] the "basis of knowledge" prong and the "veracity" prong are treated as entirely separate requirements, which must be independently satisfied in every case in order to sustain a determination of probable cause. Some ancillary doctrines are relied on to satisfy certain of the foregoing requirements. For example, the "self-verifying detail" of a tip may satisfy the "basis of knowledge" requirement, although not the "credibility" spur of the "veracity" prong. Conversely, corroboration would seem not capable of supporting the "basis of knowledge" prong, but only the "veracity" prong. * * *

Bloomingdale Police Department] was credible." The court indicated that corroboration by police of details contained in the letter might never satisfy the "veracity" prong, and in any event, could not do so [if] only "innocent" details are corroborated. In addition, the letter gave no indication of the basis of its writer's knowledge of the Gates' activities. The Illinois court understood *Spinelli* as permitting the detail contained in a tip to be used to infer that the informant had a reliable basis for his statements, but it thought that the anonymous letter failed to provide sufficient detail to permit such an inference. Thus, it concluded that no showing of probable cause had been made.

We agree with the Illinois Supreme Court that an informant's "veracity," "reliability" and "basis of knowledge" are all highly relevant in determining the value of his report. We do not agree, however, that these elements should be understood as entirely separate and independent requirements to be rigidly exacted in every case, which the opinion of the Supreme Court of Illinois would imply. Rather [they] should be understood simply as closely intertwined issues that may usefully illuminate the commonsense, practical question whether there is "probable cause" to believe that contraband or evidence is located in a particular place.

[This] totality of the circumstances approach is far more consistent with our prior treatment of probable cause than is any rigid demand that specific "tests" be satisfied by every informant's tip. Perhaps the central teaching of our decisions bearing on the probable cause standard is that it is a "practical, nontechnical conception." *Brinegar v. United States*, 338 U.S. 160 (1949). "In dealing with probable cause, [as] the very name implies, we deal with probabilities. These are not technical; they are the factual and practical considerations of everyday life on which reasonable and prudent men, not legal technicians, act." Our observation in *United States v. Cortez*, 449 U.S. 411, 418 (1981), regarding "particularized suspicion," is also applicable to the probable cause standard:

> The process does not deal with hard certainties, but with probabilities. Long before the law of probabilities was articulated as such, practical people formulated certain common-sense conclusions about human behavior; jurors as fact finders are permitted to do the same—and so are law enforcement officers. Finally, the evidence thus collected must be seen and weighed not in terms of library analysis by scholars, but as understood by those versed in the field of law enforcement.

As these comments illustrate, probable cause is a fluid concept—turning on the assessment of probabilities in particular factual contexts—not readily, or even usefully, reduced to a neat set of legal rules. Informants' tips doubtless come in many shapes and sizes from many different types of persons. As we said in *Adams v. Williams*, 407 U.S. 143, 147 (1972), "Informants' tips, like all other clues and evidence coming to a policeman on the scene may vary greatly in their value and reliability." Rigid legal rules are ill-suited to an area of such diversity. "One simple rule will not cover every situation."

Moreover, the "two-pronged test" directs analysis into two largely independent channels—the informant's "veracity" or "reliability" and his "basis of knowledge." There are persuasive arguments against according these two elements such independent status. Instead, they are better understood as relevant considerations in the totality of circumstances analysis that traditionally has guided probable cause determinations: a deficiency in one may be compensated for, in determining the overall reliability of a tip, by a strong showing as to the other, or by some other indicia of reliability.

If, for example, a particular informant is known for the unusual reliability of his predictions of certain types of criminal activities in a locality, his failure, in a particular case, to thoroughly set forth the basis of his knowledge surely should not serve as an absolute bar to a finding of probable cause based on his tip. Likewise, if an unquestionably honest citizen comes forward with a report of criminal activity—which if fabricated would subject him to criminal liability—we have found rigorous scrutiny of the basis of his knowledge unnecessary. Conversely, even if we entertain some doubt as to an informant's motives, his explicit and detailed description of alleged wrongdoing, along with a statement that the event was observed first-hand, entitles his tip to greater weight than might otherwise be the case. Unlike a totality of circumstances analysis, which permits a balanced assessment of the relative weights of all the various indicia of reliability (and unreliability) attending an informant's tip, the "two-pronged test" has encouraged an excessively technical dissection of informants' tips, with undue attention being focused on isolated issues that cannot sensibly be divorced from the other facts presented to the magistrate.

[Finely-tuned] standards such as proof beyond a reasonable doubt or by a preponderance of the evidence, useful in formal trials, have no place in the magistrate's decision. While an effort to fix some general, numerically precise degree of certainty corresponding to "probable cause" may not be helpful, it is clear that "only the probability, and not a prima facie showing, of criminal activity is the standard of probable cause."

We also have recognized that affidavits "are normally drafted by nonlawyers in the midst and haste of a criminal investigation. Technical requirements of elaborate specificity once exacted under common law pleading have no proper place in this area." Likewise, search and arrest warrants long have been issued by persons who are neither lawyers nor judges, and who certainly do not remain abreast of each judicial refinement of the nature of "probable cause." The rigorous inquiry into the *Spinelli* prongs and the complex superstructure of evidentiary and analytical rules that some have seen implicit in our *Spinelli* decision, cannot be reconciled with the fact that many warrants are—quite properly—issued on the basis of nontechnical, common-sense judgments of laymen applying a standard less demanding than those used in more formal legal proceedings. Likewise, given the informal, often hurried context in which it must be applied, the "built-in subtleties" of the "two-pronged test" are particularly unlikely to assist magistrates in determining probable cause.

Similarly, we have repeatedly said that after-the-fact scrutiny by courts of the sufficiency of an affidavit should not take the form of de novo review. A magistrate's "determination of probable cause should be paid great deference by reviewing courts." "A grudging or negative attitude by reviewing courts toward warrants," is inconsistent with the Fourth Amendment's strong preference for searches conducted pursuant to a warrant, "courts should not [invalidate] warrant[s] by interpreting affidavit[s] in a hyper technical, rather than a commonsense, manner."

If the affidavits submitted by police officers are subjected to the type of scrutiny some courts have deemed appropriate, police might well resort to warrantless searches, with the hope of relying on consent or some other exception to the warrant clause that might develop at the time of the search. In addition, the possession of a warrant by officers conducting an arrest or search greatly reduces the perception of unlawful or intrusive police conduct, by assuring "the individual whose property is searched or seized of the lawful authority of the executing officer, his need to search, and the limits of his power to search." Reflecting this preference for the warrant process, the traditional standard for review of an issuing magistrate's probable cause determination has been that so long as the magistrate had a "substantial basis [for] conclud[ing]" that a search would uncover evidence of wrongdoing, the Fourth Amendment requires no more. We think reaffirmation of this standard better serves the purpose of encouraging recourse to the warrant procedure and is more consistent with our traditional deference to the probable cause determinations of magistrates than is the "two-pronged test."

Finally, the direction taken by decisions following *Spinelli* poorly serves "the most basic function of any government": "to provide for the security of the individual and of his property." The strictures that inevitably accompany the "two-pronged test" cannot avoid seriously impeding the task of law enforcement. If, as the Illinois Supreme Court apparently thought, that test must be rigorously applied in every case, anonymous tips seldom would be of greatly diminished value in police work. Ordinary citizens, like ordinary witnesses, generally do not provide extensive recitations of the basis of their everyday observations. Likewise, [the] veracity of persons supplying anonymous tips is by hypothesis largely unknown, and unknowable. As a result, anonymous tips seldom could survive a rigorous application of either of the *Spinelli* prongs. Yet, such tips, particularly when supplemented by independent police investigation, frequently contribute to the solution of otherwise "perfect crimes." While a conscientious assessment of the basis for crediting such tips is required by the Fourth Amendment, a standard that leaves virtually no place for anonymous citizen informants is not.

For all these reasons, we conclude that it is wiser to abandon the "two-pronged test" established by our decisions in *Aguilar* and *Spinelli*. In its place we reaffirm the totality of the circumstances analysis that traditionally has informed probable cause determinations. The task of the issuing magistrate is simply to make a practical, common-sense decision whether, given all the circumstances set forth in the affidavit before him, including the "veracity" and "basis of knowledge" of persons supplying hearsay information, there is a fair probability that contraband or evidence of a crime will be found in a particular place. And the duty of a reviewing court is simply to ensure that the magistrate had a "substantial basis [for] conclud[ing]" that probable cause existed. We are convinced that this flexible, easily applied standard will better achieve the accommodation of public and private interests that the Fourth Amendment requires than does the approach that has developed from *Aguilar* and *Spinelli*.

Our earlier cases illustrate the limits beyond which a magistrate may not venture in issuing a warrant. A sworn statement of an affiant that "he has cause to suspect and does believe that" liquor illegally brought into the United States is located on certain premises will not do. *Nathanson v. United States*, 290 U.S. 41 (1933). An affidavit must provide the magistrate with a substantial basis for determining the existence of probable cause, and the wholly conclusory statement at issue in *Nathanson* failed to meet this requirement. An officer's statement that "affiants have received reliable information from a credible person and believe" that heroin is stored in a home, is likewise inadequate. *Aguilar v. Texas*, 378 U.S. 108 (1964). As in *Nathanson*, this is a mere conclusory statement that gives the magistrate virtually no basis at all for making a judgment regarding probable cause. Sufficient information must be presented to the magistrate to allow that official to determine probable cause; his action cannot be a mere ratification of the bare conclusions of others. In order to ensure that such an abdication of the magistrate's duty does not occur, courts must continue to conscientiously review the sufficiency of affidavits on which warrants are issued. But when we move beyond the "bare bones" affidavits present in cases such as *Nathanson* and *Aguilar*, this area simply does not lend itself to a prescribed set of rules, like that which had developed from *Spinelli*. Instead, the flexible, common-sense standard articulated in [prior precedent] better serves the purposes of the Fourth Amendment's probable cause requirement.

Justice Brennan's dissent suggests in several places that the approach we take today somehow downgrades the role of the neutral magistrate, because *Aguilar* and *Spinelli* "preserve the role of magistrates as independent arbiters of probable [cause]." [Nothing] in our opinion in any way lessens the authority of the magistrate to draw such reasonable inferences as he will from the material supplied to him by applicants for a warrant; indeed, he is freer than under the regime of *Aguilar* and *Spinelli* to draw such inferences, or to refuse to draw them if he is so minded.

The real gist of Justice Brennan's criticism seems to be a second argument, somewhat at odds with the first, that magistrates should be restricted in their authority to make probable cause determinations by the standards laid down in *Aguilar* and *Spinelli*, and that such findings "should not be authorized unless there is some assurance that the information on which they are based has been obtained in a reliable way by an honest or credible person." However, under our opinion magistrates remain perfectly free to exact such assurances as they deem necessary, as well as those required by this opinion, in making probable cause determinations. Justice BRENNAN would apparently prefer that magistrates be restricted in their findings of probable cause by the development of an elaborate body of case law dealing with the "veracity" prong of the *Spinelli* test, which in turn is broken down into two "spurs"—the informant's "credibility" and the "reliability" of his information, together with the "basis of knowledge" prong of the *Spinelli* test. That such a labyrinthine body of judicial refinement bears any relationship to familiar definitions of probable cause is hard to imagine. Probable cause deals "with probabilities. These are not technical; they are the factual and practical considerations of everyday life on which reasonable and prudent men, not legal technicians, act."

Justice Brennan's dissent also suggests that "words such as 'practical,' 'nontechnical,' and 'common sense,' as used in the Court's opinion, are but code words for an overly-permissive attitude towards police practices in derogation of the rights secured by the Fourth Amendment." * * * "Fidelity" to the commands of the Constitution suggests balanced judgment rather than exhortation. The highest "fidelity" is achieved neither by the judge who instinctively goes furthest in upholding even the most bizarre claim of individual constitutional rights, any more than it is achieved by a judge who instinctively goes furthest in accepting the most restrictive claims of governmental authorities. The task of this Court, as of other courts, is to "hold the balance true," and we think we have done that in this case.

Our decisions applying the totality of circumstances analysis outlined above have consistently recognized the value of corroboration of details of an informant's tip by independent police work. In *Jones v. United States*, 362 U.S., at 269, we held that an affidavit relying on hearsay "is not to be deemed insufficient on that score, so long as a substantial basis for crediting the hearsay is presented." We went on to say that even in making a warrantless arrest an officer "may rely upon information received through an informant, rather than upon his direct observations, so long as the informant's statement is reasonably corroborated by other matters within the officer's knowledge." Likewise, we recognized the probative value of corroborative efforts of police officials in *Aguilar*—the source of the "two-pronged test"—by observing that if the police had made some effort to corroborate the informant's report at issue, "an entirely different case" would have been presented.

Our decision in *Draper v. United States*, 358 U.S. 307 (1959), however, is the classic case on the value of corroborative efforts of police officials. [The] showing of probable cause in the present case was fully as compelling as that in *Draper*. Even standing alone, the facts obtained through the independent investigation of Mader and the DEA at least suggested that the Gates were involved in drug trafficking. In addition to being a popular vacation site, Florida is well-known as a source of narcotics and other illegal drugs. Lance Gates' flight to Palm Beach, his brief, overnight stay in a motel, and apparent immediate return north to Chicago in the family car, conveniently awaiting him in West Palm Beach, is as suggestive of a pre-arranged drug run, as it is of an ordinary vacation trip.

In addition, the magistrate could rely on the anonymous letter, which had been corroborated in major part by Mader's efforts—just as had occurred in *Draper*. The Supreme Court of Illinois reasoned that *Draper* involved an informant who had given reliable information on previous occasions, while the honesty and reliability of the anonymous informant in this case were unknown to the Bloomingdale police. While this distinction might be an apt one at the time the police department received the anonymous letter, it became far less significant after Mader's independent investigative work occurred. The corroboration of the letter's predictions that the Gates' car would be in Florida, that Lance Gates would fly to Florida in the next day or so, and that he would drive the car north toward Bloomingdale all indicated, albeit not with certainty, that the informant's other assertions also were true. "Because an informant is right about some things, he is more probably right about other facts"—including the claim regarding the Gates' illegal activity. This may well not be the type of "reliability" or "veracity" necessary to satisfy some views of the "veracity prong" of *Spinelli*, but we think it suffices for the practical, common-sense judgment called for in making a probable cause determination. It is enough, for purposes of assessing probable cause, that "corroboration through other sources of information reduced the chances of a reckless or prevaricating tale," thus providing "a substantial basis for crediting the hearsay."

Finally, the anonymous letter contained a range of details relating not just to easily obtained facts and conditions existing at the time of the tip, but to future actions of third parties ordinarily not easily predicted. The letter writer's accurate information as to the travel plans of each of the Gates was of a character likely obtained only from the Gates themselves, or from someone familiar with their not entirely ordinary travel plans. If the informant had access to accurate information of this type a magistrate could properly conclude that it was not unlikely that he also had access to reliable information of the Gates' alleged illegal activities.[9] Of course, the Gates' travel plans might have been learned

---

9. The dissent seizes on one inaccuracy in the anonymous informant's letter—its statement that Sue Gates would fly from Florida to Illinois, when in fact she drove— and argues that the probative value of the entire tip was undermined by this allegedly "material mistake." [T]he dissent apparently attributes to the magistrate who issued the warrant in this case the rather implausible notion that persons dealing in drugs always stay at home, apparently out of fear that to leave might risk intrusion by

from a talkative neighbor or travel agent; under the "two-pronged test" developed from *Spinelli*, the character of the details in the anonymous letter might well not permit a sufficiently clear inference regarding the letter writer's "basis of knowledge." [But] probable cause does not demand the certainty we associate with formal trials. It is enough that there was a fair probability that the writer of the anonymous letter had obtained his entire story either from the Gates or someone they trusted. And corroboration of major portions of the letter's predictions provides just this probability. It is apparent, therefore, that the judge issuing the warrant had a "substantial basis [for] conclud[ing]" that probable cause to search the Gates' home and car existed. The judgment of the Supreme Court of Illinois therefore must be

Reversed.

JUSTICE WHITE, concurring in the judgment.

[Although] I agree that the warrant should be upheld, I reach this conclusion in accordance with the *Aguilar-Spinelli* framework. [The Gates' activity] was quite suspicious. I agree with the Court that Lance Gates' flight to Palm Beach, an area known to be a source of narcotics, the brief overnight stay in a motel, and apparent immediate return North, suggest a pattern that trained law-enforcement officers have recognized as indicative of illicit drug-dealing activity.

Even, however, had the corroboration related only to completely innocuous activities, this fact alone would not preclude the issuance of a valid warrant. The critical issue is not whether the activities observed by the police are innocent or suspicious. [T]he proper focus should be on whether the actions of the suspects, whatever their nature, give rise to an inference that the informant is credible and that he obtained his information in a reliable manner.

[In *Draper*, the] fact that the informer was able to predict, two days in advance, the exact clothing Draper would be wearing dispelled the possibility that his tip was just based on rumor or "an off-hand remark heard at a neighborhood bar." Probably Draper had planned in advance to wear these specific clothes so that an accomplice could identify him. A clear inference could therefore be drawn that the informant was either involved in the criminal scheme himself or that he otherwise had access to reliable, inside information.

As in *Draper*, the police investigation in the present case satisfactorily demonstrated that the informant's tip was as trustworthy as one that would alone satisfy the *Aguilar* tests. The tip predicted that Sue Gates would drive to Florida, that Lance Gates would fly there a few days after May 3, and that Lance would then drive the car back. After

criminals. [The] magistrate's determination that there might be drugs or evidence of criminal activity in the Gates' home was well-supported by the less speculative theory [that] if the informant could predict with considerable accuracy the somewhat unusual travel plans of the Gates, he probably also had a reliable basis for his statements that the Gates' kept a large quantity of drugs in their home and frequently were visited by other drug traffickers there.

the police corroborated these facts, the magistrate could reasonably have inferred, as he apparently did, that the informant, who had specific knowledge of these unusual travel plans, did not make up his story and that he obtained his information in a reliable way. * * *

[I]t is not at all necessary to overrule *Aguilar-Spinelli* in order to reverse the judgment below. [A]s I read the majority opinion, [the] question whether the probable cause standard is to be diluted is left to the common-sense judgments of issuing magistrates. I am reluctant to approve any standard that does not expressly require, as a prerequisite to issuance of a warrant, some showing of facts from which an inference may be drawn that the informant is credible and that his information was obtained in a reliable way. The Court is correctly concerned with the fact that some lower courts have been applying *Aguilar-Spinelli* in an unduly rigid manner. I believe [that] with clarification of the rule of corroborating information, the lower courts are fully able to properly interpret *Aguilar-Spinelli* and avoid such unduly-rigid applications. [I]t ultimately may prove to be the case that the only profitable instruction we can provide to magistrates is to rely on common sense. But the question whether a particular anonymous tip provides the basis for issuance of a warrant will often be a difficult one, and I would at least attempt to provide more precise guidance by clarifying *Aguilar-Spinelli* and the relationship of those cases with *Draper* before totally abdicating our responsibility in this area. * * *

JUSTICE BRENNAN, with whom JUSTICE MARSHALL joins, dissenting.

Although I [believe] that the warrant is invalid even under the Court's newly announced "totality of the circumstances" test, I write separately to dissent from the Court's unjustified and ill-advised rejection of the two-prong test for evaluating the validity of a warrant based on hearsay announced in *Aguilar* and refined in *Spinelli*.

[In] recognition of the judiciary's role as the only effective guardian of Fourth Amendment rights, this Court has developed over the last half century a set of coherent rules governing a magistrate's consideration of a warrant application and the showings that are necessary to support a finding of probable cause. We start with the proposition that a neutral and detached magistrate, and not the police, should determine whether there is probable cause to support the issuance of a warrant. * * *

In order to emphasize the magistrate's role as an independent arbiter of probable cause and to insure that searches or seizures are not effected on less than probable cause, the Court has insisted that police officers provide magistrates with the underlying facts and circumstances that support the officers' conclusions. * * *

[The] use of hearsay to support the issuance of a warrant presents special problems because informants, unlike police officers, are not regarded as presumptively reliable or honest. Moreover, the basis for an informant's conclusions is not always clear from an affidavit that merely reports those conclusions. If the conclusory allegations of a police officer are insufficient to support a finding of probable cause, surely the conclusory allegations of an informant should a fortiori be insufficient.

[Properly] understood, [*Spinelli*] stands for the proposition that corroboration of certain details in a tip may be sufficient to satisfy the veracity, but not the basis of knowledge, prong of *Aguilar*. [*Spinelli*] also suggests that in some limited circumstances considerable detail in an informant's tip may be adequate to satisfy the basis of knowledge prong of *Aguilar*.

Although the rules drawn from the cases discussed above are cast in procedural terms, they advance an important underlying substantive value: Findings of probable cause, and attendant intrusions, should not be authorized unless there is some assurance that the information on which they are based has been obtained in a reliable way by an honest or credible person. As applied to police officers, the rules focus on the way in which the information was acquired. As applied to informants, the rules focus both on the honesty or credibility of the informant and on the reliability of the way in which the information was acquired. Insofar as it is more complicated, an evaluation of affidavits based on hearsay involves a more difficult inquiry. This suggests a need to structure the inquiry in an effort to insure greater accuracy. The standards announced in *Aguilar*, as refined by *Spinelli*, fulfill that need. The standards inform the police of what information they have to provide and magistrates of what information they should demand. The standards also inform magistrates of the subsidiary findings they must make in order to arrive at an ultimate finding of probable cause. *Spinelli*, properly understood, directs the magistrate's attention to the possibility that the presence of self-verifying detail might satisfy *Aguilar's* basis of knowledge prong and that corroboration of the details of a tip might satisfy *Aguilar's* veracity prong. By requiring police to provide certain crucial information to magistrates and by structuring magistrates' probable cause inquiries, *Aguilar* and *Spinelli* assure the magistrate's role as an independent arbiter of probable cause, insure greater accuracy in probable cause determinations, and advance the substantive value identified above.

[Both] *Aguilar* and *Spinelli* dealt with tips from informants known at least to the police. And surely there is even more reason to subject anonymous informants' tips to the tests established by *Aguilar* and *Spinelli*. By definition nothing is known about an anonymous informant's identity, honesty, or reliability. [T]here certainly is no basis for treating anonymous informants as presumptively reliable. Nor is there any basis for assuming that the information provided by an anonymous informant has been obtained in a reliable way. If we are unwilling to accept conclusory allegations from the police, who are presumptively reliable, or from informants who are known, at least to the police, there cannot possibly be any rational basis for accepting conclusory allegations from anonymous informants.

[It] is conceivable that police corroboration of the details of the tip might establish the reliability of the informant under *Aguilar's* veracity prong, as refined in *Spinelli*, and that the details in the tip might be sufficient to qualify under the "self-verifying detail" test established by *Spinelli* as a means of satisfying *Aguilar's* basis of knowledge prong. The *Aguilar* and *Spinelli* tests must be applied to anonymous informants' tips, however, if we are to continue to insure that findings of probable cause, and attendant intrusions, are based on information provided by an honest or credible person who has acquired the information in a reliable way.

In light of the important purposes served by *Aguilar* and *Spinelli*, I would not reject the standards they establish. If anything, I simply would make more clear that *Spinelli*, properly understood, does not depart in any fundamental way from the test established by [*Aguilar*.]

In rejecting the *Aguilar-Spinelli* standards, the Court suggests that a "totality of the circumstances approach is far more consistent with our prior treatment of probable cause than is any rigid demand that specific 'tests' be satisfied by every informant's tip." [O]ne can concede that probable cause is a "practical, nontechnical" concept without betraying the values that *Aguilar* and *Spinelli* reflect. As noted, *Aguilar* and *Spinelli* require the police to provide magistrates with certain crucial information. They also provide structure for magistrates' probable cause inquiries. [Once] a magistrate has determined that he has information before him that he can reasonably say has been obtained in a reliable way by a credible person, he has ample room to use his common sense and to apply a practical, nontechnical conception of probable cause.

[The] Court also insists that the *Aguilar-Spinelli* standards must be abandoned because they are inconsistent with the fact that non-lawyers frequently serve as magistrates. To the contrary, the standards help to structure probable cause inquiries and, properly interpreted, may actually help a non-lawyer magistrate in making a probable cause determination. * * *

[O]f particular concern to all Americans must be that the Court gives virtually no consideration to the value of insuring that findings of probable cause are based on information that a magistrate can reasonably say has been obtained in a reliable way by an honest or credible person. I share Justice White's fear that the Court's rejection of *Aguilar* and *Spinelli* and its adoption of a new totality of the circumstances test, "may foretell an evisceration of the probable cause [standard]."

[Words] such as "practical," "nontechnical," and "commonsense," as used in the Court's opinion, are but code words for an overly permissive attitude towards police practices in derogation of the rights secured by the Fourth Amendment. Everyone shares the Court's concern over the horrors of drug trafficking, but under our Constitution only measures consistent with the Fourth Amendment may be employed by government to cure this evil. * * *

[By] replacing *Aguilar* and *Spinelli* with a test that provides no assurance that magistrates, rather than the police, or informants, will make determinations of probable cause; imposes no structure on magistrates' probable cause inquiries; and invites the possibility that intrusions may be justified on less than reliable information from an honest or credible person, today's decision threatens to "obliterate one of the most fundamental distinctions between our form of government, where officers are under the law, and the police-state where they are the law."

JUSTICE STEVENS, with whom JUSTICE BRENNAN joins, dissenting.

The fact that Lance and Sue Gates made a 22–hour nonstop drive from West Palm Beach, Florida, to Bloomingdale, Illinois, only a few hours after Lance had flown to Florida provided persuasive evidence that they were engaged in illicit activity. That fact, however, was not known to the magistrate when he issued the warrant to search their home.

What the magistrate did know at that time was that the anonymous informant had not been completely accurate in his or her predictions. The informant had indicated that "Sue drives their car to Florida *where she leaves it to be loaded up with [drugs]. Sue flies back after she drops the car off in Florida*." (emphasis added) Yet Detective Mader's affidavit reported that she "left the West Palm Beach area driving the Mercury northbound."

The discrepancy between the informant's predictions and the facts known to Detective Mader is significant for three reasons. First, it cast doubt on the informant's hypothesis that the Gates already had "over $100,000 worth of drugs in their basement." The informant had predicted an itinerary that always kept one spouse in Bloomingdale, suggesting that the Gates did not want to leave their home unguarded because something valuable was hidden within. That inference obviously could not be drawn when it was known that the pair was actually together over a thousand miles from home.

Second, the discrepancy made the Gates' conduct seem substantially less unusual than the informant had predicted it would be. It would have been odd if, as predicted, Sue had driven down to Florida on Wednesday, left the car, and flown right back to Illinois. But the mere facts that Sue was in West Palm Beach with the car,[10] that she was joined by her husband at the Holiday Inn on Friday,[11] and that the couple drove north together the next morning[12] are neither unusual nor probative of criminal activity.

10. The anonymous note suggested that she was going down on Wednesday, but for all the officers knew she had been in Florida for a month.

11. Lance does not appear to have behaved suspiciously in flying down to Florida. He made a reservation in his own name and gave an accurate home phone number to the airlines. And Detective Mader's affidavit does not report that he did any of the other things drug couriers are notorious for doing, such as paying for the ticket in cash, dressing casually, looking pale and nervous, improperly filling out baggage tags, carry-

ing American Tourister luggage, not carrying any luggage, or changing airlines en route.

12. Detective Mader's affidavit hinted darkly that the couple had set out upon "that interstate highway commonly used by travelers to the Chicago area." But the same highway is also commonly used by travelers to Disney World, Sea World, and Ringling Brothers and Barnum and Bailey Circus World. It is also the road to Cocoa Beach, Cape Canaveral, and Washington, D.C. I would venture that each year dozens of perfectly innocent people fly to Florida,

Third, the fact that the anonymous letter contained a material mistake undermines the reasonableness of relying on it as a basis for making a forcible entry into a private home.

Of course, the activities in this case did not stop when the magistrate issued the warrant. The Gates drove all night to Bloomingdale, the officers searched the car and found 400 pounds of marijuana, and then they searched the house. However, none of these subsequent events may be considered in evaluating the warrant, and the search of the house was legal only if the warrant was valid. I cannot accept the Court's casual conclusion that, before the Gates arrived in Bloomingdale, there was probable cause to justify a valid entry and search of a private home. No one knows who the informant in this case was, or what motivated him or her to write the note. Given that the note's predictions were faulty in one significant respect, and were corroborated by nothing except ordinary innocent activity, I must surmise that the Court's evaluation of the warrant's validity has been colored by subsequent events.[13] * * *

Notes

1. *Analyzing Gates.* Does *Gates* abandon the *Aguilar-Spinelli* two-part test, or does it just modify that test? What does the Court suggest in *Gates*? In thinking about this issue, consider *Massachusetts v. Upton*, 466 U.S. 727 (1984), decided the following year. That case also involved an anonymous tip, but the Massachusetts Supreme Judicial Court narrowly construed *Gates* and reversed Upton's conviction. The U.S. Supreme Court summarized the Massachusetts court's decision as follows: "[The] Massachusetts court apparently viewed *Gates* as merely adding a new wrinkle to [the *Aguilar-Spinelli*] two-pronged test: where an informant's veracity and/or basis of knowledge are not sufficiently clear, substantial corroboration of the tip may save an otherwise invalid warrant...." The U.S. Supreme Court reversed: "[In *Gates*, we] did not merely refine or qualify the 'two-pronged test.' We rejected it as hyper technical and divorced from 'the factual and practical considerations of everyday life on which reasonable and prudent men, not legal technicians, act.'": "[W]e conclude that it is wiser to abandon the 'two-pronged test' established by our decisions in *Aguilar* and *Spinelli*. In its place we reaffirm the totality-of-the-circumstances analysis that traditionally has informed probable-cause determinations."

2. *Informer's Privilege.* If a defendant whose home was searched wants to challenge the probable cause determination, he might seek to discover the names of all informants relied on by the police. In *McCray v. Illinois*, 386 U.S. 300 (1967), petitioner was arrested for possession of narcotics. Petitioner moved to suppress the evidence. Since the arrest was based on an informant's tip, petitioner sought to learn the informant's identity. The trial court denied the motion for disclosure, and the Court upheld the denial: "[T]he informer is a vital part of society's defensive arsenal. The basic rule protecting his identity rests upon that belief. [W]e have repeatedly made

meet a waiting spouse, and drive off together in the family car.

13. *Draper* affords no support for today's holding. That case did not involve an anonymous informant.* * *

clear that federal officers need not disclose an informer's identity in applying for an arrest or search warrant."

In *Roviaro v. United States*, 353 U.S. 53 (1957), defendant was convicted under the Narcotic Drugs Import and Export Act. Again, the government refused to reveal the identity of an informant. Although the Court suggested that the decision to disclose should be made on a case-by-case basis, the identity should have been revealed in that case:

The scope of the privilege is limited by its underlying purpose. Thus, where the disclosure of the contents of a communication will not tend to reveal the identity of an informer, the contents are not privileged. Likewise, once the identity of the informer has been disclosed to those who would have cause to resent the communication, the privilege is no longer applicable.

[A] further limitation on the applicability of the privilege arises from the fundamental requirements of fairness. Where the disclosure of an informer's identity, or of the contents of his communication, is relevant and helpful to the defense of an accused, or is essential to a fair determination of a cause, the privilege must give way. In these situations the trial court may require disclosure and, if the Government withholds the information, dismiss the action. Most of the federal cases involving this limitation on the scope of the informer's privilege have arisen where the legality of a search without a warrant is in issue and the communications of an informer are claimed to establish probable cause. In these cases the Government has been required to disclose the identity of the informant unless there was sufficient evidence apart from his confidential communication.

[The] problem is one that calls for balancing the public interest in protecting the flow of information against the individual's right to prepare his defense. Whether a proper balance renders nondisclosure erroneous must depend on the particular circumstances of each case, taking into consideration the crime charged, the possible defenses, the possible significance of the informer's testimony, and other relevant factors.

The circumstances of this case demonstrate that John Doe's possible testimony was highly relevant and might have been helpful to the defense. So far as petitioner knew, he and John Doe were alone and unobserved during the crucial occurrence for which he was indicted. Unless petitioner waived his constitutional right not to take the stand in his own defense, John Doe was his one material witness. [His] testimony might have disclosed an entrapment. He might have thrown doubt upon petitioner's identity or on the identity of the package. He was the only witness who might have testified to petitioner's possible lack of knowledge of the contents of the package that he "transported" from the tree to John Doe's car. The desirability of calling John Doe as a witness, or at least interviewing him in preparation for trial, was a matter for the accused rather than the Government to decide.

Finally, the Government's use against petitioner of his conversation with John Doe while riding in Doe's car particularly emphasizes the unfairness of the nondisclosure in this case. The only person, other than petitioner himself, who could controvert, explain or amplify Bryson's report of this important conversation was John Doe. Contradiction or amplification might have borne upon petitioner's knowledge of the contents of the package or might have tended to show an entrapment.

See also Kentucky Rule of Evidence 508 which codifies *Roviaro*.

Problems

1. *Reconsidering Spinelli.* In light of the *Gates'* holding, would *Spinelli* be decided the same way today? In other words, applying *Gates'* "totality of the circumstances" test, rather than the two-pronged *Aguilar-Spinelli* test, would the Court be inclined to find that probable cause exists on the *Spinelli* facts?

2. *The Tip.* The police receive an anonymous phone "tip" which states that a house is rented to Gary Moore; that Keith Umfleet has drugs stored in the refrigerator at the house; that Moore and Umfleet are eating a meal and afterwards plan to travel to Illinois to dispose of the drugs; that the parties own a red Volkswagen which they might drive to Illinois; that there is an incinerator located in the back of the apartment. After receiving the call, a police officer verified that the house was rented and lived-in by Moore; that red Volkswagen was parked outside; that there was an incinerator in the back of the apartment. The officer knew that Umfleet had a reputation as a previously arrested drug trafficker. Following the verification, the police staked out the house. While they did not see either Moore or Umfleet, they did see David Hill, a known drug user, walk "in and about the house." The officers also saw an orange car pull into the parking lot, begin to look for a parking place, but drive off "in a very big hurry" when the occupants spotted the police. After a few hours, several officers went to the door of the house. The officers knocked on the door, announced that the occupants were under arrest for the possession of controlled substances and advised them of their rights. One officer then "opened the refrigerator in the kitchen" and removed a "white plastic bag of drugs from the lower compartment of the refrigerator." The bag was a white zipper top plastic bag about eight by ten inches in size containing glass bottles. Did the police have "probable cause" to believe that the occupants of the apartment were in possession of drugs? What arguments might be made on behalf of the police? How might the occupants respond? Do not concern yourself with the question of whether, even if probable cause existed, the police could enter the house without a warrant. *See State v. Wiley*, 522 S.W.2d 281 (Mo., En Banc, 1975).

3. *The Break–Ins.* Certain businesses were broken into, including the Rustic Bar and Shively's Hardware. A police officer, acting on a tip, obtained an arrest warrant charging defendant and another with breaking and entering based on an affidavit which stated that: "I, C. W. Ogburn, do solemnly swear that on or about the 23 day of November, A.D. 1964, in the County of Carbon and State of Wyoming, the said Harold Whiteley and Jack Daley, defendants did then and there unlawfully break and enter a locked and sealed building (describing the location and ownership of the building)." The actual basis for Sheriff Ogburn's conclusion was an informer's tip, but that fact was omitted from the affidavit.

The officer then issued a statewide radio request to pick up and hold defendant and the other. The request, which the officer put on the radio, led to petitioner's arrest and search provided as follows: "P & H for B & E Saratoga, early A.M. 11–24–64. Subj. #1. Jack Daley, WMA, 38, D.O.B. 2–29–(26), 5 10, 175, med. build, med. comp., blonde and blue. Tat. left shoulder: 'Love Me or Leave Me.' #2. Harold Whitley, WMA, 43, D.O.B. 6–22–21, 5 11, 180, med. build, fair comp. brown eyes. Tat. on right arm 'Bird.' Poss. driving 1953 or 1954 Buick, light green bottom, dark top. Wyo. lic. 2–bal. unknown. Taken: $281.71 in small change, numerous old coins ranging from .5 cents pieces to silver dollars, dated from 1853 to 1908. Warrant issues, will extradite. Special attention [Denver]." Late that same day, an officer in another city, in reliance on the information in the request, arrested the defendant and his companion. The officer did not possess either an arrest warrant or a search warrant. In searching the vehicle, the officer found a number of items introduced in evidence such as tools and old coins that were ultimately identified as coming from Shively's Hardware.

Were the warrant and the arrest based on probable cause? *See Whiteley v. Warden*, 401 U.S. 560 (1971).

4. *Mistaken Information*. A policeman responding to a disorderly crowd complaint saw defendant shouting and carrying a large radio which he was playing loudly. The officer approached defendant, placed him in a patrol car, and requested identification. The officer then checked defendant's name through the National Crime Information Center (NCIC), a computer data base, which reported that defendant was wanted on an outstanding arrest warrant. In fact, the NCIC computer was incorrect because the outstanding arrest warrant had been satisfied four days earlier. Unaware of the mistake, the officer arrested defendant. Subsequently, the officer noticed that defendant had picked up a wanted poster bearing artists' sketches of three robbery suspects. After defendant stated that he knew two of the suspects, the officer compared the third composite sketch and printed description to defendant. Finding a similarity, the officer arranged to have defendant transported to another police station where detectives were investigating the robbery. Defendant was ultimately indicted for the robbery. When the original arrest occurred, did the police have probable cause to arrest defendant? In other words, was the police officer entitled to rely on the computer data even though it ultimately proved to be incorrect? If you conclude that the arrest was not based on probable cause, how does that fact affect the robbery indictment? *See Arizona v. Evans*, 514 U.S. 1 (1995); *Commonwealth v. Riley*, 284 Pa.Super. 280, 425 A.2d 813 (1981).

5. *Staleness*. Most search warrants are not limited, by their terms, to execution on a particular day. Suppose that the police have probable cause to search a house on the day a warrant is issued, does this finding of probable cause carry over to subsequent days? [On] March 30, a magistrate issued a warrant for the search of a Lincoln Continental. This warrant was based on the affidavit of Agent Maffett who stated that, on March 29, he saw a pistol in defendant's trunk. Since defendant was a convicted felon, it was illegal for him to possess a gun. The police were unable to execute the warrant which expired by its terms two days later. A second warrant, issued on April 2, 1973, was successfully executed resulting in the seizure of the pistol that Agent Maffett saw in the trunk of defendant's car on March 29th. Defendant

objects that "by limiting the time in which the first warrant could be executed 'Magistrate Mitchell clearly indicated that probable cause to search Defendant's automobile did not exist beyond March 31, 1973.' " Is defendant correct? Had the probable cause gone stale by April 2? Why? Why not? *See United States v. Jones*, 366 F.Supp. 237 (W.D.Pa. 1973).

6. *Disappearing Probable Cause.* On September 15, 2000, an informant bought methamphetamine from Christopher Maddox, at Maddox's home. The informant asked if Maddox had any more methamphetamine to sell. Maddox told the informant "maybe," if the informant would bring back cash. On September 18, 2000, the police obtained a search warrant to search Maddox's residence. The affidavit for the search warrant described the September 15 controlled buy. The affidavit also stated that the informant had purchased methamphetamine from Maddox approximately 35 times over the prior four years. The State did not execute the warrant immediately out of fear that it would jeopardize other investigations in which the informant was participating. On September 21, 2000, the informant made another controlled buy from Maddox at Maddox's home. This time the informant did not have enough money to purchase the prepackaged one-ounce methamphetamine, and Maddox refused to split a package into smaller quantities. Therefore, Maddox accepted the informant's money as partial payment for one ounce of methamphetamine and "fronted" the informant the balance. On September 27, 2000, Maddox demanded by phone that the informant pay the balance of money owed to him "now." The informant went to Maddox's home with $1,000 cash to pay the drug debt and also to complete a third controlled buy of methamphetamine. Maddox collected $720 as payment of the informant's debts. Maddox told the informant that he did not have any methamphetamine to sell to the informant; he said that "he was out and that he would have some in a couple of days." On September 28, 2000, the task force executed the search warrant. Officers seized an electronic scale, 881.6 grams of marijuana, 45 pills of ecstasy, and $2,100 in cash. No methamphetamine was found. Did probable cause still exist to search for methamphetamine at the time the search warrant was actually executed? *See State v. Maddox*, 152 Wash.2d 499, 98 P.3d 1199 (2004).

D. WARRANTLESS SEARCHES AND SEIZURES

Despite the preference for a warrant, the courts have established numerous exceptions to the warrant requirement. As we shall see, the courts distinguish between warrantless arrests and warrantless searches. Even though warrantless arrests are generally permissible, warrantless searches are disfavored and are "per se unreasonable subject only to a few specifically established and well-delineated exceptions." *Katz v. United States*, 389 U.S. 347, 357 (1967). In this section, we examine the exceptions and the justifications that underlie them.

1. *Plain View Exception*

The "plain view" exception is an important exception to the warrant requirement. When the police are conducting a lawful search, and are in a place where they have the right to be, this exception allows them to seize items that they find in plain view. However, there have been debates about the limits of the exception.

HORTON v. CALIFORNIA

496 U.S. 128 (1990).

JUSTICE STEVENS delivered the opinion of the Court.

[Pursuant to a warrant, an experienced police officer (Sergeant LaRault) searched Petitioner's home for the proceeds of a robbery and the weapons used by the robbers. The officer] did not find the stolen property. [He did discover] weapons in plain view and seized them. Specifically, he seized an Uzi machine gun, a .38–caliber revolver, two stun guns, a handcuff key, a San Jose Coin Club advertising brochure [the victim was the Treasurer of the Club], and a few items of clothing identified by the victim. LaRault testified that while he was searching for the [stolen] rings, he also was interested in finding other evidence connecting petitioner to the robbery. Thus, the seized evidence was not discovered "inadvertently." * * *

[The] "plain-view" doctrine is often considered an exception to the general rule that warrantless searches are presumptively unreasonable, but this characterization overlooks the important difference between searches and seizures. If an article is already in plain view, neither its observation nor its seizure would involve any invasion of privacy. A seizure of the article, however, would obviously invade the owner's possessory interest. If "plain view" justifies an exception from an otherwise applicable warrant requirement, therefore, it must be an exception that is addressed to the concerns that are implicated by seizures rather than by searches.

The [scope of the plain view exception] as it had developed in earlier cases was fairly summarized [in] Justice Stewart's opinion:

> What the "plain view" cases have in common is that the police officer in each of them had a prior justification for an intrusion in the course of which he came inadvertently across a piece of evidence incriminating the accused. The doctrine serves to supplement the prior justification—whether it be a warrant for another object, hot pursuit, search incident to lawful arrest, or some other legitimate reason for being present unconnected with a search directed against the accused—and permits the warrantless seizure. Of course, the extension of the original justification is legitimate only where it is immediately apparent to the police that they have evidence before them; the "plain view" doctrine may not be used to extend a general exploratory search from one object to another until something incriminating at last emerges.

Justice Stewart then described the two limitations on the doctrine that he found implicit in its rationale: First, that "plain view *alone* is never enough to justify the warrantless seizure of evidence," and second, that "the discovery of evidence in plain view must be inadvertent."

Justice Stewart's analysis of the "plain-view" doctrine did not command a majority, and a plurality of the Court has since made clear that the discussion is "not a binding precedent."

[A]n essential predicate to any valid warrantless seizure of incriminating evidence that the officer did not violate the Fourth Amendment in arriving at the place from which the evidence could be plainly viewed. There are, moreover, two additional conditions that must be satisfied to justify the warrantless seizure. First, not only must the item be in plain view; its incriminating character must also be "immediately apparent." Thus, in *Coolidge*, the cars were obviously in plain view, but their probative value remained uncertain until after the interiors were swept and examined microscopically. Second, not only must the officer be lawfully located in a place from which the object can be plainly seen, but he or she must also have a lawful right of access to the object itself. [In] *Coolidge* [seizure] of the cars was accomplished by means of a warrantless trespass on the defendant's property. In all events, we are satisfied that the absence of inadvertence was not essential to the Court's rejection of the State's "plain-view" argument in *Coolidge*.

Justice Stewart concluded that the inadvertence requirement was necessary to avoid a violation of the express constitutional requirement that a valid warrant must particularly describe the things to be seized. He explained: "[The] requirement of a warrant to seize imposes no inconvenience whatever, or at least none which is constitutionally cognizable in a legal system that regards warrantless searches as *'per se* unreasonable' in the absence of 'exigent circumstances.' "

If the initial intrusion is bottomed upon a warrant that fails to mention a particular object, though the police know its location and intend to seize it, then there is a violation of the express constitutional requirement of "Warrants [particularly] describing [the] things to be seized."

We find two flaws in this reasoning. First, evenhanded law enforcement is best achieved by the application of objective standards of conduct, rather than standards that depend upon the subjective state of mind of the officer. The fact that an officer is interested in an item of evidence and fully expects to find it in the course of a search should not invalidate its seizure if the search is confined in area and duration by the terms of a warrant or a valid exception to the warrant requirement. If the officer has knowledge approaching certainty that the item will be found, we see no reason why he or she would deliberately omit a particular description of the item to be seized from the application for a search warrant. Specification of the additional item could only permit the officer to expand the scope of the search. On the other hand, if he or she has a valid warrant to search for one item and merely a suspicion concerning the second, whether or not it amounts to probable cause, we fail to see why that suspicion should immunize the second item from seizure if it is found during a lawful search for the [first].

Second, the suggestion that the inadvertence requirement is necessary to prevent the police from conducting general searches, or from converting specific warrants into general warrants, is not persuasive because that interest is already served by the requirements that no warrant issue unless it "particularly describ[es] the place to be searched and the persons or things to be seized," and that a warrantless search be circumscribed by the exigencies which justify its initiation. Scrupulous adherence to these requirements serves the interests in limiting the area and duration of the search that the inadvertence requirement inadequately protects. Once those commands have been satisfied and the officer has a lawful right of access, however, no additional Fourth Amendment interest is furthered by requiring that the discovery of evidence be inadvertent. If the scope of the search exceeds that permitted by the terms of a validly issued warrant or the character of the relevant exception from the warrant requirement, the subsequent seizure is unconstitutional without [more].

In this case, the scope of the search was not enlarged in the slightest by the omission of any reference to the weapons in the warrant. Indeed, if the three rings and other items named in the warrant had been found at the outset—or if petitioner had them in his possession and had responded to the warrant by producing them immediately—no search for weapons could have taken [place].

[T]he seizure of an object in plain view does not involve an intrusion on privacy. If the interest in privacy has been invaded, the violation must have occurred before the object came into plain view and there is no need for an inadvertence limitation on seizures to condemn it. The prohibition against general searches and general warrants serves primarily as a protection against unjustified intrusions on privacy. But reliance on privacy concerns that support that prohibition is misplaced when the inquiry concerns the scope of an exception that merely authorizes an officer with a lawful right of access to an item to seize it without a warrant.

In this case the items seized from petitioner's home were discovered during a lawful search authorized by a valid warrant. When they were discovered, it was immediately apparent to the officer that they constituted incriminating evidence. He had probable cause, not only to obtain a warrant to search for the stolen property, but also to believe that the weapons and handguns had been used in the crime he was investigating. The search was authorized by the warrant; the seizure was authorized by the "plain-view" doctrine. The judgment is affirmed.

It is so ordered.

JUSTICE BRENNAN, with whom JUSTICE MARSHALL joins, dissenting.

[The] inadvertent discovery requirement is essential if we are to take seriously the Fourth Amendment's protection of possessory interests as well as privacy interests. . . .

[T]he Court is not confronted today with what lower courts have described as a "pretextual" search. [I]f an officer enters a house pursuant to a warrant to search for evidence of one crime when he is really interested only in seizing evidence relating to another crime, for which he does not have a warrant, his search is "pretextual" and the fruits of that search should be suppressed. Similarly, an officer might use an exception to the generally applicable warrant requirement, such as "hot pursuit," as a pretext to enter a home to seize items he knows he will find in plain view. Such conduct would be a deliberate attempt to circumvent the constitutional requirement of a warrant "particularly describing the place to be searched, and the persons or things to be seized," and cannot be [condoned].

Note

1. The plain view exception is frequently applied in situations like the one involved in *Horton*: a police officer has lawfully entered a house and finds evidence laying in plain view. The officer uses the exception to justify the seizure of the evidence. Illustrative is the holding in *Washington v. Chrisman*, 455 U.S. 1 (1982), in which a university police officer arrested a student for carrying a half-gallon bottle of gin on campus (state law prohibited the possession of alcoholic beverages by individuals under 21). After the student was handcuffed, the officer asked the student for identification which the student was unable to produce. The student then asked for permission to return to his dormitory room to retrieve his identification, and the officer accompanied the student to the room. At the room, the officer observed what appeared to be a pipe and marijuana seeds in plain view and seized them. The seizure was upheld.

2. *Immediately Apparent Requirement.* In *Minnesota v. Dickerson*, 508 U.S. 366 (1993), police officers stopped Dickerson and forced him to submit to a frisk. The frisk revealed no weapons, but the officer found a small lump in respondent's nylon jacket. The officer examined the lump with his fingers. By sliding the lump, the officer determined that it was crack cocaine in cellophane. The officer then reached into respondent's pocket and retrieved a small plastic bag containing one fifth of one gram of crack cocaine. Respondent was arrested and charged with possession of a controlled substance. The Court held that the seizure was invalid:

> [If] a police officer lawfully pats down a suspect's outer clothing and feels an object whose contour or mass makes its identity immediately apparent, there has been no invasion of the suspect's privacy beyond that already authorized by the officer's search for weapons; if the object is contraband, its warrantless seizure would be justified by the same practical considerations that inhere in the plain-view context. [Here, the] officer determined that the lump was contraband only after "squeezing, sliding and otherwise manipulating the contents of the defendant's pocket"—a pocket which the officer already knew contained no weapon. [The officer's] exploration of respondent's pocket after having concluded that it contained no weapon was unrelated to "[t]he

sole justification of the search [under *Terry*: the] protection of the police officer and others nearby."

3. *More on Immediate Apparency.* In *Texas v. Brown*, 460 U.S. 730 (1983), Brown was stopped at a driver's license checkpoint, and was found holding an opaque, green party balloon between his two middle fingers. The balloon was knotted about one half inch from the tip. When Brown reached across the passenger seat and opened the glove compartment, the officer noticed that the compartment contained several small plastic vials, quantities of loose white powder, and an open bag of party balloons. The officer reached into the car and picked up the green balloon which seemed to contain a powdery substance within the tied-off portion of the balloon. Subsequent analysis revealed that the balloon contained heroin. The Court concluded that the heroin was "immediately apparent":

> [Officer] Maples possessed probable cause to believe that the balloon in Brown's hand contained an illicit substance. Maples testified that he was aware, both from his participation in previous narcotics arrests and from discussions with other officers, that balloons tied in the manner of the one possessed by Brown were frequently used to carry narcotics. This testimony was corroborated by that of a police department chemist who noted that it was "common" for balloons to be used in packaging narcotics. In addition, Maples was able to observe the contents of the glove compartment of Brown's car, which revealed further suggestions that Brown was engaged in activities that might involve possession of illicit substances. The fact that Maples could not see through the opaque fabric of the balloon is all but irrelevant: the distinctive character of the balloon itself spoke volumes as to its contents—particularly to the trained eye of the officer.

Justice Stevens concurred: "[T]he balloon could be one of those rare single-purpose containers which 'by their very nature cannot support any reasonable expectation of privacy because their contents can be inferred from their outward appearance.' "

4. *May an Officer Move an Object to Confirm its Status as Contraband?* In *Arizona v. Hicks*, 480 U.S. 321 (1987), a bullet was fired through the floor of respondent's apartment, striking and injuring a man in the apartment below. Police officers entered respondent's apartment to search for the shooter, for other victims, and for weapons. They found and seized three weapons, including a sawed-off rifle and a stocking-cap mask. Then, one of the officers noticed expensive stereo components which seemed out of place in the squalid apartment. Suspecting that they were stolen, the officer moved some of the components so that he could read and record their serial numbers. He then reported by phone to his headquarters. On being advised that the turntable had been taken in an armed robbery, he seized it and respondent was indicted for robbery. The Court concluded that the "moving" of the stereo equipment to view the serial numbers could not be justified under the plain view exception:

> [I]nspecting those parts of the turntable that came into view during [the] search would not have constituted an independent search, because it would have produced no additional invasion of respondent's privacy interest. But taking action, unrelated to the objectives of the authorized

intrusion, which exposed to view concealed portions of the apartment or its contents, did produce a new invasion of respondent's privacy unjustified by the exigent circumstance that validated the entry. [A] search is a search, even if it happens to disclose nothing but the bottom of a turntable. "[The] 'plain view' doctrine may not be used to extend a general exploratory search from one object to another until something incriminating at last [emerges]."

Justice Powell dissented: "[The majority's] distinction between "looking" at a suspicious object in plain view and "moving" it even a few inches trivializes the Fourth Amendment." Justice O'Connor also dissented: "[I]f police officers have a reasonable, articulable suspicion that an object they come across during the course of a lawful search is evidence of crime, [they] may make a cursory examination of the object to verify their suspicion. [The] additional intrusion caused by an inspection of an item in plain view for its serial number is [minuscule]."

Problems

1. *Smoking Joints in Public.* Rambo Royster is walking down a public street smoking a marijuana joint. A police officer sees Royster and the joint. Does the plain view doctrine come into play in a situation like this? If so, how?

2. *Marijuana on the Window Sill.* A police officer is walking down a public sidewalk when he observes three marijuana plants growing on the window sill inside a townhouse. May the officer use the plain view doctrine to enter the house and seize the plants?

3. *Plain Smell Doctrine?* Is there a "plain smell" doctrine analogous to the "plain view" doctrine? Suppose that a police officer stops a car that is traveling at excessive speed. When the occupant of the car rolls down the window, the officer smells marijuana smoke emanating from the window. Would the "plain smell" doctrine justify a search of the car? Might the officer be able to justify the search on other grounds?

4. *Computers and Plain View.* The police have reason to believe that defendant is a child pornographer, and obtain a warrant to search his home for books, magazines and other documents containing child pornography. On entering defendant's house, the police find a computer that is linked to the internet. On the assumption that many pornographers now use the internet to obtain pictures of children, the police seize the computer on the basis that it reflects "evidence" of child pornography found in "plain view." Is the seizure valid? After the seizure, can the police enter the hard drive of the computer and search for evidence of child pornography?

5. *More on Computers and Plain View.* Suppose that, in the prior problem, the police have probable cause to believe that defendant is using his computer to seek out and download child pornography, and particularly describe the computer as an item to be seized under the warrant. Following the seizure, as the police are going through defendant's computer files, they find evidence that he is involved in illegal bookmaking operations. Can the police use the bookmaking information on the assumption that it was found in "plain view" during the computer search? Does it matter whether the

police are generally searching through the entire computer, or only examining files with titles suggesting that they might contain child pornography?

2. Search Incident to Legal Arrest

The search incident to legal arrest exception is one of the oldest and well-established exceptions to the warrant requirement. It provides that, when the police make a legal arrest, they have the right to make a search incident to that arrest.

An arrest is the most serious form of seizure, and it occurs when the police take a suspect into custody in order to bring charges. Until 1976, there was uncertainty about the requirements for an arrest. Could an arrest be based solely on probable cause? Or, as under the search prong of the Fourth Amendment, is a warrant required?

UNITED STATES v. WATSON

423 U.S. 411 (1976).

MR. JUSTICE WHITE delivered the opinion of the Court.

[Based on information received from an informant, a federal postal inspector had reason to believe that Watson was in possession of credit cards stolen from the U.S. mail. The informant arranged to meet Watson in a restaurant. On the informant's signal (which indicated that Watson was in possession of the cards), federal inspectors closed in and arrested Watson (for possession of stolen mail). After the arrest, Watson consented to a search of his car which revealed two more stolen credit cards. The court of appeals held that Watson's arrest was unconstitutional because the inspector acted without a warrant and granted Watson's motion to suppress the credit cards.]

[Under] the Fourth Amendment, the people are to be "secure in their persons, houses, papers, and effects, against unreasonable searches and seizures, [and] no Warrants shall issue, but upon probable [cause]." [The statute under which Watson was arrested] represents a judgment by Congress that it is not unreasonable under the Fourth Amendment for postal inspectors to arrest without a warrant provided they have probable cause to do so. This was not an isolated or quixotic judgment of the legislative branch. Other federal law enforcement officers have been expressly authorized by statute for many years to make felony arrests on probable cause but without a warrant. This is true of United States marshals, and of agents of the Federal Bureau of Investigation, the Drug Enforcement Administration, the Secret Service, and the Customs Service.

[T]here is nothing in the Court's prior cases indicating that under the Fourth Amendment a warrant is required to make a valid arrest for a felony. Indeed, the relevant prior decisions are uniformly to the contrary. "The usual rule is that a police officer may arrest without warrant one believed by the officer upon reasonable cause to have been guilty of a [felony]." *Carroll v. United States*, 267 U.S. 132, 156 (1925). * * *

The cases construing the Fourth Amendment thus reflect the ancient common-law rule that a peace officer was permitted to arrest without a warrant for a misdemeanor or felony committed in his presence as well as for a felony not committed in his presence if there was reasonable ground for making the arrest. 10 HALSBURY'S LAWS OF ENGLAND 344–345 (3d ed. 1955). This has also been the prevailing rule under state constitutions and [statutes].

Because the common-law rule authorizing arrests without a warrant generally prevailed in the States, it is important for present purposes to note that in 1792 Congress invested United States marshals and their deputies with "the same powers in executing the laws of the United States, as sheriffs and their deputies in the several states have by law, in executing the laws of their respective states." The Second Congress thus saw no inconsistency between the Fourth Amendment and legislation giving United States marshals the same power as local peace officers to arrest for a felony without a warrant. This provision equating the power of federal marshals with those of local sheriffs was several times re-enacted and is today § 570 of Title 28 of the United States Code. * * *

The balance struck by the common law in generally authorizing felony arrests on probable cause, but without a warrant, has survived substantially intact. It appears in almost all of the States in the form of express statutory authorization. [The American Law Institute's model arrest statute] authorizes an officer to take a person into custody if the officer has reasonable cause to believe that the person to be arrested has committed a felony, or has committed a misdemeanor or petty misdemeanor in his presence. The commentary to this section said: "The Code thus adopts the traditional and almost universal standard for arrest without a warrant."

This is the rule Congress has long directed its principal law enforcement officers to follow. Congress has plainly decided against conditioning warrantless arrest power on proof of exigent circumstances. Law enforcement officers may find it wise to seek arrest warrants where practicable to do so, and their judgments about probable cause may be more readily accepted where backed by a warrant issued by a magistrate. But we decline to transform this judicial preference into a constitutional rule when the judgment of the Nation and Congress has for so long been to authorize warrantless public arrests on probable cause rather than to encumber criminal prosecutions with endless litigation with respect to the existence of exigent circumstances, whether it was practicable to get a warrant, whether the suspect was about to flee, and the like.

Watson's arrest did not violate the Fourth Amendment, and the Court of Appeals erred in holding to the contrary. * * *

MR. JUSTICE POWELL, concurring.

[The] historical momentum for acceptance of warrantless arrests, already strong at the adoption of the Fourth Amendment, has gained strength during the ensuing two centuries. Both the judiciary and the legislative bodies of this Nation repeatedly have placed their imprimaturs upon the practice and, as the Government emphasizes, law enforcement agencies have developed their investigative and arrest procedures upon an assumption that warrantless arrests were valid so long as based upon probable cause. * * *

[A] constitutional rule permitting felony arrests only with a warrant or in exigent circumstances could severely hamper effective law enforcement. Good police practice often requires postponing an arrest, even after probable cause has been established, in order to place the suspect under surveillance or otherwise develop further evidence necessary to prove guilt to a jury. Under the holding of the Court of Appeals such additional investigative work could imperil the entire prosecution. Should the officers fail to obtain a warrant initially, and later be required by unforeseen circumstances to arrest immediately with no chance to procure a last-minute warrant, they would risk a court decision that the subsequent exigency did not excuse their failure to get a warrant in the interim since they first developed probable cause. If the officers attempted to meet such a contingency by procuring a warrant as soon as they had probable cause and then merely held it during their subsequent investigation, they would risk a court decision that the warrant had grown stale by the time it was used. Law enforcement personnel caught in this squeeze could ensure validity of their arrests only by obtaining a warrant and arresting as soon as probable cause existed, thereby foreclosing the possibility of gathering vital additional evidence from the suspect's continued actions. * * *

MR. JUSTICE MARSHALL, with whom MR. JUSTICE BRENNAN joins, dissenting.

The Court [relies] on the English common-law rule of arrest and the many state and federal statutes following it. [T]he substance of the ancient common-law rule provides no support for the far-reaching modern rule that the Court fashions on its model. [A] felony at common law and a felony today bear only slight resemblance. [At common law], "No crime was considered a felony which did not occasion a total forfeiture of the offender's lands or goods or both." [Today,] "Any offense punishable by death or imprisonment for a term exceeding one year is a felony." 18 U.S.C. § 1(1).

This difference reflects more than changing notions of penology. [Only] the most serious crimes were felonies at common law, and many crimes now classified as felonies under federal or state law were treated as misdemeanors. [To] make an arrest for any of these crimes at common law, the police officer was required to obtain a warrant, unless the crime was committed in his presence. Since many of these same crimes are commonly classified as felonies today[, a] warrant is no longer needed to make such arrests. [T]he balance struck by the common law [decreed] that only in the most serious of cases could the warrant be dispensed with. This balance is not recognized when the common-law rule is unthinkingly transposed to our present classifications of criminal offenses. [T]he only clear lesson of history is contrary to the one the Court draws: the common law considered the arrest warrant far more important than today's decision leaves it. [T]he Court relies on the numerous state and federal statutes codifying the common-law rule. [T]he mere existence of statutes or practice, even of long standing, is no defense to an unconstitutional practice. * * *

[The] privacy guaranteed by the Fourth Amendment is quintessentially personal. [A] warrant is required in search situations not because of some high regard for property, but because of our regard for the individual, and his interest in his possessions and person. [T]here can be no less invasion of privacy when the individual himself, rather than his property, is searched and seized. [A]n unjustified arrest that forces the individual temporarily to forfeit his right to control his person and movements and interrupts the course of his daily business may be more intrusive than an unjustified search. "Being arrested and held by the police, even if for a few hours, is for most persons, awesome and frightening. . . ." ALI, Model Code of Pre-arraignment Procedure, Commentary 290–291 (1975).

A warrant requirement for arrests would, of course, minimize the possibility that such an intrusion [would] occur on less than probable cause. [F]or this reason, a warrant is required for searches. Surely there is no reason to place greater trust in the partisan assessment of a police officer that there is probable cause for an arrest than in his determination that probable cause exists for a search. * * *

[T]he suggested concerns [that the warrant requirement would unduly burden law enforcement interests] are wholly illusory. "[I]t is the standard practice of the Federal Bureau of Investigation (FBI) to [obtain a warrant] before making an arrest." * * * The Government's assertion that a warrant requirement would impose an intolerable burden stems [from] the specious supposition that procurement of an arrest warrant would be necessary as soon as probable cause ripens. There is no requirement that a search warrant be obtained the moment police have probable cause to search. [Police] would not have to cut their investigation short the moment they obtain probable cause to arrest, nor would undercover agents be forced suddenly to terminate their work and forfeit their covers. Moreover, if in the course of the continued police investigation exigent circumstances develop that demand an immediate arrest, the arrest may be made without fear of unconstitutionality, so long as the exigency was unanticipated and not used to avoid the arrest warrant requirement.

[I] respectfully dissent.

Notes

1. *Misdemeanor Arrests.* In *Atwater v. City of Lago Vista*, 532 U.S. 318 (2001), Atwater was subjected to a full custodial arrest for a misdemeanor seatbelt violation punishable only by a fine. In upholding the arrest, the Court noted that early English statutes allowed the police to make warrantless misdemeanor arrests "for all sorts of relatively minor offenses unaccompanied by violence." Similar statutes existed in the District of Columbia and all 50 states, and the Court concluded that "the fact that many of the original States with such constitutional limitations continued to grant their own peace officers broad warrantless misdemeanor arrest authority undermines Atwater's contention that the founding generation meant to bar federal law enforcement officers from exercising the same authority." The Court found that there had been "two centuries of uninterrupted (and largely unchallenged) state and federal practice permitting warrantless arrests for misdemeanors not amounting to or involving breach of the peace."

Justice O'Connor dissented noting that "[justifying] a full arrest by the same quantum of evidence that justifies a traffic stop [defies] any sense of proportionality and is in serious tension with the Fourth Amendment's proscription of unreasonable seizures." She noted that a "custodial arrest exacts an obvious toll on an individual's liberty and privacy, even when the period of custody is relatively brief." In her view, "the penalty that may attach to any particular offense seems to provide the clearest and most consistent indication of the State's interest in arresting individuals suspected of committing that offense." Since the state imposed only a fine for driving without a seatbelt, "the State's interest in taking a person suspected of committing that offense into custody is surely limited, at best."

2. *Pretext Arrests.* In *Arkansas v. Sullivan*, 532 U.S. 769 (2001), an officer stopped Sullivan for speeding as well as for having an improperly tinted windshield. After reviewing Sullivan's license, the officer realized that he was aware of "intelligence on [Sullivan] regarding narcotics." While Sullivan was trying unsuccessfully to locate his registration and insurance papers, the officer noticed a rusted roofing hatchet on the car's floorboard. The officer then arrested Sullivan for speeding, driving without registration and insurance documentation, carrying a weapon (the roofing hatchet), and improper window tinting. The officer then searched the car and found a substance that appeared to be methamphetamine as well as drug paraphernalia. Sullivan was charged with various state-law drug offenses, unlawful possession of a weapon, and speeding, and moved to suppress the evidence on the basis that his arrest was merely a "pretext and sham to search" him. The Court rejected the challenge noting that "[s]ubjective intentions play no role in ordinary, probable-cause Fourth Amendment analysis."

3. *Arrests at Private Residences.* In *Payton v. New York*, 445 U.S. 573 (1980), the Court struck down a New York law which authorized police officers to enter private residences without warrants, by force if necessary, to make a routine felony arrest:

> [The] Fourth Amendment has drawn a firm line at the entrance to the house. Absent exigent circumstances, that threshold may not reason-

ably be crossed without a warrant. [A]n arrest warrant requirement may afford less protection than a search warrant requirement, but it will suffice to interpose the magistrate's determination of probable cause between the zealous officer and the citizen. If there is sufficient evidence of a citizen's participation in a felony to persuade a judicial officer that his arrest is justified, it is constitutionally reasonable to require him to open his doors to the officers of the law. [A]n arrest warrant founded on probable cause implicitly carries with it the limited authority to enter a dwelling in which the suspect lives when there is reason to believe the suspect is within.

Mr. Justice White dissented: "[W]arrantless arrest entries [were] firmly accepted at common [law]."

4. *More on Private Residences.* In *Steagald v. United States*, 451 U.S. 204 (1981), the Court held that a law enforcement officer may not search for the subject of an arrest warrant in the home of a third party without first obtaining a search warrant. *See also Minnesota v. Olson*, 495 U.S. 91 (1990).

5. *Using Deadly Force to Effect an Arrest.* Does the Fourth Amendment preclude the police from using deadly force to effect an arrest? In *Tennessee v. Garner*, 471 U.S. 1 (1985), the Court held that the Constitution prohibits the use of deadly force in most instances: "[The] use of deadly force is a self-defeating way of apprehending a suspect and so setting the criminal justice mechanism in motion. If successful, it guarantees that that mechanism will not be set in motion. [W]hile the meaningful threat of deadly force might be thought to lead to the arrest of more live suspects by discouraging escape attempts, the presently available evidence does not support this thesis." The Court did hold that deadly force is permissible when the suspect "poses a threat of serious physical harm either to the officer or to others." In *Garner*, the suspect's youth, slightness, and lack of a weapon suggested that he did not pose a threat of physical danger to himself or others. As a result, the use of deadly force was deemed inappropriate. Justice O'Connor dissented: "The public interest involved in the use of deadly force as a last resort to apprehend a fleeing burglary suspect relates primarily to the serious nature of the crime. Household burglaries not only represent the illegal entry into a person's home, but also 'pos[e] real risk of serious harm to others.' [I]f apprehension is not immediate, it is likely that the suspect will not be caught."

6. *Stated Basis for Arrest.* In *Devenpeck v. Alford*, 543 U.S. 146 (2004), a police officer possessed probable cause to believe that defendant had been impersonating a police officer. However, when the officer realized that defendant had a tape recorder and was recording their conversation, the officer decided to arrest defendant for violating the Washington Privacy Act, Wash. Rev.Code § 9.73.030 (1994). When the charges was dismissed, defendant file suit under 42 U.S.C. § 1983 and a state cause of action for unlawful arrest and imprisonment. The Court refused to accept the proposition that the probable-cause inquiry is confined to the facts actually invoked at the time of arrest, and that (in addition) the offense supported by these known facts must be "closely related" to the offense that the officer invoked. The Court emphasized that the officer had probable cause to arrest defendant for impersonating a police officer, and chose not to charge for that offense solely

because of a departmental policy against "stacking" charges. "We have consistently rejected a conception of the Fourth Amendment that would produce such haphazard results." "Subjective intent of the arresting officer, *however* it is determined (and of course subjective intent is *always* determined by objective means), is simply no basis for invalidating an arrest. Those are lawfully arrested whom the facts known to the arresting officers give probable cause to arrest."

———

Once a legal arrest occurs, the police are allowed to make a search incident to arrest. While the right to search is clear enough, the following case discusses the scope of the search.

CHIMEL v. CALIFORNIA

395 U.S. 752 (1969).

MR. JUSTICE STEWART delivered the opinion of the Court.

[The] relevant facts are essentially undisputed. Late in the afternoon of September 13, 1965, three police officers arrived at [petitioner's home] with a warrant authorizing his arrest for the burglary of a coin shop. The officers knocked on the door, identified themselves to the petitioner's wife, and asked if they might come inside. She ushered them into the house, where they waited 10 or 15 minutes until the petitioner returned home from work. When the petitioner entered the house, one of the officers handed him the arrest warrant and asked for permission to "look around." The petitioner objected, but was advised that "on the basis of the lawful arrest," the officers would nonetheless conduct a search. No search warrant had been issued.

[T]he officers then looked through the entire three-bedroom house, including the attic, the garage, and a small workshop. In some rooms the search was relatively cursory. In the master bedroom and sewing room, however, the officers directed the petitioner's wife to open drawers and "to physically move contents of the drawers from side to side so that [they] might view any items that would have come from [the] burglary." [The police] seized numerous items—primarily coins, but also several medals, tokens, and a few other objects. The entire search took between 45 minutes and an hour.

[T]he items taken from [petitioner's] house were admitted into evidence against him, over his objection that they had been unconstitutionally seized. He was convicted and the judgments [were] affirmed.

[This] brings us directly to the question whether the warrantless search of the petitioner's entire house can be constitutionally justified as incident to that arrest. [*United States v. Rabinowitz*, 339 U.S. 56 (1950)] has come to stand for the proposition, *inter alia*, that a warrantless search "incident to a lawful arrest" may generally extend to the area that is considered to be in the "possession" or under the "control" of the person arrested. And it was on the basis of that proposition that the California courts upheld the search of the petitioner's entire house in this case. That doctrine, however, at least in the broad sense in which it was applied by the California courts[,] can withstand neither historical nor rational analysis.

[Justice] Frankfurter wisely pointed out in his *Rabinowitz* dissent that the Amendment's proscription of "unreasonable searches and seizures" must be read in light of "the history that gave rise to the words"—a history of "abuses so deeply felt by the Colonies as to be one of the potent causes of the [Revolution]." The Amendment was in large part a reaction to the general warrants and warrantless searches that had so alienated the colonists and had helped speed the movement for independence. In the scheme of the Amendment, therefore, the requirement that "no Warrants shall issue, but upon probable cause," plays a crucial [part].

Only last Term in *Terry v. Ohio*, 392 U.S. 1, we emphasized that "[t]he scope of [a] search must be 'strictly tied to and justified by' the circumstances which rendered its initiation permissible." [A] similar analysis underlies the "search incident to arrest" principle, and marks its proper extent. When an arrest is made, it is reasonable for the arresting officer to search the person arrested in order to remove any weapons that the latter might seek to use in order to resist arrest or effect his escape. Otherwise, the officer's safety might well be endangered, and the arrest itself frustrated. In addition, it is entirely reasonable for the arresting officer to search for and seize any evidence on the arrestee's person in order to prevent its concealment or destruction. And the area into which an arrestee might reach in order to grab a weapon or evidentiary items must, of course, be governed by a like rule. A gun on a table or in a drawer in front of one who is arrested can be as dangerous to the arresting officer as one concealed in the clothing of the person arrested. There is ample justification, therefore, for a search of the arrestee's person and the area "within his immediate control"—construing that phrase to mean the area from within which he might gain possession of a weapon or destructible evidence.

There is no comparable justification, however, for routinely searching any room other than that in which an arrest occurs—or, for that matter, for searching through all the desk drawers or other closed or concealed areas in that room itself. Such searches, in the absence of well-recognized exceptions, may be made only under the authority of a search warrant. The "adherence to judicial processes" mandated by the Fourth Amendment requires no less.

[It] is argued [that] it is "reasonable" to search a man's house when he is arrested in it. * * * Under such an unconfined analysis, Fourth Amendment protection in this area would approach the evaporation point. It is not easy to explain why, for instance, it is less subjectively "reasonable" to search a man's house when he is arrested on his front lawn—or just down the street—than it is when he happens to be in the house at the time of arrest. [A]lthough "[t]he recurring questions of the reasonableness of searches" depend upon "the facts and circumstances— the total atmosphere of the case," those facts and circumstances must be viewed in the light of established Fourth Amendment principles.

[No] consideration relevant to the Fourth Amendment suggests any point of rational limitation, once the search is allowed to go beyond the area from which the person arrested might obtain weapons or evidentiary items. The only reasoned distinction is one between a search of the person arrested and the area within his reach on the one hand, and more extensive searches on the other.[14]

Application of sound Fourth Amendment principles to the facts of this case produces a clear result. The search here went far beyond the petitioner's person and the area from within which he might have obtained either a weapon or something that could have been used as evidence against him. There was no constitutional justification, in the absence of a search warrant, for extending the search beyond that area. The scope of the search was, therefore, "unreasonable" under the Fourth and Fourteenth Amendments and the petitioner's conviction cannot stand.

Reversed.

MR. JUSTICE WHITE, with whom MR. JUSTICE BLACK joins, dissenting.

[The] justifications which make [a] search [incident to legal arrest] reasonable obviously do not apply to the search of areas to which the accused does not have ready physical access. [W]hen there are exigent circumstances, and probable cause, then the search may be made without a warrant, reasonably. An arrest itself may often create an emergency situation making it impracticable to obtain a warrant before embarking on a related search. [A]ssuming that there is probable cause to search premises at the spot where a suspect is arrested, it seems to me unreasonable to require the police to leave the scene in order to obtain a search warrant when they are already legally there to make a valid arrest, and when there must almost always be a strong possibility that confederates of the arrested man will in the meanwhile remove the items for which the police have probable cause to search. This must so often be

---

14. It is argued in dissent that so long as there is probable cause to search the place where an arrest occurs, a search of that place should be permitted even though no search warrant has been obtained. This position seems to be based principally on two premises: first, that once an arrest has been made, the additional invasion of privacy stemming from the accompanying search is "relatively minor"; and second, that the victim of the search may "shortly thereafter" obtain a judicial determination of whether the search was justified by probable cause. [We] cannot accept the view that Fourth Amendment interests are vindicated so long as "the rights of the criminal" are "protect[ed] [against] introduction of evidence seized without probable cause." The Amendment is designed to prevent, not simply to redress, unlawful police action. In any event, we cannot join in characterizing the invasion of privacy that results from a top-to-bottom search of a man's house as "minor." And we can see no reason why, simply because some interference with an individual's privacy and freedom of movement has lawfully taken place, further intrusions should automatically be allowed despite the absence of a warrant that the Fourth Amendment would otherwise require.

the case that it seems to me as unreasonable to require a warrant for a search of the premises as to require a warrant for search of the person and his very immediate surroundings.

This case provides a good illustration of my point. . . . Petitioner was arrested in his home. . . . There was doubtless probable cause not only to arrest petitioner, but also to search his house. He had obliquely admitted, both to a neighbor and to the owner of the burglarized store, that he had committed the burglary. In light of this, and the fact that the neighbor had seen other admittedly stolen property in petitioner's house, there [was] probable cause on which a warrant could have issued to search the house for the stolen coins. Moreover, had the police simply arrested petitioner, taken him off to the station house, and later returned with a warrant,[15] it seems very likely that petitioner's wife, who in view of petitioner's generally garrulous nature must have known of the robbery, would have removed the coins. For the police to search the house while the evidence they had probable cause to search out and seize was still there cannot be considered unreasonable.

[I] would follow past cases and permit [a] search to be carried out without a warrant, since the fact of arrest supplies an exigent circumstance justifying police action before the evidence can be removed, and also alerts the suspect to the fact of the search so that he can immediately seek judicial determination of probable cause in an adversary proceeding, and appropriate redress. * * *

Notes

1. In *Maryland v. Dyson*, 527 U.S. 465 (1999), the police had probable cause to believe that a vehicle contained illegal drugs, and they searched it without a warrant even though there was time to obtain one. The Maryland Court of Special Appeals invalidated the search on the basis that there were no exigent circumstances justifying the warrantless search. The United States Supreme Court reversed noting that automobiles should be treated differently than homes.

2. *Search before Arrest?* As a general rule, a "search incident to arrest" cannot be justified based on evidence revealed during the search itself. However, in *Rawlings v. Kentucky*, 448 U.S. 98 (1980), after petitioner admitted ownership of a sizeable quantity of drugs, the police searched his person (the search revealed money and a knife) and placed him under arrest. The Court viewed the search as "incident to arrest" even though it preceded the arrest: "Once petitioner admitted ownership of the sizable quantity of drugs found in Cox's purse, the police clearly had probable cause to place petitioner under arrest. Where the formal arrest followed quickly on the

---

15. There were three officers at the scene of the arrest. . . . Assuming that one policeman from each city would be needed to bring the petitioner in and obtain a search warrant, one policeman could have been left to guard the house. However, if he not only could have remained in the house against petitioner's wife's will, but followed her about to assure that no evidence was being tampered with, the invasion of her privacy would be almost as great as that accompanying an actual search. Moreover, had the wife summoned an accomplice, one officer could not have watched them both.

heels of the challenged search of petitioner's person, we do not believe it particularly important that the search preceded the arrest rather than vice versa."

3. *Intention to Cite.* In *Knowles v. Iowa*, 525 U.S. 113 (1998), defendant was stopped for speeding (43mph in a 25mph zone). Although the officer only intended to cite defendant, rather than arrest him, the officer conducted a full search of the vehicle which revealed the existence of marijuana. The Court concluded that the search was invalid: "Here we are asked to extend [the search incident to legal arrest] exception to a situation where the concern for officer safety is not present to the same extent and the concern for destruction or loss of evidence is not present at all. We decline to do so."

4. *Booking Searches.* When the police "book" a suspect, and place the suspect in jail, the police usually conduct a so-called "detention search" or "booking search." This type of search was upheld in *Illinois v. Lafayette*, 462 U.S. 640 (1983), in which respondent was arrested for disturbing the peace after fighting with the manager of a theater. The search occurred in the booking room where the police found ten amphetamine pills inside a cigarette case in respondent's shoulder bag. The Court upheld the search:

> [I]t is reasonable for police to search the personal effects of a person under lawful arrest as part of the routine administrative procedure at a police stationhouse incident to booking and jailing the suspect. The justification [does] not rest on probable cause [or] a warrant. * * *

> [The] governmental interests underlying a stationhouse search of the arrestee's person and possessions may in some circumstances be even greater than those supporting a search immediately following arrest. [For] example, the interests supporting a search incident to arrest would hardly justify disrobing an arrestee on the street, but the practical necessities of routine jail administration may even justify taking a prisoner's clothes before confining him, although that step would be rare. * * *

> At the stationhouse, it is entirely proper for police to remove and list or inventory property found on the person or in the possession of an arrested person who is to be jailed. A range of governmental interests support an inventory process. It is not unheard of for persons employed in police activities to steal property taken from arrested persons; similarly, arrested persons have been known to make false claims regarding what was taken from their possession at the stationhouse. A standardized procedure for making a list or inventory as soon as reasonable after reaching the stationhouse not only deters false claims but also inhibits theft or careless handling of articles taken from the arrested person. Arrested persons have also been known to injure themselves—or others—with belts, knives, drugs or other items on their person while being detained. Dangerous instrumentalities—such as razor blades, bombs, or weapons—can be concealed in innocent-looking articles taken from the arrestee's possession. [These] realities justif[y] reasonable measures by police to limit these risks—either while the items are in police possession or at the time they are returned to the arrestee upon his release. Examining all the items removed from the arrestee's person or possession and listing or inventorying them is an entirely reasonable adminis-

trative procedure. It is immaterial whether the police actually fear any particular package or container; the need to protect against such risks arises independent of a particular officer's subjective concerns. Finally, inspection of an arrestee's personal property may assist the police in ascertaining or verifying his identity. In short, every consideration of orderly police administration benefiting both police and the public points toward the appropriateness of the examination of respondent's shoulder bag prior to his incarceration.

In *United States v. Edwards*, 415 U.S. 800 (1974), the Court upheld a booking search which took place nearly 10 hours after a defendant's arrest: "searches and seizures that could be made on the spot at the time of arrest may legally be conducted later when the accused arrives at the place of detention."

Problems

1. *Arrests for Minor Offenses.* Should a "search incident to legal arrest" be permitted when the suspect is arrested for a minor traffic offense, but there is no indication that the suspect is in possession of a weapon or evidence of illegal activity? There has been considerable debate regarding the permissibility of detention searches for minor offenses. For example, in Arlington, Virginia, a woman was arrested for eating a ham sandwich on the subway. She was taken to the Arlington County jail and subjected to a strip search. The woman sued claiming that, given the nature of her offense, a strip search was unreasonable. Despite the minor nature of the woman's offense, how might the state try to justify the strip search? How might the woman respond to the state's arguments?

2. *More on Minor Offenses.* Similarly, in *United States v. Robinson*, 414 U.S. 218 (1973), a police officer saw respondent driving in the District of Columbia. Based on a stop that had occurred four days earlier, the officer had reason to believe that respondent was driving without a driver's license (an offense which carries a mandatory minimum jail term, a mandatory minimum fine, or both). The officer stopped respondent and ultimately arrested him. The officer then subjected respondent to a "pat down" search which led to the discovery of heroin. Respondent was convicted of possession and facilitation of concealment in heroin. Given the nature of the stop, should a search incident to arrest have been permitted? How might respondent argue that the search was improper? How might the state respond to those arguments? How should the court rule? *See also Gustafson v. Florida*, 414 U.S. 260 (1973).

3. *The Contemporaneousness Requirement.* Four police officers enter a hotel room (legally) to arrest a suspect. After the police handcuff her, and move her to the hallway outside the room, two officers re-enter the room and search it. The search extends to the dresser drawer and the suspect's purse (which was lying on the bed). In the drawer and in the purse, the police find contraband. Suppose that you represent the suspect, how can you argue that this search does not fit within the scope of the search incident to arrest exception? How might the state respond to these arguments? How would you expect the court to rule? *See People v. Perry*, 47 Ill.2d 402, 266 N.E.2d 330 (Ill.1971).

4. *More on Contemporaneousness.* In the prior problem, would you reach a different result if, as the police entered the room, they saw the suspect place something in a dresser drawer?

5. *Plain View?* Defendant was arrested for driving under the influence. The officer searched defendant, found an unlabeled bottle containing capsules and pills, and seized them. Subsequent lab analysis revealed that the pills contained methadone, a prohibited substance. Did the officer have the right to seize the pills and subject them to analysis? What arguments might be made on defendant's behalf? How might the state respond? *See State v. Elkins*, 245 Or. 279, 422 P.2d 250 (In Banc, 1966).

NEW YORK v. BELTON

453 U.S. 454 (1981).

JUSTICE STEWART, delivered the opinion of the Court.

[Trooper] Douglas Nicot, a New York State policeman driving an unmarked car on the New York Thruway, was passed by another automobile traveling at an excessive rate of speed. Nicot gave chase, overtook the speeding vehicle, and ordered its driver to pull [over] and stop. There were four men in the car, one of whom was Roger Belton, the respondent[.] The policeman asked to see the driver's license and automobile registration, and discovered that none of the men owned the vehicle or was related to its owner. Meanwhile, the policeman had smelled burnt marihuana and had seen on the floor of the car an envelope marked "Supergold" that he associated with marihuana. He therefore directed the men to get out the car, and placed them under arrest for the unlawful possession of marihuana. He patted down each of the men and "split them up into four separate areas of the Thruway at this time so they would not be in physical touching area of each other." He then picked up the envelope marked "Supergold" and found that it contained marihuana. After giving the arrestees the warnings required by *Miranda v. Arizona*, 384 U.S. 436, [the] policeman searched each one of them. He then searched the passenger compartment of the car. On the back seat he found a black leather jacket belonging to Belton. He unzipped one of the pockets of the jacket and discovered cocaine. Placing the jacket in his automobile, he drove the four arrestees to a nearby police station.

[Although] the principle that limits a search incident to a lawful custodial arrest may be stated clearly enough, courts have discovered the principle difficult to apply in specific cases. Yet, as one commentator has pointed out, the protection of the Fourth and Fourteenth Amendments "can only be realized if the police are acting under a set of rules which, in most instances, makes it possible to reach a correct determination beforehand as to whether an invasion of privacy is justified in the interest of law enforcement." LaFave, *"Case–By–Case Adjudication" Versus "Standardized Procedures": The Robinson Dilemma*, 1974 S.Ct. Rev. 127, 142. This is because "Fourth Amendment doctrine, given force and effect by the exclusionary rule, is primarily intended to regulate the police in their day-to-day activities and thus ought to be expressed in terms that are readily applicable by the police in the context of the law enforcement activities in which they are necessarily engaged. A highly sophisticated set of rules, qualified by all sorts of ifs, ands, and buts and requiring the drawing of subtle nuances and hairline distinctions, may be the sort of heady stuff upon which the facile minds of lawyers and judges eagerly feed, but they may be 'literally impossible of application by the officer in the field.' " *Id.*, at 141. In short, "[a] single, familiar standard is essential to guide police officers, who have only limited time and expertise to reflect on and balance the social and individual interests involved in the specific circumstances they confront." *Dunaway v. New York*, 442 U.S. 200.

[N]o straightforward rule has emerged from the litigated cases respecting the question involved here—the question of the proper scope of a search of the interior of an automobile incident to a lawful custodial arrest of its occupants. The difficulty courts have had is reflected in the conflicting views of the New York judges who dealt with the problem in the present case.... When a person cannot know how a court will apply a settled principle to a recurring factual situation, that person cannot know the scope of his constitutional protection, nor can a policeman know the scope of his authority. While the *Chimel* case established that a search incident to an arrest may not stray beyond the area within the immediate control of the arrestee, courts have found no workable definition of "the area within the immediate control of the arrestee" when that area arguably includes the interior of an automobile and the arrestee is its recent occupant. Our reading of the cases suggests the generalization that articles inside the relatively narrow compass of the passenger compartment of an automobile are in fact generally, even if not inevitably, within "the area into which an arrestee might reach in order to grab a weapon or evidentiary ite[m]." In order to establish the workable rule this category of cases requires, we read *Chimel's* definition of the limits of the area that may be searched in light of that generalization. Accordingly, we hold that when a policeman has made a lawful custodial arrest of the occupant of an automobile, he may, as a contemporaneous incident of that arrest, search the passenger compartment of that automobile.

It follows from this conclusion that the police may also examine the contents of any containers found within the passenger compartment, for if the passenger compartment is within reach of the arrestee, so also will containers in it be within his reach.[16] Such a container may, of course, be searched whether it is open or closed, since the justification for the search is not that the arrestee has no privacy interest in the container, but that the lawful custodial arrest justifies the infringement of any

---

16. "Container" here denotes any object capable of holding another object. It thus includes closed or open glove compartments, consoles, or other receptacles located anywhere within the passenger compart- ment, as well as luggage, boxes, bags, cloth- ing, and the like. Our holding encompasses only the interior of the passenger compart- ment of an automobile and does not encom- pass the trunk.

privacy interest the arrestee may have. [W]hile the Court in *Chimel* held that the police could not search all the drawers in an arrestee's house simply because the police had arrested him at home, the Court noted that drawers within an arrestee's reach could be searched because of the danger their contents might pose to the police. * * * It is true, of course, that these containers will sometimes be such that they could hold neither a weapon nor evidence of the criminal conduct for which the suspect was arrested. * * *

It is not questioned that the respondent was the subject of a lawful custodial arrest on a charge of possessing marihuana. The search of the respondent's jacket followed immediately upon that arrest. The jacket was located inside the passenger compartment of the car in which the respondent had been a passenger just before he was arrested. The jacket was thus within the area which we have concluded was "within the arrestee's immediate control" within the meaning of the *Chimel* case. The search of the jacket, therefore, was a search incident to a lawful custodial arrest, and it did not violate the Fourth and Fourteenth Amendments. Accordingly, the judgment is reversed.

It is so ordered.

Justice Brennan, with whom Justice Marshall joins, dissenting.

[The] Court [today] adopts a fiction—that the interior of a car is always within the immediate control of an arrestee who has recently been in the car. [In] so holding, the Court ignores both precedent and principle and fails to achieve its objective of providing police officers with a more workable standard for determining the permissible scope of searches incident to arrest.

[T]he Court today substantially expands the permissible scope of searches incident to arrest by permitting police officers to search areas and containers the arrestee could not possibly reach at the time of arrest. These facts demonstrate that at the time Belton and his three companions were placed under custodial arrest—which was after they had been removed from the car, patted down, and separated—none of them could have reached the jackets that had been left on the back seat of the car. * * *

[Disregarding] the principle "that the scope of a warrantless search must be commensurate with the rationale that excepts the search from the warrant requirement," the Court for the first time grants police officers authority to conduct a warrantless "area" search under circumstances where there is no chance that the arrestee "might gain possession of a weapon or destructible evidence." [T]he result would presumably be the same even if Officer Nicot had handcuffed Belton and his companions in the patrol car before placing them under arrest, and even if his search had extended to locked luggage or other inaccessible containers located in the back seat of the car.

[The] Court seeks to justify its departure from the principles underlying *Chimel* by proclaiming the need for a new "bright-line" rule to guide the officer in the field. [H]owever, "the mere fact that law enforcement may be made more efficient can never by itself justify disregard of the Fourth Amendment." Moreover, the Court's attempt to forge a "bright-line" rule fails on its own terms. While the "interior/trunk" distinction may provide a workable guide in certain routine cases—for example, where the officer arrests the driver of a car and then immediately searches the seats and floor—in the long run, I suspect it will create far more problems than it solves. The Court's new approach leaves open too many questions and, more important, it provides the police and the courts with too few tools with which to find the answers.

[A]lthough the Court concludes that a warrantless search of a car may take place even though the suspect was arrested outside the car, it does not indicate how long after the suspect's arrest that search may validly be conducted. Would a warrantless search incident to arrest be valid if conducted five minutes after the suspect left his car? Thirty minutes? Three hours? Does it matter whether the suspect is standing in close proximity to the car when the search is conducted? Does it matter whether the police formed probable cause to arrest before or after the suspect left his car? And why is the rule announced today necessarily limited to searches of cars? What if a suspect is seen walking out of a house where the police, peering in from outside, had formed probable cause to believe a crime was being committed? Could the police then arrest that suspect and enter the house to conduct a search incident to arrest? Even assuming today's rule is limited to searches of the "interior" of cars—an assumption not demanded by logic—what is meant by "interior"? Does it include locked glove compartments, the interior of door panels, or the area under the floorboards? Are special rules necessary for station wagons and hatchbacks, where the luggage compartment may be reached through the interior, or taxicabs, where a glass panel might separate the driver's compartment from the rest of the car? Are the only containers that may be searched those that are large enough to be "capable of holding another object"? Or does the new rule apply to any container even if it "could hold neither a weapon nor evidence of the criminal conduct for which the suspect was arrested"?

The Court does not give the police any "bright-line" answers to these questions. More important, because the Court's new rule abandons the justifications underlying *Chimel*, it offers no guidance to the police officer seeking to work out these answers for himself. [T]he Court has undermined rather than furthered the goal of consistent law enforcement: it has failed to offer any principles to guide the police and the courts in their application of the new rule to nonroutine situations.

The standard announced in *Chimel* is not nearly as difficult to apply as the Court suggests. [While] it may be difficult in some cases to measure the exact scope of the arrestee's immediate control, relevant factors would surely include the relative number of police officers and arrestees, the manner of restraint placed on the arrestee, and the ability of the arrestee to gain access to a particular area or container. [W]hen in doubt the police can always turn to the rationale underlying *Chimel*—

the need to prevent the arrestee from reaching weapons or contraband—before exercising their judgment. A rule based on that rationale should provide more guidance than the rule announced by the Court today. Moreover, unlike the Court's rule, it would be faithful to the Fourth Amendment.

JUSTICE WHITE, with whom JUSTICE MARSHALL joins, dissenting.

[Today's holding] seems to me an extreme extension of *Chimel* and one to which I cannot subscribe. [S]earches of luggage, briefcases, and other containers in the interior of an auto are authorized in the absence of any suspicion whatsoever that they contain anything in which the police have a legitimate interest. * * * I dissent.

Notes: Temporal & Spatial Limitations

Both *Chimel* and *Belton* are subject to temporal and spatial limitations. *Chimel* involved a search that exceeded "spatial limitations" in that the search extended beyond the area within Chimel's "immediate control." Temporal limitations are illustrated by the holding in *Preston v. United States*, 376 U.S. 364 (1964). In that case, petitioner and his companions were arrested while riding in an automobile, and taken to the police station for booking. The car was driven by an officer to the station and then towed to a garage. After the men were booked, police officers searched the car in the garage and found two loaded revolvers in the glove compartment. They were unable to open the trunk and returned to the station where a detective told one of the officers to try again. In the trunk, the officers found caps, women's stockings (one with mouth and eye holes), rope, pillow slips, and an illegally manufactured license plate equipped to be snapped over another plate. Respondents were charged with conspiracy to rob a bank. The Court invalidated the search: Petitioners "had been arrested [and] the car had been towed to the garage. At this point there was no danger that any of the men [could] have used any weapons in the car or could have destroyed any evidence.... Nor, since [the car] was in police custody at a garage, was there any danger that the car would be moved out of the locality or jurisdiction. We think that the search was too remote in time or place to have been made as incidental to the arrest." *See Thomas v. State,* 761 So.2d 1010 (Fla.1999), cert. granted, 531 U.S. 1069 (2001) (whether *Belton* applies when occupant is no longer in or near the vehicle).

Problems

1. *Applying Belton.* Suppose that the police decide to arrest Belton. Before they make a search incident to arrest, they remove Belton from the car, handcuff him, and place him in the back of a patrol car (with back doors that can only be opened from the outside). Is the ensuing search incident to legal arrest valid?

2. *Belton's Scope.* What is the scope of the search authorized in *Belton*? Suppose that Belton is arrested while driving a hatchback, or for that matter a van. Where are the police allowed to search? What if the police decide to search the glove compartment, but discover that it is locked? Can they pry it open?

3. *More on Applying Belton.* Coolidge was arrested for murdering a 14–year–old girl at Coolidge's home in his living room. At the time of the arrest, Coolidge's automobiles were sitting on the driveway in front of the house. The police searched the vehicles as a "search incident to legal arrest" on the theory that they were within the "immediate control" of Coolidge at the time of his arrest. On what basis might Coolidge argue that the search was invalid? How might the state respond? How should the court rule? *See Coolidge v. New Hampshire*, 403 U.S. 443 (1971).

4. *Belton and Departed Motorists.* A police officer saw J. Johnson driving a car with no front license plate (in a state requiring both front and back tags). Unaware that the police were planning to stop him, Johnson parks and exits his car. When he is approximately fifteen feet from the car, an officer approaches him about the license plate and asks Johnson for his driver's license. Johnson states that he has no license and starts to flee. The officer catches Johnson and arrests him. Once a transport vehicle arrives, the officer places Johnson in it and then searches the car. The officer later admits that he suspected that Johnson might be involved with illegal drugs based on an incident that occurred a week before. In the car, the officer found 100 bags of heroin. The prosecution seeks to justify the search as "incident to a legal arrest." How might Johnson argue that the search was illegal? How might the State respond to such arguments? Should the search be upheld? *See Thornton v. United States*, 541 U.S. 615 (2004).

5. *More on Departed Motorists.* In the prior problem, assume that the suspect parked his car and left to attend a two hour rock concert. After the concert, but before the suspect reaches his car, he is arrested. At that moment, he is approximately 50 feet from the car. Can the police justify a search of the car under *Belton*?

6. *Should a Booking Search be Permitted When the Police Do Not Plan to Incarcerate an Arrestee (either because the arrestee has the money to post bail or because the police do not incarcerate for that crime)?* Suppose that a truck driver was stopped because his truck emitted excess smoke. In checking the driver's license, a state trooper learned that there were two warrants for the driver's arrest (one for failure to appear on a misdemeanor charge and the other for failure to pay a $25 fine for possession of marijuana). The trooper arrested the driver and took him to the city jail. Jail procedure required complete processing of all arrestees, including a property inventory, whether or not the arrestee is able to post bail when the arrestee arrives at jail. On the driver's behalf, argue that any evidence found during the booking search should be excluded since the driver planned to immediately post bail. Does the state have a valid response to these arguments? Would it matter what was turned up by the search (*i.e.*, credit cards that implicated the driver in a rape)? *See Zehrung v. State*, 569 P.2d 189 (Alaska 1977).

7. *"Less Intrusive Alternatives?"* Everett Hoffman is arrested. At the station, the police want to search his back pack. Hoffman objects claiming that the police can serve their interest in "preservation of the defendant's property and protection of police from claims of lost or stolen property" by sealing the back pack in a plastic bag or box and placing it in a secure locker. Do the police have to accept Hoffman's suggestion or should they be allowed

to search the back pack? What arguments can be made on Hoffman's behalf? How might the police respond to those arguments?

3. Automobile Exception

The automobile exception is one of the oldest exceptions to the warrant requirement. It provides that, when the police have probable cause to believe that an automobile contains the fruits, instrumentalities or evidence of crime, they may search the vehicle without a warrant.

CALIFORNIA v. CARNEY

471 U.S. 386 (1985).

CHIEF JUSTICE BURGER delivered the opinion of the Court.

[On] May 31, 1979, Drug Enforcement Agency Agent Robert Williams watched respondent, Charles Carney, approach a youth in downtown San Diego. The youth accompanied Carney to a Dodge Mini Motor Home parked in a nearby lot. Carney and the youth closed the window shades in the motor home * * *. Agent Williams had previously received uncorroborated information that the same motor home was used by another person who was exchanging marihuana for sex. Williams, with assistance from other agents, kept the motor home under surveillance for the entire one and one-quarter hours that Carney and the youth remained inside. When the youth left the motor home, the agents followed and stopped him. The youth told the agents that he had received marijuana in return for allowing Carney sexual contacts.

At the agents' request, the youth returned to the motor home and knocked on its door; Carney stepped out. The agents identified themselves as law enforcement officers. Without a warrant or consent, one agent entered the motor home and observed marihuana, plastic bags, and a scale of the kind used in weighing drugs on a table. Agent Williams took Carney into custody and took possession of the motor home. A subsequent search of the motor home at the police station revealed additional marihuana in the cupboards and refrigerator.

Respondent was [convicted of] possession of marihuana for sale. [The] California Supreme Court reversed the conviction. [We] granted certiorari. We reverse.

[There are] exceptions to the general rule that a warrant must be secured before a search is undertaken; one is the so-called "automobile exception" at issue in this case. This exception to the warrant requirement was first set forth by the Court 60 years ago in *Carroll v. United States*, 267 U.S. 132 (1925). There, the Court recognized that the privacy interests in an automobile are constitutionally protected; however, it held that the ready mobility of the automobile justifies a lesser degree of protection of those interests. [O]ur cases have consistently recognized ready mobility as one of the principal bases of the automobile exception. [O]ur later cases have made clear that ready mobility is not the only basis for the exception. The reasons for the vehicle exception, we have said, are twofold. "Besides the element of mobility, less rigorous warrant requirements govern because the expectation of privacy with respect to one's automobile is significantly less than that relating to one's home or office."

Even in cases where an automobile was not immediately mobile, the lesser expectation of privacy resulting from its use as a readily mobile vehicle justified application of the vehicular exception. In some cases, the configuration of the vehicle contributed to the lower expectations of privacy; for example, we held in *Cardwell v. Lewis, supra*, 417 U.S., at 590, that, because the passenger compartment of a standard automobile is relatively open to plain view, there are lesser expectations of privacy. But even when enclosed "repository" areas have been involved, we have concluded that the lesser expectations of privacy warrant application of the exception. We have applied the exception in the context of a locked car trunk, a sealed package in a car trunk, a closed compartment under the dashboard, the interior of a vehicle's upholstery, or sealed packages inside a covered pickup truck.

These reduced expectations of privacy derive not from the fact that the area to be searched is in plain view, but from the pervasive regulation of vehicles capable of traveling on the public highways. As we explained in *South Dakota v. Opperman*, [428 U.S. 364 (1976),] an inventory search case: "Automobiles, unlike homes, are subjected to pervasive and continuing governmental regulation and controls, including periodic inspection and licensing requirements. As an everyday occurrence, police stop and examine vehicles when license plates or inspection stickers have expired, or if other violations, such as exhaust fumes or excessive noise, are noted, or if headlights or other safety equipment are not in proper working order."

The public is fully aware that it is accorded less privacy in its automobiles because of this compelling governmental need for regulation. [In] short, the pervasive schemes of regulation, which necessarily lead to reduced expectations of privacy, and the exigencies attendant to ready mobility justify searches without prior recourse to the authority of a magistrate so long as the overriding standard of probable cause is met.

When a vehicle is being used on the highways, or if it is readily capable of such use and is found stationary in a place not regularly used for residential purposes—temporary or otherwise—the two justifications for the vehicle exception come into play. First, the vehicle is obviously readily mobile by the turn of an ignition key, if not actually moving. Second, there is a reduced expectation of privacy stemming from its use as a licensed motor vehicle subject to a range of police regulation inapplicable to a fixed dwelling. At least in these circumstances, the overriding societal interests in effective law enforcement justify an immediate search before the vehicle and its occupants become unavailable.

While it is true that respondent's vehicle possessed some, if not many of the attributes of a home, it is equally clear that the vehicle falls clearly within the scope of the exception laid down in *Carroll* and applied in succeeding cases. Like the automobile in *Carroll*, respondent's motor home was readily mobile. Absent the prompt search and seizure, it could readily have been moved beyond the reach of the police. Furthermore, the vehicle was licensed to "operate on public streets; [was] serviced in public places; [and was] subject to extensive regulation and inspection." *Rakas v. Illinois*, 439 U.S. 128, 154, n. 2 (1978) (Powell, J., concurring). And the vehicle was so situated that an objective observer would conclude that it was being used not as a residence, but as a vehicle.

Respondent urges us to distinguish his vehicle from other vehicles within the exception because it was capable of functioning as a home. In our increasingly mobile society, many vehicles used for transportation can be and are being used not only for transportation but for shelter, *i.e.*, as a "home" or "residence." To distinguish between respondent's motor home and an ordinary sedan for purposes of the vehicle exception would require that we apply the exception depending upon the size of the vehicle and the quality of its appointments. Moreover, to fail to apply the exception to vehicles such as a motor home ignores the fact that a motor home lends itself easily to use as an instrument of illicit drug traffic and other illegal activity. In *United States v. Ross*, 456 U.S., at 822, we declined to distinguish between "worthy" and "unworthy" containers, noting that "the central purpose of the Fourth Amendment forecloses such a distinction." We decline today to distinguish between "worthy" and "unworthy" vehicles which are either on the public roads and highways, or situated such that it is reasonable to conclude that the vehicle is not being used as a residence.

Our application of the vehicle exception has never turned on the other uses to which a vehicle might be put. The exception has historically turned on the ready mobility of the vehicle, and on the presence of the vehicle in a setting that objectively indicates that the vehicle is being used for transportation.[17] These two requirements for application of the exception ensure that law enforcement officials are not unnecessarily hamstrung in their efforts to detect and prosecute criminal activity, and that the legitimate privacy interests of the public are protected. Applying the vehicle exception in these circumstances allows the essential purposes served by the exception to be fulfilled, while assuring that the exception will acknowledge legitimate privacy interests.

[This] search was not unreasonable; it was plainly one that the magistrate could authorize if presented with these facts. The DEA agents had fresh, direct, uncontradicted evidence that the respondent was distributing a controlled substance from the vehicle, apart from evidence of other possible offenses. The agents thus had abundant

---

17. We need not pass on the application of the vehicle exception to a motor home that is situated in a way or place [that] indicates that it is being used as a residence. Among the factors that might be relevant in determining whether a warrant would be required in such a circumstance is its location, whether the vehicle is readily mobile [or] elevated on blocks, whether the vehicle is licensed, whether it is connected to utilities, and whether it has convenient access to a public road.

probable cause to enter and search the vehicle for evidence of a crime notwithstanding its possible use as a dwelling place.

The judgment of the California Supreme Court is *reversed.*

JUSTICE STEVENS, with whom JUSTICE BRENNAN and JUSTICE MARSHALL join, dissenting.

[It] is hardly unrealistic to expect experienced law enforcement officers to obtain a search warrant when one can easily be secured. The ascendancy of the warrant requirement in our system of justice must not be bullied aside by extravagant claims of necessity * * *.

[Our] prior cases teach us that inherent mobility is not a sufficient justification for the fashioning of an exception to the warrant requirement, especially in the face of heightened expectations of privacy in the location searched. Motor homes, by their common use and construction, afford their owners a substantial and legitimate expectation of privacy when they dwell within. When a motor home is parked in a location that is removed from the public highway, I believe that society is prepared to recognize that the expectations of privacy within it are not unlike the expectations one has in a fixed dwelling. As a general rule, such places may only be searched with a warrant based upon probable cause. Warrantless searches of motor homes are only reasonable when the motor home is traveling on the public streets or highways, or when exigent circumstances otherwise require an immediate search without the expenditure of time necessary to obtain a warrant.

[In] this case, the motor home was parked in an off-the-street lot only a few blocks from the courthouse in downtown San Diego where dozens of magistrates were available to entertain a warrant application.[18] The officers clearly had the element of surprise with them, and with curtains covering the windshield, the motor home offered no indication of any imminent departure. The officers plainly had probable cause to arrest the respondent and search the motor home, and [it] is inexplicable why they eschewed the safe harbor of a warrant.

[The] motor home in this case [was] designed to accommodate a breadth of ordinary everyday living. [I]ts height, length, and beam provided substantial living space inside: stuffed chairs surround a table; cupboards provide room for storage of personal effects; bunk beds provide sleeping space; and a refrigerator provides ample space for food and beverages. Moreover, curtains and large opaque walls inhibit viewing the activities inside from the exterior of the vehicle. The interior configuration of the motor home establishes that the vehicle's size, shape, and mode of construction should have indicated to the officers that it was a vehicle containing mobile living quarters.

The State contends that officers in the field will have an impossible task determining whether or not other vehicles contain mobile living

---

18. In addition, a telephonic warrant was only 20 cents and the nearest phone booth away.

quarters. [C]ommon English usage suggests that we already distinguish between a "motor home" which is "equipped as a self-contained traveling home," a "camper" which is only equipped for "casual travel and camping," and an automobile which is "designed for passenger transportation." Surely the exteriors of these vehicles contain clues about their different functions which could alert officers in the field to the necessity of a warrant.

[S]earches of places that regularly accommodate a wide range of private human activity are fundamentally different from searches of automobiles which primarily serve a public transportation function. Although it may not be a castle, a motor home is usually the functional equivalent of a hotel room, a vacation and retirement home, or a hunting and fishing cabin. These places may be as spartan as a humble cottage[,] but the highest and most legitimate expectations of privacy associated with these temporary abodes should command the respect of this Court. [A] warrantless search of living quarters in a motor home is "presumptively unreasonable absent exigent circumstances."

Notes

1. *Delayed Automobile Searches.* Arguably, if the search of an automobile is delayed, the police have time to obtain a warrant and should be required to do so. However, in *Chambers v. Maroney*, 399 U.S. 42 (1970), the Court upheld a delayed search. Petitioner was riding in an automobile at the time of his arrest, but the vehicle was searched later at the police station rather than at the scene:

> Arguably, because of the preference for a magistrate's judgment, only the immobilization of the car should be permitted until a search warrant is obtained; arguably, only the "lesser" intrusion is permissible until the magistrate authorizes the "greater." * * * For constitutional purposes, we see no difference between on the one hand seizing and holding a car before presenting the probable cause issue to a magistrate and on the other hand carrying out an immediate search without a warrant. Given probable cause to search, either course is reasonable under the Fourth Amendment.

> [T]he blue station wagon could have been searched on the spot when it was stopped since there was probable cause to search and it was a fleeting target for a search. The probable-cause factor still obtained at the station house and so did the mobility of the car.... In that event there is little to choose in terms of practical consequences between an immediate search without a warrant and the car's immobilization until a warrant is obtained. * * *

In *United States v. Johns*, 469 U.S. 478 (1985), the police stopped and searched a vehicle based on probable cause. The police removed packages from the vehicle, and searched the packages several days later. The Court upheld the search: "We do not think that delay in the execution of the warrantless search is necessarily unreasonable. We do not suggest that police officers may indefinitely retain possession of a vehicle and its contents before they complete a vehicle search. [R]espondents have not even alleged, much less proved, that the delay in the search of packages adversely affected legitimate interests protected by the Fourth Amendment." Justice Brennan dissented: "[A] warrantless search occurring three days after seizure of a package found in an automobile violates the Fourth Amendment. [There] is simply no justification for departing from the Fourth Amendment warrant requirement under the circumstances of this case; no exigency precluded reasonable efforts to obtain a warrant prior to the search of the packages in the warehouse."

Problem: Coolidge v. N.H. (again)

In *Coolidge v. New Hampshire*, 403 U.S. 443 (1971), petitioner was arrested for murder at his home. His car, which was sitting on the front driveway, was impounded and towed to the police station. The car was searched two days later, as well as a year later. Evidence obtained from the search was admitted at petitioner's trial. In a plurality opinion, the Court held that the trial court erred in admitting the evidence:

> [T]he police had known for some time of the probable role of the Pontiac car in the crime. Coolidge was aware that he was a suspect[,] but he had been extremely cooperative throughout the investigation, and there was no indication that he meant to flee. He had already had ample opportunity to destroy any evidence he thought incriminating. There is no suggestion that, on the night in question, the car was being used for any illegal purpose, and it was regularly parked in the driveway of his house. The opportunity for search was thus hardly "fleeting." The objects that the police are assumed to have had probable cause to search for in the car were neither stolen nor contraband nor dangerous.

> [The] word "automobile" is not a talisman in whose presence the Fourth Amendment fades away and disappears. And surely there is nothing in this case to invoke the meaning and purpose of the *Carroll* [rule]—no alerted criminal bent on flight, no fleeting opportunity on an open highway after a hazardous chase, no contraband or stolen goods or weapons, no confederates waiting to move the evidence, not even the inconvenience of a special police detail to guard the immobilized automobile. In short, by no possible stretch of the legal imagination can this be made into a case where "it is not practicable to secure a warrant," and the "automobile exception," despite its label, is simply irrelevant.

> Since *Carroll* would not have justified a warrantless search of the Pontiac at the time Coolidge was arrested, the later search at the station house was plainly illegal, at least so far as the automobile exception is concerned. * * *

In light of later decisions, would you expect *Coolidge* to be decided the same way if it arose today?

CALIFORNIA v. ACEVEDO

500 U.S. 565 (1991).

JUSTICE BLACKMUN delivered the opinion of the Court.

[On] October 28, 1987, Officer Coleman of the Santa Ana, Cal., Police Department received a telephone call from a federal drug enforcement agent in Hawaii. The agent informed Coleman that he had seized a package containing marijuana which was to have been delivered to the Federal Express Office in Santa Ana and which was addressed to J.R. Daza at 805 West Stevens Avenue in that city. The agent arranged to send the package to Coleman instead. Coleman then was to take the package to the Federal Express office and arrest the person who arrived to claim it.

Coleman received the package on October 29, verified its contents, and took it to the Senior Operations Manager at the Federal Express office. At about 10:30 a.m. on October 30, a man, who identified himself as Jamie Daza, arrived to claim the package. He accepted it and drove to his apartment on West Stevens. He carried the package into the apartment.

At 11:45 a.m., officers observed Daza leave the apartment and drop the box and paper that had contained the marijuana into a trash bin. Coleman at that point left the scene to get a search warrant. About 12:05 p.m., the officers saw Richard St. George leave the apartment carrying a blue knapsack which appeared to be half full. The officers stopped him as he was driving off, searched the knapsack, and found 1 ½ pounds of marijuana.

At 12:30 p.m., respondent Charles Steven Acevedo arrived. He entered Daza's apartment, stayed for about 10 minutes, and reappeared carrying a brown paper bag that looked full. The officers noticed that the bag was the size of one of the wrapped marijuana packages sent from Hawaii. Acevedo walked to a silver Honda in the parking lot. He placed the bag in the trunk of the car and started to drive away. Fearing the loss of evidence, officers in a marked police car stopped him. They opened the trunk and the bag, and found marijuana.

[Respondent was charged with possession of marijuana for sale. When his motion to suppress was denied, he pleaded guilty but appealed the denial of his suppression motion.] The California Court of Appeal['s] concluded that the marijuana found in the paper bag in the car's trunk should have been suppressed. [We] granted certiorari to reexamine the law applicable to a closed container in an automobile, a subject that has troubled courts and law enforcement officers since it was first considered in [*United States v. Chadwick*, 433 U.S. 1 (1977)].

II

In *United States v. Ross*, [456 U.S. 798 (1982)] we held that a warrantless search of an automobile [could] include a search of a container or package found inside the car when such a search was supported by probable cause. The warrantless search of Ross' car occurred after an informant told the police that he had seen Ross complete a drug transaction using drugs stored in the trunk of his car. The police stopped the car, searched it, and discovered in the trunk a brown paper bag containing drugs. We decided that the search of Ross' car was not unreasonable under the Fourth Amendment: "The scope of a warrantless search based on probable cause is no narrower—and no broader— than the scope of a search authorized by a warrant supported by probable cause." Thus, "[i]f probable cause justifies the search of a lawfully stopped vehicle, it justifies the search of every part of the vehicle and its contents that may conceal the object of the search." In *Ross*, therefore, we clarified the scope of the *Carroll* doctrine as properly including a "probing search" of compartments and containers within the automobile so long as the search is supported by probable cause.

[*Ross*] distinguished the *Carroll* doctrine from the separate rule that governed the search of closed containers. The Court had announced this separate rule, unique to luggage and other closed packages, bags, and containers, in *United States v. Chadwick*, 433 U.S. 1 (1977). In *Chadwick*, federal narcotics agents had probable cause to believe that a 200–pound double-locked footlocker contained marijuana. The agents tracked the locker as the defendants removed it from a train and carried it through the station to a waiting car. As soon as the defendants lifted the locker into the trunk of the car, the agents arrested them, seized the locker, and searched it. In this Court, the United States did not contend that the locker's brief contact with the automobile's trunk sufficed to make the *Carroll* doctrine applicable. Rather, the United States urged that the search of movable luggage could be considered analogous to the search of an automobile.

The Court rejected this argument because, it reasoned, a person expects more privacy in his luggage and personal effects than he does in his automobile. Moreover, it concluded that as "may often not be the case when automobiles are seized," secure storage facilities are usually available when the police seize luggage.

In *Arkansas v. Sanders*, 442 U.S. 753 (1979), the Court extended *Chadwick's* rule to apply to a suitcase actually being transported in the trunk of a car. In *Sanders*, the police had probable cause to believe a suitcase contained marijuana. They watched as the defendant placed the suitcase in the trunk of a taxi and was driven away. The police pursued the taxi for several blocks, stopped it, found the suitcase in the trunk, and searched it. Although the Court had applied the *Carroll* doctrine to searches of integral parts of the automobile itself, (indeed, in *Carroll*, contraband whiskey was in the upholstery of the seats), it did not extend the doctrine to the warrantless search of personal luggage "merely because it was located in an automobile lawfully stopped by the police." Again, the *Sanders* majority stressed the heightened privacy expectation in personal luggage and concluded that the presence of luggage in an automobile did not diminish the owner's expectation of privacy in his personal items.

In *Ross*, the Court endeavored to distinguish between *Carroll*, which governed the *Ross* automobile search, and *Chadwick*, which governed the *Sanders* automobile search. It held that the *Carroll* doctrine covered searches of automobiles when the police had probable cause to search an entire vehicle, but that the *Chadwick* doctrine governed searches of luggage when the officers had probable cause to search only a container within the vehicle. Thus, in a *Ross* situation, the police could conduct a reasonable search under the Fourth Amendment without obtaining a warrant, whereas in a *Sanders* situation, the police had to obtain a warrant before they searched.

[*Ross*] involved the scope of an automobile search. *Ross* held that closed containers encountered by the police during a warrantless search of a car pursuant to the automobile exception could also be searched. Thus, this Court in *Ross* took the critical step of saying that closed containers in cars could be searched without a warrant because of their presence within the automobile. Despite the protection that *Sanders* purported to extend to closed containers, the privacy interest in those closed containers yielded to the broad scope of an automobile search.

The facts in this case closely resemble the facts in *Ross*. In *Ross*, the police had probable cause to believe that drugs were stored in the trunk of a particular car. Here, [the] police had probable cause to believe that respondent was carrying marijuana in a bag in his car's trunk. Furthermore, [in] *Ross*, as here, the drugs in the trunk were contained in a brown paper bag.

[*Ross*] rejected *Chadwick's* distinction between containers and cars. It concluded that the expectation of privacy in one's vehicle is equal to one's expectation of privacy in the container, and noted that "the privacy interests in a car's trunk or glove compartment may be no less than those in a movable container." It also recognized that it was arguable that the same exigent circumstances that permit a warrantless search of an automobile would justify the warrantless search of a movable container. In deference to the rule of *Chadwick* and *Sanders*, however, the Court put that question to one side. It concluded that the time and expense of the warrant process would be misdirected if the police could search every cubic inch of an automobile until they discovered a paper sack, at which point the Fourth Amendment required them to take the sack to a magistrate for permission to look inside. We now must decide the question deferred in *Ross*: whether the Fourth Amendment requires the police to obtain a warrant to open the sack in a movable vehicle simply because they lack probable cause to search the entire car. We conclude that it does not.

Dissenters in *Ross* asked why the suitcase in *Sanders* was "more private, less difficult for police to seize and store, or in any other relevant respect more properly subject to the warrant requirement, than a container that police discover in a probable-cause search of an entire automobile?" We now agree that a container found after a general search of the automobile and a container found in a car after a limited search for the container are equally easy for the police to store and for the suspect to hide or destroy. [W]e see no principled distinction in terms of either the privacy expectation or the exigent circumstances between the paper bag found by the police in *Ross* and the paper bag found by the police here. Furthermore, by attempting to distinguish between a container for which the police are specifically searching and a container which they come across in a car, we have provided only minimal protection for privacy and have impeded effective law enforcement.

The line between probable cause to search a vehicle and probable cause to search a package in that vehicle is not always clear, and separate rules that govern the two objects to be searched may enable the police to broaden their power to make warrantless searches and disserve privacy interests. [If] the police know that they may open a bag only if they are actually searching the entire car, they may search more extensively than they otherwise would in order to establish the general probable cause required by *Ross*.

[To] the extent that the *Chadwick-Sanders* rule protects privacy, its protection is minimal. Law enforcement officers may seize a container and hold it until they obtain a search warrant. "Since the police, by hypothesis, have probable cause to seize the property, we can assume that a warrant will be routinely forthcoming in the overwhelming majority of cases." And the police often will be able to search containers without a warrant, despite the *Chadwick-Sanders rule*, as a search incident to a lawful arrest. [Under] *Belton*, the same probable cause to believe that a container holds drugs will allow the police to arrest the person transporting the container and search it.

Finally, the search of a paper bag intrudes far less on individual privacy than does the incursion sanctioned long ago in *Carroll*. In that case, prohibition agents slashed the upholstery of the automobile. This Court nonetheless found their search to be reasonable under the Fourth Amendment. If destroying the interior of an automobile is not unreasonable, we cannot conclude that looking inside a closed container is. In light of the minimal protection to privacy afforded by the *Chadwick-Sanders* rule, and our serious doubt whether that rule substantially serves privacy interests, we now hold that the Fourth Amendment does not compel separate treatment for an automobile search that extends only to a container within the vehicle.

The *Chadwick-Sanders* rule not only has failed to protect privacy but also has confused courts and police officers and impeded effective law enforcement. The discrepancy between the two rules has led to confusion for law enforcement officers. For example, when an officer, who has developed probable cause to believe that a vehicle contains drugs, begins to search the vehicle and immediately discovers a closed container, which rule applies? The defendant will argue that the fact that the officer first chose to search the container indicates that his probable cause extended only to the container and that *Chadwick* and *Sanders* therefore require a warrant. On the other hand, the fact that the officer first chose to search in the most obvious location should not restrict the propriety of the search. The *Chadwick* rule, as applied in *Sanders*, has devolved into an anomaly such that the more likely the police are to discover drugs in a container, the less authority they have to search it. We have noted the virtue of providing " 'clear and unequivocal' guidelines to the law enforcement profession." The *Chadwick-Sanders* rule is the antithesis of a " 'clear and unequivocal' guideline."

[The] *Chadwick* dissenters predicted that the container rule would have "the perverse result of allowing fortuitous circumstances to control the outcome" of various searches. The rule also was so confusing that within two years after *Chadwick*, this Court found it necessary to expound on the meaning of that decision and explain its application to luggage in general. [We] conclude that it is better to adopt one clear-cut rule to govern automobile searches and eliminate the warrant requirement for closed containers set forth in *Sanders*. [The] interpretation of the *Carroll* doctrine set forth in *Ross* now applies to all searches of containers found in an automobile. In other words, the police may search without a warrant if their search is supported by probable cause. * * *

Our holding today neither extends the *Carroll* doctrine nor broadens the scope of the permissible automobile search delineated in *Carroll*, *Chambers*, and *Ross*. It remains a "cardinal principle that 'searches conducted outside the judicial process, without prior approval by judge or magistrate, are *per se* unreasonable under the Fourth Amendment— subject only to a few specifically established and well-delineated exceptions.' " We held in *Ross*: "The exception recognized in *Carroll* is unquestionably one that is 'specifically established and well delineated.' "

Until today, this Court has drawn a curious line between the search of an automobile that coincidentally turns up a container and the search of a container that coincidentally turns up in an automobile. The protections of the Fourth Amendment must not turn on such coincidences. We therefore interpret *Carroll* as providing one rule to govern all automobile searches. The police may search an automobile and the containers within it where they have probable cause to believe contraband or evidence is contained. * * *

JUSTICE STEVENS, with whom JUSTICE MARSHALL joins, dissenting.

[In] *Chadwick*, [we] concluded that neither of the justifications for the automobile exception could support a similar exception for luggage. We first held that the privacy interest in luggage is "substantially greater than in an automobile." [W]e reasoned, "[l]uggage contents are not open to public view, except as a condition to a border entry or common carrier travel; nor is luggage subject to regular inspections and official scrutiny on a continuing basis." Indeed, luggage is specifically intended to safeguard the privacy of personal effects, unlike an automobile, "whose primary function is transportation."

We then held that the mobility of luggage did not justify creating an additional exception to the Warrant Clause. Unlike an automobile, luggage can easily be seized and detained pending judicial approval of a search. Once the police have luggage "under their exclusive control, there [i]s not the slightest danger that the [luggage] or its contents could [be] removed before a valid search warrant could be obtained. [It is] unreasonable to undertake the additional and greater intrusion of a search without a warrant".

[C]oncerns that justified our holding in *Ross* are not implicated in cases like *Chadwick* and *Sanders* in which the police have probable cause to search a particular container rather than the entire vehicle. Because the police can seize the container which is the object of their search, they have no need either to search or to seize the entire vehicle. Indeed, as even the Court today recognizes, they have no authority to do so.

[T]he Court recognizes that the police did not have probable cause to search respondent's vehicle and that a search of anything but the paper bag [would] have been unconstitutional. [T]he Court assumes that the police could not have made a warrantless inspection of the bag before it was placed in the car. [T]he Court also does not question the fact that [it] would have been lawful for the police to seize the container and detain it (and respondent) until they obtained a search warrant. Thus, all of the relevant facts that governed our decisions in *Chadwick* and *Sanders* are present here whereas the relevant fact that justified the vehicle search in *Ross* is not present.

[To] the extent there was any "anomaly" in our prior jurisprudence, the Court has "cured" it at the expense of creating a more serious paradox. For surely it is anomalous to prohibit a search of a briefcase while the owner is carrying it exposed on a public street yet to permit a search once the owner has placed the briefcase in the locked trunk of his car. One's privacy interest in one's luggage can certainly not be diminished by one's removing it from a public thoroughfare and placing it— out of sight—in a privately owned vehicle. Nor is the danger that evidence will escape increased if the luggage is in a car rather than on the street. In either location, if the police have probable cause, they are authorized to seize the luggage and to detain it until they obtain judicial approval for a search. * * *

[Even] if the warrant requirement does inconvenience the police to some extent, that fact does not distinguish this constitutional requirement from any other procedural protection secured by the Bill of Rights. It is merely a part of the price that our society must pay in order to preserve its freedom. * * *

Problems

1. *Scope of the Automobile Exception.* Does the automobile exception authorize a broader search than would be permitted under the search

incident to legal arrest exception, or a more narrow one? Does the answer to this question depend on circumstances? Consider the following facts in which the police have probable cause to believe that a suspect is carrying drugs: a) in his glove compartment; b) in the trunk of his car; c) in the left front wheel well; d) in the engine compartment; e) somewhere in the vehicle. Where may the police search in each of these situations?

2. *Purse Searches.* Suppose that the police have probable cause to believe that a woman in this criminal procedure class is carrying heroin in her purse. Absent exigent circumstances, may the police make a warrantless search of the purse when the woman is outside her vehicle? Does the situation change when she enters the vehicle with the purse?

4. Inventory Exception

There is also an "inventory" exception to the warrant requirement. The most common inventory search occurs when the police impound a vehicle. The following case analyzes this type of search.

COLORADO v. BERTINE

479 U.S. 367 (1987).

Chief Justice Rehnquist delivered the opinion of the Court.

[A] police officer in Boulder, Colorado, arrested respondent Steven Lee Bertine for driving while under the influence of alcohol. After Bertine was taken into custody and before the arrival of a tow truck to take Bertine's van to an impoundment lot,[19] a backup officer inventoried the contents of the van. The officer opened a closed backpack in which he found controlled substances, cocaine paraphernalia, and a large amount of cash. Bertine was subsequently charged with driving while under the influence of alcohol, unlawful possession of cocaine with intent to dispense, sell, and distribute, and unlawful possession of methaqualone. We are asked to decide whether the Fourth Amendment prohibits the State from proving these charges with the evidence discovered during the inventory of Bertine's van. We hold that it does not.

The backup officer inventoried the van in accordance with local police procedures, which require a detailed inspection and inventory of impounded vehicles. He found the backpack directly behind the frontseat of the van. Inside the pack, the officer observed a nylon bag containing metal canisters. Opening the canisters, the officer discovered that they contained cocaine, methaqualone tablets, cocaine paraphernalia, and $700 in cash. In an outside zippered pouch of the backpack, he also found $210 in cash in a sealed envelope. After completing the inventory of the van, the officer had the van towed to an impound lot and brought the backpack, money, and contraband to the police station.

[The Supreme Court of Colorado affirmed a lower court ruling granting Bertine's motion to suppress]. The Colorado Supreme Court

19. Section 7–7–2(a)(4) of the Boulder Revised Code authorizes police officers to impound vehicles when drivers are taken into custody. * * *

premised its ruling on the United States Constitution. The court recognized that in *South Dakota v. Opperman*, 428 U.S. 364 (1976), we had held inventory searches of automobiles to be consistent with the Fourth Amendment, and that in *Illinois v. Lafayette*, 462 U.S. 640 (1983), we had held that the inventory search of personal effects of an arrestee at a police station was also permissible under that Amendment. The Supreme Court of Colorado felt, however, that our decisions in *Arkansas v. Sanders*, 442 U.S. 753 (1979), and *United States v. Chadwick*, 433 U.S. 1 (1977), holding searches of closed trunks and suitcases to violate the Fourth Amendment, meant that *Opperman* and *Lafayette* did not govern this case. [We] granted certiorari.

[I]nventory searches are now a well-defined exception to the warrant requirement of the Fourth Amendment. [An] inventory search may be "reasonable" under the Fourth Amendment even though it is not conducted pursuant to a warrant based upon probable cause. In *Opperman*, this Court assessed the reasonableness of an inventory search of the glove compartment in an abandoned automobile impounded by the police. We found that inventory procedures serve to protect an owner's property while it is in the custody of the police, to insure against claims of lost, stolen, or vandalized property, and to guard the police from danger. In light of these strong governmental interests and the diminished expectation of privacy in an automobile, we upheld the search. In reaching this decision, we observed that our cases accorded deference to police caretaking procedures designed to secure and protect vehicles and their contents within police custody.

[In] the present case, as in *Opperman* and *Lafayette*, there was no showing that the police, who were following standardized procedures, acted in bad faith or for the sole purpose of investigation. In addition, the governmental interests justifying the inventory searches in *Opperman* and *Lafayette* are nearly the same as those which obtain here. In each case, the police were potentially responsible for the property taken into their custody. By securing the property, the police protected the property from unauthorized interference. Knowledge of the precise nature of the property helped guard against claims of theft, vandalism, or negligence. Such knowledge also helped to avert any danger to police or others that may have been posed by the property.

The Supreme Court of Colorado opined that *Lafayette* was not controlling here because there was no danger of introducing contraband or weapons into a jail facility. Our opinion in *Lafayette*, however, did not suggest that the station-house setting of the inventory search was critical to our holding in that case. Both in the present case and in *Lafayette*, the common governmental interests described above were served by the inventory searches.

The Supreme Court of Colorado also expressed the view that the search in this case was unreasonable because Bertine's van was towed to a secure, lighted facility and because Bertine himself could have been offered the opportunity to make other arrangements for the safekeeping

of his property. But the security of the storage facility does not completely eliminate the need for inventorying; the police may still wish to
protect themselves or the owners of the lot against false claims of theft
or dangerous instrumentalities. And while giving Bertine an opportunity
to make alternative arrangements would undoubtedly have been possible, we said in *Lafayette*: "[T]he real question is not what 'could have
been achieved,' but whether the Fourth Amendment requires such
[steps]. The reasonableness of any particular governmental activity does
not necessarily or invariably turn on the existence of alternative 'less
intrusive' means." *Lafayette*, 462 U.S., at 647. We conclude that here, as
in *Lafayette*, reasonable police regulations relating to inventory procedures administered in good faith satisfy the Fourth Amendment, even
though courts might as a matter of hindsight be able to devise equally
reasonable rules requiring a different procedure.[20]

The Supreme Court of Colorado also thought it necessary to require
that police, before inventorying a container, weigh the strength of the
individual's privacy interest in the container against the possibility that
the container might serve as a repository for dangerous or valuable
items. We think that such a requirement is contrary to our decisions in
Opperman and *Lafayette* [and *Ross*]: "When a legitimate search is under
way, and when its purpose and its limits have been precisely defined,
nice distinctions between closets, drawers, and containers, in the case of
a home, or between glove compartments, upholstered seats, trunks, and
wrapped packages, in the case of a vehicle, must give way to the interest
in the prompt and efficient completion of the task at hand." *United
States v. Ross*, 456 U.S., at 821.

We reaffirm these principles here: " '[a] single familiar standard is
essential to guide police officers, who have only limited time and expertise to reflect on and balance the social and individual interests involved
in the specific circumstances they confront.' " *Lafayette, supra*, 462 U.S.,
at 648 (*quoting New York v. Belton*, 453 U.S. 454, 458 (1981)).

Bertine finally argues that the inventory search of his van was
unconstitutional because departmental regulations gave the police officers discretion to choose between impounding his van and parking and
locking it in a public parking place. [Nothing] in *Opperman* or *Lafayette*
prohibits the exercise of police discretion so long as that discretion is
exercised according to standard criteria and on the basis of something
other than suspicion of evidence of criminal activity. Here, the discretion
afforded the Boulder police was exercised in light of standardized criteria, related to the feasibility and appropriateness of parking and locking
a vehicle rather than impounding it.[21] There was no showing that the

---

20. [T]he trial court found that the Police Department's procedures mandated the
opening of closed containers and the listing
of their contents. Our decisions have always
adhered to the requirement that inventories
be conducted according to standardized criteria. * * *

21. [Boulder] Police Department procedures [establish] several conditions that
must be met before an officer may pursue
the park-and-lock alternative. For example,
police may not park and lock the vehicle
where there is reasonable risk of damage or
vandalism to the vehicle or where the ap-

police chose to impound Bertine's van in order to investigate suspected criminal activity.

While both *Opperman* and *Lafayette* are distinguishable from the present case on their facts, we think that the principles enunciated in those cases govern the present one. The judgment of the Supreme Court of Colorado is therefore

Reversed.

JUSTICE BLACKMUN, with whom JUSTICE POWELL and JUSTICE O'CONNOR join, concurring.

[A]bsence of discretion ensures that inventory searches will not be used as a purposeful and general means of discovering evidence of crime. Thus, it is permissible for police officers to open closed containers in an inventory search only if they are following standard police procedures that mandate the opening of such containers in every impounded vehicle. [T]he Police Department's standard procedures did mandate the opening of closed containers and the listing of their contents.

JUSTICE MARSHALL, with whom JUSTICE BRENNAN joins, dissenting.

[N]o standardized criteria limit a Boulder police officer's discretion. According to a departmental directive, after placing a driver under arrest, an officer has three options for disposing of the vehicle. First, he can allow a third party to take custody. Second, the officer or the driver (depending on the nature of the arrest) may take the car to the nearest public parking facility, lock it, and take the keys. Finally, the officer can do what was done in this case: impound the vehicle, and search and inventory its contents, including closed containers.

Under the first option, the police have no occasion to search the automobile. Under the "park and lock" option, "[c]losed containers that give no indication of containing either valuables or a weapon may not be opened and the contents searched (*i.e.*, inventoried)." Only if the police choose the third option are they entitled to search closed containers in the vehicle. Where the vehicle is not itself evidence of a crime, as in this case, the police apparently have totally unbridled discretion as to which procedure to use. Consistent with this conclusion, Officer Reichenbach testified that such decisions were left to the discretion of the officer on the scene.

Once a Boulder police officer has made this initial completely discretionary decision to impound a vehicle, he is given little guidance as to which areas to search and what sort of items to inventory. The arresting officer, Officer Toporek, testified at the suppression hearing as to what items would be inventoried: "That would I think be very individualistic as far as what an officer may or may not go into." In application, these so-called procedures left the breadth of the "inventory" to the whim of the individual officer. * * *

proval of the arrestee cannot be obtained. Not only do such conditions circumscribe the discretion of individual officers, but they also protect the vehicle and its contents and minimize claims of property loss.

Inventory searches are not subject to the warrant requirement because they are conducted by the government as part of a "community caretaking" function, "totally divorced from the detection, investigation, or acquisition of evidence relating to the violation of a criminal statute." *Cady v. Dombrowski*, 413 U.S., at 441. Standardized procedures are necessary to ensure that this narrow exception is not improperly used to justify, after the fact, a warrantless investigative foray. Accordingly, to invalidate a search that is conducted without established procedures, it is not necessary to establish that the police actually acted in bad faith, or that the inventory was in fact a "pretext." [Boulder's] discretionary scheme [is] unreasonable because of the " 'grave danger' of abuse of discretion."

[The] Court greatly overstates the justifications for the inventory exception to the Fourth Amendment. [*Opperman*] relied on three governmental interests to justify the inventory search of an unlocked glove compartment in an automobile impounded for overtime parking: (I) "the protection of the owner's property while it remains in police custody"; (ii) "the protection of the police against claims or disputes over lost or stolen property"; and (iii) "the protection of the police from potential danger." The majority finds that "nearly the same" interests obtain in this case. [O]nly the first of these interests is actually served by an automobile inventory search.

The protection-against-claims interest did not justify the inventory search either in *Opperman* or in this case. As the majority apparently concedes, the use of secure impoundment facilities effectively eliminates this concern.[22] As to false claims, "inventories are [not] a completely effective means of discouraging false claims, since there remains the possibility of accompanying such claims with an assertion that an item was stolen prior to the inventory or was intentionally omitted from the police records."

Officer Reichenbach's inventory in this case would not have protected the police against claims lodged by respondent, false or otherwise. Indeed, the trial court's characterization of the inventory as "slip-shod" is the height of understatement. For example, Officer Reichenbach failed to list $150 in cash found in respondent's wallet or the contents of a sealed envelope marked "rent," $210 * * *. His reports make no reference to other items of value, including respondent's credit cards, and a converter, a hydraulic jack, and a set of tire chains, worth a total of $125. The $700 in cash found in respondent's backpack, along with the contraband, appeared only on a property form completed later by someone other than Officer Reichenbach. * * *

The third interest—protecting the police from potential danger— failed to receive the endorsement of a majority of the Court in *Opperman*. [T]here is nothing in the nature of the offense for which respon-

---

22. [R]espondent's vehicle was taken to a lighted, private storage lot with a locked 6–foot fence. The lot was patrolled by private security officers and police, and nothing had ever been stolen from a vehicle in the lot.

dent was arrested that suggests he was likely to be carrying weapons, explosives, or other dangerous items. [Moreover,] opening closed containers to inventory the contents can only increase the risk. "[No] sane individual inspects for booby-traps by simply opening the container."

Thus, only the government's interest in protecting the owner's property actually justifies an inventory search of an impounded vehicle. [I] fail to see how preservation can even be asserted as a justification for the search in this case. [T]he owner was "present to make other arrangements for the safekeeping of his belongings," yet the police made no attempt to ascertain whether in fact he wanted them to "safeguard" his property. [S]ince respondent was charged with a traffic offense, he was unlikely to remain in custody for more than a few hours. He might well have been willing to leave his valuables unattended in the locked van for such a short period of time.

[T]he Court completely ignores respondent's expectation of privacy in his backpack. Whatever his expectation of privacy in his automobile generally, our prior decisions clearly establish that he retained a reasonable expectation of privacy in the backpack and its contents. Indeed, the Boulder police officer who conducted the inventory acknowledged that backpacks commonly serve as repositories for personal effects. Thus, even if the governmental interests in this case were the same as those in *Opperman*, they would nonetheless be outweighed by respondent's comparatively greater expectation of privacy in his luggage.

Notes

1. *Departmental Policies.* In *Florida v. Wells*, 495 U.S. 1 (1990), Wells was arrested for driving under the influence and his car was impounded. An inventory search at the impoundment facility revealed two marijuana cigarettes. It also turned up a locked suitcase which was found to contain a considerable quantity of marijuana. The record contained no evidence of any Highway Patrol policy on the opening of closed containers during inventory searches. The Court upheld the Florida Supreme Court's decision to exclude the evidence:

> [A]n inventory search must not be a ruse for a general rummaging in order to discover incriminating evidence. [T]here is no reason to insist that [inventory searches] be conducted in a totally mechanical "all or nothing" fashion. [A] police officer may be allowed [latitude] to determine whether a particular container should or should not be opened in light of the nature of the search and characteristics of the container itself. [W]hile policies of opening all containers or of opening no containers are unquestionably permissible, it would be equally permissible [to] allow the opening of closed containers whose contents officers [are] unable to ascertain from examining the containers' exteriors. [The] Florida Highway Patrol had no policy whatever with respect to the opening of closed containers encountered during an inventory search. [A]bsent such a policy, the instant search was not sufficiently regulated to satisfy the Fourth Amendment. * * *

2. *Requirements for Impoundment.* In order for an inventory search to be legal, the vehicle must have been legally impounded. Rules vary regarding the circumstances under which an impoundment is permitted. In *Cardwell v. Commonwealth*, 639 S.W.2d 549 (Ky.App.1982), defendant burglarized a home and stole guns and knives. Fleeing the scene, when defendant was involved in an automobile accident and taken to a hospital, his car was left by the side of the road. Although defendant told the police that his father would retrieve the car, the officer towed the vehicle since it protruded onto the road and constituted a hazard. Because the trunk's lock was broken, the officer searched the trunk to remove valuables and found two shotguns and a rifle marked with the name of the burglary victim. The officer then went to the victim's house where he found evidence of a break-in. When the officer returned to the car, he found one of the burglary victim's knives. Cardwell was arrested at the hospital where he later confessed to the crimes. The Court concluded that the impoundment was proper:

> [The] vehicle was a safety hazard and had to be removed from the scene as soon as possible because of its damaged condition, its close proximity to the roadway, and its location on a curve with short visibility. [T]hese circumstances causes other motorists to be distracted, to look and gawk out of concerns for rendering aid or curiosity. It impedes traffic flow and constitutes a hazard upon the highway. [The] arrangement whereby his father would come from Louisville would create several hours delay while the vehicle was abandoned and exposed to the public on the roadway. [The officer] acted properly by ordering the impoundment and removal by a local wrecker * * *. With the vehicle impounded and in a position to be removed from the scene, the trooper innocently discovered the fruits of the appellant's crimes. [Finding] the trunk lid loose, without a lock, the trooper did what we would expect a peace officer to do under like circumstances: to protect property as well as citizens. Keep in mind, the appellant was not present. He was on his way to the hospital by ambulance. * * *

In *Florida v. White*, 526 U.S. 559 (1999), the police had probable cause to believe that a vehicle contained contraband. They seized the vehicle and subjected it to an inventory search. The Court held that the police do not need a warrant to seize an automobile from a public place when they have probable cause to believe that it contains forfeitable contraband.

Problems

1. *Inventorying Suspicious Vehicles.* At 3:00 a.m., a police officer spots a heavily loaded car in a residential area. May the police officer pull the motorist over and inventory the contents of the car? Why? Why not?

2. *Probable Cause or Reasonable Suspicion?* Do the police need either probable cause or reasonable suspicion in order to conduct an inventory search?

3. *Are State Approaches Preferable?* Some state supreme courts restrict the availability of inventory searches under their state constitutions. *Wagner v. Commonwealth*, 581 S.W.2d 352 (Ky.1979), involved a rape that occurred in Wagner's car. Shortly after the rape, the police apprehended Wagner and

allowed him to lock and secure his car. At this time, the victim pointed to her scarves and a spot of blood on the seat which she said was her blood. The police took Wagner to police headquarters for questioning and impounded his car. After Wagner was formally arrested, the police conducted an "inventory" search of his car "looking for evidence." The Kentucky Supreme Court invalidated the impoundment and the inventory search:

[A] vehicle may be impounded without a warrant in only four situations:

1.   The owner or permissive user consents to the impoundment;

2.   The vehicle, if not removed, constitutes a danger to other persons or property or the public safety[23] and the owner or permissive user cannot reasonably arrange for alternate means of removal;

3.   The police have probable cause to believe both that the vehicle constitutes an instrumentality or fruit of a crime and that absent immediate impoundment the vehicle will be removed by a third party; or

4.   The police have probable cause to believe both that the vehicle contains evidence of a crime and that absent immediate impoundment the evidence will be lost or destroyed.

So long as the only potential danger that might ensue from non-impoundment is danger to the safety of the vehicle and its contents no public interest exists to justify impoundment of the vehicle without the consent of its owner or permissive user. Because the vehicle is legally in his custody the driver, even though in police custody, is competent to decide whether to park the vehicle in a "bad" neighborhood and risk damage through vandalism or allow the police to take custody. Only when the vehicle if not removed poses a danger to other persons, property or the public safety does there exist a public interest to justify impoundment if the owner or permissive user is unable to reasonably arrange for a third party to provide for the vehicle's removal.

[Mere] legal custody of an automobile by law enforcement officials does not automatically create a right to rummage about its interior. A routine police inventory of the contents of an impounded vehicle constitutes a substantial invasion of the zone of privacy of its owner or permissive user. It is an invasion additional to the intrusion upon his privacy interests occasioned by the impoundment itself. [S]uch an inventory is impermissible unless the owner or permissive user consents or substantial necessities grounded upon public safety justify the search.

If a vehicle is legally impounded and its owner or permissive user is present or otherwise known at the time the vehicle is seized no such need is ordinarily manifest. If the owner or permissive user does not consent to the routine inventory he will assume the risk that items obtained in the vehicle will be lost or stolen. The police in such a case merely lock up the vehicle and leave it in place until the owner or permissive user makes suitable arrangements for its removal. Concomitant with this right to prevent a routine inventory is the owner's or permissive user's right to have a representative present during any inventory that is authorized and his right to limit the inventory to only specific portions of the vehicle.

23. An illegally parked vehicle would constitute a danger to public safety under this exception to the warrant requirement and could be lawfully impounded.

If the police have probable cause[, they can] prevent the removal of the vehicle until a reasonable time has elapsed in which a warrant can be secured. Because the vehicle is in police custody there is no danger that any evidence it contains will be lost or stolen and hence no necessity to depart from the warrant requirement. If a warrant cannot be obtained no inventory can be undertaken unless the owner or permissive user consents. In this case the owner-driver of the seized vehicle was at police headquarters at the time of impoundment. Because neither a search warrant nor his consent was obtained prior [rummaging] through the interior of the car constituted an illegal search even though the car had been lawfully impounded. The evidence [will] be suppressed. * * *

Do you agree with the majority or with dissenting Justice Clayton who stated that "[I] see no reason why [the] Kentucky Constitution should be interpreted so as to impose a more stringent standard than the Fourth Amendment of the Federal Constitution"?

4. *Departmental Policies.* Ford was arrested and jailed for driving on a suspended driver's license. Since Ford's vehicle was obstructing traffic, the police officer called a tow truck to remove it. In conformity with Charleston Police Department "policy," Officer Sisson conducted an inventory search of the vehicle before releasing it to the custody of the tow truck driver. This search yielded a sawed-off shotgun, with a barrel length of 9 ½ inches and an overall length of 17 ½ inches. Subsequent investigation revealed that this weapon was not registered, and Ford was charged with violating the National Firearms Act. Ford challenges the inventory search on the basis that it was "a guise to justify a criminal investigatory search." Ford points to the fact that the Department had no written policies regarding inventory searches, but rather only "customary" policies followed in doing such searches. Must a departmental policy be in writing to satisfy *Bertine*? On behalf of Ford, how can you argue that the policy must be in writing? How might the state respond? *See United States v. Ford*, 986 F.2d 57 (4th Cir.1993), and *Clark v. Commonwealth*, 868 S.W.2d 101 (Ky.App.1993).

5. *Permissible Impoundment?* As Boyd exited his Camaro, which was parked on the street in front of his house, he was arrested and charged with kidnaping. The Camaro was impounded and driven to the city impoundment lot at the police station. Shortly after the arrest, Boyd stated that the clothes he wore while committing the crime could be found in the Camaro. Four days after the arrest, the police inventoried the Camaro. The department did not have a standard practice of inventorying impounded vehicles, and it had not adopted an inventory procedure. The officer who conducted the search testified that he did not "know where in the city's policy regarding inventory procedures the criteria for conducting inventories was located. He did not know where the list compiled as the result of the inventory was located, and no such list was introduced at trial." Can this search be upheld as an inventory search? *See Ex parte Boyd*, 542 So.2d 1276 (Ala. 1989).

6. *More on Impoundment.* A drug store was robbed of money and restricted drugs. The next morning, two police officers saw an automobile make a quick turn into an intersection and travel past them in the opposite direction. The officers followed the car which sped up and disappeared. Shortly thereafter the officers saw Helm walking on the sidewalk and

stopped him. After learning Helm's name, the officers asked him about the location of the car that he had been driving. Helm replied, "What car?" When the police ran a computer check and determined that there was an outstanding robbery warrant for Helm's arrest, they arrested him and took him to jail where a search revealed a single car key. Afterwards, the officers returned to the area and found a 1978 silver Monte Carlo with a warm motor less than a block from the place of arrest. The key operated the ignition. Clothing and paraphernalia were observed lying in the back seat. The officers stated that they towed the vehicle for "safekeeping" based on police policy, as well as because they had no way to contact the owner and the vehicle was in a high crime area. The officers searched the trunk, which did not contain a lock, and found a paper bag containing money and bottles of restricted drugs from the recently robbed drug store. Was the vehicle properly impounded? *See Helm v. Commonwealth*, 813 S.W.2d 816 (1991).

5. *Consent*

The consent exception is not really an "exception" to the warrant requirement. Any constitutional right can be waived, and citizens can waive their Fourth Amendment right to be free from governmental searches and seizures. The courts have struggled to determine what constitutes "consent."

SCHNECKLOTH v. BUSTAMONTE

412 U.S. 218 (1973).

MR. JUSTICE STEWART delivered the opinion of the Court.

[While] on routine patrol in Sunnyvale, California, at approximately 2:40 in the morning, Police Officer James Rand stopped an automobile when he observed that one headlight and its license plate light were burned out. Six men were in the vehicle. Joe Alcala and the respondent, Robert Bustamonte, were in the front seat with Joe Gonzales, the driver. Three older men were seated in the rear. [When] Gonzales could not produce a driver's license, Officer Rand asked if any of the other five had any evidence of identification. Only Alcala produced a license, and he explained that the car was his brother's. After the six occupants had stepped out of the car at the officer's request and after two additional policemen had arrived, Officer Rand asked Alcala if he could search the car. Alcala replied, "Sure, go ahead." Prior to the search no one was threatened with arrest and, according to Officer Rand's uncontradicted testimony, it "was all very congenial at this time." Gonzales testified that Alcala actually helped in the search of the car, by opening the trunk and glove compartment. In Gonzales' words: "[T]he police officer asked Joe (Alcala), he goes, 'Does the trunk open?' And Joe said, 'Yes.' He went to the car and got the keys and opened up the trunk." Wadded up under the left rear seat, the police officers found three checks that had previously been stolen from a car wash.

The trial judge denied the motion to suppress, and the checks in question were admitted in evidence at Bustamonte's trial. [H]e was convicted.

II

[A] search authorized by consent is wholly valid [but the State] has the burden of proving that the consent was, in fact, freely and voluntarily given. *Bumper v. North Carolina*, 391 U.S. 543, 548. The precise question in this case, then, is what must the prosecution prove to demonstrate that a consent was "voluntarily" given. * * *

[The] most extensive judicial exposition of the meaning of "voluntariness" has been developed in those cases in which the Court has had to determine the "voluntariness" of a defendant's confession for purposes of the Fourteenth Amendment. [It] is to that body of case law to which we turn for initial guidance on the meaning of "voluntariness" in the present context.

[The] significant fact about all of these decisions is that none of them turned on the presence or absence of a single controlling criterion; each reflected a careful scrutiny of all the surrounding circumstances. In none of them did the Court rule that the Due Process Clause required the prosecution to prove as part of its initial burden that the defendant knew he had a right to refuse to answer the questions that were put. While the state of the accused's mind, and the failure of the police to advise the accused of his rights, were certainly factors to be evaluated in assessing the "voluntariness" of an accused's responses, they were not in and of themselves determinative.

Similar considerations lead us to agree with the courts of California that the question whether a consent to a search was in fact "voluntary" or was the product of duress or coercion, express or implied, is a question of fact to be determined from the totality of all the circumstances. While knowledge of the right to refuse consent is one factor to be taken into account, the government need not establish such knowledge as the *sine qua non* of an effective consent. As with police questioning, two competing concerns must be accommodated in determining the meaning of a "voluntary" consent—the legitimate need for such searches and the equally important requirement of assuring the absence of coercion.

In situations where the police have some evidence of illicit activity, but lack probable cause to arrest or search, a search authorized by a valid consent may be the only means of obtaining important and reliable evidence. In the present case[,] while the police had reason to stop the car for traffic violations, the State does not contend that there was probable cause to search the vehicle or that the search was incident to a valid arrest of any of the occupants. Yet, the search yielded tangible evidence that served as a basis for a prosecution, and provided some assurance that others, wholly innocent of the crime, were not mistakenly brought to trial. And in those cases where there is probable cause to arrest or search, but where the police lack a warrant, a consent search may still be valuable. If the search is conducted and proves fruitless, that in itself may convince the police that an arrest with its possible stigma and embarrassment is unnecessary, or that a far more extensive search pursuant to a warrant is not justified. In short, a search pursuant to consent may result in considerably less inconvenience for the subject of the search, and, properly conducted, is a constitutionally permissible and wholly legitimate aspect of effective police activity.

But the Fourth and Fourteenth Amendments require that a consent not be coerced, by explicit or implicit means, by implied threat or covert force. For, no matter how subtly the coercion was applied, the resulting "consent" would be no more than a pretext for the unjustified police intrusion against which the Fourth Amendment is directed. * * *

The problem of reconciling the recognized legitimacy of consent searches with the requirement that they be free from any aspect of official coercion cannot be resolved by any infallible touchstone. To approve such searches without the most careful scrutiny would sanction the possibility of official coercion; to place artificial restrictions upon such searches would jeopardize their basic validity. Just as was true with confessions, the requirement of a "voluntary" consent reflects a fair accommodation of the constitutional requirements involved. In examining all the surrounding circumstances to determine if in fact the consent to search was coerced, account must be taken of subtly coercive police questions, as well as the possibly vulnerable subjective state of the person who consents. Those searches that are the product of police coercion can thus be filtered out without undermining the continuing validity of consent searches. In sum, there is no reason for us to depart in the area of consent searches, from the traditional definition of "voluntariness."

The approach of the Court of Appeals [finds] no support in any of our decisions that have attempted to define the meaning of "voluntariness." Its ruling, that the State must affirmatively prove that the subject of the search knew that he had a right to refuse consent, would, in practice, create serious doubt whether consent searches could continue to be conducted. There might be rare cases where it could be proved [that] a person in fact affirmatively knew of his right to refuse—such as a case where he announced to the police that if he didn't sign the consent form, "you [police] are going to get a search warrant;" or a case where by prior experience and training a person had clearly and convincingly demonstrated such knowledge. But more commonly where there was no evidence of any coercion, explicit or implicit, the prosecution would nevertheless be unable to demonstrate that the subject of the search in fact had known of his right to refuse consent.

The very object of the inquiry—the nature of a person's subjective understanding—underlines the difficulty of the prosecution's burden under the rule applied by the Court of Appeals in this case. Any defendant who was the subject of a search authorized solely by his consent could effectively frustrate the introduction into evidence of the fruits of that search by simply failing to testify that he in fact knew he could refuse to consent. And the near impossibility of meeting this prosecutorial burden suggests why this Court has never accepted any such litmus-paper test of voluntariness. * * *

One alternative that would go far toward proving that the subject of a search did know he had a right to refuse consent would be to advise him of that right before eliciting his consent. That, [is] a suggestion that has been almost universally repudiated by both federal and state courts, and, we think, rightly so. For it would be thoroughly impractical to impose on the normal consent search the detailed requirements of an effective warning. Consent searches are part of the standard investigatory techniques of law enforcement agencies. They normally occur on the highway, or in a person's home or office, and under informal and unstructured conditions. The circumstances that prompt the initial request to search may develop quickly or be a logical extension of investigative police questioning. The police may seek to investigate further suspicious circumstances or to follow up leads developed in questioning persons at the scene of a crime. These situations are a far cry from the structured atmosphere of a trial where, assisted by counsel if he chooses, a defendant is informed of his trial rights. And, while surely a closer question, these situations are still immeasurably, far removed from "custodial interrogation" where, in *Miranda v. Arizona, supra*, we found that the Constitution required certain now familiar warnings as a prerequisite to police interrogation. * * *

Consequently, we cannot accept the position [that] proof of knowledge of the right to refuse consent is a necessary prerequisite to demonstrating a "voluntary" consent. Rather it is only by analyzing all the circumstances of an individual consent that it can be ascertained whether in fact it was voluntary or coerced. It is this careful sifting of the unique facts and circumstances of each case that is evidenced in our prior decisions involving consent searches.

[It] is argued that to establish [a] "waiver" the State must demonstrate "an intentional relinquishment or abandonment of a known right or privilege." [Our] cases do not reflect an uncritical demand for a knowing and intelligent waiver in every situation where a person has failed to invoke a constitutional protection. Almost without exception, the requirement of a knowing and intelligent waiver has been applied only to those rights which the Constitution guarantees to a criminal defendant in order to preserve a fair trial. Hence, [the] standard of a knowing and intelligent waiver has most often been applied to test the validity of a waiver of counsel, either at trial, or upon a guilty plea. And the Court has also applied the [criteria] to assess the effectiveness of a waiver of other trial rights such as the right to confrontation, to a jury trial, and to a speedy trial, and the right to be free from twice being placed in jeopardy. Guilty pleas have been carefully scrutinized to determine whether the accused knew and understood all the rights to which he would be entitled at trial, and that he had intentionally chosen to forgo them. And the Court has evaluated the knowing and intelligent nature of the waiver of trial rights in trial-type situations, such as the waiver of the privilege against compulsory self-incrimination before an administrative agency or a congressional committee, or the waiver of counsel in a juvenile proceeding.

The guarantees afforded a criminal defendant at trial also protect him at certain stages before the actual trial, and any alleged waiver must meet the strict standard of an intentional relinquishment of a "known" right. But the "trial" guarantees that have been applied to the "pretrial" stage of the criminal process are similarly designed to protect the fairness of the trial itself.

[There] is a vast difference between those rights that protect a fair criminal trial and the rights guaranteed under the Fourth Amendment. Nothing, either in the purposes behind requiring a "knowing" and "intelligent" waiver of trial rights, or in the practical application of such a requirement suggests that it ought to be extended to the constitutional guarantee against unreasonable searches and seizures.

A strict standard of waiver has been applied to those rights guaranteed to a criminal defendant to insure that he will be accorded the greatest possible opportunity to utilize every facet of the constitutional model of a fair criminal trial. Any trial conducted in derogation of that model leaves open the possibility that the trial reached an unfair result precisely because all the protections specified in the Constitution were not provided. A prime example is the right to counsel. For without that right, a wholly innocent accused faces the real and substantial danger that simply because of his lack of legal expertise he may be convicted. [The] Constitution requires that every effort be made to see to it that a defendant in a criminal case has not unknowingly relinquished the basic protections that the Framers thought indispensable to a fair trial.

The protections of the Fourth Amendment are of a wholly different order, and have nothing whatever to do with promoting the fair ascertainment of truth at a criminal trial. Rather, as Mr. Justice Frankfurter's opinion for the Court put it in *Wolf v. Colorado*, 338 U.S. 25, 27, the Fourth Amendment protects the "security of one's privacy against arbitrary intrusion by the [police]." [Nor] can it even be said that a search, as opposed to an eventual trial, is somehow "unfair" if a person consents to a search. While the Fourth and Fourteenth Amendments limit the circumstances under which the police can conduct a search, there is nothing constitutionally suspect in a person's voluntarily allowing a search. The actual conduct of the search may be precisely the same as if the police had obtained a warrant. And, unlike those constitutional guarantees that protect a defendant at trial, it cannot be said every reasonable presumption ought to be indulged against voluntary relinquishment. [T]he community has a real interest in encouraging consent, for the resulting search may yield necessary evidence for the solution and prosecution of crime, evidence that may insure that a wholly innocent person is not wrongly charged with a criminal offense.

[I]t would be next to impossible to apply to a consent search the standard of "an intentional relinquishment or abandonment of a known right or privilege." [T]here must be examination into the knowing and understanding nature of the waiver, an examination that was designed for a trial judge in the structured atmosphere of a courtroom. [It] would be unrealistic to expect that in the informal, unstructured context of a consent search, a policeman, upon pain of tainting the evidence obtained, could make the detailed type of examination demanded[.] And, if for this reason a diluted form of "waiver" were found acceptable, that would itself be ample recognition of the fact that there is no universal standard that must be applied in every situation where a person forgoes a constitutional right.[24]

[In] short, there is nothing in the purposes or application of the waiver requirements of *Johnson v. Zerbst* that justifies, much less compels, the easy equation of a knowing waiver with a consent search. To make such an equation is to generalize from the broad rhetoric of some of our decisions, and to ignore the substance of the differing constitutional guarantees. We decline to follow what one judicial scholar has termed "the domino method of constitutional adjudication [wherein] every explanatory statement in a previous opinion is made the basis for extension to a wholly different situation."

Much of what has already been said disposes of the argument that the Court's decision in the *Miranda* case requires the conclusion that knowledge of a right to refuse is an indispensable element of a valid consent. * * * In *Miranda* the Court found that the techniques of police questioning and the nature of custodial surroundings produce an inherently coercive situation. The Court concluded that "[u]nless adequate protective devices are employed to dispel the compulsion inherent in custodial surroundings, no statement obtained from the defendant can truly be the product of his free choice." And at another point the Court noted that "without proper safeguards the process of in-custody interrogation of persons suspected or accused of crime contains inherently compelling pressures which work to undermine the individual's will to resist and to compel him to speak where he would not otherwise do so freely."

In this case, there is no evidence of any inherently coercive tactics—either from the nature of the police questioning or the environment in which it took place. Indeed, since consent searches will normally occur on a person's own familiar territory, the specter of incommunicado police interrogation in some remote station house is simply inapposite. There is no reason to believe, under circumstances such as are present here, that the response to a policeman's question is presumptively coerced; and there is, therefore, no reason to reject the traditional test for determining the voluntariness of a person's response. *Miranda*, of course, did not

---

24. It seems clear that even a limited view of the demands of "an intentional relinquishment or abandonment of a known right or privilege" standard would inevitably lead to a requirement of detailed warnings before any consent search—a requirement all but universally rejected to date. As the Court stated in *Miranda* with respect to the privilege against compulsory self-incrimination: "[W]e will not pause to inquire in individual cases whether the defendant was aware of his rights without a warning being given. Assessments of the knowledge the defendant possessed, based on information as to his age, education, intelligence, or prior contact with authorities, can never be more than speculation; a warning is a clear-cut fact." *Miranda v. Arizona*, 384 U.S., at 468–469.

reach investigative questioning of a person not in custody, which is most directly analogous to the situation of a consent search, and it assuredly did not indicate that such questioning ought to be deemed inherently coercive.

It is also argued that the failure to require the Government to establish knowledge as a prerequisite to a valid consent, will relegate the Fourth Amendment to the special province of "the sophisticated [versus the] knowledgeable and the privileged." We cannot agree. The traditional definition of voluntariness we accept today has always taken into account evidence of minimal schooling, low intelligence, and the lack of any effective warnings to a person of his rights; and the voluntariness of any statement taken under those conditions has been carefully scrutinized to determine whether it was in fact voluntarily given.

Our decision today is a narrow one. We hold only that when the subject of a search is not in custody and the State attempts to justify a search on the basis of his consent, the Fourth and Fourteenth Amendments require that it demonstrate that the consent was in fact voluntarily given, and not the result of duress or coercion, express or implied. Voluntariness is a question of fact to be determined from all the circumstances, and while the subject's knowledge of a right to refuse is a factor to be taken into account, the prosecution is not required to demonstrate such knowledge as a prerequisite to establishing a voluntary consent.

[The] judgment must be *reversed*.

Mr. Justice Brennan, dissenting.

[It] wholly escapes me how our citizens can meaningfully be said to have waived something as precious as a constitutional guarantee without ever being aware of its existence. [T]he Court's conclusion is supported neither by "linguistics," nor by "epistemology," nor [by] "common sense." I respectfully dissent.

Mr. Justice Marshall, dissenting.

[This] Court has always scrutinized with great care claims that a person has foregone the opportunity to assert constitutional rights. I see no reason to give the claim that a person consented to a search any less rigorous scrutiny. * * *

[C]onsent searches are permitted, not because such an exception to the requirements of probable cause and warrant is essential to proper law enforcement, but because we permit our citizens to choose whether or not they wish to exercise their constitutional rights. Our prior decisions simply do not support the view that a meaningful choice has been made solely because no coercion was brought to bear on the subject.

[I] am at a loss to understand why consent "cannot be taken literally to mean a 'knowing' choice." In fact, I have difficulty in comprehending how a decision made without knowledge of available alternatives can be treated as a choice at all.

If consent to search means that a person has chosen to forgo his right to exclude the police from the place they seek to search, it follows that his consent cannot be considered a meaningful choice unless he knew that he could in fact exclude the police. [I] can think of no other situation in which we would say that a person agreed to some course of action if he convinced us that he did not know that there was some other course he might have pursued. I would therefore hold, at a minimum, that the prosecution may not rely on a purported consent to search if the subject of the search did not know that he could refuse to give consent. * * *

If one accepts this view, the question then is a simple one: must the Government show that the subject knew of his rights, or must the subject show that he lacked such knowledge? I think that any fair allocation of the burden would require that it be placed on the prosecution. * * *

If the burden is placed on the defendant, all the subject can do is to testify that he did not know of his rights. And I doubt that many trial judges will find for the defendant simply on the basis of that testimony. Precisely because the evidence is very hard to come by, courts have traditionally been reluctant to require a party to prove negatives such as the lack of knowledge.

In contrast, there are several ways by which the subject's knowledge of his rights may be shown. The subject may affirmatively demonstrate such knowledge by his responses at the time the search took place. Where [the] person giving consent is someone other than the defendant, the prosecution may require him to testify under oath. Denials of knowledge may be disproved by establishing that the subject had, in the recent past, demonstrated his knowledge of his rights, for example, by refusing entry when it was requested by the police. The prior experience or training of the subject might in some cases support an inference that he knew of his right to exclude the police.

The burden on the prosecutor would disappear, of course, if the police, at the time they requested consent to search, also told the subject that he had a right to refuse consent and that his decision to refuse would be respected. [T]here is nothing impractical about this method of satisfying the prosecution's burden of proof. It must be emphasized that the decision about informing the subject of his rights would lie with the officers seeking consent. If they believed that providing such information would impede their investigation, they might simply ask for consent, taking the risk that at some later date the prosecutor would be unable to prove that the subject knew of his rights or that some other basis for the search existed.

The Court contends that if an officer paused to inform the subject of his rights, the informality of the exchange would be destroyed. I doubt that a simple statement by an officer of an individual's right to refuse consent would do much to alter the informality of the exchange, except to alert the subject to a fact that he surely is entitled to know. [F]or many years the agents of the Federal Bureau of Investigation have routinely informed subjects of their right to refuse consent when they request consent to search. The [information] can be given without disrupting the casual flow of events. [N]othing disastrous would happen if the police, before requesting consent, informed the subject that he had a right to refuse consent and that his refusal would be respected.

[W]hen the Court speaks of practicality, what it really is talking of is the continued ability of the police to capitalize on the ignorance of citizens so as to accomplish by subterfuge what they could not achieve by relying only on the knowing relinquishment of constitutional rights. * * *

[I believe that] "[u]nder many circumstances a reasonable person might read an officer's 'May I' as the courteous expression of a demand backed by force of law." Consent is ordinarily given as acquiescence in an implicit claim of authority to search. Permitting searches in such circumstances, without any assurance at all that the subject of the search knew that, by his consent, he was relinquishing his constitutional rights, is something that I cannot believe is sanctioned by the Constitution. * * *

Notes

1. *The Duty to Advise.* In *Ohio v. Robinette*, 519 U.S. 33 (1996), Robinette was lawfully stopped for speeding on an interstate highway and given a verbal warning. The officer then asked Robinette whether he was carrying contraband. When Robinette answered in the negative, the officer asked for (and obtained) permission to search Robinette's car. The search revealed a small amount of marijuana and a contraband pill. The Court held that the officer was not required to tell Robinette that he was "free to go" before asking for consent to search the vehicle: "The Fourth Amendment test for a valid consent to search is that the consent be voluntary, and 'voluntariness is a question of fact to be determined from all the circumstances.'" Justice Stevens dissented: "[W]hen the officer had completed his task of either arresting or reprimanding the driver of the speeding car, his continued detention of that person constituted an illegal seizure. [Because] Robinette's consent to the search was the product of an unlawful detention, 'the consent was tainted by the illegality and was ineffective to justify the search.'" In Justice Stevens' view, had the officer told Robinette that he was "free to go", this warning would have terminated the seizure and rendered the consent valid.

2. *The Scope of a Consent Search.* In *Florida v. Jimeno*, 500 U.S. 248 (1991), believing that respondent was carrying narcotics, a police officer asked for permission to search his car. Respondent consented stating that he had nothing to hide. The officer found a folded brown paper bag containing a kilogram of cocaine on the floorboard. The trial court held that the consent did not extend to the paper bag, and the Court reversed: "Respondent granted Officer Trujillo permission to search his car, and did not place any explicit limitation on the scope of the search. [I]t was objectively reasonable for the police to conclude that the general consent to search respondent's car

included consent to search containers within that car which might bear drugs [including] the paper bag lying on the car's floor." Justice Marshall dissented: "[A]n individual has a heightened expectation of privacy in the contents of a closed container. [I]t follows that an individual's consent to a search of the interior of his car cannot necessarily be understood as extending to containers in the car."

Problems

1. *Consent and Reasonable Suspicion.* Must the Police have a "reasonable suspicion of criminal activity," or for that matter "probable cause," before requesting consent to search?

2. *What Constitutes Consent?* After *Schneckloth,* when will consent be invalid? A narcotics detective received a tip from a known narcotics user that unknown persons were smoking opium in the Europe Hotel. At the hotel, the detective smelled a strong odor of burning opium emanating from Room #1. The officers knocked on the door and a voice inside asked who was there. "Lieutenant Belland," was the reply. There was a slight delay, some "shuffling or noise" in the room and then the defendant opened the door. The officer said, "I want to talk to you a little bit." She then, as he describes it, "stepped back acquiescently and admitted us." He said, "I want to talk to you about the opium smell in the room here." She denied that there was such a smell. Then he said, "I want you to consider yourself under arrest because we are going to search the room." The search turned up opium and a smoking apparatus, the latter being warm, apparently from recent use. Did defendant "consent" to the officers entry and search? Based on *Schneckloth,* how might defendant argue that she did not consent? How might the prosecution respond to that argument? How should the court rule? *See Johnson v. United States,* 333 U.S. 10 (1948).

3. *Police Misrepresentations & Consent.* Petitioner lived with his grandmother, a 66-year-old black widow, in a house located in a rural area at the end of an isolated road. Four white law enforcement officers went to this house and found the grandmother there with some young children. One of the officers stated that "I have a warrant to search your house." The grandmother responded, "Go ahead," and opened the door. In the kitchen the officers found a rifle that was later used as evidence against petitioner. Should it matter that the officers did not have a warrant? What arguments would you make on behalf of the prosecution? How might the State respond? What is the proper result? Would it matter whether the police had probable cause to obtain a warrant? *See Bumper v. State of North Carolina,* 391 U.S. 543 (1968).

4. *More on Misrepresentations & Consent.* In the prior problem, should it matter how the grandmother responded? Suppose that she had stated: a) "You don't need a warrant. I'd be happy to let you search"; b) "Well, if you have a warrant, I guess I'll have to let you search"; c) "I have no objection to you searching my house. I am willing to let you look in any room or drawer in my house that you desire." In which of these situations is there valid consent?

5. *The Nature of the Misrepresentation.* Suppose that an undercover narcotics agent, after misrepresenting himself as a drug purchaser, was invited into John Preston's home to make a purchase. After the deal was consummated, the agent arrested Preston. At Preston's trial, the prosecution seeks to admit the drugs that were purchased against him. Preston moves to suppress. Should the motion be granted? *See Lewis v. United States*, 385 U.S. 206 (1966).

6. *The Student Dorm Room.* A police officer arrested a student for carrying alcohol on a university campus (state law prohibited the possession of alcohol by individuals under 21), and asked for identification which the student was unable to produce. When the student asked for permission to return to his dormitory room to retrieve his identification, the officer accompanied the student to the room with the student's consent. While waiting at the door, the officer noticed seeds and a small pipe lying on a desk. From his training and experience, the officer believed that the seeds were marihuana and that the pipe was of a type used to smoke marihuana. The officer entered the room and examined the pipe and seeds, confirming that the seeds were marihuana and observing that the pipe smelled of marihuana. After *Mirandizing* the students and obtaining a waiver of their rights, the officer asked for permission to search the room. Both students consented. The search yielded more marihuana and a quantity of LSD, both controlled substances. Was the consent valid? If you were hired to represent respondent, how would you argue that it is invalid? How might the state respond? *See Washington v. Chrisman*, 455 U.S. 1 (1982).

7. *The Scope of Consent.* Police stopped defendant's vehicle because of "excessively tinted" windows. When the officer noticed fresh undercoating on the car, he asked for and obtained permission to search. When the officer pulled up some non-factory carpeting on the floor, and noticed a small cut or hole in the floorboard, the officer took a crowbar and pried open the gas tank where he found cocaine. Did defendant's consent justify the officer's use of the crowbar? Does it matter that the car was returned to defendant in a "materially different" condition with an effect on its "structural integrity?" Was the officer required to obtain additional permission before using the crowbar? *See People v. Gomez*, 5 N.Y.3d 416, 838 N.E.2d 1271, 805 N.Y.S.2d 24 (2005).

8. *The Burglar's Consent.* A burglar breaks into a home. While the burglar is in the house, the police knock at the door. The burglar, being rather bold, opens the door. The police, assuming that the burglar is the owner of the house (or, otherwise, he wouldn't have opened the door) tell the burglar that they would like to search the house and ask for permission to do so. The burglar responds that he doesn't object to the search, but that he is just leaving for an urgent appointment. The burglar (whom the police still assume is the owner of the house) agrees to the search provided that two conditions are met: the burglar is free to leave for his appointment, and the police agree to lock up the house as they leave. If the police search the home and find illegal narcotics, can the evidence be admitted against the owner? On behalf of the owner, what arguments might you make? How might the state respond to those arguments? Does the following case affect your analysis?

ILLINOIS v. RODRIGUEZ

497 U.S. 177 (1990).

JUSTICE SCALIA delivered the opinion of the Court.

[T]he present case presents [the following] issue: Whether a warrantless entry is valid when based upon the consent of a third party whom the police, at the time of the entry, reasonably believe to possess common authority over the premises, but who in fact does not do so.

I

Respondent Edward Rodriguez was arrested in his apartment by law enforcement officers and charged with possession of illegal drugs. The police gained entry to the apartment with the consent and assistance of Gail Fischer, who had lived there with respondent for several months. The relevant facts [are] as follows.

On July 26, 1985, police were summoned to the residence of Dorothy Jackson on South Wolcott in Chicago. They were met by Ms. Jackson's daughter, Gail Fischer, who showed signs of a severe beating. She told the officers that she had been assaulted by respondent Edward Rodriguez earlier that day in an apartment on South California. Fischer stated that Rodriguez was then asleep in the apartment, and she consented to travel there with the police in order to unlock the door with her key so that the officers could enter and arrest him. * * * Fischer several times referred to the apartment on South California as "our" apartment, and said that she had clothes and furniture there. It is unclear whether she indicated that she currently lived at the apartment, or only that she used to live there.

The police officers drove to the apartment * * * accompanied by Fischer. They did not obtain an arrest warrant for Rodriguez, nor did they seek a search warrant for the apartment. At the apartment, Fischer unlocked the door with her key and gave the officers permission to enter. They moved through the door into the living room, where they observed in plain view drug paraphernalia and containers filled with white powder that they believed (correctly) to be cocaine. They proceeded to the bedroom, where they found Rodriguez asleep and discovered additional containers of white powder in two open attache cases. The officers arrested Rodriguez and seized the drugs and related paraphernalia.

Rodriguez was charged with possession of a controlled substance with intent to deliver. [The trial court's decision to grant Rodriguez's motion to suppress was affirmed on appeal.]

The Fourth Amendment generally prohibits the warrantless entry of a person's home, whether to make an arrest or to search for specific objects. The prohibition does not apply, however, to situations in which voluntary consent has been obtained, either from the individual whose property is searched, or from a third party who possesses common authority over the premises. The State of Illinois contends that that exception applies in the present case.

As we stated in [*United States v. Matlock*, 415 U.S. 164 (1974),] "[c]ommon authority" rests "on mutual use of the property by persons generally having joint access or control for most [purposes]" The burden of establishing that common authority rests upon the State. On the basis of this record, it is clear that burden was not sustained. [A]lthough Fischer, with her two small children, had lived with Rodriguez[,] she had moved out [almost] a month before the search at issue here, and had gone to live with her mother. She took her and her children's clothing with her, though leaving behind some furniture and household effects. During the period after July 1 she sometimes spent the night at Rodriguez's apartment, but never invited her friends there, and never went there herself when he was not home. Her name was not on the lease nor did she contribute to the rent. She had a key to the apartment, which she said at trial she had taken without Rodriguez's knowledge (though she testified at the preliminary hearing that Rodriguez had given her the key). On these facts the State has not established [that] Fischer had "joint access or control for most purposes." * * *

[R]espondent asserts that permitting a reasonable belief of common authority to validate an entry would cause a defendant's Fourth Amendment rights to be "vicariously waived." We disagree. * * * What Rodriguez is assured [by] the Fourth Amendment [is] not that no government search of his house will occur unless he consents; but that no such search will occur that is "unreasonable." There are various elements, of course, that can make a search of a person's house "reasonable"—one of which is the consent of the person or his cotenant. The essence of respondent's argument is that we should impose upon this element a requirement that we have not imposed upon other elements that regularly compel government officers to exercise judgment regarding the facts: namely, the requirement that their judgment be not only responsible but correct.

The fundamental objective that alone validates all unconsented government searches is, of course, the seizure of persons who have committed or are about to commit crimes, or of evidence related to crimes. But "reasonableness," with respect to this necessary element, does not demand that the government be factually correct in its assessment that that is what a search will produce. Warrants need only be supported by "probable cause," which demands no more than a proper "assessment of probabilities in particular factual contexts. . . ." *Illinois v. Gates*, 462 U.S. 213, 232 (1983). If a magistrate, based upon seemingly reliable but factually inaccurate information, issues a warrant for the search of a house in which the sought-after felon is not present, has never been present, and was never likely to have been present, the owner of that house suffers one of the inconveniences we all expose ourselves to as the cost of living in a safe society; he does not suffer a violation of the Fourth Amendment.

Another element often, though not invariably, required in order to render an unconsented search "reasonable" is, of course, that the officer be authorized by a valid warrant. Here also we have not held that "reasonableness" precludes error with respect to those factual judgments that law enforcement officials are expected to make. [In this case, the search] unquestionably was [objectively understandable and reasonable]. The objective facts available to the officers at the time suggested no distinction between [the suspect's] apartment and the third-floor premises.

[It] is apparent that in order to satisfy the "reasonableness" requirement of the Fourth Amendment, what is generally demanded of the many factual determinations that must regularly be made by agents of the government—whether the magistrate issuing a warrant, the police officer executing a warrant, or the police officer conducting a search or seizure under one of the exceptions to the warrant requirement—is not that they always be correct, but that they always be reasonable. As we put it in *Brinegar v. United States*, 338 U.S. 160, 176 (1949): "Because many situations which confront officers in the course of executing their duties are more or less ambiguous, room must be allowed for some mistakes on their part. But the mistakes must be those of reasonable men, acting on facts leading sensibly to their conclusions of probability."

We see no reason to depart from this general rule with respect to facts bearing upon the authority to consent to a search. Whether the basis for such authority exists is the sort of recurring factual question to which law enforcement officials must be expected to apply their judgment; and all the Fourth Amendment requires is that they answer it reasonably. The Constitution is no more violated when officers enter without a warrant because they reasonably (though erroneously) believe that the person who has consented to their entry is a resident of the premises, than it is violated when they enter without a warrant because they reasonably (though erroneously) believe they are in pursuit of a violent felon who is about to escape.

[W]hat we hold today does not suggest that law enforcement officers may always accept a person's invitation to enter premises. Even when the invitation is accompanied by an explicit assertion that the person lives there, the surrounding circumstances could conceivably be such that a reasonable person would doubt its truth and not act upon it without further inquiry. As with other factual determinations bearing upon search and seizure, determination of consent to enter must "be judged against an objective standard: would the facts available to the officer at the [moment] 'warrant a man of reasonable caution in the belief' " that the consenting party had authority over the premises? If not, then warrantless entry without further inquiry is unlawful unless authority actually exists. But if so, the search is valid.

[T]he Appellate Court found it unnecessary to determine whether the officers reasonably believed that Fischer had the authority to consent. [Since] we find that ruling to be in error, we remand for consideration of that question. * * *

So ordered.

JUSTICE MARSHALL, with whom JUSTICE BRENNAN and JUSTICE STEVENS join, dissenting.

[A]n individual's decision to permit another "joint access [to] or control [over the property] for most purposes," limits that individual's reasonable expectation of privacy and to that extent limits his Fourth Amendment protections. If an individual has not so limited his expectation of privacy, the police may not dispense with the safeguards established by the Fourth Amendment.

[Because] the sole law enforcement purpose underlying third-party consent searches is avoiding the inconvenience of securing a warrant, a departure from the warrant requirement is not justified simply because an officer reasonably believes a third party has consented to a search of the defendant's home.

[T]hird-party consent searches are not based on an exigency and therefore serve no compelling social goal. Police officers, when faced with the choice of relying on consent by a third party or securing a warrant, should secure a warrant and must therefore accept the risk of error should they instead choose to rely on consent.

[T]hird-party consent limits a person's ability to challenge the reasonableness of the search only because that person voluntarily has relinquished some of his expectation of privacy by sharing access or control over his property with another person. [A] search conducted pursuant to an officer's reasonable but mistaken belief that a third party had authority to consent is thus on an entirely different constitutional footing from one based on the consent of a third party who in fact has such authority. Even if the officers reasonably believed that Fischer had authority to consent, she did not, and Rodriguez's expectation of privacy was therefore undiminished. Rodriguez accordingly can challenge the warrantless intrusion into his home as a violation of the Fourth Amendment. * * *

Problems

1. *Reconsidering the Burglar's Consent.* In light of the holding in *Rodriguez*, reconsider problem #6, *supra*, entitled "The Burglar's Consent."

2. *Supervisors and Employees.* May a supervisor consent to a search of an employee's desk? Appellee was arrested for suspicion of petty larceny. The police suspected that he stashed some of the loot in a drawer in his office. With the consent of appellee's supervisor, the police search the desk (which was used only by defendant and was not shared with anyone else). The police find the loot in the drawer. Is a supervisor entitled to consent to the search of an employee's desk under these circumstances? What arguments might be made on behalf of appellee? How might the government

respond to these arguments? *See United States v. Blok*, 188 F.2d 1019, 88 U.S.App.D.C. 326 (D.C.Cir.1951).

3. *More on Supervisor's and Employees.* May a supervisor consent to the search of an area allocated exclusively to an employee? At the U.S. Mint in D.C., there occurred a loud noise which sounded like an explosion. An investigation revealed that a firecracker or other explosive had gone off. In an effort to find other fireworks possessed by Mint employees, the Captain of the security guard decided to search all employee lockers. In Donato's locker, he found a bag of quarters. Donato was charged with embezzlement. Was the search illegal? Did the security guard, acting on behalf of Donato's employer, need Donato's consent to search the locker? Would it matter whether Mint regulations expressly stated that "No mint lockers in mint institutions shall be considered to be private lockers", that all employee lockers were subject to inspection, were regularly inspected by the Mint security guards for sanitation purposes, and that Mint security guards had a master key which opened all the employee lockers. *See United States v. Donato*, 269 F.Supp. 921 (E.D.Pa. 1967).

4. *The Metal Box.* Following a bank robbery, an FBI investigation led to petitioner's arrest. Previously, petitioner had given a small metal box to Mrs. Bradley stating that it contained "stocks and bonds and silver paper and important papers that he had saved up for his children" and asked her to keep it for them "so they wouldn't be tempted to spend it." Mrs. Bradley placed the box in a bedroom closet. No key to the box or instructions concerning it were given to the Bradleys who did not then know that it was locked. After the robbery, the Bradleys turned the locked box over to FBI agents who opened it and found $17,080 stolen in the robbery. Did Mrs. Bradley have the right to turn over the box and its contents to the police? Could she authorize them to open the box? *See United States v. Diggs*, 544 F.2d 116 (3d Cir.1976).

5. *The Pat–Down Search.* A police officer validly stops a motorist for turning without using his signals. The officer issues a warning and authorizes the motorist to return to his vehicle. As the motorist does, the officer asks whether the motorist has drugs or alcohol in his possession. When the motorist answers "no," the officer asks for permission to search the motorist's vehicle, and the motorist consents. Before the officer conducts the search, he subjects the motorist to a pat-down search. Does the motorist's consent to a vehicle search necessarily include consent to a pat-down search of his person? *See United States v. Manjarrez*, 348 F.3d 881 (10th Cir.2003).

GEORGIA v. RANDOLPH
___ U.S. ___, 126 S.Ct. 1515 (2006).

JUSTICE SOUTER delivered the opinion of the Court.

The Fourth Amendment recognizes a valid warrantless entry and search of premises when police obtain the voluntary consent of an occupant who shares, or is reasonably believed to share, authority over the area in common with a co-occupant who later objects to the use of evidence so obtained. *Illinois v. Rodriguez*, 497 U.S. 177 (1990); *United*

States v. Matlock, 415 U.S. 164 (1974). The question here is whether such an evidentiary seizure is likewise lawful with the permission of one occupant when the other, who later seeks to suppress the evidence, is present at the scene and expressly refuses to consent. * * *

I

Respondent Scott Randolph and his wife, Janet, separated in late May 2001, when she left the marital residence [in] Georgia, and went to stay with her parents[,] taking their son and some belongings. In July, she returned to the Americus house with the child, though the record does not reveal whether her object was reconciliation or retrieval of remaining possessions.

On the morning of July 6, she complained to the police that after a domestic dispute her husband took their son away, and when officers reached the house she told them that her husband was a cocaine user whose habit had caused financial troubles. [A]fter the police arrived, Scott Randolph returned and explained that he had removed the child to a neighbor's house out of concern that his wife might take the boy out of the country again; he denied cocaine use, and countered that it was in fact his wife who abused drugs and alcohol.

One of the officers, Sergeant Murray, went with Janet Randolph to reclaim the child, and when they returned she not only renewed her complaints about her husband's drug use, but also volunteered that there were "items of drug evidence" in the house. Sergeant Murray asked Scott Randolph for permission to search the house, which he unequivocally refused.

The sergeant turned to Janet Randolph for consent to search, which she readily gave. She led the officer upstairs to a bedroom that she identified as Scott's, where the sergeant noticed [a] drinking straw with a powdery residue he suspected was cocaine. He then left the house to get an evidence bag from his car and to call the district attorney's office, [who] instructed him to stop the search and apply for a warrant. When Sergeant Murray returned to the house, Janet Randolph withdrew her consent. The police took the straw to the police station, along with the Randolphs. After getting a search warrant, they returned to the house and seized further evidence of drug use, on the basis of which Scott Randolph was indicted for possession of cocaine.

He moved to suppress the evidence, as products of a warrantless search of his house unauthorized by his wife's consent over his express refusal. [The trial court denied the motion. The Court of Appeals of Georgia reversed, and was sustained by the State Supreme Court.] We granted certiorari [and] affirm.

II

To the Fourth Amendment rule ordinarily prohibiting the warrantless entry of a person's house as unreasonable *per se,* one "jealously and carefully drawn" exception recognizes the validity of searches with the voluntary consent of an individual possessing authority. That person might be the householder against whom evidence is sought, or a fellow occupant who shares common authority over property, when the suspect is absent, and the exception for consent extends even to entries and searches with the permission of a co-occupant whom the police reasonably, but erroneously, believe to possess shared authority as an occupant, *Rodriguez, supra,* at 186. None of our co-occupant consent-to-search cases, however, has presented the further fact of a second occupant physically present and refusing permission to search, and later moving to suppress evidence so obtained.[2] The significance of such a refusal turns on the underpinnings of the co-occupant consent rule, as recognized since *Matlock*.

The defendant in that case was arrested in the yard of a house where he lived with a Mrs. Graff and several of her relatives, and was detained in a squad car parked nearby. When the police went to the door, Mrs. Graff admitted them and consented to a search of the house. [W]e said that "the consent of one who possesses common authority over premises or effects is valid as against the absent, nonconsenting person with whom that authority is shared." Consistent with our prior understanding that Fourth Amendment rights are not limited by the law of property, we explained that the third party's "common authority" is not synonymous with a technical property interest:

> "The authority which justified the third-party consent does not rest upon the law of property, with its attendant historical and legal refinement, but rests rather on mutual use of the property by persons generally having joint access or control for most purposes, so that it is reasonable to recognize that any of the co-inhabitants has the right to permit the inspection in his own right and that the others have assumed the risk that one of their number might permit the common area to be searched."

[The] constant element in assessing Fourth Amendment reasonableness in the consent cases, then, is the great significance given to widely shared social expectations, which are naturally enough influenced by the law of property, but not controlled by its rules. *Matlock* [not] only holds that a solitary co-inhabitant may sometimes consent to a search of shared premises, but stands for the proposition that the reasonableness of such a search is in significant part a function of commonly held understanding about the authority that co-inhabitants may exercise in ways that affect each other's interests.

[When] someone comes to the door of a domestic dwelling with a baby at her hip, as Mrs. Graff did, she shows that she belongs there, and that fact standing alone is enough to tell a law enforcement officer or any other visitor that if she occupies the place along with others, she probably lives there subject to the assumption tenants usually make about their common authority when they share quarters. They under-

---

2. Mindful of the multiplicity of living arrangements, [we] do not mean [to] sug- gest that the rule to be applied to them [is] varied.

stand that any one of them may admit visitors, with the consequence that a guest obnoxious to one may nevertheless be admitted in his absence by another. As *Matlock* put it, shared tenancy is understood to include an "assumption of risk," on which police officers are entitled to rely, and although some group living together might make an exceptional arrangement that no one could admit a guest without the agreement of all, the chance of such an eccentric scheme is too remote to expect visitors to investigate a particular household's rules before accepting an invitation to come in. So, *Matlock* relied on what was usual and placed no burden on the police to eliminate the possibility of atypical arrangements, in the absence of reason to doubt that the regular scheme was in place.

It is also easy to imagine different facts on which, if known, no common authority could sensibly be suspected. [A] landlord or a hotel manager calls up no customary understanding of authority to admit guests without the consent of the current occupant. See *Chapman v. United States, supra* (landlord); *Stoner v. California,* 376 U.S. 483 (1964) (hotel manager). A tenant in the ordinary course does not take rented premises subject to any formal or informal agreement that the landlord may let visitors into the dwelling, and a hotel guest customarily has no reason to expect the manager to allow anyone but his own employees into his room. In these circumstances, neither state-law property rights, nor common contractual arrangements, nor any other source points to a common understanding of authority to admit third parties generally without the consent of a person occupying the premises. And when it comes to searching through bureau drawers, there will be instances in which even a person clearly belonging on premises as an occupant may lack any perceived authority to consent; "a child of eight might well be considered to have the power to consent to the police crossing the threshold into that part of the house where any caller, such as a pollster or salesman, might well be admitted," 4 LaFave 8.4(c), at 207 (4th ed.2004), but no one would reasonably expect such a child to be in a position to authorize anyone to rummage through his parents' bedroom.
* * *

[I]t is fair to say that a caller standing at the door of shared premises would have no confidence that one occupant's invitation was a sufficiently good reason to enter when a fellow tenant stood there saying, "stay out." Without some very good reason, no sensible person would go inside under those conditions. Fear for the safety of the occupant issuing the invitation, or of someone else inside, would be thought to justify entry, but the justification then would be the personal risk, the threats to life or limb, not the disputed invitation.

The visitor's reticence without some such good reason would show not timidity but a realization that when people living together disagree over the use of their common quarters, a resolution must come through voluntary accommodation, not by appeals to authority. Unless the people living together fall within some recognized hierarchy, like a household of parent and child or barracks housing military personnel of different grades, there is no societal understanding of superior and inferior, a fact reflected in a standard formulation of domestic property law, that "[e]ach cotenant [has] the right to use and enjoy the entire property as if he or she were the sole owner, limited only by the same right in the other cotenants." 7 R. POWELL, POWELL ON REAL PROPERTY 50.03[1], p. 50–14 (M. Wolf gen. ed.2005). [The] law does not ask who has the better side of the conflict; it simply provides a right to any co-tenant, even the most unreasonable, to obtain a decree partitioning the property (when the relationship is one of co-ownership) and terminating the relationship. [In] sum, there is no common understanding that one co-tenant generally has a right or authority to prevail over the express wishes of another, whether the issue is the color of the curtains or invitations to outsiders.

Since the co-tenant wishing to open the door to a third party has no recognized authority in law or social practice to prevail over a present and objecting co-tenant, his disputed invitation, without more, gives a police officer no better claim to reasonableness in entering than the officer would have in the absence of any consent at all. [We] have, after all, lived our whole national history with an understanding of "the ancient adage that a man's home is his castle [to the point that t]he poorest man may in his cottage bid defiance to all the forces of the Crown," *Miller v. United States,* 357 U.S. 301 (1958). Disputed permission is thus no match for this central value of the Fourth Amendment[. W]e recognize the consenting tenant's interest as a citizen in bringing criminal activity to light. And we understand a co-tenant's legitimate self-interest in siding with the police to deflect suspicion raised by sharing quarters with a criminal.

But society can often have the benefit of these interests without relying on a theory of consent that ignores an inhabitant's refusal to allow a warrantless search. The co-tenant acting on his own initiative may be able to deliver evidence to the police, and can tell the police what he knows, for use before a magistrate in getting a warrant.[6] The reliance on a co-tenant's information instead of disputed consent accords with the law's general partiality toward "police action taken under a warrant [as against] searches and seizures without one * * *," *United States v. Lefkowitz,* 285 U.S. 452 (1932).

[No] question has been raised, or reasonably could be, about the authority of the police to enter a dwelling to protect a resident from domestic violence; so long as they have good reason to believe such a threat exists.... (And since the police would then be lawfully in the premises, there is no question that they could seize any evidence in plain view or take further action supported by any consequent probable cause)

---

6. [The] very exchange of information like this in front of the objecting inhabitant may render consent irrelevant by creating an exigency that justifies immediate action on the police's part; if the objecting tenant cannot be incapacitated from destroying easily disposable evidence during the time required to get a warrant, a fairly perceived need to act on the spot to preserve evidence may justify entry and search under the exigent circumstances exception * * *.

[The] undoubted right of the police to enter in order to protect a victim [has] nothing to do with the question in this case, whether a search with the consent of one co-tenant is good against another, standing at the door and expressly refusing consent.[7] [None] of the cases cited by the dissent support its improbable view that recognizing limits on merely evidentiary searches would compromise the capacity to protect a fearful occupant. [We] therefore hold that a warrantless search of a shared dwelling for evidence over the express refusal of consent by a physically present resident cannot be justified as reasonable as to him on the basis of consent given to the police by another resident.

[If] *Matlock's*s co-tenant is giving permission "in his own right," how can his "own right" be eliminated by another tenant's objection? [T]o ask whether the consenting tenant has the right to admit the police when a physically present fellow tenant objects is not to question whether some property right may be divested by the mere objection of another. It is, rather, the question whether customary social understanding accords the consenting tenant authority powerful enough to prevail over the co-tenant's objection. [If] a potential defendant with self-interest in objecting is in fact at the door and objects, the co-tenant's permission does not suffice for a reasonable search, whereas the potential objector, nearby but not invited to take part in the threshold colloquy, loses out.

[So] long as there is no evidence that the police have removed the potentially objecting tenant from the entrance for the sake of avoiding a possible objection, there is practical value in the simple clarity of complementary rules, one recognizing the co-tenant's permission when there is no fellow occupant on hand, the other according dispositive weight to the fellow occupant's contrary indication when he expresses it. [It] would needlessly limit the capacity of the police to respond [if] we were to hold that reasonableness required the police to take affirmative steps to find a potentially objecting co-tenant before acting on the permission they had already received. [E]very co-tenant consent case would turn into a test about the adequacy of the police's efforts to consult with a potential objector. * * *

This case invites a straightforward application of the rule that a physically present inhabitant's express refusal of consent to a police search is dispositive as to him, regardless of the consent of a fellow occupant. [The] State does not argue that she gave any indication to the police of a need for protection inside the house that might have justified entry into the portion of the premises where the police found the powdery straw[.] Nor does the State claim that the entry and search should be upheld under the rubric of exigent circumstances * * *.

The judgment of the Supreme Court of Georgia is therefore affirmed.

---

7. We understand the possibility that a battered individual will be afraid to express fear candidly, but this does not seem to be a reason to think such a person would invite the police into the dwelling to search for evidence against another....

It is so ordered.

JUSTICE ALITO took no part in the consideration or decision of this case.

JUSTICE STEVENS, concurring.

[I]n the absence of exigent circumstances, a government agent has no right to enter a "house" or "castle" unless authorized to do so by a valid warrant. See *Semayne's Case,* 5 Co. Rep. 91a, 77 Eng. Rep. 194 (K.B.). [When] the Fourth Amendment was adopted, [g]iven the then-prevailing dramatic differences between the property rights of the husband and the far lesser rights of the wife, only the consent of the husband would matter. [Thus] if "original understanding" were to govern the outcome of this case, the search was clearly invalid because the husband did not consent. [I]t is now clear, as a matter of constitutional law, that the male and the female are equal partners. *Reed v. Reed,* 404 U.S. 71 (1971). Assuming that both spouses are competent, neither one is a master possessing the power to override the other's constitutional right to deny entry to their castle. With these observations, I join the Court's opinion.

JUSTICE BREYER, concurring.

[The] search at issue was a search solely for evidence. The objecting party was present and made his objection known clearly and directly to the officers seeking to enter the house. The officers did not justify their search on grounds of possible evidence destruction. [The] officers might easily have secured the premises and sought a warrant permitting them to enter. Thus, the "totality of the circumstances" [here] do not suffice to justify abandoning the Fourth Amendment's traditional hostility to police entry into a home without a warrant. [T]he risk of an ongoing crime or other exigent circumstance can make a critical difference. [If] a possible abuse victim invites a responding officer to enter a home or consents to the officer's entry request, that invitation (or consent) itself could reflect the victim's fear about being left alone with an abuser. [In] that context, an invitation (or consent) would provide a special reason for immediate, rather than later, police entry. And, entry following invitation or consent by one party ordinarily would be reasonable even in the face of direct objection by the other. [T]oday's decision will not adversely affect ordinary law enforcement practices. * * *

CHIEF JUSTICE ROBERTS, with whom JUSTICE SCALIA joins, dissenting.

[The] rule the majority fashions [provides] protection on a random and happenstance basis, protecting, for example, a co-occupant who happens to be at the front door when the other occupant consents to a search, but not one napping or watching television in the next room. [The] correct approach [recognizes that the] Fourth Amendment protects privacy. If an individual shares information, papers, *or places* with another, he assumes the risk that the other person will in turn share access to that information or those papers *or places* with the government. And just as an individual who has shared illegal plans or incriminating documents with another cannot interpose an objection when that other person turns the information over to the government, just because the individual happens to be present at the time, so too someone who shares a place with another cannot interpose an objection when that person decides to grant access to the police, simply because the objecting individual happens to be present.

A warrantless search is reasonable if police obtain the voluntary consent of a person authorized to give it. Co-occupants have "assumed the risk that one of their number might permit [a] common area to be searched." *United States v. Matlock,* 415 U.S. 164 (1974). Just as Mrs. Randolph could walk upstairs, come down, and turn her husband's cocaine straw over to the police, she can consent to police entry and search of what is, after all, her home, too. * * *

[T]he majority describes [the] "widely shared social expectations" that "when people living together disagree over the use of their common quarters, a resolution must come through voluntary accommodation." [T]he majority [assumes that] an invited social guest who arrives at the door of a shared residence, and is greeted by a disagreeable co-occupant shouting "stay out," would simply go away. [A] wide variety of differing social situations can readily be imagined, giving rise to quite different social expectations. A relative or good friend of one of two feuding roommates might well enter the apartment over the objection of the other roommate. [A] guest who came to celebrate an occupant's birthday, or one who had traveled some distance for a particular reason, might not readily turn away simply because of a roommate's objection. The nature of the place itself is also pertinent: Invitees may react one way if the feuding roommates share one room, differently if there are common areas from which the objecting roommate could readily be expected to absent himself. [The] possible scenarios are limitless, and slight variations in the fact pattern yield vastly different expectations about whether the invitee might be expected to enter or to go away. Such shifting expectations are not a promising foundation on which to ground a constitutional rule * * *.

The majority suggests that "widely shared social expectations" are a "constant element in assessing Fourth Amendment reasonableness," but [the] Fourth Amendment precedents the majority cites refer instead to a "legitimate expectation of *privacy*." [If] two roommates share a computer and one keeps pirated software on a shared drive, [the one] person has given up his privacy with respect to his roommate by saving the software on their shared computer. [A] wide variety of often subtle social conventions may shape expectations about how we act when another shares with us what is otherwise private, and those conventions go by a variety of labels-courtesy, good manners, custom, protocol, even honor among thieves. The Constitution, however, protects not these but privacy, and once privacy has been shared, the shared information, documents, or places remain private only at the discretion of the confidant. * * *

The same analysis applies to the question whether our privacy can be compromised by those with whom we share common living space. If a person keeps contraband in common areas of his home, he runs the risk that his co-occupants will deliver the contraband to the police. [A] person "assume[s] the risk" that those who have access to and control over his shared property might consent to a search. In *Matlock,* we explained that this assumption of risk is derived from a third party's "joint access or control for most purposes" of shared property. And we concluded that shared use of property makes it "reasonable to recognize that any of the co-inhabitants has the right to permit the inspection in his own right." [If] a person wants to ensure that his possessions will be subject to a consent search only due to his *own* consent, he is free to place these items in an area over which others do *not* share access and control, be it a private room or a locked suitcase under a bed. * * *

[The] majority repeats several times that a present co-occupant's refusal to permit entry renders the search unreasonable and invalid "as to him." This implies entry and search would be reasonable "as to" someone else, presumably the consenting co-occupant and any other absent co-occupants. The normal Fourth Amendment rule is that items discovered in plain view are admissible if the officers were legitimately on the premises; if the entry and search were reasonable "as to" Mrs. Randolph, based on her consent, it is not clear why the cocaine straw should not be admissible "as to" Mr. Randolph, as discovered in plain view during a legitimate search * * *.

The question presented often arises when innocent cotenants seek to disassociate or protect themselves from ongoing criminal activity. [Under] the majority's rule, there will be many cases in which a consenting co-occupant's wish to have the police enter is overridden by an objection from another present co-occupant. What does the majority imagine will happen, in a case in which the consenting co-occupant is concerned about the other's criminal activity, once the door clicks shut? The objecting co-occupant may pause briefly to decide whether to destroy any evidence of wrongdoing or to inflict retribution on the consenting co-occupant first, but there can be little doubt that he will attend to both in short order. [Perhaps] the most serious consequence of the majority's rule is its operation in domestic abuse situations.... [The] majority's rule apparently forbids police from entering to assist with a domestic dispute if the abuser whose behavior prompted the request for police assistance objects. [I]t is far from clear that an exception for emergency entries suffices to protect the safety of occupants in domestic disputes. [I] respectfully dissent.

JUSTICE SCALIA, dissenting.

[The issue] is what to do when there is a *conflict* between two equals. [It] does not follow that the spouse who *refuses* consent should be the winner of the contest. Given the usual patterns of domestic violence, how often can police be expected to encounter the situation in which a man urges them to enter the home while a woman simultaneously demands that they stay out? The most common practical effect of today's decision [is] to give men the power to stop women from allowing police into their homes-which is, curiously enough, *precisely* the power that Justice STEVENS disapprovingly presumes men had in 1791. * * *

JUSTICE THOMAS, dissenting.

[*Coolidge v. New Hampshire,* 403 U.S. 443 (1971)] held that when a citizen leads police officers into a home shared with her spouse to show them evidence relevant to their investigation [no] Fourth Amendment search has occurred. * * *

Problems

1. *Randolph's Meaning.* How does the Court's decision apply to a defendant, who happens to be asleep when his wife agrees to allow the police to enter their residence, wakes up and immediately objects to the search. May the police continue with the search, or must they discontinue their efforts? How would you advise the police to act?

2. *The Co–Occupant in the Patrol Car.* Defendant has been arrested, placed in handcuffs, and seated in the back of a patrol car. How should the police act in the following situations: a) the police ask defendant's wife for permission to search the house, and she consents, but defendant (realizing what is going on) yells out an objection; b) defendant, who was present when the police arrived, has been taken to the police station by the time that the police ask his wife for consent to search and therefore is not present to object; c) defendant (who has not yet been taken to the station) is fearful that the police will ask his wife for consent to search, and yells out an objection to a search before the police cruiser pulls away. After defendant has been taken away to the station, the police ask the wife for consent, and she gives it. In which of these situations might the police be entitled to search?

3. *The Meth Lab.* Defendant, who was present when the police ask her husband for permission to search her house for evidence of a meth lab, objects loudly. However, the husband pleads with the police to enter anyway because he fears that the meth chemicals are dangerous to his house, to him, and to their kids. May the police enter the house anyway? See, *e.g., United States v. Hendrix,* 595 F.2d 883 (D.C.Cir.1979) (wife asked police "to get her baby and take [a] sawed-off shotgun out of her house").

4. *Consent and Children.* In *Randolph,* the Court indicates that an eight year old child might not be permitted to consent to the search of his parent's house. Would the same be true for a babysitter who is in charge of the eight year old child? What about a 16 year old? Does the analysis change? An adult child who is living at home with the parent?

5. *The Guest's Consent.* Believing that criminals are using a house to traffic narcotics, the police ask Chambers (who does not own the house, but is simply staying there with the permission of the owner's) for permission to search the house for evidence of money laundering and drug trafficking. Is the search valid if it reveals cocaine in the living room? What if the police find a boarded-up attic entryway, and Chambers consents to using a sledge-

hammer to dislodge the boards. In the attic, the police find nearly $1,000,000 in cash, more drugs, and ledgers. Did Chambers have the power to consent to a search of the boarded-up attic? If you represent Ibarra, the owner of the house, how would you argue that the search is invalid? How might the state respond? *See United States v. Ibarra*, 948 F.2d 903 (5th Cir.1991).

6. *The Grandmother's Consent.* In *Bumper v. State of North Carolina*, 391 U.S. 543 (1968), the police searched a grandmother's home in search of a rifle allegedly used by her grandson in committing a rape. If the grandmother owns the house, can she consent to a search of her grandson's bedroom? Does it matter whether the grandson is present and objecting?

6. Administrative Inspections

A number of agencies regularly inspect buildings and worksites. Health inspectors enter restaurants to determine whether food preparation and service areas are clean, as well as to see whether food is being kept under healthy conditions. For example, OSHA inspectors examine construction and factory sites to make sure that workers are employed in safe and healthy conditions. In some instances, administrative officials even seek to enter people's homes or yards (*e.g.*, child welfare officials enter a house looking for abused or neglected children).

Although the Fourth Amendment prohibits unreasonable searches and seizures, and therefore seems to provide homeowners and businessmen with some protection against administrative prying, until the 1960s there was doubt about whether the Fourth Amendment applied to administrative inspections. The Fourth Amendment clearly applies when the police search homes or businesses for evidence of criminal activity. However, prior to the following decision, many believed that administrative inspections are fundamentally different than police searches, and are not therefore subject to Fourth Amendment requirements.

CAMARA v. MUNICIPAL COURT
387 U.S. 523 (1967).

MR. JUSTICE WHITE delivered the opinion of the Court.

[Appellant Camara leased a ground floor apartment. City inspectors sought to inspect the apartment under § 503 of a San Francisco ordinance which authorized them to enter buildings "to perform any duty imposed upon them by the Municipal Code." When Camara refused to allow the inspectors to enter his apartment without a warrant, he was charged with violating § 507 of the ordinance which made it illegal to refuse to permit a lawful inspection.]

[The Fourth Amendment was designed] to safeguard the privacy and security of individuals against arbitrary invasions by governmental officials. [E]xcept in certain carefully defined classes of cases, a search of private property without proper consent is "unreasonable" unless it has been authorized by a valid search warrant. * * *

In *Frank v. State of Maryland*, [359 U.S. 360 (1959),] this Court upheld the conviction of one who refused to permit a warrantless inspection of private premises for the purposes of locating and abating a suspected public [nuisance]. [To] the *Frank* majority, municipal fire, health, and housing inspection programs "touch at most upon the periphery of the important interests safeguarded by the Fourteenth Amendment's protection against official intrusion," because the inspections are merely to determine whether physical conditions exist which do not comply with minimum standards prescribed in local regulatory ordinances. Since the inspector does not ask that the property owner open his doors to a search for "evidence of criminal action" which may be used to secure the owner's criminal conviction, historic interests of "self-protection" jointly protected by the Fourth and Fifth Amendments are said not to be involved, but only the less intense "right to be secure from intrusion into personal privacy."

We may agree that a routine inspection of the physical condition of private property is a less hostile intrusion than the typical policeman's search for the fruits and instrumentalities of crime. [But] we cannot agree that the Fourth Amendment interests at stake in these inspection cases are merely "peripheral." It is surely anomalous to say that the individual and his private property are fully protected by the Fourth Amendment only when the individual is suspected of criminal behavior. [E]ven the most law-abiding citizen has a very tangible interest in limiting the circumstances under which the sanctity of his home may be broken by official authority, for the possibility of criminal entry under the guise of official sanction is a serious threat to personal and family security. And even accepting *Frank's* rather remarkable premise, inspections of the kind we are here considering do in fact jeopardize "self-protection" interests of the property owner. Like most regulatory laws, fire, health, and housing codes are enforced by criminal processes. In some cities, discovery of a violation by the inspector leads to a criminal complaint. Even in cities where discovery of a violation produces only an administrative compliance order, refusal to comply is a criminal offense, and the fact of compliance is verified by a second inspection, again without a warrant. Finally[,] refusal to permit an inspection is itself a crime, punishable by fine or even by jail sentence.

[Appellee asserts that] the warrant process could not function effectively in this field. The decision to inspect an entire municipal area is based upon legislative or administrative assessment of broad factors such as the area's age and condition. Unless the magistrate is to review such policy matters, he must issue a "rubber stamp" warrant which provides no protection at all to the property owner.

[T]hese arguments unduly discount the purposes behind the warrant machinery contemplated by the Fourth Amendment. [W]hen the inspector demands entry, the occupant has no way of knowing whether enforcement of the municipal code involved requires inspection of his premises, no way of knowing the lawful limits of the inspector's power to search, and no way of knowing whether the inspector himself is acting under proper authorization. These are questions which may be reviewed by a neutral magistrate without any reassessment of the basic agency decision to canvass an area. Yet, only by refusing entry and risking a criminal conviction can the occupant ... challenge the inspector's decision to search. And even if the occupant possesses sufficient fortitude to take this risk[,] he may never learn any more about the reason for the inspection than that the law generally allows housing inspectors to gain entry. The practical effect of this system is to leave the occupant subject to the discretion of the official in the field. This is precisely the discretion to invade private property which we have consistently circumscribed by a requirement that a disinterested party warrant the need to [search].

The final justification suggested for warrantless administrative searches is that the public interest demands such a rule: it [is] argued that the health and safety of entire urban populations is dependent upon enforcement of minimum fire, housing, and sanitation standards, and that the only effective means of enforcing such codes is by routine systematized inspection of all physical structures. [I]n applying any reasonableness standard, including one of constitutional dimension, an argument that the public interest demands a particular rule must receive careful consideration. But [the] question is not [whether] these inspections may be made, but whether they may be made without a warrant. [In] assessing whether the public interest demands creation of a general exception to the Fourth Amendment's warrant requirement, the question is not whether the public interest justifies the type of search in question, but whether the authority to search should be evidenced by a warrant, which in turn depends in part upon whether the burden of obtaining a warrant is likely to frustrate the governmental purpose behind the search. It has nowhere been urged that fire, health, and housing code inspection programs could not achieve their goals within the confines of a reasonable search warrant requirement. Thus, we do not find the public need argument dispositive.

[W]e hold that administrative searches of the kind at issue here are significant intrusions upon the interests protected by the Fourth Amendment, that such searches when authorized and conducted without a warrant procedure lack the traditional safeguards which the Fourth Amendment guarantees to the individual, and that the reasons put forth in *Frank* [and] other cases for upholding these warrantless searches are insufficient to justify so substantial a weakening of the Fourth Amendment's protections. Because of the nature of the municipal programs under consideration, [these] conclusions must be the beginning, not the end, of our [inquiry].

[In] cases in which the Fourth Amendment requires that a warrant to search be obtained, "probable cause" is the standard by which a particular decision to search is tested against the constitutional mandate of reasonableness. To apply this standard, it is obviously necessary first to focus upon the governmental interest which allegedly justifies official intrusion upon the constitutionally protected interests of the private citizen. For example, in a criminal investigation, the police may undertake to recover specific stolen or contraband goods. But that public interest would hardly justify a sweeping search of an entire city [in] the hope that these goods might be found. [A] search for these goods, even with a warrant, is "reasonable" only when there is "probable cause" to believe that they will be uncovered in a particular dwelling.

[T]he inspection programs at issue here are aimed at securing city-wide compliance with minimum physical standards for private property. The primary governmental interest at stake is to prevent even the unintentional development of conditions which are hazardous to public health and safety. Because fires and epidemics may ravage large urban areas, because unsightly conditions adversely affect the economic values of neighboring structures, numerous courts have upheld the police power of municipalities to impose and enforce such minimum standards even upon existing structures. In determining whether a particular inspection is reasonable—and thus in determining whether there is probable cause to issue a warrant for that inspection—the need for the inspection must be weighed in terms of these reasonable goals of code enforcement.

There is unanimous agreement among those most familiar with this field that the only effective way to seek universal compliance with the minimum standards required by municipal codes is through routine periodic inspections of all structures. It is here that the probable cause debate is focused, for the agency's decision to conduct an area inspection is unavoidably based on its appraisal of conditions in the area as a whole, not on its knowledge of conditions in each particular building. Appellee contends that, if the probable cause standard [is] adopted, the area inspection will be eliminated as a means of seeking compliance with code standards and the reasonable goals of code enforcement will be dealt a crushing blow.

[T]here can be no ready test for determining reasonableness other than by balancing the need to search against the invasion which the search entails. [A] number of persuasive factors combine to support the reasonableness of area code-enforcement inspections. First, such programs have a long history of judicial and public acceptance. Second, the public interest demands that all dangerous conditions be prevented or abated, yet it is doubtful that any other canvassing technique would achieve acceptable results. Many such conditions—faulty wiring[—]are not observable from outside the building and indeed may not be apparent to the inexpert occupant himself. Finally, because the inspections are neither personal in nature nor aimed at the discovery of evidence of crime, they involve a relatively limited invasion of the urban citizen's [privacy].

Having concluded that the area inspection is a "reasonable" search of private property within the meaning of the Fourth Amendment, it is obvious that "probable cause" to issue a warrant to inspect must exist if reasonable legislative or administrative standards for conducting an area inspection are satisfied with respect to a particular dwelling. Such standards, which will vary with the municipal program being enforced, may be based upon the passage of time, the nature of the building (*e.g.*, a multifamily apartment house), or the condition of the entire area, but they will not necessarily depend upon specific knowledge of the condition of the particular dwelling. It has been suggested that so to vary the probable cause test from the standard applied in criminal cases would be to authorize a "synthetic search warrant" and thereby to lessen the overall protections of the Fourth Amendment. [W]e do not agree. The warrant procedure is designed to guarantee that a decision to search private property is justified by a reasonable governmental interest. But reasonableness is still the ultimate standard. If a valid public interest justifies the intrusion contemplated, then there is probable cause to issue a suitably restricted search warrant. Such an approach neither endangers time-honored doctrines applicable to criminal investigations nor makes a nullity of the probable cause requirement in this area. It merely gives full recognition to the competing public and private interests here at stake and, in so doing, best fulfills the historic purpose behind the constitutional right to be free from unreasonable government invasions of privacy.

Since our holding emphasizes the controlling standard of reasonableness, nothing we say today is intended to foreclose prompt inspections, even without a warrant, that the law has traditionally upheld in emergency situations. *See North American Cold Storage Co. v. City of Chicago*, 211 U.S. 306 (seizure of unwholesome food); *Jacobson v. Commonwealth of Massachusetts*, 197 U.S. 11 (compulsory smallpox vaccination); *Compagnie Francaise de Navigation a Vapeur v. Louisiana State Board of Health*, 186 U.S. 380 (health quarantine); *Kroplin v. Truax*, 119 Ohio St. 610, 165 N.E. 498 (summary destruction of tubercular cattle). On the other hand, in the case of most routine area inspections, there is no compelling urgency to inspect at a particular time or on a particular day. Moreover, most citizens allow inspections of their property without a warrant. Thus, as a practical matter and in light of the Fourth Amendment's requirement that a warrant specify the property to be searched, it seems likely that warrants should normally be sought only after entry is refused unless there has been a citizen complaint or there is other satisfactory reason for securing immediate entry. Similarly, the requirement of a warrant procedure does not suggest any change in what seems to be the prevailing local policy, in most situations, of authorizing entry, but not entry by force, to inspect.

In this case, appellant has been charged with a crime for his refusal to permit housing inspectors to enter his leasehold without a warrant. There was no emergency demanding immediate access; in fact, the inspectors made three trips to the building in an attempt to obtain appellant's consent to search. Yet no warrant was obtained and thus appellant was unable to verify either the need for or the appropriate limits of the inspection. [We] therefore conclude that appellant had a constitutional right to insist that the inspectors obtain a warrant to search and that appellant may not constitutionally be convicted for refusing to consent to the [inspection].

Judgment vacated and case remanded.

Problems

1. *Applying Camara.* Although *Camara* involved a person's home, its holding extends to government inspections of business property. Suppose that you are an attorney for the Occupational Safety & Health Administration (OSHA). You just received a call from Ms. Grace Harlow, a workplace inspector, assigned to the inspection of poultry factories. Tomorrow morning, Ms. Harlow plans to visit the Ajax Poultry Co. (Ajax). She wants to know whether she needs to obtain a warrant before going to the factory, or whether she can just show up. How would you advise Ms. Harlow? Does *Camara* force an inspector to begin every day at a judge's office seeking a warrant authorizing the search of a business or home?

2. *The Factory Owner's Response.* Now, assume that you represent the Ajax rather than OSHA. You receive a call from Ajax's President Herb Deets indicating that a Ms. Harlow, an OSHA inspector, just "showed up" at Ajax's factory—unannounced and without a warrant. (OSHA's attorneys advised Ms. Harlow that a warrant was not necessary.) Mr. Deets wants to know whether he should allow the inspector to enter without a warrant. Mr. Deets feels that his plant is in compliance with OSHA regulations. However, OSHA regulations are so strict that an overzealous inspector can always find a violation of OSHA. Would it be advisable to give, or to refuse, consent? Advise Mr. Deets?

3. *The Elevator Inspector and the Cocaine.* Suppose that an elevator inspector enters an office building to inspect an elevator. While there, he happens to notice crack cocaine lying in plain view. You are the lawyer for the agency for which the inspector works, and he calls you for advice. May the inspector seize the cocaine? Can he make arrests? If not, what can he do? How should he proceed?

NEW YORK v. BURGER

482 U.S. 691 (1987).

JUSTICE BLACKMUN delivered the opinion of the Court.

[Respondent] Joseph Burger is the owner of a junkyard in Brooklyn, N.Y. His business consists, in part, of dismantling of automobiles and selling their parts. [The junkyard is an open lot, filled with vehicles and vehicle parts, with no buildings, surrounded by a high fence. Police officers,] all members of the Auto Crimes Division of the New York City Police Department, entered respondent's junkyard to conduct an inspection pursuant to N.Y.Veh. & Traf.Law § 415–a5 (McKinney 1986). On any given day, the Division conducts from 5 to 10 inspections of vehicle dismantlers, automobile junkyards, and related businesses.

Upon entering the junkyard, the officers asked to see Burger's license and his "police book"—the record of the automobiles and vehicle parts in his possession. Burger replied that he had neither a license nor a police book. The officers then announced their intention to conduct a § 415–a5 inspection. Burger did not object. In accordance with their practice, the officers copied down the Vehicle Identification Numbers

(VINs) of several vehicles and parts of vehicles that were in the junkyard. After checking these numbers against a police computer, the officers determined that respondent was in possession of stolen vehicles and parts. Accordingly, Burger was arrested and charged with five counts of possession of stolen property and one count of unregistered operation as a vehicle dismantler, in violation of § 415–a1.

[Burger] moved to suppress the evidence obtained [from] the inspection, primarily on the ground that § 415–a5 was unconstitutional. [W]e granted certiorari.

II

The Court long has recognized that the Fourth Amendment's prohibition on unreasonable searches and seizures is applicable to commercial premises, as well as to private homes. An owner or operator of a business thus has an expectation of privacy in commercial property which society is prepared to consider to be reasonable. This expectation exists not only with respect to traditional police searches conducted for the gathering of criminal evidence but also with respect to administrative inspections designed to enforce regulatory statutes. An expectation of privacy in commercial premises, however, is different from, and indeed less than, a similar expectation in an individual's home. This expectation is particularly attenuated in commercial property employed in "closely regulated" industries. The Court observed in *Marshall v. Barlow's, Inc.*: "Certain industries have such a history of government oversight that no reasonable expectation of privacy could exist for a proprietor over the stock of such an enterprise."

The Court first examined the "unique" problem of inspections of "closely regulated" businesses in two enterprises that had "a long tradition of close government supervision." In *Colonnade Corp. v. United States*, 397 U.S. 72 (1970), it considered a warrantless search of a catering business pursuant to several federal revenue statutes authorizing the inspection of the premises of liquor dealers. Although the Court disapproved the search because the statute provided that a sanction be imposed when entry was refused, and because it did not authorize entry without a warrant as an alternative[,] it recognized that "the liquor industry [was] long subject to close supervision and inspection." [*United States v. Biswell*, 406 U.S. 311 (1972)], involved a warrantless inspection of the premises of a pawnshop operator, who was federally licensed to sell sporting weapons pursuant to the Gun Control Act of 1968, 18 U.S.C. § 921 *et seq.* While noting that "[f]ederal regulation of the interstate traffic in firearms is not as deeply rooted in history as is governmental control of the liquor industry," we nonetheless concluded that the warrantless inspections authorized by the Gun Control Act would "pose only limited threats to the dealer's justifiable expectations of privacy." We observed: "When a dealer chooses to engage in this pervasively regulated business and to accept a federal license, he does so with the knowledge that his business records, firearms, and ammunition will be subject to effective inspection."

Because the owner or operator of commercial premises in a "closely regulated" industry has a reduced expectation of privacy, the warrant and probable-cause requirements, which fulfill the traditional Fourth Amendment standard of reasonableness for a government search have lessened application in this context. Rather, we conclude that, as in other situations of "special need," where the privacy interests of the owner are weakened and the government interests in regulating particular businesses are concomitantly heightened, a warrantless inspection of commercial premises may well be reasonable within the meaning of the Fourth Amendment.

This warrantless inspection, however, even in the context of a pervasively regulated business, will be deemed to be reasonable only so long as three criteria are met. First, there must be a "substantial" government interest that informs the regulatory scheme pursuant to which the inspection is made. *See Donovan v. Dewey*, 452 U.S., at 602 ("substantial federal interest in improving the health and safety conditions in the Nation's underground and surface mines").

Second, the warrantless inspections must be "necessary to further [the] regulatory scheme." *Donovan v. Dewey*, 452 U.S., at 600. For example, in *Dewey* we recognized that forcing mine inspectors to obtain a warrant before every inspection might alert mine owners or operators to the impending inspection, thereby frustrating the purposes of the Mine Safety and Health Act—to detect and thus to deter safety and health violations.

Finally, "the statute's inspection program, in terms of the certainty and regularity of its application, [must] provid[e] a constitutionally adequate substitute for a warrant." In other words, the regulatory statute must perform the two basic functions of a warrant: it must advise the owner of the commercial premises that the search is being made pursuant to the law and has a properly defined scope, and it must limit the discretion of the inspecting officers. To perform this first function, the statute must be "sufficiently comprehensive and defined that the owner of commercial property cannot help but be aware that his property will be subject to periodic inspections undertaken for specific purposes." *Donovan v. Dewey*, 452 U.S., at 600. [In addition, the] discretion [of] inspectors [must] be "carefully limited in time, place, and scope." *United States v. Biswell*, 406 U.S., at 315.

III

Searches made pursuant to § 415–a5 [fall] within this established exception to the warrant requirement for administrative inspections in "closely regulated" businesses. First, the nature of the regulatory statute reveals that the operation of a junkyard, part of which is devoted to vehicle dismantling, is a "closely regulated" business in the State of New York. The provisions regulating . . . vehicle dismantling are extensive. An operator cannot engage in this industry without first obtaining a license, which means that he must meet the registration requirements and must pay a fee. Under § 415–a5(a), the operator must maintain a police book recording the acquisition and disposition of motor vehicles and vehicle parts, and make such records and inventory available for inspection by the police or any agent of the Department of Motor Vehicles. The operator also must display his registration number prominently at his place of business, on business documentation, and on vehicles and parts that pass through his business. Moreover, the person engaged in this activity is subject to criminal penalties, as well as to loss of license or civil fines, for failure to comply with these provisions. That other States besides New York have imposed similarly extensive regulations on automobile junkyards further supports the "closely regulated" status of this industry.

In determining whether vehicle dismantlers constitute a "closely regulated" industry, the "duration of [this] particular regulatory scheme," *Donovan v. Dewey*, 452 U.S., at 606, has some relevancy. [B]ecause the automobile is a relatively new phenomenon in our society and because its widespread use is even newer, automobile junkyards and vehicle dismantlers have not been in existence very long and thus do not have an ancient history of government oversight. [The] automobile-junkyard business, however, is simply a new branch of an industry that has existed, and has been closely regulated, for many years. The automobile junkyard is closely akin to the secondhand shop or the general junkyard. Both share the purpose of recycling salvageable articles and components of items no longer usable in their original form. As such, vehicle dismantlers represent a modern, specialized version of a traditional activity. In New York, general junkyards and secondhand shops long have been subject to regulation. [I]n light of the regulatory framework governing his business and the history of regulation of related industries, an operator of a junkyard engaging in vehicle dismantling has a reduced expectation of privacy in this "closely regulated" business.

The New York regulatory scheme satisfies the three criteria necessary to make reasonable warrantless inspections pursuant to § 415–a5. First, the State has a substantial interest in regulating the vehicle-dismantling and automobile-junkyard industry because motor vehicle theft has increased in the State and because the problem of theft is associated with this industry. [A]utomobile theft has become a significant social problem, placing enormous economic and personal burdens upon the citizens of different States. * * *

Second, regulation of the vehicle-dismantling industry reasonably serves the State's substantial interest in eradicating automobile theft. [T]he theft problem can be addressed effectively by controlling the receiver of, or market in, stolen property. [T]he State rationally may believe that it will reduce car theft by regulations that prevent automobile junkyards from becoming markets for stolen vehicles and that help trace the origin and destination of vehicle parts.

Moreover, the warrantless administrative inspections pursuant to § 415–a5 "are necessary to further [the] regulatory scheme." [We] see no difference between these inspections and those approved by the Court in *United States v. Biswell* and *Donovan v. Dewey*. [I]n the present case, a warrant requirement would interfere with the statute's purpose of deterring automobile theft accomplished by identifying vehicles and parts as stolen and shutting down the market in such items. Because stolen cars and parts often pass quickly through an automobile junkyard, "frequent" and "unannounced" inspections are necessary in order to detect them. In sum, surprise is crucial if the regulatory scheme aimed at remedying this major social problem is to function at all.

Third, § 415–a5 provides a "constitutionally adequate substitute for a warrant." The statute informs the operator of a vehicle dismantling business that inspections will be made on a regular basis. Thus, the vehicle dismantler knows that the inspections to which he is subject do not constitute discretionary acts by a government official but are conducted pursuant to statute. Section 415–a5 also sets forth the scope of the inspection [and] places the operator on notice as to how to comply with the statute. In addition, it notifies the operator as to who is authorized to conduct an inspection.

Finally, the "time, place, and scope" of the inspection is limited to place appropriate restraints upon the discretion of the inspecting officers. The officers are allowed to conduct an inspection only "during [the] regular and usual business hours." The inspections can be made only of vehicle-dismantling and related industries. And the permissible scope of these searches is narrowly defined: the inspectors may examine the records, as well as "any vehicles or parts of vehicles which are subject to the record keeping requirements of this section and which are on the premises."

IV

A search conducted pursuant to § 415–a5, therefore, clearly falls within the well-established exception to the warrant requirement for administrative inspections of "closely regulated" businesses. The Court of Appeals, nevertheless, struck down the statute as violative of the Fourth Amendment because, in its view, the statute had no truly administrative purpose but was "designed simply to give the police an expedient means of enforcing penal sanctions for possession of stolen property." The court rested its conclusion that the administrative goal of the statute was pretextual and that § 415–a5 really "authorize[d] searches undertaken solely to uncover evidence of criminality" particularly on the fact that, even if an operator failed to produce his police book, the inspecting officers could continue their inspection for stolen vehicles and parts. The court also suggested that the identity of the inspectors—police officers—was significant in revealing the true nature of the statutory scheme.

[T]he Court of Appeals failed to recognize that a State can address a major social problem both by way of an administrative scheme and through penal sanctions. Administrative statutes and penal laws may have the same ultimate purpose of remedying the social problem, but they have different subsidiary purposes and prescribe different methods of addressing the problem. An administrative statute establishes how a particular business in a "closely regulated" industry should be operated, setting forth rules to guide an operator's conduct of the business and allowing government officials to ensure that those rules are followed. Such a regulatory approach contrasts with that of the penal laws, a major emphasis of which is the punishment of individuals for specific acts of behavior.

[This] case, too, reveals that an administrative scheme may have the same ultimate purpose as penal laws, even if its regulatory goals are narrower. . . . New York, like many States, faces a serious social problem in automobile theft and has a substantial interest in regulating the vehicle-dismantling industry because of this problem. The New York penal laws address automobile theft by punishing it or the possession of stolen property, including possession by individuals in the business of buying and selling property. In accordance with its interest in regulating the automobile-junkyard industry, the State also has devised a regulatory manner of dealing with this problem. Section 415–a, as a whole, serves the regulatory goals of seeking to ensure that vehicle dismantlers are legitimate businesspersons and that stolen vehicles and vehicle parts passing through automobile junkyards can be identified. In particular, § 415–a5 was designed to contribute to these goals * * *.

Nor do we think that this administrative scheme is unconstitutional simply because, in the course of enforcing it, an inspecting officer may discover evidence of crimes, besides violations of the scheme itself. [The] discovery of evidence of crimes in the course of an otherwise proper administrative inspection does not render that search illegal or the administrative scheme suspect.

Finally, we fail to see any constitutional significance in the fact that police officers, rather than "administrative" agents, are permitted to conduct the § 415–a5 inspection. [S]tate police officers [have] numerous duties in addition to those associated with traditional police work. [S]o long as a regulatory scheme is properly administrative, it is not rendered illegal by the fact that the inspecting officer has the power to arrest individuals for violations other than those created by the scheme itself. * * *

JUSTICE BRENNAN, with whom JUSTICE MARSHALL joins, and with whom JUSTICE O'CONNOR joins as to all but Part III, dissenting.

[A]lthough historical supervision may help to demonstrate that close regulation exists, it is "the pervasiveness and regularity [of] regulation that ultimately determines whether a warrant is necessary to render an inspection program reasonable under the Fourth Amendment."

The provisions governing vehicle dismantling in New York simply are not extensive. A vehicle dismantler must register and pay a fee, display the registration in various circumstances, maintain a police book, and allow inspections. [R]egistration and recordkeeping requirements [cannot] be characterized as close regulation. [Few] substantive qualifications are required of an aspiring vehicle dismantler; no regulation governs the condition of the premises, the method of operation, the hours of operation, the equipment utilized, etc. This scheme stands in marked contrast to, *e.g.*, the mine safety regulations relevant in *Donovan v. Dewey*. [If] New York City's administrative scheme renders the vehicle-dismantling business closely regulated, few businesses will escape such a finding. Under these circumstances, the warrant requirement is the exception not the rule * * *.

Even if vehicle dismantling were a closely regulated industry, I would nonetheless conclude that this search violated the Fourth Amendment. [Section] 415–a5 does not approach the level of "certainty and regularity [of] application" necessary to provide "a constitutionally adequate substitute for a warrant." [The] statute does not inform the operator of a vehicle-dismantling business that inspections will be made on a regular basis; in fact, there is no assurance that any inspections at all will occur. There is neither an upper nor a lower limit on the number of searches that may be conducted at any given operator's establishment in any given time period. Neither the statute, nor any regulations, nor any regulatory body, provides limits or guidance on the selection of vehicle dismantlers for inspection. * * *

The Court also maintains that this statute effectively limits the scope of the search. [This] statute fails to tailor the scope of administrative inspection to the particular concerns posed by the regulated business. [The] conduct of the police in this case underscores this point. The police removed identification numbers from a walker and a wheelchair, neither of which fell within the statutory scope of a permissible administrative search. [The] sole limitation I see on a police search of the premises of a vehicle dismantler is that it must occur during business hours; otherwise it is open season. The unguided discretion afforded police in this scheme precludes its substitution for a warrant.

III

The fundamental defect in § 415–a5 is that it authorizes searches intended solely to uncover evidence of criminal acts. [T]he State has used an administrative scheme as a pretext to search without probable cause for evidence of criminal violations. It thus circumvented the requirements of the Fourth Amendment by altering the label placed on the search. [Moreover,] it is factually impossible that the search was intended to discover wrongdoing subject to administrative sanction. Burger stated that he was not registered to dismantle vehicles as required by § 415–a1, and that he did not have a police book, as required by § 415–a5(a). At that point he had violated every requirement of the administrative scheme. There is no administrative provision forbidding possession of stolen automobiles or automobile parts. The inspection became a search for evidence of criminal acts when all possible administrative violations had been uncovered.

The State contends that acceptance of this argument would allow a vehicle dismantler to thwart its administrative scheme simply by failing to register and keep records. This is false. A failure to register or keep required records violates the scheme and results in both administrative sanctions and criminal penalties. Neither is the State's further criminal investigation thwarted; the police need only obtain a warrant and then proceed to search the premises. * * *

[The] implications of the Court's opinion, if realized, will virtually eliminate Fourth Amendment protection of commercial entities in the context of administrative searches. No State may require, as a condition of doing business, a blanket submission to warrantless searches for any purpose. I respectfully dissent.

Problem: McCown Iron

The Occupational Safety and Health Administration (OSHA) officials have a long and complicated history with McCown Iron Works (McCown Iron), an iron foundry in Coeur d'Alene, Idaho. When OSHA attempted an inspection in 2004, John McCown, CEO and principal owner, refused to permit inspectors to enter. OSHA aborted the attempted search. Later that year, in response to an employee complaint, OHSA made an unannounced visit to the foundry with a warrant. McCown Iron barred entry and was held in contempt of court. The next year, when OSHA sent letters of inquiry to McCown Iron, after receiving letters of complaint from McCown Iron employees, John McCown responded aggressively. In one letter to OSHA, McCown stated that: "You have wasted my time and taxpayer money without improving safety. This is the problem with OSHA. You are a tool for disgruntled ex-employees who make anonymous phone calls and cause trouble. It makes you look like fools and wastes everyone's time and money. Why don't you try to help the employers by providing information about unsafe products and processes rather than acting like the Gestapo with secret informants and star courts." Despite the letters of inquiry, OSHA did not attempt to inspect McCown Iron.

In early 2006, OSHA sought a search warrant to inspect McCown Iron's foundry. In its application to a federal court, OSHA stated that the inspection was selected pursuant to its General Schedule System (GSS) which outlines OSHA's search policies and assigns each industry a nationwide Standard Industrial Classification (SIC) Code. OSHA then complies lists which show each industry employer with a lost work day injury rate (LWDI) at or above the national LWDI rate for their industries. From this list, inspection sites are selected randomly for each high rate industry. Based on the GSS, SIC and LWDI, a federal court issued a warrant authorizing a search of McCown Iron. This morning, the warrant was served on John McCown.

Suppose that you represent McCown Iron, and John McCown has called you for advice. The company would like to resist the subpoena. May it do so? On what grounds? Will McCown Iron suffer any special risks if it refuses to admit OSHA inspectors? How is OSHA likely to respond to McCown Iron's arguments, and how would you expect the court to rule?

———————

Even though *Camara* loosened the probable cause requirements for administrative searches, illegal inspections do occur. Sometimes, an agency obtains a warrant but the warrant was invalidly issued. In other cases, as in *Barlow*, the agency searches without a warrant when one is required. Or, as sometimes happens, the police conduct an illegal search and give the results to administrative officials.

7. *Stop and Frisk*

Although the "stop and frisk" exception is one of the more recent exceptions to the warrant requirement, it has reshaped Fourth Amendment law in important respects.

TERRY v. STATE OF OHIO

392 U.S. 1 (1968).

MR. CHIEF JUSTICE WARREN delivered the opinion of the Court.

[Petitioner] Terry was convicted of carrying a concealed weapon and sentenced [to] one to three years in the penitentiary. Following the denial of a pretrial motion to suppress, the prosecution introduced in evidence two revolvers and a number of bullets seized from Terry and a codefendant by Cleveland Police Detective Martin McFadden. At the hearing on the motion to suppress this evidence, Officer McFadden testified that while he was patrolling in plain clothes in downtown Cleveland at approximately 2:30 in the afternoon of October 31, 1963, his attention was attracted by two men, Chilton and Terry, standing on the corner of Huron Road and Euclid Avenue. He had never seen the two men before, and he was unable to say precisely what first drew his eye to them. However, he testified that he had been a policeman for 39 years and a detective for 35 and that he had been assigned to patrol this vicinity of downtown Cleveland for shoplifters and pickpockets for 30 years. He explained that he had developed routine habits of observation over the years and that he would "stand and watch people or walk and watch people at many intervals of the day." He added: "Now, in this case when I looked over they didn't look right to me at the time."

His interest aroused, Officer McFadden took up a post of observation in the entrance to a store 300 to 400 feet away from the two men. "I get more purpose to watch them when I seen their movements," he testified. He saw one of the men leave the other one and walk southwest on Huron Road, past some stores. The man paused for a moment and looked in a store window, then walked on a short distance, turned around and walked back toward the corner, pausing once again to look in the same store window. He rejoined his companion at the corner, and the two conferred briefly. Then the second man went through the same series of motions, strolling down Huron Road, looking in the same window, walking on a short distance, turning back, peering in the store window again, and returning to confer with the first man at the corner. The two men repeated this ritual alternately between five and six times apiece—in all, roughly a dozen trips. At one point, while the two were standing together on the corner, a third man approached them and engaged them briefly in conversation. This man then left the two others and walked west on Euclid Avenue. Chilton and Terry resumed their measured pacing, peering and conferring. After this had gone on for 10 to 12 minutes, the two men walked off together, heading west on Euclid Avenue, following the path taken earlier by the third man.

By this time Officer McFadden had become thoroughly suspicious. He testified that after observing their elaborately casual and oft-repeated reconnaissance of the store window[,] he suspected the two men of "casing a job, a stick-up," and that he considered it his duty as a police officer to investigate further. [He] feared "they may have a gun." Thus, Officer McFadden followed Chilton and Terry and saw them stop in front of Zucker's store to talk to the same man who had conferred with them earlier on the street corner. Deciding that the situation was ripe for direct action, Officer McFadden approached the three men, identified himself as a police officer and asked for their names. At this point his knowledge was confined to what he had observed. He was not acquainted with any of the three men by name or by sight, and he had received no information concerning them from any other source. When the men "mumbled something" in response to his inquiries, Officer McFadden grabbed petitioner Terry, spun him around so that they were facing the other two, with Terry between McFadden and the others, and patted down the outside of his clothing. In the left breast pocket of Terry's overcoat Officer McFadden felt a pistol. He reached inside the overcoat[,] but was unable to remove the gun. At this point, keeping Terry between himself and the others, the officer ordered all three men to enter Zucker's store. As they went in, he removed Terry's overcoat completely, removed a .38–caliber revolver from the pocket and ordered all three men to face the wall with their hands raised. Officer McFadden proceeded to pat down the outer clothing of Chilton and the third man, Katz. He discovered another revolver in the outer pocket of Chilton's overcoat, but no weapons were found on Katz. The officer testified that he only patted the men down to see whether they had weapons, and that he did not put his hands beneath the outer garments of either Terry or Chilton until he felt their guns. [H]e never placed his hands beneath Katz' outer garments. Officer McFadden seized Chilton's gun, asked the proprietor of the store to call a police wagon, and took all three men to the station, where Chilton and Terry were formally charged with carrying concealed weapons.

[We] granted certiorari to determine whether the admission of the revolvers in evidence violated petitioner's rights under the Fourth Amendment, made applicable to the States by the [Fourteenth].

I.

[P]etitioner was entitled to the protection of the Fourth Amendment as he walked down the street in Cleveland. The question is whether in all the circumstances of this on-the-street encounter, his right to personal security was violated by an unreasonable search and seizure.

[T]his question thrusts to the fore difficult and troublesome issues regarding a sensitive area of police activity. [On] the one hand, it is frequently argued that in dealing with the rapidly unfolding and often dangerous situations on city streets the police are in need of an escalating set of flexible responses, graduated in relation to the amount of information they possess. For this purpose it is urged that distinctions should be made between a "stop" and an "arrest" (or a "seizure" of a person), and between a "frisk" and a "search." Thus, it is argued, the police should be allowed to "stop" a person and detain him briefly for questioning upon suspicion that he may be connected with criminal activity. Upon suspicion that the person may be armed, the police should have the power to "frisk" him for weapons. If the "stop" and the "frisk" give rise to probable cause to believe that the suspect has committed a crime, then the police should be empowered to make a formal "arrest," and a full incident "search" of the person. This scheme is justified in part upon the notion that a "stop" and a "frisk" amount to a mere "minor inconvenience and petty indignity," which can properly be imposed upon the citizen in the interest of effective law enforcement on the basis of a police officer's suspicion.

On the other side the argument is made that the authority of the police must be strictly circumscribed by the law of arrest and search as it has developed to date in the traditional jurisprudence of the Fourth Amendment. It is contended with some force that there is not—and cannot be—a variety of police activity which does not depend solely upon the voluntary cooperation of the citizen and yet which stops short of an arrest based upon probable cause to make such an arrest. The heart of the Fourth Amendment, the argument runs, is a severe requirement of specific justification for any intrusion upon protected personal security, coupled with a highly developed system of judicial controls to enforce upon the agents of the State the commands of the [Constitution].

[W]e approach the issues in this case mindful of the limitations of the judicial function in controlling the myriad daily situations in which policemen and citizens confront each other on the [street].

[We] turn our attention to the quite narrow question posed by the facts before us: whether it is always unreasonable for a policeman to seize a person and subject him to a limited search for weapons unless there is probable cause for an arrest. [Our] first task is to establish at what point in this encounter the Fourth Amendment becomes relevant. That is, we must decide whether and when Officer McFadden "seized" Terry and whether and when he conducted a "search." There is some suggestion in the use of such terms as "stop" and "frisk" that such police conduct is outside the purview of the Fourth Amendment because neither action rises to the level of a "search" or "seizure" within the meaning of the Constitution. We emphatically reject this notion. It is quite plain that the Fourth Amendment governs "seizures" of the person which do not eventuate in a trip to the station house and prosecution for crime—"arrests" in traditional terminology. [W]henever a police officer accosts an individual and restrains his freedom to walk away, he has "seized" that person. And it is nothing less than sheer torture of the English language to suggest that a careful exploration of the outer surfaces of a person's clothing all over his or her body in an attempt to find weapons is not a "search." Moreover, it is simply fantastic to urge that such a procedure performed in public by a policeman while the citizen stands helpless, perhaps facing a wall with his hands raised, is a "petty indignity." It is a serious intrusion upon the sanctity of the person, which may inflict great indignity and arouse strong resentment, and it is not to be undertaken lightly.

The danger in the logic which proceeds upon distinctions between a "stop" and an "arrest," or "seizure" of the person, and between a "frisk" and a "search" is twofold. It seeks to isolate from constitutional scrutiny the initial stages of the contact between the policeman and the citizen. And by suggesting a rigid all-or-nothing model of justification and regulation under the Amendment, it obscures the utility of limitations upon the scope, as well as the initiation, of police action as a means of constitutional regulation. This Court has held in the past that a search which is reasonable at its inception may violate the Fourth Amendment by virtue of its intolerable intensity and scope. The scope of the search must be "strictly tied to and justified by" the circumstances which rendered its initiation permissible.

The distinctions of classical "stop-and-frisk" theory thus serve to divert attention from the central inquiry under the Fourth Amendment—the reasonableness in all the circumstances of the particular governmental invasion of a citizen's personal security. "Search" and "seizure" are not talismans. We therefore reject the notions that the Fourth Amendment does not come into play at all as a limitation upon police conduct if the officers stop short of something called a "technical arrest" or a "full-blown search."

In this case there can be no question [that] Officer McFadden "seized" petitioner and subjected him to a "search" when he took hold of him and patted down the outer surfaces of his clothing. We must decide whether at that point it was reasonable for Officer McFadden to have interfered with petitioner's personal security as he did. And in determining whether the seizure and search were "unreasonable" our inquiry is a dual one—whether the officer's action was justified at its inception, and whether it was reasonably related in scope to the circumstances which justified the interference in the first place.

[We] do not retreat from our holdings that the police must, whenever practicable, obtain advance judicial approval of searches and seizures through the warrant procedure, or that in most instances failure to comply with the warrant requirement can only be excused by exigent circumstances. But we deal here with an entire rubric of police conduct—necessarily swift action predicated upon the on-the-spot observations of the officer on the beat—which historically has not been, and as a practical matter could not be, subjected to the warrant procedure. Instead, the conduct involved in this case must be tested by the Fourth Amendment's general proscription against unreasonable searches and seizures.

Nonetheless, the notions which underlie both the warrant procedure and the requirement of probable cause remain fully relevant in this context. In order to assess the reasonableness of Officer McFadden's conduct as a general proposition, it is necessary "first to focus upon the governmental interest which allegedly justifies official intrusion upon the constitutionally protected interests of the private citizen," for there is "no ready test for determining reasonableness other than by balancing the need to search (or seize) against the invasion which the search (or seizure) entails." *Camara v. Municipal Court*, 387 U.S. 523, 534–535 (1967). And in justifying the particular intrusion the police officer must be able to point to specific and articulable facts which, taken together with rational inferences from those facts, reasonably warrant that intrusion. The scheme of the Fourth Amendment becomes meaningful only when it is assured that at some point the conduct of those charged with enforcing the laws can be subjected to the more detached, neutral scrutiny of a judge who must evaluate the reasonableness of a particular search or seizure in light of the particular circumstances. And in making that assessment it is imperative that the facts be judged against an objective standard: would the facts available to the officer at the moment of the seizure or the search "warrant a man of reasonable caution in the belief" that the action taken was appropriate? Anything less would invite intrusions upon constitutionally guaranteed rights based on nothing more substantial than inarticulate hunches, a result this Court has consistently refused to sanction. And simple "good faith on the part of the arresting officer is not enough. [If] subjective good faith alone were the test, the protections of the Fourth Amendment would evaporate, and the people would be 'secure in their persons, houses, papers and effects,' only in the discretion of the police."

Applying these principles to this case, we consider first the nature and extent of the governmental interests involved. One general interest is [that] of effective crime prevention and detection; it is this interest which underlies the recognition that a police officer may in appropriate circumstances and in an appropriate manner approach a person for purposes of investigating possibly criminal behavior even though there is no probable cause to make an arrest. It was this legitimate investigative function Officer McFadden was discharging when he decided to approach petitioner and his companions [after] he had observed Terry, Chilton, and Katz go through a series of acts, each of them perhaps innocent in itself, but which taken together warranted further investigation. There is nothing unusual in two men standing together on a street corner, perhaps waiting for someone. Nor is there anything suspicious about people in such circumstances strolling up and down the street, singly or in pairs. Store windows, moreover, are made to be looked in. But the story is quite different where, as here, two men hover about a street corner for an extended period of time, at the end of which it becomes apparent that they are not waiting for anyone or anything; where these men pace alternately along an identical route, pausing to stare in the same store window roughly 24 times; where each completion of this route is followed immediately by a conference between the two men on the corner; where they are joined in one of these conferences by a third man who leaves swiftly; and where the two men finally follow the third and rejoin him a couple of blocks away. It would have been poor police work indeed for an officer of 30 years' experience in the detection of thievery from stores in this same neighborhood to have failed to investigate this behavior further.

The crux of this case, however, is not the propriety of Officer McFadden's taking steps to investigate petitioner's suspicious behavior, [but] whether there was justification for McFadden's invasion of Terry's personal security by searching him for weapons in the course of that investigation. We are now concerned with more than the governmental interest in investigating crime; [there] is the more immediate interest of the police officer in taking steps to assure himself that the person with whom he is dealing is not armed with a weapon that could unexpectedly and fatally be used against him. Certainly it would be unreasonable to require that police officers take unnecessary risks in the performance of their duties. American criminals have a long tradition of armed violence, and every year in this country many law enforcement officers are killed in the line of duty, and thousands more are wounded. Virtually all of these deaths and a substantial portion of the injuries are inflicted with guns and knives.

In view of these facts, we cannot blind ourselves to the need for law enforcement officers to protect themselves and other prospective victims of violence in situations where they may lack probable cause for an arrest. When an officer is justified in believing that the individual whose suspicious behavior he is investigating at close range is armed and presently dangerous to the officer or to others, it would appear to be clearly unreasonable to deny the officer the power to take necessary measures to determine whether the person is in fact carrying a weapon and to neutralize the threat of physical harm.

We must still consider, however, the nature and quality of the intrusion on individual rights which must be accepted if police officers are to be conceded the right to search for weapons in situations where probable cause to arrest for crime is lacking. Even a limited search of the outer clothing for weapons constitutes a severe, though brief, intrusion upon cherished personal security, and it must surely be an annoying, frightening, and perhaps humiliating experience. Petitioner contends that such an intrusion is permissible only incident to a lawful arrest, either for a crime involving the possession of weapons or for a crime the commission of which led the officer to investigate in the first place. However, this argument must be closely examined.

Petitioner does not argue that a police officer should refrain from making any investigation of suspicious circumstances until such time as he has probable cause to make an arrest; nor does he deny that police officers in properly discharging their investigative function may find themselves confronting persons who might well be armed and dangerous. Moreover, he does not say that an officer is always unjustified in searching a suspect to discover weapons. Rather, he says it is unreasonable for the policeman to take that step until such time as the situation evolves to a point where there is probable cause to make an arrest. When that point has been reached, petitioner would concede the officer's right to conduct a search of the suspect for weapons, fruits or instrumentalities of the crime, or "mere" evidence, incident to the arrest.

There are two weaknesses in this line of reasoning however. First, it fails to take account of traditional limitations upon the scope of searches, and thus recognizes no distinction in purpose, character, and extent between a search incident to an arrest and a limited search for weapons. The former, although justified in part by the acknowledged necessity to protect the arresting officer from assault with a concealed weapon, is also justified on other grounds, and can therefore involve a relatively extensive exploration of the person. A search for weapons in the absence of probable cause to arrest, however, must, like any other search, be strictly circumscribed by the exigencies which justify its initiation. Thus it must be limited to that which is necessary for the discovery of weapons which might be used to harm the officer or others nearby, and may realistically be characterized as something less than a "full" search, even though it remains a serious intrusion.

A second, and related, objection to petitioner's argument is that it assumes that the law of arrest has already worked out the balance between the particular interests involved here—the neutralization of danger to the policeman in the investigative circumstance and the sanctity of the individual. But this is not so. An arrest is a wholly different kind of intrusion upon individual freedom from a limited search for weapons, and the interests each is designed to serve are likewise quite different. An arrest is the initial stage of a criminal prosecution. It is intended to vindicate society's interest in having its laws obeyed, and it is inevitably accompanied by future interference with the individual's freedom of movement, whether or not trial or conviction ultimately follows. The protective search for weapons, on the other hand, constitutes a brief, though far from inconsiderable, intrusion upon the sanctity of the person. It does not follow that because an officer may lawfully arrest a person only when he is apprised of facts sufficient to warrant a belief that the person has committed or is committing a crime, the officer is equally unjustified, absent that kind of evidence, in making any intrusions short of an arrest. Moreover, a perfectly reasonable apprehension of danger may arise long before the officer is possessed of adequate information to justify taking a person into custody for the purpose of prosecuting him for a crime. Petitioner's reliance on cases which have worked out standards of reasonableness with regard to "seizures" constituting arrests and searches incident thereto is thus misplaced. It assumes that the interests sought to be vindicated and the invasions of personal security may be equated in the two cases, and thereby ignores a vital aspect of the analysis of the reasonableness of particular types of conduct under the Fourth Amendment.

Our evaluation of the proper balance that has to be struck in this type of case leads us to conclude that there must be a narrowly drawn authority to permit a reasonable search for weapons for the protection of the police officer, where he has reason to believe that he is dealing with an armed and dangerous individual, regardless of whether he has probable cause to arrest the individual for a crime. The officer need not be absolutely certain that the individual is armed; the issue is whether a reasonably prudent man in the circumstances would be warranted in the belief that his safety or that of others was in danger. And in determining whether the officer acted reasonably in such circumstances, due weight must be given, not to his inchoate and unparticularized suspicion or "hunch," but to the specific reasonable inferences which he is entitled to draw from the facts in light of his experience.

We must now examine the conduct of Officer McFadden in this case to determine whether his search and seizure of petitioner were reasonable, both at their inception and as conducted. He had observed Terry, together with Chilton and another man, acting in a manner he took to be preface to a "stick-up." We think on the facts and circumstances Officer McFadden detailed before the trial judge a reasonably prudent man would have been warranted in believing petitioner was armed and thus presented a threat to the officer's safety while he was investigating his suspicious behavior. The actions of Terry and Chilton were consistent with McFadden's hypothesis that these men were contemplating a daylight robbery—which, it is reasonable to assume, would be likely to involve the use of weapons—and nothing in their conduct from the time he first noticed them until the time he confronted them and identified himself as a police officer gave him sufficient reason to negate that hypothesis. Although the trio had departed the original scene, there was nothing to indicate abandonment of an intent to commit a robbery at some point. Thus, when Officer McFadden approached the three men gathered before the display window at Zucker's store he had observed enough to make it quite reasonable to fear that they were armed; and nothing in their response to his hailing them, identifying himself as a police officer, and asking their names served to dispel that reasonable belief. We cannot say his decision at that point to seize Terry and pat his clothing for weapons was the product of a volatile or inventive imagination, or was undertaken simply as an act of harassment; the record evidences the tempered act of a policeman who in the course of an investigation had to make a quick decision as to how to protect himself and others from possible danger, and took limited steps to do so.

The manner in which the seizure and search were conducted is, of course, as vital a part of the inquiry as whether they were warranted at [all]. We need not develop at length in this case, however, the limitations which the Fourth Amendment places upon a protective seizure and search for weapons. These limitations will have to be developed in the concrete factual circumstances of individual cases. Suffice it to note that such a search, unlike a search without a warrant incident to a lawful arrest, is not justified by any need to prevent the disappearance or destruction of evidence of crime. The sole justification of the search in the present situation is the protection of the police officer and others nearby, and it must therefore be confined in scope to an intrusion reasonably designed to discover guns, knives, clubs, or other hidden instruments for the assault of the police officer.

The scope of the search in this case presents no serious problem in light of these standards. Officer McFadden patted down the outer clothing of petitioner and his two companions. He did not place his hands in their pockets or under the outer surface of their garments until he had felt weapons, and then he merely reached for and removed the guns. He never did invade Katz' person beyond the outer surfaces of his clothes, since he discovered nothing in his patdown which might have been a weapon. Officer McFadden confined his search strictly to what was minimally necessary to learn whether the men were armed and to disarm them once he discovered the weapons. He did not conduct a general exploratory search for whatever evidence of criminal activity he might find.

We conclude that the revolver seized from Terry was properly admitted in evidence against him. At the time he seized petitioner and searched him for weapons, Officer McFadden had reasonable grounds to believe that petitioner was armed and dangerous, and it was necessary for the protection of himself and others to take swift measures to discover the true facts and neutralize the threat of harm if it materialized. The policeman carefully restricted his search to what was appropriate to the discovery of the particular items which he sought. Each case of this sort will, of course, have to be decided on its own facts. We merely hold today that where a police officer observes unusual conduct which leads him reasonably to conclude in light of his experience that criminal activity may be afoot and that the persons with whom he is dealing may be armed and presently dangerous, where in the course of investigating this behavior he identifies himself as a policeman and makes reasonable inquiries, and where nothing in the initial stages of the encounter serves to dispel his reasonable fear for his own or others' safety, he is entitled for the protection of himself and others in the area to conduct a carefully limited search of the outer clothing of such persons in an attempt to discover weapons which might be used to assault him. Such a search is a reasonable search under the Fourth Amendment, and any weapons seized may properly be introduced in evidence against the person from whom they were taken.

Affirmed.

MR. JUSTICE HARLAN, concurring.

[A] limited frisk incident to a lawful stop must often be rapid and routine. There is no reason why an officer, rightfully but forcibly confronting a person suspected of a serious crime, should have to ask one question and take the risk that the answer might be a [bullet].

MR. JUSTICE DOUGLAS, dissenting.

[The] infringement on personal liberty of any "seizure" of a person can only be "reasonable" under the Fourth Amendment if we require the police to possess "probable cause" before they seize him. Only that line draws a meaningful distinction between an officer's mere inkling and the presence of facts within the officer's personal knowledge which would convince a reasonable man that the person seized has committed, is committing, or is about to commit a particular crime.... To give the police greater power than a magistrate is to take a long step down the totalitarian path. Perhaps such a step is desirable to cope with modern forms of lawlessness. But if it is taken, it should be the deliberate choice of the people through a constitutional amendment. Until the Fourth Amendment [is] rewritten, the person and the effects of the individual are beyond the reach of all government agencies until there are reasonable grounds to believe (probable cause) that a criminal venture has been launched or is about to be launched. * * *

Notes

1. *More on Frisks.* In *Florida v. J.L.*, 529 U.S. 266 (2000), the police received an anonymous tip that a young black male at a bus stop wearing a plaid shirt was carrying a gun. At the stop, the police found three young black males including one who was wearing a plaid shirt. Apart from the tip, the officers had no reason to believe that any of the males was engaged in illegal conduct. The officers immediately frisked defendant and found a gun in his pocket, and charged him with carrying a concealed firearm. The Court invalidated the search: "All the police had to go on in this case was the bare report of an unknown, unaccountable informant who neither explained how he knew about the gun nor supplied any basis for believing he had inside information about J.L. An accurate description of a subject's readily observable location and appearance is of course reliable in this limited sense: It will help the police correctly identify the person whom the tipster means to accuse. Such a tip, however, does not show that the tipster has knowledge of concealed criminal activity. The reasonable suspicion here at issue requires that a tip be reliable in its assertion of illegality, not just in its tendency to identify a determinate person." The Court also rejected the state's contention that *Terry* should encompass a "firearms exception" permitting police to stop and frisk individuals for firearms.

2. *Defining "Armed and Dangerous."* In *Michigan v. Long*, 463 U.S. 1032 (1983), the police saw a car traveling "erratically" and at excessive speed. When the car turned down a side road and swerved off into a shallow ditch, the officers stopped to investigate. Long (the driver) appeared to be "under the influence of something," and both officers observed a large

hunting knife on the floorboard of the driver's side of the car. The officers then subjected Long to a *Terry* frisk which revealed no weapons, and searched his car where they found marijuana. The Court upheld Long's conviction for possession:

> [R]oadside encounters between police and suspects are especially hazardous, and that danger may arise from the possible presence of weapons in the area surrounding a suspect. [T]he search of the passenger compartment of an automobile, limited to those areas in which a weapon may be placed or hidden, is permissible if the police officer possesses a reasonable belief based on "specific and articulable facts which, taken together with the rational inferences from those facts, reasonably warrant" the officers in believing that the suspect is dangerous and the suspect may gain immediate control of weapons. . . . The circumstances of this case clearly justified [the officers] in their reasonable belief that Long posed a danger if he were permitted to reenter his vehicle. The hour was late and the area rural. Long was driving his automobile at excessive speed, and his car swerved into a ditch. The officers had to repeat their questions to Long, who appeared to be "under the influence" of some intoxicant. Long was not frisked until the officers observed that there was a large knife in the interior of the car into which Long was about to reenter. The subsequent search of the car was restricted to those areas to which Long would generally have immediate control, and that could contain a weapon. [The] leather pouch containing marijuana could have contained a weapon. It is clear that the intrusion was "strictly circumscribed by the exigencies which justifi[ed] its initiation." [A] *Terry* suspect in Long's position [might] break away from police control and retrieve a weapon from his automobile. In addition, if the suspect is not placed under arrest, he will be permitted to reenter his automobile, and he will then have access to any weapons inside. [Or] the suspect may be permitted to reenter the vehicle before the *Terry* investigation is over, and again, may have access to weapons. . . .

3. *A different standard for schoolchildren?* In *New Jersey v. T.L.O.*, 469 U.S. 325 (1985), a teacher found two girls smoking in a lavatory. Both girls were taken to the Principal's office where they met with the Assistant Vice Principal, Mr. Choplick. When T.L.O. denied that she had been smoking, Choplick demanded to see her purse. In the purse, he found cigarettes, rolling papers, marijuana and a substantial number of one-dollar bills. Afterwards, T.L.O. confessed to the crime of selling marijuana. Based on the confession and the evidence found during the search, delinquency charges were brought against T.L.O. The Court upheld the search after holding that the Fourth Amendment applies to searches by public school officials, but held that such officials had greater latitude:

> Against the child's interest in privacy must be set the substantial interest of teachers and administrators in maintaining discipline in the classroom and on school grounds. [I]n recent years, school disorder has often taken particularly ugly forms: drug use and violent crime in the schools have become major social problems. * * *

[T]he school setting requires some easing of the restrictions to which searches by public authorities are ordinarily subject. The warrant requirement, [would] unduly interfere with the maintenance of the swift and informal disciplinary procedures needed in the schools. [T]he legality of a search of a student should depend simply on the reasonableness, under all the circumstances, of the search. Determining the reasonableness of any search involves a twofold inquiry: first, one must consider "whether the [action] was justified at its inception," [and] whether the search as actually conducted "was reasonably related in scope to the circumstances which justified the interference in the first place." Under ordinary circumstances, a search of a student by a teacher or other school official will be "justified at its inception" when there are reasonable grounds for suspecting that the search will turn up evidence that the student has violated or is violating either the law or the rules of the school. Such a search will be permissible in its scope when the measures adopted are reasonably related to the objectives of the search and not excessively intrusive in light of the age and sex of the student and the nature of the infraction.

[This] search was in no sense unreasonable for Fourth Amendment purposes. [A] teacher had reported that T.L.O. was smoking in the lavatory. [T]his report gave Mr. Choplick reason to suspect that T.L.O. was carrying cigarettes with her; and if she did have cigarettes, her purse was the obvious place in which to find them. [The] suspicion upon which the search for marihuana was founded was provided when Mr. Choplick observed a package of rolling papers in the purse as he removed the pack of cigarettes. [The] discovery of the rolling papers concededly gave rise to a reasonable suspicion that T.L.O. was carrying marihuana as well as cigarettes in her purse. This suspicion justified further exploration of T.L.O.'s purse, which turned up more evidence of drug-related [activities]. [I]t was not unreasonable to extend the search to a separate zippered compartment of the purse; and when a search of that compartment revealed an index card containing a list of "people who owe me money" as well as two letters, the inference that T.L.O. was involved in marihuana trafficking was substantial enough to justify Mr. Choplick in examining the letters to determine whether they contained any further evidence. In short, we cannot conclude that the search for marihuana was unreasonable in any respect.

Justice Powell concurred: "[S]tudents within the school environment have a lesser expectation of privacy than members of the population generally. [The] special relationship between teacher and student also distinguishes the setting within which schoolchildren operate. The] primary duty of school officials and teachers [is] the education and training of young people. A State has a compelling interest in assuring that the schools meet this responsibility. [Also,] the school has the obligation to protect pupils from mistreatment by other children, and also to protect teachers themselves from violence by the few students whose conduct in recent years has prompted national concern."

Justice Brennan concurred in part and dissented in part: "Mr. Choplick's suspicion of marihuana possession at this time was based solely on the presence of the package of cigarette papers. The mere presence without more of such a staple item of commerce is insufficient to warrant [the inference] both that T.L.O. had violated the law by possessing marihuana and that evidence of that violation would be found in her purse." Justice Stevens also concurred in part and dissented in part: "[I] would view this case differently if the Assistant Vice Principal had reason to believe T.L.O.'s purse contained evidence of criminal activity, or of an activity that would seriously disrupt school discipline. There was, however, absolutely no basis for any such assumption—not even a 'hunch.' "

Problems

1. *Justifying the Stop and Frisk Exception.* Was it really necessary for the Court to create the stop and frisk exception? Did Officer McFadden have probable cause to arrest Terry and his cohorts? Did he have probable cause to search them? Even if McFadden possessed probable cause to search, based on what you have studied thus far, could he have searched Terry without a warrant? Should Officer McFadden have been forced to wait until Terry and his cohorts "made their move?"

2. *Suspicious Men.* Police receive a phone tip at 3:00 a.m. that "three suspicious men" have been seated in a motorcar parked in a business district since 10:00 p.m. the prior evening. Police officers investigate and observe three men in the car. The officers ask the three men why they are parked there, but receive evasive answers. All three men admit that they are unemployed; all of them together have only 25 cents. One of the men says that he bought the car the day before, but he is unable to produce a title. The men say that they plan to meet a truck driver who will pass through the city that night, but they cannot identify the company he works for, cannot say what the truck will look like, and do not know what time he will arrive. The officers search the passenger compartment for weapons and find two loaded revolvers in the glove compartment. Did the police act properly in searching the passenger compartment of the vehicle? *See Preston v. United States*, 376 U.S. 364 (1964).

3. *More on the Suspicious Men.* In the prior problem, suppose that it is illegal to carry concealed weapons. As a result, the officers place the men under arrest. The police then search the trunk where they find women's stockings (one with mouth and eye holes), rope, pillow slips, and an illegally manufactured license plate equipped to be snapped over another plate. Should the items found in the trunk be suppressed?

4. *Investigative Stops.* In *Fields v. Swenson*, 459 F.2d 1064 (8th Cir. 1972), late at night, two police officers observed a station wagon at rest in an unlighted section of a parking lot near a hardware store. All nearby business establishments were closed. One of the officers was familiar with the area

and had never seen the car before, but he recognized the license number as belonging to a David Montgomery, whom he knew as a suspect in some prior burglaries. At 11:40 p.m., the officers saw three persons approach the car "carrying something." One entered the car's back seat while the other two walked back into the parking lot. When one drove the car away, the police followed for several blocks and saw the occupant of the rear seat take off a red jacket. When the officers stopped the car, they observed a lady's handbag containing tools (hammers and other large tools) on the floor. The occupants of the car were then placed under arrest for "investigation of burglary and larceny" and possession of burglary tools. The Rambler was searched, and the police found pistols under the front and back seats, ammunition, chisels and other small tools, a hunting cap and some cotton gloves. Some of the items had "Peer Hardware" stickers attached. About this time, a radio report was made to police headquarters that Peer Hardware had been burglarized. Should the court uphold the stop and the search?

5. *Drug Activity?* A police officer is patrolling when he observes Sibron "continually from the hours of 4:00 p.m. to midnight [in] the vicinity of 742 Broadway." During this period, the officer sees Sibron in conversation with 6 to 8 people whom the officer knows from past experience to be narcotics addicts. The officer does not overhear any of these conversations, and did not see anything pass between Sibron and the others. Late in the evening, Sibron enters a restaurant and speaks with three more known addicts. Again, nothing is overheard and nothing is seen to pass between Sibron and the addicts. After Sibron sits down and began eating, the officer approaches and asks him to come outside. There, the officer says to Sibron, "You know what I am after." Sibron "mumbled something and reached into his pocket." Simultaneously, the officer thrust his hand into the same pocket, discovering several glassine envelopes which contained heroin. Did the officer have adequate grounds to frisk Sibron? Was the scope of the frisk permissible? *See Sibron v. New York*, 392 U.S. 40 (1968).

6. The "Bulge." Police officers observe Bill Andris driving a car with an expired license plate. The officers stop Andris to issue a traffic summons. The officers approach the car, and ask Andris to step out to produce his owner's card and operator's license. When Andris alights, the officer notices a large bulge under Andris' sports jacket. Fearing that the bulge might be a weapon, the officer frisks Andris and discovers in his waistband a .38–caliber revolver loaded with five rounds of ammunition. Andris is immediately arrested and subsequently indicted for carrying a concealed deadly weapon and for unlawfully carrying a firearm without a license. Under the circumstances, was a frisk appropriate? Would it matter whether it was legal to carry a concealed weapon in the subject jurisdiction? Did the police act properly in searching Andris? *See Pennsylvania v. Mimms*, 434 U.S. 106 (1977).

7. *The Fleeing Suspect.* While police officers are patrolling in a heavy narcotics trafficking area, they see defendant flee when he sees them. The officers chase defendant, catch him, and subject him to a pat-down search for

weapons. During the frisk, an officer squeeze the bag defendant is carrying and feels a heavy, hard object similar to the shape of a gun. The officer then opens the bag and discovers a .38–caliber handgun with five live rounds of ammunition. Did the officer exceed the proper scope of a frisk? *See Illinois v. Wardlow*, 528 U.S. 119 (2000).

8. *The Seated Suspect.* At 2:00 a.m., a police officer in a high crime area is informed that an individual seated in a nearby vehicle is carrying narcotics and has a gun at his waist. The officer approaches the vehicle, taps on the window, and asks the driver to open the door. When the driver rolls down the window instead, the officer reaches into the car and removes a fully loaded revolver from the driver's waistband. The gun was not visible to the officer from outside the car, but it was in precisely the place indicated by the informant. The officer then arrests the driver for unlawful possession of the pistol. A search incident to arrest reveals heroin on the driver's person and in the car, as well as a machete and a second revolver hidden in the automobile. Did the officer have adequate grounds for a frisk? Did he exceed the permissible scope of a frisk? *See Adams v. Williams*, 407 U.S. 143 (1972).

a. Other Investigatory Searches and Seizures

In addition to authorizing a "frisk," *Terry* also authorizes police to make a "stop" which is a form of seizure. The Fourth Amendment prohibits not only unreasonable searches, but also unreasonable "seizures." The Court has recognized many different types of seizures ranging from an investigatory stop to an arrest. These seizures are subject to differing constitutional requirements.

Most seizures are investigative in nature and can be relatively brief. Roadside stops usually fit this description. But police also "seize" individuals for fingerprinting, lineups or interrogation purposes. What constitutes a seizure? When are such seizures valid? Consider the following cases.

UNITED STATES v. MENDENHALL

446 U.S. 544 (1980).

MR. JUSTICE STEWART announced the judgment of the Court and delivered an opinion, in which MR. JUSTICE REHNQUIST joined.

[R]espondent arrived at the Detroit Metropolitan Airport on a commercial airline flight from Los Angeles early in the morning on February 10, 1976. As she disembarked from the airplane, she was observed by two agents of the DEA, who were present at the airport for the purpose of detecting unlawful traffic in narcotics. After observing the respondent's conduct, which appeared to the agents to be characteristic of persons unlawfully carrying narcotics, the agents approached her as she was walking through the concourse, identified themselves as federal agents, and asked to see her identification and airline ticket. The respondent produced her driver's license, which was in the name of Sylvia Mendenhall, and, in answer to a question of one of the agents, stated that she resided at the address appearing on the license. The airline ticket was issued in the name of "Annette Ford." When asked why the ticket bore a name different from her own, the respondent stated that she "just felt like using that name." In response to a further question, the respondent indicated that she had been in California only two days. Agent Anderson then specifically identified himself as a federal narcotics agent [and] the respondent "became quite shaken, extremely nervous. She had a hard time speaking."

After returning the airline ticket and driver's license to her, Agent Anderson asked the respondent if she would accompany him to the airport DEA office for further questions. She did so, although the record does not indicate a verbal response to the request. The office, which was located up one flight of stairs about 50 feet from where the respondent had first been approached, consisted of a reception area adjoined by three other rooms. At the office the agent asked the respondent if she would allow a search of her person and handbag and told her that she had the right to decline the search if she desired. She responded: "Go ahead." She then handed Agent Anderson her purse, which contained a receipt for an airline ticket that had been issued to "F. Bush" three days earlier for a flight from Pittsburgh through Chicago to Los Angeles. The agent asked whether this was the ticket that she had used for her flight to California, and the respondent stated that it was.

A female police officer then arrived to conduct the search of the respondent's person. She asked the agents if the respondent had consented to be searched. The agents said that she had, and the respondent followed the policewoman into a private room. There the policewoman again asked the respondent if she consented to the search, and the respondent replied that she did. The policewoman explained that the search would require that the respondent remove her clothing. The respondent stated that she had a plane to catch and was assured by the policewoman that if she were carrying no narcotics, there would be no problem. The respondent then began to disrobe without further comment. As the respondent removed her clothing, she took from her undergarments two small packages, one of which appeared to contain heroin, and handed both to the policewoman. The agents then arrested the respondent for possessing heroin. [At her trial, respondent moved to suppress the heroin. The motion was denied.]

[T]he Government concedes that its agents had neither a warrant nor probable cause to believe that the respondent was carrying narcotics when the agents conducted a search of the respondent's person. It is the Government's position [that] the search was conducted pursuant to the respondent's consent, and thus was excepted from the requirements of both a warrant and probable cause. * * *

The Fourth Amendment's requirement that searches and seizures be founded upon an objective justification, governs all seizures of the person, "including seizures that involve only a brief detention short of traditional arrest." Accordingly, if the respondent was "seized" when the DEA agents approached her on the concourse and asked questions of her, the agents' conduct in doing so was constitutional only if they reasonably suspected the respondent of wrongdoing. But "[o]bviously, not all personal intercourse between policemen and citizens involves 'seizures' of persons. Only when the officer, by means of physical force or show of authority, has in some way restrained the liberty of a citizen may we conclude that a 'seizure' has occurred."

[A] person is "seized" only when, by means of physical force or a show of authority, his freedom of movement is restrained. Only when such restraint is imposed is there any foundation whatever for invoking constitutional safeguards. The purpose of the Fourth Amendment is not to eliminate all contact between the police and the citizenry, but "to prevent arbitrary and oppressive interference by enforcement officials with the privacy and personal security of individuals." As long as the person to whom questions are put remains free to disregard the questions and walk away, there has been no intrusion upon that person's liberty or privacy as would under the Constitution require some particularized and objective justification.

[C]haracterizing every street encounter between a citizen and the police as a "seizure," while not enhancing any interest secured by the Fourth Amendment, would impose wholly unrealistic restrictions upon a wide variety of legitimate law enforcement practices. The Court [has] referred to the acknowledged need for police questioning as a tool in the effective enforcement of the criminal laws. "Without such investigation, those who were innocent might be falsely accused, those who were guilty might wholly escape prosecution, and many crimes would go unsolved. In short, the security of all would be diminished." *Schneckloth v. Bustamonte*, 412 U.S., at 225.

We conclude that a person has been "seized" within the meaning of the Fourth Amendment only if, in view of all of the circumstances surrounding the incident, a reasonable person would have believed that he was not free to leave.[8] Examples of circumstances that might indicate a seizure, even where the person did not attempt to leave, would be the threatening presence of several officers, the display of a weapon by an officer, some physical touching of the person of the citizen, or the use of language or tone of voice indicating that compliance with the officer's request might be compelled. In the absence of some such evidence, otherwise inoffensive contact between a member of the public and the police cannot, as a matter of law, amount to a seizure of that person.

8. [T]he subjective intention of the DEA agent in this case to detain the respondent, had she attempted to leave, is irrelevant except insofar as that may have been conveyed to the respondent.

On the facts of this case, no "seizure" of the respondent occurred. The events took place in the public concourse. The agents wore no uniforms and displayed no weapons. They did not summon the respondent to their presence, but instead approached her and identified themselves as federal agents. They requested, but did not demand to see the respondent's identification and ticket. Such conduct without more, did not amount to an intrusion upon any constitutionally protected interest. The respondent was not seized simply by reason of the fact that the agents approached her, asked her if she would show them her ticket and identification, and posed to her a few questions. Nor was it enough to establish a seizure that the person asking the questions was a law enforcement official. In short, nothing in the record suggests that the respondent had any objective reason to believe that she was not free to end the conversation in the concourse and proceed on her way, and for that reason we conclude that the agents' initial approach to her was not a seizure.

Our conclusion that no seizure occurred is not affected by the fact that the respondent was not expressly told by the agents that she was free to decline to cooperate with their inquiry, for the voluntariness of her responses does not depend upon her having been so informed. We also reject the argument that the only inference to be drawn from the fact that the respondent acted in a manner so contrary to her self-interest is that she was compelled to answer the agents' questions. It may happen that a person makes statements to law enforcement officials that he later regrets, but the issue in such cases is not whether the statement was self-protective, but rather whether it was made voluntarily.

[Although] we have concluded that the initial encounter between the DEA agents and the respondent on the concourse at the Detroit Airport did not constitute an unlawful seizure, it is still arguable that the respondent's Fourth Amendment protections were violated when she went from the concourse to the DEA office. Such a violation might in turn infect the subsequent search of the respondent's person.

[W]hether the respondent's consent to accompany the agents was in fact voluntary or was the product of duress or coercion, express or implied, is to be determined by the totality of all the circumstances, and is a matter which the Government has the burden of proving. [The] Government's evidence showed that the respondent was not told that she had to go to the office, but was simply asked if she would accompany the officers. There were neither threats nor any show of force. The respondent had been questioned only briefly, and her ticket and identification were returned to her before she was asked to accompany the officers.

[I]t is argued that the incident would reasonably have appeared coercive to the respondent, who was 22 years old and had not been graduated from high school. It is additionally suggested that the respondent, a female and a Negro, may have felt unusually threatened by the officers, who were white males. While these factors were not irrelevant, neither were they decisive, and the totality of the evidence in this case was plainly adequate to support [the] finding that the respondent voluntarily consented to accompany the officers to the DEA office.

Because the search of the respondent's person was not preceded by an impermissible seizure of her person, it cannot be contended that her apparent consent to the subsequent search was infected by an unlawful detention. There remains to be considered whether the respondent's consent to the search was for any other reason invalid. The District Court [found] that the "consent was freely and voluntarily given." There was more than enough evidence in this case to sustain that view. First, we note that the respondent, who was 22 years old and had an 11th-grade education, was plainly capable of a knowing consent. Second, it is especially significant that the respondent was twice expressly told that she was free to decline to consent to the search, and only thereafter explicitly consented to it. Although the Constitution does not require "proof of knowledge of a right to refuse as the *sine qua non* of an effective consent to a search," such knowledge was highly relevant to the determination that there had been consent. And, perhaps more important for present purposes, the fact that the officers themselves informed the respondent that she was free to withhold her consent substantially lessened the probability that their conduct could reasonably have appeared to her to be coercive.

Counsel for the respondent has argued that she did in fact resist the search, relying principally on the testimony that when she was told that the search would require the removal of her clothing, she stated to the female police officer that "she had a plane to catch." But the trial court was entitled to view the statement as simply an expression of concern that the search be conducted quickly. The respondent had twice unequivocally indicated her consent to the search, and when assured by the police officer that there would be no problem if nothing were turned up by the search, she began to undress without further comment.

Counsel for the respondent has also argued that because she was within the DEA office when she consented to the search, her consent may have resulted from the inherently coercive nature of those surroundings. But [there] is little or no evidence that she was in any way coerced. [I]n response to the argument that the respondent would not voluntarily have consented to a search that was likely to disclose the narcotics that she carried, we repeat that the question is not whether the respondent acted in her ultimate self-interest, but whether she acted voluntarily.[9]

We conclude that the District Court's determination that the respondent consented to the search of her person "freely and voluntarily" was sustained by the [evidence].

It is so ordered.

---

9. [R]espondent may have thought she was acting in her self-interest by voluntarily cooperating with the officers in the hope of receiving more lenient treatment.

MR. JUSTICE WHITE, with whom MR. JUSTICE BRENNAN, MR. JUSTICE MARSHALL, and MR. JUSTICE STEVENS join, dissenting.

[Ms. Mendenhall] undoubtedly was "seized" within the meaning of the Fourth Amendment when the agents escorted her from the public area of the terminal to the DEA office for questioning and a strip-search of her person. [Although] Ms. Mendenhall was not told that she was under arrest, she in fact was not free to refuse to go to the DEA office and was not told that she was. Furthermore, once inside the office, Ms. Mendenhall would not have been permitted to leave without submitting to a strip-search. [The Court's conclusion] that the "totality of evidence was plainly adequate" to support a finding of consent [can] only be based on the notion that consent can be assumed from the absence of proof that a suspect resisted police authority. This is a notion that we have squarely rejected. [T]he Government [cannot] rely solely on acquiescence to the officers' wishes to establish the requisite consent. [Because] Ms. Mendenhall was being illegally detained at the time of the search of her person, her suppression motion should have been granted in the absence of evidence to dissipate the taint.

Notes

1. *Bus Sweeps.* In *Florida v. Bostick*, 501 U.S. 429 (1991), two police officers, with badges, insignia and holstered pistols, boarded a bus bound from Miami to Atlanta during a stopover in Fort Lauderdale. Without any articulable suspicion, the officers picked out defendant passenger and asked to inspect his ticket and identification. The ticket matched the defendant's identification and both were immediately returned to him. The officers then explained their presence as narcotics agents on the lookout for illegal drugs, and requested consent to search his luggage. The police specifically advised defendant that he had the right to refuse consent, and they did not threaten him with their weapons. The Court concluded that defendant had not been "seized" within the meaning of the Fourth Amendment, and that his consent was therefore valid: "[When] police attempt to question a person who is walking down the street or through an airport lobby, it makes sense to inquire whether a reasonable person would feel free to continue walking. But when the person is seated on a bus and has no desire to leave, the degree to which a reasonable person would feel that he or she could leave is not an accurate measure of the coercive effect of the encounter." Justice Marshall dissented: "[O]fficers who conduct suspicionless, dragnet-style sweeps put passengers to the choice of cooperating or of exiting their buses and possibly being stranded in unfamiliar locations. It is exactly because this 'choice' is no 'choice' at all that police engage this technique. [The police may] continue to confront passengers without suspicion so long as they [take] simple steps, like advising the passengers confronted of their right to decline to be questioned, to dispel the aura of coercion and intimidation that pervades such encounters."

2. *Factory Sweeps.* In *Immigration and Naturalization Service v. Delgado*, 466 U.S. 210 (1984), under a warrant based on probable cause, the INS surveyed the work force at a plant looking for illegal aliens. Some agents

positioned themselves near the buildings' exits, while other agents dispersed throughout the factory to question employees at their work stations. The agents displayed badges, carried walkie-talkies, and carried holstered weapons. The agents approached employees and, after identifying themselves, asked one to three questions relating to their citizenship. If an employee gave a credible reply that he was a United States citizen, the questioning ended, and the agent moved on to another employee. If the employee gave an unsatisfactory response or admitted that he was an alien, the employee was asked to produce his immigration papers. During the survey, employees continued with their work and were free to walk about the factory. The Court rejected the employees' claim that they had been "seized":

> [W]hen people are at work their freedom to move about has been meaningfully restricted, not by the actions of law enforcement officials, but by the workers' voluntary obligations to their employers. [Respondents argue that] the stationing of agents near the factory doors showed the INS's intent to prevent people from leaving. But there is nothing in the record indicating that this is what the agents at the doors actually did. The obvious purpose of the agents' presence at the factory doors was to insure that all persons in the factories were questioned. [If] mere questioning does not constitute a seizure when it occurs inside the factory, it is no more a seizure when it occurs at the exits.

> Respondents argue that the manner in which the surveys were conducted and the attendant disruption caused by the surveys created a psychological environment which made them reasonably afraid they were not free to leave. [I]t was obvious from the beginning of the surveys that the INS agents were only questioning people. Persons such as respondents who simply went about their business in the workplace were not detained in any way; nothing more occurred than that a question was put to them. While persons who attempted to flee or evade the agents may eventually have been detained for questioning, respondents did not do so and were not in fact detained. The manner in which respondents were questioned, given its obvious purpose, could hardly result in a reasonable fear that respondents were not free to continue working or to move about the factory. [T]he encounters with the INS agents [were] classic consensual encounters rather than Fourth Amendment seizures.

Justice Brennan concurred in part and dissented in part:

> [T]he surveys were carried out by surprise by relatively large numbers of agents, generally from 15 to 25, who moved systematically through the rows of workers who were seated at their work stations. [A]s the INS agents discovered persons whom they suspected of being illegal aliens, they would handcuff these persons and lead them away to waiting vans outside the factory. [A]ll of the factory exits were conspicuously guarded by INS agents, stationed there to prevent anyone from leaving while the survey was being conducted. Finally, as the INS agents moved through the rows of workers, they would show their badges and direct pointed questions at the workers. [It is] fantastic to conclude that a reasonable person could ignore all that was occurring throughout the factory and, when the INS agents reached him, have the temerity to believe that he was at liberty to refuse to answer their questions and

walk away. [R]espondents' testimony paints a frightening picture of people subjected to wholesale interrogation under conditions designed not to respect personal security and privacy, but rather to elicit prompt answers from completely intimidated workers. [T]hese tactics amounted to seizures of respondents under the Fourth Amendment.

Problems

1. *Applying Mendenhall.* What additional facts, or changes in fact, would have been sufficient to transform the *Mendenhall* situation into a "seizure?"

2. *Evaluating Mendenhall.* Do you agree with the holding in *Mendenhall*? Would an ordinary person (one not schooled in criminal procedure), who is approached by the police in an airport, believe that she is "free to leave? Would the average traveler believe that she could respond to a police request by saying "Sorry, I'd love to chat with you, but I need to get a cup of coffee and don't really have time to chat. Perhaps next time." Or would the ordinary person more likely believe that she was required to submit to police questioning?

3. *More on Mendenhall.* Given that Mendenhall must have known that she was carrying drugs in her clothes, how do you explain her decision to submit to a strip search? Was she acting voluntarily, or out of public spirit? Or did she not realize that she had the right to refuse?

4. *Applying Mendenhall.* On your way home from this class, a police cruiser follows you for three blocks when the officer turns on his lights and siren. Believing that the officer wants you to stop, you pull off the road. The officer pulls over behind you and approaches your car. Under *Mendenhall*, have you been seized?

5. *More on Applying Mendenhall.* A robbery occurs at the campus book store. Shortly afterwards, the police search the campus for the robbers as well as for evidence. About this time, you are walking across campus on your way to this class. A police officer approaches you and says: "A robbery has just occurred at the campus book store. I'm looking for witnesses and would like to ask you a few questions." Have you been "seized" within the meaning of the Fourth Amendment?

6. *Yet More on Applying Mendenhall.* In the prior problem, would you conclude that you had been "seized" if the officer regarded you as a possible suspect rather than as a witness? Is the officer's subjective intent relevant? What arguments can you make in support of the position that you have been "seized"? Does the State have any counter arguments?

CALIFORNIA v. HODARI D.
499 U.S. 621 (1991).

Justice Scalia delivered the opinion of the Court.

Late one evening[,] Officers Brian McColgin and Jerry Pertoso were on patrol in a high-crime area of Oakland, California. They were dressed in street clothes but wearing jackets with "Police" embossed on both front and back. Their unmarked car proceeded west on Foothill Boulevard, and turned south onto 63rd Avenue. As they rounded the corner, they saw four or five youths huddled around a small red car parked at the curb. When the youths saw the officers' car approaching they apparently panicked, and took flight. The respondent[,] Hodari D., and one companion ran west through an alley; the others fled south. The red car also headed south, at a high rate of speed.

The officers were suspicious and gave chase. McColgin remained in the car and continued south on 63rd Avenue; Pertoso left the car, ran back north along 63rd, then west on Foothill Boulevard, and turned south on 62nd Avenue. Hodari, meanwhile, emerged from the alley onto 62nd and ran north. Looking behind as he ran, he did not turn and see Pertoso until the officer was almost upon him, whereupon he tossed away what appeared to be a small rock. A moment later, Pertoso tackled Hodari, handcuffed him, and radioed for assistance. Hodari was found to be carrying $130 in cash and a pager; and the rock he had discarded was found to be crack cocaine. In the juvenile proceeding brought against him, Hodari moved to suppress the evidence relating to the cocaine. The court denied the motion. * * *

[T]he only issue [is] whether, at the time he dropped the drugs, Hodari had been "seized" within the meaning of the Fourth Amendment. If so, respondent argues, the drugs were the fruit of that seizure and the evidence concerning them was properly excluded. If not, the drugs were abandoned by Hodari and lawfully recovered by the police, and the evidence should have been admitted.

[T]he Fourth Amendment's protection against "unreasonable [seizures]" includes seizure of the person. From the time of the founding to the present, the word "seizure" has meant a "taking possession." For most purposes at common law, the word connoted not merely grasping, or applying physical force to, the animate or inanimate object in question, but actually bringing it within physical control. A ship still fleeing, even though under attack, would not be considered to have been seized as a war prize. A res capable of manual delivery was not seized until "tak[en] into custody." To constitute an arrest, however—the quintessential "seizure of the person" under our Fourth Amendment jurisprudence—the mere grasping or application of physical force with lawful authority, whether or not it succeeded in subduing the arrestee, was sufficient. As one commentator has described it: "There can be constructive detention, which will constitute an arrest, although the party is never actually brought within the physical control of the party making an arrest. This is accomplished by merely touching, however slightly, the body of the accused, by the party making the arrest and for that purpose, although he does not succeed in stopping or holding him even for an instant; as where the bailiff had tried to arrest one who fought him off by a fork, the court said, 'If the bailiff had touched him, that had been an [arrest]'"A. CORNELIUS, SEARCH AND SEIZURE 163–164 (2d ed. 1930).

To say that an arrest is effected by the slightest application of physical force, despite the arrestee's escape, is not to say that for Fourth Amendment purposes there is a continuing arrest during the period of fugitivity. If, for example, Pertoso had laid his hands upon Hodari to arrest him, but Hodari had broken away and had then cast away the cocaine, it would hardly be realistic to say that that disclosure had been made during the course of an arrest. The present case, however, is even one step further removed. It does not involve the application of any physical force; Hodari was untouched by Officer Pertoso at the time he discarded the cocaine. His defense relies instead upon the proposition that a seizure occurs "when the officer, by means of physical force or show of authority, has in some way restrained the liberty of a citizen." Hodari contends (and we accept as true for purposes of this decision) that Pertoso's pursuit qualified as a "show of authority" calling upon Hodari to halt. The narrow question before us is whether, with respect to a show of authority as with respect to application of physical force, a seizure occurs even though the subject does not yield. We hold that it does not.

The language of the Fourth Amendment [cannot] sustain respondent's contention. The word "seizure" readily bears the meaning of a laying on of hands or application of physical force to restrain movement, even when it is ultimately unsuccessful. ("She seized the purse-snatcher, but he broke out of her grasp.") It does not remotely apply, however, to the prospect of a policeman yelling "Stop, in the name of the law!" at a fleeing form that continues to flee. That is no seizure. Nor can the result respondent wishes to achieve be produced—indirectly by suggesting that Pertoso's uncomplied—with show of authority was a common-law arrest, and then appealing to the principle that all common-law arrests are seizures. An arrest requires either physical force [or], where that is absent, submission to the assertion of authority.

"Mere words will not constitute an arrest, while, on the other hand, no actual, physical touching is essential. The apparent inconsistency in the two parts of this statement is explained by the fact that an assertion of authority and purpose to arrest followed by submission of the arrestee constitutes an arrest. There can be no arrest without either touching or submission." Perkins, *The Law of Arrest*, 25 Iowa L.Rev. 201, 206 (1940).

We do not think it desirable, even as a policy matter, to stretch the Fourth Amendment beyond its words and beyond the meaning of arrest[.] Street pursuits always place the public at some risk, and compliance with police orders to stop should therefore be encouraged. Only a few of those orders [will] be without adequate basis, and since the addressee has no ready means of identifying the deficient ones it almost invariably is the responsible course to comply. Unlawful orders will not be deterred, moreover, by sanctioning through the exclusionary rule those of them that are not obeyed. Since policemen do not command "Stop!" expecting to be ignored, or give chase hoping to be outrun, it fully suffices to apply the deterrent to their genuine, successful seizures.

Respondent contends that his position is sustained by [the] *Mendenhall* [test] [*United States v. Mendenhall*, 446 U.S. 544 (1980)]. [That test] says that a person has been seized "only if," not that he has been seized "whenever"; it states a necessary, but not a sufficient, condition for seizure—or, more precisely, for seizure effected through a "show of authority." *Mendenhall* establishes that the test for existence of a "show of authority" is an objective one: not whether the citizen perceived that he was being ordered to restrict his movement, but whether the officer's words and actions would have conveyed that to a reasonable person. Application of this objective test was the basis for our decision in the other case principally relied upon by respondent where we concluded that the police cruiser's slow following of the defendant did not convey the message that he was not free to disregard the police and go about his business. We did not address in *Chesternut*, however, the question whether, if the *Mendenhall* test was met—if the message that the defendant was not free to leave had been conveyed—a Fourth Amendment seizure would have occurred.

In sum, assuming that Pertoso's pursuit in the present case constituted a "show of authority" enjoining Hodari to halt, since Hodari did not comply with that injunction he was not seized until he was tackled. The cocaine abandoned while he was running was in this case not the fruit of a seizure, and his motion to exclude evidence of it was properly denied. We reverse the decision of the California Court of Appeal, and remand for further proceedings not inconsistent with this opinion.

It is so ordered.

JUSTICE STEVENS, with whom JUSTICE MARSHALL joins, dissenting.

[The] test for a "seizure," as formulated by the Court in *Mendenhall*, was whether, "in view of all of the circumstances surrounding the incident, a reasonable person would have believed that he was not free to leave." [T]he officer's show of force—taking the form of a head-on chase—adequately conveyed the message that respondent was not free to leave. [H]ere, respondent attempted to end "the conversation" before it began and soon found himself literally "not free to leave" when confronted by an officer running toward him head-on who eventually tackled him to the ground. There was an interval of time between the moment that respondent saw the officer fast approaching and the moment when he was tackled, and thus brought under the control of the officer. The question is whether the Fourth Amendment was implicated at the earlier or the later moment.

[T]he same issue would arise if the show of force took the form of a command to "freeze," a warning shot, or the sound of sirens accompanied by a patrol car's flashing lights. In any of these situations, there may be a significant time interval between the initiation of the officer's show of force and the complete submission by the citizen. [T]he Court concludes that the timing of the seizure is governed by the citizen's reaction, rather than by the officer's conduct. One consequence of this conclusion is that the point at which the interaction between citizen and police officer becomes a seizure occurs, not when a reasonable citizen believes he or she is no longer free to go, but, rather, only after the officer exercises control over the citizen.

[O]ur interests in effective law enforcement and in personal liberty would be better served by adhering to a standard that "allows the police to determine in advance whether the conduct contemplated will implicate the Fourth Amendment." The range of possible responses to a police show of force, and the multitude of problems that may arise in determining whether, and at which moment, there has been "submission," can only create uncertainty and generate litigation. [In] some cases, of course, it is immediately apparent at which moment the suspect submitted to an officer's show of force. * * *

[T]he constitutionality of a police officer's show of force should be measured by the conditions that exist at the time of the officer's action. [The] character of the citizen's response should not govern the constitutionality of the officer's conduct. [In] the present case, if Officer Pertoso had succeeded in tackling respondent before he dropped the rock of cocaine, the rock unquestionably would have been excluded as the fruit of the officer's unlawful seizure. [U]nder the Court's logic-chopping analysis, the exclusionary rule has no application because an attempt to make an unconstitutional seizure is beyond the coverage of the Fourth Amendment, no matter how outrageous or unreasonable the officer's conduct may be. * * *

Notes

1. *The Fleeing Motorist.* A similar decision was rendered in *Hester v. United States*, 265 U.S. 57 (1924). During Prohibition, federal agents saw a moonshiner hand a customer a quart of whiskey. The agents tried to arrest both the moonshiner and the customer, but both fled. During the chase, both the moonshiner and the customer dropped various items of contraband. The police recovered the items and used them to convict the moonshiner of concealing alcohol in violation of federal law. The Court concluded that the items were properly admitted in evidence: "[t]he defendant's own acts [disclosed the contraband] and there was no seizure in the sense of the law when the officers examined the contents of each after they had been abandoned."

2. *The Police Cruiser.* In *Michigan v. Chesternut*, 486 U.S. 567 (1988), police officers were engaged in routine patrol in a marked police cruiser. When respondent saw the patrol car nearing the corner where he stood, he turned and began to run. The patrol car followed respondent "to see where he was going." The cruiser quickly caught up with respondent, drove alongside him for a short distance, and saw him discard a number of packets. The officers retrieved the packets, found that they contained pills which appeared to be codeine, and arrested respondent for possession of narcotics. During an ensuing search, the police discovered another packet of pills, a packet containing heroin, and a hypodermic needle. The Court upheld respondent's conviction for possession of illegal narcotics:

[R]espondent was not seized [before] he discarded the packets containing the controlled substance. [T]he police conduct involved here would not have communicated to the reasonable person an attempt to capture or otherwise intrude upon respondent's freedom of movement. The record does not reflect that the police activated a siren or flashers; or that they commanded respondent to halt, or displayed any weapons; or that they operated the car in an aggressive manner to block respondent's course or otherwise control the direction or speed of his movement. While the very presence of a police car driving parallel to a running pedestrian could be somewhat intimidating, this kind of police presence does not, standing alone, constitute a seizure. The police therefore were not required to have "a particularized and objective basis for suspecting [respondent] of criminal activity," in order to pursue him.
* * *

Problems

1. *Applying Hodari D.* Suppose that the officer shot Hodari to prevent his escape. Hodari was seriously wounded and immediately fell to the ground. Before the officer could get to Hodari, Hodari discarded a chunk of rock cocaine. The officer retrieved the cocaine and then subdued Hodari. At what point was Hodari seized? Was the cocaine obtained as a result of the seizure or afterwards? Was the seizure valid? *See Tennessee v. Garner*, 471 U.S. 1 (1985).

2. *More on Fleeing Motorists.* Johnson stole an automobile and eluded police by traveling at high speeds for 20 miles. During this time, Johnson was followed by police cars with flashing lights. The chase ended when Johnson slammed the car into a police roadblock killing himself. The roadblock consisted of 18–wheel tractor-trailers placed across both lanes of a two-lane highway. The roadblock was "effectively concealed" by the fact that it was around a bend in the road and was unilluminated. The roadblock was also concealed by the fact that a police car, with its headlights on, had been placed between Johnson's oncoming vehicle and the truck, so that Johnson was "blinded." Johnson's heirs sued claiming that the police had effected an unreasonable seizure in violation of the Fourth Amendment. In light of the holdings in *Mendenhall* and *Hodari D*, do you agree that Johnson was seized? If so, when did the seizure occur? What arguments might you make on behalf of Johnson's estate? How might the State respond? How should the Court rule? *See Brower v. County of Inyo*, 489 U.S. 593 (1989).

FLORIDA v. ROYER
460 U.S. 491 (1983).

JUSTICE WHITE announced the judgment of the Court and delivered an opinion in which JUSTICES MARSHALL, POWELL and STEVENS joined.

[Royer] was observed at Miami International Airport by two plainclothes detectives of the Dade County, Florida, Public Safety Department assigned to the County's Organized Crime Bureau, Narcotics Investigation Section. [The detectives] believed that Royer's appearance, mannerisms, luggage, and actions fit the so-called "drug courier profile."[10] Royer, [unaware] of the attention he had attracted, purchased a one-way ticket to New York City and checked his two suitcases, placing on each suitcase an identification tag bearing the name "Holt" and the destination, "LaGuardia". As Royer made his way to [the] boarding area, [two] detectives approached him, identified themselves as policemen[,] and asked if Royer had a "moment" to speak with them; Royer said "Yes."

Upon request, but without oral consent, Royer produced for the detectives his airline ticket and his driver's license. The airline ticket, like the baggage identification tags, bore the name "Holt," while the driver's license carried respondent's correct name, "Royer." When the detectives asked about the discrepancy, Royer explained that a friend had made the reservation in the name of "Holt." Royer became noticeably more nervous during this conversation, whereupon the detectives informed Royer that they were in fact narcotics investigators and that they had reason to suspect him of transporting narcotics.

The detectives did not return his airline ticket and identification but asked Royer to accompany them to a room, approximately forty feet away, adjacent to the concourse. Royer said nothing in response but went with the officers as he had been asked to do. The room was later described by Detective Johnson as a "large storage closet," located in the stewardesses' lounge and containing a small desk and two chairs. Without Royer's consent or agreement, Detective Johnson, using Royer's baggage check stubs, retrieved the "Holt" luggage from the airline and brought it to the room where respondent and [a detective] were waiting. Royer was asked if he would consent to a search of the suitcases. Without orally responding to this request, Royer produced a key and unlocked one of the suitcases, which the detective then opened without seeking further assent from Royer. Drugs were found in that suitcase. [Royer] stated that he did not know the combination to the lock on the second suitcase. When asked if he objected to the detective opening the second suitcase, Royer said "no, go ahead," and did not object when the detective explained that the suitcase might have to be broken open. The suitcase was pried open by the officers and more marihuana was found. Royer was then told that he was under arrest. Approximately fifteen minutes had elapsed from the time the detectives initially approached respondent until his arrest upon the discovery of the contraband. [Royer was convicted and appealed.]

[*Terry*] and its progeny [created] only limited exceptions to the general rule that seizures of the person require probable cause to arrest.

---

10. The "drug courier profile" [includes] characteristics found to be typical of persons transporting illegal drugs. In Royer's case, the detectives' attention was attracted by the following facts which were considered to be within the profile: a) Royer was carrying American Tourister luggage, which appeared to be heavy, b) he was young, apparently between 25–35, c) he was casually dressed, d) Royer appeared pale and nervous, looking around at other people, e) Royer paid for his ticket in cash with a large number of bills, and f) rather than completing the airline identification tag to be attached to checked baggage, which had space for a name, address, and telephone number, Royer wrote only a name and the destination.

[The] predicate permitting seizures on suspicion short of probable cause is that law enforcement interests warrant a limited intrusion on the personal security of the suspect. The scope of the intrusion permitted will vary to some extent with the particular facts and circumstances of each case. [A]n investigative detention must be temporary and last no longer than is necessary to effectuate the purpose of the stop. [T]he investigative methods employed should be the least intrusive means reasonably available to verify or dispel the officer's suspicion in a short period of time. It is the State's burden to demonstrate that the seizure it seeks to justify on the basis of a reasonable suspicion was sufficiently limited in scope and duration to satisfy the conditions of an investigative seizure.

[Our prior decisions] hold that statements given during a period of illegal detention are inadmissible even though voluntarily given if they are the product of the illegal detention and not the result of an independent act of free will. [W]hen the officers discovered that Royer was traveling under an assumed name, this fact, and the facts already known to the officers—paying cash for a one-way ticket, the mode of checking the two bags, and Royer's appearance and conduct in general— were adequate grounds for suspecting Royer of carrying drugs and for temporarily detaining him and his luggage while they attempted to verify or dispel their suspicions in a manner that did not exceed the limits of an investigative detention. [H]ad Royer voluntarily consented to the search of his luggage while he was justifiably being detained on reasonable suspicion, the products of the search would be admissible against him. [H]owever, [at] the time Royer produced the key to his suitcase, the detention to which he was then subjected was a more serious intrusion on his personal liberty than is allowable on mere suspicion of criminal activity.

[What] had begun as a consensual inquiry [escalated] into an investigatory procedure in a police interrogation room, where the police, unsatisfied with previous explanations, sought to confirm their suspicions. The officers had Royer's ticket, they had his identification, and they had seized his luggage. Royer was never informed that he was free to board his plane if he so chose, and he reasonably believed that he was being detained. At least as of that moment, any consensual aspects of the encounter had evaporated, [and] *Terry* and the cases following it did not justify the restraint to which Royer was then subjected. As a practical matter, Royer was under arrest. [Royer] would not have been free to leave the interrogation room had he asked to do so. [H]ad Royer refused to consent to a search of his luggage, the officers would have held the luggage and sought a warrant to authorize the search.

[The] courts are not strangers to the use of trained dogs to detect the presence of controlled substances in luggage. There is no indication here that this means was not feasible and available. If it had been used, Royer and his luggage could have been momentarily detained while this investigative procedure was carried out. Indeed, it may be that no detention at all would have been necessary. A negative result would have freed Royer in short order; a positive result would have resulted in his justifiable arrest on probable cause.

We do not suggest that there is a litmus-paper test for distinguishing a consensual encounter from a seizure or for determining when a seizure exceeds the bounds of an investigative stop. Even in the discrete category of airport encounters, there will be endless variations in the facts and circumstances, so much variation that it is unlikely that the courts can reduce to a sentence or a paragraph a rule that will provide unarguable answers to the question whether there has been an unreasonable search or seizure in violation of the Fourth Amendment. * * *

[The State argues] that Royer was not being illegally held when he gave his consent because there was probable cause to [arrest]. [H]owever, [probable] cause to arrest Royer did not exist at the time he consented to the search of his luggage. The facts are that a nervous young man with two American Tourister bags paid cash for an airline ticket to a "target city". These facts led to inquiry, which in turn revealed that the ticket had been bought under an assumed name. The proffered explanation did not satisfy the officers. We cannot agree with the State [that] every nervous young man paying cash for a ticket to New York City under an assumed name and carrying two heavy American Tourister bags may be arrested and held to answer for a serious felony charge.

[Because] Royer was being illegally detained when he consented to the search of his luggage, we agree that the consent was tainted by the illegality and was ineffective to justify the search. The judgment of the Florida Court of Appeal is accordingly

Affirmed.

JUSTICE BRENNAN, concurring in the result.

[A]ny suggestion that the *Terry* reasonable suspicion standard justifies anything but the briefest of detentions or the most limited of searches finds no support in the *Terry* [decision]. I interpret the plurality's requirement that the investigative methods employed pursuant to a *Terry* stop be "the least intrusive means reasonably available to verify or dispel the officer's suspicion in a short period of time," to mean that the availability of a less intrusive means may make an otherwise reasonable stop unreasonable. I do not interpret it to mean that the absence of a less intrusive means can make an otherwise unreasonable stop reasonable. * * *

JUSTICE BLACKMUN, dissenting.

[As any] detention continues or escalates, a greater degree of reasonable suspicion is necessary to sustain it, and at some point probable cause will be required. [H]ere, the intrusion was short [and] minimal. Only 15 minutes transpired from the initial approach to the opening of the suitcases. The officers were polite, and sought and immediately obtained Royer's consent at each significant step of the process. Royer knew that if the search of the suitcases did not turn up contraband, he would be free to go on his way. Thus, " 'the police [were] diligently pursuing a means of investigation which [was] likely to resolve the matter one way or another very [soon].' " [In] light of the extraordinary and well-documented difficulty of identifying drug couriers, the minimal intrusion in this case, based on particularized suspicion, was eminently reasonable.

JUSTICE REHNQUIST, with whom THE CHIEF JUSTICE and JUSTICE O'CONNOR join, dissenting.

[T]he articulable suspicion which concededly focused upon Royer justified the length and nature of his detention. [The] presence of consent further justifies the action taken. [Royer] consented to go to the room in the first instance. [Royer] was not told that he had to go to the room, but was simply asked, after a brief period of questioning, if he would accompany the detectives to the room. Royer was informed [why] the officers wished to question him further. There were neither threats nor any show of force. [The detectives] were not in uniform and did not display weapons. The detectives did not touch Royer and made no demands. [Royer] admits that the detectives were quite polite. [R]oyer, who was in his fourth year of study at Ithaca College [and] has since graduated with a degree in communications, [continued] to cooperate with the detectives as he had from the beginning of the encounter. Absent any evidence of objective indicia of coercion, [the] size of the room itself does not transform a voluntary consent to search into a coerced consent. * * *

Notes

1. *Distinguishing "Reasonable Suspicion" & "Probable Cause."* In *United States v. Sokolow*, 490 U.S. 1 (1989), the Court held that "reasonable suspicion" involves "something more than an 'inchoate' and unparticularized suspicion or 'hunch,' " but "considerably less than proof of wrongdoing by a preponderance of the evidence." "[P]robable cause means 'a fair probability that contraband or evidence of a crime will be found,' and the level of suspicion required for a *Terry* stop is obviously less demanding than that for probable cause."

2. *"Totality of Circumstances" Test.* In *United States v. Cortez*, 449 U.S. 411 (1981), the Court held that "reasonable suspicion" should be determined using a "totality of the circumstances" standard: "Based upon that whole picture the detaining officers must have a particularized and objective basis for suspecting the particular person stopped of criminal activity."

3. *Reliance on Anonymous Tips.* In *Alabama v. White*, 496 U.S. 325 (1990), the Court held that police could rely on an anonymous tip in developing "reasonable suspicion":

> Reasonable suspicion is a less demanding standard than probable cause not only in the sense that reasonable suspicion can be established with information that is different in quantity or content than that required to establish probable cause, but also in the sense that reason-

able suspicion can arise from information that is less reliable than that required to show probable cause[.] Reasonable suspicion, like probable cause, is dependent upon both the content of information possessed by police and its degree of reliability. Both factors—quantity and quality— are considered in the "totality of the circumstances—the whole picture," that must be taken into account when evaluating whether there is reasonable suspicion. Thus, if a tip has a relatively low degree of reliability, more information will be required to establish the requisite quantum of suspicion than would be required if the tip were more reliable.

4. *Pretextual Stops.* In *Whren v. United States*, 517 U.S. 806 (1996), two undercover police officers were patrolling in a "high drug area" when they saw respondent driving in an unusual manner (he sat for an unusually long time at a stop sign, and then took off at a high rate of speed), and stopped him. Although respondent conceded that the officers had probable cause to stop him for traffic violations, he argued that it was a pretextual stop designed to search for drugs. The Court upheld the stop: "[Prior] cases foreclose any argument that the constitutional reasonableness of traffic stops depends on the actual motivations of the individual officers involved. [T]he Constitution prohibits selective enforcement [based] on considerations such as race. But the constitutional basis for objecting to intentionally discriminatory application of laws is the [Equal Protection Clause]. Subjective intentions play no role in ordinary, probable-cause Fourth Amendment analysis."

5. *Drug Courier Profiles.* In *United States v. Sokolow*, 490 U.S. 1 (1989), the Court upheld the use of so-called "drug courier profiles" like the one used in *Royer*: "A court sitting to determine the existence of reasonable suspicion must require the agent to articulate the factors leading to that conclusion, but the fact that these factors may be set forth in a 'profile' does not somehow detract from their evidentiary significance as seen by a trained agent."

6. *Duration of Stop.* In *United States v. Sharpe*, 470 U.S. 675 (1985), the Court rejected a court of appeals decision holding that investigative stops could not last longer than twenty minutes noting that there is:

"no rigid time limitation on *Terry* stops. While it is clear that 'the brevity of the invasion of the individual's Fourth Amendment interests is an important factor in determining whether the seizure is so minimally intrusive as to be justifiable on reasonable suspicion,' we [need] to consider the law enforcement purposes to be served by the stop as well as the time reasonably needed to effectuate those purposes." The Court went on: "In assessing whether a detention is too long [to] be justified as an investigative stop, [it is] appropriate to examine whether the police diligently pursued a means of investigation that was likely to confirm or dispel their suspicions quickly, during which time it was necessary to detain the defendant. A court making this assessment should [consider] whether the police are acting in a swiftly developing situation, [and] not indulge in unrealistic second-guessing. [The] question is not simply whether some other alternative was available, but whether the police acted unreasonably in failing to recognize or to pursue it."

7. *Custodial Questioning.* When may the police force a suspect to go to the police station for questioning? In *Dunaway v. New York*, 442 U.S. 200 (1979), the police focused on Dunaway as the prime suspect in a murder case. Detectives decided to "pick up" Dunaway and "bring him in" for questioning. Dunaway was not told that he was under arrest, but the police stated that he would have been physically restrained had he attempted to leave. The Court held that probable cause was required for this action:

> In contrast to the brief and narrowly circumscribed intrusions involved in [*Terry*], the detention of petitioner was in important respects indistinguishable from a traditional arrest. The application of the Fourth Amendment's requirement of probable cause does not depend on whether an intrusion of this magnitude is termed an "arrest" under state law. [A]ny "exception" that could cover a seizure as intrusive as that in this case would threaten to swallow the general rule that Fourth Amendment seizures are "reasonable" only if based on probable cause. [The] central importance of the probable-cause requirement to the protection of a citizen's privacy afforded by the Fourth Amendment's guarantees cannot be compromised in that a multifactor balancing test of "reasonable police conduct under the circumstances" to cover all seizures that do not amount to technical arrests.

8. *Fingerprinting.* In *Davis v. Mississippi*, 394 U.S. 721 (1969), Davis was convicted of rape and sentenced to life imprisonment based on fingerprints taken after a forced trip to the police station. The Court held that probable cause was required. Mr. Justice Stewart dissented: "[Like] the color of a man's eyes, his height, or his very physiognomy, the tips of his fingers are an inherent and unchanging characteristic of the man. [We] do not deal here with a confession wrongfully obtained or with property wrongfully seized. [We] deal, instead, with "evidence" that can be identically reproduced and lawfully used at any subsequent trial."

In *Hayes v. Florida*, 470 U.S. 811 (1985), in dicta, the Court suggested the following qualification to *Davis'* holding: "None of the foregoing implies that a brief detention in the field for the purpose of fingerprinting, where there is only reasonable suspicion not amounting to probable cause, is necessarily impermissible under the Fourth Amendment. [If] there are articulable facts supporting a reasonable suspicion that a person has committed a criminal offense, that person may be stopped in order to identify him, to question him briefly, or to detain him briefly while attempting to obtain additional information."

Problems

1. *Drug Courier Profiles.* In recent years, narcotics agents have increasingly relied on so-called "drug courier profiles." In *Mendenhall*, detectives claimed that the profile focused their attention on Mendenhall:

> The agent testified that the respondent's behavior fit the so-called "drug courier profile"—an informally compiled abstract of characteristics thought typical of persons carrying illicit drugs. In this case the agents thought it relevant that (1) the respondent was arriving on a flight from Los Angeles, a city believed by the agents to be the place of

origin for much of the heroin brought to Detroit; (2) the respondent was the last person to leave the plane, "appeared to be very nervous," and "completely scanned the whole area where [the agents] were standing"; (3) after leaving the plane the respondent proceeded past the baggage area without claiming any luggage; and (4) the respondent changed airlines for her flight out of Detroit.

[Mendenhall] engaged in behavior that the agents believed was designed to evade detection. She deplaned only after all other passengers had left the aircraft. Agent Anderson testified that drug couriers often disembark last in order to have a clear view of the terminal so that they more easily can detect government agents. Once inside the terminal, the respondent scanned the entire gate area and walked "very, very slowly" toward the baggage area. When she arrived there, she claimed no baggage. Instead, she asked a skycap for directions to the Eastern Airlines ticket counter located in a different terminal. . . . Although she carried an American Airlines ticket for a flight from Detroit to Pittsburgh, she asked for an Eastern Airlines ticket. An airline employee gave her an Eastern Airlines boarding pass. Agent Anderson testified that drug couriers frequently travel without baggage and change flights en route to avoid surveillance. On the basis of these observations, the agents stopped and questioned the respondent.

Do you agree that Mendenhall's conduct was "suspicious?" In thinking about that issue, consider Justice White's dissent:

[No] aspects of Ms. Mendenhall's conduct, either alone or in combination, were sufficient to provide reasonable suspicion that she was engaged in criminal activity. The fact that Ms. Mendenhall was the last person to alight from a flight originating in Los Angeles was plainly insufficient to provide a basis for stopping her. Nor was the fact that her flight originated from a "major source city," for the mere proximity of a person to areas with a high incidence of drug activity or to persons known to be drug addicts, does not provide the necessary reasonable suspicion for an investigatory stop. [T]he DEA agents' observations that Ms. Mendenhall claimed no luggage and changed airlines were also insufficient to provide reasonable suspicion. Unlike [*Terry*], where "nothing in [the suspects'] conduct from the time [the officer] first noticed them until the time he confronted them and identified himself as a police officer gave him sufficient reason to negate [his] hypothesis" of criminal behavior, Ms. Mendenhall's subsequent conduct negated any reasonable inference that she was traveling a long distance without luggage or changing her ticket to a different airline to avoid detection. Agent Anderson testified that he heard the ticket agent tell Ms. Mendenhall that her ticket to Pittsburgh already was in order and that all she needed was a boarding pass for the flight. Thus it should have been plain to an experienced observer that Ms. Mendenhall's failure to claim luggage was attributable to the fact that she was already ticketed through to Pittsburgh on a different airline. Because Agent Anderson's suspicion that Ms. Mendenhall was transporting narcotics could be based only on "his inchoate and unparticularized suspicion or 'hunch,'" rather than "specific reasonable inferences which he is entitled to draw from the facts in light of his experience," he was not justified in "seizing" Ms. Mendenhall.

2. *More on Profiles.* Is there a "reasonable suspicion of criminal activity" when a suspect (1) pays $2,100 for two airplane tickets from a roll of $20 bills; (2) travels under a name that does not match the name under which his telephone number is listed; (3) his original destination is Miami, a source city for illicit drugs; (4) he stayed in Miami for only 48 hours, even though a round-trip flight from Honolulu to Miami takes 20 hours; (5) he appeared nervous during his trip; and (6) he checked none of his luggage? *See United States v. Sokolow*, 490 U.S. 1 (1989).

3. *Automobile Profiles?* Suppose that the police create a "drug courier" profile for suspects that transport drugs between Miami and New York City or Boston by automobile. The profile focuses on cars coming from a "source city" (Miami) using a major "drug highway" (I–95). Because so many drivers on this highway tend to exceed the speed limit, and because drug couriers are anxious about not being stopped, the profile includes a reference to drivers who are traveling at or below the speed limit. Do the police have a "reasonable suspicion" that anyone meeting this profile is a "drug courier?"

4. *Applying Royer.* After *Mendenhall* and *Royer*, do narcotics agents have clear guidance about how they may act in airport situations? Suppose that the officers had approached Royer in the airport, and sought to ask him some questions, but Royer had refused to answer them. In light of the holding in *Royer*, what could the officers do next?

5. *More on Pretextual Stops.* When the driver of a late model convertible Buick sees the police, he abruptly turns away and slides down, causing the police to become "suspicious" that the car is "a stolen vehicle." As the police tail the vehicle, and run a registration check, the driver of the Buick "reaches way down, as if to obtain an object or place an object under the right front seat." The movement causes the Buick to abruptly swerve to its left across the center line, and the officers decide to conduct a traffic stop. The police later admit that they did not stop the driver for a traffic offense, but rather because they were suspicious that the vehicle might be stolen and that the driver might have a weapon. As the officers approach the car, the driver "gets low in the seat" with his right arm positioned "low in his lap". At that point, the police order the driver to place his hands where they could see them and pull him from the car. The officers then frisk the driver and find an object in defendant's right jacket pocket which "felt like the butt of a small automatic." An officer then reaches into the pocket and finds only a "considerable sum of money folded in half," and a "plastic Baggi with a white powdery substance." Defendant was then placed under arrest for possession of a controlled substance. Did the police act properly? *See State v. Cotterman*, 544 S.W.2d 322 (Mo.App. 1976).

6. *A Drug Deal?* Police officers were parked in an unmarked van in an area known for drug dealing when they observe two cars pull over about 150 feet away. The driver and passenger of one car exit, approach the other car, and are handed some money. The driver of the other car then takes took a white bag from the glove compartment and hands it to the waiting men. After the two men re-enter their car and drive away, the police forced the man in the other car to exit his vehicle. The officers open the glove

compartment with a key (was found lying in the front seat) and find a white plastic bag containing cocaine base and $931 in cash. Did the officers act properly? *See United States v. Brown*, 913 F.2d 570 (8th Cir.1990).

HIIBEL v. SIXTH JUDICIAL DISTRICT COURT
542 U.S. 177 (2004).

JUSTICE KENNEDY delivered the opinion of the Court.

[The] sheriff's department in Humboldt County, Nevada, received an afternoon telephone call reporting an assault [by a man] in a red and silver GMC truck [and] dispatched [an officer] to investigate. When the officer arrived at the scene, he found the truck parked on the side of the road. A man was standing by the truck, and a young woman was sitting inside it. The officer observed skid marks in the gravel behind the vehicle, leading him to believe it had come to a sudden stop.

The officer approached the man and explained that he was investigating a report of a fight. The man appeared to be intoxicated. The officer asked him if he had "any identification on [him]," which we understand as a request to produce a driver's license or some other form of written identification. The man refused and asked why the officer wanted to see identification. The officer responded that he was conducting an investigation and needed to see some identification. The [man] became agitated and insisted he had done nothing wrong. The officer explained that he wanted to find out who the man was and what he was doing there. After continued refusals to comply with the officer's request for identification, the man began to taunt the officer by placing his hands behind his back and telling the officer to arrest him and take him to jail. This routine kept up for several minutes: the officer asked for identification 11 times and was refused each time. After warning the man that he would be arrested if he continued to refuse to comply, the officer placed him under arrest.

[The man, Larry Hiibel,] was charged with "willfully resist[ing], delay[ing], or obstruct[ing] a public officer in discharging or attempting to discharge any legal duty of his office" in violation of Nev.Rev.Stat. (NRS) § 199.280 (2003). [A] Nevada statute [defines] the legal rights and duties of a police officer in the context of an investigative stop. Section 171.123 provides in relevant part: "1. Any peace officer may detain any person whom the officer encounters under circumstances which reasonably indicate that the person has committed, is committing or is about to commit a crime.... 3. The officer may detain the person pursuant to this section only to ascertain his identity and the suspicious circumstances surrounding his presence abroad. Any person so detained shall identify himself, but may not be compelled to answer any other inquiry of any peace officer." [Hiibel] was convicted and fined $250. [T]he Supreme Court of Nevada [affirmed.] We granted certiorari.

NRS § 171.123(3) is an enactment sometimes referred to as a "stop and identify" statute. Stop and identify statutes often combine elements of traditional vagrancy laws with provisions intended to regulate police behavior in the course of investigatory stops. The statutes vary[,] but all permit an officer to ask or require a suspect to disclose his identity. A few States model their statutes on the Uniform Arrest Act, a model code that permits an officer to stop a person reasonably suspected of committing a crime and "demand of him his name, address, business abroad and whither he is going." Warner, *The Uniform Arrest Act*, 28 VA. L.REV. 315, 344 (1942). Other statutes are based on the text proposed by the American Law Institute as part of the Institute's Model Penal Code. The provision [provides] that a person who is loitering "under circumstances which justify suspicion that he may be engaged or about to engage in crime commits a violation if he refuses the request of a peace officer that he identify himself and give a reasonably credible account of the lawfulness of his conduct and purposes." In some States, a suspect's refusal to identify himself is a misdemeanor offense or civil violation; in others, it is a factor to be considered in whether the suspect has violated loitering laws. In other States, a suspect may decline to identify himself without penalty.

Stop and identify statutes have their roots in early English vagrancy laws that required suspected vagrants to face arrest unless they gave "a good Account of themselves," a power that itself reflected common-law rights of private persons to "arrest any suspicious night-walker, and detain him till he give a good account of himself...." 2 W. HAWKINS, PLEAS OF THE CROWN, ch. 13, § 6, p. 130. (6th ed. 1787). In recent decades, the Court has found constitutional infirmity in traditional vagrancy laws. In *Papachristou v. Jacksonville,* 405 U.S. 156 (1972), the Court held that a traditional vagrancy law was void for vagueness. Its broad scope and imprecise terms denied proper notice to potential offenders and permitted police officers to exercise unfettered discretion in the enforcement of the law.

The Court has recognized similar constitutional limitations on the scope and operation of stop and identify statutes. In *Brown v. Texas,* 443 U.S. 47 (1979), the Court invalidated a conviction for violating a Texas stop and identify statute on Fourth Amendment grounds. The Court ruled that the initial stop was not based on specific, objective facts establishing reasonable suspicion to believe the suspect was involved in criminal activity. Absent that factual basis for detaining the defendant, the Court held, the risk of "arbitrary and abusive police practices" was too great and the stop was impermissible. [L]ater, the Court invalidated a modified stop and identify statute on vagueness grounds. [In] *Kolender v. Lawson,* 461 U.S. 352 (1983)[, a] California law [required] a suspect to give an officer " 'credible and reliable' " identification when asked to identify himself. The Court held that the statute was void because it provided no standard for determining what a suspect must do to comply with it, resulting in "virtually unrestrained power to arrest and charge persons with a violation."

[Here] there is no question that the initial stop was based on reasonable suspicion, satisfying the Fourth Amendment requirements noted in *Brown*. Further, the petitioner has not alleged that the statute is unconstitutionally vague. [T]he Nevada statute is narrower and more precise. [In contrast to *Kolender*,] the Nevada Supreme Court has interpreted NRS § 171.123(3) to require only that a suspect disclose his name. As we understand it, the statute does not require a suspect to give the officer a driver's license or any other document. Provided that the suspect either states his name or communicates it to the officer by other means—a choice, we assume, that the suspect may make—the statute is satisfied and no violation occurs.

Hiibel argues that his conviction cannot stand because the officer's conduct violated his Fourth Amendment rights. We disagree.... Beginning with *Terry v. Ohio,* 392 U.S. 1 (1968), the Court has recognized that a law enforcement officer's reasonable suspicion that a person may be involved in criminal activity permits the officer to stop the person for a brief time and take additional steps to investigate further. To ensure that the resulting seizure is constitutionally reasonable, a *Terry* stop must be limited. The officer's action must be "justified at its inception, [and] reasonably related in scope to the circumstances which justified the interference in the first place." [T]he seizure cannot continue for an excessive period of time or resemble a traditional arrest.

[Q]uestions concerning a suspect's identity are a routine and accepted part of many *Terry* stops. Obtaining a suspect's name in the course of a *Terry* stop serves important government interests. Knowledge of identity may inform an officer that a suspect is wanted for another offense, or has a record of violence or mental disorder. On the other hand, knowing identity may help clear a suspect and allow the police to concentrate their efforts elsewhere. Identity may prove particularly important in cases such as this, where the police are investigating what appears to be a domestic assault. Officers called to investigate domestic disputes need to know whom they are dealing with in order to assess the situation, the threat to their own safety, and possible danger to the potential victim.

[It] has been an open question whether the suspect can be arrested and prosecuted for refusal to answer.... The reasonableness of a seizure under the Fourth Amendment is determined "by balancing its intrusion on the individual's Fourth Amendment interests against its promotion of legitimate government interests." *Delaware v. Prouse,* 440 U.S. 648 (1979). The Nevada statute satisfies that standard. The request for identity has an immediate relation to the purpose, rationale, and practical demands of a *Terry* stop. The threat of criminal sanction helps ensure that the request for identity does not become a legal nullity. On the other hand, the Nevada statute does not alter the nature of the stop itself: it does not change its duration or its location....

Petitioner argues that the Nevada statute circumvents the probable cause requirement, in effect allowing an officer to arrest a person for being suspicious.... Petitioner's concerns are met by the requirement that a *Terry* stop must be justified at its inception and "reasonably related in scope to the circumstances which justified" the initial stop. . . . It is clear in this case that the request for identification was "reasonably related in scope to the circumstances which justified" the stop. The officer's request was a commonsense inquiry, not an effort to obtain an arrest for failure to identify after a *Terry* stop yielded insufficient evidence. The stop, the request, and the State's requirement of a response did not contravene the guarantees of the Fourth Amendment.

Petitioner further contends that his conviction violates the Fifth Amendment's prohibition on compelled self-incrimination. . . . As we stated in *Kastigar v. United States,* 406 U.S. 441 (1972), the Fifth Amendment privilege against compulsory self-incrimination "protects against any disclosures that the witness reasonably believes could be used in a criminal prosecution or could lead to other evidence that might be so used." [P]etitioner's refusal to disclose his name was not based on any articulated real and appreciable fear that his name would be used to incriminate him, or that it "would furnish a link in the chain of evidence needed to prosecute" him. [P]etitioner refused to identify himself only because he thought his name was none of the officer's business. . . . While we recognize petitioner's strong belief that he should not have to disclose his identity, the Fifth Amendment does not override the Nevada Legislature's judgment to the contrary absent a reasonable belief that the disclosure would tend to incriminate him.

The narrow scope of the disclosure requirement is also important. One's identity is, by definition, unique; yet it is, in another sense, a universal characteristic. Answering a request to disclose a name is likely to be so insignificant in the scheme of things as to be incriminating only in unusual circumstances. In every criminal case, it is known and must be known who has been arrested and who is being tried. Even witnesses who plan to invoke the Fifth Amendment privilege answer when their names are called to take the stand. Still, a case may arise where there is a substantial allegation that furnishing identity at the time of a stop would have given the police a link in the chain of evidence needed to convict the individual of a separate offense. . . . We need not resolve those questions here.

The judgment of the Nevada Supreme Court is

Affirmed.

JUSTICE STEVENS, dissenting.

[Given] our statements to the effect that citizens are not required to respond to police officers' questions during a *Terry* stop, it is no surprise that petitioner assumed [that] he had a right not to disclose his identity. [T]he Court reasons that we should not assume that the disclosure of petitioner's name would be used to incriminate him or that it would furnish a link in a chain of evidence needed to prosecute him. But why else would an officer ask for it? And why else would the Nevada Legislature require its disclosure only when circumstances "reasonably indicate that the person has committed, is committing or is about to commit a crime"? If the Court is correct, then petitioner's refusal to cooperate did not impede the police investigation. [T]he Nevada Legislature intended to provide its police officers with a useful law enforcement tool, and that the very existence of the statute demonstrates the value of the information it demands. . . .

JUSTICE BREYER, with whom JUSTICE SOUTER and JUSTICE GINSBURG join, dissenting.

[Can] a State, in addition to requiring a stopped individual to answer "What's your name?" also require an answer to "What's your license number?" or "Where do you live?" [A]nswers to any of these questions may, or may not, incriminate, depending upon the circumstances. [A] name [will] sometimes provide the police with "a link in the chain of evidence needed to convict the individual of a separate offense."

. . .

Problems

1. *Requiring Proof of Identity.* In *Hibbel*, the Court emphasizes that Nevada only requires a suspect to state his name and does not require him/her to produce credible proof of identity (e.g., a driver's license). Would the result in this case have been different had Nevada required proof of identity as well?

2. *Requiring More Information.* A dissenting Justice Breyer inquired whether a state, "in addition to requiring a stopped individual to answer 'What's your name?,' the police can also require an answer to 'What's your license number?' or 'Where do you live?'" How would you answer Justice Breyer's questions?

3. *Hiibel's Limits.* In light of the Court's holding, consider the validity of the following laws mentioned in the majority opinion:

    A. The Uniform Arrest Act's provisions which allow a police officer to stop a person reasonably suspected of committing a crime and "demand of him his name, address, business abroad and whither he is going."

    B. The Model Penal Code's provisions which state that a person who is loitering "under circumstances which justify suspicion that he may be engaged or about to engage in crime commits a violation if he refuses the request of a peace officer that he identify himself and give a reasonably credible account of the lawfulness of his conduct and purposes."

    C. The rule in some States that a suspect's refusal to identify himself is a misdemeanor offense or civil violation.

    D. The rule in some states that a suspect's refusal to identify himself is a factor to be considered in whether the suspect has violated loitering laws.

4. *More on Hiibel.* Following *Hibbel*, when can the police demand identification? Consider the following scenarios:

A. In an effort to be pro-active and "nip crime in the bud," a police officer decides to make routine stops of motorists to demand identification.

B. At 3:00am, a policeman sees a carload of teenagers driving in a residential neighborhood. The officer stops the teenagers to demand identification and information about their activities.

5. *The Men in the Alley.* Suppose that two officers are cruising in a patrol car when they observe Brown and another man walking in opposite directions away from one another in an alley. Although the men are a few feet apart when first observed, the officers believe that the two have been together or were about to meet until the patrol car appeared. The officers stop one of the men, and ask him to identify himself and explain what he is doing. The other man is not questioned or detained. The officer testifies that he stopped appellant because the situation "looked suspicious and we had never seen that subject in that area before." The area of El Paso where appellant was stopped has a high incidence of drug traffic. However, the officers did not claim to suspect appellant of any specific misconduct, nor did they have any reason to believe that he was armed. Appellant refused to identify himself and angrily asserted that the officers had no right to stop him. Officer Venegas replied that he was in a "high drug problem area." The man was then arrested under a state law which made it a crime for a person to refuse to give his name and address to an officer "who has lawfully stopped him and requested the information." In light of the holding in *Brown*, was the arrest for failure to produce identification legal and proper?

6. *Forcibly Taking Identification.* Police receive a report of a break-in at a sporting goods store by a man between 5' and 6' tall with dark hair dressed in dark clothing. At the scene, an officer observes two men emerge from a nearby alley. One of the men fits the description of the suspect. The officer approaches the men and requests identification. Although one man identifies himself, the other (Roberts) refuses to do so. The officer explains his reason for requesting identification, but Roberts persists in his refusal even though he admits having identification in his wallet. The officer then tells Roberts that if he does not identify himself he will be taken to the police station. When Roberts again refuses, the officer frisks Roberts and removes Robert's wallet and a pair of long-nosed pliers from his pocket. At this point, a flashlight falls from Robert's sleeve onto the ground. The pliers and the flashlight are seized, and the officer then leafs through Robert's wallet and finds identification. After radioing headquarters, the officer learns that a "pick-up" order has been issued for Roberts. Roberts is placed under arrest and conveyed to the police station. It is later learned that a bar, located in the same general area, had also been broken into. Long-nosed pliers and a flashlight were among the items that had been taken in that burglary. Roberts is charged with the burglary of the bar, and files a motion to suppress all oral and physical evidence on the ground that it had been obtained in an illegal search. Should the motion be granted? *See State v. Flynn*, 92 Wis.2d 427, 285 N.W.2d 710 (1979).

MARYLAND v. BUIE

494 U.S. 325 (1990).

JUSTICE WHITE delivered the opinion of the Court.

[On] February 3, 1986, two men committed an armed robbery of a Godfather's Pizza restaurant in Prince George's County, Maryland. One of the robbers was wearing a red running suit. That same day, Prince George's County police obtained arrest warrants for respondent Jerome Edward Buie and his suspected accomplice in the robbery, Lloyd Allen. Buie's house was placed under police surveillance.

On February 5, the police executed the arrest warrant for Buie. They first had a police department secretary telephone Buie's house to verify that he was home. The secretary spoke to a female first, then to Buie himself. Six or seven officers proceeded to Buie's house. Once inside, the officers fanned out through the first and second floors. Corporal James Rozar announced that he would "freeze" the basement so that no one could come up and surprise the officers. With his service revolver drawn, Rozar twice shouted into the basement, ordering anyone down there to come out. When a voice asked who was calling, Rozar announced three times: "this is the police, show me your hands." Eventually, a pair of hands appeared around the bottom of the stairwell and Buie emerged from the basement. He was arrested, searched, and handcuffed. Thereafter, Detective Joseph Frolich entered the basement "in case there was someone else" down there. He noticed a red running suit lying in plain view on a stack of clothing and seized it.

The trial court denied Buie's motion to suppress the running [suit], but the Court of Appeals of Maryland reversed. We granted certiorari.

II

[U]ntil the point of Buie's arrest the police had the right, based on the authority of the arrest warrant, to search anywhere in the house that Buie might have been found, including the basement. [I]f Detective Frolich's entry into the basement was lawful, the seizure of the red running suit, which was in plain view and which the officer had probable cause to believe was evidence of a crime, was also lawful under the Fourth Amendment. The issue in this case is what level of justification the Fourth Amendment required before Detective Frolich could legally enter the basement to see if someone else was there.

[The] ingredients to apply the balance struck in *Terry* and *Long* are present in this case. Possessing an arrest warrant and probable cause to believe Buie was in his home, the officers were entitled to enter and to search anywhere in the house in which Buie might be found. Once he was found, however, the search for him was over, and there was no longer that particular justification for entering any rooms that had not yet been searched.

That Buie had an expectation of privacy in those remaining areas of his house [does] not mean such rooms were immune from entry. In *Terry* and *Long* we were concerned with the immediate interest of the police officers in taking steps to assure themselves that the persons with whom they were dealing were not armed with, or able to gain immediate control of, a weapon that could unexpectedly and fatally be used against them. In the instant case, there is an analogous interest [in] taking steps to assure [that] the house in which a suspect is being, or has just been, arrested is not harboring other persons who are dangerous and who could unexpectedly launch an attack. The risk of danger in the context of an arrest in the home is as great as, if not greater than, it is in an on-the-street or roadside investigatory encounter. A *Terry* or *Long* frisk occurs before a police-citizen confrontation has escalated to the point of arrest. A protective sweep, in contrast, occurs as an adjunct to the serious step of taking a person into custody for the purpose of prosecuting him for a crime. [U]nlike an encounter on the street or along a highway, an in-home arrest puts the officer at the disadvantage of being on his adversary's "turf." An ambush in a confined setting of unknown configuration is more to be feared than it is in open, more familiar surroundings.

We recognized in *Terry* that "[e]ven a limited search of the outer clothing for weapons constitutes a severe, though brief, intrusion upon cherished personal security, and it must surely be an annoying, frightening, and perhaps humiliating experience." But we permitted the intrusion, which was no more than necessary to protect the officer from harm. Nor do we here suggest [that] entering rooms not examined prior to the arrest is a *de minimis* intrusion that may be disregarded. We are quite sure [that] the arresting officers are permitted in such circumstances to take reasonable steps to ensure their safety after, and while making, the arrest. That interest is sufficient to outweigh the intrusion such procedures may entail.

[A] warrant was not required. We also hold that as an incident to the arrest the officers could, as a precautionary matter and without probable cause or reasonable suspicion, look in closets and other spaces immediately adjoining the place of arrest from which an attack could be immediately launched. Beyond that, [we] hold that there must be articulable facts which, taken together with the rational inferences from those facts, would warrant a reasonably prudent officer in believing that the area to be swept harbors an individual posing a danger to those on the arrest scene. [A] protective sweep, aimed at protecting the arresting officers, if justified by the circumstances, is nevertheless not a full search of the premises, but may extend only to a cursory inspection of those spaces where a person may be found. The sweep lasts no longer than is necessary to dispel the reasonable suspicion of danger and in any event no longer than it takes to complete the arrest and depart the premises.

[B]y requiring a protective sweep to be justified by probable cause to believe that a serious and demonstrable potentiality for danger existed, the Court of Appeals of Maryland applied an unnecessarily strict Fourth

Amendment standard. The Fourth Amendment permits a properly limited protective sweep in conjunction with an in-home arrest when the searching officer possesses a reasonable belief based on specific and articulable facts that the area to be swept harbors an individual posing a danger to those on the arrest scene. We therefore vacate the judgment below and remand this case to the Court of Appeals [for] further proceedings not inconsistent with this opinion.

It is so ordered.

JUSTICE STEVENS, concurring.

[The] fact that respondent offered no resistance when he emerged from the basement [is] inconsistent with the hypothesis that the danger of an attack by a hidden confederate persisted after the arrest. Moreover, Officer Rozar testified that he was not worried about any possible danger when he arrested Buie. Officer Frolich [supplied] no explanation for why he might have thought another person was in the basement. He said only that he "had no idea who lived there." [But] Officer Frolich's participat[ed] in the 3–day prearrest surveillance of Buie's home. [N]o reasonable suspicion of danger justified the entry into the basement. [If the officers were] concerned about safety, one would expect them to do what Officer Rozar did before the arrest: guard the basement door to prevent surprise attacks. [Officer] Frolich [might] reasonably have "look[ed] in" the already open basement door to ensure that no accomplice had followed Buie to the stairwell. But Officer Frolich did not merely "look in" the basement; he entered it. That strategy is [a] surprising choice for an officer, worried about safety, who need not risk entering the stairwell at [all].

JUSTICE BRENNAN, with whom JUSTICE MARSHALL joins, dissenting.

[*Terry*] "permit[ted] only brief investigative stops and extremely limited searches based on reasonable suspicion." [T]his Court more recently has applied the rationale underlying *Terry* to a wide variety of more intrusive searches and seizures, prompting my continued criticism of the " 'emerging tendency on the part of the Court to convert the *Terry* decision' " from a narrow exception into one that " 'swallow[s] the general rule that [searches] are "reasonable" only if based on probable cause.' "

[The] majority offers no support for its assumption that the danger of ambush during planned home arrests approaches the danger of unavoidable "on-the-beat" confrontations in "the myriad daily situations in which policemen and citizens confront each other on the street." [T]he Court's implicit judgment that a protective sweep constitutes a "minimally intrusive" search akin to that involved in *Terry* markedly undervalues the nature and scope of the privacy interests involved. [A] protective sweep would bring within police purview virtually all personal possessions within the house not hidden from view in a small enclosed space. Police officers searching for potential ambushers might enter every room including basements and attics; open up closets, lockers, chests, wardrobes, and cars; and peer under beds and behind furniture.

The officers will view letters, documents, and personal effects that are on tables or desks or are visible inside open drawers; books, records, tapes, and pictures on shelves; and clothing, medicines, toiletries and other paraphernalia not carefully stored in dresser drawers or bathroom cupboards. While perhaps not a "full-blown" or "top-to-bottom" search, a protective sweep is much closer to it than to a "limited patdown for weapons" or a " 'frisk' of an automobile." [T]he nature and scope of the intrusion sanctioned here are far greater than those upheld in *Terry* and *Long*. . . .   In light of the special sanctity of a private residence and the highly intrusive nature of a protective sweep, [police] officers must have probable cause to fear that their personal safety is threatened by a hidden confederate of an arrestee before they may sweep through the entire home. [I] would affirm the state court's decision to suppress the incriminating evidence. I respectfully dissent.

Notes

1.   *Temporary Detention During Execution of Search Warrant.* In *Michigan v. Summers*, 452 U.S. 692 (1981), the occupant of a house was detained while a search warrant for the house was being executed. The Court held that the warrant made the occupant sufficiently suspicious to justify his temporary seizure: the "limited intrusion on the personal security" of the person detained was justified "by such substantial law enforcement interests" that the seizure could be made on articulable suspicion not amounting to probable cause.

2.   *Securing the Premises.* In *Illinois v. McArthur*, 531 U.S. 326 (2001), a woman asked police to accompany her to a trailer that she shared with her husband so that she could retrieve her belongings. As the woman was leaving, she told police that her husband, "Chuck had dope in there" and that she had seen him "slid[e] some dope underneath the couch." The officer then asked Chuck for permission to search the trailer and he refused. The officer then sent another officer to obtain a warrant, and told Chuck that he could not reenter the trailer unless accompanied by a police officer. Chuck reentered the trailer two or three times (to get cigarettes and to make phone calls), and each time the officer stood just inside the door to see what Chuck did. A couple of hours later, when a warrant was obtained, the police searched and found a marijuana pipe, a box for marijuana (a "one-hitter" box), and a small amount of marijuana. Chuck was convicted and claimed that he was unlawfully seized when the officer refused to allow him to enter the trailer unaccompanied. The Court disagreed:

> [We] cannot say that the warrantless seizure was *per se* unreasonable. It involves [a] claim of specially pressing or urgent law enforcement need, *i.e.,* "exigent circumstances." Moreover, the restraint [was] tailored to that need, being limited in time and scope, and avoiding significant intrusion into the home itself. [R]ather than employing a *per se* rule of unreasonableness, we balance the privacy-related and law enforcement-related concerns to determine if the intrusion was reasonable. [T]he restriction [was] reasonable, and hence lawful, in light of the following circumstances, which we consider in combination. First, the

police had probable cause to believe that McArthur's trailer home contained evidence of a crime and contraband, namely, unlawful drugs.... Second, the police had good reason to fear that, unless restrained, McArthur would destroy the drugs before they could return with a warrant.... Third, the police made reasonable efforts to reconcile their law enforcement needs with the demands of personal privacy. They neither searched the trailer nor arrested McArthur before obtaining a warrant. Rather, they imposed a significantly less restrictive restraint, preventing McArthur only from entering the trailer unaccompanied. They left his home and his belongings intact—until a neutral Magistrate, finding probable cause, issued a warrant.... Fourth, the police imposed the restraint for a limited period of time, namely, two hours. [T]his time period was no longer than reasonably necessary for the police, acting with diligence, to obtain the warrant....

Justice Stevens dissented. "[Illinois] has decided that the possession of less than 2.5 grams of marijuana is a class C misdemeanor" and therefore is not "a law enforcement priority in the State of Illinois." Balancing the need versus the intrusion, he concluded that the majority got "the balance wrong" given McArthur's interest in the sanctity of his home.

3. *Length of Seizure.* In *United States v. Sokolow*, 490 U.S. 1 (1989), believing that Sokolow was a drug courier, DEA agents approached him during a stopover in Los Angeles. Sokolow "appeared to be very nervous...." Later that day, at 6:30 p.m., Sokolow arrived in Honolulu. He had not checked any luggage and proceeded directly to the street and tried to hail a cab, where Agent Richard Kempshall and three other DEA agents approached him. Kempshall displayed his credentials, grabbed Sokolow by the arm, and moved him back onto the sidewalk. Kempshall asked Sokolow for his airline ticket and identification; Sokolow said that he had neither. He told the agents that his name was "Sokolow," but that he was traveling under his mother's maiden name, "Kray." Sokolow was escorted to the DEA office at the airport. There, his luggage was examined by "Donker," a narcotics detector dog, which alerted on Sokolow's brown shoulder bag. The agents arrested respondent. The agents obtained a warrant to search the shoulder bag. They found no illicit drugs, but the bag did contain several suspicious documents indicating respondent's involvement in drug trafficking. The agents had Donker reexamine the remaining luggage, and this time the dog alerted on a medium-sized Louis Vuitton bag. By now, it was 9:30 p.m., too late for the agents to obtain a second warrant. They allowed respondent to leave for the night, but kept his luggage. The next morning, the agents obtained a warrant and found 1,063 grams of cocaine inside the bag.

Respondent challenged the search on the basis that the police failed to use "the least intrusive means available to verify or dispel their suspicions that he was smuggling narcotics." The Court rejected the challenge: "[Respondent] points to the statement in *Royer*, that 'the investigative methods employed should be the least intrusive means reasonably available to verify or dispel the officer's suspicion in a short period of time.' That statement, however, was directed at the length of the investigative stop, not at whether the police had a less intrusive means to verify their suspicions before stopping Royer. The reasonableness of the officer's decision to stop a suspect does not turn on the availability of less intrusive investigatory techniques. Such a rule would unduly hamper the police's ability to make swift, on-the-spot decisions—here, respondent was about to get into a taxicab—and it would require courts to indulge in 'unrealistic second-guessing.'"

4. *Relying on "Wanted Flyers" to Establish "Reasonable Suspicion"* In *United States v. Hensley*, 469 U.S. 221 (1985), following an armed robbery, an informant told police that Hensley had driven the getaway car. Based on this information, the officer issued a "wanted flyer" which stated that Hensley was wanted for investigation of an aggravated robbery, described Hensley, stated the date and location of the alleged robbery, and asked other departments to pick up and hold Hensley in the event he were located. The flyer also warned other departments to use caution and to consider Hensley armed and dangerous. Based on the flyer, officers from another department stopped Hensley. When the officers spotted a revolver in plain view, they arrested Hensley. A search revealed other weapons. Based on the weapons, respondent was convicted of being a convicted felon in possession of firearms. The Court upheld the stop:

[A]dmissibility turns on whether the officers who issued the flyer possessed probable cause to make the arrest. It does not turn on whether those relying on the flyer were themselves aware of the specific facts which led their colleagues to seek their assistance. In an era when criminal suspects are increasingly mobile and increasingly likely to flee across jurisdictional boundaries, this rule [minimizes] the volume of information concerning suspects that must be transmitted to other jurisdictions and enables police in one jurisdiction to act promptly in reliance on information from another jurisdiction. [The] law enforcement interests promoted by allowing one department to make investigatory stops based upon another department's bulletins or flyers are considerable, while the intrusion on personal security is minimal. [R]eliance on [a] flyer or bulletin justifies a stop to check identification, to pose questions to the person, or to detain the person briefly while attempting to obtain further information. If the flyer has been issued in the absence of a reasonable suspicion, then a stop in the objective reliance upon it violates the Fourth Amendment. [O]f course, the officers making the stop may have a good-faith defense to any civil suit.

5. *Can an Officer Order the Driver and Passengers to Exit a Lawfully-Stopped Vehicle?* In *Pennsylvania v. Mimms*, 434 U.S. 106 (1977), the Court held that a police officer may as a matter of course order the driver of a lawfully stopped car to exit the vehicle. In *Maryland v. Wilson*, 519 U.S. 408 (1997), the Court extended this rule to passengers. In *Wilson*, an officer attempted to stop a speeding vehicle, but the driver refused to stop. During the pursuit, the officer noticed that there were three occupants in the car and that the two passengers turned to look at him several times, repeatedly ducking below sight level and then reappearing. As the officer approached the car on foot, the driver alighted and met him halfway. The driver was trembling and appeared extremely nervous, but nonetheless produced a valid Connecticut driver's license. Hughes instructed him to return to the car and retrieve the rental documents, and he complied. During this encounter, Hughes noticed that the front-seat passenger (Wilson) was sweating and appeared extremely nervous. While the driver was looking for the rental papers, Hughes ordered Wilson out of the car. When Wilson exited the car, a

quantity of crack cocaine fell to the ground. Wilson was then arrested and charged with possession of cocaine with intent to distribute. The Court held that the officer validly ordered Wilson to exit the vehicle:

> [T]he same weighty interest in officer safety is present regardless of whether the occupant of the stopped car is a driver or passenger. [In] 1994 alone, there were 5,762 officer assaults and 11 officers killed during traffic pursuits and stops. [T]he fact that there is more than one occupant of the vehicle increases the possible sources of harm to the officer.
>
> On the personal liberty side of the balance, the case for the passengers is in one sense stronger than that for the driver. There is probable cause to believe that the driver has committed a minor vehicular offense, but there is no such reason to stop or detain the passengers. But as a practical matter, the passengers are already stopped by virtue of the stop of the vehicle. Outside the car, the passengers will be denied access to any possible weapon that might be concealed in the interior of the passenger compartment. [T]he possibility of a violent encounter stems not from the ordinary reaction of a motorist stopped for a speeding violation, but from the fact that evidence of a more serious crime might be uncovered during the stop. [T]he motivation of a passenger to employ violence to prevent apprehension of such a crime is every bit as great as that of the driver. [While] there is not the same basis for ordering the passengers out of the car as there is for ordering the driver out, the additional intrusion on the passenger is minimal. We therefore hold that an officer making a traffic stop may order passengers to get out of the car pending completion of the stop.

Justice Stevens dissented: "[I]f a police officer [has] an articulable suspicion of possible danger, the officer may order passengers to exit the vehicle as a defensive tactic without running afoul of the Fourth Amendment. [But] the Court's ruling [applies] equally to traffic stops in which there is not even a scintilla of evidence of any potential risk to the police officer. [T]he Fourth Amendment prohibits routine and arbitrary seizures of obviously innocent citizens." Justice Kennedy also dissented: "Traffic stops, even for minor violations, can take upwards of 30 minutes. When an officer commands passengers innocent of any violation to leave the vehicle and stand by the side of the road in full view of the public, the seizure is serious, not trivial. [T]he command to exit ought not to be given unless there are objective circumstances making it reasonable for the officer to issue the order."

Problems

1. *The Cigarette Pack.* A warrant authorized police to search the Aurora Tavern and the person of "Greg," a white male who worked at the tavern, for possession of controlled substances. Police officers went to the tavern to execute the warrant, announced their purpose, and advised all present that they were going to conduct a "cursory search for weapons." The officers patted down each of the 13 customers. In patting down Gregory, the officer felt what he described as "a cigarette pack with objects in it." The officer retrieved the cigarette pack from Gregory's pants pocket. Inside the

pack he found tinfoil packets containing a brown powdery substance which later turned out to be heroin. Was the search of Gregory constitutional? What arguments might be made on behalf of the police? How might Gregory respond to these arguments? How should the Court rule? *See Ybarra v. Illinois*, 444 U.S. 85 (1979).

2. *Checking the House.* Police officers have a warrant to arrest Johnson, but do not have a search warrant for his residence. An informant tells police that Johnson is staying in a particular house, is armed, and might have accomplices with him. The officers stake out the apartment. When Johnson's fiancee emerged, she tells the police that Johnson is inside alone. When Johnson steps outside leaving the door ajar behind him, the police place him under arrest. While handcuffing Johnson, the officer notice that James Hamilton is observing from a distance, and Johnson tells Hamilton "they got me." Hamilton disappears. When other officers arrive, an officer conducts a "security check" of the house including the bedroom, bathroom, and kitchen to verify that there are no armed individuals present who might threaten the officers. In the bedroom, the officer discovers and seizes a gun sitting on a dresser and two bags of heroin lying in an open drawer. Did the police act properly in entering the apartment? *See United States v. Henry*, 48 F.3d 1282, 310 U.S.App.D.C. 431 (D.C.Cir.1995).

3. *The Investigation.* Police officers are "investigating gambling establishments" based on complaints of noise and disorderly conduct. An unidentified man walks out of one building "smelling like drink." The man, who had "supplied reliable information" to police in the past, states that he bought the drink at 56 Albany Street. The officers go to that address and enter without a warrant. They find themselves in a big room containing a pool table, barber chairs, a shoeshine stand and a showcase. An officer asks the owner whether he is selling drinks, and he denies it. The officers then "looks through everything." Seeing nothing incriminating, they search the women's room, a storage room and a wash room before reaching a large room at the back. In the back room, the officers find a four foot bar, two stools, a table with six chairs, and a refrigerator loaded with beer. On the bar are whisky bottles. No one is present. The officers place the owner under arrest for the illegal sale of alcohol, and then search his person and find two marijuana cigarettes in a vest pocket. The whole episode takes 30 minutes. Did the police act properly in searching the establishment without a warrant? Is the marijuana admissible? *See State v. Baker*, 112 N.J.Super. 351, 271 A.2d 435 (1970).

4. *The Law Student.* About midnight, a law student at Tulane University Law School leaves his French Quarter apartment in New Orleans to get something to eat. Two police officers stop him because he fits the description of a murder suspect. The student tells the officers that he has identification at home but not on his person. He gives them his name and address, and informs them he is a law student and is on his way to get some food. The officers tell the student that he resembles a murder suspect, and ask him to remove his jacket so they can check his forearm for a tattoo (the suspect has a tattoo on his left forearm that reads "born to raise hell"). The student refuses, saying he will not allow himself "to be molested by a bunch of cops," and he "doesn't want to be humiliated by the police." When the student tries to walk away, he is charged with resisting an officer. Did the police act

properly in stopping petitioner? *See Wainwright v. City of New Orleans*, 392 U.S. 598 (1968).

DELAWARE v. PROUSE

440 U.S. 648 (1979).

MR. JUSTICE WHITE delivered the opinion of the Court.

[A] patrolman in a police cruiser stopped the automobile occupied by respondent. The patrolman smelled marihuana smoke as he was walking toward the stopped vehicle, and he seized marihuana in plain view on the car floor. Respondent was subsequently indicted for illegal possession of a controlled substance. At a hearing on respondent's motion to suppress[,] the patrolman testified that prior to stopping the vehicle he had observed neither traffic or equipment violations nor any suspicious activity, and that he made the stop only in order to check the driver's license and registration. The patrolman was not acting pursuant to any standards, guidelines, or procedures pertaining to document spot checks, promulgated by either his department or the State Attorney General. Characterizing the stop as "routine," the patrolman explained, "I saw the car in the area and wasn't answering any complaints, so I decided to pull them off." The trial court granted the motion to [suppress].

[T]he permissibility of a particular law enforcement practice is judged by balancing its intrusion on the individual's Fourth Amendment interests against its promotion of legitimate governmental interests. Implemented in this manner, the reasonableness standard usually requires, at a minimum, that the facts upon which an intrusion is based be capable of measurement against "an objective standard," whether this be probable cause or a less stringent test. * * *

[T]he State of Delaware urges that [these] stops are reasonable under the Fourth Amendment because the State's interest in the practice as a means of promoting public safety upon its roads more than outweighs the intrusion entailed. Although the record discloses no statistics concerning [a] lack of highway safety, in Delaware or in the Nation as a whole, we are aware of the danger to life and property posed by vehicular traffic and of the difficulties that even a cautious and an experienced driver may encounter. We agree that the States have a vital interest in ensuring that only those qualified to do so are permitted to operate motor vehicles, that these vehicles are fit for safe operation, and hence that licensing, registration, and vehicle inspection requirements are being observed. Automobile licenses are issued periodically to evidence that the drivers holding them are sufficiently familiar with the rules of the road and are physically qualified to operate a motor vehicle. The registration requirement [and] the related annual inspection requirement in Delaware are designed to keep dangerous automobiles off the road. Unquestionably, these provisions, properly administered, are essential elements in a highway safety program. Furthermore, we note that the State of Delaware requires a minimum amount of insurance coverage as a condition to automobile registration, implementing its legitimate interest in seeing to it that its citizens have protection when involved in a motor vehicle accident.

The question remains, however, whether in the service of these important ends the discretionary spot check is a sufficiently productive mechanism to justify the intrusion upon Fourth Amendment interests which such stops entail. [T]hat question must be answered in the negative. Given the alternative mechanisms available, both those in use and those that might be adopted, we are unconvinced that the incremental contribution to highway safety of the random spot check justifies the practice under the Fourth Amendment.

The foremost method of enforcing traffic and vehicle safety regulations, it must be recalled, is acting upon observed violations. Vehicle stops for traffic violations occur countless times each day; and on these occasions, licenses and registration papers are subject to inspection and drivers without them will be ascertained. Furthermore, drivers without licenses are presumably the less safe drivers whose propensities may well exhibit themselves. Absent some empirical data to the contrary, it must be assumed that finding an unlicensed driver among those who commit traffic violations is a much more likely event than finding an unlicensed driver by choosing randomly from the entire universe of drivers. [The] contribution to highway safety made by discretionary stops selected from among drivers generally will therefore be marginal at best. Furthermore, [we] find it difficult to believe that the unlicensed driver would not be deterred by the possibility of being involved in a traffic violation or having some other experience calling for proof of his entitlement to drive but that he would be deterred by the possibility that he would be one of those chosen for a spot check. In terms of actually discovering unlicensed drivers or deterring them from driving, the spot check does not appear sufficiently productive to qualify as a reasonable law enforcement practice under the Fourth Amendment.

Much the same can be said about the safety aspects of automobiles as distinguished from drivers. Many violations of minimum vehicle-safety requirements are observable, and something can be done about them by the observing officer, directly and immediately. Furthermore, in Delaware, as elsewhere, vehicles must carry and display current license plates, which themselves evidence that the vehicle is properly registered; and, under Delaware law, to qualify for annual registration a vehicle must pass the annual safety inspection and be properly insured. It does not appear, therefore, that a stop of a Delaware-registered vehicle is necessary in order to ascertain compliance with the State's registration requirements; and, because there is nothing to show that a significant percentage of automobiles from other States do not also require license plates indicating current registration, there is no basis for concluding that stopping even out-of-state cars for document checks substantially promotes the State's interest.

The marginal contribution to roadway safety possibly resulting from a system of spot checks cannot justify subjecting every occupant of every vehicle on the roads to a seizure—limited in magnitude compared to other intrusions but nonetheless constitutionally cognizable—at the unbridled discretion of law enforcement officials. [By] hypothesis, stopping apparently safe drivers is necessary only because the danger presented by some drivers is not observable at the time of the stop. When there is not probable cause to believe that a driver is violating any one of the multitude of applicable traffic and equipment regulations—or other articulable basis amounting to reasonable suspicion that the driver is unlicensed or his vehicle unregistered—we cannot conceive of any legitimate basis upon which a patrolman could decide that stopping a particular driver for a spot check would be more productive than stopping any other driver. This kind of standardless and unconstrained discretion is the evil the Court has discerned when in previous cases it has insisted that the discretion of the official in the field be circumscribed, at least to some extent.

The "grave danger" of abuse of discretion does not disappear simply because the automobile is subject to state regulation resulting in numerous instances of police-citizen contact. [There] are certain "relatively unique circumstances" in which consent to regulatory restrictions is presumptively concurrent with participation in the regulated enterprise. Otherwise, regulatory inspections unaccompanied by any quantum of individualized, articulable suspicion must be undertaken pursuant to previously specified "neutral criteria."

An individual operating or traveling in an automobile does not lose all reasonable expectation of privacy simply because the automobile and its use are subject to government regulation. Automobile travel is a basic, pervasive, and often necessary mode of transportation to and from one's home, workplace, and leisure activities. Many people spend more hours each day traveling in cars than walking on the streets. Undoubtedly, many find a greater sense of security and privacy in traveling in an automobile than they do in exposing themselves by pedestrian or other modes of travel. Were the individual subject to unfettered governmental intrusion every time he entered an automobile, the security guaranteed by the Fourth Amendment would be seriously circumscribed. * * *

Accordingly, we hold that except in those situations in which there is at least articulable and reasonable suspicion that a motorist is unlicensed or that an automobile is not registered, or that either the vehicle or an occupant is otherwise subject to seizure for violation of law, stopping an automobile and detaining the driver in order to check his driver's license and the registration of the automobile are unreasonable under the Fourth Amendment. * * *

MR. JUSTICE REHNQUIST, dissenting.

[No] one questions that the State may require the licensing of those who drive on its highways and the registration of vehicles which are driven on those highways. If it may insist on these requirements, it obviously may take steps necessary to enforce compliance. The reasonableness of the enforcement measure chosen by the State is tested by

weighing its intrusion on the motorists' Fourth Amendment interests against its promotion of the State's legitimate interests. [The] State's primary interest, however, is in traffic safety, not in apprehending unlicensed motorists for the sake of apprehending unlicensed motorists. The whole point of enforcing motor vehicle safety regulations is to remove from the road the unlicensed driver before he demonstrates why he is unlicensed. The Court would apparently prefer that the State check licenses and vehicle registrations as the wreckage is being towed away.
* * *

Notes

1. *Defining "Reasonable Suspicion."* In *United States v. Cortez*, 449 U.S. 411 (1981), border patrol agents stopped a van which they suspected contained illegal aliens. The Court held that the suspicion was "reasonable":

> [W]hen used by trained law enforcement officers, objective facts, meaningless to the untrained, can be combined with permissible deductions from such facts to form a legitimate basis for suspicion of a particular person and for action on that suspicion. [T]he officers knew that the area was a crossing point for illegal aliens. They knew that it was common practice for persons to lead aliens through the desert from the border to Highway 86, where they could—by prearrangement—be picked up by a vehicle. Moreover, based upon clues they had discovered in the 2–month period prior to the events at issue here, they believed that one such guide, whom they designated "Chevron," had a particular pattern of operations.... By piecing together the information at their disposal, the officers tentatively concluded that there was a reasonable likelihood that "Chevron" would attempt to lead a group of aliens on the night of Sunday, January 30–31. Someone with chevron-soled shoes had led several groups of aliens in the previous two months, yet it had been two weeks since the latest crossing. "Chevron," they deduced, was therefore due reasonably soon. "Chevron" tended to travel on clear weekend nights. Because it had rained on the Friday and Saturday nights of the weekend involved here, Sunday was the only clear night of that weekend * * *.

> [T]he officers drew upon other objective facts known to them to deduce a time frame within which "Chevron" and the aliens were likely to arrive. [They] knew the time when sunset would occur; they knew about how long the trip would take. They were thus able to deduce that "Chevron" would likely arrive at the pickup point on Highway 86 in the time frame between 2 a.m. and 6 a.m. From objective facts, the officers also deduced the probable point on the highway—milepost 122—at which "Chevron" would likely rendezvous with a pickup vehicle. They deduced from the direction taken by the sets of "Chevron" footprints they had earlier discovered that the pickup vehicle would approach the aliens from, and return with them to, a point east of milepost 122. They therefore staked out a position east of milepost 122 and watched for vehicles that passed them going west and then, approximately one and a half hours later, passed them again, this time going east.

From what they had observed about the previous groups guided by the person with "chevron" shoes, they deduced that "Chevron" would lead a group of 8 to 20 aliens. They therefore focused their attention on enclosed vehicles of that passenger capacity. [I]n a 4–hour period the officers observed only one vehicle meeting that description. And it is not surprising that when they stopped the vehicle on its return trip it contained "Chevron" and several illegal aliens.

The limited purpose of the stop in this case was to question the occupants of the vehicle about their citizenship and immigration status and the reasons for the round trip in a short timespan in a virtually deserted area. No search of the camper or any of its occupants occurred until after respondent Cortez voluntarily opened the back door of the [camper]. The intrusion upon privacy associated with this stop was limited and [reasonable].

2. *Canine Sniffs.* In *Illinois v. Caballes*, 543 U.S. 405 (2005), Caballes was stopped for speeding. While stopped, the police brought in a drug sniffing dog to "sniff" his car. The sniff revealed the presence of illegal drugs. The Court assumed that the sniff did not prolong the stop and held that Caballes' rights were not violated.

Problems

1. *The Evasive Camper.* A federal agent observes a pickup truck with a camper shell traveling in tandem with another vehicle for 20 miles in an area near the coast known to be frequented by drug traffickers. The agent testifies that campers are often used to transport large quantities of marihuana. The pickup truck in question appears to be heavily loaded, and the windows of the camper are covered with a quilted bed-sheet material rather than curtains. When the officer begins following the vehicles in a marked police car, both vehicles take evasive actions and starts speeding. Was there sufficient cause to stop the camper? *See United States v. Sharpe*, 470 U.S. 675 (1985).

2. *"Reasonable Suspicion."* In *Alabama v. White*, 496 U.S. 325 (1990), police receive an anonymous call stating that Vanessa White will be leaving Lynwood Terrace Apartments at a particular time in a brown Plymouth station wagon with the right taillight lens broken, that she will be going to Dobey's Motel, and that she will be carrying an ounce of cocaine in a brown attache case. Officers go to the apartments, find a brown Plymouth station wagon with a broken right taillight, observe respondent leave the building (carrying nothing in her hands) and enter the station wagon. They follow the vehicle as it drives the most direct route to Dobey's Motel. When the vehicle is stopped just short of the motel, the officer asks respondent to step to the rear of her car, where he informs her that she has been stopped because she is suspected of carrying cocaine. He asks if they may look for cocaine, and respondent consents. The officers find a locked brown attache case in the car, and, upon request, respondent provides the combination to the lock. The officers find cocaine in the attache case and place respondent under arrest. Did the police have reasonable suspicion for the stop?

3. *Canine Sniffs*. Defendant motorist was stopped for weaving across lines. After checking defendant's license and registration, the officer wrote a citation but did not give it to defendant. Instead, the officer told defendant that he would give him a "courtesy warning." The officer then asked defendant whether he was carrying narcotics. Defendant responded in the negative. When the officer then asked for permission to search the vehicle, defendant refused. The officer immediately requested a drug canine unit and ran a criminal history check on defendant. About six minutes later, the canine unit arrived and reacted positively to defendant's vehicle. Did the officer act permissibly in detaining the motorist long enough to run a background check and bring in a canine unit? *See United States v. Boyce*, 351 F.3d 1102 (11th Cir.2003).

4. *More on Canine Sniffs*. In the prior problem, would you reach a different result if the officer had stopped the motorist based on a valid drug courier profile (suggesting that the suspect was transporting narcotics)?

5. *The Lost Motorist*. A police officer concludes that the driver of an automobile is lost, and stops the driver to offer help. As the officer approaches the vehicle, he spots a bomb in plain view in the backseat. How might you argue that the officer acted properly? How might the driver respond? Are there instances when the police should stop someone to offer help (*i.e.*, a bridge is out and an officer wants to stop the motorist to inform him of this fact)?

6. *"Good Driving" Programs*. In some areas, the police have instituted "good driving" programs designed to reward "good" drivers. Under these programs, officers pull drivers over (using their sirens and lights), and present the drivers with gift certificates and coupons for prizes. The purpose of these programs is to encourage better driving. Are "good driving" programs constitutional? Suppose, for example, that an officer pulls a driver over to award a certificate, notices contraband in the car, and arrests the driver. Can the state use the evidence against the driver? How might you argue that the evidence should be suppressed? How might the state respond?

7. *More on "Good Driving" Programs*. Is a "good driving" program more likely to be constitutional if the police provide drivers with bumper stickers designed to signal their participation in the "good driver" program, and only pull over cars that have such stickers on their bumpers?

8. *"Stops" for Completed Crimes*. Days after a business is robbed, the police learn the identity of the robber and issue a "wanted flyer." Relying on the flyer, an officer pulls defendant over. The officer approaches Hensley's car with his service revolver drawn, and orders Hensley and a passenger to step out of the car. The officer recognizes the passenger as a convicted felon. The officer then steps up to the open passenger door and observes the butt of a revolver protruding from underneath the passenger's seat. The felon is then arrested. A search of the car uncovers a second handgun in the middle of the front seat and a third handgun in a bag in the back seat. After the discovery of these weapons, defendant is also arrested, and moves to suppress arguing that a *Terry* stop can only be justified for a "crime in progress." If you represent the State, how might you respond to Hensley's argument? On behalf of Hensley, what flaws do you see in the State's position? *See United States v. Hensley*, 469 U.S. 221 (1985).

CITY OF INDIANAPOLIS v. EDMOND
531 U.S. 32 (2000).

JUSTICE O'CONNOR delivered the opinion of the Court.

In *Michigan Dept. of State Police v. Sitz*, 496 U.S. 444 (1990), and *United States v. Martinez–Fuerte*, 428 U.S. 543 (1976), we held that brief, suspicionless seizures at highway checkpoints for the purposes of combating drunk driving and intercepting illegal immigrants were constitutional. We now consider the constitutionality of a highway checkpoint program whose primary purpose is the discovery and interdiction of illegal narcotics.

I

In August 1998, the city of Indianapolis began to operate vehicle checkpoints on Indianapolis roads in an effort to interdict unlawful drugs. The city conducted six such roadblocks between August and November that year, stopping 1,161 vehicles and arresting 104 motorists. Fifty-five arrests were for drug-related crimes, while 49 were for offenses unrelated to drugs. The overall "hit rate" of the program was thus approximately nine percent.

[At] each checkpoint location, the police stop a predetermined number of vehicles. Approximately 30 officers are stationed at the checkpoint. Pursuant to written directives issued by the chief of police, at least one officer approaches the vehicle, advises the driver that he or she is being stopped briefly at a drug checkpoint, and asks the driver to produce a license and registration. The officer also looks for signs of impairment and conducts an open-view examination of the vehicle from the outside. A narcotics-detection dog walks around the outside of each stopped vehicle.

The directives instruct the officers that they may conduct a search only by consent or based on the appropriate quantum of particularized suspicion. The officers must conduct each stop in the same manner until particularized suspicion develops, and the officers have no discretion to stop any vehicle out of sequence. The city agreed [to] operate the checkpoints in such a way as to ensure that the total duration of each stop, absent reasonable suspicion or probable cause, would be five minutes or less.

[According to] Indianapolis Police Sergeant Marshall DePew[, checkpoint] locations are selected weeks in advance based on such considerations as area crime statistics and traffic flow. The checkpoints are generally operated during daylight hours and are identified with lighted signs reading, "NARCOTICS CHECKPOINT ___ MILE AHEAD, NARCOTICS K–9 IN USE, BE PREPARED TO STOP." Once a group of cars has been stopped, other traffic proceeds without interruption until all the stopped cars have been processed or diverted for further processing.

[T]he average stop for a vehicle not subject to further processing lasts two to three minutes or less.

Respondents James Edmond and Joell Palmer were each stopped at a narcotics checkpoint in late September 1998. Respondents then filed [suit] on behalf of themselves and the class of all motorists who had been stopped or were subject to being stopped in the future at [the] checkpoints. [The trial court] denied the motion for a preliminary injunction.... A [divided] United States Court of Appeals for the Seventh Circuit reversed.... We granted certiorari, and now affirm.

II

The Fourth Amendment requires that searches and seizures be reasonable. A search or seizure is ordinarily unreasonable in the absence of individualized suspicion of wrongdoing. While such suspicion is not an "irreducible" component of reasonableness, we have recognized only limited circumstances in which the usual rule does not apply. For example, we have upheld certain regimes of suspicionless searches where the program was designed to serve "special needs, beyond the normal need for law enforcement." *See, e.g., Vernonia School Dist. 47J v. Acton*, 515 U.S. 646 (1995) (random drug testing of student-athletes); *Treasury Employees v. Von Raab*, 489 U.S. 656 (1989) (drug tests for United States Customs Service employees seeking transfer or promotion to certain positions); *Skinner v. Railway Labor Executives' Assn.*, 489 U.S. 602 (1989) (drug and alcohol tests for railway employees involved in train accidents or found to be in violation of particular safety regulations). We have also allowed searches for certain administrative purposes without particularized suspicion of misconduct, provided that those searches are appropriately limited. *See, e.g., New York v. Burger*, 482 U.S. 691 (1987) (warrantless administrative inspection of premises of "closely regulated" business); *Michigan v. Tyler*, 436 U.S. 499 (1978) (administrative inspection of fire-damaged premises to determine cause of blaze); *Camara v. Municipal Court*, 387 U.S. 523 (1967) (administrative inspection to ensure compliance with city housing code).

We have also upheld brief, suspicionless seizures of motorists at a fixed Border Patrol checkpoint designed to intercept illegal aliens, and at a sobriety checkpoint aimed at removing drunk drivers from the road. In addition, in *Delaware v. Prouse*, 440 U.S. 648 (1979), we suggested that a similar type of roadblock with the purpose of verifying drivers' licenses and vehicle registrations would be permissible. In none of these cases, however, did we indicate approval of a checkpoint program whose primary purpose was to detect evidence of ordinary criminal wrongdoing.

In *Martinez–Fuerte*, we entertained Fourth Amendment challenges to stops at two permanent immigration checkpoints located on major United States highways less than 100 miles from the Mexican border. We noted [the] "formidable law enforcement problems" posed by the northbound tide of illegal entrants into the United States. [W]e found that the balance tipped in favor of the Government's interests in policing the Nation's borders[, and] emphasized the difficulty of effectively containing illegal immigration at the border itself. We also stressed the impracticality of the particularized study of a given car to discern whether it was transporting illegal aliens, as well as the relatively modest degree of intrusion entailed by the stops.... Although the stops in [did] not occur at the border itself, the checkpoints were located near the border and served a border control function made necessary by the difficulty of guarding the border's entire length.

In *Sitz*, we evaluated the constitutionality of a Michigan highway sobriety checkpoint program [involving] brief suspicionless stops of motorists so that police officers could detect signs of intoxication and remove impaired drivers from the road. Motorists who exhibited signs of intoxication were diverted for a license and registration check and, if warranted, further sobriety tests. This checkpoint program was clearly aimed at reducing the immediate hazard posed by the presence of drunk drivers on the highways, and there was an obvious connection between the imperative of highway safety and the law enforcement practice at issue. The gravity of the drunk driving problem and the magnitude of the State's interest in getting drunk drivers off the road weighed heavily in our determination that the program was constitutional.

In *Prouse*, we invalidated a discretionary, suspicionless stop for a spot check of a motorist's driver's license and vehicle registration.... We nonetheless acknowledged the States' "vital interest in ensuring that only those qualified to do so are permitted to operate motor vehicles, that these vehicles are fit for safe operation, and hence that licensing, registration, and vehicle inspection requirements are being observed." Accordingly, we suggested that "[q]uestioning of all oncoming traffic at roadblock-type stops" would be a lawful means of serving this interest in highway safety.

We [indicated] in *Prouse* that we considered the purposes of such a hypothetical roadblock to be distinct from a general purpose of investigating crime. The State proffered the additional interests of "the apprehension of stolen motor vehicles and of drivers under the influence of alcohol or narcotics" in its effort to justify the discretionary spot check. We attributed the entirety of the latter interest to the State's interest in roadway safety. We also noted that the interest in apprehending stolen vehicles may be partly subsumed by the interest in roadway safety. We observed, however, that "[t]he remaining governmental interest in controlling automobile thefts is not distinguishable from the general interest in crime control." Not only does the common thread of highway safety thus run through *Sitz* and *Prouse*, but *Prouse* itself reveals a difference in the Fourth Amendment significance of highway safety interests and the general interest in crime control.

It is well established that a vehicle stop at a highway checkpoint effectuates a seizure within the meaning of the Fourth Amendment. The fact that officers walk a narcotics-detection dog around the exterior of each car at the Indianapolis checkpoints does not transform the seizure into a search. *See United States v. Place*, 462 U.S. 696 (1983). Just as in *Place*, an exterior sniff of an automobile does not require entry into the car and is not designed to disclose any information other than the presence or absence of narcotics. [A] sniff by a dog that simply walks around a car is "much less intrusive than a typical search."

[T]he Indianapolis checkpoint program unquestionably has the primary purpose of interdicting illegal narcotics. [T]he parties repeatedly refer to the checkpoints as "drug checkpoints" and describe them as "being operated by the City of Indianapolis in an effort to interdict unlawful drugs in Indianapolis." [We] have never approved a checkpoint program whose primary purpose was to detect evidence of ordinary criminal wrongdoing. Rather, our checkpoint cases have recognized only limited exceptions to the general rule that a seizure must be accompanied by some measure of individualized suspicion. We suggested in *Prouse* that we would not credit the "general interest in crime control" as justification for a regime of suspicionless stops. Consistent with this suggestion, each of the checkpoint programs that we have approved was designed primarily to serve purposes closely related to the problems of policing the border or the necessity of ensuring roadway safety. Because the primary purpose of the Indianapolis narcotics checkpoint program is to uncover evidence of ordinary criminal wrongdoing, the program contravenes the Fourth Amendment.

Petitioners propose several ways in which the narcotics-detection purpose of the instant checkpoint program may instead resemble the primary purposes of the checkpoints in *Sitz* and *Martinez–Fuerte*. Petitioners state that the checkpoints in those cases had the same ultimate purpose of arresting those suspected of committing crimes. Securing the border and apprehending drunk drivers are, of course, law enforcement activities, and law enforcement officers employ arrests and criminal prosecutions in pursuit of these goals. If we were to rest the case at this high level of generality, there would be little check on the ability of the authorities to construct roadblocks for almost any conceivable law enforcement purpose. [T]he Fourth Amendment would do little to prevent such intrusions from becoming a routine part of American life.

Petitioners also emphasize the severe and intractable nature of the drug problem as justification for the checkpoint program. There is no doubt that traffic in illegal narcotics creates social harms of the first magnitude. The law enforcement problems that the drug trade creates likewise remain daunting and complex, particularly in light of the myriad forms of spin-off crime that it spawns. The same can be said of various other illegal activities, if only to a lesser degree. But the gravity of the threat alone cannot be dispositive of questions concerning what means law enforcement officers may employ to pursue a given purpose. Rather, in determining whether individualized suspicion is required, we must consider the nature of the interests threatened and their connection to the particular law enforcement practices at issue. We are particularly reluctant to recognize exceptions to the general rule of individualized suspicion where governmental authorities primarily pursue their general crime control ends.

Nor can the narcotics-interdiction purpose of the checkpoints be rationalized in terms of a highway safety concern similar to that present in *Sitz*. The detection and punishment of almost any criminal offense serves broadly the safety of the community, and our streets would no doubt be safer but for the scourge of illegal drugs. Only with respect to a smaller class of offenses, however, is society confronted with the type of immediate, vehicle-bound threat to life and limb that the sobriety checkpoint in *Sitz* was designed to eliminate.

Petitioners also liken the anticontraband agenda of the Indianapolis checkpoints to the antismuggling purpose of the checkpoints in *Martinez–Fuerte*. Petitioners cite this Court's conclusion in *Martinez–Fuerte* that the flow of traffic was too heavy to permit "particularized study of a given car that would enable it to be identified as a possible carrier of illegal aliens," and claim that this logic has even more force here. The problem [is] that the same logic prevails any time a vehicle is employed to conceal contraband or other evidence of a crime.... Further, the Indianapolis checkpoints are far removed from the border context that was crucial in *Martinez–Fuerte*. [We] must look more closely at the nature of the public interests that such a regime is designed principally to serve.

The primary purpose of the Indianapolis [checkpoints is] to advance "the general interest in crime control." We decline to suspend the usual requirement of individualized suspicion where the police seek to employ a checkpoint primarily for the ordinary enterprise of investigating crimes. We cannot sanction stops justified only by the generalized and ever-present possibility that interrogation and inspection may reveal that [a] given motorist has committed some crime.

Of course, there are circumstances that may justify a law enforcement checkpoint where the primary purpose would otherwise, but for some emergency, relate to ordinary crime control. For example, [the] Fourth Amendment would almost certainly permit an appropriately tailored roadblock set up to thwart an imminent terrorist attack or to catch a dangerous criminal who is likely to flee by way of a particular route. The exigencies created by these scenarios are far removed from the circumstances under which authorities might simply stop cars as a matter of course to see if there just happens to be a felon leaving the jurisdiction. While we do not limit the purposes that may justify a checkpoint program to any rigid set of categories, we decline to approve a program whose primary purpose is ultimately indistinguishable from the general interest in crime control....

Petitioners argue that the Indianapolis checkpoint program is justified by its lawful secondary purposes of keeping impaired motorists off the road and verifying licenses and registrations. If this were the case, however, law enforcement authorities would be able to establish checkpoints for virtually any purpose so long as they also included a license or sobriety check. [W]e examine the available evidence to determine the primary purpose of the checkpoint program. [A] program driven by an impermissible purpose may be proscribed while a program impelled by licit purposes is permitted, even though the challenged conduct may be outwardly similar. [Our] holding today does nothing to alter the constitutional status of the sobriety and border checkpoints that we approved in *Sitz* and *Martinez–Fuerte*, or of the type of traffic checkpoint that we suggested would be lawful in *Prouse*. [Our] holding also does not affect the validity of border searches or searches at places like airports and government buildings, where the need for such measures to ensure public safety can be particularly acute. Nor does our opinion speak to other intrusions aimed primarily at purposes beyond the general interest in crime control. Our holding also does not impair the ability of police officers to act appropriately upon information that they properly learn during a checkpoint stop justified by a lawful primary purpose, even where such action may result in the arrest of a motorist for an offense unrelated to that purpose. Finally, we caution that the purpose inquiry in this context is to be conducted only at the programmatic level and is not an invitation to probe the minds of individual officers acting at the scene.

Because the primary purpose of the Indianapolis checkpoint program is ultimately indistinguishable from the general interest in crime control, the checkpoints violate the Fourth Amendment. The judgment of the Court of Appeals is accordingly affirmed.

It is so ordered.

CHIEF JUSTICE REHNQUIST, with whom JUSTICE THOMAS joins, and with whom JUSTICE SCALIA joins as to Part I, dissenting.

[Because] these seizures serve the State's accepted and significant interests of preventing drunken driving and checking for driver's licenses and vehicle registrations, and because there is nothing in the record to indicate that the addition of the dog sniff lengthens these otherwise legitimate seizures, I dissent.

[Roadblock seizures] are consistent with the Fourth Amendment if they are "carried out pursuant to a plan embodying explicit, neutral limitations on the conduct of individual officers." Specifically, the constitutionality of a seizure turns upon "a weighing of the gravity of the public concerns served by the seizure, the degree to which the seizure advances the public interest, and the severity of the interference with individual liberty." [This] case follows naturally from *Martinez–Fuerte* and *Sitz* [and] it is constitutionally irrelevant that petitioners also hoped to interdict drugs. . . .

With these checkpoints serving two important state interests, the remaining prongs of the *Brown v. Texas* balancing test are easily met. The seizure is objectively reasonable as it lasts, on average, two to three minutes and does not involve a search. The subjective intrusion is likewise limited as the checkpoints are clearly marked and operated by uniformed officers who are directed to stop every vehicle in the same manner. The only difference between this case and *Sitz* is the presence of the dog. We have already held, however, that a "sniff test" by a trained narcotics dog is not a "search" within the meaning of the Fourth Amendment.... And there is nothing in the record to indicate that the dog sniff lengthens the stop. Finally, the checkpoints' success rate—49 arrests for offenses unrelated to drugs—only confirms the State's legitimate interests in preventing drunken driving and ensuring the proper licensing of drivers and registration of their vehicles....

[The] "special needs" doctrine, which has been used to uphold certain suspicionless searches performed for reasons unrelated to law enforcement, is an exception to the general rule that a search must be based on individualized suspicion of wrongdoing. *See, e.g., Skinner v. Railway Labor Executives' Assn.*, 489 U.S. 602 (1989) (drug test search). The doctrine permits intrusions into a person's body and home, areas afforded the greatest Fourth Amendment protection. But there were no such intrusions here....

Note

In dicta, *Prouse* sanctioned roadside truck weigh-stations and inspection checkpoints. The Court recognized that some vehicles may be subjected to longer detention and more intrusive inspections than others.

Problems

1. *Sobriety Checkpoints.* On New Year's Eve, the police establish a sobriety checkpoint on a divided interstate highway about a mile beyond an exit. Approximately one-half mile beyond the exit is a large sign which reads: "Sobriety checkpoint one mile ahead. Prepare to stop." On seeing the sign, some drivers make a u-turn over the median and head in the opposite direction. (State law permits u-turns on divided highways provided that the driver makes the turn in a "careful and prudent" manner) Do the police have reasonable suspicion to stop drivers who make u-turns? What arguments might be made on behalf of the police? How might the driver respond to those arguments?

2. *Sobriety Checkpoints with Drug Sniffing Dogs.* Suppose that the police establish sobriety checkpoints rather than drug interdiction checkpoints. However, during the sobriety checks, officers walk drug sniffing dogs around the cars. Is the procedure permissible if it is "primarily" justified as a sobriety check?

ILLINOIS v. LIDSTER

540 U.S. 419 (2004).

JUSTICE BREYER delivered the opinion of the Court.

[On] August 23, 1997, just after midnight, an unknown motorist traveling eastbound on a highway in Lombard, Illinois, struck and killed a 70–year-old bicyclist. The motorist drove off without identifying himself. About one week later at about the same time of night and at about the same place, local police set up a highway checkpoint designed to obtain more information about the accident from the motoring public.

Police cars with flashing lights partially blocked the eastbound lanes of the highway. The blockage forced traffic to slow down, leading to lines of up to 15 cars in each lane. As each vehicle drew up to the checkpoint, an officer would stop it for 10 to 15 seconds, ask the occupants whether they had seen anything happen there the previous weekend, and hand each driver a flyer. The flyer said "ALERT ... FATAL HIT & RUN ACCIDENT" and requested "assistance in identifying the vehicle and driver in this accident which killed a 70 year old bicyclist."

Robert Lidster, the respondent, drove a minivan toward the checkpoint. As he approached the checkpoint, his van swerved, nearly hitting one of the officers. The officer smelled alcohol on Lidster's breath. He directed Lidster to a side street where another officer administered a sobriety test and then arrested Lidster. Lidster was tried and convicted in Illinois state court of driving under the influence of alcohol.

Lidster challenged the lawfulness of his arrest and conviction on the ground that the government had obtained much of the relevant evidence through use of a checkpoint stop that violated the Fourth Amendment. The trial court rejected that challenge. But an Illinois appellate reached the opposite conclusion. The Illinois Supreme Court [held] that our decision in *Indianapolis v. Edmond*, 531 U.S. 32 (2000), required it to find the stop unconstitutional. [W]e granted certiorari [and] now reverse. . . .

The checkpoint stop here differs significantly from that in *Edmond.* The stop's primary law enforcement purpose was *not* to determine whether a vehicle's occupants were committing a crime, but to ask vehicle occupants, as members of the public, for their help in providing information about a crime in all likelihood committed by others. The police expected the information elicited to help them apprehend, not the vehicle's occupants, but other individuals.

Edmond's language, as well as its context, makes clear that the constitutionality of this latter, information-seeking kind of stop was not then before the Court. *Edmond* refers to the subject matter of its holding as "stops justified only by the generalized and ever-present possibility that interrogation and inspection may reveal that *any given motorist has committed some crime.*" We concede that *Edmond* describes the law enforcement objective there in question as a "general interest in crime control," but it specifies that the phrase "general interest in crime control" does not refer to every "law enforcement" objective. . . .

Neither do we believe [that] the Fourth Amendment would have us apply an *Edmond*-type rule of automatic unconstitutionality to brief, information-seeking highway stops of the kind now before us. [T]he fact that such stops normally lack individualized suspicion cannot by itself determine the constitutional outcome. . . . The Fourth Amendment does not treat a motorist's car as his castle. See, *e.g., New York v. Class,* 475

U.S. 106 (1986). And special law enforcement concerns will sometimes justify highway stops without individualized suspicion. See *Michigan Dept. of State Police v. Sitz,* 496 U.S. 444 (1990) (sobriety checkpoint); *Martinez-Fuerte, supra* (Border Patrol checkpoint). [U]nlike *Edmond,* the context here (seeking information from the public) is one in which, by definition, the concept of individualized suspicion has little role to play. Like certain other forms of police activity, say, crowd control or public safety, an information-seeking stop is not the kind of event that involves suspicion, or lack of suspicion, of the relevant individual.

For another thing, information-seeking highway stops are less likely to provoke anxiety or to prove intrusive. The stops are likely brief. The police are not likely to ask questions designed to elicit self-incriminating information. And citizens will often react positively when police simply ask for their help as "responsible citizen[s]" to "give whatever information they may have to aid in law enforcement." *Miranda v. Arizona,* 384 U.S. 436 (1966).

Further, the law ordinarily permits police to seek the voluntary cooperation of members of the public in the investigation of a crime. [V]oluntary requests play a vital role in police investigatory work.

The importance of soliciting the public's assistance is offset to some degree by the need to stop a motorist to obtain that help—a need less likely present where a pedestrian, not a motorist, is involved. The difference is significant in light of our determinations that such an involuntary stop amounts to a "seizure" in Fourth Amendment terms. That difference, however, is not important enough to justify an *Edmond*-type rule here. [T]he motorist stop will likely be brief. Any accompanying traffic delay should prove no more onerous than many that typically accompany normal traffic congestion. And the resulting voluntary questioning of a motorist is as likely to prove important for police investigation as is the questioning of a pedestrian. Given these considerations, it would seem anomalous were the law (1) ordinarily to allow police freely to seek the voluntary cooperation of pedestrians but (2) ordinarily to forbid police to seek similar voluntary cooperation from motorists.

[W]e do not believe that an *Edmond*-type rule is needed to prevent an unreasonable proliferation of police checkpoints. Practical considerations—namely, limited police resources and community hostility to related traffic tie-ups—seem likely to inhibit any such proliferation. And [the] Fourth Amendment's normal insistence that the stop be reasonable in context will still provide an important legal limitation on police use of this kind of information-seeking checkpoint.

These considerations, taken together, convince us that an *Edmond*-type presumptive rule of unconstitutionality does not apply here. [We] must judge its reasonableness, hence, its constitutionality, on the basis of the individual circumstances. And as this Court said in *Brown v. Texas,* 443 U.S. 47 (1979), in judging reasonableness, we look to "the gravity of the public concerns served by the seizure, the degree to which the seizure advances the public interest, and the severity of the interference with individual liberty."

[We] hold that the stop was constitutional.... The relevant public concern was grave. Police were investigating a crime that had resulted in a human death. [T]he stop's objective was to help find the perpetrator of a specific and known crime, not of unknown crimes of a general sort.... The stop advanced this grave public concern to a significant degree. The police appropriately tailored their checkpoint stops to fit important criminal investigatory needs. The stops took place about one week after the hit-and-run accident, on the same highway near the location of the accident, and at about the same time of night. And police used the stops to obtain information from drivers, some of whom might well have been in the vicinity of the crime at the time it occurred.

Most importantly, the stops interfered only minimally with liberty of the sort the Fourth Amendment seeks to protect. [E]ach stop required only a brief wait in line—a very few minutes at most. Contact with the police lasted only a few seconds. Cf. *Martinez–Fuerte*, 428 U.S., at 547 (upholding stops of three-to-five minutes). Police contact consisted simply of a request for information and the distribution of a flyer. Viewed subjectively, the contact provided little reason for anxiety or alarm. The police stopped all vehicles systematically. And there is no allegation here that the police acted in a discriminatory or otherwise unlawful manner while questioning motorists during stops.

For these reasons we conclude that the checkpoint stop was constitutional.

The judgment of the Illinois Supreme Court is

Reversed.

Justice Stevens, with whom Justice Souter and Justice Ginsburg join, concurring in part and dissenting in part.

There is a valid and important distinction between seizing a person to determine whether she has committed a crime and seizing a person to ask whether she has any information about an unknown person who committed a crime a week earlier.... In contrast to pedestrians, who are free to keep walking when they encounter police officers handing out flyers or seeking information, motorists who confront a roadblock are required to stop, and to remain stopped for as long as the officers choose to detain them. Such a seizure may seem relatively innocuous to some, but annoying to others who are forced to wait.... Still other drivers may find an unpublicized roadblock at midnight on a Saturday somewhat alarming.

On the other side of the equation, the likelihood that questioning a random sample of drivers will yield useful information about a hit-and-run accident that occurred a week earlier is speculative at best. To be sure, the sample in this case was not entirely random: [The] police knew that the victim had finished work at the Post Office shortly before the fatal accident, and hoped that other employees of the Post Office or the nearby industrial park might work on similar schedules and, thus, have been driving the same route at the same time the previous week. That is a plausible theory, but there is no evidence [that] the police did anything to confirm that the nearby businesses in fact had shift changes at or near midnight on Saturdays, or [that] a roadblock would be more effective than, say, placing flyers on the employees' cars. . . .

Problems

1. *The Limits of "Need" Versus "Intrusion."* How far can *Terry's* "need" versus "intrusion" test be pushed? Suppose that, over the last five months, seven gruesome murders have been committed in Gainesville, Florida near the University of Florida campus. Even though the police have reason to believe that all 7 murders were committed by a single person who lives in the Gainesville area, they are not close to making an arrest and they believe that more murders will be committed in the near future. Desperate for information, the police establish roadblocks for the purpose of interviewing motorists. The police hope that one or more motorists will provide information that will lead to a break in the case. Given the "need" to find the murderer before another crime is committed, are the roadblocks constitutional?

2. *More on the Limits of "Need" Versus "Intrusion."* In the prior problem, if the roadblocks prove unsuccessful, and another murder is committed, would the police be justified in making house-to-house searches in hopes of finding relevant evidence?

b.   Investigatory Seizures of Property

Do different rules apply when the government seizes property rather than people?

UNITED STATES v. PLACE

462 U.S. 696 (1983).

JUSTICE O'CONNOR delivered the opinion of the Court.

[Respondent] Place's behavior aroused the suspicions of law enforcement officers as he waited in line at the Miami International Airport to purchase a ticket to New York's LaGuardia Airport. As Place proceeded to the gate for his flight, the agents approached him and requested his airline ticket and some identification. Place complied with the request and consented to a search of the two suitcases he had checked. Because his flight was about to depart, however, the agents decided not to search the luggage.

Prompted by Place's parting remark that he had recognized that they were police, the agents inspected the address tags on the checked luggage and noted discrepancies in the two street addresses. Further investigation revealed that neither address existed and that the telephone number Place had given the airline belonged to a third address on the same street. On the basis of their encounter with Place and this information, the Miami agents called Drug Enforcement Administration (DEA) authorities in New York to relay their information about Place.

Two DEA agents waited for Place at the arrival gate at LaGuardia Airport in New York. There again, his behavior aroused the suspicion of the agents. After he had claimed his two bags and called a limousine, the agents decided to approach him. They identified themselves as federal narcotics agents, to which Place responded that he knew they were "cops" and had spotted them as soon as he had deplaned. One of the agents informed Place that, based on their own observations and information obtained from the Miami authorities, they believed that he might be carrying narcotics. [The] agents requested and received identification from Place—a New Jersey driver's license, on which the agents later ran a computer check that disclosed no offenses, and his airline ticket receipt. When Place refused to consent to a search of his luggage, one of the agents told him that they were going to take the luggage to a federal judge to try to obtain a search warrant and that Place was free to accompany them. Place declined, but obtained from one of the agents telephone numbers at which the agents could be reached.

The agents then took the bags to Kennedy Airport, where they subjected the bags to a "sniff test" by a trained narcotics detection dog. The dog reacted positively to the smaller of the two bags but ambiguously to the larger bag. Approximately 90 minutes had elapsed since the seizure of respondent's luggage. Because it was late on a Friday afternoon, the agents retained the luggage until Monday morning, when they secured a search warrant from a magistrate for the smaller bag. Upon opening that bag, the agents discovered 1,125 grams of cocaine.

Place was indicted for possession of cocaine with intent to distribute. [The District Court denied Place's motion to suppress, but the court of appeals reversed].

II

[The] Court has viewed a seizure of personal property as *per se* unreasonable within the meaning of the Fourth Amendment unless it is accomplished pursuant to a judicial warrant issued upon probable cause and particularly describing the items to be seized. Where law enforcement authorities have probable cause to believe that a container holds contraband or evidence of a crime, but have not secured a warrant, the Court has interpreted the Amendment to permit seizure of the property, pending issuance of a warrant to examine its contents, if the exigencies of the circumstances demand it or some other recognized exception to the warrant requirement is present. For example, "objects such as weapons or contraband found in a public place may be seized by the police without a warrant," because, under these circumstances, the risk of the item's disappearance or use for its intended purpose before a warrant may be obtained outweighs the interest in possession.

[T]he Government asks us to recognize the reasonableness under the Fourth Amendment of warrantless seizures of personal luggage from the custody of the owner on the basis of less than probable cause, for the purpose of pursuing a limited course of investigation, short of opening the luggage, that would quickly confirm or dispel the authorities' suspicion. Specifically, we are asked to apply the principles of *Terry v. Ohio* to [permit] seizures on the basis of reasonable, articulable suspicion, premised on objective facts, that the luggage contains contraband or evidence of a crime. In our view, such application is appropriate.

[The] Government contends that, where the authorities possess specific and articulable facts warranting a reasonable belief that a traveler's luggage contains narcotics, the governmental interest in seizing the luggage briefly to pursue further investigation is substantial. "[T]he public has a compelling interest in detecting those who would traffic in deadly drugs for personal profit." Respondent suggests that, absent some special law enforcement interest such as officer safety, a generalized interest in law enforcement cannot justify an intrusion on an individual's Fourth Amendment interests in the absence of probable cause. Our prior cases [do] not support this proposition. In *Terry*, we described the governmental interests supporting the initial seizure of the person as "effective crime prevention and detection; it is this interest which underlies the recognition that a police officer may in appropriate circumstances and in an appropriate manner approach a person for purposes of investigating possibly criminal behavior even though there is no probable cause to make an arrest." Similarly, in *Michigan v. Summers* we identified three law enforcement interests that justified limited detention of the occupants of the premises during execution of a valid search warrant: "preventing flight in the event that incriminating evidence is found," "minimizing the risk of harm" both to the officers and the occupants, and "orderly completion of the search." The test is whether those interests are sufficiently "substantial," not whether they are independent of the interest in investigating crimes effectively and apprehending suspects. The context of a particular law enforcement practice [may] affect the determination whether a brief intrusion on Fourth Amendment interests on less than probable cause is essential to effective criminal investigation. Because of the inherently transient nature of drug courier activity at airports, allowing police to make brief investigative stops of persons at airports on reasonable suspicion of drug-trafficking substantially enhances the likelihood that police will be able to prevent the flow of narcotics into distribution channels.

Against this strong governmental interest, we must weigh the nature and extent of the intrusion upon the individual's Fourth Amendment rights when the police briefly detain luggage for limited investigative purposes. [The] intrusion on possessory interests occasioned by a seizure of one's personal effects can vary both in its nature and extent. The seizure may be made after the owner has relinquished control of the property to a third party or, as here, from the immediate custody and control of the owner. Moreover, the police may confine their investigation to an on-the-spot inquiry—for example, immediate exposure of the luggage to a trained narcotics detection dog—or transport the property to another location. Given the fact that seizures of property can vary in intrusiveness, some brief detentions of personal effects may be so minimally intrusive of Fourth Amendment interests that strong countervailing governmental interests will justify a seizure based only on specific articulable facts that the property contains contraband or evidence of a crime.

[We] conclude that when an officer's observations lead him reasonably to believe that a traveler is carrying luggage that contains narcotics, the principles of *Terry* and its progeny would permit the officer to detain the luggage briefly to investigate the circumstances that aroused his suspicion, provided that the investigative detention is properly limited in scope.

The purpose for which respondent's luggage was seized, of course, was to arrange its exposure to a narcotics detection dog. Obviously, if this investigative procedure is itself a search requiring probable cause, the initial seizure of respondent's luggage for the purpose of subjecting it to the sniff test—no matter how brief—could not be justified on less than probable cause. [We] have affirmed that a person possesses a privacy interest in the contents of personal luggage that is protected by the Fourth Amendment. A "canine sniff" by a well-trained narcotics detection dog, however, does not require opening the luggage. It does not expose noncontraband items that otherwise would remain hidden from public view, as does, for example, an officer's rummaging through the contents of the luggage. Thus, the manner in which information is obtained through this investigative technique is much less intrusive than a typical search. Moreover, the sniff discloses only the presence or absence of narcotics, a contraband item. [D]espite the fact that the sniff tells the authorities something about the contents of the luggage, the information obtained is limited. This limited disclosure also ensures that the owner of the property is not subjected to the embarrassment and inconvenience entailed in less discriminate and more intrusive investigative methods.

In these respects, the canine sniff is *sui generis*. We are aware of no other investigative procedure that is so limited both in the manner in which the information is obtained and in the content of the information revealed by the procedure. Therefore, we conclude that the particular course of investigation that the agents intended to pursue here—exposure of respondent's luggage, which was located in a public place, to a trained canine—did not constitute a "search" within the meaning of the Fourth Amendment.

There is no doubt that the agents made a "seizure" of Place's luggage for purposes of the Fourth Amendment when, following his refusal to consent to a search, the agent told Place that he was going to take the luggage to a federal judge to secure issuance of a warrant. [We] reject the Government's suggestion that the point at which probable cause for seizure of luggage from the person's presence becomes necessary is more distant than in the case of a *Terry* stop of the person himself. The premise of the Government's argument is that seizures of property are generally less intrusive than seizures of the person. While true in some circumstances, [the] precise type of detention we confront here is seizure of personal luggage from the immediate possession of the suspect for the purpose of arranging exposure to a narcotics detection dog. Particularly in the case of detention of luggage within the traveler's immediate possession, the police conduct intrudes on both the suspect's possessory interest in his luggage as well as his liberty interest in proceeding with his itinerary. The person whose luggage is detained is technically still free to continue his travels or carry out other personal activities pending release of the luggage. Moreover, he is not subjected to the coercive atmosphere of a custodial confinement or to the public indignity of being personally detained. Nevertheless, such a seizure can effectively restrain the person since he is subjected to the possible disruption of his travel plans in order to remain with his luggage or to arrange for its return. Therefore, when the police seize luggage from the suspect's custody, we think the limitations applicable to investigative detentions of the person should define the permissible scope of an investigative detention of the person's luggage on less than probable cause. Under this standard, it is clear that the police conduct here exceeded the permissible limits of a *Terry*-type investigative stop.

The length of the detention of [Place's] luggage [precludes a] conclusion that the seizure was reasonable in the absence of probable cause. [T]he brevity of the invasion of the individual's Fourth Amendment interests is an important factor in determining whether the seizure is so minimally intrusive as to be justifiable on reasonable suspicion. Moreover, in assessing the effect of the length of the detention, we take into account whether the police diligently pursue their investigation. [H]ere the New York agents knew the time of Place's scheduled arrival at LaGuardia, had ample time to arrange for their additional investigation[,] and thereby could have minimized the intrusion on respondent's Fourth Amendment interests. [A]lthough we decline to adopt any outside time limitation for a permissible *Terry* stop,[11] we have never approved a seizure of the person for the prolonged 90–minute period involved here and cannot do so on the facts presented by this case.

Although the 90–minute detention of respondent's luggage is sufficient to render the seizure unreasonable, the violation was exacerbated by the failure of the agents to accurately inform respondent of the place to which they were transporting his luggage, of the length of time he might be dispossessed, and of what arrangements would be made for return of the luggage if the investigation dispelled the suspicion. [We] hold that the detention of respondent's luggage in this case went beyond the narrow authority possessed by police to detain briefly luggage reasonably suspected to contain narcotics. [We] conclude that, under all of the circumstances of this case, the seizure of respondent's luggage was unreasonable under the Fourth Amendment. Consequently, the evidence

---

11. *Cf.* ALI, Model Code of Pre–Arraignment Procedure § 110.2(1) 1975)(recommending a maximum of 20 minutes for a *Terry* stop).

obtained from the subsequent search of his luggage was inadmissible, and Place's conviction must be reversed. * * *

JUSTICE BRENNAN, with whom JUSTICE MARSHALL joins, concurring in the result.

[T]he use of a balancing test in this case is inappropriate. First, the intrusion involved in this case is no longer the "narrow" one contemplated by the *Terry* line of cases. In addition, the intrusion [involves] not only the seizure of a person, but also the seizure of property.... *Terry* and the cases that followed it established "isolated exceptions to the general rule that the Fourth Amendment itself has already performed the constitutional balance between police objectives and personal privacy." "[T]he Court today has employed a balancing test 'to swallow the general rule that [seizures of property] are "reasonable" only if based on probable cause.'" Justice Blackmun's concern over "an emerging tendency on the part of the Court to convert the *Terry* decision into a general statement that the Fourth Amendment requires only that any seizure be reasonable," is certainly justified. * * *

Note: Seizing Mail

In *United States v. Van Leeuwen*, 397 U.S. 249 (1970), respondent mailed two 12–pound packages at a post office in the State of Washington, about 60 miles from the Canadian border, declaring that the packages contained coins. One package was addressed to a post office box in California, and the other to a post office box in Tennessee. Each package was sent airmail registered and insured for $10,000, a type of mailing that did not subject them to discretionary inspection. When the postal clerk told police that he was suspicious of the packages, an officer noticed that the return address on the packages was a vacant housing area and that the license plates of respondent's car were British Columbia. Further investigation revealed that the California address was under investigation in Van Nuys for trafficking in illegal coins. Due to the time differential, Seattle customs was unable to reach Nashville until the following morning, but it was then learned that the Tennessee address was also being investigated for the same crime. A customs official in Seattle thereupon obtained a search warrant, and the packages were opened and inspected. Respondent was subsequently tried for illegally importing gold coins. The Court upheld the seizure: "No interest protected by the Fourth Amendment was invaded by forwarding the packages the following day rather than the day when they were deposited. The significant Fourth Amendment interest was in the privacy of this first-class mail; and that privacy was not disturbed or invaded until the approval of the magistrate was obtained. [O]n the facts of this case—the nature of the mailings, their suspicious character, the fact that there were two packages going to separate destinations, the unavoidable delay in contacting the more distant of the two destinations, the distance between Mt. Vernon and Seattle—a 29–hour delay between the mailings and the service of the warrant cannot be said to be 'unreasonable' within the meaning of the Fourth Amendment."

Problems

1.   In *Place*, suppose that you had been asked to advise the police about how to handle the Place investigation. What would you have advised them to do differently?

2.   Police detain a suspect at his home while they search his home. Because the weather is chilly, and the police intend to take defendant outside, the police unilaterally decide to provide the suspect with a jacket and they choose the jacket from his closet. Before the police actually hand the jacket to the suspect, may they "frisk" the jacket to make sure that it does not contain a weapon or evidence? How would you respond to defendant's argument that, since the police have chosen to place the jacket within the area of defendant's "immediate control," they commit "serious abuse" when they also search it? *See State v. Peterson*, 110 P.3d 699 (Utah 2005).

8.   Border Searches

The government has always exercised broad authority to stop individuals seeking to enter the United States, to demand identification, and to search their persons and effects to make sure that contraband is not being smuggled. However, there have been questions about the scope of governmental authority. Consider the following case.

UNITED STATES v. FLORES–MONTANO
541 U.S. 149 (2004).

CHIEF JUSTICE REHNQUIST delivered the opinion of the Court.

Customs officials seized 37 kilograms—a little more than 81 pounds—of marijuana from respondent Manuel Flores–Montano's gas tank at the international border. The Court of Appeals [held] that the Fourth Amendment forbade the fuel tank search absent reasonable suspicion. We hold that the search in question did not require reasonable suspicion.

Respondent, driving a 1987 Ford Taurus station wagon, attempted to enter the United States at the Otay Mesa Port of Entry in southern California. A customs inspector conducted an inspection of the station wagon, and requested respondent to leave the vehicle. The vehicle was then taken to a secondary inspection station [where] a second customs inspector inspected the gas tank by tapping it, and noted that the tank sounded solid. [T]he inspector requested a mechanic under contract with Customs to come to the border station to remove the tank. Within 20 to 30 minutes, the mechanic arrived. He raised the car on a hydraulic lift, loosened the straps and unscrewed the bolts holding the gas tank to the undercarriage of the vehicle, and then disconnected some hoses and electrical connections. After the gas tank was removed, the inspector hammered off bondo (a putty-like hardening substance that is used to seal openings) from the top of the gas tank. The inspector opened an access plate underneath the bondo and found 37 kilograms of marijuana bricks. The process took 15 to 25 minutes.

A grand jury [indicted] respondent on one count of unlawfully importing marijuana, in violation of 21 U.S.C. § 952, and one count of possession of marijuana with intent to distribute, in violation of § 841(a)(1).... The District Court [held] that reasonable suspicion was required to justify the search and, accordingly, granted respondent's motion to suppress. The Court of Appeals [affirmed.] We granted certiorari and now reverse.

[T]he reasons that might support a requirement of some level of suspicion in the case of highly intrusive searches of the person—dignity and privacy interests of the person being searched—simply do not carry over to vehicles. Complex balancing tests to determine what is a "routine" search of a vehicle, as opposed to a more "intrusive" search of a person, have no place in border searches of vehicles.

The Government's interest in preventing the entry of unwanted persons and effects is at its zenith at the international border. Time and again, we have stated that "searches made at the border, pursuant to the longstanding right of the sovereign to protect itself by stopping and examining persons and property crossing into this country, are reasonable simply by virtue of the fact that they occur at the border." *United States v. Ramsey,* 431 U.S. 606 (1977). Congress, since the beginning of our Government, "has granted the Executive plenary authority to conduct routine searches and seizures at the border, without probable cause or a warrant, in order to regulate the collection of duties and to prevent the introduction of contraband into this country." *Montoya de Hernandez, supra,* at 537. The modern statute that authorized the search in this case, 19 U.S.C. § 1581(a),[12] derived from a statute passed by the First Congress, and reflects the "impressive historical pedigree" of the Government's power and interest. It is axiomatic that the United States, as sovereign, has the inherent authority to protect, and a paramount interest in protecting, its territorial integrity.

That interest in protecting the borders is illustrated in this case by the evidence that smugglers frequently attempt to penetrate our borders with contraband secreted in their automobiles' fuel tank. Over the past 5 ½ fiscal years, there have been 18,788 vehicle drug seizures at the southern California ports of entry. Of those 18,788, gas tank drug seizures have accounted for 4,619 of the vehicle drug seizures, or approximately 25%. In addition, instances of persons smuggled in and around gas tank compartments are discovered at the ports of entry of San Ysidro and Otay Mesa at a rate averaging 1 approximately every 10 days.

12. Section 1581(a) provides: "Any officer of the customs may at any time go on board [any] vehicle at any place in the United States [or], as he may be authorized, within a customs-enforcement area established under the Anti–Smuggling Act, or at any other authorized place, without as well as within his district, and examine [and] examine, inspect, and search the vessel or vehicle and every part thereof and any person, trunk, package, or cargo on board, and to this end may hail and stop such vessel or vehicle, and use all necessary force to compel compliance."

Respondent [urges] that he has a privacy interest in his fuel tank, and that the suspicionless disassembly of his tank is an invasion of his privacy. [We] have noted that the expectation of privacy is less at the border than it is in the interior. *Montoya de Hernandez, supra,* at 538. We have long recognized that automobiles seeking entry into this country may be searched. It is difficult to imagine how the search of a gas tank, which should be solely a repository for fuel, could be more of an invasion of privacy than the search of the automobile's passenger compartment.

Second, respondent argues that the Fourth Amendment "protects property as well as privacy," *Soldal v. Cook County,* 506 U.S. 56 (1992), and that the disassembly and reassembly of his gas tank is a significant deprivation of his property interest because it may damage the vehicle. He [cannot], truly contend that the procedure of removal, disassembly, and reassembly of the fuel tank in this case [has] resulted in serious damage to, or destruction of, the property. [In] fiscal year 2003, 348 gas tank searches conducted along the southern border were negative (*i.e.,* no contraband was found), the gas tanks were reassembled, and the vehicles continued their entry into the United States without incident.... Respondent cites not a single accident involving the vehicle or motorist in the many thousands of gas tank disassemblies that have occurred at the border. A gas tank search involves a brief procedure that can be reversed without damaging the safety or operation of the vehicle. If damage to a vehicle were to occur, the motorist might be entitled to recovery. While the interference with a motorist's possessory interest is not insignificant when the Government removes, disassembles, and reassembles his gas tank, it nevertheless is justified by the Government's paramount interest in protecting the border.[3]

For the reasons stated, we conclude that the Government's authority to conduct suspicionless inspections at the border includes the authority to remove, disassemble, and reassemble a vehicle's fuel tank. While it may be true that some searches of property are so destructive as to require a different result, this was not one of them. The judgment of the United States Court of Appeals for the Ninth Circuit is therefore reversed, and the case is remanded for further proceedings consistent with this opinion.

It is so ordered.

JUSTICE BREYER, concurring.

[Customs] keeps track of the border searches its agents conduct, including the reasons for the searches. This administrative process should help minimize concerns that gas tank searches might be undertaken in an abusive manner.

---

3. Respondent also argued that he has [a] Fourth Amendment right not to be subject to delay at the international border and that the need for the use of specialized labor, as well as the hour actual delay here and the potential for even greater delay for reassembly are an invasion of that right. Respondent points to no cases indicating the Fourth Amendment shields entrants from inconvenience or delay at the international border. [D]elays of one to two hours at international borders are to be expected.

Notes

1. *Roving Border Patrols.* In *United States v. Brignoni–Ponce*, 422 U.S. 873 (1975), the Court held that: "Except at the border and its functional equivalents, officers on roving patrol may stop vehicles only if they are aware of specific articulable facts, together with rational inferences from those facts, that reasonably warrant suspicion that the vehicles contain aliens who may be illegally in the country."

2. *Fixed Checkpoints Inside the United States.* In *United States v. Martinez–Fuerte*, 428 U.S. 543 (1976), the Court upheld immigration road-blocks located within 100 miles of the United States border.

Problems

1. *More on Border Searches of Property.* Following the holding in *Flores–Montano*, what powers may customs officials exercise at international borders? Rip out the seats? Tear luggage apart? Strip searches? Body cavity searches?

2. *Roving Border Patrols.* In *United States v. Brignoni–Ponce*, 422 U.S. 873 (1975), the Court held that a roving patrol of law enforcement officers could stop motorists near an international border to briefly inquire about their residence status provided that the officers "reasonably suspect that vehicles contain aliens who are illegally in the country." But what constitutes "reasonable suspicion" that vehicles contain illegal aliens? Near the Mexican border, is there sufficient cause if an officer spots someone of Hispanic descent driving a vehicle? What more should be required?

9. Special Needs

In a number of recent cases, the Court has established and developed a "special needs" exception to the warrant requirement. This exception, which especially applies in safety and administrative cases, allows the government to search or seize without probable cause and sometimes even without reasonable suspicion.

Illustrative is the holding in *Skinner v. Railway Labor Executives' Association*, 489 U.S. 602 (1989). In that case, the Court upheld Federal Railroad Administration (FRA) regulations mandating blood and urine tests of railroad employees involved in "major" train accidents, and authorizing railroads to administer breath and urine tests to employees who violate certain safety rules. The regulations were designed to combat the problem of drug and controlled substance abuse by railroad employees. The Court upheld the regulations noting that the "governmental interest in ensuring the safety of the traveling public and of the employees themselves plainly justifies prohibiting covered employees from using alcohol or drugs on duty, or while subject to being called for duty." The Court emphasized that "[A]lcohol and other drugs are eliminated from the bloodstream at a constant rate, and blood and breath samples taken to measure whether these substances were in the bloodstream when a triggering event occurred must be obtained as soon as possible. [T]he delay necessary to procure a warrant nevertheless may result in the destruction of valuable evidence." As a result, the Court concluded that the "Government interest in testing without a showing of individualized suspicion is compelling." Finally, the Court held that covered employees had a diminished expectation of privacy due to the nature of their jobs, and that the "the privacy interests implicated by the search are minimal" because of the manner in which the tests were performed.

BOARD OF EDUCATION OF INDEPENDENT SCHOOL DISTRICT NO. 92 OF POTTA- WATOMIE COUNTY v. EARLS

536 U.S. 822 (2002).

JUSTICE THOMAS delivered the opinion of the Court.

[Tecumseh, Oklahoma,] is a rural community [about] 40 miles southeast of Oklahoma City. [In] 1998, the School District adopted the Student Activities Drug Testing Policy (Policy), which requires all middle and high school students to consent to drug testing in order to participate in any extracurricular activity. In practice, the Policy has been applied only to competitive extracurricular activities sanctioned by the Oklahoma Secondary Schools Activities Association, such as the Academic Team, Future Farmers of America, Future Homemakers of America, band, choir, pom pom, cheerleading, and athletics. Under the Policy, students are required to take a drug test before participating in an extracurricular activity, must submit to random drug testing while participating in that activity, and must agree to be tested at any time upon reasonable suspicion. The urinalysis tests are designed to detect only the use of illegal drugs, including amphetamines, marijuana, cocaine, opiates, and barbituates, not medical conditions or the presence of authorized prescription medications.

[Lindsay Earls] was a member of the show choir, the marching band, the Academic Team, and the National Honor Society.... Daniel James sought to participate in the Academic Team. [Both] brought [suit challenging] the Policy [on Fourth Amendment grounds. The district court rejected respondents' claim and the court of appeals reversed.] We granted certiorari....

II

[Searches] by public school officials, such as the collection of urine samples, implicate Fourth Amendment interests. *See Vernonia School Dist. 47J v. Acton,* 515 U. S. 646 (1995). We must therefore review the School District's Policy for "reasonableness," which is the touchstone of the constitutionality of a governmental search.

[R]easonableness usually requires a showing of probable cause. The probable-cause standard, however, "is peculiarly related to criminal investigations" and may be unsuited to determining the reasonableness of administrative searches where the "Government seeks to *prevent* the development of hazardous conditions." *Treasury Employees v. Von Raab,* 489 U. S. 656 (1989). [A] warrant and finding of probable cause are unnecessary in the public school context because such requirements " 'would unduly interfere with the maintenance of the swift and informal disciplinary procedures [that are] needed.' " *Vernonia, supra,* at 653.

Given that the School District's Policy is [not] related to the conduct of criminal investigations, respondents do not contend that the School District requires probable cause before testing students for drug use. Respondents instead argue that drug testing must be based at least on some level of individualized suspicion. [We] generally determine the reasonableness of a search by balancing the nature of the intrusion on the individual's privacy against the promotion of legitimate governmental interests. But we have long held that "the Fourth Amendment imposes no irreducible requirement of [individualized] suspicion." *United States v. Martinez–Fuerte,* 428 U. S. 543 (1976). "[I]n certain limited circumstances, the Government's need to discover such latent or hidden conditions, or to prevent their development, is sufficiently compelling to justify the intrusion on privacy entailed by conducting such searches without any measure of individualized suspicion." *Von Raab, supra,* at 668. [In] the context of safety and administrative regulations, a search unsupported by probable cause may be reasonable "when 'special needs, beyond the normal need for law enforcement, make the warrant and probable-cause requirement impracticable.' " *Griffin v. Wisconsin,* 483 U. S. 868 (1987) (quoting *T.L.O., supra,* at 351 (Blackmun, J., concurring)).

Significantly, this Court has previously held that "special needs" inhere in the public school context. While schoolchildren do not shed their constitutional rights when they enter the schoolhouse, "Fourth Amendment rights [are] different in public schools than elsewhere; the 'reasonableness' inquiry cannot disregard the schools' custodial and tutelary responsibility for children." In particular, a finding of individualized suspicion may not be necessary when a school conducts drug testing.

In *Vernonia,* this Court held that the suspicionless drug testing of athletes was constitutional. The Court, however, did not simply authorize all school drug testing, but rather conducted a fact-specific balancing of the intrusion on the children's Fourth Amendment rights against the promotion of legitimate governmental interests. [Applying] *Vernonia* to [the] facts of this case, we conclude that Tecumseh's Policy is also constitutional.

We first consider the nature of the privacy interest allegedly compromised by the drug testing. [A] student's privacy interest is limited in a public school environment where the State is responsible for maintaining discipline, health, and safety. Schoolchildren are routinely required to submit to physical examinations and vaccinations against disease. Securing order in the school environment sometimes requires that students be subjected to greater controls than those appropriate for adults.

Respondents argue that because children participating in nonathletic extracurricular activities are not subject to regular physicals and communal undress, they have a stronger expectation of privacy than the athletes tested in *Vernonia*. This distinction [was] not essential to our decision in *Vernonia*, which depended primarily upon the school's custodial responsibility and authority.... In any event, students who participate in competitive extracurricular activities voluntarily subject themselves to many of the same intrusions on their privacy as do athletes. Some of these clubs and activities require occasional off-campus travel and communal undress. All of them have their own rules and requirements for participating students that do not apply to the student body as a whole [and] a faculty sponsor monitors [students] for compliance [with these] rules.... This regulation of extracurricular activities further diminishes the expectation of privacy among schoolchildren. [We] conclude that the students affected by this Policy have a limited expectation of privacy.

Next, we consider the character of the intrusion imposed by the Policy. Urination is "an excretory function traditionally shielded by great privacy." But the "degree of intrusion" on one's privacy caused by collecting a urine sample "depends upon the manner in which production of the urine sample is monitored." Under the Policy, a faculty monitor waits outside the closed restroom stall for the student to produce a sample and must "listen for the normal sounds of urination in order to guard against tampered specimens and to insure an accurate chain of custody." The monitor then pours the sample into two bottles that are sealed and placed into a mailing pouch along with a consent form signed by the student. This procedure is virtually identical to that reviewed in *Vernonia*, except that it additionally protects privacy by allowing male students to produce their samples behind a closed stall. Given that we considered the method of collection in *Vernonia* a "negligible" intrusion, the method here is even less problematic.

In addition, the Policy clearly requires that the test results be kept in confidential files separate from a student's other educational records and released to school personnel only on a "need to know" basis. Respondents nonetheless contend that the intrusion on students' privacy is significant because the Policy fails to protect effectively against the disclosure of confidential information and, specifically, that the school "has been careless in protecting that information: for example, the Choir teacher looked at students' prescription drug lists and left them where other students could see them." But the choir teacher is someone with a "need to know," because during off-campus trips she needs to know what medications are taken by her students.... In any event, there is no allegation that any other student did see such information. This one example of alleged carelessness hardly increases the character of the intrusion.

Moreover, the test results are not turned over to any law enforcement authority. Nor do the test results here lead to the imposition of discipline or have any academic consequences. [T]he only consequence of a failed drug test is to limit the student's privilege of participating in extracurricular activities. Indeed, a student may test positive for drugs twice and still be allowed to participate in extracurricular activities. After the first positive test, the school contacts the student's parent or guardian for a meeting. The student may continue to participate in the activity if within five days of the meeting the student shows proof of receiving drug counseling and submits to a second drug test in two weeks. For the second positive test, the student is suspended from participation in all extracurricular activities for 14 days, must complete four hours of substance abuse counseling, and must submit to monthly drug tests. Only after a third positive test will the student be suspended from participating in any extracurricular activity for the remainder of the school year, or 88 school days, whichever is longer.

Given the minimally intrusive nature of the sample collection and the limited uses to which the test results are put, we conclude that the invasion of students' privacy is not significant.

Finally, this Court must consider the nature and immediacy of the government's concerns and the efficacy of the Policy in meeting them. This Court has already articulated [the] importance of the governmental concern in preventing drug use by schoolchildren. The drug abuse problem among our Nation's youth has hardly abated since *Vernonia* was decided in 1995. In fact, evidence suggests that it has only grown worse. As in *Vernonia*, "the necessity for the State to act is magnified by the fact that this evil is being visited not just upon individuals at large, but upon children for whom it has undertaken a special responsibility of care and direction." The health and safety risks identified in *Vernonia* apply with equal force to Tecumseh's children. Indeed, the nationwide drug epidemic makes the war against drugs a pressing concern in every school.

Additionally, the School District in this case has presented specific evidence of drug use at Tecumseh schools. Teachers testified that they had seen students who appeared to be under the influence of drugs and that they had heard students speaking openly about using drugs. A drug dog found marijuana cigarettes near the school parking lot. Police officers once found drugs or drug paraphernalia in a car driven by a Future Farmers of America member. And the school board president reported that people in the community were calling the board to discuss the "drug situation." We decline to second-guess the finding of the District Court that "[the School District] was faced with a 'drug problem' when it adopted the Policy."

Respondents consider the proffered evidence insufficient and argue that there is no "real and immediate interest" to justify a policy of drug testing nonathletes. We have recognized [that] "[a] demonstrated problem of drug abuse [is] not in all cases necessary to the validity of a testing regime," but that some showing does "shore up an assertion of special need for a suspicionless general search program." The School District has provided sufficient evidence to shore up the need for its drug testing program.

Furthermore, this Court has not required a particularized or pervasive drug problem before allowing the government to conduct suspicionless drug testing. [In] *Von Raab* the Court upheld the drug testing of customs officials on a purely preventive basis, without any documented history of drug use by such officials. In response to the lack of evidence relating to drug use, the Court noted [that] "drug abuse is one of the most serious problems confronting our society today," and that programs to prevent and detect drug use among customs officials could not be deemed unreasonable. Likewise, the need to prevent and deter the substantial harm of childhood drug use provides the necessary immediacy for a school testing policy. [It] would make little sense to require a school district to wait for a substantial portion of its students to begin using drugs before it was allowed to institute a drug testing program designed to deter drug use. . . . Given the nationwide epidemic of drug use, and the evidence of increased drug use in Tecumseh schools, it was entirely reasonable for the School District to enact this particular drug testing policy. . . .

Respondents also argue that the testing of nonathletes does not implicate any safety concerns, and that safety is a "crucial factor" in applying the special needs framework. They contend that there must be "surpassing safety interests," or "extraordinary safety and national security hazards," in order to override the usual protections of the Fourth Amendment. Respondents are correct that safety factors into the special needs analysis, but the safety interest furthered by drug testing is undoubtedly substantial for all children, athletes and nonathletes alike. We know all too well that drug use carries a variety of health risks for children, including death from overdose.

We also reject [the] argument that drug testing must presumptively be based upon an individualized reasonable suspicion of wrongdoing because such a testing regime would be less intrusive. In this context, the Fourth Amendment does not require a finding of individualized suspicion, and we decline to impose such a requirement on schools attempting to prevent and detect drug use by students. Moreover, we question whether testing based on individualized suspicion in fact would be less intrusive. Such a regime would place an additional burden on public school teachers who are already tasked with the difficult job of maintaining order and discipline [and] might unfairly target members of unpopular groups. The fear of lawsuits resulting from such targeted searches may chill enforcement of the program, rendering it ineffective in combating drug use. In any case, this Court has repeatedly stated that reasonableness under the Fourth Amendment does not require employing the least intrusive means, because "[t]he logic of such elaborate less-restrictive-alternative arguments could raise insuperable barriers to the exercise of virtually all search-and-seizure powers." *Martinez–Fuerte*, 428 U. S., at 556–557, n. 12.

Finally, we find that testing students who participate in extracurricular activities is a reasonably effective means of addressing the School District's legitimate concerns in preventing, deterring, and detecting drug use. While in *Vernonia* there might have been a closer fit between the testing of athletes and the trial court's finding that the drug problem was "fueled by the 'role model' effect of athletes' drug use," such a finding was not essential to the holding. [D]rug testing of Tecumseh students who participate in extracurricular activities effectively serves the School District's interest in protecting the safety and health of its students.

Within the limits of the Fourth Amendment, local school boards must assess the desirability of drug testing schoolchildren. In upholding the constitutionality of the Policy, we express no opinion as to its wisdom. [W]e hold only that Tecumseh's Policy is a reasonable means of furthering the School District's important interest in preventing and deterring drug use among its schoolchildren. [We] reverse the judgment of the Court of Appeals.

It is so ordered.

JUSTICE BREYER, concurring.

[T]he drug problem in our Nation's schools is serious in terms of size, the kinds of drugs being used, and the consequences of that use both for our children and the rest of us. [T]he program at issue here seeks to discourage demand for drugs by changing the school's environment in order to combat the single most important factor leading school children to take drugs, namely, peer pressure. It offers the adolescent a nonthreatening reason to decline his friend's drug-use invitations, namely, that he intends to play baseball, participate in debate, join the band, or engage in any one of half a dozen useful, interesting, and important activities.

[N]ot everyone would agree with this Court's characterization of the privacy-related significance of urine sampling as "negligible." [But the] testing program avoids subjecting the entire school to testing [and] it preserves an option for a conscientious objector. He can refuse testing while paying a price (nonparticipation) that is serious, but less severe than expulsion from the school. [R]equiring "individualized suspicion" in this public school context [could] well lead schools to push the boundaries of "individualized suspicion" to its outer limits, using subjective criteria that may "unfairly target members of unpopular groups," or leave those whose behavior is slightly abnormal stigmatized in the minds of others.... I cannot know whether the school's drug testing program will work. But [the] Constitution does not prohibit the effort....

JUSTICE GINSBURG, with whom JUSTICE STEVENS, JUSTICE O'CONNOR, and JUSTICE SOUTER join, dissenting.

[The] particular testing program upheld today is not reasonable. . . . Petitioners' policy targets for testing a student population least likely to be at risk from illicit drugs and their damaging effects. I therefore dissent. . . .

This case presents circumstances dispositively different from those of *Vernonia*. . . . Concern for student health and safety is basic to the school's caretaking, and it is undeniable that "drug use carries a variety of health risks for children, including death from overdose." [Those] risks, however, are present for *all* schoolchildren. *Vernonia* cannot be read to endorse invasive and suspicionless drug testing of all students upon any evidence of drug use, solely because drugs jeopardize the life and health of those who use them. Many children, like many adults, engage in dangerous activities on their own time; that the children are enrolled in school scarcely allows government to monitor all such activities. If a student has a reasonable subjective expectation of privacy in the personal items she brings to school, surely she has a similar expectation regarding the chemical composition of her urine. . . .

[While] extracurricular activities are "voluntary" in the sense that they are not required for graduation, [p]articipation in such activities is a key component of school life, essential in reality for students applying to college, and, for all participants, a significant contributor to the breadth and quality of the educational experience. . . .

Voluntary participation in athletics has a distinctly different dimension: Schools regulate student athletes discretely because competitive school sports by their nature require communal undress and, more important, expose students to physical risks that schools have a duty to mitigate. [S]chools cannot offer a program of competitive athletics without intimately affecting the privacy of students. . . . Interscholastic athletics [require] close safety and health regulation; a school's choir, band, and academic team do not.

[*Vernonia*] applied [the] principle that "the legality of a search of a student should depend simply on the reasonableness, *under all the circumstances*, of the search." Enrollment in a public school,and election to participate in school activities beyond the bare minimum that the curriculum requires, are indeed factors relevant to reasonableness, but they do not on their own justify intrusive, suspicionless searches. [S]tudent athletes' expectations of privacy are necessarily attenuated. . . . On "occasional out-of-town trips," students like Lindsay Earls "must sleep together in communal settings and use communal bathrooms." But those situations are hardly equivalent to the routine communal undress associated with athletics; the School District itself admits that when such trips occur, "public-like restroom facilities," which presumably include enclosed stalls, are ordinarily available for changing, and that "more modest students" find other ways to maintain their privacy.

[In] this case, [respondents] allege that the School District handled personal information collected under the policy carelessly, with little regard for its confidentiality. . . .

[The] "nature and immediacy of the governmental concern," faced by the Vernonia School District dwarfed that confronting Tecumseh administrators. Vernonia initiated its drug testing policy in response to "[a] large segment of the student body, particularly those involved in interscholastic athletics, [in] a state of rebellion...." Tecumseh, by contrast, repeatedly reported to the Federal Government [that drug use was not a major problem. [T]he *Vernonia* Court emphasized that "the particular drugs screened by [Vernonia's] Policy have been demonstrated to pose substantial physical risks to athletes." [Despite] nightmarish images [of] colliding tubas[,] the great majority of students the School District seeks to test [are] engaged in activities that are not safety sensitive to an unusual degree. There is a difference between imperfect tailoring and no tailoring....

Nationwide, students who participate in extracurricular activities are significantly less likely to develop substance abuse problems than are their less-involved peers.... Tecumseh's policy thus falls short doubly if deterrence is its aim: It invades the privacy of students who need deterrence least, and risks steering students at greatest risk for substance abuse away from extracurricular involvement that potentially may palliate drug problems.

[It] is a sad irony that the petitioning School District seeks to justify its edict here by trumpeting "the schools' custodial and tutelary responsibility for children." ... "That [schools] are educating the young for citizenship is reason for scrupulous protection of Constitutional freedoms of the individual, if we are not to strangle the free mind at its source and teach youth to discount important principles of our government as mere platitudes." *West Virginia Bd. of Ed. v. Barnette,* 319 U.S. 624, 637 (1943). [I] would affirm the judgment of the Tenth Circuit declaring the testing policy at issue unconstitutional.

Notes: Probationers and "Special Needs"

In *Griffin v. Wisconsin,* 483 U.S. 868 (1987), the Court upheld probationer searches conducted pursuant to a Wisconsin regulation permitting "any probation officer to search a probationer's home without a warrant as long as his supervisor approves and as long as there are 'reasonable grounds' to believe the presence of contraband." The Court held that a probation system presented a "special need" for the "exercise of supervision to assure that [probation] restrictions are in fact observed" and therefore the search was reasonable. Likewise, in *United States v. Knights,* 534 U.S. 112 (2001), when a judge imposed a similar restriction as a condition of probation, the Court upheld a search of the probationer's residence based on a reasonable suspicion that he was involved in criminal activity. The Court balanced the need for the search against the intrusion, and held that the search was justified. In assessing the intrusion, the Court held that probationers do not enjoy the same liberties as other citizens, "a court granting probation may impose reasonable conditions that deprive the offender of some freedoms enjoyed by law-abiding citizens," and that a probationer "is more likely than the ordinary citizen to violate the law." The Court held that the search could be justified based on a finding of reasonable suspicion that the probationer is involved in criminal activity.

Problems

1. *Extending Earls*. Following the favorable decision in this case, suppose that the Tecumseh school district decides to adopt a drug testing program applicable to all students, and not just those involved in extracurricular activities. Based on the evidence before the Court, would such a program be constitutional?

2. *Modifying Earls*. In the program referred to in the prior problem, would it matter whether the program involved only "random" drug testing (10 students were chosen per week based on their names' position in the alphabet), or whether it also involved an annual drug test of each student?

3. *Direct Observation*. In an effort to ensure the integrity of the program referred to in the *Pottawatomie* case, could a school require that all urine samples be collected under the direct observation of school employees (rather than in a closed stall)?

4. A public school district adopts a new drug interdiction policy. Under that policy, at the beginning of each school year, every student is issued a handbook which states that the district reserves the right to subject all secondary school students and their belongings to random suspicionless searches. Under the policy, students are directed to place their purses and backpacks on their desks and to leave the room while school officials conduct the search. Under existing precedent, can the searches be justified as a "special needs" search?

5. The City of Mesa, Arizona, wishes to adopt a random drug testing program for firefighters in an effort to deter drug and alcohol use. In order to adopt a valid program, what kind of findings must the City make in order to justify the program? How should the program be administered?

FERGUSON v. CITY OF CHARLESTON

532 U.S. 67 (2001).

Justice Stevens delivered the opinion of the Court.

[W]e must decide whether a state hospital's performance of a diagnostic test to obtain evidence of a patient's criminal conduct for law enforcement purposes is an unreasonable search if the patient has not consented to the procedure. More narrowly, the question is whether the interest in using the threat of criminal sanctions to deter pregnant women from using cocaine can justify a departure from the general rule that an official nonconsensual search is unconstitutional if not authorized by a valid warrant.

I

[In] 1988, staff members at the public hospital operated in the city of Charleston by the Medical University of South Carolina (MUSC) became concerned about [an] increase in the use of cocaine by patients who were receiving prenatal treatment. [MUSC] began to order drug screens [performed] on urine samples from maternity patients who were suspected of using cocaine. If a patient tested positive, she was [referred] to the county substance abuse commission for counseling and treatment. [T]he incidence of cocaine use among the patients at MUSC did not appear to change.

[F]our months later, Nurse Shirley Brown, [case] manager for the MUSC obstetrics department, heard [that] the [police] were arresting pregnant users of cocaine [for] child abuse.[6] Nurse Brown discussed the story with MUSC's general counsel [who] contacted Charleston['s] Solicitor [to] offer [cooperation] in prosecuting mothers whose children tested positive for drugs at birth.... Solicitor Condon [appointed a] task force [with] representatives of MUSC, the police, the County Substance Abuse Commission and the Department of Social Services. Their deliberations led to MUSC's adoption of a 12–page document entitled "POLICY M–7," dealing with the subject of "Management of Drug Abuse During Pregnancy.".

The first three pages of Policy M–7 set forth the procedure to be followed by the hospital staff to "identify/assist pregnant patients suspected of drug abuse." The first section[,] the "Identification of Drug Abusers," provided that a patient should be tested for cocaine through a urine drug screen if she met one or more of nine criteria.[4] It also stated that a chain of custody should be followed when obtaining and testing urine samples [to] make sure that the results could be used in subsequent criminal proceedings. The policy also provided for education and referral to a substance abuse clinic for patients who tested positive. [I]t added the threat of law enforcement intervention [which was regarded as] essential to the program's success in getting women into treatment and keeping them there.

The threat of law enforcement involvement was set forth in two protocols, the first dealing with the identification of drug use during pregnancy, and the second with identification of drug use after labor. Under the latter protocol, the police were to be notified without delay and the patient promptly arrested. Under the former, after the initial positive drug test, the police were to be notified (and the patient arrested) only if the patient tested positive for cocaine a second time or if she missed an appointment with a substance abuse counselor. In 1990, [the] policy was modified at the behest of the solicitor's office to give the patient who tested positive during labor, like the patient who tested

---

6. Under South Carolina law, a viable fetus [has] been regarded as a person [and] the ingestion of cocaine during the third trimester of pregnancy constitutes criminal child neglect.

4. Those criteria were as follows: 1. No prenatal care; 2. Late prenatal care after 24 weeks gestation; 3. Incomplete prenatal care; 4. Abruptio placentae; 5. Intrauterine fetal death; 6. Preterm labor 'of no obvious cause'; 7. IUGR [intrauterine growth retardation] 'of no obvious cause'; 8. Previously known drug or alcohol abuse; 9. Unexplained congenital anomalies.

positive during a prenatal care visit, an opportunity to avoid arrest by consenting to substance abuse treatment.

[The] policy contained forms for the patients to sign, as well as procedures for the police to follow when a patient was arrested. The policy [prescribed] in detail the precise offenses with which a woman could be charged.... If the pregnancy was 27 weeks or less, the patient was to be charged with simple possession. If it was 28 weeks or more, she was to be charged with possession and distribution to a person under the age of 18 [the fetus]. If she delivered "while testing positive for illegal drugs," she was also to be charged with unlawful neglect of a child. Under the policy, the police were instructed to interrogate the arrestee in order "to ascertain the identity of the subject who provided illegal drugs to the suspect." [T]he policy made no mention of any change in the prenatal care of such patients, nor did it prescribe any special treatment for the newborns.

Petitioners [are] women who received obstetrical care at MUSC and who were arrested after testing positive for cocaine.... Respondents include the city of Charleston, law enforcement officials[,] and representatives of MUSC.... Petitioners' [challenged] the validity of the policy under various theories, including the claim that warrantless and nonconsensual drug tests conducted for criminal investigatory purposes were unconstitutional searches. [Lower courts] found for respondents.... We granted certiorari....

III

[Because] the hospital seeks to justify its authority to conduct drug tests and to turn the results over to law enforcement agents without the knowledge or consent of the patients, this case differs from the four previous cases in which we have considered whether comparable drug tests "fit within the closely guarded category of constitutionally permissible suspicionless searches." In three of those cases, we sustained drug tests for railway employees involved in train accidents, *Skinner v. Railway Labor Executives' Assn.*, 489 U.S. 602 (1989), for United States Customs Service employees seeking promotion to certain sensitive positions, *Treasury Employees v. Von Raab*, 489 U.S. 656 (1989), and for high school students participating in interscholastic sports, *Vernonia School Dist. 47J v. Acton*, 515 U.S. 646 (1995). In the fourth case, we struck down such testing for candidates for designated state offices as unreasonable. *Chandler v. Miller*, 520 U.S. 305 (1997).

[Those] cases [balanced] the intrusion on the individual's interest in privacy against the "special needs" that supported the program. [T]he invasion of privacy in this case is far more substantial.... In the previous four cases, there was no misunderstanding about the purpose of the test or the potential use of the test results, and there were protections against the dissemination of the results to third parties. The use of an adverse test result to disqualify one from eligibility for a particular benefit, such as a promotion or an opportunity to participate in an extracurricular activity, involves a less serious intrusion on privacy than the unauthorized dissemination of such results to third parties. The reasonable expectation of privacy enjoyed by the typical patient undergoing diagnostic tests in a hospital is that the results of those tests will not be shared with nonmedical personnel without her consent. In none of our prior cases was there any intrusion upon that kind of expectation.

The critical difference between those four drug-testing cases and this one [lies] in the nature of the "special need" asserted as justification for the warrantless searches. In [the] earlier cases, the "special need" [advanced] as a justification for the absence of a warrant or individualized suspicion was one divorced from the State's general interest in law enforcement. [In] this case, [the] central and indispensable feature of the policy from its inception was the use of law enforcement to coerce the patients into substance abuse treatment. This fact distinguishes this case from circumstances in which physicians or psychologists, in the course of ordinary medical procedures aimed at helping the patient herself, come across information that under rules of law or ethics is subject to reporting requirements. . . .

Respondents argue [that] their ultimate purpose—[protecting] the health of both mother and child—is a beneficent one. In *Chandler*, [we] did not simply accept the State's invocation of a "special need." Instead, we carried out a "close review" of the scheme [before] concluding that the need [was] not "special," as that term has been defined . . . . In this case, a review of the M–7 policy [reveals] that the purpose [served] by the MUSC searches "[is] indistinguishable from the general interest in crime control."

In looking to the programmatic purpose, "[it] is clear [that] an initial and continuing focus of the policy was on the arrest and prosecution of drug-abusing mothers. . . ." [T]he document codifying the policy incorporates the police's operational guidelines. It devotes its attention to the chain of custody, the range of possible criminal charges, and the logistics of police notification and arrests. Nowhere [does] the document discuss [medical] treatment for either mother or infant, aside from treatment for the mother's addiction.

[T]hroughout the development and application of the policy, the Charleston prosecutors and police were extensively involved in the day-to-day administration of the policy. Police and prosecutors decided who would receive the reports of positive drug screens and what information would be included with those reports. Law enforcement officials [helped] determine the procedures to be followed when performing the screens. In the course of the policy's administration, they had access [to] medical files on the women who tested positive, routinely attended the substance abuse team's meetings, and regularly received copies of team documents discussing the women's progress. Police took pains to coordinate the timing and circumstances of the arrests with MUSC staff. . . .

While the ultimate goal of the program may well have been to get the women [into] substance abuse treatment and off of drugs, the immediate objective of the searches was to generate evidence for law enforcement purposes in order to reach that goal.[21] The threat of law enforcement may ultimately have been intended as a means to an end, but the direct and primary purpose of MUSC's policy was to ensure the use of those means. [T]his distinction is critical. Because law enforcement involvement always serves some broader social purpose or objective[,] virtually any nonconsensual suspicionless search could be immunized under the special needs doctrine by defining the search solely in terms of its ultimate, rather than immediate, purpose. Such an approach is inconsistent with the Fourth Amendment. Given the primary purpose of the Charleston program, which was to use the threat of arrest and prosecution in order to force women into treatment, and given the extensive involvement of law enforcement officials at every stage of the policy, this case simply does not fit within the closely guarded category of "special needs."[23]

The fact that positive test results were turned over to the police does not merely provide a basis for distinguishing our prior cases applying the "special needs" balancing approach to the determination of drug use. It also provides an affirmative reason for enforcing the strictures of the Fourth Amendment. While state hospital employees, like other citizens, may have a duty to provide the police with evidence of criminal conduct that they inadvertently acquire in the course of routine treatment, when they undertake to obtain such evidence from their patients *for the specific purpose of incriminating those patients,* they have a special obligation to make sure that the patients are fully informed about their constitutional rights, as standards of knowing waiver require.

[Respondents] motive was benign rather than punitive. Such a motive, however, cannot justify a departure from Fourth Amendment protections, given the pervasive involvement of law enforcement with the development and application of the MUSC policy. The stark and unique fact that characterizes this case is that Policy M–7 was designed to obtain evidence of criminal conduct by the tested patients that would be turned over to the police and that could be admissible in subsequent criminal prosecutions. [While] drug abuse [is] a serious problem, "the gravity of the threat alone cannot be dispositive of questions concerning what means law enforcement officers may employ to pursue a given purpose." The Fourth Amendment's general prohibition against nonconsensual, warrantless, and suspicionless searches necessarily applies to such a policy.

21. [T]his case differs from *New York v. Burger,* 482 U.S. 691 (1987), [because the] discovery of evidence of other violations would have [been] incidental to the purposes of the administrative search. [This policy] was specifically designed to gather evidence of violations of penal laws. This case also differs from [the roadblock] seizure cases [which did not involve] "intrusive search of the body or the home" [and distinguished] checkpoints from [cases] dealing with "special needs."

23. It is especially difficult to argue that the program here was designed simply to save lives. *Amici* claim a near consensus in the medical community that programs of the sort at issue, by discouraging women who use drugs from seeking prenatal care, harm, rather than advance, the cause of prenatal health.

[The] judgment of the Court of Appeals is reversed, and the case is remanded for further proceedings consistent with this opinion.

It is so ordered.

JUSTICE KENNEDY, concurring in the judgment.

[I]n almost every case the immediate purpose of a search policy will be to obtain evidence. [None] of our special needs precedents has sanctioned the routine inclusion of law enforcement, both in the design of the policy and in using arrests, either threatened or real, to implement the system designed for the special needs objectives. [The] traditional warrant and probable-cause requirements are waived [on] the explicit assumption that the evidence [is] not intended [for] law enforcement purposes. [T]he hospital acted [as] an institutional arm of law enforcement for purposes of the policy. [W]hile the policy may well have served legitimate needs unrelated to law enforcement, it had as well a penal character with a far greater connection to law enforcement than other searches sustained under our special needs rationale.

[We recognize] the legitimacy of the State's interest in fetal life and of the grave risk to the life and health of the fetus, and later the child, caused by cocaine ingestion. [South Carolina] can impose punishment upon an expectant mother who has so little regard for her own unborn that she risks [causing] lifelong damage and suffering. . . .

An essential, distinguishing feature of the special needs cases is that the person searched has consented, though the usual voluntariness analysis is altered because adverse consequences, (*e.g.,* dismissal from employment or disqualification from playing on a high school sports team), will follow from refusal. . . . The consent, and the circumstances in which it was given, bear upon the reasonableness of the whole special needs program . . . . .

JUSTICE SCALIA, with whom THE CHIEF JUSTICE and JUSTICE THOMAS join as to Part II, dissenting.

[The] hospital's reporting of positive drug-test results to police [is] obviously not a search. At most it may be a "derivative use of the product of a past unlawful search," [which] "work[s] no new Fourth Amendment wrong" and "presents a question, not of rights, but of remedies." There is only one act that could conceivably be regarded as a search of petitioners in the present case: the *taking* of the urine sample. . . . Some [may] argue [that] testing of the urine is prohibited by some generalized privacy [right]; but it is not [arguable] that the testing of urine that has been lawfully obtained is [a] search. . . .

[A] search which has been consented to is not unreasonable. There is no contention [that] the urine samples were extracted forcibly. The only conceivable bases for saying that they were obtained without consent are the contentions (1) that the consent was coerced by the patients' need for medical treatment, (2) that the consent was uninformed because the patients were not told that the tests would include testing for drugs, and (3) that the consent was uninformed because the patients were not told that the results of the tests would be provided to the police.... Abuse of trust is surely a sneaky and ungentlemanly thing.... That, however, is immaterial for Fourth Amendment purposes. [We] have *never* held—or even suggested—that material which a person voluntarily entrusts to someone else cannot be given by that person to the police, and used for whatever evidence it may contain. [P]laintiffs claim that they] were coerced to produce their urine samples by their necessitous circumstances, to-wit, their need for medical treatment of their pregnancy. If that was coercion, it was not coercion applied by the government. [I] think it clear [that] there is no basis for saying that obtaining of the urine sample was unconstitutional. The special-needs doctrine is [quite] irrelevant, since it operates [to] validate searches and seizures that are otherwise unlawful....

The [Court's conclusion] that the special-needs doctrine is inapplicable rests upon its contention that respondents "undert[ook] to obtain [drug] evidence from their patients" ... *"for the specific purpose of incriminating those patients."* [In] their origin—before the police were in any way involved—the tests had an immediate, not merely an "ultimate," purpose of improving maternal and infant health. [There is] no basis [to] "distinguis[h] this case from circumstances in which physicians or psychologists, in the course of ordinary medical procedures aimed at helping the patient herself, come across information that [is] subject to reporting requirements ..." [S]ince the special-needs doctrine was developed, and is ordinarily employed, precisely to enable searches *by law enforcement officials* who, of course, ordinarily have a law enforcement objective. [T]oday's judgment, authorizing the assessment of damages against the county solicitor and individual doctors and nurses who participated in the program, proves once again that no good deed goes unpunished. [I] respectfully dissent.

Problems

1. *Advising MUSC.* Suppose that you are the legal adviser to MUSC. Following the decision in this case, you are asked for advice about how to establish a constitutionally permissible program for expectant mothers. How would you advise MUSC to proceed?

2. *"Special Needs" and Future Crimes?* The Commonwealth of Kentucky declares a "special need" to protect its citizens from future crimes, and requires convicted felons to provide DNA samples for inclusion in a crime database. DNA samples are to be collected from all convicts regardless of whether there is probable cause or even a reasonable suspicion to believe that individual convicts continue to be involved in criminal activity. Is Kentucky's collection system constitutional? Should it matter that the samples are not being collected to solve existing or unsolved crimes, but future crimes? Does this fact separate the collection and make it "removed from the normal need for law enforcement?" Could Kentucky extend the DNA collection to all citizens, convicted or not? *See State v. Martinez*, 276 Kan. 527, 78 P.3d 769 (2003); *United States v. Kincade,* 345 F.3d 1095 (9th Cir.2003).

3. A city fire department adopts a program of random suspicionless drug testing in an effort to control drug and alcohol use among firemen. The Program requires testing of firefighters in four situations: (1) if the Department has reasonable suspicion to believe an individual firefighter has abused drugs or alcohol; (2) after a firefighter is involved in an accident on the job; (3) following a firefighter's return to duty or as a follow-up to "a determination that a covered member is in need of assistance"; and (4) "on an unannounced and random basis spread reasonably throughout the calendar year." Under the Program, a computer selects the firefighters to be tested. The Department notifies firefighters of their selection for random testing immediately before, during, or after work; the firefighters are to be tested within thirty minutes of their notification, with allowance for travel time to the laboratory for collection. Once at the laboratory, firefighters are permitted to use private bathroom stalls when providing urine samples, which are then inspected by a monitor for the proper color and temperature.

The laboratory tests the sample for the presence of marijuana, cocaine, opiates, amphetamines, and phencyclidine. The laboratory initially tests the specimens by using an immunoassay test that meets the requirements of the Food and Drug Administration for commercial distribution. The laboratory then confirms all positive test results using the gas chromatography/mass spectrometry technique and reports positive results to a Medical Review Officer (MRO), who has a "detailed knowledge of possible alternate medical explanations." The MRO reviews the results before giving the information to the Department's administrative official. Only confirmed tests are reported to the Department as positive for a specific drug. Before verifying a positive result, however, the MRO must contact the firefighter on a confidential basis.

The Department does not release information in a firefighter's drug testing record outside the Department without the firefighter's consent. A firefighter whose test reveals a blood alcohol concentration in excess of that allowed under the Program or who tests positive for any of several specified drugs is removed from all covered positions and is evaluated by a substance abuse professional. The Department may discipline or terminate the employment of a firefighter who tests positive a second time or who refuses to submit to a required test. According to section 8 of the Program, the primary purpose of the random testing component "is to deter prohibited alcohol and controlled substance use and to detect prohibited use for the purpose of removing identified users from the safety-sensitive work force." This purpose advances the City's goal of establishing "a work environment that is totally free of the harmful effects of drugs and the misuse of alcohol." Is the program constitutional?

4. In the prior problem, which of the following facts might be determinative regarding the constitutionality of the program:

A. The City asserts that it has a "special need" to test firefighters because they occupy safety-sensitive positions. The City alleges that random testing furthers this interest by deterring "prohibited alcohol and controlled substance use" and detecting "prohibited use for the purpose of removing identified users from the safety-sensitive work force." We agree that the City has an interest in deterring and detecting prohibited alcohol and drug use among the City's firefighters

B.   The fact that the record is devoid of any indication that the City has ever encountered any problem involving drug use by its firefighters. The record lacks not only evidence of even a single instance of drug use among the firefighters to be tested but also any evidence of accidents, fatalities, injuries, or property damage that can be attributed to drug or alcohol use by the City's firefighters.

C.   Can it be argued that it is reasonable to assume that anyone applying for a safety-sensitive position in a heavily regulated field of activity not to anticipate—and implicitly agree to—a probing inquiry into the applicant's capacity to perform job-related duties; the same would hold true for any employee who might be promoted, demoted, transferred, or become involved in a job-related accident.

10.   *Exigent Circumstances*

The police can also dispense with a warrant when they are faced with "exigent circumstances." For example, when a police officer on the street hears shots followed by cries for help from a nearby apartment, the officer can enter the apartment to render emergency help and assistance. *See McDonald v. United States*, 335 U.S. 451 (1948). Likewise, "a warrant is not required to break down a door to enter a burning home to rescue occupants or extinguish a fire, [or] to bring emergency aid to an injured person." *See Wayne v. United States*, 318 F.2d 205 (D.C.Cir.1963). Under what other circumstances may police search without a warrant? Consider the following cases.

BRIGHAM CITY v. STUART

___ U.S. ___, 126 S.Ct. 1943 (2006).

CHIEF JUSTICE ROBERTS delivered the opinion of the Court.

[This] case arises out of a melee that occurred in a Brigham City, Utah, home in the early morning hours of July 23, 2000. At about 3 a.m., four police officers responded to a call regarding a loud party at a residence. Upon arriving at the house, they heard shouting from inside, and proceeded down the driveway to investigate. There, they observed two juveniles drinking beer in the backyard. They entered the backyard, and saw-through a screen door and windows-an altercation taking place in the kitchen of the home. [F]our adults were attempting, with some difficulty, to restrain a juvenile. The juvenile eventually "broke free, swung a fist and struck one of the adults in the face." The officer [observed] the victim of the blow spitting blood into a nearby sink. The other adults continued to try to restrain the juvenile, pressing him up against a refrigerator with such force that the refrigerator began moving across the floor. At this point, an officer opened the screen door and announced the officers' presence. Amid the tumult, nobody noticed. The officer entered the kitchen and again cried out, and as the occupants slowly became aware that the police were on the scene, the altercation ceased.

The officers subsequently arrested respondents and charged them with contributing to the delinquency of a minor, disorderly conduct, and intoxication. In the trial court, respondents filed a motion to suppress all evidence obtained after the officers entered the home, arguing that the warrantless entry violated the Fourth Amendment. The court granted the motion, and the Utah Court of Appeals affirmed.... We granted certiorari in light of differences among state courts and the Courts of Appeals concerning the appropriate Fourth Amendment standard governing warrantless entry by law enforcement in an emergency situation.

It is a "basic principle of Fourth Amendment law that searches and seizures inside a home without a warrant are presumptively unreasonable." *Groh v. Ramirez,* 540 U.S. 551 (2004). Nevertheless, because the ultimate touchstone of the Fourth Amendment is "reasonableness," the warrant requirement is subject to certain exceptions. *Flippo v. West Virginia,* 528 U.S. 11 (1999) (per curiam). We have held, for example, that law enforcement officers may make a warrantless entry onto private property to fight a fire and investigate its cause, *Michigan v. Tyler,* 436 U.S. 499 (1978), to prevent the imminent destruction of evidence, *Ker v. California,* 374 U.S. 23 (1963), or to engage in "hot pursuit" of a fleeing suspect, *United States v. Santana,* 427 U.S. 38 (1976). "[W]arrants are generally required to search a person's home or his person unless 'the exigencies of the situation' make the needs of law enforcement so compelling that the warrantless search is objectively reasonable under the Fourth Amendment." *Mincey v. Arizona,* 437 U.S. 385 (1978).

One exigency obviating the requirement of a warrant is the need to assist persons who are seriously injured or threatened with such injury. "The need to protect or preserve life or avoid serious injury is justification for what would be otherwise illegal absent an exigency or emergency." *Id.,* at 392. Accordingly, law enforcement officers may enter a home without a warrant to render emergency assistance to an injured occupant or to protect an occupant from imminent injury. *Mincey, supra,* at 392.

Respondents [advance] two reasons why the officers' entry here was unreasonable. First, they argue that the officers were more interested in making arrests than quelling violence. They urge us to consider, in assessing the reasonableness of the entry, whether the officers were "indeed motivated primarily by a desire to save lives and property."

[Our] cases have repeatedly rejected this approach. An action is "reasonable" under the Fourth Amendment, regardless of the individual officer's state of mind, "as long as the circumstances, viewed *objectively*, justify [the] action." *Scott v. United States*, 436 U.S. 128 (1978) (emphasis added). The officer's subjective motivation is irrelevant. It therefore does not matter here-even if their subjective motives could be so neatly unraveled-whether the officers entered the kitchen to arrest respondents and gather evidence against them or to assist the injured and prevent further violence.

[We] have held in the context of programmatic searches conducted without individualized suspicion-such as checkpoints to combat drunk driving or drug trafficking-that "an inquiry into *programmatic* purpose" is sometimes appropriate. *Indianapolis v. Edmond*, 531 U.S. 32 (2000) (emphasis added). But this inquiry is directed at ensuring that the purpose behind the *program* is not "ultimately indistinguishable from the general interest in crime control." *Edmond*, 531 U.S., at 44. It has nothing to do with discerning what is in the mind of the individual officer conducting the search.

Respondents further contend that their conduct was not serious enough to justify the officers' intrusion into the home. They rely on *Welsh v. Wisconsin*, 466 U.S. 740 (1984), in which we held that "an important factor to be considered when determining whether any exigency exists is the gravity of the underlying offense for which the arrest is being made." * * * *Welsh* involved a warrantless entry by officers to arrest a suspect for driving while intoxicated. There, the "only potential emergency" confronting the officers was the need to preserve evidence (*i.e.,* the suspect's blood-alcohol level)-an exigency that we held insufficient under the circumstances to justify entry into the suspect's home. Here, the officers were confronted with *ongoing* violence occurring *within* the home. *Welsh* did not address such a situation.

We think the officers' entry here was plainly reasonable under the circumstances. The officers were responding, at 3 o'clock in the morning, to complaints about a loud party. As they approached the house, they could hear from within "an altercation occurring, some kind of a fight." "It was loud and it was tumultuous." The officers heard "thumping and crashing" and people yelling "stop, stop" and "get off me." "[It] was obvious [that] knocking on the front door" would have been futile. The noise seemed to be coming from the back of the house; after looking in the front window and seeing nothing, the officers proceeded around back to investigate further. They found two juveniles drinking beer in the backyard. From there, they could see that a fracas was taking place inside the kitchen. A juvenile, fists clenched, was being held back by several adults. As the officers watch, he breaks free and strikes one of the adults in the face, sending the adult to the sink spitting blood.

In these circumstances, the officers had an objectively reasonable basis for believing both that the injured adult might need help and that the violence in the kitchen was just beginning. Nothing in the Fourth

Amendment required them to wait until another blow rendered someone "unconscious" or "semi-conscious" or worse before entering. The role of a peace officer includes preventing violence and restoring order, not simply rendering first aid to casualties; an officer is not like a boxing (or hockey) referee, poised to stop a bout only if it becomes too one-sided.

The manner of the officers' entry was also reasonable. After witnessing the punch, one of the officers opened the screen door and "yelled in police." When nobody heard him, he stepped into the kitchen and announced himself again. Only then did the tumult subside. The officer's announcement of his presence was at least equivalent to a knock on the screen door. Indeed, it was probably the only option that had even a chance of rising above the din. Under these circumstances, there was no violation of the Fourth Amendment's knock-and-announce rule. Furthermore, once the announcement was made, the officers were free to enter; it would serve no purpose to require them to stand dumbly at the door awaiting a response while those within brawled on, oblivious to their presence.

Accordingly, we reverse the judgment of the Supreme Court of Utah, and remand the case for further proceedings not inconsistent with this opinion.

It is so ordered.

JUSTICE STEVENS, concurring.

The Utah Supreme Court [has] made clear that the Utah Constitution provides greater protection to the privacy of the home than does the Fourth Amendment.... "[A] policy of judicial restraint-one that allows other decisional bodies to have the last word in legal interpretation until it is truly necessary for this Court to intervene-enables this Court to make its most effective contribution to our federal system of government." *Michigan v. Long,* 463 U.S. 1032 (1983) (STEVENS, J., dissenting).... I remain persuaded that my vote to deny the State's petition for certiorari was correct.

Notes

1. *Hot Pursuit.* In *Warden v. Hayden,* 387 U.S. 294 (1967), following a hold-up, cab drivers followed the robber to a nearby house. The police arrived at the house minutes later, knocked, and announced their presence. The woman who answered the door did not object to allowing the police to search. In the ensuring search, the police found Hayden in an upstairs bedroom feigning sleep, a shotgun and a pistol in a flush tank in a bathroom (where water was heard to be running), a jacket and trousers (matching the description of those worn by the robber) in a washing machine in the basement, and ammunition under the mattress of Hayden's bed. The Court ultimately upheld the search on the theory that the police were in "hot pursuit" of the robber:

> "[T]he exigencies of the situation made [a warrantless entry and search] imperative." The police were informed that an armed robbery

had taken place, and that the suspect had entered [the house] less than five minutes before they reached it.... The Fourth Amendment does not require police officers to delay in the course of an investigation if to do so would gravely endanger their lives or the lives of others. Speed here was essential, and only a thorough search of the house for persons and weapons could have insured that Hayden was the only man present and that the police had control of all weapons which could be used against them or to effect an escape. [T]he seizures occurred prior to or immediately contemporaneous with Hayden's arrest, as part of an effort to find a suspected felon, armed, within the house into which he had run only minutes before the police arrived. The permissible scope of search must, therefore, at the least, be as broad as may reasonably be necessary to prevent the dangers that the suspect at large in the house may resist or escape. [The] officer who found the clothes in the washing machine [knew] that the robber was armed and he did not know that some weapons had been found at the time he opened the machine. In these circumstances the inference that he was in fact also looking for weapons is fully justified.

2. *More on Hot Pursuit.* In *United States v. Santana*, 427 U.S. 38 (1976), after an undercover drug buy, the police went to "Mom" Santana's home to arrest her (Santana provided drugs to the seller), and found her standing in the doorway with a brown paper bag in her hand. When the officers shouted "police," and displayed their identification, Santana retreated into her house. The officers followed through the open door and caught her in the vestibule. As she tried to pull away, the bag tilted and "two bundles of glazed paper packets with a white powder" fell to the floor. The Court upheld the entry into the house as a "hot pursuit": " '[H]ot pursuit' means some sort of a chase, but it need not be an extended hue and cry 'in and about [the] public streets.' The fact that the pursuit here ended almost as soon as it began did not render it any the less a 'hot pursuit' sufficient to justify the warrantless entry into Santana's house. Once Santana saw the police, there was likewise a realistic expectation that any delay would result in destruction of evidence. Once she had been arrested the search, incident to that arrest, which produced the drugs and money was clearly justified."

3. *Homicide Scenes.* In *Flippo v. West Virginia*, 528 U.S. 11 (1999), after Flippo's wife was found dead at a cabin in a state park, and Flippo was taken to a hospital (he claimed that he and his wife had been attacked), officers returned and searched the cabin where the two had been staying. In the cabin, they found photographs that were later used at Flippo's trial. The Court rejected the argument that the police had an automatic right to make a warrantless search of a "homicide crime scene."

4. *Political Assassination.* In *People v. Sirhan*, 7 Cal.3d 710, 102 Cal.Rptr. 385, 497 P.2d 1121 (Cal. 1972), after Senator Robert Kennedy was murdered, the police took Sirhan Sirhan into custody, and searched his home where they found several items that were ultimately used against him (*e.g.*, pages from his notebooks and an envelope). The government justified the search on the basis that "there was a pressing emergency to ascertain the existence of a possible conspiracy to assassinate presidential candidates or high government officials...." The court upheld the search: "[The] officers believed that there might be a conspiracy [to] assassinate political leaders in

this country. [T]hey believed that an emergency existed and that prompt action on their part was necessary. [Their] beliefs were entirely reasonable. The crime was one of enormous gravity. . . . The victim was a major presidential candidate, and a crime of violence had already been committed against him. . . . Although the officers did not have reasonable cause to believe that the house contained evidence of a conspiracy to assassinate prominent political leaders, [the] mere possibility that there might be such evidence in the house fully warranted the officers' actions. It is not difficult to envisage what would have been the effect on this nation if several more political assassinations had followed that of Senator Kennedy. Today when assassinations of persons of prominence have repeatedly been committed in this country, it is essential that law enforcement officers be allowed to take fast action in their endeavors to combat such crimes."

Problems

1. *The Dead Body.* Police receive a tip that there is "a dead body in apartment 618 of the Rhode Island Avenue Plaza." The police knock repeatedly and identify themselves as police officers. After ten minutes of knocking and identifying themselves, the police enter the apartment and find the body. Was it permissible for the police to enter without a warrant on the report of a "dead body?" How might the owner of the premises argue that the entry was improper? How might the state respond? Would it make a difference if the police had received a report of an "unconscious" rather than a "dead" body? *See Wayne v. United States*, 318 F.2d 205, 115 U.S.App.D.C. 234 (D.C.Cir.1963).

2. *The "Foaming" Driver.* The police find Dunavan in a disabled car foaming at the mouth and unable to talk. The police remove Dunavan, send him to the hospital, and search the automobile for identification. The search reveals a Social Security card, $961 in cash, a motel key, a car rental agreement and two locked briefcases. Fearing for Dunavan's safety, and hopeful that they can find medical information, the police enter Dunavan's motel room and find two small keys which fit the briefcases. After questioning a woman in an adjoining motel room, the officers learn that Dunavan is a diabetic and that he keeps insulin in one of the briefcases. Both briefcases are opened. The first is full of money, banded with Green Hills Branch Bank bands (that bank had been robbed earlier that day), marked with red dye and smelling of gas. Some of the money is "bait" money (identifiable) and the dye and gas result from a bank anti-robbery device. In the second brief case, the police find insulin and a syringe, along with a lot more money marked like the money in the first case. Based on the evidence found in the two briefcases, the police charge Dunavan with the bank robbery. Dunavan moves to suppress the evidence. Can the police justify the search under the "exigent circumstances" exception? How might Dunavan argue that the exception does not apply? *See United States v. Dunavan*, 485 F.2d 201 (6th Cir.1973).

3. *The Light in the Vacant House.* Police respond to a call indicating that the lights are on in a house which is believed to be vacant. The police enter the house, believing that a burglary might be in progress, in order to investigate. Inside, while conducting a protective sweep, the police discover

marijuana plants growing in the basement. Can the entry and the search be justified under the "exigent circumstances" exception? *See United States v. McClain*, 430 F.3d 299 (6th Cir.2005).

4. *Marijuana Smoke.* A police report indicates that the occupants of a hotel room are smoking marijuana. The officers go to the hall outside the room and detect a marijuana smell. Do exigent circumstances exist so that the police can enter the room without a warrant? If you answered "no," what additional facts are necessary to establish a sufficient exigency? *See Johnson v. United States*, 333 U.S. 10 (1948).

5. *The Screams.* Early afternoon, police officers hear screams emanating from a hotel. An officer goes inside, determines that the screams are coming from room #7, and knocks on that door. When a male voice inquires as to who is knocking, the officers answer "the police." After several repetitions of this interchange a woman opens the door. The woman and another woman, the lessee of the room, state that they do not know of any cause for the screams, and one woman states that she might have had a nightmare. The officers then hear the flushing of a toilet in the bathroom, and see defendant emerge from the bathroom in his undershorts. An officer immediately enters the bathroom, observes pieces of currency floating in the commode, and retrieves them. The officer then pulls the chain of the water closet and recovers additional pieces of currency which have floated to the surface. Defendant is charged with counterfeiting, and the police seek to admit the currency from the commode against him. Can the state justify the admission of this evidence? How might defendant respond to the state's justifications? *See United States v. Barone*, 330 F.2d 543 (2d Cir.1964).

MINNESOTA v. OLSON

495 U.S. 91 (1990).

JUSTICE WHITE delivered the opinion of the Court.

[Shortly] before 6 a.m. on Saturday, July 18, 1987, a lone gunman robbed an Amoco gasoline station in Minneapolis, Minnesota, and fatally shot the station manager. A police officer heard the police dispatcher report and suspected Joseph Ecker. The officer and his partner drove immediately to Ecker's home, arriving at about the same time that an Oldsmobile arrived. The driver of the Oldsmobile took evasive action, and the car spun out of control and came to a stop. Two men fled the car on foot. Ecker, who was later identified as the gunman, was captured shortly thereafter inside his home. The second man escaped.

Inside the abandoned Oldsmobile, police found a sack of money and the murder weapon. They also found a title certificate with the name Rob Olson crossed out as a secured party, a letter addressed to a Roger R. Olson of 3151 Johnson Street, and a videotape rental receipt made out to Rob Olson and dated two days earlier. The police verified that a Robert Olson lived at 3151 Johnson Street.

The next morning, [a] woman identifying herself as Dianna Murphy called the police and said that a man by the name of Rob drove the car in which the gas station killer left the scene and that Rob was planning to leave town by bus. About noon, the same woman called again, gave her address and phone number, and said that a man named Rob had told a Maria and two other women, Louanne and Julie, that he was the driver in the Amoco robbery. The caller stated that Louanne was Julie's mother and that the two women lived at 2406 Fillmore Northeast. The detective-in-charge who took the second phone call sent police officers to 2406 Fillmore to check out Louanne and Julie. When police arrived they determined that the dwelling was a duplex and that Louanne Bergstrom and her daughter Julie lived in the upper unit but were not home. Police spoke to Louanne's mother, Helen Niederhoffer, who lived in the lower unit. She confirmed that a Rob Olson had been staying upstairs but was not then in the unit. She promised to call the police when Olson returned. At 2 p.m., a pickup order, or "probable cause arrest bulletin," was issued for Olson's arrest. The police were instructed to stay away from the duplex.

At approximately 2:45 p.m., Niederhoffer called police and said Olson had returned. The detective-in-charge instructed police officers to go to the house and surround it. He then telephoned Julie from headquarters and told her Rob should come out of the house. The detective heard a male voice say, "tell them I left." Julie stated that Rob had left, whereupon at 3 p.m. the detective ordered the police to enter the house. Without seeking permission and with weapons drawn, the police entered the upper unit and found respondent hiding in a closet. Less than an hour after his arrest, respondent made an inculpatory statement at police headquarters.

[This] case requires us to determine whether the Minnesota Supreme Court was correct in holding that there were no exigent circumstances that justified the warrantless entry into the house to make the arrest.

The Minnesota Supreme Court applied essentially the correct standard in determining whether exigent circumstances existed. The court observed that "a warrantless intrusion may be justified by hot pursuit of a fleeing felon, or imminent destruction of evidence, or the need to prevent a suspect's escape, or the risk of danger to the police or to other persons inside or outside the dwelling." The court also apparently thought that in the absence of hot pursuit there must be at least probable cause to believe that one or more of the other factors justifying the entry were present and that in assessing the risk of danger, the gravity of the crime and likelihood that the suspect is armed should be considered. Applying this standard, the state court determined that exigent circumstances did not exist.

We are not inclined to disagree with this fact-specific application of the proper legal standard. [A]lthough a grave crime was involved, respondent "was known not to be the murderer but thought to be the driver of the getaway car," [and] the police had already recovered the murder weapon. "The police knew that Louanne and Julie were with the suspect in the upstairs duplex with no suggestion of danger to them.

Three or four Minneapolis police squads surrounded the house. The time was 3 p.m., Sunday.... It was evident the suspect was going nowhere. If he came out of the house he would have been promptly apprehended." We do not disturb the state court's judgment that these facts do not add up to exigent circumstances.

Notes: Exigent Circumstances Following Arrest

In *Vale v. Louisiana*, 399 U.S. 30 (1970), officers possessed a warrant for Vale's arrest and had information that he was residing at a specified address. After surveilling the house, the officers observed a car drive up and sound the horn. Vale, who was known to the officers, came out of the house and had a brief conversation with the driver. After looking up and down the street, he returned to the house and reappeared a few minutes later. He again cautiously looked up and down the street, went to the car, and leaned through the window. From this the officers were convinced a narcotics sale had taken place. They immediately drove toward Vale. As he saw them, he turned and walked quickly toward the house. The officers called for Vale to stop as he reached the front steps of the house. Once the officers subdued Vale, they told him that they were going to search the house. After entering, the officers made a cursory inspection to ascertain if anyone else was present. At that point, Mrs. Vale and James Vale, mother and brother of defendant, returned home carrying groceries and were informed of the arrest and impending search. The search of a rear bedroom revealed a quantity of narcotics. The Court held that the search could not be justified under the "exigent circumstances" exception: "[The] officers were not responding to an emergency. They were not in hot pursuit of a fleeing felon. The goods ultimately seized were not in the process of destruction. Nor were they about to be removed from the jurisdiction. The officers were able to procure two warrants for Vale's arrest. They also had information that he was residing at the address where they found him. There is thus no reason [to] suppose that it was impracticable for them to obtain a search warrant as well. We decline to hold that an arrest on the street can provide its own 'exigent circumstance' so as to justify a warrantless search of the arrestee's house." Mr. Justice Black dissented: "[Vale's] arrest took place near the house, and anyone observing from inside would surely have been alerted to destroy the stocks of contraband which the police believed Vale had left there. [T]he police were faced with the choice of risking the immediate destruction of evidence or entering the house and conducting a search. I cannot say that their decision to search was unreasonable."

Problems

1. *The Trap.* Aware (based on a tip) that Hendrix is selling drugs from his house, two officers stake out the house while another telephones the residence. The telephoning officer asks for "Hendrix," receives an affirmative response, and warns him that the police are on their way to the house with a search warrant. The lights in the house go off, and there is a great deal of activity within the house for three or four minutes, then the lights come back on. Hendrix exits the residence, jumps in his Lincoln Continental,

and drives away. An officer follows the Lincoln which travels a short distance and turns into a driveway on another street. Did the officer have adequate cause to stop Hendrix and search the vehicle? How would you argue the case for the State? How might Hendrix respond?

2. *More on the Trap.* In the prior problem, suppose that the officer did not stop the vehicle and search it, but rather simply followed it. They see Hendrix stop and hurriedly exit. The officer goes to the car, peers in, and sees a set of scales commonly used for weighing cocaine, a lock box, a large suitcase, and a bottle of Inositol powder (used to dilute cocaine). The officer then enters the car, opens the suitcase and finds weapons inside. When he removes the scales and lock box from the back seat he observes a plastic bag of cocaine. A search warrant is subsequently obtained to open the lock box which contains a larger quantity of cocaine in plastic bags. Assume that defendants file motions seeking to suppress the drugs and drug paraphernalia seized by the police at the time of their arrest. What arguments might defendants make that the search and seizure were illegal? How might the state respond to these arguments? How should the court rule? *See State v. Hendrix,* 782 S.W.2d 833 (Tenn.1989).

3. *The Deal.* In the prior problem, suppose that police do not call the house. Instead, they simply observe it. While they are watching, they see Bradshaw enter the house, remain a short time, enter his van and drive away. An officer stops him a short distance from the house. A vial of cocaine and a package of cigarette papers are observed lying on top of the engine box in the front of the van. Assume that Bradshaw moves to suppress the drugs and drug paraphernalia. What arguments might Bradshaw make in favor of suppression? How might the state respond to these arguments? How should the court rule? *See State v. Hendrix,* 782 S.W.2d 833 (Tenn.1989).

ROCHIN v. CALIFORNIA
342 U.S. 165 (1952).

MR. JUSTICE FRANKFURTER delivered the opinion of the Court.

Having "information that [petitioner] was selling narcotics," [deputy sheriffs] of the County of Los Angeles, [went to] the two-story dwelling house in which Rochin lived.... Finding the outside door open, they entered and then forced open the door to Rochin's room on the second floor. Inside they found petitioner sitting partly dressed on the side of the bed, upon which his wife was lying. On a "night stand" beside the bed the deputies spied two capsules. When asked "Whose stuff is this?" Rochin seized the capsules and put them in his mouth. A struggle ensued [during] which [the officers] attempted to extract the capsules. The force they applied proved unavailing against Rochin's resistance. He was handcuffed and taken to a hospital. At the direction of one of the officers a doctor forced an emetic solution through a tube into Rochin's stomach against his will. This "stomach pumping" produced vomiting. In the vomited matter were found two capsules which proved to contain morphine.

[Regard] for the requirements of the Due Process Clause "inescapably imposes upon this Court an exercise of judgment upon the whole course of the proceedings (resulting in a conviction) in order to ascertain whether they offend those canons of decency and fairness which express the notions of justice of English-speaking peoples even toward those charged with the most heinous offenses." These standards of justice are not authoritatively formulated anywhere as though they were specifics. Due process of law is a summarized constitutional guarantee of respect for those personal immunities which, as Mr. Justice Cardozo twice wrote for the Court, are "so rooted in the traditions and conscience of our people as to be ranked as fundamental", or are "implicit in the concept of ordered liberty". *Palko v. State of Connecticut*, 302 U.S. 319.

[The] vague contours of the Due Process Clause do not leave judges at large. We may not draw on our merely personal and private notions and disregard the limits that bind judges in their judicial function. Even though the concept of due process of law is not final and fixed, these limits are derived from considerations that are fused in the whole nature of or judicial process. *See* Cardozo, The Nature of the Judicial Process; The Growth of the Law; The Paradoxes of Legal Science. These are considerations deeply rooted in reason and in the compelling traditions of the legal profession. The Due Process Clause places upon this Court the duty of exercising a judgment, within the narrow confines of judicial power in reviewing State convictions, upon interests of society pushing in opposite directions.

Due process of law thus conceived is not to be derided as resort to a revival of "natural law." To believe that this judicial exercise of judgment could be avoided by freezing "due process of law" at some fixed stage of time or thought is to suggest that the most important aspect of constitutional adjudication is a function for inanimate machines and not for judges, for whom the independence safeguarded by Article III of the Constitution was designed and who are presumably guided by established standards of judicial behavior. * * *

Applying these general considerations to [the] present case, we are compelled to conclude that the proceedings by which this conviction was obtained do more than offend some fastidious squeamishness or private sentimentalism about combating crime too energetically. This is conduct that shocks the conscience. Illegally breaking into the privacy of the petitioner, the struggle to open his mouth and remove what was there, the forcible extraction of his stomach's contents—this course of proceeding by agents of government to obtain evidence is bound to offend even hardened sensibilities. They are methods too close to the rack and the screw to permit of constitutional differentiation.

[On] the facts of this case the conviction of the petitioner has been obtained by methods that offend the Due Process Clause. The judgment below must be reversed.

Reversed.

Mr. Justice Black, concurring.

[If] the Due Process Clause does vest this Court with such unlimited power to invalidate laws, I am still in doubt as to why we should consider only the notions of English-speaking peoples to determine what are immutable and fundamental principles of justice. [O]ne may well ask what avenues of investigation are open to discover "canons" of conduct so universally favored that this Court should write them into the Constitution? All we are told is that the discovery must be made by an "evaluation based on a disinterested inquiry pursued in the spirit of science, on a balanced order of facts." * * *

MR. JUSTICE DOUGLAS, concurring.

The evidence obtained from this accused's stomach would be admissible in the majority of states where the question has been raised. [Yet] the Court now says that the rule which the majority of the states have fashioned violates the "decencies of civilized conduct." To that I cannot agree. It is a rule formulated by responsible courts with judges as sensitive as we are to the proper standards for law administration. * * *

SCHMERBER v. CALIFORNIA

384 U.S. 757 (1966).

MR. JUSTICE BRENNAN delivered the opinion of the Court.

Petitioner was convicted in Los Angeles [of] the criminal offense of driving an automobile while under the influence of intoxicating liquor. He had been arrested at a hospital while receiving treatment for injuries suffered in an accident involving the automobile that he [had] been driving. At the direction of a police officer, a blood sample was then withdrawn from petitioner's body by a physician at the hospital. The chemical analysis of this sample revealed a percent by weight of alcohol in his blood at the time of the offense which indicated intoxication, and the report of this analysis was admitted in evidence at the trial. Petitioner objected to receipt of this evidence of the analysis on the ground that the blood had been withdrawn despite his refusal, on the advice of his counsel, to consent to the test. * * *

[The] overriding function of the Fourth Amendment is to protect personal privacy and dignity against unwarranted intrusion by the State. In *Wolf* we recognized "[t]he security of one's privacy against arbitrary intrusion by the police as being "at the core of the Fourth Amendment" and "basic to a free society." [C]ompulsory administration of a blood test [plainly] involves the broadly conceived reach of a search and seizure under the Fourth Amendment. [Such] testing procedures plainly constitute searches of "persons," and depend antecedently upon seizures of "persons," within the meaning of that Amendment.

Because we are dealing with intrusions into the human body rather than with state interferences with property relationships or private papers—"houses, papers, and effects"—we write on a clean slate. Limitations on the kinds of property which may be seized under warrant, as distinct from the procedures for search and the permissible scope of search, are not instructive in this context. We begin with the assumption that once the privilege against self-incrimination has been found not to bar compelled intrusions into the body for blood to be analyzed for alcohol contest, the Fourth Amendment's proper function is to constrain, not against all intrusions as such, but against intrusions which are not justified in the circumstances, or which are made in an improper manner. In other words, the questions we must decide in this case are whether the police were justified in requiring petitioner to submit to the blood test, and whether the means and procedures employed in taking his blood respected relevant Fourth Amendment standards of reasonableness.

In this case, as [is] often [true of] charges of driving under the influence of alcohol[,] these questions arise in the context of an arrest made by an officer without a warrant. Here, there was plainly probable cause [to] arrest petitioner and charge him with driving an automobile while under the influence of intoxicating liquor. The police officer who arrived at the scene shortly after the accident smelled liquor on petitioner's breath, and testified that petitioner's eyes were "bloodshot, watery, sort of a glassy appearance." The officer saw petitioner again at the hospital, within two hours of the accident. There he noticed similar symptoms of drunkenness. He thereupon informed petitioner "that he was under arrest and that he was entitled to the services of an attorney, and that he could remain silent, and that anything that he told me would be used against him in evidence."

While early cases suggest that there is an unrestricted "right on the part of the government always recognized under English and American law, to search the person of the accused when legally arrested, to discover and seize the fruits or evidences of crime," the mere fact of a lawful arrest does not end our inquiry. The suggestion of these cases [rests] on two factors—first, there may be more immediate danger of concealed weapons or of destruction of evidence under the direct control of the accused; second, once a search of the arrested person for weapons is permitted, it would be both impractical and unnecessary to enforcement of the Fourth Amendment's purpose to attempt to confine the search to those objects alone. Whatever the validity of these considerations in general, they have little applicability [to] searches involving intrusions beyond the body's surface. The interests in human dignity and privacy which the Fourth Amendment protects forbid any such intrusions on the mere chance that desired evidence might be obtained. In the absence of a clear indication [that] such evidence will be found, these fundamental human interests require law officers to suffer the risk that such evidence may disappear unless there is an immediate search.

Although the facts which established probable cause to arrest in this case also suggested the required relevance and likely success of a test of petitioner's blood for alcohol, the question remains whether the arresting officer was permitted to draw these inferences himself, or was required instead to procure a warrant before proceeding with the test. Search warrants are ordinarily required for searches of dwellings, and absent an emergency, no less could be required where intrusions into the human body are concerned. The requirement that a warrant be obtained is a requirement that inferences to support the search "be drawn by a neutral and detached magistrate instead of being judged by the officer engaged in the often competitive enterprise of ferreting out crime." *Johnson v. United States*, 333 U.S. 10. The importance of informed, detached and deliberate determinations of the issue whether or not to invade another's body in search of evidence of guilt is indisputable and great.

The officer in the present case [might] reasonably have believed that he was confronted with an emergency, in which the delay necessary to obtain a warrant, under the circumstances, threatened "the destruction of evidence," *Preston v. United States*, 376 U.S. 364. We are told that the percentage of alcohol in the blood begins to diminish shortly after drinking stops, as the body functions to eliminate it from the system. [I]n a case such as this, where time had to be taken to bring the accused to a hospital and to investigate the scene of the accident, there was no time to seek out a magistrate and secure a warrant. [We] conclude that the attempt to secure evidence of blood-alcohol content in this case was an appropriate incident to petitioner's arrest.

Similarly, we are satisfied that the test chosen to measure petitioner's blood-alcohol level was a reasonable one. Extraction of blood samples for testing is a highly effective means of determining the degree to which a person is under the influence of alcohol. Such tests are a commonplace in these days of periodic physical examination and experience with them teaches that the quantity of blood extracted is minimal, and that for most people the procedure involves virtually no risk, trauma, or pain. Petitioner is not one of the few who on grounds of fear, concern for health, or religious scruple might prefer some other means of testing, such as the "Breathalyzer" test petitioner refused. We need not decide whether such wishes would have to be respected.

Finally, [the] test was performed in a reasonable manner. Petitioner's blood was taken by a physician in a hospital environment according to accepted medical practices. We are thus not presented with the serious questions which would arise if a search involving use of a medical technique, even of the most rudimentary sort, were made by other than medical personnel or in other than a medical environment—for example, if it were administered by police in the privacy of the stationhouse. To tolerate searches under these conditions might be to invite an unjustified element of personal risk of infection and pain.

We thus conclude that [the] record shows no violation of petitioner's right under the Fourth and Fourteenth Amendments to be free of unreasonable searches and seizures. It bears repeating [that] we reach this judgment only on the facts of the present record. The integrity of an individual's person is a cherished value of our society. That we today told that the Constitution does not forbid the States minor intrusions into an individual's body under stringently limited conditions in no way indicates that it permits more substantial intrusions, or intrusions under other conditions.

Affirmed.

MR. JUSTICE DOUGLAS, dissenting.

[T]he Fifth Amendment marks "a zone of privacy" which the Government may not force a person to surrender. Likewise the Fourth Amendment recognizes that right when it guarantees the right of the people to be secure "in their persons." No clearer invasion of this right of privacy can be imagined than forcible bloodletting of the kind involved here.

Notes

1. *Fingernail Scrapings.* In *Cupp v. Murphy*, 412 U.S. 291 (1973), Murphy's wife died by strangulation at her home with abrasions and lacerations on her throat, but no indication of a break-in. When Murphy, who did not live with his wife, agreed to come to the police station for questioning, the police noticed a dark spot on his finger. Suspecting that the spot might be dried blood, and aware that strangulation often leaves evidence under the assailant's fingernails, the police requested permission to take a sample of the spot. When Murphy refused, and was seen trying to remove the blood, the police took the sample without a warrant. The samples were found to include fabric from the victim's nightgown as well as traces of her skin and blood. The Court upheld the search: "[Murphy] was motivate[d] to attempt to destroy what evidence he could without attracting further attention. [C]onsidering the existence of probable cause, the very limited intrusion undertaken incident to the station house detention, and the ready destructibility of the evidence, we cannot say that this search violated the Fourth and Fourteenth Amendments." Mr. Justice Marshall concurred: "If the Fourth Amendment permits a stop-and-frisk[,] it also [permits] fingernail scrapings in the circumstances of this case." Mr. Justice Douglas dissented in part: "[Scraping] a man's fingernails is an invasion of that privacy and it is tolerable, constitutionally speaking, only if there is a warrant for a search or seizure issued by a magistrate on a showing of 'probable cause' that the suspect had committed the crime. [Murphy] could have been detained while one was sought; and that detention would have preserved the perishable evidence the police sought."

2. *Seizure for Breathalyzer Test.* In *Welsh v. Wisconsin*, 466 U.S. 740 (1984), the police received reports indicating that Welsh had been driving under the influence. When Welsh's stepdaughter answered the door of his home, the police entered and proceeded upstairs to Welsh's bedroom where they found him lying naked in bed. The police arrested Welsh and took him to the police station where he refused to submit to a breathalyzer test. The Court concluded that the police acted improperly:

> [Before the] government may invade the sanctity of the home, the burden is on the government to demonstrate exigent circumstances that overcome the presumption of unreasonableness that attaches to all warrantless home entries. When the government's interest is only to

arrest for a minor offense, that presumption of unreasonableness is difficult to rebut, and the government usually should be allowed to make such arrests only with a warrant issued upon probable cause by a neutral and detached magistrate. [T]he claim of hot pursuit is unconvincing because there was no immediate or continuous pursuit of the petitioner from the scene of a crime. Moreover, because the petitioner had already arrived home, and had abandoned his car at the scene of the accident, there was little remaining threat to the public safety. [T]he only potential emergency claimed by the State was the need to ascertain the petitioner's blood-alcohol level. [The] similarity to other cases involving the imminent destruction of evidence is not sufficient. The State of Wisconsin has chosen to classify the first offense for driving while intoxicated as a noncriminal, civil forfeiture offense for which no imprisonment is possible. [Given] this expression of the State's interest, a warrantless home arrest cannot be upheld simply because evidence of the petitioner's blood-alcohol level might have dissipated while the police obtained a warrant. * * *

Justice White dissented: "A test under which the existence of exigent circumstances turns on the perceived gravity of the crime would significantly hamper law enforcement and burden courts with pointless litigation concerning the nature and gradation of various crimes.... Nevertheless, this Court has long recognized the compelling state interest in highway safety."

3. *Benzidine Test.* In *United States v. Smith*, 470 F.2d 377 (D.C.Cir. 1972), defendant was charged with assault with intent to commit rape against a six year-old girl who was raped and left bleeding. The police then asked defendant to undergo a benzidine test "to see if there was a show of blood". The mechanics of the test were outlined, and defendant was advised that if the test results were positive he would be charged with the offense; if negative, he would be released. Defendant replied that "he had no fear about the test because he knew it would be negative." The test was performed and there was a positive reaction. The court held that the test results had been properly admitted: "[The] search was reasonable since it was necessary to conduct the test as promptly as possible because of the ease with which the evidence could be destroyed by a thorough washing. The simplicity of the test makes it unnecessary to have it conducted by a physician. It is a chemical test not a medical test and was properly administered by a trained police technician."

Problems

1. *Surgical Bullet Removal.* During a robbery of a shop, the assailant was wounded and flees. Twenty minutes later, police find defendant eight blocks from the robbery scene suffering from a gunshot wound to the chest. He tells police that he was shot when a man tried to rob him. When defendant arrives at the emergency room, the victim of his robbery sees defendant, and exclaims "[t]hat's the man that shot me." The police decide that defendant's story of himself being a robbery victim is untrue. Since the bullet in defendant's stomach constitutes evidence, the state seeks an order forcing him to undergo surgery to remove the bullet (lodged under his left collarbone). Defendant objects to the procedure which would take 45 minutes

and involve a three to four percent chance of temporary nerve damage, a one percent chance of permanent nerve damage, and a one-tenth of one percent chance of death. The surgeon states that a general anesthetic would be desirable for medical reasons, and that the risks described above derive from the anesthetic. In light of *Rochin* and *Schmerber*, may a court order defendant to undergo the surgical procedure under a general anesthetic for removal of the bullet lodged in his chest? What arguments might you make on defendant's behalf? How might the state respond? *See Winston v. Lee*, 470 U.S. 753 (1985).

2.   *Searching the Pregnant Woman*. Defendant was arrested at home on a warrant charging her with selling cocaine. During the arrest, the officers see paraphernalia used in the heating and administering of heroin (*e.g.*, hypodermic needles, an eyedropper, water, copper wire, a "cooker" (a burned bottle cap with a wad of cotton) and white residue). Two policewomen take defendant (clad only in a nightgown and underpants) into the bathroom to search her, and tell her to strip, bend over, and spread her buttocks. It was difficult for defendant to bend over because she was seven months pregnant. The police women then looked into her privates and found nothing. Because of cramped quarters and poor lighting in the bathroom, the officers decided that defendant should be searched a second time at the station. The detectives had been told by a "reliable informer" that defendant was known to carry heroin in her vagina. At the station, defendant was again forced to disrobe and bend over (this time leaning on a chair), and a policewomen using rubber gloves spread her buttocks. A second policewoman, using a flashlight, found a plastic container protruding from defendant's vagina. The container was found to contain heroin. How might defendant argue that the strip search was invalid? How might the state respond to these arguments? How should the court rule? *See United States v. McCauley*, 385 F.Supp. 193 (E.D.Wis.1974).

Chapter 5

ENTRAPMENT

When government agents conduct investigations of criminal activity, they sometimes participate in criminal acts. This participation may be minimal, as where an undercover agent offers to buy drugs from a person who has been arrested for selling drugs in the past. Or, a "sting" operation may involve numerous contacts and extend over several years, and the "target" may be a person who has no criminal record. These law enforcement activities often may be used for prosecuting so-called victimless crimes, such as prostitution, or drug and weapons offenses. But agents also participate in crimes ranging from attempted homicide to money laundering, and including conspiracies of many kinds.

The Supreme Court has endorsed the entrapment defense for almost 70 years in all federal prosecutions, and state supreme courts have established their own versions of this defense. The Supreme Court became committed to a "subjective" test for entrapment in all federal cases in the 1930s. This test requires the defendant to produce some evidence of government "inducement," and imposes the burden of persuasion for negating this defense on the prosecutor, who must prove that the defendant had the "predisposition" to commit the crime beyond a reasonable doubt. While the federal constitution is not the source of the criminal law defense of entrapment, the Court's entrapment opinions do reflect policy concerns that are frequently found in other Due Process fields in criminal procedure. The Court also has recognized that outrageous government conduct in an entrapment scenario might be held to violate Due Process, and some lower courts have recognized the validity of particular Due Process claims despite the Supreme Court's failure to establish standards in this area. Therefore, defendants may seek to avoid conviction by presenting both an entrapment defense and a Due Process claim at trial.

A. THE ENTRAPMENT DEFENSE

1. *The Early Foundations*

SHERMAN v. UNITED STATES

356 U.S. 369 (1958).

MR. CHIEF JUSTICE WARREN delivered the opinion of the [Court].

In late August 1951, Kalchinian, a government informer, first met petitioner at a doctor's office where apparently both were being treated to be cured of narcotics addiction. Several accidental meetings followed, either at the doctor's office or at the pharmacy where both filled their prescriptions from the doctor. From mere greetings, conversation progressed to a discussion of mutual experiences and problems, including their attempts to overcome addiction to narcotics. Finally Kalchinian asked petitioner if he knew of a good source of narcotics. He asked petitioner to supply him with a source because he was not responding to treatment. From the first, petitioner tried to avoid the issue. Not until after a number of repetitions of the request, predicated on Kalchinian's presumed suffering, did petitioner finally acquiesce. Several times thereafter he obtained a quantity of narcotics which he shared with Kalchinian. Each time petitioner told Kalchinian that the total cost of narcotics he obtained was twenty-five dollars and that Kalchinian owed him fifteen dollars. The informer thus bore the cost of his share of the narcotics plus the taxi and other expenses necessary to obtain the drug. After several such sales Kalchinian informed agents of the Bureau of Narcotics that he had another seller for them. On three occasions during November 1951 Government agents observed petitioner give narcotics to Kalchinian in return for money supplied by the Government.

At the trial the factual issue was whether the informer had convinced an otherwise unwilling person to commit a criminal act or whether petitioner was already predisposed to commit the act and exhibited only the natural hesitancy of one acquainted with the narcotics trade. The issue of entrapment went to the jury, and a conviction resulted. Petitioner was sentenced to imprisonment for ten years. The Court of Appeals for the Second Circuit affirmed.

In *Sorrells v. United States*, 287 U.S. 435 [1932], this Court firmly recognized the defense of entrapment in the federal courts. The intervening years have in no way detracted from the principles underlying that decision. The function of law enforcement is the prevention of crime and the apprehension of criminals. Manifestly, that function does not include the manufacturing of crime. Criminal activity is such that stealth and strategy are necessary weapons in the arsenal of the police officer. However, "A different question is presented when the criminal design originates with the officials of the government, and they implant in the mind of an innocent person the disposition to commit the alleged offense and induce its commission in order that they may prosecute." The stealth and strategy become as objectionable police methods as the coerced confession and the unlawful search. Congress could not have intended that its statutes were to be enforced by tempting innocent persons into violations.

However, the fact that government agents "merely afford opportunities or facilities for the commission of the offense does not" constitute entrapment. Entrapment occurs only when the criminal conduct was "the product of the creative activity" of law enforcement officials. To determine whether entrapment has been established, a line must be drawn between the trap for the unwary innocent and the trap for the unwary criminal. The principles by which the courts are to make this determination were outlined in *Sorrells*. On the one hand, at trial the accused may examine the conduct of the government agent; and on the other hand, the accused will be subjected to an "appropriate and searching inquiry into his own conduct and predisposition" as bearing on his claim of innocence.

We conclude from the evidence that entrapment was established as a matter of law. In so holding, we are not choosing between conflicting witnesses, nor judging credibility. Aside from recalling Kalchinian, who was the Government's witness, the defense called no witnesses. We reach our conclusion from the undisputed testimony of the prosecution's witnesses.

It is patently clear that petitioner was induced by Kalchinian. The informer himself testified that, believing petitioner to be undergoing a cure for narcotics addiction, he nonetheless sought to persuade petitioner to obtain for him a source of narcotics. In Kalchinian's own words we are told of the accidental, yet recurring, meetings, the ensuing conversations concerning mutual experiences in regard to narcotics addiction, and then of Kalchinian's resort to sympathy. One request was not enough, for Kalchinian tells us that additional ones were necessary to overcome, first, petitioner's refusal, then his evasiveness, and then his hesitancy in order to achieve capitulation. Kalchinian not only procured a source of narcotics but apparently also induced petitioner to return to the habit. Finally, assured of a catch, Kalchinian informed the authorities so that they could close the net. The Government cannot disown Kalchinian and insist it is not responsible for his actions. Although he was not being paid, Kalchinian was an active government informer who had but recently been the instigator of at least two other prosecutions. Undoubtedly the impetus for such achievements was the fact that in 1951 Kalchinian was himself under criminal charges for illegally selling narcotics and had not yet been sentenced. It makes no difference that the sales for which petitioner was convicted occurred after a series of sales. They were not independent acts subsequent to the inducement but part of a course of conduct which was the product of the inducement. In his testimony the federal agent in charge of the case admitted that he never bothered to question Kalchinian about the way he had made contact with petitioner. The Government cannot make such use of an informer and then claim disassociation through ignorance.

The Government sought to overcome the defense of entrapment by claiming that petitioner evinced a "ready complaisance" to accede to Kalchinian's request. Aside from a record of past convictions, [the] Government's case is unsupported. There is no evidence that petitioner himself was in the trade. When his apartment was searched after arrest, no narcotics were found. There is no significant evidence that petitioner even made a profit on any sale to Kalchinian. The Government's characterization of petitioner's hesitancy to Kalchinian's request as the natural wariness of the criminal cannot fill the evidentiary void.

The Government's additional evidence in the second trial to show that petitioner was ready and willing to sell narcotics should the opportunity present itself was petitioner's record of two past narcotics convictions. In 1942 petitioner was convicted of illegally selling narcotics; in 1946 he was convicted of illegally possessing them. However, a nine-year-old sales conviction and a five-year-old possession conviction are insufficient to prove petitioner had a readiness to sell narcotics at the time Kalchinian approached him, particularly when we must assume from the record he was trying to overcome the narcotics habit at the time.

The case at bar illustrates an evil which the defense of entrapment is designed to overcome. The government informer entices someone attempting to avoid narcotics not only into carrying out an illegal sale but also into returning to the habit of use. Selecting the proper time, the informer then tells the government agent. The set-up is accepted by the agent without even a question as to the manner in which the informer encountered the seller. Thus the Government plays on the weaknesses of an innocent party and beguiles him into committing crimes which he otherwise would not have attempted. Law enforcement does not require methods such as this.

Mr. Justice Frankfurter, whom Mr. Justice Douglas, Mr. Justice Harlan, and Mr. Justice Brennan join, concurring in the result.

[Today's] opinion [fails] to give the doctrine of entrapment the solid foundation that the decisions of the lower courts and criticism of learned writers have clearly shown is [needed]. It is surely sheer fiction to suggest that a conviction cannot be had when a defendant has been entrapped by government officers or informers because "Congress could not have intended that its statutes were to be enforced by tempting innocent persons into violations." In these cases raising claims of entrapment, the only legislative intention that can with any show of reason be extracted from the statute is the intention to make criminal precisely the conduct in which the defendant has engaged. * * *

The courts refuse to convict an entrapped defendant, not because his conduct falls outside the proscription of the statute, but because, even if his guilt be admitted, the methods employed on behalf of the Government to bring about conviction cannot be countenanced. As Mr. Justice Holmes said in *Olmstead v. United States*, 277 U.S. 438, 470 (dissenting), in another connection, "[F]or my part I think it a less evil that some criminals should escape than that the government should play an ignoble part." Insofar as they are used as instrumentalities in the administration of criminal justice, the federal courts have an obligation to set their face against enforcement of the law by lawless means or means that violate rationally vindicated standards of justice, and to refuse to sustain such methods by effectuating them. They do this in the exercise of a recognized jurisdiction to formulate and apply "proper standards for the enforcement of the federal criminal law in the federal courts," an obligation that goes beyond the conviction of the particular defendant before the court. Public confidence in the fair and honorable administration of justice, upon which ultimately depends the rule of law, is the transcending value at stake.

[The] crucial question, not easy of answer, to which the court must direct itself is whether the police conduct revealed in the particular case falls below standards, to which common feelings respond, for the proper use of governmental power. For answer it is wholly irrelevant to ask if the "intention" to commit the crime originated with the defendant or government officers, or if the criminal conduct was the product of "the creative activity" of law enforcement officials. Yet in the present case the Court repeats and purports to apply these unrevealing tests. Of course in every case of this kind the intention that the particular crime be committed originates with the police, and without their inducement the crime would not have occurred. But it is perfectly clear [that,] where the police in effect simply furnished the opportunity for the commission of the crime, that this is not enough to enable the defendant to escape conviction.

The intention referred to, therefore, must be a general intention or predisposition to commit, whenever the opportunity should arise, crimes of the kind solicited, and in proof of such a predisposition evidence has often been admitted to show the defendant's reputation, criminal activities, and prior disposition. The danger of prejudice in such a situation, particularly if the issue of entrapment must be submitted to the jury and disposed of by a general verdict of guilty or innocent, is evident. The defendant must either forego the claim of entrapment or run the substantial risk that, in spite of instructions, the jury will allow a criminal record or bad reputation to weigh in its determination of guilt of the specific offense of which he stands charged. Furthermore, a test that looks to the character and predisposition of the defendant rather than the conduct of the police loses sight of the underlying reason for the defense of entrapment. No matter what the defendant's past record and present inclinations to criminality, or the depths to which he has sunk in the estimation of society, certain police conduct to ensnare him into further crime is not to be tolerated by an advanced society. And in the present case it is clear that the Court in fact reverses the conviction because of the conduct of the informer Kalchinian, and not because the Government has failed to draw a convincing picture of petitioner's past criminal conduct. Permissible police activity does not vary according to the particular defendant concerned; surely if two suspects have been solicited at the same time in the same manner, one should not go to jail simply because he has been convicted before and is said to have a criminal disposition. No more does it vary according to the suspicions, reasonable or unreasonable, of the police concerning the defendant's activities. Appeals to sympathy, friendship, the possibility of exorbitant gain, and so forth, can no more be tolerated when directed against a past offender than against an ordinary law-abiding citizen. A contrary view runs afoul of fundamental principles of equality under law, and would espouse the notion that when dealing with the criminal classes anything goes. The possibility that no matter what his past crimes and general disposition the defendant might not have committed the particular crime unless confronted with inordinate inducements, must not be ignored. Past crimes do not forever outlaw the criminal and open him to police practices, aimed at securing his repeated conviction, from which the ordinary citizen is protected. The whole ameliorative hopes of modern penology and prison administration strongly counsel against such a view.

This does not mean that the police may not act so as to detect those engaged in criminal conduct and ready and willing to commit further crimes should the occasion arise. Such indeed is their obligation. It does mean that in holding out inducements they should act in such a manner as is likely to induce to the commission of crime only these persons and not others who would normally avoid crime and through self-struggle resist ordinary temptations. This test shifts attention from the record and predisposition of the particular defendant to the conduct of the police and the likelihood, objectively considered, that it would entrap only those ready and willing to commit crime. It is as objective a test as the subject matter permits, and will give guidance in regulating police conduct that is lacking when the reasonableness of police suspicions must be judged or the criminal disposition of the defendant retrospectively appraised. It draws directly on the fundamental intuition that led in the first instance to the outlawing of "entrapment" as a prosecutorial instrument. The power of government is abused and directed to an end for which it was not constituted when employed to promote rather than detect crime and to bring about the downfall of those who, left to themselves, might well have obeyed the law. Human nature is weak enough and sufficiently beset by temptations without government adding to them and generating crime.

What police conduct is to be condemned, because likely to induce those not otherwise ready and willing to commit crime, must be picked out from case to case as new situations arise involving different crimes and new methods of detection. The *Sorrells* case involved persistent solicitation in the face of obvious reluctance, and appeals to sentiments aroused by reminiscences of experiences as companions in arms in the World War. Particularly reprehensible in the present case was the use of repeated requests to overcome petitioner's hesitancy, coupled with appeals to sympathy based on mutual experiences with narcotics addiction. Evidence of the setting in which the inducement took place is of course highly relevant in judging its likely effect, and the court should also consider the nature of the crime involved, its secrecy and difficulty of detection, and the manner in which the particular criminal business is usually carried on. * * *

Notes

1. *The Evolution of the "Objective" Test.* Soon after *Sherman* was decided, the drafters of the Model Penal Code endorsed an objective test for entrapment, rejecting the Supreme Court's subjective test and turning instead to the approach used by the concurring justices in *Sherman*. The objective test does not focus on predisposition, but instead addresses the question whether the government conduct is likely to cause an ordinary person to commit a crime. The MPC defines entrapment as occurring when "a public law enforcement official or person acting in cooperation with such an official [for] the purpose of obtaining evidence of the commission of an offense [induces] or encourages another person to engage in [criminal conduct by] employing methods of persuasion or inducement which create a substantial risk that such an offense will be committed by persons other than those who are ready to commit it."

About one third of the state courts now use some version of the objective test. Yet for more than three decades after *Sherman*, the Supreme Court has remained committed to the subjective test for all federal prosecutions, seemingly ignoring the criticisms of commentators and state judges who supported the objective test. After *Sherman* most federal courts found it relatively easy to accept government claims of predisposition on the part of defendants who participated willingly in criminal activities, and this made the entrapment defense difficult to win. Not until 1992 did the Court signal its willingness to scrutinize predisposition evidence more closely in the *Jacobson* case.

2. *What Is an Inducement?* Both the subjective and objective tests require some definition of an "inducement" in the sense of a threshold event that triggers an entrapment claim. (Once that threshold is crossed, Justice Frankfurter's concurrence provides some factors for identifying the kinds of inducements that violate the objective test standard.) All the judges in *Sherman* agreed that providing "mere opportunity" for crime does not create the threshold inducement that allows a defendant to raise the entrapment defense. One federal court has explained the meaning of the inducement concept in *United States v. Gendron*, 18 F.3d 955 (1st Cir. 1994):

An "inducement" consists of an "opportunity" *plus* something else— typically, excessive pressure by the government upon the defendant or the government's taking advantage of an alternative, non-criminal type of motive. * * *

Some of examples of improper "inducement" may help. Courts have found a basis for sending the entrapment issue to the jury (or finding entrapment established as a matter of law) where government officials: (1) used "intimidation" and "threats" against a defendant's family; (2) called every day, "began threatening" the defendant, and were belligerent; (3) engaged in "forceful" solicitation and "dogged insistence until [defendant] capitulated"; (4) played upon defendant's sympathy for informant's common narcotics experience and withdrawal symptoms; (5)

played upon sentiment of "one former war buddy ... for another" to get liquor (during prohibition); (6) used "repeated suggestions" which succeeded only when defendant had lost his job and needed money for his family's food and rent; (7) told defendant that she (the agent) was suicidal and in desperate need of money.

3. *Factors that Bear on Predisposition for the "Subjective" Test.* One federal court summarized the post-*Sherman* law as follows in *United States v. Dion*, 762 F.2d 674 (8th Cir.1985), *rev'd on other grounds*, 476 U.S. 734 (1986):

> The lower courts have looked to a variety of factors in determining predisposition, including: (1) whether the defendant readily responded to the inducement offered; (2) the circumstances surrounding the illegal conduct; (3) the state of mind of a defendant before government agents make any suggestion that he shall commit a crime; (4) whether the defendant was engaged in an existing course of conduct similar to the crime for which he is charged; (5) whether the defendant had already formed the "design" to commit the crime for which he is charged; (6) the defendant's reputation; (7) the conduct of the defendant during the negotiations with the undercover agent; (8) whether the defendant has refused to commit similar acts on other occasions; (9) the nature of the crime charged; and (10) "[t]he degree of coercion present in the instigation law officers have contributed to the transaction" relative to the "defendant's criminal background."

Problems

1. *The Policy Objectives Animating Each Test.* Suppose, for example, that a drug dealer desperately needs a drug courier. Unable to find one, the dealer offers someone $10 million to make a single trip to another city to pick-up and transport a large quantity of drugs. Suppose that the likelihood of getting caught is very low. Would the average person accept? Of course, some people will never commit a crime no matter what the inducement. But these people do not need the entrapment defense since they never engage in criminal activity. If the entrapment defense is to have meaning, it must apply to those who actually commit crimes they would not otherwise have committed absent the governmental inducement. What policy concerns help to explain the widespread support for the "subjective" test, and what concerns motivate the critics of that test who prefer the "objective" test? How are the tests similar and how are they different? In what way does each test reflect different ideals of Due Process expressed through non-constitutional doctrine? *See generally* Seidman, *The Supreme Court, Entrapment, and the Criminal Justice Dilemma*, 1981 SUP.CT.REV. 111; P. Marcus, THE ENTRAPMENT DEFENSE (1989).

2. *Contrasting the Tests.* Suppose that a police officer, Jill, learns from an informant that Bob has purchased drugs from the informant every week during the past two months. Jill pretends to be the informant's agent when she calls on Bob and asks whether he would like to make his usual purchase. Bob says "yes." Jill comes by later with the drugs and, when Bob buys them, she arrests him. In a jurisdiction that uses the "subjective" test for entrap-

ment, would Bob have much chance of proving entrapment? What his chances be any better in a jurisdiction that uses the "objective" test?

3. *The High Value Temptation.* Suppose that Anne regularly sells heroin, crack and marijuana, but only to close friends. She refuses to sell to others for fear that she will get caught. A government agent, Nick, tries to befriend Anne in order to purchase narcotics. Anne rebuffs the advance. Nick then tells Anne that he is "desperate" to get drugs and is willing to pay twice the normal price. Anne again refuses to help him. Only when the agent offers Anne four times the normal price does she agree to sell. Would Anne argue the case differently in a "subjective" jurisdiction than in an "objective" jurisdiction? If Anne is prosecuted for the sale and pleads an entrapment defense that is rejected at trial, would she have a better chance of success with the defense on appeal in a "subjective" jurisdiction or an "objective" jurisdiction?

2. *Modern Developments*

JACOBSON v. UNITED STATES

503 U.S. 540 (1992).

WHITE, J., delivered the opinion of the Court, in which BLACKMUN, STEVENS, SOUTER and THOMAS, JJ., joined.

[In] February 1984, petitioner, a 56–year-old veteran-turned-farmer who supported his elderly father in Nebraska, ordered two magazines and a brochure from a California adult bookstore. The magazines, entitled Bare Boys I and Bare Boys II, contained photographs of nude preteen and teenage boys. The contents of the magazines startled petitioner, who testified that he had expected to receive photographs of "young men 18 years or older."

[The] young men depicted in the magazines were not engaged in sexual activity, and petitioner's receipt of the magazines was legal under both federal and Nebraska law. Within three months, the law with respect to child pornography changed; Congress passed the Act illegalizing the receipt through the mails of sexually explicit depictions of children. In the very month that the new provision became law, postal inspectors found petitioner's name on the mailing list of the California bookstore that had mailed him Bare Boys I and II. There followed over the next 2 1/2 years repeated efforts by two Government agencies, through five fictitious organizations and a bogus pen pal, to explore petitioner's willingness to break the new law by ordering sexually explicit photographs of children through the mail.

The Government began its efforts in January 1985 when a postal inspector sent petitioner a letter supposedly from the American Hedonist Society, which in fact was a fictitious organization. The letter included a membership application and stated the Society's doctrine: that members had the "right to read what we desire, the right to discuss similar interests with those who share our philosophy, and finally that we have the right to seek pleasure without restrictions being placed on us by outdated puritan morality." Petitioner enrolled in the organization and returned a sexual attitude questionnaire that asked him to rank on a scale of one to four his enjoyment of various sexual materials, with one being "really enjoy," two being "enjoy," three being "somewhat enjoy," and four being "do not enjoy." Petitioner ranked the entry "[p]re-teen sex" as a two, but indicated that he was opposed to pedophilia.

For a time, the Government left petitioner alone. But then a new "prohibited mailing specialist" in the Postal Service found petitioner's name in a file, and in May 1986, petitioner received a solicitation from a second fictitious consumer research company, "Midlands Data Research," seeking a response from those who "believe in the joys of sex and the complete awareness of those lusty and youthful lads and lasses of the neophite [sic] age." The letter never explained whether "neophite" referred to minors or young adults. Petitioner responded: "Please feel free to send me more information, I am interested in teenage sexuality. Please keep my name confidential."

Petitioner then heard from yet another Government creation, "Heartland Institute for a New Tomorrow" (HINT), which proclaimed that it was "an organization founded to protect and promote sexual freedom and freedom of choice. We believe that arbitrarily imposed legislative sanctions restricting your sexual freedom should be rescinded through the legislative process." The letter also enclosed a second survey. Petitioner indicated that his interest in "[p]reteen sex-homosexual" material was above average, but not high. In response to another question, petitioner wrote: "Not only sexual expression but freedom of the press is under attack. We must be ever vigilant to counter attack right wing fundamentalists who are determined to curtail our freedoms."

HINT replied, portraying itself as a lobbying organization seeking to repeal "all statutes which regulate sexual activities, except those laws which deal with violent behavior, such as rape. HINT is also lobbying to eliminate any legal definition of 'the age of consent.'" These lobbying efforts were to be funded by sales from a catalog to be published in the future "offering the sale of various items which we believe you will find to be both interesting and stimulating." HINT also provided computer matching of group members with similar survey responses; and, although petitioner was supplied with a list of potential "pen pals," he did not initiate any correspondence.

Nevertheless, the Government's "prohibited mailing specialist" began writing to petitioner, using the pseudonym "Carl Long." The letters employed a tactic known as "mirroring," which the inspector described as "reflect[ing] whatever the interests are of the person we are writing to." Petitioner responded at first, indicating that his interest was primarily in "male-male items." Inspector "Long" wrote back:

"My interests too are primarily male-male items. Are you satisfied with the type of VCR tapes available? Personally, I like the amateur stuff better if its [sic] well produced as it can get more kinky and also seems more real. I think the actors enjoy it more.''

Petitioner responded:

> "As far as my likes are concerned, I like good looking young guys (in their late teens and early 20's) doing their thing together.''

Petitioner's letters to "Long" made no reference to child pornography. After writing two letters, petitioner discontinued the correspondence.

By March 1987, 34 months had passed since the Government obtained petitioner's name from the mailing list of the California bookstore, and 26 months had passed since the Postal Service had commenced its mailings to petitioner. Although petitioner had responded to surveys and letters, the Government had no evidence that petitioner had ever intentionally possessed or been exposed to child pornography. The Postal Service had not checked petitioner's mail to determine whether he was receiving questionable mailings from persons—other than the Government—involved in the child pornography industry.

At this point, a second Government agency, the Customs Service, included petitioner in its own child pornography sting, "Operation Borderline," after receiving his name on lists submitted by the Postal Service. Using the name of a fictitious Canadian company called "Produit Outaouais," the Customs Service mailed petitioner a brochure advertising photographs of young boys engaging in sex. Petitioner placed an order that was never filled.

The Postal Service also continued its efforts in the Jacobson case, writing to petitioner as the "Far Eastern Trading Company Ltd." The letter began:

> "As many of you know, much hysterical nonsense has appeared in the American media concerning 'pornography' and what must be done to stop it from coming across your borders. This brief letter does not allow us to give much comments; however, why is your government spending millions of dollars to exercise international censorship while tons of drugs, which makes yours the world's most crime ridden country are passed through easily.''

The letter went on to say:

> "[W]e have devised a method of getting these to you without prying eyes of U.S. Customs seizing your [mail]. After consultations with American solicitors, we have been advised that once we have posted our material through your system, it cannot be opened for any inspection without authorization of a judge.''

The letter invited petitioner to send for more information. It also asked petitioner to sign an affirmation that he was "not a law enforcement officer or agent of the U.S. Government acting in an undercover capacity for the purpose of entrapping Far Eastern Trading Company, its agents or customers." Petitioner responded. A catalog was sent, and petitioner ordered Boys Who Love Boys, a pornographic magazine depicting young boys engaged in various sexual activities. Petitioner was arrested after a controlled delivery of a photocopy of the magazine.

When petitioner was asked at trial why he placed such an order, he explained that the Government had succeeded in piquing his curiosity:

> "Well, the statement was made of all the trouble and the hysteria over pornography and I wanted to see what the material was. It didn't describe the—I didn't know for sure what kind of sexual action they were referring to in the Canadian letter."

In petitioner's home, the Government found the Bare Boys magazines and materials that the Government had sent to him in the course of its protracted investigation, but no other materials that would indicate that petitioner collected, or was actively interested in, child pornography.

Petitioner was indicted for violating 18 U.S.C. § 2252(a)(2)(A). The trial court instructed the jury on the petitioner's entrapment defense, [and] petitioner was convicted.

II

There can be no dispute about the evils of child pornography or the difficulties that laws and law enforcement have encountered in eliminating it. Likewise, there can be no dispute that the Government may use undercover agents to enforce the law. "It is well settled that the fact that officers or employees of the Government merely afford opportunities or facilities for the commission of the offense does not defeat the prosecution. Artifice and stratagem may be employed to catch those engaged in criminal enterprises." *Sorrells v. United States*, 287 U.S. 435, 441 (1932).

In their zeal to enforce the law, however, Government agents may not originate a criminal design, implant in an innocent person's mind the disposition to commit a criminal act, and then induce commission of the crime so that the Government may prosecute. Where the Government has induced an individual to break the law and the defense of entrapment is at issue, as it was in this case, the prosecution must prove beyond reasonable doubt that the defendant was disposed to commit the criminal act prior to first being approached by Government agents.

Thus, an agent deployed to stop the traffic in illegal drugs may offer the opportunity to buy or sell drugs and, if the offer is accepted, make an arrest on the spot or later. In such a typical case, or in a more elaborate "sting" operation involving government-sponsored fencing where the defendant is simply provided with the opportunity to commit a crime, the entrapment defense is of little use because the ready commission of the criminal act amply demonstrates the defendant's predisposition. Had the agents in this case simply offered petitioner the opportunity to order child pornography through the mails, and petitioner—who must be presumed to know the law—had promptly availed himself of this criminal opportunity, it is unlikely that his entrapment defense would have warranted a jury instruction.

But that is not what happened here. By the time petitioner finally placed his order, he had already been the target of 26 months of repeated mailings and communications from Government agents and fictitious organizations. Therefore, although he had become predisposed to break the law by May 1987, it is our view that the Government did not prove that this predisposition was independent and not the product of the attention that the Government had directed at petitioner since January 1985.

The prosecution's evidence of predisposition falls into two categories: evidence developed prior to the Postal Service's mail campaign, and that developed during the course of the investigation. The sole piece of preinvestigation evidence is petitioner's 1984 order and receipt of the Bare Boys magazines. But this is scant if any proof of petitioner's predisposition to commit an illegal act, the criminal character of which a defendant is presumed to know. It may indicate a predisposition to view sexually oriented photographs that are responsive to his sexual tastes; but evidence that merely indicates a generic inclination to act within a broad range, not all of which is criminal, is of little probative value in establishing predisposition.

Furthermore, petitioner was acting within the law at the time he received these magazines. Receipt through the mails of sexually explicit depictions of children for noncommercial use did not become illegal under federal law until May 1984, and Nebraska had no law that forbade petitioner's possession of such material until 1988. Evidence of predisposition to do what once was lawful is not, by itself, sufficient to show predisposition to do what is now illegal, for there is a common understanding that most people obey the law even when they disapprove of it. This obedience may reflect a generalized respect for legality or the fear of prosecution, but for whatever reason, the law's prohibitions are matters of consequence. Hence, the fact that petitioner legally ordered and received the Bare Boys magazines does little to further the Government's burden of proving that petitioner was predisposed to commit a criminal act. This is particularly true given petitioner's unchallenged testimony that he did not know until they arrived that the magazines would depict minors.

The prosecution's evidence gathered during the investigation also fails to carry the Government's burden. Petitioner's responses to the many communications prior to the ultimate criminal act were at most indicative of certain personal inclinations, including a predisposition to view photographs of preteen sex and a willingness to promote a given agenda by supporting lobbying organizations. Even so, petitioner's responses hardly support an inference that he would commit the crime of receiving child pornography through the mails. Furthermore, a person's inclinations and "fantasies [are] his own and beyond the reach of [government]."

On the other hand, the strong arguable inference is that, by waving the banner of individual rights and disparaging the legitimacy and constitutionality of efforts to restrict the availability of sexually explicit materials, the Government not only excited petitioner's interest in sexually explicit materials banned by law but also exerted substantial pressure on petitioner to obtain and read such material as part of a fight against censorship and the infringement of individual rights. For instance, HINT described itself as "an organization founded to protect and promote sexual freedom and freedom of choice" and stated that "the most appropriate means to accomplish [its] objectives is to promote honest dialogue among concerned individuals and to continue its lobbying efforts with State Legislators." These lobbying efforts were to be financed through catalog sales. Mailings from the equally fictitious American Hedonist Society, and the correspondence from the nonexistent Carl Long, endorsed these themes.

Similarly, the two solicitations in the spring of 1987 raised the spectre of censorship while suggesting that petitioner ought to be allowed to do what he had been solicited to do. The mailing from the Customs Service referred to "the worldwide ban and intense enforcement on this type of material," observed that "what was legal and commonplace is now an 'underground' and secretive service," and emphasized that "[t]his environment forces us to take extreme measures" to ensure delivery. The Postal Service solicitation described the concern about child pornography as "hysterical nonsense," decried "international censorship," and assured petitioner, based on consultation with "American solicitors," that an order that had been posted could not be opened for inspection without authorization of a judge. It further asked petitioner to affirm that he was not a Government agent attempting to entrap the mail order company or its customers. In these particulars, both Government solicitations suggested that receiving this material was something that petitioner ought to be allowed to do.

Petitioner's ready response to these solicitations cannot be enough to establish beyond reasonable doubt that he was predisposed, prior to the Government acts intended to create predisposition, to commit the crime of receiving child pornography through the mails. The evidence that petitioner was ready and willing to commit the offense came only after the Government had devoted 2 1/2 years to convincing him that he had or should have the right to engage in the very behavior proscribed by law. Rational jurors could not say beyond a reasonable doubt that petitioner possessed the requisite predisposition prior to the Government's investigation and that it existed independent of the Government's many and varied approaches to petitioner. As was explained in *Sherman*, where entrapment was found as a matter of law, "the Government [may not] pla[y] on the weaknesses of an innocent party and beguil[e] him into committing crimes which he otherwise would not have attempted."

Law enforcement officials go too far when they "implant in the mind of an innocent person the disposition to commit the alleged offense and induce its commission in order that they may prosecute." Like the *Sorrells* Court, we are "unable to conclude that it was the intention of the Congress in enacting this statute that its processes of detection and enforcement should be abused by the instigation by government officials of an act on the part of persons otherwise innocent in order to lure them to its commission and to punish them." When the Government's quest for convictions leads to the apprehension of an otherwise law-abiding citizen who, if left to his own devices, likely would have never run afoul of the law, the courts should intervene.

Because we conclude that this is such a case and that the prosecution failed, as a matter of law, to adduce evidence to support the jury verdict that petitioner was predisposed, independent of the Government's acts and beyond a reasonable doubt, to violate the law by receiving child pornography through the mails, we reverse the Court of Appeals' judgment affirming the conviction of Keith Jacobson.

Justice O'CONNOR, with whom THE CHIEF JUSTICE and Justice KENNEDY join, and with whom Justice SCALIA joins except as to Part II, dissenting.

Keith Jacobson was offered only two opportunities to buy child pornography through the mail. Both times, he ordered. Both times, he asked for opportunities to buy more. He needed no Government agent to coax, threaten, or persuade him; no one played on his sympathies, friendship, or suggested that his committing the crime would further a greater good. In fact, no Government agent even contacted him face to face. The Government contends that from the enthusiasm with which Mr. Jacobson responded to the chance to commit a crime, a reasonable jury could permissibly infer beyond a reasonable doubt that he was predisposed to commit the crime. I agree.

The first time the Government sent Mr. Jacobson a catalog of illegal materials, he ordered a set of photographs advertised as picturing "young boys in sex action fun." He enclosed the following note with his order: "I received your brochure and decided to place an order. If I like your product, I will order more later." For reasons undisclosed in the record, Mr. Jacobson's order was never delivered.

The second time the Government sent a catalog of illegal materials, Mr. Jacobson ordered a magazine called "Boys Who Love Boys," described as: "11 year old and 14 year old boys get it on in every way possible. Oral, anal sex and heavy masturbation. If you love boys, you will be delighted with this." Along with his order, Mr. Jacobson sent the following note: "Will order other items later. I want to be discreet in order to protect you and me."

Government agents admittedly did not offer Mr. Jacobson the chance to buy child pornography right away. Instead, they first sent questionnaires in order to make sure that he was generally interested in the subject matter. Indeed, a "cold call" in such a business would not only risk rebuff and suspicion, but might also shock and offend the uninitiated, or expose minors to suggestive materials. Mr. Jacobson's responses to the questionnaires gave the investigators reason to think he would be interested in photographs depicting preteen sex.

The Court, however, concludes that a reasonable jury could not have found Mr. Jacobson to be predisposed beyond a reasonable doubt on the basis of his responses to the Government's catalogs, even though it admits that, by that time he was predisposed to commit the crime. The Government, the Court holds, failed to provide evidence that Mr. Jacobson's obvious predisposition at the time of the crime "was independent and not the product of the attention that the Government had directed at petitioner." In so holding, I believe the Court fails to acknowledge the reasonableness of the jury's inference from the evidence, redefines "predisposition," and introduces a new requirement that Government sting operations have a reasonable suspicion of illegal activity before contacting a suspect.

This Court has held previously that a defendant's predisposition is to be assessed as of the time the Government agent first suggested the crime, not when the Government agent first became involved. Until the Government actually makes a suggestion of criminal conduct, it could not be said to have "implant[ed] in the mind of an innocent person the disposition to commit the alleged offense and induce its [commission]."
* * *

Today, the Court holds that Government conduct may be considered to create a predisposition to commit a crime, even before any Government action to induce the commission of the crime. In my view, this holding changes entrapment doctrine. Generally, the inquiry is whether a suspect is predisposed before the Government induces the commission of the crime, not before the Government makes initial contact with him. There is no dispute here that the Government's questionnaires and letters were not sufficient to establish inducement; they did not even suggest that Mr. Jacobson should engage in any illegal activity. If all the Government had done was to send these materials, Mr. Jacobson's entrapment defense would fail. Yet the Court holds that the Government must prove not only that a suspect was predisposed to commit the crime before the opportunity to commit it arose, but also before the Government came on the scene.

The rule that preliminary Government contact can create a predisposition has the potential to be misread by lower courts as well as criminal investigators as requiring that the Government must have sufficient evidence of a defendant's predisposition before it ever seeks to contact him. Surely the Court cannot intend to impose such a requirement, for it would mean that the Government must have a reasonable suspicion of criminal activity before it begins an investigation, a condition that we have never before imposed. The Court denies that its new rule will affect run-of-the-mill sting operations, and one hopes that it means what it says. Nonetheless, after this case, every defendant will claim that something the Government agent did before soliciting the crime "created" a predisposition that was not there before. For example, a bribetaker will claim that the description of the amount of money available was so enticing that it implanted a disposition to accept the bribe later offered. A drug buyer will claim that the description of the drug's purity and effects was so tempting that it created the urge to try it for the first time. In short, the Court's opinion could be read to prohibit the Government from advertising the seductions of criminal activity as part of its sting operation, for fear of creating a predisposition in its suspects. That limitation would be especially likely to hamper sting operations such as this one, which mimic the advertising done by genuine purveyors of pornography. No doubt the Court would protest that its opinion does not stand for so broad a proposition, but the apparent lack of a principled basis for distinguishing these scenarios exposes a flaw in the more limited rule the Court today adopts. * * *

[The] second puzzling thing about the Court's opinion is its redefinition of predisposition. The Court acknowledges that "[p]etitioner's responses to the many communications prior to the ultimate criminal act [were] indicative of certain personal inclinations, including a predisposition to view photographs of preteen [sex]." If true, this should have settled the matter; Mr. Jacobson was predisposed to engage in the illegal conduct. Yet, the Court concludes, "petitioner's responses hardly support an inference that he would commit the crime of receiving child pornography through the mails."

The Court seems to add something new to the burden of proving predisposition. Not only must the Government show that a defendant was predisposed to engage in the illegal conduct, here, receiving photographs of minors engaged in sex, but also that the defendant was predisposed to break the law knowingly in order to do so. The statute violated here, however, does not require proof of specific intent to break the law; it requires only knowing receipt of visual depictions produced by using minors engaged in sexually explicit conduct. Under the Court's analysis, however, the Government must prove more to show predisposition than it need prove in order to convict.

The Court ignores the judgment of Congress that specific intent is not an element of the crime of receiving sexually explicit photographs of minors. The elements of predisposition should track the elements of the crime. The predisposition requirement is meant to eliminate the entrapment defense for those defendants who would have committed the crime anyway, even absent Government inducement. Because a defendant might very well be convicted of the crime here absent Government inducement even though he did not know his conduct was illegal, a specific intent requirement does little to distinguish between those who would commit the crime without the inducement and those who would not. In sum, although the fact that Mr. Jacobson's purchases of Bare Boys I and Bare Boys II were legal at the time may have some relevance to the question of predisposition, it is not, as the Court suggests, dispositive.

The crux of the Court's concern in this case is that the Government went too far and "abused" the " 'processes of detection and enforcement' " by luring an innocent person to violate the law. Consequently, the Court holds that the Government failed to prove beyond a reasonable doubt that Mr. Jacobson was predisposed to commit the crime. It was, however, the jury's task, as the conscience of the community, to decide whether Mr. Jacobson was a willing participant in the criminal activity here or an innocent dupe. The jury is the traditional "defense against arbitrary law enforcement." Indeed, in *Sorrells*, in which the Court was also concerned about overzealous law enforcement, the Court did not decide itself that the Government conduct constituted entrapment, but left the issue to the jury. There is no dispute that the jury in this case was fully and accurately instructed on the law of entrapment, and nonetheless found Mr. Jacobson guilty. Because I believe there was sufficient evidence to uphold the jury's verdict, I respectfully dissent.

Notes

1. *Predisposition and Readiness.* Some judges argue that *Jacobson* has created a new interpretation of predisposition by shifting from a concept of psychological willingness to something different. For example, in *United States v. Hollingsworth*, 27 F.3d 1196, 1200 (7th Cir. 1994) (en banc), Judge Posner reasoned:

> We do not suggest that *Jacobson* adds a new element to the entrapment defense—"readiness" or "ability" or "dangerousness" on top of inducement and, most important, predisposition. ([I]nducement is significant chiefly as evidence bearing on predisposition: the greater the inducement, the weaker the inference that in yielding to it the defendant demonstrated that he was predisposed to commit the crime in question.) Rather, the Court clarified the meaning of predisposition. Predisposition is not a purely mental state, the state of being willing to swallow the government's bait. It has positional as well as dispositional force. The dictionary definitions of the word include "tendency" as well as "inclination." The defendant must be so situated by reason of previous training or experience or occupation or acquaintances that it is likely that if the government had not induced him to commit the crime some criminal would have done so; only then does a sting or other arranged crime take a dangerous person out of circulation. A public official is in a position to take bribes; a drug addict to deal drugs; a gun dealer to engage in illegal gun sales. For these and other traditional targets of stings all that must be shown to establish predisposition and thus defeat the defense of entrapment is willingness to violate the law without extraordinary inducements; ability can be presumed. It is different when the defendant is not in a position without the government's help to become involved in illegal activity.

For further analysis of *Jacobson*'s interpretation of the predisposition inquiry, see P. Marcus, *Presenting, Back From the (Almost) Dead, the Entrapment Defense*, 47 Fla. L. Rev. 205 (1995).

2. *The Willing but Incompetent Defendant.* Judge Posner's interpretation of *Jacobson* was criticized by the *Hollingsworth* dissenters. Judge Ripple opined:

[By] this decision, the majority treats "ready" as a new word of art. It has changed the "ready" defendant from one who is inclined, feeling or exhibiting no reluctance, to one on the point of acting. * * *

[The] holding in this case [will] benefit not only the pathetic incompetents of the criminal world but also the very competent criminal who is sufficiently studied in his way of doing business so as to appear not too organized. [Perhaps] the most problematic application of the new rule will come when a sting operation attracts a very willing but also not very well organized or inept first offender. A defendant's prior arrests and convictions, as well as his previous associations with drug traffickers, are strong indications of predisposition. Without that past record, however, would the neophyte's quick reply to an agent's invitation to "talk business" count as predisposition? Would his agreement to distribute drugs show a willingness, but not a readiness?

There is, of course, no constitutional requirement that the Congress punish only activity that *is immediately* dangerous. Nor can the majority point to any expression by the Congress of such an intent. If such a criterion is appropriate, it is the members of Congress, not the judges of an intermediate appellate court, who ought to make that decision.

Hollingsworth, 27 F.3d at 1196, 1215–1217 (Ripple, J., dissenting) (emphasis in original)

Problems

1. *Evidence of Predisposition.* The implications of *Jacobson* are the subject of debate among lower court judges. Justice Breyer, when he was a circuit court judge, interpreted its reasoning in *United States v. Gendron*, 18 F.3d 955 (1st Cir.1994):

In three respects [the agents] did more than provide an ordinary opportunity to buy child pornography: First, the solicitations reflected a psychologically "graduated" set of responses to Jacobson's own non-criminal responses, beginning with innocent lures and progressing to frank offers. [Second,] the government's soliciting letters sometimes depicted their senders as "free speech" lobbying organizations and fighters for the "right to read what we desire"; they asked Jacobson to "fight against censorship and the infringement of individual rights. Third, the government's effort to provide an "opportunity" to buy child pornography stretched out over two and a half years. * * *

[Placing orders for pornography] could not show how Jacobson would have acted had the solicitation lacked the three elements we just mentioned, namely, the improper appeals to anti-censorship motives, the graduated response, and the lengthy time frame. The government therefore failed to show "predisposition" (beyond a reasonable doubt). This means (as we understand it) that the government's evidence did not show how Jacobson would have acted had he been faced with an ordinary "opportunity" to commit the crime rather than a special "inducement."

What kinds of evidence would the government have needed to win in *Jacobson* in order to satisfy the burden described by Justice Breyer?

2. *The Normal Sale Price.* Detective Paul Andry, an undercover Indiana policeman, purchased cocaine from Nelson. When Andry called to make a follow-up purchase, prefatory to arresting Nelson, he learned that Nelson had been sent to jail on a burglary charge. Nelson's roommate, Farland, stated that he might be able to "do [Andry] some good," but that he could not talk on the phone. Later that evening, Andry met Farland at a prearranged place. Farland stated, "I can't do you any good tonight, but I'm getting ready to head to New York either tonight or tomorrow morning." Farland told Andry about his supplier and about the quality of the drugs. Andry gave Farland $300.00 as a down payment for the purchase of an ounce of cocaine. A week later, Andry contacted Farland, and they arranged to meet. Andry wore a transmitter to the meeting. When Andry arrived, Farland gave him a plastic bag containing 27.054 grams of cocaine. The men discussed future purchases, and Farland stated that he normally sold "eight balls" for $300.00. Farland also indicated that he was planning to make another trip to New York in two to three weeks. As a result of the prior sale, Farland was charged with dealing in cocaine. Assuming that the court applies a subjective test for entrapment, how might defendant argue that he was entrapped? How might the prosecution respond? *See McGowan v. State,* 671 N.E.2d 872 (Ind.App.1996).

3. *The Amateur Financiers.* Pickard (an orthodontist) and Hollingsworth (a farmer and businessman) tried to augment their incomes by business ventures, all of which failed. The last and most disastrous failure began when the two decided to become international financiers—a vocation for which neither had any training, contacts, aptitude, or experience. Pickard formed a Virgin Islands corporation, CIAL (Compagnie d'Investement de Les Antilles Limitee), to conduct international banking. The company obtained a Grenadan banking license and advertised for customers. No customers were obtained. With the enterprise steadily losing money the corporation decided to sell the Grenadan license to raise working capital. Pickard placed a classified ad in USA Today offering to sell the unused license for $29,950. U.S. customs agent Thomas Rothrock, read the ad and, knowing that foreign banks are sometimes used for money laundering, called the phone number listed in the ad and spoke with Pickard. Using the pseudonym of "Tom Hinch," Rothrock told Pickard that he had money that he wanted to deposit it offshore. Pickard responded that he had a bank for sale, and other vehicles or instruments for achieving "Hinch's" purposes that might be less expensive than a bank; and he described a variety of lawful international financial services. Hinch explained that his organization had a lot of cash, that the profit margin generated by the organization's activities was very large, and that the organization wanted to deposit it somewhere. Pickard pointed out that a cash deposit of less than $10,000 would not have to be reported to federal banking authorities and hence that a larger sum could be broken up into smaller ones and deposited in different banks. Rothrock expressed interest in this maneuver. There is no evidence that Pickard realized that "structuring" a large cash deposit to avoid federal reporting requirements would violate the law. "Structuring" is a specific-intent crime so that, unless the "structurer" knows that what he is doing is illegal, he is not guilty.

Pickard asked "Hinch" for assurance that the cash wasn't from drug sales and that Hinch himself was not a federal agent or informer, and Hinch gave him the requested assurances. In another telephone conversation, Pickard asked Hinch whether he wanted Pickard merely to "clean and polish" funds or for "extended services"; Hinch was evasive. In subsequent conversations Pickard turned coy, indicating that he was interested only in a long-term banking relationship.

Matters were at a standstill between August 20, 1990, the date of the last of the conversations in which Pickard expressed his lack of interest in providing spot services, and February 9, 1991, when Rothrock, having obtained $200,000 in sting money from his superiors, called Pickard, and told him he was "getting overwhelmed." "Hinch" explained that the source of his cash was the smuggling of guns to South Africa. They agreed that Pickard would travel to a hotel room where he would be shown $20,000 plus Pickard's fee of $2,405 in cash. Pickard would arrange a wire transfer of $20,000 to Hinch's bank account and after the transfer was confirmed would take possession of the cash. The transaction took place two days later, and subsequent transactions brought the total transferred in this manner to $200,000. Hollingsworth made one of the trips to Indianapolis, bringing back $30,000 in cash in exchange for $405 in fee and expenses. A further transaction was scheduled for September 13, at which Pickard was to transfer $235,000 for Hinch, but when Pickard showed up he was arrested. When arrested Pickard was carrying false-name passports for himself and Hollingsworth issued by the mythical "Dominion of Melchizedek." Before becoming involved with Hinch neither Pickard nor Hollingsworth had ever engaged in financial or for that matter any other wrongdoing, the Melchizedekian passports having been obtained after Hinch appeared on the scene. Nor did CIAL ever attract a single customer other than Hinch—who also was the only person who responded to the ad for the Grenadan banking license. What arguments will be made on appeal about entrapment by the prosecutor and defense counsel? *See United States v. Hollingsworth*, 27 F.3d 1196 (7th Cir.1994) (en banc).

4. *The Rhetoric of Laundering.* In the prior problem, suppose that, when Pickard called Hinch the second time, he told him that he had a "tap light" to monitor whether anyone was listening in on the conversation. Pickard also initiated two further calls and sent two letters to Hinch describing his business and providing a business address. When Hinch called to ask for Pickard's help with his illegal cash in February, Pickard said that he would first have to do a background check on Hinch with a private investigator. At the St. Louis meeting Hinch mentioned the word "launder" for the first time and Pickard assured him he could get Hinch's cash into the banking system while avoiding any reporting requirements. Pickard asked Hinch whether he was "wired" and patted him down to see if Hinch was wearing a recording device. When Hinch said that he wished he hadn't gotten his "hands dirty," Pickard said, "I didn't even hear you say [that]." The next month, Pickard sent Hinch a fee schedule for his services, asked for his social security number, and a "release" to perform the background check. Pickard then met with Hinch on April 3, April 18, May 21, June 21, July 19 and September 13. During each meeting cash was exchanged for wire transfers and fees were charged by Hinch. At these meetings Pickard once commented that he didn't want to end up in jail, and once again sought assurances that Hinch was not a government agent. During an August

phone call, Pickard said he wanted to handle larger and larger transactions and used the term, "smurfing," which is slang for breaking down large sums into units of under ten thousand dollars. Finally, during their last meeting, when Pickard showed Hinch his false passport, he also told Hinch about his plans to create a check cashing business to launder money in the future. How do these additional facts affect the outcome of the case? *See Hollingsworth*, 27 F.3d at 1205, 1207–1210 (Coffey, J., dissenting).

5. *Loneliness and Entrapment.* Jon is an undercover police officer and a very attractive man. His supervisor instructs him to go to a bar known to be popular with gay men, and to conduct a sting operation there. The bar is known to police as a location where customers have used drugs on the premises in the past. Jon goes to the bar and approaches a bar customer named Henry. When Jon finds out that Henry is gay, Jon repeatedly asks Henry to obtain some cocaine for him so that the two of them can "party." There is no evidence suggesting that Henry has cocaine or any knowledge of how to obtain it. There is evidence suggesting that Henry is very lonely. After an hour spent asking other bar customers about how to buy cocaine, Henry obtains the cocaine and gives it to Jon, who arrests him for drug possession. Was Henry entrapped? See *State v. Blanco*, 896 So.2d 900 (Fla.App.2005).

6. *Reluctance to Violate the Law.* Doug did not know that it was illegal to export military encryption devices and he thought he could make money exporting them to China. When he called the manufacturer of the devices, he was referred to a "sales representative" who actually was an undercover U. S. Customs agent named Amanda. Amanda met with Doug and told him that his plan to export the devices was illegal under the Arms Export Control Act (AECA), and then she said that "off the record," she was willing to work with Doug to "make the sale happen." Doug's immediate response was that he didn't want to "do anything illegal" and so the meeting ended. However, a few weeks later, Doug called Amanda and they went ahead with a transaction that resulted in Doug's prosecution for the crime of attempt to violate the AECA. When Doug's defense counsel sought an entrapment instruction at Doug's trial, the trial judge denied this request. Was the trial judge correct? See *United States v. Hsu*, 364 F.3d 192 (4th Cir.2004).

7. *Proof of Lack of Predisposition.* Undercover agents noticed Stan, who was standing on the sidewalk; Stan appeared to be a narcotics addict suffering from withdrawal because he was pale, twitching, shaking, and vomiting as the agents approached him. The agents decided to use Stan as a decoy. When the agents gave Stan $50 and asked him to buy drugs for them, the man led the agents to a nearby intersection where he expected to find drug sellers. Finding no sellers at the intersection, Stan called out to a passing stranger, Ricardo, saying, "I need a fix, I need your help, I'm really hurting. Please, just find me someone who can sell me something right away." Ricardo told Stan that he was sorry to see Stan in such terrible shape, and that he had heard some people say that drug sellers sometimes came to a nearby park. So Ricardo and Stan walked to the park, with the agents trailing them at a distance. At the park, Stan collapsed on a bench, while Ricardo took Stan's $50 and approached a woman who appeared to be selling drugs. Ricardo bought the drugs for Stan and when he gave them to Stan, Ricardo was arrested and charged with drug crimes. Ricardo's defense

counsel asks for an entrapment instruction at trial. Was there sufficient evidence of inducement? See *Bradley v. Duncan*, 315 F.3d 1091 (9th Cir. 2002). If so, should Ricardo be required to come forward with some evidence of lack of predisposition in order to receive an entrapment instruction? See *United States v. Hsu*, 364 F.3d 192, 202 n.4 (4th Cir.2004) (describing circuit split on issue).

B. DUE PROCESS AND "OUTRAGEOUS GOVERNMENT CONDUCT"

Although *Sherman* settled the debate in the federal courts over whether to adopt the subjective or objective test, some judges remained concerned about the danger that government agents might engage in extreme types of inducement strategies against predisposed defendants. As one judge noted, it would be "unthinkable, for example, to permit government agents to instigate robberies and beatings merely to gather evidence to convict other members of a gang of hoodlums." *United States v. Archer*, 486 F.2d 670, 676–77 (2d Cir.1973) (Friendly, J.). Therefore, some federal courts looked to Due Process principles as a source for reversing convictions in cases of "outrageous government conduct" in scenarios involving predisposed entrapped defendants. The Supreme Court responded to this development by its rulings in the cases that follow, particularly *Russell* and *Hampton*. In neither case did the Court find that a Due Process violation had occurred. In the years following these cases some courts that use the subjective test have taken on the task of articulating standards for Due Process claims in the absence of Supreme Court guidance. Any defendant may make entrapment and Due Process arguments in the same case. However, it is predisposed defendants in subjective test jurisdictions who have the most at stake in arguing Due Process.

UNITED STATES v. RUSSELL

411 U.S. 423 (1973).

MR. JUSTICE REHNQUIST delivered the opinion of the Court.

[On] December 7, 1969, Joe Shapiro, an undercover agent for the Federal Bureau of Narcotics and Dangerous Drugs, went to respondent's home on Whidbey Island in the State of Washington where he met with respondent and his two codefendants, John and Patrick Connolly. Shapiro's assignment was to locate a laboratory where it was believed that methamphetamine was being manufactured illicitly. He told the respondent and the Connollys that he represented an organization in the Pacific Northwest that was interested in controlling the manufacture and distribution of methamphetamine. He then made an offer to supply the defendants with the chemical phenyl–2–propanone, an essential ingredient in the manufacture of methamphetamine, in return for one-half of the drug produced. This offer was made on the condition that Agent Shapiro be shown a sample of the drug which they were making and the laboratory where it was being produced.

During the conversation, Patrick Connolly revealed that he had been making the drug since May 1969 and since then had produced three pounds of it. John Connolly gave the agent a bag containing a quantity of methamphetamine that he represented as being from "the last batch that we made." Shortly thereafter, Shapiro and Patrick Connolly left respondent's house to view the laboratory which was located in the Connolly house on Whidbey Island. At the house, Shapiro observed an empty bottle bearing the chemical label phenyl–2–propanone.

By prearrangement, Shapiro returned to the Connolly house on December 9, 1969, to supply 100 grams of propanone and observe the manufacturing process. When he arrived he observed Patrick Connolly and the respondent cutting up pieces of aluminum foil and placing them in a large flask. There was testimony that some of the foil pieces accidentally fell on the floor and were picked up by the respondent and Shapiro and put into the flask. Thereafter, Patrick Connolly added all of the necessary chemicals, including the propanone brought by Shapiro, to make two batches of methamphetamine. The manufacturing process having been completed the following morning, Shapiro was given one-half of the drug and respondent kept the remainder. Shapiro offered to buy, and the respondent agreed to sell, part of the remainder for $60. Shapiro did not otherwise participate in the manufacture of the drug or direct any of the work.

About a month later, Shapiro returned to the Connolly house and met with Patrick Connolly to ask if he was still interested in their "business arrangement." Connolly replied that he was interested but that he had recently obtained two additional bottles of phenyl–2–propanone and would not be finished with them for a couple of days. He provided some additional methamphetamine to Shapiro at that time. Three days later Shapiro returned to the Connolly house with a search warrant and, among other items, seized an empty 500–gram bottle of propanone and a 100–gram bottle, not the one he had provided, that was partially filled with the chemical.

There was testimony at the trial of respondent and Patrick Connolly that phenyl–2–propanone was generally difficult to obtain. At the request of the Bureau of Narcotics and Dangerous Drugs, some chemical supply firms had voluntarily ceased selling the chemical.

[A]fter receiving the District Judge's standard entrapment instruction, the jury found the respondent guilty on all counts charged. On appeal, the respondent conceded that the jury could have found him predisposed to commit the offenses, but argued that on the facts presented there was entrapment as a matter of law. The Court of Appeals agreed, although it did not find the District Court had misconstrued or misapplied the traditional standards governing the entrapment defense. Rather, the court in effect expanded the traditional notion of entrapment, which focuses on the predisposition of the defendant, to mandate dismissal of a criminal prosecution whenever the court determines that there has been "an intolerable degree of governmental participation in the criminal enterprise." In this case the court decided that the conduct of the agent in supplying a scarce ingredient essential for the manufacture of a controlled substance established that defense.

This new defense was held to rest on either of two alternative theories. One theory is based on two lower court decisions which have found entrapment, regardless of predisposition, whenever the government supplies contraband to the defendants. The second theory, a nonentrapment rationale, is based on a recent Ninth Circuit decision that reversed a conviction because a government investigator was so enmeshed in the criminal activity that the prosecution of the defendants was held to be repugnant to the American criminal justice system. The court below held that these two rationales constitute the same defense, and that only the label distinguishes them. In any event, it held that "[b]oth theories are premised on fundamental concepts of due process and evince the reluctance of the judiciary to countenance 'overzealous law enforcement.' "

[Respondent would have this] Court adopt a rigid constitutional rule that would preclude any prosecution when it is shown that the criminal conduct would not have been possible had not an undercover agent "supplied an indispensable means to the commission of the crime that could not have been obtained otherwise, through legal or illegal channels." Even if we were to surmount the difficulties attending the notion that due process of law can be embodied in fixed rules, and those attending respondent's particular formulation, the rule he proposes would not appear to be of significant benefit to him. For, on the record presented, it appears that he cannot fit within the terms of the very rule he proposes.

The record discloses that although the propanone was difficult to obtain, it was by no means impossible. The defendants admitted making the drug both before and after those batches made with the propanone supplied by Shapiro. Shapiro testified that he saw an empty bottle labeled phenyl–2–propanone on his first visit to the laboratory on December 7, 1969. And when the laboratory was searched pursuant to a search warrant on January 10, 1970, two additional bottles labeled phenyl–2–propanone were seized. Thus, the facts in the record amply demonstrate that the propanone used in the illicit manufacture of methamphetamine not only could have been obtained without the intervention of Shapiro but was in fact obtained by these defendants.

While we may some day be presented with a situation in which the conduct of law enforcement agents is so outrageous that due process principles would absolutely bar the government from invoking judicial processes to obtain a conviction, the instant case is distinctly not of that breed. Shapiro's contribution of propanone to the criminal enterprise already in process was scarcely objectionable. The chemical is by itself a harmless substance and its possession is legal. While the Government may have been seeking to make it more difficult for drug rings, such as that of which respondent was a member, to obtain the chemical, the evidence described above shows that it nonetheless was obtainable. The law enforcement conduct here stops far short of violating that "fundamental fairness, shocking to the universal sense of justice," mandated by the Due Process Clause of the Fifth Amendment.

The illicit manufacture of drugs is not a sporadic, isolated criminal incident, but a continuing, though illegal, business enterprise. In order to obtain convictions for illegally manufacturing drugs, the gathering of evidence of past unlawful conduct frequently proves to be an all but impossible task. Thus in drug-related offenses law enforcement personnel have turned to one of the only practicable means of detection: the infiltration of drug rings and a limited participation in their unlawful present practices. Such infiltration is a recognized and permissible means of investigation; if that be so, then the supply of some item of value that the drug ring requires must, as a general rule, also be permissible. For an agent will not be taken into the confidence of the illegal entrepreneurs unless he has something of value to offer them. Law enforcement tactics such as this can hardly be said to violate "fundamental fairness" or "shocking to the universal sense of justice."

Sorrells and *Sherman* both recognize "that the fact that officers or employees of the Government merely afford opportunities or facilities for the commission of the offense does not defeat the prosecution." Nor will the mere fact of deceit defeat a prosecution for there are circumstances when the use of deceit is the only practicable law enforcement technique available. It is only when the Government's deception actually implants the criminal design in the mind of the defendant that the defense of entrapment comes into play.

[Reversed.]

MR. JUSTICE DOUGLAS, with whom MR. JUSTICE BRENNAN concurs, dissenting.

[In] my view, the fact that the chemical ingredient supplied by the federal agent might have been obtained from other sources is quite irrelevant. Supplying the chemical ingredient used in the manufacture of this batch of "speed" made the United States an active participant in the unlawful activity.

[May] the federal agent supply the counterfeiter with the kind of paper or ink that he needs in order to get a quick and easy arrest? The Court of Appeals in *Greene v. United States*, 9 Cir., 454 F.2d 783, [said] "no" in a case where the federal agent treated the suspects "as partners" with him, offered to supply them with a still, a still site, still equipment, and an operator and supplied them with sugar.

[Federal] agents play a debased role when they become the instigators of the crime, or partners in its commission, or the creative brain behind the illegal scheme. That is what the federal agent did here when he furnished the accused with one of the chemical ingredients needed to manufacture the unlawful drug.

MR. JUSTICE STEWART, with whom MR. JUSTICE BRENNAN and MR. JUSTICE MARSHALL join, dissenting.

[W]hen the agents' involvement in criminal activities goes beyond the mere offering of such an opportunity and when their conduct is of a kind that could induce or instigate the commission of a crime by one not ready and willing to commit it, then—regardless of the character or propensities of the particular person induced—I think entrapment has occurred. For in that situation, the Government has engaged in the impermissible manufacturing of crime, and the federal courts should bar the prosecution in order to preserve the institutional integrity of the system of federal criminal justice.

[It] is the Government's duty to prevent crime, not to promote it. Here, the Government's agent asked that the illegal drug be produced for him, solved his quarry's practical problems with the assurance that he could provide the one essential ingredient that was difficult to obtain, furnished that element as he had promised, and bought the finished product from the respondent—all so that the respondent could be prosecuted for producing and selling the very drug for which the agent had asked and for which he had provided the necessary component. Under the objective approach that I would follow, this respondent was entrapped, regardless of his predisposition or "innocence."

HAMPTON v. UNITED STATES

425 U.S. 484 (1976).

MR. JUSTICE REHNQUIST announced the judgment of the Court in an opinion in which THE CHIEF JUSTICE and MR. JUSTICE WHITE join.

[Petitioner] was convicted of two counts of distributing heroin [and] sentenced to concurrent terms of five years' imprisonment (suspended). The case arose from two sales of heroin by petitioner to agents of the Federal Drug Enforcement Administration (DEA) in St. Louis on February 25 and 26, 1974. The sales were arranged by one Hutton, who was a pool-playing acquaintance of petitioner at the Pud bar in St. Louis and also a DEA informant.

According to the Government's witnesses, in late February 1974, Hutton and petitioner were shooting pool at the Pud when petitioner, after observing "track" [needle] marks on Hutton's arms told Hutton that he needed money and knew where he could get some heroin. Hutton responded that he could find a buyer and petitioner suggested that he "get in touch with those people." Hutton then called DEA Agent Terry Sawyer and arranged a sale for 10 p.m. on February 25.

At the appointed time, Hutton and petitioner went to a prearranged meeting place and were met by Agent Sawyer and DEA Agent McDowell, posing as narcotics dealers. Petitioner produced a tinfoil packet from his cap and turned it over to the agents who tested it, pronounced it "okay," and negotiated a price of $145 which was paid to petitioner. Before they parted, petitioner told Sawyer that he could obtain larger quantities of heroin and gave Sawyer a phone number where he could be reached.

The next day Sawyer called petitioner and arranged for another "buy" that afternoon. Petitioner got Hutton to go along and they met the agents again near where they had been the previous night. [Petitioner was arrested after producing tinfoil packet of heroin from his cap and asking for $500.]

Petitioner's version of events was quite different. [He testified that] Hutton said that he had a friend who was a pharmacist who could produce a non-narcotic counterfeit drug which would give the same reaction as heroin. Hutton proposed selling this drug to gullible acquaintances. [They] successfully duped one buyer with this fake drug and [the] sales which led to the arrest were solicited by petitioner in an effort to profit further from this ploy.

Petitioner contended that he neither intended to sell, nor knew that he was dealing in heroin and that all of the drugs he sold were supplied by Hutton. [But the] guilty verdict necessarily implies that the jury rejected petitioner's claim that he did not know the substance was heroin, and petitioner himself admitted both soliciting and carrying out sales.

[The trial court rejected petitioner's proposed jury instruction that predisposition should be disregarded because as a matter of law acquittal was required if the jury believed that a government agent had supplied the drugs on these particular facts where the drugs also had been sold to an agent. On appeal petitioner renewed this claim and the Court of Appeals affirmed the conviction, relying on *Russell*.]

[P]etitioner correctly recognizes that his case does not qualify as one involving "entrapment" at all. He instead relies on the language in *Russell* that "we may some day be presented with a situation in which the conduct of law enforcement agents is so outrageous that due process principles would absolutely bar the government from invoking judicial processes to obtain a conviction."

[Admittedly] petitioner's case is different from *Russell*'s but the difference is one of degree not of kind. In *Russell* the ingredient supplied by the Government agent was a legal drug which the defendants demonstrably could have obtained from other sources besides the Government. Here the drug which the Government informant allegedly supplied to petitioner both was illegal and constituted the *corpus delicti* for the sale of which the petitioner was convicted. The Government obviously played a more significant role in enabling petitioner to sell contraband in this case than it did in *Russell*.

But in each case the Government agents were acting in concert with the defendant, and in each case either the jury found or the defendant conceded that he was predisposed to commit the crime for which he was convicted. The remedy of the criminal defendant with respect to the acts of Government agents, which, far from being resisted, are encouraged by him, lies solely in the defense of entrapment. But, as noted, petitioner's conceded predisposition rendered this defense unavailable to him.

To sustain petitioner's contention here would run directly contrary to our statement in *Russell* that the defense of entrapment is not intended "to give the federal judiciary a 'chancellor's foot' veto over law enforcement practices of which it did not approve."

[The] limitations of the Due Process Clause of the Fifth Amendment come into play only when the Government activity in question violates some protected right of the defendant. Here, the police, the Government informant, and the defendant acted in concert with one another. If the result of the governmental activity is to "implant in the mind of an innocent person the disposition to commit the alleged offense and induce its [commission]," the defendant is protected by the defense of entrapment. If the police engage in illegal activity in concert with a defendant beyond the scope of their duties the remedy lies, not in freeing the equally culpable defendant, but in prosecuting the police under the applicable provisions of state or federal law. But the police conduct here no more deprived defendant of any right secured to him by the United States Constitution than did the police conduct in *Russell* deprive Russell of any rights.

Affirmed.

MR. JUSTICE POWELL, with whom MR. JUSTICE BLACKMUN concurring in the judgment.

Petitioner, Charles Hampton, contends that the Government's supplying of contraband to one later prosecuted for trafficking in contraband constitutes a *per se* denial of due process. As I do not accept this proposition, I concur in the judgment of the Court and much of the plurality opinion directed specifically to Hampton's contention. I am not able to join the remainder of the plurality opinion, as it would unnecessarily reach and decide difficult questions not before us.

[The] plurality [says] that the concept of fundamental fairness inherent in the guarantee of due process would never prevent the conviction of a predisposed defendant, regardless of the outrageousness of police behavior in light of the surrounding circumstances.

I do not understand *Russell* or earlier cases [to] have gone so far. [I] am not unmindful of the doctrinal and practical difficulties of delineating limits to police involvement in crime that do not focus on predisposition, as Government participation ordinarily will be fully justified in society's "war with the criminal classes." *Sorrells v. United States*, 287 U.S. 435 (1932). This undoubtedly is the concern that prompts the plurality to embrace an absolute rule. But we left these questions open in *Russell*, and this case is controlled completely by *Russell*. I therefore am unwilling to join the plurality in concluding that, no matter what the circumstances, neither due process principles nor our supervisory power could support a bar to conviction in any case where the Government is able to prove predisposition.

MR. JUSTICE BRENNAN, with whom MR. JUSTICE STEWART and MR. JUSTICE MARSHALL concur, dissenting.

[Justice Brennan notes that petitioner's claims "would plainly be held to constitute entrapment as a matter of law" under the "objective" test and then says,] I think that reversal of petitioner's conviction is [compelled] for those who follow the "subjective" approach to the defense of entrapment. As Mr. Justice Rehnquist notes, the Government's role in the criminal activity involved in this case was more pervasive than the Government involvement in *Russell*. In addition, I agree with Mr. Justice Powell that *Russell* does not foreclose imposition of a bar to conviction—based on our supervisory power or due process principles—where the conduct of law enforcement authorities is sufficiently offensive, even though the individuals entitled to invoke such a defense might be "predisposed." In my view, the police activity in this case was beyond permissible limits.

Two facts sufficiently distinguish this case from *Russell*. First, the chemical supplied in that case was not contraband. [In] contrast, petitioner claims that the very narcotic he is accused of selling was supplied by an agent of the government.

Second, the defendant in *Russell* "was an active participant in an illegal drug manufacturing enterprise which began before the Government agent appeared on the scene and continued after the Government agent had left the scene." [In] contrast, the two sales for which petitioner was convicted were allegedly instigated by Government agents and completed by the Government's purchase. The beginning and end of this crime thus coincided exactly with the Government's entry into and withdrawal from the criminal activity in this case, while the Government was not similarly involved in Russell's crime.

Whether the differences from the *Russell* situation are of degree or of kind, I think they clearly require a different result. Where the Government's agent deliberately sets up the accused by supplying him with contraband and then bringing him to another agent as a potential purchaser, the Government's role has passed the point of toleration. The Government is doing nothing less than buying contraband from itself through an intermediary and jailing the intermediary. There is little, if any, law enforcement interest promoted by such conduct; plainly it is not designed to discover ongoing drug traffic. Rather, such conduct deliberately entices an individual to commit a crime. That the accused is "predisposed" cannot possibly justify the action of government officials in purposefully creating the crime. No one would suggest that the police could round up and jail all "predisposed" individuals, yet that is precisely what set-ups like the instant one are intended to accomplish. Thus, this case is nothing less than an instance of "the Government [seeking] to punish for an alleged offense which is the product of the creative activity of its own officials."

Note

Totality of Circumstances Test. Not surprisingly, given the uncertain state of Due Process doctrine, defendants have difficulty winning a claim of "outrageous government conduct." One state court has summarized the development of Due Process standards after *Russell* and *Hampton*, and has created a list of factors that can be used to resolve Due Process claims. Consider the reasoning of the court in *State v. Lively*, 130 Wash.2d 1, 921 P.2d 1035 (1996):

> In determining whether police conduct violates due process, this court has held that the conduct must be so shocking that it violates fundamental fairness. A due process claim based on outrageous conduct requires more than a mere demonstration of flagrant police conduct. Public policy allows for some deceitful conduct and violation of criminal laws by the police in order to detect and eliminate criminal activity. Dismissal based on outrageous conduct is reserved for only the most egregious circumstances. * * *

> Following the *Hampton* decision, courts have continued to recognize the rights of defendants to claim a due process violation based on outrageous government conduct without requiring a separate constitutional violation. To require defendants to prove a separate violation of a constitutional right effectively negates the claim of outrageous conduct. Either outrageous conduct may be raised independently of other constitutional restrictions, as we recognize here, or the defense is essentially nonexistent.

> While some courts have read the United States Supreme Court decisions to limit the outrageous conduct defense to a "slim category of cases in which the police have been brutal, employing physical or psychological coercion against the defendant," other courts have not accepted this limited application of the defense. Also violating due process standards are those cases where the government conduct is so integrally involved in the offense that the government agents direct the crime from beginning to end, or where the crime is fabricated by the police to obtain a defendant's conviction, rather than to protect the public from criminal behavior.

> We agree with those courts which hold that in reviewing a defense of outrageous government conduct, the court should evaluate the conduct based on the "totality of the circumstances." Each case must be resolved on its own unique set of facts and each component of the conduct must be submitted to scrutiny bearing in mind "proper law enforcement objectives—the prevention of crime and the apprehension of violators, rather than the encouragement of and participation in sheer lawlessness." The government conduct may be so extensive that even a predisposed defendant may not be prosecuted based on "the ground of deprivation of due process."

> In evaluating whether the State's conduct violated due process, we focus on the State's behavior and not the defendant's predisposition. There are several factors which courts consider when determining whether police conduct offends due process: whether the police conduct

instigated a crime or merely infiltrated ongoing criminal activity, whether the defendant's reluctance to commit a crime was overcome by pleas of sympathy, promises of excessive profits, or persistent solicitation, whether the government controls the criminal activity or simply allows for the criminal activity to occur, whether the police motive was to prevent crime or protect the public; and whether the government conduct itself amounted to criminal activity or conduct "repugnant to a sense of justice."

Problems

1. *Defining Due Process.* One problem for federal judges is how to articulate a Due Process concept of outrageous government conduct that does not simply mimic the standards of the objective test jurisdictions. As one judge noted, "the language used in both *Russell* and *Hampton* indicates that no such back-door reincarnation of the objective approach was intended." *United States v. Twigg*, 588 F.2d 373, 385 (3d Cir. 1978) (Adams, J., dissenting). How many different versions of Due Process are expressed in the opinions in *Russell* and *Hampton*?

2. *Government Supplies for Drug Lab Operation.* Kubica agrees to help the D.E.A. in exchange for a guilty plea to the crime of manufacturing methamphetamine hydrochloride (speed) and a recommendation for a reduced sentence. The D.E.A. asks Kubica to reestablish contact with people who were involved in his numerous illegal drug activities in the past, and so he calls Neville and asks whether he can help Kubica set up a laboratory to manufacture speed. Neville had helped him set up a speed lab four years earlier, but had not been involved in criminal activities since that time. Neville is willing to help Kubica and it takes several months to set up the lab. DEA agents gave Kubica two and one-half gallons of the essential chemical, cphenyl–2–propanone, as well as 20 percent of the glassware needed for the lab. The D.E.A. also rents a farmhouse for Kubica to use for the lab, and make arrangements with chemical supply houses to facilitate the purchase of the balance of the needed materials. Kubica buys all these supplies with $1500 supplied by Neville. The day that the lab is finally ready to operate, Neville introduces Kubica to Twigg, who gets involved in the operation in order to repay a debt to Neville. Kubica is in charge of the lab because only he has the necessary expertise to operate it. Neville and Twigg provide minor assistance under his direction. Twigg accompanies Kubica on a trip to several chemical supply houses, and runs errands for groceries or coffee. After one week of operation, Kubica produces six pounds of speed in the lab, and Neville and Twigg are arrested and charged with manufacture of a controlled substance, possession with intent to distribute, and related crimes. Neville raises the entrapment defense at trial and also claims that the government violated Due Process. Twigg is not eligible for the entrapment defense because he was not brought into the criminal enterprise by a government agent, so he makes only a Due Process argument at trial. Both defendants are convicted. On appeal, Neville and Twigg decide to renew their Due Process arguments. What arguments will they make and how will the prosecutor respond? See *United States v. Twigg*, 588 F.2d 373 (3d Cir.1978).

3. *The Government Fencing Operation.* In an attempt to uncover information about illegal activity, the police set-up an undercover fencing operation in New York City. The operation accepts stolen property from people who steal the property or know that it is stolen, and resells it to others who know the property is stolen. Because of the fencing operation, the police are able to crack a major theft ring. Eventually, the police shut down the operation and make a number of arrests for burglary, possession of stolen property, receiving stolen property, and other related crimes. The defendants claim that the government violated Due Process by establishing and operating the fencing operation. Did the government embroil itself to an intolerable degree in the criminal enterprise?

4. *The Two-year Solicitation.* The Bald and Golden Eagle Act, the Migratory Bird Treaty Act, and the Endangered Species Act, all prohibit the "taking" or "selling" of eagles and other protected migratory bird parts. Undercover government agents were charged with investigating violations of the acts on an Indian reservation. In 1981, the agents developed reason to believe that Dion may have sold eagle parts in the past. The agents offered Dion, described as an unsophisticated individual living in poverty, a "large sum of money" ($30,000) to "get some birds." Dion refused. The agents continued to solicit Dion over the next two years. Eventually, Dion agreed and killed a bald eagle. Has Dion been entrapped? Whether or not he has been entrapped, should the Due Process defense apply? *See United States v. Dion*, 762 F.2d 674 (8th Cir.1985).

5. *The Child Prostitute Operation.* Recognizing that child sexual abuse is a major problem, the police recruit young boys to work as prostitutes. The boys are encouraged to cooperate with the "johns" and to place themselves in revealing situations. At the appropriate point, the police break-in and arrest the "johns." Given the compelling nature of the child abuse problem, is this sting operation justifiable, or would it violate Due Process?

6. *Targeting Addicts in Treatment.* An undercover drug investigation was assisted by a police informant, Koby Desai. Desai phoned a drug unit detective to arrange a delivery of cocaine from the Defendant, Amy Lively. The detective went to Desai's residence and gave Lively $70. Defendant left in Desai's automobile and returned fifteen minutes later. She told the detective, whom she knew as Rick, a friend of Desai, that she would have the cocaine later that day. The detective left and, after receiving a call from Desai, returned to Desai's apartment three hours later. At that time, the Defendant delivered a packet of cocaine weighing 1.3 grams to the detective.

One week later, the same detective responded to a telephone call from Desai regarding another delivery of cocaine. He arrived at Desai's apartment at 8:30 p.m. and paid the purchase price. Again, she left in Desai's car. Defendant called to say that her connection was delayed, and she did not return until after midnight. When she did not have either the cocaine or the money, the detective claimed that she was trying to steal his money. Lively retrieved a packet of cocaine weighing .9 grams from the kitchen and handed it to him. Lively then stated that she wanted to get high and have sex with one of them. In addition, she asked for $10 to put gas in Desai's car.

Lively was charged with two counts of delivering a controlled substance. At her trial, she did not dispute the cocaine deliveries, but claimed entrap-

ment. She testified that by the time she was fourteen years old she was
drinking alcohol and using cocaine. She stopped using cocaine at fifteen
when she learned she was pregnant. At age eighteen, when she was raising
two children and her husband was stationed in Korea, she began drinking
alcohol heavily. She attempted alcohol withdrawal, admitted herself into a
detoxification program, and began attending Alcoholics Anonymous/Narcot-
ics Anonymous (AA/NA) meetings. In March 1991, she had an alcoholic
relapse and entered a 28–day inpatient detoxification program. Prior to
meeting Desai, the Defendant testified that she had never sold or offered to
sell drugs, and had never been arrested or convicted of any crime other than
the charges for delivery of cocaine in June 1991. She also testified that she
was not using drugs at the time of the offenses and had not used cocaine
since her first pregnancy.

In 1991, Desai began working as a police informant and was given an
apartment, including utilities, a car, and other living expenses, in exchange
for his work. He signed a contract with the drug unit which required that he
not break any criminal laws, not use narcotics, and stay in daily communication with the drug unit. Desai began attending AA/NA meetings with the
knowledge and approval of detectives from the drug unit. He attended these
meetings in order to identify repeat drug addicts continuing to sell illegal
drugs. Defendant met Desai at an AA/NA meeting following her completion
of the inpatient hospital program. She tried to kill herself after completing
the program and remained emotionally distraught. She testified that Desai
asked her out on a date about two weeks after they met. She maintained the
relationship because he was very supportive and responsive to her emotional
needs.

Defendant then began a sexual relationship with Desai, and she moved
in with him for two months. The two spoke of their plans to marry, of his
assistance to her in obtaining a divorce, and of his offer to fly her friends to
California for the wedding. Defendant lived with Desai at the time the
offenses occurred. About four to six weeks after the two met, Desai said he
had a very good friend who wanted to buy cocaine and asked if she had a
connection. Desai asked her to get drugs for Rick (the detective) each day for
two weeks before she finally agreed to purchase cocaine and she did so only
because she was emotionally reliant on Desai.

Desai, who was called only as a rebuttal witness, disagreed with much of
the Defendant's testimony. He stated that she was the first to discuss drugs
by mentioning she had a connection and could get marijuana and cocaine.
He denied asking her to obtain cocaine for his friend Rick. He testified that
they never dated and never had a sexual relationship. He admitted, however,
allowing her to stay at his apartment, but said that she used a separate
bedroom during her stay. He also admitted that marriage was discussed, but
that he never proposed to her and that she initiated the discussion. Desai
claimed that he regarded the marriage plans as a joke. He denied offering to
assist her in obtaining a divorce, and testified that he saw her use cocaine on
three separate occasions.

Desai admitted lying repeatedly about his background in a deposition
taken by the defense. He stated that he thought it was all right to lie to
maintain his cover story and said he did not believe he was under oath

during the deposition. How would defendant argue that the Due Process defense applies? How should the prosecution respond? Who should win? *State v. Lively*, 130 Wash.2d 1, 921 P.2d 1035 (1996) (en banc).

7. *Testing the Virtue of Congressmen with Bribes.* The Federal Bureau of Investigation (FBI), in an effort to recover stolen art and securities, set up an undercover operation—"Abscam"—designed to catch red-handed those who dealt in such items. In due time the FBI altered the character of the operation to target government corruption, and began offering bribes to congressman in exchange for helping fictitious Arabs gain asylum in the United States. In the *Kelly* case, although the court recognized that the police may need to use undercover investigative techniques to detect "diabolical criminal conduct so sophisticated as to be nearly impossible to detect," it concluded that the Abscam investigation was not the type of carefully devised and supervised covert operation generally accepted by the courts. The district court was concerned that Abscam was not triggered by any suspicion of corruption in government and that, unlike ordinary, passive sting operations, it utilized legal and illegal bait promoted by a "recruiting agent" "to persuade the Congressman to become a sting patron." In addition, in that case, Congressman Kelly rejected the bribe on two separate occasions. As a result, the district court concluded that the sole purpose of the asylum scenario was to test the virtue of members of Congress and concluded that the investigation exceeded the outer limits of any concept of fundamental fairness. The district court concluded that:

> [I]n the circumstances of this case, any further pursuit and pressure on the part of government agents was nothing short of outrageous.... If the government had no knowledge of Kelly doing anything wrong up to his rejection of illicit money, its continuing role as the third man in a fight between his conscience and temptation rises above the level of mere offensiveness to that of being "outrageous." No concept of fundamental fairness can accommodate what happened to Kelly in this case.

Do you agree? See *United States v. Kelly,* 707 F.2d 1460 (D.C.Cir.), *cert. denied,* 464 U.S. 908 (1983), and *United States v. Williams,* 705 F.2d 603 (2d Cir.), *cert. denied,* 464 U.S. 1007 (1983).

8. *Sentencing Manipulation.* An informant's tip leads undercover police agents to Wally, who engages in "ripping off" drug dealers. The agents meet with Wally and they pretend to be organized crime figures who want to punish Michele for failing to pay them illegal kickbacks. The agents offer to give Wally information about how to steal drugs from Michele, in return for Wally giving them a portion of the drugs that he steals. When Wally agrees to this plan, the agents tell him that they believe that Michele has 85 kilograms of cocaine in the trunk of her car, which is parked in her driveway. Michele is actually an undercover agent and the 85 kilos of cocaine are planted by the agents in her car trunk. When Wally steals the cocaine from the trunk, the agents arrest him for drug crimes. After Wally is convicted, he is sentenced under the state sentencing guidelines to 15 years for the drug crimes, with an additional 25 years added to his sentence as an "enhancement" because he attempted to transport more than 80 kilos of drugs. On appeal, Wally's defense counsel argues that the agents engaged in a type of entrapment known as sentencing manipulation. Therefore, Wally's

sentence should be reduced to 15 years because the agents selected the "enhancement-triggering drug quantity" of 85 kilos for "no legitimate law enforcement purpose but solely to maximize Wally's sentence." Should the appellate court endorse the sentencing manipulation doctrine and reduce Wally's sentence? Compare *People v. Claypool*, 470 Mich. 715, 684 N.W.2d 278 (2004) with *People v. Smith*, 31 Cal.4th 1207, 7 Cal.Rptr.3d 559, 80 P.3d 662 (2003).

9. *Entrapment of Terrorists*. Three men come to the attention of federal authorities when they approach an FBI undercover agent named Mo. Mo is a terrorism investigator who meets the men in a warehouse where religious services are conducted in Miami's Liberty City neighborhood. When Mo presents himself to the men as an agent of al-Qaida, the men tell Mo that they want to build an Islamic Army to wage jihad and that they need boots, uniforms, guns, radios, vehicles, and $50,000 in cash. Mo provides the men only with boots and a video camera, which one of the men uses to record video footage of federal buildings in Miami. Mo persuades the men to take an oath of allegiance to al-Qaida, and Mo and the men discuss the topics of bombing the Sears Tower in Chicago and the F.B.I. Office in Miami. The men never formulate a plan of action and they have no known contact with al-Qaida. They drive old cars and are self-employed; their main source of income is from selling shampoo and hair tonic on the street. All of the men are U. S. citizens. When the men are arrested and charged with federal crimes based on the conduct of planning to blow up the Sears Tower and other buildings, they are described by the federal prosecutor as a "home-grown terrorist cell." Should the federal trial judge grant the defendants an entrapment instruction at trial? Can the defendants claim successfully that Mo violated Due Process?

Chapter 6

POLICE INTERROGATIONS & CONFESSIONS

A. PRE-*MIRANDA* DOCTRINES

Prior to the landmark decision in *Miranda v. Arizona* in 1966, the Supreme Court created three doctrines to regulate police interrogations. In 1936, the Court recognized the Due Process Clause of the Fourteenth Amendment as a source for standards to govern the admissibility of confessions in state courts; the same analysis came to be used for the Fifth Amendment Due Process standards applied in federal courts. The Court also developed the non-constitutional *McNabb-Mallory* doctrine to exclude some confessions by using its supervisory powers to create evidence rules for federal courts. In 1964 the Court relied on Sixth Amendment right-to-counsel doctrine to limit post-indictment interrogations by undercover government agents. The doctrines established in Due Process and Sixth Amendment confession precedents remain good law today. However, the modern scope of each doctrine has been influenced in significant ways by *Miranda* doctrine, which delineates the rights of persons interrogated in police custody, and thereby serves to protect the exercise of the Fifth Amendment privilege against self-incrimination.

1. Pre-Miranda Due Process

BROWN v. MISSISSIPPI

297 U.S. 278 (1936).

MR. CHIEF JUSTICE HUGHES delivered the opinion of the Court.

[The violent acts used to procure the confessions of three African-American defendants were admitted at trial by the white sheriff and white men who helped him. After arrest, one defendant was "hanged by a rope to the limb of a tree" three times, "tied to a tree and whipped," and then released, "suffering intense pain and agony." A day or two later, the same man was arrested again, "severely whipped," and told

425

that the whipping would continue "until he confessed" to murder, which he did. When the two other defendants were arrested and taken to jail, they were made to strip, "and they were laid over chairs and their backs were cut to pieces with a leather strap with buckles on it." They were told that the whipping would continue until they confessed. When they did confess, they "changed or adjusted their confession in all particulars of detail so as to conform to the demands of their torturers." The two-day trial began the day after the arraignment when the defendants received appointed counsel; the defendants testified that their confessions were false, but they were convicted of murder and sentenced to death. They challenged their convictions on Due Process grounds.]

The question in this case is whether convictions, which rest solely upon confessions shown to have been extorted [by] brutality and violence, are consistent with the due process of law required by the Fourteenth [Amendment]. The state stresses [that] "exemption from compulsory self-incrimination in the courts of the states is not secured by any part of the Federal Constitution," and that "the privilege against self-incrimination may be withdrawn and the accused put upon the stand as a witness for the state." But the question of the right of the state to withdraw the privilege against self-incrimination is not here involved. The compulsion to which the [Fifth Amendment refers] is that of the processes of justice by which the accused may be called as a witness and required to testify. Compulsion by torture to extort a confession is a different matter.

The state is free to regulate the procedure of its courts in accordance with its own conceptions of policy, unless in so doing it "offends some principle of justice so rooted in the traditions and conscience of our people as to be ranked as fundamental." [The] freedom of the state in establishing its policy [is] limited by the requirement of due process of law. Because a state may dispense with a jury trial, it does not follow that it may substitute trial by ordeal. The rack and torture chamber may not be substituted for the witness stand. The state may not permit an accused to be hurried to conviction under mob domination—where the whole proceeding is but a mask—without supplying corrective process. *Moore v. Dempsey*, 261 U.S. 86 (1923). The state may not deny to the accused the aid of counsel. *Powell v. Alabama*, 287 U.S. 45 (1932). Nor may a state, through the action of its officers, contrive a conviction through the pretense of a trial [which] "depriv[es] a defendant of liberty through a deliberate deception of court and jury by the presentation of testimony known to be perjured." *Mooney v. Holohan*, 294 U.S. 103, 112 (1935). And the trial equally is a mere pretense where the state authorities have contrived a conviction resting solely upon confessions obtained by violence. The due process clause requires [that government action] "shall be consistent with the fundamental principles of liberty and justice which lie at the base of all our civil and political institutions." *Hebert v. Louisiana*, 272 U.S. 312 (1926). It would be difficult to conceive of methods more revolting to the sense of justice than those taken to procure the confessions of these [defendants], and the use of the confessions thus obtained as the basis for conviction and sentence was a clear denial of due process. * * *

Note

Evolution of the "Coercion" Concept. The purposes of the Due Process ban on involuntary confessions overlapped with the purpose of common law evidence doctrine that prohibits the admission of such evidence. The evidence doctrine was intended to insure the inadmissibility of "presumptively false evidence," whereas an additional purpose of the Due Process doctrine was to prevent unfairness "in the use of evidence whether true or false." *Lisenba v. California*, 314 U.S. 219, 236 (1941). The vocabulary and rules of evidence doctrine came to be incorporated into Due Process law, as illustrated by the requirements that only "voluntary" confessions are admissible, produced by the "free will" of the defendant, rather than police "coercion" that includes inducements, threats, or deceptive stratagems. *See, e.g., Spano v. New York*, 360 U.S. 315 (1959) (involuntary confession obtained by tricks of lying police officer); *Lynumn v. Illinois*, 372 U.S. 528 (1963) (involuntary confession obtained by threat that defendant's children could be taken away from her if she did not cooperate). During the thirty years between *Brown* and *Miranda*, the Court relied on Due Process doctrine to invalidate confessions in more than twenty cases, while upholding confessions in fewer than half that number. Most of these decisions reveal sharp disagreements among the justices concerning the interpretation of the "voluntariness" concept. Over time, the Court expanded this concept to encompass various types of psychologically coercive interrogation strategies, and came to focus upon the customs of incommunicado police questioning as the ultimate source of the coercion problem.

HAYNES v. WASHINGTON

373 U.S. 503 (1963).

Mr. Justice Goldberg delivered the opinion of the Court.

[Haynes was arrested at night for robbing a gas station; he was taken to the police station and booked for "investigation" on the "small book," which meant that he was not allowed to make phone calls or to have visitors. During the first interrogation that night, Haynes asked to call an attorney and to call his wife, but the police refused these requests, telling him that "he might make a call if he confessed." The next day, the police continued to reject his requests to call his wife during the second interrogation, while telling Haynes that after he "made a statement and cooperated with" the police, they "would see to it" that he could call his wife. Then during a third interrogation in the prosecutor's office, Haynes made further requests to call his wife, which were rejected again. He made incriminating statements during all three interrogations, and his second and third statements were transcribed. Haynes signed the second statement but refused to sign the third one, telling the prosecutor that "all the promises of all the officers I had talked to had not been fulfilled and [so] I would sign nothing under any

conditions until I was allowed to call my wife to see about legal counsel."
After he appeared at a preliminary hearing on the day after arrest,
Haynes was returned to jail and held incommunicado while the police
made repeated efforts to obtain his signature on the third statement. He
was not allowed to call his wife until "some five or seven days after his
arrest." The signed statement was admitted at his trial, and he was
convicted of robbery; he argued that this statement was involuntary
under Due Process standards.]

[It] is uncontroverted that Haynes was not taken before a magistrate and granted a preliminary hearing until he had acceded to demands that he give and sign the written statement. Nor is there any
indication [that] prior to signing the written confession, or even thereafter, Haynes was advised by authorities of his right to remain silent,
warned that his answers might be used against him, or told of his rights
respecting consultation with an attorney. [W]hether the confession was
obtained by coercion or improper inducement can be determined only by
an examination of all of the attendant circumstances. Haynes' undisputed testimony as to the making and signing of the challenged confession
[permits] no doubt that it was obtained under a totality of circumstances
evidencing an involuntary written admission of guilt. [Haynes] was alone
in the hands of the police, with no one to advise or aid him, and he had
"no reason not to believe that the police had ample power to carry out
their threats," to continue, for a much longer period if need be, the
incommunicado detention—as in fact was actually done. [Confronted]
with the express threat of continued incommunicado detention and
induced by the promise of communication with and access to family,
Haynes understandably chose to make and sign the damning written
[statement].

We cannot blind ourselves to what experience unmistakably teaches:
that even apart from the express threat, the basic techniques present
here—the secret and incommunicado detention and interrogation—are
devices adapted and used to extort confessions from suspects. [The] line
between proper and permissible police conduct and techniques and
methods offensive to due process is, at best, a difficult one to draw,
particularly in cases such as this where it is necessary to make fine
judgments as to the effect of psychologically coercive pressures and
inducements on the mind and will of an accused. But [we] are here
impelled to the conclusion, from all of the facts presented, that the
bounds of due process have been exceeded. [Moreover,] history amply
shows that confessions have often been extorted to save law enforcement
officials the trouble and effort of obtaining valid and independent evidence[;] the coercive devices used here were designed to obtain admissions [to] complete a case in which there had already been obtained, by
proper investigative efforts, competent evidence sufficient to sustain a
conviction. The procedures here are no less constitutionally impermissible, and perhaps more unwarranted because so unnecessary. * * *

Official overzealousness of the type which vitiates [a conviction] has
only deleterious effects. Here it has put the State to the substantial

additional expense of prosecuting the case through the appellate courts and, now, will require even a greater expenditure in the event of retrial, as is likely. But it is the deprivation of the protected rights themselves which is fundamental and the most regrettable, not only because of the effect on the individual defendant, but because of the effect on our system of law and justice. Whether there is involved the brutal "third degree," or the more subtle, but no less offensive, methods here obtaining, official misconduct cannot but breed disrespect for law, as well as for those charged with its enforcement. * * *

MR. JUSTICE CLARK, with whom MR. JUSTICE HARLAN, MR. JUSTICE STEWART and MR. JUSTICE WHITE, join, dissenting.

[Haynes] is neither youthful in age [nor] lacking in experience in law breaking. He is married and was a skilled sheet-metal worker temporarily unemployed. [He] had not only served time but had been on parole for two [years]. He cannot [be] placed in the category of those types of people with whom [our Due Process] cases have ordinarily dealt, such as the mentally subnormal accused, the youthful offender, or the naive and impressionable defendant. [He] is a mature adult who appears [to] be of at least average intelligence and who is neither a stranger to police techniques and custodial procedures nor unaware of his rights on arrest. [Here] there is no contention [of] physical [abuse], no extended or repeated interrogation, no deprivation of sleep or food, no use of psychiatric [techniques,] and no [threat] of mob [violence]. In light of [his] age, intelligence and experience with the police, [the] comparative absence of any coercive circumstances, and [the] fact that [he] never [evidenced] a will to deny his guilt, [his] written confession was not involuntary.

Notes

1. *Defendant's Attributes.* The Court's Due Process precedents that invalidated confessions before *Haynes* often relied on the defendant's special vulnerability to police coercion, based on physical and mental attributes and life experiences. One notable example is *Spano v. New York*, 360 U.S. 315 (1959), where the Court relied on many factors in a "totality of circumstances" to invalidate a confession, including the factor of the defendant's attributes:

> [Spano] was a foreign-born young man of 25 with no past history of law [violation]. He had progressed only one-half year into high school and the record indicates that he had a history of emotional instability. [He had suffered a cerebral concussion, and was found unacceptable for military service primarily because of psychiatric disorder. He had also failed the Army's intelligence test.] [He] was subjected to questioning [from early evening into the night by many officials, including fifteen police officers, prosecutors, and others] for virtually eight straight hours before he confessed. [The] questioners persisted in the face of his repeated refusals to answer on the advice of his attorney, and they ignored his reasonable requests to contact [his retained attorney]. The

use of Bruno, [a police cadet and] "childhood friend" of [Spano's] is another factor which deserves mention [because] Bruno's was the one face visible to [Spano] in which he could put some trust. [The police officers] instructed Bruno falsely to state [that] his job was in jeopardy [unless Spano confessed], and that loss of his job would be disastrous to his three children, his wife and his unborn child. And Bruno played this part of a worried father, harried by his superiors, in not one, but four different acts, the final one lasting an hour. [Spano ultimately] yielded to his false friend's entreaties. We conclude that [Spano's] will was overborne by official pressure, fatigue and sympathy falsely aroused after considering all the [facts.]

2. *Inherent Coercion and the Search for Alternatives to Due Process.* By contrast with *Spano*, in *Stein v. New York*, 346 U.S. 156 (1953), the Court opined that some defendants might be especially resistant to police coercion, reasoning that, "What would be overpowering to the weak of will or mind might be utterly ineffective against an experienced criminal." But the *Stein* Court noted that the defendant's attributes were irrelevant in some cases, as where "physical violence or threat of [it] invalidates confessions [and] is universally condemned by law," so "there is no need to weigh or measure its effects on the will of the individual victim." Another decision based on the inherently coercive nature of an interrogation strategy is *Ashcraft v. Tennessee*, 322 U.S. 143 (1944), where the Court determined that 36 hours of "third degree" interrogation inevitably would produce an involuntary confession.

The "inherent coercion" approach appealed to those justices who were dissatisfied with the Due Process "totality" doctrine because it could not provide clear, predictable, and uniform guidelines as to the boundaries of acceptable police conduct during interrogations. Moreover, the difficulties of defining "voluntariness" were magnified, as one justice observed, because "the trial on the issue of coercion is seldom helpful," as police "usually testify one way, the accused another," and the secrecy of interrogations gives defendants "little chance to prove coercion at trial." *Crooker v. California*, 357 U.S. 433 (1958) (Douglas, J., dissenting). The creation of *per se* rules for interrogations offered the promise of clearer guidelines for police and greater protections from coercion for interrogated people. One such rule was proposed by those justices in *Spano* who endorsed a *per se* Due Process right for an indicted defendant who asks for counsel during interrogation to be allowed to consult with counsel. *See Spano*, 360 U.S. at 324 (Douglas, J., concurring, joined by Justices Black and Brennan).

Problems

1. *The Role of Rights in Due Process Analysis.* The *Haynes* Court emphasizes that the defendant was never "advised by authorities of his right to remain silent, warned that his answers might be used against him, or told of his rights respecting consultation with an attorney." What is the source of these "rights" and the relevance of the lack of "advice" about these rights to the Due Process analysis?

2. *The Juvenile and His Mother.* Robert Gallegos, a 14–year–old boy, is arrested for assault, and when the victim dies from his injuries, Gallegos

becomes a potential defendant in a homicide prosecution. During his detention in a juvenile jail facility, his mother attempts to visit him; she is told that she must either wait at least three more days until the next visiting day occurs on a Monday, or wait six more days and visit on the next Thursday. By the time she visits Gallegos as allowed on Thursday, he has signed a confession. He is detained incommunicado during this entire period. Before his confession, police tell Gallegos that he may ask to have his parents or an attorney present during the interrogation, but he does not make this request. Police also warn him that he does not have to make a statement and that he faces the possibility of a murder charge. His mother is informed by police that Gallegos has a right to counsel, but she does not obtain a lawyer for him before his confession occurs. Gallegos later testifies that he was not threatened by the police and not questioned for long periods of time. Do the circumstances of his interrogation violate Due Process? Argue the pros and cons. *See Gallegos v. Colorado*, 370 U.S. 49 (1962).

2.   *The McNabb–Mallory Rule*

During the post-*Brown* era, the Court supplemented Due Process doctrine with the *McNabb-Mallory* rule that applied only to federal courts. The Court repeatedly rejected the argument that this rule should be incorporated into Due Process doctrine and applied to the states, but some state courts chose to incorporate the rule into state law. The rule was legislatively superceded by Congress in Title II of the Omnibus Crime Control and Safe Streets Act of 1968. The holdings in the *McNabb* and *Mallory* cases rested on the Supreme Court's supervisory authority over the federal courts. In *McNabb v. United States*, 318 U.S. 332 (1943), the Court created an exclusionary rule to enforce the command of 18 U.S.C. § 595, which requires that a federal officer who arrests any person must "take the defendant before [the] nearest judicial officer having jurisdiction [for] a hearing, commitment, or taking bail for [trial]." The *McNabb* rule allowed courts to exclude confessions obtained in a suspicious context, where a federal officers delayed an arrestee's appearance in court so as to perform interrogation before counsel could be appointed. The *McNabb* Court acknowledged that, "Congress has not explicitly forbidden the use of evidence" procured in this way, but declared that the admission of such a confession "would stultify the policy" of that of § 595.

Similarly, in *Mallory v. United States*, 354 U.S. 449 (1957), the Court created an exclusionary rule to enforce the mandate of Rule 5(a) of the Federal Rules of Criminal Procedure, which requires arraignment of federal arrestees without "unnecessary delay." The *Mallory* Court reasoned that the purpose of this requirement was to insure that a person "may be advised of his rights" by a judicial officer "as quickly as possible" after arrest. Therefore, a court should invalidate a confession in a case such as *Mallory*, where the officers delayed arraignment for over four hours, used that time to procure a confession at police headquarters, and refrained from informing the arrestee "of his rights to counsel," his right "to a preliminary examination before a magistrate," his right "to keep silent," and his right to know that "any statement made by him may be used against him." The *McNabb-Mallory* rule expressed the Court's concern that arrestees could be interrogated while remaining ignorant of their rights, as long as information about those rights was communicated only by judges at a hearing that came too late for arrestees to learn of those rights and exercise them. In effect, the *McNabb-Mallory* doctrine was based on the assumption that the exclusion of some confessions would have a deterrent effect on police decisions to delay the access of arrestees to hearings and consultations with counsel.

3. The Sixth Amendment Right to Counsel at Interrogations

After the Sixth Amendment right to counsel was incorporated into Due Process and applied to the states in 1963, two different approaches for regulating police interrogations appeared the next year in two Sixth Amendment decisions. One approach called for a ban on the admission of confessions obtained from an indicted defendant by undercover government agents; the other allowed police officers to perform interrogations if they would supply some of the "cautions" to an arrestee in custody that otherwise would be supplied later by judges at a post-arrest hearing.

MASSIAH v. UNITED STATES

377 U.S. 201 (1964).

MR. JUSTICE STEWART delivered the opinion of the Court.

[Massiah] was indicted for violating the federal narcotics laws. He retained a lawyer, pleaded not guilty, and was released on bail. While he was free on bail a federal agent succeeded by surreptitious means in listening to incriminating statements made by him. [The agent listened to conversations with a co-defendant who had agreed to hide a radio transmitter under his car seat to broadcast the conversations to the agent. These statements were introduced at Massiah's trial for the narcotics crime, and he was convicted. He argued that his Sixth Amendment rights were violated by the agent's deliberate elicitation of his statements, after indictment and in the absence of his counsel.]

[Some justices opined in *Spano*] that a confession is inadmissible when it is deliberately elicited by the police after the defendant [has] been indicted, and therefore at a time when he [is] clearly entitled to a lawyer's help. [A] Constitution which guarantees a defendant the aid of counsel at [a public] trial could surely vouchsafe no less to an indicted defendant under interrogation by the police in a completely extrajudicial proceeding. Anything less [might] deny a defendant "effective representation by counsel at the only stage when legal aid and advice would help him." [Since *Spano*, the] New York courts [have] followed this rule: "Any secret interrogation of the defendant, from and after the finding of the indictment, without the protection afforded by the presence of counsel, contravenes the basic dictates of fairness in the conduct of criminal causes and the fundamental rights of person charged with crime." This view no more than reflects a constitutional principle established as long ago as *Powell v. Alabama,* 287 U.S. 45 (1932), where the Court noted that "[during] perhaps the most critical period of the proceedings [from] the time of their arraignment until the beginning of their trial, when consultation, thorough-going investigation and preparation [are] vitally important, the defendants [are] as much entitled to [the] aid [of counsel] during that period as at the trial itself." * * *

[We] hold that [Massiah] was denied the basic protections of [the Sixth Amendment] when there was used against him at his trial evidence of his own incriminating words, which federal agents had deliberately elicited from him after he had been indicted and in the absence of his counsel. It is true that in the *Spano* case the defendant was interrogated in a police station, while here the damaging testimony was elicited from the defendant without his knowledge while he was free on bail. [But] "if such a rule is to have any efficacy it must apply to indirect and surreptitious interrogations as well as those conducted in the jailhouse." [We] do not question that in this case [it] was entirely proper to continue an investigation of the suspected criminal activities of the defendant and his alleged confederates, even though the defendant had already been indicted. All that we hold is that the defendant's own incriminating statements [could] not constitutionally be used by the prosecution as evidence against him at his trial [on the narcotics charge].

Mr. Justice White, with whom Mr. Justice Clark and Mr. Justice Harlan join, dissenting.

[T]oday's rule promises to have wide application well beyond the facts of this case. The reason given for the result here [would] seem equally pertinent to statements obtained at any time after the right to counsel attaches, [at] least where the defendant has counsel or asks for [it]. [I] am unable to see how this case presents an unconstitutional interference with Massiah's right to counsel. Massiah was not prevented from consulting with counsel as often as he wished. No meetings with counsel were disturbed or spied upon. Preparation for trial was in no way obstructed. It is [unsound] to say that because Massiah had a right to counsel's aid before and during the trial, his out-of-court conversations and admissions must be excluded if obtained without counsel's consent or presence. [The] right to counsel has never meant as much [before]. [Had] there been no prior arrangements between [Massiah's co-defendant] and the police, [his] testimony [would] be readily admissible at [Massiah's trial]. But [because the co-defendant] had been cooperating with the police prior to his meeting with Massiah, [his] evidence [is] somehow transformed into inadmissible evidence despite the fact that the hazard to Massiah remains precisely the same—the defection of a confederate in crime.

Notes

1. *Temporary Extension of the Sixth Amendment to Pre–Indictment Arrestees.* The Court decided *Massiah* in an era before the right to counsel was limited to "critical stages" of a criminal prosecution that occur after the

initiation of "adversary judicial proceedings," such as an indictment or formal charge by a prosecutor, against a defendant,. See *Kirby v. Illinois*, 406 U.S. 682 (1972). Soon after *Massiah*, the Court extended *Massiah*'s Sixth Amendment protection to interrogated arrestees who are not yet indicted, but limited that protection in *Escobedo v. Illinois*, 378 U.S. 478 (1964), to circumstances where the investigation has "begun to focus on a particular suspect" who is "in custody," the police elicit incriminating statements during interrogation, the suspect "has requested and been denied an opportunity to consult with his lawyer," and the police have not "effectively warned" the suspect of "the right to remain silent." The *Escobedo* defendant met these criteria; even after his lawyer arrived at the police station, the lawyer was repeatedly refused access to his client, and Escobedo was repeatedly refused access to his lawyer, although they did come "into each other's view for a few moments."

The *Escobedo* Court reasoned that the right to counsel for indicted defendants was necessary both at trial and during the "completely extrajudicial proceeding" of police interrogation, and held that it "should make no difference" that the *Escobedo* defendant was not yet indicted. For the "right to use counsel at the formal trial" would be "a very hollow thing" if "for all practical purposes, the conviction is already assured" by pre-indictment interrogation of an arrestee. The Court noted that "[t]he fact that many confessions are obtained" during "the period between arrest and indictment" "points up its critical nature as a 'stage when legal aid and advice' are surely needed." The *Escobedo* Court acknowledged that the police need to use interrogations to investigate "an unsolved crime," but concluded that once the police "process shifts from investigatory to accusatory" so that the purpose of that process "is to elicit a confession," then the "adversary system begins to operate" for Sixth Amendment purposes. Therefore, the police failure to warn *Escobedo* of his right to remain silent during custodial interrogation, coupled with the police refusals to stop the interrogation after his requests to consult counsel, required the exclusion of Escobedo's statements at his trial on homicide charges not yet filed at the time of interrogation.

2. *Escobedo as a "Fifth Amendment" Precedent.* The elements of the *Escobedo* holding prefigure some elements of *Miranda's* holding two years later, but the Court allowed *Miranda's* Fifth Amendment doctrine to supplant *Escobedo's* Sixth Amendment holding by remaining silent as to *Escobedo's* implications. Six years after *Miranda*, *Escobedo's* extension of the Sixth Amendment counsel right to pre-indictment arrestees lost its legitimacy when the Court held that this right attached only after "adversary judicial proceedings" commenced. Later, instead of overruling *Escobedo*, the Court adopted the fiction in *Oregon v. Elstad*, 470 U.S. 298 (1985), that *Escobedo* was decided on Fifth Amendment grounds. By contrast, *Massiah's* Sixth Amendment foundation remained intact, as the *Massiah* facts and holding involved an indicted defendant. Moreover, *Massiah* was never displaced by *Miranda*. *Miranda* rights do not apply to people who are not in custody, or to people who are interrogated by undercover government agents. *Massiah* rights apply to people in both situations, as long as they are indicted or charged before interrogation. During the post-*Miranda* era, the *Massiah*

doctrine also came to provide some further protections, beyond those provided by *Miranda*, for indicted persons interrogated by police.

Problem

Massiah Rights at the Police Station. Assume that a defendant is indicted, but she is in police custody and is never released on bail. Does the defendant qualify for the Sixth Amendment right to counsel under *Massiah* when she is interrogated by the police while in custody? If so, explain the consequences that follow from the existence of this right, and the conditions under which the defendant may be interrogated by the police.

B.   THE FIFTH AMENDMENT AND *MIRANDA*

The Court's recognition of the shortcomings of Due Process doctrine led to the articulation of Fifth Amendment protections for interrogated persons in custody.

MIRANDA v. ARIZONA

384 U.S. 436 (1966).

Mr. Chief Justice Warren delivered the opinion of the Court.

I

[The question in these cases is whether the Fifth Amendment privilege "is fully applicable during a period of custodial interrogation."] More specifically, we deal with the admissibility of statements obtained from an individual who is subjected to custodial police interrogation and the necessity for procedures which assure that the individual is accorded his privilege under the Fifth Amendment [not] to be compelled to incriminate [himself or herself]. [The] modern practice of in-custody interrogation is psychologically rather than physically oriented. [Interrogation] still takes place in privacy. Privacy results in secrecy and this in turn results in a gap in our knowledge as to what in fact goes on in the interrogation rooms. A valuable source of information about present police practices, however, may be found in various police manuals and texts which document procedures employed with success in the [past]. These texts are used by law enforcement agencies themselves as guides.[1] [The] officers are told by the manuals that the "principal psychological factor contributing to a successful interrogation is privacy—being alone with the person under interrogation." The efficacy of this tactic has been explained as follows:

> "If at all practicable, the interrogation should take place in the investigator's office or at least in a room of his own choice. [In] his own home he may be confident, indignant, or recalcitrant. He is more keenly aware of his rights and more reluctant to tell of his

---

1.   [The Court cited Inbau & Reid, Criminal Interrogation and Confessions (1962), and O'Hara, Fundamentals of Criminal Investigation (1956), as having "extensive use among law enforcement agencies."]

indiscretions of criminal behavior within the walls of his home. Moreover his family and other friends are nearby, their presence lending moral support. In his office, the investigator possesses all the advantages. The atmosphere suggests the invincibility of the forces of the law."

[The] manuals instruct the police to display an air of confidence in the suspect's guilt and from outward appearance to maintain only an interest in confirming certain details. [The] interrogator should direct his comments toward the reasons why the subject committed the act, rather than court failure by asking the subject whether he did it. [The] officers are instructed to minimize the moral seriousness of the offense, to cast blame on the victim or on society. These tactics are designed to put the subject in a psychological state where his story is but an elaboration of what the police purport to know already—that he is guilty. Explanations to the contrary are dismissed and discouraged. The texts thus stress that the major qualities an interrogator should possess are patience and perseverance: "[The] investigator [will] encounter many situations where the sheer weight of his personality will be the deciding factor. Where emotional appeals and tricks are employed to no avail, he must rely on an oppressive atmosphere of dogged persistence. He must interrogate steadily and without relent, leaving the subject no prospect of surcease. He must dominate his subject and overwhelm him with his inexorable will to obtain the truth. He should interrogate for a spell of several hours pausing only for the subject's necessities in acknowledgment of the need to avoid a charge of duress that can be technically substantiated. In a serious case, the interrogation may continue for days, with the required intervals for food and sleep, but with no respite from the atmosphere of domination. It is possible in this way to induce the subject to talk without resorting to duress or [coercion]."

The manuals suggest that the suspect be offered legal excuses for his actions in order to obtain an initial admission of guilt. Where there is a suspected revenge-killing, for example, the interrogator may say: "Joe, you probably didn't go out looking for this fellow with the purpose of shooting him. My guess is, however, that you expected something from him and that's why you carried a gun—for your own protection. You knew him for what he was, no good. Then when you met him he probably started using foul, abusive language and he gave some indication that he was about to pull a gun on you, and that's when you had to act to save your own life. That's about it, isn't it, Joe?" Having then obtained the admission of shooting, the interrogator is advised to refer to circumstantial evidence which negates the self-defense explanation. This should enable him to secure the entire story. One text notes that "Even if he fails to do so, the inconsistency between the subject's original denial of the shooting and his present admission of at least doing the shooting will serve to deprive him of a self-defense 'out' at the time of trial."

When the techniques described above prove unavailing, the texts recommend they be alternated with a show of some hostility. One ploy often used has been termed the "friendly-unfriendly" or the "Mutt and

Jeff" act: "[In] this technique, two agents are employed. Mutt, the relentless investigator, who knows the subject is guilty and is not going to waste any time. He's sent a dozen men away for this crime and he's going to send the subject away for the full term. Jeff, on the other hand, is obviously a kindhearted man. [He] disapproves of Mutt and his tactics and will arrange to get him off the case if the subject will cooperate. He can't hold Mutt off for very long. The subject would be wise to make a quick decision. The technique is applied by having both investigators present while Mutt acts out his role. Jeff may stand by quietly and demur at some of Mutt's tactics. When Jeff makes his plea for cooperation, Mutt is not present in the room."

The interrogators sometimes are instructed to induce a confession out of trickery. [In] the identification situation, the interrogator may take a break in his questioning to place the subject among a group of men in a line-up. "The witness or complainant (previously coached, if necessary) studies the line-up and confidently points out the subject as the guilty party." Then the questioning resumes "as though there were now no doubt about the guilt of the subject." A variation on this technique is called the "reverse line-up": "The accused is placed in a line-up, but this time he is identified by several fictitious witnesses or victims who associated him with different offenses. It is expected that the subject will become desperate and confess to the offense under investigation in order to escape from the false accusations."

The manuals also contain instructions for police on how to handle the individual who refuses to discuss the matter entirely, or who asks for an attorney or relatives. The examiner is to concede him the right to remain silent. "This usually has a very undermining effect. First of all, he is disappointed in his expectation of an unfavorable reaction on the part of the interrogator. Secondly, a concession of this right to remain silent impresses the subject with the apparent fairness of his interrogator." After this psychological conditioning, however, the officer is told to point out the incriminating significance of the suspect's refusal to talk:

> "Joe, you have a right to remain silent. That's your privilege and I'm the last person in the world who'll try to take it away from you. If that's the way you want to leave this, O.K. But let me ask you this. Suppose you were in my shoes and I were in yours and you called me in to ask me about this and I told you, 'I don't want to answer any of your questions.' You'd think I had something to hide, and you'd probably be right in thinking that. That's exactly what I'll have to think about you, and so will everybody else. So let's sit here and talk this whole thing over."

Few will persist in their initial refusal to talk, it is said, if this monologue is employed correctly. In the event that the subject wishes to speak to a relative or an attorney, the following advice is tendered: "[T]he interrogator should respond by suggesting that the subject first tell the truth to the interrogator himself rather than get anyone else involved in the matter. If the request is for an attorney, the interrogator may suggest that the subject save himself or his family the expense of any such professional service, particularly if he is innocent of the offense under investigation. The interrogator may also add, 'Joe, I'm only looking for the truth, and if you're telling the truth, that's it. You can handle this by yourself.' "

From these representative samples of interrogation techniques, the setting prescribed by the manuals and observed in practice becomes clear. In essence, it is this: To be alone with the subject is essential to prevent distraction and to deprive him of any outside support. The aura of confidence in his guilt undermines his will to resist. [To] obtain a confession, the interrogator must "patiently maneuver himself or his quarry into a position from which the desired objective may be attained." When normal procedures fail to produce the needed result, the police may resort to deceptive stratagems such as giving false legal advice. It is important to keep the subject off balance, for example, by trading on his insecurity about himself or his surroundings. The police then persuade, trick, or cajole him out of exercising his constitutional rights. Even without employing brutality, the "third degree" or the specific stratagems described [here], the very fact of custodial interrogation exacts a heavy toll on individual liberty and trades on the weakness of individuals. * * *

In the [four] cases before us today, [we] concern ourselves primarily with this interrogation atmosphere and the evils it can bring. [In] these cases, we might not find the defendants' statements to have been involuntary in traditional terms. [However, in] each of the cases, the defendant was thrust into an unfamiliar atmosphere and run through menacing police interrogation procedures. [To] be sure, the records do not evince overt physical coercion or patent psychological ploys. The fact remains that in none of these cases did the officers undertake to afford appropriate safeguards at the outset of the interrogation to insure that the statements were truly the product of free choice.

It is obvious that such an interrogation environment is created for no purpose other than to subjugate the individual to the will of his examiner. This atmosphere carries its own badge of intimidation. To be sure, this is not physical intimidation, but it is equally destructive of human dignity. The current practice of incommunicado interrogation is at odds with one of our Nation's most cherished principles—that the individual may not be compelled to incriminate himself. Unless adequate protective devices are employed to dispel the compulsion inherent in custodial surroundings, no statement obtained from the defendant can truly be the product of his free choice. From the foregoing, we can readily perceive an intimate connection between the privilege against self-incrimination and police custodial questioning.

II

[T]he privilege against self-incrimination—the essential mainstay of our adversary system—is founded on a complex of values. All these policies point to one overriding thought: the constitutional foundation underlying the privilege is the respect a government—state or federal— must accord to the dignity and integrity of its citizens. To maintain a "fair state-individual balance," to require the government "to shoulder the entire load," to respect the inviolability of the human personality, our accusatory system of criminal justice demands that the government seeking to punish an individual produce the evidence against him by its own independent labors, rather than by the cruel, simple expedient of compelling it from his own mouth. In sum, the privilege is fulfilled only when the person is guaranteed the right "to remain silent unless he chooses to speak in the unfettered exercise of his own will." *Malloy v. Hogan*, 378 U.S. 1, 8 (1964).

[We] are satisfied that all the principles embodied in the privilege apply to informal compulsion exerted by law-enforcement officers during in-custody questioning. An individual swept from familiar surroundings into police custody, surrounded by antagonistic forces, and subjected to the techniques of persuasion described above cannot be otherwise than under compulsion to speak. As a practical matter, the compulsion to speak in the isolated setting of the police station may well be greater than in courts or other official investigations, where there are often impartial observers to guard against intimidation or trickery. * * *

III

[Today] there can be no doubt that the Fifth Amendment privilege is available outside of criminal court proceedings and serves to protect persons in all settings in which their freedom of action is curtailed in any significant way from being compelled to incriminate themselves. We have concluded that without proper safeguards the process of in-custody interrogation of persons suspected or accused of crime contains inherently compelling pressures which work to undermine the individual's will to resist and to compel him to speak where he would not otherwise do so freely. In order to combat these pressures and to permit a full opportunity to exercise the privilege against self-incrimination, the accused must be adequately and effectively apprised of his rights and the exercise of those rights must be fully honored. It is impossible for us to foresee the potential alternatives for protecting the privilege which might be devised by Congress or the States in the exercise of their creative rule-making [capacities]. Our decision in no way creates a constitutional straitjacket which will handicap sound efforts at reform, nor is it intended to have this effect. We encourage Congress and the States to continue their laudable search for increasingly effective ways of protecting the rights of the individual while promoting efficient enforcement of our criminal laws. However, unless we are shown other procedures which are at least as effective in apprising accused persons of their right of silence and in assuring a continuous opportunity to exercise it, the following safeguards must be observed.

[First, at] the outset, if a person in custody is to be subjected to interrogation, he must first be informed in clear and unequivocal terms that he has the right to remain silent. For those unaware of the privilege, the warning is needed simply to make them aware of it—the threshold requirement for an intelligent decision as to its exercise. More important, such a warning is an absolute prerequisite in overcoming the inherent pressures of the interrogation atmosphere. [Further], the warning will show the individual that his interrogators are prepared to recognize his privilege should he choose to exercise it. The Fifth Amendment privilege is so fundamental to our system of constitutional rule and the expedient of giving an adequate warning as to the availability of the privilege so simple, we will not pause to inquire in individual cases whether the defendant was aware of his rights without a warning being [given].

[Second, the] warning of the right to remain silent must be accompanied by the explanation that anything said can and will be used against the individual in court. This warning is needed in order to make him aware not only of the privilege, but also of the consequences of forgoing it. It is only through an awareness of these consequences that there can be any assurance of real understanding and intelligent exercise of the privilege. Moreover, this warning may serve to make the individual more acutely aware that he is faced with a phase of the adversary system—that he is not in the presence of persons acting solely in his interest.

[Third, the] right to have counsel present at the interrogation is indispensable to the protection of the Fifth Amendment privilege under the system we delineate today. [A] once-stated warning, delivered by those who will conduct the interrogation, cannot itself suffice to that end among those who most require knowledge of their rights. [Even] preliminary advice given to the accused by his own attorney can be swiftly overcome by the secret interrogation process. Thus, the need for counsel to protect the Fifth Amendment privilege comprehends not merely a right to consult with counsel prior to questioning, but also to have counsel present during any questioning if the defendant so desires. [An] individual need not make a pre-interrogation request for a lawyer. While such request affirmatively secures his right to have one, his failure to ask for a lawyer does not constitute a waiver. No effective waiver of the right to counsel during interrogation can be recognized unless specifically made after the warnings we here delineate have been given. The accused who does not know his rights and therefore does not make a request may be the person who most needs [counsel]. Accordingly we hold that an individual held for interrogation must be clearly informed that he has the right to consult with a lawyer and to have the lawyer with him during interrogation under the system for protecting the privilege we delineate today. As with the warnings of the right to remain silent and that anything stated can be used in evidence against him, this warning is an absolute prerequisite to [interrogation].

[Fourth, if] an individual indicates that he wishes the assistance of counsel before any interrogation occurs, the authorities cannot rationally ignore [his] request on the basis that the individual does not have or cannot afford a retained attorney. [The] privilege against self-incrimination secured by the Constitution applies to all individuals. The need for counsel in order to protect the privilege exists for the indigent as well as the [affluent]. [The] vast majority of confession cases with which we have dealt [involve] those unable to retain [counsel]. [Therefore], it is necessary to warn [an interrogated person] that if he is indigent a lawyer will be appointed to represent him. Without this additional warning, the admonition of the right to consult with counsel would often be understood as meaning only that he can consult with a lawyer if he has one or has the funds to obtain one. The warning of a right to counsel would be hollow if not couched in terms that would convey to the indigent [the] knowledge that he too has a right to have counsel present. As with the warnings of the right to remain silent and of the general right to counsel, only by effective and express explanation to the indigent of this right can there be assurance that he was truly in a position to exercise it.

[Fifth, once] warnings have been given, the subsequent procedure is clear. If the individual indicates in any manner, at any time prior to or during questioning, that he wishes to remain silent, the interrogation must cease. At this point he has shown that he intends to exercise his Fifth Amendment privilege; any statement taken after the person invokes his privilege cannot be other than the product of compulsion, subtle or otherwise. Without the right to cut off questioning, the setting of in-custody interrogation operates on the individual to overcome free choice in producing a statement after the privilege has been once invoked. If the individual states that he wants an attorney, the interrogation must cease until an attorney is present. At that time, the individual must have an opportunity to confer with the attorney and to have him present during any subsequent questioning. If the individual cannot obtain an attorney and he indicates that he wants one before speaking to police, they must respect his decision to remain silent. This does not mean, as some have suggested, that each police station must have a "station house lawyer" present at all times to advise prisoners. It does mean, however, that if police [authorities] conclude that they will not provide counsel during a reasonable period of time in which investigation in the field is carried out, they may refrain from doing so without violating the person's Fifth Amendment privilege so long as they do not question him during that time.

[Sixth, if] the interrogation continues without the presence of an attorney and a statement is taken, a heavy burden rests on the government to demonstrate that the defendant knowingly and intelligently waived his privilege against self-incrimination and his right to retained or appointed counsel. [An] express statement that the individual is willing to make a statement and does not want an attorney followed closely by a statement could constitute a waiver. But a valid waiver will not be presumed simply from the silence of the accused after warnings are given or simply from the fact that a confession was in fact eventually obtained. [The] fact of lengthy interrogation or incommunicado incarceration before a statement is made is strong evidence that the accused did not validly waive his rights [because] the fact that the individual eventually made a statement is consistent with the conclusion that the compelling influence of the interrogation finally forced him to do so. [Moreover], any evidence that the accused was threatened, tricked, or cajoled into a waiver will, of course, show that the defendant did not voluntarily waive his [privilege].

[Finally, no] distinction can be drawn between statements which are direct confessions and statements which amount to "admissions" of part or all of an offense. The privilege against self-incrimination [does] not distinguish degrees of incrimination. Similarly, [no] distinction may be drawn between inculpatory statements and statements alleged to be merely "exculpatory." If a statement made were in fact truly exculpatory it would, of course, never be used by the [prosecution]. [When] an individual is in custody on probable cause, the police may, of course, seek out evidence in the field to be used at trial against him. Such investigation may include inquiry of persons not under restraint. General on-the-scene questioning as to facts surrounding a crime or other general questioning of citizens in the fact-finding process is not affected by our [holding].

To summarize, we hold that when an individual is taken into custody or otherwise deprived of his freedom by the authorities in any significant way and is subjected to questioning, the privilege against self-incrimination is jeopardized. Procedural safeguards must be employed to protect the privilege and [in the absence of other fully effective measures, the] following measures are required. He must be warned prior to any questioning that he has the right to remain silent, that anything he says can be used against him in a court of law, that he has the right to the presence of an attorney, and that if he cannot afford an attorney one will be appointed for him prior to any questioning if he so desires. Opportunity to exercise these rights must be afforded to him throughout the interrogation. After such warnings have been given, and such opportunity afforded him, the individual may knowingly and intelligently waive these rights and agree to answer questions or make a statement. But unless and until such warnings and waiver are demonstrated by the prosecution at trial, no evidence obtained as a result of interrogation can be used against him.

IV

A recurrent argument made in these cases is that society's need for interrogation outweighs the [privilege]. [But] the Constitution has prescribed the rights of the individual [when] it provided in the Fifth Amendment that an individual cannot be compelled to be a witness against himself. That right cannot be [abridged].[O]ur decision does not in any way preclude police from carrying out their traditional investigatory functions. Although confessions may play an important role in some convictions, the cases before us present graphic examples of the overstatement of the "need" for confessions [because even after police officers obtained "considerable" independent evidence against each defendant, they still conducted interrogations].

It is also urged that an unfettered right to detention for interrogation should be allowed because it will often redound to the benefit of the person questioned. [But the] person who has committed no offense [will] be better able to clear himself after warnings with counsel present than without. [Moreover, custodial] interrogation, [does] not necessarily afford the innocent an opportunity to clear themselves. [A] serious consequence of the present practice [is] that many arrests "for investigation" subject large numbers of innocent persons to detention and interrogation. [In one case here,] police held four persons [in] jail for five days until one defendant [confessed,] although [the police] stated [later] that there was "no evidence to connect them with any crime." * * *

Over the years the Federal Bureau of Investigation has compiled an exemplary record of effective law enforcement while advising any suspect or arrested person, at the outset of an interview, that he is not required to make a statement, that any statement may be used against him in court, that the individual may obtain the services of an attorney of his own choice and, more recently, that he has a right to free counsel if he is unable to pay. [The] practice of the FBI can readily be emulated by state and local enforcement [agencies]. * * *

[Judicial] solutions to problems of constitutional dimension have evolved decade by decade. As courts have been presented with the need to enforce constitutional rights, they have found means of doing so. [Where] rights secured by the Constitution are involved, there can be no rule making or legislation which would abrogate them.

Mr. Justice Clark, dissenting in [three cases] and concurring in the result in [one case].

[I] would continue to follow [the Due Process] rule. [I] would consider in each case whether the police officer prior to custodial interrogation added the warning that the suspect might have counsel present at the interrogation and, further, [the warning] that a court would appoint one at his request if he was too poor to employ counsel. In the absence of warnings, the burden would be on the State to prove that counsel was knowingly and intelligently waived or that in the totality of the circumstances, including the failure to give the necessary warnings, the confession was clearly voluntary.

Mr. Justice Harlan, whom Mr. Justice Stewart and Mr. Justice White join, dissenting.

[The] new rules are not designed to guard against police brutality or other unmistakably banned forms of coercion. Those who use third-degree tactics and deny them in court are equally able and destined to lie as skillfully about warnings and waivers. Rather, the thrust of the new rules is to negate all pressures, to reinforce the nervous or ignorant suspect, and ultimately to discourage any confession at [all]. [What] the Court largely ignores is that its rules impair, if they will not eventually serve wholly to frustrate, an instrument of law enforcement that has long and quite reasonably been thought worth the price paid for it. There can be little doubt that the Court's new code would markedly decrease the number of confessions. To warn the suspect that he may remain silent and remind him that his confession may be used in court are minor obstructions. To require also an express waiver by the suspect and an end to questioning whenever he demurs must heavily handicap questioning. And to suggest or provide counsel for the suspect simply invites the end of the interrogation.

[How] much harm this decision will inflict on law enforcement cannot fairly be predicted with accuracy. [We] do know that some crimes cannot be solved without confessions, that ample expert testimony attests to their importance in crime control, and that the Court is taking a real risk with society's welfare in imposing its new regime on the country. The social costs of crime are too great to call the new rules anything but a hazardous experimentation. While passing over the costs and risks of its experiment, the Court portrays the evils of normal police questioning [in] exaggerated [terms]. [I]nterrogation is no doubt often inconvenient and unpleasant for the suspect. However, it is no less so for a man to be arrested and jailed, to have his house searched, or to stand trial in court, yet all this may properly happen to the most innocent given probable cause, a warrant, or an indictment. Society has always paid a stiff price for law and order, and peaceful interrogation is not one of the dark moments of the law. * * *

MR. JUSTICE WHITE, with whom MR. JUSTICE HARLAN and MR. JUSTICE STEWART join, dissenting.

[Even] if one were to postulate that the Court's concern is [that some] confessions are coerced and present judicial procedures are believed to be inadequate to identify the confessions that are coerced and those that are not, it would still not be essential to impose the rule that the Court has now fashioned. Transcripts or observers could be required, specific time limits, tailored to fit the cause, could be imposed, or other devices could be utilized to reduce the chances that otherwise indiscernible coercion will produce an inadmissible confession. [By] considering any answers to any interrogation to be compelled [and] by escalating the requirements to prove waiver, the [Court,] for all practical [purposes,] forbids interrogation except in the presence of counsel. [I]nstead of confining itself to protection of the right against compelled self-incrimination the Court has created a limited Fifth Amendment right to counsel—or, as the Court expresses it, a "need for counsel to protect the Fifth Amendment privilege." * * *

[There] is, in my view, every reason to believe that a good many criminal defendants who otherwise would have been convicted [will] now under this new version of the Fifth Amendment, either not be tried at all or will be acquitted if the State's evidence, minus the confession, is put to the test of [litigation]. [Furthermore,] today's decision leaves open such questions as whether the accused was in custody, whether his statements were spontaneous or the product of interrogation, [and] whether the accused has effectively waived his rights, [all] of which are certain to prove productive of uncertainty during investigation and litigation during prosecution. * * *

Notes

1. *The Concept of "Safeguards."* Prior to *Miranda*, the Court sometimes referred to certain trial rights and procedures as "safeguards" that protect the right to a fair trial. For example, the Court described its judge-made exclusionary rule in *Brown* as one of the "procedural safeguards of due process" for the pre-trial stage of a criminal prosecution. *Chambers v. Florida*, 309 U.S. 227, 238 (1940). Later the Court identified the theory underlying Due Process doctrine as "a compound of two influences": first, the idea that the right to a fair trial with "procedural safeguards" should be viewed as an antidote to inquisitorial procedures like police interrogation, and second, the idea that the Fourteenth Amendment prohibition on coercion and the Fifth Amendment prohibition on compulsion are linked together. *Gallegos v. Colorado*, 370 U.S. 49, 55 (1962). The *Miranda* Court continued to use the Due Process metaphor of "safeguards" in fashioning new methods for effectuating the Fifth Amendment privilege, and subsequent decisions reveal differing perspectives concerning the consequences of the labeling of *Miranda's* requirements as "prophylactic safeguards." *Compare Withrow v. Williams*, 507 U.S. 680 (1993) ("[p]rophylactic" though it may be, in protecting a defendant's Fifth Amendment privilege against self-incrimination *Miranda* safeguards "a fundamental trial right") with *United States v. Patane*, 542 U.S. 630 (2004) (plurality opinion) (*Miranda's* "prophylactic rules" necessarily "sweep beyond the actual protections of the Self-Incrimination Clause").

2. *Can Congress Overrule Miranda?* In 1968 Congress enacted 18 U.S.C. § 3501 which provided that confessions are admissible in federal courts if they are voluntarily given. In *Dickerson v. United States*, 530 U.S. 428 (2000), the Court held that § 3501 is unconstitutional. The Court noted that the *Miranda* opinion "is replete with statements indicating that the majority thought it was announcing a constitutional rule," and concluded that, "Congress may not legislatively supersede our decisions interpreting and applying the Constitution." However, the *Dickerson* Court declined to hold that "the *Miranda* warnings are required by the Constitution, in the sense that nothing else will suffice to satisfy constitutional requirements." Instead, the Court found that, "[We] need not go farther than *Miranda*" to find that the *Miranda* decision was based on the assumption that "something more than the [Due Process] totality test was necessary" to prevent involuntary custodial confessions. Therefore, the totality test of § 3501 "cannot be sustained if *Miranda* is to remain the law." The *Dickerson* Court found no justification for overruling *Miranda* because the decision "has become embedded in routine police practice to the point where the warnings have become part of our national culture" and because principles of *stare decisis* "weigh heavily against overruling it."

3. *Miranda Violations and Civil Damage Actions.* In *Chavez v. Martinez*, 538 U.S. 760 (2003), Martinez alleged that he was coercively interroga-

ted in violation of *Miranda*. Since he was never prosecuted, he could not seek the suppression of his statements at trial; instead, he brought a civil suit under 42 U.S.C. § 1983 and claimed that the officer's actions violated his Fifth Amendment privilege, as well as his Due Process right to be free from coercive questioning. The Chavez Court concluded that Martinez could not establish a violation of his Fifth Amendment rights because the privilege only prevents a defendant from being "compelled in any criminal case to be a witness against himself." This right could not have been violated since "Martinez was never prosecuted for a [crime]."

4. *Miranda and Habeas Review*. In *Withrow v. Williams*, 507 U.S. 680 (1993), the Court held that even when a defendant has received a "full and fair chance to litigate" a *Miranda* claim in state court, the doctrine of *Stone v. Powell*, 428 U.S. 465 (1976), does not bar habeas review of that claim. However, *Miranda* habeas claims are subject to the requirements of the Antiterrorism and Effective Death Penalty Act of 1996 (AEDPA), so that a defendant must show that the state-court ruling on the *Miranda* claim "was contrary to, or involved an unreasonable application of, clearly established" federal law as determined by the Supreme Court precedents under 28 U.S.C. § 2254(d)(1).

Problems

1. *Miranda and the Interrogation Manuals*. Consider the *Miranda* Court's use of police interrogation manuals to support its reasoning. The Court did not find that any of the techniques in those manuals were used in any of the four cases under review. Explain how the manuals were relevant to *Miranda's* reasoning, and the role that the Court's analysis of the manuals could play in later *Miranda* litigation.

2. *Alternatives to Miranda*. Consider Justice White's proposal in his dissent that specific alternatives, such as transcripts or observers, could serve as substitutes for the *Miranda* remedies; consider also the A.C.L.U. proposal in its amicus brief, advocating that only "the presence of counsel in custodial interrogation" would provide adequate protection for a person's Fifth Amendment privilege. Explain the pros and cons of each of these proposals, as compared to the remedies provided in *Miranda*.

3. *Explaining and Understanding Miranda*. If the custodial interrogation environment is inherently coercive, then arguably a waiver cannot be valid because it is infected with the same inherent coercion that is present during all incommunicado communications in custody, according to Justice White's dissent in *Miranda*. Explain how the *Miranda* majority might defend its waiver requirement in response to Justice White's criticism, and explain Justice White's implied preferences concerning the solutions for inherent coercion.

C. *MIRANDA'S* APPLICATION

In extending the privilege against self-incrimination to custodial interrogations, *Miranda* raised a host of questions regarding the scope of its requirements, and years of litigation produced many precedents defining such terms as "custody," "interrogation," adequate warnings,"

"voluntary, knowing and intelligent" waiver, "unambiguous invocations" of the rights to silence and counsel, and post-invocation "initiation" that nullifies an invocation.

1. Custody

The duty to give *Miranda* warnings arises only when police interrogate a person who is in custody. The concepts of "custody" and "interrogation" are distinct and must coexist during "custodial interrogation" in
order to give rise to *Miranda* rights and duties. In *Thompson v. Keohane*,
516 U.S. 99 (1995), the Court summarized the custody inquiry as
follows:

> Two discrete inquiries are essential to the determination: first, what
> were the circumstances surrounding the interrogation; and second,
> given those circumstances, would a reasonable person have felt he or
> she was not at liberty to terminate the interrogation and leave. Once
> the scene is set and the players' lines and actions are reconstructed,
> the court must apply an objective test to resolve the ultimate
> inquiry: was there a formal arrest or restraint on freedom of
> movement of the degree associated with a formal arrest.

STANSBURY v. CALIFORNIA
511 U.S. 318 (1994).

PER CURIAM.

[Our] decisions make clear that the initial determination of custody
depends on the objective circumstances of the interrogation, not on the
subjective views harbored by either the interrogating officers or the
person being questioned. In *Beckwith v. United States*, 425 U.S. 341
(1976), for example, the defendant, without being advised of his *Miranda*
rights, made incriminating statements to Government agents during an
interview in a private home. He later asked that *Miranda* "be extended
to cover interrogation in non-custodial circumstances after a police
investigation has focused on the suspect." We found his argument
unpersuasive, explaining that it "was the compulsive aspect of custodial
interrogation, and not the strength or content of the government's
suspicions at the time the questioning was conducted, which led the
Court to impose the *Miranda* requirements with regard to custodial
questioning."

[In] *Berkemer v. McCarty*, 468 U.S. 420 (1984), [the Court] reaffirmed the conclusions reached in *Beckwith*. *Berkemer* concerned the roadside questioning of a motorist detained in a traffic stop. We decided that
the motorist was not in custody for purposes of *Miranda* even though
the traffic officer "apparently decided as soon as [the motorist] stepped
out of his car that [the motorist] would be taken into custody and
charged with a traffic offense." The reason [was] that the officer "never
communicated his intention to" the motorist during the relevant ques-

tioning. [U]nder *Miranda* "[a] policeman's unarticulated plan has no bearing on the question whether a suspect was 'in custody' at a particular time"; rather, "the only relevant inquiry is how a reasonable man in the suspect's shoes would have understood his situation."

It is well settled, then, that a police officer's subjective view that the individual under questioning is a suspect, if undisclosed, does not bear upon the question whether the individual is in custody for purposes of *Miranda*. The same principle obtains if an officer's undisclosed assessment is that the person being questioned is not a suspect. In either instance, one cannot expect the person under interrogation to probe the officer's innermost thoughts. Save as they are communicated or otherwise manifested to the person being questioned, an officer's evolving but unarticulated suspicions do not affect the objective circumstances of an interrogation or interview, and thus cannot affect the *Miranda* custody [inquiry]. An officer's knowledge or beliefs may bear upon the custody issue if they are conveyed, by word or deed, to the individual being questioned. Those beliefs are relevant only to the extent they would affect how a reasonable person in the position of the individual being questioned would gauge the breadth of his or her " 'freedom of action.' " Even a clear statement from an officer that the person under interrogation is a prime suspect is not, in itself, dispositive of the custody issue, for some suspects are free to come and go until the police decide to make an arrest. The weight and pertinence of any communications regarding the officer's degree of suspicion will depend upon the facts and circumstances of the particular case. [The Court remanded the case for the state supreme to resolve the custody issue in light of the standard articulated in its opinion.]

Notes

1. *Relevance of Defendant's Personal Characteristics and Experiences.* The *Stansbury* Court refers to the perspective of the "reasonable person in the suspect's shoes." In *Yarborough v. Alvarado*, 541 U.S. 652 (2004), the Court explained that the "objective" aspect of the "reasonable person" standard is meant to further the clarity of the custody test, so that the police officers do not have "to make guesses" about a person's subjective experiences before deciding how they may interrogate a person. The Court acknowledged that "the line between permissible objective facts and impermissible subjective experiences can be indistinct in some cases." However, the Court held that a person's "prior history with law enforcement" is irrelevant to the custody inquiry, reasoning as follows:

> In most cases, police officers will not know a suspect's interrogation history. Even if they do, the relationship between a suspect's past experiences and the likelihood a reasonable person with that experience would feel free to leave often will be speculative. True, suspects with prior law enforcement experience may understand police procedures and reasonably feel free to leave unless told otherwise. On the other hand, they may view past as prologue and expect another in a string of arrests. We do not ask police officers to consider these contingent psychological

factors when deciding when suspects should be advised of their *Miranda* rights. The inquiry turns too much on the suspect's subjective state of mind and not enough on the "objective circumstances of the interrogation."

Regarding the personal characteristic of age, the *Yarborough* Court held that it was not unreasonable for a reviewing court to ignore the seventeen-year-old defendant's youth in reaching a finding of no custody. Justice Breyer's dissent took a contrary position, and was joined by Justices Souter, Stevens, and Ginsburg. Breyer argued that age is "an objective circumstance known to the police" that must be relevant to the custody inquiry because it "is not a special quality, but rather a widely shared characteristic that generates commonsense conclusions about behavior and perception." The *Yarborough* dissenters viewed age as a factor that supported a finding of custody on the facts, because the defendant's youth made it more likely that he could not ignore his parents' request to comply with the police request for him to come to the station. The dissenters also thought his youth made him more likely to defer to police authority, which was invoked to exclude his parents from his interrogation. Although she supported the Court's holding on the facts, Justice O'Connor's concurring opinion acknowledged that, "there may be cases in which a suspect's age will be relevant to the *Miranda* 'custody' inquiry."

2. *No Miranda Warning during Routine Traffic Stop.* The *Stansbury* Court relied on *Berkemer* in rejecting a finding of custody. In *Berkemer*, the Court found that routine traffic stops do not create "custody," and reasoned as follows:

> Two features of an ordinary traffic stop mitigate the danger that a person questioned will be induced "to speak where he would not otherwise do so freely." First, detention of a motorist pursuant to a traffic stop is presumptively temporary and brief. [A] motorist's expectations [are] that he will be obliged to spend a short period of time answering questions and waiting while the officer checks his license and registration, that he may then be given a citation, but that in the end he most likely will be allowed to continue on his way. In this respect, questioning incident to an ordinary traffic stop is quite different from station house interrogation, which frequently is prolonged, and in which the detainee often is aware that questioning will continue until he provides his interrogators the answers they seek. Second, circumstances associated with the typical traffic stop are not such that the motorist feels completely at the mercy of the police. To be sure, the aura of authority surrounding an armed, uniformed officer and the knowledge that the officer has some discretion in deciding whether to issue a citation, in combination, exert some pressure on the detainee to respond to questions. But [the] typical traffic stop is public, at least to some degree. [This] exposure to public view both reduces the ability of an unscrupulous policeman to use illegitimate means to elicit self-incriminating statements and diminishes the motorist's fear that, if he does not cooperate, he will be subjected to abuse. The fact that the detained motorist typically is confronted by only one or at most two [officers] further mutes his sense of vulnerability. In short, the atmosphere surrounding an ordinary traffic stop is substantially less "police domi-

nated" than that surrounding the kinds of interrogation at issue in *Miranda* itself, and in the subsequent cases in which we have applied *Miranda*.

3. *The Non-custodial Interview.* In *Mathiason*, the Court found that a station house interrogation might not be regarded as custodial if it is the equivalent of a voluntary interview:

> [T]here is no indication that the questioning took place in a context where [Mathiason's] freedom to depart was restricted in any way. He came voluntarily to the police station, where he was immediately informed that he was not under arrest. At the close of a 1/2–hour interview [Mathiason] did in fact leave the police station without hindrance. It is clear from these facts that Mathiason was not in [custody]. [A] noncustodial situation is not converted to [one] simply because a reviewing court concludes that, even in the absence of any formal arrest or restraint on freedom of movement, the questioning took place in a "coercive environment." Any interview of one suspected of a crime by a police officer will have coercive aspects to [it]. But the requirement of warnings [is not] to be imposed simply because the questioning takes place in the station house, or because the questioned person is one whom the police suspect. [The lower court found that the] officer's false statement about having discovered Mathiason's fingerprints at the scene was [another] circumstance contributing to the coercive environment. [Whatever] relevance this fact may have to other issues in the case, it has nothing to do with whether [Mathiason] was in custody for purposes of the *Miranda* rule.

Justice Marshall dissented in *Mathiason*, arguing that *Miranda* "requires us to distinguish situations that resemble the "coercive aspects" of custodial interrogation from those that more nearly resemble "[g]eneral on-the-scene questioning [or] other general questioning of citizens in the fact-finding process." He concluded that since Mathiason was interrogated in "private" and in "unfamiliar surroundings," and was subject to "deceptive stratagems" condemned in *Miranda*, he was in custody during the interview and should have received *Miranda* warnings. Justice Stevens also dissented on the ground that a parolee like Mathiason "should always be warned" during a police interview because "parolee is technically in legal custody continuously until his sentence has been served."

Problems

1. *When a Seizure Creates "Custody."* A Fourth Amendment "seizure" occurs when an individual is subjected to either an investigative stop or a custodial arrest. Assume that a motorist dutifully stops at a police roadblock set up to catch drunk drivers. Has the motorist been "seized" within the meaning of the Fourth Amendment? Does the seizure rise to the level of "custody" for purposes of the Fifth Amendment?

2. *Restraint of Freedom of Movement.* Police officers Pam and Sue observe a car parked at a street corner with its engine running, and they notice that the man in the driver's seat passes something through the open window to a woman on the sidewalk. Pam recognizes the woman as someone

who has been arrested in the past for drug crimes. The officers watch the woman open the front passenger door and get into the car. Then the driver moves the vehicle around the corner into a dark alley. Pam and Sue approach unnoticed from behind the car, tiptoe around to the front of the car, and shine their flashlights through the windshield, with Pam standing near the driver's door and Sue standing near the passenger door. The car occupants are startled, and Pam and Sue observe that the driver is holding a small box. The driver exits the car quickly, identifies himself to Pam as Hugh Robinson, and asks her, "So, what is going on?" Pam says, "We're wondering the same thing, Mr. Robinson. This is a very dark alley. Are you having any car problems?" Hugh replies, "No, officer, everything is fine." While this conversation is going on, Sue talks quietly to the woman passenger in the front seat of the car. Hugh looks over at Sue, and then he asks Pam, "Am I under arrest?" Pam replies, "It all depends on what my partner decides." At this point, Hugh takes his cell phone out of his pocket, and starts to make a call. Pam puts her hand on the phone and says, "I'm sorry, but the call will have to wait." About thirty seconds later, Sue walks over to where Pam and Hugh are standing, and Sue says to Pam, "It's what we thought. He paid in advance. So we've got probable cause. The question is, should we leave the car here?" Hugh interrupts Sue and declares sheepishly, "Look, I've got some marijuana in my glove compartment, but it's only a small amount, so I hope you'll let it go this time." Pam says, "No, and you are under arrest." Assume that Hugh is arrested and that the prosecutor wants to introduce his statement about the marijuana at his trial for the crime of drug possession. Hugh's defense counsel argues that the statement about marijuana is inadmissible because the police failed to give *Miranda* warnings to Hugh when he was in custody before he made the statement. First, explain the arguments that will be made on both sides concerning the existence of "custody." Second, assuming that custody existed, explain how can the defense counsel argue that the statement about marijuana occurred after custodial "interrogation."

3. *Unreasonable Beliefs.* In its custody precedents the Court assumes that *Miranda* does not apply when a suspect honestly, but unreasonably, believes that he is in police custody during an interview or an interrogation. Is this result consistent with *Miranda*?

4. *Freedom to Leave an Interview.* In *Stansbury*, four police officers went to the defendant's home near midnight, and asked him to accompany them to the police station for questioning as a possible witness in a homicide case. They offered him the choice of riding in the patrol car or driving himself to the station. Stansbury accepted the ride. At the station, he had to pass through a locked parking structure and a locked jail entrance, in order to reach the jail area where he was questioned in an interview room. He was not restrained in the interview room, but he would have needed assistance to leave the facility because of the security. The interviewing officer told Stansbury that he wanted to question him as a possible witness. Then the officer asked Stansbury about his movements the previous day, and their discussion lasted about 20 to 30 minutes. The discussion was terminated and Stansbury was given *Miranda* warnings as soon as he described his use of a turquoise car that matched the description of a car observed at the scene of the homicide. Stansbury's pre-warning statements were admitted at his

murder trial. What arguments would be made by both sides as to whether Stansbury was in custody before the warnings were given? *See People v. Stansbury*, 9 Cal.4th 824, 38 Cal.Rptr.2d 394, 889 P.2d 588 (Ca.1995).

5. *The Two–Hour Interview.* In *Yarborough*, Alvarado's parents were informed that the police wanted to talk to their seventeen-year-old son, so they brought him to the police station for an interview. The police refuse to allow the parents to be present for the interview, telling them, "we are going to question a suspect." Police officials initially tell Alvarado and his parents that the interview is "not going to be long," and do not say that Alvarado is (or is not) under arrest. The detective questions Alvarado alone in an interview room without *Miranda* warnings, and when Alvarado denies knowledge about an attempted carjacking and related homicide, the detective tells him that, "we have witnesses that are saying quite the opposite," that "the very best thing is to be honest," and that "all I'm simply doing is giving you the opportunity to tell the truth." As Alvarado slowly changes his story and makes incriminating statements, the detective continues to appeal to his "sense of honesty," and "the need to bring the man who killed the victim to justice." Toward the end of the two hour interrogation, the detective twice gives Alvarado permission to take a break, but Alvarado declines. The police allow Alvarado to go home when the interview ends, but arrest and charge him a few weeks later. What arguments could be made by both sides as to whether Alvarado was in "custody" when his statements were obtained without *Miranda* warnings? *See Yarborough v. Alvarado*, 541 U.S. 652 (2004).

6. *The Barricaded Suspect.* Police officers have probable cause to believe that Mack shot and wounded his wife and daughter, and obtain a warrant for his arrest. Mack barricades himself in a motel room with hostages and high-powered weapons. The agents surround Mack's room. When Mack does not respond to police requests to give himself up, which are communicated to him via bullhorn, the police bring in an FBI hostage negotiator who calls Mack on the phone. For three and one-half hours, the FBI agent converses with Mack without giving him *Miranda* warnings. At Mack's trial, the prosecution seeks to introduce Mack's statements at his trial for assault. Was Mack in "custody" during the hostage negotiation? *See United States v. Mesa*, 638 F.2d 582 (3d Cir.1980).

7. *Border Encounters.* After a chase, border patrol agents detain several men on suspicion of being illegal immigrants. The detention takes place at a remote location just inside the U. S. border, and the men are ordered to sit in a circle with other detainees. Are the men in "custody" so that a *Miranda* warning is required? How would you argue the case for the detainees? How might the prosecution respond? *See United States v. Galindo–Gallegos*, 244 F.3d 728 (9th Cir.2001).

2. *Interrogation*

Police may violate a *Miranda* by impermissible "interrogation" in three contexts. First, they may interrogate a person in custody without giving *Miranda* warnings; second, they may interrogate improperly after warnings without obtaining a valid waiver of rights; third, they may violate the duty to cut off questioning and interrogate in violation of

Miranda after the person in custody invokes the right to remain silent, the right to counsel, or both. The same standard is used to define the concept of "interrogation" in each of these contexts.

RHODE ISLAND v. INNIS

446 U.S. 291 (1980).

MR. JUSTICE STEWART delivered the opinion of the Court.

[A taxi driver was robbed shortly after midnight by a man with a sawed-off shotgun; the driver identified Innis as the robber from a photo array, and reported that he had dropped Innis off in the Mount Pleasant section of Providence. Five days earlier, another Providence taxi driver had been killed by a man with a shotgun. Around 4:30 a.m., Patrolman Lovell was cruising in a patrol car when he spotted Innis standing in the street. Lovell arrested Innis, who was unarmed, and advised him of his *Miranda* rights. Lovell and Innis waited in the patrol car and Lovell did not converse with Innis. A sergeant soon arrived and read Innis the *Miranda* warnings; minutes later Captain Leyden arrived with other officers and advised Innis again of his *Miranda* rights.] [Innis] stated that he understood those rights and wanted to speak with a lawyer. Captain Leyden then directed that [Innis should] be placed in a "caged wagon," a four-door police car with a wire screen mesh between the front and rear seats, and be driven to the central police station. Three officers [were] assigned to accompany [Innis] to the [police station]. Captain Leyden then instructed the officers not to question [Innis] or intimidate or coerce him in any [way].

[While] en route to the central station, Patrolman Gleckman initiated a conversation with Patrolman McKenna concerning the missing shotgun. [Gleckman later testified :] "At this point, I was talking back and forth with Patrolman McKenna stating that I frequent this area while on patrol and [that because a school for handicapped children is located nearby,] there's a lot of handicapped children running around in this area, and God forbid one of them might find a weapon with shells and they might hurt themselves." Patrolman McKenna [testified:] "I more or less concurred with [Gleckman] that it was a safety factor and that we [should] continue to search for the [weapon]." [Patrolman] Williams [testified that he heard Gleckman say,] "it would be too bad if the little—I believe he said a girl—would pick up the gun, maybe kill herself." [Innis] then interrupted the conversation, stating that the officers should turn the car around so he could show them where the gun was located. [At] the time, they had traveled no more than a mile, a trip encompassing only a few minutes. The police vehicle then returned to the scene of the arrest where a search for the shotgun was in progress. There, Captain Leyden again advised [Innis] of his *Miranda* rights [and Innis] replied that he understood those rights but that he "wanted to get the gun out of the way because of the kids in the area in the school." [Innis] then led the police to a nearby field, where he pointed out the shotgun under some rocks by the side of the road. [The gun and his statements were introduced at his trial for kidnaping, robbery, and murder, and Innis was convicted of these crimes. He argued that the gun and statements were inadmissible because of improper police interrogation after he invoked his right to counsel under *Miranda*.]

[The] starting point for defining "interrogation" [is the] *Miranda* opinion [where] the Court observed that "[by custodial interrogation, we mean questioning initiated by law enforcement officers after a person has been taken into custody or otherwise deprived of his freedom of action in any significant way." This passage [might] suggest that the *Miranda* rules were to apply only to those police interrogation practices that involve express questioning of a defendant while in custody.

We do not, however, construe the *Miranda* opinion so narrowly. The concern of the Court in *Miranda* was that the "interrogation environment" created by the interplay of interrogation and custody would "subjugate the individual to the will of his examiner" and thereby undermine the privilege against compulsory self-incrimination. The police practices that evoked this concern included several that did not involve express questioning. For example, one of the practices [was] the use of line-ups in which a coached witness would pick the defendant as the perpetrator. This was designed to establish that the defendant was in fact guilty as a predicate for further interrogation. A variation on this theme [was] the so-called "reverse line-up" in which a defendant would be identified by coached witnesses as the perpetrator of a fictitious crime, with the object of inducing him to confess to the actual crime of which he was suspected in order to escape the false prosecution. The Court in *Miranda* also included in its survey of interrogation practices the use of psychological ploys, such as to "posit]" "the guilt of the subject," to "minimize the moral seriousness of the offense," and "to cast blame on the victim or on society." It is clear that these techniques of persuasion, no less than express questioning, were thought, in a custodial setting, to amount to interrogation. This is not to say [that] all statements obtained by the police after a person has been taken into custody are to be considered the product of interrogation. As the Court in *Miranda* noted: "[Volunteered] statements of any kind are not barred by the Fifth [Amendment]." [The] special procedural safeguards outlined in *Miranda* are required not where a suspect is simply taken into custody, but rather where a suspect in custody is subjected to interrogation. 'Interrogation,' as conceptualized in the *Miranda* opinion, must reflect a measure of compulsion above and beyond that inherent in custody itself."

We conclude that the *Miranda* safeguards come into play whenever a person in custody is subjected to either express questioning or its functional equivalent. That is to say, the term "interrogation" [refers] also to any words or actions on the part of the police (other than those normally attendant to arrest and custody) that the police should know are reasonably likely to elicit an incriminating response from the suspect. The latter portion of this definition focuses primarily upon the perceptions of the suspect, rather than the intent of the police. This focus reflects the fact that the *Miranda* safeguards were designed to vest a suspect in custody with an added measure of protection against coercive police practices, without regard to objective proof of the underlying intent of the [police]. * * *

Turning to the facts of the present case, we conclude that [Innis] was not "interrogated" within the meaning of *Miranda*. It is undisputed [that] the conversation [between] Gleckman and McKenna included no express questioning of [Innis]. Rather, that conversation was, at least in form, nothing more than a dialogue between the two officers to which no response from [Innis] was invited. Moreover, it cannot be fairly concluded that [Innis] was subjected to the "functional equivalent" of questioning. It cannot be said [that] Gleckman and McKenna should have known that their conversation was reasonably likely to elicit an incriminating response from [Innis]. There is nothing in the record to suggest that the officers were aware that [Innis] was peculiarly susceptible to an appeal to his conscience concerning the safety of handicapped children. Nor is there anything in the record to suggest that the police knew that [he] was unusually disoriented or upset at the time of his arrest.

The case thus boils down to whether, in the context of a brief conversation, the officers should have known that [Innis] would suddenly be moved to make a self-incriminating response. Given the fact that the entire conversation appears to have consisted of no more than a few off hand remarks, we cannot say that the officers should have known that it was reasonably likely that Innis would so respond. This is not a case where the police carried on a lengthy harangue in the presence of the suspect. Nor does the record support [the] contention [by Innis] that, under the circumstances, the officers' comments were particularly "evocative." It is our view, therefore, that [Innis] was not subjected by the police to words or actions that the police should have known were reasonably likely to elicit an incriminating response from [him].

MR. JUSTICE MARSHALL, with whom MR. JUSTICE BRENNAN joins, dissenting.

[I agree] with the Court's definition of "interrogation" within the meaning of *Miranda*. [I] am utterly at a loss, however, to understand how this objective standard as applied to the facts before us can rationally lead to the conclusion that there was no interrogation. If the statements had been addressed to [Innis], it would be impossible to draw such a conclusion. The simple message of the "talking back and forth" between Gleckman and McKenna was that they had to find the shotgun to avert a child's death. One can scarcely imagine a stronger appeal to the conscience of a suspect—any suspect—than the assertion that if the weapon is not found an innocent person will be hurt or killed. And not just any innocent person, but an innocent child—a little girl—a helpless, handicapped little girl on her way to school. The notion that such an appeal could not be expected to have any effect unless the suspect were known to have some special interest in handicapped children verges on the ludicrous. As a matter of fact, the appeal to a suspect to confess for the sake of others, to "display some evidence of decency and honor," is a classic interrogation technique. See, e.g., F. INBAU & J. REID, CRIMINAL INTERROGATION AND CONFESSIONS 60–62 (2d ed. 1967). [This] is not a case where police officers speaking among themselves are accidentally overheard by a suspect. These officers were "talking back and forth" in close quarters with the handcuffed suspect, traveling past the very place where they believed the weapon was located. They knew respondent would hear and attend to their conversation, and they are chargeable with knowledge of and responsibility for the pressures to speak which they created. * * *

Notes

1. *The Public Safety Exception.* In *New York v. Quarles*, 467 U.S. 649 (1984), the Court held that police officers may sometimes withhold the *Miranda* warnings until after they ask an arrestee questions that are "necessary to secure their own safety or the safety of the public." In *Quarles*, police received information from a rape victim, describing the clothing and height of her assailant, and reporting that the man had just entered a nearby supermarket carrying a gun. When the officers entered the store, a man matching the victim's description turned and ran. The officers pursued and caught the man, after losing sight of him briefly. When they stopped him at gunpoint and frisked him, the police discovered that man was wearing an empty shoulder holster. One officer handcuffed the man in presence of three other officers, and then asked the man about the location of the gun. When the man nodded in the direction of some empty cartons and said, "Over there," the police located the gun and then recited the *Miranda* warnings. The *Quarles* Court held that the gun and the defendant's statement about its location should be admissible at his trial for criminal possession of the weapon, under a "public safety" exception to *Miranda*, reasoning as follows:

> [The] police in this case, in the very act of apprehending a suspect, were confronted with the immediate necessity of ascertaining the whereabouts of a gun which they had every reason to believe the suspect had just removed from his empty holster and discarded in the supermarket. So long as the gun was concealed somewhere in the supermarket, [it] obviously posed more than one danger to the public safety: an accomplice might make use of it, a customer or employee might later come upon it. [I]f the police are required to recite the familiar *Miranda* warnings before asking the whereabouts of the gun, suspects in Quarles' position might well be deterred from responding. Procedural safeguards which deter a suspect from responding were deemed acceptable in *Miranda* in order to protect the Fifth Amendment privilege; when the primary social cost of those added protections is the possibility of fewer convictions, the *Miranda* majority was willing to bear that cost. Here, had *Miranda* warnings deterred Quarles from responding to [the] question about the whereabouts of the gun, [the police could not have] insure[d] that further danger to the public did not result from the concealment of the gun in a public [area]. [The officer] asked only the question necessary to locate the missing gun before advising [Quarles] of

his rights. It was only after securing the loaded revolver and giving the warnings that [the officer] continued with investigatory questions about the ownership and place of purchase of the gun. The exception which we recognize today, far from complicating the thought processes and the on-the-scene judgments of police officers, will simply free them to follow their legitimate instincts when confronting situations presenting a danger to the public safety.

Justice Marshall dissented, and Justices Brennan and Stevens joined his opinion, arguing that no public safety exception should be recognized, and that no danger to public safety was shown on the facts. The *Quarles* dissenters emphasized that *Miranda* was not informed by a cost-benefit analysis, but by the conclusion that "society's need for interrogation" cannot "outweigh" the privilege. In addition, the *Quarles* dissenters challenged the Court's "factual assumption that the public was at risk" as "speculative" and "completely in conflict" with state court findings, reasoning as follows:

> [Before] the interrogation began, Quarles had been "reduced to a condition of physical powerlessness" [and he] was not believed to have [an] accomplice to come to his rescue. When the questioning began, the arresting officers were sufficiently confident of their safety to put away their guns. Based on [the interrogating officer's] own testimony [that "the situation was under control"], the [lower court] found that "[n]othing suggests that any of the officers was by that time concerned for his own physical safety." [The] conclusion that neither Quarles nor his missing gun posed a threat to the public's safety is amply supported by the evidence that [no] customers or employees were wandering about the store, [and that] Quarles' arrest took place during the middle of the night when the store was apparently deserted except for the clerks at the checkout counter. The police could easily have cordoned off the store and searched for the missing gun. Had they done so, they would have found the gun [quickly because they] were well aware that Quarles had discarded his weapon somewhere near the scene of the arrest.

2. *The Routine Booking Question Exception.* The *Miranda* Court noted that police questions that are "normally attendant to arrest and custody" do not qualify as "interrogation." In *Pennsylvania v. Muniz*, 496 U.S. 582 (1990), the Court noted that "routine booking questions" typically are asked to secure "the biographical data necessary to complete booking or pretrial services," and held that an intoxicated driver could be asked booking questions about his or her "name, address, height, weight, eye color, date of birth, and current age." The government conceded that a sixth question for the driver was not a "routing booking question": "Do you know what the date was of your sixth birthday?" The *Muniz* Court held that asking the driver this question violated the Fifth Amendment because it called for a "testimonial response": it called for the defendant to "explicitly or implicitly relate a factual assertion or disclose information," and it subjected the defendant to the "cruel trilemma" of "self-accusation, perjury, or contempt." The Court reasoned as follows:

> When [Muniz could] not remember [the date of his sixth birthday,] he was confronted with the trilemma. [T]he inherently coercive environment created by the custodial interrogation precluded the option of

remaining silent. Muniz was left with the choice of incriminating himself by admitting that he did not then know the date of his sixth birthday, or answering untruthfully by reporting a date that he did not then believe to be accurate (an incorrect guess would be incriminating as well as untruthful). The content of his truthful answer supported an inference that his mental faculties were [impaired]. Hence, the incriminating inference of impaired mental faculties stemmed [from] a testimonial aspect of that [response, and] and the response should have been suppressed.

Chief Justice Rehnquist dissented, joined by Justices White, Blackmun, and Stevens, arguing that the "sixth birthday" question would allow the police officers to determine whether Muniz "was able to do a simple mathematical exercise," and that "there is no reason why [they] should not be able to require [Muniz] "to speak or write in order to determine his mental coordination."

3. *The Undercover Agent Exception.* In *Illinois v. Perkins*, 496 U.S. 292 (1990), the Court held that when an undercover agent questions a suspect in custody, such questioning does not qualify as "interrogation" under *Miranda*, reasoning as follows:

Conversations between suspects and undercover agents do not implicate the concerns underlying *Miranda*. The essential ingredients of a "police-dominated atmosphere" and compulsion are not present when an incarcerated person speaks freely to someone whom he believes to be a fellow inmate. Coercion is determined from the perspective of the [suspect]. It is the premise of *Miranda* that the danger of coercion results from the interaction of custody and official interrogation. [Questioning] by captors, who appear to control the suspect's fate, may create mutually reinforcing pressures that the Court has assumed will weaken the suspect's will, but where a suspect does not know that he is conversing with a government agent, these pressures do not exist. [When] the suspect has no reason to think that the listeners have official power over him, it should not be assumed that his words are motivated by the reaction he expects from his listeners. "[W]hen the agent carries neither badge nor gun and wars not 'police blue,' but the same prison gray" as the suspect, there is no "interplay between police interrogation and police [custody]." [The] use of undercover agents is a recognized law enforcement technique, often employed in the prison context to detect violence against correctional officials or inmates, as well as for the purposes [of gathering evidence] here.

Problems

1. *Stolen Furs.* Defendant is arrested for the murder of a woman and the theft of her furs and invokes his right to silence. After defendant is placed in a jail cell, the police place the stolen furs in front of his cell, about a foot away. At this point, defendant makes several incriminating statements. Was defendant subjected to "interrogation" within the meaning of *Miranda*? How might you argue the case for defendant? How might prosecution respond? *See People v. Ferro*, 63 N.Y.2d 316, 472 N.E.2d 13, 482 N.Y.S.2d 237 (1984).

2. *Defining Interrogation.* Fraser and Vecchio arrest Nan for murder, and take her to an interview room. Fraser brings two forms into the room, including a "waiver form" with the printed *Miranda* warnings, and a "probable cause form" used by police to record facts during an investigation. After Vecchio recites the *Miranda* warnings, Nan responds, "I want to remain silent now. I don't want to talk to either of you. I also want to talk to a lawyer now." Fraser notes this statement on the *Miranda* waiver form and both officers leave the room. However, they leave the probable cause form on the table next to Nan. A few minutes later, Fraser returns. He sits down at the table with Nan. He says nothing and starts writing on the probable cause form. When Nan says, "I thought I told you I don't want to talk to you," Fraser replies, "I'm simply filling out the probable cause form. I left it in here earlier, and I might as well fill it out now. It says here that you were arrested after you were identified in a photo array and that you are being charged with murder. I'm supposed to write down on this form what you said to us earlier." Assuming that Nan makes incriminating statements in response to Fraser's comments, do Fraser's words and conduct constitute "interrogation"? Explain the arguments on both sides.

3. *Exposing the Suspect to Potentially Evocative People.* Hal is arrested after he tells police that he killed his son David. After Hal is given *Miranda* warnings, he tells police that he would like to remain silent, and that he wants to talk to a lawyer. When Hal's wife Bea is brought in for questioning, she asks for permission to speak to Hal and the police agree to allow her to do so on condition that a police officer remain in the room. When Bea enters the room, Hal objects to her presence, but Officer Don responds that Bea insists on talking to him. Officer Don places a tape recorder on the desk in front of Hal and Bea, and stays in the room while recording the following conversation: Bea: We should have put David in the hospital. We should have gone for help. Hal: You tried as best you could to stop it. Just please shut up. Bea: We should have taken him to a hospital or something. What'll we do now? Hal: Shut up. Don't answer questions until you have an attorney. You tried the best you can to stop me. Bea: I don't, we don't, have money. Hal: There's a public attorney. Why don't you just be quiet. Bea: I don't have any money to bury him. All I got is enough money for the rent and that's it. Hal: Don't talk to me. Get out. [End of recording.] Assume that the prosecutor wants to use all the statements by Hal and Bea at Hal's trial for murder. Did the police obtain these statements by impermissible "interrogation" of Hal in violation of *Miranda*? If Bea is later prosecuted for a homicide crime, are the statements admissible at her trial? *See Arizona v. Mauro*, 481 U.S. 520 (1987).

4. *Defining the Public Safety Exception.* Suppose that a series of murders occurs in a community. Although the police are unable to locate the murderer, they do have a number of suspects. Given the severity of the crimes, would/should the *Quarles* public safety exception allow the police to interrogate each of the suspects without giving *Miranda* warnings? How might you argue the case for the prosecution? How might the defense respond?

5. *A Routine Question about Weapons.* Suppose that police arrest a defendant pursuant to an arrest warrant, and that the warrant is based on a witness's identification of the defendant as a person involved in a shooting.

The arrest takes place outside the defendant's apartment building in a parking lot, and the defendant's car is not far away. Immediately after the arrest, the police ask the defendant, without initially providing *Miranda* warnings: "Do you have anything on you that would hurt me—any guns or sharp objects?" The defendant replies, "No, but I have a gun in my car." Does the admission of the defendant's statement violate *Miranda*? Would it matter if the arrest warrant was for a traffic crime? *Compare United States v. Lackey*, 334 F.3d 1224 (10th Cir. 2003) with *United States v. DeSumma*, 272 F.3d 176 (3d Cir. 2001).

3. Adequate Warnings

Whenever custodial interrogation takes place, the prosecution must prove that the *Miranda* warnings were given before interrogation occurred. *Tague v. Louisiana*, 444 U.S. 469 (1980). Even when warnings are given, a defendant may argue that the warnings were "inadequate" because they did not "reasonably convey" the *Miranda* rights. The warnings may be inadequate if they are phrased so as to provide incomplete or misleading information about the rights. Or properly phrased warnings may be inadequate if they are "non-functional" in context; this may be true when the police fail to warn at the outset of an interrogation, and then deliver "midstream" warnings and continue the interrogation. If a court determines that the *Miranda* warnings were inadequate, then the post-warning statement is inadmissible; in this case, the issue of the validity of a defendant's waiver need not be addressed. Thus, any claim that warnings were "inadequate" is distinct from a claim that an invalid waiver was obtained after adequate warnings were provided.

CALIFORNIA v. PRYSOCK

453 U.S. 355 (1981).

[A juvenile was arrested for murder, and his parents were present during the interrogation, when the following warnings were given]: "Sgt. Byrd: Number One, you have the right to remain silent. This means you don't have to talk to me at all unless you so desire. Do you understand this?" "Randall P.: Yeh." "Sgt. Byrd: If you give up your right to remain silent, anything you say can and will be used as evidence against you in a court of law. Do you understand this?" "Randall P.: Yes." "Sgt. Byrd: You have the right to talk to a lawyer before you are questioned, have him present with you while you are being questioned, and all during the questioning. Do you understand this?" "Randall P.: Yes." "Sgt. Byrd: [A]lso, being a juvenile, you have the right to have your parents present, which they are. Do you understand this?" "Randall P.: Yes." "Sgt. Byrd: Even if they weren't here, you'd have this right. Do you understand this?" "Randall P.: Yes." "Sgt. Byrd: You have the right to have a lawyer appointed to represent you at no cost to yourself. Do you understand this?" "Randall P.: Yes." "Sgt. Byrd: Now, having all these legal rights in mind, do you wish to talk to me at this time?" "Randall

P.: Yes." At this [point,] Mrs. Prysock asked if [Randall] could still have an attorney at a later time if he gave a statement now without one. Sgt. Byrd assured Mrs. Prysock that [Randall] would have an attorney when he went to court and that "he could have one at this time if he wished one." [Prysock waived his rights and made incriminating statements that were admitted as his trial. He argued that the warnings were inadequate because he was not "properly advised of his right to the services of a free attorney before and during interrogation," since "he was not explicitly informed of his right to have an attorney appointed before further questioning."]

[*Miranda*] itself indicated that no talismanic incantation was required to satisfy its strictures. [Lower] courts [have] not required a verbatim recital of the words of the *Miranda* opinion but rather have examined the warnings given to determine if the reference to the right to appointed counsel was linked with some future point in time after the police interrogation. [N]othing in the warnings given [to Prysock] suggested any limitation on the right to the presence of appointed counsel different from the clearly conveyed rights to a lawyer in general, including the "right to a lawyer before you are questioned . . . while you are being questioned, and all during the questioning." [T]he police [fully] conveyed to [Prysock] his rights as required by *Miranda*. He was told of his right to have a lawyer present prior to and during interrogation, and his right to have a lawyer appointed at no cost if he could not afford one. These warnings conveyed to [Prysock] his right to have a lawyer appointed if he could not afford one prior to and during interrogation. * * *

JUSTICE STEVENS, with whom JUSTICE BRENNAN and JUSTICE MARSHALL join, dissenting.

[The] police sergeant informed [Prysock] that he had the right to have counsel present during questioning and, after a brief interlude, informed him that he had the right to appointed counsel. [This] warning was constitutionally inadequate, not because it deviated from the precise language of *Miranda*, but because [Prysock] "was not given the crucial information that the services of the free attorney were available prior to the impending questioning." [The] ambiguity in the warning [is] further demonstrated by the colloquy between the [sergeant] and [Prysock's] parents [after Prysock] was told that he had the "right to have a lawyer appointed to represent you at no cost to yourself." Because lawyers are normally "appointed" by judges, [the] reference to appointed counsel could reasonably have been understood to refer to trial counsel. That is what [Prysock's] parents must have assumed, because [the] colloquy with the sergeant related to their option "to hire a lawyer." * * *

Problem

Warning variations. The *Miranda* opinion states that "the following measures are required," and then describes the warnings for a person in custody as follows: "He must be warned prior to any questioning that he has the right to remain silent, that anything he says can be used against him in a court of law, that he has the right to the presence of an attorney and that if he cannot afford an attorney one will be appointed for him prior to any questioning if he so desires." Do you see a difference between these warnings and the ones given in *Prysock*? As the prosecutor assigned to argue the *Prysock* case in the Supreme Court, explain how you could have defended the officer's use of the ambiguous warnings that he was trained to use in Tulare County, California, and his failure to use the less ambiguous warnings described in *Miranda*. What policy arguments could be used to counter the *Prysock* dissent's position?

DUCKWORTH v. EAGAN

492 U.S. 195 (1989).

[Eagan was arrested for attempted murder, and given a waiver form, which police read to him and asked him to sign. The form included the following warnings:] Before we ask you any questions, you must understand your rights. You have the right to remain silent. Anything you say can be used against you in court. You have a right to talk to a lawyer for advice before we ask you any questions, and to have him with you during questioning. You have this right to the advice and presence of a lawyer even if you cannot afford to hire one. We have no way of giving you a lawyer, but one will be appointed for you, if you wish, if and when you go to court. If you wish to answer questions now without a lawyer present, you have the right to stop answering questions at any time. You also have the right to stop answering at any time until you've talked to a lawyer. [After reading this form, Eagan signed a waiver and made an initial statement. The next day, the officers arranged to question Eagan again, and this time they provided a form with the standard *Miranda* warnings. This time Eagan read the form, signed a waiver, and made a second statement. Both statements were admitted at his trial, and he was convicted. The lower appellate court concluded that the warnings on the first form did not adequately inform Eagan of right to receive appointed counsel before interrogation, and also impermissibly linked his right to counsel before interrogation with a future event, as prohibited by *Prysock*.]

[We] have never insisted that *Miranda* warnings be given in the exact form described in that decision. [*Miranda*] has not been limited to station house questioning, [and] the officer in the field may not always have access to printed *Miranda* warnings, or [may] inadvertently depart from routine practice, particularly if a suspect requests an elaboration of the warnings. [The necessary] inquiry is simply whether the warnings reasonably "conve[y] to [a suspect his] rights as required by *Miranda*. [Here] the initial warnings given to [Eagan] touched all of the bases required by *Miranda*. [The] police also added that they could not provide [Eagan] with a lawyer, but that one would be appointed "if and when you go to court." The Court of Appeals thought this "if and when you go to court" language suggested that "only those accused who can afford an attorney have the right to have one present before answering any questions," and "implie[d] that if the accused does not 'go to court,' i.e.[,] the government does not file charges, the accused is not entitled to [counsel] at all."

[T]he Court of Appeals misapprehended the effect of the inclusion of [the "if and when" language] in *Miranda* warnings. First, this instruction accurately described the procedure for the appointment of counsel in Indiana. [C]ounsel is appointed at the defendant's initial appearance in court, and formal charges must be filed at or before that hearing. [I]t must be relatively commonplace for a suspect, after receiving *Miranda* warnings, to ask when he will obtain counsel. The "if and when you go to court" advice simply anticipates that question. Second, *Miranda* does not require that attorneys be producible on call, but only that the suspect be informed [that] he has the right to an attorney before and during questioning, and that an attorney would be appointed for him if he could not afford [one]. [If] the police cannot provide appointed counsel, *Miranda* requires only that the police not question a suspect unless he waives his right to counsel. Here, [the police officers] did just that.

[The] Court of Appeals also referred to *Prysock* in finding deficient the initial warning given to [Eagan]. But the vice referred to in *Prysock* was [that the] warnings [used there] would not apprise the accused of his right to have an attorney present if he chose to answer questions. The warnings in this case did not suffer from that defect. Of the eight sentences in the initial warnings, one described respondent's right to counsel "before [the police] ask[ed] [him] questions," while another stated his right to "stop answering at any time until [he] talk[ed] to a lawyer." We hold that the initial warnings given to [Eagan], in their totality, satisfied *Miranda*, and therefore that his first statement [was] properly admitted into evidence.

Mr. Justice Marshall, with whom Mr. Justice Brennan, Mr. Justice Blackmun and Mr. Justice Stevens join, dissenting.

[Eagan] could easily have concluded [that] only "those accused who can afford an attorney have the right to have one present before answering any questions; those who are not so fortunate must wait." [He] was, after all, never told that questioning would be delayed until a lawyer was appointed "if and when" [he did] go to court. Thus, the "if and when" caveat may well have had the effect of negating the initial promise that counsel could be [present]. [The majority] finds that the most plausible interpretation is that [Eagan] would not be questioned until a lawyer was appointed when he later appeared in court. What goes [overlooked] is that the recipients of police warnings are often frightened suspects unlettered in the law, not lawyers or judges or others schooled in interpreting legal or semantic nuance. [Even] if the typical suspect could draw the inference the majority [draws], a warning qualified by an "if and when" caveat still fails to give a suspect any indication of when he will be taken to court. [A] suspect [who hears the warnings] would likely conclude that no lawyer would be provided until trial. In common parlance, "going to court" is synonymous with "going to trial." [T]he negative implication of the caveat is that, if the suspect is never taken to court, he "is not entitled to an attorney at all." An unwitting suspect harboring uncertainty on this score is precisely the sort of person who may feel compelled to talk "voluntarily" to the police, without the presence of [counsel]. [Such a suspect may believe] that he can talk now or remain in custody [for] an indeterminate length of time. To the average accused, still hoping [to] be home on time for dinner or to make it to work on time, the implication that his [two choices are] to answer questions right away or remain in custody until that nebulous time "if and when" he goes to court is a coerced choice of the most obvious [kind]. [It] poses no great burden on law enforcement officers to eradicate the confusion stemming from the "if and when" caveat. Deleting the sentence containing the offending language is all that needs to be done. * * *

Problems

1. *When a Suspect Knows the Warnings.* A police officer arrests Jane for a drug crime and takes her into custody. The officer attempts to advise Jane of her *Miranda* rights. Suppose that the police officer gets no further than reciting, "You have the right to remain silent" when Jane interrupts and tells the officer, "I know my rights, you don't have to tell me any more." The officer then asks Jane whether she is willing to waive her rights and identify her source of drugs, and Jane immediately says yes, and names Dan (a drug dealer) as her source. The prosecutor wants to introduce Jane's statement at her trial. Is this statement inadmissible because of inadequate *Miranda* warnings? *See United States v. Patane*, 542 U.S. 630 (2004).

2. *The "Anything You Say" Warning.* In the prior problem, what if Jane does not interrupt the officer who gives her the following warning: "You have the right to remain silent, the right to the presence of an attorney if you so wish, you are not required to answer any questions and if you decide to answer questions you can stop and do so, and if you cannot afford an attorney one will be appointed before you answer any questions." How can Jane's counsel argue that these *Miranda* warnings are inadequate? *See United States v. Tillman*, 963 F.2d 137 (6th Cir.1992).

3. *The Appointment of Counsel at a Future Event.* At a suppression hearing, a police officer gives the following testimony: "Q: After the defendant was read his rights, Detective, did you ask him if he was willing to speak to you? A: Yes, I did. Q: What did he say? A: His initial statement was, "What about No.3?" directing our attention to the number 3 sentence on the Rights Advice Form. A: Yes. The No. 3. Q: Go ahead. A: His statement to us then was, "Do I get an attorney now?" And he followed that up by saying, "I don't have the money to pay for one." He continued speaking. He didn't stop after that point and wait for either of us to respond to his questions. He continued his statement and told us, "I know what this is about. I just kind of freaked out. I only stabbed him once." Q: After he made the statement, did you answer his questions concerning his rights? A: Yes. Q: What did you tell him about his rights at that point? A: I told him that he would be

arraigned tomorrow, which would be the 21st at two o'clock in the afternoon, and that an attorney then would be routinely appointed for him. If he didn't have the money [to] pay for one, he needn't be concerned about it. This would be no expense. Q: Go ahead. A: Then I asked him if he would make a statement regarding the murder. He said he would. Then I asked him if we could make a tape-recorded statement and he consented." Are the defendant's statements inadmissible? *See Pope v. Zenon*, 69 F.3d 1018 (9th Cir.1995).

4. *Post-waiver Break and Interrogation without New Warnings.* A police officer gives Larry a *Miranda* warning, and obtains a valid waiver. In response to questioning, Larry then makes a statement denying any involvement in a homicide. Larry is returned to his cell. The next morning, the same officer drives Larry from the jail to his first appearance hearing. The officer says to Larry, "if you have anything to say, now is the time to do it, because once we get to the hearing it will be too late." Larry makes an incriminating statement. Is this statement admissible? How would the defense argue for suppression? *See United States v. Pruden*, 398 F.3d 241 (3d Cir.2005).

MISSOURI v. SEIBERT

542 U.S. 600 (2004).

JUSTICE SOUTER announced the judgment of the Court and delivered an opinion, in which JUSTICE STEVENS, JUSTICE GINSBURG, and JUSTICE BREYER join.

[A police officer testified that he made a "conscious decision" to withhold *Miranda* warnings from Seibert when interrogating her at the station, using an interrogation technique that he had been taught, to "question first, then give the warnings, and then repeat the question" until "I get the answer that [the suspect has] already provided once." Seibert made incriminating statements about her knowledge that her sons burned her mobile home with the expectation that an unrelated teenager living with the family would not be rescued from the fire. The initial interrogation lasted for 30 to 40 minutes, and then stopped for 20 minutes; then the same officer gave Seibert *Miranda* warnings and she signed a waiver. During the interrogation that followed, the officer obtained incriminating statements that repeated the information in the pre-warnings statement. The pre-warning statement was suppressed at Seibert's trial, but the post-warning statement was admitted and Seibert was convicted of murder.]

This case tests a police protocol for custodial interrogation that calls for giving no warnings of the rights to silence and counsel until interrogation has produced a confession. [Then] the interrogating officer follows it with *Miranda* warnings and [leads] the suspect to cover the same ground a second [time]. Because this midstream recitation of warnings [following an] interrogation and unwarned confession could not effectively comply with *Miranda's* constitutional requirement, we hold that a statement repeated after a warning in such circumstances is inadmissible.

[The] technique of interrogating in successive, unwarned and warned phases raises a new challenge to *Miranda*. [One officer here] testified that the strategy of withholding *Miranda* warnings until after interrogating and drawing out a confession was promoted not only by his own department, but by a national police training organization and other departments in which he had worked. [T]he Police Law Institute, for example, instructs that "officers may conduct a two-stage interrogation [so that at] any point during the pre-*Miranda* interrogation, usually after arrestees have confessed, officers may then read the *Miranda* warnings and ask for a waiver. If the arrestees waive their *Miranda* rights, officers will be able to repeat any subsequent incriminating statements later in court." Police Law Institute, Illinois Police Law Manual 83 (Jan.2001–Dec.2003) (Police Law Manual).[2] * * *

[Just] as "no talismanic incantation [is] required to satisfy [*Miranda's*] strictures," it would be absurd to think that mere recitation of the litany suffices to satisfy *Miranda* in every conceivable circumstance. "The inquiry is simply whether the warnings reasonably 'conve[y] to [a suspect] his rights as required by *Miranda.*'" *Duckworth v. Eagan*, 492 U.S. 195 (1989). The threshold issue when interrogators question first and warn later [is] whether it would be reasonable to find that in these circumstances the warnings could function "effectively" as *Miranda* requires. Could the warnings effectively advise the suspect that he had a real choice about giving an admissible statement [or] that he could choose to stop talking if he had talked earlier? For unless the warnings could place a suspect who has just been interrogated in a position to [make such] informed choice[s], there is no practical justification for accepting the formal warnings as compliance with *Miranda*, or for treating the second stage of interrogation as distinct from the first, unwarned and inadmissible segment.[4]

[By] any objective measure, [it] is likely that if the interrogators employ the technique of withholding warnings until after interrogation succeeds in eliciting a confession, the warnings will be ineffective in preparing the suspect for successive interrogation, close in time and similar in content. [Upon] hearing warnings only in the aftermath of interrogation and just after making a confession, a suspect would hardly think he had a genuine right to remain silent, let alone persist in so believing once the police began to lead him over the same ground again.

---

2. Emphasizing the impeachment exception to the *Miranda* rule approved by this Court, *Harris v. New York*, 401 U.S. 222 (1971), some training programs advise officers to omit *Miranda* warnings altogether or to continue questioning after the suspect invokes his [rights.]

4. [In] a sequential confession case, clarity is served if the later confession is approached by asking whether in the circumstances the *Miranda* warnings given could reasonably be found effective. If yes, a court can take up the standard issues of voluntary waiver and voluntary statement; if no, the subsequent statement is inadmissible for want of adequate *Miranda* warnings, because the earlier and later statements are realistically seen as parts of a single, unwarned sequence of questioning.

A more likely reaction on a suspect's part would be perplexity about the reason for discussing rights at that [point]. What is worse, telling a suspect that "anything you say can and will be used against you," without expressly excepting the statement just given, could lead to an entirely reasonable inference that what he has just said will be used, with subsequent silence being of no avail. Thus, when *Miranda* warnings are inserted in the midst of coordinated and continuing interrogation, they are likely to mislead and "depriv[e] a defendant of knowledge essential to his ability to understand the nature of his rights and the consequences of abandoning them." By the same token, it would ordinarily be unrealistic to treat two spates of integrated and proximately conducted questioning as independent interrogations subject to independent evaluation simply because *Miranda* warnings formally punctuate them in the middle.

[Also by] any objective measure [the facts here] reveal a police strategy adapted to undermine the *Miranda* warnings.[6] The unwarned interrogation was conducted in the station house, and the questioning was systematic, exhaustive, and managed with psychological skill. [The] warned phase of questioning proceeded after a pause of only 15 to 20 minutes, in the same place as the unwarned segment. When the same officer who had conducted the first phase recited the *Miranda* warnings, he said nothing to counter the probable misimpression that the advice that anything Seibert said could be used against her also applied to the details of the inculpatory statement previously elicited. In particular, the police did not advise that her prior statement could not be used.[7] Nothing was said or done to dispel the oddity of warning about legal rights to silence and counsel right after the police had led her through a systematic [interrogation]. The impression that the further questioning was a mere continuation of the earlier questions and responses was fostered by references back to the confession already given. It would have been reasonable to regard the two sessions as parts of a continuum, in which it would have been unnatural to refuse to repeat at the second stage what had been said before. These circumstances must be seen as challenging the comprehensibility and efficacy of the *Miranda* warnings to the point that a reasonable person in the suspect's shoes would not have understood them to convey a message that she retained a choice about continuing to talk.[8] [Because] the question-first tactic effectively threatens to thwart *Miranda's* purpose of reducing the risk that a coerced confession would be admitted, and because the facts here do not reasonably support a conclusion that the warnings given could have

---

6. Because the intent of the officer will rarely be as candidly admitted as it was [here, our] focus is on facts apart from intent that show the question-first tactic at work.

7. We do not hold that a formal addendum warning that a previous statement could not be used would be sufficient to change the character of the question-first procedure to the point of rendering an ensuing statement admissible, but its absence is clearly a factor that blunts the efficacy of the warnings and points to a continuing, not a new, interrogation.

8. Because we find that the warnings were inadequate, there is no need to assess the actual voluntariness of the statement.

served their purpose, Seibert's postwarning statements are inadmissible. The judgment of the Supreme Court of Missouri is affirmed.

JUSTICE O'CONNOR, with whom THE CHIEF JUSTICE, JUSTICE SCALIA and JUSTICE THOMAS join, dissenting.

[We have previously rejected a theory that is] indistinguishable from the one today's plurality adopts: [that the] "coercive impact of [an] unconstitutionally obtained [pre-warning] statement remains [to influence a post-warning statement], because in a defendant's mind [the pre-warning statement] has sealed his fate." We rejected this theory outright [in *Oregon v. Elstad*, 470 U.S. 298 (1985),] not because we refused to recognize the "psychological impact of the suspect's conviction that he has let the cat out of the bag," but because we refused to "endo[w] those "psychological effects" with "constitutional implications." To do so [would] "effectively immuniz[e] a suspect who responds to [pre-warning] questions from the consequences of his subsequent informed waiver," an immunity that "comes at a high cost to legitimate law enforcement [activity]." I would analyze the two-step interrogation procedure under the [voluntary waiver] standard [of] *Elstad* [and] leave this analysis for the Missouri courts to conduct on remand. * * *

Notes

1. *Elstad and Midstream Warnings.* The *Seibert* Court held that there was "no need to assess the actual voluntariness" of the defendant's post-warning waiver and statement, and thus made no reference to the "voluntary waiver" standard prescribed in *Oregon v. Elstad*, 470 U.S. 298 (1985). Instead, *Seibert* relied on *Elstad* as a precedent that revealed how midstream warnings "could be effective enough to accomplish their object" under certain circumstances. In *Elstad*, police went to a young suspect's house to arrest him on a burglary charge. Before the arrest, one officer spoke with Elstad's mother, while the other one joined the suspect in a "brief stop in the living room," where the officer stated that he "felt" that Elstad was involved in a burglary and the suspect acknowledged that he was present at the scene. The Court held that any causal connection between the pre-warning admission (in the living room) and the post-warning confession (at the station) was "speculative and attenuated." The Court treated the living room conversation as a "good-faith *Miranda* mistake, [open] to correction by careful warnings before systematic [station-house] questioning [and] posing no threat to the [*Miranda's*] warn-first practice generally." The Court viewed the post-warning questioning as presenting a markedly different experience from the short conversation in the living room. "[S]ince a reasonable person in the suspect's shoes could have seen the station house questioning as a new and distinct experience, the *Miranda* warnings could have made sense as presenting a genuine choice whether to follow up on the earlier admission." By contrast, the *Seibert* dissenters rejected the *Seibert* Court's interpretation of *Elstad* as an "adequate warnings" precedent, and Justice O'Connor argued that *Elstad* required the Court to address the "voluntary waiver" issue in *Seibert*. Seibert's post-warning statement would be inadmissible only if she could show either that "actual coercion" by police

produced that statement, or that "actual coercion" produced her initial unwarned statement and was "carried over" into her post-warning statement. No such "carried-over" coercion would be recognized if any initial coercion were "dissipated" through "the passing of time or a change in circumstances," such as "the change in place of interrogations," or "the change in identity of the interrogators."

2. *Alternate Solutions for Midstream Warning Cases.* Justice Breyer's concurring opinion in *Seibert* endorsed the plurality's opinion "in full," and he opined that its approach "in practice will function as a "fruit of the poisonous tree" test analysis like that used for Fourth Amendment violations under *Wong Sun v. United States*, 371 U.S. 471 (1963), notwithstanding the fact that the *Wong Sun* fruits test was rejected in *Elstad* for *Miranda* violations. Breyer predicted that "effective" *Miranda* warnings will occur in midstream-warning cases "only when certain circumstances—a lapse in time, a change in location or interrogating officer, or a shift in the focus of the questioning—intervene between the unwarned questioning and any postwarning statement." Breyer also proposed that whenever police use a two-stage interrogation technique, courts should find that any post-warning statement is a tainted "fruit" of inadmissible pre-warning statements, and exclude the post-warning statement "unless the failure to warn was in good faith." Justice Kennedy's opinion, concurring in the judgment, proposed that *Seibert's* "effective warnings" analysis should be limited to situations where police deliberately employ the "question first" strategy. In other midstream-warning cases, Kennedy proposed that post-warning statements "that are related to the substance" of pre-warning statements should be excluded unless police undertake "curative measures" to ensure that "a reasonable person in the suspect's situation would understand the import and effect" of the warnings and of waiver. Kennedy envisioned that an extra warning explaining "the likely inadmissibility" of the pre-warning statement "might be" a sufficient cure; alternatively, a "substantial break in time and circumstances" between the pre-warning statement and the midstream warnings "may suffice."

Problems

1. *Questioning First in Good Faith.* In *Seibert* the police admitted that they deliberately used the "question-first" approach. Suppose that, in future midstream-warnings cases, the police deny that they are using this strategy and argue that they are acting in good faith when they fail to give initial warnings. Under *Seibert*, what factors might a reviewing court consider in deciding whether to apply *Seibert* or *Elstad*?

2. *Police Chatting with Arrestee without Warnings.* Assume that police go to Sarah's home to arrest her pursuant to an arrest warrant. During the arrest, the police chat with Sarah without giving her *Miranda* warnings, and she makes incriminating statements. When defendant arrives at the jail, she is given *Miranda* warnings, waives her rights, and makes further incriminating statements. In evaluating whether this case resembles *Seibert* or *Elstad*, what else would you like to know about the initial incriminating statements and the comments made by the police to the defendant?

3. *Comparing Solutions.* Compare the four different doctrinal solutions to the midstream warnings problem offered by the *Seibert* plurality, the *Seibert* dissenters, Justice Breyer, and Justice Kennedy. Which solution is preferable?

4. Waiver

Even when the required *Miranda* warnings are given, the prosecution must prove by a preponderance of the evidence that the suspect "voluntarily, knowingly and intelligently" waived his or her *Miranda* rights. In *Moran v. Burbine*, 475 U.S. 412 (1986), the Court summarized the waiver requirement as follows: "The inquiry has two distinct dimensions. First, the relinquishment of the right must have been voluntary in the sense that it was the product of a free and deliberate choice rather than intimidation, coercion, or deception. Second, the waiver must have been made [knowingly and intelligently,] with a full awareness of both the nature of the right being abandoned and the consequences of the decision to abandon it. Only if the "totality of the circumstances surrounding the interrogation" reveal both an uncoerced choice and the requisite level of comprehension may a court properly conclude that the *Miranda* rights have been waived." Most of the Court's waiver precedents address the claim that a particular interrogation practice produces invalid waivers in all cases, and therefore must be modified in light of *Miranda's* policies.

COLORADO v. SPRING

479 U.S. 564 (1987).

JUSTICE POWELL delivered the opinion of the Court.

[An informant's tip provided ATF agents with the information that Spring, a dealer in illegal firearms, had committed an unrelated homicide in Colorado. The ATF agents created a sting operation to catch Spring, and they arrested him for selling illegal firearms in Kansas City. He was given *Miranda* rights at the scene of arrest, [and] at the ATF office. Then Spring signed a waiver form stating "that he understood and waived his rights, and that he was willing to make a statement and answer questions." When the interrogation began, the ATF agents first questioned Spring about the firearms transactions that led to his arrest. Then they asked him if he had a criminal record, and he admitted that he has "a juvenile record for shooting his aunt" when he was 10 years old. Then the agents asked Spring if he had ever shot anyone else. Spring mumbled, "I shot another guy once." But when the agents asked Spring if he had ever been to Colorado, he said no. Then when they asked, "if he had shot a man named Walker in Colorado and thrown his body in a snowbank," Spring said no again, and the interrogation ended. Two months later, Colorado police came to question Spring in the Kansas City jail about the homicide. They gave Spring *Miranda* warnings and he waived his rights, and made incriminating statements about the Colorado crime. The trial court admitted Spring's statements to the

ATF agents at his murder trial, rejecting his argument that the waiver obtained by those agents violated *Miranda* because they did not tell him that they planned to question him about the homicide crime as well as the firearms crime.]

[This] case presents the question whether the suspect's awareness of all the crimes about which he may be questioned is relevant to determining the validity of his decision to waive the Fifth Amendment privilege. [There] is no doubt that Spring's decision to waive his Fifth Amendment privilege was voluntary. [His] allegation that the police failed to supply him with certain information does not relate to any of the traditional indicia of coercion: "the duration and conditions of [detention], the manifest attitude of the police toward him, his physical and mental state, the diverse pressures which sap or sustain his powers of resistance and self-control." *Culombe v. Connecticut*, 367 U.S. 568, 602 (1961) (opinion of Frankfurter, J.). Absent evidence that Spring's "will [was] overborne and his capacity for self-determination critically impaired" because of coercive police conduct, his waiver of his Fifth Amendment privilege was voluntary [under] *Miranda*.

There also is no doubt that Spring's waiver of his Fifth Amendment privilege was knowingly and intelligently [made]. The Constitution does not require that a criminal suspect know and understand every possible consequence of a waiver of the Fifth Amendment privilege. *Miranda* warnings ensure that a waiver of [the privilege] is knowing and intelligent by requiring that the suspect be fully advised of [his rights,] including the critical advice that whatever he chooses to say may be used as evidence against him. [In] this case there is no allegation that Spring failed to understand the basic [privilege, nor] is there any allegation that he misunderstood the consequences of speaking freely to the law enforcement officials. In sum, we think that [his] waiver was made knowingly and intelligently within the meaning of *Miranda*.

Spring relies on this Court's statement in *Miranda* that "any evidence that the accused was threatened, tricked, or cajoled into a waiver will [show] that the defendant did not voluntarily waive his privilege." He contends that the failure to inform him of the potential subjects of interrogation constitutes the police trickery and deception condemned in *Miranda*, thus rendering his waiver of *Miranda* rights invalid. [This] Court has never held that mere silence by law enforcement officials as to the subject matter of an interrogation is "trickery" sufficient to invalidate a suspect's waiver of *Miranda* rights, and we expressly decline so to hold today. [However, "we are not confronted with an affirmative representation by law enforcement officials as to the scope of the interrogation and do not reach the question whether a waiver of *Miranda* rights would be valid in such a circumstance."]

[O]nce *Miranda* warnings are given, it is difficult to see how official silence could cause a suspect to misunderstand the nature of his constitutional [rights]. [A] valid waiver does not require that an individual be informed of all information "useful" in making his decision or all information that "might [affect] his decision to confess." *Moran v. Burbine*, 475 U.S., at 422. Here, the additional information could affect only the wisdom of a *Miranda* waiver, not [its] knowing [nature]. [*Miranda*] specifically required that the police inform a criminal suspect that he has the right to remain silent and that anything he says may be used against him. There is no qualification of this broad and explicit warning. Accordingly, we hold that a suspect's awareness of all the possible subjects of questioning in advance of interrogation is not relevant to determining whether the suspect voluntarily, knowingly, and intelligently waived his Fifth Amendment privilege.

JUSTICE MARSHALL, with whom JUSTICE BRENNAN joins, dissenting.

[The] interrogation tactics utilized in this case demonstrate the relevance of the information Spring did not receive. The agents evidently hoped to obtain from Spring a valid confession to the federal firearms charge for which he was arrested and then parlay this admission into an additional confession of first-degree murder. Spring could not have expected questions about the latter, separate offense when he agreed to waive his rights, as it occurred in a different State and was a violation of state law outside the normal investigative focus of federal [ATF] agents. [The] coercive aspects of the psychological ploy intended in this case, when combined with an element of surprise which may far too easily rise to a level of deception, cannot be justified in light of *Miranda's* strict requirements that the suspect's waiver and confession be voluntary, knowing, and [intelligent]. Once [a] waiver is given and [a] statement made, the protections afforded by *Miranda* against the "inherently compelling pressures" of the custodial interrogation have effectively dissipated. Additional questioning about entirely separate and more serious suspicions of criminal activity can take unfair advantage of the suspect's psychological state, as the unexpected questions cause the compulsive pressures suddenly to reappear. * * *

Notes

1. *Proving Waiver.* In *North Carolina v. Butler*, 441 U.S. 369 (1979), the Court held that an explicit oral or written waiver is not necessary under *Miranda*. The Court reasoned as follows: "An express written or oral statement of waiver of the right to remain silent or of the right to counsel is usually strong proof of the validity of that waiver, but is not inevitably either necessary or sufficient to establish waiver. The question is not one of form, but rather whether the defendant in fact knowingly and voluntarily waived the rights delineated [in *Miranda*]. [*Miranda* held that] mere silence is not enough. That does not mean that the defendant's silence, coupled with an understanding of his rights and a course of conduct indicating waiver, may never support a conclusion that a defendant has waived his rights. [In] at least some cases waiver can be clearly inferred from the actions and words of the person interrogated."

2. *Conditional Waivers with Limited–Purpose Invocations.* In *Connecticut v. Barrett*, 479 U.S. 523 (1987), the defendant was arrested for sexual

assault and given *Miranda* warnings. Barrett said that "he would not give the police any written statements but he had no problem in talking about the incident." Then he made incriminating statements. Thirty minutes later, the police gave him warnings again and this time Barrett said that he would not make a written statement unless his attorney was present, and then after repeating his comment that he had "no problem" talking about the crime, he made a second oral statement. He also made a third oral statement that was tape-recorded after he received additional warnings, and after he stated again that he had no problem with talking but would not put anything in writing until his attorney arrived. The Court upheld the admissibility of all Barrett's statements:

> Barrett's limited requests for counsel [were] accompanied by affirmative announcements of his willingness to speak the authorities. [Here] Barrett made clear his intentions, and they were honored by police. To conclude that [he] invoked his right to counsel for all purposes requires [a] disregard of the ordinary meaning of his statement. [We] reject the contention that [Barrett's] distinction between oral and written statements indicates an understanding of the consequences so incomplete that we should deem his limited invocation of the right to counsel effective for all purposes. [The] warnings made clear to Barrett that "[I]f you talk to any police officers, anything you say can and will be used against you in court." [We] have never embraced the theory that a defendant's ignorance of the full consequences of his decisions vitiates their voluntariness.

3. *Efforts by Counsel to Contact a Custodial Defendant.* In *Moran v. Burbine*, 475 U.S. 412 (1986) defendant was in custody when his sister obtained a lawyer for him and the lawyer telephoned the police in an effort to obtain contact Burbine prior to his interrogation. The lawyer was told that Burbine was not going to be interrogated because the police "were through with him for the night." Nevertheless, officers interrogated Burbine an hour later without informing him about the lawyer's phone call. After receiving warnings, he waived his rights and made incriminating statements. The *Moran* Court held that his waiver was valid because he made the "voluntary decision to speak" with "full awareness and comprehension of all the information *Miranda* requires, reasoning as follows:

> Events occurring outside of the presence of the suspect and entirely unknown to him surely can have no bearing on the capacity to comprehend and knowingly relinquish a constitutional right. [Although] the "deliberate or reckless" withholding of information is objectionable as a matter of ethics, such conduct is only relevant to the constitutional validity of a waiver if it deprives a defendant of knowledge essential to his ability to understand the nature of his rights and the consequences of abandoning them. [We are not] prepared to adopt a rule requiring that police inform a suspect of an attorney's efforts to reach him. While such a rule might add marginally to *Miranda's* goal of dispelling the compulsion inherent in custodial interrogation, overriding practical considerations counsel against its adoption. [T]he [proposed rule] would have the inevitable consequence of muddying *Miranda's* otherwise relatively clear waters. The legal questions it would spawn are legion: To what extent should the police be held accountable for knowing that the

accused has counsel? Is it enough that someone in the station house knows, or must the interrogating officer himself know of counsel's efforts to contact the suspect? Do counsel's efforts to talk to the suspect concerning one criminal investigation trigger the obligation to inform [on] a wholly separate [matter]? [A] rule requiring the police to inform the suspect of an attorney's efforts to contact him [would] come at a substantial cost to society's legitimate and substantial interest in securing admissions of guilt.

Justice Stevens dissented, joined by Justices Brennan and Marshall, pointing out that the *Moran* police violated the ABA Standards for Criminal Justice, as well as the *Miranda* standards established by a "near-consensus of state courts." He argued that there should be "no constitutional distinction," between "a deceptive misstatement and the concealment by the police of the critical fact that an attorney retained by the accused or his family has offered assistance, either by telephone or in person."

4. *Unwarned Questioning after Midstream Warnings.* In *Oregon v. Elstad*, 470 U.S. 298 (1985), the Court held that a *Miranda* waiver obtained after midstream warnings in sequential interrogations was "voluntary" in the absence of proof of "actual coercion" by police:

The failure of police to administer *Miranda* warnings does not mean that [either the pre-warning or post-warning statements have] actually been coerced, but only that courts will presume the privilege against compulsory self-incrimination has not been intelligently exercised. [Absent] deliberately coercive or improper tactics in obtaining the initial [pre-warning] statement, the mere fact that a suspect has made an unwarned admission does not warrant a presumption of compulsion. A subsequent administration of *Miranda* warnings to a suspect who has given a voluntary but unwarned statement ordinarily should suffice to remove the conditions that precluded admission of [that] statement. [The] relevant inquiry is whether, in fact, the second [post-warning] statement was also voluntarily [made]. [A court] must examine the surrounding circumstances and the entire course of police conduct with respect to the suspect in evaluating the voluntariness of his statements. The fact that a suspect chooses to speak after being informed of his rights [is] highly probative.

It should be noted that *Elstad* rejected the argument that a person cannot make a "knowing and intelligent" waiver in a midstream warnings scenario unless police provide *Miranda* warnings and an extra warning that the prior statement cannot be used against the person. *Elstad* reasoned that such an extra warning was "neither practicable nor constitutionally necessary" because police "are ill-equipped to pinch-hit for counsel, construing the murky and difficult questions of when "custody" begins or whether a given unwarned statement will ultimately be held admissible." By contrast, the *Seibert* Court observed that in a sequential interrogation case, when a defendant argues that midstream warnings are not "adequate" to convey the *Miranda* rights, the absence of "a formal addendum warning that a previous statement could not be used" is "a factor that blunts the efficacy" of the midstream warnings. Further, the *Seibert* Court noted that even if police give such an addendum warning, this is not sufficient alone to "change the character of the question-first [without warnings] procedure to the point of rendering an ensuing [post-warning] statement admissible.''

Problems

1. *State Constitutional Solutions.* Some state courts have rejected various Supreme Court interpretations of *Miranda*, and adopted more protective rules for interrogated persons based on state constitutional law. Assume that you are the law clerk for a state supreme court justice who tells you that the court is considering whether to reject *Spring* and *Moran*. Your judge asks for your analysis of the possible alternative rules that could be adopted instead of the rules endorsed by the Court in these cases.

a. *Extra Warnings for Spring.* Describe the various kinds of extra warnings that should be provided to a person like the *Spring* defendant, in order to satisfy *Miranda* policies, and explain any problems that you imagine may arise if police are required to provide some kind of warning concerning the subject matter of a planned interrogation.

b. *Extra Warnings for Moran.* Describe the possible duties that might be imposed on police to inform an interrogated person that his attorney (either his previously retained attorney or one obtained for him by friends or family) is trying to contact him. Explain how the state court could resolve the problems that are likely to arise if such a duty is created, including the problems mentioned by the *Moran* majority. Compare *Commonwealth v. Mavredakis*, 430 Mass. 848, 725 N.E.2d 169 (2000); *People v. Bender*, 452 Mich. 594, 551 N.W.2d 71 (1996); *State v. Stoddard*, 206 Conn. 157, 537 A.2d 446 (1988).

2. *The Blurted–Out Confession.* Assume that Mike is in custody in an interrogation room with Kira, a police officer. Kira tells Mike that he has been arrested for the crime of bank robbery. After Kira gives Mike the *Miranda* warnings, Mike says immediately, ''I did it—I robbed the bank.'' Is Mike's statement admissible? Why?

3. *The Inquisitive Arrestee.* In the prior problem, after Kira gives Mike the *Miranda* warnings, she asks him if he understands his rights and if he wants to waive them. Mike says that he does not understand his rights, and that he has three questions: 1) what the police will do if he says he wants to remain silent or that he wants to talk to a lawyer, 2) are police required to let him actually talk to a lawyer before interrogation if he says he wants to do so, and 3) whether Kira thinks it is a good idea for him to talk to a lawyer now. You are the prosecuting attorney, and Kira has asked for your advice. How would you advise her to respond to these questions in order to create a valid waiver?

4. *God's Command.* Sam walks into a police station in Denver and announces that he wants to confess to a murder that occurred ten years earlier. Sam is lawfully taken into custody, receives *Miranda* warnings, and signs a waiver stating that he understands his rights. Then Sam makes incriminating statements. Later that day, counsel is appointed for Sam at his first appearance hearing. Sam tells counsel that the voice of God commanded him to come to Denver and either confess to the murder or commit suicide. Sam's counsel consults Dr. Joely, who examines Sam and determines that he

is a schizophrenic who was in a psychotic state when he made his statement to police. Later she provides expert testimony that, "Sam is incapable of making a free decision to exercise his legal rights," because he suffers from "command hallucinations" that interfere with his volitional abilities to make free and rational choices, and also interfere with his cognitive abilities to understand his rights. Was Sam's waiver "voluntary"? Was Sam's waiver "knowing and intelligent"? Explain. *See Colorado v. Connelly*, 479 U.S. 157 (1986).

5. *Drafting Warnings*. Assume that you are a defense lawyer. Draft a comprehensive set of warnings that will communicate all the rules that you have learned about *Miranda*, and try to provide as much information as possible to assist someone who is about to undergo interrogation. Then take the role of a prosecutor, and criticize these warnings based on case law and policy.

6. *Drafting Guidelines*. Assume that you are a prosecutor. You are asked by the police chief to draw up some guidelines for obtaining waivers from people who are juveniles, who may be intoxicated, who may have language problems, or who may suffer from mental illness. What guidelines would you suggest in order to insure that valid waivers be obtained from these persons?

5. Invocations of Miranda Rights

If a person in custody receives *Miranda* warnings and "invokes" either the Fifth Amendment right to remain silent, or the "Fifth Amendment right to counsel," *Miranda* requires the police to cease questioning immediately. However, this duty is not described in the *Miranda* warnings, nor does *Miranda* require a police officer to ask a person, "Would you like to invoke your rights?" Instead, the *Miranda* Court assumed that once a person is notified of her rights, she can be expected to notify the interrogating officer, in reciprocal fashion, that she wishes to exercise these rights; in the absence of such notice, the officer may assume that she does not wish to exercise them and may attempt safely to procure a waiver. Thus, the threshold issue in invocation litigation is whether the defendant effectively communicated an invocation to the interrogating officer after warnings. If so, then a court must address the question whether the officer cut off questioning immediately without further waiver-seeking or interrogation. If so, then a third question remains, which is whether later circumstances may establish the lawfulness of a subsequent attempt to seek a waiver. After *Miranda*, the Court decided that an invocation does not necessarily establish permanent immunity from interrogation. Instead, the Court decided that the consequences of an invocation depend upon whether a person invokes the right to silence or the right to counsel. Later opportunities for officers to obtain waivers may arise after each type of invocation, but for different reasons, as demonstrated by the cases that follow.

a. Unambiguous Invocation Requirement

DAVIS v. UNITED STATES

512 U.S. 452 (1994).

JUSTICE O'CONNOR delivered the opinion of the Court.

[Navy authorities suspected Davis of murder. After receiving *Miranda* warnings, Davis initially waived his right to remain silent and his right to counsel, both orally and in writing. After an hour and a half of questioning, Davis said, "Maybe I should talk to a lawyer." The interrogating officer testified that he responded by telling Davis "that if he wants a lawyer, then we will stop any kind of questioning with him, that we weren't going to pursue the matter unless we have it clarified is he asking for a lawyer or is he just making a comment about a lawyer, and he said, 'No, I'm not asking for a lawyer,' [and] "I don't want a lawyer." After a short break, the officers reminded Davis of his rights to silence and to counsel. Then the questioning continued for another hour until Davis stated, "I think I want a lawyer before I say anything else." Then the questioning ceased. Davis sought to suppress his statements on the theory that he invoked his right to counsel when he said, "Maybe I should talk to a lawyer"; therefore, the subsequent comments by the officer violated the *Miranda* duty to cut off questioning, and statements made by Davis after these comments were inadmissible. The trial court rejected this argument and ruled that the statements were admissible; Davis was convicted of murder and appealed on *Miranda* grounds.]

[If] a suspect requests counsel at any time during [an] interview, he is not subject to further [questioning, and this rule] requires courts to "determine whether the accused actually invoked his right to counsel." *Smith v. Illinois*, 469 U.S. [91,] 98 [1984]. To avoid difficulties of proof and to provide guidance to officers conducting interrogations, this is an objective inquiry. [If] a suspect makes a reference to an attorney that is ambiguous or equivocal in that a reasonable officer in light of the circumstances would have understood only that the suspect might be invoking the right to counsel, our precedents do not require the cessation of questioning.

Rather, the suspect must unambiguously request counsel. As we have observed, "a statement either is such an assertion of the right to counsel or it is not." *Smith*[,] 469 U.S. at 97–98. Although a suspect need not "speak with the discrimination of an Oxford don," he must articulate his desire to have counsel present sufficiently clearly that a reasonable police officer in the circumstances would understand the statement to be a request for an attorney. If the statement fails to meet the requisite level of clarity, [the] officers [need not] stop questioning the suspect. [When officers] reasonably do not know whether or not the suspect wants a lawyer, [a] cessation of questioning [would] needlessly prevent [them] from questioning [when] the suspect did not wish to have a lawyer present.

We recognize that requiring a clear assertion of the right to counsel might disadvantage some suspects—who because of fear, intimidation, lack of linguistic skills, or a variety of other reasons—will not articulate their right to counsel although they actually want to have a lawyer present. [But] if we were to require questioning to cease [based on an ambiguous invocation,] officers would be forced to make difficult judgment calls [with] the threat of suppression if they guess wrong. [Of] course, when a suspect makes an ambiguous or equivocal statement it will often be good police practice for the [officers] to clarify whether or not he actually wants an [attorney, in order to] help protect the rights of the suspect [and] to minimize the chance of a confession being [suppressed]. But we decline to adopt a rule requiring officers to ask clarifying questions. * * *

The courts below found that [the] remark to the [agents] was not a request for counsel, and we see no reason to disturb that conclusion. The agents therefore were not required to stop questioning [Davis,] though it was entirely proper for them to clarify whether [he] wanted a lawyer. Because there is no ground for the suppression of [his] statements, the judgment of the Court of Military Appeals is

Affirmed.

JUSTICE SOUTER, with whom JUSTICES BLACKMUN, STEVENS and GINSBURG join, concurring in the judgment.

[W]hen law enforcement officials "reasonably do not know whether or not the suspect wants a lawyer," they should stop their interrogation and ask him to make his choice clear. [A] rule barring government agents from further interrogation until they determine whether a suspect's ambiguous statement was meant as a request for counsel [assures] that a suspect's choice whether or not to deal with police through counsel will be "scrupulously honored" [under *Miranda*]. [Moreover, this rule] would relieve the officer for any responsibility for guessing "whether in fact the suspect wants a lawyer even though he hasn't said so" [by assuring that] the "judgment call" will be made by the party most competent to resolve the ambiguity, [the] individual suspect. [I] am not persuaded by [Davis's] contention that even ambiguous statements require an end to all police questioning. [The] costs to society of losing confessions would be hard to bear where the suspect, if asked for his choice, would have chosen to continue. [Here Davis's invocation was ambiguous and the officers properly] confined [their questions] to verifying whether [he] meant to ask for a lawyer [and so no *Miranda* violation occurred.]* * *

Problems

1. *Ambiguous Invocations of Counsel.* Suppose that after Della is placed in custody, she is given *Miranda* warnings, and when police officer asks her if she understands her rights and wants to waive them, she replies: a) "I'm scared to say anything without talking to a lawyer"; b) "I think I

would rather have an attorney here to speak for me''; c) ''You did say I could have an attorney if I wanted one?''; d) ''Well, what good is an attorney going to do?''; or e) ''Maybe I should talk to a lawyer,'' and then she gives the police officer the business card of a lawyer. Note that unlike the scenario in *Davis*, Della has not waived her rights and answered questions for an hour and a half. How will this fact be relevant to a court's determination whether an unambiguous invocation occurred? Are any of Della's responses sufficiently unambiguous to invoke the right to counsel under *Davis*?

2. *Ambiguous Invocations of Silence*. After *Davis*, lower courts assumed that the unambiguous invocation requirement applies to invocations of the right to silence as well as the right to counsel. Suppose that after Joachim is placed in custody by two officers, he is given *Miranda* warnings, and when he is asked whether he understands his rights and is willing to speak to the officers, Joachim says: a) ''not right now''; b) ''I ain't got nothing to say to y'all''; or c) ''I can't talk about it.'' Do any of these responses qualify as unambiguous invocations of the right to silence under the *Davis* standard? If you are the legal adviser to the police department, and the Police Chief seeks your advice regarding these arguable invocations, what advice would you give the Chief as to how police should respond when persons in custody make statements like these?

3. *Invocation Interrupting Warnings*. Smith is arrested on suspicion of armed robbery, and taken to an interrogation room. The police officer gives Smith the *Miranda* warnings as follows: ''Q. You have a right to remain silent. You do not have to talk to me unless you want to do so. Do you understand that? A. Uh. She told me to get my lawyer. She said you guys would railroad me. Q. If you do want to talk to me I must advise you that whatever you say can and will be used against you in court. Do you understand that? A. Yeah. Q. You have a right to consult with a lawyer and to have a lawyer present with you when you're being questioned. Do you understand that? A. Uh, yeah. I'd like to do that. Q. Okay.'' At this point, the interrogating officer does not cut off questioning; instead, he finishes reading Smith the warnings: ''Q. [If] you want a lawyer and you're unable to pay for one a lawyer will be appointed to represent you free of cost, do you understand that? A. Okay. Q. Do you wish to talk to me at this time without a lawyer being present? A. Yeah and no, uh, I don't know what's what, really. Q. Well. You either have [to agree] to talk to me at this time without a lawyer being present and if you do agree to talk with me without a lawyer being present you can stop at any time you want to. Q. All right. I'll talk to you then.'' Smith makes incriminating statements, but then declares, ''I wanta get a lawyer.'' Now the interrogation ends. The prosecutor wants to use the incriminating statements but Smith's defense counsel argues that the police officer violated *Miranda*. How will each side use the *Davis* standard in making arguments about the invocation of counsel? *Compare Smith v. Illinois*, 469 U.S. 91 (1984) (for analysis predating *Davis*).

b. Waiver–Seeking after Invocation

i. *Invocation of Right to Silence*

MICHIGAN v. MOSLEY

423 U.S. 96 (1975).

MR. JUSTICE STEWART delivered the opinion of the Court.

[Mosley was arrested in the afternoon based on a tip that he had participated in two robberies at bars in Detroit. Detective Cowie brought Mosley to the Robbery Bureau on the fourth floor of the police headquarters, and gave him *Miranda* warnings. Mosley signed a "rights notification" form and then he said he did not want to answer any questions about the robberies. Cowie ceased the questioning, and took Mosley to a ninth-floor cell block. A few hours later, Detective Hill brought Mosley from the cell block to the fifth-floor office of the Homicide Bureau for questioning about the fatal shooting of Williams, who had been killed during an attempted holdup at a different bar. Hill read and explained the *Miranda* warnings to Mosley, and this time Mosley waived his rights. When Hill told Mosley that another man had implicated Mosley in the Williams homicide, Mosley made incriminating statements during the 15 minute interrogation that followed. These statements were admitted at Mosley's murder trial and he was convicted.]

[The] issue in this case [is] whether the conduct of the Detroit police that led to Mosley's incriminating statement [violated *Miranda*]. Resolution of the question turns almost entirely on the interpretation of a single passage in the *Miranda* [opinion]: "Once warnings have been given, the subsequent procedure is clear. If the individual indicates in any manner, at any time prior to or during questioning, that he wishes to remain silent, the interrogation must cease. At this point he has shown that he intends to exercise his Fifth Amendment privilege; any statement taken after the person invokes his privilege cannot be other than the product of compulsion, subtle or otherwise. Without the right to cut off questioning, the setting of in-custody interrogation operates on the individual to overcome free choice in producing a statement after the privilege has been once invoked."

[This] passage could be literally read to mean that a person who has invoked his "right to silence" can never again be subjected to custodial interrogation by any police officer at any time or place on any subject. Another possible construction of the passage would characterize "any statement taken after the person invokes his privilege" as [inadmissible], even if it were volunteered by the person in [custody]. Or the passage could be interpreted to require only the immediate cessation of questioning, and to permit a resumption of interrogation after a momentary respite. It is evident that any of these possible literal interpretations would lead to absurd and unintended results. To permit the continuation of custodial interrogation after a momentary cessation would clearly frustrate the purposes of *Miranda* by allowing repeated rounds of questioning to undermine the will of the person being questioned. At the other extreme, a blanket prohibition against the taking of voluntary statements or a permanent immunity from further interrogation, regardless of the circumstances, would transform the *Miranda* safeguards into wholly irrational obstacles to legitimate police investigative activity, and deprive suspects of an opportunity to make informed and intelligent assessments of their [interests]. [Moreover, *Miranda* prescribes different consequences for different kinds of invocations: an invocation of silence does not trigger the requirement of a lawyer's presence before interrogation can occur, but if "the individual states that he wants an attorney," then "the interrogation must cease until an attorney is present."]

A reasonable and faithful interpretation of the *Miranda* opinion must rest on the intention of the Court in that case to adopt "fully effective means [to] notify the person of his right of silence and to assure that the exercise of the right will be scrupulously [honored]." The critical safeguard identified in the passage at issue is a person's "right to cut off questioning." Through the exercise of his option to terminate questioning he can control the time at which questioning occurs, the subjects discussed, and the duration of the interrogation. The requirement that law enforcement authorities must respect a person's exercise of that option counteracts the coercive pressures of the custodial [setting].

A review of the circumstances leading to Mosley's confession reveals that his "right to cut off questioning" was [scrupulously honored] in this case. Before his initial interrogation, Mosley [received warnings,] orally acknowledged that he understood them, and signed a notification-of-rights form. When Mosley stated that he did not want to discuss the robberies, Detective Cowie immediately ceased the interrogation and did not try either to resume the questioning or in any way to persuade Mosley to reconsider his position. After an interval of more than two hours, Mosley was questioned by another police officer at another location about an unrelated holdup murder. He was given full and complete *Miranda* warnings at the outset of the second interrogation. The subsequent questioning did not undercut Mosley's previous decision not to answer Detective Cowie's inquiries. Detective Hill did not resume the interrogation about [the robberies], but instead focused exclusively on the [homicide], a crime different in nature and in time and place of occurrence from the [robberies]. [The] questioning of Mosley about an unrelated homicide was quite consistent with a reasonable interpretation of Mosley's earlier refusal to answer any questions about the robberies. [For] these reasons, we conclude that the admission in evidence of Mosley's incriminating statement did not violate the principles of *Miranda*. * * *

MR. JUSTICE BRENNAN, with whom MR. JUSTICE MARSHALL joins, dissenting.

[*Miranda*] is not to be read [to] impose an absolute ban on resumption of questioning "at any time or place on any subject," [or] "to permit

a resumption of interrogation after a momentary respite." [*Miranda's*] terms, however, are not so uncompromising as to preclude the fashioning of guidelines to govern this case. [Adequate] procedures are readily available. Michigan law requires that the suspect be arraigned before a judicial officer "without unnecessary delay," certainly not a burdensome requirement. Alternatively, a requirement that resumption of questioning should await appointment and arrival of counsel for the suspect would be an acceptable and readily satisfied precondition to resumption. [The] Court expediently bypasses this alternative in its search for circumstances where renewed questioning would be permissible. [Today's] decision, however, virtually empties *Miranda* of principle, for plainly the decision encourages police asked to cease interrogation to continue the suspect's detention until the police station's coercive atmosphere does its work and the suspect responds to resumed questioning.
* * *

Problems

1. *Waiver Seeking about Same Crime.* Kevin is arrested for theft, receives *Miranda* warnings and says, "I wish to exercise my right to remain silent." Kevin is returned to his cell, but the same police officer returns two hours later and wants to talk to Kevin about the same theft. The officer gives Kevin the *Miranda* warnings again, and again seeks a waiver. This time, Kevin does not invoke his right to silence and instead waives his rights and makes incriminating statements. How can his defense counsel argue that the police officer violated *Mosley*? How might the prosecutor respond? If the officer gave Kevin the warnings again after only 20 minutes, how would this change the arguments?

2. *New Evidence.* Suppose that the officer's justification for returning to seek a waiver in problem 1 after two hours is based on his discovery of new evidence about the same theft crime, and now the officer wants to find out if Kevin is interested in hearing about the new evidence in order to reconsider his decision to remain silent. How does this change the arguments?

3. *No Additional Warnings.* If the officer in problem 1 does not give Kevin the *Miranda* warnings again before seeking a waiver about the same theft crime two hours after Kevin's invocation of silence, how does this change the arguments?

4. *Repeated Requests for Waiver.* How would Kevin's defense counsel argue that *Mosley* was violated if the officer in problem 1 came back every two hours for the next 12 hours to give Kevin the warnings again and to seek a waiver about the same theft crime? Assume that Kevin continued to invoke his right to silence each time the officer sought a waiver, and then during the seventh visit by the officer, Kevin waived his rights and made incriminating statements?

5. *Invocation of Silence with Conditions.* Assume that border patrol agents in San Diego arrest several occupants of a house for the crime of smuggling illegal immigrants into the country. When the agents find Jerry standing across the street from the house, they arrest him lawfully and give

him the *Miranda* warnings. One officer asks Jerry whether he is willing to waive his rights, so that he can be questioned about his own citizenship and about his knowledge concern the people in the house. Jerry says, "I'll make a statement about my citizenship, but I won't talk about the people in the house." The agent says, "No, we want to talk about both your citizenship and the people in the house." Then Jerry says, "I will only talk about my citizenship." Then the agent asks Jerry questions about his citizenship and about the people in the house and Jerry answers all the questions. Did the agent violate *Miranda* and *Mosley* by ignoring Jerry's attempt to invoke his right to silence on the subject of the people in the house? *See United States v. Soliz*, 129 F.3d 499 (9th Cir.1997).

6. *Asserting the Right to Counsel.* Assume that after the defendant in *Mosley* received *Miranda* warnings from Detective Cowie, the defendant responded by saying, "I want a lawyer before I talk about the robberies." Should this invocation of the right to counsel change the result in *Mosley*? Why or why not?

ii. *Invocation of Right to Counsel*

EDWARDS v. ARIZONA

451 U.S. 477 (1981).

JUSTICE WHITE delivered the opinion of the Court.

[Edwards was arrested for theft and homicide crimes and he was given *Miranda* warnings at the police station. Initially, Edwards said that he understood his rights and would submit to questioning. Then he was told that another suspect in custody had implicated him, and he denied involvement in the crimes, gave a taped statement presenting an alibi defense, and said he wanted to "make a deal." One interrogating officer replied that he had no authority to do that, and gave *Edwards* the telephone number of the county prosecutor. *Edwards* made the call but hung up after a few moments and declared, "I want an attorney before making a deal." At that point, questioning ceased and *Edwards* was taken to jail. The next morning, two detectives asked to see *Edwards*, and the guard told *Edwards* that "he had" to talk to them, even though *Edwards* told the guard that he did not want to talk to anyone. Then the detectives told *Edwards* that they wanted to question him, and they gave him *Miranda* warnings. *Edwards* said that he was willing to talk, but first he wanted to hear the taped statement of the alleged suspect who had implicated him. After listening to the statement for several minutes, *Edwards* agreed to make a statement as long as it was not recorded. When the detectives explained that they could testify in court about any unrecorded statement he made, *Edwards* replied, "I'll tell you anything you want to know, but I don't want it on tape." He made incriminating statements that were admitted at the trial that led to his conviction.]

[A]lthough we have held that after initially being advised of his *Miranda* rights, the accused may himself validly waive his rights and respond to interrogation, the Court has strongly indicated that additional safeguards are necessary when the accused asks for counsel; and we now hold that when an accused has invoked his right to have counsel present during custodial interrogation, a valid waiver of that right cannot be established by showing only that he responded to further police-initiated custodial interrogation even if he has been advised of his rights. We further hold that an accused, [having] expressed his desire to deal with the police only through counsel, is not subject to further interrogation by the authorities until counsel has been made available to him, unless the accused himself initiates further communication, exchanges, or conversations with the police. *Miranda* itself indicated that the assertion of the right to counsel was a significant event and that once exercised by the accused, "the interrogation must cease until an attorney is present." Our later cases have [maintained] that view. In *Michigan v. Mosley*, 423 U.S. 96 (1975), the Court noted that *Miranda* had distinguished between the procedural safeguards triggered by a request to remain silent and a request for an attorney [and] required that interrogation cease until an attorney was present only if the individual stated that he wanted counsel.

[Had] *Edwards* initiated the meeting [with the detectives,] nothing [would] prohibit [them] from merely listening to his voluntary, volunteered statements and using them against him at the trial. [Absent] interrogation, there would have been no infringement of the right that *Edwards* [invoked]. [Here], the officers conducting the [first] interrogation ceased [their questions] when *Edwards* requested counsel as he had been advised he had the right to do. [But without] making counsel available to *Edwards*, the police returned to him the next day. This was not at his suggestion or request. Indeed, *Edwards* informed the detention officer that he did not want to talk to anyone. At the meeting, the detectives told *Edwards* that they wanted to talk to him and again advised him of his *Miranda* rights. *Edwards* stated that he would talk, but what prompted this action does not appear. He listened at his own request to part of the taped statement made by one of his alleged accomplices and then made an incriminating statement, which was used against him at his trial. We think it is clear that *Edwards* was subjected to custodial interrogation [within] the meaning of *Innis*, and that this occurred at the instance of the authorities. His statement made without having had access to counsel, did not amount to a valid waiver and hence was [inadmissible].

Notes

1. *"Initiation" that Nullifies Invocation.* In *Oregon v. Bradshaw*, 462 U.S. 1039 (1983), the defendant was arrested for furnishing liquor to a juvenile who died in a car accident. After Bradshaw was given *Miranda* warnings, he denied involvement in the accident, and he invoked his right to counsel by saying, "I do want an attorney before it goes very much further." The police officer cut off questioning, but soon thereafter, Bradshaw lost the benefits of his invocation under *Edwards* because of his subsequent conversation with the officer:

[A few minutes after his invocation, when Bradshaw was being transferred from the police station to the county jail, some ten to fifteen miles away, Bradshaw] inquired of a police officer, "Well, what is going to happen to me now?" The officer answered by saying "You do not have to talk to me. You have requested an attorney and I don't want you talking to me unless you so desire because anything you say—because—since you have requested an attorney, you know, it has to be at your own free will." [Bradshaw] said he understood. There followed a discussion between [Bradshaw] and the officer concerning where [Bradshaw] was being taken and the offense with which he would be charged. The officer suggested that [Bradshaw] might help himself by taking a polygraph examination. [Bradshaw agreed to do so, and he made incriminating statements during the examination the next day, after receiving warnings and waiving his rights during the polygraph procedure.]

There can be no doubt [that] in asking, "Well, what is going to happen to me now?", [Bradshaw] "initiated" further conversation in the ordinary dictionary sense of that word. [T]here are undoubtedly situations where a bare inquiry by either a defendant or by a police officer should not be held to "initiate" any conversation or dialogue. There are some inquiries, such as a request for a drink of water or a request to use a telephone that are so routine that they cannot be fairly said to represent a desire on the part of an accused to open up a more generalized discussion relating directly or indirectly to the investigation. Such inquiries or statements, by either an accused or a police officer, relating to routine incidents of the custodial relationship, will not generally 'initiate' a conversation in the sense in which that word was used in *Edwards*. [Although] ambiguous, [Bradshaw's] question in this case as to what was going to happen to him evinced a willingness and a desire for a generalized discussion about the investigation; it was not merely a necessary inquiry arising out of the incidents of the custodial relationship. [Since] there was no violation of the *Edwards* rule in this case, the next inquiry was "whether a valid waiver of the right to counsel and the right to silence had [occurred]. As we have said many times before, this determination depends "upon the particular facts and circumstances surrounding the case, including the background, experience, and conduct of the accused."

Justice Marshall dissented in *Bradshaw*, joined by Justices Brennan, Blackmun, and Stevens, arguing that Bradshaw's question, which "came only minutes after invocation," was "a normal reaction to being taken from the police station and placed in a police car, obviously for transport to some destination." They determined that the *Edwards* "initiation" concept was designed for "communication or dialogue about the subject matter of the criminal investigation," and concluded that "a question or statement which does not invite further interrogation" cannot qualify as "initiation."

2. *Edwards and Different Crimes.* In *Arizona v. Roberson*, 486 U.S. 675 (1988), the defendant was arrested for burglary and given *Miranda* warnings. He invoked his right to counsel by saying that he "wanted a lawyer before answering any questions." Three days later Roberson was still in custody, and a different police officer, who was unaware of the earlier invocation, sought to interrogate him about a different burglary. After this

officer gave Roberson the *Miranda* warnings, he waived his rights and made incriminating statements about the different burglary. The Court rejected the prosecutor's argument that police should be allowed to seek a waiver after invocation of counsel in order to discuss different crimes. Instead, the Court interpreted *Edwards* as prohibiting such a violation of the duty to cut off questioning, reasoning as follows:

> [The State argues that the reasoning of *Mosley* supports the police-initiated interrogation here, but a person's invocation of silence], unlike his request for counsel, does not raise the presumption that he is unable to proceed without a lawyer's advice. [Roberson's] unwillingness to answer any questions without the advice of counsel, without limiting his request for counsel, indicated that he did not feel sufficiently comfortable with the pressures of custodial interrogation to answer questions without an attorney. This discomfort is precisely the state of mind that *Edwards* presumes to persist unless the suspect himself initiates further conversation about the investigation; [otherwise,] there is no reason to assume that a suspect's state of mind is in any way investigation-specific. [*Edwards*] laid down [a rule] designed to protect an accused [from] being badgered by police officers[.] [After a person invokes the right to consult counsel,] any further interrogation without counsel having been provided will surely exacerbate whatever compulsion to speak the suspect may be feeling. [Even if a suspect may wish] to learn from the police what the new investigation is about so that he can decide whether [to] make a statement [about it,] the suspect [can] determine how to deal with the separate investigations with counsel's advice. [Police] are free to inform the suspect of the facts of the second investigation as long as such communication does not constitute interrogation. [Finally,] we attach no significance to the fact that the officer who conducted the second interrogation did not know that [Roberson] had made a request for counsel. [Whether] a contemplated reinterrogation concerns the same or a different offense, or whether the same or different law enforcement authorities are involved in the second investigation, the same need to determine whether the suspect has requested counsel exists. The police department's failure to honor that request cannot be justified by the lack of diligence of a particular officer.

Justice Kennedy, joined by Chief Justice Rehnquist, dissented in *Roberson*, arguing that the Court's extension of *Edwards* to bar waiver-seeking for "separate and independent investigations" will deprive the law enforcement network of a useful investigative technique "routinely used to resolve major crimes." When a person is arrested, his name and fingerprints are checked, and police frequently discover that this person "is wanted for questioning" for unrelated crimes. No *Edwards* protection is necessary from such questioning after invocation of counsel because "the danger of badgering is minimal"; it is unlikely that "fresh teams of police are regularly turning up to question the suspect." The *Roberson* dissenters also emphasized that *Mosley* supports the use of fresh *Miranda* warnings as sufficient protection before police engage in waiver-seeking and interrogation about a different crime; the warnings show a suspect that police respect his right to invoke, and remind him that he may invoke his rights again.

3. *The Duty to Cut off Questioning after Consultation with Counsel.* In *Minnick v. Mississippi*, 498 U.S. 146 (1990), the defendant was arrested in San Diego for a murder in Mississippi committed after his escape from jail. Although he refused to be interviewed by FBI agents, he was required to do so. After he received *Miranda* warnings from the agents, he refused to sign a waiver and told the agents, "Come back Monday when I have a lawyer." The agents cut off questioning, and an appointed attorney then met with Minnick, warned him not to talk to anybody, and promised to get a court order to stop police from interrogating him. Three days later, a Mississippi sheriff came to the San Diego jail to question Minnick, and the jailer told Minnick that he could not refuse to talk to the sheriff. After receiving *Miranda* warnings, Minnick again refused to sign a waiver, but then he started to talk to the sheriff "about how everybody was back in the county jail and what everybody was doing, had he heard from Mama and had he went and talked to Mama and had he seen my brother, Tracy, and several different other questions pertaining to such things as [that, and] then we went off into how the escape went down at the county jail." Minnick made further incriminating statements, which were admitted at his murder trial; he was convicted and received the death penalty. The *Minnick* Court rejected the prosecutor's argument that after a defendant invokes the right to counsel and then consults with counsel, the police no longer have duty to cut off questioning, and may renew the attempt to seek a waiver. Instead, the Court held that this duty remains in effect during the post-consultation period, and reasoned as follows:

> [When] counsel is requested, interrogation must cease, and officials may not reinitiate interrogation without counsel present, whether or not the accused has consulted with his attorney. [The] case before us well illustrates the pressures, and abuses, that may be concomitants of custody. [Minnick] testified that though he resisted, he was required to submit to both the FBI and the Denham interviews. [The] compulsion to submit to interrogation followed [his] unequivocal request during the FBI interview that questioning cease until counsel was present. The case illustrates also that consultation is not always effective in instructing the suspect of his rights. One plausible interpretation of the record is that [Minnick] thought he could keep his admissions out of evidence by refusing to sign a formal waiver of rights. If the authorities had complied with Minnick's request to have counsel present during interrogation, the attorney could have corrected Minnick's misunderstanding, or indeed counseled him that he need not make a statement at all. We decline to remove protection from police-initiated questioning based on isolated consultations with counsel who is absent when the interrogation resumes.

Justice Scalia dissented, joined by Chief Justice Rehnquist, arguing that after consultation with counsel, a suspect will have a heightened awareness of his or her rights, especially of the right to remain silent, so that any police-initiated waiver and confession should no longer be presumed to be based on the suspect's ignorance of rights or on police coercion. Scalia concluded that the *Minnick* Court's extension of the *Edwards* rule was unjustified because it "makes it impossible" for police to ask a prisoner who invokes and consults counsel whether "he has changed his mind" about waiving his rights.

Problems

1. *Refusal to Honor Invocation.* Suppose that Ted is given *Miranda* warnings during interrogation and invokes his right to counsel by saying, "I want a lawyer now." The interrogating officers ignore Ted's invocation and continue to interrogate. Ted refuses to sign a waiver and repeatedly invokes his right to counsel during a three-hour interrogation during which he makes no incriminating statements. He is taken back to the jail. Five hours later he is brought back to the interrogation room for more questioning. Before he is given more warnings, Ted says, "What is going to happen to me now?" The police officer responds by saying, "We're going to resume our interrogation." At this point Ted makes incriminating statements. Are they admissible under *Miranda*? *See Hill v. Brigano*, 199 F.3d 833 (6th Cir.1999).

2. *Interrogation before Initiation.* Assume that Fraser and Vecchio arrest Nan for a murder that occurred in New York, and as in problem 2 after *Perkins*, Nan receives warnings and invokes her rights to silence and counsel. This time when Fraser returns to the room, he sits down at the table with a different form that has the words, Death Penalty, printed in large letters, at the top. When Fraser sits down next to Nan, she notices the large print words and asks, "Why does that form say, Death Penalty?" Fraser says, "You have to waive your rights if you want to discuss the case. All I can tell you is that this form says that you can get the death penalty for this crime. Over there in that bookcase you'll find a copy of the state penal code, and if you want to look up the penalty, you can look it up yourself." Nan says, "Uh-oh. Do you know anything about extradition?" Fraser says, "Well, you can get extradited to any other state, if you've committed a crime in that state and if the prosecutor there has evidence that is sufficient to charge you, like the evidence we have in this case against you based on the photo array and the eyewitness identification." Nan blurts out, "I might as well tell you, yesterday I left Massachusetts because I killed a guy in Boston." The prosecutor argues that this statement is admissible because Nan "initiated" a "generalized discussion" under *Bradshaw*. Nan's defense counsel argues that her conversation does not qualify as "initiation" and so her two statements are inadmissible because Fraser violated *Edwards* when he made the comments about the death penalty and about extradition. Explain the arguments on both sides.

6.   *The Uses of Evidence Obtained in Violation of Miranda*

a.   **When Unwarned Confessions Precede Warnings**

In *Oregon v. Elstad*, 470 U.S. 298 (1985), the Court rejected the application of the Fourth Amendment "fruit of the poisonous tree" doctrine to the *Miranda* context of sequential confessions with midstream warnings. That "fruits" doctrine requires police to show that the "taint" of an illegal search or seizure has become so "attenuated" that subsequently obtained evidence should not be treated as the inadmissible "poisoned fruit" of the primary illegality. When police can show that they are not exploiting the original constitutional violation to obtain further evidence, then there is no need to exclude the "fruits" evidence to deter police from engaging in the original violation. In order to determine whether "attenuation" has occurred, courts examine a totality of factors, including "the strength of the causal connection between the illegal police action and the evidence, the proximity in time and place, the presence of intervening factors, and the purpose and flagrancy of official misconduct." Before *Elstad*, most lower courts relied on the "fruits" analysis in assuming that "(1) there is a rebuttable presumption that a confession obtained in violation of *Miranda* taints subsequent confessions" unless the prosecution can show that the taint is "attenuated," and that (2) such taint cannot be dissipated solely by giving *Miranda* warnings." *Oregon v. Elstad*, 470 U.S. 298, 318 (Brennan, J., dissenting). The *Elstad* Court rejected these assumptions, and endorsed the propositions that (1) when errors are made by police in administering *Miranda* procedures, "they should not breed the same irremediable consequences as police infringement of the Fifth Amendment itself," and that (2) after an unwarned statement is obtained, the administration of *Miranda* warnings usually should be sufficient to allow a post-warning statement to be admitted, assuming that police have obtained a "voluntary, knowing, and intelligent" waiver. More narrowly, the *Elstad* Court held that a defendant's statement following midstream warnings would not be tainted by the *Miranda* error of the failure to give warnings at the outset of interrogation, as long as no "actual coercion" occurred.

In *Michigan v. Tucker*, 417 U.S. 433 (1974), the Court held that police may obtain the identity of a witness from a defendant's statement that is inadmissible under *Miranda*, and the testimony of that witness is admissible in the prosecution's case in chief at the defendant's trial. The *Tucker* defendant did not receive complete *Miranda* warnings, and therefore the statement he made after waiver, describing his alibi and the name of an alibi witness, was inadmissible at his rape trial. However, the *Tucker* Court held that the testimony of that witness was admissible in the state's case-in-chief. The Court reasoned that where the police violated *Miranda* in good faith, the "deterrent effect" on future police violations of *Miranda* would not be "significantly augmented" by excluding the testimony of "a third party who was subject to no custodial pressures." *See United States v. Patane*, 542 U.S. 630 (2004) (the *Dickerson* Court's "reliance on our *Miranda* precedents, including both *Tucker* and *Elstad*, further demonstrates the continuing validity of those decisions").

Note

Under *Missouri v. Seibert*, 542 U.S. 600, 617, n.8 (2004), a defendant in a midstream warnings case may avoid the need to produce the showing of actual coercion to prove that a waiver is involuntary under *Elstad* by arguing that a court should resolve the threshold issue whether the warnings were not adequate in communicating the *Miranda* rights according to the *Seibert* criteria. If the warnings were not adequate, then the defendant's post-warning statement will be inadmissible under *Seibert*, and no inquiry will be necessary concerning the voluntariness of the waiver that occurred before the statement was made.

Problems

1. *Edwards Violations and Elstad.* Assume that a police officer fails to cut off questioning when a person in custody invokes the right to counsel after adequate warnings are given; instead, the officer violates *Miranda* by interrogating the person and obtains an inadmissible statement in violation of *Edwards* and *Innis*. Then the interrogation ends. One hour later, the person in custody "initiates" a generalized discussion of the offense with a different officer. This officer provides *Miranda* warnings to the person, obtains a waiver, and interrogates the person so as to obtain a second statement. Should this post-warning statement be admissible under *Elstad's* standard defining the validity of the waiver? How would the defense argue the case? How might the prosecution respond?

2. *Actual Coercion and Sequential Interrogations.* Lyons, a murder suspect, was illegally arrested by police officers who erroneously believed that they had probable cause, and interrogated for two hours at the county jail without *Miranda* warnings, starting at midnight. A confession was obtained at 2:00 a.m., and Lyons later testified that police gave him a black eye and subjected him to threats of further harm unless he confessed. Lyons stayed in jail for a week, and then a second unwarned interrogation occurred, which began at noon; Lyons testified that during questioning, the police placed a pan of bones in his lap and told him that the bones were those of the victim. This time after twelve hours of questioning, a second confession was obtained at midnight. Finally, the next morning, Lyons was taken to the prosecutor's office and given *Miranda* warnings by the same police officers who questioned him during the two previous interrogations. He stated that he understood the warnings and he agreed to waive his rights and speak to the police. He made a third confession. What arguments may be made by the defense counsel as to the inadmissibility of each of the three confessions? How should the prosecutor respond to the arguments relating to each confession? *Compare Lyons v. Oklahoma*, 322 U.S. 596 (1944).

3. *The Impact of Miranda Warnings in an "Actual Coercion" Scenario.* Assume that in problem 2, the initial arrest was valid, that Lyons was given *Miranda* warnings at the outset of each of the three interrogations, and that he agreed to waive his rights each time before making statements. Assume that the facts remain the same in all other respects. Under the *Elstad* "actual coercion" standard, are all three confessions admissible? If not, what is the admissibility status of each one and why?

4. *Seibert's Application.* Assume that in problem 3, the defense counsel for Lyons argues that each time the *Miranda* warnings were provided, they were "inadequate" under *Seibert* standards, and so irrespective of whether the three waivers were voluntary, each of the three statements is inadmissible. Will the defendant win this argument? Explain.

b. Physical Fruits of Unwarned Statements

In *United States v. Patane*, 542 U.S. 630 (2004) a plurality of the Court held that police failure to give the prescribed *Miranda* warnings did not require suppression of the physical fruits of a defendant's unwarned but voluntary statements. Patane was arrested at his home for violating a restraining order, but he was warned only about the "right to remain silent" before he was asked about a gun that he was believed to possess illegally as a convicted felon. When Patane told the officers that the gun was in his bedroom, they retrieved it, and it was offered in evidence at his trial for a firearms crime. The police failure to provide complete *Miranda* warnings made Patane's statement about gun inadmissible, but the *Patane* Court ruled that the gun itself should be admissible because *Miranda* should not be interpreted to require exclusion of physical evidence that is obtained as a result of *Miranda* violations. This decision repudiated the view of some lower courts that *Dickerson v. United States*, 530 U.S. 428 (2000), implicitly undermined the Court's prior holdings that rejected the *Wong Sun* Fourth Amendment "fruits" doctrine for *Miranda* violations. The *Patane* plurality justified its holding as follows:

> [The] characterization of *Miranda* [in *Dickerson*] as a constitutional rule does not lessen the need to maintain the closest possible fit between the Self–Incrimination Clause and any judge-made rule designed to protect it. And there is no such fit here. Introduction of the nontestimonial fruit of a voluntary statement, such as [Patane's gun], does not implicate the Self–Incrimination Clause. The admission of such fruit presents no risk that a defendant's coerced statements [will] be used against him at a criminal trial. In any case, "[t]he exclusion of unwarned statements [is] a complete and sufficient remedy" for any perceived *Miranda* violation. There is simply no need to extend [the] prophylactic rule of *Miranda* to [require the exclusion of physical evidence]. Similarly, because police cannot violate the Self–Incrimination Clause by taking unwarned though voluntary statements, an exclusionary rule cannot be justified by reference to a deterrence effect on law [enforcement]. Our decision not to apply *Wong Sun* to mere failures to give *Miranda* warnings was sound at the time [when *Oregon v. [Elstad[*, 470 U.S. 298 (1985)] and *[Michigan v.] Tucker[*, 417 U.S. 433 (1974)] were decided, and we decline to apply *Wong Sun* to such failures now. [W]e have held that "[t]he word 'witness' in the constitutional text limits the" scope of the Self–Incrimination Clause to testimonial evidence. [And] although it is true that the Court requires the exclusion of the physical fruit of actually coerced statements, it must be remembered that statements taken without sufficient *Miranda* warnings are presumed to have been coerced only for certain purposes and then only when necessary to protect the privilege against self-incrimination. [We] decline to extend that presumption further.

Justices Kennedy, joined by Justice O'Connor, concurred in the judgment, opining that "the important probative value of reliable physical evidence" made it "doubtful that exclusion can be justified by a deterrence rationale." But Justice Souter's dissent, joined by Justices Stevens and Ginsburg, argued that the *Patane* rule is an "invitation to law enforcement officers to flout *Miranda* when there may be physical evidence to be gained," and that when a *Miranda* violation leads police to discover "derivative evidence" that includes physical evidence, such evidence should be excluded. Justice Breyer's dissent advocated the same position, with an exception for good faith violations of *Miranda*.

c.   The Miranda Impeachment Exception

In *Harris v. New York*, 401 U.S. 222 (1971), the Court upheld the use of *Miranda*-defective statements for purposes of impeaching a defendant's credibility at trial. The prosecutor conceded that the police violated *Miranda* by interrogating Harris without giving him warnings; therefore, his incriminating statements were inadmissible in the state's case-in-chief. However, after undercover agents testified that Harris sold heroin to one agent, Harris took the stand and testified that he sold the agent baking powder in a glassine bag. Therefore, the prosecutor sought to use Harris's statements to police to impeach his testimony on cross-examination; the trial judge allowed this use of the statements, but told the jury that the statements could be considered only in passing on the Harris's credibility. The *Harris* Court upheld this use of the *Miranda*-defective statements, reasoning that the *Miranda* Court did not intend to bar the use of such evidence "for all purposes," and that "the impeachment process [in *Harris*] undoubtedly provided valuable aid to the jury in assessing [the defendant's] credibility." The Court opined that "the benefits" of the impeachment process "should not be lost" merely "because of the speculative possibility that impermissible police conduct will encouraged thereby"; moreover, the Court determined that "sufficient deterrence" of police violations of Fifth Amendment rights could be obtained by making *Miranda*-defective statements "unavailable to the prosecution in its case in chief." The Court emphasized that a defendant who takes the stand is "under an obligation to speak truthfully and accurately," and that a bar to the impeachment use of *Miranda*-defective statements would cause "[t]he shield provided by *Miranda*" to be "perverted into a license to use perjury by way of defense, free from the risk of confrontation with prior inconsistent utterances." Justice Brennan's dissent, joined by Justices Douglas and Marshall, argued that courts should not "aid or abet the law-breaking police officer" by validating an impeachment exception to *Miranda*. The dissenters predicted that the *Harris* rule "will seriously undermine" *Miranda's* objective of deterring unconstitutional police practices.

Problems

1.   *The Thief and the Bicycle*. Suppose that Hass is arrested for bicycle theft, taken into custody by the arresting officer, and given *Miranda* warnings. Then Hass waives his rights, admits that he has stolen three bicycles and tells the arresting officer where to find two of them. The officer

drives Hass to find the bicycles and takes custody of them. Then Hass states that he thinks he is "in a lot of trouble at this point," and that he "wants to phone his attorney now." The arresting officer tells Hass that he can phone his attorney only after he shows the officer where the third stolen bicycle is located. Then Hass tells the officer where to find the third bicycle, and the officer drives there and seizes it as evidence. The prosecutor offers all the statements by Hass as evidence in her case-in-chief. The trial judge rules that the statements about the first two bicycles are admissible, but that the statement about the location of the third bicycle is inadmissible. When Hass takes the stand and denies his guilt, the trial judge allows the prosecutor to introduce his statement about the location of the third bicycle for purposes of impeachment. Explain how these decisions of the trial court are justified. *See Oregon v. Hass*, 420 U.S. 714 (1975).

2. *The Drug Smuggler.* Assume that when Mac is searched lawfully by customs officials, they discover cocaine sewn into the makeshift pockets of his homemade T-shirt. Mac makes a statement implicating his traveling companion Havens, so police arrest Havens and search his luggage, finding no drugs, but finding the T-shirt from which the pocket pieces were cut to sew the extra pockets on Mac's T-shirt full of drugs. Assume that the evidence from the luggage search is suppressed, and that Mac pleads guilty and testifies against Havens at his trial for drug crimes, asserting that Havens supplied him with the pocket material, filled the pockets with drugs, and sewed the pockets shut. After Havens takes the stand and says that Mac is lying, the prosecutor persuades the trial judge to allow her to ask Havens on cross-examination about the T-shirt found in his luggage. Then when Havens denies that any T-shirt was in his luggage, the prosecutor persuades the trial judge to allow her to offer the T-shirt in evidence against Havens, and to call as a rebuttal witness the customs agent who can testify that the T-shirt was found in the luggage. Havens is convicted and argues on appeal that the admission of the rebuttal-witness testimony of the customs agent violated his constitutional rights. What reasoning can be used to uphold the admission of this testimony? Explain. *See United States v. Havens*, 446 U.S. 620 (1980).

d.   Due Process Limits on Impeachment Based on Silence

In *Doyle v. Ohio*, 426 U.S. 610 (1976), the Court held that it is a Due Process violation for a prosecutor to use an arrestee's silence after *Miranda* warnings to impeach her testimony at trial. The defendants were charged with selling marijuana to an undercover agent. After their arrest, they were given *Miranda* warnings and remained silent. At their trial, the agent testified that the defendants sold him marijuana and then went looking for him and demanded more money, claiming that he had underpaid them; therefore, the agent gave them the money that was found in their car after arrest. The defendants took the stand and testified that the agent attempted to sell them marijuana and then threw money into their car to frame them when they refused to buy the drugs from the agent. On cross-examination, the prosecutor asked each defendant repeatedly why he had not told the police officers about the "frame up" by the agent, after they were arrested. The objections by defense counsel to these questions were overruled. The *Doyle* Court granted a new trial on the grounds that the prosecutor's questions violated Due Process, rejecting the prosecutor's argument that the jury's need for complete information outweighed the Due Process concerns. The Court reasoned that "every post-arrest silence is insolubly ambiguous because of what the State is required to advise the person arrested," namely, the right to remain silent under *Miranda*. Therefore, an arrestee's "[s]ilence in the wake of [the *Miranda* warnings] may be nothing more than the arrestee's exercise of [the] *Miranda* rights." The *Doyle* Court acknowledged that "the *Miranda* warnings contain no express assurance that silence will carry no penalty," and therefore refrained from creating a new *Miranda* duty for police to add such an assurance to the *Miranda* warnings. Instead, the Court held that it would violate Due Process "to allow the arrested person's silence to be used to impeach an explanation subsequently offered at trial," because an assurance that silence will carry no penalty "is implicit to any person who receives the warnings."

Problems

1. *Jury Instruction to Disregard a Doyle Violation.* When Randy is arrested and immediately given his *Miranda* warnings by police, he invokes his right to silence and right to counsel, and tells the police nothing. Before Randy's trial, his co-defendant Pierre pleads guilty and agrees to testify as a prosecution witness at Randy's trial. According to Pierre's testimony, it was Randy's idea to kidnap the victim and Randy agreed to allow Pierre to bring the victim to Randy's home for confinement. When Randy takes the stand, he testifies that he had no knowledge of the kidnapping until Pierre showed up at Randy's home with the victim, and that Pierre threatened Randy with a gun in order to force him to confine the victim there. On cross-examination, the prosecutor asks Randy, "Why didn't you tell your story to the police after you were arrested?" The defense counsel objects to this question and moves for a mistrial. The trial judge denies the motion but sustains the objection, telling the jury, "Please ignore the prosecutor's question for the time being." Then during general jury instructions at the end of the trial, the judge tells the jury to "disregard questions to which objections were sustained." Randy is convicted, and argues on appeal that the conviction must be reversed because the prosecutor violated *Doyle*. What result? Would it matter if the prosecutor also made references in closing argument to Randy's failure to tell his story to the police, which references then provoked objections by defense counsel that were sustained by the trial judge? Explain. *See Greer v. Miller*, 483 U.S. 756 (1987).

2. *Impeaching a Defendant Who Talks after Warnings.* Assume that in problem 1, instead of invoking his right to silence and right to counsel after receiving *Miranda* warnings, Randy told the police that he tried to tell Pierre that the kidnaping was a bad idea before Pierre showed up at Randy's house with the victim. At trial, Pierre testifies as in problem 1, and when Randy takes the stand and tells his story as in problem 1, the prosecutor asks Randy on cross-examination, "Isn't it true that the story you are telling now is inconsistent with the comments about Pierre that you made to the police?" The defense counsel objects to this question, arguing that the

prosecutor has violated *Doyle*. What result? *See Anderson v. Charles*, 447 U.S. 404 (1980).

3.   *Pre-arrest Silence.* Assume that Jake is an undercover police agent who is posing as a drug buyer in a sting operation, and that he approaches Lenora because he believes her to be a drug seller, based on an informant's tip. Jake asks Lenora, "Do you have any drugs that you can get right now and sell to me?" Lenora remains silent in response to this question. Jake reveals his identity and makes a lawful arrest of Lenora based on probable cause provided by the informant. Then Jake gives Lenora the *Miranda* warnings and she tells him nothing. Would the impeachment use of Lenora's silence before her arrest, in response to Jake's question, violate Due Process under *Doyle*? Explain. *See Jenkins v. Anderson*, 447 U.S. 231 (1980).

4.   *Post-arrest, Pre-warning Silence.* Assume that in problem 3, Lenora remains silent not only in response to Jake's pre-arrest question, but also remains silent after he takes her into custody and before he gives her the *Miranda* warnings. Would the impeachment use of Lenora's silence after arrest and before the warnings violate Due Process under *Doyle*? Explain. *See Fletcher v. Weir*, 455 U.S. 603 (1982).

D.   POST–*MIRANDA* SIXTH AMENDMENT LAW

For eleven years after *Miranda*, the Court's decisions on police interrogations refrained from addressing the potential implications of *Massiah*'s Sixth Amendment doctrine. But in 1977 the Court turned back to that doctrine as an alternative grounds to *Miranda* for resolving a controversial case. This decision required the Court to embark upon the process of articulating the similarities and differences between the constitutional protections provided by *Miranda* and *Massiah*.

1.   *Reliance on Counsel and Waiver*

BREWER v. WILLIAMS

430 U.S. 387 (1977).

MR. JUSTICE STEWART delivered the opinion of the Court.

[An arrest warrant was issued for the arrest of Williams for the crime of abduction, based on a report that he was seen carrying a child to his car in Des Moines on Christmas Eve; the next day, his car was found abandoned in Davenport, 160 miles away. Based on the advice of counsel in Des Moines, Williams turned himself in to the police in Davenport; during his arraignment there, local counsel was appointed. Two police officers from Des Moines traveled to Davenport to pick up Williams, and police officials promised that he would not be questioned during the return trip. Williams received *Miranda* warnings from the Davenport police, the arraignment judge, and the Des Moines police upon their arrival in Davenport. Both his Davenport counsel and his Des Moines counsel told him not to talk to the police until after he returned to Des Moines and consulted with counsel there. On arrival in Davenport, Detective Leaming informed Williams and his lawyer that "we'll be visiting [on the ride] between here and Des Moines," prompting the lawyer to remind Leaming of the official promise not to interrogate Williams. When the Davenport counsel asked Leaming to allow him to accompany Williams on the road trip back to Des Moines, Leaming refused, and set off in the patrol car with Williams and the other officer. During the trip, Williams told Leaming several times, "[w]hen I get to Des Moines and see [my lawyer], I am going to tell you the whole story." Leaming knew that Williams was a former mental patient and was deeply religious.]

The detective and his prisoner soon embarked on a wide-ranging conversation covering a variety of topics, including the subject of religion. [N]ot long after leaving Davenport and reaching the interstate highway, Detective Leaming delivered what has been referred to [as] the "Christian burial speech." Addressing Williams as "Reverend," the detective said: "I want to give you something to think about while we're traveling down the [road]. Number one, I want you to observe the weather conditions, it's raining, it's sleeting, it's freezing, driving is very treacherous, visibility is poor, it's going to be dark early this evening. They are predicting several inches of snow for tonight, and I feel that you yourself are the only person that knows where this little girl's body is, that you yourself have only been there once, and if you get a snow on top of it you yourself may be unable to find it. And, since we will be going right past the area on the way into Des Moines, I feel that we could stop and locate the body, that the parents of this little girl should be entitled to a Christian burial for the little girl who was snatched away from them on Christmas Eve and murdered. And I feel we should stop and locate it on the way in rather than waiting until morning and trying to come back out after a snow storm and possibly not being able to find it at all." Williams asked Detective Leaming why he thought their route to Des Moines would be taking them past the girl's body, and Leaming responded that he knew the body was in the area of Mitchellville, a town they would be passing on the way to Des Moines. Leaming then stated: "I do not want you to answer me. I don't want to discuss it any further. Just think about it as we're riding down the road."

As the car approached Grinnell, a town approximately 100 miles west of Davenport, Williams asked whether the police had found the victim's shoes. When Detective Leaming replied that he was unsure, Williams directed the officers to a service station where he said he had left the shoes; a search for them proved unsuccessful. As they continued towards Des Moines, Williams asked whether the police had found the blanket, and directed the officers to a rest area where he said he had disposed of the blanket. Nothing was found. The car continued towards Des Moines, and as it approached Mitchellville, Williams said that he would show the officers where the body was. He then directed the police to the body of Pamela Powers. [His statements were admitted into evidence at his murder trial and he was convicted.]

[Whatever] else it may mean, the right to counsel granted by the Sixth and Fourteenth Amendments means at least that a person is entitled to the help of a lawyer at or after the time that judicial proceedings have been initiated against him "whether by way of formal charge, preliminary hearing, indictment, information, or arraignment." *Kirby v. Illinois*, 406 U.S. at 689. There can be no doubt in the present case that judicial proceedings had been initiated against Williams before the start of the automobile ride from Davenport to Des Moines. A warrant had been issued for his arrest, he had been arraigned on that warrant before a judge in a Davenport courtroom, and he had been committed by the court to confinement in [jail].

There can be no serious doubt [that] Detective Leaming deliberately and designedly set out to elicit information from Williams just as surely as and perhaps more effectively than if he had formally interrogated him. Detective Leaming was fully aware before departing for Des Moines that Williams was being represented [by counsel] in Davenport [and by counsel] in Des Moines[,] [yet Leaming] purposely sought during Williams' isolation from his lawyers to obtain as much incriminating information as possible. Indeed, Detective Leaming conceded as much when he testified at Williams' trial: "Q. In fact, Captain, [you] were trying to get all the information you could before he got to his lawyer, weren't you? 'A. I was sure hoping to find out where that little girl was, yes, sir.' " [The] clear rule of *Massiah* is that once adversary proceedings have commenced against an individual, he has a right to legal representation when the government interrogates him. It thus requires [no] technical application of the *Massiah* doctrine to conclude that Williams was entitled to the assistance of counsel guaranteed to him by the Sixth and Fourteenth Amendments.

[The prosecutor argues that Williams waived his Sixth Amendment right.] [I]t was incumbent upon the State to prove "an intentional relinquishment or abandonment of a known right or privilege." *Johnson v. Zerbst*, 304 U.S., at 464. [C]ourts indulge [every] reasonable presumption against waiver. This strict standard applies [to] an alleged waiver [at] trial or at a critical stage of pretrial proceedings. [T]he record in this case falls far short of sustaining [the state's] burden. [Williams] had been informed of and appeared to understand his right to counsel. But waiver requires not merely comprehension but relinquishment, and Williams' consistent reliance upon the advice of counsel in dealing with the authorities refutes any suggestion that he waived that right. [Williams] was advised not to make any statements before seeing [his counsel] in Des Moines, and was assured that the police had agreed not to question him. His statements while in the car that he would tell the whole story after seeing [his counsel] in Des Moines were the clearest expressions by Williams himself that he desired the presence of an attorney before any interrogation took place. [E]ven before making these statements, Williams had effectively asserted his right to counsel by having secured attorneys at both ends of the automobile trip, both of whom [had] made clear to the police that no interrogation was to occur during the journey. Williams knew of that agreement and, particularly in view of his consistent reliance on counsel, there is no basis for concluding that he disavowed it.

Despite Williams' express and implicit assertions of his right to counsel, Detective Leaming proceeded to elicit incriminating statements from Williams. Leaming did not preface this effort by telling Williams that he had a right to the presence of a lawyer, and made no effort at all to ascertain whether Williams wished to relinquish that right. The circumstances [thus] provide no reasonable basis for finding that Williams waived his right to the assistance of counsel.

MR. CHIEF JUSTICE BURGER, dissenting.

[It] is very clear that Williams had made a valid waiver of his Fifth Amendment right to silence and his Sixth Amendment right to counsel when he led police to the [body]. [One] unarticulated basis for the result [is] that once a suspect has asserted his right [to counsel] it becomes legally impossible for him to waive that right until he has seen an attorney. [The Court does not explain] why police conduct—whether good or bad—should operate to suspend Williams' right to change his mind and "tell all" at once rather than waiting until he reached Des Moines. [Even] if there was no waiver, [the] Court errs gravely in mechanically applying the exclusionary rule [and] fails even to consider whether the benefits secured by application of the exclusionary rule in this case outweigh its obvious social [costs]. [U]se of Williams' disclosures and their fruits carries no risk [of unreliability]. [The] fundamental purpose of the Sixth Amendment is to safeguard the fairness of the trial and the integrity of the factfinding process. [It] appears suppression is mandated here for no other reason than the Court's general impression that it may have a beneficial effect on future police [conduct]. * * *

MR. JUSTICE WHITE, with whom MR. JUSTICE BLACKMUN and MR. JUSTICE REHNQUIST join, dissenting.

[Waiver] is not a formalistic concept. Waiver is shown whenever the facts establish that an accused knew of a right and intended to relinquish it. Such waiver, even if not express, was plainly shown here. [The] majority believes that the law enforcement officers acted in a way which involves some risk of injury to society and that such conduct should be deterred. However, the officers' conduct did [not] jeopardize the fairness of respondent's trial or in any way risk the conviction of an innocent man, the risk against which the Sixth Amendment guarantee of assistance of counsel is designed to protect. [T]he result in this case seems utterly [senseless]. * * *

Notes

1. *Postscript to Brewer.* After the case was remanded to the lower courts, the prosecutor argued that the evidence should be admissible despite the *Massiah* violation because the police "inevitably" would have discovered the body given the search procedures then underway. Ultimately the Court endorsed this concept and upheld the conviction on this theory on the record in *Brewer. See Nix v. Williams*, 467 U.S. 431 (1984).

2. *Potential Borrowing of Miranda Doctrines for Sixth Amendment Rules.* While the Court could have decided *Brewer* on *Miranda* grounds, the Court's reliance on *Massiah* allowed it to avoid resolving some difficult *Miranda* issues. For example, *Brewer* was decided before *Innis* established the *Miranda* definition of interrogation, before *Edwards* and *Minnick* established the prohibition on waiver-seeking after invocation of counsel and consultation with counsel, and before *Davis* established the requirement for unambiguous invocations of counsel. However, *Brewer*'s Sixth Amendment rationale raised questions about the potential similarities and differences between *Miranda* doctrines and *Massiah* doctrines in the making. More specifically, it was unclear whether the Sixth Amendment concept of "deliberate elicitation" was different from the *Miranda* concept of "interrogation," whether the Sixth Amendment standard of "intentional relinquishment" was different from the "voluntary, knowing and intelligent" waiver standard of *Miranda*, and whether a *Massiah* defendant in custody needed a *"Massiah* warning" about Sixth Amendment rights as well as *Miranda* warnings about Fifth Amendment rights. The *Brewer* Court appeared to endorse one difference between Fifth and Sixth Amendment rights, in observing that for indicted defendants, "[We] have said that the right to counsel does not depend upon a request by the defendant." But the Court also emphasized the defendant's "assertions" of his right to counsel in *Brewer* and "his consistent reliance on counsel"; such comments implied that *Miranda's* Fifth Amendment invocation requirements might be used to require a *Massiah* invocation requirement for indicted defendants faced not with questioning by undercover agents, but with police interrogation. Soon after *Brewer* the Court began to address and resolve the issues related to the interplay between *Miranda* and *Massiah* rights.

Problems

1. *Brewer and Massiah.* Is *Brewer's* analysis of the Sixth Amendment right to counsel consistent with *Massiah's* analysis? Explain the differences you see, as well as the ambiguities and potential similarities of each analysis.

2. *Comments Not Directed at Arrestee.* Assume that unlike Detective Leaming, the police officers in *Brewer* know nothing about Williams' past experiences or beliefs. Also assume that the officers talk between themselves in the police car on the ride between Des Moines and Davenport, but they do not address Williams directly. They comment briefly on the weather because a heavy snow is falling; they mention the fact that people are searching for the body of the victim. But they make no other references to these subjects and no Christian Burial Speech occurs. Suddenly, Williams blurts out the location of the body. Did the police officers violate Williams' Sixth Amendment right? Did they violate his modern Fifth Amendment *Miranda* rights? Explain.

3. *The Christian Burial Conversation among Officers.* Assume that like Detective Leaming, the officers know that Williams is a very religious man and suffers from mental problems. This time their conversation between themselves in the police car laments the fact that the body of a little girl is out there somewhere in the snow where no one can find her on Christmas Eve, so that her grieving parents will be unable to give her a decent

Christian burial. Again, Williams suddenly blurts out the location of the body. Did the police officers violate the Sixth Amendment? Did they violate *Miranda*? Why? Why not?

4. *Brewer Today.* Assume that the facts of *Brewer* arise in a case today, and that the prosecutor argues that Williams' statements are admissible because he did not invoke his rights, and because even if he invoked his rights, he waived his rights. Describe the arguments that will be made by both sides on these issues, using modern *Miranda* precedents to fit the *Brewer* facts.

2. *Deliberate Elicitation*

KUHLMANN v. WILSON

477 U.S. 436 (1986).

JUSTICE POWELL announced the judgment of the Court and delivered the opinion of the Court.

[Kuhlmann was arraigned on charges of robbery and murder and placed in a cell with Lee, a prisoner who had agreed to act as a police informant. Lee agreed to listen to Kuhlmann's conversations and report his remarks to Detective Cullen, who wished to discover the identities of Kuhlmann's confederates. Cullen told Lee not to ask any questions, but simply to "keep his ears open." Kuhlmann first spoke to Lee about the crimes after he noticed that their cellblock window overlooked the Star Taxicab Garage, where the crimes had occurred. He said, "someone's messing with me," and told Lee the same story about the robbery that he gave the police at the time of his arrest. Lee advised Kuhlmann that his explanation "didn't sound too good," but Kuhlmann did not alter his story immediately. After a few days, Kuhlmann received a visit from his brother, who mentioned that members of his family were upset because they believed that Kuhlmann was guilty of murder. After the visit, Kuhlmann admitted to Lee that he and two other men had planned and carried out the robbery and murder. Lee reported Kuhlmann's statements to Detective Cullen, and gave Cullen the notes that he had written surreptitiously while sharing the cell with Kuhlmann.] The trial court found that Cullen had instructed Lee "to ask no questions of [Kuhlmann] about the crime but merely to listen as to what [Kuhlmann] might say in his presence." The court determined that Lee obeyed these instructions, that he "at no time asked any questions with respect to the crime," and that he "only listened to [Kuhlmann] and made notes regarding what [he] had to say." The trial court also found that [Kuhlmann's] statements to Lee were "spontaneous" and "unsolicited."

[T]he primary concern of the *Massiah* [precedents] is secret interrogation by investigatory techniques that are the equivalent of direct police interrogation. Since "the Sixth Amendment is not violated whenever—by luck or happenstance—the State obtains incriminating statements from the accused after the right to counsel has attached," a defendant does not make out a violation of that right simply by showing that an informant, either through prior arrangement or voluntarily, reported his incriminating statements to the police. Rather, the defendant must demonstrate that the police and their informant took some action, beyond merely listening, that was designed deliberately to elicit incriminating remarks. [Cullen] instructed Lee [only] to listen to [Kuhlmann] and Lee followed these instructions[;] "at no time [did he ask] any questions" of [Kuhlmann] concerning the pending charges [and he] "only listened" to [Kuhlmann's] statements. [The] only remark made by Lee [was] his comment that [Kuhlmann's] initial version of his participation in the crimes "didn't sound too good." [The Court concluded that on the record there was no "deliberate elicitation" by Lee that violated the Sixth Amendment. The Court also noted that "for all the record shows," it was "sheer coincidence" that Kuhlmann was placed in a cell overlooking the crime scene, and opined that there is no reason "to require police to isolate one charged with crime so that he cannot view the scene, whatever it may be, from his cell window."]

JUSTICE BRENNAN, with whom JUSTICE MARSHALL joins, dissenting.

[U]nder [*Massiah*] it is irrelevant whether the informant asks pointed questions about the crime or "merely engage[s] in general conversation about it." [Lee] encouraged [Kuhlmann] to talk about his crime by conversing with him on the subject over the course of several days and by telling [him] that his exculpatory story would not convince anyone without more work. [A] disturbing visit from [his] brother, rather than a conversation with the informant, seems to have been the immediate catalyst for [Kuhlmann's confession]. [But] the deliberate-elicitation standard requires consideration of the entire course of government behavior. [Here the] State intentionally created a situation in which it was foreseeable that [Kuhlmann] would make incriminating statements without the assistance of counsel—it assigned [him] to a cell overlooking the scene of the crime and designated a secret informant to be [his] cellmate. The informant, while avoiding direct questions, nonetheless developed a relationship of cellmate camaraderie with [Kuhlmann] and encouraged him to talk about his crime. [Clearly] the State's actions had a sufficient nexus with [Kuhlmann's] admission of guilt to constitute deliberate [elicitation]. * * *

Note

Continuing Investigations after Indictment. The *Massiah* Court observed that it was "entirely proper to continue an investigation of the suspected criminal activities of the defendant," and held only that statements obtained in violation of the Sixth Amendment could not be admitted at Massiah's trial for the crime charged in the indictment. In *Maine v. Moulton*, 474 U.S. 159 (1985), the prosecutor argued that the Court should allow statements elicited in violation of *Massiah* to be admitted at trial whenever there is a legitimate reason for this use of the agent that is different from simple need to investigate the charged crime. In *Moulton*, the defendant was indicted for a theft crime, and the police received a report from a co-conspirator that the defendant was planning to kill a witness who was to supposed to testify at the theft trial. The co-conspirator agreed to wear a body wire transmitter to record his meeting with the defendant, and prosecutor sought to use incriminating statements made by the defendant during that meeting as evidence in the theft trial. The *Moulton* Court rejected the proposed exception to *Massiah* because it would be too difficult to define the parameters of a "legitimate reason" for conducting investigations that would be exempt from the *Massiah* exclusionary rule. Rather, the exception would invite "abuse by law enforcement personnel in the form of fabricated investigations and [would risk] the evisceration of the Sixth Amendment right recognized in *Massiah*." The Court noted, however, that the statements obtained by the co-conspirator in Moulton would be admissible at future trials for other crimes.

Problems

1. *Defense Strategy*. What additional facts might the defense counsel have offered in *Kuhlmann* to show that deliberate elicitation occurred in violation of the Sixth Amendment? For example, what if the defense could show that the informant had been promised leniency in exchange for information, although the informant had also been instructed not to initiate a conversation but only to listen for incriminating statements?

2. *Evaluating Jail Plants*. Suppose that a jail inmate regularly has given information to the government authorities in the past. Is this sufficient evidence for the inmate to be regarded as a government agent, assuming that the inmate has been advised in the past not to focus on any particular inmate and not to "elicit" information from any inmate? *See United States v. Johnson*, 338 F.3d 918 (8th Cir. 2003).

3. *Warnings and Waivers*

PATTERSON v. ILLINOIS

487 U.S. 285 (1988).

JUSTICE WHITE delivered the opinion of the Court.

[Patterson was arrested for battery and mob action and was suspected of murder. He was given *Miranda* warnings and initially he answered questions about the battery and mob action crimes, but denied knowing about the murder. The next day he was indicted for murder, taken from the lockup, and told that because he was now indicted, he was being transferred to another jail. When Patterson started to make incriminating statements, Officer Gresham interrupted him, gave him a *Miranda* form, and read the warnings aloud as Patterson read along with him. Patterson signed a waiver form and made incriminating statements to Gresham; during a later interview with a prosecutor, he received *Miranda* warnings again, waived his rights again, and made further incriminating statements.]

[Patterson's] principal [claim] is that questioning him without counsel present violated the Sixth Amendment because he did not validly

waive his right to have counsel present during the interviews. [In] the past, this Court has held that a waiver of the Sixth Amendment right to counsel is valid only when it reflects "an intentional relinquishment or abandonment of a known right or privilege." *Johnson v. Zerbst, supra,* at 464. In a case arising under the Fifth Amendment, we described this requirement as "a full awareness of both the nature of the right being abandoned and the consequences of the decision to abandon it." *Moran v. Burbine,* 475 U.S. 412, 421 (1986). Whichever of these formulations is used, the key inquiry in a case such as this one must be: Was the accused, who waived his Sixth Amendment rights during postindictment questioning, made sufficiently aware of his right to have counsel present during the questioning, and of the possible consequences of a decision to forgo the aid of counsel? In this case, we are convinced that by admonishing [Patterson] with the *Miranda* warnings, [the state] has met this burden and that petitioner's waiver of his right to counsel at the questioning was valid.

First, the *Miranda* warnings given [Patterson] made him aware of his right to have counsel present during the questioning. [Second,] the *Miranda* warnings also served to make [Patterson] aware of the consequences of a decision by him to waive his Sixth Amendment rights during postindictment questioning. [He] knew that any statement that he made could be used against him in subsequent criminal proceedings. This is the ultimate adverse consequence [Patterson] could have suffered by virtue of his choice to make uncounseled admissions to the authorities. This warning also sufficed [to] let [him] know what a lawyer could "do for him" during the postindictment questioning: namely, advise [Patterson] to refrain from making any such statements.

We reject [the] argument [that] a waiver of an accused's Sixth Amendment right to counsel should be "more difficult" to effectuate than waiver of a suspect's Fifth Amendment rights. [We] have never suggested that one right is "superior" or "greater" than the [other]. [Instead,] we have taken a more pragmatic approach to the waiver question—asking what purposes a lawyer can serve at the particular stage of the proceedings in question, and what assistance he could provide to an accused at that stage—to determine the scope of the Sixth Amendment right to counsel, and the type of warnings and procedures that should be required before a waiver of that right will be [recognized]. Applying this approach, it is our view that whatever warnings suffice for *Miranda's* purposes will also be sufficient in the context of postindictment questioning. The State's decision to take an additional step and commence formal adversarial proceedings against the accused does not substantially increase the value of counsel to the accused at questioning, or expand the limited purpose that an attorney serves when the accused is questioned by authorities. [B]ecause the role of counsel at questioning is relatively simple and limited, we see no problem in having a waiver procedure at that stage which is likewise simple and limited. So long as the accused is made aware of the "dangers and disadvantages of self-representation" during postindictment questioning by use of the *Mi-*

randa warnings, his waiver of his Sixth Amendment right to counsel at such questioning is "knowing and intelligent."

JUSTICE BLACKMUN, dissenting.

[A]fter formal adversary proceedings against a defendant have been commenced, the Sixth Amendment mandates that the defendant not be "subject to further interrogation by the authorities until counsel has been made available to him, unless the accused [initiates] further communication, exchanges, or conversations with the police." [T]he Sixth Amendment does not allow the prosecution to take undue advantage of any gap between the commencement of the adversary process and the time at which counsel is appointed for a defendant.

JUSTICE STEVENS, with whom JUSTICE BRENNAN and JUSTICE MARSHALL join, dissenting.

[To say that the *Miranda* warnings] lay a sufficient basis for accepting a waiver of the [Sixth Amendment] right to counsel [because they] make clear to an accused [that] a lawyer could [advise him] to refrain from making any [incriminating] statements [is] a gross understatement of the disadvantage of proceeding without a lawyer and an understatement of what a defendant must understand to know a knowing waiver. The *Miranda* warnings do not [inform] the accused that a lawyer might examine the indictment for legal sufficiency [or] that a lawyer is likely to be considerably more skillful at negotiating a plea bargain [and] that such negotiations may be most fruitful if initiated prior to any interrogation. [The] warnings do not even go so far as to explain to the accused the nature of the charges pending against him— advice that a court would insist upon before allowing a defendant to enter a guilty plea with or without the presence of an attorney. [A]fter indictment the adversary relationship between the state and the accused has solidified, [so] it inescapably follows that a prosecutor may not conduct private interviews with a charged defendant. [Even] the *Miranda* warnings themselves are a species of legal advice that is improper when given by the prosecutor [or his or her agents, the police] after [indictment].

Problem

Elstad and the Sixth Amendment. When police officers go to Jon's home, they tell him that they have a federal warrant for his arrest, and that a grand jury has indicted him for a drug crime. When they also tell him that the indictment refers to his involvement with four named individuals, Jon responds that he knows the four people and has used drugs with them. After 15 minutes in Jon's home, the officers transport him to the jail and provide *Miranda* warnings. Then Jon signs a *Miranda*-style waiver form and reiterates his earlier incriminating statements. The trial court excludes the pre-warning statement from Jon's trial but rules that the post-warning statement is admissible on the theory that Jon validly waived his rights because there was no police "actual coercion" as required by *Elstad*. Jon is convicted

and on appeal his counsel argues that the post-warning statements should be excluded as the "fruit" of the Sixth Amendment violation that occurred when police failed to provide *Miranda*-style warnings to communicate Jon's Sixth Amendment rights before he made the unwarned statements in his home. The Supreme Court remanded to the lower court for a resolution of whether *Elstad's* waiver definition applies in the Sixth Amendment context. *See Fellers v. United States*, 540 U.S. 519 (2004). Another issue in *Fellers* is whether the *Seibert* "effective warnings" doctrine applies to the Sixth Amendment "midstream warnings" problem, so as to require exclusion of the post-warning statements. Discuss the arguments on both sides of the two issues that must be resolved in *Fellers*.

4. Invocations, Waivers, and the Interplay Between Massiah and Miranda Rights

MICHIGAN v. JACKSON
475 U.S. 625 (1986).

JUSTICE WHITE delivered the opinion of the Court.

[Two defendants were arrested for murder in two consolidated cases; each made admissible statements to the police prior to arraignment. When each defendant was arraigned, each asked for appointed counsel on the basis of indigency. The police who were handling the murder investigations were present at the arraignments and heard the requests. Soon after the arraignment hearings, and before each defendant had a chance to consult with appointed counsel, police officers came to the jail to question them. Each defendant received *Miranda* warnings, waived his rights, and made incriminating statements. The defendants argued that the "deliberate elicitation" of the statements by police violated the Sixth Amendment rights provided by *Massiah*.]

[T]he reasons for prohibiting the interrogation of an uncounseled prisoner who has asked for the help of a lawyer are even stronger after he has been formally charged with an offense than [before]. "It is only at that time [after the initiation of adversary judicial proceedings] that the government has committed itself to prosecute, and only then that the adverse positions of government and defendant have solidified. It is then that a defendant finds himself faced with the prosecutorial forces of organized society, and immersed in the intricacies of substantive and procedural criminal law. As a result, the 'Sixth Amendment guarantees the accused, at least after the initiation of formal charges, the right to rely on counsel as a "medium" between him and the State.' Thus, the Sixth Amendment right to counsel at a postarraignment interrogation requires at least as much protection as the Fifth Amendment right to counsel at any custodial interrogation."

[A]fter a formal accusation has been made—and a person who had previously been just a "suspect" has become an "accused" within the meaning of the Sixth Amendment—the constitutional right to the assistance of counsel is of such importance that the police may no longer employ techniques for eliciting information from an uncounseled defendant that might have been entirely proper at an earlier stage of their investigation. Thus, the surreptitious employment of a cellmate [may] violate the defendant's Sixth Amendment right to counsel even though the same methods of investigation might have been permissible before arraignment or [indictment].

[I]t is the State that has the burden of establishing a valid waiver here. Doubts must be resolved in favor of protecting the constitutional claim. This settled approach to questions of waiver requires us to give a broad, rather than a narrow, interpretation to a defendant's request for counsel—we presume that the defendant requests the lawyer's services at every critical stage of the [prosecution]. [T]he State maintains that each of the [defendants] made a valid waiver of his Sixth Amendment rights by signing a postarraignment confession after again being advised of his constitutional rights. In *Edwards*, [we] rejected the notion that, after a suspect's request for counsel, advice of rights and acquiescence in police-initiated questioning could establish a valid waiver. We find no warrant for a different view under Sixth Amendment [analysis]. [The Court also notes that "we do not suggest that the right to counsel turns on [a] request [but rather,] we construe the defendant's request for counsel as an extremely important fact in considering the validity of a subsequent waiver in response to police-initiated interrogation.]

JUSTICE REHNQUIST, with whom JUSTICE POWELL, and JUSTICE O'CONNOR, join, dissenting.

[Police] do not commonly deny defendants their Sixth Amendment right to counsel. [The justification for *Miranda* and *Edwards* is] the perceived widespread problem that the police were violating, and would probably continue to violate, the Fifth Amendment rights of defendants during the course of custodial interrogations [but this justification] is conspicuously missing in the Sixth Amendment context. [Moreover,] the Court ultimately limits its holding to those situations where the police "initiate interrogation after a defendant's assertion, at an arraignment or similar proceeding, of his right to counsel." [But] the Court provides no satisfactory explanation for its decision to extend the *Edwards* rule to the Sixth Amendment, yet limits that rule to those defendants foresighted enough, or just plain lucky enough, to have made an explicit request for counsel which we have always understood to be completely unnecessary for Sixth Amendment [purposes].

Notes

1. *Impeachment with Jackson—Defective Statement.* In *Michigan v. Harvey*, 494 U.S. 344 (1990), the Court held that statements obtained in violation of *Jackson* could be used to impeach a defendant who testifies at trial. The Court reasoned that *"Jackson* simply superimposed the Fifth Amendment analysis of *Edwards* onto the Sixth Amendment," and that therefore, the *Harris* rule allowing impeachment with *Miranda*-defective statements should be superimposed onto the Sixth Amendment as well.

2. *Massiah Invocation Is "Offense Specific."* In *McNeil v. Wisconsin*, 501 U.S. 171 (1991), McNeil was arrested and charged with armed robbery. He received *Miranda* warnings, and refused to answer questions, but did not invoke his right to counsel. When he went to court for his "initial appearance," bail was set and a public defender was appointed to represent him. Later that evening, a detective visited McNeil to talk about other uncharged crimes, including a murder. McNeil was again given *Miranda* warnings, and this time he waived his rights and denied involvement in the murder and other crimes. When the detective returned two days later and gave McNeil warnings again, McNeil provided another waiver and made incriminating statements; two more days passed and the same events of warnings, waiver, and incriminating statements occurred again. All McNeil's statements to police were admitted at his murder trial, and he was convicted. On appeal, he argued that his waivers were invalid because his earlier *Massiah-Jackson* request for an attorney during his "initial appearance" on the armed robbery crime should be treated as an invocation of his *Miranda-Edwards* right to counsel during his interrogation about the other crimes. The Court rejected this argument, reasoning as follows:

> The Sixth Amendment right [is] offense specific. It cannot be invoked once for all future prosecutions, for it does not attach until a prosecution is commenced [by] the initiation of adversary judicial [proceedings]. [J]ust as the right is offense specific, so also its [*Jackson*] effect of invalidating subsequent waivers in police initiated interviews is offense specific. "[T]o exclude evidence pertaining to charges as to which the Sixth Amendment right to counsel had not attached at the time the evidence was obtained, [would] unnecessarily frustrate the public's interest in the investigation of criminal [activities]." *Maine v. Moulton*, 474 U.S. 159, 179–180 (1985). Because *McNeil* provided the statements [before] his Sixth Amendment right to counsel with respect to the [murder and other crimes] had been (or even could have been) invoked, that right poses no bar to the admission of the statements in this [case].

> [To] invoke the Sixth Amendment interest is [not] to invoke the *Miranda Edwards* [Fifth Amendment] interest. [Even if] it is likely that one who has asked for counsel's assistance in defending against a prosecution would want counsel present for all custodial interrogation, even interrogation unrelated to the charge, the likelihood that a suspect would wish counsel to be present is not the test for applicability of *Edwards*. The rule of [*Edwards*] requires, at a minimum, [an] expression of a desire for the assistance of an attorney in dealing with custodial interrogation by the police. Requesting the assistance of an attorney at a bail hearing does not bear that [construction]. [If] we were to adopt [*McNeil*'s argument], most persons in pretrial custody for serious offenses would be unapproachable by police officers suspecting them of involvement in other crimes, even though they have never expressed any unwillingness to be questioned. Since the ready ability to obtain uncoerced confessions is not an evil but an unmitigated good, society would be the loser."

Justice Stevens, joined by Justices Marshall and Blackmun, dissented, arguing that there is no rational basis for "afford[ing] relief from further interrogation to a defendant who asks a police officer for an attorney," but not affording such relief to "a defendant who makes an identical request to a judge." He also noted that "the scope of the relationship" between a client and attorney "is as broad as the subject matter that might reasonably be encompassed by negotiations for a plea bargain or the contents of a presentence investigation report." Thus, defining the Sixth Amendment as "offense specific" so as to limit the *Jackson* protection for a defendant's invocation of counsel to a "pending charge" is "both unrealistic and invidious."

3. *No Massiah–Jackson Protection for Factually–Related Uncharged Crimes.* In *Brewer* the defendant's Sixth Amendment right attached at his arraignment on an abduction charge, and the Court held that the police violated the Sixth Amendment when Detective Leaming deliberately elicited incriminating statements from him concerning an uncharged murder, by making the "Christian Burial Speech" that provoked the defendant to show the officers the location of the murder victim's body. But in *Texas v. Cobb*, 532 U.S. 162 (2001), the Court held that a *Massiah* defendant's *Jackson* invocation only protects a defendant from police questioning about the charged offense and not from questioning about uncharged offenses that are "factually related" to the charged offense. The *Cobb* Court borrowed the definition of "offense" from the Double Jeopardy context, citing *Blockburger v. United States*, 284 U.S. 299, 304 (1932): "[W]here the same act or transaction constitutes a violation of two distinct statutory provisions," a court must "determine whether there are two offenses or only one" by determining "whether each provision requires proof of a fact which the other does not." The *Cobb* dissenters advocated that the *Jackson* ban on deliberate elicitation should cover police questioning about offenses that are "closely related to" or "inextricably intertwined" with a charged offense to which the Sixth Amendment has attached. They noted that their test was commonly accepted by lower courts and based on "common sense," and predicted that because prosecutors can so easily "spin out [a] series of offenses from a [single] criminal transaction," the *Cobb* majority's rule will "remove a significant portion of the protection" that the Court "has found inherent in the Sixth Amendment."

Problems

1. *Evaluating Jackson and McNeil.* Examine the differences between the scenarios in *Jackson* and in *McNeil*, and explain why the defendant in *Jackson* won and the defendant in *McNeil* lost.

2. *Custody and Jackson.* The *Jackson* Court noted that in the proceedings below, the state supreme court found that the defendants' request for the appointment of counsel implicated only their Sixth Amendment right to counsel because the request was not made during custodial interrogation. The Court then stated, "We express no comment on the validity of the [state] court's Fifth Amendment analysis." Can it be argued that the defendants were in custody at arraignment in *Jackson*, so that their request for the assistance of counsel constituted a *Miranda* invocation of counsel under *Edwards*? Explain.

3. *Protecting Clients with Anticipatory Invocations.* Justice Stevens's *McNeil* dissent observed that defense counsel could insure that their clients

did not lose their confession claims by making sure "that they, or their clients, make a statement on the record" invoking the client's *Miranda-Edwards* right to counsel. Justice Scalia's opinion for the Court rebutted this observation by noting that the Court had "never held that a person can invoke his *Miranda* rights anticipatorily," and declared that the Court's willingness to adopt the *Edwards* rule "does not necessarily mean that we will allow [*Miranda*] rights to be asserted initially outside the context of custodial interrogation, with similar future effect." Should the *McNeil* dissenters' proposal be adopted? Explain. *See People v. Avila*, 75 Cal.App.4th 416, 89 Cal.Rptr.2d 320 (1999).

4. *Applying Massiah.* Max is arrested in Florida after being indicted in Wisconsin for homicide. The Wisconsin detectives who are dispatched to bring him back know about the indictment and arrest. They also know that an attorney purports to represent Max, and has asked the police not to talk to Max about the crime unless she is present. When the Wisconsin detectives meet Max at the jail, he says, "My lawyer told me I shouldn't talk to you guys." However, a detective tells Max that there are witnesses to his crime, and that they are willing to give him a chance to tell his side of the story. The detective then gives Max the *Miranda* warnings. He signs a waiver and makes incriminating statements. Assume that Max seeks to have his statements excluded on *Massiah* grounds. Was the Sixth Amendment violated? *See State v. Dagnall*, 228 Wis.2d 495, 596 N.W.2d 482 (App.1999).

E.   POST-*MIRANDA* DUE PROCESS LAW

In the post-*Miranda* era, defendants continue to challenge their confessions based on police violations of Due Process; for those defendants who do not have viable *Miranda* or *Massiah* claims, a Due Process claim be the only basis for an argument that their statements to police are inadmissible at trial. These defendants lack *Miranda* arguments when they waive their rights, when they confess while not in "custody," when they are interrogated by secret agents, and when they face impeachment on the stand with *Miranda*-defective statements. Even defendants who qualify for *Massiah* rights may lose them through waivers provided to police interrogators. The Court's modern Due Process precedents continue to rely on a "totality" test, which now incorporates the factor of police compliance with *Miranda*. As in the pre-*Miranda* era, the Court remains divided about the meaning of coercion and about the appropriate interpretation of the "involuntariness" standard.

MINCEY v. ARIZONA

437 U.S. 385 (1978).

MR. JUSTICE STEWART delivered the opinion of the Court.

[Mincey was wounded during an exchange of fire with officers entering his house to arrest him for narcotics crimes; he was taken to the hospital and treated in intensive care. An officer died in the shootout, and that evening, Detective Hust came to interrogate Mincey about the shooting. Hust gave *Miranda* warnings to Mincey and told him that he was under arrest. Mincey could not talk because of the tube in his mouth, and so he wrote out his answers to Hust's questions. The interrogation lasted until almost midnight, and Hust repeatedly violated *Miranda* by ignoring Mincey's repeated invocations of the right to counsel. However, Mincey took the stand at his murder trial, and so his *Miranda*-defective statements could be used to impeach his testimony under *Harris*. Mincey's statements were admitted and he was convicted, despite his counsel's argument that his hospital statements were inadmissible for impeachment purposes because they were involuntary under Due Process standards.]

[If] Mincey's statements [were not the] "product of a rational intellect and a free will," his conviction cannot stand. [This] Court is under a duty to make an independent evaluation of the record. [Mincey] had been seriously wounded [and] had arrived at the hospital "depressed almost to the point of coma," according to his [physician]. He complained to [Detective] Hust that the pain in his leg was "unbearable." He was evidently confused and unable to think clearly [because] some of his written answers were [not] entirely coherent. Finally, while Mincey was being questioned he was lying on his back on a hospital bed, encumbered by tubes, needles, and breathing apparatus. He was [at] "the complete mercy" of Detective Hust, unable to escape or resist the thrust of Hust's interrogations. In this debilitated and helpless condition, Mincey clearly expressed his wish not to be interrogated. As soon as Hust's questions turned to the details of the afternoon's events, Mincey wrote: "This is all I can say without a lawyer." Hust nonetheless continued to question him, and a nurse who was present suggested it would be best if Mincey answered. Hust ignored [Mincey's second] request [for a lawyer] and [his third request] made immediately thereafter. [But] despite Mincey's entreaties to be let alone, Hust ceased the interrogation only during intervals when Mincey lost consciousness or received medical treatment, and after each such interruption returned relentlessly to his task. * * *

There were not present in this case some of the gross abuses that have led the Court in other cases to find confessions involuntary, such as beatings, or "truth serums." But "the blood of the accused is not the only hallmark of an unconstitutional inquisition." [It] is apparent from the record [that] Mincey's statements were [involuntary]. [Mincey] was weakened by pain and shock, isolated from family, friends, and legal counsel, and barely conscious, and his will was simply overborne. Due process of law requires that statements obtained as these were cannot be used in any way against a defendant at his trial.

Mr. Justice Rehnquist [dissenting in part]:

The Court [ignores] entirely some evidence of [voluntariness]. As the [state supreme court observed], Mincey's nurse "testified that she had not given [Mincey] any medication and that [he] was alert and able to understand the officer's [questions]. She said that [Mincey] was in moderate pain but was very cooperative with everyone. The interrogating officer also testified that [Mincey] did not appear to be under the influence of drugs and that [his] answers were generally responsive to the questions. [While] the interviews took place over a three-hour time span, [they] were not "very long; probably not more than an hour total for everything." Hust would leave the room whenever Mincey received medical treatment "or if it looked like he was getting a little bit exhausted." According to Detective Hust, Mincey never "los[t] consciousness at any time." [It] was the testimony of both Detective Hust and Nurse Graham "that neither mental or physical force nor abuse was used on [Mincey]. Nor were any promises made." [Mincey] did not claim that he felt compelled by Detective Hust to answer the questions propounded. [The] trial court was entitled to conclude that notwithstanding Mincey's medical condition, his statements were [admissible.]

ARIZONA v. FULMINANTE

499 U.S. 279 (1991).

JUSTICE WHITE delivered [the] opinion [of] the Court.

[Fulminante was serving a sentence for a firearms crime, and Sarivola was serving a short sentence for extortion, when they became friends and "came to spend several hours a day together" in a federal prison in New York. Sarivola was a former police officer with organized crime experience in loansharking, and as a paid informant for the FBI he was "masquerading" in prison as an organized crime figure. When he asked Fulminante about a prison rumor that Fulminante had killed a child in Arizona, Fulminante repeatedly denied the allegation. When Sarivola passed this information to an FBI agent, he was instructed to "find out more."] Sarivola learned more one evening [as] he and Fulminante walked together around the prison track. Sarivola said that he knew Fulminante was "starting to get some tough treatment and whatnot" from other inmates because of the rumor. Sarivola offered to protect Fulminante from his fellow inmates, but told him, " 'You have to tell me about it,' you know. I mean, in other words, 'For me to give you any help.' " [Fulminante then made incriminating statements to Sarivola, which were admitted at Mincey's murder trial; Mincey was convicted, and argued on appeal that his statements were involuntary under Due Process standards.]

In applying the totality of the circumstances test to determine that the confession to Sarivola was coerced, the state supreme court focused on a number of relevant facts. First, the court noted that "because [Fulminante] was an alleged child murderer, he was in danger of physical harm at the hands of other inmates." [Using] his knowledge of these threats [of receiving "rough treatment from the guys"], Sarivola offered to protect Fulminante in exchange for a confession to [the crime], and "[i]n response to Sarivola's offer of protection, [Fulminante] confessed." [The state court] declared: "[T]he confession was obtained as a direct result of extreme coercion and was tendered in the belief that the defendant's life was in jeopardy if he did not confess. This is a true coerced confession in every sense of the word." [The Court also noted that Fulminante dropped out of school in the fourth grade, that he is short in stature and slight of build, that he requested protective custody when he was in prison in his mid-twenties, and that he was once admitted to a psychiatric hospital in prison because he was unable to cope with the isolation.] We normally give great deference to the factual findings of the state court [and] we agree [that] Fulminante's confession was coerced. [Our] cases have made clear that a finding of coercion need not depend upon actual violence by a government agent; a credible threat is sufficient. As we have said, "coercion can be mental as well as physical, [and] the blood of the accused is not the only hallmark of an unconstitutional inquisition." *Blackburn v. Alabama*, 361 U.S. 199, 206 (1960). As in *Payne [v. Arkansas*, 356 U.S. 560 (1958),] where the Court found that a confession was coerced because the interrogating police officer had promised that if the accused confessed, the officer would protect the accused from an angry mob outside the jailhouse door, so too here, [it] was fear of physical violence, absent protection from his friend (and Government agent) Sarivola, which motivated Fulminante to confess. [Given the] credible threat of physical violence, we agree [that] Fulminante's will was overborne in such a way as to render his confession the product of coercion. * * *

The dissenting opinion of Chief Justice Rehnquist, with whom Justices O'Connor Kennedy and Souter join:

[The] presentence report [showed] that Fulminante was no stranger to the criminal justice system: He had six prior felony convictions and had been imprisoned on three prior occasions. Exercising our responsibility to make "[an] independent examination of the [record], I am at a loss to see how the [state supreme court found the confession involuntary]. [Since] Fulminante was unaware that Sarivola was an FBI informant, there existed none of "the danger of coercion result[ing] from the interaction of custody and official interrogation." [The] conversations between Sarivola and Fulminante were not lengthy, and the defendant was free at all times to leave Sarivola's company. Sarivola at no time threatened him or demanded that he confess; he simply requested that he speak the truth about the matter. Fulminante was an experienced habitué of prisons, and presumably able to fend for himself. In concluding on these facts that Fulminante's confession was involuntary, the Court today embraces a more expansive definition of that term than is warranted by any of our decided [cases]. * * *

COLORADO v. CONNELLY

479 U.S. 157 (1986).

Chief Justice Rehnquist delivered the opinion of the Court.

[Connelly approached an officer in Denver and said without prompting that he had killed someone. The officer gave him *Miranda* warnings, and Connelly said he understood his rights and wanted to talk. In response to the officer's questions, Connelly denied that he had been taking drugs or drinking, but mentioned that he had been a patient in several mental hospitals. He told the officer he wanted to talk because his conscience had been bothering him. A detective gave *Miranda* warnings to Connelly again, and then asked him "what he had on his mind." Connelly told the officers that he killed a woman in November 1982 and he took the officers to the location of the killing. The officers did not perceive that Connelly was suffering from mental illness when he confessed. But after Connelly was held overnight, he became disoriented during an interview with the public defender the next morning and explained that "God's voice" told him to go to Denver and either confess to the murder or commit suicide. Experts at Connelly's preliminary hearing testified that he was suffering from chronic schizophrenia and was in a psychotic state at least as of the day before he confessed. Connelly argued that he did not confess voluntarily of his own "free will" but his confession was admitted at his trial and he was convicted of murder.]

[The Due Process] cases [since] *Brown* have focused upon the crucial element of police overreaching. [Absent] police conduct causally related to the confession, there is simply no basis for concluding that any state actor has deprived a criminal defendant of due process of law. [We do not agree] that a defendant's mental condition, by itself and apart from its relation to official coercion, should ever dispose of the inquiry into constitutional "voluntariness." [Connelly] relies on *Blackburn v. Alabama*, 361 U.S. 199 (1960), and *Townsend v. Sain*, 372 U.S. 293 (1963), for the proposition that the "deficient mental condition of the defendants in those cases was sufficient to render their confessions involuntary." [In] Blackburn, the Court found that the [defendant] was probably insane at the time of his confession and the police learned during the interrogation that he had a history of mental problems. The police exploited this weakness with coercive tactics [and these] tactics supported a finding that the confession was involuntary. [*Townsend*] presented a similar instance of police wrongdoing. In that case, a police physician had given Townsend a drug with truth-serum properties. [These] two cases demonstrate that while mental condition is surely relevant to an individual's susceptibility to police coercion, mere examination of the confessant's state of mind can never conclude the due process [inquiry]. [The] purpose of excluding evidence seized in violation of the Constitution is to substantially deter future violations of the Constitution. Only if we were to establish a brand new constitutional right—the right of a criminal defendant to confess to his crime only when totally rational and properly motivated—could [Connelly's] present claim be sustained. We hold that coercive police activity is a necessary predicate to the finding that a confession is not "voluntary" within the meaning of the Due Process Clause of the Fourteenth Amendment. We also conclude that the taking of [Connelly's] statements, and their admission into evidence, constitute no violation of that [Clause].

JUSTICE BRENNAN, with whom JUSTICE MARSHALL joins, dissenting.

[The] Court's failure to recognize all forms of involuntariness or coercion as antithetical to due process reflects a refusal to acknowledge free will as a value of constitutional consequence. [We] have never confined our focus to police [coercion]. [While] police overreaching has been an element of every confession case to date, [the] Court has made clear that ensuring that a confession is a product of free will is an independent [concern in our Due Process cases]. [No] physical evidence links the defendant to the alleged crime. Police did not identify the alleged victim's body as the woman named by the defendant. Mr. Connelly identified the alleged scene of the crime, but it has not been verified that the unidentified body was found there or that a crime actually occurred there. There is not a shred of competent evidence in this record linking the defendant to the charged homicide. There is only Mr. Connelly's confession. Minimum standards of due process should require that the trial court find substantial indicia of reliability, on the basis of evidence extrinsic to the confession itself, before admitting the confession of a mentally ill person into evidence. [To] hold otherwise allows the State to imprison and possibly to execute a mentally ill defendant based solely upon an inherently unreliable confession. [The dissent also noted that the officer and the detective were both aware of Connelly's five hospitalizations in mental institutions and this should be sufficient knowledge about Connelly's mental incapacity to render it "involuntary."]

Note

Proof Standards for Voluntariness. Before *Miranda*, some states allowed a jury to determine the "voluntariness" of a confession at trial, but the Court invalidated this procedure in *Jackson v. Denno*, 378 U.S. 368 (1964). The Court held that a pre-trial judicial hearing is required to determine voluntariness because a jury cannot be expected to produce a fair and reliable finding on this question during the trial on the issue of guilt. The prosecutor bears the burden of proving that a confession does not violate Due Process by a preponderance of the evidence. *See Lego v. Twomey*, 404 U.S. 477 (1972). If a confession is admitted at trial, and is later held to be unconstitutional under Due Process standards, its admission may be found to be harmless error only if the prosecution shows that it was harmless beyond a reasonable doubt. The *Fulminante* Court held that the admission of the defendant's confession made to an undercover agent was not harmless in that case; the Court also advised judges to "exercise extreme caution" before finding that the admission of a confession was harmless error, given "the risk that [a given] confession is unreliable, coupled with the profound impact that the confession has upon the jury."

Problems

1. *Evaluating Modern Due Process Standards.* Examine the pre-*Miranda* Due Process cases and compare them to the post-*Miranda* cases. What

new elements do you see in the modern cases, and what elements remain unchanged?

2. *"Mutt and Jeff" Today.* Suppose that you are a legal adviser to the local police department. The Chief wants to know whether, in light of the Supreme Court's Due Process decisions, police interrogators may continue to use the "Mutt and Jeff" treatment described in *Miranda.* How would you advise the Chief?

3. *Making Promises.* Doug was arrested for drug offenses and given *Miranda* warnings. He signed the standard advice of rights form and acknowledged that he waived all of his rights. Officer Nick then advised Doug to "come clean." Doug made a statement, while Nick accurately wrote down what Doug said and permitted Doug to review and sign the statement. At trial, Nick admitted that before Doug made the statement, Doug asked Nick what he could do to stay out of jail. Nick told Doug "that he could help us with the source, and we wouldn't have to arrest him on the spot, but he would sooner or later be arrested for the charges." After Doug gave Nick his statement, Nick told Doug that "whatever he did to help us in our investigation would be made known to the District Attorney's office, and it would be up to them to make a recommendation to the Court." Another officer testified that after Doug made the statement, Nick told Doug, "that he would have to be truthful to us in all regards before he could expect any kind of recommendation based on what he did to assist us." Assume that Doug does not argue that *Miranda* was violated but tries to get his statements excluded as involuntary. Did the police violate Due Process? *See Harper v. State*, 722 So.2d 1267 (Miss. App. 1998).

4. *Applying Miranda, Massiah and Due Process Standards.* Defendant Roy is arrested and indicted with burglary; he posts bail, and is released. While he is out on bail, the police develop evidence suggesting that Roy committed a murder in an unrelated case. A police detective goes to Roy's home and knocks on the door. When Roy opens the door, the detective identifies himself, tells Roy that he is investigating a murder case, and asks whether he and Roy can "talk." The detective speaks in a normal voice, keeps his gun holstered, and does not make any threatening movements. Roy agrees to talk and remains standing at his front door. The detective continues to talk in a normal voice, and asks questions about the murder. Do *Miranda*, *Massiah*, or Due Process precedents require exclusion if Roy makes incriminating statements? Does your answer change if the detective suddenly changes the subject and asks Roy questions about the burglary? Explain.

5. *Vulnerable Arrestee.* Assume that an arrested person suffers from both alcohol withdrawal and mental health problems. In light of the suspect's condition, would it be improper for the interrogating officer to focus on emotionally laden topics and ask leading questions? Under what circumstances could interrogation tactics constitute a Due Process violation when questioning such a person? See *State v. Hoppe*, 261 Wis.2d 294, 661 N.W.2d 407 (2003).

6. *Fabricating Evidence.* Would it violate Due Process for the police to fabricate evidence (such as a bogus gunshot residue test or a lineup at which the purported victim (in reality, a police officer) "identifies" defendant as the perpetrator of the crime) in order to obtain a confession? Why or why

not? *See, e.g., State v. Patton*, 362 N.J.Super. 16, 826 A.2d 783 (App.Div. 2003); *Whittington v. State*, 147 Md.App. 496, 809 A.2d 721 (Md.Spec.App. 2002).

7.   *Threatening Arrest.* Police officers discover crack cocaine in Johnson's sister's house where Johnson is temporarily living. The officers interrogate both Johnson and his sister about the cocaine. When Johnson refuses to admit that the cocaine is his, the officers threaten to arrest his sister, and then he confesses. Is this confession inadmissible because of a Due Process violation by the police? Is it relevant that the police can argue that they had probable cause to arrest the sister anyway because the discovery of the cocaine gave them probable cause to do so? *See United States v. Johnson*, 351 F.3d 254 (6th Cir. 2003).

Chapter 7

IDENTIFICATION PROCEDURES

A. THE NATURE AND CONSTITUTIONAL IMPLICATIONS OF IDENTIFICATION PROCESSES

Eyewitness identification may be a particularly potent form of evidence in a criminal proceeding. Inherent in such evidentiary methods, however, are significant reliability risks. Accurate identification depends upon perception and recall that are free of distortion. A multiplicity of factors, individually or collectively, may operate under a given set of circumstances to impair either process. The ability to perceive may be skewed by physical realities such as distance, observation time, light and the field or content of activity. Stereotypes and cultural assumptions also may interfere with perceptual acuity. Even accurate perception may be undermined by suggestive questioning, faded memory and mental tendencies to convert assumption or expectation into reality.

Did Your Eyes Deceive You? Expert Psychological Testimony on the Unreliability of Eyewitness Identification, 29 STAN. L. REV. 970, 971–89 (1977).

* * *

1. The Problem: The Unreliability of Eyewitness Identification

a. A Typical Scenario

Mary Smith, a white female, age 30, is walking home at 1:00 a.m., having finished working the night shift at the phone company. As Mary passes a tavern, she hears someone step away from the entrance and follow her, causing her to quicken her pace.

Suddenly, in a dark stretch of the street, the footsteps catch up with her. Mary is knocked to the ground and, looking up, sees a tall black man. Waving a gun in front of her face, he demands her purse and jewelry; she obediently complies. Following her assailant's commands, Mary remains lying on her stomach until she no longer hears his fleeing footsteps. In a panic, Mary runs into her apartment and locks the door.

She immediately calls the police and, in an agitated state, quickly explains the incident.

When the police arrive 10 minutes later, Mary is still shaking but is not injured seriously. She tells the officers what she can of the event and tries to describe the man but can offer little help: The police ascertain that the assailant was a tall, fairly dark-complexioned black man in his late twenties, of medium build, with a large, flat nose and medium Afro. Under police pressure to "remember something else," Mary offers: "Well he might have had a beard or something, like a goatee. [Yeah,] I think he had a goatee."

The police Drive Mary to the station house, where the investigation continues. Again she describes what happened, and then she helps the police to construct a composite picture of her attacker. Throughout the process, the officer using the "photo-kit" implores Mary for more details, concentrating on differing types of noses, eyes and mouths. Exhausted they finally produce a composite photo that satisfies Mary. At last, the police take Mary home, leaving her with the comment, "We'll get back to you as soon as anything comes up."

Meanwhile, another police officer has gone to the tavern near where Mary first noticed she was being followed. Although the tavern is still quite crowded, no patrons remember anyone matching the description Mary first gave of the assailant. The bartender, John Williams, however, vaguely remembers someone fitting the suspect's general description. Although he cannot add anything to it, John suggests that he might recognize the man if he saw him again.

At first, the police investigation turns up no new information. Five weeks after the robbery, however, a parole officer reports that the composite photo resembles one of his parolees, Jimmy Jones, who has three prior burglary convictions. This information leads a detective to pull Jimmy's year-old photo from police files along with seven others. The detective brings the eight photos to the phone company and asks Mary to examine them one at a time. Under the detective's careful scrutiny, she picks up Jimmy's picture and states: "This is the only one it could be."

The officer probes, "Could you be any more positive?"

"Well, of course, I can't tell how tall this guy is from this picture," Mary replies, "but if he's about six feet tall, it could be him. It looks like him, all right."

On the basis of this identification, the police detain Jimmy Jones and include him in a corporeal lineup. Jones is 6'2", weighs 165 pounds, sports a full beard, and has a long scar over his right eye. The police choose five other men, all from the county jail and all dressed in orange jumpsuits, to complete the lineup. Jimmy is forced to attire himself in a new jumpsuit taken from the jail storeroom.

The police bring Mary Smith and John Williams down to view the lineup. Asked by the detective if she recognizes the man who had attacked her, Mary replies, pointing to Jimmy Jones, "Number three looks familiar."

"Are you certain that's the man?" asks the detective.

"I'm pretty sure. [Yeah,] that's him," she announces.

The officer then turns to John. "And how about you, Mr. Williams? Do you recognize the man?" John pauses for a moment and then announces emphatically, "She's right. That's the guy."

On the basis of the two identifications, the police charge Jones with armed robbery. In court, Mary Smith relates her harrowing experience to the jury and identifies Jimmy Jones as her attacker. John Williams testifies that he remembers seeing Jones in his bar that same night. Despite Jones' claim of innocence, his wife's testimony that Jones was with her and asleep at the time of the robbery, and the police's inability to find any physical evidence of the crime, the jury convicts Jones and the judge sentences him to 7 years in prison.

Two years later, while searching the apartment of a man accused of another armed robbery, the police find Mary Smith's checkbook. Under police questioning, the suspect in that case admits that he robbed Mary Smith 2 years earlier.

Although the exact events described above are fictitious, the scenario is probably familiar to any experienced criminal defense attorney. Unfortunately, it is the rare case in which the police can discover that a jury wrongfully has convicted a Jimmy Jones, and many innocent persons may be sent to prison because of mistaken identifications. In order to prevent these miscarriages of justice, however, it is first necessary to specify and examine the various factors that contribute to the unreliability of eyewitness testimony

B.   PSYCHOLOGICAL RESEARCH FINDINGS

Research on the psychological dimensions of eyewitness identification has emerged from a combination of somewhat distinct fields of specialization within experimental psychology, including perception, memory and social psychology. Although experimental psychologists traditionally have concentrated their efforts on pure research and only occasionally have alluded to the practical effects of their findings, some of their earliest work in applied psychology, dating back to the 19th century, explored relevant areas of "legal psychology." In particular, having observed that major discrepancies often existed between different eyewitness accounts of the same event, many psychologists began to study the psychology of testimony and later to examine experimentally the fallibility of perception, the unreliability of memory and the inaccuracy of eyewitness identification.

The need for scientific study in this area was occasioned by the earlier "sensationalist" thinking in the field, which assumed that the human brain operates more or less as a mechanical recording device: A person sees everything and records this information on a memory "tape." When necessary to describe a past event, the person simply selects the appropriate memory tape and plays it back, producing a faithful recounting of the original perception.

Over the past half-century, however, psychological research emphatically has demonstrated the invalidity of this conception and has revealed that the "videotape recorder" analogy is misleading in three respects.... First, perception is not a mere passive recording of an event but instead is a constructive process by which people consciously and unconsciously use decisional strategies to attend selectively to only a minimal number of environmental stimuli. Second, over time, the representation of an event stored in memory undergoes constant change; some details are added or altered unconsciously to conform the original memory representation to new information about the event, while others simply are forgotten. Finally, the manner in which information is retrieved from memory almost always distorts the remembered image; most often, very powerful-yet imperceptibly subtle-suggestions shape the resulting recollection.

1. Perception of the Original Event

Perceptual Selectivity. The inherent limitations of the human brain are the major source of inaccuracy in perception. People can perceive only a limited number of the simultaneous stimuli in the environment at any time; the number of these that can be encoded in memory is even smaller. In order to cope with these innate limitations, an observer develops unconscious strategies to aid in the selectivity of perceptual processes and ultimately to concentrate attention on the most necessary and useful details. In short, a human must "learn" how to perceive efficiently.

Unfortunately, the resulting perceptual shortcuts and strategies, although generally effective in daily life, often lead to inaccurate perceptions when the eye must make the fine distinctions necessary to observe and recognize faces accurately. Furthermore, witnesses generally are unaware of the distortions produced by these perceptual strategies and may appreciate the resulting inaccuracies only when confronted with something like a classic optical illusion.

The major difficulty that selective perceptual processes cause is the failure to observe the details of an event, especially those that are at first unimportant but later assume great significance. The ability to perceive and recall such details plays a crucial role in eyewitness identifications, yet numerous studies have confirmed that even trained observers find it difficult to describe such obvious physical characteristics as height, weight and age. Lay witnesses surely must recognize and relate specific details of physiognomy much more inaccurately than these trained, objective observers. Moreover, perceptual inaccuracy is magnified if the observer does not realize that a detail will become significant later, as happens when a witness such as John Williams learns only after the fact that a crime has been committed.

Time perception. Humans also find it especially difficult to perceive time accurately, that is, to estimate either the duration of an event or the interval between successive events. Studies have shown that people tend to judge time by the amount of activity occurring; during sudden, action-packed events such as crimes, people almost always overestimate the length of time involved because the flurry of activity leads them to conclude that a significant amount of time has passed. Time is also perceived to pass more slowly when the observer is caught in an anxiety-producing situation; the desire to "escape" makes it seem as if the unpleasant event is lasting longer than it actually is. Thus, the witness or victim who, like Mary Smith, may claim to have observed her attacker 1 or 2 minutes, in reality probably saw him for only 10 or 15 seconds.

Poor observation conditions. In addition to perceptual inaccuracies caused by the brain's inherent limitations, many identification errors are due to the circumstances of the observation. A major variable influencing perception is the duration of the observation period. Crimes in which the primary evidence is an eyewitness identification characteristically are brief, fast-moving events; the victim and witnesses consequently will have difficulty getting a sufficiently good "look" to allow them to process enough visual features of the event and the offender to make a reliable subsequent recognition. This durational constraint has particularly deleterious effects when the crime occurs suddenly, and the witness is thus unprepared to focus perceptual attention on the important features of the event.

Furthermore, visual efficiency drops markedly when the observation occurs under poor or rapidly changing lighting conditions or over great distances, reducing the absolute amount of visual information implying on the retina, or in conjunction with distracting noises or other activity, forcing the already limited attentional capacities to be spread even thinner. Each of these conditions frequently accompanies the observation of crimes and may reduce the reliability of a witness identification.

Stressful situation. Another important environmental factor limiting the accuracy of perception is the stressful situation facing the victim. Although judges and juries often may be convinced by the victim's assertion that "I was so frightened that his face is etched in my memory forever," psychological research demonstrates that perceptual abilities actually *decrease* significantly when the observer is in a fearful or anxiety-provoking situation.

Studies have shown that an increase in anxiety generally produces a cluster of certain physiological responses. The frightened victim or eyewitness may report increases in heart rate, rapid breathing and excessive perspiration, but usually does not notice that the anxiety also has caused fixation of the eyes. Yet, because visual information is processed by contrasting successive retinal images, this fixation reduces visual acuity, particularly for details on the periphery of the environment.

Excessive anxiety also produces involuntary cognitive reactions in the observer, who often will attempt to cope with a frightening situation simply by rejecting it. This phenomenon of "perceptual defense" may cause a frightened victim such as Mary Smith to "close" her mind—and eyes—in order to block out and avoid recognition of stimuli that might produce anxiety. Even when still able to attend to the environment, the witness will concentrate only on possible escape alternatives or the gun in her face; despite the proximity, she may not observe the attacker's face well enough to allow an accurate identification. Perception is so narrowed to one aspect of the experience that all others are missed.

Expectancy. Although many of the organic and environmental limitations on perceptual abilities come quickly to mind, other social psychological factors operate more subtly, if quite powerfully, to distort perception. In order to compensate for the perceptual selectivity made necessary by the brain's limitations, observers make extensive use of expectancy, not only in developing strategies for determining what to look at, but also in interpreting what they see. Because the human mind can process only small portions of what is visible at any given time, it develops the ability to form conclusions about what has been perceived based on limited amounts of sensory information. It accomplishes this task by integrating fragmentary visual information into existing conceptual schemata based upon a fund of general knowledge acquired over time. In essence, witnesses unconsciously reconstruct what *has* occurred from what they assume *must have* occurred. Consequently, they exhibit a pronounced tendency to perceive the expected.

Various factors shape these expectancies. Studies using so-called "ambiguous figures" show that the context in which witnesses view the same object or individual may cause them to view and interpret it differently. Furthermore, once they have classified an ambiguous figure, they tend to conform their continuing perception of it to their idea of what such an object should look like, encouraging even more errors in their perception. Thus, having Mary Smith make a composite photo of her attacker in a context differing from that of the original observation is likely to introduce errors, and once Mary has that picture in her mind, she will minimize the differences in appearance between the composite and a suspect resembling it.

Personal needs and biases. In addition to expectancies caused by prior experience and information about the world the personal needs and motives of the observer also distort perception. In short, witnesses tend to see what they *want* to see. Thus, the need and desire to produce a complete description of an assailant may foster perception that is more the product of an unconscious imagination than a keen eye.

Personal biases and latent prejudices also shape expectancies, often distorting perceptions to fit the various stereotypes that all humans possess. Social psychology experiments indicate that people tend to correlate physical characteristics with personality traits, and that perceptual distortion increases when the viewer regards objects unfavorably.

These findings imply that a victim may unwittingly distort her perception of an assailant to include physical features that the victim associates with the personality traits typified by the criminal's behavior.

Cross-racial identifications. Finally, considerable evidence indicates that people are poorer at identifying members of another race than of their own. Some studies have found that, in the United States at least, whites have greater difficulty recognizing black faces than vice versa. Moreover, counter intuitively, the ability to perceive the physical characteristics of a person from another racial group apparently does not improve significantly upon increased contact with other members of that race.

Because many crimes are cross-racial, these factors may play an important part in reducing the accuracy of eyewitness perception.

2. Encoding and Storage in Memory

Memory decays over time. Even if someone accurately perceived an event, its representation in the observer's memory would not remain entirely intact for very long. People forget both quickly and easily. The phenomenon of forgetting what once has been perceived and encoded in memory, known as "retroactive inhibition," is one of the earliest and most consistent findings of cognitive psychology. Simply put, the more time that has elapsed since the perception of some event—and, therefore, the more intervening occurrences that must be stored in memory—the poorer a person's memory is of that event. Particularly with visual images, memory begins to decay within minutes of the event, so that considerable memory loss probably occurs during the many days-and often months—that typically elapse between the offense and an eyewitness identification of the suspect in a criminal case.

Filling gaps in memory. Many psychologists once thought that automatic decay of the memory trace caused all distortions of memory. More recently, however, they have discovered that memory, like perception, is an active, constructive process that often introduces inaccuracies by adding details not present in the initial representation or in the event itself. The mind combines all the information required about a particular event into a single storage "bin," making it difficult to distinguish what the witness saw originally from what she learned later. Because all of the research on human memory indicates that the actual memorial representation must decay in accuracy over time, any reported increases in the completeness of a description come only at the risk of a reduction in the description's correctness. If a witness' description of a suspect becomes more detailed as the investigation proceeds from the police report through the preliminary hearing to trial, the witness in this situation probably unconsciously has changed the image in memory to include details subsequently acquired from, for example, newspaper reports of the event or a mug shot of the defendant.

Moreover, because of a psychological need to reduce uncertainty and eliminate inconsistencies, witnesses have a tendency not only to fill any gaps in memory by adding extraneous details but also to change mental representations unconsciously so that they "all make sense." This mental process of adding and changing little details is an efficient strategy in everyday life, where the total sum of information contained in memory usually matters more than the specific circumstances surrounding its acquisition. In the context of an eyewitness identification of a criminal defendant, such unconscious modifications of memory can have tragic consequences.

Although a careful defense attorney and a scrupulous prosecutor might take measures to shield a witness from exposure to certain types of information obtained after the event itself, such as viewing the defendant in custody prior to identification, recent experiments have demonstrated that some suggestions work so subtly as virtually to make it impossible to prevent their incorporation into the witness' memory. The leading series of experiments in this area suggests that the mere wording of a question put to an eyewitness during a deposition, an interview or at the trial itself may affect not only the immediate answer but also the witness' memory of the original event as well as any answers to subsequent questions about that event. By implication, therefore, even routine police interrogation of the witness immediately after the crime may plant subtle suggestions that unconsciously become incorporated into the witness' memory of the event. If, as with Mary Smith, the police constantly pressure the witness to produce more and more details, she is even more likely to seize any information contained in the questions asked her and include it in her resulting description.

False feelings of confidence. Psychological research also indicates that a witness' feeling of confidence in the details of a memory concerning a particular event generally does not measure validly the accuracy of that recollection. In fact, a negative correlation sometimes exists between accuracy and confidence. Surprisingly, witnesses—particularly victims—often become more confident of the correctness of their identification as time progresses. For example, a victim who originally voiced grave doubts as to any ability to identify the assailant and who showed some hesitancy in making a pretrial identification commonly may exude and express absolute certainty in testifying on the witness stand that the defendant committed the crime.

3. *Retrieval of Information From Memory*

Inadequacy of verbal descriptions. The final source of errors in identification, and the one discussed most thoroughly in the legal literature, is the process by which information is retrieved from memory for purposes of making an identification. Because few eyewitnesses have the artistic ability to draw an accurate representation of the criminal-the closest analogy to free recall-the criminal justice system must rely upon the eyewitness' vocabulary. Initially, therefore, the recall process suffers from the inadequacy of the witness' memory of the offender. Moreover, numerous studies have shown that even the most free and accurate form of verbal recall—a narrative description unprompted by questions—

results in exceedingly incomplete information retrieval. On the other hand, as the questions become more structured in order to achieve completeness, the resulting responses become more inaccurate, because witnesses may feel compelled to answer questions completely in spite of incomplete knowledge. Faced with this inverse relationship between accuracy and completeness of a description, law enforcement officials generally opt for the latter at the expense of the former.

Suggestion in the composition of an identification test. In order to obtain identifications, police must rely on structured "recognition" tests, such as lineups and photo arrays, even though these procedures are notoriously unreliable because of their potential for exposing the witness to suggestive influences. Much already has been written on the dangers involved in the use of such techniques for identification purposes, so this section of the Note will discuss only their most obvious defects from a psychological perspective.

The lineup is a multiple-choice recognition test. Moreover, witnesses very likely will perceive it as a multiple-choice test that lacks a "none of the above" alternative because, despite contrary admonitions, there is always the implicit suggestion that the lineup includes the criminal. Thus, the witness often may treat the task as one of identifying the individual who best matches the witness' recollection of the culprit, even if that match is not perfect, rather than as one of identifying the true criminal.

The reliability of an identification made at a lineup, therefore, depends upon the similarity between the "target" item, the suspect, and the "distractor" items, the other members of the lineup. If, for example, the witness described the assailant as "tall," and only one of the participants in the lineup could be considered tall, then the choice of that one individual has little meaning for the purpose of identifying the true criminal. In addition to the tendency of the defendant in a lineup to be dangerously dissimilar in overall physical characteristics to the other participants, he may also have one distinctive feature, which generally suffices to bias the witness toward identifying him. Some of the more common factors potentially exerting suggestive influences include any unusual physical characteristics such as scars or tattoos, differences in the clothing worn by the participants and their demeanor and facial expressions.

The common practice of securing identifications by first using a photo array and subsequently conducting a corporeal lineup further tends to reduce reliability. From the standpoint of memory recall, the crucial identification is that made from the photo array, because a witness most likely will not identify anyone at a later corporeal lineup other than the individual chosen from the photo array. Obtaining identifications by using photographs is particularly dangerous, however, for they exclude a multitude of characteristics typically relied upon in recognizing people, such as views of the whole body or from varying angles, or any individual mannerisms or gestures, and therefore cause a greater number of mistaken identifications.

Suggestion in the administration of an identification test. In addition to the possibility that the police will make and reinforce suggestions as to the "proper" choice by the manner in which they construct the lineup or photo array, police officers while conducting the identification procedure often themselves provide more or less unwitting clues. An officer who is cognizant of the identity of the prime suspect may subtly influence the witness' choice simply by changes in voice intonation, increased attention to the response, the hint of a smile, or by more obvious gestures such as nodding agreement or asking the witness to take another, more careful, look if the "correct" identification has not been made. It is very difficult, if not impossible, to avoid unknowingly giving such clues; even trained psychologists who design their investigations to avoid these effects occasionally pass on their own expectations to the participants in their experiments.

Social psychological influences. Various social psychological factors also increase the danger of suggestibility in a lineup confrontation. Witnesses, like other people, are motivated by a desire to be correct and to avoid looking foolish. By arranging a lineup, the police have evidenced their belief that they have caught the criminal; witnesses realizing this probably will feel foolish if they cannot identify anyone and therefore may choose someone despite residual uncertainty. Moreover, the need to reduce psychological discomfort often motivates the victim of a crime to find a likely target for feelings of hostility.

Finally, witnesses are highly motivated to behave like those around them. This desire to conform produces an increased need to identify someone in order to show the police that they, too, feel that the criminal is in the lineup, and makes the witnesses particularly vulnerable to any clues conveyed by the police or other witnesses as to whom they suspect of the crime. When John Williams, for example, hears Mary Smith identify Jimmy Jones as her attacker, he may make a similar choice in order to conform to her judgment.

Exertion of suggestive influences by such authority figures as police officers tends to magnify these other social psychological pressures. Any witnesses who have agreed to cooperate with the police may be especially desirous of doing what they think the authority figure wishes. In Professor Milgram's classic experiments on compliance, for example, subjects went so far as to administer apparently lethal doses of electrical shock to other subjects—actually confederates of the experimenter—in order to please the psychologist.

Like searches, seizures and custodial interrogation, identification procedures constitute a basic methodology for building a criminal case. Compulsory generation of an identifying characteristic, such as a writing exemplar, voice sample or fingerprint, could be understood as a seizure or self-incrimination. However, case law establishes that unlike searches and seizures, identification processes are not governed by the Fourth

Amendment. Nor do they implicate the Fifth Amendment guarantee against self-incrimination.

Critical to the distinction between methods of seizure and identification is the concept of privacy. Referencing *Katz v. United States*, the Supreme Court has determined that no reasonable expectation of privacy exists in publicly exposed traits. Responding to arguments that required disclosure of a person's voice implicated Fourth Amendment interests, the Court in *United States v. Dionisio*, 410 U.S. 1, 14 (1973), observed that:

> [t]he physical characteristics of a person's voice, its tone and manner, as opposed to the content of a specific conversation, are constantly exposed to the public. Like a man's facial characteristics, or handwriting, his voice is repeatedly produced for others to hear. No person can have a reasonable expectation that others will not know the sound of his voice any more than he can reasonably expect that his face will be a mystery to the world.

Although acknowledging that identification procedures elicit incriminating information, the Court has determined that they do not implicate the Fifth Amendment. In repulsing a privilege against self-incrimination claim in the context of identification procedures, the Court characterized such evidence as nontestimonial. In *Gilbert v. California*, 388 U.S. 263, 266–67 (1967), it found that:

> taking of [handwriting] exemplars did not violate petitioner's Fifth Amendment privilege against self-incrimination. The privilege reaches only compulsion of "an accused's communications, whatever form they might take, and the compulsion of responses which are also communications, for example, compliance with a subpoena to produce one's papers," and not "compulsion which mutes a suspect or accused the source of real or physical evidence." One's voice and handwriting are, of course, means of communications. It by no means follows, however, that every compulsion of an accused to use his voice or write (compel) a communication within the cover of the privilege. A mere handwriting exemplar, in contrast to the content of what is written, like the voice or body itself, is an identifying physical characteristic outside its protection.

Despite the general irrelevance of the Fourth and Fifth Amendments to them (although Fourth Amendment interests may be implicated when a person must be seized for purposes of obtaining identification. *Hayes v. Florida*, 470 U.S. 811 (1985)), identification procedures are not without significant constitutional protection. Like other criminal investigative methods, identification processes may implicate due process. Case law also has established that the right to counsel may attach to identification proceedings. Contrasted with the pervasive applicability of the due process clause, however, Sixth Amendment protection is limited to identification procedures employed "at or after the time that adversarial judicial proceedings have been initiated." *Kirby v. Illinois*, 406 U.S. 682, 688 (1972)(plurality opinion).

C. THE SIXTH AMENDMENT

The right to counsel in an identification context is dependent upon whether the proceeding occurs at a stage of the process that is critical enough so that counsel's presence "is necessary to preserve the defendant's basic right to a fair trial." *United States v. Wade*, 388 U.S. 218, 227 (1967). Seminal case law reflected the Court's sense that post-indictment line-ups not only satisfied the "critical stage" requirement but presented profound risks to a fair trial.

UNITED STATES v. WADE

388 U.S. 218 (1967).

MR. JUSTICE BRENNAN delivered the opinion of the Court.

[The] federally insured bank in Eustace, Texas, was robbed on September 21, 1964. A man with a small strip of tape on each side of his face entered the bank, pointed a pistol at the female cashier and the vice president, the only persons in the bank at the time, and forced them to fill a pillowcase with the bank's money. The man then drove away with an accomplice who had been waiting in a stolen car outside the bank. On March 23, 1965, an indictment was returned against respondent, Wade, and two others for conspiring to rob the bank, and against Wade and the accomplice for the robbery itself. Wade was arrested [and] counsel was appointed to represent [him]. Fifteen days later an FBI agent, without notice to Wade's lawyer, arranged to have the two bank employees observe a lineup made up of Wade and five or six other prisoners and conducted in a courtroom of the local county courthouse. Each person in the line wore strips of tape such as allegedly worn by the robber and upon direction each said something like "put the money in the bag," the words allegedly uttered by the robber. Both bank employees identified Wade in the lineup as the bank robber.

At trial the two employees, when asked on direct examination if the robber was in the courtroom, pointed to Wade. The prior lineup identification was then elicited from both employees on cross-examination. [Wade] was convicted. * * *

Neither the lineup itself nor anything shown by this record that Wade was required to do in the lineup violated his privilege against self-incrimination. [T]he privilege "protects an accused only from being compelled to testify against himself, or otherwise provide the State with evidence of a testimonial or communicative [nature]."

The fact that the lineup involved no violation of Wade's privilege against self-incrimination does not, however, dispose of his contention that the courtroom identifications should have been excluded because the lineup was conducted without notice to and in the absence of his counsel. [I]t is urged that the assistance of counsel at the lineup was indispensable to protect Wade's most basic right as a criminal defendant—his right to a fair trial at which the witnesses against him might be meaningfully cross-examined. * * *

The Government characterizes the lineup as a mere preparatory step in the gathering of the prosecution's evidence, not different—for Sixth Amendment purposes—from various other preparatory steps, such as systematized or scientific analyzing of the accused's fingerprints, blood sample, clothing, hair, and the like. We think there are differences which preclude such stages being characterized as critical stages at which the accused has the right to the presence of his counsel. Knowledge of the techniques of science and technology is sufficiently available, and the variables in techniques few enough, that the accused has the opportunity for a meaningful confrontation of the Government's case at trial through the ordinary processes of cross-examination of the Government's expert witnesses and the presentation of the evidence of his own experts. The denial of a right to have his counsel present at such analyses does not therefore violate the Sixth Amendment; they are not critical stages since there is minimal risk that his counsel's absence at such stages might derogate from his right to a fair trial.

But the confrontation compelled by the State between the accused and the victim or witnesses to a crime to elicit identification evidence is peculiarly riddled with innumerable dangers and variable factors which might seriously, even crucially, derogate from a fair trial. The vagaries of eyewitness identification are well-known; the annals of criminal law are rife with instances of mistaken identification. Mr. Justice Frankfurter once said: "What is the worth of identification testimony even when uncontradicted? The identification of strangers is proverbially untrustworthy. The hazards of such testimony are established by a formidable number of instances in the records of English and American trials. These instances are recent—not due to the brutalities of ancient criminal procedure." A major factor contributing to the high incidence of miscarriage of justice from mistaken identification has been the degree of suggestion inherent in the manner in which the prosecution presents the suspect to witnesses for pretrial identification. [Suggestion] can be created intentionally or unintentionally in many subtle ways. And the dangers for the suspect are particularly grave when the witness' opportunity for observation was insubstantial, and thus his susceptibility to suggestion the greatest. Moreover, "[i]t is a matter of common experience that, once a witness has picked out the accused at the line-up, he is not likely to go back on his word later on, so that in practice the issue of identity may (in the absence of other relevant evidence) for all practical purposes be determined there and then, before the trial."

The pretrial confrontation for purpose of identification may take the form of a lineup, also known as an "identification parade" or "showup," as in the present case, or presentation of the suspect alone to the witness. It is obvious that risks of suggestion attend either form of confrontation and increase the dangers inhering in eyewitness identification. But as is the case with secret interrogations, there is serious difficulty in depicting what transpires at lineups and other forms of identification confrontations. "Privacy results in secrecy and this in turn results in a gap in our knowledge as to what in fact goes on." [T]he defense can seldom reconstruct the manner and mode of lineup identification for judge or jury at trial. Those participating in a lineup with the accused may often be police officers; in any event, the participants' names are rarely recorded or divulged at trial. The impediments to an objective observation are increased when the victim is the witness. Lineups are prevalent in rape and robbery prosecutions and present a particular hazard that a victim's understandable outrage may excite vengeful or spiteful motives. In any event, neither witnesses nor lineup participants are apt to be alert for conditions prejudicial to the suspect. And if they were, it would likely be of scant benefit to the suspect since neither witnesses nor lineup participants are likely to be schooled in the detection of suggestive influences. Improper influences may go undetected by a suspect, guilty or not, who experiences the emotional tension which we might expect in one being confronted with potential accusers. Even when he does observe abuse, if he has a criminal record he may be reluctant to take the stand and open up the admission of prior convictions. Moreover any protestations by the suspect of the fairness of the lineup made at trial are likely to be in vain; the jury's choice is between the accused's unsupported version and that of the police officers present. In short, the accused's inability effectively to reconstruct at trial any unfairness that occurred at the lineup may deprive him of his only opportunity meaningfully to attack the credibility of the witness' courtroom identification.

[The] potential for improper influence is illustrated by the circumstances, insofar as they appear, surrounding the prior identifications in the three cases we decide today. In the present case, the testimony of the identifying witnesses elicited on cross-examination revealed that those witnesses were taken to the courthouse and seated in the courtroom to await assembly of the lineup. The courtroom faced on a hallway observable to the witnesses through an open door. The cashier testified that she saw Wade "standing in the hall" within sight of an FBI agent. Five or six other prisoners later appeared in the hall. The vice president testified that he saw a person in the hall in the custody of the agent who "resembled the person that we identified as the one that had entered the bank."

[The] vice of suggestion created by the identification in *Stovall [v. Denno*, 388 U.S. 293, 302 (1967),] was the presentation to the witness of the suspect alone handcuffed to police officers. It is hard to imagine a situation more clearly conveying the suggestion to the witness that the one presented is believed guilty by the police.

The few cases that have surfaced therefore reveal the existence of a process attended with hazards of serious unfairness to the criminal accused and strongly suggest the plight of the more numerous defendants who are unable to ferret out suggestive influences in the secrecy of the confrontation. We do not assume that these risks are the result of police procedures intentionally designed to prejudice an accused. Rather we assume they derive from the dangers inherent in eyewitness identification and the suggestibility inherent in the context of the pretrial identification. Williams & Hammelmann, in one of the most comprehensive studies of such forms of identification, said, "[T]he fact that the police themselves have, in a given case, little or no doubt that the man put up for identification has committed the offense, and that their chief pre-occupation is with the problem of getting sufficient proof, because he has not 'come clean,' involves a danger that this persuasion may communicate itself even in a doubtful case to the witness in some [way]." Williams & Hammelmann, *Identification Parades*, Part I, (1963) Crim. L.Rev. 479, 483

Insofar as the accused's conviction may rest on a courtroom identification in fact the fruit of a suspect pretrial identification which the accused is helpless to subject to effective scrutiny at trial, the accused is deprived of that right of cross-examination which is an essential safeguard to his right to confront the witnesses against him. And even though cross-examination is a precious safeguard to a fair trial, it cannot be viewed as an absolute assurance of accuracy and reliability. Thus in the present context, where so many variables and pitfalls exist, the first line of defense must be the prevention of unfairness and the lessening of the hazards of eyewitness identification at the lineup itself. The trial which might determine the accused's fate may well not be that in the courtroom but that at the pretrial confrontation, with the State aligned against the accused, the witness the sole jury, and the accused unprotected against the overreaching, intentional or unintentional, and with little or no effective appeal from the judgment there rendered by the witness—"that's the man."

Since it appears that there is grave potential for prejudice, intentional or not, in the pretrial lineup, which may not be capable of reconstruction at trial, and since presence of counsel itself can often avert prejudice and assure a meaningful confrontation at trial, there can be little doubt that for Wade the postindictment lineup was a critical stage of the prosecution at which he was "as much entitled to such aid [of counsel as] at the trial itself." Thus both Wade and his counsel should have been notified of the impending lineup, and counsel's presence should have been a requisite to conduct of the lineup, absent an "intelligent waiver." No substantial countervailing policy considerations have been advanced against the requirement of the presence of counsel. Concern is expressed that the requirement will forestall prompt identifications and result in obstruction of the confrontations. As for the first, we note that in the two cases in which the right to counsel is today held to apply, counsel had already been appointed and no argument is made in either case that notice to counsel would have prejudicially delayed the confrontations. Moreover, we leave open the question whether the presence of substitute counsel might not suffice where notification and presence of the suspect's own counsel would result in prejudicial delay. And to refuse to recognize the right to counsel for fear that counsel will obstruct the course of justice is contrary to the basic assumptions upon which this Court has operated in Sixth Amendment cases. We rejected similar logic in *Miranda* concerning presence of counsel during custodial interrogation.

In our view counsel can hardly impede legitimate law enforcement; on the contrary, for the reasons expressed, law enforcement may be assisted by preventing the infiltration of taint in the prosecution's identification evidence. That result cannot help the guilty avoid conviction but can only help assure that the right man has been brought to justice.

Legislative or other regulations, such as those of local police departments, which eliminate the risks of abuse and unintentional suggestion at lineup proceedings and the impediments to meaningful confrontation at trial may also remove the basis for regarding the stage as "critical." But neither Congress nor the federal authorities have seen fit to provide a solution. What we hold today "in no way creates a constitutional straitjacket which will handicap sound efforts at reform, nor is it intended to have this effect."

We come now to the question whether the denial of Wade's motion to strike the courtroom identification by the bank witnesses at trial because of the absence of his counsel at the lineup required [the] grant of a new trial at which such evidence is to be excluded. We do not think this disposition can be justified without first giving the Government the opportunity to establish by clear and convincing evidence that the in-court identifications were based upon observations of the suspect other than the lineup identification. Where, as here, the admissibility of evidence of the lineup identification itself is not involved, a *per se* rule of exclusion of courtroom identification would be unjustified. A rule limited solely to the exclusion of testimony concerning identification at the lineup itself, without regard to admissibility of the courtroom identification, would render the right to counsel an empty one. The lineup is most often used [to] crystallize the witnesses' identification of the defendant for future reference. We have already noted that the lineup identification will have that effect. The State may then rest upon the witnesses' unequivocal courtroom identifications, and not mention the pretrial identification as part of the State's case at trial. Counsel is then in the predicament in which Wade's counsel found himself—realizing that possible unfairness at the lineup may be the sole means of attack upon the unequivocal courtroom identification, and having to probe in the dark in an attempt to discover and reveal unfairness, while bolstering the government witness' courtroom identification by bringing out and dwelling upon his prior identification. Since counsel's presence at the lineup would equip him to attack not only the lineup identification but the courtroom identification as well, limiting the impact of violation of the right to counsel to exclusion of evidence only of identification at the lineup itself disregards a critical element of that right.

We think it follows that the proper test to be applied in these situations is "[W]hether, granting establishment of the primary illegality, the evidence to which instant objection is made has been come at by exploitation of that illegality or instead by means sufficiently distinguishable to be purged of the primary taint.'' Application of this test in the present context requires consideration of various factors; for example, the prior opportunity to observe the alleged criminal act, the existence of any discrepancy between any pre-lineup description and the defendant's actual description, any identification prior to lineup of another person, the identification by picture of the defendant prior to the lineup, failure to identify the defendant on a prior occasion, and the lapse of time between the alleged act and the lineup identification. It is also relevant to consider those facts which, despite the absence of counsel, are disclosed concerning the conduct of the lineup.

[On] the record now before us we cannot make the determination whether the in-court identifications had an independent origin. [We] therefore [vacate] the conviction pending a hearing to determine whether the in-court identifications had an independent source, or whether, in any event, the introduction of the evidence was harmless error, and for the District Court to reinstate the conviction or order a new trial, as may be [proper].

MR. JUSTICE BLACK, dissenting in part and concurring in part.

[T]he Government forced [Wade] to stand in a lineup, wear strips on his face, and speak certain words, in order to make it possible for government witnesses to identify him as a criminal. [Being] forced by the Government to help convict himself and to supply evidence against himself by talking outside the courtroom is equally violative of his constitutional right not to be compelled to be a witness against himself. [T]he assistance of counsel at the lineup is also necessary to protect the defendant's in-custody assertion of his privilege against self-incrimination, for [counsel] may advise the defendant not to participate in the lineup or to participate only under certain conditions.

MR. JUSTICE WHITE, whom MR. JUSTICE HARLAN and MR. JUSTICE STEWART join, dissenting in part and concurring in part.

[The] premise for the Court's rule is not the general unreliability of eyewitness identifications nor the difficulties inherent in observation, recall, and recognition. The Court assumes a narrower evil as the basis for its rule—improper police suggestion which contributes to erroneous identifications. [I] do not share this pervasive distrust of all official investigations. None of the materials the Court relies upon supports it. * * *

[I]t may be asked, what possible state interest militates against requiring the presence of defense counsel at lineups? After all, the argument goes, he *may* do some good, he *may* upgrade the quality of identification evidence in state courts and he can scarcely do any harm. [Absent] some reliably established constitutional violation, the processes by which the States enforce their criminal laws are their own prerogative. * * *

[I] would [not] require counsel's presence at pretrial identification procedures. [Some] counsel may advise their clients to refuse to make any movements or to speak any words in a lineup or even to appear in one. To that extent the impact on truthful factfinding is quite obvious. Others will not only observe what occurs and develop possibility for later cross-examination but will hover over witnesses and begin their cross-examination then, menacing truthful factfinding as thoroughly as the Court fears the police now do. Certainly there is an implicit invitation to counsel to suggest rules for the lineup and to manage and produce it as best he can. [I] doubt that the Court's new rule, at least absent some clearly defined limits on counsel's role, will measurably contribute to more reliable pretrial identifications. [T]he State is entitled to investigate and develop its case outside the presence of defense counsel. This includes the right to have private conversations with identification [witnesses].

MR. JUSTICE FORTAS, with whom THE CHIEF JUSTICE and MR. JUSTICE DOUGLAS join, concurring in part and dissenting in part.

[T]he accused may not be compelled in a lineup to speak the words uttered by the person who committed the crime. [It] is more than passive, mute assistance to the eyes of the victim or of witnesses. It is the kind of volitional act—the kind of forced cooperation by the accused—which is within the historical perimeter of the privilege against compelled self-incrimination.

[I] completely agree that the accused must be advised of and given the right to counsel before a lineup—and I join in that part of the Court's [opinion]. * * *

Notes

1. Crucial to *Wade's* outcome was the Court's recognition that lineups could be managed or manipulated in innumerable ways. The logical extension of that understanding is that identification methods which are a function of scientific review, such as fingerprinting, blood sampling, and hair, fiber or DNA analysis, do not trigger the right to counsel. Given the standardization of analysis characterizing such testing, the *Wade* Court stressed "that the accused has the opportunity for a meaningful confrontation of the Government's case at trial through the ordinary processes of cross-examination of the Government's expert witnesses and the presentation of the evidence of his own experts." Such analysis and distinction illuminates an overarching concern with the right to counsel not independently but as a means of facilitating a fair trial when other protections would be inadequate. Elaborating on this theme, the Court in *Gilbert v. California*, 388 U.S. 263, 266–67 (1967), concluded that

The taking of handwriting exemplars was not a "critical" stage of the criminal proceedings entitling petitioner to the assistance of counsel. Putting aside the fact that the exemplars were taken before the indictment and appointment of counsel, there is minimal risk that the absence of counsel might derogate from his right to a fair trial. If [an] unrepresentative exemplar is taken, this can be brought out and corrected through the adversary process at trial since the accused can make an unlimited number of additional exemplars for analysis and comparison by government and defense handwriting experts. Thus, "the accused has the opportunity for a meaningful confrontation of the [State's] case at trial through the ordinary processes of cross-examination of the [State's] expert [handwriting] witnesses and the presentation of the evidence of his own [handwriting] experts."

2. In *Kirby v. Illinois*, 406 U.S. 682 (1972), the Court was asked to extend the exclusionary rule to identification testimony (a showup) that took place *before* the defendant had been indicted or otherwise formally charged with any criminal offense. The Court refused:

[A] person's Sixth and Fourteenth Amendment right to counsel attaches only at or after the time that adversary judicial proceedings have been initiated against him. [The] initiation of judicial criminal proceedings is far from a mere formalism. It is the starting point of our whole system of adversary criminal justice. For it is only then that the government has committed itself to prosecute, and only then that the adverse positions of government and defendant have solidified. It is then that a defendant finds himself faced with the prosecutorial forces of organized society, and immersed in the intricacies of substantive and procedural criminal law. * * *

Mr. Justice Brennan dissented:

[Counsel] is required [at] confrontations because "the dangers inherent in eyewitness identification and the suggestibility inherent in the context of the pretrial identification," mean that protection must be afforded to the "most basic right [of] a criminal defendant—his right to a fair trial at which the witnesses against him might be meaningfully cross-examined." [Hence,] "the initiation of adversary judicial criminal proceedings," is completely [irrelevant]. [T]here inhere in a confrontation for identification conducted after arrest the identical hazards to a fair trial that inhere in such a confrontation conducted "after the onset of formal prosecutional proceedings."

Problems

1. Is counsel really necessary in a lineup situation? What isn't it possible for the suspect to "observe" and "report" to his/her attorney? Based on such observations, would it be possible for the attorney to cross-examine witnesses at trial?

2. You have been hired to represent a suspect who is going to be placed in a lineup. After *Wade*, you know that you have to be concerned about the possibility of "suggestiveness" in the lineup. How is suggestiveness created? In other words, when you go to the lineup, what sorts of problems should you look for?

3. You attend the actual lineup and find that it is unduly suggestive. What is your role? Do you object? Do you remain silent and take notes?

4. If the lineup is suggestive, but you were present, you probably won't be able to challenge the result of the identification on Sixth Amendment right to counsel grounds. So, on what basis do you challenge it?

5. Suppose that a lineup occurs before the suspect has been indicted or formally charged, and the suspect is forced to appear without the benefit of counsel. The suspect is identified by the witness, and the suspect is ultimately indicted. You have been appointed to represent him. After *Wade*, you know that you cannot object to the pre-trial identification (or, for that matter, an in-court identification by the same witness) on Sixth Amendment right to counsel grounds. On what basis might you object if you felt that the process was tainted?

UNITED STATES v. ASH

413 U.S. 300 (1973).

MR. JUSTICE BLACKMUN delivered the opinion of the Court.

[On] the morning of August 26, 1965, a man with a stocking mask entered a bank in Washington, D.C., and began waving a pistol. He ordered an employee to hang up the telephone and instructed all others present not to move. Seconds later a second man, also wearing a stocking mask, entered the bank, scooped up money from tellers' drawers into a bag, and left. The gunman followed, and both men escaped through an alley. The robbery lasted three or four minutes.

A Government informer, Clarence McFarland, told authorities that he had discussed the robbery with Charles J. Ash, Jr., the respondent here. Acting on this information, an FBI agent, in February 1966, showed five black-and-white mug shots of Negro males of generally the same age, height, and weight, one of which was of Ash, to four witnesses. All four made uncertain identifications of Ash's picture. At this time Ash was not in custody and had not been charged. On April 1, 1966, an indictment was returned charging Ash and a codefendant, John L. Bailey, in five counts related to this bank robbery. * * *

[In] preparing for trial, the prosecutor decided to use a photographic display to determine whether the witnesses he planned to call would be able to make in-court identifications. Shortly before the trial, an FBI agent and the prosecutor showed five color photographs to the four witnesses who previously had tentatively identified the black-and-white photograph of Ash. Three of the witnesses selected the picture of Ash, but one was unable to make any selection. None of the witnesses selected the picture of Bailey which was in the group. This post-indictment identification provides the basis for respondent Ash's claim that he was denied the right to counsel at a "critical stage" of the prosecution.

[The] Government [argued] in *Wade* that if counsel was required at a lineup, the same forceful considerations would mandate counsel at other preparatory steps in the "gathering of the prosecution's evidence," such as, for particular example, the taking of fingerprints or blood samples.

The Court concluded that there were differences. Rather than distinguishing these situations from the lineup in terms of the need for counsel to assure an equal confrontation at the time, the Court recognized that there were times when the subsequent trial would cure a one-sided confrontation between prosecuting authorities and the uncounseled defendant. In other words, such stages were not "critical." Referring to fingerprints, hair, clothing, and other blood samples, the Court explained: "Knowledge of the techniques of science and technology is sufficiently available, and the variables in techniques few enough, that the accused has the opportunity for a meaningful confrontation of the Government's case at trial through the ordinary processes of cross-examination of the Government's expert witnesses and the presentation of the evidence of his own experts."

The structure of *Wade*, viewed in light of the careful limitation of the Court's language to "confrontations," makes it clear that lack of scientific precision and inability to reconstruct an event are not the tests for requiring counsel in the first instance. These are, instead, the tests to determine whether confrontation with counsel at trial can serve as a substitute for counsel at the pretrial confrontation. If accurate reconstruction is possible, the risks inherent in any confrontation still remain, but the opportunity to cure defects at trial causes the confrontation to cease to be "critical."

[A] substantial departure from the historical test would be necessary if the Sixth Amendment were interpreted to give Ash a right to counsel at the photographic identification in this case. Since the accused himself is not present at the time of the photographic display, and asserts no right to be present, no possibility arises that the accused might be misled by his lack of familiarity with the law or overpowered by his professional adversary. Similarly, the counsel guarantee would not be used to produce equality in a trial-like adversary confrontation. Rather, the guarantee was used by the Court of Appeals to produce confrontation at an event that previously was not analogous to an adversary trial.

Even if we were willing to view the counsel guarantee in broad terms as a generalized protection of the adversary process, we would be unwilling to go so far as to extend the right to a portion of the prosecutor's trial-preparation interviews with witnesses. Although photography is relatively new, the interviewing of witnesses before trial is a procedure that predates the Sixth Amendment. In England in the 16th and 17th centuries counsel regularly interviewed witnesses before trial. The traditional counterbalance in the American adversary system for these interviews arises from the equal ability of defense counsel to seek and interview witnesses himself.

That adversary mechanism remains as effective for a photographic display as for other parts of pretrial interviews. No greater limitations are placed on defense counsel in constructing displays, seeking witnesses, and conducting photographic identifications than those applicable to the prosecution. Selection of the picture of a person other than the accused, or the inability of a witness to make any selection, will be useful to the defense in precisely the same manner that the selection of a picture of the defendant would be useful to the prosecution. In this very case, for example, the initial tender of the photographic display was by Bailey's counsel, who sought to demonstrate that the witness had failed to make a photographic identification. Although we do not suggest that equality of access to photographs removes all potential for abuse, it does remove any inequality in the adversary process itself and thereby fully satisfies the historical spirit of the Sixth Amendment's counsel guarantee.

The argument has been advanced that requiring counsel might compel the police to observe more scientific procedures or might encourage them to utilize corporeal rather than photographic displays. This Court has recognized that improved procedures can minimize the dangers of suggestion. [Pretrial] photographic identifications, however, are hardly unique in offering possibilities for the actions of the prosecutor unfairly to prejudice the accused. Evidence favorable to the accused may be withheld; testimony of witnesses may be manipulated; the results of laboratory tests may be contrived. In many ways the prosecutor, by accident or by design, may improperly subvert the trial. The primary safeguard against abuses of this kind is the ethical responsibility of the prosecutor, who, as so often has been said, may "strike hard blows" but not "foul ones." If that safeguard fails, review remains available under due process standards.

We are not persuaded that the risks inherent in the use of photographic displays are so pernicious that an extraordinary system of safeguards is required.

We hold, then, that the Sixth Amendment does not grant the right to counsel at photographic displays conducted by the Government for the purpose of allowing a witness to attempt an identification of the offender. * * *

MR. JUSTICE STEWART, concurring in the judgment.

[A] photographic identification is quite different from a lineup, for there are substantially fewer possibilities of impermissible suggestion when photographs are used, and those unfair influences can be readily reconstructed at trial. It is true that the defendant's photograph may be markedly different from the others displayed, but this unfairness can be demonstrated at trial from an actual comparison of the photographs used or from the witness' description of the display. Similarly, it is possible that the photographs could be arranged in a suggestive manner, or that by comment or gesture the prosecuting authorities might single out the defendant's picture. But these are the kinds of overt influence that a witness can easily recount and that would serve to impeach the identification testimony. In short, there are few possibilities for unfair suggestiveness—and those rather blatant and easily reconstructed. Accordingly, an accused would not be foreclosed from an effective cross-examination of an identification witness simply because his counsel was not present at the photographic display. For this reason, a photographic display cannot fairly be considered a "critical stage" of the prosecution. * * *

MR. JUSTICE BRENNAN, with whom MR. JUSTICE DOUGLAS and MR. JUSTICE MARSHALL join, dissenting.

[T]he "dangers of mistaken identification [set] forth in *Wade* are applicable in large measure to photographic as well as corporeal identifications." To the extent that misidentification may be attributable to a witness' faulty memory or perception, or inadequate opportunity for detailed observation during the crime, the risks are obviously as great at a photographic display as at a lineup. "[B]ecause of the inherent limitations of photography, which presents its subject in two dimensions rather than the three dimensions of reality, [a] photographic identification, even when properly obtained, is clearly inferior to a properly obtained corporeal identification." [I]n this sense at least, the dangers of misidentification are even greater at a photographic display than at a lineup.

[A]s in the lineup situation, the possibilities for impermissible suggestion in the context of a photographic display are manifold. Such suggestion, intentional or unintentional, may derive from three possible sources. First, the photographs themselves might tend to suggest which of the pictures is that of the suspect. For example, differences in age, pose, or other physical characteristics of the persons represented, and variations in the mounting, background, lighting, or markings of the photographs all might have the effect of singling out the accused. Second, impermissible suggestion may inhere in the manner in which the photographs are displayed to the witness. [If] the photographs are arranged in an asymmetrical pattern, or if they are displayed in a time sequence that tends to emphasize a particular photograph, "any identification of the photograph which stands out from the rest is no more reliable than an identification of a single photograph, exhibited alone."

Third, gestures or comments of the prosecutor at the time of the display may lead an otherwise uncertain witness to select the "correct" photograph. "[R]egardless of how the initial misidentification comes about, the witness [is] apt to retain in his memory the image of the photograph rather than of the person actually [seen]." As a result, "the issue of identity may [in the absence of other relevant evidence] for all practical purposes by determined there and then, before the trial."

Moreover, as with lineups, the defense can "seldom reconstruct" at trial the mode and manner of photographic identification. [P]reservation of the photographs affords little protection to the unrepresented accused. For, although retention of the photographs may mitigate the dangers of misidentification due to the suggestiveness of the photographs themselves, it cannot in any sense reveal to defense counsel the more subtle, and therefore more dangerous, suggestiveness that might derive from the manner in which the photographs were displayed or any accompanying comments or gestures. [T]he accused cannot rely upon the witnesses themselves to expose these latter sources of suggestion, for the witnesses are not "apt to be alert for conditions prejudicial to the suspect. And if they were, it would likely be of scant benefit to the suspect" since the witnesses are hardly "likely to be schooled in the detection of suggestive influences."

Finally, [the] accused himself is not even present at the photographic identification, thereby reducing the likelihood that irregularities in the procedures will ever come to [light]. Thus, the difficulties of reconstructing at trial an uncounseled photographic display are at least equal to, and possibly greater than, those involved in reconstructing an uncounseled lineup. * * *

[T]his Court's decisions [suggest] that a "stage" of the prosecution must be deemed "critical" for the purposes of the Sixth Amendment if it is one at which the presence of counsel is necessary "to protect the fairness of the trial itself." Indeed, to exclude counsel from a pretrial proceeding at which his presence might be necessary to assure the fairness of the subsequent trial would, in practical effect, render the Sixth Amendment guarantee virtually meaningless, for it would "deny a defendant 'effective representation by counsel at the only stage when legal aid and advice would help him.' "

[*Wade*] envisioned counsel's function at the lineup to be primarily that of a trained observer, able to detect the existence of any suggestive influences and capable of understanding the legal implications of the events that transpire. Having witnessed the proceedings, counsel would then be in a position effectively to reconstruct at trial any unfairness that occurred at the lineup, thereby preserving the accused's fundamental right to a fair trial on the issue of identification.

[T]here simply is no meaningful difference, in terms of the need for attendance of counsel, between corporeal and photographic identifications. And applying established and well-reasoned Sixth Amendment principles, I can only conclude that a pretrial photographic display, like a pretrial lineup, is a "critical stage" of the prosecution at which the accused is constitutionally entitled to the presence of counsel.

Notes

Post-*Ash* law establishes the continuing vitality of *Wade* in post-charging circumstances. In *Moore v. Illinois*, 434 U.S. 220, 224–25 (1977), the Court reiterated the basic premise that counsel must be present for a showup or one-on-one confrontation. The *Wade-Ash–Moore* line of decisions indicates that the right of counsel extends only to post-charging procedures requiring presence and identification of the defendant. Prior to charging, counsel is not required even at a line-up or show-up. The distinction between pre-charging and post-charging circumstances is rooted in Sixth Amendment text that references "criminal prosecutions." In reviewing arguments for extending the *Wade* rule to pre-charging circumstances, the Court in *Kirby v. Illinois* reiterated the significance of actual judicial criminal proceedings rather than police investigations.

D. DUE PROCESS CONSIDERATIONS

Even though the Sixth Amendment may not govern an identification proceeding, because of its timing or circumstance, constitutional review is not necessarily precluded. As a guarantor of procedural fairness, due process claims may be asserted in any investigative or adjudicative context. Standards of review impose upon due process claimants a significant task of demonstrating that identification methods were "unnecessarily suggestive and conducive to mistaken identification." *Stovall v. Denno*, 388 U.S. 293, 302 (1967). Unlike *Gilbert* and *Wade*, which referenced the Sixth Amendment's relevance to defendants identified in person, the companion case of *Stovall v. Denno* concerned a pre-indictment one-on-one identification. The *Stovall* decision represents the seminal articulation of due process principles governing identification procedures.

In *Stovall v. Denno*, 388 U.S. 293 (1967), Dr. Paul Behrendt was stabbed to death in the kitchen of his home. During the murder, Behrendt's wife was stabbed 11 times. She was hospitalized for major surgery, and the following occurred:

> Mrs. Behrendt was hospitalized for major surgery to save her life. The police, without affording petitioner time to retain counsel, arranged with her surgeon to permit them to bring petitioner to her hospital room about noon of August 25, the day after the surgery. Petitioner was handcuffed to one of five police officers who, with two members of the staff of the District Attorney, brought him to the hospital room. Petitioner was the only Negro in the room. Mrs. Behrendt identified him from her hospital bed after being asked by an officer whether he "was the man" and after petitioner repeated at the direction of an officer a "few words for voice identification." None of the witnesses could recall the words that were used. Mrs. Behrendt and the officers testified at the trial to her identification of the petitioner in the hospital room, and she also made an in-court identification of petitioner in the courtroom.

Petitioner claimed that the in-hospital identification was unconstitutionally obtained. The Court disagreed: "[A] claimed violation of due process of law in the conduct of a confrontation depends on the totality of the circumstances surrounding it, and the record in the present case reveals that the showing of Stovall to Mrs. Behrendt in an immediate hospital confrontation was imperative." The Court quoted from the court of appeals' opinion:

> Here was the only person in the world who could possibly exonerate Stovall. Her words, and only her words, "He is not the man" could have resulted in freedom for Stovall. The hospital was not far distant from the courthouse and jail. No one knew how long Mrs. Behrendt might live. Faced with the responsibility of identifying the attacker, with the need for immediate action and with the knowledge that Mrs. Behrendt could not visit the jail, the police followed the only feasible procedure and took Stovall to the hospital room. Under these circumstances, the usual police station line-up, which Stovall now argues he should have had, was out of the question.

See also Simmons v. United States, 390 U.S. 377, 384–85 (1968) (although the identification process included repetitive use of the suspect's picture, the Court found a need for swift police action there was a need to determine whether police "were on the right track" and the risk of misidentification was insignificant).

A year later, in *Foster v. California*, the Court determined that an identification procedure was so suggestive, and reliability so undermined, that due process was denied.

FOSTER v. CALIFORNIA

394 U.S. 440 (1969).

MR. JUSTICE FORTAS delivered the opinion of the Court.

Petitioner was charged by information with the armed robbery of a Western Union office. [The] day after the robbery one of the robbers, Clay, surrendered to the police and implicated Foster and [Grice].

Except for the robbers themselves, the only witness to the crime was Joseph David, the late-night manager of the Western Union office. After Foster had been arrested, David was called to the police station to view a lineup. There were three men in the lineup. One was petitioner. He is a tall man—close to six feet in height. The other two men were short—five feet, five or six inches. Petitioner wore a leather jacket which David said was similar to the one he had seen underneath the coveralls worn by the robber. After seeing this lineup, David could not positively identify petitioner as the robber. He "thought" he was the man, but he was not sure. David then asked to speak to petitioner, and petitioner was brought into an office and sat across from David at a table. Except for prosecuting officials there was no one else in the room. Even after this one-to-one confrontation David still was uncertain whether petitioner was one of the robbers: "truthfully—I was not sure," he testified at trial. A week or 10 days later, the police arranged for David to view a second lineup. There were five men in that lineup. Petitioner was the only person in the second lineup who had appeared in the first lineup. This time David was "convinced" petitioner was the man.

At trial, David testified to his identification of petitioner in the lineups, as summarized above. He also repeated his identification of petitioner in the courtroom. The only other evidence against petitioner which concerned the particular robbery with which he was charged was the testimony of the alleged accomplice Clay.

Judged by that standard, this case presents a compelling example of unfair lineup procedures. In the first lineup arranged by the police, petitioner stood out from the other two men by the contrast of his height and by the fact that he was wearing a leather jacket similar to that worn by the robber. When this did not lead to positive identification, the police permitted a one-to-one confrontation between petitioner and the witness. This Court pointed out in Stovall that "[t]he practice of showing suspects singly to persons for the purpose of identification, and not as part of a lineup, has been widely condemned." Even after this the witness' identification of petitioner was tentative. So some days later another lineup was arranged. Petitioner was the only person in this lineup who had also participated in the first lineup. This finally produced a definite identification.

The suggestive elements in this identification procedure made it all but inevitable that David would identify petitioner whether or not he was in fact "the man." In effect, the police repeatedly said to the witness, *"This* is the man." This procedure so undermined the reliability of the eyewitness identification as to violate due process. * * *

Notes

Determining whether an identification procedure is "impermissible", even if suggestive, requires attention to concerns that compete with and may supersede optimum integrity and regularity. The *Simmons* Court referenced reliability and terminal prejudice factors as a potential offset to suggestive procedures. In *Neil v. Biggers*, the Court stressed that "irreparable misidentification" was "the primary evil to be avoided."

NEIL v. BIGGERS
409 U.S. 188 (1972).

MR. JUSTICE POWELL delivered the opinion of the Court.

[A]fter a jury [trial], respondent was convicted of rape and was sentenced to 20 years' imprisonment. The State's evidence consisted in part of testimony concerning a station-house identification of respondent by the victim. The Tennessee Supreme Court affirmed. On certiorari, the judgment of the Tennessee Supreme Court was affirmed by an equally divided Court. Respondent then brought a federal habeas corpus action raising several claims. * * *

The District Court held that the claims were not barred and, after a hearing, held in an unreported opinion that the station-house identification procedure was so suggestive as to violate due process. The Court of Appeals affirmed. We granted certiorari to decide [whether] the identification procedure violated due process.

[The] victim testified at trial that on the evening of January 22, 1965, a youth with a butcher knife grabbed her in the doorway to her kitchen:

"A. (H)e grabbed me from behind, and grappled—twisted me on the floor. Threw me down on the floor.

"Q. And there was no light in that kitchen?

"A. Not in the kitchen.

"Q. So you couldn't have seen him then?

"A. Yet, I could see him, when I looked up in his face.

"Q. In the dark?

"A.   He was right in the doorway—it was enough light from the bedroom shining through. Yes, I could see who he was.

"Q.   You could see? No light? And you could see him and know him then?

"A.   Yes."

[When] the victim screamed, her 12–year-old daughter came out of her bedroom and also began to scream. The assailant directed the victim to "tell her [the daughter] to shut up, or I'll kill you both." She did so, and was then walked at knifepoint about two blocks along a railroad track, taken into a woods, and raped there. She testified that "the moon was shining brightly, full moon." After the rape, the assailant ran off, and she returned home, the whole incident having taken between 15 minutes and half an hour.

She then gave the police what the [trial court] characterized as "only a very general description," describing him as "being fat and flabby with smooth skin, bushy hair and a youthful voice." Additionally, [she] testified at the habeas corpus hearing that she had described her assailant as being between 16 and 18 years old and between five feet ten inches and six feet tall, as weighing between 180 and 200 pounds, and as having a dark brown complexion. This testimony was substantially corroborated by that of a police officer who was testifying from his notes.

On several occasions over the course of the next seven months, she viewed suspects in her home or at the police station, some in lineups and others in showups, and was shown between 30 and 40 photographs. She told the police that a man pictured in one of the photographs had features similar to those of her assailant, but identified none of the suspects. On August 17, the police called her to the station to view respondent, who was being detained on another charge. In an effort to construct a suitable lineup, the police checked the city jail and the city juvenile home. Finding no one at either place fitting respondent's unusual physical description, they conducted a showup instead.

The showup itself consisted of two detectives walking respondent past the victim. At the victim's request, the police directed respondent to say "shut up or I'll kill you." The testimony at trial was not altogether clear as to whether the victim first identified him and then asked that he repeat the words or made her identification after he had spoken. In any event, the victim testified that she had "no doubt" about her identification.

[We] turn [to] the central question, whether under the "totality of the circumstances" the identification was reliable even though the confrontation procedure was suggestive. As indicated by our cases, the factors to be considered in evaluating the likelihood of misidentification include the opportunity of the witness to view the criminal at the time of the crime, the witness' degree of attention, the accuracy of the witness' prior description of the criminal, the level of certainty demonstrated by the witness at the confrontation, and the length of time between the crime and the confrontation. Applying these factors, we disagree with the District Court's conclusion.

In part, as discussed above, we think the District Court focused unduly on the relative reliability of a lineup as opposed to a showup, the issue on which expert testimony was taken at the evidentiary hearing. * * *

We find that the District Court's conclusions on the critical facts are unsupported by the record and clearly erroneous. The victim spent a considerable period of time with her assailant, up to half an hour. She was with him under adequate artificial light in her house and under a full moon outdoors, and at least twice, once in the house and later in the woods, faced him directly and intimately. She was no casual observer, but rather the victim of one of the most personally humiliating of all crimes. Her description to the police, which included the assailant's approximate age, height, weight, complexion, skin texture, build, and voice, might not have satisfied Proust but was more than ordinarily thorough. She had "no doubt" that respondent was the person who raped her. In the nature of the crime, there are rarely witnesses to a rape other than the victim, who often has a limited opportunity of observation. The victim here, a practical nurse by profession, had an unusual opportunity to observe and identify her assailant. She testified at the habeas corpus hearing that there was something about his face "I don't think I could ever forget."

There was, to be sure, a lapse of seven months between the rape and the confrontation. This would be a seriously negative factor in most cases. Here, however, the testimony is undisputed that the victim made no previous identification at any of the showups, lineups, or photographic showings. Her record for reliability was thus a good one, as she had previously resisted whatever suggestiveness inheres in a showup. Weighing all the factors, we find no substantial likelihood of misidentification. The evidence was properly allowed to go to the jury.

Notes

The *Biggers* decision stressed that, even if an identification procedure is unnecessarily suggestive, the due process inquiry does not end. The *Stovall* Court intimated that suggestiveness itself might be sufficient to make an identification inadmissible. *Stovall v. Denno*, 388 U.S. 293, 302 (1967). *Biggers* previewed a redirection of case law emphasizing that suggestiveness is merely a factor, and that due process inquiry will be driven primarily by considerations of reliability.

MANSON v. BRATHWAITE
432 U.S. 98 (1977).

MR. JUSTICE BLACKMUN delivered the opinion of the Court.

[Jimmy D. Glover], a full-time trooper of the Connecticut State Police, in 1970 was assigned to the Narcotics Division in an undercover capacity. On May 5 of that year, about 7:45 p.m., and while there was still daylight, Glover and Henry Alton Brown, an informant, went to an apartment building at 201 Westland, in Hartford, for the purpose of purchasing narcotics from "Dickie Boy" Cicero, a known narcotics dealer. Cicero, it was thought, lived on the third floor of that apartment building. Glover and Brown entered the building, observed by back-up Officers D'Onofrio and Gaffey, and proceeded by stairs to the third floor. Glover knocked at the door of one of the two apartments served by the stairway. The area was illuminated by natural light from a window in the third floor hallway. The door was opened 12 to 18 inches in response to the knock. Glover observed a man standing at the door and, behind him, a woman. Brown identified himself. Glover then asked for "two things" of narcotics. The man at the door held out his hand, and Glover gave him two $10 bills. The door closed. Soon the man returned and handed Glover two glassine bags. While the door was open, Glover stood within two feet of the person from whom he made the purchase and observed his face. Five to seven minutes elapsed from the time the door first opened until it closed the second time.

Glover and Brown then left the building. This was about eight minutes after their arrival. Glover drove to headquarters where he described the seller to D'Onofrio and Gaffey. Glover at that time did not know the identity of the seller. He described him as being "a colored man, approximately five feet eleven inches tall, dark complexion, black hair, short Afro style, and having high cheekbones, and of heavy build. He was wearing at the time blue pants and a plaid shirt." D'Onofrio, suspecting from this description that respondent might be the seller, obtained a photograph of respondent from the Records Division of the Hartford Police Department. He left it at Glover's office. D'Onofrio was not acquainted with respondent personally but did know him by sight and had seen him "[s]everal times" prior to May 5. Glover, when alone, viewed the photograph for the first time upon his return to headquarters on May 7; he identified the person shown as the one from whom he had purchased the narcotics.

[Respondent] was charged, in a two-count information, with possession and sale of heroin. At his [trial], the photograph from which Glover had identified respondent was received in evidence without objection on the part of the defense. Glover also testified that, although he had not seen respondent in the eight months that had elapsed since the sale, "there [was] no doubt whatsoever" in his mind that the person shown on the photograph was respondent. Glover also made a positive in-court identification without objection. [No] explanation was offered by the prosecution for the failure to utilize a photographic array or to conduct a lineup.

[The] jury found respondent guilty on both counts of the information [and] was affirmed [by the Connecticut Supreme Court]. [Thereafter, respondent filed a petition for habeas corpus which the court of appeals granted.] [T]he court felt that evidence as to the photograph should have been excluded, regardless of reliability, because the examination of the single photograph was unnecessary and suggestive. And, in the court's view, the evidence was unreliable in any event.

[Petitioner] at the outset acknowledges that "the procedure in the instant case was suggestive [because only one photograph was used] and unnecessary" [because there was no emergency or exigent circumstance]. The respondent [proposes] a *per se* rule of exclusion that he claims is dictated by the demands of the Fourteenth Amendment's guarantee of due process. * * *

Since the decision in *Biggers*, the Courts of Appeals appear to have developed at least two approaches to such evidence. The first, or *per se* approach [focuses] on the procedures employed and requires exclusion of the out-of-court identification evidence, without regard to reliability, whenever it has been obtained through unnecessarily suggestive confrontation procedures. The justifications advanced are the elimination of evidence of uncertain reliability, deterrence of the police and prosecutors, [and] "assurance against the awful risks of misidentification."

The second, or more lenient, approach is one that continues to rely on the totality of the circumstances. It permits the admission of the confrontation evidence if, despite the suggestive aspect, the out-of-court identification possesses certain features of reliability. Its adherents feel that the *per se* approach is not mandated by the Due Process Clause of the Fourteenth Amendment. This second approach, in contrast to the other, is ad hoc and serves to limit the societal costs imposed by a sanction that excludes relevant evidence from consideration and evaluation by the trier of fact.

There are, of course, several interests to be considered and taken into account. The driving force behind [our prior holdings] was the Court's concern with the problems of eyewitness identification. Usually the witness must testify about an encounter with a total stranger under circumstances of emergency or emotional stress. The witness' recollection of the stranger can be distorted easily by the circumstances or by later actions of the police. Thus, *Wade* and its companion cases reflect the concern that the jury not hear eyewitness testimony unless that evidence has aspects of reliability. It must be observed that both approaches before us are responsive to this concern. The *per se* rule, however, goes too far since its application automatically and peremptorily, and without consideration of alleviating factors, keeps evidence from the jury that is reliable and relevant.

The second factor is deterrence. Although the *per se* approach has the more significant deterrent effect, the totality approach also has an influence on police behavior. The police will guard against unnecessarily suggestive procedures under the totality rule, as well as the *per se* one, for fear that their actions will lead to the exclusion of identifications as unreliable.

The third factor is the effect on the administration of justice. Here the *per se* approach suffers serious drawbacks. Since it denies the trier reliable evidence, it may result, on occasion, in the guilty going free.

Also, because of its rigidity, the per se approach may make error by the trial judge more likely than the totality approach. And in those cases in which the admission of identification evidence is error under the *per se* approach but not under the totality approach—cases in which the identification is reliable despite an unnecessarily suggestive identification procedure reversal is a Draconian sanction. Certainly, inflexible rules of exclusion that may frustrate rather than promote justice have not been viewed recently by this Court with unlimited enthusiasm.

It is true [that] the Court in *Biggers* referred to the pre-*Stovall* character of the confrontation in that case. But that observation was only one factor in the judgmental process. It does not translate into a holding that post-*Stovall* confrontation evidence automatically is to be excluded.

[We] therefore conclude that reliability is the linchpin in determining the admissibility of identification testimony for both pre-and post-*Stovall* confrontations. The factors to be considered are set out in *Biggers*. These include the opportunity of the witness to view the criminal at the time of the crime, the witness' degree of attention, the accuracy of his prior description of the criminal, the level of certainty demonstrated at the confrontation, and the time between the crime and the confrontation. Against these factors is to be weighed the corrupting effect of the suggestive identification itself.

[We] turn, then, to the facts of this case and apply the analysis: 1. *The opportunity to view*. Glover testified that for two to three minutes he stood at the apartment door, within two feet of the respondent. The door opened twice, and each time the man stood at the door. The moments passed, the conversation took place, and payment was made. Glover looked directly at his vendor. It was near sunset, to be sure, but the sun had not yet set, so it was not dark or even dusk or twilight. Natural light from outside entered the hallway through a window. There was natural light, as well, from inside the apartment.

2. *The degree of attention*. Glover was not a casual or passing observer, as is so often the case with eyewitness identification. Trooper Glover was a trained police officer on duty and specialized and dangerous duty when he called at the third floor of 201 Westland in Hartford on May 5, 1970. Glover himself was a Negro and unlikely to perceive only general features of "hundreds of Hartford black males," as the Court of Appeals stated. It is true that Glover's duty was that of ferreting out narcotics offenders and that he would be expected in his work to produce results. But it is also true that, as a specially trained, assigned, and experienced officer, he could be expected to pay scrupulous attention to detail, for he knew that subsequently he would have to find and arrest his vendor. In addition, he knew that his claimed observations would be subject later to close scrutiny and examination at any trial.

3. *The accuracy of the description*. Glover's description was given to D'Onofrio within minutes after the transaction. It included the vendor's race, his height, his build, the color and style of his hair, and

the high cheekbone facial feature. It also included clothing the vendor wore. No claim has been made that respondent did not possess the physical characteristics so described. D'Onofrio reacted positively at once. Two days later, when Glover was alone, he viewed the photograph D'Onofrio produced and identified its subject as the narcotics seller.

4. *The witness' level of certainty.* There is no dispute that the photograph in question was that of respondent. Glover, in response to a question whether the photograph was that of the person from whom he made the purchase, testified: "There is no question whatsoever." This positive assurance was repeated.

5. *The time between the crime and the confrontation.* Glover's description of his vendor was given to D'Onofrio within minutes of the crime. The photographic identification took place only two days later. We do not have here the passage of weeks or months between the crime and the viewing of the photograph.

These indicators of Glover's ability to make an accurate identification are hardly outweighed by the corrupting effect of the challenged identification itself. Although identifications arising from single-photograph displays may be viewed in general with suspicion, we find in the instant case little pressure on the witness to acquiesce in the suggestion that such a display entails. D'Onofrio had left the photograph at Glover's office and was not present when Glover first viewed it two days after the event. There thus was little urgency and Glover could view the photograph at his leisure. And since Glover examined the photograph alone, there was no coercive pressure to make an identification arising from the presence of another. The identification was made in circumstances allowing care and reflection.

Although it plays no part in our analysis, all this assurance as to the reliability of the identification is hardly undermined by the facts that respondent was arrested in the very apartment where the sale had taken place, and that he acknowledged his frequent visits to that apartment.

Surely, we cannot say that under all the circumstances of this case there is "a very substantial likelihood of irreparable misidentification." Short of that point, such evidence is for the jury to weigh. We are content to rely upon the good sense and judgment of American juries, for evidence with some element of untrustworthiness is customary grist for the jury mill. Juries are not so susceptible that they cannot measure intelligently the weight of identification testimony that has some questionable feature.

Of course, it would have been better had D'Onofrio presented Glover with a photographic array including "so far as practicable [a] reasonable number of persons similar to any person then suspected whose likeness is included in the array." The use of that procedure would have enhanced the force of the identification at trial and would have avoided the risk that the evidence would be excluded as unreliable. But we are not disposed to view D'Onofrio's failure as one of constitutional dimension to be enforced by a rigorous and unbending exclusionary rule. The defect, if there be one, goes to weight and not to substance.

We conclude that the criteria laid down in *Biggers* are to be applied in determining the admissibility of evidence offered by the prosecution concerning a post-*Stovall* identification, and that those criteria are satisfactorily met and complied with here.

The judgment of the Court of Appeals is reversed.

MR. JUSTICE STEVENS, concurring.

[I] am persuaded that this rulemaking function [the Court's decision to fashion new rules to minimize the danger of convicting the innocent on the basis of unreliable eyewitness testimony] can be performed "more effectively by the legislative process than by a somewhat clumsy judicial fiat," and that the Federal Constitution does not foreclose experimentation by the States in the development of such rules. * * *

MR. JUSTICE MARSHALL, with whom MR. JUSTICE BRENNAN joins, dissenting.

[T]he Court wrongly evaluates the impact of [the *Biggers*] factors. First, the Court acknowledges that one of the factors, deterrence of police use of unnecessarily suggestive identification procedures, favors the *per se* rule. Indeed, it does so heavily, for such a rule would make it unquestionably clear to the police they must never use a suggestive procedure when a fairer alternative is available. I have no doubt that conduct would quickly conform to the rule.

Second, the Court gives passing consideration to the dangers of eyewitness identification recognized in the *Wade* trilogy. [T]he dangers of mistaken identification [are] too great to permit unnecessarily suggestive identifications. Neither *Biggers* nor the Court's opinion today points to any contrary empirical evidence. * * *

Finally, the Court errs in its assessment of the relative impact of the two approaches on the administration of justice. The Court relies most heavily on this factor, finding that "reversal is a Draconian sanction" in cases where the identification is reliable despite an unnecessarily suggestive procedure used to obtain it. Relying on little more than a strong distaste for "inflexible rules of exclusion," the Court rejects the *per se* test. In so doing, the Court disregards two significant distinctions between the per se rule advocated in this case and the exclusionary remedies for certain other constitutional violations.

First, the *per se* rule here is not "inflexible." Where evidence is suppressed, for example, as the fruit of an unlawful search, it may well be forever lost to the prosecution. Identification evidence, however, can by its very nature be readily and effectively reproduced. The in-court identification, permitted under *Wade* and *Simmons* if it has a source independent of an uncounseled or suggestive procedure, is one example. Similarly, when a prosecuting attorney learns that there has been a suggestive confrontation, he can easily arrange another lineup conducted under scrupulously fair [conditions].

Second, other exclusionary rules have been criticized for preventing jury consideration of relevant and usually reliable evidence in order to serve interest unrelated to guilt or innocence, such as discouraging illegal searches or denial of counsel. Suggestively obtained eyewitness testimony is excluded, in contrast, precisely because of its unreliability and concomitant irrelevance. Its exclusion both protects the integrity of the truth-seeking function of the trial and discourages police use of needlessly inaccurate and ineffective investigatory methods.

Indeed, impermissibly suggestive identifications are not merely worthless law enforcement tools. They pose a grave threat to society at large in a more direct way than most governmental disobedience of the law. For if the police and the public erroneously conclude, on the basis of an unnecessarily suggestive confrontation, that the right man has been caught and convicted, the real outlaw must still remain at large. Law enforcement has failed in its primary function and has left society unprotected from the depredations of an active criminal.

[T]he Court's totality test will allow seriously unreliable and misleading evidence to be put before juries. Equally important, it will allow dangerous criminals to remain on the streets while citizens assume that police action has given them protection. According to my calculus, all three of the factors upon which the Court relies point to acceptance of the *per se* approach.

[Despite] my strong disagreement with the Court over the proper standards to be applied in this case, I am pleased that its application of the totality test does recognize the continuing vitality of *Stovall*. In assessing the reliability of the identification, the Court mandates weighing "the corrupting effect of the suggestive identification itself" against the "indicators of (a witness') ability to make an accurate identification." The Court holds, as *Neil v. Biggers* failed to, that a due process identification inquiry must take account of the suggestiveness of a confrontation and the likelihood that it led to misidentification, as recognized in *Stovall* and *Wade*. Thus, even if a witness did have an otherwise adequate opportunity to view a criminal, the later use of a highly suggestive identification procedure can render his testimony inadmissible. Indeed, it is my view that, assuming applicability of the totality test enunciated by the Court, the facts of the present case require that result.

I consider first the opportunity that Officer Glover had to view the suspect. Careful review of the record shows that he could see the heroin seller only for the time it took to speak three sentences of four or five short words, to hand over some money, and later after the door re-opened, to receive the drugs in return. The entire face-to-face transaction could have taken as little as 15 or 20 seconds. But during this time, Glover's attention was not focused exclusively on the seller's face. He observed that the door was opened 12 to 18 inches,that there was a window in the room behind the door, and, most importantly, that there was a woman standing behind the man. Glover was, of course, also concentrating on the details of the transaction he must have looked away from the seller's face to hand him the money and receive the drugs. The observation during the conversation thus may have been as brief as 5 or 10 seconds.

As the Court notes, Glover was a police officer trained in and attentive to the need for making accurate identifications. Nevertheless, both common sense and scholarly study indicate that while a trained observer such as a police officer "is somewhat less likely to make an erroneous identification than the average untrained observer, the mere fact that he has been so trained is no guarantee that he is correct in a specific case. His identification testimony should be scrutinized just as carefully as that of the normal witness." Moreover, "identifications made by policemen in highly competitive activities, such as undercover narcotic [agents], should be scrutinized with special care." Yet it is just such a searching inquiry that the Court fails to make here.

Another factor on which the Court relies the witness' degree of certainty in making the identification is worthless as an indicator that he is correct. Even if Glover had been unsure initially about his identification of respondent's picture, by the time he was called at trial to present a key piece of evidence for the State that paid his salary, it is impossible to imagine his responding negatively to such questions as "is there any doubt in your mind whatsoever" that the identification was correct. As the Court noted in Wade: " 'It is a matter of common experience that, once a witness has picked out the accused at the [pretrial confrontation], he is not likely to go back on his word later on.' " Next, the Court finds that because the identification procedure took place two days after the crime, its reliability is enhanced. While such temporal proximity makes the identification more reliable than one occurring months later, the fact is that the greatest memory loss occurs within hours after an event. After that, the dropoff continues much more slowly. Thus, the reliability of an identification is increased only if it was made within several hours of the crime. If the time gap is any greater, reliability necessarily decreases.

Finally, the Court makes much of the fact that Glover gave a description of the seller to D'Onofrio shortly after the incident. Despite the Court's assertion that because "Glover himself was a Negro and unlikely to perceive only general features of 'hundreds of Hartford black males,' as the Court of Appeals stated," the description given by Glover was actually no more than a general summary of the seller's appearance. We may discount entirely the seller's clothing, for that was of no significance later in the proceeding. Indeed, to the extent that Glover noticed clothes, his attention was diverted from the seller's face. Otherwise, Glover merely described vaguely the seller's height, skin color, hairstyle, and build. He did say that the seller had "high cheekbones," but there is no other mention of facial features, nor even an estimate of age. Conspicuously absent is any indication that the seller was a native of the West Indies, certainly something which a member of the black community could immediately recognize from both appearance and accent.

From all of this, I must conclude that the evidence of Glover's ability to make an accurate identification is far weaker than the Court finds it. In contrast, the procedure used to identify respondent was both extraordinarily suggestive and strongly conducive to error. In dismissing "the corrupting effect of the suggestive identification" procedure here, the Court virtually grants the police license to convict the innocent. By displaying a single photograph of respondent to the witness Glover under the circumstances in this record almost everything that could have been done wrong was done wrong.

In the first place, there was no need to use a photograph at all. Because photos are static, two-dimensional, and often outdated, they are "clearly inferior in reliability" to corporeal [procedures].

Worse still than the failure to use an easily available corporeal identification was the display to Glover of only a single picture, rather than a photo array. With good reason, such single-suspect procedures have "been widely condemned." They give no assurance that the witness can identify the criminal from among a number of persons of similar appearance, surely the strongest evidence that there was no [misidentification].

The use of a single picture (or the display of a single live suspect, for that matter) is a grave error, of course, because it dramatically suggests to the witness that the person shown must be the culprit. Why else would the police choose the person? And it is deeply ingrained in human nature to agree with the expressed opinions of others particularly others who should be more knowledgeable when making a difficult decision. In this case, moreover, the pressure was not limited to that inherent in the display of a single photograph. Glover, the identifying witness, was a state police officer on special assignment. He knew that D'Onofrio, an experienced Hartford narcotics detective, presumably familiar with local drug operations, believed respondent to be the seller. There was at work, then, both loyalty to another police officer and deference to a better-informed colleague. Finally, of course, there was Glover's knowledge that without an identification and arrest, government funds used to buy heroin had been wasted.

The Court discounts this overwhelming evidence of suggestiveness, however. It reasons that because D'Onofrio was not present when Glover viewed the photograph, there was "little pressure on the witness to acquiesce in the suggestion." That conclusion blinks psychological reality. There is no doubt in my mind that even in D'Onofrio's absence, a clear and powerful message was telegraphed to Glover as he looked at respondent's photograph. He was emphatically told that "this is the man," and he responded by identifying respondent then and at trial "whether or not he was in fact 'the man.'"

I must conclude that this record presents compelling evidence that there was "a very substantial likelihood of misidentification" of respondent Brathwaite. The suggestive display of respondent's photograph to the witness Glover likely erased any independent memory that Glover had retained of the seller from his barely adequate opportunity to observe the criminal.

Notes

Review of identification procedures has been characterized by less demanding criteria than those governing confessions. Even if found reliable, an involuntary confession is inadmissible. *Jackson v. Denno*, 378 U.S. 368, 376 (1964). Relevant case law, when involuntary confessions are concerned, reflects not only an inclination to exclude such evidence but an insistence upon excusing the jury when arguments on admissibility are heard. Although the impact of an inadmissible identification may be as profound as that of a confession, the admissibility question may be resolved with the jury present. *Watkins v. Sowders*, 449 U.S. 341, 349 (1981). Beyond finding reliability an offset to suggestiveness, the Court also may reference an independent source of identification or harmless error as factors that support admissibility.

Problems

1. Recall the earlier problem in which a lineup occurs before the suspect has been indicted or formally charged, and the suspect is forced to appear without the benefit of counsel. When the suspect is identified by the witness, and the suspect is ultimately indicted, you are appointed to represent him. You object that neither identification should be permitted. Now you need to develop proof to support your objection. What type of proof would be convincing and probative? How would you develop it?

2. As we have seen, even though a defendant cannot object to a prior photographic identification on Sixth Amendment right to counsel grounds, he might be able to raise a due process objection. If you are appointed to represent a defendant confronted by this situation, what types of evidence might help you establish a due process violation? How might you develop the evidence?

3. Shortly after noon, the victim awakened from a nap to find a man holding a knife in the doorway to her bedroom. The man entered the bedroom, threw her face down on the bed, and choked her until she was quiet. After covering his face with a bandana, the intruder partially undressed the victim, forced her to commit oral sodomy, raped her and left. When police arrived, the victim gave them a description of her assailant. Although she did not know who he was and had seen his face for only 10 to 15 seconds during the attack, she thought he was the same man who had made offensive remarks to her in a neighborhood bar the night before. In the week that followed, police showed the victim two groups of photographs of men. From the first group of 200 she picked about 30 who resembled her assailant in height, weight, and build. From the second group of about 10, she picked two or three. One of these was of petitioner.

On the evening of December 20, 1967, police arrested petitioner at his apartment and held him overnight pending a preliminary hearing to determine whether he should be bound over to the grand jury and to set bail. The next morning, a policeman accompanied the victim to the court for the hearing. The policeman told her she was going to view a suspect and should identify him if she could. He also had her sign a complaint that named petitioner as her assailant. At the hearing, petitioner's name was called and he was led before the bench. The judge told petitioner that he was charged with rape and deviate sexual behavior. The judge then called the victim, who had been in the courtroom waiting for the case to be called, to come before the bench. The State's Attorney stated that police had found evidence linking petitioner with the offenses charged. He asked the victim whether she saw her assailant in the courtroom, and she pointed at petitioner.

At trial, the victim testified on direct examination by the prosecution that she had identified petitioner as her assailant at the preliminary hearing. She also testified that petitioner was the man who had raped her. Was petitioner's right to counsel, or his right to due process, violated by the pretrial identification? Should the witness be allowed to make an in-court identification of petitioner or to testify regarding the pre-trial identification? What arguments might be made on the defendant's behalf? How might the state respond to those arguments? *See Moore v. Illinois*, 434 U.S. 220 (1977).

Chapter 8

EAVESDROPPING AND WIRETAPPING

This chapter presents an opportunity to reexamine the scope of the Fourth Amendment as it relates directly to governmental eavesdropping on the varied forms of human communication, whether oral, telephonic, or electronic. The federal government's War on Terror has raised public awareness as well as criticism of the vast and sophisticated forms of "listening" that have been developed to seek out terrorist, as well as ordinary criminal, activity. By and large, the United States Supreme Court has left the arena and Congress has filled the void with legislation.

This chapter is divided into three sections. First, it covers warrantless eavesdropping, with or without electronic devices, by government informants or undercover agents who are present at the conversations. The Court bases its Fourth Amendment analysis in these cases upon concepts of implied consent and assumption of the risk when a third party is invited to the conversation.

The second section discusses nonconsensual interceptions of communications, whether oral, wire, or electronic. After the Court's brief foray into the constitutional requirements of a warrant, Congress stepped in and legislated the area with Title III of the Omnibus Crime Control Act of 1968, as amended by the Electronic Communications Privacy Act of 1986 and the USA PATRIOT Act of 2001, and with the Foreign Intelligence Surveillance Act of 1978. This section discusses the broad coverage of that legislation, and poses questions as to the constitutionality of these and recent measures to gain access to private communications.

The third section discusses the constitutional and statutory implications of silent video surveillance, a lesser discussed and lesser litigated, but powerful investigative tool.

A. EAVESDROPPING THROUGH SECRET GOVERNMENT AGENTS

HOFFA v. UNITED STATES

385 U.S. 293 (1966).

JUSTICE STEWART delivered the opinion of the Court.

* * * The controlling facts can be briefly stated. The Test Fleet trial, in which James Hoffa was the sole individual defendant, was in progress between October 22 and December 23, 1962, in Nashville, Tennessee. James Hoffa was president of the International Brotherhood of Teamsters. During the course of the trial he occupied a three-room suite in the Andrew Jackson Hotel in Nashville. One of his constant companions throughout the trial was the petitioner King, president of the Nashville local of the Teamsters Union. Edward Partin, a resident of Baton Rouge, Louisiana, and a local Teamsters Union official there, made repeated visits to Nashville during the period of the trial. On these visits he frequented the Hoffa hotel suite, and was continually in the company of Hoffa and his associates, including King, in and around the hotel suite, the hotel lobby, the courthouse, and elsewhere in Nashville. During this period Partin made frequent reports to a federal agent named Sheridan concerning conversations he said Hoffa and King had had with him and with each other, disclosing endeavors to bribe members of the Test Fleet jury. Partin's reports and his subsequent testimony at the petitioners' trial unquestionably contributed, directly or indirectly, to the convictions of all four of the petitioners.

* * *

[W]e proceed upon the premise that Partin was a government informer from the time he first arrived in Nashville on October 22, and that the Government compensated him for his services as such. It is upon that premise that we consider the constitutional issues presented. * * * [Defendant's] argument is that Partin's failure to disclose his role as a government informer vitiated the consent that the petitioner gave to Partin's repeated entries into the suite, and that by listening to the petitioner's statements Partin conducted an illegal "search" for verbal evidence. * * *

In the present case, however, it is evident that no interest legitimately protected by the Fourth Amendment is involved. It is obvious that the petitioner was not relying on the security of his hotel suite when he made the incriminating statements to Partin or in Partin's presence. Partin did not enter the suite by force or by stealth. He was not a surreptitious eavesdropper. Partin was in the suite by invitation, and every conversation which he heard was either directed to him or knowingly carried on in his presence. The petitioner, in a word, was not relying on the security of the hotel room; he was relying upon his misplaced confidence that Partin would not reveal his wrongdoing. * * * Neither this Court nor any member of it has ever expressed the view that the Fourth Amendment protects a wrongdoer's misplaced belief that a person to whom he voluntarily confides his wrongdoing will not reveal it.

* * *

Adhering to these views, we hold that no right protected by the Fourth Amendment was violated in the present case.

Notes and Questions

1.   In his dissenting opinion in *Hoffa*, 385 U.S. 323, Justice Douglas indicated that Partin's status as a "turn-coat friend" or a "government spy" should have been the determinative factor in negating any consent to governmental intrusion:

> We are rapidly entering the age of no privacy, where everyone is open to surveillance at all times; where there are no secrets from government. The aggressive breaches of privacy by the Government increase by geometric proportions. Wiretapping and "bugging" run rampant, without effective judicial or legislative control. * * *

> A householder who admits a government agent, knowing that he is such, waives of course any right to privacy. One who invites or admits an old "friend" takes, I think, the risk that the "friend" will tattle and disclose confidences or that the Government will wheedle them out of him. The case for me, however, is different when government plays an ignoble role of "planting" an agent in one's living room or uses fraud and deception in getting him there. These practices are at war with the constitutional standards of privacy which are parts of our choicest tradition.

> The formula approved today by the Court in *Hoffa* * * * makes it possible for the Government to use willy-nilly, son against father, nephew against uncle, friend against friend to undermine the sanctity of the most private and confidential of all conversations. The Court takes the position that whether or not the Government "placed" Partin in Hoffa's councils is immaterial. The question of whether the Government planted Partin or whether Hoffa was merely the victim of misplaced confidence is dismissed as a "verbal controversy … unnecessary to a decision of the constitutional issues." * * * But, very real differences underlie the "verbal controversy." As I have said, a person may take the risk that a friend will turn on him and report to the police. But that is far different from the Government's "planting" a friend in a person's entourage so that he can secure incriminating evidence. In the one case, the Government has merely been the willing recipient of information supplied by a fickle friend. In the other, the Government has actively encouraged and participated in a breach of privacy by sending an undercover agent. * * * [T]he Government unlawfully enters a man's home when its agent crawls through a window, breaks down a door, enters surreptitiously, or, as alleged here, gets in by trickery and fraud. I therefore do not join in the *Hoffa* opinion.

2. Suppose you ask to speak to your professor in strictest confidence, and the professor assures you that she would never repeat what you say. You disclose your commission of a recent crime, and the professor, through a pre-arranged agreement with the police, promptly informs the police. If this type of communication is to be protected, should it be protected by the Fourth Amendment or by creation of a student-teacher communication privilege?

Note, however, that communication privileges generally do not encompass a derivative use rule. Thus even if a privilege bars the professor from testifying to your confidential communication in the courtroom, nothing prevents the professor from disclosing your statement to the police, who then may use your statement to direct an investigation that uncovers independent evidence of your crime. *See United States v. Friedemann*, 210 F.3d 227 (4th Cir.2000) ("The question whether a document is privileged has nothing at all to do with the separate question whether there existed probable cause to justify the issuance of a warrant to seize that document.").

Exercise

Your client is charged with selling narcotics to John Smith. The client admits the sale but contends that it was a non-profit, "accommodation" sale based on your client's long standing friendship with Smith. Smith refuses to talk to you, but indicates that he would be willing to discuss the situation with your client. Your client feels that if given the opportunity to confront Smith face-to-face, he can convince Smith to corroborate the accommodation nature of the sale. In light of *Hoffa*, is there any way your client could have a confidential conversation with someone who is presently or may in the future cooperate with the government? Should you permit your client to talk to Smith? If so, how would you structure the meeting to minimize the dangers of Smith reporting the conversations to the police?

UNITED STATES v. WHITE

401 U.S. 745 (1971).

JUSTICE WHITE announced the judgment of the Court and an opinion in which THE CHIEF JUSTICE, JUSTICE STEWART, and JUSTICE BLACKMUN join.

* * * The issue before us is whether the Fourth Amendment bars from evidence the testimony of governmental agents who related certain conversations which had occurred between defendant White and a government informant, Harvey Jackson, and which the agents overheard by monitoring the frequency of a radio transmitter carried by Jackson and concealed on his person.

* * *

Hoffa v. United States, * * * which was left undisturbed by *Katz,* held that however strongly a defendant may trust an apparent colleague, his expectations in this respect are not protected by the Fourth Amendment when it turns out that the colleague is a government agent regularly communicating with the authorities. In these circumstances, "no interest legitimately protected by the Fourth Amendment is involved," for that amendment affords no protection to "a wrongdoer's misplaced belief that a person to whom he voluntarily confides his wrongdoing will not reveal it."

* * *

If the conduct and revelations of an agent operating without electronic equipment do not invade the defendant's constitutionally justifiable expectations of privacy, neither does a simultaneous recording of the same conversations made by the agent or by others from transmissions received from the agent to whom the defendant is talking and whose trustworthiness the defendant necessarily risks.

Our problem is not what the privacy expectations of particular defendants in particular situations may be or the extent to which they may in fact have relied on the discretion of their companions. Very probably, individual defendants neither know nor suspect that their colleagues have gone or will go to the police or are carrying recorders or transmitters. Otherwise, conversation would cease and our problem with these encounters would be nonexistent or far different from those now before us. Our problem, in terms of the principles announced in *Katz*, is what expectations of privacy are constitutionally "justifiable"—what expectations the Fourth Amendment will protect in the absence of a warrant. * * *

Inescapably, one contemplating illegal activities must realize and risk that his companions may be reporting to the police. If he sufficiently doubts their trustworthiness, the association will very probably end or never materialize. But if he has no doubts, or allays them, or risks what doubt he has, the risk is his. In terms of what his course will be, what he will or will not do or say, we are unpersuaded that he would distinguish between probable informers on the one hand and probable informers with transmitters on the other. Given the possibility or probability that one of his colleagues is cooperating with the police, it is only speculation to assert that the defendant's utterances would be substantially different or his sense of security any less if he also thought it possible that the suspected colleague is wired for sound. At least there is no persuasive evidence that the difference in this respect between the electronically equipped and the unequipped agent is substantial enough to require discrete constitutional recognition, particularly under the Fourth Amendment which is ruled by fluid concepts of "reasonableness."

* * * The judgment of the Court of Appeals is reversed.

Justice HARLAN, dissenting.

* * * Authority is hardly required to support the proposition that words would be measured a good deal more carefully and communication inhibited if one suspected his conversations were being transmitted and transcribed. Were third-party bugging a prevalent practice, it might well smother that spontaneity—reflected in frivolous, impetuous, sacrilegious, and defiant discourse—that liberates daily life. Much off-hand exchange is easily forgotten and one may count on the obscurity of his remarks, protected by the very fact of a limited audience, and the likelihood that the listener will either overlook or forget what is said, as well as the listener's inability to reformulate a conversation without having to contend with a documented record. All these values are sacrificed by a rule of law that permits official monitoring of private discourse limited only by the need to locate a willing assistant. * * *

By casting its "risk analysis" solely in terms of the expectations and risks that "wrongdoers" or "one contemplating illegal activities" ought to bear, the plurality opinion, I think, misses the mark entirely. [The Court] does not simply mandate that criminals must daily run the risk of unknown eavesdroppers prying into their private affairs; it subjects each and every law-abiding member of society to that risk. * * * Interposition of a warrant requirement is designed not to shield "wrongdoers," but to secure a measure of privacy and a sense of personal security throughout our society. * * * [T]hird-party electronic monitoring, subject only to the self-restraint of law enforcement officials, has no place in our society.

Notes and Questions

1. The *White* decision was rendered 13 years prior to "1984," George Orwell's date for a society controlled by Big Brother. With the benefit of hindsight, does our technologically advanced society bear out or refute the diabolical images of Big Brother? In Justice Harlan's words, has technology smothered "that spontaneity—reflected in frivolous, impetuous, sacrilegious, and defiant discourse—that liberates daily life?"

The plurality in *White* countered Justice Harlan's concerns by stating that "it is only speculation to assert that the defendant's utterances would be substantially different or his sense of security any less if he also thought it possible that the suspect colleague is wired for sound." Would your spontaneity be affected if you were asked to express your opinions of your least favorite professor in an on-line chat room?

2. In *Belmer v. Commonwealth*, 36 Va.App. 448, 553 S.E.2d 123 (2001), the court noted: "Simply leaving a suspect alone with another individual while in police custody does not create a reasonable expectation of privacy that society is prepared to recognize." Thus electronic interception of an oral communication between a minor and his mother in the police interrogation room did not violate the Fourth Amendment.

Most courts considering the issue have held that prisoners generally have no expectation of privacy in conversations with visitors because routine monitoring and recording of such conversations is a reasonable means of maintaining prison security.... Generally, the federal courts continue to find a suspect has no reasonable expectation of privacy in areas controlled by the police.... The whispered conversation between appellant, his mother, and her boyfriend occurred in the police station's interview room, a room designed for the disclosure, not the hiding, of information. The room had a one-way glass mirror. Detective Gandy did not suggest appellant could speak freely to his mother and her boyfriend without fear of eavesdropping. The police were in the middle of an investigation into an armed robbery and appellant knew he was an object of that inquiry. He had no reason to believe this interrogation room was a 'sanctuary for private discussions.'

Compare State v. Munn, 56 S.W.3d 486 (Tenn.2001) ("When viewed with the circumstances indicating that the officers both deceived and assured the defendant and his parents that they were free to talk in private, we conclude that the expectation of privacy was reasonable and justified.").

3. In *United States v. Hammond*, 286 F.3d 189 (4th Cir.2002), the court noted that the Federal Bureau of Prisons routinely tapes inmates' telephone conversations which are permissible under the "law enforcement" and "consent" exceptions to Title III (discussed *infra*). Once such tapes are made, a law enforcement agency may acquire the tapes by means of a subpoena (which does not require a showing of probable cause).

4. *Monitoring of attorney-client communications*. The Federal Bureau of Prisons rule [printed in Federal Register at 66 Fed. Reg. 55062] provides that if the Attorney General receives information from the head of a federal law enforcement or intelligence agency that "reasonable suspicion exists to believe that a particular inmate may use communications with attorneys or their agents to further or facilitate acts of terrorism," the Attorney General may order the implementation of "appropriate procedures for the monitoring or review of communications between that inmate and attorneys who are traditionally covered by the attorney-client privilege, for the purpose of deterring future acts that could result in death or serious bodily injury to persons, or substantial damage to property that would entail the risk of death or serious bodily injury to persons."

Unless a court order is obtained [the rule doesn't address procedures for getting a court order], the inmate and attorney must be notified of the monitoring and of the crime/fraud exception to disclosure of confidential communications. If monitoring occurs, a "privilege team" consisting of attorneys not involved in the investigation will prevent privileged communications from being revealed to prosecutors.

The electronic monitoring of communications between Sheik Omar Rahman and his attorney, Lynne Stewart, were pursuant to court order and led to her prosecution for conspiring with her client, a suspected terrorist. *See United States v. Sattar*, 2003 WL 22137012 (S.D.N.Y. Sept. 15, 2003).

In *Weatherford v. Bursey*, 429 U.S. 545 (1977), an undercover agent participated in two conversations with defendant and counsel. The conversation was never communicated to anyone on the prosecution team. The Court held that there is no *per se* Sixth Amendment rule against monitoring attorney-client communication. The Court, however, also noted that "[t]he Sixth Amendment's assistance-of-counsel guarantee can be meaningfully implemented only if a criminal defendant knows that his communications with his attorney are private and that his lawful preparations for trial are secure against intrusion by the government, his adversary in the criminal proceeding."

B. NONCONSENSUAL INTERCEPTION OF COMMUNICATIONS: CONSTITUTIONAL AND STATUTORY LIMITS

1. *The Supreme Court's Fourth Amendment Foray*

In *Katz v. United States*, 389 U.S. 347 (1967), the Supreme Court made clear that nonconsensual governmental intrusion on a private conversation—"the uninvited ear"—is a "search," and therefore requires a warrant. The Court suggested that the surveillance of the conversation in the telephone booth in *Katz* was "so narrowly circumscribed" that a magistrate could have authorized the search.

In *Berger v. New York*, 388 U.S. 41 (1967), the Court had an opportunity to review the New York wiretap statute and found it to be the equivalent of an unconstitutional "general warrant, contrary to the command of the Fourth Amendment." Specifically, the Court found that the statute "lays down no requirement for particularity in the warrant as to what specific crime has been or is being committed, nor 'the place to be searched,' or 'the persons or things to be seized' as specifically required by the Fourth Amendment. The statute places no termination date on the eavesdrop once the conversation sought is seized. This is left entirely in the discretion of the officer. Finally, the statute's procedure, necessarily because its success depends on secrecy, has no requirement for notice as do conventional warrants, nor does it overcome this defect by requiring some showing of special facts. Nor does the statute provide for a return on the warrant thereby leaving full discretion in the officer as to the use of seized conversations of innocent as well as guilty parties. In short, the statute's blanket grant of permission to eavesdrop is without adequate judicial supervision or protective procedures."

Although the *Berger* Court observed that "it is said that no ... statute authorizing eavesdropping can be drawn so as to meet the Fourth Amendment's requirements," the decision set the stage for the requirements of any legislation. Indeed, *Katz* and *Berger* helped to mobilize Congress to enact Title III of the Omnibus Crime Control Act of 1968, which set parameters for the interception of nonconsensual oral, wire, and ultimately, electronic communications.

2. *Title III of the Omnibus Crime Control and Safe Streets Act of 1968 (Title III), as amended by the Electronic Communications Privacy Act of 1986 (ECPA) and the USA PATRIOT Act (Uniting and Strengthening America by Providing Appropriate Tools Required to Intercept and Obstruct Terrorism Act) of 2001*

Title III prohibits the interception of "wire, oral or electronic communications" by both private and governmental parties. Electronic communications were added by the ECPA in 1986 to cover forms of communication that had emerged since 1968, such as e-mail and facsimiles. Title III does not cover communications where one of the parties has consented to the interception. The Court's previously-described Fourth Amendment analysis in *Hoffa* and *White* continues to guide the legality of such interceptions.

Title III sets out the manner in which federal law enforcement agents may apply to get a court order for such interception. Originally, Title III required that applications to a federal judge had to be authorized by the Attorney General or one of several designated Deputy, Associate or Assistant Attorneys General, 18 U.S.C. § 2516(1), but this requirement was loosened by the 1986 amendments which allow "any attorney for the Government" to authorize such an application, 18 U.S.C. § 2516(3). Also, while Title III originally required that the application must involve an investigation of one of the enumerated offenses set out in the statute, 18 U.S.C. § 2516(1), in 1986, it was expanded so that an application was authorized when the interception may provide evidence of "any Federal felony," 18 U.S.C. § 2516(3). A separate provision in Title III also invites the principal prosecuting authority in any state to apply for an order for interception in conformity with the requirements of Title III. 18 U.S.C. § 2516(2). As a result, most states have adopted legislation mirroring Title III.

The application for an order authorizing interception of wire, oral, or electronic communication must be made in writing and under oath and provide:

- the identity of the law enforcement officer making the application and the officer authorizing it;

- a "full and complete statement of the facts and circumstances," including details of the particular offense, a particular description of the nature and location of the facilities where the communication is to be intercepted, a particular description of the type of communications to be intercepted, and the identity of the person, if known, committing the offense and whose communications are to be intercepted;

- a "full and complete statement as to whether or not other investigative procedures have been tried and failed or why they reasonably appear to be unlikely to succeed if tried or to be too dangerous";

- a statement of the period of time for which the interception is to be maintained.

18 U.S.C. § 2518(1).

The federal judge may then issue the order upon findings that:

- there is probable cause to believe an individual has committed or is committing one of the enumerated offenses;

- there is probable cause to believe that particular communications concerning the offense will be obtained through the interception;

- there is probable cause to believe that the facilities from which the communication is to be intercepted are being used in connection with the offense or are commonly used by the targeted person;

- normal investigative procedures have been tried and failed or reasonably appear unlikely to succeed or are too dangerous.

18 U.S.C. § 2518(3).

The judge's order must then set out the particularities of the time, place and manner of the interception, along the same parameters as required for the application (*i.e.*, identity of persons, if known, nature and location of facilities, description of type of communication, identity of agency and person authorized to intercept). 18 U.S.C. § 2518(4). The judge may not authorize a period of interception longer than thirty days, but may entertain applications to extend the order. 18 U.S.C. § 2518(5). In addition, every order to intercept "shall be conducted in a way as to minimize the interception of communications not otherwise subject to interception under this chapter[.]" 18 U.S.C. § 2518(5).

The legislation provides for the contents of the interception, preferably recorded, to be placed in the custody of the judge and placed under seal. 18 U.S.C. § 2518(8). In addition, within ninety days of the termination of the period of the order (unless postponement for good cause is shown), the judge shall notify the persons named in the order, and, in the judge's discretion, any other parties to the intercepted communication, of the fact of the order and the fact of the interception. 18 U.S.C. § 2518(8).

There is an emergency exception to the requirement of seeking an order, if it involves "immediate danger of death or serious physical injury to any person," "conspiratorial activities threatening the national security interest," or "conspiratorial activities characteristic of organized crime," that requires a wire, oral, or electronic interception before an order can be obtained. An order must be sought and approved within 48 hours. 18 U.S.C. § 2518(7).

Title III has an exclusionary rule. If an oral or wire communication was intercepted in violation of Title III, then the contents of the communication and the evidence derived therefrom shall not be used in any "trial, hearing, or proceeding in or before any court, department, officer, agency, regulatory body, or other authority of the United States, a State, or a political subdivision thereof." 18 U.S.C. § 2518(10)(a). When Title III was amended in 1986 to add electronic communications, this section was not updated as well, so there is no exclusionary remedy for electronic communications intercepted in violation of Title III.

Notes and Questions

1. The Supreme Court has never ruled on the constitutionality of Title III. The Court has relegated itself thus far to interpreting the statute, and has not generally re-entered the field of nonconsensual eavesdropping with a Fourth Amendment analysis. What might be the advantages and disadvantages to allowing a legislature to take over an area of law traditionally policed and shepherded by the Court through constitutional interpretation? Does Title III adequately deal with the constitutional objections of the Court in *Berger* to the New York wiretapping statute?

2. **Minimization.** Perhaps one of the ripest areas for concern is Title III's minimization requirement. How can interceptions of wire, oral, and electronic communications be conducted "in such a way as to minimize the interception of [unauthorized] communications"? With spoken conversations, law enforcement personnel can, in theory, stop listening when the conversation meanders away from the relevant criminal matter. With electronic communication, such as e-mail over the Internet, however, can law enforcement personnel do anything short of an after-the-fact sifting of authorized and unauthorized communications? Should that be lawful, and, if so, what sort of rules should guide them?

The FBI developed an Internet surveillance program called "Carnivore" (much to the horror of its critics, and hence renamed the innocuous "DCS–1000" in 2001), designed to filter out relevant from irrelevant communications as they are en route from the sender to the recipient. How well the program minimized communications unauthorized by Title III is unknown, however, since the FBI has not disclosed how the program works.

What happens if law enforcement personnel do not make attempts to minimize? In *Scott v. United States*, 436 U.S. 128 (1978), the agent conducting the wiretap admitted that he was aware of the minimization requirement "but made no attempt to comply therewith." The Court was unconcerned with the particular agent's lack of good-faith efforts to comply with the minimization requirement. Instead, the Court applied an objective assessment of the officer's actions and concluded that in light of the fact that criminal conversations often involve guarded or coded language, the officer "can hardly be expected to know [which] calls are not pertinent prior to their termination." While only 40% of the calls were narcotics related, the remaining calls were very short, and the wide-ranging conspiracy meant "even a seasoned listener would have been hard pressed to determine with any precision the relevancy of many of the calls before they were completed." Is this explanation for the agent's flouting the minimization requirement satisfactory? What should or can agents do to minimize in such a case?

3. Title III's requirement of a showing that "normal investigative procedures have been tried and have failed or reasonably appear to be unlikely to succeed if tried or to be too dangerous" has also lacked teeth in the application. *See* W. LaFave et al., Criminal Procedure § 4.4(b)(2d ed. 1984), at 372 ("the requisite showing is 'not great' and is to be 'tested in a practical and commonsense fashion,' and in practice the standard has been watered down to 'one of investigatory utility, rather than necessity'") (citations omitted).

The federal district court in *In re Application for Interception of Wire Communications*, 2 F.Supp.2d 177 (D.Mass.1998), however, warned that it would be taking the requirement seriously:

> The government's statutory obligation to make a full and complete statement concerning the necessity of the powerful but intrusive weapon that electronic surveillance constitutes is unqualified; the government is obligated to inform the court of all its information on this issue.
>
> Although there has been no suggestion, nor does the Court harbor any suspicion, that either the affiant or anyone connected with this investigation has been anything other than forthright in the preparation

of this application, recent events in this District give this Court pause when reviewing an application such as this one. It has come to light in an unrelated prosecution now pending before another judge of this District that the government failed to reveal the existence of confidential government informants in its application to intercept and record wire communication. As that court has observed, "applications which are later found to be incomplete or materially misleading regarding the necessity for electronic surveillance may result in the suppression of intercepted communications." With a caution born out of these revelations, the Court predicated its own order in this case on the representation that the United States had no knowledge of undisclosed informants in a position to assist this investigation.

The Court is mindful of and sensitive to the enormous administrative difficulties involved in ascertaining the existence of potential informants employed by various agencies within the government, as well as the attendant danger both to the informants and to law enforcement personnel. Accordingly, the demands made by the Court are not designed to exhaust every avenue of inquiry or eliminate every possibility of error. It is enough that the government agent who applies for the order has made "a reasonable, good faith effort to run the gamut of normal investigative procedures before resorting to means so intrusive as electronic interception of telephone calls."

4. **The Exclusionary Remedy**. Title III's exclusionary rule is broader than the exclusionary rule of the Fourth Amendment, as it applies to many more types of legal proceedings. As previously mentioned, however, the ECPA did not explicitly extend the exclusionary rule to electronic communications, so that an aggrieved party's only remedies under Title III are civil actions for damages and criminal punishment of any person who "intentionally discloses, or endeavors to disclose, to any other person the contents of" any communication obtained through illegal interception.

The reach of the exclusionary remedy is further limited by the Supreme Court's interpretation of it in *United States v. Giordano*, 416 U.S. 505 (1974). There, the Court specified that exclusion was only required when the statutory provision violated "was intended to play a central role in the statutory scheme." *See, e.g., United States v. Donovan*, 429 U.S. 413 (1977) (holding that suppression was not required where the agents did not name all persons they had probable cause to believe were involved in the communications, as the "naming" requirement did not play a central role in the regulatory scheme) (cited in W. LaFave, *supra*, § 4.6(a), at 390).

Unlike the Fourth Amendment, Title III appears to require suppression of evidence illegally obtained by *private* parties as well as by government agents. Nonetheless, the courts have read a number of exceptions into Title III's exclusionary rule. The divergent views of various Circuits are discussed in *United States v. Murdock*, 63 F.3d 1391 (6th Cir.1995), which identified the principle exceptions as:

(1) The ordinary course of business exception—"when an employee's supervisor has particular suspicions about confidential information being disclosed to a business competitor, has warned the employee not to disclose the information, has reason to believe that the employee is

continuing to disclose the information and knows that a particular phone call is to an agent of the competition, it is within the ordinary course of business to listen in on an extension phone for at least as long as the call involves the type of information the supervisor fears is being disclosed'';

(2) Interspousal wiretaps used in preparation for divorce litigation—some courts have distinguished between unaided surveillance by a spouse and surveillance involving a third-party, even if instigated by the spouse; and

(3) Family settings involving children. See the exercise following the Notes and Problems.

Why does Title III extend its suppression remedy to violations by private parties? Are the exceptions all justified?

5. **Stored Communications.** Title III, as originally conceived, prohibits the interception of communications *as they are being made*. Until the ECPA in 1986, when Congress amended the statute's application to add electronic communications, the statute did not apply to stored communications, such as e-mails sitting in a person's "In box". The ECPA regulates electronic communications stored by electronic communications service providers, such as Internet service providers like "America Online". The statute does not regulate privately generated storage, such as e-mails stored on computer hard drives, leaving such regulation to the Fourth Amendment.

Should the government wish to access stored communications covered under ECPA, the procedures depend upon the status of the communication and its time in storage. Government agents can only access communications that have been in storage for less than 180 days by obtaining a warrant based on probable cause. However, for communications in storage longer than 180 days or for opened e-mails, the government can access them by subpoena (which has no requirement of probable cause). What is the rationale for the distinction? Does the receiver of the e-mail have a "reasonable expectation of privacy" in opened e-mail or unopened e-mail stored for more than six months? Also, what is the rationale for the distinction between e-mail in transit and e-mail received? Why does Title III treat them differently? Can you conceive of a reason based upon implied consent or assumption of the risk?

As with other electronic communications intercepted under Title III, there is no exclusionary remedy for violation of these provisions of the statute.

6. **Pen Registers.** Title III, as originally enacted, only prohibited the interception of the *contents* of any communication, 18 U.S.C. § 2510(4) (emphasis added), and did not cover "pen registers." A pen register is a recording of the numbers dialed from a phone. Recall that in *Smith v. Maryland*, 442 U.S. 735 (1979), the Court held that collecting information from pen registers did not constitute a "search" under the Fourth Amendment. Nonetheless, in 1986, the ECPA added a separate chapter to Title 18 prohibiting the use of pen registers without a court order. 18 U.S.C. §§ 3121–3127. The requirement for obtaining the order is lowered from

probable cause—the government need only certify that the information sought through the pen register is "relevant." 18 U.S.C. § 3127.

In 2001, the Patriot Act amended the definition of a pen register to make it applicable to the Internet, thereby covering "dialing, routing, addressing, or signaling information." 18 U.S.C. § 3127(3)-(4). This does not involve intercepting the contents of the communication, but merely the "routing" and "addressing" information, *i.e.,* the TO and FROM lines on email; not the SUBJECT box or the text of the email. What standard for obtaining pen register information makes the most sense—the Court's in *Smith*, the requirement of "relevance" under the ECPA, or a requirement of probable cause, as is required for interception of the contents of the communications under Title III? Do you have the same or lesser expectation of privacy in the addressee of your e-mail as you do in the contents of that e-mail?

7. Title III did not explicitly address the issue of how and whether governments agents may intercept communications when it requires entry into a private structure. In *Dalia v. United States*, 441 U.S. 238 (1979), the Court stated that the Fourth Amendment does not prohibit a covert entry performed for the purpose of installing otherwise legal electronic bugging equipment. According to the Court, nothing in the language of the Fourth Amendment suggests that search warrants "must include a specification of the precise manner in which they are to be executed. On the contrary, it is generally left to the discretion of the executing officers to determine the details of how best to proceed with the performance of a search authorized by warrant—subject of course to the general Fourth Amendment protection 'against unreasonable searches and seizures.' "

8. **Dissemination of Intercepted Communications.** Title III limits the ability of law enforcement officials to disseminate intercepted communications. They may only disclose the contents of the communications "to another investigative or law enforcement officer to the extent that such disclosure is appropriate to the proper performance of the official duties of the officer making or receiving the disclosure." 18 U.S.C. § 2517(1).

The Patriot Act loosened these restrictions, by expanding the list of officials to whom the contents may be disclosed and the reasons for disclosure. Disclosure may be made to any "Federal law enforcement, intelligence, protective, immigration, national defense, or national security official to the extent that such contents includes foreign intelligence" for performance of their official duties. 18 U.S.C. § 2517(6). Also, disclosure may be made to any Federal, State, local or foreign government official when the contents reveal a threat of actual or potential attack or other grave hostile acts by foreign powers or their agents, domestic international sabotage, or domestic or international terrorism, in order to prevent or respond to the threats. The provisions of the Patriot Act were drafted to sunset on December 31, 2005, but Congress has recently re-authorized the Act.

9. **Roving wiretaps.** While the requirements of Title III are that the court order specify the particular location or facility at which communications are to be intercepted, the ECPA added an exception to that requirement. ECPA authorizes a "roving wiretap," a wiretap that follows a person rather than a specific phone or computer terminal, when the application

"contains a full and complete statement as to why such specification [of a surveillance site] is not practical," and the judge so finds. 18 U.S.C. § 2518(11)(a). For wire and electronic communications, the applicant must also demonstrate "probable cause to believe that the person's actions could have the effect of thwarting interception from a specified facility." 18 U.S.C. § 2518(11)(b). In order to obtain authorization for a roving wiretap, the application and order must specify the identity of the target (as opposed to Title III's usual requirement of identifying persons "if known"). Does the lack of designation of a place to be searched violate the Fourth Amendment's "particularity" requirement? How would you answer that question if you were representing the government?

10. The 1994 Communications Assistance for Law Enforcement Act (CALEA) required telephone companies to rewire their networks and switches to accommodate wiretapping by law enforcement. In June 2006, a federal appeals court, 2–1, upheld the extension of the Act to also require providers of broadband Internet access to accommodate the government's surveillance of electronic communications. *American Council on Educ. v. F.C.C.*, 451 F.3d 226 (D.C. Cir. 2006). Are Justice Harlan's concerns in *White* becoming more real?

11. The Administrative Office of the U.S. Courts provides annual reports gathering statistics on the number of interceptions authorized under Title III. According to its 2005 report, 1,773 interceptions of wire, oral and electronic communications were authorized by state and federal courts. Only one application was denied. The number of interceptions has increased each year, from 1,442 in 2003, and 1,710 in 2004.

Problems

1. The defendant is known on the street as the "Dominos of narcotics" because he responds within thirty minutes to any call to his pager. The police, without court approval, obtain a duplicate pager used to intercept messages to the defendant's digital pager. The police rely on *Smith v. Maryland*, *supra*, which held that a pen register which merely records the caller's phone number is not a "listening device" within the meaning of Title III. Is the duplicate pager a pen register or a listening device? See *Brown v. Waddell*, 50 F.3d 285 (4th Cir. 1995) (holding duplicate pager was a "full-fledged eavesdropping device" because it obtained not only the caller's phone number but also additional numeric characters that could be used to convey coded messages).

2. When your client was stopped for a traffic violation he consented to a search of his vehicle for guns, drugs, money, or illegal contraband. The police took a cellular telephone found in the car and removed the cover of the battery compartment. In the compartment they found a small quantity of cocaine. The police then accessed the cellular phone's computer memories and discovered the telephone numbers of your client's suppliers and customers. What evidence would you move to suppress; on what grounds; and what result?

In *Smith v. State*, 713 N.E.2d 338 (Ind.Ct.App.1999) the court held that a reasonable person would have understood the defendant's consent to include permission to search any containers inside the vehicle that might reasonably contain the items specified by the troopers. "A cellular phone is a container capable of hiding such items as drugs or money. Therefore, it was proper for the troopers to seize the cellular phone long enough to determine whether it was truly an operating cellular phone or merely a pretense for hiding the expressed objects of their search." However, the troopers went too far in accessing the phone's internal memory. The Fourth Amendment "affords protection from the unreasonable search and seizure of the computer memory of a cellular phone to retrieve its electronic contents," and no reasonable person would believe that the troopers might reasonably find guns, drugs, money, or other contraband by retrieving the electronic contents of the telephone.

Exercise

The parents of a 13–year–old girl became suspicious of the girl's relationship with an adult neighbor. They listened in on a phone conversation between their daughter and the defendant and heard the pair talking in sexual terms and discussing killing the girl's parents. The parents purchased a tape recorder and surreptitiously taped numerous conversations between their daughter and the defendant. The parents submitted a compilation tape to the police, but the defendant was not charged until after the girl received extensive counseling for depression and finally accused the defendant of molesting her. By the time of trial, the girl states that she is glad her parents made the recordings.

At the defendant's trial for child molesting, is the tape admissible under federal law? What provisions of Title III would you cite? Should there be judicial recognition of a parent's vicarious consent on behalf of a child? What use would you make of the cases discussed in *Murdock, supra?*

3.   *The Foreign Intelligence Surveillance Act of 1978 (FISA)*

Title III originally did not appear to regulate national security surveillance. Section 2511(3) stated that nothing in the statute "shall limit the constitutional power of the President to take such measures as he deems necessary to protect the Nation against actual or potential attack or other hostile acts of a foreign power, to obtain foreign intelligence deemed essential to the security of the United States, or to protect national security information against foreign intelligence activities." The provision also stated that the statute did not "limit the constitutional power of the President to take such measures as he deems necessary to protect the United States against the overthrow of the Government [by] unlawful means or against any other clear and present danger to the structure or existence of the Government."

The Court made short order of what the latter provision meant for citizens of the United States in *United States v. United States District Court,* 407 U.S. 297 (1972). The Court held that the provision did not authorize the government to engage in a warrantless surveillance of a domestic radical group, made up of only U.S. citizens, accused of conspiring to overthrow the government—the Fourth Amendment required a warrant. The Court, however, did suggest that different standards may be reasonable under the Fourth Amendment when engaged in domestic security surveillance, as opposed to the surveillance of ordinary criminal wrongdoing.

Congress responded with the Foreign Intelligence Surveillance Act of 1978 (50 U.S.C. §§ 1801–1811) (FISA). FISA established the Foreign Intelligence Surveillance Court (FISC), comprised of eleven federal district judges. Judges in the FISC take applications for electronic surveillance. The hearings on the applications are *ex parte*. The judge must find probable cause to believe that the target of the electronic surveillance is "a foreign power or an agent of a foreign power" and that the places where the surveillance is to occur are used by "a foreign power or an agent of a foreign power." 50 U.S.C. § 1804. The judge does *not* need to find probable cause that the surveillance will lead to finding foreign intelligence information. FISA also contains application requirements similar to those of Title III, such as a showing that the "information cannot reasonably be obtained by normal investigative techniques" and that procedures will be used to minimize interceptions of communications by U.S. citizens. Upon proper findings, the judge may enter an *ex parte* order for surveillance for no longer than 120 days.

Notes and Questions

1. The *ex parte* nature of the hearing, as well as any review of a denial of an application, means that only the government is privy to the process. The existence of FISC was not known to the public until recently, and its secrecy has drawn extensive criticism. Is the *ex parte* nature of the procedures here any different from the application for a warrant under the Fourth Amendment? What are the possibilities for abuse and how may they be guarded against?

2. FISA defines a "foreign power" as including a "foreign government" or a "foreign-based political organization not substantially comprised of United States persons," and a "foreign agent" as including a foreign national employed by a "foreign power." 50 U.S.C. § 1801. Critics of FISA therefore note that these definitions do not require that such organization or individual be suspected of terrorist activities or any illegal activities. Combined with the fact that the judge does not need to find probable cause that foreign intelligence will be gathered as a result of the surveillance, does FISA pass constitutional muster?

3. In 2001, the Patriot Act, enacted six weeks after the September 11th attacks, amended FISA and expanded its reach. Prior to 2001, FISA procedures required that a government official certify that the collection of foreign intelligence was "the purpose" of the surveillance. After 2001, the certification need only be that the collection be "a significant purpose" of the surveillance. The result is law enforcement officials have more flexibility when investigating activities that have both a criminal investigation component and a foreign intelligence component, and criminal wrongdoing can be the primary purpose of the investigation. Increasingly, the Attorney General has sought and achieved more ability for foreign intelligence officials to

consult and coordinate with U.S. attorneys prosecuting crime. Does the inclusion of an ordinary criminal law enforcement primary purpose change the role the Fourth Amendment should play in regulating surveillance under FISA?

4. **Roving wiretaps**. The Patriot Act also amended FISA to allow "roving wiretaps" under the same procedures as allowed under Title III.

Problem

In December 2005, the American public learned that, in 2002, the Bush Administration had secretly authorized the National Security Agency (NSA) to monitor the international telephone calls and international e-mails of U.S. citizens. Over the past four years, NSA has collected the phone call records of tens of millions of Americans, using data provided by AT & T, Verizon and BellSouth. Most of these Americans were not suspected of any crime, and the data gathered includes both domestic and international calls. Note that the program does not monitor the content of the calls. The call records are sorted in an attempt to uncover patterns which indicate communications with Al Qaeda, the terrorist group responsible for the 9/11 attacks. NSA is a leading expert in this sort of "data mining."

The Bush Administration did not seek a warrant from the FISC before proceeding with this secret program. If you were counsel to the Bush Administration, how might you defend the program as within constitutional and statutory limits? How would you respond as counsel to the A.C.L.U.?

C. ELECTRONIC VIDEO SURVEILLANCE

Title III does not cover video surveillance. Use of video surveillance in public areas like an airport may not constitute a search within the *Katz* definition. *See, e.g., Vega–Rodriguez v. Puerto Rico Telephone Co.*, 110 F.3d 174 (1st Cir.1997) (holding that employees of a quasi-public telephone company had no legitimate expectation to be free from video-taping in an "open and undifferentiated work area"). *Compare United States v. Cuevas–Sanchez*, 821 F.2d 248 (5th Cir.1987) (holding that the installation of a surveillance camera on a power pole to videotape activities in a suspect's backyard constitutes a "search" within the meaning of the Fourth Amendment).

Courts have cautioned that "hidden video surveillance is one of the most intrusive investigative mechanisms available to law enforcement. The sweeping, indiscriminate manner in which video surveillance can intrude upon us, regardless of where we are, dictates that its use be approved only in limited circumstances." *United States v. Nerber*, 222 F.3d 597 (9th Cir.2000).

Note and Questions

1. In *Nerber, supra*, the Ninth Circuit distinguished between "silent" videos and those that record sound as well as visual images. The court concluded that, while neither Title III nor FISA prohibits domestic silent

video and Title III does not regulate such surveillance, video recording is still subject to the Fourth Amendment. The court then looked to Title III "for guidance." The court adopted the following four requirements, in addition to the ordinary requirement of a finding of probable cause:

> (1) the judge issuing the warrant must find that "normal investigative procedures have been tried and have failed or reasonably appear to be unlikely to succeed if tried or to be too dangerous,"; (2) the warrant must contain "a particular description of the type of [activity] sought to be [videotaped], and a statement of the particular offense to which it relates,"; (3) the warrant must not allow the period of [surveillance] to be "longer than is necessary to achieve the objective of the authorization, [ ]or in any event longer than thirty days" (though extensions are possible); and (4) the warrant must require that the [surveillance] "be conducted in such a way as to minimize the [videotaping] of [activity] not otherwise subject to [surveillance.]"

Do these requirements satisfy the Fourth Amendment? Should video surveillance be treated differently than wire, oral and electronic surveillance?

2. More than 60 urban centers in the United States use video surveillance in public places. The process has been used for a decade in England, and it was used at the 2001 Super Bowl in Tampa (subsequently know as the "Snooper Bowl"). Face scanners, which plug into existing cameras, are increasingly used in airports. A face scanner grabs images of faces while the camera is recording. Software extracts the unique characteristics of each face and creates a template, a compressed digital file that can then be sent over the Internet to several databases at once. [There are 80 unique landmarks on a face: *e.g.,* eye sockets, cheekbones and the bridge of the nose. The computer only has to match 14 of these 80 landmarks to make a reliable identification. The software ignores changeable characteristics like hair color, hair style, facial expression]. Further software installed alongside each database sifts through a million photos per second and signals when it finds a match.

Should the use of face scanners require a warrant? Do you expose those facial features to the public or do you retain a "reasonable expectation of privacy" in the details scanned?

Chapter 9

THE EXCLUSIONARY RULE

The exclusionary evidence rule precludes the state from using evidence seized in violation of a defendant's constitutional rights to convict the defendant of a crime. Although the rule is frequently applied when the police conduct an illegal search or seizure, it is also applied to violations of other constitutional rights (*e.g.*, evidence obtained from unconstitutional lineups and interrogations).

A. THE RULE'S APPLICATION TO FEDERAL AND STATE PROCEEDINGS

Although the United States Supreme Court's 1914 decision in *Weeks v. United States*, 232 U.S. 383 (1914), held that the exclusionary rule applies to federal courts proceedings, that decision failed to extend the rule to state court proceedings.

WOLF v. COLORADO
338 U.S. 25 (1949).

MR. JUSTICE FRANKFURTER delivered the opinion of the Court.

[The] security of one's privacy against arbitrary intrusion by the police—which is at the core of the Fourth Amendment—is basic to a free society. It is therefore implicit in "the concept of ordered liberty" and as such enforceable against the States through the Due Process Clause. The knock at the door, whether by day or by night, as a prelude to a search, without authority of law but solely on the authority of the police, did not need the commentary of recent history to be condemned as inconsistent with the conception of human rights enshrined in the history and the basic constitutional documents of English-speaking peoples.

Accordingly, we have no hesitation in saying that were a State affirmatively to sanction such police incursion into privacy it would run counter to the guaranty of the Fourteenth Amendment. But the ways of enforcing such a basic right raise questions of a different order. How such arbitrary conduct should be checked, what remedies against it should be afforded, the means by which the right should be made effective, are all questions that are not to be so dogmatically answered as to preclude the varying solutions which spring from an allowable range of judgment on issues not susceptible of quantitative solution.

In *Weeks v. United States*, [232 U.S. 383 (1914)], this Court held that in a federal prosecution the Fourth Amendment barred the use of evidence secured through an illegal search and seizure. This ruling [was] not derived from the explicit requirements of the Fourth [Amendment]. The decision was a matter of judicial implication. Since then it has been frequently applied and we stoutly adhere to it. But the immediate question is whether the basic right to protection against arbitrary intrusion by the police demands the exclusion of logically relevant evidence obtained by an unreasonable search and seizure because, in a federal prosecution for a federal crime, it would be excluded. [O]ne would suppose this to be an issue to which men with complete devotion to the protection of the right of privacy might give different answers. When we find that in fact most of the English-speaking world does not regard as vital to such protection the exclusion of evidence thus obtained, we must hesitate to treat this remedy as an essential ingredient of the right. The contrariety of views of the States is particularly impressive.... I. Before the *Weeks* decision 27 States had passed on the admissibility of evidence obtained by unlawful search and seizure. (a) Of these, 26 States opposed the *Weeks* doctrine. (b) Of these, 1 State anticipated the *Weeks* doctrine. II. Since the *Weeks* decision 47 States [have] passed on the *Weeks* doctrine. (a) Of these, 20 passed on it for the first time. (1) Of the foregoing States, 6 followed the *Weeks* doctrine. (2) Of the foregoing States, 14 rejected the *Weeks* doctrine. (b) Of these, 26 States reviewed prior decisions contrary to the *Weeks* doctrine. (1) Of these, 10 States have followed *Weeks*, overruling or distinguishing their prior decisions. (2) Of these, 16 States adhered to their prior decisions against *Weeks*. (c) Of these, 1 State adhered to its prior formulation of the *Weeks* doctrine. III. As of today 30 States reject the *Weeks* doctrine, 17 States are in agreement with it. IV. Of 10 jurisdictions within the United Kingdom and the British Commonwealth of Nations which have passed on the question, none has held evidence obtained by illegal search and seizure inadmissible.

The jurisdictions which have rejected the *Weeks* doctrine have not left the right to privacy without other means of protection.[1] Indeed, the exclusion of evidence is a remedy which directly serves only to protect

---

1. The common law provides actions for damages against the searching officer; against one who procures the issuance of a warrant maliciously and without probable cause; against a magistrate who has acted without jurisdiction in issuing a warrant, against persons assisting in the execution of an illegal search. One may also without liability use force to resist an unlawful search. Statutory sanctions [provide] for the punishment of one maliciously procuring a search warrant or willfully exceeding his authority in exercising it. Some statutes more broadly penalize unlawful searches. Virginia also makes punishable one who issues a general search warrant or a warrant unsupported by affidavit. A few States have provided statutory civil remedies. And in one State, misuse of a search warrant may be an abuse of process punishable as contempt of court.

those upon whose person or premises something incriminating has been found. We cannot, therefore, regard it as a departure from basic standards to remand such persons, together with those who emerge scatheless from a search, to the remedies of private action and such protection as the internal discipline of the police, under the eyes of an alert public opinion, may afford. Granting that in practice the exclusion of evidence may be an effective way of deterring unreasonable searches, it is not for this Court to condemn as falling below the minimal standards assured by the Due Process Clause a State's reliance upon other methods which, if consistently enforced, would be equally effective. [We] cannot brush aside the experience of States which deem the incidence of such conduct by the police too slight to call for a deterrent remedy not by way of disciplinary measures but by overriding the relevant rules of evidence. There are, moreover, reasons for excluding evidence unreasonably obtained by the federal police which are less compelling in the case of police under State or local authority. The public opinion of a community can far more effectively be exerted against oppressive conduct on the part of police directly responsible to the community itself than can local opinion, sporadically aroused, be brought to bear upon remote authority pervasively exerted throughout the country.

We hold, therefore, that in a prosecution in a State court for a State crime the Fourteenth Amendment does not forbid the admission of evidence obtained by an unreasonable search and seizure. * * *

Affirmed.

Mr. JUSTICE BLACK, concurring.

[T]he federal exclusionary rule is not a command of the Fourth Amendment but is a judicially created rule of evidence which Congress might negate. * * *

Mr. JUSTICE RUTLEDGE, dissenting.

[I] reject the Court's [conclusion] that the mandate embodied in the Fourth Amendment, although binding on the states, does not carry with it the one sanction—exclusion of evidence taken in violation of the Amendment's terms—failure to observe which means that "the protection of the 4th Amendment [might] as well be stricken from the Constitution." *Weeks v. United States*, 232 U.S. 383. [T]he Amendment without the sanction is a dead letter. Twenty-nine years ago this Court, speaking through Justice Holmes, refused to permit the Government to subpoena documentary evidence which it had stolen, copied and then returned, for the reason that such a procedure "reduces the Fourth Amendment to a form of words." *Silverthorne Lumber Co. v. United States*, 251 U.S. 385, 392. But the version of the Fourth Amendment today held applicable to the states hardly rises to the dignity of a form of words; at best it is a pale and frayed carbon copy of the original, bearing little resemblance to the Amendment the fulfillment of whose command I had heretofore thought to be "an indispensable need for a democratic society." [The] view that the Fourth Amendment itself forbids the introduction of evidence illegally obtained in federal prosecutions is one of long standing and firmly established. It is too late in my judgment to question it now. * * *

Mr. Justice Murphy, with whom Mr. Justice Rutledge joins, dissenting.

[T]here is but one alternative to the rule of exclusion. That is no sanction at all. [This] has been perfectly clear since 1914, when a unanimous Court decided *Weeks*. "If letters and private documents can thus be seized and held and used in evidence against a citizen accused of an offense," we said, "the protection of the 4th Amendment, declaring his right to be secure against such searches and seizures, is of no value, and [might] as well be stricken from the Constitution." "It would reduce the Fourth Amendment to a form of words." Holmes, J., for the Court, in *Silverthorne Lumber Co. v. United States*, 251 U.S. 385.

Today the Court wipes those statements from the books with this bland citation of "other remedies." Little need be said concerning the possibilities of criminal prosecution. Self-scrutiny is a lofty ideal, but its exaltation reaches new heights if we expect a District Attorney to prosecute himself or his associates for well-meaning violations of the search and seizure clause during a raid the District Attorney or his associates have ordered.... A trespass action for damages is a venerable means of securing reparation for unauthorized invasion of the home. Why not put the old writ to a new use? [But] what an illusory remedy this is, if by "remedy" we mean a positive deterrent to police and prosecutors tempted to violate the Fourth Amendment. [The] measure of damages is simply the extent of the injury to physical property. If the officer searches with care, he can avoid all but nominal damages.... Are punitive damages possible? Perhaps. But a few states permit none, whatever the circumstances. In those that do, the plaintiff must show [malice], and surely it is not unreasonable to assume that one in honest pursuit of crime bears no malice toward the search victim. If that burden is carried, recovery may yet be defeated by the rule that there must be physical damages before punitive damages may be awarded. In addition, some states limit punitive damages to the actual expenses of litigation. Others demand some arbitrary ratio between actual and punitive damages.... Even assuming the ill will of the officer, his reasonable grounds for belief that the home he searched harbored evidence of crime is admissible in mitigation of punitive damages. The bad reputation of the plaintiff is likewise admissible. If the evidence seized was actually used at a trial, that fact has been held a complete justification of the search, and a defense against the trespass action. And even if the plaintiff hurdles all these obstacles, and gains a substantial verdict, the individual officer's finances may well make the judgment useless—for the municipality, of course, is not liable without its consent. Is it surprising that there is so little in the books concerning trespass actions for violation of the search and seizure clause?

[But] one remedy exists to deter violations of the search and seizure clause. That is the rule which excludes illegally obtained evidence. Only by exclusion can we impress upon the zealous prosecutor that violation of the Constitution will do him no good. And only when that point is driven home can the prosecutor be expected to emphasize the importance of observing constitutional demands in his instructions to the police.

If proof of the efficacy of the federal rule were needed, there is testimony in abundance in the recruit training programs and in-service courses provided the police in states which follow the federal rule. [T]his is an area in which judicial action has positive effect upon the breach of law; and that without judicial action, there are simply no effective sanctions presently available.

[Today's] decision will do inestimable harm to the cause of fair police methods in our cities and states. Even more important, [it] must have tragic effect upon public respect for our judiciary. For the Court now allows that is indeed shabby business: lawlessness by officers of the law. . . . Since the evidence admitted was secured in violation of the Fourth Amendment, the judgment should be reversed.

Problems

1. *The Serial Murder.* Serial murders are committed in the New Orleans area. The police search for the murderer, trying to find him before he kills again. Weeks pass, more murders occur, and still the murderer has not been found. The police suspect Yoplait of the crimes, but do not have probable cause to arrest him. In a desperate attempt to solve the crime and prevent further murders, the police illegally search Yoplait's apartment (the police lacked both a search warrant and probable cause), and find conclusive evidence of Yoplait's involvement in the murders (Yoplait liked to keep gory pictures of the people he killed). Suppose that, under *Wolf*, the exclusionary rule does not apply in state court proceedings. Does Yoplait have adequate alternative remedies available to him? Consider the following possibilities:

    A. Suppose that Yoplait brings a civil suit against the police officers claiming that the police officers trespassed, as well as that they converted his property. If Yoplait prevails, is a jury likely to award him substantial damages?

    B. Of course, it is possible for the jury to award punitive damages. Is the jury likely to award punitive damages against the police in a case like this?

    C. Public opinion can provide a powerful deterrent to police misconduct. Is the public likely to rise up in outrage over the illegal search?

    D. Is the prosecutor likely to criminally prosecute the police for this illegal search (or, for that matter, is the police disciplinary board likely to bring disciplinary charges)?

2. *More on the Serial Murderer.* Would you answer the same questions differently if the evidence showed a pervasive pattern of police misconduct? Suppose that there is evidence that New Orleans police routinely violate citizens' civil rights by illegally stopping motorists, "roughing them up," and

illegally searching cars. Suppose that a motorist brings a civil suit against the police officers claiming that intentional violations of his rights (e.g., assault, battery, kidnaping). Consider the following avenues for relief: a) damages in a tort action; b) punitive damages c) public opinion; d) criminal prosecution of the offending police. Are any of these remedies likely to provide an effective deterrent to misconduct?

3. *The Innocent Suspect.* Now, let's consider one more scenario. Suppose that the police intentionally search someone else's home without a warrant or probable cause. Would it matter that the subject of the search was innocent, and that the police were completely mistaken about the subject's involvement in criminal activity? For example, suppose that the police illegally search a medical doctor's home believing that he is involved in illicit drug trafficking. The police are in error about this fact because, while listening to a wiretap, they *thought* they heard a reference to the doctor. Are the following remedies likely to be effective for this violation: a) Civil suit for damages? b) Punitive damages? c) Public opinion? d) Criminal prosecution? e) Disciplinary sanctions?

4. *§ 1983 Actions.* Are there other, more effective, remedies for Fourth Amendment violations? For example, would the § 1983 remedy provide an effective deterrent for police misconduct? That statute provides as follows: "Every person who, under color of any statute, ordinance, regulation, custom or usage, of any State or Territory, subjects, or causes to be subjected, any citizen of the United States or other person within the jurisdiction thereof to the deprivation of any rights, privileges, or immunities secured by the Constitution and laws, shall be liable to the party injured in an action at law, suit in equity, or other proper proceeding for redress."

It is difficult to recover under § 1983 when the governing law is uncertain. *Monroe v. Pape,* 365 U.S. 167 (1961), construed § 1983 as applicable to suits against individual governmental officials. However, in *Pierson v. Ray,* 386 U.S. 547 (1967), the Court held that police officers are protected by qualified immunity "if they act [in] good faith and with probable cause in making an arrest under a statute that they believe to be valid." In *Gomez v. Toledo,* 446 U.S. 635 (1980), the Court held that defendant has the burden of proving qualified immunity in a 1983 action.

Monell v. Department of Social Services of the City of New York, 436 U.S. 658 (1978), held that a local government is liable under § 1983 only to the extent that its "policy or custom, whether made by its lawmakers or by those whose edicts or acts may fairly be said to represent official policy, inflicts the injury that the government as an entity is responsible under § 1983." In *Pembaur v. Cincinnati,* 475 U.S. 469 (1986), the Court held that a single decision by a prosecutor could satisfy the official "policy or custom" requirement. *Owen v. City of Independence,* 445 U.S. 622 (1980), held that municipalities are not entitled to qualified immunity even though their officials act in "good faith and without malice": "[T]he public will be forced to bear only the costs of injury inflicted by the 'execution of a government's policy or custom, whether made by its lawmakers or by those whose edicts or acts may fairly be said to represent official policy.' " Justice Powell dissented: "[M]unicipalities [have] gone in two short years from absolute immunity under § 1983 to strict liability."

Given this precedent, is the § 1983 action a viable remedy for Fourth Amendment violations?

5. *Would Bivens Actions Provide an Effective Remedy?* Since § 1983 actions are generally unavailable when the offending official is a federal agent or employee, suits against such officials are often based directly on the Constitution itself. These so-called *"Bivens"* actions, named for the holding in *Bivens v. Six Unknown Named Agents*, 403 U.S. 388 (1971), are claims based directly on the Fourth Amendment itself: "[It is] well settled that where legal rights have been invaded, and a federal statute provides for a general right to sue for such invasion, federal courts may use any available remedy to make good the wrong done." In *Carlson v. Green*, 446 U.S. 14 (1980), the Court held that the availability of relief under the Federal Tort Claims Act did not bar a *Bivens* action. Finally, in *Anderson v. Creighton*, 483 U.S. 635 (1987), the Court imposed a good faith defense in *Bivens* actions which provided that "a federal law enforcement officer may [not] be held personally liable for money damages if a reasonable officer could have believed that the search comported with the Fourth Amendment." Do *Bivens* actions against federal officials, coupled with § 1983 actions against state officials, provide an effective remedy?

6. *The Possibility of Injunctive Relief?* The injunctive remedy might seem particularly appropriate when the police have engaged in a pattern of misconduct. However, in *Rizzo v. Goode*, 423 U.S. 362 (1976), the Court imposed significant barriers to injunctive relief against police officials. That case involved a claim that the police had engaged in an "assertedly pervasive pattern of illegal and unconstitutional mistreatment" against "minority citizens in particular and against all Philadelphia residents in general." Plaintiffs presented 250 witnesses who described some 40–odd incidents. The trial court ordered petitioners to draft "a comprehensive program for dealing adequately with civilian complaints" for its approval. The Supreme Court concluded that injunctive relief was inappropriate:

> [We doubt whether an Art. III case or controversy exists.] In *O'Shea v. Littleton*, 414 U.S. 488 (1974), [plaintiffs] alleged that [a] county magistrate and judge, had embarked on a continuing, intentional practice of racially discriminatory bond setting, sentencing, and assessing of jury fees. No specific instances involving the individual respondents were set forth in the prayer for injunctive [relief]. [E]ven though [some] of the named respondents had in fact "suffered from the alleged unconstitutional practices," the Court concluded that "[p]ast exposure to illegal conduct does not in itself show a present case or controversy regarding injunctive relief, however, if unaccompanied by any continuing, present adverse effects." The Court further recognized that while "past wrongs are evidence bearing on whether there is a real and immediate threat of repeated injury", the attempt to anticipate under what circumstances the respondents there would be made to appear in the future before petitioners "takes us into the area of speculation and conjecture." These observations apply here with even more force, for the individual respondents' claim to "real and immediate" injury rests not upon what the named petitioners might do to them in the future such as set a bond on the basis of race but upon what one of a small, unnamed minority of policemen might do to them in the future because of that

unknown policeman's perception of departmental disciplinary procedures. This hypothesis is even more attenuated than those allegations of future injury found insufficient in *O'Shea* to warrant invocation of federal jurisdiction. Thus, insofar as the individual respondents were concerned, we think they lacked the requisite "personal stake in the outcome"; *i.e.*, the order overhauling police disciplinary procedures.

[C]onsiderations of federalism are additional factors weighing against [the granting of relief]. The District Court's injunctive order here, significantly revising the internal procedures of the Philadelphia police department, was indisputably a sharp limitation on the department's "latitude in the 'dispatch of its own internal affairs.' " [P]rinciples of federalism [also] have applicability where injunctive relief is sought, not against the judicial branch of the state government, but against those in charge of an executive branch of an agency of state or local governments such as petitioners here. * * *

MAPP v. OHIO

367 U.S. 643 (1961).

Mr. Justice Clark delivered the opinion of the Court.

[Appellant was convicted of possession of lewd and lascivious books, pictures, and photographs in violation of Ohio law.] [T]he Supreme Court of Ohio [upheld the] conviction [though] "based [upon evidence] seized during an unlawful search of defendant's [home]."

[The] State says that even if the search were made without authority, or otherwise unreasonably, it is not prevented from using the unconstitutionally seized evidence at trial, citing *Wolf v. People of State of Colorado*.... While in 1949, prior to the *Wolf* case, almost two-thirds of the States were opposed to the use of the exclusionary rule, now, despite the *Wolf* case, more than half of those since passing upon it, by their own legislative or judicial decision, have wholly or partly adopted or adhered to the *Weeks* rule. Significantly, among those now following the rule is California, which, according to its highest court, was "compelled to reach that conclusion because other remedies have completely failed to secure compliance with the constitutional [provisions]." *People v. Cahan*, 1955, 44 Cal.2d 434, 282 P.2d 905. [T]he second basis elaborated in *Wolf* [was] that "other means of protection" have been afforded "the right to privacy." The experience of California that such other remedies have been worthless and futile is buttressed by the experience of other States. The obvious futility of relegating the Fourth Amendment [to] the protection of other remedies has [been] recognized by this Court since *Wolf*.... Likewise, time has set its face against what *Wolf* called the "weighty testimony" of *People v. Defore*, 1926, 242 N.Y. 13, 150 N.E. 585. There Justice (then Judge) Cardozo, rejecting adoption of the *Weeks* exclusionary rule in New York, had said that "[t]he Federal rule as it stands is either too strict or too lax." [T]he force of that reasoning has been largely vitiated by later decisions of this Court. * * *

It, therefore, plainly appears that the factual considerations supporting the failure of the *Wolf* Court to include the *Weeks* exclusionary rule when it recognized the enforceability of the right to privacy against the States in 1949, while not basically relevant to the constitutional consideration, could not, in any analysis, now be deemed controlling.

[Today] we once again examine *Wolf's* constitutional documentation of the right to privacy free from unreasonable state intrusion, and [are led] to close the only courtroom door remaining open to evidence secured by official lawlessness in flagrant abuse of that basic right, reserved to all persons as a specific guarantee against that very same unlawful conduct. We hold that all evidence obtained by searches and seizures in violation of the Constitution is, by that same authority, inadmissible in a state court.

Since the Fourth Amendment's right of privacy has been declared enforceable against the States through the Due Process Clause of the Fourteenth, it is enforceable against them by the same sanction of exclusion as is used against the Federal Government. Were it otherwise, [the] assurance against unreasonable federal searches and seizures would be "a form of words", valueless and undeserving of mention in a perpetual charter of inestimable human liberties, so too, without that rule the freedom from state invasions of privacy would be so ephemeral and so neatly severed from its conceptual nexus with the freedom from all brutish means of coercing evidence as not to merit this Court's high regard as a freedom "implicit in the concept of ordered liberty." At the time that the Court held in *Wolf* that the Amendment was applicable to the States through the Due Process Clause, the cases of this Court [had] steadfastly held that as to federal officers the Fourth Amendment included the exclusion of the evidence seized in violation of its provisions. Even *Wolf* "stoutly adhered" to that proposition. The right to privacy, when conceded operatively enforceable against the States, was not susceptible of destruction by avulsion of the sanction upon which its protection and enjoyment had always been deemed dependent under the *Boyd*, *Weeks* and *Silverthorne* cases. Therefore, in extending the substantive protections of due process to all constitutionally unreasonable searches—state or federal—it was logically and constitutionally necessary that the exclusion doctrine—an essential part of the right to privacy—be also insisted upon as an essential ingredient of the right newly recognized by the *Wolf* case. In short, the admission of the new constitutional right by *Wolf* could not consistently tolerate denial of its most important constitutional privilege, namely, the exclusion of the evidence which an accused had been forced to give by reason of the unlawful seizure. To hold otherwise is to grant the right but in reality to withhold its privilege and enjoyment. Only last year the Court itself recognized that the purpose of the exclusionary rule "is to deter—to compel respect for the constitutional guaranty in the only effectively available way—by removing the incentive to disregard it." *Elkins v. United States*, *supra*, 364 U.S. at page 217.

[We] are aware of no restraint, similar to that rejected today, conditioning the enforcement of any other basic constitutional right. The right to privacy, no less important than any other right carefully and particularly reserved to the people, would stand in marked contrast to all other rights declared as "basic to a free society." This Court has not hesitated to enforce as strictly against the States [the] rights of free speech and of a free press, the rights to notice and to a fair, public trial, including [the] right not to be convicted by use of a coerced confession, however logically relevant it be, and without regard to its reliability. And nothing could be more certain that when a coerced confession is involved, "the relevant rules of evidence" are overridden without regard to "the incidence of such conduct by the police," slight or frequent. Why should not the same rule apply to what is tantamount to coerced testimony by way of unconstitutional seizure of goods, papers, effect, documents, etc.? [As] to the Federal Government, the Fourth and Fifth Amendments and, as to the States, the freedom from unconscionable invasions of privacy and the freedom from convictions based upon coerced confessions do enjoy an "intimate relation" in their perpetuation of "principles of humanity and civil liberty (secured) [only] after years of struggle." *Bram v. United States*, 1897, 168 U.S. 532. They express "supplementing phases of the same constitutional purpose—to maintain inviolate large areas of personal privacy." *Feldman v. United States*, 1944, 322 U.S. 487. The philosophy of each Amendment and of each freedom is complementary to, although not dependent upon, that of the other in its sphere of influence—the very least that together they assure in either sphere is that no man is to be convicted on unconstitutional evidence.

[Our] holding that the exclusionary rule is an essential part of both the Fourth and Fourteenth Amendments is not only the logical dictate of prior cases, but it also makes very good sense. There is no war between the Constitution and common sense. Presently, a federal prosecutor may make no use of evidence illegally seized, but a State's attorney across the street may, although he supposedly is operating under the enforceable prohibitions of the same Amendment. Thus the State, by admitting evidence unlawfully seized, serves to encourage disobedience to the Federal Constitution which it is bound to uphold. [In] non-exclusionary States, federal officers, being human, were by it invited to and [did] step across the street to the State's attorney with their unconstitutionally seized evidence. Prosecution on the basis of that evidence was then had in a state court in utter disregard of the enforceable Fourth Amendment. If the fruits of an unconstitutional search had been inadmissible in both state and federal courts, this inducement to evasion would have been sooner eliminated. * * * Federal-state cooperation in the solution of crime under constitutional standards will be promoted, if only by recognition of their now mutual obligation to respect the same fundamental criteria in their approaches. [Denying] shortcuts to only one of two cooperating law enforcement agencies tends naturally to breed legitimate suspicion of "working arrangements" whose results are equally tainted.

There are those who say, as did Justice (then Judge) Cardozo, that under our constitutional exclusionary doctrine "[t]he criminal is to go free because the constable has blundered." *People v. Defore*, 242 N.Y. at page 21, 150 N.E. at page 587. In some cases this will undoubtedly be the result. But, as was said in *Elkins*, "there is another consideration—the imperative of judicial integrity." The criminal goes free, if he must, but it is the law that sets him free. Nothing can destroy a government more quickly than its failure to observe its own laws, or worse, its disregard of the charter of its own existence. As Mr. Justice Brandeis, dissenting, said in *Olmstead v. United States*, 1928, 277 U.S. 438: "Our government is the potent, the omnipresent teacher. For good or for ill, it teaches the whole people by its example. [If] the government becomes a lawbreaker, it breeds contempt for law; it invites every man to become a law unto himself; it invites anarchy." Nor can it lightly be assumed that, as a practical matter, adoption of the exclusionary rule fetters law enforcement. Only last year this Court expressly considered that contention and found that "pragmatic evidence of a sort" to the contrary was not wanting. *Elkins v. United States, supra*, 364 U.S. at page 218. The Court noted that "The federal courts themselves have operated under the exclusionary rule of *Weeks* for almost half a century; yet it has not been suggested either that the Federal Bureau of Investigation has thereby been rendered ineffective, or that the administration of criminal justice in the federal courts has thereby been disrupted. Moreover, the experience of the states is [impressive]. The movement towards the rule of exclusion has been halting but seemingly inexorable."

The ignoble shortcut to conviction left open to the State tends to destroy the entire system of constitutional restraints on which the liberties of the people rest. Having once recognized that the right to privacy embodied in the Fourth Amendment is enforceable against the States, and that the right to be secure against rude invasions of privacy by state officers is, therefore, constitutional in origin, we can no longer permit that right to remain an empty promise. Because it is enforceable in the same manner and to like effect as other basic rights secured by the Due Process Clause, we can no longer permit it to be revocable at the whim of any police officer who [chooses] to suspend its enjoyment. Our decision, founded on reason and truth, gives to the individual no more than that which the Constitution guarantees him, to the police officer no less than that to which honest law enforcement is entitled, and, to the courts, that judicial integrity so necessary in the true administration of justice.

The judgment of the Supreme Court of Ohio is reversed and the cause remanded for further proceedings not inconsistent with this opinion.

Reversed and remanded.

MR. JUSTICE BLACK, concurring.

[T]he Fourth Amendment, standing alone, would [not] be enough to bar the introduction into evidence against an accused of papers and effects seized from him in violation of its commands. For the Fourth Amendment does not itself contain any provision expressly precluding the use of such evidence, and I am extremely doubtful that such a provision could properly be inferred from nothing more than the basic command against unreasonable searches and seizures. [W]hen the Fourth Amendment's ban against unreasonable searches and seizures is considered together with the Fifth Amendment's ban against compelled self-incrimination, a constitutional basis emerges which not only justifies but actually requires the exclusionary rule. [I]n *Boyd v. United States*[,] the Court [declared] itself "unable to perceive that the seizure of a man's private books and papers to be used in evidence against him is substantially different from compelling him to be a witness against himself." * * *

MR. JUSTICE DOUGLAS, concurring.

[The facts of this case] show—as would few other cases—the casual arrogance of those who have the untrammeled power to invade one's home and to seize one's person. * * *

MR. JUSTICE HARLAN, whom MR. JUSTICE FRANKFURTER and MR. JUSTICE WHITTAKER join, dissenting.

[I] would not impose upon the States this federal exclusionary remedy. [I]t is said that "the factual grounds upon which *Wolf* was based" have since changed, in that more States now follow the *Weeks* exclusionary [rule]. While that is true, [one-half] of the States still adhere to the common-law non-exclusionary [rule]. The preservation of a proper balance between state and federal responsibility in the administration of criminal justice demands patience on the part of those who might like to see things move faster among the States in this respect. Problems of criminal law enforcement vary widely from State of State. One State [may] conclude that the need for embracing the *Weeks* rule is pressing because other remedies are unavailable or inadequate to secure compliance with the substantive Constitutional principle involved. Another, though equally solicitous of Constitutional rights, may choose to pursue one purpose at a time, allowing all evidence relevant to guilt to be brought into a criminal trial, and dealing with Constitutional infractions by other means. [T]his Court should continue to forbear from fettering the States with an adamant [rule] in criminal law enforcement.

[In *Weeks*], in implementing the Fourth Amendment, we occupied the position of a tribunal having the ultimate responsibility for developing the standards and procedures of judicial administration within the judicial system over which it presides. Here we review state procedures whose measure is to be taken not against the specific substantive commands of the Fourth Amendment but under the flexible contours of the Due Process Clause. I do not believe that the Fourteenth Amendment empowers this Court to mold state remedies effectuating the right to freedom from "arbitrary intrusion by the police" * * *.

[I]n requiring exclusion of an involuntary statement of an accused, we are concerned not with an appropriate remedy for what the police have done, but with something which is regarded as going to the heart of our concepts of fairness in judicial procedure. The operative assumption of our procedural system is that "Ours is the accusatorial as opposed to the inquisitorial system...." *Watts v. State of Indiana*, 338 U.S. 49. [What] is crucial is that the trial defense to which an accused is entitled should not be rendered an empty formality by reason of statements wrung from him, for then "a prisoner [has been] made the deluded instrument of his own conviction." 2 HAWKINS, PLEAS OF THE CROWN (8th ed., 1824), c. 46, § 34.... I think the coerced confession analogy works strongly against what the Court does today.

[I] think this Court can increase respect for the Constitution only if it rigidly respects the limitations which the Constitution places upon it, and respects as well the principles inherent in its own processes. In the present case I think we exceed both, and that our voice becomes only a voice of power, not of reason.

Note: Forfeiture Proceedings

In *One 1958 Plymouth Sedan v. Commonwealth of Pennsylvania*, 380 U.S. 693 (1965), the Court applied the exclusionary rule to a forfeiture proceeding because of the "quasi-criminal" nature of that proceeding. That case involved the forfeiture of an automobile found to be carrying liquor without Pennsylvania tax seals.

Problem: An "Experiment" That Failed?

Consider then Chief Justice Burger's dissent in *Bivens v. Six Unknown Named Agents*, 403 U.S. 388 (1971):

> Rejection of the evidence does nothing to punish the wrong-doing official, while it may, and likely will, release the wrong-doing defendant. It deprives society of its remedy against one lawbreaker because he has been pursued by another. It protects one against whom incriminating evidence is discovered, but does nothing to protect innocent persons who are the victims of illegal but fruitless searches.

> [Instead] of continuing to enforce the suppression doctrine inflexibly, rigidly, and mechanically, we should [discontinue] what the experience of over half a century has shown neither deters errant officers nor affords a remedy to the totally innocent victims of official misconduct. I do not propose [that] we abandon the suppression doctrine until some meaningful alternative can be developed. [T]he public interest would be poorly served if law enforcement officials were suddenly to gain the impression [that] all constitutional restraints on police had somehow been removed—that an open season on "criminals" had been declared. [The] problems of both error and deliberate misconduct by law enforcement officials call for a workable remedy. Private damage actions against individual police officers concededly have not adequately met this requirement.

> [A]n entirely different remedy is necessary but it [is] beyond judicial [power]. Congress should develop an administrative or quasi-judicial

remedy against the government itself to afford compensation and restitution for persons whose Fourth Amendment rights have been violated. The venerable doctrine of respondeat superior in our tort law provides an entirely appropriate conceptual basis for this remedy. * * * Such a statutory scheme would have the added advantage of providing some remedy to the completely innocent persons who are sometimes the victims of illegal police conduct—something that the suppression doctrine, of course, can never accomplish.

A simple structure would suffice. For example, Congress could enact a statute along the following lines: (a) a waiver of sovereign immunity as to the illegal acts of law enforcement officials committed in the performance of assigned duties; (b) the creation of a cause of action for damages sustained by any person aggrieved by conduct of governmental agents in violation of the Fourth Amendment or statutes regulating official conduct; (c) the creation of a tribunal, quasi judicial in nature or perhaps patterned after the United States Court of Claims to adjudicate all claims under the statute; (d) a provision that this statutory remedy is in lieu of the exclusion of [evidence]; and (e) a provision directing that no evidence, otherwise admissible, shall be excluded from any criminal proceeding because of violation of the Fourth Amendment.

I doubt that lawyers serving on such a tribunal would be swayed either by undue sympathy for officers or by the prejudice against "criminals" that has sometimes moved lay jurors to deny claims. In addition to awarding damages, the record of the police conduct [would] become a relevant part of an officer's personnel file so that the need for additional training or disciplinary action could be identified or his future usefulness as a public official evaluated. Finally, appellate judicial review could be made available on much the same basis that it is now provided as to district courts and regulatory agencies. This would leave to the courts the ultimate responsibility for determining and articulating standards.

Once the constitutional validity of such a statute is established, it can reasonably be assumed that the States would develop their own remedial systems on the federal model. [Steps] along these lines would move our system toward more responsible law enforcement on the one hand and away from the irrational and drastic results of the suppression doctrine on the other. * * *

Does Chief Justice Burger's proposal make sense?

HUDSON v. MICHIGAN

___ U.S. ___, 126 S.Ct. 2159 (2006).

JUSTICE SCALIA delivered the opinion of the Court, except as to Part IV.

[This] case is before us only because of the method of entry into the house. When the police arrived to execute [a] warrant, they announced their presence, but waited only a short time-perhaps "three to five seconds" before turning the knob of the unlocked front door and entering Hudson's home. Hudson moved to suppress all the inculpatory evidence [drugs and a loaded gun], arguing that the premature entry violated his Fourth Amendment rights. [However, the evidence was admitted and Hudson's appeal was rejected.] We granted certiorari.

The common-law principle that law enforcement officers must announce their presence and provide residents an opportunity to open the door is an ancient one. See *Wilson v. Arkansas,* 514 U.S. 927 (1995). Since 1917, [this] traditional protection has been part of federal statutory law and is currently codified at 18 U.S.C. § 3109. [*Wilson* concluded that it] was also a command of the Fourth Amendment.... It is not necessary [to knock and announce] when "circumstances presen[t] a threat of physical violence," or if there is "reason to believe that evidence would likely be destroyed if advance notice were given," or if knocking and announcing would be "futile," *Richards v. Wisconsin,* 520 U.S. 385 (1997). We require only that police "have a reasonable suspicion [under] the particular circumstances" that one of these grounds for failing to knock and announce exists, and we have acknowledged that "[t]his showing is not high."

When the knock-and-announce rule does apply, it is not easy to determine precisely what officers must do. How many seconds' wait are too few? Our "reasonable wait time" standard, see *United States v. Banks,* 540 U.S. 31 (2003), is necessarily vague. *Banks* (a drug case, like this one) held that the proper measure was not how long it would take the resident to reach the door, but how long it would take to dispose of the suspected drugs-but that such a time (15 to 20 seconds in that case) would necessarily be extended when, for instance, the suspected contraband was not easily concealed. If our *ex post* evaluation is subject to such calculations, it is unsurprising that, *ex ante,* police officers about to encounter someone who may try to harm them will be uncertain how long to wait.

[Michigan] has conceded that the entry was a knock-and-announce violation. The issue here is remedy.... In *Weeks v. United States,* 232 U.S. 383 (1914), we adopted the federal exclusionary rule for evidence that was unlawfully seized from a home without a warrant in violation of the Fourth Amendment. We began applying the same rule to the States, through the Fourteenth Amendment, in *Mapp v. Ohio,* 367 U.S. 643 (1961).

Suppression of evidence, however, has always been our last resort, not our first impulse. The exclusionary rule generates "substantial social costs," *United States v. Leon,* 468 U.S. 897 (1984), which sometimes include setting the guilty free and the dangerous at large. We have therefore been "cautio[us] against expanding" it, and "have repeatedly emphasized that the rule's 'costly toll' upon truth-seeking and law enforcement objectives presents a high obstacle for those urging [its] application," *Pennsylvania Bd. of Probation and Parole v. Scott,* 524 U.S. 357 (1998). We have rejected "[i]ndiscriminate application" of the rule, and have held it to be applicable only "where its remedial objectives are thought most efficaciously served,"—that is, "where its deterrence bene-fits outweigh its 'substantial social costs,' " *Scott, supra,* at 363 (quoting *Leon, supra,* at 907).

We did not always speak so guardedly. [D]icta in *Mapp* [suggested] wide scope for the exclusionary rule. But we have long since rejected that approach. [I]n *Leon,* [we] explained that "[w]hether the exclusionary sanction is appropriately imposed in a particular case, [is] 'an issue separate from the question whether the Fourth Amendment rights of the party seeking to invoke the rule were violated by police conduct.' " 468 U.S., at 906 (quoting *Illinois v. Gates,* 462 U.S. 213 (1983)).

[E]xclusion may not be premised on the mere fact that a constitu-tional violation was a "but-for" cause of obtaining evidence. [B]ut-for causality is only a necessary, not a sufficient, condition for suppression. In this case, [the] constitutional violation of an illegal *manner* of entry was *not* a but-for cause.... Whether that preliminary misstep had occurred *or not,* the police would have executed the warrant they had obtained, and would have discovered the gun and drugs inside the house. [Regardless,] we have "never held that evidence is 'fruit of the poisonous tree' simply because 'it would not have come to light but for the illegal actions of the police.' " *Segura v. United States,* 468 U.S. 796 (1984). Rather, but-for cause, or "causation in the logical sense alone," can be too attenuated to justify exclusion. Even in the early days of the exclusionary rule, we declined to "hold that all evidence is 'fruit of the poisonous tree' simply because it would not have come to light *but for* the illegal actions of the police. Rather, the more apt question in such a case is 'whether, granting establishment of the primary illegality, the evidence to which instant objection is made has been come at by exploitation of that illegality or instead by means sufficiently distin-guishable to be purged of the primary taint.' " *Wong Sun v. United States,* 371 U.S. 471 (1963) (quoting J. Maguire, Evidence of Guilt 221 (1959) (emphasis added)).

Attenuation can occur [when] the causal connection is remote. Attenuation also occurs when, even given a direct causal connection, the interest protected by the constitutional guarantee that has been violated would not be served by suppression of the evidence obtained. "The penalties visited upon the Government, and in turn upon the public, because its officers have violated the law must bear some relation to the purposes which the law is to serve." [I]n *New York v. Harris,* 495 U.S. 14 (1990), where an illegal warrantless arrest was made in Harris' house, we held that "suppressing [Harris'] statement taken outside the house would not serve the purpose of the rule that made Harris' in-house arrest illegal. The warrant requirement for an arrest in the home is imposed to protect the home, and anything incriminating the police gathered from arresting Harris in his home, rather than elsewhere, has been excluded, as it should have been; the purpose of the rule has thereby been vindicated."

For this reason, cases excluding the fruits of unlawful warrantless searches say nothing about the appropriateness of exclusion to vindicate the interests protected by the knock-and-announce requirement. Until a valid warrant has issued, citizens are entitled to shield "their persons, houses, papers, and effects," U.S. Const., Amdt. 4, from the government's scrutiny. Exclusion of the evidence obtained by a warrantless search vindicates that entitlement. The interests protected by the knock-and-announce requirement are quite different-and do not include the shielding of potential evidence from the government's eyes.

One of those interests is the protection of human life and limb, because an unannounced entry may provoke violence in supposed self-defense by the surprised resident. Another interest is the protection of property. Breaking a house (as the old cases typically put it) absent an announcement would penalize someone who " 'did not know of the process, of which, if he had notice, it is to be presumed that he would obey it. . . . ' " *Wilson,* 514 U.S., at 931–932 (quoting *Semayne's Case,* 77 Eng. Rep. 194, 195–196 (K.B.1603)). The knock-and-announce rule gives individuals "the opportunity to comply with the law and to avoid the destruction of property occasioned by a forcible entry." *Richards,* 520 U.S., at 393, n. 5. And thirdly, the knock-and-announce rule protects those elements of privacy and dignity that can be destroyed by a sudden entrance. It gives residents the "opportunity to prepare themselves for" the entry of the police. "The brief interlude between announcement and entry with a warrant may be the opportunity that an individual has to pull on clothes or get out of bed." In other words, it assures the opportunity to collect oneself before answering the door.

What the knock-and-announce rule has never protected, however, is one's interest in preventing the government from seeing or taking evidence described in a warrant. Since the interests that *were* violated in this case have nothing to do with the seizure of the evidence, the exclusionary rule is inapplicable.

Quite apart from the requirement of unattenuated causation, the exclusionary rule has never been applied except "where its deterrence benefits outweigh its 'substantial social costs,' " *Scott,* 524 U.S., at 363 (quoting *Leon,* 468 U.S., at 907). The costs here are considerable. In addition to the grave adverse consequence that exclusion of relevant incriminating evidence always entails (viz., the risk of releasing dangerous criminals into society), imposing that massive remedy for a knock-and-announce violation would generate a constant flood of alleged failures to observe the rule, and claims that any asserted *Richards* justification for a no-knock entry had inadequate support. The cost of entering this lottery would be small, but the jackpot enormous: suppression of all evidence, amounting in many cases to a get-out-of-jail-free card. Courts would experience as never before the reality that "[t]he exclusionary rule frequently requires extensive litigation to determine whether particular evidence must be excluded." *Scott, supra,* at 366. Unlike the warrant or *Miranda* requirements, compliance with which is readily determined[,] what constituted a "reasonable wait time" in a particular case (or, for that matter, how many seconds the police in fact waited), or whether there was "reasonable suspicion" of the sort that would invoke the *Richards* exceptions, is difficult for the trial court to determine and even more difficult for an appellate court to review.

Another consequence of the incongruent remedy Hudson proposes would be police officers' refraining from timely entry after knocking and announcing. [T]he amount of time they must wait is necessarily uncertain. If the consequences of running afoul of the rule were so massive, officers would be inclined to wait longer than the law requires—producing preventable violence against officers in some cases, and the destruction of evidence in many others. We deemed these consequences severe enough to produce our unanimous agreement that a mere "reasonable suspicion" that knocking and announcing "under the particular circumstances, would be dangerous or futile, or that it would inhibit the effective investigation of the crime," will cause the requirement to yield. *Richards, supra,* at 394.

Next to these "substantial social costs" we must consider the deterrence benefits, existence of which is a necessary condition for exclusion. (It is not, of course, a sufficient condition: "[I]t does not follow that the Fourth Amendment requires adoption of every proposal that might deter police misconduct." *Calandra,* 414 U.S., at 350) [T]he value of deterrence depends upon the strength of the incentive to commit the forbidden act. Viewed from this perspective, deterrence of knock-and-announce violations is not worth a lot. Violation of the warrant requirement sometimes produces incriminating evidence that could not otherwise be obtained. But ignoring knock-and-announce can realistically be expected to achieve absolutely nothing except the prevention of destruction of evidence and the avoidance of life-threatening resistance by occupants of the premises-dangers which, if there is even "reasonable suspicion" of their existence, *suspend the knock-and-announce requirement anyway.* Massive deterrence is hardly required.

It seems to us not [true] that without suppression there will be no deterrence of knock-and-announce violations at all. Of course even if this assertion were accurate, it would not necessarily justify suppression. Assuming [that] civil suit is not an effective deterrent, one can think of many forms of police misconduct that are similarly "undeterred." When, for example, a confessed suspect in the killing of a police officer, arrested (along with incriminating evidence) in a lawful warranted search, is subjected to physical abuse at the station house, would it seriously be suggested that the evidence must be excluded, since that is the only "effective deterrent"? And what, other than civil suit, is the "effective deterrent" of police violation of an already-confessed suspect's Sixth Amendment rights by denying him prompt access to counsel? Many would regard these violated rights as more significant than the right not to be intruded upon in one's nightclothes-and yet nothing but "ineffective" civil suit is available as a deterrent. And the police incentive for those violations is arguably greater than the incentive for disregarding the knock-and-announce rule.

We cannot assume that exclusion in this context is necessary deterrence simply because we found that it was necessary deterrence in different contexts and long ago.... Hudson complains that "it would be very hard to find a lawyer to take a case such as this," but ... Congress has authorized attorney's fees for civil-rights plaintiffs. This remedy was unavailable in the heydays of our exclusionary-rule jurisprudence.... Hudson points out that few published decisions to date announce huge awards for knock-and-announce violations.... Even if we thought that only large damages would deter police misconduct (and that police somehow are deterred by "damages" but indifferent to the prospect of large s. 1988 attorney's fees), we do not know how many claims have been settled, or indeed how many violations have occurred that produced anything more than nominal injury. [L]ower courts are allowing colorable knock-and-announce suits to go forward, unimpeded by assertions of qualified immunity. As far as we know, civil liability is an effective deterrent here....

Another development over the past half-century that deters civil-rights violations is the increasing professionalism of police forces, including a new emphasis on internal police discipline. [We] have increasing evidence that police forces across the United States take the constitutional rights of citizens seriously. There have been "wide-ranging reforms in the education, training, and supervision of police officers." S. WALKER, TAMING THE SYSTEM: THE CONTROL OF DISCRETION IN CRIMINAL JUSTICE 1950–1990, p. 51 (1993). Numerous sources are now available to teach officers and their supervisors what is required of them under this Court's cases, how to respect constitutional guarantees in various situations, and how to craft an effective regime for internal discipline. Failure to teach and enforce constitutional requirements exposes municipalities to financial liability. [I]t is not credible to assert that internal discipline, which can limit successful careers, will not have a deterrent effect. There is also evidence that the increasing use of various forms of citizen review can enhance police accountability.

In sum, the social costs of applying the exclusionary rule to knock-and-announce violations are considerable; the incentive to such violations is minimal to begin with, and the extant deterrences against them are substantial—incomparably greater than the factors deterring warrantless entries when *Mapp* was decided. Resort to the massive remedy of suppressing evidence of guilt is unjustified.

A trio of cases—*Segura v. United States,* 468 U.S. 796 (1984); *New York v. Harris,* 495 U.S. 14 (1990); and *United States v. Ramirez,* 523 U.S. 65 (1998)—confirms our conclusion that suppression is unwarranted in this case. [*Segura*] involved a concededly illegal entry. [Police] had neither a warrant nor consent to enter, [and] stayed in the apartment for *19 hours* awaiting a search warrant.... We recognized that only the evidence gained from the particular violation could be excluded, and therefore distinguished the effects of the illegal entry from the effects of the legal search. [If] the probable cause backing a warrant that was issued *later in time* could be an "independent source" for a search that proceeded after the officers illegally entered and waited, a search warrant obtained *before* going in must have at least this much effect. [In] *Harris,* the police violated the defendant's Fourth Amendment rights by arresting him at home without a warrant.... While Harris's statement was "the product of an arrest and being in custody," it "was not the fruit of the fact that the arrest was made in the house rather than someplace else." Likewise here: While acquisition of the gun and drugs was the product of a search pursuant to warrant, it was not the fruit of the fact that the entry was not preceded by knock and announce. *Ramirez* involved a claim that police entry violated the Fourth Amendment because it was effected by breaking a window. [We] concluded that the property destruction [was] reasonable, but [we] unanimously said the following: "[D]estruction of property in the course of a search may violate the Fourth Amendment, even though the entry itself is lawful and the fruits of the search are not subject to suppression." ...

For the foregoing reasons we affirm the judgment of the Michigan Court of Appeals.

It is so ordered.

JUSTICE KENNEDY, concurring in part and concurring in the judgment.

[T]he knock-and-announce requirement protects rights and expectations linked to ancient principles in our constitutional order [and the] Court's decision should not be interpreted as suggesting that violations of the requirement are trivial or beyond the law's concern. [Also,] the continued operation of the exclusionary rule [is] not in doubt. Today's decision determines only that in the specific context of the knock-and-announce requirement, a violation is not sufficiently related to the later discovery of evidence to justify suppression.

JUSTICE BREYER, with whom JUSTICE STEVENS, JUSTICE SOUTER, and JUSTICE GINSBURG join, dissenting.

[In] *Wilson,* [we traced] the lineage of the knock-and-announce rule back to the 13th century [and] concluded that there was "[the] Framers of the Fourth Amendment thought that the method of an officer's entry into a dwelling was among the factors to be considered in assessing the reasonableness of a search or seizure." ... Thus, "a search or seizure of a dwelling might be constitutionally defective if police officers enter without prior announcement."

[An] unreasonable search or seizure is, constitutionally speaking, an illegal search or seizure. [E]ver since *Weeks* (in respect to federal prosecutions) and *Mapp* (in respect to state prosecutions), "the use of evidence secured through an illegal search and seizure" is "barred" in criminal trials. [T]he driving legal purpose underlying the exclusionary rule, namely, the deterrence of unlawful government behavior, argues strongly for suppression. [F]ailure to apply the exclusionary rule would make [the Fourth Amendment's] promise a hollow one, reducing it to "a form of words," "of no value" to those whom it seeks to protect.... *Mapp* held that the exclusionary rule applies to the States in large part due to its belief that alternative state mechanisms for enforcing the Fourth Amendment's guarantees had proved "worthless and futile."

[What] reason is there to believe that [alternative] remedies (such as private damages actions under 42 U.S.C. § 1983), which the Court found inadequate in *Mapp,* can adequately deter unconstitutional police behavior here? [T]he majority [has] failed to cite a single [case] in which a plaintiff has collected more than nominal damages solely as a result of a knock-and-announce violation. [T]he need for deterrence-the critical factor driving this Court's Fourth Amendment cases for close to a century-argues with at least comparable strength for evidentiary exclusion here.

[The] Court has declined to apply the exclusionary rule only: (1) where there is a specific reason to believe that application of the rule would "not result in appreciable deterrence," or (2) where admissibility in proceedings other than criminal trials was at issue. Neither of these two exceptions applies here. The second does not apply because this case is an ordinary criminal trial. The first does not apply because . . . there is no reason to think that, in the case of knock-and-announce violations by the police, "the exclusion of evidence at trial would not sufficiently deter future errors," or " 'further the ends of the exclusionary rule in any appreciable way.' " . . .

The majority [argues] that "the constitutional violation of an illegal *manner* of entry was *not* a but-for cause of obtaining the evidence." . . . Although the police might have entered Hudson's home lawfully, they did not in fact do so. Their unlawful behavior inseparably characterizes their actual entry; that entry was a necessary condition of their presence in Hudson's home; and their presence in Hudson's home was a necessary condition of their finding and seizing the evidence. [W]e have described a failure to comply with the knock-and-announce rule, not as an independently unlawful event, but as a factor that renders the *search* "constitutionally defective." *Wilson,* 514 U.S., at 936.

[The] government cannot [avoid] suppression of evidence seized without a warrant (or pursuant to a defective warrant) simply by showing that it could have obtained a valid warrant had it sought one. Instead, it must show that the same evidence "inevitably *would* have been discovered *by lawful means.*" *Nix v. Williams,* 467 U.S., at 444 (emphasis added). . . . It is difficult for me to see how the presence of a warrant that does not authorize the entry in question has anything to do with the "inevitable discovery" exception or otherwise diminishes the need to enforce the knock-and-announce requirement through suppression.

The majority and the United States [argue] that the constitutional purpose of the knock-and-announce rule is to prevent needless destruction of property (such as breaking down a door) and to avoid unpleasant surprise. And it concludes that the exclusionary rule should suppress evidence of, say, damage to property, the discovery of a defendant in an "intimate or compromising moment," or an excited utterance from the occupant caught by surprise, but nothing more.... There are three serious problems with this argument. First, it does not fully describe the constitutional values, purposes, and objectives underlying the knock-and-announce requirement. That rule does help to protect homeowners from damaged doors; it does help to protect occupants from surprise. But it does more than that. It protects the occupants' privacy by assuring them that government agents will not enter their home without complying with those requirements (among others) that diminish the offensive nature of any such intrusion.... The knock-and-announce requirement is no less a part of the "centuries-old principle" of special protection for the privacy of the home than the warrant requirement. The Court is therefore wrong to reduce the essence of its protection to "the right not to be intruded upon in one's nightclothes." Second, ... failure to comply with the knock-and-announce rule renders the related search unlawful. And where a search is unlawful, the law insists upon suppression of the evidence consequently discovered, even if that evidence or its possession has little or nothing to do with the reasons underlying the unconstitutionality of a search.... Third, [o]rdinarily a court will simply look to see if the unconstitutional search produced the evidence....

B. THE "GOOD FAITH" EXCEPTION

Because of the perceived "costs" associated with the exclusionary rule (*i.e.*, the loss of evidence, the reversal of convictions, and difficulty of convicting without suppressed evidence), some police and law enforcement officials pressed for a "good faith" exception to the exclusionary rule. That issue was presented in the following case.

UNITED STATES v. LEON

468 U.S. 897 (1984).

JUSTICE WHITE delivered the opinion of the Court.

This case presents the question whether the Fourth Amendment exclusionary rule should be modified so as not to bar the use in the prosecution's case in chief of evidence obtained by officers acting in reasonable reliance on a search warrant issued by a detached and neutral magistrate but ultimately found to be unsupported by probable cause. * * *

[The] Fourth Amendment contains no provision expressly precluding the use of evidence obtained in violation of its commands, and an examination of its origin and purposes makes clear that the use of fruits of a past unlawful search or seizure "work[s] no new Fourth Amendment wrong." *United States v. Calandra*, 414 U.S. 338 (1974). The wrong condemned by the Amendment is "fully accomplished" by the unlawful search or seizure itself, and the exclusionary rule is neither intended nor able to "cure the invasion of the defendant's rights which he has already suffered." *Stone v. Powell, supra*, 428 U.S., at 540 (WHITE, J., dissenting). The rule thus operates as "a judicially created remedy designed to safeguard Fourth Amendment rights generally through its deterrent effect, rather than a personal constitutional right of the party aggrieved." *United States v. Calandra*, 414 U.S., at 348.

Whether the exclusionary sanction is appropriately imposed in a particular case [is] "an issue separate from the question whether the Fourth Amendment rights of the party seeking to invoke the rule were violated by police conduct." Only the former question is currently before us, and it must be resolved by weighing the costs and benefits of preventing the use in the prosecution's case in chief of inherently trustworthy tangible evidence obtained in reliance on a search warrant issued by a detached and neutral magistrate that ultimately is found to be defective.

The substantial social costs exacted by the exclusionary rule [have] long been a source of concern. "Our cases have consistently recognized that unbending application of the exclusionary sanction to enforce ideals of governmental rectitude would impede unacceptably the truth-finding functions of judge and jury." *United States v. Payner*, 447 U.S. 727 (1980). An objectionable collateral consequence of this interference [is] that some guilty defendants may go free or receive reduced sentences as a result of favorable plea bargains.[2] Particularly when law enforcement officers have acted in objective good faith or their transgressions have been minor, the magnitude of the benefit conferred on such guilty defendants offends basic concepts of the criminal justice system. Indiscriminate application of the exclusionary rule, therefore, may well "generat[e] disrespect for the law and administration of justice." "[As] with any remedial device, the application of the rule has been restricted to those areas where its remedial objectives are thought most efficaciously served." *United States v. Calandra*, 414 U.S., at 348.

Close attention to those remedial objectives has characterized our recent decisions concerning the scope of the Fourth Amendment exclusionary rule. The Court has, to be sure, not seriously questioned, "in the absence of a more efficacious sanction, the continued application of the rule to suppress evidence from the [prosecution's] case where a Fourth Amendment violation has been substantial and [deliberate]." *Franks v. Delaware*, 438 U.S. 154 (1978). Nevertheless, the balancing [approach] "forcefully suggest[s] that the exclusionary rule be more generally modified to permit the introduction of evidence obtained in the reasonable good-faith belief that a search or seizure was in accord with the Fourth

---

2. [One] study suggests that the rule results in the nonprosecution or nonconviction of between 0.6% and 2.35% of individuals arrested for felonies. The estimates are higher for particular crimes the prosecution of which depends heavily on physical evidence. Thus, the cumulative loss [of] felony drug charges is probably in the range of 2.8% to 7.1%. [Many] researchers have concluded that the impact of the exclusionary rule is insubstantial, but the small percentages with which they deal mask a large absolute number of felons who are re-

leased. . . . "[A]ny rule of evidence that denies the jury access to clearly probative and reliable evidence must bear a heavy burden of justification, and must be carefully limited to the circumstances in which it will pay its way by deterring official unlawlessness." *Illinois v. Gates*, 462 U.S., at 257–258 (White, J., concurring in judgment). Because we find that the rule can have no substantial deterrent effect in the sorts of situations under consideration in this case, we conclude that it cannot pay its way in those situations.

Amendment." *Illinois v. Gates*, 462 U.S., at 255 (White, J., concurring in judgment).

In *Stone v. Powell*, the Court emphasized the costs of the exclusionary rule, expressed its view that limiting the circumstances under which Fourth Amendment claims could be raised in federal habeas corpus proceedings would not reduce the rule's deterrent effect, and held that a state prisoner who has been afforded a full and fair opportunity to litigate a Fourth Amendment claim may not obtain federal habeas relief on the ground that unlawfully obtained evidence had been introduced at his trial. Proposed extensions of the exclusionary rule to proceedings other than the criminal trial itself have been evaluated and rejected under the same analytic approach. In *Calandra*, [we] declined to allow grand jury witnesses to refuse to answer questions based on evidence obtained from an unlawful search or seizure since "[a]ny incremental deterrent effect which might be achieved by extending the rule to grand jury proceedings is uncertain at best." Similarly, in *United States v. Janis*, [428 U.S. 433 (1976),] we permitted the use in federal civil proceedings of evidence illegally seized by state officials since the likelihood of deterring police misconduct through such an extension of the exclusionary rule was insufficient to outweigh its substantial social costs. In so doing, we declared that, "[i]f [the] exclusionary rule does not result in appreciable deterrence, then, clearly, its use in the instant situation is unwarranted."

[It] does not follow from the emphasis on the exclusionary rule's deterrent value that "anything which deters illegal searches is thereby commanded by the Fourth Amendment." In determining whether persons aggrieved solely by the introduction of damaging evidence unlawfully obtained from their co-conspirators or co-defendants could seek suppression, for example, we found that the additional benefits of such an extension of the exclusionary rule would not outweigh its costs. Standing to invoke the rule has thus been limited to cases in which the prosecution seeks to use the fruits of an illegal search or seizure against the victim of police misconduct.

Even defendants with standing to challenge the introduction in their criminal trials of unlawfully obtained evidence cannot prevent every conceivable use of such evidence. Evidence obtained in violation of the Fourth Amendment and inadmissible in the prosecution's case in chief may be used to impeach a defendant's direct testimony. A similar assessment of the "incremental furthering" of the ends of the exclusionary rule led us to conclude in *United States v. Havens*, 446 U.S. 620 (1980), that evidence [may] be used to impeach statements made by a defendant in response to "proper cross-examination reasonably suggested by the defendant's direct examination."

When considering the use of evidence obtained in violation of the Fourth Amendment in the prosecution's case in chief, moreover, we have declined to adopt a per se or "but for" rule that would render inadmissible any evidence that came to light through a chain of causation that began with an illegal arrest. We also have held that a witness' testimony may be admitted even when his identity was discovered in an unconstitutional search. The perception underlying these decisions—that the connection between police misconduct and evidence of crime may be sufficiently attenuated to permit the use of that evidence at trial—is a product of considerations relating to the exclusionary rule and the constitutional principles it is designed to protect.[3] [I]n view of this purpose, an assessment of the flagrancy of the police misconduct constitutes an important step in the calculus.

[W]e have not recognized any form of good-faith exception to the Fourth Amendment exclusionary rule. But the balancing approach that has evolved during the years of experience with the rule provides strong support for the modification currently urged upon us. * * *

Because a search warrant "provides the detached scrutiny of a neutral magistrate, which is a more reliable safeguard against improper searches than the hurried judgment of a law enforcement officer 'engaged in the often competitive enterprise of ferreting out crime,' " we have expressed a strong preference for warrants and declared that "in a doubtful or marginal case a search under a warrant may be sustainable where without one it would fall." *United States v. Ventresca*, 380 U.S. 102 (1965). Reasonable minds frequently may differ on the question whether a particular affidavit establishes probable cause, and [the] preference for warrants is most appropriately effectuated by according "great deference" to a magistrate's determination.

Deference to the magistrate, however, is not boundless. It is clear, first, that the deference accorded to a magistrate's finding of probable cause does not preclude inquiry into the knowing or reckless falsity of the affidavit on which that determination was based. Second, the courts must also insist that the magistrate purport to "perform his 'neutral and detached' function and not serve merely as a rubber stamp for the police." A magistrate failing to "manifest that neutrality and detachment demanded of a judicial officer when presented with a warrant application" and who acts instead as "an adjunct law enforcement officer" cannot provide valid authorization for an otherwise unconstitutional search.

Third, reviewing courts will not defer to a warrant based on an affidavit that does not "provide the magistrate with a substantial basis for determining the existence of probable cause." [Even] if the warrant application was supported by more than a "bare bones" affidavit, a reviewing court may properly conclude that, notwithstanding the deference that magistrates deserve, the warrant was invalid because the magistrate's probable-cause determination reflected an improper analy-

---

3. *"Brown's* focus on 'the causal connection between the illegality and the confession' reflected the two policies behind the use of the exclusionary rule to effectuate the Fourth Amendment. Where there is a close causal connection between the illegal seizure and the confession, not only is exclusion of the evidence more likely to deter similar police misconduct in the future, but use of the evidence is more likely to compromise the integrity of the courts." *Dunaway v. New York*, 442 U.S., at 217–218.

sis of the totality of the circumstances, or because the form of the warrant was improper in some respect.

Only in the first of these three situations, however, has the Court set forth a rationale for suppressing evidence obtained pursuant to a search warrant; in the other areas, it has simply excluded such evidence without considering whether Fourth Amendment interests will be advanced. To the extent that proponents of exclusion rely on its behavioral effects on judges and magistrates in these areas, their reliance is misplaced. First, the exclusionary rule is designed to deter police misconduct rather than to punish the errors of judges and magistrates. Second, there exists no evidence suggesting that judges and magistrates are inclined to ignore or subvert the Fourth Amendment or that lawlessness among these actors requires application of the extreme sanction of exclusion.

Third, [we] discern no basis, and are offered none, for believing that exclusion of evidence seized pursuant to a warrant will have a significant deterrent effect on the issuing judge or magistrate. Many of the factors that indicate that the exclusionary rule cannot provide an effective "special" or "general" deterrent for individual offending law enforcement officers apply as well to judges or magistrates. [To] the extent that the rule is thought to operate as a "systemic" deterrent on a wider audience, it clearly can have no such effect on individuals empowered to issue search warrants. Judges and magistrates are not adjuncts to the law enforcement team; as neutral judicial officers, they have no stake in the outcome of particular criminal prosecutions. The threat of exclusion [cannot] be expected significantly to deter them. Imposition of the exclusionary sanction is not necessary meaningfully to inform judicial officers of their errors, and we cannot conclude that admitting evidence obtained pursuant to a warrant while at the same time declaring that the warrant was somehow defective will in any way reduce judicial officers' professional incentives to comply with the Fourth Amendment, encourage them to repeat their mistakes, or lead to the granting of all colorable warrant requests.[4]

If exclusion of evidence obtained pursuant to a subsequently invalidated warrant is to have any deterrent effect, [it] must alter the behavior of individual law enforcement officers or the policies of their departments. One could argue that applying the exclusionary rule in cases where the police failed to demonstrate probable cause in the warrant application deters future inadequate presentations or "magistrate shopping" and thus promotes the ends of the Fourth Amendment. Suppressing evidence obtained pursuant to a technically defective warrant supported by probable cause also might encourage officers to scrutinize more closely the form of the warrant and to point out suspected judicial errors. We find such arguments speculative and conclude that suppression of evidence obtained pursuant to a warrant

---

4. [If] a magistrate serves merely as a "rubber stamp" for the police or is unable to exercise mature judgment, closer supervision or removal provides a more effective remedy than the exclusionary rule.

should be ordered only [in] those unusual cases in which exclusion will further the purposes of the exclusionary rule.

We have frequently questioned whether the exclusionary rule can have any deterrent effect when the offending officers acted in the objectively reasonable belief that their conduct did not violate the Fourth Amendment. [E]ven assuming that the rule effectively deters some police misconduct and provides incentives for the law enforcement profession as a whole to conduct itself in accord with the Fourth Amendment, it cannot be expected, and should not be applied, to deter objectively reasonable law enforcement activity. [This] is particularly true [when] an officer acting with objective good faith has obtained a search warrant from a judge or magistrate and acted within its scope. In most such cases, there is no police illegality and thus nothing to deter. It is the magistrate's responsibility to determine whether the officer's allegations establish probable cause and, if so, to issue a warrant comporting in form with the requirements of the Fourth Amendment. In the ordinary case, an officer cannot be expected to question the magistrate's probable-cause determination or his judgment that the form of the warrant is technically sufficient. [Penalizing] the officer for the magistrate's error, rather than his own, cannot logically contribute to the deterrence of Fourth Amendment violations.[5]

We conclude that the marginal or nonexistent benefits produced by suppressing evidence obtained in objectively reasonable reliance on a subsequently invalidated search warrant cannot justify the substantial costs of exclusion. We do not suggest [that] exclusion is always inappropriate in cases where an officer has obtained a warrant and abided by its terms. "[S]earches pursuant to a warrant will rarely require any deep inquiry into reasonableness" for "a warrant issued by a magistrate normally suffices to establish" that a law enforcement officer has "acted in good faith in conducting the search." *United States v. Ross*, 456 U.S. 798 (1982). Nevertheless, the officer's reliance on the magistrate's probable-cause determination and on the technical sufficiency of the warrant he issues must be objectively reasonable,[6] and it is clear that in some circumstances the officer[7] will have no reasonable grounds for believing that the warrant was properly issued.

---

5. [When] a Fourth Amendment violation has occurred because the police have reasonably relied on a warrant issued by a detached and neutral magistrate but ultimately found to be defective, "the integrity of the courts is not implicated." *Illinois v. Gates,* 462 U.S., at 259, n.14 (White, J., concurring in judgment).

6. [We] eschew inquiries into the subjective beliefs of law enforcement officers who seize evidence pursuant to a subsequently invalidated warrant. [Our] good-faith inquiry is confined to the objectively ascertainable question whether a reasonably well trained officer would have known that the search was illegal despite the magistrate's authorization. In making this determination, all of the circumstances—including whether the warrant application had previously been rejected by a different magistrate—may be considered.

7. [We] consider the objective reasonableness, not only of the officers [who] executed a warrant, but also of the officers [who] obtained it or who provided information material to the probable-cause determination. Nothing [suggests that] an officer could obtain a warrant on the basis of a "bare bones" affidavit and then rely on colleagues who are ignorant of the circumstances under which the warrant was obtained to conduct the search.

Suppression therefore remains an appropriate remedy if the magistrate or judge in issuing a warrant was misled by information in an affidavit that the affiant knew was false or would have known was false except for his reckless disregard of the truth. The exception [will] also not apply [where] the issuing magistrate wholly abandoned his judicial role in the manner condemned in *Lo-Ji Sales, Inc. v. New York*, 442 U.S. 319 (1979); in such circumstances, no reasonably well trained officer should rely on the warrant. Nor would an officer manifest objective good faith in relying on a warrant based on an affidavit "so lacking in indicia of probable cause as to render official belief in its existence entirely unreasonable." Finally, depending on the circumstances of the particular case, a warrant may be so facially deficient—*i.e.*, in failing to particularize the place to be searched or the things to be seized—that the executing officers cannot reasonably presume it to be valid.

In so limiting the suppression remedy, we leave untouched the probable-cause standard and the various requirements for a valid warrant. [The] good-faith exception for searches conducted pursuant to warrants is not intended to signal our unwillingness strictly to enforce the requirements of the Fourth Amendment, and we do not believe that it will have this effect. [The] good-faith exception, turning as it does on objective reasonableness, should not be difficult to apply in practice. When officers have acted pursuant to a warrant, the prosecution should ordinarily be able to establish objective good faith without a substantial expenditure of judicial time.

Nor are we persuaded that application of a good-faith exception to searches conducted pursuant to warrants will preclude review of the constitutionality of the search or seizure, deny needed guidance from the courts, or freeze Fourth Amendment law in its present state.[8] There is no need for courts to adopt the inflexible practice of always deciding whether the officers' conduct manifested objective good faith before turning to the question whether the Fourth Amendment has been violated. [If] resolution of a particular Fourth Amendment question is necessary to guide future action by law enforcement officers and magistrates, nothing will prevent reviewing courts from deciding that question before turning to the good-faith issue. Indeed, it frequently will be difficult to determine whether the officers acted reasonably without resolving the Fourth Amendment issue. Even if the Fourth Amendment question is not one of broad import, reviewing courts could decide in particular cases that magistrates under their supervision need to be informed of their errors and so evaluate the officers' good faith only after finding a violation. In other circumstances, those courts could reject suppression motions posing no important Fourth Amendment questions

---

8. The argument that defendants will lose their incentive to litigate meritorious Fourth Amendment claims as a result of the good-faith exception [is] unpersuasive. Although the exception might discourage presentation of insubstantial suppression motions, the magnitude of the benefit conferred on defendants by a successful motion makes it unlikely that litigation of colorable claims will be substantially diminished.

by turning immediately to a consideration of the officers' good faith. * * *

When the principles we have enunciated today are applied to the facts of this case, it is apparent that the judgment of the Court of Appeals cannot stand. [Leon] has contended that no reasonably well trained police officer could have believed that there existed probable cause to search his [house]. Officer Rombach's application for a warrant clearly was supported by much more than a "bare bones" affidavit. The affidavit related the results of an extensive investigation [and] provided evidence sufficient to create disagreement among thoughtful and competent judges as to the existence of probable cause. Under these circumstances, the officers' reliance on the magistrate's determination of probable cause was objectively reasonable, and application of the extreme sanction of exclusion is inappropriate.

Accordingly, the judgment of the Court of Appeals is

Reversed.

JUSTICE BRENNAN, with whom JUSTICE MARSHALL joins, dissenting.

[I] have witnessed the Court's gradual but determined strangulation of the [exclusionary] rule. It now appears that the Court's victory over the Fourth Amendment is complete. [T]oday the Court sanctions the use in the prosecution's case in chief of illegally obtained evidence against the individual whose rights have been [violated].

[T]he language of deterrence and of cost/benefit analysis [can] have a narcotic effect. It creates an illusion of technical precision and ineluctability. [When] the Court's analysis is examined carefully, [it] is clear that we have not been treated to an honest assessment of the merits of the exclusionary rule, but have instead been drawn into a curious world where the "costs" of excluding illegally obtained evidence loom to exaggerated heights and where the "benefits" of such exclusion are made to disappear with a mere wave of the hand.

[The Court treats] the exclusionary rule [as] merely a " 'judicially created remedy designed to safeguard Fourth Amendment rights [through] its deterrent effect, rather than a personal constitutional right.' " [I] had thought that such a narrow conception of the rule had been forever put to [rest]. [T]he [Fourth] Amendment, like other provisions of the Bill of Rights, restrains the power of the government as a whole. . . . The judiciary is responsible, no less than the executive, for ensuring that constitutional rights are respected. [Because] seizures are executed principally to secure evidence, and because such evidence generally has utility in our legal system only in the context of a [trial, the] admission of illegally obtained evidence implicates the same constitutional concerns as the initial seizure of that evidence. [B]y admitting unlawfully seized evidence, the judiciary becomes a part of what is [a] single governmental action prohibited by the terms of the Amendment. * * *

[The] right to be free from the initial invasion of privacy and the right of exclusion are coordinate components of the central embracing right to be free from unreasonable searches and seizures. [*Weeks* recognized] that, if the Amendment is to have any meaning, police and the courts cannot be regarded as constitutional strangers to each other; because the evidence-gathering role of the police is directly linked to the evidence-admitting function of the courts, an individual's Fourth Amendment rights may be undermined as completely by one as by the other.

[F]rom *Weeks to Olmstead*[,] the Court plainly understood that the exclusion of illegally obtained evidence was compelled not by judicially fashioned remedial purposes, but rather by a direct constitutional command. * * *

[T]he deterrence theory is both misguided and unworkable. First, the Court has frequently bewailed the "cost" of excluding reliable evidence. [T]he Amendment directly contemplates that some reliable and incriminating evidence will be lost to the government; therefore, it is not the exclusionary rule, but the Amendment itself that has imposed this cost. [T]he entire enterprise of attempting to assess the benefits and costs of the exclusionary rule in various contexts is a virtually impossible task for the judiciary to perform honestly or accurately. [To] the extent empirical data are available regarding the general costs and benefits of the exclusionary rule, such data have shown, on the one hand, [that] the costs are not as substantial as critics have asserted[, and] that while the exclusionary rule may well have certain deterrent effects, it is extremely difficult to determine with any degree of precision whether the incidence of unlawful conduct by police is now lower than it was prior to *Mapp*. The Court has sought to turn this uncertainty to its advantage by casting the burden of proof upon proponents of the rule. * * *

[Rather] than seeking to give effect to the liberties secured by the Fourth Amendment through guesswork about deterrence, the Court should restore to its proper place the principle framed 70 years ago in *Weeks* that an individual whose privacy has been invaded in violation of the Fourth Amendment has a right grounded in that Amendment to prevent the government from subsequently making use of any evidence so obtained.

[In this case, the] affidavit filed by the police officers [failed] to provide [a] basis on which a neutral and detached magistrate could conclude that there was probable cause to issue the warrant. [The] application for a warrant was based in part on information supplied by a confidential informant of unproven reliability that was over five months [old]. Although the police conducted an independent [investigation, the] additional information [failed] to corroborate the details of [the] tip and was "as consistent with innocence as [with] guilt." The warrant, therefore, should never have issued. Stripped of the authority of the warrant, the conduct of these officers was plainly unconstitutional—it amounted to nothing less than a naked invasion of the privacy of respondents' homes without the requisite justification demanded by the Fourth Amendment. [I]t was necessary that the evidence be suppressed. * * *

[The] tenor of the Court's opinion suggests that this order somehow imposed a grave and presumably unjustifiable cost on society. Such a suggestion, however, is a gross exaggeration. [S]ince the bulk of the evidence seized [was] plainly [admissible], the Government would clearly still be able to present a strong case to the jury following the court's suppression order. * * *

[T]he Court suggests that society has been asked to pay a high price—in terms either of setting guilty persons free or of impeding the proper functioning of trials—as a result of excluding relevant physical evidence in cases where the police, in conducting searches and seizing evidence, have made only an "objectively reasonable" mistake concerning the constitutionality of their actions. But what evidence is there to support such a claim? [The] Court points to none, [and] recent studies have demonstrated that the "costs" of the exclusionary rule—calculated in terms of dropped prosecutions and lost convictions—are quite low. [F]ederal and state prosecutors very rarely drop cases because of potential search and seizure problems. [A] 1979 study [reported] that only 0.4% of all cases actually declined for prosecution by federal prosecutors were declined primarily because of illegal search problems. [T]he study shows that only 0.2% of all felony arrests are declined for prosecution because of potential exclusionary rule problems.[9] Of course, these data describe only the costs attributable to the exclusion of evidence in all cases; the costs due to the exclusion of evidence in the narrower category of cases where police have made objectively reasonable mistakes must necessarily be even smaller. The Court [ignores] this distinction and mistakenly weighs the aggregated costs of exclusion in all cases, irrespective of the circumstances that led to exclusion against the potential benefits associated with only those cases in which evidence is excluded because police reasonably but mistakenly believe that their conduct does not violate the Fourth Amendment. When such faulty scales are used, it is little wonder that the balance tips in favor of restricting the application of the rule.

[The] key to the Court's [holding] is [the] belief that the prospective deterrent effect of the exclusionary rule operates only in those situations in which police officers, when deciding whether to go forward with some particular search, have reason to know that their planned conduct will violate the requirements of the Fourth Amendment. [The] Court's argument [captures] only one comparatively minor element of the generally acknowledged deterrent purposes of the exclusionary rule. To be sure, the rule operates [to] deter future misconduct by individual officers who

9. [A] recent National Institute of Justice [NIJ] study [showed] that 4.8% of all cases that were declined for prosecution by California prosecutors were rejected because of illegally seized evidence [—] only 0.8% of all [arrests]. [The] number of prose-cutions that are dismissed or result in acquittals in cases where evidence has been excluded—the [data] show that the Court's [assessment] of the rule's costs has [been] exaggerated. * * *

have had evidence suppressed in their own cases. [W]hat the Court overlooks is that the deterrence rationale [is] not designed to be [a] form of "punishment" of individual police officers for their failures to obey the restraints imposed by the Fourth Amendment. Instead, the chief deterrent function of the rule is its tendency to promote institutional compliance with Fourth Amendment requirements on the part of law enforcement agencies generally. [As] the Court has previously recognized, "[the] demonstration [provided by the exclusionary rule] that our society attaches serious consequences to violation of constitutional rights is thought to encourage those who formulate law enforcement policies, and the officers who implement them, to incorporate Fourth Amendment ideals into their value system." *Stone v. Powell*, 428 U.S., at 492. It is only through such an institution wide mechanism that information concerning Fourth Amendment standards can be effectively communicated to rank-and-file officers.

If the overall educational effect of the exclusionary rule is considered, application of the rule to even those situations in which individual police officers have acted on the basis of a reasonable but mistaken belief that their conduct was authorized can still be expected to have a considerable long-term deterrent effect. If evidence is consistently excluded in these circumstances, police departments will surely be prompted to instruct their officers to devote greater care and attention to providing sufficient information to establish probable cause when applying for a warrant, and to review with some attention the form of the warrant that they have been issued, rather than automatically assuming that whatever document the magistrate has signed will necessarily comport with Fourth Amendment requirements.

After today's decisions, [that] institutional incentive will be lost. [T]he Court's "reasonable mistake" exception to the exclusionary rule will tend to put a premium on police ignorance of the law. Armed with the assurance provided by today's decisions that evidence will always be admissible whenever an officer has "reasonably" relied upon a warrant, police departments will be encouraged to train officers that if a warrant has simply been signed, it is reasonable, without more, to rely on it. [T]here will no longer be any incentive to err on the side of constitutional [behavior].

Moreover, the good-faith exception will encourage police to provide only the bare minimum of information in future warrant applications. The police will now know that if they can secure a warrant, so long as the circumstances of its issuance are not "entirely unreasonable," all police conduct pursuant to that warrant will be protected from further judicial review. The clear incentive that operated in the past to establish probable cause adequately because reviewing courts would examine the magistrate's judgment carefully, has now been so completely vitiated that the police need only show that it was not "entirely unreasonable" under the circumstances of a particular case for them to believe that the warrant they were issued was valid. The long-run effect unquestionably will be to undermine the integrity of the warrant process.

[G]iven the relaxed standard for assessing probable cause established just last Term in *Illinois v. Gates*, 462 U.S. 213 (1983), the Court's newly fashioned good-faith exception, when applied in the warrant context, will rarely, if ever, offer any greater flexibility for police than the *Gates* standard already supplies. * * *

When the public [demands] that those in government increase their efforts to combat crime, it is all too easy for those government officials to seek expedient solutions. In contrast to such costly and difficult measures as building more prisons, improving law enforcement methods, or hiring more prosecutors and judges to relieve the overburdened court systems in the country's metropolitan areas, the relaxation of Fourth Amendment standards seems a tempting, costless means of meeting the public's demand for better law enforcement. In the long run, however, we as a society pay a heavy price for such [expediency]. Once lost, [rights] are difficult to recover. * * *

Justice Stevens, concurring in the judgment in No. 82–963, and dissenting in No. 82–1771.

[T]he Amendment was actually motivated by the practice of issuing general warrants—warrants which did not satisfy the particularity and probable-cause requirements. [T]he Framers of the Fourth Amendment were deeply suspicious of warrants; in their minds the paradigm of an abusive search was the execution of a warrant not based on probable cause. The fact that colonial officers had magisterial authorization for their conduct when they engaged in general searches surely did not make their conduct "reasonable." The Court's view that it is consistent with our Constitution to adopt a rule that it is presumptively reasonable to rely on a defective warrant is the product of constitutional amnesia.

[The] exclusionary rule is designed to prevent violations of the Fourth Amendment. [Today's] decisions do grave damage to that deterrent function. Under the majority's new rule, even when the police know their warrant application is probably insufficient, they retain an incentive to submit it to a magistrate, on the chance that he may take the bait. No longer must they hesitate and seek additional evidence in doubtful cases. * * *

The Court is of course correct that the exclusionary rule cannot deter when the authorities have no reason to know that their conduct is unconstitutional. But when probable cause is lacking, [a] reasonable person [would] not believe there is a fair likelihood that a search will produce evidence of a crime. Under such circumstances well-trained professionals must know that they are violating the Constitution. The Court's approach—[which] encourages the police to seek a warrant even if they know the existence of probable cause is doubtful—can only lead to an increased number of constitutional violations.

[The Court's decision] tarnishes the role of the judiciary in enforcing the Constitution. [Courts] simply cannot escape their responsibility for redressing constitutional violations if they admit evidence obtained through unreasonable searches and seizures, since the entire point of police conduct that violates the Fourth Amendment is to obtain evidence for use at trial. . . . It is of course true that the exclusionary rule exerts a high price—the loss of probative evidence of guilt. But that price is one courts have often been required to pay to serve important social goals. That price is also one the Fourth Amendment requires us to pay, assuming as we must that the Framers intended that its strictures "shall not be violated." . . . We [could] facilitate the process of administering justice [by] ignoring the entire Bill of Rights—but it is the very purpose of a Bill of Rights to identify values that may not be sacrificed to expediency. In a just society those who govern, as well as those who are governed, must obey the law. * * *

Notes

1. *Good Faith and "Technical Errors." Massachusetts v. Sheppard*, 468 U.S. 981 (1984) was a "companion case" to *Leon*, i.e. it was handed down by the Supreme Court at the same time. In *Sheppard*, the Court extended *Leon* to a case involving a warrant invalidated because of a technical error on the part of the issuing judge: "Suppressing evidence because the judge failed to make all the necessary clerical corrections despite his assurances that such changes would be made will not serve the deterrent function that the exclusionary rule was designed to achieve."

2. *Good Faith Reliance on an Invalid Statute.* In *Illinois v. Krull*, 480 U.S. 340 (1987), the Court extended the good faith exception to situations where the police act in objectively reasonable reliance upon a statute authorizing warrantless administrative searches, but where the statute is ultimately found to violate the Fourth Amendment: "The application of the exclusionary rule to suppress evidence obtained by an officer acting in objectively reasonable reliance on a statute would have as little deterrent effect on the officer's actions as would the exclusion of evidence when an officer acts in objectively reasonable reliance on a warrant. Unless a statute is clearly unconstitutional, an officer cannot be expected to question the judgment of the legislature that passed the law. If the statute is subsequently declared unconstitutional, excluding evidence obtained pursuant to it prior to such a judicial declaration will not deter future Fourth Amendment violations by an officer who has simply fulfilled his responsibility to enforce the statute as written." Justice O'Connor dissented: "Statutes authorizing unreasonable searches were the core concern of the Framers of the Fourth Amendment. [B]oth the history of the Fourth Amendment and this Court's later interpretations of it, support application of the exclusionary rule to [this situation]."

Problems

1. *Evaluating the Underpinnings of the Exclusionary Rule.* Reread *Mapp v. Ohio.* Does your reading suggest that the exclusionary rule is premised solely on principles of deterrence, or does it suggest that the rule is based on other considerations as well (e.g., the "imperative" of judicial integrity, or the Fourth Amendment itself—in other words, that the rule is "constitutionally required")?

2. *Do you agree that the exclusionary rule should be subject to a "good faith" defense?* About one-third of the states have rejected the good faith exception to the exclusionary rule under their own state constitutions. In construing the New Jersey Constitution, for example, the New Jersey Supreme Court rejected *Leon's* reasoning. In *State v. Novembrino*, 105 N.J. 95, 519 A.2d 820 (1987), the court offered the following reasons:

> [T]he good-faith exception will inevitably and inexorably diminish the quality of evidence presented in search-warrant applications [because it eliminates the] cost for noncompliance with the constitutional requirement of probable cause. [The] exclusionary rule['s] function is not merely to deter police misconduct. The rule also serves as the indispensable mechanism for vindicating the constitutional right to be free from unreasonable searches. Because [the] good-faith exception [would] tend to undermine the constitutionally-guaranteed standard of probable cause, and in the process disrupt the highly effective procedures employed by our criminal justice system to accommodate that constitutional guarantee without impairing law enforcement, we decline to recognize a good-faith exception to the exclusionary rule. [We] see no need in New Jersey to experiment with the fundamental rights protected by the fourth-amendment counterpart of our State Constitution.
> * * *

Is the holding in *Novembrino* preferable to the holding in *Leon*?

3. *More state court disagreements.* Consider also *State v. Marsala*, 216 Conn. 150, 579 A.2d 58 (1990), another state court decision rejecting *Leon*:

> [T]he *Leon* court "consistently and repeatedly refers to the costs of the exclusionary rule as if they were somehow a matter quite distinct from the Fourth Amendment itself." 1 W. LaFave, *supra*, § 1.3(C), p. 53. "[The] inevitable result of the Constitution's prohibition against unreasonable searches and seizures and its requirement that no warrant shall issue but upon probable cause is that police officers who obey its strictures will catch fewer criminals. [It] is the price the framers anticipated and were willing to pay to ensure the sanctity of the person, the home, and property against unrestrained governmental power." P. Stewart, *"The Road to Mapp v. Ohio and Beyond: The Origins, Development and Future of the Exclusionary Rule in Search-and-Seizure Cases,"* 83 Col.L.Rev. 1365, 1392–93 (1983).
>
> [T]he rule as it stood before *Leon* was [a] significant factor inducing judges to take seriously their obligation to ensure that the probable cause requirement [had] been met before issuing search [warrants]. [S]earch warrants failing to meet the probable cause requirement more often "result from carelessness than from intentional constitutional violations, and just as surely the exclusionary rule is logically directed to those more common violations." [T]he issuing authority, when the determination of probable cause is overturned on appeal, is not being "punished" for a mistake, but is, rather, being informed that a constitutional violation has taken place and is also being instructed in how to avoid such violations in the future. "[The] exclusionary rule [has] served [to] influence judicial behavior [by] creating an 'incentive to err on the

side of constitutional behavior.' " *Id., quoting United States v. Johnson*, 457 U.S. 537, 561 (1982). * * *

[A] good faith exception to the exclusionary rule would have several negative [effects]. First, [the] good faith exception would encourage some police officers to expend less effort in establishing the necessary probable cause [and] more effort in locating a judge who might be less exacting than some others when ruling on whether an affidavit has established the requisite level of probable cause. Second, the "exception [implicitly] tells magistrates that they need not take much care in reviewing warrant applications, since their mistakes will from now on have virtually no [consequence]." Finally, [it] is unlikely "that overburdened trial and appellate courts will take the time and effort to write advisory opinions on [search and seizure] law when they can just as easily admit the evidence under the good faith exception." * * *

[T]he exclusionary rule is not designed to "punish" anyone. It [is] designed to deter future police misconduct and [ensure] institutional compliance with the warrant issuing requirements [of] our state constitution. The relevant inquiry, therefore, is [whether] the sanction of the exclusionary rule is appropriate in cases where the officer in question believed that he was doing everything correctly, but in fact had not supplied the issuing authority with information sufficient to meet the constitutional requirement of probable cause. We conclude that the rule is appropriate in these situations. [I]f evidence is consistently [excluded], police departments will surely be prompted to instruct their officers to devote greater care and attention to providing sufficient information to establish probable cause when applying for a warrant, and to review with some attention the form of the warrant that they have been issued, rather than automatically assuming that whatever document the magistrate has signed will necessarily comport with Fourth Amendment requirements. * * *

Do you agree?

4. *Is Leon's impact mitigated by the holding in Malley v. Briggs*, 475 U.S. 335 (1986)? *Malley* involved a police officer who unconstitutionally arrested plaintiffs by presenting a judge with a complaint and a supporting affidavit which failed to establish probable cause. Plaintiffs sued the officers for damages. The Court held that the officers were protected by qualified immunity, but only if they acted "reasonably": "[The] question in this case is whether a reasonably well-trained officer in petitioner's position would have known that his affidavit failed to establish probable cause and that he should not have applied for the warrant. If such was the case, the officer's application for a warrant was not objectively reasonable, because it created the unnecessary danger of an unlawful arrest. . . ." Does the possibility of a civil suit sufficiently deter police misconduct?

5. *Applying Leon to Warrantless Searches?* Would *Leon's* logic suggest that the good faith exception should apply when an officer makes a warrantless search in "good faith" (not in reliance on an invalid statute)? For example, the officer believes that he has probable cause to search a vehicle, and therefore can invoke the automobile exception to the warrant require-

ment, but he is wrong in concluding that probable cause exists. Does *Leon's* rationale extend to warrantless searches of this type?

6. *More on Applying Leon.* Should *Leon* apply when a warrant is based on probable cause, but the police relied on the fruits of prior illegal conduct to establish probable cause. Police responded to a call indicating that the lights were on in a house which was believed to be vacant. The police entered the house, believing that a burglary was in progress in order to investigate. Inside, while conducting a protective sweep, the police discovered marijuana plants growing in the basement. The police reported their findings to a narcotics task force which obtained a warrant to search the house and seized the plants. Assuming that the prior investigation was illegal, should *Leon* be extended to permit the fruits of the search to be admitted under the good faith exception? *See United States v. McClain,* 430 F.3d 299 (6th Cir. 2005).

7. *Erroneous Arrest Warrants.* Should the good faith exception apply when a police officer makes an arrest based on a police record indicating the existence of an outstanding arrest warrant—a record that was later determined to be erroneous. The erroneous record led to an arrest during which the existence of marijuana was discovered. How would the defense argue for exclusion? How might the prosecution respond? *See Arizona v. Evans,* 514 U.S. 1 (1995).

GROH v. RAMIREZ

540 U.S. 551 (2004).

JUSTICE STEVENS delivered the opinion of the Court.

[R]espondents, Joseph Ramirez and members of his family, live on a large ranch in Butte–Silver Bow County, Montana. Petitioner, Jeff Groh, has been a Special Agent for the Bureau of Alcohol, Tobacco and Firearms (ATF) since 1989. In February 1997, a concerned citizen informed petitioner that on a number of visits to respondents' ranch the visitor had seen a large stock of weaponry, including an automatic rifle, grenades, a grenade launcher, and a rocket launcher. Based on that information, petitioner prepared and signed an application for a warrant to search the ranch. The application stated that the search was for "any automatic firearms or parts to automatic weapons, destructive devices to include but not limited to grenades, grenade launchers, rocket launchers, and any and all receipts pertaining to the purchase or manufacture of automatic weapons or explosive devices or launchers." Petitioner supported the application with a detailed affidavit, which he also prepared and executed, that set forth the basis for his belief that the listed items were concealed on the ranch. Petitioner then presented these documents to a Magistrate, along with a warrant form that petitioner also had completed. The Magistrate signed the warrant form.

Although the application particularly described the place to be searched and the contraband petitioner expected to find, the warrant itself was less specific; it failed to identify any of the items that petitioner intended to seize. In the portion of the form that called for a description of the "person or property" to be seized, petitioner typed a description of respondents' two-story blue house rather than the alleged stockpile of firearms. The warrant did not incorporate by reference the itemized list contained in the application. It did, however, recite that the Magistrate was satisfied the affidavit established probable cause to believe that contraband was concealed on the premises, and that sufficient grounds existed for the warrant's issuance.

The day after the Magistrate issued the warrant, petitioner led a team of law enforcement officers, including both federal agents and members of the local sheriff's department, in the search of respondents' premises. Although respondent Joseph Ramirez was not home, his wife and children were. Petitioner states that he orally described the objects of the search to Mrs. Ramirez in person and to Mr. Ramirez by telephone. According to Mrs. Ramirez, however, petitioner explained only that he was searching for " 'an explosive device in a box.' " At any rate, the officers' search uncovered no illegal weapons or explosives. When the officers left, petitioner gave Mrs. Ramirez a copy of the search warrant, but not a copy of the application, which had been sealed. The following day, in response to a request from respondents' attorney, petitioner faxed the attorney a copy of the page of the application that listed the items to be seized. No charges were filed against the Ramirezes.

Respondents sued petitioner and the other officers under *Bivens v. Six Unknown Fed. Narcotics Agents*, 403 U.S. 388 (1971), and Rev. Stat. § 1979, 42 U.S.C. § 1983, raising eight claims, including violation of the Fourth Amendment. The District Court entered summary judgment for all defendants.... We granted certiorari.

The warrant was plainly invalid. The Fourth Amendment states unambiguously that "no Warrants shall issue, but upon probable cause, supported by Oath or affirmation, and *particularly describing* the place to be searched, and *the persons or things to be seized*." (Emphasis added.) The warrant in this case complied with the first three of these requirements: It was based on probable cause and supported by a sworn affidavit, and it described particularly the place of the search. On the fourth requirement, however, the warrant failed altogether. Indeed, petitioner concedes that "the warrant ... was deficient in particularity because it provided no description of the type of evidence sought."

The fact that the *application* adequately described the "things to be seized" does not save the *warrant* from its facial invalidity. The Fourth Amendment by its terms requires particularity in the warrant, not in the supporting documents. See *Massachusetts v. Sheppard*, 468 U.S. 981 (1984). And for good reason: "The presence of a search warrant serves a high function," and that high function is not necessarily vindicated when some other document, somewhere, says something about the objects of the search, but the contents of that document are neither known to the person whose home is being searched nor available for her inspection. We do not say that the Fourth Amendment forbids a warrant from cross-referencing other documents. Indeed, [a] court may construe a warrant with reference to a supporting application or affidavit if the warrant uses appropriate words of incorporation, and if the supporting document accompanies the warrant. But in this case the warrant did not incorporate other documents by reference, nor did either the affidavit or the application (which had been placed under seal) accompany the warrant. . . .

Petitioner argues that even though the warrant was invalid, the search nevertheless was "reasonable" within the meaning of the Fourth Amendment. He notes that a Magistrate authorized the search on the basis of adequate evidence of probable cause, that petitioner orally described to respondents the items to be seized, and that the search did not exceed the limits intended by the Magistrate and described by petitioner. Thus, petitioner maintains, his search of respondents' ranch was functionally equivalent to a search authorized by a valid warrant.

We disagree. This warrant did not simply omit a few items from a list of many to be seized, or misdescribe a few of several items. Nor did it make what fairly could be characterized as a mere technical mistake or typographical error. Rather, in the space set aside for a description of the items to be seized, the warrant stated that the items consisted of a "single dwelling residence . . . blue in color." In other words, the warrant did not describe the items to be seized *at all*. In this respect the warrant was so obviously deficient that we must regard the search as "warrantless" within the meaning of our case law. "We are not dealing with formalities." Because "the right of a man to retreat into his own home and there be free from unreasonable governmental intrusion" stands "[a]t the very core of the Fourth Amendment," our cases have firmly established the " 'basic principle of Fourth Amendment law' that searches and seizures inside a home without a warrant are presumptively unreasonable," *Payton v. New York,* 445 U.S. 573 (1980). Thus, "absent exigent circumstances, a warrantless entry to search for weapons or contraband is unconstitutional even when a felony has been committed and there is probable cause to believe that incriminating evidence will be found within." * * * Because petitioner did not have in his possession a warrant particularly describing the things he intended to seize, proceeding with the search was clearly "unreasonable" under the Fourth Amendment. . . .

Having concluded that a constitutional violation occurred, we turn to the question whether petitioner is entitled to qualified immunity despite that violation. The answer depends on whether the right that was transgressed was "clearly established"—that is, "whether it would be clear to a reasonable officer that his conduct was unlawful in the situation he confronted." *Saucier v. Katz,* 533 U.S. 194 (2001). . . . Given that the particularity requirement is set forth in the text of the Constitution, no reasonable officer could believe that a warrant that plainly did not comply with that requirement was valid. Moreover, because petitioner himself prepared the invalid warrant, he may not argue that he reasonably relied on the Magistrate's assurance that the warrant contained an adequate description of the things to be seized and was therefore valid. In fact, the guidelines of petitioner's own department placed him on notice that he might be liable for executing a manifestly invalid warrant. An ATF directive in force at the time of this search warned: "Special agents are liable if they exceed their authority while executing a search warrant and must be sure that a search warrant is sufficient on its face even when issued by a magistrate." And even a cursory reading of the warrant in this case—perhaps just a simple glance—would have revealed a glaring deficiency that any reasonable police officer would have known was constitutionally fatal.

No reasonable officer could claim to be unaware of the basic rule, well established by our cases, that, absent consent or exigency, a warrantless search of the home is presumptively unconstitutional. . . .

Petitioner contends that the search in this case was the product, at worst, of a lack of due care, and that our case law requires more than negligent behavior before depriving an official of qualified immunity. See *Malley v. Briggs*, 475 U.S. 335 (1986). [But] "a warrant may be so facially deficient—*i.e.*, in failing to particularize the place to be searched or the things to be seized—that the executing officers cannot reasonably presume it to be valid." This is such a case.

Accordingly, the judgment of the Court of Appeals is affirmed.

It is so ordered.

JUSTICE KENNEDY, with whom the CHIEF JUSTICE joins, dissenting.

I agree [that] the Fourth Amendment was violated in this case. . . . I disagree [on] whether the officer who obtained the warrant and led the search team is entitled to qualified immunity for his role in the search. . . . An officer conducting a search is entitled to qualified immunity if "a reasonable officer could have believed" that the search was lawful "in light of clearly established law and the information the searching officers possessed." *Anderson v. Creighton*, 483 U.S. 635 (1987). . . . The present case involves a straightforward mistake of fact. [T]he officer simply made a clerical error when he filled out the proposed warrant and offered it to the Magistrate Judge. The officer used the proper description of the property to be seized when he completed the affidavit. He also used the proper description in the accompanying application. When he typed up the description a third time for the proposed warrant, however, the officer accidentally entered a description of the place to be searched in the part of the warrant form that called for a description of the property to be seized. No one noticed the error before the search was executed. [T]he officer trained the search team and executed the warrant based on his mistaken belief that the warrant contained the proper description of the items to be seized.

The question is whether the officer's mistaken belief that the warrant contained the proper language was a reasonable belief. In my view, it was. A law enforcement officer charged with leading a team to execute a search warrant for illegal weapons must fulfill a number of serious responsibilities. The officer must establish probable cause to believe the crime has been committed and that evidence is likely to be found at the place to be searched; must articulate specific items that can be seized, and a specific place to be searched; must obtain the warrant from a magistrate judge; and must instruct a search team to execute the warrant within the time allowed by the warrant. The officer must also oversee the execution of the warrant in a way that protects officer safety, directs a thorough and professional search for the evidence, and avoids unnecessary destruction of property. These difficult and important tasks demand the officer's full attention in the heat of an ongoing and often dangerous criminal investigation. . . . An officer who complies fully with all of these duties can be excused for not being aware that he had made a clerical error in the course of filling out the proposed warrant. See *Maryland v. Garrison,* 480 U.S. 79 (1987). An officer who drafts an affidavit, types up an application and proposed warrant, and then obtains a judge's approval naturally assumes that he has filled out the warrant form correctly. Even if the officer checks over the warrant, he may very well miss a mistake. . . . In the context of an otherwise proper search, however, an officer's failure to recognize his clerical error on a warrant form can be a reasonable mistake. * * *

The language the Court quotes from *Leon* [notes] that there are some cases in which "no reasonably well trained officer should rely on the warrant." The passage also includes several examples, among them the one that the Court relies on in this case: "depending on the circumstances of the particular case, a warrant may be so facially deficient—*i.e.,* in failing to particularize the place to be searched or the things to be seized—that the executing officers cannot reasonably presume it to be valid." [No] one suggests that the officer reasonably could have relied on the defective language in the warrant. This is a case about an officer being unaware of a clerical error, not a case about an officer relying on one. . . . The Court's opinion [requires] our Nation's police officers to concentrate more on the correctness of paper forms than substantive rights. . . . I dissent.

JUSTICE THOMAS with whom JUSTICE SCALIA joins, and with whom the CHIEF JUSTICE joins as to Part III, dissenting.

[In] the instant case, the items to be seized were clearly specified in the warrant application and set forth in the affidavit, both of which were given to the Judge (Magistrate). The Magistrate reviewed all of the documents and signed the warrant application and made no adjustment or correction to this application. . . . Under these circumstances, I would not hold that any ensuing search constitutes a presumptively unreasonable warrantless search. . . . Because the search was not unreasonable, I would conclude that it was constitutional. . . .

Even assuming a constitutional violation, I would find that petitioner is entitled to qualified immunity. . . . Even if it were true that no reasonable officer could believe that a search of a home pursuant to a warrant that fails the particularity requirement is lawful absent exigent circumstances[,] petitioner did not know when he carried out the search that the search warrant was invalid—let alone legally nonexistent.... Petitioner's belief surely was reasonable.... [It] is inevitable that officers acting reasonably and entirely in good faith will occasionally make such errors.... In my view, petitioner's actions were objectively reasonable, and thus he should be entitled to qualified immunity.... For the foregoing reasons, I respectfully dissent.

C. THE RULE'S APPLICATION IN OTHER CONTEXTS

Should the exclusionary rule apply in other contexts (*e.g.*, civil proceedings)? Consider the following case.

UNITED STATES v. JANIS
428 U.S. 433 (1976).

MR. JUSTICE BLACKMUN delivered the opinion of the Court.

[In] November 1968 the Los Angeles police obtained a warrant directing a search for bookmaking paraphernalia at two specified apartment locations in the city and, as well, on the respective persons of Morris Aaron Levine and respondent Max Janis. The warrant was issued by a judge of the Municipal Court of the Los Angeles Judicial District. It was based upon the affidavit of Officer Leonard Weissman. After the search, made pursuant to the warrant, both the respondent and Levine were arrested and the police seized from respondent property consisting of $4,940 in cash and certain wagering records.

Soon thereafter, Officer Weissman telephoned an agent of the United States Internal Revenue Service and informed the agent that Janis had been arrested for bookmaking activity. With the assistance of Weissman, who was familiar with bookmakers' codes, the revenue agent analyzed the wagering records that had been seized and determined from them the gross volume of respondent's gambling activity for the five days immediately preceding the seizure. Weissman informed the agent that he had conducted a surveillance of respondent's activities that indicated that respondent had been engaged in bookmaking during the 77–day period from September 14 through November 30, 1968, the day of the arrest.

Respondent had not filed any federal wagering tax return pertaining to bookmaking activities for that 77–day period. Based exclusively upon its examination of the evidence so obtained by the Los Angeles police, the Internal Revenue Service made an assessment jointly against respondent and Levine for wagering taxes, under § 4401 of the Internal Revenue Code of 1954, in the amount of $89,026.09, plus interest. [The] assessment having been made, the Internal Revenue Service exercised its statutory authority, under 26 U.S.C. § 6331, to levy upon the $4,940 in cash in partial satisfaction of the assessment against respondent.

Charges were filed in due course against respondent and Levine in Los Angeles Municipal Court for violation of the local gambling laws.

[The judge concluded that the evidence had been illegally obtained, and granted a motion to quash the warrant.]

In June 1969 respondent filed a claim for refund of the $4,940. The claim was not honored, [and] respondent filed suit for that [amount]. The Government [counterclaimed] for the substantial unpaid balance of the assessment. In pretrial proceedings, it was agreed that the "sole basis of the computation of the civil tax assessment [was] the items obtained pursuant to the search warrant [and] the information furnished to (the revenue agent) by Officer Weissman with respect to the duration of (respondent's) alleged wagering activities." Respondent then moved to suppress the evidence seized, and all copies thereof in the possession of the Service, and to quash the assessment. [The District Court granted the motion to suppress.] Because of the obvious importance of the question, we granted certiorari.

[In] the complex and turbulent history of the rule, the Court never has applied it to exclude evidence from a civil proceeding, federal or state. In the present case we are asked to create judicially a deterrent sanction by holding that evidence obtained by a state criminal law enforcement officer in good-faith reliance on a warrant that later proved to be defective shall be inadmissible in a federal civil tax proceeding. Clearly, the enforcement of admittedly valid laws would be hampered by so extending the exclusionary rule, [and] concededly relevant and reliable evidence would be rendered unavailable.

In evaluating the need for a deterrent sanction, one must first identify those who are to be deterred. In this case it is the state officer who is the primary object of the sanction.... Two factors suggest that a sanction in addition to those that presently exist is unnecessary. First, the local law enforcement official is already "punished" by the exclusion of the evidence in the state criminal trial. That, necessarily, is of substantial concern to him. Second, the evidence is also excludable in the federal criminal trial so that the entire criminal enforcement process, which is the concern and duty of these officers, is frustrated.

Jurists and scholars uniformly have recognized that the exclusionary rule imposes a substantial cost on the societal interest in law enforcement by its proscription of what concededly is relevant evidence. And alternatives that would be less costly to societal interests have been the subject of extensive discussion and exploration. [If] the exclusionary rule is the "strong medicine" that its proponents claim it to be, then its use in the situations in which it is now applied (resulting, for example, in this case in frustration of the Los Angeles police officers' good-faith duties as enforcers of the criminal laws) must be assumed to be a substantial and efficient deterrent. Assuming this efficacy, the additional marginal deterrence provided by forbidding a different sovereign from using the evidence in a civil proceeding surely does not outweigh the cost to society of extending the rule to that situation. If, on the other hand, the exclusionary rule does not result in appreciable deterrence, then, clearly, its use in the instant situation is unwarranted....

In short, we conclude that exclusion from federal civil proceedings of evidence unlawfully seized by a state criminal enforcement officer has not been shown to have a sufficient likelihood of deterring the conduct of the state police so that it outweighs the societal costs imposed by the exclusion. This Court, therefore, is not justified in so extending the exclusionary rule.... [I]mposition of the exclusionary rule [in] this case is unlikely to provide significant, much less substantial, additional deterrence. It falls outside the offending officer's zone of primary interest. The extension of the exclusionary rule [would] be an unjustifiably drastic action by the courts in the pursuit of what is an undesired and undesirable supervisory role over police officers.

[In] the situation before us, we do not find sufficient justification for the drastic measure of an exclusionary rule. There comes a point at which courts, consistent with their duty to administer the law, cannot continue to create barriers to law enforcement in the pursuit of a supervisory role that is properly the duty of the Executive and Legislative Branches.... We therefore hold that the judicially created exclusionary rule should not be extended to forbid the use in the civil proceeding of one sovereign of evidence seized by a criminal law enforcement agent of another sovereign.

The judgment of the Court of Appeals is reversed, and the case is remanded for further proceedings consistent with this opinion.

It is so ordered.

MR. JUSTICE BRENNAN, with whom MR. JUSTICE MARSHALL concurs, dissenting.

[T]he exclusionary rule is a necessary and inherent constitutional ingredient of the protections of the Fourth Amendment....

MR. JUSTICE STEWART, dissenting.

[Federal] officials responsible for the enforcement of the wagering tax provisions regularly cooperate with federal and local officials responsible for enforcing criminal laws restricting or forbidding wagering. Similarly, federal and local law enforcement personnel regularly provide federal tax officials with information, obtained in criminal investigations, indicating liability under the wagering tax. The pattern is one of mutual cooperation and coordination, with the federal wagering tax provisions buttressing state and federal criminal sanctions. [If] state police officials can effectively crack down on gambling law violators by the simple expedient of violating their constitutional rights and turning the illegally seized evidence over to Internal Revenue Service agents on the proverbial "silver platter," then the deterrent purpose of the exclusionary rule is wholly frustrated. "If, on the other hand, it is understood that the fruit of an unlawful search by state agents will be inadmissible in a federal trial, there can be no inducement to subterfuge and evasion with respect to federal-state cooperation in criminal investigation." *Elkins v. United States, supra,* 364 U.S., at 222.

Notes

1. *Janis* was followed by the Court's decision in *Immigration and Naturalization Service v. Lopez–Mendoza*, 468 U.S. 1032 (1984), where the Court refused to apply the exclusionary rule in a deportation proceeding. The Court justified its decision as follows:

> The likely deterrence value of the exclusionary rule in deportation proceedings is difficult to assess. [O]nly a very small percentage of arrests of aliens are intended or expected to lead to criminal prosecutions. Thus the arresting officer's primary objective, in practice, will be to use evidence in the civil deportation proceeding. Moreover, here, in contrast to *Janis*, the agency officials who effect the unlawful arrest are the same officials who subsequently bring the deportation action. As recognized in *Janis*, the exclusionary rule is likely to be most effective when applied to such "intrasovereign" violations.

> Nonetheless, several other factors significantly reduce the likely deterrent value of the exclusionary rule in a civil deportation proceeding. First, [deportation] will still be possible when evidence not derived directly from the arrest is sufficient to support deportation. "[T]he sole matters necessary for the Government to establish are the respondent's identity and alienage—at which point the burden shifts to the respondent to prove the time, place and manner of entry." Since the person and identity of the respondent are not themselves suppressible, the INS must prove only alienage, and that will sometimes be possible using evidence gathered independently of, or sufficiently attenuated from, the original arrest. The INS's task is simplified in this regard by the civil nature of the proceeding. [There] is no provision which forbids drawing an adverse inference from the fact of standing mute. * * *

> The second factor is a practical one. In the course of a year the average INS agent arrests almost 500 illegal aliens. Over 97.5% apparently agree to voluntary deportation without a formal hearing. Among the [remainder] (a dozen or so in all, per officer, per year) very few challenge the circumstances of their arrests. [Every] INS agent knows, therefore, that it is highly unlikely that any particular arrestee will end up challenging the lawfulness of his arrest in a formal deportation proceeding. When an occasional challenge is brought, the consequences from the point of view of the officer's overall arrest and deportation record will be trivial. In these circumstances, the arresting officer is most unlikely to shape his conduct in anticipation of the exclusion of evidence at a formal deportation hearing.

> Third, and perhaps most important, the INS has its own comprehensive scheme for deterring Fourth Amendment violations by its officers. [T]he INS has developed rules restricting stop, interrogation, and arrest practices. These regulations require that no one be detained without reasonable suspicion of illegal alienage, and that no one be arrested unless there is an admission of illegal alienage or other strong evidence thereof. New immigration officers receive instruction and examination in Fourth Amendment law, and others receive periodic re-

fresher courses in law. Evidence seized through intentionally unlawful conduct is excluded by Department of Justice policy from the proceeding for which it was obtained. The INS also has in place a procedure for investigating and punishing immigration officers who commit Fourth Amendment violations. The INS's attention to Fourth Amendment interests cannot guarantee that constitutional violations will not occur, but it does reduce the likely deterrent value of the exclusionary rule. Deterrence must be measured at the margin.

Finally, the deterrent value of the exclusionary rule in deportation proceedings is undermined by the availability of alternative remedies for institutional practices by the INS that might violate Fourth Amendment rights. The INS is a single agency, under central federal control, and engaged in operations of broad scope but highly repetitive character. The possibility of declaratory relief against the agency thus offers a means for challenging the validity of INS practices, when standing requirements for bringing such an action can be met.

[On] the other side of the scale, the social costs of applying the exclusionary rule in deportation proceedings are both unusual and significant. The first cost is one that is unique to continuing violations of the law. Applying the exclusionary rule in proceedings that are intended not to punish past transgressions but to prevent their continuance or renewal would require the courts to close their eyes to ongoing violations of the law. This Court has never before accepted costs of this character in applying the exclusionary rule.

[Sandoval] is a person whose unregistered presence in this country, without more, constitutes a crime. His release within our borders would immediately subject him to criminal penalties. His release would clearly frustrate the express public policy against an alien's unregistered presence in this country. Even the objective of deterring Fourth Amendment violations should not require such a result. The constable's blunder may allow the criminal to go free, but we have never suggested that it allows the criminal to continue in the commission of an ongoing crime. * * *

Other factors also weigh against applying the exclusionary rule in deportation proceedings. The INS currently operates a deliberately simple deportation hearing system, streamlined to permit the quick resolution of very large numbers of deportation actions, and it is against this backdrop that the costs of the exclusionary must be assessed. The costs of applying the exclusionary rule, like the benefits, must be measured at the margin.

[Finally], the INS advances the credible argument that applying the exclusionary rule to deportation proceedings might well result in the suppression of large amounts of information that had been obtained entirely lawfully. INS arrests occur in crowded and confused circumstances. Though the INS agents are instructed to follow procedures that adequately protect Fourth Amendment interests, agents will usually be able to testify only to the fact that they followed INS rules. [In] these circumstances we are persuaded that the *Janis* balance between costs and benefits comes out against applying the exclusionary rule in civil deportation hearings held by the INS. * * *

There were three dissents. Justice Brennan argued that "[the] Government [has] an obligation to obey the Fourth Amendment; that obligation is not lifted simply because [the evidence] was to be used in civil deportation proceedings." Justice White took the position that: "Because INS agents are law enforcement officials whose mission is closely analogous to that of police officers and because civil deportation proceedings are to INS agents what criminal trials are to police officers, [the] costs and benefits of applying the exclusionary rule in civil deportation proceedings do not differ in any significant way from the costs and benefits of applying the rule in ordinary criminal proceedings." Justice Marshall pointed out that: "[T]here is no other way [than exclusion] to achieve 'the twin goals of enabling the judiciary to avoid the taint of partnership in official lawlessness and of assuring the people—all potential victims of unlawful government conduct— that the government would not profit from its lawless behavior, thus minimizing the risk of seriously undermining popular trust in government.' "

2. *Should the Exclusionary Rule Apply in Grand Jury Proceedings?* In *United States v. Calandra*, 414 U.S. 338 (1974), the Court refused to apply the exclusionary rule to a witness summoned to appear and testify before a grand jury who refused to answer questions on the ground that they were based on evidence obtained from an unlawful search and seizure. The Court justified its decision as follows:

> [T]his extension of the exclusionary rule would seriously impede the grand jury. Because the grand jury does not finally adjudicate guilt or innocence, it has traditionally been allowed to pursue its investigative and accusatorial functions unimpeded by the evidentiary and procedural restrictions applicable to a criminal trial. [Any] incremental deterrent effect which might be achieved by extending the rule to grand jury proceedings is uncertain at best. [Such] an extension would deter only police investigation consciously directed toward the discovery of evidence solely for use in a grand jury investigation. The incentive to disregard the requirement of the Fourth Amendment solely to obtain an indictment from a grand jury is substantially negated by the inadmissibility of the illegally seized evidence in a subsequent criminal prosecution of the search victim. [A] prosecutor would be unlikely to request an indictment where a conviction could not be obtained. * * *

Justice Brennan dissented: "[T]he exclusionary rule is 'an essential part of both the Fourth and Fourteenth Amendments,' that 'gives to the individual no more than that which the Constitution guarantees him, to the police officer no less than that to which honest law enforcement is entitled, and, to the courts, that judicial integrity so necessary in the true administration of justice.' "

Problems

1. *Might the Exclusionary Rule Apply in Other Civil Contexts?* Does *Janis* suggest that the exclusionary rule should *never* be applied in administrative proceedings? Suppose that the *Janis* search had been conducted by IRS investigators rather than by the police. Would the Court's "cost-benefit"

analysis require exclusion of the evidence? Suppose that IRS investigators enter Grace Harlow's home in hopes of finding evidence of illegal gambling. The police, acting without a warrant even though one is required, enter without knocking. When Harlow confronts the investigators, they beat and restrain her. Ultimately, the investigators uncover evidence of illegal gambling and seek to use that evidence against Harlow in a civil tax proceeding. If you are hired to represent Harlow, how can you distinguish *Janis* and *Lopez–Mendoza* and argue that the exclusionary rule should be applied to Harlow's case? How might the IRS respond to those arguments? In light of *Lopez–Mendoza*, is the Court likely to apply the exclusionary rule in administrative proceedings? When will the "benefits" of the exclusionary rule outweigh the "costs" in a way that justifies application of the exclusionary rule in an administrative proceeding?

2. *Cooperative Investigations*. Commonly, the police and the IRS work together on criminal investigations. Suppose that Janis could produce proof that the police and the IRS were working together in investigating him? Under such circumstances, should the Court apply the exclusionary rule? Would it matter whether the IRS was actually involved, or helped plan, the illegal search?

3. *Evaluating Calandra*. Do you agree with *Calandra's* conclusion that a prosecutor would have no incentive to seek an indictment based on evidence that could not be admitted at trial? Suppose that the prosecutor believes that defendant is part of a conspiracy to commit bank robberies, and uses the illegal evidence to indict one of the conspirators. What advantage might the prosecutor gain from the indictment?

D. THE SCOPE OF THE EXCLUSIONARY RULES

The exclusionary rule is subject to various rules and doctrines that expand or limit the scope of the rule.

1. Standing

Standing concepts also limit the exclusionary rule's application. In the Fifth Amendment area, the Court treats the privilege against self-incrimination as "personal" and has held that it can only be asserted by the person whose rights have been violated. This limitation is seemingly implicit in the Fifth Amendment itself which states that "no person shall be [compelled] in any criminal case to be a witness against himself." U.S. Constitution, Amendment V. As the Court stated in *Hale v. Henkel*, 201 U.S. 43 (1906): "[The] right of a person under the 5th Amendment to refuse to incriminate himself is purely a personal privilege of the witness. It was never intended to permit him to plead the fact that some third person might be incriminated by his testimony, even though he were the agent of such person. A privilege so extensive might be used to put a stop to the examination of every witness who was called upon to testify before the grand jury with regard to the doings or business of his principal, whether such principal were an individual or a corporation."

Even though the Fourth Amendment is not phrased in such personal terms, the Court has also applied the standing requirement to Fourth

Amendment violations. In *Alderman v. United States*, 394 U.S. 165 (1969), the Court stated:

> Fourth Amendment rights are personal rights which, like some other constitutional rights, may not be vicariously asserted.... No rights of the victim of an illegal search are at stake when the evidence is offered against some other party. The victim can and very probably will object for himself when and if it becomes important for him to do so. [If] the police make an unwarranted search of a house and seize tangible property belonging to third parties—even a transcript of a third-party conversation—the homeowner may object to its use against him, not because he had any interest in the seized items as "effects" protected by the Fourth Amendment, but because they were the fruits of an unauthorized search of his house, which is itself expressly protected by the Fourth Amendment. Nothing seen or found on the premises may legally form the basis for an arrest or search warrant or for testimony at the homeowner's trial, since the prosecution would be using the fruits of a Fourth Amendment violation.

However, for a period, the standing requirement was modified by an "automatic standing" rule articulated in *Jones v. United States*, 362 U.S. 257 (1960). Jones, who was prosecuted for crimes involving the possession of narcotics, moved to suppress evidence obtained via a search warrant on the basis that the warrant had been issued without probable cause. The judge denied the motion for lack of standing, and the Supreme Court reversed:

> [Since] narcotics charges [may] be established through proof solely of possession of narcotics, a defendant seeking to comply with [the] conventional standing requirement has been forced to allege facts the proof of which would tend, if indeed not be sufficient, to convict him. [He] has been faced, not only with the chance that the allegations made on the motion to suppress may be used against him at the trial, [but] also with the encouragement that he perjure himself if he seeks to establish "standing" while maintaining a defense to the charge of possession.

> [Petitioner's] conviction flows from his possession of the narcotics at the time of the search. Yet the fruits of that search, upon which the conviction depends, were admitted into evidence on the ground that petitioner did not have possession of the narcotics at that time. The prosecution here thus subjected the defendant to the penalties meted out to one in lawless possession while refusing him the remedies designed for one in that situation. It is not consonant with the amenities [of] the administration of criminal justice to sanction such squarely contradictory assertions of power by the Government. The possession on the basis of which petitioner is to be and was convicted suffices to give him standing under any fair and rational conception of the requirements of Rule 41(e).

RAKAS v. ILLINOIS

439 U.S. 128 (1978).

MR. JUSTICE REHNQUIST delivered the opinion of the Court.

[A] police officer on a routine patrol received a radio call notifying him of a robbery of a clothing store [and] describing the getaway car. Shortly thereafter, the officer spotted an automobile which he thought might be the getaway car. After following the car for some time[,] he and several other officers stopped the vehicle. The occupants of the automobile, petitioners and two female companions, were ordered out of the car and [two] officers searched the interior of the vehicle. They discovered a box of rifle shells in the glove compartment, which had been locked, and a sawed-off rifle under the front passenger seat. After discovering the rifle and the shells, the officers [placed petitioners] under arrest.

[P]etitioners moved to suppress the rifle and shells [on] the ground that the search violated the Fourth and Fourteenth Amendments. They conceded that they did not own the automobile and were simply passengers; the owner of the car had been the driver of the vehicle at the time of the search. Nor did they assert that they owned the rifle or the shells seized. The prosecutor challenged petitioners' standing to object to the lawfulness of the search of the car.... The trial court [held] that petitioners lacked standing and denied the motion to suppress the evidence. [Petitioners were convicted and the conviction was affirmed.]

Petitioners [urge] us to relax or broaden the rule of standing enunciated in *Jones v. United States*, 362 U.S. 257 (1960), so that any criminal defendant at whom a search was "directed" would have standing to contest the legality of that search and object to the admission [of] evidence obtained as a result of the search. Alternatively, petitioners argue that they have standing to object to the search under *Jones* because they were "legitimately on [the] premises" at the time of the search.

[*Jones*] focuses on whether the person seeking to challenge the legality of a search [was] himself the "victim" of the search or seizure. Adoption of the so-called "target" theory advanced by petitioners would in effect permit a defendant to assert that a violation of the Fourth Amendment rights of a third party entitled him to have evidence suppressed at his trial. [We] decline to extend the rule of standing [in] the manner suggested by petitioners. As we stated in *Alderman v. United States*, 394 U.S. 165, 174 (1969), "Fourth Amendment rights are personal rights which, like some other constitutional rights, may not be vicariously asserted." A person who is aggrieved by an illegal search and seizure only through the introduction of damaging evidence secured by a search of a third person's premises or property has not had any of his Fourth Amendment rights infringed. [S]ince the exclusionary rule is an attempt to effectuate the guarantees of the Fourth Amendment, it is proper to permit only defendants whose Fourth Amendment rights have been violated to benefit from the rule's protections. There is no reason to think that a party whose rights have been infringed will not, if evidence is used against him, have ample motivation to move to suppress it. Even if such a person is not a defendant in the action, he may be able to recover damages for the violation of his Fourth Amendment rights, or seek redress under state law for invasion of privacy or trespass.

In support of their target theory, petitioners rely on the following quotation from *Jones*: "In order to qualify as a 'person aggrieved by an unlawful search and seizure' one must have been a victim of a search or seizure, one against whom the search was directed, as distinguished from one who claims prejudice only through the use of evidence gathered as a consequence of a search or seizure directed at someone else." [This] statement from *Jones* suggests that [the] language was meant merely as a parenthetical equivalent of the previous phrase "a victim of a search or seizure." To the extent that the language might be read more broadly, it is dictum which was impliedly repudiated in *Alderman* and which we now expressly reject. In *Alderman*, Mr. Justice Fortas [argued] that the Court should "include within the category of those who may object to the introduction of illegal evidence 'one against whom the search was directed.' "The Court [rejected] this theory [holding] that persons who were not parties to unlawfully overheard conversations or who did not own the premises on which such conversations took place did not have standing to contest the legality of the surveillance, regardless of whether or not they were the "targets" of the surveillance. Mr. Justice Harlan ... identified administrative problems posed by the target theory: "[T]he [target] rule would entail very substantial administrative difficulties. In the majority of cases, [the] police plant a bug with the expectation that it may well produce leads to a large number of crimes. A lengthy hearing would then [be] necessary in order to determine whether the police knew of an accused's criminal activity at the time the bug was planted and whether the police decision to plant a bug was motivated by an effort to obtain information against the accused or some other individual. I do not believe that this administrative burden is justified in any substantial degree by the hypothesized marginal increase in Fourth Amendment protection." [We] cannot but give weight to practical difficulties such as those foreseen by Mr. Justice Harlan in the quoted language.

Conferring standing to raise vicarious Fourth Amendment claims would necessarily mean a more widespread invocation of the exclusionary rule during criminal trials. The Court's opinion in *Alderman* counseled against such an extension of the exclusionary rule: "The deterrent values of preventing the incrimination of those whose rights the police have violated have been considered sufficient to justify the suppression of probative evidence even though the case against the defendant is weakened or destroyed. We adhere to that judgment. But we are not convinced that the additional benefits of extending the exclusionary rule to other defendants would justify further encroachment upon the public interest in prosecuting those accused of crime and having them acquitted

or convicted on the basis of all the evidence which exposes the truth."
Each time the exclusionary rule is applied it exacts a substantial social
cost for the vindication of Fourth Amendment rights. Relevant and
reliable evidence is kept from the trier of fact and the search for truth at
trial is deflected. Since our cases generally have held that one whose
Fourth Amendment rights are violated may successfully suppress evidence obtained in the course of an illegal search and seizure, misgivings
as to the benefit of enlarging the class of persons who may invoke that
rule are properly considered when deciding whether to expand standing
to assert Fourth Amendment violations.

[We] can think of no decided cases [that] would have come out
differently had we concluded, as we do now, that the type of standing
requirement discussed in *Jones* and reaffirmed today is more properly
subsumed under substantive Fourth Amendment doctrine. [We] think
the better analysis forthrightly focuses on the extent of a particular
defendant's rights under the Fourth Amendment, rather than on any
theoretically separate, but invariably intertwined concept of standing.
* * *

[T]he issue of standing involves two inquiries: first, whether the
proponent of a particular legal right has alleged "injury in fact," and,
second, whether the proponent is asserting his own legal rights and
interests rather than basing his claim for relief upon the rights of third
parties. [T]he question is whether the challenged search or seizure
violated the Fourth Amendment rights of a criminal defendant who
seeks to exclude the evidence obtained during it. That inquiry in turn
requires a determination of whether the disputed search and seizure has
infringed an interest of the defendant which the Fourth Amendment was
designed to protect. We are under no illusion that by dispensing with the
rubric of standing used in *Jones* we have rendered any simpler the
determination of whether the proponent of a motion to suppress is
entitled to contest the legality of a search and seizure. But [we] think the
decision of this issue will rest on sounder logical footing.

Here petitioners, who were passengers occupying a car which they
neither owned nor leased, seek to analogize their position to that of the
defendant in *Jones*. In *Jones*, petitioner was present at the time of the
search of an apartment which was owned by a friend. The friend had
given Jones permission to use the apartment and a key to it, with which
Jones had admitted himself on the day of the search. He had a suit and
shirt at the apartment and had slept there "maybe a night," but his
home was elsewhere. At the time of the search, Jones was the only
occupant of the apartment because the lessee was away for a period of
several days. Under these circumstances, this Court stated that while
one wrongfully on the premises could not move to suppress evidence
obtained as a result of searching them, "anyone legitimately on premises
where a search occurs may challenge its legality." Petitioners argue that
their occupancy of the automobile in question was comparable to that of
Jones in the apartment and that they therefore have standing to contest
the legality of the search—or as we have rephrased the inquiry, that

they, like Jones, had their Fourth Amendment rights violated by the search.

We do not question the conclusion in *Jones*.... Nonetheless, we believe that the phrase "legitimately on premises" coined in *Jones* creates too broad a gauge for measurement of Fourth Amendment rights. [A]pplied literally, this statement would permit a casual visitor who has never seen, or been permitted to visit, the basement of another's house to object to a search of the basement if the visitor happened to be in the kitchen of the house at the time of the search. Likewise, a casual visitor who walks into a house one minute before a search of the house commences and leaves one minute after the search ends would be able to contest the legality of the search. The first visitor would have absolutely no interest or legitimate expectation of privacy in the basement, the second would have none in the house, and it advances no purpose served by the Fourth Amendment to permit either of them to object to the lawfulness of the search.

We think that *Jones* [stands] for the unremarkable proposition that a person can have a legally sufficient interest in a place other than his own home so that the Fourth Amendment protects him from unreasonable governmental intrusion into that place. In defining the scope of that interest, [arcane] distinctions developed in property and tort law between guests, licensees, invitees, and the like, ought not to control. But the *Jones* statement that a person need only be "legitimately on premises" in order to challenge the validity of the search of a dwelling place cannot be taken in its full sweep beyond the facts of that case.

[*Katz*] held that capacity to claim the protection of the Fourth Amendment depends not upon a property right in the invaded place but upon whether the person who claims the protection of the Amendment has a legitimate expectation of privacy in the invaded place.... *Jones* can best be explained by the fact that Jones had a legitimate expectation of privacy in the premises he was using and therefore could claim the protection of the Fourth Amendment with respect to a governmental invasion of those premises, even though his "interest" in those premises might not have been a recognized property interest at common law.[10]

10. [A] "legitimate" expectation of privacy by definition means more than a subjective expectation of not being discovered. A burglar plying his trade in a summer cabin [may] have [a] subjective expectation of privacy, but it is not one which the law recognizes as "legitimate." [Legitimate] expectations [must] have a source outside of the Fourth Amendment, either by reference to concepts of real or personal property law or to understandings that are recognized and permitted by society. [Expectations] of privacy [need] not be based on a common-law interest in real or personal property, or on the invasion of such an interest. [But] the Court has not altogether abandoned use of property concepts in determining the presence or absence of the privacy interests protected by that Amendment. [I]n *Alderman*, [the] Court held that an individual's property interest in his own home was so great as to allow him to object to electronic surveillance of conversations emanating from his home, even though he himself was not a party to the conversations. On the other hand, even a property interest in premises may not be sufficient to establish a legitimate expectation of privacy with respect to particular items located on the premises or activity conducted thereon.

[In] abandoning "legitimately on premises" for the doctrine that we announce today, [we] are rejecting blind adherence to a phrase which at most has superficial clarity and which conceals underneath that thin veneer all of the problems of line drawing which must be faced in any conscientious effort to apply the Fourth Amendment. [We] would not wish to be understood as saying that legitimate presence on the premises is irrelevant to one's expectation of privacy, but it cannot be deemed controlling.

Judged by [this] analysis, petitioners' claims must fail. They asserted neither a property nor a possessory interest in the automobile, nor an interest in the property seized. [The] fact that they were "legitimately on [the] premises" in the sense that they were in the car with the permission of its owner is not determinative of whether they had a legitimate expectation of privacy in the particular areas of the automobile searched. It is unnecessary [to] decide here whether the same expectations of privacy are warranted in a car [as] in a dwelling place in analogous circumstances. [P]etitioners' claim is one which would fail even in an analogous situation in a dwelling place, since they made no showing that they had any legitimate expectation of privacy in the glove compartment or area under the seat of the car in which they were merely passengers. Like the trunk of an automobile, these are areas in which a passenger qua passenger [would] not normally have a legitimate expectation of privacy.

Jones and *Katz* involved significantly different factual circumstances. Jones not only had permission to use the apartment of his friend, but also had a key to the apartment with which he admitted himself on the day of the search and kept possessions in the apartment. Except with respect to his friend, Jones had complete dominion and control over the apartment and could exclude others from it. Likewise in *Katz*, the defendant occupied the telephone booth, shut the door behind him to exclude all others and paid the toll, which "entitled [him] to assume that the words he utter[ed] into the mouthpiece [would] not be broadcast to the world." Katz and Jones could legitimately expect privacy in the areas which were the subject of the search and seizure each sought to contest. No such showing was made [by] petitioners with respect to those portions of the automobile which were [searched].[11]

The Illinois courts were therefore correct in concluding that it was unnecessary to decide whether the search of the car might have violated the rights secured to someone else by the Fourth and Fourteenth Amendments to the United States Constitution. Since it did not violate any rights of these petitioners, their judgment of conviction is

Affirmed.

11. [O]ur dissenting Brethren repeatedly criticize our "holding" that unless one has a common-law property interest in the premises searched, one cannot object to the search. . . . To the contrary, we have taken pains to reaffirm the statements in *Jones* and *Katz* that "arcane distinctions developed in property [law] ought not to control." * * *

MR. JUSTICE POWELL, with whom THE CHIEF JUSTICE joins, concurring.

[None] of the passengers is said to have had control of the vehicle or the keys. It is unrealistic—as the shared experience of us all bears witness—to suggest that these passengers had any reasonable expectation that the car in which they had been riding would not be searched after they were lawfully stopped and made to get out. The minimal privacy that existed simply is not comparable to that, for example, of an individual in his place of abode * * *.

MR. JUSTICE WHITE, with whom MR. JUSTICE BRENNAN, MR. JUSTICE MARSHALL, and MR. JUSTICE STEVENS join, dissenting.

[W]hen a person is legitimately present in a private place, his right to privacy is protected from unreasonable governmental interference even if he does not own the premises. [An] expectation of privacy does not hinge on [ownership]. In *Alderman*, Mr. Justice Harlan, concurring in part and dissenting in part, noted that "our own past decisions [have] decisively rejected the notion that the accused must necessarily have a possessory interest in the premises before he may assert a Fourth Amendment claim." * * *

[S]urely a person riding in an automobile next to his friend the owner, or a child or wife with the father or spouse, must have some [protection]. [If] a nonowner may consent to a search merely because he is a joint user or occupant of a "premises," then that same nonowner must have a protected privacy interest. The scope of the authority sufficient to grant a valid consent can hardly be broader than the contours of protected privacy. And why should the owner of a vehicle be entitled to challenge the seizure from it of evidence even if he is absent at the time of the search while a nonowner enjoying in person, and with the owner's permission, the privacy of an automobile is not so entitled?

[T]he Court asserts that it is not limiting [the] bar against unreasonable searches to the protection of property rights, but in reality it is doing exactly that.[12] Petitioners were in a private place with the permission of the [owner]. [I]f that is not sufficient, what would be? [I]t is hard to imagine anything short of a property interest that would satisfy the majority. Insofar as the Court's rationale is concerned, no passenger in an automobile, without an ownership or possessory interest and regardless of his relationship to the owner, may claim Fourth Amendment protection against illegal stops and searches of the automobile in which he is rightfully present. The Court approves the result in *Jones*, but it fails to give any explanation why the facts in *Jones* differ, in a fashion

---

12. The Court's reliance on property law concepts is additionally shown by its suggestion that visitors could "contest the lawfulness of the seizure of evidence or the search if their own property were seized during the search." What difference should that property interest make to constitutional protection against unreasonable searches, which is concerned with privacy? [A] passenger in a car expects to enjoy the privacy of the vehicle whether or not he happens to carry some item along for the ride. We have never before limited our concern for a person's privacy to those situations in which he is in possession of personal property. Even a person living in a barren room without possessions is entitled to expect that the police will not intrude without cause.

material to the Fourth Amendment, from the facts here.[13] More importantly, how is the Court able to avoid answering the question why presence in a private place with the owner's permission is insufficient? * * *

As a control on governmental power, the Fourth Amendment assures that some expectations of privacy are justified and will be protected from official intrusion. [If] protected zones of privacy can only be purchased or obtained by possession of property, then much of our daily lives will be unshielded from unreasonable governmental prying, and the reach of the Fourth Amendment will have been narrowed to protect chiefly those with possessory interests in real or personal property. [Katz] firmly established that the Fourth Amendment was intended as more than simply a trespass law applicable to the government. Katz had no possessory interest in the public telephone booth, at least no more than petitioners had in their friend's car; Katz was simply legitimately present. And the decision in Katz was based not on property rights, but on the theory that it was essential to securing "conditions favorable to the pursuit of happiness" that the expectation of privacy in question be recognized. [O]ne could say that perhaps the Constitution provides some degree less protection for the personal freedom from unreasonable governmental intrusion when one does not have a possessory interest in the invaded private place. But that would only change the extent of the protection; it would not free police to do the unreasonable. * * *

The Court's holding is contrary [to] the everyday expectations of privacy that we all share. [If] the owner of the car had not only invited petitioners to join her but had said to them, "I give you a temporary possessory interest in my vehicle so that you will share the right to privacy that [I] own," then apparently the majority would reverse. But people seldom say such things, though they may mean their invitation to encompass them if only they had thought of the problem. If the nonowner were the spouse or child of the owner, would the Court recognize a sufficient interest? If so, would distant relatives somehow have more of an expectation of privacy than close friends? What if the nonowner were driving with the owner's permission? [Katz] expressly recognized protection for such passengers. Why should Fourth Amendment rights be present when one pays a cabdriver for a ride but be absent when one is given a ride by a friend?

[This] decision invites police to engage in patently unreasonable searches every time an automobile contains more than one occupant.

13. Jones had permission to use the apartment, had slept in it one night, had a key, had left a suit and a shirt there, and was the only occupant at the time of the search. Petitioners here had permission to be in the car and were occupying it at the time of the search. Thus the only distinguishing fact is that Jones could exclude others from the apartment by using his friend's key. But petitioners and their friend the owner had excluded others by entering the automobile and shutting the doors. Petitioners did not need a key because the owner was present. Similarly, the Court attempts to distinguish Katz on the theory that Katz had "shut the door behind him to exclude all others," but petitioners here did exactly the same. The car doors remained closed until the police ordered them opened at gunpoint.

Should something be found, only the owner of the vehicle, or of the item, will have standing to seek suppression, and the evidence will presumably be usable against the other occupants. The danger of such bad faith is especially high in cases [where] the officers are only after the [passengers]. . . .

Note

1. *Automatic Standing after Rakas?* The concept of "automatic standing," first articulated in *Jones*, did not survive long after the *Rakas* decision. The Court laid the groundwork for the rule's demise in *Simmons v. United States*, 390 U.S. 377 (1968), a case in which petitioner was arrested for armed robbery based on an illegal search of a house. Petitioner testified that he thought he was the owner of the seized items. Using a self-incrimination analysis, the Court held that petitioner's testimony could not be used against him: "[w]hen a defendant testifies in support of a motion to suppress evidence on Fourth Amendment grounds, his testimony may not [be] admitted against him at trial on the issue of guilt unless he makes no objection." *But see United States v. Kahan*, 415 U.S. 239 (1974) (Court refused to apply *Simmons* to a prosecution for perjury: "*Simmons* barred the use of pretrial testimony at trial to prove its incriminating content. Here, by contrast, the incriminating component of respondent's pretrial statements derives not from their content, but from respondent's knowledge of their falsity.").

2. Following *Simmons* and *Rakas*, the Court reconsidered *Jones'* automatic standing rule in *United States v. Salvucci*, 448 U.S. 83 (1980): "[D]efendants charged with crimes of possession may only claim the benefits of the exclusionary rule if their own Fourth Amendment rights have in fact been violated. The automatic standing rule of *Jones* is therefore overruled. [The] 'dilemma' identified in *Jones*, that a defendant charged with a possessory offense might only be able to establish his standing to challenge a search and seizure by giving self-incriminating testimony admissible as evidence of his guilt, was eliminated by our decision in *Simmons*. [*Simmons*] grants a form of 'use immunity' to those defendants charged with nonpossessory crimes. [We] decline to use possession of a seized good as a substitute for a factual finding that the owner of the good had a legitimate expectation of privacy in the area searched." Justice Marshall dissented: "[*Simmons* does not provide] complete protection against the 'self-incrimination dilemma.' [The] use of the testimony for impeachment purposes would subject a defendant to precisely the same dilemma, unless he was prepared to relinquish his constitutional right to testify in his own defense, and would thereby create a strong deterrent to asserting Fourth Amendment claims. One of the purposes of *Jones* and *Simmons* was to remove such obstacles. Moreover, the opportunity for cross-examination at the suppression hearing may enable the prosecutor to elicit incriminating information beyond that offered on direct examination to establish the requisite Fourth Amendment interest. Even if such information could not be introduced at the subsequent trial, it might be helpful to the prosecution in developing its case or deciding its trial strategy. The furnishing of such a tactical advantage to the prosecution should not be the price of asserting a Fourth Amendment claim."

Problems

1. *Evaluating Rakas.* Does Rakas use any standard other than property principles to define the expectation of privacy test? If so, what are those principles?

2. *Standing—The Fortas Position.* Consider Justice Fortas' opinion, concurring in part and dissenting in part, in *Alderman*:

> [In] recognition of the principle that lawlessness on the part of the Government must be stoutly condemned, this Court has ruled that [the] Government may not profit from its fruits. [F]or reasons which [are] related more to convenience and judicial prudence than to constitutional principles, courts of all states except California and of the federal system [have] allowed in evidence material obtained by police agents in direct and acknowledged violation of the Fourth Amendment. They have allowed this evidence except [where] a defendant who moves for suppression of the material can show that his personal right of privacy was violated by the unlawful search or seizure. [I]f the exclusionary rule follows from the Fourth Amendment itself, there is no basis for confining its invocation to persons whose right of privacy has been violated by an illegal search. The Fourth Amendment [is] couched in terms of a guarantee that the Government will not engage in unreasonable searches and seizures. It is a general prohibition, a fundamental part of the constitutional compact, the observance of which is essential to the welfare of all persons. Accordingly, [the] necessary implication [is] that any defendant against whom illegally acquired evidence is offered, whether or not it was obtained in violation of his right to privacy, may have the evidence excluded. [The] Fourth Amendment [is] an assurance to all that the Government will exercise its formidable powers to arrest and to investigate only subject to the rule of law.

Do you agree with Justice Fortas?

3. *Katz and Rakas.* Does *Rakas* apply the "expectation of privacy" test in the same manner as *Katz*? If not, how do you explain the difference in application?

4. In *Rakas*, Justice White asks whether the Court would have reached the opposite result (in other words, it would have found that "standing" existed), had the passengers been related to the driver. Suppose that you were hired to represent the driver's teenage son. Following a search of the car, the police found illegal drugs under the seat (rather than a shotgun). Would the son have standing to challenge the search? In light of the *Rakas* decision, how would you argue the case on his behalf?

5. *More on Passenger Standing.* In *Rakas*, the police also found shotgun shells in the glove compartment. Would a passenger have standing to challenge the search if the glove compartment were locked, and he was in possession of the key? Would it matter whether the owner/driver also had a key? If you were a prosecutor, how would you argue that the passenger does not have standing under these circumstances? How would you expect the defense to respond?

6. *Challenging the Stop.* Would the result in *Rakas* have been different if, instead of challenging the search, the passengers had claimed that the police illegally stopped the car in which they were riding? How might Rakas have argued that he has standing to challenge the illegal stop? Would his standing to challenge the stop also give him standing to challenge the subsequent search?

7. *Standing in an Internet Age.* The police believe that defendant is transmitting child pornography. In an effort to catch defendant, the police obtain a warrant to search Google's computer records regarding defendant's internet search requests. When the Google search uncovers information that incriminates defendant, defendant moves to suppress on the basis that the Google search was a "fishing expedition" that was not justified based on probable cause. Does defendant have standing to challenge the Google search?

MINNESOTA v. OLSON

495 U.S. 91 (1990).

JUSTICE WHITE delivered the opinion of the Court.

[Shortly] before 6 a.m. on Saturday, July 18, 1987, a lone gunman robbed an Amoco gasoline station in Minneapolis, Minnesota, and fatally shot the station manager. A police officer heard the police dispatcher report and suspected Joseph Ecker. The officer and his partner drove immediately to Ecker's home, arriving at about the same time that an Oldsmobile arrived. The driver of the Oldsmobile took evasive action, and the car spun out of control and came to a stop. Two men fled the car on foot. Ecker, who was later identified as the gunman, was captured shortly thereafter inside his home. The second man escaped.

Inside the abandoned Oldsmobile, police found a sack of money and the murder weapon. They also found a title certificate with the name Rob Olson crossed out as a secured party, a letter addressed to a Roger R. Olson of 3151 Johnson Street, and a videotape rental receipt made out to Rob Olson and dated two days earlier. The police verified that a Robert Olson lived at 3151 Johnson Street.

The next morning, Sunday, July 19, a woman identifying herself as Dianna Murphy called the police and said that a man by the name of Rob drove the car in which the gas station killer left the scene and that Rob was planning to leave town by bus. About noon, the same woman called again, gave her address and phone number, and said that a man named Rob had told a Maria and two other women, Louanne and Julie, that he was the driver in the Amoco robbery. The caller stated that Louanne was Julie's mother and that the two women lived at 2406 Fillmore Northeast. [Police officers were sent] to 2406 Fillmore to check out Louanne and Julie. When police arrived they determined that the dwelling was a duplex and that Louanne Bergstrom and her daughter Julie lived in the upper unit but were not home. Police spoke to Louanne's mother, Helen Niederhoffer, who lived in the lower unit. She confirmed that a Rob

Olson had been staying upstairs but was not then in the unit. She promised to call the police when Olson returned. At 2 p.m., [a] "probable cause arrest bulletin," was issued for Olson's arrest. The police were instructed to stay away from the duplex.

At approximately 2:45 p.m., Niederhoffer called police and said Olson had returned. The detective-in-charge instructed police officers to go to the house and surround it. He then telephoned Julie from headquarters and told her Rob should come out of the house. The detective heard a male voice say, "tell them I left." Julie stated that Rob had left, whereupon at 3 p.m. the detective ordered the police to enter the house. Without seeking permission and with weapons drawn, the police entered the upper unit and found respondent hiding in a closet. Less than an hour after his arrest, respondent made an inculpatory statement at police headquarters.

[The] trial court [denied] respondent's motion to suppress his statement [which] was admitted into evidence [and Olson] was convicted on one count of first-degree murder, three counts of armed robbery, and three counts of second-degree assault. [T]he Minnesota Supreme Court reversed [holding] that respondent had a sufficient interest in the Bergstrom home to challenge the legality of his warrantless arrest there, that the arrest was illegal because there were no exigent circumstances to justify a warrantless entry, and that respondent's statement was tainted by that illegality and should have been suppressed. [We] granted the State's petition for certiorari and now affirm.

It was held in *Payton v. New York*, 445 U.S. 573 (1980), that a suspect should not be arrested in his house without an arrest warrant, even though there is probable cause to arrest him. The purpose of the decision was not to protect the person of the suspect but to protect his home from entry in the absence of a magistrate's finding of probable cause. [The] State argues that Olson's relationship to the premises does not satisfy the 12 factors which in its view determine whether a dwelling is a "home." Aside from the fact that it is based on the mistaken premise that a place must be one's "home" in order for one to have a legitimate expectation of privacy there, the State's proposed test is needlessly complex. We need go no further than to conclude [that] Olson's status as an overnight guest is alone enough to show that he had an expectation of privacy in the home that society is prepared to recognize as reasonable.

[T]he facts of this case are similar to those in *Jones v. United States*, 362 U.S. 257 (1960). In *Jones*, the defendant was arrested in a friend's apartment during the execution of a search warrant and sought to challenge the warrant as not supported by probable cause. "[Jones] testified that the apartment belonged to a friend, Evans, who had given him the use of it, and a key, with which [Jones] had admitted himself on the day of the arrest. [Jones] testified that he had a suit and shirt at the apartment, that his home was elsewhere, that he paid nothing for the use of the apartment, that Evans had let him use it 'as a friend,' that he had slept there 'maybe a night,' and that at the time of the search Evans had been away in Philadelphia for about five days."[14]

The Court ruled that Jones could challenge the search of the apartment because he was "legitimately on [the] premises." Although the "legitimately on [the] premises" standard was rejected in *Rakas* as too broad, [*Rakas*] explicitly reaffirmed the factual holding in [*Jones*]. *Rakas* thus recognized that, as an overnight guest, Jones was much more than just legitimately on the premises.

The distinctions relied on by the State between this case and *Jones* are not legally determinative. The State emphasizes that in this case Olson was never left alone in the duplex or given a key, whereas in Jones the owner of the apartment was away and Jones had a key with which he could come and go and admit and exclude others.... We do not understand *Rakas* [to] hold that an overnight guest can never have a legitimate expectation of privacy except when his host is away and he has a key.... To hold that an overnight guest has a legitimate expectation of privacy in his host's home merely recognizes the everyday expectations of privacy that we all share. Staying overnight in another's home is a longstanding social custom that serves functions recognized as valuable by society. [S]ociety recognizes that a houseguest has a legitimate expectation of privacy in his host's home.

From the overnight guest's perspective, he seeks shelter in another's home precisely because it provides him with privacy, a place where he and his possessions will not be disturbed by anyone but his host and those his host allows inside. We are at our most vulnerable when we are asleep because we cannot monitor our own safety or the security of our belongings. It is for this reason that, although we may spend all day in public places, when we cannot sleep in our own home we seek out another private place to sleep, whether it be a hotel room, or the home of a friend. Society expects at least as much privacy in these places as in a telephone booth—"a temporarily private place whose momentary occupants' expectations of freedom from intrusion are recognized as reasonable," *Katz*, 389 U.S., at 361 (Harlan, J., concurring).

That the guest has a host who has ultimate control of the house is not inconsistent with the guest having a legitimate expectation of privacy. The houseguest is there with the permission of his host, who is willing to share his house and his privacy with his guest. It is unlikely that the guest will be confined to a restricted area of the house; and when the host is away or asleep, the guest will have a measure of control over the premises. The host may admit or exclude from the house as he prefers, but it is unlikely that he will admit someone who wants to see or meet with the guest over the objection of the guest. On the other hand, few houseguests will invite others to visit them while they are guests without consulting their hosts; but the latter, who have the authority to

---

14. Olson, who had been staying at Ecker's home for several days before the robbery, spent the night of the robbery on the floor of the Bergstroms' home, with their permission. He had a change of clothes with him at the duplex.

exclude despite the wishes of the guest, will often be accommodating. The point is that hosts will more likely than not respect the privacy interests of their guests, who are entitled to a legitimate expectation of privacy despite the fact that they have no legal interest in the premises and do not have the legal authority to determine who may or may not enter the household. If the untrammeled power to admit and exclude were essential to Fourth Amendment protection, an adult daughter temporarily living in the home of her parents would have no legitimate expectation of privacy because her right to admit or exclude would be subject to her parents' veto.

Because respondent's expectation of privacy in the Bergstrom home was rooted in "understandings that are recognized and permitted by society," it was legitimate, and respondent can claim the protection of the Fourth Amendment. [We] therefore affirm the judgment of the Minnesota Supreme Court.

It is so ordered.

Notes

1. *Short, Non–Overnight Visits.* In *Minnesota v. Carter*, 525 U.S. 83 (1998), a police officer peered through a gap in a closed window blind into a ground floor apartment, and observed respondent bagging cocaine. The Court held that respondent lacked standing to challenge the officer's action because he was a temporary out-of-state visitor to the apartment: "If we regard the overnight guest in *Minnesota v. Olson* as typifying those who may claim the protection of the Fourth Amendment in the home of another, and one merely 'legitimately on the premises' as typifying those who may not do so, the present case is obviously somewhere in between. [The] purely commercial nature of the transaction engaged in here, the relatively short period of time on the premises, and the lack of any previous connection between respondents and the householder, all lead us to conclude that respondents' situation is closer to that of one simply permitted on the premises. [Any] search which may have occurred did not violate their Fourth Amendment rights."

2. *Controlled Substances in Another's Purse.* In *Rawlings v. Kentucky*, 448 U.S. 98 (1980), petitioner was convicted of trafficking in, and possession of, various controlled substances based on evidence seized during the search of a purse. Petitioner, who was staying at a friend's home, carried drugs in a green bank bag. He asked a woman friend whether she would carry it for him and she said "yes." Shortly after she did so, the police arrived. In response to a police request, Cox poured the contents of her purse onto a coffee table, and told petitioner to "to take what was his." Petitioner immediately claimed ownership of the controlled substances. Over petitioner's objection, the trial court admitted the drugs against him. The Court upheld the search: "[At] the time petitioner dumped thousands of dollars worth of illegal drugs into Cox's purse, he had known her for only a few days. [P]etitioner had never sought or received access to her purse prior to that sudden bailment. Nor did petitioner have any right to exclude other persons from access to Cox's purse. In fact, Cox testified that [a] longtime

acquaintance and frequent companion of Cox's [had] free access to her purse on the very morning of the arrest [and] had rummaged through its contents in search of a hairbrush. [E]ven assuming that petitioner's version of the bailment is correct and that Cox did consent to the transfer of possession, the precipitous nature of the transaction hardly supports a reasonable inference that petitioner took normal precautions to maintain his privacy. [The record] contains a frank admission by petitioner that he had no subjective expectation that Cox's purse would remain free from governmental [intrusion]. [While] petitioner's ownership of the drugs is undoubtedly one fact to be [considered], *Rakas* emphatically rejected the notion that "arcane" concepts of property law ought to control the ability to claim the protections of the Fourth Amendment. Had petitioner placed his drugs in plain view, he would still have owned them, but he could not claim any legitimate expectation of privacy. [P]etitioner had no legitimate expectation of privacy in Cox's purse at the time of the search."

Justice Marshall dissented: "When the government seizes a person's property, it interferes with his constitutionally protected right to be secure in his effects. That interference gives him the right to challenge the reasonableness of the government's conduct, including the seizure. If the defendant's property was seized as the result of an unreasonable search, the seizure cannot be other than unreasonable.... *Jones* and *Katz* expanded our view of the protections afforded by the Fourth Amendment by recognizing that privacy interests are protected even if they do not arise from property rights. But that recognition was never intended to exclude interests that had historically been sheltered by the Fourth Amendment from its protection."

3. *A Search of a Union Office.* In *Mancusi v. DeForte*, 392 U.S. 364 (1968), respondent was convicted of conspiracy, coercion and extortion. The conviction was based on evidence seized from a union office where DeForte and several other union officials worked. The search was conducted without a warrant and over DeForte's objections. The Court concluded that DeForte had standing to object to the search even though the papers belonged to the union: "[One] has standing to object to a search of his office, as well as of his home. [I]f DeForte had occupied a "private" office in the union headquarters, and union records had been seized from a desk or a filing cabinet in that office, he would have had standing. In such a "private" office, DeForte would have been entitled to expect that he would not be disturbed except by personal or business invitees, and that records would not be taken except with his permission or that of his union superiors. [T]he situation was not fundamentally changed because DeForte shared an office with other union officers. DeForte still could reasonably have expected that only those persons and their personal or business guests would enter the office, and that records would not be touched except with their permission or that of union higher-ups. This expectation was inevitably defeated by the entrance of state officials, their conduct of a general search, and their removal of records which were in DeForte's custody. It [is] irrelevant that the Union or some of its officials might validly have consented to a search of the area where the records were kept, regardless of DeForte's wishes, for it is not claimed that any such consent was [given]."

Justice Black dissented: "[A] corporate or union official suffers no personal injury when the business office he occupies as an agent of the corporation or union is invaded and when records he has prepared and safeguarded as an agent are seized. . . . The organization has every right to challenge such intrusions whenever they occur—if the seizure is illegal, the records obtained can be suppressed in a prosecution against the organization, and if no prosecution is initiated, the organization can obtain return of all the documents by bringing a civil action. Such intrusions, however, involve absolutely no invasion of the 'personal privacy' or security of the agent or employee as an individual, and he accordingly has no right to seek suppression of records that the corporation or union itself has made no effort to regain.''

UNITED STATES v. PAYNER

447 U.S. 727 (1980).

Mr. Justice Powell delivered the opinion of the Court.

[Respondent] Payner was indicted [on] a charge of falsifying his 1972 federal income tax return in violation of 18 U.S.C. § 1001. The indictment alleged that respondent denied maintaining a foreign bank account at a time when he knew that he had such an account at the Castle Bank and Trust Company of Nassau, Bahama Islands. The Government's case rested heavily on a loan guarantee agreement dated April 28, 1972, in which respondent pledged the funds in his Castle Bank account as security for a $100,000 loan.

[The] events [are] not in dispute. [T]he Internal Revenue Service launched an investigation into the financial activities of American citizens in the Bahamas. The project, known as "Operation Trade Winds," was headquartered in Jacksonville, Fla. Suspicion focused on the Castle Bank in 1972, when investigators learned that a suspected narcotics trafficker had an account there. Special Agent Richard Jaffe of the Jacksonville office asked Norman Casper, a private investigator and occasional informant, to learn what he could about the Castle Bank and its depositors. . . . Casper cultivated his friendship with Castle Bank vice president Michael Wolstencroft. Casper introduced Wolstencroft to Sybol Kennedy, a private investigator and former employee. When Casper discovered that the banker intended to spend a few days in Miami in January 1973, he devised a scheme to gain access to the bank records he knew Wolstencroft would be carrying in his briefcase. Agent Jaffe approved the basic outline of the plan.

Wolstencroft arrived in Miami on January 15 and went directly to Kennedy's apartment. At about 7:30 p.m., the two left for dinner at a Key Biscayne restaurant. Shortly thereafter, Casper entered the apartment using a key supplied by Kennedy. He removed the briefcase and delivered it to Jaffe. While the agent supervised the copying of approximately 400 documents taken from the briefcase, a "lookout" observed Kennedy and Wolstencroft at dinner. The observer notified Casper when the pair left the restaurant, and the briefcase was replaced. The documents photographed that evening included papers evidencing a close working relationship between the Castle Bank and the Bank of Perrine,

Fla. Subpoenas issued to the Bank of Perrine ultimately uncovered the loan guarantee agreement at issue in this case.

The District Court found that the United States, acting through Jaffe, "knowingly and willfully participated in the unlawful seizure of Michael Wolstencroft's [briefcase]." According to that court, "the Government affirmatively counsels its agents that the Fourth Amendment standing limitation permits them to purposefully conduct an unconstitutional search and seizure of one individual in order to obtain evidence against third [parties]." [The] documents seized from Wolstencroft provided the leads that ultimately led to the discovery of the critical loan guarantee agreement. Although the search did not impinge upon the respondent's Fourth Amendment rights, the District Court believed that the Due Process Clause of the Fifth Amendment and the inherent supervisory power of the federal courts required it to exclude evidence tainted by the Government's "knowing and purposeful bad faith hostility to any person's fundamental constitutional rights." The Court of Appeals for the Sixth Circuit [affirmed]. We granted certiorari, and we now reverse.

[R]espondent lacks standing under the Fourth Amendment to suppress the documents illegally seized from Wolstencroft.... The District Court and the Court of Appeals believed, however, that a federal court should use its supervisory power to suppress evidence tainted by gross illegalities that did not infringe the defendant's constitutional rights. [We] understand the District Court's commendable desire to deter deliberate intrusions into the privacy of persons who are unlikely to become defendants in a criminal prosecution. No court should condone the unconstitutional and possibly criminal behavior of those who planned and executed this "briefcase caper." [But our cases] do not command the exclusion of evidence in every case of illegality. [The illegality] must be weighed against the considerable harm that would flow from indiscriminate application of an exclusionary rule.

[T]he exclusionary rule "has been restricted to those areas where its remedial objectives are most efficaciously served." The Court has acknowledged that the suppression of probative but tainted evidence exacts a costly toll upon the ability of courts to ascertain the truth in a criminal case. Our cases have consistently recognized that unbending application of the exclusionary sanction to enforce ideals of governmental rectitude would impede unacceptably the truth-finding functions of judge and jury. After all, it is the defendant, and not the constable, who stands trial.

The same societal interests are at risk when a criminal defendant invokes the supervisory power to suppress evidence seized in violation of a third party's constitutional rights. The supervisory power is applied with some caution even when the defendant asserts a violation of his own rights. In *United States v. Caceres*, 440 U.S. 741 (1979), we refused to exclude all evidence tainted by violations of an executive department's rules. And in *Elkins v. United States*, 364 U.S. 206 (1960), the Court called for a restrained application of the supervisory power. "[A]ny apparent limitation upon the process of discovering truth in a federal trial ought to be imposed only upon the basis of considerations which outweigh the general need for untrammeled disclosure of competent and relevant evidence in a court of justice."

We conclude that the supervisory power does not authorize a federal court to suppress otherwise admissible evidence on the ground that it was seized unlawfully from a third party not before the court. Our Fourth Amendment decisions have established beyond any doubt that the interest in deterring illegal searches does not justify the exclusion of tainted evidence at the instance of a party who was not the victim of the challenged practices. The values assigned to the competing interests do not change because a court has elected to analyze the question under the supervisory power instead of the Fourth Amendment. In either case, the need to deter the underlying conduct and the detrimental impact of excluding the evidence remain precisely the same.

The District Court erred, therefore, when it concluded that "society's interest in deterring [bad faith] conduct by exclusion outweigh[s] society's interest in furnishing the trier of fact with all relevant evidence." [Were] we to accept this use of the supervisory power, we would confer on the judiciary discretionary power to disregard the considered limitations of the law it is charged with enforcing. We hold that the supervisory power does not extend so far.

The judgment of the Court of Appeals is

Reversed.

MR. JUSTICE MARSHALL, with whom MR. JUSTICE BRENNAN and MR. JUSTICE BLACKMUN join, dissenting.

[This] Court has on several occasions exercised its supervisory powers over the federal judicial system in order to suppress evidence that the Government obtained through misconduct. The rationale for such suppression of evidence is twofold: to deter illegal conduct by Government officials, and to protect the integrity of the federal courts. The Court has particularly stressed the need to use supervisory powers to prevent the federal courts from becoming accomplices to such misconduct.

The need to use the Court's supervisory powers to suppress evidence obtained through governmental misconduct was perhaps best expressed by Mr. Justice Brandeis in his famous dissenting opinion in *Olmstead v. United States*, 277 U.S. 438 (1928): "Decency, security and liberty alike demand that government officials shall be subjected to the same rules of conduct that are commands to the citizen. In a government of laws, existence of the government will be imperilled if it fails to observe the law scrupulously. [If] the Government becomes a lawbreaker, it breeds contempt for law; it invites every man to become a law unto himself; it invites anarchy. To declare that in the administration of the criminal law the end justifies the means—to declare that the Government may commit crimes in order to secure the conviction of a private criminal—

would bring terrible retribution. Against that pernicious doctrine this Court should resolutely set its face." [If] the federal court permits [the introduction of] evidence, the intended product of deliberately illegal Government action, to be used to obtain a conviction, it places its imprimatur upon such lawlessness and thereby taints its own integrity.

The present case falls within that category. The District Court found [a] deliberate decision by Government agents to violate the constitutional rights of Wolstencroft for the explicit purpose of obtaining evidence against persons such as Payner. The actions of the Government agents— stealing the briefcase, opening it, and photographing all the documents inside—were both patently in violation of the Fourth Amendment rights of Wolstencroft and plainly in violation of the criminal law. The Government knew exactly what information it wanted. . . . Similarly, the Government knew that it wanted to prosecute persons such as Payner, and it made a conscious decision to forgo any opportunity to prosecute Wolstencroft in order to obtain illegally the evidence against Payner and others.

Since the supervisory powers are exercised to protect the integrity of the court, rather than to vindicate the constitutional rights of the defendant, it is hard to see why the Court today bases its analysis entirely on Fourth Amendment standing rules. [T]he federal judiciary should not be made accomplices to the crimes of Casper, Jaffe, and others. * * *

2. *"Fruit of the Poisonous Tree" Doctrine*

When the exclusionary rule is applied, it prohibits the prosecution from using evidence directly obtained from a constitutional violation. Thus, if the police coerce a suspect into confessing, the exclusionary rule prohibits the use of that confession. The "derivative evidence rule," also known as the "Fruit of the Poisonous Tree" doctrine, prohibits the police from using other evidence "derived" from the direct evidence. For example, if a confession alerts the police to the whereabouts of the murder weapon, the derivative evidence rule prohibits the prosecution from using the weapon as evidence. As the Court stated in *Nardone v. United States*, 308 U.S. 338 (1939), "[t]he essence of a provision forbidding the acquisition of evidence in a certain way is that not merely evidence so acquired shall not be used before the Court but that it shall not be used at all."

BROWN v. ILLINOIS

422 U.S. 590 (1975).

MR. JUSTICE BLACKMUN delivered the opinion of the Court.

[Petitioner Richard Brown was arrested for murder while attempting to enter his Chicago apartment. The arrest was illegal because the police lacked probable cause. The police then took] petitioner to [the] police station. During the 20–minute drive Nolan again asked Brown, who then was sitting with him in the back seat of the car, whether his name was Richard Brown and whether he owned a 1966 Oldsmobile. Brown alternately evaded these questions or answered them falsely. Upon arrival at the station house Brown was placed in the second-floor central interrogation room. The room was bare, except for a table and four chairs. He was left alone, apparently without handcuffs, for some minutes while the officers obtained the file on [the] homicide. They returned with the file, sat down at the table, one across from Brown and the other to his left, and spread the file on the table in front of him.

The officers warned Brown of his rights under *Miranda*. They then informed him that they knew of an incident that had occurred in a poolroom on May 5, when Brown, angry at having been cheated at dice, fired a shot from a revolver into the ceiling. Brown answered: "Oh, you know about that." Lenz informed him that a bullet had been obtained from the ceiling of the poolroom and had been taken to the crime laboratory to be compared with bullets taken from [the victim's] body. Brown responded: "Oh, you know that, too." At this point—it was about 8:45 p.m.—Lenz asked Brown whether he wanted to talk about [the] homicide. Petitioner answered that he did. For the next 20 to 25 minutes Brown answered questions put to him by Nolan, as Lenz typed.

This questioning produced a two-page statement in which Brown acknowledged that he and a man named Jimmy Claggett visited Corpus on the evening of May 5; that the three for some time sat drinking and smoking marihuana; that Claggett ordered him at gunpoint to bind Corpus' hands and feet with cord from the headphone of a stereo set; and that Claggett, using a .38–caliber revolver sold to him by Brown, shot Corpus three times through a pillow. The statement was signed by Brown.

[Later that night, after the police apprehended Claggett,] Brown was again placed in the interrogation room. He was given coffee and was left alone, for the most part, until 2 a.m. when Assistant State's Attorney Crilly arrived.... Crilly, too, informed Brown of his *Miranda* rights. After a half hour's conversation, a court reporter appeared. Once again the *Miranda* warnings were given: "I read him the card." Crilly told him that he "was sure he would be charged with murder." Brown gave a second statement, providing a factual account of the murder substantially in accord with his first statement, but containing factual inaccuracies with respect to his personal background. When the statement was completed, at about 3 a.m., Brown refused to sign it. An hour later he made a phone call to his mother. At 9:30 that morning, about 14 hours after his arrest, he was taken before a magistrate.

[At trial, the] State introduced evidence of both statements, and [the] jury found petitioner guilty of murder. [The conviction was affirmed on appeal.]

[In] *Wong Sun v. United States*, 371 U.S. 471 (1963), [the] Court pronounced the principles to be applied where the issue is whether statements and other evidence obtained after an illegal arrest or search should be excluded. In that case, federal agents elicited an oral statement from defendant Toy after forcing entry at 6 a.m. into his laundry, at the back of which he had his living quarters. The agents had followed Toy down the hall to the bedroom and there had placed him under arrest. This Court [agreed with the Court of Appeals that there was no probable cause for the arrest.] Toy's statement, which bore upon his participation in the sale of narcotics, led the agents to question another person, Johnny Yee, who actually possessed narcotics. Yee stated that heroin had been brought to him earlier by Toy and another Chinese known to him only as "Sea Dog." Under questioning, Toy said that "Sea Dog" was Wong Sun. Toy led agents to a multifamily dwelling where, he said, Wong Sun lived. Gaining admittance to the building through a bell and buzzer, the agents climbed the stairs and entered the apartment. One went into the back room and brought Wong Sun out in handcuffs. After arraignment, Wong Sun was released on his own recognizance. Several days later, he returned voluntarily to give an unsigned confession.

This Court ruled that Toy's declarations and the contraband taken from Yee were the fruits of the agents' illegal action and should not have been admitted as evidence against Toy. [The] statement did not result from "an intervening independent act of a free will," [and] was not "sufficiently an act of free will to purge the primary taint of the unlawful invasion." With respect to Wong Sun's confession, however, the Court held that in the light of his lawful arraignment and release on his own recognizance, and of his return voluntarily several days later to make the statement, the connection between his unlawful arrest and the statement "had become so attenuated as to dissipate the taint." The Court said: "We need not hold that all evidence is 'fruit of the poisonous tree' simply because it would not have come to light but for the illegal actions of the police. Rather, the more apt question in such a case is 'whether, granting establishment of the primary illegality, the evidence to which instant objection is made has been come at by exploitation of that illegality or instead by means sufficiently distinguishable to be purged of the primary taint.' MAGUIRE, EVIDENCE OF GUILT, 221 (1959)."

The exclusionary rule thus was applied in *Wong Sun* primarily to protect Fourth Amendment rights. Protection of the Fifth Amendment right against self-incrimination was not the Court's paramount concern there. To the extent that the question whether Toy's statement was voluntary was considered, it was only to judge whether it "was sufficiently an act of free will to purge the primary taint of the unlawful invasion."

The Court in *Wong Sun*, as is customary, emphasized that application of the exclusionary rule on Toy's behalf protected Fourth Amendment guarantees in two respects: "in terms of deterring lawless conduct by federal officers," and by "closing the doors of the federal courts to any use of evidence unconstitutionally obtained." These considerations of deterrence and of judicial integrity, by now, have become rather commonplace in the Court's cases.

[The] Illinois courts refrained from resolving the question [whether] Brown's statements were obtained by exploitation of the illegality of his arrest. They assumed that the *Miranda* warnings, by themselves, assured that the statements (verbal acts, as contrasted with physical evidence) were of sufficient free will as to purge the primary taint of the unlawful arrest. . . .

This Court has described the *Miranda* warnings as a "prophylactic rule," and as a "procedural safeguard," employed to protect Fifth Amendment rights against "the compulsion inherent in custodial surroundings." The function of the warnings relates to the Fifth Amendment's guarantee against coerced self-incrimination, and the exclusion of a statement made in the absence of the warnings, [serves] to deter the taking of an incriminating statement without first informing the individual of his Fifth Amendment rights.

Although, almost 90 years ago, the Court observed that the Fifth Amendment is in "intimate relation" with the Fourth, the *Miranda* warnings thus far have not been regarded as a means either of remedying or deterring violations of Fourth Amendment rights. Frequently[,] rights under the two Amendments may appear to coalesce since "the 'unreasonable searches and seizures' condemned in the Fourth Amendment are almost always made for the purpose of compelling a man to give evidence against himself, which in criminal cases is condemned in the Fifth Amendment." The exclusionary rule, however, when utilized to effectuate the Fourth Amendment, serves interests and policies that are distinct from those it serves under the Fifth. It is directed at all unlawful searches and seizures, and not merely those that happen to produce incriminating material or testimony as fruits. In short, exclusion of a confession made without *Miranda* warnings might be regarded as necessary to effectuate the Fifth Amendment, but it would not be sufficient fully to protect the Fourth. *Miranda* warnings, and the exclusion of a confession made without them, do not alone sufficiently deter a Fourth Amendment violation.

Thus, even if the statements in this case were found to be voluntary under the Fifth Amendment, the Fourth Amendment issue remains. In order for the causal chain, between the illegal arrest and the statements made subsequent thereto, to be broken, *Wong Sun* requires not merely that the statement meet the Fifth Amendment standard of voluntariness but that it be "sufficiently an act of free will to purge the primary taint." *Wong Sun* thus mandates consideration of a statement's admissibility in light of the distinct policies and interests of the Fourth Amendment.

If *Miranda* warnings, by themselves, were held to attenuate the taint of an unconstitutional arrest, regardless of how wanton and purposeful the Fourth Amendment violation, the effect of the exclusionary rule would be substantially diluted. Arrests made without warrant or without probable cause, for questioning or "investigation," would be encouraged by the knowledge that evidence derived therefrom could well be made admissible at trial by the simple expedient of giving *Miranda* warnings. Any incentive to avoid Fourth Amendment violations would be eviscerated by making the warnings, in effect, a "cure-all," and the constitutional guarantee against unlawful searches and seizures could be said to be reduced to "a form of words."

It [is] possible, of course, [that] persons arrested illegally [may] decide to confess, as an act of free will unaffected by the initial illegality. But the *Miranda* warnings, alone and *per se*, cannot always make the act sufficiently a product of free will to break, for Fourth Amendment purposes, the causal connection between the illegality and the confession. They cannot assure [that] the Fourth Amendment violation has not been unduly exploited.

[The] question whether a confession is the product of a free will under *Wong Sun* must be answered on the facts of each case. No single fact is dispositive. The workings of the human mind are too complex, and the possibilities of misconduct too diverse, to permit protection of the Fourth Amendment to turn on such a talismanic test. The *Miranda* warnings are an important factor [in] determining whether the confession is obtained by exploitation of an illegal arrest. But they are not the only factor to be considered. The temporal proximity of the arrest and the confession, the presence of intervening circumstances, and, particularly, the purpose and flagrancy of the official misconduct are all relevant. The voluntariness of the statement is a threshold requirement. And the burden of showing admissibility rests [on] the prosecution.

[We] conclude that the State failed to sustain the burden of showing that the evidence in question was admissible under *Wong Sun*.... Brown's first statement was separated from his illegal arrest by less than two hours, and there was no intervening event of significance whatsoever. [His] situation is remarkably like that of James Wah Toy in *Wong Sun*.... And the second statement was clearly the result and the fruit of the first.[15]

The illegality here, moreover, had a quality of purposefulness. The impropriety of the arrest was obvious; awareness of that fact was virtually conceded by the two detectives when they repeatedly acknowledged [that] the purpose of their action was "for investigation" or for "questioning." [The] detectives embarked upon this expedition for evidence in the hope that something might turn up. The manner in which Brown's arrest was affected gives the appearance of having been calculated to cause surprise, fright, and confusion.

[We] decide only that the Illinois courts were in error in assuming that the *Miranda* warnings, by themselves, under *Wong Sun* always purge the taint of an illegal arrest.

---

15. The fact that Brown had made one statement, believed by him to be admissible, and his cooperation with the arresting and interrogating officers in the search for Claggett, with his anticipation of leniency, bolstered the pressures for him to give the second, or at least vitiated any incentive on his part to avoid self-incrimination.

The judgment of the Supreme Court of Illinois is reversed and the case is remanded for further proceedings not inconsistent with this opinion.

It is so ordered.

MR. JUSTICE POWELL, with whom MR. JUSTICE REHNQUIST joins, concurring in part.

[In] my view, the point at which the taint can be said to have dissipated should be related, in the absence of other controlling circumstances, to the nature of that taint.

That police have not succeeded in coercing the accused's confession through willful or negligent misuse of the power of arrest does not remove the fact that they may have tried. The impermissibility of the attempt, and the extent to which such attempts can be deterred by the use of the exclusionary rule, are of primary relevance in determining whether exclusion is an appropriate remedy. The basic purpose of the rule [is] to remove possible motivations for illegal arrests. Given this purpose the notion of voluntariness has practical value in deciding whether the rule should apply to statements removed from the immediate circumstances of the illegal arrest. If an illegal arrest merely provides the occasion of initial contact between the police and the accused, and because of time or other intervening factors the accused's eventual statement is the product of his own reflection and free will, application of the exclusionary rule can serve little purpose: the police normally will not make an illegal arrest in the hope of eventually obtaining such a truly volunteered statement. In a similar manner, the role of the *Miranda* warnings in the *Wong Sun* inquiry is indirect. To the extent that they dissipate the psychological pressures of custodial interrogation, *Miranda* warnings serve to assure that the accused's decision to make a statement has been relatively unaffected by the preceding illegal arrest. Correspondingly, to the extent that the police perceive *Miranda* warnings to have this equalizing potential, their motivation to abuse the power of arrest is diminished. Bearing these considerations in mind, and recognizing that the deterrent value of the Fourth Amendment exclusionary rule is limited to certain kinds of police conduct, the following general categories can be identified.

Those most readily identifiable are on the extremes: the flagrantly abusive violation of Fourth Amendment rights, on the one hand, and "technical" Fourth Amendment violations, on the other. In my view, these extremes call for significantly different judicial responses.... I would require the clearest indication of attenuation in cases in which official conduct was flagrantly abusive of Fourth Amendment rights. [In such cases,] I would consider the equalizing potential of *Miranda* warnings rarely sufficient to dissipate the taint. In such cases the deterrent value of the exclusionary rule is most likely to be effective, and the corresponding mandate to preserve judicial integrity, most clearly demands that the fruits of official misconduct be denied. I thus would require some demonstrably effective break in the chain of events leading from the illegal arrest to the statement, such as actual consultation with counsel or the accused's presentation before a magistrate for a determination of probable cause, before the taint can be deemed removed. . . . At the opposite end of the spectrum lie "technical" violations of Fourth Amendment rights where, for example, officers in good faith arrest an individual in reliance on a warrant later invalidated or pursuant to a statute that subsequently is declared unconstitutional. . . . I would not require more than proof that effective *Miranda* warnings were given and that the ensuing statement was voluntary in the Fifth Amendment sense. Absent aggravating circumstances, I would consider a statement given at the station house after one has been advised of *Miranda* rights to be sufficiently removed from the immediate circumstances of the illegal arrest to justify its admission at trial.

Notes

1. *Dunaway.* After *Brown*, the Court has decided several similar cases. In *Dunaway v. New York*, 442 U.S. 200 (1979), the Court held that the police violated petitioner's rights when they seized him and took him to the stationhouse for custodial questioning absent probable cause. Because of the illegal seizure, the Court refused to admit petitioner's incriminating statements at the stationhouse: "The situation in this case is virtually a replica of the situation in *Brown*. Petitioner [was] seized without probable cause in the hope that something might turn up, and confessed without any intervening event of significance." Chief Justice Rehnquist dissented: "[T]he connection between petitioner's allegedly, unlawful detention and the incriminating statements and sketches is sufficiently attenuated to permit their use at trial. . . . Where police have acted in good faith and not in a flagrant manner, I would require no more than that proper *Miranda* warnings be given and that the statement be voluntary within the meaning of the Fifth Amendment." *See also Taylor v. Alabama*, 457 U.S. 687 (1982) (Court suppressed confession when "petitioner was arrested without probable cause in the hope that something would turn up, and he confessed shortly thereafter without any meaningful intervening event" even though petitioner was given three *Miranda* warnings).

2. *Rawlings.* In *Rawlings v. Kentucky*, 448 U.S. 98 (1980), petitioner was convicted of trafficking in, and possession of, various controlled substances. The conviction was based, in part, on statements made by petitioner at the scene of the arrest. Even though the Court concluded that petitioner was illegally detained at the time he made the statements, the Court felt that the connection between the seizure and the statements was sufficiently attenuated: "First[,] petitioner received *Miranda* warnings only moments before he made his incriminating statements. . . . Second[,] petitioner and his companions were detained for a period of approximately 45 minutes. [T]he three people [sat] quietly in the living room, or at least initially, moved freely about the first floor of the house. Third, petitioner's admissions were apparently spontaneous reactions to the discovery of his drugs in Cox's purse, [and] this factor weighs heavily in favor of a finding that petitioner acted 'of free will unaffected by the initial illegality.' Fourth[,] the conduct of the police here does not rise to the level of conscious or flagrant miscon-

duct.... Finally[,] petitioner has not argued [that] his admission to owner-ship of the drugs was anything other than voluntary." Justice Marshall dissented: "Petitioner's admissions, far from being 'spontaneous' were made in response to Vanessa Cox's demand that petitioner 'take what was his.' [Her] statement was the direct product of the illegal search of her purse. And that search was made possible only because the police refused to let anyone in the house depart unless they 'consented' to a body search; that detention the Court has assumed was illegal."

Problems

1. *Evaluating Brown.* What might the police have done differently in *Brown* that might have altered the result?

2. *An Identification as the "Fruit" of an Unlawful Arrest?* A woman was accosted and robbed at gunpoint by a young man in the women's restroom on the grounds of the Washington Monument. Six days later, two other women were assaulted and robbed in the same restroom. All three women gave the same description of the robber: "a young black male, 15–18 years old, approximately 5'5" to 5'8" tall, slender in build, with a very dark complexion and smooth skin." When an officer spied respondent (who matched the description) in the vicinity of the Washington Monument restrooms, the officer took him into custody (ostensibly for truancy) and transported him to the station where he was photographed and released. Afterwards, the police showed the victim of the first robbery an array of eight photographs. Although she had failed to identify the robber after previously viewing more than 100 pictures, she immediately identified respondent as her assailant. Afterwards, respondent was then taken into custody and forced to participate in a lineup where he was positively identified by two victims. At respondent's trial, should the court suppress the photographic identifications and the lineup identification? How would you argue the case for defendant? How might the prosecution respond? *See United States v. Crews*, 445 U.S. 463 (1980).

3. *More on Identifications as "Fruits."* Suppose that, instead of offer-ing the photographic and lineup identifications in court, the prosecution seeks to have the witnesses identify respondent in court on the basis of their independent recollections. Should the witnesses be allowed to do so? How would you argue the case for the defendant? How might the prosecution respond? How should the court hold? *See United States v. Crews*, 445 U.S. 463 (1980).

4. *The Effect of Suggestivity.* In the prior problem, would the result be different if the photographic identification and the lineup had been conduct-ed in a highly suggestive manner? Or, given the circumstances, was there sufficient evidence of reliability?

5. *A Witness as the "Fruit" of an Illegal Search?* While the police were investigating illegal gambling, a uniformed police officer entered respon-dent's place of business (a flower shop), went behind the customer counter and spent his break talking with his friend, an employee of the shop. During the conversation, he spotted an envelope with money lying on the cash register. The officer picked up the envelope, examined its contents, and

discovered that it contained not only money but betting slips. He placed the envelope back on the register and, without telling his fried what he had seen, asked her who owned it. She replied that the envelope belonged to respondent, and that he had instructed her to give it to someone. Later, when respondent testified before a federal grand jury that he had never taken bets, the officer's friend gave contrary testimony. The grand jury indicted respondent for perjury. The case is now before the trial court. Should the court suppress the betting slips and the envelopes and the testimony of the officer's friend? How would you argue the case for the defense? How might the prosecution respond? Who should prevail? *See United States v. Ceccolini*, 435 U.S. 268 (1978).

6. *A Confession as the "Fruit" of a Payton Violation?* The police had probable cause to arrest Harris, but they arrested him at his home without an arrest warrant in contravention of *Payton v. New York, supra*. Harris was *Mirandized* and admitted committing a murder. Harris was then taken to the stationhouse where he was given a second *Miranda* warning and made a written incriminating statement. After reading Harris his rights a third time, the police videotaped his confession. Should the confession be suppressed as the "fruit" of an illegal arrest? *See New York v. Harris*, 495 U.S. 14 (1990).

NIX v. WILLIAMS

467 U.S. 431 (1984).

CHIEF JUSTICE BURGER delivered the opinion of the Court.

[In *Brewer v. Williams*, the Court reversed Williams' murder conviction because it was based on a confession obtained in violation of his Sixth Amendment right to counsel. The Court found that the confession was deliberately elicited by the "Christian burial speech" that a police officer gave to respondent on route from Davenport to Des Moines.]

At Williams' second [trial], the prosecution did not offer Williams' statements into evidence, nor did it seek to show that Williams had directed the police to the child's body. However, evidence of the condition of her body as it was found, articles and photographs of her clothing, and the results of post mortem medical and chemical tests on the body were admitted. The trial court concluded that the State had proved by a preponderance of the evidence that, if the search had not been suspended and Williams had not led the police to the victim, her body would have been discovered "within a short time" in essentially the same condition as it was actually found. The trial court also ruled that if the police had not located the body, "the search would clearly have been taken up again where it left off, given the extreme circumstances of this case and the body would [have] been found in short order." [In] finding that the body would have been discovered in essentially the same condition as it was actually found, the court noted that freezing temperatures had prevailed and tissue deterioration would have been suspended. The challenged evidence was admitted and the jury again found Williams guilty of first-degree murder; he was sentenced to life in prison.

[After respondent's conviction was affirmed on appeal, he sought a writ of habeas corpus challenging his conviction. The court denied the writ.... The Eighth Circuit Court of Appeals reversed finding that, whether or not the body would have been discovered, suppression was required because the police acted in bad faith]. We granted the State's petition for certiorari and we reverse.

[The] "vast majority" of all courts, both state and federal, recognize an inevitable discovery exception to the exclusionary rule. We are now urged to adopt and apply the so-called ultimate or inevitable discovery exception to the exclusionary rule.

Williams contends that evidence of the body's location and condition is "fruit of the poisonous tree," *i.e.*, the "fruit" or product of Detective Leaming's plea to help the child's parents give her "a Christian burial," which this Court had already held equated to interrogation. He contends that admitting the challenged evidence violated the Sixth Amendment whether it would have been inevitably discovered or not. Williams also contends that, if the inevitable discovery doctrine is constitutionally permissible, it must include a threshold showing of police good faith.

The doctrine requiring courts to suppress evidence as the tainted "fruit" of unlawful governmental conduct had its genesis in *Silverthorne Lumber Co. v. United States*, 251 U.S. 385 (1920); there, the Court held that the exclusionary rule applies not only to the illegally obtained evidence itself, but also to other incriminating evidence derived from the primary evidence. The holding of *Silverthorne* was carefully limited [for] the Court emphasized that such information does not automatically become "sacred and inaccessible." "If knowledge of [such facts] is gained from an independent source, they may be proved like any [others]."

[The] core rationale consistently advanced by this Court for extending the exclusionary rule to evidence that is the fruit of unlawful police conduct has been that this admittedly drastic and socially costly course is needed to deter police from violations of constitutional and statutory protections. This Court has accepted the argument that the way to ensure such protections is to exclude evidence seized as a result of such violations notwithstanding the high social cost of letting persons obviously guilty go unpunished for their crimes. On this rationale, the prosecution is not to be put in a better position than it would have been in if no illegality had transpired.

By contrast, the derivative evidence analysis ensures that the prosecution is not put in a worse position simply because of some earlier police error or misconduct. The independent source doctrine allows admission of evidence that has been discovered by means wholly independent of any constitutional violation. That doctrine, although closely related to the inevitable discovery doctrine, does not apply here; Williams' statements to Leaming indeed led police to the child's body.... The independent source doctrine teaches us that the interest of society in deterring unlawful police conduct and the public interest in having juries receive all probative evidence of a crime are properly balanced by putting the police in the same, not a worse, position than they would have been in if no police error or misconduct had occurred. When the challenged evidence has an independent source, exclusion of such evidence would put the police in a worse position than they would have been in absent any error or violation. There is a functional similarity between these two doctrines in that exclusion of evidence that would inevitably have been discovered would also put the government in a worse position, because the police would have obtained that evidence if no misconduct had taken place. Thus, while the independent source exception would not justify admission of evidence in this case, its rationale is wholly consistent with and justifies our adoption of the ultimate or inevitable discovery exception to the exclusionary rule.

[Cases] implementing the exclusionary rule "begin with the premise that the challenged evidence [is] the product of illegal governmental activity." *United States v. Crews*, 445 U.S. 463 (1980). [This] does not end the inquiry. If the prosecution can establish by a preponderance of the evidence that the information ultimately or inevitably would have been discovered by lawful means—here the volunteers' search—then the deterrence rationale has so little basis that the evidence should be received.[16] Anything less would reject logic, experience, and common sense.

The requirement that the prosecution must prove the absence of bad faith [would] place courts in the position of withholding from juries relevant and undoubted truth that would have been available to police absent any unlawful police activity. [That] view would put the police in a worse position than they would have been in if no unlawful conduct had transpired. [Of] equal importance, it wholly fails to take into account the enormous societal cost of excluding truth in the search for truth in the administration of justice. Nothing in this Court's prior holdings supports any such formalistic, pointless, and punitive approach.

The Court of Appeals concluded [that] if an absence-of-bad-faith requirement were not imposed, "the temptation to risk deliberate violations of the Sixth Amendment would be too great, and the deterrent effect of the Exclusionary Rule reduced too far." We reject that view. A police officer who is faced with the opportunity to obtain evidence illegally will rarely, if ever, be in a position to calculate whether the evidence sought would inevitably be discovered. On the other hand, when an officer is aware that the evidence will inevitably be discovered[,]

---

16. [Williams] argues that the preponderance-of-the-evidence standard [is] inconsistent with *United States v. Wade*, 388 U.S. 218 (1967). In requiring clear and convincing evidence of an independent source for an in-court identification, the Court gave weight to the effect an uncounseled pretrial identification has in "crystalliz[ing] the witnesses' identification of the defendant for future reference." The Court noted as well that possible unfairness at the lineup "may be the sole means of attack upon the un-equivocal courtroom identification," and recognized the difficulty of determining whether an in-court identification was based on independent recollection unaided by the lineup identification. By contrast, inevitable discovery involves no speculative elements but focuses on demonstrated historical facts capable of ready verification or impeachment and does not require a departure from the usual burden of proof at suppression hearings.

there will be little to gain from taking any dubious "shortcuts" to obtain the evidence. Significant disincentives to obtaining evidence illegally— including the possibility of departmental discipline and civil liability— also lessen the likelihood that the ultimate or inevitable discovery exception will promote police misconduct. In these circumstances, the societal costs of the exclusionary rule far outweigh any possible benefits to deterrence that a good-faith requirement might produce.

Williams contends that because he did not waive his right to the assistance of counsel, the Court may not balance competing values in deciding whether the challenged evidence was properly admitted. He argues that [the] Sixth Amendment exclusionary rule is designed to protect the right to a fair trial and the integrity of the factfinding process. Williams contends that, when those interests are at stake, the societal costs of excluding evidence obtained from responses presumed involuntary are irrelevant in determining whether such evidence should be excluded. We disagree. Exclusion of physical evidence that would inevitably have been discovered adds nothing to either the integrity or fairness of a criminal trial. [Here], Detective Leaming's conduct did nothing to impugn the reliability of the evidence in question—the body of the child and its condition as it was found, articles of clothing found on the body, and the autopsy.... Suppression, in these circumstances, would do nothing whatever to promote the integrity of the trial process, but would inflict a wholly unacceptable burden on the administration of criminal justice.

Nor would suppression ensure fairness on the theory that it tends to safeguard the adversary system of justice. [I]f the government can prove that the evidence would have been obtained inevitably and, therefore, would have been admitted regardless of any overreaching by the police, there is no rational basis to keep that evidence from the jury in order to ensure the fairness of the trial proceedings. [The] State has gained no advantage at trial and the defendant has suffered no prejudice. Indeed, suppression of the evidence would operate to undermine the adversary system by putting the State in a worse position than it would have occupied without any police misconduct....

More than a half century ago, Judge, later Justice, Cardozo made his seminal observation that under the exclusionary rule "[t]he criminal is to go free because the constable has blundered." Prophetically, he went on to consider "how far-reaching in its effect upon society" the exclusionary rule would be when "[t]he pettiest peace officer would have it in his power through overzeal or indiscretion to confer immunity upon an offender for crimes the most flagitious." Some day, Cardozo speculated, some court might press the exclusionary rule to the outer limits of its logic—or beyond—and suppress evidence relating to the "body of a murdered" victim because of the means by which it was found. [When], as here, the evidence in question would inevitably have been discovered without reference to the police error or misconduct, there is no nexus sufficient to provide a taint and the evidence is admissible.

The Court of Appeals did not find it necessary to consider whether the record fairly supported the finding that the volunteer search party would ultimately or inevitably have discovered the victim's body. However, three courts independently reviewing the evidence have found that the body of the child inevitably would have been found by the searchers. [The] prosecution offered the testimony of Agent Ruxlow of the Iowa Bureau of Criminal Investigation. Ruxlow had organized and directed some 200 volunteers who were searching for the child's body. The searchers were instructed "to check all the roads, the ditches, any [culverts]. If they came upon any abandoned farm buildings, they were instructed to go onto the property and search those abandoned farm buildings or any other places where a small child could be secreted." Ruxlow testified that he marked off highway maps of Poweshiek and Jasper Counties in grid fashion, divided the volunteers into teams of four to six persons, and assigned each team to search specific grid areas. Ruxlow also testified that, if the search had not been suspended because of Williams' promised cooperation, it would have continued into Polk County, using the same grid system. Although he had previously marked off into grids only the highway maps of Poweshiek and Jasper Counties, Ruxlow had obtained a map of Polk County, which he said he would have marked off in the same manner had it been necessary for the search to continue.

The search had commenced at approximately 10 a.m. and moved westward through Poweshiek County into Jasper County. At approximately 3 p.m., after Williams had volunteered to cooperate with the police, Detective Leaming, who was in the police car with Williams, sent word to Ruxlow and the other Special Agent directing the search [and] the search was suspended at that time. . . . The search was not resumed once it was learned that Williams had led the police to the body, which was found two and one-half miles from where the search had stopped in what would have been the easternmost grid to be searched in Polk County. There was testimony that it would have taken an additional three to five hours to discover the body if the search had continued; the body was found near a culvert, one of the kinds of places the teams had been specifically directed to search.

On this record it is clear that the search parties were approaching the actual location of the body, and we are satisfied [that] the volunteer search teams would have resumed the search had Williams not earlier led the police to the body and the body inevitably would have been found. The evidence asserted by Williams as newly discovered, *i.e.*, certain photographs of the body and deposition testimony of Agent Ruxlow made in connection with the federal habeas proceeding, does not demonstrate that the material facts were inadequately developed in the suppression hearing in state court or that Williams was denied a full, fair, and adequate opportunity to present all relevant facts at the suppression hearing.

The judgment of the Court of Appeals is reversed, and the case is remanded for further proceedings consistent with this opinion.

It is so ordered.

JUSTICE STEVENS, concurring in the judgment.

[This] was a case "in which the police deliberately took advantage of an inherently coercive setting in the absence of counsel, contrary to their express agreement." * * * *Williams I* grew out of a line of cases in which this Court made it clear that the adversarial process protected by the Sixth Amendment may not be undermined by the strategems [sic] of the police. [T]he now-familiar plaint that " '[t]he criminal is to go free because the constable has blundered,' " is entirely beside the point. More pertinent is what THE CHIEF JUSTICE wrote for the Court on another occasion: "This is not a case where, in Justice Cardozo's words, 'the constable [blundered],' rather, it is one where the 'constable' planned an impermissible interference with the right to the assistance of counsel."

[Admission] of the victim's body, if it would have been discovered anyway, means that the trial in this case was not the product of an inquisitorial process; that process was untainted by illegality. The good or bad faith of Detective Leaming is therefore simply irrelevant. If the trial process was not tainted as a result of his conduct, this defendant received the type of trial that the Sixth Amendment [envisions]. [The] prosecution can [not] escape responsibility for a constitutional violation through speculation. [The] need to adduce proof sufficient to discharge its burden, and the difficulty in predicting whether such proof will be available or sufficient, means that the inevitable discovery rule does not permit state officials to avoid the uncertainty they would have faced but for the constitutional violation.

The majority refers to the "societal cost" of excluding probative evidence. In my view, the more relevant cost is that imposed on society by police officers who decide to take procedural shortcuts instead of complying with the law. What is the consequence of the shortcut that Detective Leaming took when he decided to question Williams in this case and not to wait an hour or so until he arrived in Des Moines? The answer is years and years of unnecessary but costly litigation. Instead of having a 1969 conviction affirmed in routine fashion, the case is still alive 15 years later. Thanks to Detective Leaming, the State of Iowa has expended vast sums of money and countless hours of professional labor in his defense. That expenditure surely provides an adequate deterrent to similar violations; the responsibility for that expenditure lies not with the Constitution, but rather with the constable. Accordingly, I concur in the Court's judgment.

JUSTICE BRENNAN, with whom JUSTICE MARSHALL joins, dissenting.

[The] "inevitable discovery" exception to the exclusionary rule is consistent with the requirements of the Constitution. In its zealous efforts to emasculate the exclusionary rule, however, the Court loses sight of the crucial difference between the "inevitable discovery" doctrine and the "independent source" exception from which it is derived. [The] inevitable discovery exception necessarily implicates a hypothetical finding that differs in kind from the factual finding that precedes application of the independent source rule. To ensure that this hypothetical finding is narrowly confined to circumstances that are functionally equivalent to an independent source, and to protect fully the fundamental rights served by the exclusionary rule, I would require clear and convincing evidence before concluding that the government had met its burden of proof on this issue. Increasing the burden of proof serves to impress the fact finder with the importance of the decision and thereby reduces the risk that illegally obtained evidence will be admitted. [I] would remand this case for application of this heightened burden of proof by the lower courts in the first instance. . . .

Note: Independent Source

In *Segura v. United States*, 468 U.S. 796 (1984), the police had probable cause to search Segura's apartment. However, because it was evening, they decided to secure the apartment until a warrant could be obtained the next day. After entering, the police made a limited check to make sure that no one was present who might pose a threat to their safety or destroy evidence. During this search, the police found evidence of drug trafficking in plain view, but did not disturb it. Because of administrative delays, the warrant was not obtained until 5 p.m. the next day, and the apartment was not searched until 6 p.m. (approximately 19 hours after the initial entry). The search turned up the items discovered the night before, as well as cocaine, 18 rounds of ammunition, more than $50,000 cash, and records of narcotics transactions. Defendants were convicted of conspiring to distribute cocaine, and of distributing and possessing with intent to distribute cocaine based, in part, on the evidence seized. The Court concluded that the initial seizure of the apartment was "reasonable." It then held that there was an "independent source" for the evidence: "[Whether] the initial entry was illegal or not is irrelevant to the admissibility of the challenged evidence because there was an independent source for the warrant under which that evidence was seized. . . . None of the information on which the warrant was secured was derived from or related in any way to the initial entry into petitioners' apartment; the information came from sources wholly unconnected with the entry and was known to the agents well before the initial entry. . . . It is therefore beyond dispute that the information possessed by the agents before they entered the apartment constituted an independent source for the discovery and seizure of the evidence now challenged. . . . The valid warrant search was a 'means sufficiently distinguishable' to purge the evidence of any 'taint' arising from the entry. Had police never entered the apartment, but instead conducted a perimeter stakeout to prevent anyone from entering the apartment and destroying evidence, the contraband now challenged would have been discovered and seized precisely as it was here." The Court rejected the argument that "if the agents had not entered the apartment, petitioners might have arranged for the removal or destruction of the evidence, and that in this sense the agents' actions could be considered the 'but for' cause for discovery of the evidence." The Court concluded: "The essence of the dissent is that there is some 'constitutional right' to destroy evidence. This concept defies both logic and common sense."

Justice Stevens, joined by three other justices, dissented, arguing that "the agents' access to the fruits of the authorized search, rather than the information which led to that search, was a product of illegal conduct.... If Segura had not returned home at all that night, or during the next day, it is probable that the occupants of the apartment would have become concerned and might at least have destroyed the records of their illegal transactions, or removed some of the evidence. If [so,] then obviously that evidence would not have been accessible to the agents when the warrant finally was executed. [If] the evidence would not have been available to the agents at the time they finally executed the warrant had they not illegally entered and impounded petitioners' apartment, then it cannot be said that the agents' access to the evidence was 'independent' of the prior illegality.... [If] we are to give more than lipservice to protection of the core constitutional interests that were twice violated in this case, some effort must be made to isolate and then remove the advantages the Government derived from its illegal conduct."

Problems

1. *Applying Nix.* In *Nix,* the Court emphasized the fact that the weather was sub-freezing and that the victim's body was preserved by the cold against deterioration. Had the search taken place in mid-summer, should the Court have reached a different result? Would that fact make the discovery less "inevitable?"

2. *Proving Inevitable Discovery* In a murder case like *Nix,* the prosecution is able to prove inevitability by pointing to the fact that a search was already underway, and demonstrating that this search was likely to have uncovered the body. But suppose that the search had not begun at the time of the Christian Burial Speech. Would it still have been possible for the prosecution to show inevitability? If so, how?

3. *Limits of "Inevitable Discovery."* Suppose that a police officer randomly pulls a motorist over and illegally searches his car (without a warrant, probable cause, or any other basis for the search). The trial court suppresses the evidence as the fruit of an illegal search. Would it be possible for the prosecution to prove inevitable discovery? If so, how?

E. HARMLESS ERROR

CRAWFORD v. WASHINGTON

541 U.S. 36 (2004).

JUSTICE SCALIA delivered the opinion of the Court.

[On] August 5, 1999, Kenneth Lee was stabbed at his apartment. Police arrested petitioner later that night. After giving petitioner and his wife *Miranda* warnings, detectives interrogated each of them twice. Petitioner eventually confessed that he and Sylvia had gone in search of Lee because he was upset over an earlier incident in which Lee had tried to rape her. The two had found Lee at his apartment, and a fight ensued in which Lee was stabbed in the torso and petitioner's hand was cut.

[Petitioner claimed that he saw something in Lee's hand, possibly a weapon, right before he stabbed him.] Sylvia generally corroborated petitioner's story about the events leading up to the fight, but her account of the fight itself was arguably different—particularly with respect to whether Lee had drawn a weapon before petitioner assaulted him[. She denied seeing anything in Lee's hands.]

The State charged petitioner with assault and attempted murder. At trial, he claimed self-defense. Sylvia did not testify because of the state marital privilege, which generally bars a spouse from testifying without the other spouse's consent. In Washington, this privilege does not extend to a spouse's out-of-court statements admissible under a hearsay exception, so the State sought to introduce Sylvia's tape-recorded statements to the police as evidence that the stabbing was not in self-defense. Noting that Sylvia had admitted she led petitioner to Lee's apartment and thus had facilitated the assault, the State invoked the hearsay exception for statements against penal interest.

Petitioner countered that, state law notwithstanding, admitting the evidence would violate his federal constitutional right to be "confronted with the witnesses against him." Amdt. 6. According to our description of that right in *Ohio v. Roberts,* 448 U.S. 56 (1980), it does not bar admission of an unavailable witness's statement against a criminal defendant if the statement bears "adequate 'indicia of reliability.' " To meet that test, evidence must either fall within a "firmly rooted hearsay exception" or bear "particularized guarantees of trustworthiness." The trial court here admitted the statement on the latter ground, offering several reasons why it was trustworthy.... The Washington Court of Appeals reversed [concluding] that, although Sylvia's statement did not fall under a firmly rooted hearsay exception, it bore guarantees of trustworthiness.... We granted certiorari to determine whether the State's use of Sylvia's statement violated the Confrontation Clause.

The Sixth Amendment's Confrontation Clause provides that, "[i]n all criminal prosecutions, the accused shall enjoy the right ... to be confronted with the witnesses against him." We have held that this bedrock procedural guarantee applies to both federal and state prosecutions.... *Roberts* says that an unavailable witness's out-of-court statement may be admitted so " 'long as it has adequate indicia of reliability—*i.e.,* falls within a "firmly rooted hearsay exception" or bears "particularized guarantees of trustworthiness." Petitioner argues that this test strays from the original meaning of the Confrontation Clause....

The Constitution's text does not alone resolve this case. One could plausibly read "witnesses against" a defendant to mean those who actually testify at trial, those whose statements are offered at trial, or something in-between. We must therefore turn to the historical background of the Clause to understand its meaning....

English common law ... tradition is one of live testimony in court subject to adversarial testing.... See 3 W. Blackstone, Commentaries on the Laws of England 373–374 (1768).... Many declarations of rights adopted around the time of the Revolution guaranteed a right of confrontation. See Virginia Declaration of Rights § 8 (1776). The proposed Federal Constitution, however, did not. [When there was an outcry against this omission, the] First Congress responded by including the Confrontation Clause in the proposal that became the Sixth Amendment.... Early state decisions shed light upon the original understanding of the common-law right. *State v. Webb,* 2 N.C. 103 (1794) *(per curiam),* [held]: "[I]t is a rule of the common law, founded on natural justice, that no man shall be prejudiced by evidence which he had not the liberty to cross examine." ...

This history supports two inferences about the meaning of the Sixth Amendment.... First, the principal evil at which the Confrontation Clause was directed was the civil-law mode of criminal procedure, and particularly its use of *ex parte* examinations as evidence against the accused. It was these practices that the Crown deployed in notorious treason cases [and] that the founding-era rhetoric decried. The Sixth Amendment must be interpreted with this focus in mind.

[We] reject the view that the Confrontation Clause applies of its own force only to in-court testimony, and that its application to out-of-court statements introduced at trial depends upon "the law of Evidence for the time being." Leaving the regulation of out-of-court statements to the law of evidence would render the Confrontation Clause powerless to prevent even the most flagrant inquisitorial practices....

This focus also suggests that not all hearsay implicates the Sixth Amendment's core concerns. An off-hand, overheard remark might be unreliable evidence and thus a good candidate for exclusion under hearsay rules, but it bears little resemblance to the civil-law abuses the Confrontation Clause targeted. On the other hand, *ex parte* examinations might sometimes be admissible under modern hearsay rules, but the Framers certainly would not have condoned them.

The text of the Confrontation Clause reflects this focus. It applies to "witnesses" against the accused—in other words, those who "bear testimony." "Testimony," in turn, is typically "[a] solemn declaration or affirmation made for the purpose of establishing or proving some fact." An accuser who makes a formal statement to government officers bears testimony in a sense that a person who makes a casual remark to an acquaintance does not. The constitutional text, like the history underlying the common-law right of confrontation, thus reflects an especially acute concern with a specific type of out-of-court statement.

Various formulations of this core class of "testimonial" statements exist: "*ex parte* in-court testimony or its functional equivalent—that is, material such as affidavits, custodial examinations, prior testimony that the defendant was unable to cross-examine, or similar pretrial statements that declarants would reasonably expect to be used prosecutorially," "extrajudicial statements ... contained in formalized testimonial materials, such as affidavits, depositions, prior testimony, or confessions," *White v. Illinois,* 502 U.S. 346 (1992) (THOMAS, J., joined by SCALIA, J., concurring in part and concurring in judgment); "statements that were made under circumstances which would lead an objective witness reasonably to believe that the statement would be available for use at a later trial." These formulations all share a common nucleus and then define the Clause's coverage at various levels of abstraction around it. Regardless of the precise articulation, some statements qualify under any definition—for example, *ex parte* testimony at a preliminary hearing.

Statements taken by police officers in the course of interrogations are also testimonial under even a narrow standard.... That interrogators are police officers rather than magistrates does not change the picture.... The involvement of government officers in the production of testimonial evidence presents the same risk, whether the officers are police or justices of the peace. [E]ven if the Sixth Amendment is not solely concerned with testimonial hearsay, that is its primary object, and interrogations by law enforcement officers fall squarely within that class.

The historical record also supports a second proposition: that the Framers would not have allowed admission of testimonial statements of a witness who did not appear at trial unless he was unavailable to testify, and the defendant had had a prior opportunity for cross-examination. The text of the Sixth Amendment does not suggest any open-ended exceptions from the confrontation requirement to be developed by the courts. Rather, the "right ... to be confronted with the witnesses against him" is most naturally read as a reference to the right of confrontation at common law, admitting only those exceptions established at the time of the founding. As the English authorities above reveal, the common law in 1791 conditioned admissibility of an absent witness's examination on unavailability and a prior opportunity to cross-examine. The Sixth Amendment therefore incorporates those limitations....

We do not read the historical sources to say that a prior opportunity to cross-examine was merely a sufficient, rather than a necessary, condition for admissibility of testimonial statements. They suggest that this requirement was dispositive, and not merely one of several ways to establish reliability. This is not to deny [that] "[t]here were always exceptions to the general rule of exclusion" of hearsay evidence.... But there is scant evidence that exceptions were invoked to admit *testimonial* statements against the accused in a *criminal* case....

Our case law has been largely consistent with these two principles. [In] *Mattox v. United States,* 156 U.S. 237 (1895)[,] we relied on the fact that the defendant had had, at the first trial, an adequate opportunity to confront the witness.... Our later cases conform to *Mattox's* holding that prior trial or preliminary hearing testimony is admissible only if the defendant had an adequate opportunity to cross-examine. Even where the defendant had such an opportunity, we excluded the testimony where the government had not established unavailability of the wit-

ness.... Even our recent cases, in their outcomes, hew closely to the
traditional line. *Ohio v. Roberts,* 448 U.S., at 67–70, admitted testimony
from a preliminary hearing at which the defendant had examined the
witness. *Lilly v. Virginia,* excluded testimonial statements that the
defendant had had no opportunity to test by cross-examination. And
Bourjaily v. United States, 483 U.S. 171 (1987), admitted statements
made unwittingly to an FBI informant after applying a more general test
that did *not* make prior cross-examination an indispensable requirement....

Our cases have thus remained faithful to the Framers' understanding: Testimonial statements of witnesses absent from trial have been
admitted only where the declarant is unavailable, and only where the
defendant has had a prior opportunity to cross-examine. [W]hen the
declarant appears for cross-examination at trial, the Confrontation
Clause places no constraints at all on the use of his prior testimonial
statements. See *Tennessee v. Street,* 471 U.S. 409 (1985).

Although the results of our decisions have generally been faithful to
the original meaning of the Confrontation Clause, the same cannot be
said of our rationales. *Roberts* conditions the admissibility of all hearsay
evidence on whether it falls under a "firmly rooted hearsay exception"
or bears "particularized guarantees of trustworthiness." This test de-
parts from the historical principles identified above in two respects....
It applies the same mode of analysis whether or not the hearsay consists
of *ex parte* testimony. This often results in close constitutional scrutiny
in cases that are far removed from the core concerns of the Clause. At
the same time, however, the test is too narrow: It admits statements
that *do* consist of *ex parte* testimony upon a mere finding of reliability.
This malleable standard often fails to protect against paradigmatic
confrontation violations....

Where testimonial statements are involved, we do not think the
Framers meant to leave the Sixth Amendment's protection to the
vagaries of the rules of evidence, much less to amorphous notions of
"reliability." ... Admitting statements deemed reliable by a judge is
fundamentally at odds with the right of confrontation.... The Clause
[reflects] a judgment, not only about the desirability of reliable evidence[,] but about how reliability can best be determined. Cf. M. Hale,
History and Analysis of the Common Law of England 258 (1713)....
The *Roberts* test allows a jury to hear evidence, untested by the adversary process, based on a mere judicial determination of reliability. It thus
replaces the constitutionally prescribed method of assessing reliability
with a wholly foreign one....

Dispensing with confrontation because testimony is obviously reliable is akin to dispensing with jury trial because a defendant is obviously
guilty. This is not what the Sixth Amendment prescribes.

The legacy of *Roberts* in other courts vindicates the Framers'
wisdom in rejecting a general reliability exception. The framework is so

unpredictable that it fails to provide meaningful protection from even core confrontation violations.

Reliability is an amorphous, if not entirely subjective, concept. There are countless factors bearing on whether a statement is reliable.... Whether a statement is deemed reliable depends heavily on which factors the judge considers and how much weight he accords each of them. Some courts wind up attaching the same significance to opposite facts....

The unpardonable vice of the *Roberts* test, however, is not its unpredictability, but its demonstrated capacity to admit core testimonial statements that the Confrontation Clause plainly meant to exclude.... One recent study found that, after *Lilly,* appellate courts admitted accomplice statements to the authorities in 25 out of 70 cases—more than one-third of the time. Courts have invoked *Roberts* to admit other sorts of plainly testimonial statements despite the absence of any opportunity to cross-examine....

To add insult to injury, some of the courts that admit untested testimonial statements find reliability in the very factors that *make* the statements testimonial. [O]ne court relied on the fact that the witness's statement was made to police while in custody on pending charges—the theory being that this made the statement more clearly against penal interest and thus more reliable. That inculpating statements are given in a testimonial setting is not an antidote to the confrontation problem, but rather the trigger that makes the Clause's demands most urgent....

Roberts' failings were on full display in the proceedings below. Sylvia Crawford made her statement while in police custody, herself a potential suspect in the case. Indeed, she had been told that whether she would be released "depend[ed] on how the investigation continues." In response to often leading questions from police detectives, she implicated her husband in Lee's stabbing and at least arguably undermined his self-defense claim. Despite all this, the trial court admitted her statement, listing several reasons why it was reliable. In its opinion reversing, the Court of Appeals listed several *other* reasons why the statement was *not* reliable. Finally, the State Supreme Court relied exclusively on the interlocking character of the statement and disregarded every other factor the lower courts had considered. The case is thus a self-contained demonstration of *Roberts'* unpredictable and inconsistent application.

Each of the courts also made assumptions that cross-examination might well have undermined. The trial court, for example, stated that Sylvia Crawford's statement was reliable because she was an eyewitness with direct knowledge of the events. But Sylvia at one point told the police that she had "shut [her] eyes and ... didn't really watch" part of the fight, and that she was "in shock." [The] Framers would be astounded to learn that *ex parte* testimony could be admitted against a criminal defendant because it was elicited by "neutral" government officers. But even if the court's assessment of the officer's motives was accurate, it says nothing about Sylvia's perception of her situation. Only cross-examination could reveal that....

We readily concede that we could resolve this case by simply reweighing the "reliability factors" under *Roberts* and finding that Sylvia Crawford's statement falls short. [T]o reverse the Washington Supreme Court's decision after conducting our own reliability analysis would perpetuate [what] the Sixth Amendment condemns. The Constitution prescribes a procedure for determining the reliability of testimony in criminal trials, and [we] lack authority to replace it with one of our own devising.... The Framers [knew] that judges, like other government officers, could not always be trusted to safeguard the rights of the people.... They were loath to leave too much discretion in judicial hands. By replacing categorical constitutional guarantees with open-ended balancing tests, we do violence to their design....

Where nontestimonial hearsay is at issue, it is wholly consistent with the Framers' design to afford the States flexibility in their development of hearsay law—as does *Roberts,* and as would an approach that exempted such statements from Confrontation Clause scrutiny altogether. Where testimonial evidence is at issue, however, the Sixth Amendment demands what the common law required: unavailability and a prior opportunity for cross-examination. We leave for another day any effort to spell out a comprehensive definition of "testimonial." Whatever else the term covers, it applies at a minimum to prior testimony at a preliminary hearing, before a grand jury, or at a former trial; and to police interrogations. These are the modern practices with closest kinship to the abuses at which the Confrontation Clause was directed.

In this case, the State admitted Sylvia's testimonial statement against petitioner, despite the fact that he had no opportunity to cross-examine her. That alone is sufficient to make out a violation of the Sixth Amendment. *Roberts* notwithstanding, we decline to mine the record in search of indicia of reliability. Where testimonial statements are at issue, the only indicium of reliability sufficient to satisfy constitutional demands is the one the Constitution actually prescribes: confrontation.

The judgment of the Washington Supreme Court is reversed, and the case is remanded for further proceedings not inconsistent with this opinion.

It is so ordered.

CHIEF JUSTICE REHNQUIST, with whom JUSTICE O'CONNOR joins, concurring in the judgment.

I dissent from the Court's decision to overrule *Roberts*.... The Court's distinction between testimonial and nontestimonial statements [is] no better rooted in history than our current doctrine.... Testimonial statements such as accusatory statements to police officers likely would have been disapproved of in the 18th century, not necessarily because they resembled *ex parte* affidavits or depositions as the Court reasons, but more likely than not because they were not made under oath. See *King v. Woodcock,* 1 Leach 500, 503, 168 Eng. Rep. 352, 353 (1789). Without an oath, one usually did not get to the second step of whether confrontation was required.

[W]hile I agree that the Framers were mainly concerned about sworn affidavits and depositions, it does not follow that they were similarly concerned about the Court's broader category of testimonial statements. [U]nsworn testimonial statements were treated no differently at common law than were nontestimonial statements, and it seems to me any classification of statements as testimonial beyond that of sworn affidavits and depositions will be somewhat arbitrary, merely a proxy for what the Framers might have intended had such evidence been liberally admitted as substantive evidence like it is today.... I therefore see no reason why the distinction the Court draws is preferable to our precedent.... Exceptions to confrontation have always been derived from the experience that some out-of-court statements are just as reliable as cross-examined in-court testimony due to the circumstances under which they were made....

"[I]n a given instance [cross-examination may] be superfluous; it may be sufficiently clear [that] the statement offered is free enough from the risk of inaccuracy and untrustworthiness, so that the test of cross-examination would be a work of supererogation." 5 Wigmore § 1420, at 251.... In choosing the path it does, the Court of course overrules *Roberts,* a case decided nearly a quarter of a century ago.... The Court grandly declares that "[w]e leave for another day any effort to spell out a comprehensive definition of 'testimonial,' "But the thousands of federal prosecutors and the tens of thousands of state prosecutors need answers as to what beyond the specific kinds of "testimony" the Court lists is covered by the new rule. They need them now, not months or years from now. Rules of criminal evidence are applied every day in courts throughout the country, and parties should not be left in the dark in this manner.

[The] result the Court reaches follows inexorably from *Roberts* and its progeny without any need for overruling that line of cases. In *Idaho v. Wright,* 497 U.S. 805 (1990), we held that an out-of-court statement was not admissible simply because the truthfulness of that statement was corroborated by other evidence at trial.... A citation to *Wright,* would suffice. [T]his would be a far preferable course for the Court to take here.

CHAPMAN v. STATE OF CALIFORNIA
386 U.S. 18 (1967).

MR. JUSTICE BLACK delivered the opinion of the Court.

Petitioners, Ruth Elizabeth Chapman and Thomas LeRoy Teale, were convicted in a California state court upon a charge that they robbed, kidnaped, and murdered a bartender. She was sentenced to life imprisonment and he to death. At the time of the trial, Art I, § 13, of the

State's Constitution provided that "in any criminal case, whether the defendant testifies or not, his failure to explain or to deny by his testimony any evidence or facts in the case against him may be commented upon by the court and by counsel, and may be considered by the court or the jury." Both petitioners [chose] not to testify at their trial, and the State's attorney [filled] his argument to the jury from beginning to end with numerous references to their silence and inferences of their guilt resulting therefrom. The trial court also charged the jury that it could draw adverse inferences from petitioners' failure to testify. Shortly after the trial, [this] Court decided *Griffin v. State of California*, 380 U.S. 609, in which we held California's constitutional provision and practice invalid on the ground that they put a penalty on the exercise of a person's right not to be compelled to be a witness against himself, guaranteed by the Fifth Amendment to the United States Constitution and made applicable [to the] States by the Fourteenth Amendment. On appeal, the State Supreme Court [affirmed] applying the State Constitution's harmless error provision, which forbids reversal unless "the court shall be of the opinion that the error complained of has resulted in a miscarriage of justice." We granted [certiorari].

[We] are urged by petitioners to hold that all federal constitutional errors, regardless of the facts and circumstances, must always be deemed harmful. Such a holding [would] require an automatic reversal of their convictions and make further discussion unnecessary. We decline to adopt any such rule. All 50 States have harmless error statutes or rules, [and] Congress [long ago] established for [the] courts the rule that judgments shall not be reversed for "errors or defects which do not affect the substantial rights of the parties." 28 U.S.C. § 2111.... All of these rules, state or federal, serve a very useful purpose insofar as they block setting aside convictions for small errors or defects that have little, if any, likelihood of having changed the result of the trial. We conclude that there may be some constitutional errors which in the setting of a particular case are so unimportant and insignificant that they may, consistent with the Federal Constitution, be deemed harmless, not requiring the automatic reversal of the conviction.

In fashioning a harmless-constitutional-error rule, we must recognize that harmless error rules can work very unfair and mischievous results [when] highly important and persuasive evidence, or argument, though legally forbidden, finds its way into a trial in which the question of guilt or innocence is a close one. What harmless error rules all aim at is a rule that will save the good in harmless error practices while avoiding the bad, so far as possible.

The federal rule emphasizes "substantial rights" as do most others. The California constitutional rule emphasizes "a miscarriage of justice," but the California courts have neutralized this to some extent by emphasis [upon] the court's view of "overwhelming evidence." We prefer the approach of this Court in deciding what was harmless error in our recent case of *Fahy v. State of Connecticut*, 375 U.S. 85[:] "The question is whether there is a reasonable possibility that the evidence complained of might have contributed to the conviction." Although our prior cases have indicated that there are some constitutional rights so basic to a fair trial that their infraction can never be treated as harmless error, this statement [belies] any belief that all trial errors which violate the Constitution automatically call for reversal. At the same time[,] like the federal harmless error statute, it emphasizes an intention not to treat as harmless those constitutional errors that "affect substantial rights" of a party. An error in admitting plainly relevant evidence which possibly influenced the jury adversely to a litigant cannot [be] conceived of as harmless. Certainly error, constitutional error, in illegally admitting highly prejudicial evidence or comments, casts on someone other than the person prejudiced by it a burden to show that it was harmless. It is for that reason that the original common-law harmless error rule put the burden on the beneficiary of the error either to prove that there was no injury or to suffer a reversal of his erroneously obtained judgment. There is little, if any, difference between our statement in *Fahy* about "whether there is a reasonable possibility that the evidence complained of might have contributed to the conviction" and requiring the beneficiary of a constitutional error to prove beyond a reasonable doubt that the error complained of did not contribute to the verdict obtained. We, therefore, [hold] that before a federal constitutional error can be held harmless, the court must be able to declare a belief that it was harmless beyond a reasonable doubt. [It] is a familiar standard to all courts, and we believe its adoption will provide a more workable standard, although achieving the same result as that aimed at in our *Fahy*, case.

[We] have no doubt that the error in these cases was not harmless to petitioners. [One] need only glance at the prosecutorial [comments]. The California Supreme Court [summarized the] comments as follows: "Such comments went to the motives for the procurement and handling of guns purchased by Mrs. Chapman, funds or the lack thereof in Mr. Teale's possession immediately prior to the killing, the amount of intoxicating liquors consumed by defendants at the Spot Club and other taverns, the circumstances of the shooting in the automobile and the removal of the victim's body therefrom, who fired the fatal shots, why defendants used a false registration at a motel shortly after the killing, the meaning of a letter written by Mrs. Chapman several days after the killing, why Teale had a loaded weapon in his possession when apprehended, the meaning of statements made by Teale after his apprehension, why certain clothing and articles of personal property were shipped by defendants to Missouri, what clothing Mrs. Chapman wore at the time of the killing, conflicting statements as to Mrs. Chapman's whereabouts immediately preceding the killing and, generally, the overall commission of the crime." Thus, the state prosecutor's argument and the trial judge's instruction to the jury continuously and repeatedly impressed the jury that from the failure of petitioners to testify, [the] inferences from [the] evidence had to be drawn in favor of the State—[that] by their silence petitioners had served as irrefutable witnesses against themselves. And though the case [involved] a reasonably strong "circumstantial web of evidence" against petitioners, it was also a case in which, absent the constitutionally forbidden comments, honest, fair-minded jurors might very well have brought in not-guilty verdicts. Under these circumstances, it is completely impossible for us to say that the State has demonstrated, beyond a reasonable doubt, that the prosecutor's comments and the trial judge's instruction did not contribute to petitioners' convictions. Such a machine-gun repetition of a denial of constitutional rights, designed and calculated to make petitioners' version of the evidence worthless, can no more be considered harmless than the introduction against a defendant of a coerced confession. Petitioners are entitled to a trial free from the pressure of unconstitutional inferences.

Reversed and remanded.

Mr. Justice Stewart, concurring in the result.

[In] a long line of cases, involving a variety of constitutional claims[,] this Court has steadfastly rejected any notion that constitutional violations might be disregarded on the ground that they were "harmless." * * *

When involuntary confessions have been introduced at trial, the Court has always reversed convictions regardless of other evidence of guilt. As we stated in *Lynumn v. State of Illinois*, 372 U.S. 528, the argument that the error in admitting such a confession "was a harmless one [is] an impermissible doctrine." [Even] when the confession is completely "unnecessary" to the conviction, the defendant is entitled to "a new trial free of constitutional infirmity."

When a defendant has been denied counsel at trial, we have refused to consider claims that this constitutional error might have been harmless. "The right to have the assistance of counsel is too fundamental and absolute to allow courts to indulge in nice calculations as to the amount of prejudice arising from its denial." *Glasser v. United States*, 315 U.S. 60. [Even] before trial, when counsel has not been provided at a critical stage, "we do not stop to determine whether prejudice resulted." *Hamilton v. State of Alabama*, 368 U.S. 52.

A conviction must be reversed if the trial judge's remuneration is based on a scheme giving him a financial interest in the result, even if no particular prejudice is shown and even if the defendant was clearly guilty. To try a defendant in a community that has been exposed to publicity highly adverse to the defendant is per se ground for reversal of his conviction; no showing need be made that the jurors were in fact prejudiced against him. *Sheppard v. Maxwell*, 384 U.S. 333.

When a jury is instructed in an unconstitutional presumption, the conviction must be overturned, though there was ample evidence apart from the presumption to sustain the verdict. *Bollenbach v. United States*, 326 U.S. 607. Reversal is required when a conviction may have been rested on a constitutionally impermissible ground, despite the fact that there was a valid alternative ground on which the conviction could have been sustained. [It] has never been suggested that reversal of convictions because of purposeful discrimination in the selection of grand and petit jurors turns on any showing of prejudice to the defendant.

To be sure, constitutional rights are not fungible goods. The differing values which they represent and protect may make a harmless error rule appropriate for one type of constitutional error and not for another. I would not foreclose the possibility that a harmless-error rule might appropriately be applied to some constitutional violations.[17] Indeed, one source of my disagreement with the court's opinion is its implicit assumption that the same harmless-error rule should apply indiscriminately to all constitutional violations.

But I see no reason to break with settled precedent in this case, and promulgate a novel rule of harmless error applicable to clear violations of *Griffin v. State of California*, 380 U.S. 609. The adoption of any harmless error rule [commits] this Court to a case-by-case examination to determine the extent to which we think unconstitutional comment on a defendant's failure to testify influenced the outcome of a particular trial. This burdensome obligation is one that we here are hardly qualified to discharge. [For] these reasons I believe it inappropriate to inquire whether the violation of *Griffin* that occurred in this case was harmless by any standard, and accordingly I concur in the reversal of the judgment.

Proving

1. *Proving That an Error is "Harmless."* In the early 1980s, John Hinckley attempted to assassinate President Ronald Reagan. Suppose that the attempt is caught on videotape, and Hinckley is immediately apprehended by the police. After Hinckley is apprehended, the police take him to police headquarters where he is interrogated without a *Miranda* warning and makes incriminating statements. At Hinckley's trial, the statements are admitted along with other evidence. On appeal, Hinckley seeks reversal based on a violation of *Miranda*. Suppose that you represent the state and you want to argue that admission of the incriminating statements was "harmless error." How would you argue the case? How might the defense respond?

2. *Can the Admission of a Coerced Confession Ever Constitute "Harmless Error?"* While Fulminante was in prison on weapons charges, he was suspected of having murdered his step-daughter. He was befriended by a former police officer (Savriola), who was working as a paid undercover FBI informant, and who masqueraded as an organized crime figure. When the general prison population learned that Fulminante was suspected of having murdered a child, he began receiving "some tough treatment." Savriola offered to protect Fulminante, but only if Fulminante told him about the

---

17. [Q]uite different considerations are involved when evidence is introduced which was obtained in violation of the Fourth and Fourteenth Amendments. The exclusionary rule in that context balances the desirability of deterring objectionable police conduct against the undesirability of excluding relevant and reliable evidence. The resolution of these values with interests of judicial economy might well dictate a harmless-error rule for such violations.

crime. Fulminante then admitted that he had murdered the girl and the admission is used to convict him of murder. Suppose that the Court concludes that the confession was coerced. Is it possible for a coerced confession to be regarded as "harmless error?" Why? Why not? *See Arizona v. Fulminante*, 499 U.S. 279 (1991).

3. *Can a Bruton Violation be Harmless?* Four defendants were jointly tried for attempted robbery and first-degree murder. Harrington's motion to sever the prosecutions was denied. At trial, the prosecution admitted the confessions of Harrington's codefendants with limiting instructions that the jury was to consider the confession only against the confessor. Only one of the defendants took the stand and was subjected to cross-examination. Relying on *Bruton v. United States*, 391 U.S. 123 (1968), in which the Court held that the prosecution could not use the confession of codefendants who did not take the stand without violating the Confrontation Clause of the Sixth Amendment, Harrington challenged the admission of the confessions. Is the error "harmless?" Would it matter whether the case against Harrington was "overwhelming?" What if, instead of being overwhelming, the evidence was disputed? *See Harrington v. California*, 395 U.S. 250 (1969).

4. *Violation of the Sixth Amendment Right to Counsel.* After petitioner was indicted and received appointed counsel, a police officer posed as a prisoner and shared a cell with petitioner for two days. At petitioner's trial, the officer testified to incriminating statements made by petitioner. If the cell-mates actions are found to violate defendant's Sixth Amendment right to counsel, can the error be regarded as harmless? Should it matter that the evidence against defendant is "overwhelming?" What if it is not overwhelming? *See Milton v. Wainwright*, 407 U.S. 371 (1972).

5. *Flawed Jury Instructions.* Respondent was convicted of second-degree murder which required proof of malice. The trial court gave the jury an instruction which stated that "[a]ll homicides are presumed to be malicious in the absence of evidence which would rebut the implied presumption. Thus, if the State has proven beyond a reasonable [doubt] that a killing has occurred, then it is presumed that the killing was done maliciously. But this presumption may be rebutted by either direct or circumstantial evidence, or by both, regardless of whether the same be offered by the Defendant, or exists in the evidence of the State." This instruction violated the principles of *Sandstrom v. Montana*, 442 U.S. 510 (1979), and *Francis v. Franklin*, 471 U.S. 307 (1985), both of which required the prosecution to prove respondent's right to have his guilt determined beyond a reasonable doubt. Would it matter that the jury was also given another instruction which required them to find defendant guilty as to "all" elements of the crime? *See Rose v. Clark*, 478 U.S. 570 (1986).

6. *More on Flawed Jury Instructions.* A trial court gave a jury a deficient "reasonable-doubt" instruction. The jury found petitioner guilty of first-degree murder and subsequently recommended that he be sentenced to death. Is a defect in the "reasonable doubt" instruction so fundamental that it should never be regarded as "harmless?" *See Sullivan v. Louisiana*, 508 U.S. 275 (1993).

Part III

THE ADVERSARY SYSTEM

Chapter 10

INTRODUCTION TO THE ADVERSARY SYSTEM

Unlike criminal justice systems in many parts of the world, the American criminal justice system is an adversary system. A criminal defendant's guilt or innocence is determined as a result of the adversarial arguments and presentations of evidence by a prosecutor and defense counsel, overseen by a neutral and impartial judge.

While such a system has the immediate virtue of familiarity to most Americans, it is difficult if not impossible to argue that this method of adjudication is the *only* fair way to determine the guilt or innocence of criminal defendants. Indeed, some commentators argue that the American adversarial system, in practice if not in theory, is not truly fair at all. In the face of such criticisms, it is worthwhile to consider whether or not an adversary criminal adjudication model is and continues to be the most appropriate way to try criminal defendants in this country. And, even if we decide on balance that it is, what does that mean in terms of the appropriate roles of defense counsel and prosecutors?

A. COSTS AND BENEFITS

THE ROSCOE POUND–AMERICAN TRIAL LAWYERS FOUNDATION—THE AMERICAN LAWYER'S CODE OF CONDUCT

(rev. ed. 1982).

PREAMBLE

The legal system that gives context and meaning to basic American rights is the adversary system. It is the adversary system which assures each of us a "champion against a hostile world," and which thereby helps to preserve and enhance our dignity as individuals.

Recognizing that the American attorney functions in an adversary system, and that such a system expresses fundamental American values, helps us to appreciate the emptiness of some cliches of lawyers' ethics. It is said, for example, that the lawyer is an "officer of the court," or an "officer of the legal system." Out of context, such phrases are at best meaningless, and at worst misleading. In the context of the adversary system, it is clear that the lawyer for a private party is and should be an officer of a court only in the sense of serving a court as a zealous, partisan advocate of one side of the case before it, and in the sense of having been licensed by a court to play that very role.

MONROE H. FREEDMAN—LAWYERS' ETHICS IN AN ADVERSARY SYSTEM (1975)*

2–4, 9.

Let us begin [with] an understanding of the role of a criminal defense attorney in a totalitarian state. As expressed by law professors at the University of Havana, "the first job of a revolutionary lawyer is not to argue that his client is innocent, but rather to determine if his client is guilty and, if so, to seek the sanction which will best rehabilitate him".

Similarly, a Bulgarian attorney began his defense in a criminal treason trial by noting that: "In a socialist state there is no division of duty between the judge, prosecutor, and defense counsel. [The] defense must assist the prosecution to find the objective truth in a case." In that case, the defense attorney ridiculed his client's defense, and the client was convicted and executed. Sometime later the verdict was found to have been erroneous, and the defendant was "rehabilitated".

The emphasis in a free society is, of course, sharply different. Under our adversary system, the interests of the state are not absolute, or even paramount. The dignity of the individual is respected to the point that even when the citizen is known by the state to have committed a heinous offense, the individual is nevertheless accorded such rights as counsel, trial by jury, due process, and the privilege against self-incrimination.

A trial is, in part, a search for truth. Accordingly, those basic rights are most often characterized as procedural safeguards against error in the search for truth. Actually, however, a trial is far more than a search for truth, and the constitutional rights that are provided by our system of justice may well outweigh the truth-seeking value—a fact which is manifest when we consider that those rights and others guaranteed by the Constitution may well impede the search for truth rather than further it. What more effective way is there, for example, to expose a defendant's guilt than to require self-incrimination, at least to the extent of compelling the defendant to take the stand and respond to interrogation before the jury? The defendant, however, is presumed innocent; the burden is on the prosecution to prove guilt beyond a reasonable doubt, and even the guilty accused has an "absolute constitutional right" to remain silent and to put the government to its proof.

* Professor Freedman has updated and expanded his views, including discussion of the Model Rules of Professional Conduct and the Restatement of the Law Governing Lawyers. See Monroe Freedman & Abbe Smith, Understanding Lawyers' Ethics (3d ed., 2004) (Matthew Bender).

Thus, the defense lawyer's professional obligation may well be to advise the client to withhold the truth. As Justice Jackson said: "Any lawyer worth his salt will tell the suspect in no uncertain terms to make no statement to police under any circumstances." Similarly, the defense lawyer is obligated to prevent the introduction of evidence that may be wholly reliable, such as a murder weapon seized in violation of the Fourth Amendment, or a truthful but involuntary confession. Justice White has observed that although law enforcement officials must be dedicated to using only truthful evidence, "defense counsel has no comparable obligation to ascertain or present the truth. Our system assigns him a different mission. [We] insist that he defend his client whether he is innocent or guilty."

[By] emphasizing that the adversary process has its foundations in respect for human dignity, even at the expense of the search for truth, I do not mean to deprecate the search for truth or to suggest that the adversary system is not concerned with it. On the contrary, truth is a basic value, and the adversary system is one of the most efficient and fair methods for determining it. That system proceeds on the assumption that the best way to ascertain the truth is to present to an impartial judge or jury a confrontation between the proponents of conflicting views, assigning to each the task of marshalling and presenting the evidence in as thorough and persuasive a way as possible. the truth-seeking techniques used by the advocates on each side include investigation, pretrial discovery, cross-examination of opposing witnesses, and a marshalling of the evidence in summation. Thus, the judge or jury is given the strongest possible view of each side, and is put in the best possible position to make an accurate and fair judgment. Nevertheless, the point that I now emphasize is that in a society that honors the dignity of the individual, the high value that we assign to truth-seeking is not an absolute, but may on occasion be subordinated to even higher values.

[T]he adversary system assumes that the most efficient and fair way of determining the truth is by presenting the strongest possible case for each side of the controversy before an impartial judge or jury. Each advocate, therefore, must give "entire devotion to the interest of the client, warm zeal in the maintenance and defense of his rights and the exertion of his utmost learning and ability". The classic statement of that ideal is by Lord Brougham, in his representation of the Queen in *Queen Caroline's Case*. Threatening to defend his client on a ground that would, literally, have brought down the kingdom, Brougham stated:

> [A]n advocate, in the discharge of his duty, knows but one person in all the world, and that person is his client. To save that client by all means and expedients, and at all hazards and costs to other persons, and, amongst them, to himself, is his first and only duty; and in performing this duty he must not regard the alarm, the torments, the destruction which he may bring upon others. separating the duty of a patriot from that of an advocate, he must go on

reckless of the consequences, though it should be his unhappy fate to involve his country in confusion.

Let justice be done—that is, for my client let justice be done—though the heavens fall. That is the kind of advocacy that I would want as a client and that I feel bound to provide as an advocate. The rest of the picture, however, should not be ignored. the adversary system ensures an advocate on the other side, and an impartial judge over both. Despite the advocate's argument, therefore, the heavens do not really have to fall—not unless justice requires that they do.

W. WILLIAM HODES—SEEKING THE TRUTH VERSUS TELLING THE TRUTH AT THE BOUNDARIES OF THE LAW: MISDIRECTION, LYING, AND "LYING WITH AN EXPLANATION"

44 S. Tex. L. Rev. 53, 57–62 (2002).

One of the most brutal clashes between competing values is that between "truth" and "justice," with implications for the very nature of the legal system itself. Finding the truth and then resolving disputes on the basis of that truth ranks very highly in our value system. But so does achieving justice, even though justice as Peter defines it will often be purchased at Paul's expense, and even though some of the truth is frequently obscured or even sacrificed along the way. And, of course, the elusive and essentially fatuous concept of "the whole truth" is always lost in the fog of adversarial combat.

The tension between truth on the one hand, and justice on the other—the latter often equated in our culture simply with winning—has long engaged both the legal profession and the public. This clash of values arises most dramatically in the context of high profile criminal trials, which correspondingly receive the most media attention and public debate.

The public is offended enough when a criminal defense is based on suppression of evidence or some other legal or "technical" defense. But that pales in comparison to the outrage expressed when it appears that the defense lawyers knew the truth of a client's factual guilt, but nonetheless attempted to achieve an acquittal on the merits. This is often seen as a form of "lying," and it must be conceded that the lawyer's plan in such a case is to induce the jury to come to a conclusion that the lawyer knows is factually wrong, namely that someone other than the accused physically did the deeds in question.

Defense lawyers, on the other hand, and allies in the bar generally, are typically angered by such attacks, and point to a lawyer's obligation—rooted in both professional ethics and in the Sixth Amendment to the United States Constitution—to use all legal means to mount a defense, whether or not the client is known to be factually guilty. More important, for present purposes, they reject any claim that they have "lied," if no false evidence has been introduced, and if they have engaged only in argumentation, pointing out inconsistencies and trying to punch logical holes in the government's case, and suggesting alternative "narratives" that the jury is free to accept or reject.

This quarrel can be seen as no more than a variant on the distinction between active and passive behavior, but I prefer the shorthand implicit in the title of this essay—that while lawyers must tell the truth, they are not required to seek the truth or to aid in the search. Instead, they are often required by their roles to work to obscure inconvenient truths and to prevent the truth from coming out.

Moreover, although I have my moments of queasiness, like everyone else, and although I struggle along with everyone else to locate the exact boundary line between truth and justice, I am convinced that the law of lawyering has drawn this particular line roughly where it ought to be drawn.

DEBORAH L. RHODE—THE FUTURE OF THE LEGAL PROFESSION: INSTITUTIONALIZING ETHICS

44 CASE W. RES. L.REV. 665, 667–73 (1994).

The central norm of contemporary American legal practice is one of neutral partisanship; the attorney's role is to advance client interests "zealously within the bounds of the law" regardless of the attorney's own assessment of their underlying merits. Although lawyers have certain obligations as officers of the court, these are quite limited and largely track the prohibitions on criminal and fraudulent conduct that govern all participants in the legal process.

This neutral partisanship model rests on two assumptions. The first is that an adversarial clash between two zealous advocates is the best way to discover truth and to promote accurate legal decision making. A second assumption is that partisan advocacy provides the most effective protection for individual rights. [The] first assumption, that an adversarial clash yields accurate outcomes, is not self-evident. As many commentators have observed, this is not how most countries adjudicate disputes, how most professionals investigate facts, or even how most lawyers conduct inquiries outside the courtroom.

[In] an adversarial model, the merits prevail only if the contest is a balanced one—that is, if each side has roughly equal access to relevant legal information, resources, and capabilities. Yet how often a fully balanced contest occurs in practice is open to doubt. American lawyers practice in a social order that tolerates vast disparities in wealth, makes most litigation enormously expensive, and allocates civil legal assistance almost entirely through market mechanisms. Under these circumstances, one would expect that the "haves" generally come out ahead.

Among defenders of current partisan norms, the conventional "solution" to the problem of unequal advocacy "is not to impose on counsel the burden of representing interests other than those of his client, but rather to take appropriate steps to ensure that all interests are effectively represented.'' Exactly what those steps might be have never been satisfactorily elaborated. [Inequalities] in access have been seriously confronted only at a rhetorical level.

[The] unqualified pursuit of client interests carries obvious costs: It obstructs the decision-making process, imposes unnecessary delays and expense, and deters meritorious claims. [In] response to such criticisms, proponents of neutral partisanship typically invoke a second line of defense. Whatever its effectiveness or efficiency in promoting truth, this partisan framework is an indispensable safeguard of individual rights. On this view, respect for clients' autonomy implies respect for their pursuit of legal claims and demands largely undivided loyalty from their legal advisors. By absolving attorneys from accountability for clients' acts, the traditional advocacy role encourages representation of those most vulnerable to public prejudice and state oppression. The promise of non-judgmental advocacy may also encourage legal consultation by those most in need of ethical counseling. Any alternative system, it is argued, would threaten "rule by an oligarchy of lawyers." To demand that attorneys judge, rather than simply defend, their clients would be "equivalent to saying that saints must have a monopoly of lawsuits" and that the lawyers should have a monopoly of deciding who qualifies for sainthood.

From an ethical standpoint, this justification for neutral partisanship presents two central difficulties. First, it conflates legal and moral entitlements; it assumes that society wishes to permit whatever lawmakers do not prohibit. Yet some conduct that is clearly antithetical to broader public interests may nonetheless remain legal—either because prohibitions appear too difficult or costly to enforce, or because decision makers are too uninformed, overworked, or pressured by special interests. Although lawyers may have no special moral expertise, they at least have a more disinterested perspective than clients on the ethical dimensions of certain practices. Attorneys can accept moral responsibility without necessarily imposing it. Unless the lawyer is the last in town, his or her refusal of the neutral partisan role may simply impose on clients the psychological and financial cost of finding alternative counsel.

A second problem with rights-based justifications for partisanship is that they fail to explain why the rights of clients should trump those of all other parties whose interests are inadequately represented.

[Much] of the appeal of rights-based justifications for partisanship draws on the lawyer's role in criminal defense proceedings. Yet such proceedings are distinctive in their potential for governmental oppression and in their impact on individual life, liberty, and reputation. For the same reasons that our constitutional traditions impose special protections for criminal cases, most commentators suggest that the justifications for neutral partisanship are strongest in that context. To be sure, in some civil matters, the potential for state action or the constraints on fundamental rights raise concerns analogous to those at issue in criminal proceedings. Yet while zealous advocacy has been of enormous importance in such civil cases, they do not constitute the mainstay of legal work. Only a small portion of the bar is primarily involved either in criminal defense or in civil rights, civil liberties, and public interest representation. Professional norms that are appropriate in those cases can hardly serve as the paradigm for all legal practice.

GORDON VAN KESSEL—ADVERSARY EXCESSES IN THE AMERICAN CRIMINAL TRIAL

67 Notre Dame L.Rev. 403, 405–06, 407–09, 410, 413–15, 415–20, 548–51 (1992).

The American criminal justice adjudication system typically produces numerous rapid-fire convictions based on pressurized guilty pleas and a few complex, lengthy and highly adversary trials that often provide more entertainment than justice. Yet, we are unable or unwilling to make the fundamental reforms necessary to create a system that would be fair and effective for its consumers, i.e., victims, witnesses, defendants, and the general public.

In evaluating our criminal jury trial system and considering reforms, we would benefit by examining the less adversary approaches of the great majority of civilized countries today. [Examination] of our adversary system will reveal a number of unhealthy aspects that largely stem from our unquestioned worship of what we perceive to be the adversary ideal. We strive to preserve its purity by resisting all reforms in the name of defending against "inquisitorial" encroachments. Our insistence on extreme forms of the adversary model results in judicial passivity and lawyer domination of the jury trial, emphasis on the contest rather than on the outcome, over-reliance on the lay jury, and formal, restrictive evidentiary and procedural rules. The ultimate result is the most uncompromisingly adversary criminal trial structure in the world.

We pay a high price for these excesses. In the past few decades, criminal jury trials have become so lengthy and complex that we cannot, or will not, provide them to the vast majority of defendants. Instead of offering a fair and expeditious procedure in which the trier of fact has the opportunity to hear substantially all relevant evidence and come to an informed decision, our system relies on pleas of guilty that entirely displace the trial. This system requires that the accused be subjected to threats of increased punishment for going to trial. The few trials that do take place often fall short of the primary goal of achieving a fair, expeditious, and reliable resolution of the charges. Excessive trial length itself often diminishes the quality of the trial. Lawyer control, highly contentious advocacy, and rigid procedural rules tend to shift the focus of the trial from the accused and from truth-determining objectives to the contest between counsel. Over-reliance on the lay jury and on formal and technical rules of evidence and procedure hinder the prompt and reliable adjudication of guilt.

[Contrary] to many other observers who have embarked upon this comparative sea, I conclude that, at least in serious criminal cases, we should reject as both impractical and undesirable radical changes to our trial system through wholesale or piecemeal adoption of the main nonadversary procedures of Continental systems. However, less radical reforms are both possible and desirable. Without abandoning the essential adversary character of our criminal trial, we should take measured steps to restrain our lawyers, and encourage judges to exercise greater authority. Judges should control abuses by directing the course of the trial in such areas as case management, jury selection, and questioning of witnesses. We should also seek to shift the focus of the trial from the battle between the lawyers to the discovery of truth by modifying our complex rules of evidence, encouraging the defendant to contribute to the search for truth, and requiring full and open discovery from the prosecutor.

Finally, in endeavoring to moderate the extreme contentiousness of our lawyers and their desire to win at any cost, we should concentrate our efforts on changing those structural aspects of our adversary system that encourage and enable lawyers to frustrate truth-determining objectives in the pursuit of victory rather than pursuing reform primarily through modifying the ethical rules governing lawyer conduct. By reducing adversary excesses in our criminal trials, we will speed up the trial process and focus it more sharply on the central character of the trial—the accused—and on the most important issue—guilt or innocence.

[We] should * * * rid ourselves of inaccurate assumptions about the fundamental nature of adversary and nonadversary systems. American courts have suggested that our adversary system contrasts with inquisitory ones because we offer the privilege against self-incrimination, due process, and the presumption of innocence. However, these guarantees, though often in different form, also are found in most modern nonadversary systems. The essence of the modern nonadversary (Continental) system lies not in the presence of these guarantees, but in its nature as a judicial inquiry in which the primary responsibility for presenting the evidence and conducting the trial rests with the judge rather than with opposing parties. The nonadversary system is characterized by an activist judge familiar with the facts of the case who calls and first questions the witnesses. The other important characteristics of the current Continental nonadversary system include a mixed tribunal composed of professional and lay judges as the fact finder in serious cases and the absence of formal or technical rules of evidence.

A clear picture of the major distinctions between adversary and nonadversary systems makes it apparent that one system is not inherently more fair or reliable than the other; rather, each has its own particular attributes and deficiencies. [It] is arguable that by allowing the defendant full discovery of the state's case, an opportunity to give unsworn narrative testimony, and a right to written reasons supporting the fact finder's decision, the nonadversary system shows greater respect for the accused. In terms of the fundamental differences between the two systems, surely there is nothing sinister or presumptively unfair in a procedure which depends upon an "inquiry" into the facts by a neutral and informed judge rather than upon presentation of evidence by interested "advocates" to an unprepared fact finder.

Similarly, the adversary system is not by nature more reliable. Some contend that a contest is inherently more likely to reveal the truth than an inquiry. By presenting their case to an impartial judge or jury, proponents of conflicting views will be as thorough and persuasive as possible. The fact finder will be "given the strongest case that each side can present" and will be "in a position to make an informed, considered, and fair judgment." Also, some argue that a passive and uninformed judge is more likely to avoid bias, because a judge who studies the case file developed by the police and prosecutor prior to trial may tend to reach a conclusion at an early stage and be impervious to contradictory evidence later developed at trial. While these arguments appear to point out strengths of the adversary system, they fail to consider its many weaknesses. For example, the adversary system usually involves partisan advocates, burdened by a lack of discovery and restrictive rules of evidence, besieging an ignorant fact-finder.

[Yet] the American trial does serve one purpose—it is terrific entertainment.

Exercise

Spend at least half a day observing a criminal trial or hearings at your local courthouse. Write a paper briefly reporting the nature of your observations and addressing all of the following questions where they are applicable: Were defense counsel and the prosecutor contentious in their advocacy? Should they have been more zealous or adversarial in their advocacy? In what ways did the outcome of the proceedings you observed turn on the adversarial manner of presentation of arguments and/or evidence? What difference do you think it would have made if the proceedings had taken place in a more inquisitorial fashion?

B. DEFENSE COUNSEL'S ROLE

Accepting the present reality, *i.e.* that criminal trials take place in an adversary setting, what does adversariness mean in practice for defense counsel? Is it possible to be an able and effective defense attorney and to be a "good person" at the same time? Is it possible to stay emotionally healthy?

SUSAN BANDES—REPRESSION AND DENIAL IN CRIMINAL LAWYERING
9 Buff. Crim. L. Rev. 339, 339–343, 359–363, 366–369 (2006).

For criminal defense attorneys, being asked to justify defending "those people" is such a predictable part of the job it may as well be included in the job description. Laypeople "want to find out how criminal lawyers can represent people who hurt other people." Scholars are interested in the same question, albeit in more sophisticated garb. For scholars, "[t]he central question of legal ethics arises . . . because lawyers are sometimes asked or required, in their role as lawyers, to do things that strike all conscientious people . . . as morally suspect." Yet this is a topic that fascinates mostly laypeople and scholars. Defense attorneys, as a rule, are comfortable with their ethical obligation to offer a zealous defense and do not find the question, as posed, very interesting.

[A] separate though related conversation needs to occur. Its topic is how, in an emotional sense, one defends people accused of terrible crimes, and what toll such defense takes. [The] emotional costs of lawyering are rarely considered worthy of mainstream legal discussion. To the extent the topic of emotional adaptation is broached, either in the criminal defense context or more broadly, its locales tend to be psychology journals, clinical law publications, and seminars on legal education or legal writing. This marginalization is problematic. Questions about how we lawyers do our jobs cannot be neatly divided into intellectual and emotional spheres, or into doctrinal, strategic, ethical, and emotional quadrants. Such divisions manage to shortchange every aspect of lawyering: the intellectual as well as the emotional; the scholarly as well as the practical.

Most obviously, the traditional view tends to ensure that the emotional variables affecting legal practice will receive inadequate attention. There may be no other profession whose practitioners are required to deal with so much pain with so little support and guidance. And there is ample evidence that we could use the help: levels of alcoholism, drug abuse, depression, and other serious dysfunction that are well above those for other stressful professions. The problem is more basic, though, than a lack of support systems. In the conventional view the very acknowledgment of our work's emotional aspects—of the pain we cause, the pain we experience, the costs of the dissonance between role and conscience, the empathy or revulsion we may feel toward particular clients and how we ought to deal with it—seems at odds with law's essence as a rational and rigorous discipline. In short, acknowledging the role of emotion may brand one as not merely weak, but downright unlawyerlike.

The conventional division between emotion and reason shortchanges the discussion of the theory and practice of lawyering as well. [Certain] emotional strategies can be seen to affect a lawyer's ability to do a professional job for a particular client. She may become too involved at the expense of judgment, or fail to deal with her own repugnance. A recent horrifying example of this latter scenario occurred when a lawyer from North Carolina, appointed to his first capital case, was so repelled by his client that he deliberately lost his case, a deed he acknowledged to himself and others only years later. Emotional strategies may also shade into ethical issues in the long run, for example when lawyers become burned out and unable to provide adequate representation because of excessive involvement or failure to care for their own emotional well-being.

[From] an emotional perspective, criminal lawyers draw strength from many sources, not all of them lofty. Many of the lawyers who thrive in criminal defense (and perhaps this is true of any litigation-oriented practice) seem to relish the fight. They may be energized by challenging, and preferably thwarting, authority, by fighting for the underdog, or by their political commitments. Not all of these lawyers have a systemic critique of the criminal justice system and the place of capital punishment within that system. Some work for public interest organizations which fight capital punishment as part of a larger strategy of fighting for civil rights. Most do capital cases one at a time, trying to save one life at a time. In terms of ability to sustain commitment and emotional health, there are advantages and disadvantages to each approach. The burden of saving lives can be crushing; adding the imperative of "mak[ing] the world a better place" may be sustaining for some, debilitating for others. Yet my point here is that all these lawyers would describe themselves as fighting for a principle as well as a client, and would say that, in varying measures, both the abstract principle and the immense needs of the individual client were important in sustaining them.

At times, however, abstract principle may sit uneasily with concrete experience. Charles Ogeltree, for example, describes the situation he confronted when, during his time as a public defender, his sister Barbara was murdered. He says, in describing his crisis of faith:

> My determination to track down my sister's murderer and secure his conviction led me to adopt an outlook that was in many ways incompatible with the justifications I had consistently used to defend my profession.

His abstract belief in the importance of constraints on police behavior was challenged by his desire for the police to find the murderer. In addition, he was forced to consider, from a wholly new vantage point, the role of the defense attorney at the trial of his sister's killer. He says:

> Imagining the role the defense attorney would play at the trial of Barbara's killer forced me to face squarely the real consequences suffered by victims and their families as a direct result of the zealous advocacy of clever defense lawyers. I had to consider how victims feel about lawyers like myself, lawyers who secure dismissals on technicalities, or who seek to raise sufficient doubt for a jury to find the client not guilty, even in the face of strong evidence against the accused. I also imagined the impact on my mother of a defense strategy that would present Barbara's life in a negative light. I agonized over the possibility that the person responsible for my sister's death might walk away.

His faith in the criminal justice system and his commitment to criminal defense work were badly shaken. Ultimately, he found a way beyond his crisis of faith, and he gives much of the credit to the power of empathy for his clients. His ability to focus on his clients as individuals and as friends, to understand their problems and to feel compassion for their plights, became a sustaining motivation for him. He says, in relation to one such client:

> I did not think about what he had done, nor did I feel responsible for what he might do if released. I knew that at that moment I was my client's only friend, and that my friend wanted to go home.

The narrative raises important questions about the nature of a criminal defense attorney's empathy toward his clients. First, Ogeltree's discussion makes clear that empathy serves several purposes for the criminal defense lawyer. Empathy can provide a sense of meaning. It enables lawyers to care deeply about what happens to their clients, and this concern is one of the things that keep them going in difficult times. As Ogeltree explicitly recognizes, empathy for the client can also improve the quality of representation. It is a source of the passion that can transform advocacy. It is also a quality that will influence decision makers. If the judge or jury sees that the lawyer cares about her client, they will be more likely to care about him as well.

[A] broad capacity for empathy is likely an important component of emotional maturity and mental health. It may—and this is a separate question—make us better professionals by allowing us to understand what is at stake for our opponents as well as our clients. Or perhaps too much empathy will actually interfere with our ability to represent our clients. If so, the needs of our profession may diverge from our psychic and emotional needs. Both the professional and emotional effects of empathy are important to address; recognizing their divergence is equally important. [Exercising] selective empathy, shutting out awareness of the pain of victims, survivors, and witnesses may on some level be adaptive and even necessary for lawyers, and perhaps especially for criminal lawyers.

[The] ethical literature about criminal defense attorneys shows a fascination with the question of what the defense attorney knows, or chooses not to know, about her client's guilt or innocence of the crime charged. The question is often cast as the much debated "role differentiation" issue: is it ethical for lawyers knowingly to defend behavior that they would not condone in their non-professional lives? As an ethical matter, I believe Ted Schneyer's response to this argument is persuasive. Role is imbedded in situation. We have moral principles that govern various aspects of our lives, but they will not necessarily be consistent across all our complex roles in life. "[T]he lawyer-client relationship has moral value as a relationship; . . . some actions taken in [its name] will conflict with the moral principles [the participants] would follow if acting independently. . . ." It is possible for lawyers to uphold the principles of the adversary system, including the right to a fair trial and the presumption of innocence, without moral inconsistency, though they would not defend the commission of crimes in their personal lives.

[Criminal] defense attorneys are intellectually comfortable with role differentiation, but the emotional conflicts are more complex, and much farther below the radar. Barbara Babcock explains the defender's need not to know as follows:

> The defender goes down the treacherous path of burnout once she concerns herself with guilt or innocence. The defender must suspend belief (or disbelief) in every case, and must be disinterested in either freeing the guilty or protecting the innocent. Any other attitude inevitably leads to corruption of the defender's role because most of the accused are guilty. Once the defender consciously recognizes this fact, her work becomes insupportable and she is disabled.

> This justification makes clear that the act of "not knowing" is designed to protect the rights of defendants and the working of the adversary system. Abbe Smith argues that the suspension of judgment is "one of the most important things a defense lawyer can offer a client accused of a terrible crime...." It may also be protective of the defender's emotional health, or perhaps not. Smith, like Ogeltree, recognizes that even the deepest commitment to criminal defense work will not insulate defenders from emotional conflict over the pain they confront, some of it caused by their clients.

How, then, does the defender suspend disbelief? How does she maintain the presumption of innocence in any but the most abstract sense? Must she avoid knowing, or dwelling on, the crime of which her client is accused, and the pain caused by that crime? If so, how is this achieved, and at what cost?

Barbara Babcock believes that "the fundamental mind-set of most criminal defense lawyers toward defending the guilty is one of staggering indifference to the question." But, she notes, "the indifference to their clients' guilt takes its psychological toll on members of the defense bar." Lisa McIntyre says,

> Public defenders are quick to admit that they usually do not ask their clients whether they are guilty or innocent.... The lawyers claimed that it was simply not relevant.... But there seems to be more to it than that. Many said that, when it comes down to it, they do not ask because they are afraid that the client will tell them the truth.

Seymour Wishman says,

> Fighting for acquittal of guilty men ... didn't disturb me ... "society" was too abstract an idea for me.... I tried, as an act of will, to limit my vision to what I actually did in the courtroom—the trial was a fascinating process, a game.... If a crime or a criminal had been particularly offensive, I had always coped with my feelings by putting them aside, out of the way of my professional judgments. My method of dealing with these kinds of cases had seemed emotionally necessary and ethically appropriate.

James Kunen is concerned about not wanting to know. He describes thinking "What's become of me? ... I'm in it to win. It's a matter of indifference to me whether my client's guilty or not." And later he says:

> We would never know whether ... [our client] had committed the crimes, but that was beside the point. The complaining witness had lied. She was not credible. In our world, that's what mattered.

WILLIAM H. SIMON—THE ETHICS OF CRIMINAL DEFENSE

91 Mich. L. Rev. 1703, 1707–08 (June 1993).

Libertarians claim that aggressive advocacy is distinctively appropriate to the criminal sphere because it serves to check oppression by the "state." Such arguments invoke the image of the "isolated," "lone," "friendless," or "naked" individual faced with the "enormous power and resources of the state." Aggressive defense is supposed to level the playing field and turn the trial into a "contest of equals," or at least express the system's commitment to treat all citizens with respect.

Aggressive defense is also supposed to protect against the abuse of state power. The danger of abuse is most commonly attributed to the inherently corrupting nature of state power and the consequent aggression and rapacity of state officials. The aggressive defense lawyer inhibits such abuse by increasing the difficulty of conviction. In David Luban's rhetoric:

> We want to handicap the state in its power even legitimately to punish us, for we believe as a matter of political theory and historical experience that if the state is not handicapped or restrained ex ante, our political and civil liberties are jeopardized. Power-holders are inevitably tempted to abuse the criminal justice system to persecute political opponents, and overzealous police will trample civil liberties in the name of crime prevention and order.

This type of rhetoric has been exempt from critical reflection for so long that even a small amount should raise doubts. In the first place, the image of the lonely individual facing Leviathan is misleading. Let us grant the lonely part even though some defendants have lots of friends. But, what about the state? Libertarian rhetoric tends to suggest that the individual defendant takes on the entire state. But, of course, the state has other concerns besides this defendant. From the state's point of view, the defendant may be part of an enormous class of criminal defendants and suspects with which it can hardly begin to cope.

It is more plausible to portray the typical defendant as facing a small number of harassed, overworked bureaucrats. Of course, state agencies can focus their resources on particular defendants and, when they do so, their power can be formidable. But the state cannot possibly focus its power this way on all defendants or even most of them. Yet, aggressive defense treats all defendants as if they faced the full concentrated power of the state.

Second, victims do not appear in the libertarian picture. [The] "victims' rights" movement has worked for the past two decades to replace in the popular consciousness the defense lawyer's image of the criminal trial as a state-versus-defendant contest with that of a victim-versus-defendant contest. The movement is often naive, even blind, about the efficacy of criminal punishment in deterring future wrongs or aiding victims, but its imagery seems as plausible as that of the defense lawyer.

[A] frequent concomitant of the idea that aggressive defense checks the rapacity of the state is the idea that it expresses respect for the "dignity of the individual." [The] idea that helping the accused escape substantively appropriate punishment through aggressive defense serves individual dignity is hard to square with the legitimacy of punishment after conviction. A viable ideal of dignity has to make room for respect for the rights of others and, at least in our system, for acceptance of punishment when the individual violates such rights.

Problem

Two part-time public defenders, brothers George and Walter Stenhach, were appointed to represent Richard Buchanan who was charged in Potter County, Pennsylvania, with murder. In discussing the events surrounding the alleged homicide with George Stenhach, Buchanan revealed the locations of some pieces of physical evidence. An investigator for the brothers went to one of the locations and discovered a broken rifle stock which had apparently been used in the homicide. The investigator retrieved and turned the stock over to the Stenhach brothers who withheld it from the prosecution on the theory that "they were obligated to retain the rifle stock to protect their client." During Buchanan's murder trial, the prosecution learned of the existence of the rifle stock and the trial judge subsequently ordered the Stenhach brothers to produce it, which they did. After Buchanan was convicted of murder, the Stenhach brothers were themselves charged with various criminal offenses relating to obstruction of justice.

Do you think that the Stenhach brothers were guilty of criminal activity on these facts or were they, instead, simply acting zealously and professionally in the best interests of their client? Does it make any difference in your analysis that the prosecutor never asked the Stenhach brothers, formally or informally, to produce any relevant evidence that they may have had in their possession? Would it make any difference in your analysis if the evidence that the Stenhach brothers withheld was testimonial rather than physical, *e.g.* Buchanan's confidential statements to them confessing to the crime? *See Commonwealth v. Stenhach*, 356 Pa.Super. 5, 514 A.2d 114 (1986).

C. THE PROSECUTOR'S ROLE

Prosecutors, like defense counsel, often struggle with the appropriate contours of their role in the American adversarial criminal justice system. If "justice" requires that criminal defense counsel defend their clients' zealously, does the same hold true for prosecutors? Do—should—

prosecutors have professional duties that differ from those assigned to defense counsel?

FRED C. ZACHARIAS—STRUCTURING THE ETHICS OF PROSECUTORIAL TRIAL PRACTICE: CAN PROSECUTORS DO JUSTICE?

44 Vand. L. Rev. 45, 46–49, 50–53, 56–60, 109–10 (Jan. 1991).

Codes of professional responsibility take a very different approach to civil and criminal trials. In civil litigation, the codes presume that good outcomes result when lawyers represent clients aggressively. In criminal cases, the codes do not rely as fully on competitive lawyering. They treat prosecutors as advocates, but also as "ministers" having an ethical duty to "do justice."

Although the special prosecutorial duty is worded so vaguely that it obviously requires further explanation, the codes provide remarkably little guidance on its meaning. In effect, code drafters have delegated to prosecutors the task of resolving the special ethical issues prosecutors face at every stage of trial. Is a prosecutor free to seek a jury biased against the defendant? If a prosecutor becomes convinced at trial that defense counsel is overmatched because of limited resources, what are the prosecutor's options? Should she help a defendant whose lawyer is incompetent? What should she do if she believes the judge incorrectly has restricted counsel's ability to present a defense? In her own presentation, may she legitimately invite the jurors to draw false inferences from the facts? How emotional a summation may she make in her effort to sway the jury toward conviction?

[One] obvious concern underlying the prosecutor's special ethical duty is to prevent punishment of innocent defendants. At the charging, plea bargaining, and sentencing stages, the heart of the codes' mandate to do justice seems clear: the prosecutor should exercise discretion so as to prosecute only persons she truly considers guilty, and then only in a manner that fits the crime. Many codes reinforce the prosecutor's general obligation with specific rules limiting pretrial conduct along these lines.

Once a case reaches trial, this duty is no longer very meaningful. The prosecutor already has made her good faith determination that the defendant is guilty. Unless some unexpected development makes her reconsider her conclusion, she may pursue a conviction. Thus, in extending the prosecutor's justice obligation to the trial stage, the codes almost by definition intend a higher obligation than simply avoiding unjustified prosecutions.

[Reputable] scholars have advanced the proposition that the adversary system is ineffective in producing accurate verdicts. Interpreting the codes from that perspective, one might assume that "doing justice" requires prosecutors to temper their zeal. One can hypothesize open-minded prosecutors who present facts neutrally and encourage courts and jurors to emphasize defendants' procedural rights. These idealized government attorneys constantly would reevaluate the strength of their case. They would adjust the content and force of each evidentiary presentation to further the outcome that they believe the jury should reach on the current state of the evidence.

[By] including government attorneys within the general adversarial framework, the codes signal that prosecutors can achieve justice while operating within the adversary system's rules. Government trial lawyers, like defense counsel, influence jury verdicts through effective lawyering. Better performance makes conviction more likely, regardless of the defendant's guilt or innocence. That reality is consistent with the core of the adversary process: advocates are meant to do their best. To the extent prosecutors temper advocacy on the basis that adversarial contests routinely produce poor outcomes, they call into question the essential assumptions of the very system the rules codify.

[To] the extent that the adversary system works according to theory, government lawyers promote justice by playing the same role at trial as private advocates. They contribute to truth by defending their own factual hypotheses and contesting those of their opponents. Prosecutors help courts assess defendants' rights; the claims of defendants' champions must be contested to determine their validity. Prosecutors also enhance the efficiency aspects of the process by acting adversarially. By challenging defense counsels' positions at every step, prosecutors force defenders to remain vigilant and to frame the issues clearly for proper adjudication.

[While] prosecutorial autonomy helps justify a less adversarial framework, the fear of unfettered prosecutorial power is the impetus for the special ethical obligation. The prosecutor's freedom from client control gives rise to vast discretion. That, in turn, creates a risk that prejudice or self-interest will govern her decisions. She may arbitrarily favor one defendant, or type of defendant, over others. Alternatively, because her success is measured by her conviction rate, she may be tempted to ignore the rights of defendants, victims, or the community in order to obtain pleas or guilty verdicts.

Moreover, the prosecutor benefits from unique prestige and symbolic power. Because she represents the community, she commonly carries more influence with juries than attorneys allied solely with individual clients. The prosecutor can rely on jurors' natural instincts to be protected against crime. She can draw upon jurors' tendencies to believe that persons a grand jury singles out for prosecution probably are guilty.

Finally, a prosecutor enjoys practical advantages over her adversaries. She benefits from the state's hefty investigative and litigation resources. Through the police and grand jury, she monopolizes the ability to coerce testimony and obtain cooperation in the investigation of crimes. The literature is replete with discussions of ways in which a prosecutor can misuse her singular tools.

The fear of prosecutorial abuses thus explains why code drafters have chosen to adopt a "do justice" obligation. The drafters reasonably expect that, as the symbol of fair criminal justice, prosecutors should not take undue advantage of their built-in resources. Prosecutors who over-reach undermine "confidence, not only in [their] profession, but in government and the very ideal of justice itself."

Problem

ABA Standards for Criminal Justice, Prosecution Function Standard 3–3.2(h)(3d ed. 1993) provides that "[w]here practical, the prosecutor should seek to insure that victims of serious crimes or their representatives are given an opportunity to consult with and to provide information to the prosecutor prior to the decision whether or not to prosecute, to pursue a disposition by plea, or to dismiss the charges."

Since the victim of an alleged criminal offense is not the prosecutor's "client," do you think it appropriate in the following situations for a prosecutor to either consider the victim's (or the victim's representatives') input or to require the victim's (or representatives') approval before taking the action proposed:

(1) A rape victim does not want her attacker to be prosecuted because she fears the humiliation and embarrassment of having to recount the circumstances of the rape on the witness stand;

(2) A rape victim does not want her attacker to be prosecuted because she fears that he or friends of his will harm her or her family;

(3) The family of a murdered victim wants the prosecutor to seek the death penalty in a homicide prosecution;

(4) The family of a murdered victim wants the prosecutor not to seek the death penalty in a homicide prosecution;

(5) An armed robbery victim does not want the prosecution to offer the defendant a proposed plea bargain which would not include incarceration. (Should it make a difference in this situation how strong the prosecution thinks its case is?)

In addition to ethical constraints and quandries, prosecutors must operate in a setting where they often do not control their own investigative resources. In considering the following excerpt discussing this issue in the federal setting, consider the ways in which this dynamic might influence prosecutorial decision-making.

DANIEL RICHMAN—PROSECUTORS AND THEIR AGENTS, AGENTS AND THEIR PROSECUTORS

103 Colum. L. Rev. 749, 756–763, 786–790 (2003).

Although all federal prosecutors are housed within the Justice Department (either in the litigating divisions of "Main Justice" or in United States Attorneys' Offices), not all federal investigative agencies are. The Secret Service (which handles financial and computer crimes in addition to its protective duties) and the Customs Service, previously in the Treasury Department, are now both in the Department of Homeland Security, as is the enforcement arm of the Immigration and Naturalization Service, hitherto in the Justice Department. The criminal agents in the Internal Revenue Service report to the Secretary of the Treasury. Postal Inspectors—whose jurisdiction over mail fraud sweeps in a broad array of criminal activity, and who gained a new visibility in the anthrax investigation—are part of the U.S. Postal Service. And criminal investigations are also conducted by personnel within various regulatory agencies, including the Securities and Exchange Commission and the Environmental Protection Agency, and such executive departments as Agriculture, Labor, and Interior. Even within the Justice Department, special agents in the FBI, DEA, and (since the 2002 Homeland Security legislation) the renamed "Bureau of Alcohol, Tobacco, Firearms and Explosives" report not to prosecutors, but to other agency officials, with only the Attorney General and Deputy Attorney General exercising (or at least possessing) hierarchical authority over them. One often hears rookie prosecutors refer to "my agents." Most soon learn to drop the possessive.

If neither a line prosecutor nor her chief can dictate how an agency should deploy its resources or run an investigation, and agency officials cannot control the adjudicative process, how are the terms of this coordinate relationship set? Part of the answer lies in the macro policymaking that comprises an administration's criminal justice agenda. Congressional agendas may have similar effects as well. Policy formation and decisions about implementation (assuming for the moment that the two are analytically distinct) will also occur at the subcabinet level, within the Justice Department or at the upper reaches of enforcement agency hierarchies. Even specific cases, because of their importance and national ramifications, may be coordinated and controlled at the highest levels of the executive branch.

My focus here [is] on micro policymaking—the interaction between prosecutors and agents in the run-of-the-mill cases that have not been selected out for special attention by Washington. These cases are generally handled by prosecutors in the ninety-four U.S. Attorney's Offices, and by field agents scattered across the country (but concentrated in the bigger cities). In the absence of a clear bureaucratic command, how are they able to achieve a modus vivendi? What are the structures that drive agencies and prosecutors to negotiate the terms of their interaction and that set those terms?

[At] its heart, the relationship between federal prosecutors and federal enforcement agents is a bilateral monopoly. Prosecutors are the exclusive gatekeepers over federal court, but they need agents to gather evidence. Agencies control investigative resources, but they are not free to retain separate counsel. If agents want criminal charges to be pursued against the target of an investigation, they will have to convince a prosecutor to take the case. To focus on these truisms, however, is to ignore the interactions that determine how enforcement discretion is exercised on the ground.

Let us refine the prosecutorial side of the equation. Federal prosecutors would have monopoly power only if they were able to act through some central "purchasing" agent. And they aren't. Traditions of local independence, advantages of local knowledge, and the limited resources they have because of Congress's affinity for decentralized power are all barriers to the entry of litigating units from Main Justice into a district without cooperation from the U.S. Attorney. Those units remain at least potential entrants, however, offering a limited counterweight to the U.S. Attorney's Office's control over its district's criminal docket.

[One] U.S. Attorney's Office can [face] competition from another. Where a metropolitan area is divided among two or more federal districts (as when a large city lies near a district's border), flexible federal venue rules will allow an aggressive investigative agency to play one U.S. Attorney's Office off against another, steering its "best" cases to the district that has given the agency the best service by taking less alluring cases or offering the "best" (i.e., the most accommodating) legal support for investigations.

[The] possibility that another federal prosecutorial office can take cases from its jurisdiction may not be of great concern to a U.S. Attorney's Office. Disputes may occur when two offices simultaneously reach for a high-profile case holding the promise of institutional and personal glory, but ordinarily the universe of potential federal cases is large enough (and low profile enough) to allow any number of offices to pursue territorially overlapping matters with little friction. The important point for our purposes, however, is that the overlap of prosecutorial authority inevitably reduces the ability of each office to control investigative agencies' access to federal court, and consequentially reduces the extent to which an office can leverage its gatekeeping power into control of those agencies' agendas.

The overlap between state and federal criminal law also offers agencies some choice, at least in theory. Although the federal system is generally thought to offer significant procedural and resource advantages over state criminal processes, the difference will not always be significant, or, if significant, may still be outweighed by the desire to circumvent federal prosecutorial gatekeeping. A U.S. Attorney will not mourn whenever federal agencies take cases to the local D.A.'s office and will often want cases falling below some threshold level to go there. Yet an agency's interaction with local authorities will limit the U.S. Attorney's control, and even knowledge, of agency activity.

Finally, the size and organization of a single U.S. Attorney's Office can limit its power if agents can play one assistant or unit off against another. If agents can "shop" cases around until they find a sympathetic assistant, gatekeeping standards can fall victim to a "race to the bottom," in which those individual prosecutors with the lowest standards (or, from another perspective, the greatest zeal) will be the ones to whom agents most prefer to take cases. Since there are limits to how many cases even the most acquiescent assistant can take, office standards are unlikely to fall all the way to his level. But the risk is that agents will reserve for him the cases over which they want to exercise the most control—which may be precisely those cases most in need of prosecutorial oversight. If, because of their significance, these cases are among the most personally rewarding for prosecutors to work on, other assistants will be tempted to lower their standards as well. Offices can, and do, counter this problem by establishing some centralized screening mechanism. But circumvention may still be possible, as sometimes occurs when an assistant pursues a "related" matter.

[Whatever] their legal and institutional obligations to work together, prosecutors and agents [are sometimes] pushed apart by their membership in distinct, even antagonistic, professional cultures.

[The] basics are well known. Although the FBI has a long tradition of lawyer-agents, most agencies do not. And even the FBI has changed a lot since the Hoover years. As a general rule, then, most agents have not been exposed to the acculturation process at law school, which not only tends to be process oriented when it addresses criminal enforcement issues, but also exalts a norm of moral neutrality that can (but need not) lead prosecutors to distance themselves from the enforcement projects of the agents they deal with[.] Law school is only the beginning of the story, though. Far more influential are the differences in the career paths of agents and prosecutors and the aftermarkets they face. There are many career, or at least long-serving, prosecutors. But a great many view the job as a way station, a means of acquiring human capital (litigation experience, familiarity with local legal practices and personalities) that will facilitate their representation of private clients thereafter. Even those prosecutors who plan to stay with the government will often orient themselves toward their professional counterparts through participation in local bar activities and the like. In contrast, agents stay a long time. A 1994 RAND report found that "[o]verall attrition in the [FBI] is low," and that, while some agents resign in their first five years, "[m]ost agents either retire at the earliest opportunity [age 50] or remain in the bureau until mandatory retirement [age 57]."

Agents and prosecutors also have different geographical orientations. AUSAs wishing to move may try to transfer to another U.S. Attorney's Office. They may even be asked by Washington to take on jobs in another city. But the typical AUSA stays in one city and builds her professional reputation there. Life is very different for agents. According to the RAND report, upon graduation from the FBI Academy, an FBI agent starts with a three-to five-year assignment to a field office that cannot be near her home. After that, she typically will be sent to another field office—"often one of the 'top 12' offices that are larger, have broader operational requirements, and are sometimes difficult to staff—or to headquarters in Washington D.C." Reassignments are "based on the needs of the FBI and whether agents choose to compete for management positions in other locations."

[These] cultural differences can drive a powerful wedge between agents and prosecutors. Agents or even agencies seeking to justify their refusal to share information about sources and methods with prosecutors will assert a fear that such data will be misused once the prosecutors enter private practice. This tendency toward non-disclosure is bolstered by concerns that prosecutors have far less "on the line" when it comes to investigative security. An agent's promise to an informant is bonded by his and his agency's professional reputation. The prosecutor who will soon move into another world is not so bound. Agents may worry that prosecutors looking for lucrative private practice berths will be too quick to compromise cases with, or extend professional courtesies to, prospective professional allies, or, alternatively, too quick to tax agency resources by taking cases to trial unnecessarily in order to gain marketable litigation experience. Agents may also see prosecutors as all too ready to credit defense allegations of agent misconduct. Part of the problem may be sheer resentment on the part of agents at the rewards that private practice will bring prosecutors, and perhaps some disdain for the unworldliness of young prosecutors' law school experience. Prosecutors, for their part, may tend to identify with professional adversaries and see their job as reining in "cowboy" line agents who pay little heed to the niceties of due process.

Chapter 11

PRETRIAL RELEASE

A. INTRODUCTION

A defendant's pretrial release from custody typically is in exchange for a pledge of something of value that the defendant will appear in court and will comply with the court's orders in a pending criminal case. Bail is the Anglo–American criminal justice system's answer to the issue of what is to be done with an accused, whose guilt has not been proven, during the time period between arrest and trial. Conceptually, the use of bail is to accommodate the defendant's interest in pretrial liberty (consistent with the presumption of innocence) and society's interest in assuring that the accused is present for trial. In each case a judge decides whether to grant pretrial release, and if so, what monetary amount and/or conditions of release will assure the defendant's presence. A judge's discretion to make pretrial release available is limited, however, because most state constitutions expressly guarantee pretrial release before conviction.

Constitutional concerns about pretrial release concentrate on whether there is a right to release and, if so, whether the conditions of release are excessive. The Eighth Amendment states that "[e]xcessive bail shall not be required." *United States Const. Amend. VIII.* While state constitutions at least implicitly recognize the fundamental nature of the right to bail by their express prohibition of excessive bail, *United States v. Salerno,* 481 U.S. 739 (1987) found that there is no federal constitutional right to bail, holding that the Eighth Amendment is not violated by the use of pretrial detention due to the dangerousness of the defendant.

Several limited legislative or judicial exceptions exist to the general right of pretrial release. First, in states which use capital punishment, the denial of bail occurs in capital cases if the prosecution can show that the proof is evident or the presumption is great that the defendant is guilty. Second, the denial of bail frequently is authorized in cases in which a prisoner has escaped and is recaptured. Third, denial of bail also may be authorized in cases of criminal contempt. Finally, in response to a growing problem of defendants committing crimes during the period of pretrial release, some state legislatures and the Congress have enacted laws prohibiting pretrial release due to a defendant's criminal history or to the nature of the pending charges. *See* 18 U.S.C. §§ 3141–3150 for the Bail Reform Act of 1984.

Bail becomes excessive when a court sets it higher than reasonably necessary to assure a defendant's appearance at trial. In *Stack v. Boyle*, 342 U.S. 1 (1951) the Court stated that bail set at a figure higher than an amount reasonably calculated to fulfill the purpose of assuring that the defendant will stand trial and, if found guilty, submit to sentence, is excessive under the Eighth Amendment. That prohibition is not directly applicable to the states, but a comparable standard may be required as a matter of due process of law and equal protection of the laws. The equal protection approach to the issue of excessive bail is that the defendant is being detained solely on account of the economic inability to afford the monetary bail set by the court. The due process argument is two-fold: 1) the defendant is being punished without a trial and in violation of the presumption of innocence; and 2) continued pretrial detention prevents adequate trial preparation and could result in ineffective assistance of counsel.

The traditional rationale for the use of money bail and/or conditions imposed upon defendants pending trial is to ensure their appearance at trial. During the 1960s and 1970s, "bail reform" meant that nonmonetary information increasingly became an important part of the pretrial release process, in order (1) to avoid discrimination against accused persons who could not afford the monetary amount imposed for their release; as well as (2) to reemphasize the rationale of appearing for trial. Instead of focusing on whether an accused could afford an amount imposed by the court, defense counsel emphasizes that the facts of the defendant's situation demonstrate that the likelihood of appearance at trial would be increased by the imposition of nonfinancial conditions of release, e.g., that the accused not commit another crime during release, or the use of a curfew.

By the 1980s, the nature of "bail reform" changed. Increasing numbers of persons released pending trial were committing crimes—either against specific witnesses in the pending case, or against others in the community, or both. The nature of reform began to focus not on whether an accused would appear in court, but on whether and under what circumstances an accused legally could be detained and not released at all pending trial in order to prevent the accused from committing crimes.

B. TYPES OF RELEASE

Personal Recognizance. Release on personal recognizance may not fall within the technical definition of a bail bond. Upon acquiring control over the person of the defendant, the court merely allows the defendant to be at liberty in return for a written promise to return and to comply with the orders of the court throughout the case. Because the defendant has this duty anyway and the only thing the defendant pledges is the surrender of liberty which is already under the power of the court, a release on personal recognizance is not a contractual undertaking for a consideration in the classical sense.

Release on personal recognizance has long been a practice in the courts, and for good reason. If the defendant has ties to the community and will likely return to court without the imposition of liability or other conditions, the requirement of a bond accomplishes none of the purposes of bail but rather imposes a substantial hardship upon persons of limited resources. Perhaps for this reason, the law not only acknowledges the power of the courts to release a defendant on recognizance but indeed entitles a defendant to release in this manner unless the court finds that something more is required to insure the defendant's appearance in court.

Unsecured Bond. An unsecured bond is a pledge by the defendant alone to be liable for a specified sum if the defendant should breach a material condition of release. Unlike the release on personal recognizance, the unsecured bond is a contractual undertaking in the true sense. The unsecured bond undoubtedly has an advantage over the release on personal recognizance in the case of a defendant of means who has long term ties to the community. The bond gives the defendant a financial stake in obeying the orders of the court and thus helps insure the defendant's appearance. On the other hand, the theoretical civil liability of an indigent defendant upon an unsecured bond provides no real stake in the proceedings.

Release on Nonfinancial Conditions. Release on nonfinancial conditions may not technically be a separate kind of bail or undertaking. However, the court has the power to annex nonfinancial conditions to the basic bond agreement that the defendant will be responsive to the orders of the court. Courts should impose the least onerous conditions which will insure the presence of the defendant in court. Such conditions may include but are not limited to placing the defendant in the custody of a person or agency, placing restrictions upon travel, association or place of abode, or requiring confinement during specified hours.

Cash Bond. A defendant may be released from custody by depositing cash in the amount of the bail with the court. The money is deposited by the clerk in an escrow account, and is available for forfeiture or for application to indebtedness upon judgment in the case. A major advantage of the cash bond is that it gives the defendant an immediate stake in the court proceedings. The cash may be returned only if upon compliance with the terms of the bond. The defendant thus faces an immediate financial loss, rather than some sort of distant civil liability, as would be true under an unsecured bond. A further advantage of the cash bond is that it creates a visible asset which can be assigned to counsel for a fee. Thus, the money can do double duty, and the private bar is able to obtain employment in cases which are otherwise assigned to appointed counsel due to depletion of resources in order to obtain release on bail.

Percentage Bond. Instead of a total cash bond, a court may permit the defendant to deposit only a percentage of the total amount of the bond. The money deposited is generally handled in the same way as a full cash bond. However, a portion of the deposit is kept by the court for operating costs. The percentage bond can be used effectively to permit the release from custody of defendants of limited means and still provide adequate assurance that they will appear in court.

Property Bond. The pledging of real property or of stocks and bonds as security for a bail bond is permitted. The proposed pledge of security must be justified by a detailed statement filed with the court. If the pledge is of real estate, it is recorded as a lien. Upon the failure of the defendant to comply with the terms of the bond, security in the form of real property or of stocks or bonds may be forfeited in whole or in part. On the other hand, if the defendant is discharged from the obligations of the bond, the stocks or bonds are returned to their owner, and any lien on real estate is released.

Surety Bond. The court may require the bond of a defendant to be underwritten by one or more sureties. In this classic bonding situation, the surety is undertaking an indebtedness to insure the conduct of another. However, unlike the surety offering security for a property bond, the surety on a surety bond is not required to create an encumbrance on property, and enforcement of the obligation is essentially the same as any other civil action for debt. The officers before whom bail may be taken shall ascertain that the amount deposited is no less than the amount fixed by the court. In the case of a surety bond, the surety or sureties must demonstrate by affidavit a net worth at least equal to the amount of the undertaking.

Guaranteed Arrest Bond Certificate. A guaranteed arrest bond certificate is a printed card or certificate of an association obligating the association and a licensed surety to guarantee the appearance in court of the member whose signature appears on the certificate and to pay any fine or forfeiture imposed upon the member, not to exceed a certain amount of money, e.g., five hundred dollars. Such a certificate may not be accepted for certain violations, such as the laws regulating motor carriers or for the offense of driving under the influence of an intoxicant. Such a certificate may be accepted for any traffic offense in lieu of a cash bond not to exceed five hundred dollars.

C. BAIL STATUTES

Most states rely upon statutes to define the circumstances under which an accused may obtain pretrial release. The Bail Reform Act of 1984 (18 U.S.C. §§ 3141–3150) governs release determinations in federal courts, and may serve as a reference for defining various types of pretrial release. As you read the statute (set forth in the statutory supplement), assess the scheme for judicial determinations about appropriate types of pretrial release and the circumstances suggesting the need for pretrial detention.

The federal statute is not very well-organized. The statutory scheme seems to be that an initial determination is made by the court (with assistance from the prosecutor) about whether the accused is a flight or safety risk. If not, you read that § 3142(b) mandates a recognizance bond or an unsecured appearance bond. If the court believes that the accused presents either risk, the court is to inquire whether the risk can be minimized by measures short of pretrial detention, *i.e.*, by imposing conditions in § 3142(c), after considering the § 3142(g) factors. If the risk can be minimized, the court tailors conditions to address the risk posed. Under particular circumstances, including a serious risk that the defendant will not appear, the defendant may be subject to pretrial detention without the possibility of release, per § 3142(e)–(g). *See* Section F.

A uniform schedule of bail is frequently promulgated for most misdemeanors and violations. A defendant who secures release from custody pursuant to this schedule before arraignment often waives the right to be considered for release on personal recognizance or nonfinancial conditions. Except for those offenses covered by the schedule, the amount of bail is fixed upon the issuance of a warrant or upon the arraignment of the defendant.

Regardless of the type of release, it is always subject to the condition that the person not commit another crime. § 3142(b). When a defendant commits a crime while released, an independent, mandatory, consecutive, additional sentence (up to ten years for felonies and one year for misdemeanors) is imposed after conviction. § 3147. In addition, the sentencing judge may increase the sentence for crimes committed prior to or while on pretrial release. United States Sentencing Commission, Federal Sentencing Guidelines Manual, §§ 2J1.7, 4A1.3.

§ 3142(c)(2) prohibits the imposition of financial conditions that are so burdensome that the defendant is effectively subject to preventive detention. Does that mean that a court cannot set a bail that the defendant cannot meet immediately? The court in *United States v. Mantecon–Zayas*, 949 F.2d 548 (1st Cir.1991) held that a court can impose a financial condition exceeding defendant's means as long as the judge finds that the bail is reasonably necessary to assure the defendant's presence at trial.

Although the nature of the crime and the weight of the evidence are relevant to a court's decision about whether to authorize preventive detention, note that the court also must consider them in deciding the proper conditions of release. Under § 3142(g), the court determines whether the charged offense is a crime of violence or involves narcotics, and weight of the evidence against the defendant.

Exercises

In the following exercises, assume that the applicable state pretrial release law is identical to the federal Bail Reform Act of 1984. Your professor will assign you to represent the defendant or the prosecution in the following situations. Be prepared to advocate the position of your client, per the applicable statutory section.

(a) Which form of pretrial release is appropriate?

(b) What nonfinancial conditions are appropriate?

(c) As a judge, what other information would you like to have about the defendant?

(d) Do the circumstances suggest that a detention hearing is appropriate?

(e) Are the defendant's constitutional rights being violated by continued detention?

Problems

1.   After being identified by two witnesses, defendant was arrested and charged with robbery. A state judge conditioned the defendant's pretrial release on his executing a $5,000 appearance bond with an eight percent ($400) cash deposit. Unable to raise more than $200, defendant petitioned the court for release on his own recognizance or, alternatively, on nonfinancial conditions. At an evidentiary hearing, the twenty-year old, unemployed defendant, whose most serious prior offense was a conviction for burglary, testified that "for the most part" he lived with his parents, "now and then" staying with his girlfriend. The Pretrial Services Agency reported its inability to verify the defendant's address, but defense counsel explained this was because the defendant's parents had just moved and still lacked a telephone. Counsel offered to confirm the new address by arranging an interview with the defendant's parents. What statutory and/or constitutional arguments can you make on behalf of defendant? On behalf of the prosecution?

2.   Joe is a 25–year old unemployed man who has lived with his parents all of his life. He has two prior assault convictions. He was recently arrested and charged with three counts of possessing, with intent to distribute, a large quantity of narcotics. At the time of his arrest, the police searched his car and found twelve ounces of 30.9% pure cocaine, four ounces of 27.5% pure heroin and a quantity of marijuana. The drugs had an estimated street value in excess of $400,000. The judge checked her records and found that in a similar case in Louisiana, bail was set at $10,000 full cash; she set bail at the same amount for Joe. Joe has no assets, and his parents have refused to assist in obtaining his release. Joe's Public Defender moved for a recognizance bond. Should the court grant Joe's motion?

3.   The 49–year old defendant was arrested two days ago for attempted murder. He has a prior record of ten armed robberies and one attempted jailbreak while awaiting an earlier trial. Yesterday, he threatened the life of

a cellmate, and boasted that he always carries a loaded gun. He has an excellent record for his prior experience on parole, and a perfect attendance record while free on bond for his prior charges. He has been working part-time, and for the past six months has lived with his mother. Assume that the maximum sentence for the murder is ten years. What type of bail should the court consider and impose?

4. A 36–year old defendant is charged with burglary of a residence. She is a heroin addict, and has a record of seven prior burglary convictions, as well as two convictions for possession of narcotics. She is divorced, lives with her three children, and works part-time in the department store where she was arrested. Should the court release her on her own recognizance? Does your answer depend upon whether drug treatment is available, in the community or in the local jail? Does your answer depend upon whether the defendant has someone responsible with whom to leave her children?

5. Stanley was indicted on one count of conspiracy and thirty-three counts of wire fraud and telemarketing fraud. The indictment alleges that he and others engaged in illegal telemarketing practices when he solicited citizens throughout the United States by telephone to purchase merchandise by inducing them with false promises of prizes and cash awards. Stanley was released on his personal recognizance subject to several conditions imposed, including that he not be employed in the telemarketing industry. Harris seeks a modification of that employment restriction, pursuant to § 3142(c)(1)(B)(xiv). Stanley maintains that he should be permitted to work for another telemarketing company since his solicitation activity there would be monitored and remain well within the limits of the law. The evidence submitted shows that Stanley repeatedly employed high-pressure sales techniques upon elderly individuals to induce the purchase of merchandise of nominal value for exorbitant prices. Does your answer depend upon whether Stanley can be effective with a reputable telemarketing entity, e.g., a charity like United Way? Suppose Stanley does not make a good appearance and is an effective worker only when working in the telephone industry? Can he perform the job of a person who leaves wake-up calls for people, assuming that he can be relied upon to give the correct time?!

D.   OBTAINING THE DEFENDANT'S RELEASE

Invariably, the first communication that defense counsel receives about a case is a telephone call from a defendant or the defendant's friends or relatives stating that the defendant has been arrested and wants to be immediately released on bail. These telephone calls are frequently received at night when the courts and the clerk's office are closed, and therefore it may be extremely difficult to secure the immediate release of the defendant even if suitable property or money is available.

A defense attorney anticipates these problems and has a list of critical phone numbers and names of certain officials:

1. Arrest warrant issuing office.

2. Police or sheriff's office booking room.

3. Police or sheriff's office fingerprinting room.

4. Police or sheriff's office general number.

5. County jail.

6. Court clerk's office.

7. Name and office and home phone number for every judge.

8. Registrar of deeds office.

A new attorney should visit the court clerk's office and find out who "handles" bail matters. Invariably, there is an assistant clerk who has been there for twenty years who will be only too happy to explain how bonds are taken in that county. Thirty minutes with this clerk will be well spent; look at the bond book and inquire about the requirements of property bonds.

When the defendant, friend or relative calls, counsel should first determine if the caller wishes him or her to represent the charged person. If representation is unclear at this point, certain advice may be given as to bail which may then be followed by an appointment in the attorney's office the next morning to finalize the attorney-client relationship. In any event, counsel should prepare a questionnaire which may help obtain vital information critical to a bail determination.

1. What is the client's full name?

2. Does the client go by any other names or nicknames?

3. Where does the client live?

4. What is the client's relationship to the caller?

5. When did the defendant call?

6. Did he give his location?

7. What is the defendant charged with doing?

8. Did the defendant tell you anything about the crime?

9. Does counsel personally know anything about it?

10. Did the client sound drunk or high or is he injured in any way?

11. Has bond been set? If so, how much is it?

If a bond has not been set, counsel can take the following actions. Initially, the main problem at this stage will be locating the defendant and finding some officer who knows something about the defendant. Defense counsel should first call the booking room and the jail should then be called. The officer who issues warrants may also be a source of information. When someone who is familiar with the defendant is finally located, the defense attorney should find out under what name the defendant was booked, the charge or charges, the warrant number, and the amount of bond. If no bond appears on the warrant, the defense attorney should call the committing judge and inquire as to why no bond has been set. It may be that the offense is a serious felony and the judge may have refused to fix a bail. If that is the situation, the defense counsel should request that the judge set bond. This request should be made only under extreme circumstances (such as an arrest on Friday night when the courts will be closed until Monday) because the judge may set an extremely high bond in serious cases or decline to set bail until court convenes. In most instances, however, the best practical action would be to make a formal application for bail the next morning before a judge.

If bail has been set, counsel should advise the caller as to the amount of the bail. The quickest way of obtaining the defendant's release is to post a cash bail at the place where the defendant is held. Checks or credit cards are usually not acceptable. If the defendant does not have sufficient cash to make bail, the defendant can attempt to locate some friend or relative to post a cash bail. In the event it is not possible to raise cash bail, the defendant can attempt to locate a person who will qualify as surety because of the real or personal property that he or she owns. If a prospective surety who has real property to use as bail is located, the surety should be instructed to bring the deed to the real property as well as the most recent tax bill to establish the value of the property. In places with a pretrial release program, the program personnel should be contacted to begin an interview with the defendant to see if the defendant is acceptable into the program.

If the defendant or the defendant's family is unsuccessful in finding sufficient cash or property to use as bail to obtain the defendant's immediate release, the defense counsel should make application to the court to have the defendant released on an "own recognizance" release or to have the amount of bail reduced.

E. CHALLENGES TO THE BAIL DECISION

A defendant who cannot make bail as originally set may be entitled to mandatory review of bail. After the bail has been set and reviewed, it may be changed upon the motion of the court or either party following an adversary hearing and written findings by the court. Bail can be increased only when the prosecutor shows by clear and convincing evidence that there is a need to modify the existing conditions of release. Bail may not be forfeited except upon a finding based upon clear and convincing evidence that a material change of circumstances has occurred or that the defendant has violated a condition of the bail and that there is a substantial risk that the defendant will not appear unless the bail is altered.

After a motion for change in the amount of bail or nonfinancial conditions is filed, the defense attorney should be prepared to present evidence of the defendant's fitness for a low bail. The prosecutor should also come prepared to present proof if there is strong opposition to a low bail. Before the bail hearing the defense attorney should attempt to negotiate a bail agreement with the prosecuting attorney. Occasionally, the prosecutor may readily agree to a compromise figure or other bail condition.

In a bail hearing the defense attorney should realize that the judge is trying to determine what will assure the defendant's appearance at future proceedings. Twenty witnesses are not required to inform the judge that the defendant is a fine person. The defense proof should consist of three main points of information: (1) personal information about the defendant, (2) brief allusions to a possible defense to the crime, and (3) hardships to the defendant if he remains incarcerated. Counsel should be cautious about personally vouching for the defendant. If the defendant fails to appear, counsel's credibility about such matters will be seriously damaged in the future.

The defense attorney should present proof to assure that bail will be set as low as necessary. The following questions may be asked of the defendant:

1. How long have you lived in this community?

2. How long at the same address?

3. What type of house do you live in?

4. Do you have a job?

5. What type of work does it involve?

6. How long have you held this job?

7. Will you lose your job if you remain in jail?

8. What types of jobs have you held in the past?

9. How much education have you had?

10. Where were you born and raised?

11. Do you have any savings?

12. Do you own any property in this community?

13. Are you married?

14. Do you have any children?

15. What jobs do you have?

16. What is the state of your health?

17. Do you feel you enjoy a good reputation in this community?

18. Have you had any recent mental problems of any sort?

19. Have you ever been previously arrested or convicted for a criminal offense?

20. If so, have you ever forfeited bail or failed to appear in court when you were told to do so?

The prosecutor will have the opportunity to cross-examine the defendant so the defendant should be cautioned to be truthful with the court. The defense counsel should strenuously object to any questions which touch on the facts of the present case.

After the defendant testifies, defense counsel should call other witnesses to corroborate the defendant's testimony. For example, an employer may testify that, if released, the defendant will have a job notwithstanding the present charges. A court clerk from a prior arrest may testify that the defendant was always prompt in court appearances. Indeed, a prior arrest may turn out to be an asset in establishing reliability. The defense counsel may, in addition, wish to call individuals who would be responsible in a nonfinancial sense for the defendant who is released into their custody.

A factor included in any bail determination is "the nature of the offense charged." The nature of the crime appears to be the major consideration in present bail hearings. The prosecutor will stress that the crime and the degree of proof will enhance the likelihood of the defendant's flight, particularly in serious crimes.

The prosecutor's concerns in a bail hearing are: (1) the possibility of flight, and (2) the potential of future crimes. The more serious the crime the less the defendant has to lose by fleeing the jurisdiction. The prosecutor may also reason that a defendant accused of a property crime is in need of money, and the additional expenses for an attorney will only increase the defendant's motivation to perpetrate further crimes. These arguments are usually made due to bad experiences with isolated defendants who have abused the bail system.

A defense attorney may counter these arguments with specific proposals. First, even though a defendant is charged with a serious crime, the law presumes the defendant innocent of the charges. Here, a brief description of a possible defense may be helpful to the judge in assuring that the defendant will not flee. The defendant's ties to the community—family, friends and employment—are the key factors in assuring the defendant's continued presence. Second, to rebut the argument of possible future crimes, the purpose of bail is not preventive detention. Also, a defendant on bail can work and earn money to make restitution to the present victim rather than be motivated to perpetrate additional crimes.

The court has a very wide latitude in setting bail with the additional authority to make certain special conditions of bail such as refraining from contacting certain individuals or remaining within the jurisdiction. Defense counsel should propose that the court set a low bond and impose reasonable restrictions as an alternative to a high bail. After both parties have presented evidence, the court will fix bail or release the defendant on his or her own recognizance.

Once taken, bail remains in effect until the termination of the proceedings, including appeal, unless revoked, modified, or forfeited. Bail taken in any proceeding must be terminated:

(1) when the defendant is acquitted or the prosecution is dismissed;

(2) when the defendant, following conviction, fails to perfect a timely appeal;

(3) when the defendant's appeal is dismissed; or

(4) when the defendant's conviction is affirmed on appeal.

Following a conviction, the defendant's bail may be raised, lowered, revoked or modified without a hearing by the trial court, which maintains control over bail throughout any appeal. If an appellate court reverses a conviction and grants a new trial, the defendant is entitled to the rights of pretrial release granted upon an initial appearance.

F. PRETRIAL DETENTION

As you read in Section C, the Bail Reform Act of 1984 not only governs pretrial release decisions but also pretrial detention determinations. Detention is authorized if the prosecution persuades the court that the defendant poses either a danger to the community or to any other person *or* a danger of not appearing for trial. 18 U.S.C. § 3142 authorizes a judicial officer to order the detention of a defendant pending trial if the prosecution demonstrates by clear and convincing evidence that no release conditions will reasonably assure the safety of the community. Pretrial (also known as preventive) detention is constitutional, violating neither due process nor the Eighth Amendment, as long as that detention (1) serves a compelling state interest; (2) does not impose punishment before an adjudication of guilt; and (3) is implemented in a fair, nonarbitrary manner. *United States v. Salerno*, 481 U.S. 739 (1987); *Bell v. Wolfish*, 441 U.S. 520 (1979).

The *Salerno* Court stated that preventive detention does not violate due process, because it is a regulatory measure imposed to regulate the "pressing societal problem" of defendants on pretrial release endangering the community by continuing to engage in criminal activity. The Court found that the Congress did not intend to punish individuals through preventive detention. The regulatory goal of preventing danger to the community outweighed a defendant's liberty interest. The legislation is limited to specific categories of individuals arrested for specific categories of serious crimes, both of which are likely to pose a danger to the community. Preventive detention due to dangerousness is not "excessive bail" under the Eighth Amendment. The Court found that excessive bail applies only to cases which qualify for bail where the traditional concern is prevention of flight. Detention, on the other hand, is constitutionally permitted when a different compelling interest (here, the protection of the community) exists.

Detention is also authorized by the statute if the prosecution proves that the defendant poses such a risk of flight that no condition or combination of conditions will reasonably assure the defendant's presence at trial. Because the Act is silent on standard of evidence necessary to prove a risk of flight and it explicitly recognizes an increased amount of proof for dangerousness, courts have indicated that the flight risk must be shown simply by a preponderance of the evidence. *See, e.g., United States v. Jackson*, 823 F.2d 4 (2d Cir.1987). The statutory standard for assuring appearance is a reasonable likelihood of appearance rather than a guarantee of appearance. 18 U.S.C. § 3142 (b), (c), (e).

In *United States v. Watson*, 253 F.Supp.2d 1 (D.D.C.2003), the granted the government's motion that the defendant be detained pending trial. The defendant was driving a tractor both on the grass and in the pond at Constitution Gardens located on The National Mall. When police asked the defendant to leave the tractor and exit the National Mall grounds, he refused, stating that he had "organic phosphate" and that he would detonate it if approached. The United States Park Police established a command post and evacuated buildings and concession stands along Constitution Avenue and closed nearby national monuments to the public.

The defendant made additional statements about using the explosives, adding that he was "ready to fight" and "willing to die for the cause." Throughout the course of the next day, the defendant stated that he would "bring D.C. to its knees" and "leave a mark on the Mall never to be forgotten." He also requested that the District be evacuated within 82 hours, and stated that he left "Easter eggs" near the Philip Morris sign in Richmond, Columbia Island, and at the Navy/Marine Memorial in Virginia. He indicated that, if the "Easter eggs" were to get wet, they would explode. The Park Police believed that this was a reference to grenades. The defendant communicated to law enforcement that "he would shoot back" if shot at first. The standoff ended on the following day.

The court examined the factors required to be considered by 18 U.S.C.A. section 3142(g), and concluded that defendant's release on any condition or combination of conditions would not reasonably assure his appearance or the safety of the community. The defendant held the city under siege for three days uttering threats to detonate explosives on The National Mall. The crime charged was a violent offense. The defendant was from North Carolina and had no roots in the metropolitan Washington, D.C. area. The government's evidence was overwhelming and based upon personal knowledge of the events and direct personal communications with the defendant.

As you read in 18 U.S.C. § 3142(e), the statute establishes two rebuttable presumptions for proof purposes at a hearing on preventive detention. A rebuttable presumption of dangerousness arises when a judge finds that a defendant is charged with a violent crime, capital offense, or a drug felony with a maximum term of ten years imprisonment *and* within five years of the finding, the defendant was convicted of or released from prison for a similar offense. A rebuttable presumption of both dangerousness and risk of flight occurs when a defendant is charged with a drug felony with a maximum term of ten years imprisonment *or* with the use or possession of a firearm during the commission of any violent crime or drug trafficking crime, *and* there is a finding of probable cause that the defendant committed an offense enumerated in the statute.

UNITED STATES v. ABAD

350 F.3d 793 (8th Cir. 2003).

RILEY, CIRCUIT JUDGE.

Vicente Abad (Abad), a 26–year old resident alien, was arrested and indicted for traveling from his United States residence in Florida to Iowa to commit criminal sexual activity with a 13–year old girl Abad met in an Internet chat room for 13– and 14–year olds. The magistrate judge ordered Abad released pending trial. The district court denied the government's appeal of the pretrial release order. Because we conclude the government (1) met its burden, by clear and convincing evidence, to show Abad is a danger to the community and (2) met its burden, by a preponderance of the evidence, to show Abad is a flight risk, we reverse and vacate the release order.

On July 17, 2003, Abad was arrested and later was indicted for interstate travel with intent to commit criminal sexual activity with a minor in violation of 18 U.S.C. §§ 2423(b), 2243, and 2246. At Abad's detention hearing on August 25, 2003, the magistrate judge noted the Pretrial Services Report (Pretrial Report) recommended Abad be detained as a flight risk and as a danger to the community. The Pretrial Report and the hearing evidence revealed the following: (1) Abad is a 26–year old unmarried Philippine citizen who has no children and resides with his parents in Hialeah, Florida; (2) Abad is well-educated and, at the time of arrest, was working as a registered nurse in Miami Children's Hospital; (3) Abad contacted an Iowa girl through an Internet chat room for 13– and 14–year olds; (4) Abad traveled to Iowa and had various forms of sexual relations with the Iowa girl, in the girl's residence and in Abad's hotel room, over a two-day period; (5) upon arrest, Abad possessed a digital camera and sexual items; and, (6) after receiving *Miranda* warnings, Abad admitted he knew the Iowa girl was 13 years old. Abad told the Iowa 13–year old he previously had traveled to Michigan for sex with a 15–year old girl. The hearing evidence further established Abad had engaged in "web-cam sex" with the 13–year old Iowa girl before going to Iowa. * * *

The magistrate judge denied the government's motion for detention. Although the magistrate judge found there was probable cause to believe Abad committed the offense, and remarked at the hearing that the government's case against Abad was "pretty overwhelming," the magistrate judge found Abad rebutted the statutory presumption favoring detention and the government failed to demonstrate, by clear and convincing evidence, Abad was a danger to the community, or to show, by a preponderance of evidence, Abad was a flight risk. The magistrate judge noted Abad has no prior criminal history, Abad was attending college, Abad did not use subterfuge to convince the girl to meet him, and Abad's family was willing to act as third-party custodians. The magistrate judge's order required Abad to surrender his passport and imposed home detention with electronic monitoring, but permitted Abad to leave home, without supervision, to work and to attend school. The release order implicitly permits Abad to return to his nursing job at Miami Children's Hospital.

The government appealed the denial of detention to the district court. The district court stayed the release order and, on August 29, 2003, held a hearing on the appeal. The district court did not examine the photographs or video of the victim. At the hearing, Abad's attorney introduced an "Internet profile" that showed the 13–year old as a 20–year old. Abad's attorney admitted she had downloaded the profile from the Internet, and she presented no evidence showing Abad had ever seen the profile. The district court denied the detention appeal, while acknowledging that, when it initially read the indictment, the court wondered why detention had not been ordered. After the district court considered the evidence adduced about the 13–year old girl and the "advertis[ing]" she had done on the Internet, the court determined "this case is not quite as 'dangerous' as urged by the government." The district court adopted the magistrate judge's ruling, denied the government's motion for detention, and ordered execution of papers by which Abad's parents would lose the equity interest in their home if Abad failed to appear for trial.

The government appealed the district court's decision and requested a stay of the release order. After the government appealed, the district court filed another order expressing additional reasons for denying detention, saying the minor girl's active participation on the Internet "lessens the introductory contempt of the actions of the defendant," and persuaded the court this "was not the usual 'poor victim' situation."
* * *

A defendant may be detained before trial "[o]nly if the government shows by clear and convincing evidence that no release condition or set of conditions will reasonably assure the safety of the community and by a preponderance of the evidence that no condition or set of conditions . . . will reasonably assure the defendant's appearance. . . ." *United States v. Kisling*, 334 F.3d 734, 735 (8th Cir.2003); 18 U.S.C. § 3142(c), (e)–(f)).

Because the district court found probable cause Abad committed an offense under 18 U.S.C. § 2423, a statutory rebuttable presumption arises "that no condition or combination of conditions will reasonably assure the appearance of the person as required and the safety of the community." 18 U.S.C. § 3142(e). Assuring a criminal defendant's appearance at trial is a legitimate government objective. Detaining adults who prey on children for the adult's sexual gratification or for the production of child pornography is also a legitimate government objective. One of the fundamental duties of government is public safety, including protecting children from sexual predators.

In determining if release conditions exist that will reasonably assure the appearance of a defendant at trial and the safety of the community, the court considers the following: (1) the nature and circumstances of the crime; (2) the weight of the evidence against the defendant; (3) the history and characteristics of the defendant, including mental condition, family ties, employment, community ties, and past conduct; and (4) the seriousness of the danger to the community or to an individual. 18 U.S.C. § 3142(g). "In a presumption case such as this, a defendant bears a limited burden of production—not a burden of persuasion—to rebut that presumption by coming forward with evidence he does not pose a danger to the community or a risk of flight." *United States v. Mercedes*, 254 F.3d 433, 436 (2d Cir.2001). "Once a defendant has met his burden of production relating to these two factors, the presumption favoring detention does not disappear entirely, but remains a factor to be considered among those weighed by the district court." *Id.*

The government contends Abad failed to rebut the presumption favoring detention. Alternatively, the government contends, assuming Abad rebutted the presumption, the government presented sufficient evidence to establish Abad is a danger to the community and a flight risk. We agree the evidence establishes Abad is a danger to the community and a flight risk.

To rebut the presumption favoring detention, Abad introduced the Pretrial Report, letters from members of his community, and evidence Abad's family is willing to act as third-party custodians. Abad also showed, if he fails to appear for trial, his family will forfeit a $65,000 equity interest in the parents' Hialeah, Florida, home. In analyzing the factors listed in 18 U.S.C. § 3142(g), we conclude the district court did not clearly err in finding Abad met his burden of production to rebut the detention presumption. Still, the presumption favoring detention does not disappear, but remains for consideration. * * *

Abad has no prior criminal history. However, the nature of the crime charged-sexual activity with a minor-weighs heavily against release. Strong evidence links Abad to this crime of violence. At the time of Abad's arrest, the police found a digital camera, condoms, KY Jelly, used contraceptive gels, and a dildo in Abad's hotel room. Abad admitted (1) he knew the girl was 13 years old, and he had met her in an Internet chat room for 13–and 14–year olds; (2) he engaged in telephone sex and web-cam sex with the girl before traveling to Iowa; and (3) he used a digital camera to take photos and video clips of the 13–year old girl masturbating and performing oral sex on Abad. The photos and video clips were found on the digital camera. Further, the government presented testimony Abad told the Iowa girl he previously, at the age of 22, had sex with a 15–year-old in Michigan. Based upon the evidence presented, we find the district court erred in ruling Abad is not a danger to the community. In particular, releasing Abad so he may return to his nursing position at Miami Children's Hospital is a clear abuse of discretion.

Abad is not a United States citizen. Although Abad's family members are willing to pledge a $65,000 equity interest in the parents' home, such surety is insufficient to assure Abad's presence at trial. Abad faces a maximum sentence of 30 years, which reduces the significance of the surety amount and weighs strongly in favor of a finding Abad would be a flight risk. Although electronic surveillance is available, when considering all the factors at issue in the present case, there is insufficient evidence to assure Abad's appearance at trial. See *Mercedes*, 254 F.3d at 437 (noting home detention, family assurances and electronic monitoring not sufficient in face of strong evidence defendant presented flight risk and danger to community).

To counter the government's evidence regarding risk of flight, Abad offered five letters of support from family members and friends. However, none of the letters indicate the writers knew the nature of Abad's alleged crime. Two of the letters reference only the writers' familiarity with Abad's family rather than with Abad himself. Needless to say, these letters do not tip the scales when weighed against the government's damning evidence. Abad's family's willingness to supervise Abad while he is home is entitled to little weight, because Abad contacted the Iowa girl and engaged in web-cam sex with her while living at home with his family. Taking possession of Abad's passport has little flight deterrence considering the ease of travel to Mexico and Canada. Simply stated, we conclude Abad is a flight risk. * * *

We conclude the district court's factual findings when denying detention were clearly erroneous insofar as the district court relied on the "Internet profile" and the minor girl's "active participation." Based upon the record, we conclude the government proved, (1) by clear and convincing evidence, Abad is a danger to the community; and, (2) by a preponderance of the evidence, Abad is a flight risk. Accordingly, we reverse and vacate the district court's pretrial release order, and we remand for further proceedings.

Notes and Questions

1. In *United States v. Nichols*, 897 F.Supp. 542 (W.D.Okla.), affirmed 61 F.3d 917 (10th Cir.1995), the court found by a preponderance that Terry Nichols posed "a substantial risk of flight and that no condition or combination of conditions of release will reasonably assure the appearance of the Defendant as required." The Court also found that there was clear and convincing evidence that Defendant was

> a danger to the community and to federal law enforcement agents and that no condition or combination of conditions of release will reasonably assure the safety of the community and of federal employees in particular. [The] offense Defendant is charged with committing or of aiding or abetting its commission is a crime of violence unparalleled in United States history in terms of the resulting loss of lives, injuries and property destruction, of which facts the Court takes judicial notice. There is probable cause to believe and clear and convincing evidence that Defendant committed or aided or abetted the commission of the crime that he is charged with committing, even crediting as true

information that he was not in Oklahoma City at the time of the explosion. Defendant has a history of possessing a large number of firearms, ammonium nitrate, ground ammonium nitrate, diesel fuel oil, a fuel meter, detonator cord and blasting caps, which can be used in constructing bombs. Defendant has admitted that he knows how to make a bomb by combining ammonium nitrate and fuel oil. * * *

2. *Crime of violence.* The United States Attorney can seek preventive detention under § 3142(f)(1)(A) in any case that "involves a crime of violence." If a felon is arrested for possession of a firearm, is he eligible for preventive detention?

In *United States v. Dillard*, 214 F.3d 88 (2d Cir. 2000), the court found that the definition of "crime of violence" in 18 U.S.C. § 3156(a)(4)(B) encompasses felon-in-possession offenses, when it refers to "any ... felony ... that by its nature involves a substantial risk that physical force ... may be used in the course of committing the offense." Because firearms are "essential equipment of criminals engaged in violent crime," the court found that the illegal possession of a firearm produces some risk that it may be used in an act of violence. By contrast, *United States v. Twine*, 344 F.3d 987 (9th Cir.2003) held that possession of a firearm by a convicted felon does not qualify as a crime of violence, justifying a pretrial detention hearing. *Twine* looked at the "nature" of the charge in its legal rather than in its factual context.

3. *Dangerousness.* § 3142(e) raises a rebuttable presumption about whether any condition or combination of conditions will reasonably assure the defendant's presence at trial. The following cases illustrate the nature and scope of the "dangerousness" concept.

(a) Does a defendant's "dangerousness" necessarily relate to the danger of *again* committing one or more of the statutorily designated crimes while on pretrial release? *See United States v. Himler*, 797 F.2d 156 (3d Cir.1986) (no).

(b) Preventive detention may be appropriate when the defendant poses a danger to the community or to any other person. What constitutes a "community"? The place where the charges are brought? Where the defendant has ties? *See United States v. Townsend*, 897 F.2d 989 (9th Cir.1990). (both are included as a "community").

(c) Under the federal statute, may detention be based solely upon the defendant's dangerousness, without regard to the statutory language? The cases require that detention is inappropriate unless the prosecution proves at least one of the six circumstances described in § 3142(f). *See, e.g., United States v. Byrd*, 969 F.2d 106 (5th Cir.1992); *United States v. Himler, supra.*

(d) Does a presumption of dangerousness arise for multiple offenses which individually carry maximum terms of less than ten years but together carry maximum terms of ten years or more? *See United States v. Hinote*, 789 F.2d 1490 (11th Cir.1986) (no). Does the presumption arise for a felony with a maximum term of ten years if the defendant would receive a shorter sentence under the federal Sentencing Guidelines? *See United States v. Moss*, 887 F.2d 333 (1st Cir.1989) (yes).

(e) Even if a defendant is able to sufficiently rebut a presumption of dangerousness or flight, the government may still be able to carry its burden of showing that no condition or combination of conditions will reasonably assure the appearance of the Defendant. *See, e.g., United States v. Niles*, 874 F.Supp. 1372 (N.D.Ga.1994); *United States v. Eaddy*, 853 F.Supp. 592 (N.D.N.Y.1994).

4. Other legal sources for pretrial detention may be used. For example, pursuant to federal law, the Attorney General may promulgate "Special Administrative Measures" ("SAMs") on a federal prisoner for pretrial detention, if the government finds that "there is a substantial risk that a prisoner's communications or contacts with persons could result in death or serious bodily injuries to persons...." 28 C.F.R. § 501.3(a) (2001). In *United States v. Reid*, 214 F.Supp.2d 84 (D.Mass. 2002), Richard Reid, the alleged "shoe-bomber," was not an American citizen and was accused of trying to blow up a transatlantic flight by igniting bombs concealed in his shoes. The government charged Reid in federal court with a variety of federal crimes. The court found that the SAMs issued for Reid were valid. "SAMs are prisoner-specific; that is, each prisoner upon whom SAMs are imposed has a set of SAMs issued for him, and him alone, based on the circumstances of his case."

Exercises

In the following exercises, assume that the applicable state preventive detention law is identical to the federal Bail Reform Act of 1984. Your professor will assign you to represent the defendant or the prosecution in the following situations. Assume that the prosecutor is seeking preventive detention, and evaluate whether preventive detention is appropriate for the defendant. Be prepared to advocate the position of your client, per the applicable statutory sections. What additional information would you assist you in assessing each case?

1. Defendant was charged with drug trafficking and illegal possession of firearms. A firearm was present in defendant's residence when police executed a search warrant and the firearm was in close proximity to drugs that defendant was alleged to have distributed. Seven years ago, defendant was sentenced to ten years' probation for theft, burglary, and burglary of auto; that probation was subsequently revoked. He also had convictions for obstructing an officer, trafficking in marijuana and marijuana paraphernalia, public intoxication, and failure to return rental property, for which prison sentences were imposed. All of the convictions occurred at least five years ago. Defendant has threatened a confidential informant in the case. Defendant has family ties in the area, including his responsibility to care for his minor child.

2. Defendant is a 64 year old, fit, substance-free immigration consultant who has lived abroad for the past 14 years. He is accused of making false statements in passport applications and illegal procurement of citizenship. This indictment was sealed to protect the government's ongoing investigation and efforts to apprehend the defendant. Defendant was divorced from his first wife in 1979. He sold his house and moved from the United States in 1980 or 1981. Since that time, the defendant has lived in

Europe and the Bahamas. Defendant has used at least 13 different names for various purposes during the past 14 years. Defendant became a citizen of Ireland and legally changed his name. There is also some evidence that he became a citizen of Israel. Defendant maintained his United States citizenship until 1986 when he formally renounced his citizenship in a sworn affidavit filed with the United States Embassy in London. Defendant stated that he no longer wanted dual citizenship because "I have lived in Europe for the past five years and intend to continue to do so." Defendant currently works as an immigration consultant helping clients obtain second passports by becoming naturalized citizens of various countries through economic investments. He transacts business under the name of Fax International, S.A. Fax is based in London and has offices in 39 cities around the world. Defendant holds 11 credit cards issued in six different names. Defendant has one prior conviction for passport fraud.

Defendant maintains that he should be released pending trial on certain conditions. These conditions include: (1) a substantial cash bond; (2) electronic, video and telephone monitoring; (3) third-party custody with his current mother-in-law; (4) house arrest with 24–hour security; and (5) frequent supervision by pre-trial services. The government argues that detention is required because no condition or combination of conditions will reasonably assure the defendant's appearance at trial.

3. Defendant has no prior criminal record, but was recently arrested for drug trafficking. He is 27 years old, has lived his entire life in Pennsylvania, and has a history of steady employment. He has worked in his father's construction business since graduating from high school nine years ago. He has also worked as a personal fitness trainer for the past 2 years. He has close ties to his family. Until last year, he lived with his parents. His younger sister stated that since his arrest, she has maintained his apartment and would offer to help her brother post a bond and supervise her brother if he were released. She indicated that her parents were also willing to provide support. She also found someone willing to employ defendant should he be released. Finally, the DEA agents who arrested defendant said that upon his arrest, he expressed concern about his parents' reaction to his arrest because his brother had been murdered in a drug-related incident last year. Defendant's only assets are $400 in a checking account and a Pontiac valued at approximately $200. Defendant was apprehended during a government sting operation. A confidential informant, who cooperated with the government in hope of obtaining more lenient treatment, called defendant and asked him to meet him at a hotel. The informant then produced a kilo of cocaine to sell to defendant. When he indicated that he had no money, the informant gave him the kilo on consignment.

Chapter 12

PROSECUTORIAL DISCRETION

A. PROSECUTORIAL POWER

BENNETT L. GERSHMAN—THE NEW PROSECUTORS

53 U. Pitt. L. Rev. 393–94, 395–96, 405–411, 443–46 (1992).

The power and prestige of the American prosecutor have changed dramatically over the past twenty years. Three generalizations appropriately describe this change. First, prosecutors wield vastly more power than ever before. Second, prosecutors are more insulated from judicial control over their conduct. Third, prosecutors are increasingly immune to ethical restraints. Only the last point may provoke some controversy; the first two are easily documented, and generally accepted by the courts and commentators.

Several factors account for this change. The most obvious is the transition from a due process-oriented criminal justice model to a model that has placed increasing emphasis on crime control and crime prevention. Crime has grown more complex and sophisticated since the early 1970s, particularly narcotics, racketeering, official corruption, and business fraud crimes, requiring a coordinated, powerful, and equally sophisticated response. The prosecutor has emerged as the central figure with the training and experience to administer this effort.

Examples of this new prosecutor can be seen in the so-called "special prosecutors" appointed to conduct major investigations such as Watergate, Iran–Contra, and local corruption probes, as well as the expanded use of undercover sting operations led by prosecutors. To support these new prosecutorial initiatives, legislatures have armed prosecutors with broad new weapons such as RICO, Drug Enterprise, Forfeiture, and Sentencing Guidelines. The judiciary has cooperated in this new effort too. First, by relaxing constitutional protections embodied in the exclusionary rule and due process, and by interpreting statutory and evidentiary rules broadly in the prosecutor's favor, the courts have made it much easier for prosecutors to win convictions. Second, by their increasing deference to prosecutorial discretion in every form, the courts have stimulated a law enforcement mentality that the "end justifies the means." Finally, as resort to the death penalty increases, the prosecutor has become the most dominant figure on the question of who will live and who will die for crimes committed. * * *

The prosecutor has always been a major player in crime investigation, but today the prosecutor occupies the preeminent role. Traditional functions have expanded, and new powers have been added. The prosecutor develops and coordinates strategies in major undercover investigations; uses the grand jury to investigate complex crimes such as narcotics trafficking, money laundering, official corruption, white collar crime, and organized crime; applies for authorization to obtain eavesdropping warrants; subpoenas records; and obtains the cooperation of witnesses through grants of immunity. Additionally, through sometimes controversial investigative methods, the prosecutor has been able to circumvent, neutralize, or even eliminate defense counsel as an impediment to effective investigation. * * *

Mostly as a result of his crime-charging power, the prosecutor has always been regarded as one of the most powerful officials in government. Prosecutors historically have enjoyed almost unfettered discretion in bringing charges. Doctrines such as conspiracy, for example, have given prosecutors tremendous power to join parties and offenses in one indictment. The presumption that prosecutors act in good faith has made the charging power virtually immune from judicial review. However, we have witnessed recently an even larger accretion of the prosecutor's charging power through legislative enactments, bold prosecutorial initiatives, and judicial acquiescence.

1. *New Crimes*

To supplement the prosecutor's already considerable arsenal, Congress over the past twenty years has passed legislation providing prosecutors with more potent laws than ever before: Racketeer Influenced and Corrupt Organizations Act; Continuing Criminal Enterprises Act; Criminal Forfeitures Act; Armed Career Criminal Act; Money Laundering Act; Bail Reform Act; Comprehensive Thrift and Bank Fraud Act; Victims of Child Abuse Act. Moreover, the recent trend toward mandatory minimum sentencing has given prosecutors greater leverage than ever to compel plea bargaining, force cooperation, and effectively determine the length of sentences.

Faced with increasing public pressure to win the "War on Crime," lawmakers continue to add even more crimes. For example, the Senate and House recently passed a new crime bill that would allow federal capital punishment for drug kingpins and permit imposition of the death penalty for some fifty federal offenses. Chief Justice Rehnquist publicly criticized the bill, arguing that it would inundate federal prosecutors with an unmanageable caseload of offenses that traditionally have been the province of state prosecutors. Recent efforts for even stronger prosecutorial initiatives have resulted in some astonishing proposals, a striking example being a provision in President Bush's Anti–Crime Bill that would authorize prosecutors to convene special tribunals to try foreigners accused of acts of terrorism. In proceedings before those tribunals, the defendants would not be allowed to rebut or even see the evidence against them. Expanding the Criminal Code in this way produces more convictions and is politically expedient, but the administrative and individual liberty costs are great. This is not a salutary development, especially in an era of tremendous overcrowding in the nation's prisons.

2. *Uncontrolled Discretion*

Commentators have described the prosecutor's discretion as potentially "lawless," "tyrannical," and "most dangerous." The prosecutor carries out his charging function independent from the judiciary. A prosecutor cannot be compelled to bring charges, or to terminate them. A private citizen has no standing to bring a criminal complaint if the prosecutor decides not to prosecute. And the judiciary has shown a remarkable passivity when asked to review the prosecutor's charging decisions. Indeed, some courts have deferred absolutely to the prosecutor's discretion, even though that decision has been shown to be demonstrably unfair. Thus, overcharging crimes, discriminating against defendants for prosecution, improper joinder of charges or parties, vindictiveness, coercive dismissals, plea bargaining abuses, and immunity violations, continue to occur regularly, without meaningful judicial review or correction.

Uncontrolled discretion in the hands of a powerful government official has the potential for abuse. In the hands of prosecutors, this potential is now a reality. Courts are unwilling to systematically rein in the prosecutors, resulting in a decline in the fairness of, and a loss of public confidence in, the system.

A horrendous example of the prosecutor's exercise of virtually uncontrolled charging discretion is seen in capital cases. Prosecutors historically have sought the death penalty disproportionately against black defendants as opposed to white defendants. In *McCleskey v. Kemp,* [481 U.S. 279 (1987)], the Supreme Court was presented with a statistical study of the capital punishment process in Georgia that showed that prosecutors sought the death penalty in seventy percent of the cases involving black defendants and white victims, and in only nineteen percent of the cases involving white defendants and black victims. The study also showed that a defendant's odds of receiving a death sentence were 4.3 times greater if his victim was white than if the victim was black. Although expressly assuming the validity of the study, the Supreme Court found that the statistics did not prove that the death penalty was administered in a racially discriminatory manner. Other studies also have shown that killers of white persons are prosecuted more vigorously than killers of black persons, and that black defendants charged with raping white women were more likely to be executed than were white defendants charged with raping black women, yet courts do not impose any restraints on these manifestly invidious prosecutorial charging decisions.

3. Megatrials

Equally devastating as the prosecutor's unchecked power over who and what to charge is the prosecutor's power over how to charge. A graphic illustration is the new phenomenon known as the "megatrial." The megatrial is a gargantuan criminal trial that can take up to two years to try, and involves numerous defendants, a myriad of varying charges and disparate criminal acts, a vast number of witnesses and exhibits, and an accompanying large number of defense counsel. Prosecutors deliberately seek to bring these "aberrations" because the benefits are considerable. The rationale usually advanced is "efficiency" and "fairness"—judicial resources are conserved and not duplicated; the burden on witnesses to repeat testimony is alleviated; the probability of inconsistent and erratic verdicts is reduced.

There are additional reasons why prosecutors want to charge defendants together in large group trials. Usually in large conspiracy cases, some defendants are directly involved, while others are only peripherally involved. The prosecutor's proof often is disproportionately addressed to defendants in different degrees. In a joint trial, the evidence comes in against all defendants together, notwithstanding their differing degrees of involvement. Prosecutors know that in a long and complex case, it is virtually impossible for jurors to compartmentalize proof against individual defendants. Some prosecutors pin their hopes on convicting minor participants who are charged in a small proportion of the counts on the slowly accumulating evidence against the major players, and the likelihood of "spillover taint." Moreover, in complex trials, such as RICO conspiracies, evidence will be admissible against some defendants but not against others. As Federal District Judge Jack Weinstein observed, "[T]here are conspiracies within conspiracies, and conspiracies to conceal other conspiracies, conspiracies which are discrete and finite, and those which are amorphous and indefinite, involving conspirators joining and leaving the conspiracy at various times." Asking jurors to make such factual distinctions over the course of many months "would be virtually impossible without the aid of a computer." Here again, although courts have criticized the prosecutorial tactic of bringing megatrials, they usually defer to the prosecutor's discretion. This is a dangerous abdication of the judicial duty. * * *

Ethical codes attempt to regulate many areas of prosecutorial behavior. Principal among them are the prosecutor's investigative and charging functions, disclosure of evidence, plea discussions, trial conduct, trial publicity, and conflicts of interest. Ethical codes also mandate prosecutors to "seek justice." The prosecutor's violation of an ethical rule can result in disciplinary action and the imposition of sanctions. Nevertheless, despite public and professional awareness of the existence of prosecutorial conduct that often violates ethical rules, there has been for some time a sense of frustration at the failure of professional disciplinary organizations to deal with such misconduct.

Documenting the failure of bar grievance committees to invoke disciplinary sanctions against prosecutors is not difficult. There is an astonishing absence from appellate court decisions or reports by discipline groups of cases dealing with misconduct by prosecutors. For example, despite the recognized frequency of misconduct by prosecutors in argument to the jury, this writer has found only one decision involving a disciplinary proceeding against a prosecutor for such conduct. This failure to discipline prosecutors contrasts sharply with the fairly common use of disciplinary sanctions against private attorneys in civil and criminal matters.

There are practical and institutional reasons for this default by disciplinary bodies. Professional discipline rules were drafted, have developed, and are presently used to regulate the private attorney-client relationship. Grievance committees are accustomed to disciplining the private bar. The prosecutor does not have a private client and, as a public figure, is outside the ambit of many of the ethical rules that regulate attorney-client behavior. Moreover, as a governmental figure of enormous power and prestige, the prosecutor is a person who professional bar organizations would not wish to alienate. Bar associations also are aware that in today's anti-crime climate, the prosecutor is encouraged to be zealous, and bar groups do not want to be seen as chilling this prosecutorial zeal. Further, the standards regulating prosecutorial behavior—*i.e.*, to "seek justice"—are often so nebulous as to be unenforceable, which merely reinforces the institutional reluctance to enforce the rules in the first place. Finally, with limited resources, grievance committees find that it is simpler and less costly to institute disciplinary proceedings against a private lawyer for a garden variety violation, such as the theft of escrow funds, than against a prosecutor for the failure to disclose exculpatory evidence.

MICHAEL DOYLE, STARR'S PROSECUTION TEAM PLAYED TOUGH, BUT WHAT ABOUT FAIRNESS?

Sacramento Bee p. A4 (September 28, 1998).

Strike hard but strike fair.

Federal prosecutors are supposed to live by this rule. Now, lawyers and lawmakers want to know how independent counsel Kenneth Starr's actions stack up against this standard of fair-minded toughness.

With the release last week of 3,183 pages of normally secret grand jury materials, a clearer picture is developing of the undeniably tough tactics employed by Starr in his investigation of President Clinton. At the least, the documents reveal for the public what prosecutors and defense lawyers know already:

Criminal investigations are not for the faint of heart.

In the case of Starr's deputies, the documents reveal, that meant ambushing 24–year–old Monica Lewinsky in the food court of the swank Pentagon City mall. It meant discouraging her from calling her attorney or her mother, and watching impassively for hours at a time while Lewinsky cried in a hotel room and repeatedly read Psalms 21 for solace. It meant threatening Lewinsky with the possibility of 27 years in prison if she didn't cooperate, and intimating her mother might be prosecuted as well.

"I mean, that was just so frightening," Lewinsky told grand jurors when they asked her about the day Starr's investigators confronted her. "It was so incredibly frightening."

Hardball, of course, has been played by both the White House political operatives and Starr's prosecutors during the entire 4–year–long investigation. It was never more evident than the day Starr called Lewinsky's mother to testify—testimony cut short when the mother emotionally short-circuited on the stand.

"I didn't find anything wrong with that," Fresno County District Attorney Ed Hunt said. "It didn't seem like Starr did anything wrong to me, he just went forward aggressively. . . . You follow leads, and you do what you have to do."

Within the rules, Hunt emphasized. For federal prosecutors, these rules are minutely spelled out in the multivolume U.S. Attorneys' Manual. Additional guidance is provided elsewhere.

Recently, for instance, the 44 criminal prosecutors who work in the Sacramento and Fresno offices of the U.S. attorney for the Eastern District of California were given an e-mail reminder to see a training videotape titled "Use and Abuse of Informers in Criminal Investigations and Prosecutions." It's one of the tools, like partnering junior attorneys with senior mentors, meant to ensure proper behavior.

"Most prosecutors I've ever worked with take their jobs very, very seriously," said Leesa Brown, Sacramento-based spokeswoman for the U.S. Attorney's Office. "There are certain things that really make their hair stand up."

One, Brown cited, is the necessity of keeping grand jury material secret. Following a complaint filed by White House lawyers, a federal judge in Washington has ordered an investigation into whether Starr's office leaked to reporters tidbits from the seven-month probe of Lewinsky's sexual affair with Clinton.

Some criminal defense lawyers are also questioning aspects of Starr's treatment of Lewinsky last January. The questions illustrate the perennial tension between defenders and prosecutors over the rules of fair play.

For instance, the American Bar Association's Code of Professional Responsibility discourages attorneys from contacting potential witnesses without the prior consent of the individual's own attorney. The idea is to protect individuals from being taken advantage of.

Starr's team lured Lewinsky to the Pentagon City mall even though she had an attorney, and tried negotiating with her directly once they'd convinced her to accompany them to Room 1012 of the nearby Ritz–Carlton Hotel.

"This was extremely egregious," said Jack King, an attorney and spokesman for the National Association of Criminal Defense Lawyers. "I've never seen anything like it."

Prosecutors, naturally, view such complaints skeptically. The Justice Department's official position is that disregarding attorneys and contacting individuals in the course of a law enforcement investigation does not violate ABA guidelines. There are many other areas of conduct, as well, viewed differently by prosecutors and defenders.

"As a prosecutor, the last thing you'd want to hear is a defense attorney saying you'd done a good job," Hunt said.

One of the Justice Department's own guidelines prohibits prosecutors from disparaging attorneys hired by the targeted individual. The idea is to avoid driving wedges between vulnerable individuals and their lawyers: a wedge that Starr's deputies at least seemed to suggest when they talked to Lewinsky about her first lawyer, Frank Carter.

"Someone said that Frank wasn't even—Frank was a civil attorney so that he couldn't really help me anyway," Lewinsky testified. "So I asked him if at least I could call and ask him for a recommendation for a criminal attorney, and they didn't think that was a good idea."

When there are complaints about federal prosecutors, the Justice Department handles them through the Office of Professional Responsibility. In 1996, the office received 121 complaints. Of those, 34 related to alleged abuse of prosecutorial powers, 16 related to improper release of information and two related to improper contacts with represented individuals. Only about 11 percent of the time are the complaints found to be justified.

Lewinsky's attorneys, who obtained from Starr a sweeping immunity grant in exchange for her testimony, have not complained about the independent counsel's actions. But Lewinsky herself, in her Sept. 19 testimony before the grand jury, revealed herself as badly shaken by her treatment. She spoke fully about what happened only after one of Starr's chief deputies, who had led the first confrontation with her, had left the grand jury room.

Haltingly, repeatedly stopping to cry, Lewinsky told the grand jurors how two FBI agents confronted her at the mall on Jan. 16 and urged her to come with them. She said she would talk only if she had her attorney.

"They told me that was fine, but I should know I wouldn't be given as much information and wouldn't be able to help myself as much with my attorney there," Lewinsky testified. "So I agreed to go. I was so scared."

Over the next 11 hours, in a room crowded at times with investigators and prosecutors, Starr's eight-person team worked on Lewinsky. She wanted to call her mother and her attorney; they urged her not to. They assured her she could leave whenever she wanted, but she was convinced she'd be arrested if she left. Starr's deputy, Jackie Bennett, pressed her to decide, now.

"Jackie Bennett said, 'You're 24, you're smart, you're old enough, you don't need to call your mommy,' " Lewinsky said.

Starr's team informed Lewinsky that they knew she had lied when she denied, in an affidavit, her relationship with Clinton. They told her she could be charged with perjury, obstruction of justice, witness tampering, subornation of perjury. She could be thrown into prison for 27 years.

She could save herself, but only if she helped lure information from presidential secretary Betty Currie and presidential pal Vernon Jordan.

"They told me they wanted me to cooperate," Lewinsky said. "They told me that . . . I'd have to place calls or wear a wire to see, to call Betty and Mr. Jordan and possibly the president."

After many tears, Lewinsky left the Ritz–Carlton about midnight that January night. Ultimately, it took Starr's team until August to win her cooperation. And it took until September for Lewinsky to unburden herself about the day she learned firsthand what criminal law is like.

"I didn't understand why they, why they had to trap me into coming there," Lewinsky told grand jurors. "I mean, this had all been a set-up."

DAVID ROSENZWEIG, L.A. ATTORNEYS DIVIDED ON ASHCROFT DIRECTIVE; SOME DEFENSE LAWYERS FEAR THAT PLACING RESTRICTIONS ON PROSECUTORS WHO ARE SEEKING PLEA BARGAINS WILL STRAIN THE SYSTEM

L.A. TIMES p. B2 (October 17, 2003).

A recent directive by Atty. Gen. John Ashcroft aimed at limiting prosecutors' discretion in negotiating plea bargains has aroused the ire of criminal defense lawyers across the country. Los Angeles is no exception, but seasoned defense lawyers here appear divided over whether the new rules will result in any significant changes locally.

Some say, in effect, "So what's new?" They note that the U.S. attorney's office in Los Angeles has a history of hard-nosed plea bargaining, even when more liberal rules were in place throughout the nation.

Others echo the words of veteran criminal defense lawyer Donald Re, who said, "The entire court system will collapse if this new policy is applied strictly."

In Los Angeles, 97.2% of all federal criminal cases end in guilty pleas before trial, most resolved through plea bargains. Nationally, that rate is about 96%.

If only a fraction of defendants who currently plead guilty were to choose trials because prosecutors had become uncompromising, the courts would be inundated in no time, said Re and other defense lawyers.

But that is not likely to happen, according to other experienced legal practitioners.

"My feeling is that this may be a lot of hoopla," said defense lawyer Anthony Brooklier, and that when federal prosecutors "get down to cases, cooler heads will prevail."

George Cardona, chief assistant U.S. attorney in Los Angeles, said Ashcroft's directive represented no substantive change in policy for the 260 or so federal prosecutors who staff the local office, which is second in size only to the U.S. attorney's office in Manhattan.

"For many years, we've had policies that mesh with the guidelines, essentially because we're a large office and we needed to ensure consistency in sentencing recommendations," he said.

The policy change announced by Ashcroft in his Sept. 22 directive erased permissive language written into the U.S. Attorneys' Manual in 1993 by Janet Reno, attorney general in the Clinton administration. The Reno language allowed prosecutors engaged in plea negotiations to make individualized assessments of the circumstances and seriousness of a crime and whether the sentence would be appropriate.

At the same time, however, Reno left intact a requirement that prosecutors proceed on the most serious "readily provable" charges and not arrive at a plea agreement "that fails to reflect the seriousness of the defendant's conduct."

Richard E. Drooyan, who served as chief assistant U.S. attorney in Los Angeles during the Reno years, said that, despite the added flexibility given to line prosecutors, "it was a rare case when they would not charge the most serious, provable offense."

Ashcroft incorporated that same language in his Sept. 22 directive, saying "federal prosecutors must charge and pursue the most serious, readily provable offense or offenses that are supported by the facts of the case except in limited, narrow circumstances."

Those exceptions include:

* When a defendant agrees to provide "substantial assistance" in an investigation.

* When a U.S. attorney's office is overburdened with case backlogs.

* When a prosecutor decides that the original charges will be difficult to prove because of witness problems or suppression of evidence.

* When enhancements that could result in a longer sentence remove any incentive for a defendant to plead guilty.

In addition, prosecutors will retain discretion in deciding which crimes are "readily provable."

As a practical matter, said veteran defense lawyer Joel Levine, "this is not going to mean the end of plea bargaining," though he added that the Ashcroft memo could have a chilling effect on prosecutors engaged in the give and take of plea negotiations.

Levine, who tries cases around the country, said the federal prosecutor's office in Los Angeles had "always been rigid when it comes to plea negotiations. Elsewhere, they're a lot more willing to work with you."

Defense attorney John Yzurdiaga agreed. "I think there are some districts that are more liberal than Los Angeles." He mentioned Philadelphia.

Ashcroft may also have had in mind U.S. attorney's offices in New York and Connecticut. Earlier this year, he caused a stir in the legal community when he overruled prosecutors in those two states who had recommended against seeking the death penalty in a dozen cases.

He followed that with a directive in July ordering all U.S. attorneys to report the names of federal judges who impose punishments more lenient than those recommended under federal sentencing guidelines. The guidelines are set by the U.S. Sentencing Commission, which Congress established in the mid–1980s to bring uniformity to sentencing practices by federal judges.

Judges are required to follow the guidelines unless they determine there are extenuating circumstances that warrant either a more lenient or harsher punishment.

Jan Handzlik, a veteran white-collar criminal defense lawyer based in Los Angeles, said he viewed the most recent Ashcroft directive as "part of a continuing effort by the Department of Justice to assert control and authority over local U.S. attorney's offices."

Handzlik said he was particularly disturbed by the attorney general's disdain for sentences more lenient than the guidelines call for.

"His memo articulates the need for honesty in sentencing," Handzlik said, "but instead of coming out in support of following the guidelines in their totality, it sends a message to prosecutors that upward enhancements are good and downward departures are bad, even though both are part of the guideline system."

Laurie Levenson, a former federal prosecutor who teaches at Loyola Law School in Los Angeles, said the memo seems to represent a change in tone and attitude—rather than substance—when compared to the policies of previous administrations.

"This is clearly designed to clamp down on discretion . . . and centralize power in Washington," she said. "It's a shot across the bow: Washington will be really unhappy with you if you try to depart."

B. THE DECISION TO INVESTIGATE OR CHARGE

1. *Discretionary Authority*

Prosecutors have broad discretion (rather than an obligation or a duty) about when and whether to investigate and/or to prosecute. Broad discretion is required as a matter of separation of powers because prosecutors act as part of the Executive Branch. Courts have also noted repeatedly that the decision to prosecute is particularly ill-suited to judicial review. Among the discretionary factors that are not easily reviewable are the strength of the case, the prosecution's general deterrence value, the State's enforcement priorities, and the case's relationship to the State's overall enforcement plans.

UNITED STATES v. BATCHELDER

442 U.S. 114 (1979).

MR. JUSTICE MARSHALL delivered the opinion of the Court.

At issue in this case are two overlapping provisions of the Omnibus Crime Control and Safe Streets Act of 1968 (Omnibus Act). Both prohibit convicted felons from receiving firearms, but each authorizes different maximum penalties. We must determine whether a defendant convicted of the offense carrying the greater penalty may be sentenced only under the more lenient provision when his conduct violates both statutes.

I.

Respondent, a previously convicted felon, was found guilty of receiving a firearm that had traveled in interstate commerce, in violation of 18 U.S.C. § 922(h). The District Court sentenced him under 18 U.S.C. § 924(a) to five years' imprisonment, the maximum term authorized for violation of § 922(h).

The Court of Appeals affirmed the conviction but, by a divided vote, remanded for resentencing. The majority recognized that respondent had been indicted and convicted under § 922(h) and that § 924(a) permits five years' imprisonment for such violations. However, noting that the substantive elements of § 922(h) and 18 U.S.C.App. § 1202(a) are identical as applied to a convicted felon who unlawfully receives a firearm, the court interpreted the Omnibus Act to allow no more than the 2–year maximum sentence provided by § 1202(a). * * *

II.

This Court has previously noted the partial redundancy of §§ 922(h) and 1202(a), both as to the conduct they proscribe and the individuals they reach. However, we find nothing in the language, structure, or legislative history of the Omnibus Act to suggest that because of this overlap, a defendant convicted under § 992(h) may be imprisoned for no more than the maximum term specified in § 1202(a). As we read the Act, each substantive statute, in conjunction with its own sentencing provision, operates independently of the other. * * *

In construing § 1202(a) to override the penalties authorized by § 924(a), the Court of Appeals relied, we believe erroneously, on three principles of statutory interpretation. First, the court invoked the well-established doctrine that ambiguities in criminal statutes must be resolved in favor of lenity. Although this principle of construction applies to sentencing as well as substantive provisions, in the instant case there is no ambiguity to resolve. Respondent unquestionably violated § 922(h), and § 924(a) unquestionably permits five years' imprisonment for such a violation. That § 1202(a) provides different penalties for essentially the same conduct is no justification for taking liberties with unequivocal statutory language. By its express terms, § 1202(a) limits its penalty scheme exclusively to convictions obtained under that provision. Where, as here, "Congress has conveyed its purpose clearly, ... we decline to manufacture ambiguity where none exists."

Nor can § 1202(a) be interpreted as implicitly repealing § 924(a) whenever a defendant's conduct might violate both Titles. For it is "not enough to show that the two statutes produce differing results when applied to the same factual situation." Rather, the legislative intent to repeal must be manifest in the " 'positive repugnancy between the provisions.' " In this case, however, the penalty provisions are fully capable of coexisting because they apply to convictions under different statutes.

Finally, the maxim that statutes should be construed to avoid constitutional questions offers no assistance here. This " 'cardinal principle' of statutory construction ... is appropriate only when [an alternative interpretation] is 'fairly possible' " from the language of the statute We simply are unable to discern any basis in the Omnibus Act for reading the term "five" in § 924(a) to mean "two."

III.

In resolving the statutory question, the majority below expressed "serious doubts about the constitutionality of two statutes that provide different penalties for identical conduct." Specifically, the court suggested that the statutes might (1) be void for vagueness, (2) implicate "due process and equal protection interest[s] in avoiding excessive prosecutorial discretion and in obtaining equal justice," and (3) constitute an impermissible delegation of congressional authority. We find no constitutional infirmities.

It is a fundamental tenet of due process that "[n]o one may be required at peril of life, liberty or property to speculate as to the meaning of penal statutes." A criminal statute is therefore invalid if it "fails to give a person of ordinary intelligence fair notice that his contemplated conduct is forbidden." So too, vague sentencing provisions may pose constitutional questions if they do not state with sufficient clarity the consequences of violating a given criminal statute.

The provisions in issue here, however, unambiguously specify the activity proscribed and the penalties available upon conviction. That this particular conduct may violate both Titles does not detract from the notice afforded by each. Although the statutes create uncertainty as to which crime may be charged and therefore what penalties may be imposed, they do so to no greater extent than would a single statute authorizing various alternative punishments. So long as overlapping criminal provisions clearly define the conduct prohibited and the punishment authorized, the notice requirements of the Due Process Clause are satisfied.

This Court has long recognized that when an act violates more than one criminal statute, the Government may prosecute under either so long as it does not discriminate against any class of defendants.

The Court of Appeals acknowledged this "settled rule" allowing prosecutorial choice. Nevertheless, [the] court distinguished overlapping statutes with identical standards of proof from provisions that vary in some particular. In the court's view, when two statutes prohibit "exactly the same conduct," the prosecutor's "selection of which of two penalties to apply" would be "unfettered." Because such prosecutorial discretion could produce "unequal justice," the court expressed doubt that this form of legislative redundancy was constitutional. We find this analysis factually and legally unsound.

Contrary to the Court of Appeals' assertions, a prosecutor's discretion to choose between §§ 922(h) and 1202(a) is not "unfettered." Selectivity in the enforcement of criminal laws is, of course, subject to constitutional constraints. And a decision to proceed under § 922(h) does not empower the Government to predetermine ultimate criminal sanctions. Rather, it merely enables the sentencing judge to impose a longer prison sentence than § 1202(a) would permit and precludes him from imposing the greater fine authorized by § 1202(a). More importantly, there is no appreciable difference between the discretion a prosecutor exercises when deciding whether to charge under one of two statutes with different elements and the discretion he exercises when choosing one of two statutes with identical elements. In the former situation, once he determines that the proof will support conviction under either statute, his decision is indistinguishable from the one he faces in the latter context. The prosecutor may be influenced by the penalties available upon conviction, but this fact, standing alone, does not give rise to a violation of the Equal Protection or Due Process Clause. Just as a defendant has no constitutional right to elect which of two applicable federal statutes shall be the basis of his indictment and prosecution, neither is he entitled to choose the penalty scheme under which he will be sentenced.

Approaching the problem of prosecutorial discretion from a slightly different perspective, the Court of Appeals postulated that the statutes might impermissibly delegate to the Executive Branch the Legislature's responsibility to fix criminal penalties. We do not agree. The provisions at issue plainly demarcate the range of penalties that prosecutors and judges may seek and impose. In light of that specificity, the power that Congress has delegated to those officials is no broader than the authority they routinely exercise in enforcing the criminal laws. Having informed the courts, prosecutors, and defendants of the permissible punishment alternatives available under each Title, Congress has fulfilled its duty.

Accordingly, the judgment of the Court of Appeals is reversed.

2. Criteria for the Exercise of Discretion

While not formally binding on a prosecutor's decision whether or who to investigate, or whether, who, and/or what to charge, the American Bar Association has adopted detailed standards (which are in the statutory supplement) intended to assist prosecutors in the principled exercise of their investigatory and charging discretion.

Note

In *Inmates of Attica Correctional Facility v. Rockefeller*, 477 F.2d 375 (2d Cir.1973), the court held that the federal judiciary, even at the behest of crime victims, lack the authority to compel federal and state officials to investigate and prosecute persons who have violated criminal statutes. Because prosecutors possess discretion (rather than an obligation or duty) to investigate and prosecute, they are not legally bound to do either. From the perspective of the separation of powers, the Judicial Branch should not be interfering with the executive prerogatives of prosecutors who are part of the Executive Branch. As the court points out, we do not want courts to become "superprosecutors", without anyone to check the exercise (and abuse) of such authority.

Problems

If you were a prosecutor faced with the following factual scenarios, would you charge the potential accused with homicide? (If you don't feel that you can fairly make such a decision based on these limited facts, what further facts would you ask the police to obtain for you? What significance would you attach to these further facts, *i.e.* would they make you more or less likely to charge?)

1. Dr. Jack Kevorkian has flown to your jurisdiction and, at the request of his spouse, obtained drugs with which her 72–year old husband, who had terminal cancer, killed himself. (Your jurisdiction's Crimes Code contains a section which provides that "[a] person who intentionally aids or solicits another to commit suicide is guilty of a felony punishable by up to 10 years in prison if the person's conduct causes such suicide or an attempted suicide.") Do you charge Dr. Kevorkian and/or the deceased's spouse?

2. The day after a defendant has been arrested for sexual abuse of a 10 year-old boy, the boy's distraught mother shoots and kills the defendant at his arraignment. She tells you that she bought the gun that morning in order to shoot and kill the deceased. (Your jurisdiction's Crimes Code provides that: an intentional, premeditated killing is first degree murder; an otherwise malicious killing is second degree murder; and a provoked killing is voluntary manslaughter, although the provocation must be "sudden.") What, if anything, do you charge the mother with?

3.   A woman who had been abused, physically and emotionally, by her husband for a period of three years, killed him by pouring gasoline on him and lighting it while he had passed out in his bed in an alcoholic stupor. The last time he had abused her had been three days earlier. (Your jurisdiction's Crimes Code does not expressly recognize a "battered spouse" defense. Your jurisdiction's self-defense provisions require that a defendant establish, *inter alia* that he or she used defensive deadly force in response to the "imminent" use of deadly force against him or her.) Do you charge her with murder?

Exercise

Your professor will assign half of the class to Prosecution and half the class to Defense. If you are assigned to Prosecution, you should contact a lawyer in a prosecutorial office (preferably in the city where the law school is located or the city where you are from) and ask him or her just how he or she would exercise his or her discretion in one of the three settings described in the previous Problem. Similarly, if you are assigned to Defense, you should contact a lawyer in a public defender's office or in private criminal defense practice and ask him or her just how he or she thinks that prosecutors *should* exercise their discretion in one of these settings. However, where the lawyer consulted is working in a jurisdiction where the prosecutor has discretion to seek the death penalty in first-degree murder cases, instead of using one of the settings described above, you should ask either the prosecutor or defense counsel exactly what criteria prosecutors use (or in the case of defense counsel, the criteria prosecutors *should* use) in deciding whether or not to seek the death penalty. You should thereafter be prepared to report to the class on a date set by your professor. (1) the criteria for exercise of discretion used by the lawyer consulted; and (2) your analysis of the appropriateness of that criteria.

C.   PRETRIAL DIVERSION FOR DEFENDANTS

In addition to a significant measure of discretion with respect to who and when to investigate and who, what, and whether to charge, prosecutors in many jurisdictions also possess substantial authority to divert accused persons into whatever pretrial intervention (PTI) programs that may have been established in their jurisdiction. Typically, the successful completion by an accused of the conditions set upon entry into the PTI program results in the dismissal of the whatever pending charges which led to the PTI diversion. Concomitantly, failure to meet those PTI requirements results in the prosecutorial office taking the charges to trial. The National District Attorneys Association (NDAA) has created a set of model standards for the prosecutorial exercise of discretion relating to PTI referrals, standards which have not been expressly adopted in any jurisdiction, but which well illustrate the sorts of concerns and criteria prosecutors should have and use in deciding how to exercise this discretion.

NATIONAL DISTRICT ATTORNEYS ASSOCIATION— NATIONAL PROSECUTION STANDARDS

STANDARDS 44.1 through 44.8 (2d ed. 1991).

DIVERSION

44.1   Prosecutorial Discretion The decision to divert cases from the criminal justice system should be the responsibility of the prosecutor. The prosecutor should, within the exercise of his discretion, determine whether diversion of an offender to a treatment alternative best serves the interests of justice. The determination of the prosecutor of whether or not to divert a particular defendant should not be subject to judicial review.

44.2   Alternative Diversion Programs As a central figure in the diversion process, the prosecutor should be aware and informed of the scope and availability of all alternative diversion programs. It is recommended that all programs which may be non-criminal disposition alternatives maintain close liaison and the fullest flow of information with the prosecutor's office.

44.3   Information Gathering The prosecutor should have all relevant investigative information, personal data, case records, and criminal history information necessary to render sound and reasonable decisions on diversion of individuals from the criminal justice system. Legislation and court rules should enable the prosecutor to obtain relevant information from appropriate agencies for this purpose.

44.4   Factors to Consider The prosecutor should exercise discretion to divert individuals from the criminal justice system when he considers it to be in the interest of justice and beneficial to both the community and the individual. Factors which may be considered in this decision include: The nature and severity of the offense; Any special characteristics or difficulties of the offender; Whether the defendant is a first-time offender; Whether there is a probability that the defendant will cooperate with and benefit from the diversion program; Whether an available program is appropriate to the needs of the offender; The impact of diversion upon the community; Recommendations of the involved law enforcement agency; Whether the defendant is likely to recidivate; Consideration for the opinion of the victim; Provisions for restitution; and Any mitigating circumstances.

44.5   Diversion Provisions The use of non-criminal disposition should incorporate procedures which include the following provisions:

    a.   A signed agreement identifying all requirements of the accused;

    b.   A signed waiver of speedy trial requirements;

    c.   The right of the prosecutor, for a designated time period, to proceed with the criminal case when, in his judgment, such action would be in the interest of justice;

d.   A signed release by the accused of any potential civil claims against victims, witnesses, law enforcement agencies and their personnel, the prosecutor and his personnel, after the accused has had the opportunity to confer with counsel;

e.   Appropriate mechanisms to safeguard the prosecution of the case, such as admissions of guilt, stipulations of facts, and dispositions of witnesses.

44.6   **Record of Decision** A record of the non-criminal disposition, including reasons for the disposition, should be created for each case and made a part of the accused's criminal history record.

44.7   **Explanation of Decision** The prosecutor should provide adequate explanations of the noncriminal disposition to victims, witnesses, and law enforcement officials.

44.8   **Need for Programs** In jurisdictions where diversion programs are insufficient, the prosecutor should urge the establishment, maintenance, and enhancement of such programs ad may be necessary.

Commentary

An alternative available to prosecutors in the processing of a criminal complaint is that of diversion, the channeling of criminal defendants and even potential defendants, into programs that may not involve incarceration. The purposes of diversion programs include:

1.   Unburdening court dockets and conserving judicial resources for more serious cases;

2.   Reducing the incidence of offender recidivism by providing an alternative to incarceration—community-based rehabilitation—which would be more effective and less costly than incarceration; and

3.   Benefiting society by the training and placement of previously unemployed or underemployed persons.

The prosecutor is an integral part of any diversion system; indeed, he should be the central figure in such a system. The prosecutor commonly makes the decision to introduce an offender into alternative treatment and is ultimately responsible for determining the success of that alternative treatment.

The authority of the prosecutor to institute diversion proceedings is an incident of the prosecutor's discretionary authority in screening and charging. The authority of the prosecutor to control the diversion decision prior to arraignment or indictment is well substantiated. Prosecutorial authority in post-charging diversion is also clear.

Multiple factors may legitimately be considered by the prosecutor in making the diversion decision, including the willingness of a defendant to waive potential civil claims against law enforcement personnel. Basically, these factors concern the character of the defendant, the type of offense, the availability of suitable treatment or educational facilities, and the particular relation of the case to other criminal justice goals. Determination of the appropriateness of diversion in a specified case will involve a subjective determination that, after consideration of all circumstances, the offender and the community will both benefit more by diversion than by prosecution. * * *

In order for a diversion program to be beneficial both for the defendant and for the prosecution, certain safeguards must exist for each party. To adequately provide for protection of defendants' rights, the following safeguards might be considered by prosecutors in addition to those specified in the standard:

    1.   The right of the defendant, at any point, to insist on criminal prosecution;

    2.   The presence of a reviewing judge to determine if there is sufficient factual basis for a charge;

    3.   The presence of a reviewing judge to determine whether any pressure put on the defendant to accept noncriminal disposition constituted overwhelming inducement to surrender the right to trial;

    4.   The presence of counsel.

Equally important as protecting the rights of the individual is the necessity to protect the interests of society. It must be remembered that the individual involved in the diversion process is accused of having committed a criminal act and is avoiding prosecution only because an alternative procedure is thought to be more beneficial. The right of the prosecutor to successfully reinitiate prosecution should be considered and protected. Prosecution following deferment to a diversion program that has failed to produce satisfactory results faces serious problems, since the time delay raises the possibility that witnesses and other evidence will disappear, thus compromising the prosecutors ability to obtain a conviction if treatment fails.

To protect the rights of the prosecutor, the following safeguards might be considered:

    1.   The right of the prosecutor at any point to insist upon criminal prosecution;

    2.   Waiver of speedy trial requirements;

    3.   The inclusion in the diversion agreement of admissions by the defendant, stipulation of facts or depositions of witnesses, and an agreement by the defendant to cooperate with law enforcement;

    4.   Waiver of applicable statute of limitations.

The right of a prosecutor to terminate an offender's participation in a diversion program is essential. Only by retaining this option can the prosecutor guarantee continued protection of the rights of the community. If the prosecutor does not have this authority, the diversion program itself will suffer since the prosecutor will gravitate toward prosecution of questionable cases' rather than release of the offender from his supervision.

The diversion alternative to prosecution is an increasingly utilized and effective mechanism for dealing with offenders. [Since] 1977, diversion has been adopted in almost every jurisdiction in the United States. The prosecutor plays the central role in the diversion process—he initiates the movement into diversion and must judge the efficaciousness of diversionary treatment. To maximize the effectiveness of the prosecutor's role, it is important that these responsibilities be recognized and be allowed to function efficiently.

Notes and Questions

1. What is your opinion of the appropriateness of the factors set forth to guide the prosecutor's discretion in NDAA Standard 44.4? Are all of these factors appropriate for a prosecutor's consideration given the fact that there is unlikely to be any judicial review of this decision? Is it appropriate for a prosecutor, for example, to take account of the political impact of a decision to divert an accused into an otherwise available PTI program: Is the "political reaction" of individuals in the community (including, perhaps, whether or not to vote for the prosecutor in the next election) different from the "community reaction" which Standard 44.4 provides should be appropriate for the prosecutor to consider?

In your opinion, are there any other factors not set forth in Standard 44.4 which should be considered by a prosecutor in making these decisions? What are they?

2. In *State v. Rosario*, 237 N.J.Super. 63, 566 A.2d 1173 (App.Div. 1989), the court upheld the discretion of a prosecutor to refuse to consent to the defendant's participation in a diversion program. In effect, prosecutors have essentially the same unfettered discretion with respect to a diversion decision as they possess in deciding who to investigate or to charge. The prosecutor is presumed to have considered all relevant factors in making his or her decision. In Rosario's situation, evidence that his residence was used as a source of narcotics trafficking, even though he was not charged with trafficking, justified the prosecutor's refusal to consent to Rosario's diversion. "[A]bandonment of the prosecution would be more harmful to society than admission into [the diversion program] would be beneficial to defendant."

D. SELECTIVE PROSECUTION

As a result of the wide discretion prosecutors have in prosecuting criminal cases, potential exists for abuse of that discretion. Misuse of that discretion especially presents itself when a prosecutor, with the requisite amount of probable cause, purposefully chooses to pursue a case because of the defendant's race, religion, or some other arbitrary classification.

WAYTE v. UNITED STATES
470 U.S. 598 (1985).

JUSTICE POWELL delivered the opinion of the Court. The question presented is whether a passive enforcement policy under which the Government prosecutes only those who report themselves as having violated the law, or who are reported by others, violates the First and Fifth Amendments.

I.

On July 2, 1980, pursuant to his authority under § 3 of the Military Selective Service Act, the President issued Presidential Proclamation No. 4771. This Proclamation directed male citizens and certain male residents born during 1960 to register with the Selective Service System during the week of July 21, 1980. Petitioner fell within that class but did not register. Instead, he wrote several letters to Government officials, including the President, stating that he had not registered and did not intend to do so.

Petitioner's letters were added to a Selective Service file of young men who advised that they had failed to register or who were reported by others as having failed to register. For reasons we discuss, *infra*, Selective Service adopted a policy of passive enforcement under which it would investigate and prosecute only the cases of nonregistration contained in this file. In furtherance of this policy, Selective Service sent a letter on June 17, 1981, to each reported violator who had not registered and for whom it had an address. The letter explained the duty to register, stated that Selective Service had information that the person was required to register but had not done so, requested that he either comply with the law by filling out an enclosed registration card or explain why he was not subject to registration, and warned that a violation could result in criminal prosecution and specified penalties. Petitioner received a copy of this letter but did not respond.

On July 20, 1981, Selective Service transmitted to the Department of Justice, for investigation and potential prosecution, the names of petitioner and 133 other young men identified under its passive enforcement system—all of whom had not registered in response to the Service's June letter. At two later dates, it referred the names of 152 more young men similarly identified. After screening out the names of those who appeared not to be in the class required to register, the Department of Justice referred the remaining names to the Federal Bureau of Investigation for additional inquiry and to the United States Attorneys for the districts in which the nonregistrants resided. Petitioner's name was one of those referred.

Pursuant to Department of Justice policy, those referred were not immediately prosecuted. Instead, the appropriate United States Attorney was required to notify identified nonregistrants by registered mail that, unless they registered within a specified time, prosecution would be considered. In addition, an FBI agent was usually sent to interview the nonregistrant before prosecution was instituted. This effort to persuade nonregistrants to change their minds became known as the "beg" policy. Under it, young men who registered late were not prosecuted, while those who never registered were investigated further by the Government. Pursuant to the "beg" policy, the United States Attorney for the Central District of California sent petitioner a letter on October 15, 1981, urging him to register or face possible prosecution. Again petitioner failed to respond.

On December 9, 1981, the Department of Justice instructed all United States Attorneys not to begin seeking indictments against nonregistrants until further notice. On January 7, 1982, the President announced a grace period to afford nonregistrants a further opportunity to register without penalty. This grace period extended until February 28, 1982. Petitioner still did not register.

Over the next few months, the Department decided to begin prosecuting those young men who, despite the grace period and "beg" policy, continued to refuse to register. It recognized that under the passive enforcement system those prosecuted were "liable to be vocal proponents of nonregistration" or persons "with religious or moral objections." It also recognized that prosecutions would "undoubtedly result in allegations that the [case was] brought in retribution for the nonregistrant's exercise of his first amendment rights." The Department was advised, however, that Selective Service could not develop a more "active" enforcement system for quite some time. Because of this, the Department decided to begin seeking indictments under the passive system without further delay. On May 21, 1982, United States Attorneys were notified to begin prosecution of nonregistrants. On June 28, 1982, FBI agents interviewed petitioner, and he continued to refuse to register. Accordingly, on July 22, 1982, an indictment was returned against him for knowingly and willfully failing to register with the Selective Service * * *.

II.

Petitioner moved to dismiss the indictment on the ground of selective prosecution. He contended that he and the other indicted nonregistrants were "vocal" opponents of the registration program who had been impermissibly targeted (out of an estimated 674,000 nonregistrants) for prosecution on the basis of their exercise of First Amendment rights.

[The federal district court found that the government had engaged in impermissible selective prosecution; the Ninth Circuit Court of Appeals reversed.]

III.

In our criminal justice system, the Government retains "broad discretion" as to whom to prosecute. "[S]o long as the prosecutor has probable cause to believe that the accused committed an offense defined by statute, the decision whether or not to prosecute, and what charge to file or bring before a grand jury, generally rests entirely in his discretion." This broad discretion rests largely on the recognition that the decision to prosecute is particularly ill-suited to judicial review. Such factors as the strength of the case, the prosecution's general deterrence value, the Government's enforcement priorities, and the case's relationship to the Government's overall enforcement plan are not readily susceptible to the kind of analysis the courts are competent to undertake. Judicial supervision in this area, moreover, entails systemic costs of particular concern. Examining the basis of a prosecution delays the criminal proceeding, threatens to chill law enforcement by subjecting the prosecutor's motives and decisionmaking to outside inquiry, and may undermine prosecutorial effectiveness by revealing the Government's enforcement policy. All these are substantial concerns that make the courts properly hesitant to examine the decision whether to prosecute.

As we have noted in a slightly different context, however, although prosecutorial discretion is broad, it is not " 'unfettered.' Selectivity in the enforcement of criminal laws is ... subject to constitutional constraints." In particular, the decision to prosecute may not be " 'deliberately based upon an unjustifiable standard such as race, religion, or other arbitrary classification,' " including the exercise of protected statutory and constitutional rights.

It is appropriate to judge selective prosecution claims according to ordinary equal protection standards. Under our prior cases, these standards require petitioner to show both that the passive enforcement system had a discriminatory effect and that it was motivated by a discriminatory purpose. All petitioner has shown here is that those eventually prosecuted, along with many not prosecuted, reported themselves as having violated the law. He has not shown that the enforcement policy selected nonregistrants for prosecution on the basis of their speech. Indeed, he could not have done so given the way the "beg" policy was carried out. The Government did not prosecute those who reported themselves but later registered. Nor did it prosecute those who protested registration but did not report themselves or were not reported by others. In fact, the Government did not even investigate those who wrote letters to Selective Service criticizing registration unless their letters stated affirmatively that they had refused to comply with the law. The Government, on the other hand, did prosecute people who reported themselves or were reported by others but who did not publicly protest. These facts demonstrate that the Government treated all reported nonregistrants similarly. It did not subject vocal nonregistrants to any special burden. Indeed, those prosecuted in effect selected themselves for prosecution by refusing to register after being reported and warned by the Government.

Even if the passive policy had a discriminatory effect, petitioner has not shown that the Government intended such a result. The evidence he presented demonstrated only that the Government was aware that the passive enforcement policy would result in prosecution of vocal objectors and that they would probably make selective prosecution claims. As we have noted, however: " '[D]iscriminatory purpose' [implies] more [than] intent as awareness of consequences. It implies that the decisionmaker [selected] or reaffirmed a particular course of action at least in part 'because of,' not merely 'in spite of,' its adverse effects upon an identifiable group." In the present case, petitioner has not shown that the Government prosecuted him *because of* his protest activities. Absent such a showing, his claim of selective prosecution fails.

[V.]

We conclude that the Government's passive enforcement system together with its "beg" policy violated neither the First nor Fifth Amendment. Accordingly, we affirm the judgment of the Court of Appeals.

It is so ordered.

JUSTICE MARSHALL, with whom JUSTICE BRENNAN joins, dissenting.

[T]he Court correctly points out that Wayte's selective prosecution claims must be judged according to ordinary equal protection standards. Wayte presents an equal protection challenge to the "passive" enforcement system, under which Selective Service refers to the Justice Department for further investigation and possible prosecution *only* the "names of young men who fall into two categories: (1) those who wrote to Selective Service and said that they refused to register and (2) those whose neighbors and others reported them as persons who refused to register." Wayte argues that the scheme purposefully singled out these individuals as a result of their exercise of First Amendment rights.

To make out a prima facie case, Wayte must show first that he is a member of a recognizable, distinct class. Second, he must show that a disproportionate number of this class was selected for investigation and possible prosecution. Third, he must show that this selection procedure was subject to abuse or was otherwise not neutral. The inquiry then is whether Wayte has presented sufficient evidence as to each of the elements to show that the claim is not frivolous.

Wayte has clearly established the first element of a prima facie case. The record demonstrates unequivocally that Wayte is a member of a class of vocal opponents to the Government's draft registration program. All members of that class exercised a First Amendment right to speak freely and to petition the Government for a redress of grievances, and either reported themselves or were reported by others as having failed to register for the draft.

To establish the second element, Wayte must show that the "passive" enforcement policy identified for investigation and possible prosecution a disproportionate number of vocal opponents of draft registration. The record, as it stands given the Government's refusal to comply with the District Court's discovery order, does not contain a breakdown of how many of the approximately 300 young men referred by Selective Service to the Justice Department were "vocal." However, the record suggests that responsible officials in the Justice Department were aware that the vast majority of these individuals would be vocal opponents of draft registration.

[A]s to the third element, the decision to implement the "passive" enforcement system was certainly a decision susceptible to abuse. "This is indeed an exceptional area of national life where conscientious opposition to government policy has been intertwined with violations of the laws which implement the policy." The correlation between vocal opposition and violations of the law makes it relatively easy to punish speech under the guise of enforcing the laws.

Here, the enforcement scheme was implemented with full knowledge that its effects would be particularly harsh on vocal opponents of the Government's policies. Such knowledge makes the scheme directly vulnerable to the charge that its purpose was to punish individuals for the exercise of their First Amendment rights. This Court has recognized that "[a]dherence to a particular policy or practice, 'with full knowledge of the predictable effects of such adherence [is] one factor among others which may be considered by a court' " in determining whether a decision was based on an impermissible ground.

Thus, Wayte has established the first and third elements of a prima facie case, and has presented a colorable claim as to the second. As a result, there can thus be no doubt that the District Court did not abuse its discretion when it found that Wayte's equal protection claim was not frivolous.

[T]he Court errs in the manner in which it analyzes the merits of the equal protection claim. It simply focuses on the wrong problem when it states that "the Government treated all reported nonregistrants similarly" and that "those prosecuted in effect selected themselves for prosecution by refusing to register after being reported and warned by the Government." Those issues are irrelevant to the correct disposition of this case.

The claim here is not that the Justice Department discriminated among *known* violators of the draft registration law either in its administration of the "beg" policy, which gave such individuals the option of registering to avoid prosecution, or in prosecuting only some reported nonregistrants. Instead, the claim is that the system by which the Department defined the class of possible prosecutees—the "passive" enforcement system—was designed to discriminate against those who had exercised their First Amendment rights. Such governmental action cannot stand if undertaken with discriminatory intent. As this Court has clearly stated, "for an agent of the State to pursue a course of action whose objective is to penalize a person's reliance on his legal rights is 'patently unconstitutional.' " If the Government intentionally discriminated in defining the pool of potential prosecutees, it cannot immunize itself from liability merely by showing that it used permissible methods in choosing whom to prosecute from this previously tainted pool. * * *

UNITED STATES v. ARMSTRONG
517 U.S. 456 (1996).

CHIEF JUSTICE REHNQUIST delivered the opinion of the Court.

In this case, we consider the showing necessary for a defendant to be entitled to discovery on a claim that the prosecuting attorney singled him out for prosecution on the basis of his race. We conclude that respondents failed to satisfy the threshold showing: They failed to show that the Government declined to prosecute similarly situated suspects of other races.

In April 1992, respondents were indicted in the United States District Court for the Central District of California on charges of conspiring to possess with intent to distribute more than 50 grams of cocaine base (crack) and conspiring to distribute the same, in violation of 21 U.S.C. §§ 841 and 846, and federal firearms offenses. For three months prior to the indictment, agents of the Federal Bureau of Alcohol, Tobacco, and Firearms and the Narcotics Division of the Inglewood, California, Police Department had infiltrated a suspected crack distribution ring by using three confidential informants. On seven separate occasions during this period, the informants had bought a total of 124.3 grams of crack from respondents and witnessed respondents carrying firearms during the sales. The agents searched the hotel room in which the sales were transacted, arrested respondents Armstrong and Hampton in the room, and found more crack and a loaded gun. The agents later arrested the other respondents as part of the ring.

In response to the indictment, respondents filed a motion for discovery or for dismissal of the indictment, alleging that they were selected for federal prosecution because they are black. In support of their motion, they offered only an affidavit by a "Paralegal Specialist," employed by the Office of the Federal Public Defender representing one of the respondents. The only allegation in the affidavit was that, in every one of the 24 §§ 841 or 846 cases closed by the office during 1991, the defendant was black. Accompanying the affidavit was a "study" listing the 24 defendants, their race, whether they were prosecuted for dealing cocaine as well as crack, and the status of each case.

The Government opposed the discovery motion, arguing, among other things, that there was no evidence or allegation "that the Government has acted unfairly or has prosecuted non-black defendants or failed to prosecute them." The District Court granted the motion. It ordered the Government (1) to provide a list of all cases from the last three years in which the Government charged both cocaine and firearms offenses, (2) to identify the race of the defendants in those cases, (3) to identify what levels of law enforcement were involved in the investigations of those cases, and (4) to explain its criteria for deciding to prosecute those defendants for federal cocaine offenses.

The Government moved for reconsideration of the District Court's discovery order. With this motion it submitted affidavits and other evidence to explain why it had chosen to prosecute respondents and why respondents' study did not support the inference that the Government was singling out blacks for cocaine prosecution. The federal and local agents participating in the case alleged in affidavits that race played no role in their investigation. An Assistant United States Attorney explained in an affidavit that the decision to prosecute met the general criteria for prosecution, because "there was over 100 grams of cocaine base involved, over twice the threshold necessary for a ten year mandatory minimum sentence; there were multiple sales involving multiple defendants, thereby indicating a fairly substantial crack cocaine ring; ... there were multiple federal firearms violations intertwined with the narcotics trafficking; the overall evidence in the case was extremely strong, including audio and videotapes of defendants; and several of the defendants had criminal histories including narcotics and firearms violations."

The Government also submitted sections of a published 1989 Drug Enforcement Administration report which concluded that "Large-scale, interstate trafficking networks controlled by Jamaicans, Haitians and Black street gangs dominate the manufacture and distribution of crack."

In response, one of respondents' attorneys submitted an affidavit alleging that an intake coordinator at a drug treatment center had told her that there are "an equal number of Caucasian users and dealers to minority users and dealers." Respondents also submitted an affidavit from a criminal defense attorney alleging that in his experience many nonblacks are prosecuted in state court for crack offenses, and a newspaper article reporting that Federal "crack criminals ... are being punished far more severely than if they had been caught with powder cocaine, and almost every single one of them is black."

The District Court denied the motion for reconsideration. When the Government indicated it would not comply with the court's discovery order, the court dismissed the case.

A divided three-judge panel of the Court of Appeals for the Ninth Circuit reversed, holding that, because of the proof requirements for a selective-prosecution claim, defendants must "provide a colorable basis for believing that 'others similarly situated have not been prosecuted' " to obtain discovery. The Court of Appeals voted to rehear the case en banc, and the en banc panel affirmed the District Court's order of dismissal, holding that "a defendant is not required to demonstrate that the government has failed to prosecute others who are similarly situated." We granted certiorari to determine the appropriate standard for discovery for a selective-prosecution claim. * * *

A selective-prosecution claim is not a defense on the merits to the criminal charge itself, but an independent assertion that the prosecutor has brought the charge for reasons forbidden by the Constitution. Our cases delineating the necessary elements to prove a claim of selective prosecution have taken great pains to explain that the standard is a demanding one. These cases afford a "background presumption" that the showing necessary to obtain discovery should itself be a significant barrier to the litigation of insubstantial claims.

A selective-prosecution claim asks a court to exercise judicial power over a "special province" of the Executive. The Attorney General and United States Attorneys retain " 'broad discretions' 'to enforce the Nation's criminal laws.' They have this latitude because they are designated by statute as the President's delegates to help him discharge his constitutional responsibility to 'take Care that the Laws be faithfully executed.' " As a result, "[t]he presumption of regularity supports" their prosecutorial decisions and "in the absence of clear evidence to the contrary, courts presume that they have properly discharged their official duties." In the ordinary case, "so long as the prosecutor has probable cause to believe that the accused committed an offense defined by statute, the decision whether or not to prosecute, and what charge to file or bring before a grand jury, generally rests entirely in his discretion."

Of course, a prosecutor's discretion is "subject to constitutional constraints." One of these constraints, imposed by the equal protection component of the Due Process Clause of the Fifth Amendment, is that the decision whether to prosecute may not be based on "an unjustifiable standard such as race, religion, or other arbitrary classification." A defendant may demonstrate that the administration of a criminal law is "directed so exclusively against a particular class of persons ... with a mind so unequal and oppressive" that the system of prosecution amounts to "a practical denial" of equal protection of the law.

In order to dispel the presumption that a prosecutor has not violated equal protection, a criminal defendant must present "clear evidence to the contrary." We explained in *Wayte* why courts are "properly hesitant to examine the decision whether to prosecute." Judicial deference to the decisions of these executive officers rests in part on an assessment of the relative competence of prosecutors and courts. "Such factors as the strength of the case, the prosecution's general deterrence value, the Government's enforcement priorities, and the case's relationship to the Government's overall enforcement plan are not readily susceptible to the kind of analysis the courts are competent to undertake." It also stems from a concern not to unnecessarily impair the performance of a core executive constitutional function. "Examining the basis of a prosecution delays the criminal proceeding, threatens to chill law enforcement by subjecting the prosecutor's motives and decisionmaking to outside inquiry, and may undermine prosecutorial effectiveness by revealing the Government's enforcement policy."

The requirements for a selective-prosecution claim draw on "ordinary equal protection standards." The claimant must demonstrate that the federal prosecutorial policy "had a discriminatory effect and that it was motivated by a discriminatory purpose." To establish a discriminatory effect in a race case, the claimant must show that similarly situated individuals of a different race were not prosecuted.

[W]e turn to the showing necessary to obtain discovery in support of such a claim. If discovery is ordered, the Government must assemble from its own files documents which might corroborate or refute the defendant's claim. Discovery thus imposes many of the costs present when the Government must respond to a prima facie case of selective prosecution. It will divert prosecutors' resources and may disclose the

Government's prosecutorial strategy. The justifications for a rigorous standard for the elements of a selective-prosecution claim thus require a correspondingly rigorous standard for discovery in aid of such a claim.

The parties, and the Courts of Appeals which have considered the requisite showing to establish entitlement to discovery, describe this showing with a variety of phrases, like "colorable basis," "substantial threshold showing," "substantial and concrete basis," or "reasonable likelihood." However, the many labels for this showing conceal the degree of consensus about the evidence necessary to meet it. The Courts of Appeals "require some evidence tending to show the existence of the essential elements of the defense," discriminatory effect and discriminatory intent.

In this case we consider what evidence constitutes "some evidence tending to show the existence" of the discriminatory effect element. The Court of Appeals held that a defendant may establish a colorable basis for discriminatory effect without evidence that the Government has failed to prosecute others who are similarly situated to the defendant. We think it was mistaken in this view. The vast majority of the Courts of Appeals require the defendant to produce some evidence that similarly situated defendants of other races could have been prosecuted, but were not, and this requirement is consistent with our equal protection case law. As the three-judge panel explained, " '[s]elective prosecution' implies that a selection has taken place."

The Court of Appeals reached its decision in part because it started "with the presumption that people of all races commit all types of crimes—not with the premise that any type of crime is the exclusive province of any particular racial or ethnic group." It cited no authority for this proposition, which seems contradicted by the most recent statistics of the United States Sentencing Commission. Those statistics show that: More than 90% of the persons sentenced in 1994 for crack cocaine trafficking were black; 93.4% of convicted LSD dealers were white; and 91% of those convicted for pornography or prostitution were white. Presumptions at war with presumably reliable statistics have no proper place in the analysis of this issue.

The Court of Appeals also expressed concern about the "evidentiary obstacles defendants face." But all of its sister Circuits that have confronted the issue have required that defendants produce some evidence of differential treatment of similarly situated members of other races or protected classes. In the present case, if the claim of selective prosecution were well founded, it should not have been an insuperable task to prove that persons of other races were being treated differently than respondents. For instance, respondents could have investigated whether similarly situated persons of other races were prosecuted by the State of California, were known to federal law enforcement officers, but were not prosecuted in federal court. We think the required threshold—a credible showing of different treatment of similarly situated persons—

adequately balances the Government's interest in vigorous prosecution and the defendant's interest in avoiding selective prosecution.

In the case before us, respondents' "study" did not constitute "some evidence tending to show the existence of the essential elements of" a selective-prosecution claim. The study failed to identify individuals who were not black, could have been prosecuted for the offenses for which respondents were charged, but were not so prosecuted. This omission was not remedied by respondents' evidence in opposition to the Government's motion for reconsideration. The newspaper article which discussed the discriminatory effect of federal drug sentencing laws, was not relevant to an allegation of discrimination in decision prosecuted. This omission was not evidence in opposition to the reconsideration. The newspaper article, discriminatory effect of federal drug sentencing laws, was not relevant to an allegation of discrimination in decisions to prosecute. Respondents' affidavits, which recounted one attorney's conversation with a drug treatment center employee and the experience of another attorney defending drug prosecutions in state court, recounted hearsay and reported personal conclusions based on anecdotal evidence. The judgment of the Court of Appeals is therefore reversed, and the case is remanded for proceedings consistent with this opinion.

It is so ordered.

JUSTICE STEVENS, dissenting.

Federal prosecutors are respected members of a respected profession. Despite an occasional misstep, the excellence of their work abundantly justifies the presumption that "they have properly discharged their official duties." Nevertheless, the possibility that political or racial animosity may infect a decision to institute criminal proceedings cannot be ignored. For that reason, it has long been settled that the prosecutor's broad discretion to determine when criminal charges should be filed is not completely unbridled. As the Court notes, however, the scope of judicial review of particular exercises of that discretion is not fully defined. * * *

The Court correctly concludes that in this case the facts presented to the District Court in support of respondents' claim that they had been singled out for prosecution because of their race were not sufficient to prove that defense. [Like] Chief Judge Wallace of the Court of Appeals, however, I am persuaded that the District Judge did not abuse her discretion when she concluded that the factual showing was sufficiently disturbing to require some response from the United States Attorney's Office. Perhaps the discovery order was broader than necessary, but I cannot agree with the Court's apparent conclusion that no inquiry was permissible.

The District Judge's order should be evaluated in light of three circumstances that underscore the need for judicial vigilance over certain types of drug prosecutions. First, the Anti–Drug Abuse Act of 1986 and subsequent legislation established a regime of extremely high penalties for the possession and distribution of so-called "crack" cocaine. Those provisions treat one gram of crack as the equivalent of 100 grams of powder cocaine. The distribution of 50 grams of crack is thus punishable by the same mandatory minimum sentence of 10 years in prison that applies to the distribution of 5,000 grams of powder cocaine. * * *

Second, the disparity between the treatment of crack cocaine and powder cocaine is matched by the disparity between the severity of the punishment imposed by federal law and that imposed by state law for the same conduct. * * * The majority of States draw no distinction between types of cocaine in their penalty schemes; of those that do, none has established as stark a differential as the Federal Government. For example, if respondent Hampton is found guilty, his federal sentence might be as long as a mandatory life term. Had he been tried in state court, his sentence could have been as short as 12 years, less worktime credits of half that amount.

Finally, it is undisputed that the brunt of the elevated federal penalties falls heavily on blacks. While 65% of the persons who have used crack are white, in 1993 they represented only 4% of the federal offenders convicted of trafficking in crack. Eighty-eight percent of such defendants were black. During the first 18 months of full guideline implementation, the sentencing disparity between black and white defendants grew from preguideline levels: blacks on average received sentences over 40% longer than whites. Those figures represent a major threat to the integrity of federal sentencing reform, whose main purpose was the elimination of disparity (especially racial) in sentencing. The Sentencing Commission acknowledges that the heightened crack penalties are a "primary cause of the growing disparity between sentences for Black and White federal defendants."

The extraordinary severity of the imposed penalties and the troubling racial patterns of enforcement give rise to a special concern about the fairness of charging practices for crack offenses. Evidence tending to prove that black defendants charged with distribution of crack in the Central District of California are prosecuted in federal court, whereas members of other races charged with similar offenses are prosecuted in state court, warrants close scrutiny by the federal judges in that District. In my view, the District Judge, who has sat on both the federal and the state benches in Los Angeles, acted well within her discretion to call for the development of facts that would demonstrate what standards, if any, governed the choice of forum where similarly situated offenders are prosecuted. * * *

Even if respondents failed to carry their burden of showing that there were individuals who were not black but who could have been prosecuted in federal court for the same offenses, it does not follow that the District Court abused its discretion in ordering discovery. There can be no doubt that such individuals exist, and indeed the Government has never denied the same. * * *

In this case, the evidence was sufficiently disturbing to persuade the District Judge to order discovery that might help explain the conspicuous racial pattern of cases before her Court I cannot accept the majority's conclusion that the District Judge either exceeded her power or abused her discretion when she did so. I therefore respectfully dissent.

UNITED STATES v. BASS

536 U.S. 862 (2002).

PER CURIAM.

A federal grand jury sitting in the Eastern District of Michigan returned a second superseding indictment charging respondent with, *inter alia*, the intentional firearm killings of two individuals. The United States filed a notice of intent to seek the death penalty. Respondent, who is black, alleged that the Government had determined to seek the death penalty against him because of his race. He moved to dismiss the death penalty notice and, in the alternative, for discovery of information relating to the Government's capital charging practices. The District Court granted the motion for discovery, and after the Government informed the court that it would not comply with the discovery order, the court dismissed the death penalty notice. A divided panel of the United States Court of Appeals for the Sixth Circuit affirmed the District Court's discovery order. We grant the petition for a writ of certiorari and now summarily reverse.

In *United States v. Armstrong*, we held that a defendant who seeks discovery on a claim of selective prosecution must show some evidence of both discriminatory effect and discriminatory intent. We need go no further in the present case than consideration of the evidence supporting discriminatory effect. As to that, *Armstrong* says that the defendant must make a "credible showing" that "similarly situated individuals of a different race were not prosecuted." The Sixth Circuit concluded that respondent had made such a showing based on nationwide statistics demonstrating that "[t]he United States charges blacks with a death-eligible offense more than twice as often as it charges whites" and that the United States enters into plea bargains more frequently with whites than it does with blacks. Even assuming that the *Armstrong* requirement can be satisfied by a nationwide showing (as opposed to a showing regarding the record of the decisionmakers in respondent's case), raw statistics regarding overall charges say nothing about charges brought against *similarly situated defendants*. And the statistics regarding plea bargains are even less relevant, since respondent *was* offered a plea bargain but declined it. Under *Armstrong*, therefore, because respondent failed to submit relevant evidence that similarly situated persons were treated differently, he was not entitled to discovery.

The Sixth Circuit's decision is contrary to *Armstrong* and threatens the "performance of a core executive constitutional function." For that reason, we reverse.

Notes and Questions

1.   Neither *Armstrong* nor *Bass* specified how the showing of "some evidence" of discriminatory effect could be satisfied, e.g., by affidavit, by other admissible documentation, or by specific allegations. In *McNeil v. State*, 112 Md.App. 434, 685 A.2d 839 (1996), the court suggested that presentation of verifiable facts in some form would be sufficient as long as it went beyond a mere general allegation of prosecutorial misconduct. Thus, even if a defense motion to dismiss for selective prosecution was not supported by an affidavit, it would nevertheless suffice if it was verifiable by review of the court file. In *United States v. Alemeh*, 341 F.3d 167 (2d Cir.2003), statistical evidence and affidavits showed increased prosecutions of people with Arab names after September 11, 2001, but the court held that was insufficient to support discovery because most of the investigation had occurred prior to that date.

2.   When a trial court denies a defense motion to compel discovery, the standard applied by appellate courts is abuse of discretion, see, e.g., *United States v. Hirsch*, 360 F.3d 860 (8th Cir.2004), while a few courts apply a de novo standard of review, see, e.g., *United States v. James*, 257 F.3d 1173 (10th Cir.2001).

Problems

1.   "King Paradise," a/k/a George Boyd, has retained you to represent him following his federal indictment for racketeering and murder. You have filed motions to dismiss his indictment due to selective prosecution and to gain access to information about governmental charging policies. The indictment charges George and all of the "Kings" who are officers and have prior criminal histories (e.g., King Guy, King Bullet, King Humpty, King Biz); they are also the older male members of the local chapter of the Almighty Latin King Nation. Among the other members of the local chapter who were not indicted are its only three women members, who were officers and associates (commonly referred to as, you guessed it, "Queens") of the Latin Kings. In the Latin Kings organization, because women are prohibited from holding decisionmaking positions of authority, the highest office open to women is "Secretary," who is responsible for keeping records of all Latin King meetings. Your initial interview with George indicates that some of the unindicted male members and all of the female members will testify for the Government. Evaluate whether the court will probably deny your motions.

2.   Following discovery of a large and violent crack cocaine conspiracy, the United States Attorney indicted 25 persons, all of whom are African–American. Of the 55 unindicted persons who were involved in the conspiracy, 50 are African–American and five are white. Twenty-five African–Americans were granted immunity from prosecution as were three whites. Defendant Sterling moved to dismiss the indictment, claiming that he had been selected for prosecution because of his race. He argued that the five unindicted white persons were similarly situated to him and that more than 90% of those indicted in the metro area since 1992 for crack cocaine trafficking are African–Americans. An officer in the local police department testified that he

did not choose individuals to violate the law. "They choose to violate the law themselves. And when they violate the law, if we can prove it, we prosecute them, regardless of their race, sex, where they were born, or their family identity." He also testified about the reason that each white conspirator identified in Sterling's motion had not been indicted. One had agreed to work undercover, another was a target but the evidence against him was still insufficient, and the third had proven himself to be truthful and cooperative with the investigation.

The trial court concluded that Sterling had made a nonfrivolous showing in raising a claim of selective prosecution and ordered the prosecution to respond to Sterling's formal requests for discovery into its criteria for selecting whom to prosecute. The court also found that Sterling and the unindicted white conspirators were "similarly situated" for a selective prosecution claim and that Sterling's statistical data made a nonfrivolous showing of discriminatory intent. Do you agree?

E.   VINDICTIVE PROSECUTION

UNITED STATES v. GOODWIN
457 U.S. 368 (1982).

JUSTICE STEVENS delivered the opinion of the Court.

[Goodwin was charged with several misdemeanor and petty offenses, including assault on a United States Park Policeman. He initiated plea negotiations with the prosecutor, but later advised the prosecutor that he did not wish to plead guilty and desired a trial by jury in the District Court. The case was transferred from the United States Magistrate to the District Court and responsibility for the prosecution was assumed by an Assistant United States Attorney. About six weeks later, after reviewing the case, the prosecutor obtained a four-count indictment charging respondent with one felony count of forcibly assaulting a federal officer and three related counts arising from the same incident. A jury convicted respondent on the felony count and on one misdemeanor count.]

This case involves presumptions. The question presented is whether a presumption that has been used to evaluate a judicial or prosecutorial response to a criminal defendant's exercise of a right to be retried after he has been convicted should also be applied to evaluate a prosecutor's pretrial response to a defendant's demand for a jury trial. * * *

In *North Carolina v. Pearce*, the Court held that neither the Double Jeopardy Clause nor the Equal Protection Clause prohibits a trial judge from imposing a harsher sentence on retrial after a criminal defendant successfully attacks an initial conviction on appeal. * * *

> [W]henever a judge imposes a more severe sentence upon a defendant after a new trial, the reasons for his doing so must affirmatively appear. Those reasons must be based upon objective information concerning identifiable conduct on the part of the defendant occurring after the time of the original sentencing proceeding. And the factual data upon which the increased sentence is based must be

made part of the record, so that the constitutional legitimacy of the increased sentence may be fully reviewed on appeal. * * *

In *Blackledge v. Perry*, 417 U.S. 21, the Court confronted the problem of increased punishment upon retrial after appeal in a setting different from that considered in *Pearce*. Perry was convicted of assault in an inferior court having exclusive jurisdiction for the trial of misdemeanors. The court imposed a 6–month sentence. Under North Carolina law, Perry had an absolute right to a trial de novo in the Superior Court, which possessed felony jurisdiction. After Perry filed his notice of appeal, the prosecutor obtained a felony indictment charging him with assault with a deadly weapon. Perry pleaded guilty to the felony and was sentenced to a term of five to seven years in prison. * * *

Both *Pearce* and *Blackledge* involved the defendant's exercise of a procedural right that caused a complete retrial after he had been once tried and convicted. * * *

In *Bordenkircher v. Hayes*, 434 U.S. 357 (1978), the Court for the first time considered an allegation of vindictiveness that arose in a pretrial setting. In that case the Court held that the Due Process Clause of the Fourteenth Amendment did not prohibit a prosecutor from carrying out a threat, made during plea negotiations, to bring additional charges against an accused who refused to plead guilty to the offense with which he was originally charged. The prosecutor in that case had explicitly told the defendant that if he did not plead guilty and "save the court the inconvenience and necessity of a trial" he would return to the grand jury to obtain an additional charge that would significantly increase the defendant's potential punishment. The defendant refused to plead guilty and the prosecutor obtained the indictment. It was not disputed that the additional charge was justified by the evidence, that the prosecutor was in possession of this evidence at the time the original indictment was obtained, and that the prosecutor sought the additional charge because of the accused's refusal to plead guilty to the original charge.

In finding no due process violation, the Court in *Bordenkircher* considered the decisions in *Pearce* and *Blackledge*, and stated:

In those cases the Court was dealing with the State's unilateral imposition of a penalty upon a defendant who had chosen to exercise a legal right to attack his original conviction—a situation 'very different from the give-and-take negotiation common in plea bargaining between the prosecution and defense, which arguably possess relatively equal bargaining power.'

The Court stated that the due process violation in *Pearce* and *Blackledge* "lay not in the possibility that a defendant might be deterred from the exercise of a legal right ... but rather in the danger that the State might be retaliating against the accused for lawfully attacking his conviction." * * *

This case, like *Bordenkircher*, arises from a pretrial decision to modify the charges against the defendant. Unlike *Bordenkircher*, however, there is no evidence in this case that could give rise to a claim of actual vindictiveness; the prosecutor never suggested that the charge was brought to influence the respondent's conduct. The conviction in this case may be reversed only if a presumption of vindictiveness— applicable in all cases—is warranted.

There is good reason to be cautious before adopting an inflexible presumption of prosecutorial vindictiveness in a pretrial setting. In the course of preparing a case for trial, the prosecutor may uncover additional information that suggests a basis for further prosecution or he simply may come to realize that information possessed by the State has a broader significance. At this stage of the proceedings, the prosecutor's assessment of the proper extent of prosecution may not have crystallized. In contrast, once a trial begins—and certainly by the time a conviction has been obtained—it is much more likely that the State has discovered and assessed all of the information against an accused and has made a determination, on the basis of that information, of the extent to which he should be prosecuted. Thus, a change in the charging decision made after an initial trial is completed is much more likely to be improperly motivated than is a pretrial decision. * * *

Thus, the timing of the prosecutor's action in this case suggests that a presumption of vindictiveness is not warranted. A prosecutor should remain free before trial to exercise the broad discretion entrusted to him to determine the extent of the societal interest in prosecution. An initial decision should not freeze future conduct. As we made clear in *Bordenkircher*, the initial charges filed by a prosecutor may not reflect the extent to which an individual is legitimately subject to prosecution.

The nature of the right asserted by the respondent confirms that a presumption of vindictiveness is not warranted in this case. After initially expressing an interest in plea negotiation, respondent decided not to plead guilty and requested a trial by jury in District Court. In doing so, he forced the Government to bear the burdens and uncertainty of a trial. This Court in *Bordenkircher* made clear that the mere fact that a defendant refuses to plead guilty and forces the government to prove its case is insufficient to warrant a presumption that subsequent changes in the charging decision are unjustified. * * *

In declining to apply a presumption of vindictiveness, we of course do not foreclose the possibility that a defendant in an appropriate case might prove objectively that the prosecutor's charging decision was motivated by a desire to punish him for doing something that the law plainly allowed him to do. * * *

[Justice Blackmun would have presumed vindictiveness but found that the prosecutor's reasons for seeking a felony indictment adequately rebutted presumption. Justice Brennan, joined by Justice Marshall, dissented.]

Notes and Questions

1. Should a presumption of vindictiveness arise if the defendant can prove that separate prosecutors filed the related indictments? Can a persuasive argument be made that the vindictiveness is institutional rather than personal? See *Thigpen v. Roberts*, 468 U.S. 27, 31–32 (1984), where the Court stated:

> It might be argued that if two different prosecutors are involved, a presumption of vindictiveness, which arises in part from assumptions about the individual's personal stake in the proceedings, is inappropriate. On the other hand, to the extent the presumption reflects "institutional pressure that ... might ... subconsciously motivate a vindictive prosecutorial ... response to a defendant's exercise of his right to obtain a retrial of a decided question," it does not hinge on the continued involvement of a particular individual. A district attorney burdened with the retrial of an already-convicted defendant might be no less vindictive because he did not bring the initial prosecution. Indeed, *Blackledge* referred frequently to actions by "the State," rather than "the prosecutor."
>
> We need not determine the correct rule when two independent prosecutors are involved, however.

Still, the Court noted that the "addition" of another prosecutor changed "little."

2. Does a presumption of vindictiveness exist when the prosecutor brings additional charges after a mistrial but before a retrial? See, e.g., *United States v. Poole*, 407 F.3d 767 (6th Cir.2005) (no presumption of vindictiveness for adding charges following a mistrial due to a hung jury).

Problem

Three defendants were indicted for narcotics and firearms offenses. At their initial appearance, two of the defendants requested that they be released on bail pending trial, but the government was strongly opposed. Apparently, the third defendant had turned state's evidence and had been threatened. The government responded by placing her in the federal witness protection program and urged that the other two defendants not be released on bail. Based on testimony by the Assistant United States Attorney regarding the threats, the magistrate judge denied bail and remanded the two defendants to federal custody. The jailed defendants appealed that decision to the district judge who released them on bond. Two days later, the Assistant United States Attorney sought and obtained a superseding indictment charging defendants with an additional conspiracy count. Should the conspiracy charge be dismissed as vindictive?

Chapter 13

PRELIMINARY PROCEEDINGS

Following the arrest and administrative "booking" procedures, the police take the accused to a judge for a proceeding called an "initial appearance" or "preliminary arraignment." The functions of an initial appearance include informing the accused of the charge, appointing counsel, setting conditions of release, and scheduling future proceedings. The judge may combine the initial appearance with a "Gerstein hearing" for defendants who were arrested without a warrant, in order to examine the validity of their detention. Within a short period after the initial appearance, the judge conducts a preliminary hearing to determine whether there is probable cause to hold the defendant to answer the charges in a court which has jurisdiction to conduct the trial of felony cases.

A. INITIAL APPEARANCE

Most jurisdictions require that the arresting officer bring the accused before the nearest available judge without unnecessary delay. [A judge has the discretion to conduct an initial appearance by video teleconferencing, with the defendant's consent. The judge also has flexibility under Federal Rule 5 as to the district in which the initial appearance may be held.] In *United States v. Alvarez–Sanchez*, 511 U.S. 350 (1994), the Supreme Court held that the period of delay in federal courts usually is measured from the time the accused is arrested on federal charges. An unreasonable delay between arrest and the initial appearance may violate due process. In evaluating an allegation of unreasonable delay, courts analyze the amount of time that passes as well as how and why the delay occurred.

Confessions which are obtained during periods of unnecessary delay prior to the initial appearance may be inadmissible. For example, under 18 U.S.C. § 3501, delay is one of several statutory factors considered to decide whether a confession was given voluntarily during the period of unreasonable delay. See Chapter 7, on Police Interrogation and Confessions.

Fed.R.Crim.P. 5(d) is typical of most rules setting the procedures for the initial appearance in court. At the initial appearance, the judge must inform the accused about:

(1) The charges;

(2) The right to remain silent;

(3) The right to request or retain an attorney;

(4) The fact that any statement made may be used against the accused;

(5) The circumstances under which the accused may secure pretrial release;

(6) The right to a preliminary hearing;

(7) A reasonable time to consult with an attorney; and

(8) Setting or denying bail.

While the court is not required to conduct any preliminary inquiry, it is customary and desirable at the outset that the court determine that the correct person is before the court. The court should inquire whether the person is actually the person who is accused of committing the offense charged and that the defendant is actually before the court, either in person or by counsel.

The court must give the defendant notice of the charges against him. This is accomplished by informing the defendant in open court, by either reading or stating the substance of the charge. A defendant who has counsel prior to the initial appearance normally waives a formal reading of the charge, because counsel has either previously ascertained the charge (in the case of a misdemeanor) or has been provided with a copy of the indictment.

After the court gives the accused notice of the charges, the rules may require that the court ask the accused to enter a plea to those charges. Most defendants enter a plea of not guilty to felony charges, in part because defense counsel knows little about the charges at the time. If a defendant chooses to stand mute, the court, by rule or its inherent authority, enters a not guilty plea on the defendant's behalf.

Under rules like Fed.R.Crim.P. 44(a), the right of the accused to be represented by counsel begins at the initial appearance. However, the initial appearance is not regarded as a "critical stage" at which the Sixth Amendment grants a right to counsel. On the other hand, an accused's request for counsel at the initial appearance precludes subsequent police interrogation about the charged offense but does not prohibit police interrogation about other crimes. *McNeil v. Wisconsin*, 501 U.S. 171 (1991).

B. *GERSTEIN* HEARING

In *Gerstein v. Pugh*, 420 U.S. 103 (1975), the Supreme Court held that "the Fourth Amendment requires a judicial determination of probable cause as a prerequisite to extended restraint of liberty following arrest." The *Gerstein* hearing is necessary prior to the continued detention of an accused who was arrested without either a prior judicial determination of probable cause such as an arrest warrant or the return of a grand jury indictment. Because of the similarity between the timing of the initial appearance and the timing of a *Gerstein* hearing following a warrantless arrest, a judge may conduct both proceedings at the time of the initial appearance.

The only issue determined at a *Gerstein* hearing is whether there is probable cause to believe that the accused committed an offense. *Gerstein* requires a "fair and reliable determination of probable cause." *Gerstein*, 420 U.S. at 125. A hearing is nonadversarial in nature, with the accused having no right to counsel, to be present, or to question witnesses. Hearsay and written testimony are admissible. When a court determines that there is no probable cause, release from custody is the proper remedy but that finding does not foreclose a later prosecution. Similarly, the absence of a prompt decision about further detention does not invalidate a later conviction, but it may provide grounds for a § 1983 civil rights case. See, e.g., *Turner v. City of Taylor*, 412 F.3d 629 (6th Cir.2005).

The determination of probable cause ordinarily must occur within 48 hours of the warrantless arrest. *County of Riverside v. McLaughlin*, 500 U.S. 44 (1991). A hearing may violate *Gerstein* if the arrested individual can prove that his or her probable cause determination was delayed unreasonably, e.g., delays for the purpose of gathering additional evidence to justify the arrest. In evaluating whether the delay in a particular case is unreasonable, however, courts must allow a substantial degree of flexibility, e.g., unavoidable delays in transporting arrested persons from one facility to another, handling late-night bookings where no judge is readily available.

Where an arrested individual does not receive a probable cause determination within 48 hours, the calculus changes. See, e.g., *Cherrington v. Skeeter*, 344 F.3d 631 (6th Cir. 2003) (burden of demonstrating "emergency or other extraordinary circumstance" not met by showing that 72–hour delay occurred because of intervening weekend or holiday).

C. PRELIMINARY HEARING

Although *Gerstein* held that there is no constitutional right to a preliminary hearing, all jurisdictions have court rules like Fed.R.Crim.P. 5.1, statutory enactments and court decisions which provide for preliminary proceedings involving felony charges. The traditional purpose of a preliminary hearing, or examining trial, is to determine whether there is probable cause for the defendant's charge to be presented to the grand jury. The required "probable cause" is that an offense was committed and that the accused committed it. Without a finding of probable cause, the accused is released from custody. The preliminary hearing occurs shortly after arrest. Unlike a *Gerstein* hearing or the initial appearance, state rules and statutes provide that the preliminary hearing is a formal, adversarial proceeding.

A preliminary hearing is important, not only because of the protections afforded the accused but also because of its strategic position in the criminal justice system. The preliminary hearing interrelates with other aspects of the criminal process—arrest, bail, prosecutorial discretion, the grand jury, and the trial itself. For example, information disclosed at the preliminary hearing may influence a judicial decision to set bail or some other condition for pretrial release. Or, it may serve as a review of a prosecutor's decision to charge the accused at all or with a particular offense.

1. The Models and Reality of the Preliminary Hearing

Throughout the fifty states and the federal system, the preliminary hearing is used, but there are important differences as to the nature of the preliminary hearing on several issues.

Admissibility of evidence. When court rules explicitly preclude the application of the rules of evidence at a preliminary hearing, judges can consider evidentiary matters admitted in the form of hearsay, illegally obtained evidence, and other incompetent evidence in deciding the issue of probable cause.

Prosecutor's evidentiary burden. In order for the case to continue through the criminal justice system, the prosecutor has to satisfy a set proof requirement. The probable cause standard of the preliminary hearing (using the same criterion for obtaining an arrest warrant) that the accused committed the offense charged is not as demanding for the prosecutor as the trial standard. To survive a motion for a directed verdict of acquittal at trial, the prosecutor must prove that there is adequate evidence for every element of the offense charged.

Participation of the accused. Most states' rules permit the defendant to conduct an active defense at the preliminary hearing, e.g., cross-examine prosecution witnesses, testify in his own behalf, subpoena witnesses, establish affirmative defenses.

Two alternative conceptual models of the preliminary hearing assist in understanding its role in the criminal justice system. See Note, "The Function of the Preliminary Hearing in Federal Pretrial Procedure," 83 Yale L.J. 771 (1974). Neither of the models is used in its pure form by any jurisdiction.

The backward-looking model is primarily concerned with the legality of the arrest and the validity of the detention of the arrested person; the perspective is backward in time—toward the arrest. The focus of this model is on the factual (i.e., whether the accused in fact committed the crime), rather than legal, guilt or innocence of the accused. The standard for the quality of evidence required is the same as is required to justify an arrest-probable cause. Because of the focus on factual guilt, hearsay and illegally (i.e., unconstitutionally) obtained evidence are admissible. Similarly, the prosecutor need not introduce compelling evidence of every element of the offense charge—evidence to establish probable cause is sufficient. There is no right to counsel, to present evidence, or to cross-examine witnesses.

The forward-looking model of the preliminary hearing is concerned with whether there is a sufficient probability of a conviction at trial to justify further proceedings. The court should dismiss cases lacking probable cause. The perspective is forward—toward trial. The focus of the forward-looking model is upon the probability of the legal (i.e., whether the accused would be convicted), rather than factual, guilt of innocence of the accused. The accused's interests in avoiding further unnecessary proceedings are thereby protected. Trial-type standards generally are imposed under this model of a preliminary hearing. The rules of evidence apply because they are applied at trial, and because competent evidence is generally more reliable. Accordingly, most hearsay and illegally obtained evidence would be excluded. The level of proof would have to be legally sufficient to avoid a directed verdict of acquittal, i.e., the evidence if unexplained would justify a conviction. Finally, the rights of the accused would be similar to those at trial—the accused has a right to counsel, to cross-examine witnesses, to testify, to prove affirmative defenses, and to present witnesses.

For the accused, the forward-looking model is advantageous. With higher proof standards, the defendant appears to have a better opportunity to escape the anxiety of an unjustified prosecution. However, in many jurisdictions the reality is that a judicial finding of no probable cause at the preliminary hearing does not preclude the prosecutor from taking the case to the grand jury for indictment or filing an information against the accused.

The forward-looking model also permits the accused to preserve the testimony of witnesses. The "former testimony" exception to the hearsay rule admits on the merits at trial prior testimony if (1) it was given at a judicial hearing under oath; (2) the declarant is "unavailable" to testify at trial; and (3) the opposing party had a reasonable opportunity (regardless of whether the opportunity was exercised) for cross-examination on substantially the same issues at the preliminary hearing. See *Crawford v. Washington*, 541 U.S. 36 (2004), which held that the Sixth Amendment Confrontation Clause permits admission of testimonial (such as prior testimony from a preliminary hearing) hearsay when the person who made the statement is unavailable and the accused has had a prior opportunity to cross-examine the person who made the statement. *Ohio v. Roberts* is now applicable only to nontestimonial statements like casual remarks to an acquaintance. *Roberts* permits admission of out of court nontestimonial statements that are either trustworthy or a "firmly rooted" hearsay exception.

For the prosecution, the forward-looking model permits the prosecution to test its witnesses in an adversary proceeding prior to trial. The prosecutor also may use the preliminary hearing as an opportunity to record and perpetuate the testimony of its witnesses while the events are recent and clearly remembered.

What is the reality of the preliminary hearing? In most jurisdictions, the current rules and statutes about preliminary hearings approximate the backward-looking model. For example, the federal preliminary hearing requires only a showing of probable cause. That showing may be based solely on hearsay or illegally obtained evidence. The only major elements of the forward-looking model in the federal system are the trial-type rights, such as the right to counsel and to cross-examine prosecution witnesses.

It is important to note that there is no constitutional right to a preliminary hearing which involves adversary proceedings and the right to counsel. In Gerstein v. Pugh, supra, the Supreme Court held that, instead of a preliminary hearing, it is constitutional for a state to prescribe that probable cause be determined by a court informally, with only a prosecutor present. However, when state statutes and rules do provide for a preliminary hearing in the context of an adversary proceeding, there is a right to counsel and to confront witnesses.

Questions

1.   Is it an efficient use of scarce judicial resources to ignore evidentiary issues completely at a preliminary hearing? For example, would the time necessary at a preliminary hearing to consider search and seizure issues avoid relitigation at trial?

2.   If the standard of proof for conviction is proof beyond a reasonable doubt, why should prosecutors be able to maintain cases against a defendant when the best they can produce is probable cause, which falls far short of the requisite proof for conviction?

3.   If the judge is to study the prosecution's evidence in the same way it would examine a motion for a directed verdict, i.e., in the light most favorable to the prosecution, what is the purpose of the right to cross-examine witnesses and to present evidence? If the judge cannot make credibility determinations, what is the purpose of cross-examination either intended to test the presence of the elements of the crime or to produce impeachment evidence for trial? Should cross-examination be confined to proof of affirmative defenses which do not depend on challenging prosecution testimony? Is proof of affirmative defenses relevant if the sole purpose of the hearing is to determine probable cause? As the next section shows, the scope of subjects examined at a preliminary hearing may depend upon the judge's attitude toward the purpose of the hearing.

2.   *Functions of the Preliminary Hearing*

In *Coleman v. Alabama*, 399 U.S. 1 (1970), the Supreme Court concluded that, once a state authorizes a preliminary hearing, the Sixth Amendment right to counsel applies to that hearing. Counsel is necessary, the Court said, to try to rebut the showing of probable cause, discover the prosecution's case, build a record for later impeachment, preserve testimony of witnesses who are unavailable for trial, and make effective arguments on matters like the necessity for bail.

a. Screening

The primary function of a preliminary hearing is the screening of cases. The prosecutor must prove that there is probable cause to believe that a crime was committed and that the defendant committed the crime charged. Preliminary hearings save accused persons from the humiliation and anxiety involved in a public prosecution. Whether the screening function is successful depends upon:

1) The extent of screening by the prosecutor before the case reaches the preliminary hearing stage;

2) Whether the prosecutor bypasses the preliminary hearing by first obtaining an indictment;

3) Whether the prosecutor at the preliminary hearing presents all the key witnesses or relies largely on the testimony of the arresting officer; and

4) The practical impact of the judge's finding of no probable cause.

For the prosecution, the preliminary hearing provides an opportunity for the termination of weak or groundless charges without lengthy preparation and trial time. With the opportunity to discover the nature of its own evidence early in the prosecution, the government is able to conform the charge(s) to its proof before trial. In cases originating by a "private" complaint obtained by a citizen where no police investigation has occurred, the preliminary hearing provides an immediate forum for testing the strength of the case until further investigation can be conducted.

b. Pretrial Discovery

In practice, the preliminary hearing may provide defense counsel with a valuable discovery technique. In meeting the evidentiary standard for sending the case to the grand jury, the prosecutor necessarily provides the defense with some discovery of the prosecution's case. Defense counsel may obtain even more discovery by cross-examining the prosecution's witnesses at the hearing and by subpoenaing other potential trial witnesses to testify as defense witnesses at the hearing. The extent of the discovery depends upon:

1) Whether the prosecution relies entirely upon hearsay reports and thereby limits the witnesses it presents;

2) Whether the probable cause standard is satisfied by presenting a minimal amount of testimony on each element of the offense;

3) Whether the prosecutor follows a general practice of presenting most or all of the government's case; and

4) Whether the defense is limited, in both cross-examination of prosecution witnesses and in the presentation of its own witnesses, to direct rebuttal of material presented by the prosecution.

The importance to the defense of the limited discovery accessible through the preliminary hearing depends in large part on the availability of alternative discovery procedures. For example, if prior statements of prospective witnesses and the arresting officer's report are readily accessible, the hearing's discovery potential may be relatively unimportant. On the other hand, if state law and practice provide for little pretrial discovery, the preliminary hearing may serve as the primary discovery device. Similarly, if discovery does not occur until after the critical time for plea negotiations, the preliminary hearing may serve as the main discovery device for the large percentage of cases resolved by guilty pleas.

c.   Future Impeachment

Extensive cross-examination of prosecution witnesses at the preliminary hearing may be of value to the defense even though there is little likelihood of successfully challenging the prosecution's showing of probable cause and little to be gained by way of discovery. The skilled interrogation of witnesses can be a vital impeachment tool for use in cross-examination later at trial. Witnesses are more likely to make damaging admissions or contradictory statements at the preliminary hearing because they are less thoroughly briefed for that proceeding than they are for trial. In addition, the more some witnesses say before trial, the more likely that there will be some inconsistency between their trial testimony and their previous statements.

Of course, cross-examination designed to lay the foundation for future impeachment carries certain dangers for the defense. By focusing on potential weaknesses in a witness's testimony, a witness may be rehabilitated for trial and state that at the preliminary hearing she was confused but now all is clear. Cross-examination may also harden a witness's position, making the witness less able to retreat to a more friendly position. Finally, if the witness becomes unavailable at trial, the perpetuated testimony may be more damaging than that which would have existed without the cross-examination.

d.   Perpetuation of Testimony

Preliminary hearing testimony traditionally has been admitted at trial as substantive evidence under the "prior testimony" exception to the hearsay rule, where the witness is unavailable to testify. See, e.g., F.R.E. 804. The preliminary hearing thus perpetuates the testimony of witnesses so that it may be used even if the witness dies, disappears or otherwise becomes unavailable to testify. The Supreme Court has held that recorded preliminary hearing testimony may be used against the defendant as substantive evidence at trial. *Ohio v. Roberts*, 448 U.S. 56 (1980).

The admission of the preliminary hearing testimony of a prosecution witness who is unavailable for trial must be reconciled with the defendant's constitutional right of confrontation. Preliminary hearing testimony is admissible as substantive evidence at trial if: 1) it was given under oath; 2) the declarant is unavailable to testify at trial; and 3) if a reasonable opportunity, whether exercised or not, for cross-examination on substantially the same issues was afforded the opposing party at the preliminary hearing. See *Crawford v. Washington*, 541 U.S. 36 (2004), which held that the Sixth Amendment Confrontation Clause permits admission of testimonial (such as prior testimony from a preliminary hearing) hearsay when the person who made the statement is unavailable and the accused has had a prior opportunity to cross-examine the person who made the statement. *Ohio v. Roberts* is now applicable only to nontestimonial statements like casual remarks to an acquaintance. *Roberts* permits admission of out of court nontestimonial statements that are either trustworthy or a "firmly rooted" hearsay exception.

If state rules do not provide for the use of depositions in criminal cases, perpetuation of testimony is recommended. As a practical matter, the prosecution views the perpetuation of its witnesses' testimony as a significant benefit of the preliminary hearing, while the possibility of perpetuation may be viewed by the defense as a negative feature of the hearing.

e. Pretrial Release

Where bail is set at the initial appearance on the basis of sketchy facts, the preliminary hearing provides the judge with the first extensive examination of the facts of the individual case. The testimony may persuade the court to reduce or increase bail, or impose other terms or conditions of pretrial release. The hearing also insures that an accused who has been unjustifiably charged will be promptly released from custody.

f. Plea Bargaining

A preliminary hearing may be an "educational experience" for the defendant who is unpersuaded by defense counsel's opinion that the prosecution has such a strong case that a negotiated plea is in the defendant's best interest. Conversely, the proof at the hearing may be insufficient on the charged offenses, and require reduction of excessive charges. It thereby serves as a check against the prosecutorial practice of "overcharging" (by the number of charges and/or the severity of charges) in anticipation of plea negotiations.

Exercise

Based on the foregoing discussion of the functions of a preliminary hearing, read the following preliminary hearing transcript. In what way(s) was each function of the preliminary hearing served? What were the prosecutor and defense counsel trying to achieve in their questioning? Was either counsel successful in those efforts?

METRO CIRCUIT COURT DIVISION TWELVE

STATE OF COMMONWEALTH
v.

LARRY KNOX   PRELIMINARY HEARING
BILLY OLSON   TRANSCRIPT
NED LORD

(Separation of Witnesses)

Officer Joanne Davis of the Metro Division of Police was called to testify on behalf of the prosecution in the above-styled action, and after having been duly sworn was examined and testified as follows:

DIRECT EXAMINATION

BY MS. ROBERTA SMITH:

Q1 State you name, please?

A1 Officer Joanne Davis.

Q2 Officer Davis, you're an officer with the Metro Police Department, is that correct?

A2 I am.

Q3 Officer, on or about last January 28th, were you involved in the arrest of Mr. Larry Knox?

A3 That's right.

Q4 Tell the court, please, the circumstances of that arrest.

A4 My partner and I were driving north on Preston Highway at about 10:20 in the morning, when an armed robbery came out on the police radio at the Zach's Drug Store on Eastern Parkway. The radio pickup said to be on the look out for a maroon Camaro occupied by three males. We saw the car go past us as we were going north. We turned around, and proceeded in a chase after these subjects. They went south on Preston, and turned east into Audubon Parkway. After they went about three blocks, they stopped the car, and jumped out and ran. Knox was captured about three blocks from there.

Q5 Did you capture Mr. Knox, or—

A5 No, he was captured by some other officers who were in the area at the time, after we called in the chase.

Q6 Did you make an investigation of the vehicle they were driving?

A6 Yes, we did. We found a .32 caliber revolver, all the narcotics that were taken from the drug store, and the money.

Q7 How much money was that?

A7 It was $43.10, I think. I have it in my papers here. We have a list of all the narcotics that were taken also.

Q8 Was there any identification made as part of the investigation by any of the witnesses?

A8 We had a line-up downtown. The witnesses could not identify the subjects. They had masks over their faces in the drug store.

Q9 Did the witnesses make any kind of identification at the line-up?

A9 Yes, they identified the clothes that they were wearing at the time of the armed robbery.

Q10 All of this occurred in Metro City, is that correct?

A10 It did.

MS. SMITH: That's all.

CROSS–EXAMINATION

BY MR. BOB JONES:

Q11 You say no one made a facial identification of the defendant here?

A11 No, sir.

Q12 When does your report say that this robbery occurred at the drug store? What hour, or what time of day?

A12 About 10:30 in the morning.

Q13 All right, when did you first observe this car?

A13 It was about five minutes after the robbery came out on the radio.

Q14 Can you identify the people who were in that car?

A14 Yes, sir, it was Mr. Knox, a Billy Olson, and a Ned Lord.

Q15 Did you ever lose sight of the vehicle?

A15 No, sir, I never did.

Q16 From your vantage point, you can identify three of the people who were in that vehicle?

A16 When the subjects jumped out of the car and fled on foot, we saw all of them.

Q17 What period of time elapsed from the time that they jumped out until the time they were captured?

A17 Anywhere from five to ten minutes.

Q18 Did you ever lose sight of these people?

A18 Yes, sir, we lost sight of them.

Q19 So, you were not the officer who actually made the arrest?

A19 No, sir, we just were in the chase, and saw them jump out of the car and run.

Q20 Did you search that automobile?

A20 Yes, sir.

Q21 You stated on direct what was found. Did you find a mask in that car?

A21 No, sir, I did not.

Q22 Do you have any pictures of the line-up that was conducted?

A22 Yes, sir, I do.

Q23 May we have a look at those photographs? (Mr. Jones examines the photographs.) I notice that you have a picture of a gun in that collection of photographs. Were any fingerprints taken off that gun?

A23 No, sir, no fingerprints.

Q24 Were any scientific tests at all done in relation to the robbery?

A24 No, there was no shooting.

MR. JONES: I believe that's all.

Henry Zach was called to testify on behalf of the prosecution in the above-styled action, and after having been duly sworn was examined and testified as follows:

DIRECT EXAMINATION

BY MS. SMITH:

Q25 State you name, please, sir?

A25 Henry J. Zach.

Q26 Where do you live, sir?

A26 3285 Lee Avenue.

Q27 Here in Metro?

A27 Yes, ma'am.

Q28 What's your business, Mr. Zach?

A28 I'm a pharmacist.

Q29 And where is your pharmacy?

A29 947 Eastern Parkway.

Q30 On or about January 28th of this year, was there a robbery at your pharmacy?

A30 That's correct.

Q31 What time of day or night was that?

A31 Around 10:20, 10:30 in the morning.

Q32 Who was present at the time?

A32 One customer, one employee, and myself.

Q33 Would you tell the court what happened?

A33 Well, one man came in and jumped over the counter, and another one entered the door, and we assumed he had a shotgun. The other one had a .38, and he proceeded to the rear of the store and took the narcotics. He moved me to the front of the store, and took money from one register and from the front safe.

Q34 How much money was taken, Mr. Zach?

A34 It was approximately ninety some odd dollars. I forget the exact amount.

Q35 Why do you say that you assumed one of the men had a shotgun?

A35 It had the appearance of a gun, but I couldn't determine for sure. He had a mask, and the only thing I could recognize on the line-up was the type of jacket he was wearing.

Q36 Do you remember at this time which of these men you identified as wearing that particular jacket?

A36 The one who had the mask.

Q37 Just one of the men had a mask?

A37 Yes. The other one who jumped over the counter and went back into the prescription department was unmasked.

Q38 Are you able to identify the man who did not have the mask on?

A38 Yes, it's that man (pointing to Mr. Olson).

Q39 You're saying there were three men involved, is that right?

A39 Two men and the man in the getaway car. Two came in the store.

Q40 Were you able to see the man in the getaway car?

A40 No, ma'am.

Q41 Did you make a report of this incident to the police?

A41 About one or two minutes afterwards, as soon as I could get to the back phone.

Q42 Do you know what kind of car or the color of the getaway car?

A42 No, ma'am, I don't. That was determined by another witness who came in the store and gave us that information.

CROSS–EXAMINATION

BY MR. JONES:

Q43 Mr. Zach, did the police show you any photographs prior to your making an identification in court today?

A43 Yes.

Q44 And how many photographs did they show you?

A44 Three.

Q45 Did you ever attend a line-up where Mr. Olson was a participant?

A45 No, sir.

MR. JONES: I believe that's all.

REDIRECT EXAMINATION

Q46 Mr. Zach, have you identified any of the items that were taken from your drug store?

A46 Yes, I have.

Q47 Where did you see those items?

A47 At the Narcotics Bureau.

Q48 What were the items?

A48 They were drugs. They had my code, my price, and the type and size of bottle drugs that I carry.

Q49 At the time the drugs were taken, were you able to determine what was taken at that time?

A49 Within a day and a half we had the inventory complete.

Q50 And the drugs that you viewed at the police department, did they fit the description of what was taken.

A50 Absolutely.

MS. SMITH: That's all.

Kathy Frick was called to testify on behalf of the prosecution in the above-styled action, and after having been duly sworn was examined and testified as follows:

DIRECT EXAMINATION

BY MS. SMITH:

Q51 State you name please?

A51 Kathy Frick.

Q52 Ms. Frick, on January 28th, were you in the vicinity of Zach's Drug Store?

A52 Yes.

Q53 What did you observe?

A53 I saw two guys running around the corner from the drug store, into the alley, and they got into a cranberry Camaro.

Q54 Was anyone else in the vehicle when they got into it?

A54 Yeah, there was a third guy sitting in the car.

Q55 Did they have their faces covered?

A55 I really didn't notice.

Q56 Did you see their faces enough that you could make an identification?

A56 No, ma'am.

Q57 Did you tell anyone you saw the two men get in the car?

A57 Yes, I told two people who were peeping out of the drug store at the time.

CROSS–EXAMINATION

BY MR. JONES:

Q58 No questions. We will not present any witnesses at this time, Your Honor. At this time, Your Honor, the defense moves to dismiss the charges because the prosecution has failed to establish probable cause.

Notes and Questions

1. As counsel for either the prosecution or the defendants, what arguments would you make to the judge relating to the issue of probable cause? As judge, would you have found that probable cause was established? Probable cause of what crime?

2. What discovery was defense counsel able to achieve during cross-examination? Should the prosecutor have objected to any questioning which focused on discovery instead of the issue of probable cause? Even without objections by the prosecutor, should the judge have disallowed the questioning, if the judge believed that discovery was not a proper function of the hearing?

3. As defense counsel, would you have offered any proof after the prosecution presented its case for probable cause? Suppose, for example, you had a witness who is able to place at least one of the defendants at his workplace during the time when the robbery occurred. Should you present that witness's testimony or await the trial? Does the likelihood of a finding of probable cause affect your decision to forego presenting any case on behalf of your client?

4. After the court denies defense counsel's motion to dismiss the charges, defense counsel may present adverse witnesses or its own witnesses. Frequently, the prosecution does not call all of the witnesses it will present later at trial, because it may not want to reveal any more than is necessary to establish probable cause. Even if the defense is able to obtain some favorable evidence from adverse witnesses, the prosecution's questioning likely will produce additional unfavorable proof. Presenting defense witnesses may be similarly futile unless the defense believes either that the court will dismiss the charges or that it is necessary to send the prosecution a "message" about the strength of its case.

5. Does your decision about whether to present testimony on behalf of the defendant depend upon the nature of the testimony, e.g., my client did not commit this or any crime, my client has a justification defense such as self-defense, my client was suffering from a mental disease or defect at the time of the offense?

6. If counsel fails to pursue any of the functions of a preliminary hearing, should counsel be considered to have been ineffective?

Problem

The F.B.I. arrested Jack Penny for federal bank robbery on October 21 at approximately 11:00 a.m. Mr. Penny contacts you to represent him on the charge. From the documents you have been able to obtain, it appears that someone robbed the employees of a federally insured bank in a small town located about seventy-five miles from the city where your client resides. From the photographs taken by the bank camera, the F.B.I. located Mr. Penny and arrested him. In addition, several employees of the bank identified him in a line-up held on October 23 at the local Federal Building.

Mr. Penny has told you that, during the late morning of October 21, he was visiting his hometown methadone center receiving his weekly dosage. You are able to corroborate this information with the sign-in sheets at the center, and with both the receptionist and the treating doctor on duty at that time. To help Mr. Penny overcome his drug dependence, both the receptionist and the treating doctor are willing to appear at the hearing without being subpoenaed.

At the preliminary hearing, the Assistant United States Attorney presented the evidence described in the first paragraph. In addition, the bank employees identified Mr. Penny as he sat next to you at counsel table in the small courtroom where the United States Magistrate Judge was conducting the proceedings. You dutifully conduct your cross-examination of the prosecution witnesses, but you are unable to make much progress in challenging their identification. At the conclusion of the government's case, you move to dismiss the charges because there was inadequate proof of probable cause, but you are unsuccessful. Now you must decide whether to present your witnesses or even your client. What should you do?

3. Procedural Issues at the Preliminary Hearing

a. Timing of Preliminary Hearing

The preliminary hearing must occur within a reasonable time. For example, Fed.R.Crim.P. 5.1(c) requires the hearing to occur no later than ten days after the initial appearance if the accused is still in custody and no later than twenty days if the defendant has obtained pretrial release.

In many cases, the issue is not when the examination is held but whether it must be held at all. Most courts have held that there is no necessity for a preliminary hearing after a grand jury first has returned an indictment. If the only purpose of the preliminary hearing is to determine whether there is probable cause for holding the accused to answer further, this is a logical rule because the grand jury has decided the issue of probable cause and there is no need to have a court duplicate that determination. Thus, where an accused is first arrested after indictment, rather than on an arrest warrant, the accused is not entitled to a preliminary hearing. To the extent that the preliminary hearing is of benefit to the accused as an instrument of discovery, the prosecution can deny that benefit by indicting the accused prior to the scheduled time of the preliminary hearing. For example, 18 U.S.C § 3060(e) provides that no preliminary hearing is required for an arrested person if at any time subsequent to the initial appearance of that person and prior to the date fixed for the preliminary examination, an indictment is returned.

b. Waiver of Preliminary Hearing

A defendant may waive a preliminary hearing. Waiver rates vary substantially among jurisdictions and sometimes exceed 50%, even in places which provide quite extensive hearings. Despite the aforementioned advantages of the hearing, defense counsel may consider a waiver where the hearing presents a substantial danger to the defense. Defense counsel considerations may include the following:

1) An essential prosecution witness will testify at the preliminary hearing but may be unavailable at trial. Recall that the recorded preliminary hearing testimony may be used against the defendant as substantive evidence at trial.

2) A complainant is likely to "mellow" with time if he is not required to put his testimony "on the record" at this point. By contrast, a complainant who testifies under oath at a preliminary hearing may be less likely either to change the version of what happened or to consent to an interview with the defense.

3) The preliminary hearing may add to adverse publicity that will make it difficult to obtain a fair trial.

4) The preliminary hearing will call the prosecutor's attention to a curable defect in the case that otherwise would not be noticed until trial.

5) The preliminary hearing will alert the prosecutor to the fact that the defendant is undercharged, and should be charged with more serious or simply more offenses than those in the complaint.

See Anthony G. Amsterdam, Trial Manual 5 for the Defense of Criminal Cases (1988). Even if the defendant waives the hearing, a jurisdiction's criminal rules may provide that prior to indictment or information the prosecutor may be entitled to demand a preliminary hearing. The prosecutor will oppose a defense waiver and insist upon a hearing under special circumstances, e.g., where either there appears to be a need to perpetuate testimony because a particular witness is likely to become unavailable, or a particular witness's testimony is "shaky" and there would be some value in placing him under oath.

c. Dispositions Following Preliminary Hearing

At the close of the prosecution's case at a preliminary hearing, defense counsel should move to dismiss the charges, based upon the failure of the proof to establish:

1) That an offense was committed;

2) That the accused committed an offense; and

3) Venue—where the offense took place, for jurisdictional purposes.

Frequently, after the judge denies defense counsel's motion for a dismissal based upon the above grounds, counsel will move the court to reduce the original charge to a lesser offense, e.g., from a felony to a misdemeanor, have the accused plead guilty to the reduced charge, and thereby dispose of the case. If a court permits a guilty plea to an amended charge which is a lesser included offense of the original charge, double jeopardy probably will prevent the prosecution from reinstituting the original charge against the accused.

If the evidence presented at the preliminary hearing establishes probable cause to believe that the defendant has committed the offense, the court must refer the case to the grand jury for possible indictment or to the court for trial following the filing of an information on any charge supported by probable cause. If the court does not find probable cause to refer the charge, it may nevertheless find probable cause as to some other offense. In this situation, the court may permit the prosecution to amend the charge if substantial rights of the defendant are not prejudiced. If the evidence at the preliminary hearing fails to establish probable cause, the defendant is discharged from the jurisdiction of the court. However, dismissal of the charge due to the insufficiency of the evidence at a preliminary hearing does not bar a subsequent prosecution arising out of the same transaction.

Chapter 14

GRAND JURIES

A. INTRODUCTION

Both the preliminary hearings discussed in the prior chapter and
grand jury review considered in the present chapter test the government's case for the quantum of proof required to go to trial, although
each usually requires only proof of probable cause (as opposed to proof
beyond a reasonable doubt) that a crime has been committed and that a
particular defendant committed the crime. They differ, however, in
important respects. For example: preliminary hearings are public, while
grand jury proceedings are secret. Preliminary hearings are adversary
proceedings in which the defense can challenge the prosecution's case,
but grand juries normally hear only the prosecution's case, and prospective defendants and defense counsel are excluded from the grand jury
proceedings. Judges preside over preliminary hearings, while grand jury
proceedings occur without judicial participation. Finally, judges determine the sufficiency of the evidence in preliminary hearings, while grand
jurors (citizens of the local community) make this determination in
grand jury proceedings.

The grand jury is an ancient common law entity which originated as
a body of local residents who helped look into possible crimes. This
investigative function of a grand jury has been characterized as a **sword**
to root out crime. By the time of the American Revolution, however, the
grand jury assumed another function as a **shield** to protect citizens
against malicious and unfounded prosecutions. The dual functions of the
grand jury are considered separately in this Chapter.

In the federal system, the view that the grand jury acts as a "shield"
or "screen" against improper prosecutions was embodied in U.S. Constitution, Amendment V which provides: "No person shall be held to
answer for a capital, or otherwise infamous crime, unless on a presentment or indictment of a Grand Jury...." The U.S. Supreme Court,
however, has held that the States are not required to abide by the grand
jury requirement imposed on the federal courts. *See Hurtado v. California*, 110 U.S. 516 (1884) (the grand jury requirement has not been

"incorporated" against the states through the Due Process clause of the Fourteenth Amendment). About half the States have their own constitutional provisions or statutory requirements for grand jury indictment. The other half have either eliminated grand juries and permit prosecution by information, or allow the prosecutor to choose between grand jury indictment and information. Even the states which use grand juries may have rules comparable to the federal rules, permitting defendants to waive the right to indictment and proceed by information. (An information is a charge drawn up by the prosecutor and not submitted to a grand jury, although it may or may not be screened by a judicial officer at a preliminary hearing).

1. *Selection of the Grand Jury*

Grand juries in individual jurisdictions differ greatly in their composition and selection processes. At common law, the grand jury was comprised of twenty-three persons, at least twelve of whom had to agree in order to hand down an indictment for a criminal offense. Today, federal grand juries consist of between sixteen and twenty-three jurors, twelve of whom must agree to indict the defendant for any charge. Other jurisdictions utilize much smaller grand juries, although all jurisdictions require that an indictment be based on the concurrence of at least a majority of the grand jurors empaneled to review the charges.

The process of selecting grand jurors begins with the court's summoning of a number of persons qualified to serve as grand jurors. The qualifications for grand jury service are set out in the jurisdiction's statutes and normally include requirements that the prospective grand juror be: (1) a citizen of the jurisdiction; (2) reside in the jurisdiction; (3) be over eighteen years of age; (4) have no felony convictions; and (4) be a person of honesty, intelligence, and good demeanor. Purging the grand jury is the process of narrowing the number of qualified grand jurors to the number of jurors who will actually serve. The process eliminates otherwise qualified grand jurors who have legitimate excuses for not serving, such as health problems, family obligations and the like.

Defense counsel do not participate in the selection of the grand jury. Thus any deficiencies in the composition of the grand jury must be raised when the defendant is brought to trial (objections cannot be raised for the first time on appeal). A timely pretrial objection allows the trial court to void the indictment and send the prosecutor back to a lawfully constituted grand jury. Challenges to the composition of the grand jury are made by a motion to dismiss or quash the indictment returned by the grand jury. Generally, the courts have recognized only two proper grounds for objecting to the composition of the grand jury: (1) one or more of the grand jurors failed to meet the statutory qualifications for service; or (2) the process for selecting grand jurors violated constitutional standards.

Although the States are not required to utilize grand juries, if they choose to do so, the Equal Protection Clause of the U.S. Constitution requires that no State may deliberately and systematically exclude individuals because of race, class, gender, or national origin. *Taylor v. Louisiana*, 419 U.S. 522 (1975). The basic elements of an equal protection challenge to the grand jury are the same as required for challenges to the trial jury. (The U. S. Supreme Court has not determined whether the Sixth Amendment requirement that the jury be drawn from a "fair cross-section of the community" applies to grand juries). Constitutional infirmities in the composition of a grand jury may invalidate a conviction even though the trial jury was legally constituted and guilt was established beyond a reasonable doubt. *Vasquez v. Hillery*, 474 U.S. 254 (1986). [Reproduced below is a typical motion to challenge the selection of a grand jury].

Challenge to Array of Grand Jury and Objection to Grand Jury

The defendant in the above styled case challenges the array of and objects to the grand jury to be convened on ___, 2007, and states that charges against him should not be presented to said grand jury for the following reasons:

1. (a) Young adults ages 18 to 30 were systematically and purposefully excluded from the grand jury pool from which the current grand jury panel was selected. On a grand jury list of ___ people, only ___ young adults under the age of 30 or only ___% of the entire list are included. Those persons within the 18 to 30 year old age group constitute ___% of the total over 18 years of age population of ___ County. (b) The exclusion of this class is in violation of the rights guaranteed the defendant by the due process and equal protection clauses of the Fourteenth Amendment of the United States Constitution.

2. (a) Women were systematically and purposefully excluded from the grand jury pool from which the current grand jury panel was selected. Out of a population over the age of 18 in ___ County totaling some ___ persons, ___ or ___% are women. The current grand jury pool for ___ County lists the names of some ___ people. Of that number, only ___ or ___% are women.

(b) The exclusion of this class is in violation of the rights guaranteed the defendant by the due process and equal protection clauses of the Fourteenth Amendment of the United States Constitution.

3. (a) Black persons were systematically and purposefully excluded from the grand jury pool from which the current grand jury panel was selected. Out of a population of persons over the age of 18 in ___ County totaling some ___ persons, ___ or ___% are black.

(b) The exclusion of this group is in violation of the rights guaranteed the defendant by the due process and equal protection clauses of the Fourteenth Amendment of the United States Constitution.

4. In support of the foregoing allegations and to demonstrate the result of the unconstitutional composition of the current ___ County grand jury pool, a profile of the grand jury whose array is hereby challenged is attached hereto as Exhibit A. Said grand jury is made up of ___ white persons, and ___ black persons. There are ___ males and ___ females. There are ___ under the age of 31 and ___ 31 years of age or older.

5. A copy of the ___ County grand jury list with the respective classes designated thereon is attached hereto as Exhibit B; graphs depicting proportional representation on the grand jury as to age, race, and sex are attached as Exhibits C and D; a copy of the official United States census figures for ___ County, as they appear in Department of Commerce Publication pages ___ (31) ___ attached hereto as Exhibit E.

WHEREFORE, defendant prays:

(1) For a hearing at which he may introduce evidence in support of each and every allegation enumerated above;

(2) That the charges against this defendant not be presented to this grand jury panel; and

(3) That this challenge to the array of the grand jury be granted.

Exercise

The police observed defendant Jones, an African–American, proceed in the wrong direction on a one-way street. The police officer stopped defendant's vehicle and determined that defendant's driver's license was suspended. During a search of the vehicle subsequent to the stop, the police officer discovered marijuana, a nine-millimeter pistol, and drug paraphernalia. The defendant was initially slated for prosecution in state court. However, a program designated "Project Exile" resulted in the transfer of Jones' case to a federal grand jury which issued a four-count indictment against Jones. The federal indictment covered precisely the same conduct originally prosecuted in the state proceedings.

Project Exile is a project jointly undertaken by the prosecutor for the City of Richmond, Virginia and the United States Attorney for the Eastern District of Virginia. Although Richmond possesses only three percent of the State's population, it accounts for twenty-seven percent of the State's homicides. The stated goal of Project Exile is to reduce violent crime by federally prosecuting firearm-related crimes whenever possible. Under Project Exile, local police review each firearm-related offense to determine whether the conduct alleged also constitutes a federal crime. In those cases in which the conduct alleged also constitutes a federal crime, local police refer the matter to the United States Attorney for the Eastern District of Virginia. If the United States Attorney obtains an indictment charging the defendant with federal firearm-related crimes, then the Commonwealth's Attorney drops the state charges, and the case proceeds in federal court.

The parties are unable to obtain precise empirical data concerning either the race of Project Exile defendants or the racial composition of the relevant grand jury pools. However, the parties agree to these general facts: The vast majority, and perhaps as many as ninety percent of the defendants prosecuted under Project Exile are African–American. The jury pool for the Circuit Court for the City of Richmond is approximately seventy-five percent African–American. The jury pool for the Richmond Division of the Eastern District of Virginia is drawn from a broader geographic area. In contrast to the state jury pool, it is only about ten percent African–American. At a local Bench–Bar Conference discussing the issue, an Assistant United States Attorney stated that one goal of Project Exile is to avoid "Richmond juries." The Project is publicized through advertising on television, on billboards, on buses, and in other venues, all paid for by the "Project Exile Citizens Support Foundation," a private group for which the U. S. Attorney helps to solicit contributions from local merchants.

As defense counsel for Mr. Jones, draft a motion to quash the indictment issued by the federal grand jury. As the prosecutor, how would you respond to the motion to quash?

2. Scope of Grand Jury Investigation

Once the grand jury is selected and empaneled, the judge will charge the grand jury. This charge may range from the judge's statements about the general state of the Union, to suggestions about particular matters that will come before the grand jury. All judges, however, will caution the grand jury to maintain the secrecy of its proceedings. Once the judge has charged the grand jury, the grand jury independently conducts its investigation of alleged criminal offenses. Unlike preliminary hearings, the judge does not preside over grand jury proceedings.

In the absence of the judge, the prosecutor will focus the grand jury's attention on the task at hand by: (1) submitting an *indictment*, which is a written accusation of crime prepared by the prosecutor; and (2) suggesting what witnesses and evidence the grand jury should consider. If the grand jury agrees that the evidence indicates that a crime has occurred, they will return a "true bill" of indictment upon which the accused will face trial. If the grand jury concludes that the evidence does not warrant a trial they will return "no bill." The grand jury's refusal to return a true bill does not preclude the prosecutor from resubmitting the indictment to another grand jury. Until the actual trial begins, Double Jeopardy does not protect the accused from undergoing successive grand jury investigations.

Although the prosecutor may direct the grand jury's attention to the submitted indictments, the prosecutor may not limit the scope of the grand jury's investigation of other crimes because grand juries are often charged to inquire of and present all felonies, misdemeanors and violations of penal laws committed within its jurisdiction. A grand jury which goes beyond the indictments prepared by the prosecutor and launches its own investigation is often referred to as a *run away grand jury*. The charges returned by such a grand jury are referred to as presentments rather than indictments. (Indictments are submitted to the grand jury by a prosecutor; *presentments* are drawn up at the grand jury's initiative). The information necessary to return a presentment can be obtained from additional witnesses called by the grand jury or from the personal knowledge of the grand jurors. In contrast to trial jurors, grand jurors need not stand impartial in the case.

3. Grand Jury Secrecy

Unlike most stages of a criminal prosecution, grand jury proceedings are conducted in secret. The Supreme Court has explained that the secrecy requirement is designed to serve five important objectives:

> (1) to prevent the escape of those whose indictment may be contemplated; (2) to insure the utmost freedom to the grand jury in its deliberations, and to prevent persons subject to indictment or their friends from importuning the grand jurors; (3) to prevent subornation of perjury or tampering with the witnesses who may testify before the grand jury and later appear at the trial of those indicted by it; (4) to encourage free and untrammeled disclosures by persons who have information with respect to the commission of crimes; (5) to protect the innocent accused who is exonerated from disclosure of the fact that he has been under investigation, and from the expense of standing trial where there was no probability of guilt.

United States v. Procter & Gamble Co., 356 U.S. 677 (1958).

Grand jury secrecy requirements vary among jurisdictions, but generally the prosecutor and the grand jurors are prohibited from disclosing grand jury testimony except when authorized by court order. Most jurisdictions do not impose an obligation of secrecy upon grand jury witnesses, and the Supreme Court has held that a State may not prohibit grand jury witnesses from disclosing their own testimony after the term of the grand jury has ended. *Butterworth v. Smith*, 494 U.S. 624 (1990).

Rule 6(e)(3)(D) follows the Patriot Act, § 203, to allow disclosure of Grand Jury information that "involves foreign intelligence or counterintelligence" to intelligence, defense, national security, or immigration officials.

B. THE GRAND JURY AS A SHIELD

1. Sufficiency of the Evidence

Wood v. Georgia, 370 U.S. 375 (1962) described the grand jury as:

> a primary security to the innocent against hasty, malicious and oppressive persecution; it serves the invaluable function in our society of standing between the accuser and the accused, whether the latter be an individual, minority group, or other, to determine whether a charge is founded upon reason or was dictated by an intimidating power or by malice and personal ill will.

Despite this lofty view of the function of a grand jury, most states have either eliminated grand juries in favor of proceeding by information, or the state may utilize preliminary hearings as another method of screening charges brought by a prosecutor. The majority view is that the shielding function of the grand jury, while attractive rhetoric, is illusory in practice. Statistics show that grand juries rarely refuse to indict, an understandable result in light of the fact that grand jury proceedings are not adversarial. Without a defense counsel to challenge the government's evidence or to present exculpatory evidence, it's rather like a hockey game where only one team has a goalie.

The Fifth Amendment provides in part that "[n]o person shall be held to answer for a capital, or otherwise infamous crime, unless on a presentment or indictment of a Grand Jury. . . ." In the federal system, the constitutional requirement for grand jury indictment has continuing vitality. When a properly constituted grand jury returns an indictment, courts will not review the adequacy of evidence presented to a grand jury.

COSTELLO v. UNITED STATES

350 U.S. 359 (1956).

JUSTICE BLACK delivered the opinion of the Court.

We granted certiorari in this case to consider a single question: "May a defendant be required to stand trial and a conviction be sustained where only hearsay evidence was presented to the grand jury which indicted him?"

Petitioner, Frank Costello, was indicted for wilfully attempting to evade payment of income taxes due the United States. The charge was that petitioner falsely and fraudulently reported less income than he and his wife actually received during the taxable years in question. Petitioner promptly filed a motion for inspection of the minutes of the grand jury and for a dismissal of the indictment. His motion was based on an affidavit stating that he was firmly convinced there could have been no legal or competent evidence before the grand jury which indicted him since he had reported all his income and paid all taxes due. The motion was denied. At the trial which followed the Government offered evidence designed to show increases in Costello's net worth in an attempt to prove that he had received more income during the years in question than he had reported. To establish its case the Government called and examined 144 witnesses and introduced 368 exhibits. All of the testimony and documents related to business transactions and expenditures by petitioner and his wife. The prosecution concluded its case by calling three government agents. Their investigations had produced the evidence used against petitioner at the trial. They were allowed to summarize the vast amount of evidence already heard and to introduce computations showing, if correct, that petitioner and his wife had received far greater income than they had reported.

Counsel for petitioner asked each government witness at the trial whether he had appeared before the grand jury which returned the indictment. This cross-examination developed the fact that the three investigating officers had been the only witnesses before the grand jury.

After the Government concluded its case, petitioner again moved to dismiss the indictment on the ground that the only evidence before the grand jury was "hearsay," since the three officers had no firsthand knowledge of the transactions upon which their computations were based. Nevertheless the trial court again refused to dismiss the indictment, and petitioner was convicted. The Court of Appeals affirmed. * * *

Petitioner here urges: (1) that an indictment based solely on hearsay evidence violates that part of the Fifth Amendment providing that "No person shall be held to answer for a capital, or otherwise infamous crime, unless on a presentment or indictment of a Grand Jury" and (2) that if the Fifth Amendment does not invalidate an indictment based solely on hearsay we should now lay down such a rule for the guidance of federal courts. * * *

[N]either the Fifth Amendment nor any other constitutional provision prescribes the kind of evidence upon which grand juries must act. The grand jury is an English institution, brought to this country by the early colonists and incorporated in the Constitution by the Founders. There is every reason to believe that our constitutional grand jury was intended to operate substantially like its English progenitor. The basic purpose of the English grand jury was to provide a fair method for instituting criminal proceedings against persons believed to have committed crimes. Grand jurors were selected from the body of the people and their work was not hampered by rigid procedural or evidential rules. In fact, grand jurors could act on their own knowledge and were free to make their presentments or indictments on such information as they deemed satisfactory. Despite its broad power to institute criminal proceedings the grand jury grew in popular favor with the years. It acquired an independence in England free from control by the Crown or judges. Its adoption in our Constitution as the sole method for preferring charges in serious criminal cases shows the high place it held as an instrument of justice. * * *

In *Holt v. United States,* 218 U.S. 245 (1910), this Court had to decide whether an indictment should be quashed because supported in part by incompetent evidence. Aside from the incompetent evidence "there was very little evidence against the accused." The Court refused to hold that such an indictment should be quashed, pointing out that "The abuses of criminal practice would be enhanced if indictments could be upset on such a ground." The same thing is true where as here all the evidence before the grand Jury was in the nature of "hearsay." If indictments were to be held open to challenge on the ground that there was inadequate or incompetent evidence before the grand jury, the resulting delay would be great indeed. * * *

Affirmed.

JUSTICE BURTON, concurring.

I agree with the denial of the motion to quash the indictment. In my view, however, this case does not justify the breadth of the declarations made by the Court. I assume that this Court would not preclude an examination of grand jury action to ascertain the existence of bias or prejudice in an indictment. Likewise, it seems to me that if it is, shown that the grand jury had before it no substantial or rationally persuasive evidence upon which to base its indictment, that indictment should be quashed. To hold a person to answer to such an empty indictment for a capital or otherwise infamous federal crime robs the Fifth Amendment of much of its protective value to the private citizen.

Notes and Questions

1. *Costello*'s holding rests on the assumption that the "accused will get his fair, judicial, hearing at his trial." But if the grand jury is to protect the innocent against oppression and unjust prosecution, should a defendant be compelled to go to trial to prove the insufficiency of the charge?

> A wrongful indictment is no laughing matter; often it works a grievous irreparable injury to the person indicted. The stigma cannot be easily erased. In the public mind, the blot on a man's escutcheon, resulting from such a public accusation of wrongdoing, is seldom wiped out by a subsequent judgment of not guilty. Frequently, the public remembers the accusation, and still suspects guilt, even after an acquittal. *In re Fried,* 161 F.2d 453 (2d Cir.1947) (concurring opinion).

If the Supreme Court had held the *Costello* indictment invalid because it rested on incompetent evidence, would the "flood gates" have been opened to challenges to almost any indictment by a grand jury that considered evidence that would be inadmissible at trial? How effective would these challenges be? In jurisdictions rejecting *Costello* based on state law, interlocutory appellate review generally is not available. Thus a trial judge's adverse ruling on a challenged indictment ordinarily comes before the appellate court as part of the appeal following conviction. Once the defendant has been convicted at trial, should any insufficiency in the evidence before the grand jury be viewed as harmless error since the trial jury found sufficient evidence to convict?

2. In *United States v. Calandra*, 414 U.S. 338 (1974) the Supreme Court indicated that the *Costello* rationale also barred a challenge to an indictment issued on the basis of unconstitutionally obtained evidence. In *Calandra* the district court held that the defendant "need not answer any of the grand jury's questions based on" evidence obtained from an unconstitutional search. The Supreme Court reversed stating:

> It is evident that this extension of the exclusionary rule would seriously impede the grand jury. Because the grand jury does not finally adjudicate guilt or innocence, it has traditionally been allowed to pursue its investigative and accusatorial functions unimpeded by the evidentiary and procedural restrictions applicable to a criminal trial. Permitting witnesses to invoke the exclusionary rule before a grand jury would precipitate adjudication of issues hitherto reserved for the trial on the merits and would delay and disrupt grand jury proceedings.

The United States Attorneys' Manual, however, directs federal prosecutors "not [to] present to the grand jury for use against a person whose constitutional rights clearly have been violated evidence which the prosecutor personally knows was obtained as a direct result of the constitutional violation." 9 U.S. Dep't. Of Justice, *U.S. Attorneys' Manual* § 9–11.233 (Supp. 2002).

2. *Misconduct Challenges*

Following *Costello*, some federal courts employed a "prosecutorial misconduct" rationale to exert control over the type of the evidence presented to the grand jury. These cases relied upon the courts' inherent authority "to preserve the integrity of the judicial process" by dismissing indictments that were the product of "flagrantly abusive prosecutorial conduct." Prosecutor misconduct was held to include the presentation of evidence in an unfair manner. For example, the knowing presentation of false testimony; the presentation of hearsay disguised as if the witness was testifying based on personal observations; or failing to produce known exculpatory evidence that clearly was material. This use of the judiciary's supervisory power was rejected in *United States v. Williams*.

UNITED STATES v. WILLIAMS

504 U.S. 36 (1992).

JUSTICE SCALIA delivered the opinion of the Court.

The question presented in this case is whether a district court may dismiss an otherwise valid indictment because the Government failed to disclose to the grand jury "substantial exculpatory evidence", in its possession.

On May 4, 1988, respondent John H. Williams, Jr., a Tulsa, Oklahoma, investor, was indicted by a federal grand jury on seven counts of "knowingly mak[ing] [a] false statement or report . . . for the purpose of influencing . . . the action [of a federally insured financial institution]," in violation of 18 U.S.C. § 1014 (1988 ed., Supp. 11). According to the indictment, between September 1984 and November 1985 Williams supplied four Oklahoma banks with "materially false" statements that variously overstated the value of his current assets and interest income in order to influence the banks' actions on his loan requests. * * *

Shortly after arraignment, the District Court granted Williams' motion for disclosure of all exculpatory portions of the grand jury transcripts. Upon reviewing this material, Williams demanded that the District Court dismiss the indictment, alleging that the Government had failed to fulfill its obligation to present "substantial exculpatory evidence" to the grand jury. His contention was that evidence which the Government had chosen not to present to the grand jury—in particular, Williams' general ledgers and tax returns, and Williams' testimony in his contemporaneous Chapter 11 bankruptcy proceeding—disclosed that, for tax purposes and otherwise, he had regularly accounted for the "notes receivable" (and the interest on them) in a manner consistent with the Balance Sheet and the Income Statement. This, he contended, belied an intent to mislead the banks, and thus directly negated an essential element of the charged offense.

The District Court found, after a hearing, that the withheld evidence was "relevant to an essential element of the crime charged," created " 'a reasonable doubt about [respondent's] guilt,' " and thus "render[ed] the grand jury's decision to indict gravely suspect." Upon the Government's appeal, the Court of Appeals affirmed the District Court's order.... Under these circumstances, the Tenth Circuit concluded, it was not an abuse of discretion for the District Court to require the Government to begin anew before the grand jury. We granted certiorari. * * *

Bank of Nova Scotia v. United States, 487 U.S. 250 (1988) makes clear that the supervisory power can be used to dismiss an indictment because of misconduct before the grand jury, at least where that misconduct amounts to a violation of one of those "few, clear rules which were carefully drafted and approved by this Court and by Congress to ensure the integrity of the grand jury's functions."

We did not hold in *Bank of Nova Scotia,* however, that the courts' supervisory power could be used, not merely as a means of enforcing or vindicating legally compelled standards of prosecutorial conduct before the grand jury, but as a means of *prescribing* those standards of prosecutorial conduct in the first instance—just as it may be used as a means of establishing standards of prosecutorial conduct before the courts themselves. It is this latter exercise that respondent demands. Because the grand jury is an institution separate from the courts, over whose functioning the courts do not preside, we think it clear that, as a general matter at least, no such "supervisory" judicial authority exists, and that the disclosure rule applied here exceeded the Tenth Circuit's authority. * * *

"[R]ooted in long centuries of Anglo–American history," the grand jury is mentioned in the Bill of Rights, but not in the body of the Constitution. It has not been textually assigned, therefore, to any of the branches described in the first three Articles. * * * In fact the whole theory of its function is that it belongs to no branch of the institutional government, serving as a kind of buffer or referee between the Government and the people. * * * Although the grand jury normally operates, of course, in the courthouse and under judicial auspices, its institutional relationship with the judicial branch has traditionally been, so to speak, at arm's length. Judges' direct involvement in the functioning of the grand jury has generally been confined to the constitutive one of calling the grand jurors together and administering their oaths of office. * * *

[W]e have insisted that the grand jury remain "free to pursue its investigations unhindered by external influence or supervision so long as it does not trench upon the legitimate rights of any witness called before it." Recognizing this tradition of independence, we have said that the Fifth Amendment's "constitutional guarantee *presupposes* an investigative body 'acting independently of either prosecuting attorney *or judge*'...." * * *

Given the grand jury's operational separateness from its constituting court, it should come as no surprise that we have been reluctant to invoke the judicial supervisory power as a basis for prescribing modes of grand jury procedure. Over the years, we have received many requests to exercise supervision over the grand jury's evidence-taking process, but we have refused them all, including some more appealing that the one presented today. * * *

[A]ny power federal courts may have to fashion, on their own initiative, rules of grand jury procedure is a very limited one, not remotely comparable to the power they maintain over their own proceedings. It certainly would not permit judicial reshaping of the grand jury institution, substantially altering the traditional relationships between the prosecutor, the constituting court, and the grand jury itself. * * *

[R]equiring the prosecutor to present exculpatory as well as inculpatory evidence would alter the grand jury's historical role, transforming it from an accusatory to an adjudicatory body.

* * *

Imposing upon the prosecutor a legal obligation to present exculpatory evidence in his possession would be incompatible with this system. If a "balanced" assessment of the entire matter is the objective, surely the first thing to be done—rather than requiring the prosecutor to say what he knows in defense of the target of the investigation—is to entitle the target to tender his own defense. To require the former while denying (as we do) the latter would be quite absurd. It would also be quite pointless, since it would merely invite the target to circumnavigate the system by delivering his exculpatory evidence to the prosecutor, whereupon it would *have* to be passed on to the grand jury—unless the prosecutor is willing to take the chance that a court will not deem the evidence important enough to qualify for mandatory disclosure. * * *

Respondent insists . . . that courts must require the modern prosecutor to alert the grand jury to the nature and extent of the available exculpatory evidence, because otherwise the grand jury "merely functions as an arm of the prosecution." We reject the attempt to convert a nonexistent duty of the grand jury itself into an obligation of the prosecutor. The authority of the prosecutor to seek an indictment has long been understood to be "coterminous with the authority of the grand jury to entertain [the prosecutor's] charges." If the grand jury has no obligation to consider all "substantial exculpatory" evidence, we do not understand how the prosecutor can be said to have a binding obligation to present it.

There is yet another respect in which respondent's proposal not only fails to comport with, but positively contradicts, the "common law" of the Fifth Amendment grand jury. Motions to quash indictments based upon the sufficiency of the evidence relied upon by the grand jury were unheard of at common law in England. And the traditional American practice was described by Justice Nelson as follows:

"No case has been cited, nor have we been able to find any, furnishing an authority for looking into and revising the judgment of the grand jury upon the evidence, for the purpose of determining whether or not the finding was founded upon sufficient proof, or whether there was a deficiency in respect to any part of the complaint. . . . "

It would make little sense, we think, to abstain from reviewing the evidentiary support for the grand jury's judgment while scrutinizing the sufficiency of the prosecutor's presentation. A complaint about the quality or adequacy of the evidence can always be recast as a complaint that the prosecutor's presentation was "incomplete" or "misleading." Our words in *Costello* bear repeating: Review of facially valid indictments on such grounds "would run counter to the whole history of the grand jury institution, [and] [neither justice nor the concept of a fair trial requires [it]]."

Respondent argues that a rule requiring the prosecutor to disclose exculpatory evidence to the grand jury would, by removing from the docket unjustified prosecutions, save valuable judicial time. That depends, we suppose, upon what the ratio would turn out to be between unjustified prosecutions eliminated and grand jury indictments challenged—for the latter as well as the former consume "valuable judicial time." We need not pursue the matter; if there is an advantage to the proposal, Congress is free to prescribe it. For the reasons set forth above, however, we conclude that courts have no authority to prescribe such a duty pursuant to their inherent supervisory authority over their own proceedings. The judgment of the Court of Appeals is accordingly reversed and the cause remanded for further proceedings consistent with this opinion.

JUSTICE STEVENS, with whom JUSTICE BLACKMUN and JUSTICE O'CONNOR join, and with whom JUSTICE THOMAS joins as to Parts II and III, dissenting. * * * I agree with the Government that the prosecutor is not required to place all exculpatory evidence before the grand jury. A grand jury proceeding is an *ex parte* investigatory proceeding to determine whether there is probable cause to believe a violation of the criminal laws has occurred, not a trial. Requiring the prosecutor to ferret out and present all evidence that could be used at trial to create a reasonable doubt as to the defendant's guilt would be inconsistent with the purpose of the grand jury proceeding and would place significant burdens on the investigation. But that does not mean that the prosecutor may mislead the grand jury into believing that there is probable cause to indict by withholding clear evidence to the contrary. I thus agree with the Department of Justice that "when a prosecutor conducting a grand jury inquiry is personally aware of substantial evidence which directly negates the guilt of a subject of the investigation, the prosecutor must present or otherwise disclose such evidence to the grand jury before seeking an indictment against such a person." U.S. Dept. of Justice, United States Attorneys' Manual, Title 9, ch. 11, & 9–11.233, 88 (1988).

Although I question whether the evidence withheld in this case directly negates respondent's guilt, I need not resolve my doubts because the Solicitor General did not ask the Court to review the nature of the evidence withheld. Instead, he asked us to decide the legal question whether an indictment may be dismissed because the prosecutor failed to present exculpatory evidence. Unlike the Court and the Solicitor General, I believe the answer to that question is yes, if the withheld evidence would plainly preclude a finding of probable cause. 1 therefore cannot endorse the Court's opinion.

Notes and Questions

1. Despite the *Williams* decision, most state courts which have confronted the issue have imposed a duty on prosecutors to disclose exculpatory evidence to the grand jury in the unique cases where the prosecutor has evidence in her file. *See, e.g., State v. Hogan*, 144 N.J. 216, 676 A.2d 533 (1996). In order to reduce the circumstances in which a prosecutor's duty will arise, most courts rejecting the *Williams* approach have also ignored the California rule which imposed a requirement on prosecutors to disclose evidence which "reasonably tends to negate the guilt of the accused." Instead, most state courts which have imposed a limited duty on the prosecutor to inform the grand jury of evidence which directly negates the guilt of the accused and is clearly exculpatory. In the following situations, would the prosecutor have an obligation to disclose that:

A. The accused did not have a motive to commit the crime?

B. The State's witnesses have criminal records?

C. The testimony of an eyewitness is potentially biased?

D. The testimony of an eyewitness is contradicted by other witnesses?

E. The accused denied involvement in the crime?

F. A reliable alibi witness is available to testify?

G. Reliable exculpatory physical evidence is available?

H. The prosecution's main witness has recanted her testimony?

I. The target of the grand jury's investigation was insane at the time of the offense?

2. Defendant moves to dismiss the indictment, because the prosecutor's office provided prospective grand jury witnesses with a list of questions that the assistant prosecutor expected to ask them, along with the anticipated answers, based upon the witnesses' own prior statements or reports. The prosecutor also provided written instructions that the witness was to (1) notify the prosecutor if the answers were inconsistent with their recollection, and (2) tell the truth. A comparison of the submitted answers with the witnesses' answers during the grand jury proceedings showed that the witnesses did not "memorize" the submitted answers, *i.e.*, they were not "scripted automatons." In many instances the grand jury answers were far more detailed than the submitted answers. No evidence exists that either the submitted answers nor the actual testimony constituted a fabrication of the

facts. Should the judge dismiss the indictment? Has the prosecutor engaged in improper conduct?

3. *Does a prosecutor have the duty to present possible defenses to the grand jury?* In a later opinion arising from the same facts, the appellate court in *State v. Hogan*, 336 N.J.Super. 319, 764 A.2d 1012, 1025 (2001) opined:

> In our view, a prosecutor's obligation to instruct the grand jury on possible defenses is a corollary to his responsibility to present exculpatory evidence. The extent of the prosecutor's duty must be defined with reference to the role of the grand jury—to protect the innocent, and bring to trial those who may be guilty. Viewed from this perspective, the question of whether a particular defense need be charged depends upon its potential for eliminating a needless or unfounded prosecution. The appropriate distinction for this purpose is between exculpatory and mitigating defenses. An exculpatory defense is one that would, if believed, result in a finding of no criminal liability, i.e., a complete exoneration. * * *

> The rule accords with common sense and promotes the ability of a grand jury to filter out cases that should never be tried. We adopt that rule to the extent that it defines the existence of the prosecutor's duty.

> We now focus upon the scope of the prosecutor's duty. The first question is when such a duty arises. * * * We do not believe that the prosecutor has the obligation on his own meticulously to sift through the entire record of investigative files to see if some combination of facts and inferences might rationally sustain a defense or justification. The rule should be that it is only when the facts known to the prosecutor clearly indicate or clearly establish the appropriateness of an instruction that the duty of the prosecution arises.

Problems

1. Faced with the option of proceeding by information or seeking a grand jury indictment, would any prosecutor pay attention to the "shielding" function of a grand jury? Consider the following situation: in the course of an alleged robbery of an inner-city grocery store, the grocer shot and killed the fleeing robber, a member of a racial minority. Local merchant groups are insisting that no charges be brought, while various civil rights groups are demanding prosecution of the grocer. You are the prosecutor, an elected official. How will you proceed? If you opt to submit the matter to a grand jury, will you allow the local merchants association and/or the civil rights groups to address the grand jury? How would you respond to the grand jury's request that you furnish them with statistical evidence of interracial violence in the city?

2. By what means can a court control a "runaway grand jury?" May the court dismiss the grand jury? Refuse to extend its term? Refuse to issue or enforce subpoenas requested by the grand jury? Some jurisdictions permit the judge to dismiss the grand jury at any time; other jurisdictions prohibit dismissal because of fears that a judge will thwart a legitimate investigation, particularly an investigation into government corruption. The refusal to

extend the grand jury term or to enforce its subpoenas are less blatant forms of controlling a run away grand jury. During the early stages of the Watergate investigation, Federal District Judge Sirica was hailed as a hero for extending the grand jury's term until it could pierce the suspected coverup.

3. Is defense counsel at the mercy of the prosecutor in terms of presenting exculpatory evidence? Assume that as defense counsel for the "target" of an investigation, you submitted exculpatory evidence to the prosecutor who refused to pass it on to the grand jury. At this point may you ask the judge to rule on submitting this evidence to the grand jury? May you bypass both judge and prosecutor by sending the evidence directly to the grand jury foreperson? May you release the evidence to the media, (assuming the media has some interest in the subject matter)?

4. If a grand jury names someone as an "unindicted coconspirator" or otherwise criticizes a person, what can that person do to clear his or her name? Consider the following situation: A grand jury investigating the death of a child issued a report calling for the indictment and ouster of a county sheriff. The grand jury also criticized the chief deputy sheriff and a supervisor in the human services department, and recommended that they be terminated from the supervisory positions they held. The grand jury, however, did not indict them or institute ouster proceedings against them. The deputy and supervisor brought a mandamus action requiring the supervising judge to expunge the above language from the grand jury's report. They relied upon a state statute providing that "no report shall charge any public officer, or other person with willful misconduct or malfeasance, nor reflect on the management of any public office as being willful and corrupt misconduct." In *Stonecipher v. Taylor*, 970 P.2d 182 (Okla.1998), the court ordered expungement because the purpose of the statute is "to preserve to every person the right to meet his accusers in a court of competent jurisdiction and be heard, in open court, in his defense." Failure to expunge would result in the parties "being accused of willful and improper conduct without having any avenue by which to confront their accusers." In the absence of such a statute, would the deputy and supervisor be likely to obtain an expungement order from the court?

C. THE GRAND JURY AS A SWORD

The Supreme Court has often emphasized that screening charges before a grand jury creates a shield to protect innocent citizens against unfounded prosecutions. In practice, however, the grand jury's potential to "shield" innocent citizens is often subordinate to its functioning as a "sword" to root out crime through use of its investigative authority. Rather than viewing grand jury indictment as an unnecessary burden, many prosecutors favor use of grand jury proceedings in hopes of uncovering additional evidence. They seek to use the grand jury's broad subpoena powers over witnesses and documents, and in the typical grand jury proceeding the prosecutor determines what witnesses and evidence will be subpoenaed by the grand jury as part of their investigation. Unquestionably, in the clash between Special Prosecutor Kenneth Starr and President Clinton, the grand jury was not convened for the purpose of shielding the President against unwarranted charges.

Typically, the prosecutor determines what witnesses and evidence will be subpoenaed by the grand jury as part of the investigation. Unlike suspects or witnesses who are questioned by the police, an individual subpoenaed to appear before the grand jury has no general right to remain silent or to refuse to cooperate. In the absence of a constitutional provision such as the Fifth Amendment privilege against self-incrimination or a common law communication privilege, the witness "must tell what he knows" or risk being punished for contempt. *Branzburg v. Hayes*, 408 U.S. 665 (1972). The contempt sanction makes the grand jury subpoena particularly useful in obtaining statements from persons who will not voluntarily furnish information to the police. Even when a witness invokes the privilege against self-incrimination, the grand jury may, if authorized by law, grant the witness immunity and thus force an answer to its question.

The grand jury also may issue a *subpoena duces tecum*, which is a command to a person to produce writings or objects described in the subpoena. The only constitutional limitations on subpoenas duces tecum or other grand jury investigative powers are the constitutional rights of individual witnesses. The accused ultimately named in the indictment is not yet a "defendant," and thus enjoys no rights or protections beyond that afforded any witness called before the grand jury.

1. Witnesses' Rights Before a Grand Jury

The Fourth Amendment provides no protection to witnesses called to testify before a grand jury. The Fourth Amendment exclusionary rule is inapplicable at a grand jury proceeding, thus witnesses may be questioned based on evidence derived from illegal searches and seizures. *United States v. Calandra*, 414 U.S. 338 (1974). A subpoena to appear before the grand jury as a witness is not an arrest or a seizure of the person within the meaning of the Fourth Amendment, thus a subpoena for the person need not comply with the constitutional standards required for the arrest of a suspect.

UNITED STATES v. DIONISIO

410 U.S. 1 (1973).

JUSTICE STEWART delivered the opinion of the Court.

A special grand jury was convened in the Northern District of Illinois in February 1971, to investigate possible violations of federal criminal statutes relating to gambling. In the course of its investigation the grand jury received in evidence certain voice recordings that had been obtained pursuant to court orders. The grand jury subpoenaed approximately 20 persons, including the respondent Dionisio, seeking to obtain from them voice exemplars for comparison with the recorded conversations that had been received in evidence. Each witness was advised that he was a potential defendant in a criminal prosecution. Each was asked to examine a transcript of an intercepted conversation, and to go to a nearby office of the United States Attorney to read the transcript into a recording device. The witnesses were advised that they would be allowed to have their attorneys present when they read the transcripts. Dionisio and other witnesses refused to furnish the voice exemplars, asserting that these disclosures would violate their rights under the Fourth and Fifth Amendments. When Dionisio persisted in his refusal to respond to the grand jury's directive, the District Court adjudged him in civil contempt and ordered him committed to custody.

* * * Equating the procedures followed by the grand jury in the present case to the fingerprint detentions in *Davis v. Mississippi*, 394 U.S. 721 (1969) the Court of Appeals reasoned that "[t]he dragnet effect here, where approximately 30 persons were subpoenaed for purposes of identification, has the same invidious effect on fourth amendment rights as the practice condemned in *Davis*" The Court of Appeals held that the Fourth Amendment required a preliminary showing of reasonableness before a grand jury witness could be compelled to furnish a voice exemplar, and that in this case the proposed "seizures" of the voice exemplars would be unreasonable because of the large number of witnesses summoned by the grand jury and directed to produce such exemplars. We disagree.

* * * The compulsion exerted by a grand jury subpoena differs from the seizure effected by an arrest or even an investigative "stop" in more than civic obligation. For, as Judge Friendly wrote for the Court of Appeals for the Second Circuit:

> "The latter is abrupt, is effected with force or the threat of it and often in demeaning circumstances, and, in the case of arrest, results in a record involving social stigma. A subpoena is served in the same manner as other legal process; it involves no stigma whatever; if the time for appearance is inconvenient, this can generally be altered; and it remains at all times under the control and supervision of a court."

This case is thus quite different from *Davis v. Mississippi,* on which the Court of Appeals primarily relied. For in *Davis* it was the initial seizure—the lawless dragnet detention—that violated the Fourth and Fourteenth Amendments—not the taking of the fingerprints.

This is not to say that a grand jury subpoena is some talisman that dissolves all constitutional protections. The grand jury cannot require a witness to testify against himself. It cannot require the production by a person of private books and records that would incriminate him. *See Boyd v. United States*. The Fourth Amendment provides protection against a grand jury subpoena duces tecum too sweeping in its terms "to be regarded as reasonable." *Hale v. Henkel*. And last Term, in the context of a First Amendment claim, we indicated that the Constitution could not tolerate the transformation of the grand jury into an instrument of oppression: "Official harassment of the press undertaken not for purposes of law enforcement but to disrupt a reporter's relationship with his news sources would have no justification. Grand juries are subject to judicial control and subpoenas to motions to quash. We do not expect courts will forget that grand juries must operate within the limits of the First Amendment as well as the Fifth." *Branzburg v. Hayes.*

But we are here faced with no such constitutional infirmities in the subpoena to appear before the grand jury or in the order to make the voice recordings. There is no valid Fifth Amendment claim. There was no order to produce private books and papers, and no sweeping subpoena *duces tecum.* * * *

The Court of Appeals found critical significance in the fact that the grand jury had summoned approximately 20 witnesses to furnish voice exemplars. We think that fact is basically irrelevant to the constitutional issues here. The grand jury may have been attempting to identify a number of voices on the tapes in evidence, or it might have summoned the 20 witnesses in an effort to identify one voice. But whatever the case, "[a] grand jury's investigation is not fully carried out until every available clue has been run down and all witnesses examined in every proper way to find if a crime has been committed." The grand jury may well find it desirable to call numerous witnesses in the course of an investigation. It does not follow that each witness may resist a subpoena on the ground that too many witnesses have been called. Neither the order to Dionisio to appear, nor the order to make a voice recording was rendered unreasonable by the fact that many others were subjected to the same compulsion.

But the conclusion that Dionisio's compulsory appearance before the grand jury was not an unreasonable "seizure" is the answer to only the first part of the Fourth Amendment inquiry here. Dionisio argues that the grand jury's subsequent directive to make the voice recording was itself an infringement of his rights under the Fourth Amendment. We cannot accept that argument. In *Katz v. United States*, we said that the Fourth Amendment provides no protection for what "a person knowingly exposes to the public, even in his home or [office]." The physical characteristics of a person's voice, its tone and manner, as opposed to the content of a specific conversation, are constantly exposed to the public. Like a man's facial characteristics, or handwriting, his voice is repeatedly produced for others to hear. No person can have a reasonable expectation that others will not know the sound of his voice, any more than he can reasonably expect that his face will be a mystery to the world.

Since neither the summons to appear before the grand jury, nor its directive to make a voice recording infringed upon any interest protected by the Fourth Amendment, there was no justification for requiring the grand jury to satisfy even the minimal requirement of "reasonableness" imposed by the Court of Appeals. A grand jury has broad investigative powers to determine whether a crime has been committed and who has committed it. The jurors may act on tips, rumors, evidence offered by the prosecutor, or their own personal knowledge. No grand Jury witness is "entitled to set limits to the investigation that the grand jury may conduct." *Blair v. United States.* And a sufficient basis for an indictment may only emerge at the end of the investigation when all the evidence has been received. . . . Since Dionisio raised no valid Fourth Amendment claim, there is no more reason to require a preliminary showing of reasonableness here than there would be in the case of any witness who, despite the lack of any constitutional or statutory privilege, declined to answer a question or comply with a grand jury request. Neither the Constitution nor our prior cases justify any such interference with grand jury proceedings.

* * * Any holding that would saddle a grand jury with minitrials and preliminary showing would assuredly impede its investigation and frustrate the public's interest in the fair and expeditious administration of the criminal laws. The grand jury may not always serve its historic role as a protective bulwark standing solidly between the ordinary citizen and an overzealous prosecutor, but if it is even to approach the proper performance of its constitutional mission, it must be free to pursue its investigations unhindered by external influence or supervision so long as it does not trench upon the legitimate rights of any witness called before it.

The dissenting opinion of Justice Marshall is omitted.

Notes and Questions

1. In light of *Dionisio*, how would you rule on the following motion:

MOTION TO QUASH GRAND JURY SUBPOENA

1. On ____, 200_, the Movant, ____, was served with a subpoena to appear and give testimony before the grand jury of the Court of ___ on ___, 200_.

2. The appearance and testimony of Movant before the grand jury under the circumstances here presented would be in violation of the Fifth Amendment to the Constitution of the United States and the attorney-client privilege between ___ and ___, and would constitute an abuse of the grand jury process.

3. The Movant was served with the instant subpoena requiring his appearance before the grand jury on ___, 200_, and unless enforcement of the subpoena is temporarily stayed pending determination of his motion to quash said subpoena, the Movant will suffer the very legal injury he seeks to avoid.

4. If a stay is granted by this Court, the injury to the government will be de minimis in comparison to the serious and substantial injury which will be sustained by the Movant if no stay is issued.

5. The requested order to show cause is necessary because the Movant has no other relief available in time to avoid the injury which would occur if he is required to appear and testify on ___, 200_.

6. On ___, 200_, counsel for the Movant gave notice by telephone to ___, the government Attorney, who is conducting the instant grand jury proceedings on behalf of the government, of the Movant's intention to request the Court to issue a temporary stay at a hearing to be conducted in this Court on___, 200_, or as soon thereafter as counsel for Movant may be heard.

7. WHEREFORE, the Movant requests the Court to issue an order requiring the government to show cause, if any there be, why the subpoena requiring the Movant to appear and testify before the Grand Jury should not be quashed, and to stay the effect of said subpoena until the motion to quash can be heard and determined by this court.

2. In *Blair v. United States*, 250 U.S. 273 (1919) a subpoenaed witness objected to the jurisdiction of the grand jury to investigate the subject matter. The Court held that the witness "is not entitled:"

1. to urge objections of incompetency or irrelevancy,

2. to set limits to the investigation that the grand jury may conduct,

3. to take exception to the jurisdiction of the grand jury

4. to challenge the authority of the grand jury, provided it has a de facto existence and organization.

3. After *Dionisio*, can a court order a suspect to appear in a lineup at the request of the prosecutor who has not yet sought the suspect's appearance before the grand jury? *In re Melvin*, 546 F.2d 1 (1st Cir.1976) distinguished *Dionisio*, finding that the *Dionisio* order was issued only after the witnesses had appeared before a grand jury which had directed them to produce the exemplars.

4. Can a prosecutor seek an order from the trial court for a suspect to furnish a handwriting exemplar in a convoluted manner rather than in the suspect's normal writing style? *In re Layden*, 446 F.Supp. 53 (N.D.Ill.1978) found that such an order "would force the witness into the anomalous position of implicating himself accidentally by faithfully trying to comply with the order." Is a contrived handwriting sample traceable to a particular person?

2. *Fifth Amendment Rights Applicable to Testimony*

Any witness appearing before a grand jury may assert the Fifth Amendment privilege against self-incrimination, but the witness has no right to receive *Miranda* warnings.

UNITED STATES v. MANDUJANO
425 U.S. 564 (1976).

CHIEF JUSTICE BURGER announced the judgment of the Court in an opinion in which JUSTICE WHITE, JUSTICE POWELL, and JUSTICE REHNQUIST join.

This case presents the question whether the warnings called for by *Miranda v. Arizona* must be given to a grand jury witness who is called to testify about criminal activities in which he may have been personally involved; and, whether absent such warnings, false statements made to the grand jury must be suppressed in a prosecution for perjury based on those statements.

Mandujano was subpoenaed to testify before a special grand jury investigating the drug traffic in the local area. Before testifying, the prosecutor informed Mandujano of his general duty to answer, his right not to answer incriminatory questions, and of possible perjury liability for false answers. Mandujano was also told that he could have a lawyer outside the room with whom he could consult. When asked if he had a lawyer, Mandujano responded: "I don't have one. I don't have the money to get one."

During the grand jury questioning, Mandujano admitted that he had purchased heroin as recently as five months ago, but denied knowledge of the identity of any dealers, except for one street-corner source. He maintained this position notwithstanding the prosecutor's suggestion that "our information is that you can tell us more than you have today." Mandujano "steadfastly denied either selling or attempting to sell heroin since the time of his conviction 15 years before." He "specifically disclaimed having discussed the sale of heroin with anyone during the preceding year."

Mandujano subsequently was indicted for attempting to distribute heroin and for willfully and knowingly making a false material declaration to the grand jury. The prosecution sought to introduce the grand jury testimony as the basis for the false declaration charge. Mandujano argued that his grand jury testimony should be suppressed since he was not given full *Miranda* warnings prior to his testimony. The District Court sustained the motion on the ground that a "putative" or "virtual" defendant was entitled to *Miranda* warnings. The Court of Appeals affirmed.

The very availability of the Fifth Amendment privilege to grand jury witnesses suggests that occasions will often arise when potentially incriminating questions will be asked in the ordinary course of the jury's investigation. It is in keeping with the grand jury's historic function as a shield against arbitrary accusations to call before it persons suspected of criminal activity, so that the investigation can be complete. This is true whether the grand jury embarks upon an inquiry focused upon individuals suspected of wrongdoing, or is directed at persons suspected of no misconduct but who may be able to provide links in a chain of evidence relating to criminal conduct of others, or is centered upon broader problems of concern to society. It is entirely appropriate—indeed imperative—to summon individuals who may be able to illuminate the shadowy precincts of corruption and crime. Since the subject matter of the inquiry is crime, and often organized, systematic crime—as is true with drug traffic—it is unrealistic to assume that all of the witnesses capable of providing useful information will be pristine pillars of the community untainted by criminality.

Accordingly, the witness, though possibly engaged in some criminal enterprise, can be required to answer before a grand jury, so long as there is no compulsion to answer questions that are self-incriminating. * * * Absent a claim of the privilege, the duty to give testimony remains absolute.

The stage is therefore set when the question is asked. If the witness interposes his privilege, the grand jury has two choices. If the desired testimony is of marginal value, the grand jury can pursue other avenues of inquiry; if the testimony is thought sufficiently important, the grand jury can seek a judicial determination as to the bona fides of the witness' Fifth Amendment claim, in which case the witness must satisfy the presiding judge that the claim of privilege is not a subterfuge. If in fact "there is reasonable ground to apprehend danger to the witness from his being compelled to answer," the prosecutor must then determine whether the answer is of such overriding importance as to justify a grant of immunity to the witness. If immunity is sought by the prosecutor and granted by the presiding judge, the witness can then be compelled to answer, on pain of contempt, even though the testimony would implicate the witness in criminal activity. * * *

Miranda addressed extra-judicial confessions or admissions procured in a hostile, unfamiliar environment which lacked procedural safeguards. The decision expressly rested on the privilege against compulsory self-incrimination; the prescribed warnings sought to negate the "compulsion" thought to be inherent in police station interrogation. But the *Miranda* Court simply did not perceive judicial inquiries and custodial interrogation as equivalents: "the compulsion to speak in the isolated setting of the police station may well be greater than in courts or other official investigations, where there are often impartial observers to guard against intimidation or trickery."

The Court thus recognized that many official investigations, such as grand jury questioning, take place in a setting wholly different from custodial police interrogation. Indeed, the Court's opinion in *Miranda* reveals a focus on what was seen by the Court as police "coercion" derived from "factual studies [relating to] police violence and the 'third degree' physical brutality—beating, hanging, whipping—and to sustained and protracted questioning incommunicado in order to extort confessions. To extend these concepts to questioning before a grand jury inquiring into criminal activity under the guidance of a judge is an extravagant expansion never remotely contemplated by this Court in *Miranda*; the dynamics of constitutional interpretation do not compel constant extension of every doctrine announced by the Court."

* * * Under *Miranda*, a person in police custody has, of course, an absolute right to decline to answer any question, incriminating or innocuous, whereas a grand jury witness, on the contrary, has an absolute duty to answer all questions, subject only to a valid Fifth Amendment claim. And even when the grand jury witness asserts the privilege, questioning need not cease, except as to the particular subject

to which the privilege has been addressed. Other lines of inquiry may properly be pursued.

Respondent was also informed that if he desired he could have the assistance of counsel, but that counsel could not be inside the grand jury room. That statement was plainly a correct recital of the law. No criminal proceedings had been instituted against respondent, hence the Sixth Amendment right to counsel had not come into play. *Kirby v. Illinois*, 406 U.S. 682 (1972). A witness "before a grand jury cannot insist, as a matter of constitutional right, on being represented by his counsel...." *In re Groban*, 352 U.S. 330 (1957). Under settled principles the witness may not insist upon the presence of his attorney in the grand jury room. Fed.Rule Crim.Proc. 6(d).

Respondent was free at every stage to interpose his constitutional privilege against self-incrimination, but perjury was not a permissible option. The judgment of the Court of Appeals is therefore reversed.

JUSTICE BRENNAN, with whom JUSTICE MARSHALL joins, concurring in the judgment.

* * *

I would hold that, in the absence of an intentional and intelligent waiver by the individual of his known right to be free from compulsory self-incrimination, the Government may not call before a grand jury one whom it has probable cause—as measured by an objective standard—to suspect committed a crime, and by use of judicial compulsion compel him to testify with regard to that crime. In the absence of such a waiver, the Fifth Amendment requires that any testimony obtained in this fashion be unavailable to the Government for use at trial. Such a waiver could readily be demonstrated by proof that the individual was warned prior to questioning that he is currently subject to possible criminal prosecution for the commission of a stated crime, that he has a constitutional right to refuse to answer any and all questions that may tend to incriminate him, and by record evidence that the individual understood the nature of his situation and privilege prior to giving testimony. * * *

Notes and Questions

1. *United States v. Washington*, 431 U.S. 181 (1977) held that a witness need not be warned that he is a target of the grand jury investigation:

> After being sworn, respondent was explicitly advised that he had a right to remain silent and that any statements he did make could be used to convict him of crime. It is inconceivable that such a warning would fail to alert him to his right to refuse to answer any questions which might incriminate him. Even in the presumed psychologically coercive atmosphere of police custodial interrogation, *Miranda* does not require that any additional warnings be given simply because the suspect is a potential defendant; indeed, such suspects are potential defendants more

often than not. Respondent points out that unlike one subject to custodial interrogation, whose arrest should inform him only too clearly that he is a potential criminal defendant, a grand jury witness may well be unaware that he is targeted for possible prosecution. While this may be so in some situations, it is an overdrawn generalization. In any case, events here [prior questioning by the prosecutor] clearly put respondent on notice that he was a suspect in the motorcycle theft.

2.   The Supreme Court has indicated, though never explicitly held, that a witness before a grand jury has no Sixth Amendment right to be represented by counsel. *See Anonymous v. Baker*, 360 U.S. 287 (1959). Consider the following situation: You were employed to represent several witnesses who were called before a federal grand jury investigating a company's financial transactions, e.g., some of the witnesses were owners of the company, and other were employees. After designating some of the clients as targets of the investigation, the government moved to disqualify you as lawyer for the witnesses. The district court granted the motion. What action can you take to protect your clients during the grand jury proceedings? In *In re Grand Jury Investigation (Molus v. United States)*, 182 F.3d 668 (9th Cir.1999) the Ninth Circuit refused to allow the interlocutory appeal. "We see no reason why, if disqualification orders are generally unappealable in either civil or criminal proceedings, they should be appealable in the grand jury context." Besides, "whatever due process right a grand jury witness may have to the advice of counsel, it is not so broad as to encompass the right to counsel of first choice."

3.   Whatever the status of a Sixth Amendment or Due Process right to counsel at grand jury proceedings, consultation between a witness and counsel may be necessary in order that the witness may determine whether to invoke the Fifth Amendment privilege against self-incrimination in response to a particular question. In such situations, the witness has a right to consult with an attorney outside the grand jury room. Although this form of consultation is commonplace, the Supreme Court recently noted that "no decision of this Court has held that a grand jury witness has a right to have her attorney present outside the jury room." *Conn v. Gabbert*, 526 U.S. 286 (1999).

This right to consult with, but not have counsel present, often leads to almost farcical scenes where the grand jurors pose a question to a witness who then asks to be excused so that he may consult with his attorney in the hallway. The witness will repeat the question to the attorney who will advise whether the question calls for self-incrimination. The witness will return to the grand jury room, inform the grand jury of whether or not he will answer the question, and then may repeat the scenario after each question is posed. Some courts permit the witness to consult with counsel after each question, *see United States v. George*, 444 F.2d 310 (6th Cir.1971), while other courts deem this to be obstructionist tactics and limit the witness to consulting with counsel after every three or four questions. *See In re Tierney*, 465 F.2d 806 (5th Cir.1972).

4.   If defense counsel cannot be present while the client/witness testifies, and if the witness is limited to consulting with counsel only after every "three or four" questions, may counsel advise the client to claim the Fifth

Amendment in response to every question? The weakness of this approach is the possibility of a contempt citation if the privilege was not validly invoked. Can this weakness be remedied by asserting the privilege in response to every question, then following consultation with counsel (e.g. after three or four questions) the witness may return to the grand jury room and state: "Sorry about the misunderstanding, I'm now willing to answer the previous question as to which I asserted the privilege."

5. When a witness discloses any incriminating fact, she waives the Fifth Amendment privilege as to all details about that fact. *Rogers v. United States*, 340 U.S. 367 (1951). In *Rogers*, a grand jury witness testified that she was the local Communist Party treasurer. She denied having custody of other records because she had turned them over to someone else but she refused to identify that person. The Supreme Court held that once the witness had disclosed incriminating information about her activities, she could not invoke the privilege against self-incrimination to avoid disclosure of the details. However, a witness can validly claim the privilege if the answer calls for information beyond the "subject" of the prior testimony. Defense attorneys must use extreme caution when advising their clients about what questions (not) to answer during their grand jury testimony.

The issue of witness waiver arose during the early stages of the Iran–Contra investigation in the mid–1980s, when Admiral John Poindexter and Lieutenant Oliver North each invoked the Fifth Amendment in response to questions posed by members of a Congressional Committee. Admiral Poindexter's counsel noted that he did "not want it said that [his client had] waived his rights to later assert his Fifth Amendment right at another proceeding, be it before Congress or any other proceeding." *The Foreign Police Implications of Arms Sales to Iran and the Contra Connection: Hearings Before the Comm. On Foreign Affairs, House of Representatives*, 99th Cong., 2d Sess. 157, 169 (1987). *See* Leslie W. Abramson, *Witness Waiver of the Fifth Amendment Privilege: A New Look at an Old Problem*, 41 OKLA. L. REV. 235 (1988).

Exercises

1. Mary Richards, Associate Producer and Reporter for WJM–TV, reported that a local grand jury had filed a sealed report criticizing but not indicting several local government officials for their participation in a "kick-back" scheme. Ms. Richards stated that her story was based upon "inside information from a reliable source." The day after her report, Ms. Richards was subpoenaed to appear before that same grand jury to testify about the identity of her sources. As attorney for Ms. Richards, draft a motion for disclosure of the crimes the grand jury is investigating and the connection between those crimes and Ms. Richards' desired testimony. How will your motion address the holding in *Blair v. United States* that a witness may not set limits to the investigation that the grand jury may conduct, nor challenge the authority of the grand jury, provided it has a de facto existence and organization. Is it relevant whether Ms. Richards' possible breach of grand jury secrecy is a criminal offense in this jurisdiction?

2. Your client was subpoenaed to appear before a grand jury investigating an organized crime scheme to blackmail government employees who are

gay or lesbian. Your client is a suspected victim of this scheme and was asked by the grand jury whether he is gay, and whether anyone threatened to publicize this fact unless he paid "hush" money. Your client refused to answer and now faces a show cause order as to why he should not be held in contempt. What defense do you offer? Is it relevant that same gender sex acts are crimes in this jurisdiction, although no one has been prosecuted in recent times?

D. THE SUBPOENA DUCES TECUM

1. *The Reasonableness Requirement*

UNITED STATES v. R. ENTERPRISES, INC.

498 U.S. 292 (1991).

JUSTICE O'CONNOR delivered the opinion of the Court.

This case requires the Court to decide what standards apply when a party seeks to avoid compliance with a subpoena duces tecum issued in connection with a Grand Jury investigation.

Since 1986, a federal grand jury sitting in the Eastern District of Virginia has been investigating allegations of interstate transportation of obscene materials. In early 1988, the grand jury issued a series of subpoenas to three companies—Model Magazine Distributors, Inc. (Model), R. Enterprises, Inc., and MFR Court Street Books, Inc. (MFR). Model is a New York distributor of sexually oriented paperback books, magazines, and videotapes. R. Enterprises, which distributes adult materials, and MFR, which sells books, magazines, and videotapes, are also based in New York. All three companies are wholly owned by Martin Rothstein. The grand jury subpoenas sought a variety of corporate books and records and, in Model's case, copies of 193 videotapes that Model had shipped to retailers in the Eastern District of Virginia. All three companies moved to quash the subpoenas, arguing that the subpoenas called for production of materials irrelevant to the grand jury's investigation and that the enforcement of the subpoenas would likely infringe their First Amendment rights.

The District Court, after extensive hearings, denied the motions to quash. As to Model, the court found that the subpoenas for business records were sufficiently specific and that production of the videotapes would not constitute a prior restraint. As to R. Enterprises, the court found a "sufficient connection with Virginia for further investigation by the grand jury." The court relied in large part on the statement attributed to Rothstein that the three companies were "all the same thing, I'm president of all three." Additionally, the court explained in denying MFR's motion to quash that it was "inclined to agree" with "the majority of the jurisdictions," which do not require the Government to make a "threshold showing" before a grand jury subpoena will be enforced. Even assuming that a preliminary showing of relevance was required, the court determined that the Government had made such a showing. It found sufficient evidence that the companies were "related entities," at least one of which "certainly did ship sexually explicit material into the Commonwealth of Virginia." Notwithstanding these findings, the companies refused to comply with the subpoenas. The District Court found each in contempt and fined them $500 per day, but stayed imposition of the fine pending appeal.

The Court of Appeals for the Fourth Circuit upheld the business records subpoenas issued to Model, but remanded the motion to quash the subpoena for Model's videotapes. Of particular relevance here, the Court of Appeals quashed the business records subpoenas issued to R. Enterprises and MFR. In doing so, it applied the standards set out by this Court in *United States v. Nixon,* 418 U.S. 683 (1974). The court recognized that *Nixon* dealt with a trial subpoena, not a grand jury subpoena, but determined that the rule was "equally applicable" in the grand jury context. Accordingly, it required the Government to clear the three hurdles that *Nixon* established in the trial context—relevancy, admissibility, and specificity—in order to enforce the grand jury subpoenas. * * *

We granted certiorari to determine whether the Court of Appeals applied the proper standard in evaluating the grand jury subpoenas issued to respondents. We now reverse.

The grand jury occupies a unique role in our criminal justice system. [It] "can investigate merely on suspicion that the law is being violated, or even just because it wants assurance that it is not." As a necessary consequence of its investigatory function, the grand jury paints with a broad brush. A grand jury subpoena is thus much different from a subpoena issued in the context of a prospective criminal trial, where a specific offense has been identified and a particular defendant charged.

This Court has emphasized on numerous occasions that many of the rules and restrictions that apply at a trial do not apply in grand jury proceedings. This is especially true of evidentiary restrictions. The same rules that, in an adversary hearing on the merits may increase the likelihood of accurate determinations of guilt or innocence do not necessarily advance the mission of a grand jury, whose task is to conduct an *ex parte* investigation to determine whether or not there is probable cause to prosecute a particular defendant. The teaching of the Court's decisions is clear: A grand jury "may compel the production of evidence or the testimony of witnesses as it considers appropriate, and its operation generally is unrestrained by the technical procedural and evidentiary rules governing the conduct of criminal trials." *United States v. Calandra.*

This guiding principle renders suspect the Court of Appeals' holding that the standards announced in *Nixon* as to subpoenas issued in anticipation of trial apply equally in the grand jury context. The multifactor test announced in *Nixon* would invite procedural delays and detours while courts evaluate the relevancy and admissibility of documents sought by a particular subpoena. We have expressly stated that grand jury proceedings should be free of such delays. *United States v. Dionisio*. Additionally, application of the *Nixon* test in this context ignores that grand jury proceedings are subject to strict secrecy requirements. *See* Fed.Rule Crim.Proc. 6(e). Requiring the Government to explain in too much detail the particular reasons underlying a subpoena threatens to compromise "the indispensable secrecy of grand jury proceedings." Broad disclosure also affords the targets of investigation far more information about the grand jury's internal workings than the Federal Rules of Criminal Procedure appear to contemplate.

The investigatory powers of the grand jury are nevertheless not unlimited. Grand juries are not licensed to engage in arbitrary fishing expeditions, nor may they select targets of investigation out of malice or an intent to harass. In this case, the focus of our inquiry is the limit imposed on a grand jury by Federal Rule of Criminal Procedure 17(c), which governs the issuance of subpoenas *duces tecum* in federal criminal proceedings. The Rule provides that "the court on motion made promptly may quash or modify the subpoena if compliance would be unreasonable or oppressive."

This standard is not self-explanatory. As we have observed, "what is reasonable depends on the context." * * * In the grand jury context, the decision as to what offense will be charged is routinely not made until after the grand jury has concluded its investigation. One simply cannot know in advance whether information sought during the investigation will be relevant and admissible in a prosecution for a particular offense.

To the extent that Rule 17(c) imposes some reasonableness limitation on grand jury subpoenas, however, our task is to define it. In doing so, we recognize that a party to whom a grand jury subpoena is issued faces a difficult situation. As a rule, grand juries do not announce publicly the subjects of their investigations. A party who desires to challenge a grand jury subpoena thus may have no conception of the Government's purpose in seeking production of the requested information. Indeed, the party will often not know whether he or she is a primary target of the investigation or merely a peripheral witness. Absent even minimal information, the subpoena recipient is likely to find it exceedingly difficult to persuade a court that "compliance would be unreasonable." * * *

Our task is to fashion an appropriate standard of reasonableness, one that gives due weight to the difficult position of subpoena recipients but does not impair the strong governmental interests in affording grand juries wide latitude, avoiding minitrials on peripheral matters, and preserving a necessary level of secrecy. We begin by reiterating that the law presumes, absent a strong showing to the contrary, that a grand jury acts within the legitimate scope of its authority. Consequently, a grand jury subpoena issued through normal channels is presumed to be reasonable, and the burden of showing unreasonableness must be on the recipient who seeks to avoid compliance. Indeed, this result is indicated by the language of Federal Rule 17(c), which permits a subpoena to be quashed only "on motion" and "if *compliance* would be unreasonable" (emphasis added). To the extent that the Court of Appeals placed an initial burden on the Government, it committed error. Drawing on the principles articulated above, we conclude that where, as here, a subpoena is challenged on relevancy grounds, the motion to quash must be denied unless the district court determines that there is no reasonable possibility that the category of materials the Government seeks will produce information relevant to the general subject of the grand jury's investigation. Respondents did not challenge the subpoenas as being too indefinite nor did they claim that compliance would be overly burdensome. The Court of Appeals accordingly did not consider these aspects of the subpoenas, nor do we.

* * * [A] court may be justified in a case where unreasonableness is alleged in requiring the Government to reveal the general subject of the grand jury's investigation before requiring the challenging party to carry its burden of persuasion. We need not resolve this question in the present case, however, as there is no doubt that respondents knew the subject of the grand jury investigation pursuant to which the business records subpoenas were issued. In cases where the recipient of the subpoena does not know the nature of the investigation, we are confident that district courts will be able to craft appropriate procedures that balance the interests of the subpoena recipient against the strong governmental interests in maintaining secrecy, preserving investigatory flexibility, and avoiding procedural delays. For example, to ensure that subpoenas are not routinely challenged as a form of discovery, a district court may require that the Government reveal the subject of the investigation to the trial court *in camera*, so that the court may determine whether the motion to quash has a reasonable prospect for success before it discloses the subject matter to the challenging party.

Applying these principles in this case demonstrates that the District Court correctly denied respondents' motions to quash. It is undisputed that all three companies—Model, R. Enterprises, and MFR—are owned by the same person, that all do business in the same area, and that one of the three, Model, has shipped sexually explicit materials into the Eastern District of Virginia. The District Court could have concluded from these facts that there was a reasonable possibility that the business records of R. Enterprises and MFR would produce information relevant to the grand jury's investigation into the interstate transportation of obscene materials. Respondents' blanket denial of any connection to Virginia did not suffice to render the District Court's conclusion invalid. A grand jury need not accept on faith the self-serving assertions of those who may have committed criminal acts. Rather, it is entitled to determine for itself whether a crime has been committed. * * *

Problems

1. The FBI is investigating the drug trafficking activities of a large-scale cocaine distribution organization involving your client. The client filed

an affidavit of indigence with the Drug Enforcement Administration in support of his claim to contest the forfeiture of his automobile. The government obtained a grand jury subpoena duces tecum which directed your Law Firm to produce:

> Any and all documents and records concerning the payment of any moneys by, or on behalf of, the client, but not limited to, receipts, fee records, bank deposits and monetary instruments.

What motion would you file and how should the Court rule? Would it matter whether the grand jury had already returned an indictment against your client when the subpoena issued? *United States v. Crosland*, 821 F.Supp. 1123 (E.D.Va.1993) quashed such a subpoena on grounds that it constituted the type of discovery-oriented document that amounted to a mere "fishing expedition." The Court stated:

> This matter calls upon the Court to resolve questions concerning the scope of the government's subpoena powers, both in the trial and the grand jury contexts. The issues presented are particularly important given the role of the courts in maintaining the proper, delicate balance between the vital need, on the one hand, to provide the government with the means to ferret out and prosecute crime and, on the other hand, the equally vital need to protect individuals from unwarranted interference with their right to defend themselves against accusations of criminal activity. Essential in maintaining this balance is ensuring the government's strict adherence to prescribed procedures when exercising its subpoena powers.

2.   A large wholesale bookseller allegedly overcharged institutional customers, including federally funded libraries, in violation of the civil provisions of the False Claims Act. The federal government conducted an investigation to determine whether to intervene in the civil action. At the same time, the Justice Department commenced a criminal investigation to determine if the bookseller violated any federal criminal statutes. Officials working on the civil case intermittently met with their counterparts on the criminal case. When discovery in the civil case was stayed, the government sought a criminal subpoena for the bookseller's records. May the government use a criminal subpoena for the purpose of obtaining discovery for a pending civil proceeding? Government prosecutors are barred, absent judicial approval, from sharing grand jury material with government civil attorneys. *See* Fed. R. Crim. P. 6(e)(2); *United States v. Sells Eng'g, Inc.*, 463 U.S. 418 (1983). *In re Grand Jury Subpoena*, 175 F.3d 332 (4th Cir.1999) held that:

> A subpoena will ordinarily issue whenever there is a "reasonable possibility that the category of material the Government seeks will produce information relevant to the general subject of the grand jury's investigation." When such a showing of relevance can be made, a subpoena will issue even if the subpoena is also being sought for another, illegitimate purpose. A subpoena should therefore only be quashed when the illegitimate purpose is the "sole or dominant purpose of seeking the evidence."

The court also noted that "in a case in which relevant information was being sought, but in which the information was nevertheless subsequently provid-

ed to civil attorneys, the proper redress would be sanction for contempt."
See Fed. R. Crim. P. 6(e)(2) (in the statutory supplement).

2. Self-incrimination by Compliance With Subpoena Duces Tecum

The Fifth Amendment applies when three conditions are met: (1) the government seeks to "compel" compliance with its demand that the defendant produce documents or tangible items; (2) the compelled material is "testimonial" in nature; and (3) the material "incriminates" the person required to produce it. The requirement that the compelled material be "testimonial" in nature has led the Court to distinguish between the creation of and production of the document. When the government seeks documents previously created by the defendant, the act of creation is deemed to have been voluntary, not compelled. The act of producing the voluntarily created documents, however, may be "testimonial" if the act establishes incriminating aspects unrelated to the contents of the document. For example, the act of production may establish the existence of the documents; the defendant's control over the documents; or may constitute authentication of the documents.

UNITED STATES v. DOE

465 U.S. 605 (1984).

JUSTICE POWELL delivered the opinion of the Court.

This case presents the issue whether, and to what extent, the Fifth Amendment privilege against compelled self-incrimination applies to the business records of a sole proprietorship.

Respondent, the owner of several sole proprietorships objected to a series of subpoenas directing him to produce business records, including billings, ledgers, canceled checks, telephone records, contracts, and paid bills. The district court sustained the respondent's Fifth Amendment challenge, noting that the act of producing the documents had "communicative aspects" which could prove incriminating since the respondent would thereby be required to "admit that the records exist, that they are in his possession, and that they are authentic." On appeal, the Third Circuit agreed with the district court.

We granted certiorari to resolve the apparent conflict between the Court of Appeals holding and the reasoning underlying this Court's holding in *Fisher v. United States*, 425 U.S. 391 (1976). We now affirm in part, reverse in part, and remand for further proceedings.

The Court in *Fisher* expressly declined to reach the question whether the Fifth Amendment privilege protects the contents of an individual's tax records in his possession. The rationale underlying our holding in that case is, however, persuasive here. As we noted in *Fisher*, the Fifth Amendment only protects the person asserting the privilege only from *compelled* self-incrimination. Where the preparation of business records is voluntary, no compulsion is present. A subpoena that demands production of documents "does not compel oral testimony; nor would it ordinarily compel the taxpayer to restate, repeat, or affirm the truth of the contents of the documents sought." This reasoning applies with equal force here. Respondent does not contend that he prepared the documents involuntarily or that the subpoena would force him to re-state, repeat, or affirm the truth of their contents. The fact that the records are in respondent's possession is irrelevant to the determination of whether the creation of the records was compelled. We therefore hold that the contents of those records are not privileged.

Although the contents of a document may not be privileged, the act of producing the document may be. A government subpoena compels the holder of the document to perform an act that may have testimonial aspects and an incriminating effect. In *Fisher*, the Court explored the effect that the act of production would have on the taxpayer [there] and determined that the act of production would have only minimal testimo-nial value and would not operate to incriminate the taxpayer. Unlike the Court in *Fisher,* we have the explicit finding of the District Court that the act of producing the documents would involve testimonial self-incrimination. The Court of Appeals agreed. The District Court's finding essentially rests on its determination of factual issues. Therefore, we will not overturn that finding unless it has no support in the record.

We conclude that the Court of Appeals erred in holding that the contents of the subpoenaed documents were privileged under the Fifth Amendment. The act of producing the documents at issue in this case is privileged and cannot be compelled without a statutory grant of use immunity pursuant to 18 U.S.C. §§ 6002 and 6003. The judgment of the Court of Appeals is, therefore, affirmed in part, reversed in part, and the case is remanded to the District Court for further proceedings in accordance with this decision.

JUSTICE O'CONNOR, concurring.

I concur in both the result and reasoning of Justice Powell's opinion for the Court. I write separately, however, just to make explicit what is implicit in the analysis of that opinion: that the Fifth Amendment provides absolutely no protection for the contents of private papers of any kind. The notion that the Fifth Amendment protects the privacy of papers originated in *Boyd v. United States,* but our decision in *Fisher v. United States,* sounded the death-knell for *Boyd.* "Several of Boyd's express or implicit declarations [had] not stood the test of time," *Fisher,* and its privacy of papers concept "had long been a rule searching for a [rationale]. Today's decision puts a long-overdue end to that fruitless search."

JUSTICE MARSHALL, with whom JUSTICE BRENNAN joins, concurring in part and dissenting in part.

Contrary to what Justice O'Connor contends, I do not view the Court's opinion in this case as having reconsidered whether the Fifth Amendment provides protection for the contents of "private papers of any kind." * * * I would assuredly dissent. I continue to believe that under the Fifth Amendment "there are certain documents no person ought to be compelled to produce at the Government's request."

DOE v. UNITED STATES

487 U.S. 201 (1988).

JUSTICE BLACKMUN delivered the opinion of the Court.

This case presents the question whether a court order compelling a target of a grand jury investigation to authorize foreign banks to disclose records of his accounts, without identifying those documents or acknowledging their existence, violates the target's Fifth Amendment privilege against self-incrimination.

Appearing before the grand jury pursuant to subpoena directing him to produce records of transactions in accounts at three named banks in the Cayman Islands and Bermuda, petitioner produced some of the records and testified that no additional records were within his possession. When questioned about the existence of additional records, he invoked the Fifth Amendment privilege against self-incrimination. Grand jury subpoenas then were issued to United States branches of each of the banks, but the banks refused to comply because their governments' laws prohibited disclosure of account records without the customer's consent. The prosecution then filed a motion with the district court requesting that petitioner be ordered to sign forms stating that he was "directing any bank at which I may have a bank account of any kind or at which a corporation has a bank account of any kind upon which I am authorized to draw" to deliver records of those accounts to the grand jury. The form specifically noted that petitioner's directive was being made pursuant to court order, and that the directive was intended to provide compliance with the bank secrecy laws of the Cayman Islands and Bermuda. Petitioner refused to sign the consent directive on self-incrimination grounds, and after being held in contempt, sought appellate review. The Court of Appeals affirmed the contempt order.

Petitioner's sole claim is that his execution of the consent forms directing the banks to release records as to which the banks believe he has the right of withdrawal has independent testimonial significance that will incriminate him, and that the Fifth Amendment prohibits governmental compulsion of that act. The question on which this case turns is whether the act of executing the form is a "testimonial communication." The parties disagree about both the meaning of "testimonial" and whether the consent directive fits the proposed definitions.

Petitioner contends that a compelled statement is testimonial if the Government could use the content of the speech or writing, as opposed to its physical characteristics, to further a criminal investigation of the witness. The second half of petitioner's "testimonial" test is that the statement must be incriminating, which is, of course, already a separate requirement for invoking the privilege. Thus, Doe contends, in essence, that every written and oral statement significant for its content is necessarily testimonial for purposes of the Fifth Amendment. Under this view, the consent directive is testimonial because it is a declarative statement of consent made by Doe to the foreign banks, a statement that the Government will use to persuade the banks to produce potentially incriminating account records that would otherwise be unavailable to the grand jury. * * *

While the Court in *Fisher* and *Doe* did not purport to announce a universal test for determining the scope of the privilege, it also did not purport to establish a more narrow boundary applicable to acts alone. To the contrary, the Court applied basic Fifth Amendment principles. An examination of the Court's application of these principles in other cases indicates the Court's recognition that, in order to be testimonial, an accused's communication must itself, explicitly or implicitly, relate a factual assertion or disclose information. Only then is a person compelled to be a "witness" against himself.

This understanding is perhaps most clearly revealed in those cases in which the Court has held that certain acts, though incriminating, are not within the privilege. Thus, a suspect may be compelled to furnish a blood sample, to provide a handwriting exemplar or a voice exemplar, to stand in a lineup, and to wear particular clothing. These decisions are grounded on the proposition that "the privilege protects an accused only from being compelled to testify against himself, or otherwise provide the State with evidence of a testimonial or communicative nature." *Schmerber v. California.* It is the "extortion of information from the accused," the attempt to force him "to disclose the contents of his own mind," that implicates the Self–Incrimination Clause. "Unless some attempt is made to secure a communication—written, oral or otherwise—upon which reliance is to be placed as involving [the accused's] consciousness of the facts and the operations of his mind in expressing it, the demand made upon him is not a testimonial one."

It is consistent with the history of and the policies underlying the Self–Incrimination Clause to hold that the privilege may be asserted only to resist compelled explicit or implicit disclosures of incriminating information. Historically, the privilege was intended to prevent the use of legal compulsion to extract from the accused a sworn communication of facts which would incriminate him. Such was the process of the ecclesiastical courts and the Star Chamber—the inquisitorial method of putting the accused upon his oath and compelling him to answer questions designed to uncover uncharged offenses, without evidence from another source. The major thrust of the policies undergirding the privilege is to prevent such compulsion. The Court in *Murphy v. Waterfront Comm'n* explained that the privilege is founded on:

> [1] our unwillingness to subject those suspected of crime to the cruel trilemma of self-accusation, perjury or contempt; [2] our preference for an accusatorial rather than an inquisitorial system of criminal justice; [3] our fear that self-incriminating statements will be elicited by inhumane treatment and abuses; [4] our sense of fair

play which dictates "a fair state-individual balance by requiring the government to leave the individual alone until good cause is shown for disturbing him and by requiring the government in its contest with the individual to shoulder the entire load," . . .; [5] our respect for the inviolability of the human personality and of the right of each individual "to a private enclave where he may lead a private life," . . .; [6] our distrust of self-deprecatory statements; and [7] our realization that the privilege, while sometimes "a shelter to the guilty," is often "a protection to the innocent."

These policies are served when the privilege is asserted to spare the accused from having to reveal, directly or indirectly, his knowledge of facts relating him to the offense or from having to share his thoughts and beliefs with the Government.

We are not persuaded by petitioner's arguments that our articulation of the privilege fundamentally alters the power of the Government to compel an accused to assist in his prosecution. There are very few instances in which a verbal statement, either oral or written, will not convey information or assert facts. The vast majority of verbal statements thus will be testimonial and, to that extent at least, will fall within the privilege. Furthermore, it should be remembered that there are many restrictions on the Government's prosecutorial practices in addition to the Self–Incrimination Clause. Indeed, there are other protections against governmental efforts to compel an unwilling suspect to cooperate in an investigation, including efforts to obtain information from him. We are confident that these provisions, together with the Self–Incrimination Clause, will continue to prevent abusive investigative techniques.

We turn, then, to consider whether Doe's execution of the consent directive at issue here would have testimonial significance. We agree with the Court of Appeals that it would not, because neither the form, nor its execution, communicates any factual assertions, implicit or explicit, or conveys any information to the Government.

The consent directive itself is not "testimonial." It is carefully drafted not to make reference to a specific account, but only to speak in the hypothetical. Thus, the form does not acknowledge that an account in a foreign financial institution is in existence or that it is controlled by petitioner. Nor does the form indicate whether documents or any other information relating to petitioner are present at the foreign bank, assuming that such an account does exist. The form does not even identify the relevant bank. Although the executed form allows the Government access to a potential source of evidence, the directive itself does not point the Government toward hidden accounts or otherwise provide information that will assist the prosecution in uncovering evidence. The Government must locate that evidence "by the independent labor of its officers." As in *Fisher,* the Government is not relying upon the " 'truthtelling' " of Doe's directive to show the existence of, or his control over, foreign bank account records.

Given the consent directive's phraseology, petitioner's compelled act of executing the form has no testimonial significance either. By signing the form, Doe makes no statement, explicit or implicit, regarding the existence of a foreign bank account or his control over any such account. Nor would his execution of the form admit the authenticity of any records produced by the bank. Not only does the directive express no view on the issue, but because petitioner did not prepare the document, any statement by Doe to the effect that it is authentic would not establish that the records are genuine. Authentication evidence would have to be provided by bank officials. * * *

We read the directive as equivalent to a statement by Doe that, although he expresses no opinion about the existence of, or his control over, any such account, he is authorizing the bank to disclose information relating to accounts over which, in the bank's opinion, Doe can exercise the right of withdrawal. When forwarded to the bank along with a subpoena, the executed directive, if effective under local law, will simply make it possible for the recipient bank to comply with the Government's request to produce such records. As a result, if the Government obtains bank records after Doe signs the directive, the only factual statement made by anyone will be the *bank's* implicit declaration, by its act of production in response to the subpoena, that it believes the accounts to be petitioners's. *Cf. Fisher.* The fact that the bank's customer has directed the disclosure of his records "would say nothing about the correctness of the bank's representations." Indeed, the Second and Eleventh Circuits have concluded that consent directives virtually identical to the one here are inadmissible as an admission by the signator of either control or existence.

JUSTICE STEVENS, dissenting.

A defendant can be compelled to produce material evidence that is incriminating. Fingerprints, blood samples, voice exemplars, handwriting s specimens or other items of physical evidence may be extracted from a defendant against his will. But can he be compelled to use his mind to assist the prosecution in convicting him of a crime? I think not. He may in some cases be forced to surrender a key to a strong box containing incriminating documents, but I do not believe he can be compelled to reveal the combination to his wall safe—by word or deed.

The document the Government seeks to extract from John Doe purports to order third parties to take action that will lead to the discovery of incriminating evidence. The directive itself may not betray any knowledge petitioner may have about the circumstances of the offenses being investigated by the Grand Jury, but it nevertheless purports to evidence a reasoned decision by Doe to authorize action by others. The forced execution of this document differs from the forced production of physical evidence just as human beings differ from other animals.

If John Doe can be compelled to use his mind to assist the Government in developing its case, I think he will be forced "to be a witness against himself." The fundamental purpose of the Fifth Amendment was to mark the line between the kind of inquisition conducted by the Star Chamber and what we proudly describe as our accusatorial system of justice. It reflects "our respect for the inviolability of the human personality." In my opinion that protection gives John Doe the right to refuse to sign the directive authorizing access to the records of any bank account that he may control. Accordingly, I respectfully dissent.

Notes and Questions

1. What is the basis for Justice Stevens' distinction between what he concedes is permissible—forcing the defendant "to surrender a key to a strong box containing incriminating documents—and what he considers impermissible—compelling the defendant 'to reveal the combination to his wall safe by word or deed?' Does it matter if the combination to the safe has been memorized (and must be disclosed by the defendant's verbal statement) or if the combination was written on a piece of paper which the defendant is ordered to physically surrender to the government? Is there a meaningful distinction between a physical act (deemed non-testimonial) and a mental process (deemed testimonial)?"

Consider *Pennsylvania v. Muniz*, 496 U.S. 582 (1990) where the Court dealt with the Fifth Amendment's application to a videotape of the defendant's inability to perform sobriety tests and to remember the date of his sixth birthday. The majority held that: (1) the sobriety tests were admissible because "any slurring of speech and other evidence of lack of muscular coordination ... constitute nontestimonial components of those responses. Requiring a suspect to reveal the physical manner in which he articulated words, like requiring him to reveal the physical properties of the sound produced by his voice, *see Dionisio*, does not, without more, compel him to provide a 'testimonial' response for purpose of the privilege." (2) "In contrast, the sixth birthday question in this case required a testimonial response."

The dissent maintained that the sixth birthday question did not call for a testimonial response because the question was designed to test how well the defendant was able to do "a simple mathematical exercise. [The majority concedes that the defendant can be] required to perform a 'horizontal gaze nystagmus' test, the 'walk and turn' test, and the 'one leg stand' test, all of which are designed to test a suspect's physical coordination. If the police may require Muniz to use his body in order to demonstrate the level of his physical coordination, there is no reason why they should not be able to require him to speak or write in order to determine his mental coordination." *I.e.*, " 'the physiological functioning of Muniz's brain,' which is every bit as 'real or physical' as the physiological makeup of his blood and the timbre of his voice."

2. How would the Supreme Court deal with the following court orders to a defendant:

A. Tell us what is on the computer disk you prepared on September 1.

B. Surrender the disk to the U. S. Attorney.

C. Surrender the password and code used to encrypt the disk.

3. Because they are not regarded as persons, collective entities such as corporations, partnerships, and labor unions have no Fifth Amendment privilege against self-incrimination. In *Braswell v. United States*, 487 U.S. 99 (1988), the Supreme Court held that the custodian of records of a collective entity cannot resist a subpoena for entity records by claiming the privilege against self-incrimination on behalf of the corporation. The corporate custodian has no privilege as to the corporate records, even though the act of production may be personally incriminating.

Because the Court had used a fiction, i.e., the corporate employee acts only on as an agent when asked to produce corporate documents in response to a subpoena, the Court addressed the issue of personal incrimination for the custodian. To insure that the compelled act does not violate the custodian's personal Fifth Amendment privilege, the Court stated that the government cannot disclose to the jury who produced the documents. If the jury is not told that the custodian produced the records, the act of production by the custodian merely implies possession and authentication by the corporation but not by the custodian. Therefore, production of the corporate documents is not incriminating to the custodian. Although statutory immunity is irrelevant because the custodian has no ;privilege as to the documents of the corporation, the government may still prove that the documents came from the custodian's organization, and in turn permits the jury to infer that the custodian knew about the documents.

4. *Braswell* stated that "the custodian's act of production is not deemed a personal act, but rather an act of the corporation." Does the former employee of an entity have different rights from the current employee-custodian of corporate records? The cases are split. One line of cases emphasizes that when the employment relationship ends, a former employee is acting only in a personal capacity rather than as the entity's agent and therefore *Braswell* no longer applies. See, e.g., *In re Three Grand Jury Subpoenas*, 191 F.3d 173, 180–81 (2d Cir.1999). The other line of cases follows *Braswell* by focusing on the status of the documents as that of the corporation, no matter who possesses them. See, e.g., *In re Grand Jury Subpoena*, 957 F.2d 807, 810–13 (D.C.Cir.1991).

5. Under *Braswell*, can the custodian avoid turning over corporate records if he is the sole employee and officer of the corporation? At one point in *Braswell*, the Court stated that the Fifth Amendment is never implicated "regardless of how small the corporation maybe." 487 U.S. at 108. Later, the Court noted the potential that a jury would "inevitably conclude that a [corporation's sole owner] produced the records." 487 U.S. at 118, n. 11. Despite the likely accuracy of the latter observation, court have applied *Braswell* to the one-person entity. See, e.g., *United States v. Milligan*, 371 F.Supp.2d 1127 (D.Ariz.2005).

6. *Fisher* and *Doe*'s "act-of-production doctrine" requires the Court to distinguish between the mental and physical aspects of a person's response to a subpoena duces tecum. Can this sometimes

hairsplitting distinction be replaced by the dissent's suggested reexamination of the doctrine in *United States v. Hubbell*, which addressed whether the prosecution can use the contents of a document pursuant to a grant of immunity?

UNITED STATES v. HUBBELL

530 U.S. 27 (2000).

Justice Stevens delivered the opinion of the Court.

The two questions presented concern the scope of a witness' protection against compelled self-incrimination: (1) whether the Fifth Amendment privilege protects a witness from being compelled to disclose the existence of incriminating documents that the Government is unable to describe with reasonable particularity; and (2) if the witness produces such documents pursuant to a grant of immunity, whether 18 U.S.C. § 6002 prevents the Government from using them to prepare criminal charges against him.

This proceeding arises out of the second prosecution of respondent, Webster Hubbell, commenced by the Independent Counsel appointed in August 1994 to investigate possible violations of federal law relating to the Whitewater Development Corporation. The first prosecution was terminated pursuant to a plea bargain. In December 1994, respondent pleaded guilty to charges of mail fraud and tax evasion arising out of his billing practices as a member of an Arkansas law firm from 1989 to 1992, and was sentenced to 21 months in prison. In the plea agreement, respondent promised to provide the Independent Counsel with "full, complete, accurate, and truthful information" about matters relating to the Whitewater investigation.

The second prosecution resulted from the Independent Counsel's attempt to determine whether respondent had violated that promise. In October 1996, while respondent was incarcerated, the Independent Counsel served him with a subpoena duces tecum calling for the production of 11 categories of documents before a grand jury sitting in Little Rock, Arkansas. *See* Appendix, *infra*.[a] On November 19, he appeared before the grand jury and invoked his Fifth Amendment privilege against

---

a. The Subpoena Rider in the Appendix to the majority opinion identified eleven categories of documents in paragraphs A–K: "A. Any and all documents reflecting, referring, or relating to any direct or indirect sources of money or other things of value receive by or provided to Webster Hubbell, his wife, or children from January 1, 1993 to the present, including but not limited to the identity of employers or clients of legal or any other type of work. B. Any and all documents reflecting, referring, or relating to any direct or indirect sources of money or other things of value received by or provided to Webster Hubbell, his wife, or children from January 1, 1993 to the present, including but not limited to billing memoranda, draft statements, bills, final statements, and/or bills for work performed or time billed from January 1, 1993 to the present. C. Copies of all bank records of Webster Hubbell, his wife, or children for all accounts from January 1, 1993 to the present, including but not limited to all statements, registers and ledgers, cancelled checks, deposit items, and wire transfers. D. Any and all documents reflecting, referring, or relating to time worked or billed by Webster Hubbell from January 1, 1993 to the present, including but not limited to original time sheets, books, notes, papers, and/or computer records. E. Any and all documents reflecting, referring, or relating

self-incrimination. In response to questioning by the prosecutor, respondent initially refused "to state whether there are documents within my possession, custody, or control responsive to the Subpoena." Thereafter, the prosecutor produced an order, which had previously been obtained from the District Court pursuant to 18 U.S.C. § 6003(a), directing him to respond to the subpoena and granting him immunity "to the extent allowed by law." Respondent then produced 13,120 pages of documents and records and responded to a series of questions that established that those were all of the documents in his custody or control that were responsive to the commands in the subpoena, with the exception of a few documents he claimed were shielded by the attorney-client and attorney work-product privileges.

to expenses incurred by and/or disbursements of money by Webster Hubbell during the course of any work performed or to be performed by Mr. Hubbell from January 1, 1993 to the present. F. Any and all documents reflecting, referring, or relating to Webster Hubbell's schedule of activities, including but not limited to any and all calendars, day-timers, time books, appointment books, diaries, records of reverse telephone toll calls, credit card calls, telephone message slips, logs, other telephone records, minutes, databases, electronic mail messages, travel records, itineraries, tickets for transportation of any kind, payments, bills, expense backup documentation, schedules, and/or any other document or database that would disclose Webster Hubbell's activities from January 1, 1993 to the present. G. Any and all documents reflecting, referring, or relating to any retainer agreements or contracts for employment of Webster Hubbell, his wife, or his children from January 1, 1993 to the present. H. Any and all tax returns and tax return information, including but not limited to all W–2s, form 1099s, schedules, draft returns, work papers, and backup documents filed, created or held by or on behalf of Webster Hubbell, his wife, his children, and/or any business in which he, his wife, or his children holds or has held an interest, for the tax years 1993 to the present. I. Any and all documents reflecting, referring, or relating to work performed or to be performed or on behalf of the City of Los Angeles, California, the Los Angeles Department of Airports or any other Los Angeles municipal Governmental entity, Mary Leslie, and/or Alan S. Arkatov, including but not limited to correspondence, retainer agreements, contracts, time sheets, appointment calendars, activity calendars, diaries, billing statements, billing memoranda, telephone records, telephone message slips, telephone credit card statements, itineraries, tickets for transportation, payment records, ex-

pense receipts, ledgers, check registers, notes, memoranda, electronic mail, bank deposit items, cashier's checks, traveler's checks, wire transfer records and/or other records of financial transactions. J. Any and all documents reflecting, referring, or relating to work performed or to be performed by Webster Hubbell, his wife, or his children on the recommendation, counsel or other influence of Mary Leslie and/or Alan S. Arkatov, including but not limited to correspondence, retainer agreements, contracts, time sheets, appointment calendars, activity calendars, diaries, billing statements, billing memoranda, telephone records, telephone message slips, telephone credit card statements, itineraries, tickets for transportation, payment records, expense receipts, ledgers, check registers, notes, memoranda, electronic mail, bank deposit items, cashier's checks, traveler's checks, wire transfer records and/or other records of financial transactions. K. Any and all documents related to work performed or to be performed for or on behalf of Lippo Ltd. (formerly Public Finance (H.K.) Ltd.), the Lippo Group, the Lippo Bank, Mochtar Riady, James Riady, Stephen Riady, John Luen Wai Lee, John Huang, Mark W. Grobmyer, C. Joseph Giroir, Jr., or any affiliate, subsidiary, or corporation owned or controlled by or related to the aforementioned entities or individuals, including but not limited to correspondence, retainer agreements, contracts, time sheets, appointment calendars, activity calendars, diaries, billing statements, billing memoranda, telephone records, telephone message slips, telephone credit card statements, itineraries, tickets for transportation, payment records, expense receipts, ledgers, check registers, notes, memoranda, electronic mail, bank deposit items, cashier's checks, traveler's checks, wire transfer records and/or other records of financial transactions."

The contents of the documents produced by respondent provided the Independent Counsel with the information that led to this second prosecution. On April 30, 1998, a grand jury in the District of Columbia returned a 10–count indictment charging respondent with various tax-related crimes and mail and wire fraud. The District Court dismissed the indictment relying, in part, on the ground that the Independent Counsel's use of the subpoenaed documents violated § 6002 because all of the evidence he would offer against respondent at trial derived either directly or indirectly from the testimonial aspects of respondent's immunized act of producing those documents. Noting that the Independent Counsel had admitted that he was not investigating tax-related issues when he issued the subpoena, and that he had " 'learned about the unreported income and other crimes from studying the records' contents, 'the District Court characterized the subpoena as "the quintessential fishing expedition." ' "

The Court of Appeals vacated the judgment and remanded for further proceedings. The majority concluded that the District Court had incorrectly relied on the fact that the Independent Counsel did not have prior knowledge of the contents of the subpoenaed documents. The question the District Court should have addressed was the extent of the Government's independent knowledge of the documents' existence and authenticity, and of respondent's possession or control of them. It explained:

> On remand, the district court should hold a hearing in which it seeks to establish the extent and detail of the [G]overnment's knowledge of Hubbell's financial affairs (or of the paperwork documenting it) on the day the subpoena issued. It is only then that the court will be in a position to assess the testimonial value of Hubbell's response to the subpoena. Should the Independent Counsel prove capable of demonstrating with reasonable particularity a prior awareness that the exhaustive litany of documents sought in the subpoena existed and were in Hubbell's possession, then the wide distance evidently traveled from the subpoena to the substantive allegations contained in the indictment would be based upon legitimate intermediate steps. To the extent that the information conveyed through Hubbell's compelled act of production provides the necessary linkage, however, the indictment deriving therefrom is tainted.

In the opinion of the dissenting judge, the majority failed to give full effect to the distinction between the contents of the documents and the limited testimonial significance of the act of producing them. In his view, as long as the prosecutor could make use of information contained in the documents or derived therefrom without any reference to the fact that respondent had produced them in response to a subpoena, there would be no improper use of the testimonial aspect of the immunized act of production. In other words, the constitutional privilege and the statute conferring use immunity would only shield the witness from the use of any information resulting from his subpoena response "beyond what the prosecutor would receive if the documents appeared in the grand jury room or in his office unsolicited and unmarked, like manna from heaven."

On remand, the Independent Counsel acknowledged that he could not satisfy the "reasonable particularity" standard prescribed by the Court of Appeals and entered into a conditional plea agreement with respondent. In essence, the agreement provides for the dismissal of the charges unless this Court's disposition of the case makes it reasonably likely that respondent's "act of production immunity" would not pose a significant bar to his prosecution. The case is not moot, however, because the agreement also provides for the entry of a guilty plea and a sentence that will not include incarceration if we should reverse and issue an opinion that is sufficiently favorable to the Government to satisfy that condition. Ibid. Despite that agreement, we granted the Independent Counsel's petition for a writ of certiorari in order to determine the precise scope of a grant of immunity with respect to the production of documents in response to a subpoena. We now affirm.

It is useful to preface our analysis of the constitutional issue with a restatement of certain propositions that are not in dispute. The term "privilege against self-incrimination" is not an entirely accurate description of a person's constitutional protection against being "compelled in any criminal case to be a witness against himself."

The word "witness" in the constitutional text limits the relevant category of compelled incriminating communications to those that are "testimonial" in character. As Justice Holmes observed, there is a significant difference between the use of compulsion to extort communications from a defendant and compelling a person to engage in conduct that may be incriminating. Thus, even though the act may provide incriminating evidence, a criminal suspect may be compelled to put on a shirt, to provide a blood sample or handwriting exemplar, or to make a recording of his voice. The act of exhibiting such physical characteristics is not the same as a sworn communication by a witness that relates either express or implied assertions of fact or belief. * * *

More relevant to this case is the settled proposition that a person may be required to produce specific documents even though they contain incriminating assertions of fact or belief because the creation of those documents was not "compelled" within the meaning of the privilege. * * * It is clear, therefore, that respondent Hubbell could not avoid compliance with the subpoena served on him merely because the demanded documents contained incriminating evidence, whether written by others or voluntarily prepared by himself.

On the other hand, we have also made it clear that the act of producing documents in response to a subpoena may have a compelled testimonial aspect. We have held that "the act of production" itself may implicitly communicate "statements of fact." By "producing documents in compliance with a subpoena, the witness would admit that the papers existed, were in his possession or control, and were authentic." Moreover, as was true in this case, when the custodian of documents responds to a subpoena, he may be compelled to take the witness stand and answer questions designed to determine whether he has produced everything demanded by the subpoena. The answers to those questions, as well as the act of production itself, may certainly communicate information about the existence, custody, and authenticity of the documents. Whether the constitutional privilege protects the answers to such questions, or protects the act of production itself, is a question that is distinct from the question whether the unprotected contents of the documents themselves are incriminating.

Finally, the phrase "in any criminal case" in the text of the Fifth Amendment might have been read to limit its coverage to compelled testimony that is used against the defendant in the trial itself. It has, however, long been settled that its protection encompasses compelled statements that lead to the discovery of incriminating evidence even though the statements themselves are not incriminating and are not introduced into evidence. Thus, a half-century ago we held that a trial judge had erroneously rejected a defendant's claim of privilege on the ground that his answer to the pending question would not itself constitute evidence of the charged offense. As we explained:

> The privilege afforded not only extends to answers that would in themselves support a conviction under a federal criminal statute but likewise embraces those which would furnish a link in the chain of evidence needed to prosecute the claimant for a federal crime. *Hoffman v. United States*, 341 U.S. 479, 486 (1951).

Compelled testimony that communicates information that may "lead to incriminating evidence" is privileged even if the information itself is not inculpatory. *Doe v. United States*, 487 U.S. 201, 208, n. 6, 108 S.Ct. 2341, 101 L.Ed.2d 184 (1988). It is the Fifth Amendment's protection against the prosecutor's use of incriminating information derived directly or indirectly from the compelled testimony of the respondent that is of primary relevance in this case.

Acting pursuant to 18 U.S.C. § 6002, the District Court entered an order compelling respondent to produce "any and all documents" described in the grand jury subpoena and granting him "immunity to the extent allowed by law." In *Kastigar v. United States*, 406 U.S. 441 (1972), we upheld the constitutionality of § 6002 because the scope of the "use and derivative-use" immunity that it provides is coextensive with the scope of the constitutional privilege against self-incrimination.

[The] "compelled testimony" that is relevant in this case is not to be found in the contents of the documents produced in response to the subpoena. It is, rather, the testimony inherent in the act of producing those documents. The disagreement between the parties focuses entirely on the significance of that testimonial aspect.

The Government correctly emphasizes that the testimonial aspect of a response to a subpoena duces tecum does nothing more than establish the existence, authenticity, and custody of items that are produced. We assume that the Government is also entirely correct in its submission that it would not have to advert to respondent's act of production in order to prove the existence, authenticity, or custody of any documents that it might offer in evidence at a criminal trial; indeed, the Government disclaims any need to introduce any of the documents produced by respondent into evidence in order to prove the charges against him. It follows, according to the Government, that it has no intention of making improper "use" of respondent's compelled testimony.

The question, however, is not whether the response to the subpoena may be introduced into evidence at his criminal trial. That would surely be a prohibited "use" of the immunized act of production. But the fact that the Government intends no such use of the act of production leaves open the separate question whether it has already made "derivative use" of the testimonial aspect of that act in obtaining the indictment against respondent and in preparing its case for trial. It clearly has.

It is apparent from the text of the subpoena itself that the prosecutor needed respondent's assistance both to identify potential sources of information and to produce those sources. Given the breadth of the description of the 11 categories of documents called for by the subpoena, the collection and production of the materials demanded was tantamount to answering a series of interrogatories asking a witness to disclose the existence and location of particular documents fitting certain broad descriptions. The assembly of literally hundreds of pages of material in response to a request for "any and all documents reflecting, referring, or relating to any direct or indirect sources of money or other things of value received by or provided to" an individual or members of his family during a 3–year period, is the functional equivalent of the preparation of an answer to either a detailed written interrogatory or a series of oral questions at a discovery deposition. Entirely apart from the contents of the 13,120 pages of materials that respondent produced in this case, it is undeniable that providing a catalog of existing documents fitting within any of the 11 broadly worded subpoena categories could provide a prosecutor with a "lead to incriminating evidence," or "a link in the chain of evidence needed to prosecute."

Indeed, the record makes it clear that that is what happened in this case. The documents were produced before a grand jury sitting in the Eastern District of Arkansas in aid of the Independent Counsel's attempt to determine whether respondent had violated a commitment in his first plea agreement. The use of those sources of information eventually led to the return of an indictment by a grand jury sitting in the District of Columbia for offenses that apparently are unrelated to that plea agreement. What the District Court characterized as a "fishing expedition" did produce a fish, but not the one that the Independent Counsel expected to hook. It is abundantly clear that the testimonial aspect of respondent's act of producing subpoenaed documents was the first step in a chain of evidence that led to this prosecution. The documents did not magically appear in the prosecutor's office like "manna from heaven." They arrived there only after respondent asserted his constitutional privilege, received a grant of immunity, and—under the compulsion of the District Court's order—took the mental and physical steps necessary to provide the prosecutor with an accurate inventory of the many sources of potentially incriminating evidence sought by the subpoena. It was only through respondent's truthful reply to the subpoena that the Government received the incriminating documents of which it made "substantial use . . . in the investigation that led to the indictment."

For these reasons, we cannot accept the Government's submission that respondent's immunity did not preclude its derivative use of the produced documents because its "possession of the documents [was] the fruit only of a simple physical act—the act of producing the documents." It was unquestionably necessary for respondent to make extensive use of "the contents of his own mind" in identifying the hundreds of documents responsive to the requests in the subpoena. The assembly of those documents was like telling an inquisitor the combination to a wall safe, not like being forced to surrender the key to a strongbox. The Government's anemic view of respondent's act of production as a mere physical act that is principally non-testimonial in character and can be entirely divorced from its "implicit" testimonial aspect so as to constitute a "legitimate, wholly independent source" (as required by *Kastigar*) for the documents produced simply fails to account for these realities.

In sum, we have no doubt that the constitutional privilege against self-incrimination protects the target of a grand jury investigation from being compelled to answer questions designed to elicit information about the existence of sources of potentially incriminating evidence. That constitutional privilege has the same application to the testimonial aspect of a response to a subpoena seeking discovery of those sources. Before the District Court, the Government arguably conceded that respondent's act of production in this case had a testimonial aspect that entitled him to respond to the subpoena by asserting his privilege against self-incrimination. On appeal and again before this Court, however, the Government has argued that the communicative aspect of respondent's act of producing ordinary business records is insufficiently "testimonial" to support a claim of privilege because the existence and possession of such records by any businessman is a "foregone conclusion" under our decision in *Fisher v. United States*. This argument both misreads *Fisher* and ignores our subsequent decision in *United States v. Doe*, 465 U.S. 605 (1984). * * *

Whatever the scope of this "foregone conclusion" rationale, the facts of this case plainly fall outside of it. While in *Fisher* the Government already knew that the documents were in the attorneys' possession and could independently confirm their existence and authenticity through the accountants who created them, here the Government has not shown that it had any prior knowledge of either the existence or the whereabouts of the 13,120 pages of documents ultimately produced by respondent. The Government cannot cure this deficiency through the overbroad argument that a businessman such as respondent will always possess general business and tax records that fall within the broad categories described in this subpoena. The *Doe* subpoenas also sought several broad categories of general business records, yet we upheld the District Court's finding that the act of producing those records would involve testimonial self-incrimination.

Given our conclusion that respondent's act of production had a testimonial aspect, at least with respect to the existence and location of the documents sought by the Government's subpoena, respondent could not be compelled to produce those documents without first receiving a grant of immunity under § 6003. As we construed § 6002 in *Kastigar*, such immunity is co-extensive with the constitutional privilege. *Kastigar* requires that respondent's motion to dismiss the indictment on immunity grounds be granted unless the Government proves that the evidence it used in obtaining the indictment and proposed to use at trial was derived from legitimate sources "wholly independent" of the testimonial aspect of respondent's immunized conduct in assembling and producing the documents described in the subpoena. The Government, however, does not claim that it could make such a showing. Rather, it contends that its prosecution of respondent must be considered proper unless someone—presumably respondent—shows that "there is some substantial relation between the compelled testimonial communications implicit in the act of production (as opposed to the act of production standing alone) and some aspect of the information used in the investigation or the evidence presented at trial." We could not accept this submission without repudiating the basis for our conclusion in *Kastigar* that the statutory guarantee of use and derivative-use immunity is as broad as the constitutional privilege itself. This we are not prepared to do.

Accordingly, the indictment against respondent must be dismissed. The judgment of the Court of Appeals is affirmed. It is so ordered.

Notes and Questions

1. What is the nature of the foregone conclusion discussion in *Hubbell*? In *Fisher v. United States*, 425 U.S. 391 (1976) and other cases, the Court had discussed the concept of the foregone conclusion.

> It is doubtful that implicitly admitting the existence and possession of the papers rises to the level of testimony within the protection of the Fifth Amendment. The papers belong to the accountant, were prepared by him, and are the kind usually prepared by an accountant working on the tax returns of his client. Surely the Government is in no way relying on the "truthtelling" of the taxpayer to prove the existence of or his access to the documents. The existence and location of the papers are a foregone conclusion and the taxpayer adds little or nothing to the sum total of the Government's information by conceding that he in fact has the papers. Under these circumstances by enforcement of the summons "no constitutional rights are touched. The question is not of testimony but of surrender."

Besides noting that the papers were of the kind usually prepared by an accountant, the Court never explained why the existence and location of the accountant's workpapers were a foregone conclusion. *Doe I* also tied authenticity to the foregone conclusion. Authenticity concerns whether a document is genuine, rather than a forgery or fabrication. The act of production confirms that the person responding to the subpoena believes the documents are those described in the subpoena.

2. *In re Grand Jury Subpoena, Dated April 18, 2003*, 383 F.3d 905 (9th Cir.2004) held that the trial court erred in concluding that the prosecution had proved that the existence, possession, and authenticity of the documents sought was a foregone conclusion and in refusing to examine the documents in camera to determine whether the act of producing them would be incriminating.

> The government was not required to have actual knowledge of the existence and location of each and every responsive document; the government was required, however, to establish the existence of the documents sought and Doe's possession of them with "reasonable particularity" before the existence and possession of the documents could be considered a foregone conclusion and production therefore would not be testimonial. * * * Although the government possessed extensive knowledge about Doe's price-fixing activities as a result of interviews with cooperating witnesses and Doe's own incriminating statements made to federal agents on April 26, 2003, it is the government's knowledge of the existence and possession of the actual documents, not the information contained therein, that is central to the foregone conclusion inquiry. The breadth of the subpoena in this case far exceeded the government's knowledge about the actual documents that Doe created or possessed during his former employment and that he retained after he terminated his employment. The government probably could identify with sufficient particularity the existence of e-mails between Doe and some of his competitors, e-mails between Doe and his superiors regarding pricing, phone records corroborating that Doe spoke to his competitors, and records establishing meetings with certain competitors because Doe made substantial admissions to investigators during his living room interview regarding these documents. The government, however, failed to draft the subpoena narrowly to identify the documents that it could establish with reasonable particularity. Thus, on the record before us, the subpoena's breadth far exceeded the reasonably particular knowledge that the government actually possessed when it served the subpoena on Doe.

> * * *

> The authenticity prong of the foregone conclusion doctrine requires the government to establish that it can independently verify that the compelled documents "are in fact what they purport to be." Independent verification not only requires the government to show that the documents sought to be compelled would be admissible independent of the witness' production of them, but also inquires into whether the government is compelling the witness to use his discretion in selecting and assembling the responsive documents, and thereby tacitly providing identifying information that is necessary to the government's authentication of the subpoenaed documents. * * *

Although the government could probably authenticate the writing on Doe's handwritten documents through handwriting analysis, it made little effort to demonstrate how anyone beside Doe could sift through his handwritten notes, personal appointment books, and diaries to produce what Doe's attorney estimates may be 4,500 documents.... Such a response by Doe would provide the government with the identifying information that it would need to authenticate these documents. Doe's notes to himself would be difficult, if not impossible, to authenticate by anyone besides Doe. * * * In this case, the government has failed to demonstrate that it can authenticate the documents so broadly described in the subpoena without the identifying information that Doe would provide by using his knowledge and judgment to sift through, select, assemble, and produce the documents.

Chapter 15

JOINDER AND SEVERANCE

Most state criminal procedure rules as well as the Federal Rules of Criminal Procedure allow a prosecutor to combine offenses or defendants simply by charging multiple offenses of defendants in the same indictment or information.[1] In addition, if offenses or parties are charged separately but initially *could* have been joined in a single indictment or information, the criminal rules permit a trial judge the discretion, with or without a motion, to consolidate the charges for trial in a single charging document.

Joint trials have an important role in the criminal justice system by promoting efficiency and serving the interests of justice, *i.e.*, avoiding the shame and unfairness of inconsistent verdicts. They also save state funds, reduce inconvenience to witnesses and law enforcement authorities, and reduce delays in bringing defendants to trial.

Once multiple offenses of defendants are joined, either by charging document or by court order, the defense or prosecution may ask the court to sever them from one another. A motion for severance may be based upon misjoinder of either offenses or defendants because the joinder rules have not been followed. In federal courts, even if joinder is proper under the rules, a pretrial motion to sever under Fed.R.Crim.P. 14 may assert prejudicial joinder. Rule 14 leaves the determination of risk of prejudice and any remedy that may be necessary to the sound discretion of the trial court. If prejudice develops at trial after a motion to sever has been overruled, the defendant should renew the motion and move for a mistrial.

In addition to joinder and severance issues arising from the application of the criminal rules, the exercise of prosecutorial discretion to join or not to join offenses or defendants may have constitutional consequences relating to Fifth Amendment Double Jeopardy and collateral

---

1. As to multiple offenses in a single charging document, each crime must be alleged in a separate count. A prosecutor must be careful to avoid charging separate crimes in a single count because to do so will cause the count to be duplicitous.

estoppel issues, as well as Sixth Amendment Confrontation Clause problems.

A. JOINDER AND SEVERANCE OF OFFENSES

1. *Joinder and Severance of Offenses Under the Rules of Criminal Procedure*

Where a defendant is charged with multiple offenses, rules of procedure usually govern the joinder and severance of the offenses to determine whether there will be a single trial or several trials. In general, the rules give the prosecution the discretion to charge, in a single prosecution, all those offenses which a defendant allegedly committed in a closely connected series of events and within the same time sequence. Conversely, the rules permit the defendant to seek a severance of offenses that have been joined in a common prosecution. Rules like Fed.R.Crim.P. 8(a) (in the statutory supplement) are typical, allowing but not requiring joinder of offenses. It states that two or more offenses may be charged together against a defendant if they are based upon:

1) the same act or transaction (e.g., a rape and assault); or

2) a series of acts or transactions constituting a common scheme (e.g., armed robbery, auto theft, possession of weapon); or

3) the offenses being of similar character (e.g., bank robberies in same neighborhood two months apart).

Because the rule is permissive rather than mandatory, a defendant has no right to have all alleged offenses tried together. However, a defendant's motion to consolidate charges under Fed.R.Crim.P. 13 may succeed *if* the charges could have been brought together under Rule 8(a). Rule 13 states in part: "The court may order two or more indictments or informations or both to be tried together if the offenses, and the defendants if there is more than one, could have been joined in a single indictment or information."

Joinder is usually upheld when the crimes are closely related in character, circumstances and time. One example of a common scheme or plan is when the offenses show a near identical modus operandi and the offenses occur within such a close proximity of time and location to each other that there can be little doubt that the offenses were committed by the same person. A second type of case is where the crimes are somewhat similar in nature but are closely related in an overall scheme.

The efficiency to be realized from joining "same act" offenses or "same series" offenses may vanish when the only basis for the joinder is similarity of charged offenses which were committed at different places, different times or in different ways. First, when evidence of one offense is not admissible at the trial of another offense, joinder is inefficient and separate trials are preferable. Case law suggests, however, that if evidence of each crime is simple and distinct though not admissible in separate trials, joinder may be proper if the trial judge properly instructs the jury about the dangers of cumulating evidence. If evidence of one crime *is* admissible at the trial of the other, the court may not deem the joinder of offenses to be prejudicial and determine that separate trials of the similar offenses are unnecessary.

Arguably, any joinder of offenses is prejudicial to some extent, but where joinder is otherwise proper under the rules of procedure, the defendant must prove prejudice to justify and obtain a severance. There are several general discretionary considerations which may persuade a court to grant a severance. First, the jury may consider the defendant a "bad person" or infer a criminal propensity by the defendant simply because he is charged with so many offenses. Second, proof on one charge may "spill over" and assist in conviction on another charge. Unless there is a high probability of an acquittal on one count, courts will usually deny a severance on this ground. See, e.g., *United States v. Moyer*, 313 F.3d 1082 (8th Cir.2002) (joinder of crimes not prejudicial solely because evidence of some crimes is stronger than evidence of other crimes). Third, the defendant may wish to testify about one offense, but not about another offense. See, e.g., *United States v. Saadey*, 393 F.3d 669 (6th Cir.2005) (defendant failed to show trial court how testifying about one charge would violate his Fifth Amendment privilege against self-incrimination on another charge, when he had asserted that the charges were unrelated). The defendant must convince the trial court both that he has important testimony to give concerning one count but that there is a strong need to assert the Fifth Amendment Privilege Against Self–Incrimination and refrain from testifying on the other count. Finally, the defendant may wish to assert antagonistic defenses to the joinable charges. For example, if he is charged with two assaults, he may want to claim an alibi as to one assault and insanity as to the other. Because one of the defenses is likely to diminish the credibility of the other, prejudice may be asserted in support of a motion for a severance. If a court severs the offenses, what is the prejudice to the prosecution?

Problems

In the following situations, determine whether joinder is permissible under the applicable criminal procedure rule (federal, the state where you attend law school, the state where you intend to practice). If joinder is permitted, determine whether the joinder, though permissible, under that rule is nonetheless prejudicial.

1.   Tom Slime was charged in a single indictment with the rape of one of his daughters, which occurred in 1996, and a separate rape on his stepdaughter in 2006.

2.   Dick was charged with robbing Smith's Drug Store on July 1, 2006, with assaulting Jim Johnson on February 3, 2005, and with being a career criminal (two or more prior felony convictions).

3.   Harry was charged with sixteen robberies over a 28–month period. The robberies were committed in the same manner and at about the same time of day by a man wearing similar clothing.

4. In the early hours of June 19, Tom entered a convenience store, brandished a 12–inch knife, and demanded that the clerk hand over all the money in the store's two cash registers. Two weeks later, in the early morning of July 3, Tom returned to the store and demanded that another clerk hand over money from the same registers, and threatened the clerk with the jagged edge of a broken bottle. After the robberies, each clerk gave slightly different descriptions of the robber but both clerks picked Tom out of a photographic display.

(A) As defense counsel for Tom, describe the arguments you would make in a motion to the court for a severance of the two robbery counts based upon prejudicial joinder?

(B) If you were the prosecutor in the case, how would you respond to Tom's motion?

(C) As the trial judge, how would you rule on Tom's motion for a severance of the robbery charges?

2. *Double Jeopardy Implications for the Joinder of Offenses*

When the prosecution charges a defendant with multiple offenses, a constitutional issue may arise. The Double Jeopardy Clause of the Fifth Amendment shields a defendant from even the risk of being punished twice for the same offense. Double jeopardy protections depend on whether two offenses are considered to be the "same offense." That decision is important not only in the traditional double jeopardy scenario involving successive prosecutions for related acts, but also in a single prosecution involving multiple offenses and punishments.

A constitutional violation does not occur if the legislature intended to impose cumulative punishments for a single act which constitutes more than one crime. In *Missouri v. Hunter*, 459 U.S. 359 (1983), the Supreme Court held that "[w]here [a] legislature specifically authorizes cumulative punishment under two statutes, . . . the prosecutor may seek and the trial court or jury may impose cumulative punishment under such statutes in a single trial." *Hunter* held that to show legislative intent, the statutes defining the two offenses must require:

1) a "clearly expressed legislative intent" that supports the imposition of cumulative punishments; or

2) proof of different elements.

Either the legislative history of the statute or the language or organization of a statute may reveal the legislative intent. "If the offenses are set forth in different statutes or in distinct sections of a statute, and each provision or section unambiguously sets forth punishment for its violation, then courts generally infer that Congress intended to authorize multiple punishments." *United States v. Gugino*, 860 F.2d 546, 549–50 (2d Cir.1988). In your jurisdiction, how has *Hunter* been applied?

In *Brown v. Ohio*, 432 U.S. 161 (1977), the Court suggested that the legislature may divide a continuous course of conduct into separate offenses, even for conduct which occurs within a very short period of time. *See, e.g., Hennemeyer v. Commonwealth*, 580 S.W.2d 211 (Ky.1979), where the court held that six gunshots fired at police during a chase resulted in six different counts of wanton endangerment.

When the legislative intent to impose multiple charges or punishments is ambiguous, the Supreme Court test from *Blockburger v. United States*, 284 U.S. 299 (1932) governs whether multiple offenses and punishments in a single or successive prosecutions are constitutionally permissible. *Blockburger* held that two offenses do not constitute the same offense when *each* offense requires proof of elements that the other offense does not. The test may be satisfied despite substantial overlap in the evidence used to prove the offenses. In *United States v. Felix*, 503 U.S. 378 (1992), the Supreme Court held that an attempt to commit a substantive offense and a conspiracy to commit that offense are not the same offense for double jeopardy purposes even if they are based upon the same underlying facts. A conspiracy is distinct from the substantive offense that is the object of the conspiracy because the former requires proof of an agreement while the latter requires proof of an overt act.[2]

On the other hand, two offenses *do* constitute the same offense when only *one* of the offenses requires proof that the other offense does not. A lesser included offense is the same as the greater offense because by definition the greater offense includes all the elements of the lesser. Thus, multiple punishments following a single prosecution for both offenses are barred, in the absence of a clearly expressed legislative intent to the contrary. For example, in *Whalen v. United States*, 445 U.S. 684 (1980), the Supreme Court held because rape is a lesser included offense of felony-murder in the course of that rape, double jeopardy prohibited convictions in the same trial for both offenses. Only the felony-murder required evidence that proof of the rape did not: killing the same victim in the perpetration of the crime of rape. By contrast, proving that a rape had been committed by the defendant did not require the prosecutor to show anything different than what was necessary to prove the rape as to the felony-murder charge. Therefore, because rape and the felony-murder were the "same offense," cumulative punishments could not be imposed absent clear legislative intent.

UNITED STATES v. DIXON

509 U.S. 688 (1993).

JUSTICE SCALIA announced the judgment of the Court and delivered the opinion of the Court with respect to Parts I, II, and IV, and an opinion with respect to Parts III and V, in which JUSTICE KENNEDY joins.

In both of these cases, respondents were tried for criminal contempt of court for violating court orders that prohibited them from engaging in

---

2. When a single act affects multiple victims, different offenses are committed. If one person is killed and another is wounded by the same bullet, multiple criminal offenses have been committed. *See, e.g., Smith v. Commonwealth*, 734 S.W.2d 437 (Ky.1987).

conduct that was later the subject of a criminal prosecution. We consider whether the subsequent criminal prosecutions are barred by the Double Jeopardy Clause.

I

Respondent Alvin Dixon was arrested for second-degree murder and was released on bond. Consistent with the District of Columbia's bail law authorizing the judicial officer to impose any condition that "will reasonably assure the appearance of the person for trial or the safety of any other person or the community," Dixon's release form specified that he was not to commit "any criminal offense," and warned that any violation of the conditions of release would subject him "to revocation of release, an order of detention, and prosecution for contempt of court."

While awaiting trial, Dixon was arrested and indicted for possession of cocaine with intent to distribute. The court issued an order requiring Dixon to show cause why he should not be held in contempt or have the terms of his pretrial release modified. At the show-cause hearing, four police officers testified to facts surrounding the alleged drug offense; Dixon's counsel cross-examined these witnesses and introduced other evidence. The court concluded that the Government had established " 'beyond a reasonable doubt that [Dixon] was in possession of drugs and that those drugs were possessed with the intent to distribute.' " The court therefore found Dixon guilty of criminal contempt. [For] his contempt, Dixon was sentenced to 180 days in jail. He later moved to dismiss the cocaine indictment on double jeopardy grounds; the trial court granted the motion.

Respondent Michael Foster's route to this Court is similar. Based on Foster's alleged physical attacks upon her in the past, Foster's estranged wife Ana obtained a civil protection order (CPO) in Superior Court of the District of Columbia. The order, to which Foster consented, required that he not " 'molest, assault, or in any manner threaten or physically abuse' " Ana Foster * * *.

Over the course of eight months, Ana Foster filed three separate motions to have her husband held in contempt for numerous violations of the CPO. Of the 16 alleged episodes, the only charges relevant here are three separate instances of threats [and] two assaults * * *.

After issuing a notice of hearing and ordering Foster to appear, the court held a 3–day bench trial. [As] to the assault charges, the court stated that Ana Foster would have "to prove as an element, first that there was a Civil Protection Order, and then [that] … the assault as defined by the criminal code, in fact occurred." [The] court found Foster guilty beyond a reasonable doubt of four counts of criminal contempt * * *, but acquitted him on other counts. [He] was sentenced to an aggregate 600 days' imprisonment.

The United States Attorney's Office later obtained an indictment charging Foster with simple assault * * * (Count I); threatening to injure another * * * (Counts II–IV); and assault with intent to kill * * *

(Count V). Ana Foster was the complainant in all counts; the first and last counts were based on the events for which Foster had been held in contempt, and the other three were based on the alleged events for which Foster was acquitted of contempt. Like Dixon, Foster filed a motion to dismiss, claiming a double jeopardy bar to all counts, and also collateral estoppel as to Counts II–IV. The trial court denied the double-jeopardy claim and did not rule on the collateral-estoppel assertion. * * *

III

The first question before us today is whether *Blockburger* analysis permits subsequent prosecution in this new criminal contempt context, where a judicial order has prohibited a criminal act. If it does, we must then proceed to consider whether *Grady* also permits it.

We begin with Dixon. The statute applicable in Dixon's contempt prosecution provides that "[a] person who has been conditionally released . . . and who has violated a condition of release shall be subject to . . . prosecution for contempt of court." Obviously, Dixon could not commit an "offence" under this provision until an order setting out conditions was issued. The statute by itself imposes no legal obligation on anyone. Dixon's cocaine possession, although an offense under [the] D.C.Code, was not an offense under [the aforementioned contempt statute] until a judge incorporated the statutory drug offense into his release order.

In this situation, in which the contempt sanction is imposed for violating the order through commission of the incorporated drug offense, the later attempt to prosecute Dixon for the drug offense resembles the situation that produced our judgment of double jeopardy in *Harris v. Oklahoma*, 433 U.S. 682 (1977) (per curiam). There we held that a subsequent prosecution for robbery with a firearm was barred by the Double Jeopardy Clause, because the defendant had already been tried for felony-murder based on the same underlying felony. We have described our terse per curiam in *Harris* as standing for the proposition that, for double jeopardy purposes, "the crime generally described as felony murder" is not "a separate offense distinct from its various elements." *Illinois v. Vitale*, 447 U.S. 410, 420–421 (1980). Accord, *Whalen v. United States*, 445 U.S. 684, 694 (1980). So too here, the "crime" of violating a condition of release cannot be abstracted from the "element" of the violated condition. The Dixon court order incorporated the entire governing criminal code in the same manner as the *Harris* felony-murder statute incorporated the several enumerated felonies. Here, as in *Harris*, the underlying substantive criminal offense is "a species of lesser-included offense." * * *

The foregoing analysis obviously applies as well to Count I of the indictment against Foster, charging assault, based on the same event that was the subject of his prior contempt conviction for violating the provision of the CPO forbidding him to commit simple assault. The subsequent prosecution for assault fails the *Blockburger* test, and is barred.

The remaining four counts in Foster, assault with intent to kill (Count V) and threats to injure or kidnap (Counts II–IV), are not barred under *Blockburger*. As to Count V: [At] the contempt hearing, the court stated that Ana Foster's attorney, who prosecuted the contempt, would have to prove first, knowledge of a CPO, and second, a willful violation of one of its conditions, here simple assault as defined by the criminal code. On the basis of the same episode, Foster was then indicted for assault with intent to kill. Under governing law, that offense requires proof of specific intent to kill; simple assault does not. Similarly, the contempt offense required proof of knowledge of the CPO, which assault with intent to kill does not. Applying the 1 elements test, the result is clear: These crimes were different offenses and the subsequent prosecution did not violate the Double Jeopardy Clause.

Counts II, III, and IV of Foster's indictment are likewise not barred. These charged Foster under § 22–2307 (forbidding anyone to "threate[n] . . . to kidnap any person or to injure the person of another or physically damage the property of any person") for his alleged threats on three separate dates. Foster's contempt prosecution included charges that, on the same dates, he violated the CPO provision ordering that he not "in any manner threaten" Ana Foster. Conviction of the contempt required willful violation of the CPO—which conviction under § 22–2307 did not; and conviction under § 22–2307 required that the threat be a threat to kidnap, to inflict bodily injury, or to damage property—which conviction of the contempt (for violating the CPO provision that Foster not "in any manner threaten") did not. Each offense therefore contained a separate element, and the *Blockburger* test for double jeopardy was not met.

V

Dixon's subsequent prosecution, as well as Count I of Foster's subsequent prosecution, violate the Double Jeopardy Clause. For the reasons set forth in Part IV, the other Counts of Foster's subsequent prosecution do not violate the Double Jeopardy Clause. * * *

CHIEF JUSTICE REHNQUIST, with whom JUSTICE O'CONNOR and JUSTICE THOMAS join, concurring in part and dissenting in part.

[I] join Parts I [and] IV of the Court's opinion, and write separately to express my disagreement with Justice Scalia's application of *Blockburger* in Part III.

In my view, *Blockburger's* same-elements test requires us to focus not on the terms of the particular court orders involved, but on the elements of contempt of court in the ordinary sense. Relying on *Harris v. Oklahoma*, a three-paragraph per curiam in an unargued case, Justice Scalia concludes otherwise today, and thus incorrectly finds in Part III–A of his opinion that the subsequent prosecutions of Dixon for drug distribution and of Foster for assault violated the Double Jeopardy

Clause. In so doing, Justice SCALIA rejects the traditional view—shared by every federal court of appeals and state supreme court that addressed the issue prior to *Grady* [*v. Corbin,* 495 U.S. 508 (1990)]—that, as a general matter, double jeopardy does not bar a subsequent prosecution based on conduct for which a defendant has been held in criminal contempt. * * *

Our double jeopardy cases applying *Blockburger* have focused on the statutory elements of the offenses charged, not on the facts that must be proven under the particular indictment at issue—an indictment being the closest analogue to the court orders in this case. By focusing on the facts needed to show a violation of the specific court orders involved in this case, and not on the generic elements of the crime of contempt of court, Justice Scalia's double-jeopardy analysis bears a striking resemblance to that found in *Grady*—not what one would expect in an opinion that overrules *Grady*. * * *

JUSTICE SOUTER, with whom JUSTICE STEVENS joins, concurring in the judgment in part and dissenting in part.

[I] join Part I of Justice White's opinion, and I would hold, as he would, both the prosecution of Dixon and the prosecution of Foster under all the counts of the indictment against him to be barred by the Double Jeopardy Clause. * * *

[W]hile the government may punish a person separately for each conviction of at least as many different offenses as meet the *Blockburger* test, we have long held that it must sometimes bring its prosecutions for these offenses together. If a separate prosecution were permitted for every offense arising out of the same conduct, the government could manipulate the definitions of offenses, creating fine distinctions among them and permitting a zealous prosecutor to try a person again and again for essentially the same criminal conduct. While punishing different combinations of elements is consistent with the Double Jeopardy Clause in its limitation on the imposition of multiple punishments (a limitation rooted in concerns with legislative intent), permitting such repeated prosecutions would not be consistent with the principles underlying the Clause in its limitation on successive prosecution. The limitation on successive prosecution is thus a restriction on the government different in kind from that contained in the limitation on multiple punishments, and the government cannot get around the restriction on repeated prosecution of a single individual merely by precision in the way it defines its statutory offenses. * * *

An example will show why this should be so. Assume three crimes: robbery with a firearm, robbery in a dwelling and simple robbery. The elements of the three crimes are the same, except that robbery with a firearm has the element that a firearm be used in the commission of the robbery while the other two crimes do not, and robbery in a dwelling has the element that the robbery occur in a dwelling while the other two crimes do not.

If a person committed a robbery in a dwelling with a firearm and was prosecuted for simple robbery, all agree he could not be prosecuted subsequently for either of the greater offenses of robbery with a firearm or robbery in a dwelling. Under the lens of *Blockburger*, however, if that same person were prosecuted first for robbery with a firearm, he could be prosecuted subsequently for robbery in a dwelling, even though he could not subsequently be prosecuted on the basis of that same robbery for simple robbery. This is true simply because neither of the crimes, robbery with a firearm and robbery in a dwelling, is either identical to or a lesser-included offense of the other. But since the purpose of the Double Jeopardy Clause's protection against successive prosecutions is to prevent repeated trials in which a defendant will be forced to defend against the same charge again and again, and in which the government may perfect its presentation with dress rehearsal after dress rehearsal, it should be irrelevant that the second prosecution would require the defendant to defend himself not only from the charge that he committed the robbery, but also from the charge of some additional fact, in this case, that the scene of the crime was a dwelling. If, instead, protection against successive prosecution were as limited as it would be by *Blockburger* alone, the doctrine would be as striking for its anomalies as for the limited protection it would provide. * * *

Notes

1. Applying the *Blockburger* test, the Court unanimously held that a charge of conspiracy to distribute controlled substances in violation of 21 U.S.C. § 846 is a lesser included offense of conducting a continuing criminal enterprise "in concert" with others in violation of 21 U.S.C. § 848 when the "in concert" element of the latter offense is based upon the same agreement as the conspiracy offense. *Rutledge v. United States*, 517 U.S. 292 (1996). Therefore convictions of both charges in one trial violates Double Jeopardy, even when the trial court imposes concurrent life sentences. The Court remanded the case to the trial court for a determination of which conviction must be vacated.

2. In *Jeffers v. United States*, 432 U.S. 137 (1977), a plurality of the Court found:

> "If the defendant expressly asks for separate trials on the greater and the lesser offenses, or, in connection with his opposition to trial together, fails to raise the issue that one offense might be a lesser included offense of the other, [an] exception to the [same offense] rule emerges. * * * [A]lthough a defendant is normally entitled to have charges on a greater and a lesser offense resolved in one proceeding, there is no violation of the Double Jeopardy Clause when he elects to have the two offenses tried separately and persuades the trial court to honor his election."

3. Most double jeopardy cases involve the prohibition of two criminal prosecutions, but double jeopardy also may apply to a criminal charge and another type of proceeding, *e.g.*, whether respective criminal and civil actions by the government subject a defendant to penalties which violate double

jeopardy. In *Hudson v. United States*, 522 U.S. 93 (1997), the Court examined whether a civil penalty can be characterized as criminal. Bank officers were indicted for misapplication of bank funds, following imposition of monetary penalties by the Office of Comptroller of Currency (OCC). The Supreme Court held that

> whether a particular punishment is criminal or civil is, at least initially, a matter of statutory construction. A court must first ask whether the legislature, "in establishing the penalizing mechanism, indicated either expressly or impliedly a preference for one label or the other." Even in those cases where the legislature "has indicated an intention to establish a civil penalty, we have inquired further whether the statutory scheme was so punitive either in purpose or effect," as to "transfor[m] what was clearly intended as a civil remedy into a criminal penalty."
>
> In making this latter determination, the factors listed in *Kennedy v. Mendoza–Martinez*, 372 U.S. 144, 168–169 (1963), provide useful guideposts, including: (1) "[w]hether the sanction involves an affirmative disability or restraint"; (2) "whether it has historically been regarded as a punishment"; (3) "whether it comes into play only on a finding of scienter"; (4) "whether its operation will promote the traditional aims of punishment-retribution and deterrence"; (5) "whether the behavior to which it applies is already a crime"; (6) "whether an alternative purpose to which it may rationally be connected is assignable for it"; and (7) "whether it appears excessive in relation to the alternative purpose assigned." It is important to note, however, that "these factors must be considered in relation to the statute on its face," and "only the clearest proof" will suffice to override legislative intent and transform what has been denominated a civil remedy into a criminal penalty.

When the Court applied the *Kennedy* factors to *Hudson*, it concluded that the OCC penalties had been civil rather than criminal: (1) the statutory language expressly state that the penalties are civil; (2) money penalties are not historically viewed as punishment; (3) the violator's state of mind is irrelevant under the statute; (4) merely because the conduct for which OCC sanctions are imposed also may be criminal is insufficient for the penalties to be characterized as criminally punitive; and (5) deterrence as a purpose is insufficient for a sanction to be criminal, because deterrence may serve civil or criminal goals.

Because *Hudson* involved monetary penalties and occupational disbarment, it has been distinguished from cases involving confinement. In cases considering the question whether confinement is criminal or civil, the Supreme Court has looked to the actual conditions of confinement. *See, e.g., Kansas v. Hendricks*, 521 U.S. 346 (1997) (because involuntary confinement pursuant to Kansas's civil commitment statute is not punitive, that statute's operation does not raise double jeopardy concerns).

Problems

In each of the following, identify whether, under the applicable criminal law of your jurisdiction, the multiple offenses charged in one indictment, arising from the same transaction, constitute the "same offense" under the

Hunter or the *Blockburger/Dixon* cases, *i.e.*, could *each* listed offense have been committed, regardless of whether the other listed offense was committed? The prosecutor charged:

1. Basil with rape and kidnaping.

2. Boris with wanton murder and driving while under the influence of controlled substances, based on the same course of conduct.

3. Larry with theft by deception and forgery. He entered into a video cassette recorder rental agreement. The VCR was valued at approximately $150. Larry forged the name of "Earl Wheeler," his cousin, on the VCR rental agreement. After the VCR in question was not returned pursuant to the rental agreement, theft by deception and forgery charges were brought against Larry.

4. Barney was on bike patrol in front of the Mayberry Hotel at 3 a.m., when he heard tires squealing. He rode to the back of the parking lot where he saw Otis driving a white Camaro with its headlights off. Otis was speeding up to the back of a van several times as the van was leaving the parking lot. Otis then turned the Camaro in the direction of Barney, who told him twice to stop. As Barney pedalled his bike away from the Camaro, the Camaro hit the bike's back tire, spinning the bike around as Barney jumped off and hit the ground. Can Otis be convicted of DUI and attempted murder?

5. At his apartment, Cal slapped Brown several times with his gun so that the latter would empty his pockets and surrender his money. After completion of the robbery, Cal demanded more money from Brown. After looking for money and drugs for more than thirty minutes and calling a confederate on a cellular phone, Cal shot Brown once in each leg, poured bleach on Brown's wounds, and left the apartment. Can Cal be convicted of robbery and assault?

3. Collateral Estoppel Implications for Joinder of Offenses

As previously discussed, where there is a single criminal transaction or activity, it may be divided into multiple statutory crimes. If the prosecution chooses to divide the offenses into separate prosecutions or decides to bring the charges successively rather than simultaneously, an acquittal on one offense may preclude a trial on the other offense under the doctrine of collateral estoppel. This doctrine provides that determination of a factual issue in a defendant's favor at one proceeding may estop the prosecution from disputing the fact in another proceeding against the same defendant. Thus, when different offenses are charged and double jeopardy would normally not bar a second prosecution, collateral estoppel may, in effect, bar the second trial when a fact previously found in the defendant's favor is necessary to the second conviction.

For collateral estoppel to apply, the defendant must be contesting relitigation of an issue of ultimate fact previously determined in that defendant's favor by a valid and final judgment. First, the second prosecution must involve the same parties as the first trial. A defendant cannot estop the prosecution from relitigating a fact found against the prosecution in a proceeding against a different defendant. In *Standefer v.*

United States, 447 U.S. 10 (1980), a unanimous Court held that one defendant's acquittal on a bribery charge did not preclude a later prosecution of another defendant for aiding and abetting the same bribery. Second, the factfinder must have "actually and certainly" determined the issue of fact in the earlier proceeding. For example, in *Schiro v. Farley*, 510 U.S. 222 (1994), in a homicide case, the jury was given ten possible verdicts and returned a verdict on only one of the verdict sheets, convicting the defendant for rape felony murder. Defendant claimed that the state was collaterally estopped from showing intentional killing (one of the other verdict sheet possibilities) as an aggravated factor supporting a death sentence. The Court held that "failure to return a verdict does not have collateral estoppel effect.... unless the record establishes that the issue was actually and necessarily decided in the defendant's favor."

The most difficult problem in applying collateral estoppel is ascertaining what facts were established in the earlier case. Because juries render general rather than special verdicts in most criminal cases, a determination of which facts support the verdict requires careful analysis of the trial record. Only those fact determinations essential to the first decision are conclusive in later proceedings.

Not only must a court be able to determine that the fact issue was litigated in defendant's first trial, but also the nature of the reason for acquitting defendant in the earlier trial determines whether collateral estoppel applies in the current case. For example, assume that Donna Defendant is charged with assaults against two victims at the same time and place, but the offenses are not joined. If Donna is acquitted at the first trial for assaulting Victim #1 because there is doubt as to whether she was present at the time of the assaults, her acquittal acts as a collateral estoppel defense to the second assault charge. On the other hand, if the acquittal at the first trial resulted from doubt about whether Donna actually assaulted Victim #1, the prosecutor can still try to prove that Donna assaulted Victim #2.

ASHE v. SWENSON

397 U.S. 436 (1970).

MR. JUSTICE STEWART delivered the opinion of the Court. * * *

Sometime in the early hours of the morning of January 10, 1960, six men were engaged in a poker game in the basement of the home of John Gladson at Lee's Summit, Missouri. Suddenly three or four masked men, armed with a shotgun and pistols, broke into the basement and robbed each of the poker players of money and various articles of personal property. The robbers—and it has never been clear whether there were three or four of them—then fled in a car belonging to one of the victims of the robbery. Shortly thereafter the stolen car was discovered in a field, and later that morning three men were arrested by a state trooper while they were walking on a highway not far from where the abandoned car had been found. The petitioner was arrested by another officer some distance away.

The four were subsequently charged with seven separate offenses—the armed robbery of each of the six poker players and the theft of the car. In May 1960 the petitioner went to trial on the charge of robbing Donald Knight, one of the participants in the poker game. At the trial the State called Knight and three of his fellow poker players as prosecution witnesses. Each of them described the circumstances of the holdup and itemized his own individual losses. The proof that an armed robbery had occurred and that personal property had been taken from Knight as well as from each of the others was unassailable. The testimony of the four victims in this regard was consistent both internally and with that of the others. But the State's evidence that the petitioner had been one of the robbers was weak. Two of the witnesses thought that there had been only three robbers altogether, and could not identify the petitioner as one of them. Another of the victims, who was the petitioner's uncle by marriage, said that at the "patrol station" he had positively identified each of the other three men accused of the holdup, but could say only that the petitioner's voice "sounded very much like" that of one of the robbers. The fourth participant in the poker game did identify the petitioner, but only by his "size and height, and his actions."

The cross-examination of these witnesses was brief, and it was aimed primarily at exposing the weakness of their identification testimony. Defense counsel made no attempt to question their testimony regarding the holdup itself or their claims as to their losses.

Knight testified without contradiction that the robbers had stolen from him his watch, $250 in cash, and about $500 in checks. His billfold, which had been found by the police in the possession of one of the three other men accused of the robbery, was admitted in evidence. The defense offered no testimony and waived final argument.

The trial judge instructed the jury that if it found that the petitioner was one of the participants in the armed robbery, the theft of "any money" from Knight would sustain a conviction. He also instructed the jury that if the petitioner was one of the robbers, he was guilty under the law even if he had not personally robbed Knight. The jury—though not instructed to elaborate upon its verdict—found the petitioner "not guilty due to insufficient evidence."

Six weeks later the petitioner was brought to trial again, this time for the robbery of another participant in the poker game, a man named Roberts. The petitioner filed a motion to dismiss, based on his previous acquittal. The motion was overruled, and the second trial began. The witnesses were for the most part the same, though this time their testimony was substantially stronger on the issue of the petitioner's identity. For example, two witnesses who at the first trial had been wholly unable to identify the petitioner as one of the robbers, now testified that his features, size, and mannerisms matched those of one of their assailants. Another witness who before had identified the petitioner only by his size and actions now also remembered him by the unusual sound of his voice. The State further refined its case at the second trial by declining to call one of the participants in the poker game whose identification testimony at the first trial had been conspicuously negative. The case went to the jury on instructions virtually identical to those given at the first trial. This time the jury found the petitioner guilty, and he was sentenced to a 35–year term in the state penitentiary. * * *

"Collateral estoppel" is an awkward phrase, but it stands for an extremely important principle in our adversary system of justice. It means simply that when an issue of ultimate fact has once been determined by a valid and final judgment, that issue cannot again be litigated between the same parties in any future lawsuit. Although first developed in civil litigation, collateral estoppel has been an established rule of federal criminal law at least since this Court's decision more than 50 years ago in *United States v. Oppenheimer*, 242 U.S. 85. As Mr. Justice Holmes put the matter in that case, "It cannot be that the safeguards of the person, so often and so rightly mentioned with solemn reverence, are less than those that protect from a liability in debt." 242 U.S., at 87. As a rule of federal law, therefore, "(i)t is much too late to suggest that this principle is not fully applicable to a former judgment in a criminal case, either because of lack of 'mutuality' or because the judgment may reflect only a belief that the Government had not met the higher burden of proof exacted in such cases for the Government's evidence as a whole although not necessarily as to every link in the chain."

The federal decisions have made clear that the rule of collateral estoppel in criminal cases is not to be applied with the hypertechnical and archaic approach of a 19th century pleading book, but with realism and rationality. Where a previous judgment of acquittal was based upon a general verdict, as is usually the case, this approach requires a court to "examine that record of a prior proceeding, taking into account the pleadings, evidence, charge, and other relevant matter, and conclude whether a rational jury could have grounded its verdict upon an issue other than that which the defendant seeks to foreclose from consideration." The inquiry "must be set in a practical frame and viewed with an eye to all the circumstances of the proceedings." Any test more technically restrictive would, of course, simply amount to a rejection of the rule of collateral estoppel in criminal proceedings, at least in every case where the first judgment was based upon a general verdict of acquittal.

Straightforward application of the federal rule to the present case can lead to but one conclusion. For the record is utterly devoid of any indication that the first jury could rationally have found that an armed robbery had not occurred, or that Knight had not been a victim of that robbery. The single rationally conceivable issue in dispute before the jury was whether the petitioner had been one of the robbers. And the jury by its verdict found that he had not. The federal rule of law, therefore, would make a second prosecution for the robbery of Roberts wholly impermissible.

The ultimate question to be determined, then, [is] whether this established rule of federal law is embodied in the Fifth Amendment guarantee against double jeopardy. We do not hesitate to hold that it is. For whatever else that constitutional guarantee may embrace, it surely protects a man who has been acquitted from having to "run the gauntlet" a second time. * * *

Reversed and remanded.

MR. CHIEF JUSTICE BURGER, dissenting.

The Fifth Amendment to the Constitution of the United States provides in part: "nor shall any person be subject for the same offence to be twice put in jeopardy of life or limb * * *." Nothing in the language or gloss previously placed on this provision of the Fifth Amendment remotely justifies the treatment that the Court today accords to the collateral-estoppel doctrine. * * *

Notes

1. In *Ashe*, the Court believed that it was possible to identify why the first robbery trial resulted in an acquittal. Although there was no doubt that a robbery had occurred and that Knight had been a victim of that robbery, the only issue at the first trial was whether Ashe was the person who robbed Knight.

In criminal cases, statutes may effectively require the use of special verdicts. For example, in cases where the defendant has tried to prove a mental defect or mental retardation, the jury may be ordered to make a specific finding that the defendant was mentally defective or retarded. And in cases where the prosecution seeks the death penalty, the jury may need to designate in writing which aggravating circumstance it found to be applicable before the court can sentence the defendant to capital punishment.

2. Evidence of a crime for which the defendant was acquitted may be introduced at a later trial involving the same circumstances. In *Dowling v. United States*, 493 U.S. 342 (1990), while prosecuting a defendant for bank robbery, the Court held that the prosecution may introduce evidence of a burglary for which the defendant had been acquitted. The Court reasoned that the evidence was admissible at the robbery trial because the acquittal did not prove that the defendant was innocent but only that there was a reasonable doubt about the defendant's guilt. The difference in burdens of proof was the key distinction for the Court: in the first trial, the government failed to show beyond a reasonable doubt that Dowling had committed the act; to introduce evidence of the same act in another trial, the government need show only that a jury could reasonably conclude that the defendant committed the first act.

3. A prior acquittal in a criminal case does not preclude a subsequent civil forfeiture case. In both *United States v. One Assortment of 89 Firearms*, 465 U.S. 354 (1984) and *One Lot Emerald Cut Stones and One Ring v. United States*, 409 U.S. 232 (1972), the Court held that a finding of a reasonable doubt in a criminal case acquittal does not provide a bar to a civil forfeiture, which has a lesser burden of proof.

Exercise

Mel was charged with murdering his girlfriend after she was found dead in the backyard of his former girlfriend, Mary. Before his trial, Mary made a deal with the prosecution to plead guilty to the lesser crime of tampering with physical evidence in return for her testimony at his trial. At Mel's trial, Mary described how she and Mel had bound and gagged the victim, how she had taken pictures of Mel raping and abusing her, how he killed her, how they removed her jewelry, and how they together had put her body in a bag and buried her in the backyard of Mary's home. Mary testified that all of these acts occurred from 10:00 p.m. until 11:15 p.m. as a continuing course of conduct. Mel's defense attorney was so successful in challenging Mary's credibility that the jury believed nothing she said and acquitted Mel. A year later, the purchasers of Mel's home found the photographs Mary earlier had described at Mel's trial in the furnace ducts along with some of the girlfriend's jewelry. The successor prosecutor recognizes that Double Jeopardy prevents her from charging Mel again with his girlfriend's death.

You are the law clerk for the prosecutor. Advise her about whether the Double Jeopardy Clause or collateral estoppel precludes her from indicting Mel for rape in the first degree, assault in the first degree, theft, and tampering with physical evidence. Consult the criminal law statutes in your jurisdiction to assist in your evaluation.

B. JOINDER AND SEVERANCE OF DEFENDANTS

1. Joinder of Defendants Under the Rules

The rules of criminal procedure address joinder and severance procedures where multiple defendants are jointly alleged to have committed one or more crimes. The policy behind this type of rule is improved judicial economy and efficiency, since one trial is faster and less expensive than two. The joinder of defendants is permissive and severance is discretionary with the court. When multiple defendants are jointly charged, a severance may be available based upon specific allegations of prejudice. A more general request for severance may be grounded on the proposition that the defendants should not have been joined in the first place. This is similar to misjoinder of unrelated offenses.

In most jurisdictions, joinder of defendants is permitted where the defendants allegedly participated either in the same act or transaction or in the same series of acts or transactions. Unlike the rules on joinder of offenses, in order to be joined defendants must have committed offenses which are part of the same series of acts rather than being of a similar character. Joinder of defendants looks to the factual connecting link. Where the link is part of some larger plan, or there is some commonality of proof, joinder is permitted. Even where the connecting link is absent and joinder is not permitted under the rules, such a misjoinder is subject to harmless error analysis. *United States v. Lane*, 474 U.S. 438 (1986). Most rules also provide that defendants may be charged in one or more counts together or separately, but each defendant does not have to be charged in each count. *See, e.g.,* Fed.R.Crim.P. 8(b) (in the statutory supplement).

Assuming that joinder is proper under the applicable rules, severance of defendants may be based upon specific allegations of prejudice in a joint trial. The prejudicial aspects of a joint trial are commonly considered as 1) the "spill over" effect of one defendant's heinous conduct affecting the jury's view of the other co-defendants; and 2) the dangers of any one attorney not having total control over the defense. While the prosecution is unified, the defense is fragmented because each defendant has an attorney and each attorney's view of the case may differ. Specific grounds for severance of defendants for factual prejudice relate to (1) the weight or type of proof as to one defendant, (2) antagonistic defenses or positions, (3) the desire to call the codefendant as a witness; and (4) the confession of a codefendant.

Where there is a great disparity in the weight or type of the evidence against the defendants, with the evidence against one or more defendants far more damaging than the evidence against the moving defendant, a severance may be appropriate. Otherwise, the guilt of others may "rub off" on the moving defendant. For example, a defendant being tried for a single offense may seek a severance from being jointly tried with a defendant who is charged with both the same offense as the other defendant and with being a recidivist.

If antagonistic defenses are alleged as the basis for a motion for separate trials, the moving defendant must show that the antagonism with a codefendant will mislead or confuse the jury, thereby rendering his defense ineffective. In *Zafiro v. United States*, 506 U.S. 534 (1993), the Court rejected a bright line test that severance is required whenever defendants have mutually antagonistic defenses. The four *Zafiro* defendants did not articulate any specific instances of prejudice but merely argued that the "very nature of their defenses, without more, prejudiced them." Writing for the Court, Justice O'Connor responded that "it is well settled that defendants are not entitled to a severance merely because they may have a better chance of acquittal in separate trials." A court

> should grant a severance [only] if there is a serious risk that a joint trial would compromise a specific right of one of the defendants, or prevent the jury from making a reliable judgment about guilt or innocence. Such a risk might occur when evidence that the jury should not consider against a defendant and that would not be admissible if a defendant were tried alone is admitted against a codefendant. For example, evidence of a codefendant's wrongdoing in some circumstances erroneously could lead a jury to conclude that a defendant was guilty. When many defendants are tried together in a complex case and they have markedly different degrees of culpability, this risk of prejudice is heightened. Evidence that is probative of a defendant's guilt but technically admissible only against a codefendant also might present a risk of prejudice. Conversely, a defendant

might suffer prejudice if essential exculpatory evidence that would be available to a defendant tried alone were unavailable in a joint trial.

Even if there is some risk of prejudice, it may be curable with proper instructions. Justice O'Connor noted that the trial court instructed the jury to give separate consideration to each defendant, and that each defendant was entitled to have his or her case judged only on the basis of the evidence applicable to the individual defendant. Thus, the instructions "sufficed to cure any possibility of prejudice."

The problem of calling a codefendant as a witness may conflict with the codefendant's privilege against self-incrimination. Obviously, a severance where the codefendant's trial is held first might eliminate the self-incrimination problem by virtue of a conviction or acquittal. Courts faced with severance motions based on the prospect of calling a codefendant often require specific statements of 1) what the proposed testimony would contain, 2) factors which would lead the court to believe that the testimony would truly be exculpatory, and 3) concern about whether the witness would testify rather than claiming her self-incrimination privilege. See, e.g., *United States v. Lamarr*, 75 F.3d 964 (4th Cir.1996).

Questions

1. Consider whether sufficient prejudice is present in a trial of two defendants when:

a) One defendant testifies and the other does not.

b) Evidence is introduced that is competent as to one defendant but incompetent as to another.

c) One defendant claims merely to have been present at the crime scene and the other claims entrapment.

d) The chances for acquittal for one defendant are better if there are separate trials.

e) The expense or strain of a joint trial is harmful to the defendant.

2. What effect should a court give to the following when ruling on a motion to sever based upon the ground of calling a codefendant?

a) The sufficiency of a showing that the codefendant would testify at a severed trial.

b) The degree to which the exculpatory testimony would be cumulative.

c) Judicial economy.

d) The likelihood that the testimony would be substantially impeached.

Problems

In the following situations, determine whether the joinder of defendants is permissible under the applicable criminal procedure rule, and if so, determine whether the joinder, though permissible, is nonetheless prejudicial.

1.   In two counts of a ten-count indictment, the prosecutor has charged Joan and Buffy with illegally trafficking in controlled substances. In the remaining counts, Joan alone is charged with trafficking in controlled substances on eight other occasions.

2.   The prosecution charges Jill, Sally and others with trafficking illegally in controlled substances. Jill's defense is that she merely aided and abetted the other defendants; Sally's defense is entrapment.

3.   Alice and Deborah face multiple criminal tax charges arising from their business ventures. Alice is willing to give exculpatory evidence for Deborah, but without a severance of her case from Deborah's she will invoke her privilege against self-incrimination.

2.   *Constitutional Implications for the Joinder of Defendants*

In a joint trial, the admission of a codefendant's extrajudicial confession incriminating the defendant violates the defendant's Sixth Amendment right to confrontation when the codefendant does not testify at trial. This principle applies even when the trial judge instructs the jury not to consider the confession against the defendant but only against the codefendant. Where the codefendant does testify, there is no confrontation issue because the codefendant is subject to cross-examination. Normally, the codefendant's confession is not admissible even when the defendant has also confessed and even if the jury is instructed not to consider it against the defendant.

Several alternatives exist for the prosecution when a codefendant has confessed but may not testify at trial. The first alternative is to grant a severance to the nonconfessing defendant. In this way, the codefendant's confession will not be used against the defendant. In ruling on a motion for separate trials, the trial judge may order the prosecutor to deliver to the court for *in camera* inspection any statements or confessions made by defendants which the prosecutor intends to introduce in evidence at trial. The prosecution may also desire a severance where the other evidence against the codefendant is weak and a full unredacted confession is necessary as to the codefendant. In *United States v. McVeigh*, 169 F.R.D. 362 (D.Colo.1996), the court severed the Oklahoma City bombing defendants' trial because the prosecution intended to use several statements of one of the defendants against another defendant. The court granted the severance after considering and rejecting all possible mechanisms for remedying the codefendant confession problem.

A second alternative is that the prosecution not use the codefendant's confession in its case-in-chief in a joint trial. If the confessing codefendant testifies, the prosecution could then impeach the codefendant with the statements made in the confession. This would not constitute a denial of confrontation even if the codefendant denied making the statement. However, it is risky to hope the codefendant testifies in initially denying a severance and allowing introduction of the statement into evidence during the prosecution's case-in-chief.

A third alternative is a procedure called redaction, where all references to the moving, nonconfessing defendant are deleted. This may be accomplished by removing parts of or retyping the offending confession or requiring the witness to paraphrase the confession in such a manner as to avoid any references that might directly implicate other defendants. To be effective, the deletion must not call attention to the fact that the statement implicates other persons who are obviously at trial. The next case discusses these alternatives.

GRAY v. MARYLAND

523 U.S. 185 (1998).

Justice Breyer delivered the opinion of the Court.

The issue in this case concerns the application of *Bruton v. United States*, 391 U.S. 123 (1968). *Bruton* involved two defendants accused of participating in the same crime and tried jointly before the same jury. One of the defendants had confessed. His confession named and incriminated the other defendant. The trial judge issued a limiting instruction, telling the jury that it should consider the confession as evidence only against the codefendant who had confessed and not against the defendant named in the confession. *Bruton* held that, despite the limiting instruction, the Constitution forbids the use of such a confession in the joint trial.

The case before us differs from *Bruton* in that the prosecution here redacted the codefendant's confession by substituting for the defendant's name in the confession a blank space or the word "deleted." We must decide whether these substitutions make a significant legal difference. We hold that they do not and that *Bruton*'s protective rule applies.

[Bell confessed to police that he, Gray and Vanlandingham beat Stacy Williams, who died from his injuries. After Bell and Gray were indicted for murder, the trial judge permitted introduction of a redacted version of Bell's confession. Other witnesses testified that six persons, including Bell, Gray and Vanlandingham, participated in the beating. Gray denied participating. Bell did not testify. The trial judge instructed the jury not to use the confession as evidence against Gray, who was convicted along with Bell.]

Bruton, as we have said, involved two defendants—Evans and Bruton—tried jointly for robbery. Evans did not testify, but the Government introduced into evidence Evans' confession, which stated that both he (Evans) and Bruton together had committed the robbery. The trial judge told the jury it could consider the confession as evidence only against Evans, not against Bruton.

This Court held that, despite the limiting instruction, the introduction of Evans' out-of-court confession at Bruton's trial had violated Bruton's right, protected by the Sixth Amendment, to cross-examine witnesses. * * *

In *Richardson v. Marsh*, the Court considered a redacted confession. The case involved a joint murder trial of Marsh and Williams. The State had redacted the confession of one defendant, Williams, so as to "omit all reference" to his codefendant, Marsh—"indeed, to omit all indication that anyone other than . . . Williams" and a third person had "participated in the crime." The trial court also instructed the jury not to consider the confession against Marsh. As redacted, the confession indicated that Williams and the third person had discussed the murder in the front seat of a car while they traveled to the victim's house. The redacted confession contained no indication that Marsh—or any other person—was in the car. Later in the trial, however, Marsh testified that she was in the back seat of the car. For that reason, in context, the confession still could have helped convince the jury that Marsh knew about the murder in advance and therefore had participated knowingly in the crime.

The Court held that this redacted confession fell outside *Bruton*'s scope and was admissible (with appropriate limiting instructions) at the joint trial. The Court distinguished Evans' confession in *Bruton* as a confession that was "incriminating on its face," and which had "expressly implicat[ed]" *Bruton*, 481 U.S., at 208. By contrast, Williams' confession amounted to "evidence requiring linkage" in that it "became" incriminating in respect to Marsh "only when linked with evidence introduced later at trial." The Court held

> that the Confrontation Clause is not violated by the admission of a nontestifying codefendant's confession with a proper limiting instruction when, as here, the confession is redacted to eliminate not only the defendant's name, but any reference to his or her existence.

The Court added: "We express no opinion on the admissibility of a confession in which the defendant's name has been replaced with a symbol or neutral pronoun."

Originally, the codefendant's confession in the case before us, like that in *Bruton*, referred to, and directly implicated another defendant. The State, however, redacted that confession by removing the nonconfessing defendant's name. Nonetheless, unlike *Richardson*'s redacted confession, this confession refers directly to the "existence" of the nonconfessing defendant. The State has simply replaced the nonconfessing defendant's name with a kind of symbol, namely the word "deleted" or a blank space set off by commas. The redacted confession, for example, responded to the question "Who was in the group that beat Stacey," with the phrase, "Me, , and a few other guys." And when the police witness read the confession in court, he said the word "deleted" or "deletion" where the blank spaces appear. We therefore must decide a question that *Richardson* left open, namely whether redaction that replaces a defendant's name with an obvious indication of deletion, such as a blank space, the word "deleted," or a similar symbol, still falls within *Bruton*'s protective rule. We hold that it does.

Bruton, as interpreted by *Richardson*, holds that certain "powerfully incriminating extrajudicial statements of a codefendant"—those naming another defendant—considered as a class, are so prejudicial that limiting instructions cannot work. Unless the prosecutor wishes to hold separate trials or to use separate juries or to abandon use of the confession, he must redact the confession to reduce significantly or to eliminate the special prejudice that the *Bruton* Court found. Redactions that simply replace a name with an obvious blank space or a word such as "deleted" or a symbol or other similarly obvious indications of alteration, however, leave statements that, considered as a class, so closely resemble *Bruton*'s unredacted statements that, in our view, the law must require the same result.

For one thing, a jury will often react similarly to an unredacted confession and a confession redacted in this way, for the jury will often realize that the confession refers specifically to the defendant. This is true even when the State does not blatantly link the defendant to the deleted name, as it did in this case by asking whether Gray was arrested on the basis of information in Bell's confession as soon as the officer had finished reading the redacted statement. Consider a simplified but typical example, a confession that reads "I, Bob Smith, along with Sam Jones, robbed the bank." To replace the words "Sam Jones" with an obvious blank will not likely fool anyone. A juror somewhat familiar with criminal law would know immediately that the blank, in the phrase "I, Bob Smith, along with , robbed the bank," refers to defendant Jones. A juror who does not know the law and who therefore wonders to whom the blank might refer need only lift his eyes to Jones, sitting at counsel table, to find what will seem the obvious answer, at least if the juror hears the judge's instruction not to consider the confession as evidence against Jones, for that instruction will provide an obvious reason for the blank. A more sophisticated juror, wondering if the blank refers to someone else, might also wonder how, if it did, the prosecutor could argue the confession is reliable, for the prosecutor, after all, has been arguing that Jones, not someone else, helped Smith commit the crime.

For another thing, the obvious deletion may well call the jurors' attention specially to the removed name. By encouraging the jury to speculate about the reference, the redaction may overemphasize the importance of the confession's accusation—once the jurors work out the reference. That is why Judge Learned Hand, many years ago, wrote in a similar instance that blacking out the name of a codefendant not only "would have been futile. . . . [T]here could not have been the slightest doubt as to whose names had been blacked out," but "even if there had been, that blacking out itself would have not only laid the doubt, but underscored the answer."

Finally, *Bruton*'s protected statements and statements redacted to leave a blank or some other similarly obvious alteration, function the same way grammatically. They are directly accusatory. Evans' statement in *Bruton* used a proper name to point explicitly to an accused defendant. And *Bruton* held that the "powerfully incriminating" effect of what Justice Stewart called "an out-of-court accusation," 391 U.S., at 138 (Stewart, J., concurring), creates a special, and vital, need for cross-examination—a need that would be immediately obvious had the codefendant pointed directly to the defendant in the courtroom itself. The blank space in an obviously redacted confession also points directly to the defendant, and it accuses the defendant in a manner similar to Evans' use of Bruton's name or to a testifying codefendant's accusatory finger. By way of contrast, the factual statement at issue in *Richardson*—a statement about what others said in the front seat of a car—differs from directly accusatory evidence in this respect, for it does not point directly to a defendant at all.

We concede certain differences between *Bruton* and this case. A confession that uses a blank or the word "delete" (or, for that matter, a first name or a nickname) less obviously refers to the defendant than a confession that uses the defendant's full and proper name. Moreover, in some instances the person to whom the blank refers may not be clear: Although the follow-up question asked by the State in this case eliminated all doubt, the reference might not be transparent in other cases in which a confession, like the present confession, uses two (or more) blanks, even though only one other defendant appears at trial, and in which the trial indicates that there are more participants than the confession has named. Nonetheless, as we have said, we believe that, considered as a class, redactions that replace a proper name with an obvious blank, the word "delete," a symbol, or similarly notify the jury that a name has been deleted are similar enough to *Bruton*'s unredacted confessions as to warrant the same legal results.

The State, in arguing for a contrary conclusion, relies heavily upon *Richardson*. But we do not believe *Richardson* controls the result here. We concede that *Richardson* placed outside the scope of *Bruton*'s rule those statements that incriminate inferentially. 481 U.S., at 208. We also concede that the jury must use inference to connect the statement in this redacted confession with the defendant. But inference pure and simple cannot make the critical difference, for if it did, then *Richardson* would also place outside *Bruton*'s scope confessions that use shortened first names, nicknames, descriptions as unique as the "red-haired, bearded, one-eyed man-with-a-limp," and perhaps even full names of defendants who are always known by a nickname. This Court has assumed, however, that nicknames and specific descriptions fall inside, not outside, *Bruton*'s protection. * * *

That being so, *Richardson* must depend in significant part upon the kind of, not the simple fact of, inference. *Richardson*'s inferences involved statements that did not refer directly to the defendant himself and which became incriminating "only when linked with evidence introduced later at trial." The inferences at issue here involve statements that, despite redaction, obviously refer directly to someone, often obviously the defendant, and which involve inferences that a jury ordinarily could make immediately, even were the confession the very first item introduced at trial. Moreover, the redacted confession with the blank prominent on its face, in *Richardson*'s words, "facially incriminat[es]" the codefendant. Like the confession in *Bruton* itself, the accusation that the redacted confession makes "is more vivid than inferential incrimination, and hence more difficult to thrust out of mind."

Nor are the policy reasons that *Richardson* provided in support of its conclusion applicable here. *Richardson* expressed concern lest application of *Bruton*'s rule apply where "redaction" of confessions, particularly "confessions incriminating by connection," would often "not [be] possible," thereby forcing prosecutors too often to abandon use either of the confession or of a joint trial. Additional redaction of a confession that uses a blank space, the word "delete," or a symbol, however, normally is possible. Consider as an example a portion of the confession before us: The witness who read the confession told the jury that the confession (among other things) said,

"Question: Who was in the group that beat Stacey?

"Answer: Me, deleted, deleted, and a few other guys."

Why could the witness not, instead, have said:

"Question: Who was in the group that beat Stacey?

"Answer: Me and a few other guys."

Richardson itself provides a similar example of this kind of redaction. The confession there at issue had been "redacted to omit all reference to respondent—indeed, to omit all indication that anyone other than Martin and Williams participated in the crime," and it did not indicate that it had been redacted.

The *Richardson* Court also feared that the inclusion, within *Bruton*'s protective rule, of confessions that incriminated "by connection" too often would provoke mistrials, or would unnecessarily lead prosecutors to abandon the confession or joint trial, because neither the prosecutors nor the judge could easily predict, until after the introduction of all the evidence, whether or not *Bruton* had barred use of the confession. To include the use of blanks, the word "delete," symbols, or other indications of redaction, within *Bruton*'s protections, however, runs no such risk. Their use is easily identified prior to trial and does not depend, in any special way, upon the other evidence introduced in the case. We also note that several Circuits have interpreted *Bruton* similarly for many years, yet no one has told us of any significant practical difficulties arising out of their administration of that rule.

For these reasons, we hold that the confession here at issue, which substituted blanks and the word "delete" for the respondent's proper name, falls within the class of statements to which *Bruton*'s protections apply.

The judgment of the Court of Appeals is vacated, and the case is remanded for further proceedings not inconsistent with this opinion.

Justice Scalia, with whom The Chief Justice, Justice Kennedy, and Justice Thomas join, dissenting.

In *Richardson v. Marsh*, we declined to extend the "narrow exception" of *Bruton v. United States*, beyond confessions that facially incriminate a defendant. Today the Court "concede[s] that *Richardson* placed outside the scope of *Bruton's* rule those statements that incriminate inferentially," "concede[s] that the jury must use inference to connect the statement in this redacted confession with the defendant," but nonetheless extends *Bruton* to confessions that have been redacted to delete the defendant's name. Because I believe the line drawn in *Richardson* should not be changed, I respectfully dissent. * * *

We declined in *Richardson*, however, to extend *Bruton* to confessions that incriminate only by inference from other evidence. When incrimination is inferential, "it is a less valid generalization that the jury will not likely obey the instruction to disregard the evidence." Today the Court struggles to decide whether a confession redacted to omit the defendant's name is incriminating on its face or by inference. On the one hand, the Court "concede[s] that the jury must use inference to connect the statement in this redacted confession with the defendant," but later asserts, on the other hand, that "the redacted confession with the blank prominent on its face ... 'facially incriminat[es]'" him. The Court should have stopped with its concession: the statement "Me, deleted, deleted, and a few other guys" does not facially incriminate anyone but the speaker. The Court's analogizing of "deleted" to a physical description that clearly identifies the defendant (which we have assumed *Bruton* covers, *see Harrington v. California*, 395 U.S. 250, 253 (1969)) does not survive scrutiny. By "facially incriminating," we have meant incriminating independent of other evidence introduced at trial. *Richardson*. Since the defendant's appearance at counsel table is not evidence, the description "red-haired, bearded, one-eyed man-with-a-limp," would be facially incriminating—unless, of course, the defendant had dyed his hair black and shaved his beard before trial, and the prosecution introduced evidence concerning his former appearance. Similarly, the statement "Me, Kevin Gray, and a few other guys" would be facially incriminating, unless the defendant's name set forth in the indictment was not Kevin Gray, and evidence was introduced to the effect that he sometimes used "Kevin Gray" as an alias. By contrast, the person to whom "deleted" refers in "Me, deleted, deleted, and a few other guys" is not apparent from anything the jury knows independent of the evidence at trial. Though the jury may speculate, the statement expressly implicates no one but the speaker. * * *

The Court's extension of *Bruton* to name-redacted confessions "as a class" will seriously compromise "society's compelling interest in finding, convicting, and punishing those who violate the law." *Moran v. Burbine*, 475 U.S. 412, 426 (1986). We explained in *Richardson* that forgoing use of codefendant confessions or joint trials was "too high" a price to insure that juries never disregard their instructions. [In] the present case, it asks, why could the police officer not have testified that Bell's answer was "Me and a few other guys"? The answer, it seems obvious to me, is because that is not what Bell said. Bell's answer was

"Me, Tank, Kevin and a few other guys." Introducing the statement with full disclosure of deletions is one thing; introducing as the complete statement what was in fact only a part is something else. And of course even concealed deletions from the text will often not do the job that the Court demands. For inchoate offenses—conspiracy in particular—redaction to delete all reference to a confederate would often render the confession nonsensical. If the question was "Who agreed to beat Stacey?", and the answer was "Me and Kevin," we might redact the answer to "Me and [deleted]," or perhaps to "Me and somebody else," but surely not to just "Me"—for that would no longer be a confession to the conspiracy charge, but rather the foundation for an insanity defense. To my knowledge we have never before endorsed—and to my strong belief we ought not endorse—the redaction of a statement by some means other than the deletion of certain words, with the fact of the deletion shown. * * *

Notes and Questions

1.   After *Gray*, how would you describe the circumstances under which redaction is necessary?

2.   Does *Bruton* apply when a defendant's own confession, which corroborates that of his nontestifying codefendant's statement is introduced against him? Yes, said the Court in *Cruz v. New York*, 481 U.S. 186 (1987). The Supreme Court held that when the "nontestifying codefendant's confession incriminating the defendant is not directly admissible against the defendant," the nontestifying codefendant's testimony must be excluded no matter how damaging the defendant's own confession is to his own case.

3.   The major practical problem associated with the introduction of codefendant confessions is that, when the prosecutor wants to use the confession during the state's case-in-chief, it is unknown whether the codefendant will testify. As a result, during the joint trial of codefendants where one defendant has confessed and also implicated a codefendant, the prosecutor will submit for admission into evidence an edited version of the confession, possibly with blanks left to indicate the participation of others in the commission of the crime. If the confessing defendant does testify, the prosecutor tenders the unedited version of the confession during its rebuttal which follows the defense's presentation of its testimony.

4.   No matter how reliable a co-defendant's confession may be, the Court's recent examination of the Sixth Amendment Confrontation Clause precludes its admission based on reliability. In *Crawford v. Washington*, 541 U.S. 36 (2004), the Court concluded that the Confrontation Clause directs the use of testimonial statements such as prior "police interrogations." For a witness such as a confessing codefendant who does not testify at trial, that person's pretrial statement is admissible only if she is unavailable to testify and the defendant had a prior opportunity for cross-examination. In *Davis v. Washington*, 126 S.Ct. 2266 (2006), the Court defined statements as "testimonial" when the "primary purpose of the interrogation is to establish or prove past events."

Review Problem

Charles asked his friend Phil if he knew where Charles could purchase some cocaine. Phil checked with his friend Harry, who in turn found Dave who said that he would sell a kilogram of cocaine to Charles for $25,000. Late one night, the four men met in a parking lot of a shopping mall to consummate the transaction. Charles gave Dave the cash for the drugs, thinking that Dave had already given the drugs to Phil. When Dave and Harry quickly drove off in Dave's car, Charles asked Phil for the drugs. Phil replied that he did not have them and thought that Dave had given them to Charles when Charles had paid the money to Dave. Phil and Charles jumped into Phil's pickup truck and started chasing Dave and Harry. During the chase, both cars collided with another vehicle, killing the two occupants. No cocaine was found in Dave's car. Immediately after he was arrested, Charles gave the police a statement in which he described the drug-sale-gone bad, and implicated Dave as the real culprit. The prosecutor charged Charles and Dave each with two counts of wanton murder, and also charged Dave with trafficking in a controlled substance and theft by deception. The prosecutor allowed Phil and Harry to plead guilty to minor offenses in return for their testimony at Charles' and Dave's trial.

The laws of the jurisdiction define that wanton murder occurs when a defendant operates a motor vehicle under circumstances manifesting extreme indifference to human life and kills another person. Trafficking in cocaine occurs when a defendant sells, transfers or possesses with intent to sell cocaine. One way in which theft by deception may occur is when a defendant creates a false impression as to his intention and obtains the property of another with intent to deceive that person of the property. Nothing in the statutes or their legislative histories indicates that cumulative punishments for trafficking and theft by deception are permitted.

(1) As defense counsel for Charles, describe the nature of the arguments you would make in a motion to the court for a severance of his wanton murder charge from Dave's charges.

(2) If you were the prosecutor in the case, how would you respond to Charles' motion?

(3) As the trial judge, how would you rule on Charles's motion for a severance of his case from Dave's?

(4) As the trial judge, how would you rule on Dave's motion:

(a) To compel the prosecution to elect between prosecuting him for trafficking or for theft by deception because they are the same offense; and

(b) To exclude his name or any reference to his participation from Charles's statement when it is introduced during the prosecution's case-in-chief?

Chapter 16

SPEEDY TRIAL

The Sixth Amendment right states that "[i]n all criminal prosecutions, the accused shall enjoy the right to a speedy ... trial.... " This right probably is the only part of the Bill of Rights that most defendants are willing to ignore. After all, a decision by the prosecution to delay or drop criminal charges would satisfy most defendants, because no conviction may result. The defendant's concern, however, is that the prosecutor will not drop the charges, and that the delay of the trial will leave the accused in jail, without the ability to either provide for family or assist in the preparation of the defense case.

In any jurisdiction, there are frequently three sources of speedy trial rights: court rules for docket control, statutes specifying time periods especially in pretrial stages, and constitutional guarantees of a speedy trial. This chapter discusses the scope and applicability of these sources. Depending on the legal source, the issues in pre-charge delay and post-charge delay cases may vary. The speedy trial issues addressed in this chapter include the following.

1) When does the right attach, e.g, at the time of the crime, arrest, formal charge?

2) To whom does the right apply, e.g., all defendants, only defendants who have been unable to obtain pretrial release?

3) How much time must elapse for a violation? Is that lapse of time dispositive of the issue or does it serve merely as a triggering mechanism which requires inquiry into other issues?

4) Are some types of delay excusable, e.g., delay attributable to defense motions or the defendant's unavailability?

5) To assert the right to a speedy disposition, must the defendant demand that disposition? If so, does that demand trigger the running of the time period or is it merely one of several factors for analysis?

6) To obtain relief, must the defendant show prejudice to the defense case?

7) What sanctions are available for a violation, e.g., dismissal with or without prejudice to the charges being brought again?

A. DELAY IN BRINGING THE CHARGE

Fifth Amendment or Fourteenth Amendment due process protects a defendant from delay between commission of the crime and the earlier of the arrest, indictment or information. However, proving a constitutional violation is difficult. To establish a federal due process violation based on pre-charge delay, a defendant must show that 1) the delay resulted in actual prejudice to the ability of the defense to present its case; and 2) the prosecution's conduct was intentional and motivated by an intent to harass the defendant or to gain a tactical advantage over the defendant. In each case, the reasons for the delay and the prospective impact on a trial are relevant. The burden of establishing actual prejudice is a heavy one, with the defendant having to provide proof that the delay substantially prejudiced the defense. The mere passage of time is insufficient. In addition, even if the defendant is able to show actual prejudice, there must be evidence that the delay was used deliberately by the prosecution to gain a tactical advantage. As the following opinion in *United States v. Lovasco* demonstrates, the requirement of purposeful delay reflects a judicial reluctance to interfere with prosecutorial discretion.

UNITED STATES v. LOVASCO
431 U.S. 783 (1977).

Mr. Justice Marshall delivered the opinion of the Court.

[On] March 6, 1975, respondent was indicted for possessing eight firearms stolen from the United States mails, and for dealing in firearms without a license. The offenses were alleged to have occurred between July 25 and August 31, 1973, more than 18 months before the indictment was filed. Respondent moved to dismiss the indictment due to the delay.

The District Court conducted a hearing on respondent's motion at which the respondent sought to prove that the delay was unnecessary and that it had prejudiced his defense. In an effort to establish the former proposition, respondent presented a Postal Inspector's report on his investigation that was prepared one month after the crimes were committed, and a stipulation concerning the post-report progress of the probe. The report stated, in brief, that within the first month of the investigation respondent had admitted to Government agents that he had possessed and then sold five of the stolen guns, and that the agents had developed strong evidence linking respondent to the remaining three weapons. The report also stated, however, that the agents had been unable to confirm or refute respondent's claim that he had found the guns in his car when he returned to it after visiting his son, a mail handler, at work. The stipulation into which the Assistant United States Attorney entered indicated that little additional information concerning the crimes was uncovered in the 17 months following the preparation of the Inspector's report.

To establish prejudice to the defense, respondent testified that he had lost the testimony of two material witnesses due to the delay. The first witness, Tom Stewart, died more than a year after the alleged crimes occurred. At the hearing respondent claimed that Stewart had been his source for two or three of the guns. The second witness, respondent's brother, died in April 1974, eight months after the crimes were completed. Respondent testified that his brother was present when respondent called Stewart to secure the guns, and witnessed all of respondent's sales. Respondent did not state how the witnesses would have aided the defense had they been willing to testify.

The Government made no systematic effort in the District Court to explain its long delay. The Assistant United States Attorney did expressly disagree, however, with defense counsel's suggestion that the investigation had ended after the Postal Inspector's report was prepared. The prosecutor also stated that it was the Government's theory that respondent's son, who had access to the mail at the railroad terminal from which the guns were "possibly stolen," was responsible for the thefts. Finally, the prosecutor elicited somewhat cryptic testimony from the Postal Inspector indicating that the case "as to these particular weapons involves other individuals"; that information had been presented to a grand jury "in regard to this case other than [on] the day of the indictment itself"; and that he had spoken to the prosecutors about the case on four or five occasions.

Following the hearing, the District Court filed a brief opinion and order. The court found that by October 2, 1973, the date of the Postal Inspector's report, "the Government had all the information relating to defendant's alleged commission of the offenses charged against him," and that the 17–month delay before the case was presented to the grand jury "had not been explained or justified" and was "unnecessary and unreasonable." The court also found that "(a)s a result of the delay defendant has been prejudiced by reason of the death of Tom Stewart, a material witness on his behalf." Accordingly, the court dismissed the indictment. [The Eighth Circuit Court of Appeals affirmed.] * * *

We granted certiorari, and now reverse.

In *United States v. Marion*, 404 U.S. 307 (1971), this Court considered the significance, for constitutional purposes, of a lengthy preindictment delay. We held that as far as the Speedy Trial Clause of the Sixth Amendment is concerned, such delay is wholly irrelevant, since our analysis of the language, history, and purposes of the Clause persuaded us that only "a formal indictment or information or else the actual restraints imposed by arrest and holding to answer a criminal charge [engage] the particular protections" of that provision. We went on to note that statutes of limitations, which provide predictable, legislatively enacted limits on prosecutorial delay, provide "the primary guarantee, against bringing overly stale criminal charges." But we did acknowledge that the "statute of limitations does not fully define (defendants') rights with respect to the events occurring prior to indictment," and that the Due Process Clause has a limited role to play in protecting against oppressive delay.

[*Marion*] makes clear that proof of prejudice is generally a necessary but not sufficient element of a due process claim, and that the due process inquiry must consider the reasons for the delay as well as the prejudice to the accused. * * *

It requires no extended argument to establish that prosecutors do not deviate from "fundamental conceptions of justice" when they defer seeking indictments until they have probable cause to believe an accused is guilty; indeed it is unprofessional conduct for a prosecutor to recommend an indictment on less than probable cause. It should be equally obvious that prosecutors are under no duty to file charges as soon as probable cause exists but before they are satisfied they will be able to establish the suspect's guilt beyond a reasonable doubt. To impose such a duty "would have a deleterious effect both upon the rights of the accused and upon the ability of society to protect itself." From the perspective of potential defendants, requiring prosecutions to commence when probable cause is established is undesirable because it would increase the likelihood of unwarranted charges being filed, and would add to the time during which defendants stand accused but untried. [From] the perspective of law enforcement officials, a requirement of immediate prosecution upon probable cause is equally unacceptable because it could make obtaining proof of guilt beyond a reasonable doubt impossible by causing potentially fruitful sources of information to evaporate before they are fully exploited. And from the standpoint of the courts, such a requirement is unwise because it would cause scarce resources to be consumed on cases that prove to be insubstantial, or that involve only some of the responsible parties or some of the criminal acts. Thus, no one's interests would be well served by compelling prosecutors to initiate prosecutions as soon as they are legally entitled to do so.

It might be argued that once the Government has assembled sufficient evidence to prove guilt beyond a reasonable doubt, it should be constitutionally required to file charges promptly, even if its investigation of the entire criminal transaction is not complete. Adopting such a rule, however, would have many of the same consequences as adopting a rule requiring immediate prosecution upon probable cause.

First, compelling a prosecutor to file public charges as soon as the requisite proof has been developed against one participant on one charge would cause numerous problems in those cases in which a criminal transaction involves more than one person or more than one illegal act. In some instances, an immediate arrest or indictment would impair the prosecutor's ability to continue his investigation, thereby preventing society from bringing lawbreakers to justice. In other cases, the prosecutor would be able to obtain additional indictments despite an early prosecution, but the necessary result would be multiple trials involving a single set of facts. Such trials place needless burdens on defendants, law enforcement officials, and courts.

Second, insisting on immediate prosecution once sufficient evidence is developed to obtain a conviction would pressure prosecutors into resolving doubtful cases in favor of early and possibly unwarranted prosecutions. The determination of when the evidence available to the prosecution is sufficient to obtain a conviction is seldom clear-cut, and reasonable persons often will reach conflicting conclusions. In the instant case, for example, since respondent admitted possessing at least five of the firearms, the primary factual issue in dispute was whether respondent knew the guns were stolen as required by 18 U.S.C. § 1708. Not surprisingly, the Postal Inspector's report contained no direct evidence bearing on this issue. The decision whether to prosecute, therefore, required a necessarily subjective evaluation of the strength of the circumstantial evidence available and the credibility of respondent's denial. Even if a prosecutor concluded that the case was weak and further investigation appropriate, he would have no assurance that a reviewing court would agree. To avoid the risk that a subsequent indictment would be dismissed for preindictment delay, the prosecutor might feel constrained to file premature charges, with all the disadvantages that would entail.

Finally, requiring the Government to make charging decisions immediately upon assembling evidence sufficient to establish guilt would preclude the Government from giving full consideration to the desirability of not prosecuting in particular cases. The decision to file criminal charges, with the awesome consequences it entails, requires consideration of a wide range of factors in addition to the strength of the Government's case, in order to determine whether prosecution would be in the public interest. Prosecutors often need more information than proof of a suspect's guilt, therefore, before deciding whether to seek an indictment. Again the instant case provides a useful illustration. Although proof of the identity of the mail thieves was not necessary to convict respondent of the possessory crimes with which he was charged, it might have been crucial in assessing respondent's culpability, as distinguished from his legal guilt. If, for example, further investigation were to show that respondent had no role in or advance knowledge of the theft and simply agreed, out of paternal loyalty, to help his son dispose of the guns once respondent discovered his son had stolen them, the United States Attorney might have decided not to prosecute, especially since at the time of the crime respondent was over 60 years old and had no prior criminal record. Requiring prosecution once the evidence of guilt is clear, however, could prevent a prosecutor from awaiting the information necessary for such a decision.

We would be most reluctant to adopt a rule which would have these consequences absent a clear constitutional command to do so. We can find no such command in the Due Process Clause of the Fifth Amendment. In our view, investigative delay is fundamentally unlike delay undertaken by the Government solely "to gain tactical advantage over the accused," *United States v. Marion*, 404 U.S., at 324, precisely because investigative delay is not so one-sided.[17] Rather than deviating from elementary standards of "fair play and decency," a prosecutor abides by them if he refuses to seek indictments until he is completely satisfied that he should prosecute and will be able promptly to establish guilt beyond a reasonable doubt. Penalizing prosecutors who defer action for these reasons would subordinate the goal of "orderly expedition" to that of "mere speed." This the Due Process Clause does not require. We therefore hold that to prosecute a defendant following investigative delay does not deprive him of due process, even if his defense might have been somewhat prejudiced by the lapse of time. * * *

In *Marion* we conceded that we could not determine in the abstract the circumstances in which preaccusation delay would require dismissing prosecutions. More than five years later, that statement remains true. Indeed, in the intervening years so few defendants have established that they were prejudiced by delay that neither this Court nor any lower court has had a sustained opportunity to consider the constitutional significance of various reasons for delay. We therefore leave to the lower courts, in the first instance, the task of applying the settled principles of due process that we have discussed to the particular circumstances of individual cases. We simply hold that in this case the lower courts erred in dismissing the indictment.

Reversed.

MR. JUSTICE STEVENS, dissenting.

If the record presented the question which the Court decides today, I would join its well-reasoned opinion. I am unable to do so because I believe our review should be limited to the facts disclosed by the record developed in the District Court and the traditional scope of review we have exercised with regard to issues of fact. * * *

Notes and Questions

1. When and how did Justice Marshall decide that due process gives him leeway rather than restricts his ability to decide pre-charge delay cases?

2. In footnote 17, the Court leaves open the possibility that fundamental fairness may be denied in circumstances not involving prosecutorial tactics of intentional delay. The Court was prepared to recognize a due process violation when the delay occurred "in reckless disregard of circumstances, known to the prosecution, suggesting that there existed an appreciable risk that delay would impair the ability to mount an effective defense."

3. The Court also observed the impossibility of deciding in the abstract when due process relief is required, and it left to the lower courts the task of

---

17. In *Marion* we noted with approval that the Government conceded that a "tactical" delay would violate the Due Process Clause. The Government renews that concession here, and expands it somewhat by stating: "A due process violation might also be made out upon a showing of prosecutorial delay incurred in reckless disregard of circumstances, known to the prosecution, suggesting that there existed an appreciable risk that delay would impair the ability to mount an effective defense." As the Government notes, however, there is no evidence of recklessness here.

applying "settled principles of due process" to the particular circumstances of individual cases. How settled could those principles have been if the courts were lacking in the experience of deciding the significance of various reasons for delay?

4. When a defendant alleges, without substantiation, prejudice from witnesses's faded memories, the defendant's inability to locate witnesses, the loss of evidence, or the refusal of witnesses to testify, courts generally refuse to find substantial prejudice to the defendant's ability to present a defense at trial. *See, e.g., United States v. Gilbert*, 266 F.3d 1180 (9th Cir.2001) (no showing of how testimony of "lost" witnesses would have assisted defendant). If the defendant was serving a prison sentence for another crime during the delay, is it sufficient prejudice that the delay precluded the defendant from concurrently serving the prior sentence and any prospective sentence from the delayed charge concurrently?

5. Suppose a defendant is able to show prejudice from the delay between the crime and the arrest, how can the defendant prove an improper prosecutorial motive? Occasionally, courts decide that proof of prejudice to the defense is sufficient to afford the defendant a dismissal of the charge, without a showing of improper prosecutorial motive. *See, e.g., Howell v. Barker*, 904 F.2d 889 (4th Cir.1990); *State v. Cyr*, 588 A.2d 753 (Me.1991).

6. Besides constitutional restrictions on charging defendants, there may be statutes of limitations for charging defendants with felonies or misdemeanors. What is the purpose of such a statute? In *United States v. Marion, supra*, the Court stated that the

> purpose of a statute of limitations is to limit exposure to prosecution to a fixed period of time [and] to protect individuals from having to defend themselves against charges when the basic facts may have become obscured by the passage of time. [Such] a time limit may also have the salutary effect of encouraging law enforcement officials promptly to investigate suspected criminal activity.

Many states have no time limit within which felony charges must be brought. The limitations period for many federal felonies is five years. 18 U.S.C. § 3282. By contrast, misdemeanor charges typically must be commenced within a time certain, e.g., one year, from the last act constituting the offense.

Problem

In the fall of 1990, Sue acquired a building in Metro which she converted into a country-western nightclub known as Sue's. The nightclub opened in early 1991, but was damaged severely by a fire two months later. Sue was on the premises at the time the fire broke out and the evidence clearly indicates that the fire was set. Sue was alone at the time, and claims that the fire was started by a masked man who accosted her at the back door of the nightclub, collected all the money he could find, tied her to a chair, and started the fire. Sue managed to escape after she began to smell smoke, and went across the street to the Red Apple convenience store for help. The Red Apple clerks stated that Sue appeared to have been beaten and her hands were tied with wire. The police took a number of pictures of Sue's face showing cuts and bruises, but the photographs were misplaced. Local police and fire departments and Sue's insurance carrier conducted extensive investigations to determine the origin and cause of the fire. The investigations were completed in April 1991. While insurance investigators were suspicious of Sue's story, they paid her insurance claim during the summer of 1991.

During May 1996, the local grand jury indicted Sue and an associate on charges of arson. Between April 1991 and May 1996 there were no new developments in the case—no new evidence was found, no new studies were conducted, and no new witnesses or statements about the fire were made available to authorities.

Prior to trial, Sue moved to dismiss the indictment on the ground that the pre-charge delay and the State's loss of potentially exculpatory evidence had prejudiced her case. The court reserved judgment on the motion until after trial. During the trial, the State entered evidence showing that Sue was heavily in debt, and that she set the fire to her business intentionally in order to collect insurance proceeds, and then inflicted her own injuries to support her story that a robber set the fire. The jury found Sue guilty of arson. The trial judge then granted Sue's pretrial motion to dismiss the indictment on the ground of prejudicial preindictment delay. If the standard for appellate review is whether the trial judge's factual and legal findings were clearly erroneous, will the prosecutor be successful on appeal of the trial judge's grant of the dismissal?

B. DELAY IN BRINGING DEFENDANT TO TRIAL

An accused's right to a speedy trial is guaranteed by both the United States and state constitutions. The Sixth Amendment right is one of the most basic rights preserved by constitutional law, although it may be one of the least popular rights among defendants. Because the defendant has no duty to bring himself to trial, the duty of executing the right is the responsibility of the prosecution. The right is intended to spare the accused those penalties and disabilities which spring from the delay in the criminal process, as well as provide protection for society's interest in effective prosecution. *Dickey v. Florida*, 398 U.S. 30 (1970). The constitutional right to a speedy trial includes the right to speedy sentencing and a speedy appeal. *See, e.g., Pedigo v. Commonwealth*, 644 S.W.2d 355 (Ky.Ct.App.1982) (speedy sentencing); *Rheuark v. Shaw*, 477 F.Supp. 897 (N.D.Tex.1979) (speedy appeal).

In *Barker v. Wingo*, 407 U.S. 514 (1972), the Court noted that the right to a speedy trial "is generically different from any of the other rights enshrined in the Constitution for the protection of the accused" because

> there is a societal interest in providing a speedy trial which exists separate from, and at times in opposition to, the interests of the accused. The inability of the courts to provide a prompt trial has contributed to a large backlog of cases in urban courts which, among other things, enables defendants to negotiate more effectively for pleas of guilty to lesser offenses and otherwise manipulate the

system. In addition, persons released on bond for lengthy periods awaiting trial have an opportunity to commit other crimes. [Moreover,] the longer an accused is free awaiting trial, the more tempting becomes his opportunity to jump bail and escape. Finally, delay between arrest and punishment may have a detrimental effect on rehabilitation.

The right to a speedy trial attaches from the earlier of the date of the indictment or information, or the date of the arrest, *i.e.*, when the person becomes "accused." Similarly, the right to a speedy trial attaches when a detainer is lodged against an accused who is in custody on other charges. Once the right to a speedy trial attaches, it continues until the charges are dismissed. The time between the dismissal and a new related charge does not count for purposes of the right to a speedy trial, although due process may afford some protection if the defendant can identify prejudice from the delay.

In *Barker*, the Court held that any inquiry into a constitutional speedy trial claim requires a balancing on an ad hoc basis of at least four factors: (1) the length of the delay; (2) the reasons for the delay; (3) whether and how the defendant asserted the speedy trial right; and (4) the amount of prejudice suffered by the defendant. Because of this balancing approach, it is impossible to determine with precision when the constitutional right has been denied.

Barker held that the length of the delay serves as a threshold requirement or "triggering mechanism" for finding a violation of the speedy trial right. Although the length of the delay alone does not establish a constitutional violation, a court need not inquire into the other factors unless it finds the delay to be presumptively prejudicial. The *Doggett* case which follows suggested that a delay of at least twelve months triggered further analysis under *Barker* because that delay was presumptively prejudicial. *Doggett v. United States*, 505 U.S. 647, 652 n. 1.

Courts weigh delays intended to gain a trial advantage more heavily against the prosecution than unintentional delays resulting from institutional dysfunction. In the absence of a showing of bad faith or dilatory motive, the prosecution is not responsible for delays attributable to its own acts. Neutral reasons such as negligence and overcrowded calendars weigh less heavily, but are still considered because responsibility for such conditions rests with the prosecution. A period of delay attributable to tactics by the defendant is deemed a waiver of the right to a speedy trial for that period of delay. *See, e.g., United States v. Walker*, 92 F.3d 714 (8th Cir.1996) (no violation when delay caused by defendant fleeing and attempting to avoid arrest); *United States v. Occhipinti*, 998 F.2d 791 (10th Cir.1993) (no violation when most of delay caused by defendant's pretrial motions).

Despite the view that a defendant does not have the duty to bring himself to trial, the defendant's failure to demand a speedy trial undercuts the defendant's constitutional argument. By contrast, a vigorous and timely assertion of the right provides strong evidence that the defendant is interested in a speedy disposition. A court will not treat a claim seriously that a trial started too late unless the defendant continuously has sought a speedy trial. *See, e.g., United States v. Vachon*, 869 F.2d 653 (1st Cir.1989) (defendant did not assert right until two days before trial after thirteen-month delay).

Barker stated that a court must weigh any prejudice to the defendant in light of the interests protected by the speedy trial guarantee: preventing oppressive pretrial incarceration, minimizing anxiety of the accused, and limiting impairment to the defense. Courts typically do not take the first two types of allegations very seriously. The third allegation is serious, and if demonstrated usually will result in a finding of prejudice.

Barker expressly stated that dismissal with prejudice is the only possible remedy for a violation of the Sixth Amendment speedy trial right. Trial courts therefore cannot devise less extreme remedies such as a sentence reduction. *Strunk v. United States*, 412 U.S. 434 (1973). The reprosecution prohibition probably results in fewer constitutional violations. An alternative disposition is to find a violation of the relevant speedy trial statute (e.g., 18 U.S.C. § 3161 et seq.) or the relevant docket control rule (*e.g.*, Fed.R.Crim.P. 48(b)), both of which may prescribe dismissal without prejudice as an available method of enforcement. Still another remedy is to provide a writ of mandamus to compel a trial court to set a trial date for the defendant's case.

In *United States v. MacDonald*, 456 U.S. 1 (1982), the Court held that the time period between dismissal of charges and reinstatement of those charges is a part of the pre-charge period to which the Sixth Amendment right to a speedy trial is inapplicable. Once charges are dismissed, the person is no longer a subject of public accusation and has no restraints on liberty. *MacDonald* was deemed controlling in *United States v. Loud Hawk*, 474 U.S. 302 (1986), where the Court held that the time during which the prosecution appealed a dismissal, while the defendants were not incarcerated and not subject to bail, did not count. The Court stated that an interlocutory appeal is "ordinarily ... a valid reason that justifies the delay." Once the government announces that it will appeal the dismissal of an indictment, is that not a reaffirmation of the intent to prosecute, thereby requiring that the Sixth Amendment apply?

In its most recent Sixth Amendment speedy trial case, set out below, notice the extent to which the Court has altered *Barker*'s balancing test.

DOGGETT v. UNITED STATES
505 U.S. 647 (1992).

JUSTICE SOUTER delivered the opinion of the Court.

In this case we consider whether the delay of 8½ years between petitioner's indictment and arrest violated his Sixth Amendment right to a speedy trial. We hold that it did.

I

On February 22, 1980, petitioner Marc Doggett was indicted for conspiring with several others to import and distribute cocaine. Douglas Driver, the Drug Enforcement Administration's principal agent investigating the conspiracy, told the United States Marshal's Service that the DEA would oversee the apprehension of Doggett and his confederates. On March 18, 1980, two police officers set out under Driver's orders to arrest Doggett at his parents' house in Raleigh, North Carolina, only to find that he was not there. His mother told the officers that he had left for Colombia four days earlier.

To catch Doggett on his return to the United States, Driver sent word of his outstanding arrest warrant to all United States Customs stations and to a number of law enforcement organizations. He also placed Doggett's name in the Treasury Enforcement Communication System (TECS), a computer network that helps Customs agents screen people entering the country, and in the National Crime Information Center computer system, which serves similar ends. The TECS entry expired that September, however, and Doggett's name vanished from the system.

In September 1981, Driver found out that Doggett was under arrest on drug charges in Panama and, thinking that a formal extradition request would be futile, simply asked Panama to "expel" Doggett to the United States. Although the Panamanian authorities promised to comply when their own proceedings had run their course, they freed Doggett the following July and let him go to Colombia, where he stayed with an aunt for several months. On September 25, 1982, he passed unhindered through Customs in New York City and settled down in Virginia. Since his return to the United States, he has married, earned a college degree, found a steady job as a computer operations manager, lived openly under his own name, and stayed within the law.

Doggett's travels abroad had not wholly escaped the Government's notice, however. In 1982, the American Embassy in Panama told the State Department of his departure to Colombia, but that information, for whatever reason, eluded the DEA, and Agent Driver assumed for several years that his quarry was still serving time in a Panamanian prison. Driver never asked DEA officials in Panama to check into Doggett's status, and only after his own fortuitous assignment to that country in 1985 did he discover Doggett's departure for Colombia. Driver then simply assumed Doggett had settled there, and he made no effort to find out for sure or to track Doggett down, either abroad or in the United States. Thus Doggett remained lost to the American criminal justice system until September 1988, when the Marshal's Service ran a simple credit check on several thousand people subject to outstanding arrest warrants and, within minutes, found out where Doggett lived and worked. On September 5, 1988, nearly 6 years after his return to the United States and 8½ years after his indictment, Doggett was arrested.

He naturally moved to dismiss the indictment, arguing that the Government's failure to prosecute him earlier violated his Sixth Amendment right to a speedy trial. The Federal Magistrate hearing his motion applied the criteria for assessing speedy trial claims set out in *Barker v. Wingo*, 407 U.S. 514 (1972): "[l]ength of delay, the reason for the delay, the defendant's assertion of his right, and prejudice to the defendant." The Magistrate found that the delay between Doggett's indictment and arrest was long enough to be "presumptively prejudicial," that the delay "clearly [was] attributable to the negligence of the government," and that Doggett could not be faulted for any delay in asserting his right to a speedy trial, there being no evidence that he had known of the charges against him until his arrest. The Magistrate also found, however, that Doggett had made no affirmative showing that the delay had impaired his ability to mount a successful defense or had otherwise prejudiced him. In his recommendation to the District Court, the Magistrate contended that this failure to demonstrate particular prejudice sufficed to defeat Doggett's speedy trial claim.

The District Court took the recommendation and denied Doggett's motion. * * *

The Sixth Amendment guarantees that, "[i]n all criminal prosecutions, the accused shall enjoy the right to a speedy ... trial.... " On its face, the Speedy Trial Clause is written with such breadth that, taken literally, it would forbid the government to delay the trial of an "accused" for any reason at all. Our cases, however, have qualified the literal sweep of the provision by specifically recognizing the relevance of four separate enquiries: whether delay before trial was uncommonly long, whether the government or the criminal defendant is more to blame for that delay, whether, in due course, the defendant asserted his right to a speedy trial, and whether he suffered prejudice as the delay's result.

The first of these is actually a double enquiry. Simply to trigger a speedy trial analysis, an accused must allege that the interval between accusation and trial has crossed the threshold dividing ordinary from "presumptively prejudicial" delay, since, by definition, he cannot complain that the government has denied him a "speedy" trial if it has, in fact, prosecuted his case with customary promptness. If the accused makes this showing, the court must then consider, as one factor among several, the extent to which the delay stretches beyond the bare minimum needed to trigger judicial examination of the claim. This latter enquiry is significant to the speedy trial analysis because, as we discuss below, the presumption that pretrial delay has prejudiced the accused intensifies over time. In this case, the extraordinary 8½ year lag between Doggett's indictment and arrest clearly suffices to trigger the speedy trial enquiry; its further significance within that enquiry will be dealt with later.

As for *Barker*'s second criterion, the Government claims to have sought Doggett with diligence. The findings of the courts below are to the contrary, however, and we review trial court determinations of negligence with considerable deference. The Government gives us nothing to gainsay the findings that have come up to us, and we see nothing fatal to them in the record. For six years, the Government's investigators made no serious effort to test their progressively more questionable assumption that Doggett was living abroad, and, had they done so, they could have found him within minutes. While the Government's lethargy may have reflected no more than Doggett's relative unimportance in the world of drug trafficking, it was still findable negligence, and the finding stands.

The Government goes against the record again in suggesting that Doggett knew of his indictment years before he was arrested. Were this true, *Barker*'s third factor, concerning invocation of the right to a speedy trial, would be weighed heavily against him. But here again, the Government is trying to revisit the facts. At the hearing on Doggett's speedy trial motion, it introduced no evidence challenging the testimony of Doggett's wife, who said that she did not know of the charges until his arrest, and of his mother, who claimed not to have told him or anyone else that the police had come looking for him. * * *

The Government is left, then, with its principal contention: that Doggett fails to make out a successful speedy trial claim because he has not shown precisely how he was prejudiced by the delay between his indictment and trial.

We have observed in prior cases that unreasonable delay between formal accusation and trial threatens to produce more than one sort of harm, including "oppressive pretrial incarceration," "anxiety and concern of the accused," and "the possibility that the [accused's] defense will be impaired" by dimming memories and loss of exculpatory evidence. *Barker*, 407 U.S., at 532. Of these forms of prejudice, "the most serious is the last, because the inability of a defendant adequately to prepare his case skews the fairness of the entire system." Doggett claims this kind of prejudice, and there is probably no other kind that he can claim, since he was subjected neither to pretrial detention nor, he has successfully contended, to awareness of unresolved charges against him.

The Government answers Doggett's claim by citing language in three cases for the proposition that the Speedy Trial Clause does not significantly protect a criminal defendant's interest in fair adjudication. In so arguing, the Government asks us, in effect, to read part of *Barker* right out of the law, and that we will not do. In context, the cited passages support nothing beyond the principle, which we have independently based on textual and historical grounds, that the Sixth Amendment right of the accused to a speedy trial has no application beyond the confines of a formal criminal prosecution. Once triggered by arrest, indictment, or other official accusation, however, the speedy trial enquiry must weigh the effect of delay on the accused's defense just as it has to weigh any other form of prejudice that *Barker* recognized.

As an alternative to limiting *Barker*, the Government claims Doggett has failed to make any affirmative showing that the delay weakened his ability to raise specific defenses, elicit specific testimony, or produce specific items of evidence. Though Doggett did indeed come up short in this respect, the Government's argument takes it only so far: consideration of prejudice is not limited to the specifically demonstrable, and, as it concedes, affirmative proof of particularized prejudice is not essential to every speedy trial claim. *Barker* explicitly recognized that impairment of one's defense is the most difficult form of speedy trial prejudice to prove because time's erosion of exculpatory evidence and testimony "can rarely be shown." And though time can tilt the case against either side, one cannot generally be sure which of them it has prejudiced more severely. Thus, we generally have to recognize that excessive delay presumptively compromises the reliability of a trial in ways that neither party can prove or, for that matter, identify. While such presumptive prejudice cannot alone carry a Sixth Amendment claim without regard to the other *Barker* criteria, it is part of the mix of relevant facts, and its importance increases with the length of delay.

This brings us to an enquiry into the role that presumptive prejudice should play in the disposition of Doggett's speedy trial claim. We begin with hypothetical and somewhat easier cases and work our way to this one.

Our speedy trial standards recognize that pretrial delay is often both inevitable and wholly justifiable. The government may need time to collect witnesses against the accused, oppose his pretrial motions, or, if he goes into hiding, track him down. We attach great weight to such considerations when balancing them against the costs of going forward with a trial whose probative accuracy the passage of time has begun by degrees to throw into question. Thus, in this case, if the Government had pursued Doggett with reasonable diligence from his indictment to his arrest, his speedy trial claim would fail. Indeed, that conclusion would generally follow as a matter of course however great the delay, so long as Doggett could not show specific prejudice to his defense.

The Government concedes, on the other hand, that Doggett would prevail if he could show that the Government had intentionally held back in its prosecution of him to gain some impermissible advantage at trial. That we cannot doubt. *Barker* stressed that official bad faith in causing delay will be weighed heavily against the government, and a bad-faith delay the length of this negligent one would present an overwhelming case for dismissal.

Between diligent prosecution and bad-faith delay, official negligence in bringing an accused to trial occupies the middle ground. While not compelling relief in every case where bad-faith delay would make relief virtually automatic, neither is negligence automatically tolerable simply because the accused cannot demonstrate exactly how it has prejudiced him. It was on this point that the Court of Appeals erred, and on the facts before us, it was reversible error.

Barker made it clear that "different weights [are to be] assigned to different reasons" for delay. Although negligence is obviously to be weighed more lightly than a deliberate intent to harm the accused's defense, it still falls on the wrong side of the divide between acceptable and unacceptable reasons for delaying a criminal prosecution once it has begun. And such is the nature of the prejudice presumed that the weight we assign to official negligence compounds over time as the presumption of evidentiary prejudice grows. Thus, our toleration of such negligence varies inversely with its protractedness, and its consequent threat to the fairness of the accused's trial. Condoning prolonged and unjustifiable delays in prosecution would both penalize many defendants for the state's fault and simply encourage the government to gamble with the interests of criminal suspects assigned a low prosecutorial priority. The Government, indeed, can hardly complain too loudly, for persistent neglect in concluding a criminal prosecution indicates an uncommonly feeble interest in bringing an accused to justice; the more weight the Government attaches to securing a conviction, the harder it will try to get it.

To be sure, to warrant granting relief, negligence unaccompanied by particularized trial prejudice must have lasted longer than negligence demonstrably causing such prejudice. But even so, the Government's egregious persistence in failing to prosecute Doggett is clearly sufficient. The lag between Doggett's indictment and arrest was 8½ years, and he would have faced trial 6 years earlier than he did but for the Government's inexcusable oversights. The portion of the delay attributable to the Government's negligence far exceeds the threshold needed to state a speedy trial claim; indeed, we have called shorter delays "extraordinary." When the Government's negligence thus causes delay six times as long as that generally sufficient to trigger judicial review, and when the presumption of prejudice, albeit unspecified, is neither extenuated, as by the defendant's acquiescence, nor persuasively rebutted, the defendant is entitled to relief.

We reverse the judgment of the Court of Appeals and remand the case for proceedings consistent with this opinion.

JUSTICE O'CONNOR, dissenting.

I believe the Court of Appeals properly balanced the considerations set forth in *Barker v. Wingo*. Although the delay between indictment and trial was lengthy, petitioner did not suffer any anxiety or restriction on his liberty. The only harm to petitioner from the lapse of time was potential prejudice to his ability to defend his case. We have not allowed such speculative harm to tip the scales. Instead, we have required a showing of actual prejudice to the defense before weighing it in the balance. As we stated in *United States v. Loud Hawk*, 474 U.S. 302, 315 (1986), the "possibility of prejudice is not sufficient to support respondents' position that their speedy trial rights were violated. In this case, moreover, delay is a two-edged sword. It is the Government that bears the burden of proving its case beyond a reasonable doubt. The passage of time may make it difficult or impossible for the Government to carry this burden." The Court of Appeals followed this holding, and I believe we should as well. For this reason, I respectfully dissent.

JUSTICE THOMAS, with whom THE CHIEF JUSTICE and JUSTICE SCALIA join, dissenting.

Just as "bad facts make bad law," so too odd facts make odd law. Doggett's 8½–year odyssey from youthful drug dealing in the tobacco country of North Carolina, through stints in a Panamanian jail and in Colombia, to life as a computer operations manager, homeowner, and registered voter in suburban Virginia, is extraordinary. But even more extraordinary is the Court's conclusion that the Government denied Doggett his Sixth Amendment right to a speedy trial despite the fact that he has suffered none of the harms that the right was designed to prevent. I respectfully dissent. * * *

In my view, the choice presented is not a hard one. *Barker*'s suggestion that preventing prejudice to the defense is a fundamental and independent objective of the Clause is plainly dictum. Never, until today, have we confronted a case where a defendant subjected to a lengthy delay after indictment nonetheless failed to suffer any substantial impairment of his liberty. I think it fair to say that *Barker* simply did not contemplate such an unusual situation. Moreover, to the extent that the *Barker* dictum purports to elevate considerations of prejudice to the defense to fundamental and independent status under the Clause, it cannot be deemed to have survived our subsequent decisions in *MacDonald* and *Loud Hawk*. * * *

Therefore, I see no basis for the Court's conclusion that Doggett is entitled to relief under the Speedy Trial Clause simply because the Government was negligent in prosecuting him and because the resulting delay may have prejudiced his defense.

It remains to be considered, however, whether Doggett is entitled to relief under the Speedy Trial Clause because of the disruption of his life years after the criminal events at issue. In other words, does the Clause protect a right to repose, free from secret or unknown indictments? In my view, it does not, for much the same reasons set forth above. * * *

There is no basis for concluding that the disruption of an accused's life years after the commission of his alleged crime is an evil independently protected by the Speedy Trial Clause. Such disruption occurs regardless of whether the individual is under indictment during the period of delay. Thus, had Doggett been indicted shortly before his 1988 arrest rather than shortly after his 1980 crime, his repose would have been equally shattered—but he would not have even a colorable speedy-trial claim. To recognize a constitutional right to repose is to recognize a right to be tried speedily after the offense. That would, of course, convert the Speedy Trial Clause into a constitutional statute of limitations—a result with no basis in the text or history of the Clause or in our precedents. * * *

Today's opinion, I fear, will transform the courts of the land into boards of law-enforcement supervision. For the Court compels dismissal of the charges against Doggett not because he was harmed in any way by the delay between his indictment and arrest, but simply because the Government's efforts to catch him are found wanting. [Our] Constitution neither contemplates nor tolerates such a role. I respectfully dissent.

Notes and Questions

1. Does *Doggett* offer insight into the interrelationships among the *Barker* factors? For example, if the reason for the delay is the reasonable diligence of the government, a defendant's speedy trial claim probably will fail unless there is a showing of specific prejudice. Conversely, if the reason for the delay is the prosecution's attempt to gain some impermissible tactical advantage, a rebuttal presumption of prejudice exists. As a prosecutor, how would you rebut the presumption of prejudice? If the reason for the delay is the prosecution's negligence, is some showing of prejudice by the defendant necessary or is a presumption of prejudice created? Define the distinction between governmental negligence and bad faith.

2. In the absence of a demand by defense counsel, does the demand "requirement" result in the defendant paying for the omission of counsel? Is a successful claim of ineffective assistance of counsel necessary to relieve the defendant of the failure to make a demand for a speedy trial? Should the defendant's failure to request a speedy trial be treated differently when the defendant is representing herself?

3. In *Reed v. Farley*, 512 U.S. 339 (1994), the Court, citing *Barker*, asserted: "A showing of prejudice is required to establish a violation of the Sixth Amendment Speedy Trial Clause, and that necessary ingredient is entirely missing here." Does *Reed* further modify or rebalance the statements in *Doggett* about the interrelationship of the *Barker* factors?

Problems

1. In early 1996, Bob and John arranged to purchase cocaine from Sam. Sam, acting as a "middleman," set up a meeting with Bob, John and a cocaine supplier, who in fact was an undercover federal agent working with the Metro Police. The meeting took place on March 30, 1996, at which time Bob and John were arrested by the federal agent on suspicion of state law drug violations. Because of the amount of drugs involved, the Metro Police requested federal prosecution. John was soon released from custody.

A federal indictment was returned on May 8, 1996. John, however, was not arrested until October 16, 1997. Metro Police Officer Bill Green later testified that during the time between John's indictment and arrest, he spent several nights looking for John, including driving by and watching John's house, which Green said looked vacant. At one point, Green knocked on John's door, but John's wife said he was at work. Green left a message with John's wife, but did not mention that John was under federal indictment. In June, 1996, Green suspended efforts to locate John, apparently under the impression that United States Marshals would take over the case.

In October, 1997, however, Green happened to drive by John's house, saw that the lights were on, and knocked on the door. John answered, and was arrested.

John moves to dismiss the indictment because of unconstitutional delay. The United States, of course, opposes the motion. You are the judge. Write the opinion addressing John's motion.

2. Willie was indicted on April 23, 1994, for polluting the streams near his home. After indictment, the state moved for three continuances of six months each to allow the prosecutor additional time to prepare her case. In addition, the trial judge's clerk forgot to redocket the case for trial for one year. During this time of two and a half years, public opinion had become less tolerant of water pollution. In October 1996, Willie was found guilty by a jury and sentenced to ten years. Willie's counsel objected to the proceedings before and during trial, but the trial judge denied his motions to dismiss. Willie wants you to help him file an appeal. What speedy trial arguments will you make on Willie's behalf? Are they likely to be successful?

Note

In *Smith v. Hooey*, 393 U.S. 374 (1969), the Court held that an inmate in one jurisdiction has a Sixth Amendment right to a speedy trial on charges pending in another jurisdiction. A prosecutor must make a good faith and diligent effort to speedily prosecute inmates confined in other jurisdictions. Within a few years of the *Hooey* decision, Congress and most state legislatures attempted to address this issue by becoming signatories to the Interstate Agreement on Detainers. This interstate compact is enacted in 48 states, Puerto Rico, the Virgin Islands, the District of Columbia, and the United States. As a congressionally sanctioned compact, it is a federal law subject to federal construction. *Cuyler v. Adams*, 449 U.S. 433 (1981). The Interstate Agreement on Detainers is intended to enable an inmate in one state to force the expeditious disposition of outstanding charges in other states. Prosecutors also can obtain prisoners for trial under the compact. *See* Leslie W. Abramson, *The Interstate Agreement on Detainers: Narrowing Its Availability and Application*, 21 New Eng. J. Crim. & Civ. Confinement 1 (1995). When there is a pending charge in another county of the same state, separate intrastate statutes often permit the inmate to request a speedy disposition of the untried charge. *See, e.g.*, the Uniform Mandatory Disposition of Detainers Act.

C. STATUTORY PROMPT DISPOSITION PROVISIONS

In addition to the constitutional speedy trial standard and interstate compacts, many state legislatures and the Congress have enacted speedy trial legislation which establishes specific time limits for completing stages of a criminal prosecution. For example, the federal Speedy Trial Act (18 U.S.C. § 3161 et seq. in the statutory supplement) requires that an arrested defendant be formally charged within thirty days after the arrest and that the defendant's trial begin within seventy days after the formal charge was filed. In addition, the trial cannot begin earlier than thirty days from the date the defendant first appears before the court unless the defendant consents in writing to an earlier trial. Unlike the constitutional standard which makes the passage of time a "triggering mechanism," the statute makes the passage of time dispositive of whether there is a violation. Most speedy trial statutes, like the federal Act, do not require a defendant to show either that he demanded a speedy trial or that the effect of the delay was prejudicial.

Certain types of pretrial delays are automatically excluded from the computation of legislative time limits, e.g., periods of delay like the absence or unavailability of the defendant or an essential witness, delays resulting from the joinder of a codefendant, and delays resulting from other proceedings involving the defendant. In *Henderson v. United States*, 476 U.S. 321 (1986), the Court held that Congress intended the "other proceedings" provision to require exclusion of all delays attributable to pendency of pretrial motions regardless of whether the delays are reasonably necessary. Indeed, some courts have held that time for *preparation* of pretrial motions is properly excludable.

Continuances granted when the "ends of justice" outweigh the interest of the public and the defendant in a speedy trial give trial judges the flexibility to address complex or unusual cases. By contrast, a court cannot grant a continuance for delays caused by general congestion of the court calendar, or by the prosecution's failure to prepare diligently or obtain available witnesses.

To compute whether there has been a statutory violation, the court calculates the gross elapsed days and subtracts the number of days attributable to excludable time, leaving the net elapsed days. If the Act's time limits are not met, the charges against a defendant must be dismissed. The key determination for the trial judge is whether the dismissal must be with or without prejudice. As you read in 18 U.S.C. §§ 3162(a)(1)–(2), the judge is consider three factors in exercising discretion to dismiss charges with or without prejudice: 1) the seriousness of the offense; 2) the circumstances leading to dismissal; and 3) the effect of reprosecution on the administration of justice and the legislation. 18 U.S.C. § 3162(a)(1)–(2). In *United States v. Taylor*, 487 U.S. 326 (1988), the Court held that it is an abuse of discretion if the trial judge fails to consider each statutory factor and explain other factors relied upon in deciding whether to dismiss charges.

Is a defendant permitted to waive the requirements of the Speedy Trial Act? For example, can a defendant execute a written waiver of speedy trial rights based on an "ends of justice" continuance under § 3161(h)(8)? In *Zedner v. United States*, 126 S.Ct. 1976 (2006), the Supreme Court stated that, under § 3162(a)(2), a waiver of the right to dismissal for a past statutory violation occurs when a defendant fails to filed a motion for dismissal before trial or entering a guilty plea. However, that provision does not indicate the Congress intended to permit prospective waivers, i.e., a defendant cannot opt out of the Act's requirements prior to a violation. The Act was intended to serve public interests that would be subverted by an interpretation that allowed prospective waivers.

Problems

After you have read the federal Speedy Trial Act, consider the following issues.

1.   The Act requires that an information or indictment be filed within thirty days after arrest or service of a summons on the defendant.

a.   Does the thirty-day period begin to run when a defendant is arrested and released without being charged and then is indicted after the thirty-day period has run? *See United States v. Gaskin*, 364 F.3d 438 (2d Cir.2004) (no).

b.   Does the period apply to indictments for offenses for which the defendant was not charged when arrested? *See United States v. Burgos*, 254 F.3d 8 (1st Cir.2001) (no).

2.   The Act requires that the trial begin within seventy days of the filing of an information or indictment, or of the date the defendant appears before an officer of the court in which the charge is pending, whichever is later.

a.   Does the filing of a superseding indictment for offenses charged affect the seventy-day period? *See United States v. Daychild*, 357 F.3d 1082 (9th Cir.2004) (no).

b.   Does the period apply to a hearing on postconviction relief? *See United States v. Samples*, 897 F.2d 193 (5th Cir.1990).

c.   Does the period apply when a defendant withdraws a guilty plea and enters a not guilty plea? *See United States v. Solorzano–Rivera*, 368 F.3d 1073 (9th Cir.2004) (yes).

d.   What trial event constitutes the end of the pretrial period? *See United States v. Rodriguez*, 63 F.3d 1159 (1st Cir.1995) (voir dire).

3.   The Act enumerates a specific list of pretrial delays which are automatically excluded from the computation of the statutory time limits.

a.   What are the conditions under which a defendant or an essential witness is considered absent or unavailable under § 3161(h)(3)? *See United States v. Martinez–Martinez*, 369 F.3d 1076 (9th Cir.2004); *United States v. Garcia*, 995 F.2d 556 (5th Cir.1993).

b.   Are delays attributable to motions filed by codefendants excludable? *See United States v. Feurtado*, 191 F.3d 420 (4th Cir.1999) (yes).

c.   What are the consequences of a judge's failure to make explicit findings about a continuance granted when the "ends of justice" outweigh the interest of the public and the defendant in a speedy trial? *Compare United States v. Barnes*, 251 F.3d 251 (1st Cir.2001) (time not excludable) with *United States v. Stackhouse*, 183 F.3d 900 (8th Cir. 1999) (record set forth sufficient facts to support finding even though court did not make explicit finding).

Chapter 17

DISCOVERY AND DISCLOSURE

Pretrial discovery is the process of exchanging information between the prosecution and the defense. Prior to filing a pretrial motion for court ordered discovery, the defense may utilize other formal and informal methods for obtaining information from the prosecution. Prosecutors primarily look to police departments and grand jury investigations to uncover relevant facts. The grand jury offers prosecutors many of the advantages that civil litigants obtain through discovery depositions. The grand jury has the power to compel testimony and documents from many sources, and, unlike a civil deposition, the whole process occurs ex parte and in secret. The prosecutor proceeds unhampered by objections. The witness testifies without counsel at his/her side.

Defendants, on the other hand, have no control over the grand jury process and in many cases, are unaware of the grand jury's investigation until it is over. Once the investigation is complete, as a general rule defendants are not even entitled to the transcribed record of grand jury proceedings unless and until a grand jury witness later testifies for the government at trial. Defendants, however, have many other avenues for discovery. As discussed previously, a motion for a Bill of Particulars requests more specific information about the charge described in the indictment or information upon which the accused will stand trial. The charging instrument often sets forth the "bare bones" of the crime in conclusory language such as "the defendant did murder the victim at such a time and place." In order to prepare a meaningful trial defense, a Bill of Particulars might ask for a description of the particular form of murder (e.g., premeditated murder or felony murder) and the specific method by which the alleged murder was committed (e.g., with a gun, knife, or chain saw). What follows is a motion for a bill of particulars relating to a conspiracy charge.

Motion for Bill of Particulars

The Defendant, by and through counsel, moves this Court for entry of an Order directing the Government to particularize the indictment herein as requested below.

1. The exact precise date, time, location, and address at which the conspiracy is alleged to have occurred;

2. The means by which the conspiracy is alleged to have been planned and/or effectuated;

3. The relationship within the conspiracy that each alleged conspirator is alleged to have had with each other alleged conspirator;

4. The date, location and manner by which each alleged conspirator is alleged to have joined the said conspiracy as well as the like information regarding any alleged withdrawals from the said conspiracy;

5. Each and every overt act that was committed in the conspiracy;

6. The names and addresses of each conspirator (indicted or unindicted) that are known to the Government.

As grounds for the foregoing, Defendant states the following:

1. That the indictment does not contain the requested information;

2. That the information requested is necessary to avoid double jeopardy and prepare an adequate defense.

WHEREFORE, Defendant requests this Honorable Court to grant this motion and such other relief as may be deemed just.

In contrast to rules which mandate certain forms of discovery, the granting of a Bill of Particulars is largely discretionary with the judge because "the decisive consideration in each case is whether the matter claimed to be left out of the indictment has resulted in depriving the accused of a substantial right and subjects him to danger of being tried upon a charge for which he has not been indicted." *Ward v. Commonwealth*, 205 Va. 564, 138 S.E.2d 293 (1964).

As discussed previously, a preliminary hearing often yields important information about the nature of the prosecution's case. Although discovery is not an avowed purpose of preliminary hearings, discovery is an inherent byproduct of the requirement that the prosecution present at least a prima facie case to a judicial officer. Prosecutors, however, often limit the defense opportunity for discovery at the preliminary hearing by presenting the minimum evidence required to certify the case for trial, and some jurisdictions have been particularly hostile to defense counsel's efforts to expand the preliminary hearing into a discovery vehicle. For example, in *Foster v. Commonwealth*, 209 Va. 297, 163 S.E.2d 565 (1968) the defense attempted to call eleven police officers who had knowledge of the case. In the absence of any showing that such testimony would refute the prosecution's prima facie case, the court properly terminated the defendant's presentation of evidence and certified the case for trial.

Outside the confines of judicial proceedings, discovery may occur as part of the give and take of plea bargaining between defense counsel and the prosecutor. Finally, some prosecutors subscribe to an "open office" philosophy where the prosecutor voluntarily discusses the nature of the government's case and makes documentary and real evidence available for inspection by the defense. "When a prosecutor enters into an informal discovery agreement he must abide by its spirit as well as its letter." *United States v. Cole*, 857 F.2d 971 (4th Cir.1988).

In the absence of voluntary disclosure, the parties must ask the court to order pretrial discovery. When granting a motion for discovery the court will specify the time, place, and manner of making the discovery, and may prescribe such additional terms and conditions as are required to prevent confusion or misunderstandings between defense counsel and the prosecutor. Since the rise of concern for "victim's rights," statutes and court rules often authorize the court to issue protective orders barring or limiting disclosures that would otherwise be required. Once the court orders discovery, the parties have a continuing duty to disclose, as it becomes available, any additional evidence or material covered by the discovery order. The party requesting discovery is entitled to a reasonable opportunity to examine the discovery material and prepare for its use at trial. If counsel fails to provide adequate discovery, the court may order counsel to make further disclosure, grant a continuance of the trial to allow for additional discovery, or prohibit counsel from introducing evidence not disclosed. *See* section V of this chapter.

At early common law, courts lacked any inherent authority to require pretrial discovery. During the 1940's, however, discovery in civil cases was dramatically expanded to give each side pretrial access to almost all relevant information possessed by the other side. The success of this liberalized civil discovery generated proposals to similarly expand pretrial discovery in criminal cases. Proponents of expanded discovery conceded that surprising the opponent at trial created exciting Perry Mason style drama, but insisted that a criminal trial should emphasize the quest for truth rather than the gamesmanship of opposing counsel. As one commentator suggested: "The truth is more likely to emerge when each side seeks to take the other by reason rather than by surprise." Roger Traynor, "Ground Lost and Found in Criminal Discovery," 39 New York University Law Review 228, 249 (1964).

Opponents of expansive discovery contended that liberal discovery in criminal cases would give an unfair advantage to the defense because the defendant's privilege against self-incrimination would prohibit the prosecution from discovering defense evidence. *See Williams v. Florida, infra.* The issues raised in the discovery debate have been resolved in each jurisdiction by court rules or statutes which detail what discovery must or may be granted to each side. [*See* section III of this chapter]. Although the specific rules of each jurisdiction vary, most jurisdictions require the government to disclose: (1) prior statements of the defendant that are in the possession of the prosecution or other government agencies such as the police department; (2) a copy of the defendant's prior criminal record; (3) documents and tangible objects the prosecution intends to use at trial; and (4) scientific reports and tests such as autopsy reports and fingerprint analysis. In return, many jurisdictions require the defense to inform the prosecution of the defendant's intent to raise certain defenses such as alibi, insanity, self-defense or entrapment. [*See* section IV of this chapter].

A. CONSTITUTIONAL DISCOVERY

Although most discovery occurs under the authority of local statutes and court rules, the United States Constitution requires disclosure of certain information possessed by the government. In *Brady v. Maryland*, 373 U.S. 83 (1963), the Court held that "the suppression by the prosecution of evidence favorable to an accused upon request violates due process where the evidence is material either to guilt or punishment." Prosecutors sometimes boast that *Brady* never presents a problem for them because their office has an "open file" policy towards discovery, *i.e.*, "We never conceal anything. The defense can look at everything we have in our file."

UNITED STATES v. BAGLEY
473 U.S. 667 (1985).

JUSTICE BLACKMUN announced the judgment of the Court and delivered an opinion of the Court except as to Part III.

In *Brady v. Maryland*, 373 U.S. 83 (1963), this Court held that "the suppression by the prosecution of evidence favorable to an accused upon request violates due process where the evidence is material either to guilt or punishment." The issue in the present case concerns the standard of materiality to be applied in determining whether a conviction should be reversed because the prosecutor failed to disclose requested evidence that could have been used to impeach Government witnesses.

I

In October 1977, respondent Hughes Anderson Bagley was indicted in the Western District of Washington on 15 charges of violating federal narcotics and firearms statutes. On November 18, 24 days before trial, respondent filed a discovery motion. The sixth paragraph of that motion requested:

> "The names and addresses of witnesses that the government intends to call at trial. Also the prior criminal records of witnesses, and any deals, promises or inducements made to witnesses in exchange for their testimony."

The Government's two principal witnesses at the trial were James F. O'Connor and Donald E. Mitchell. O'Connor and Mitchell were state law-enforcement officers employed by the Milwaukee Railroad as private security guards. Between April and June 1977, they assisted the federal Bureau of Alcohol, Tobacco and Firearms (ATF) in conducting an undercover investigation of respondent.

The Government's response to the discovery motion did not disclose that any "deals, promises or inducements" had been made to O'Connor or Mitchell. In apparent reply to a request in the motion's ninth paragraph for "[c]opies of all Jencks Act material," the Government produced a series of affidavits that O'Connor and Mitchell had signed between April 12 and May 4, 1977, while the undercover investigation was in progress. These affidavits recounted in detail the undercover dealings that O'Connor and Mitchell were having at the time with respondent. Each affidavit concluded with the statement, "I made this statement freely and voluntarily without any threats or rewards, or promises of reward having been made to me in return for it."

Respondent waived his right to a jury trial and was tried before the court in December 1977. At the trial, O'Connor and Mitchell testified about both the firearms and the narcotics charges. On December 23, the court found respondent guilty on the narcotics charges, but not guilty on the firearms charges. * * *

[In a subsequent habeas corpus action, the district court that the prosecution had failed to disclose the existence of agreements with O'Connor and Mitchell to pay them for their testimony if it proved to be useful. These agreements would have provided impeachment material when O'Connor and Mitchell testified.]

The District Court found beyond a reasonable doubt, however, that had the existence of the agreements been disclosed to it during trial, the disclosure would have had no effect upon its finding that the Government had proved beyond a reasonable doubt that respondent was guilty of the offenses for which he had been convicted. The District Court reasoned: Almost all of the testimony of both witnesses was devoted to the firearms charges in the indictment. Respondent, however, was acquitted on those charges. The testimony of O'Connor and Mitchell concerning the narcotics charges was relatively very brief. On cross-examination, respondent's counsel did not seek to discredit their testimony as to the facts of distribution but rather sought to show that the controlled substances in question came from supplies that had been prescribed for respondent's personal use. The answers of O'Connor and Mitchell to this line of cross-examination tended to be favorable to respondent. Thus, the claimed impeachment evidence would not have been helpful to respondent and would not have affected the outcome of the trial. Accordingly, the District Court denied respondent's motion to vacate his sentence. * * *

II

The holding in *Brady v. Maryland* requires disclosure only of evidence that is both favorable to the accused and "material either to guilt or to punishment." * * *

The *Brady* rule is based on the requirement of due process. Its purpose is not to displace the adversary system as the primary means by which truth is uncovered, but to ensure that a miscarriage of justice does not occur. Thus, the prosecutor is not required to deliver his entire file to defense counsel, but only to disclose evidence favorable to the accused that, if suppressed, would deprive the defendant of a fair trial * * *.

In *Brady* and [*United States v.*] *Agurs*, the prosecutor failed to disclose exculpatory evidence. In the present case, the prosecutor failed to disclose evidence that the defense might have used to impeach the Government's witnesses by showing bias or interest. Impeachment evidence, however, as well as exculpatory evidence, falls within the *Brady* rule. Such evidence is "evidence favorable to an accused," so that, if disclosed and used effectively, it may make the difference between conviction and acquittal. * * *

The constitutional error, if any, in this case was the Government's failure to assist the defense by disclosing information that might have been helpful in conducting the cross-examination. As discussed above, such suppression of evidence amounts to a constitutional violation only if it deprives the defendant of a fair trial. Consistent with "our overriding concern with the justice of the finding of guilt," a constitutional error occurs, and the conviction must be reversed, only if the evidence is material in the sense that its suppression undermines confidence in the outcome of the trial.

III

A

It remains to determine the standard of materiality applicable to the nondisclosed evidence at issue in this case. Our starting point is the framework for evaluating the materiality of *Brady* evidence established in *United States v. Agurs*. The Court in *Agurs* distinguished three situations involving the discovery, after trial, of information favorable to the accused that had been known to the prosecution but unknown to the defense. The first situation was the prosecutor's knowing use of perjured testimony or, equivalently, the prosecutor's knowing failure to disclose that testimony used to convict the defendant was false. The Court noted the well-established rule that "a conviction obtained by the knowing use of perjured testimony is fundamentally unfair, and must be set aside if there is any reasonable likelihood that the false testimony could have affected the judgment of the jury." Although this rule is stated in terms that treat the knowing use of perjured testimony as error subject to harmless-error review, it may as easily be stated as a materiality standard under which the fact that testimony is perjured is considered material unless failure to disclose it would be harmless beyond a reasonable doubt. The Court in *Agurs* justified this standard of materiality on the ground that the knowing use of perjured testimony involves prosecutorial misconduct and, more importantly, involves "a corruption of the truth-seeking function of the trial process."

At the other extreme is the situation in *Agurs* itself, where the defendant does not make a *Brady* request and the prosecutor fails to disclose certain evidence favorable to the accused. The Court rejected a harmless-error rule in that situation, because under that rule every nondisclosure is treated as error, thus imposing on the prosecutor a constitutional duty to deliver his entire file to defense counsel. At the same time, the Court rejected a standard that would require the defendant to demonstrate that the evidence if disclosed probably would have resulted in acquittal. The Court reasoned: "If the standard applied to the usual motion for a new trial based on newly discovered evidence were the same when the evidence was in the State's possession as when it was found in a neutral source, there would be no special significance to the prosecutor's obligation to serve the cause of justice." The standard of materiality applicable in the absence of a specific Brady request is therefore stricter than the harmless-error standard but more lenient to the defense than the newly-discovered-evidence standard.

The third situation identified by the Court in *Agurs* is where the defense makes a specific request and the prosecutor fails to disclose responsive evidence. The Court did not define the standard of materiality applicable in this situation, but suggested that the standard might be more lenient to the defense than in the situation in which the defense makes no request or only a general request. The Court also noted: "When the prosecutor receives a specific and relevant request, the failure to make any response is seldom, if ever, excusable."

The Court has relied on and reformulated the *Agurs* standard for the materiality of undisclosed evidence in two subsequent cases arising outside the *Brady* context. In neither case did the Court's discussion of the *Agurs* standard distinguish among the three situations described in *Agurs*. * * * In ... *Strickland v. Washington*, 466 U.S. 668 (1984), the Court held that a new trial must be granted when evidence is not introduced because of the incompetence of counsel only if "there is a reasonable probability that, but for counsel's unprofessional errors, the result of the proceeding would have been different." The *Strickland* Court defined a "reasonable probability" as "a probability sufficient to undermine confidence in the outcome."

We find the *Strickland* formulation of the *Agurs* test for materiality sufficiently flexible to cover the "no request," "general request," and "specific request" cases of prosecutorial failure to disclose evidence favorable to the accused: The evidence is material only if there is a reasonable probability that, had the evidence been disclosed to the defense, the result of the proceeding would have been different. A "reasonable probability" is a probability sufficient to undermine confidence in the outcome.

The Government suggests that a materiality standard more favorable to the defendant reasonably might be adopted in specific request cases. The Government notes that an incomplete response to a specific request not only deprives the defense of certain evidence, but also has the effect of representing to the defense that the evidence does not exist. In reliance on this misleading representation, the defense might abandon lines of independent investigation, defenses, or trial strategies that it otherwise would have pursued.

We agree that the prosecutor's failure to respond fully to a *Brady* request may impair the adversary process in this manner. And the more specifically the defense requests certain evidence, thus putting the prosecutor on notice of its value, the more reasonable it is for the defense to assume from the nondisclosure that the evidence does not exist, and to make pretrial and trial decisions on the basis of this assumption. This possibility of impairment does not necessitate a different standard of materiality, however, for under the *Strickland* formulation the reviewing court may consider directly any adverse effect that the prosecutor's failure to respond might have had on the preparation or presentation of the defendant's case. The reviewing court should assess the possibility that such effect might have occurred in light of the totality of the circumstances and with an awareness of the difficulty of reconstructing in a post-trial proceeding the course that the defense and the trial would have taken had the defense not been misled by the prosecutor's incomplete response.

B

In the present case, we think that there is a significant likelihood that the prosecutor's response to respondent's discovery motion misleadingly induced defense counsel to believe that O'Connor and Mitchell could not be impeached on the basis of bias or interest arising from inducements offered by the Government. Defense counsel asked the prosecutor to disclose any inducements that had been made to witnesses, and the prosecutor failed to disclose that the possibility of a reward had been held out to O'Connor and Mitchell if the information they supplied led to "the accomplishment of the objective sought to be obtained . . . to the satisfaction of [the Government]." This possibility of a reward gave O'Connor and Mitchell a direct, personal stake in respondent's conviction. The fact that the stake was not guaranteed through a promise or binding contract, but was expressly contingent on the Government's satisfaction with the end result, served only to strengthen any incentive to testify falsely in order to secure a conviction. * * *

The District Court, nonetheless, found beyond a reasonable doubt that, had the information that the Government held out the possibility of reward to its witnesses been disclosed, the result of the criminal prosecution would not have been different. If this finding were sustained by the Court of Appeals, the information would be immaterial even under the standard of materiality applicable to the prosecutor's knowing use of perjured testimony. Although the express holding of the Court of Appeals was that the nondisclosure in this case required automatic reversal, the Court of Appeals also stated that it "disagreed" with the District Court's finding of harmless error. In particular, the Court of Appeals appears to have disagreed with the factual premise on which this finding expressly was based. The District Court reasoned that O'Connor's and Mitchell's testimony was exculpatory on the narcotics charges. The Court of Appeals, however, concluded, after reviewing the record, that O'Connor's and Mitchell's testimony was in fact inculpatory on those charges. Accordingly, we reverse the judgment of the Court of Appeals and remand the case to that court for a determination whether there is a reasonable probability that, had the inducement offered by the Government to O'Connor and Mitchell been disclosed to the defense, the result of the trial would have been different. * * *

JUSTICE POWELL took no part in the decision of this case.

JUSTICE WHITE, with whom THE CHIEF JUSTICE and JUSTICE REHNQUIST join, concurring in part and concurring in the judgment.

I agree with the Court that respondent is not entitled to have his conviction overturned unless he can show that the evidence withheld by the Government was "material," and I therefore join Parts I and II of the Court's opinion. I also agree with Justice Blackmun that for purposes of this inquiry, "evidence is material only if there is a reasonable probability that, had the evidence been disclosed to the defense, the result of the proceeding would have been different." As the Justice correctly observes, this standard is "sufficiently flexible" to cover all instances of prosecutorial failure to disclose evidence favorable to the accused. Given the flexibility of the standard and the inherently fact-bound nature of the cases to which it will be applied, however, I see no reason to attempt to elaborate on the relevance to the inquiry of the specificity of the defense's request for disclosure, either generally or with respect to this case. I would hold simply that the proper standard is one of reasonable probability and that the Court of Appeals' failure to apply this standard necessitates reversal. I therefore concur in the judgment.

JUSTICE MARSHALL, with whom JUSTICE BRENNAN joins, dissenting.

When the Government withholds from a defendant evidence that might impeach the prosecution's only witnesses, that failure to disclose cannot be deemed harmless error. Because that is precisely the nature of the undisclosed evidence in this case, I would affirm the judgment of the Court of Appeals and would not remand for further proceedings. * * *

Once the prosecutor suspects that certain information might have favorable implications for the defense, either because it is potentially exculpatory or relevant to credibility, I see no reason why he should not be required to disclose it. After all, favorable evidence indisputably enhances the truth-seeking process at trial. And it is the job of the defense, not the prosecution, to decide whether and in what way to use arguably favorable evidence. In addition, to require disclosure of all evidence that might reasonably be considered favorable to the defendant would have the precautionary effect of assuring that no information of potential consequence is mistakenly overlooked. * * * A clear rule of this kind, coupled with a presumption in favor of disclosure, also would facilitate the prosecutor's admittedly difficult task by removing a substantial amount of unguided discretion. * * *

The Court, however, offers a complex alternative. It defines the right not by reference to the possible usefulness of the particular evidence in preparing and presenting the case, but retrospectively, by reference to the likely effect the evidence will have on the outcome of the trial. * * *

* * * The result is to veer sharply away from the basic notion that the fairness of a trial increases with the amount of existing favorable evidence to which the defendant has access, and to disavow the ideal of full disclosure. * * *

I simply cannot agree with the Court that the due process right to favorable evidence recognized in Brady was intended to become entangled in prosecutorial determinations of the likelihood that particular information would affect the outcome of trial. * * *

In so saying, I recognize that a failure to divulge favorable information should not result in reversal in all cases. * * * [T]he benefits of disclosure may at times be tempered by the state's legitimate desire to avoid retrial when error has been harmless. However, in making the determination of harmlessness, I would apply our normal constitutional error test and reverse unless it is clear beyond a reasonable doubt that the withheld evidence would not have affected the outcome of the trial. * * *

JUSTICE STEVENS, dissenting.

* * * [T]wo situations in which the rule applies are those demonstrating the prosecution's knowing use of perjured testimony, exemplified by *Mooney v. Holohan,* and the prosecution's suppression of favorable evidence specifically requested by the defendant, exemplified by *Brady* itself. In both situations, the prosecution's deliberate nondisclosure constitutes constitutional error—the conviction must be set aside if the suppressed or perjured evidence was "material" and there was "any reasonable likelihood" that it "could have affected" the outcome of the trial. The combination of willful prosecutorial suppression of evidence and, "more importantly," the potential "corruption of the truth-seeking function of the trial process" requires that result.

[S]uppression [in response to a request] is far more serious than mere nondisclosure of evidence in which the defense has expressed no particular interest. A reviewing court should attach great significance to silence in the face of a specific request, when responsive evidence is later shown to have been in the Government's possession. Such silence actively misleads in the same way as would an affirmative representation that exculpatory evidence does not exist when, in fact, it does (i.e., perjury)—indeed, the two situations are aptly described as "sides of a single coin." Babcock, "Fair Play: Evidence Favorable to an Accused and Effective Assistance of Counsel," 34 Stan.L.Rev. 1133, 1151 (1982). * * *

Notes and Questions

1. *Prosecutors' knowing use of perjury.* One of the prohibited situations described by *Bagley* is the knowing use of perjured testimony. The defendant must prove that the witness committed perjury and that the prosecutor knew or should have known about it. Does that situation exist a witness tells the prosecutor one story before the trial which the prosecutor personally knows is true and the witness then testifies differently at trial? When the prosecutor has made a threat or promise to the witness, who denies the threat or promise while testifying? Does the prosecutor violate the *Agurs* standard by using the testimony of a witness who has made prior inconsistent statements? Is that standard violated if other evidence at trial contradicted the perjured testimony, *i.e.*, defense counsel identified inconsistencies in the witness's testimony?

2. *The materiality standard.* The standard for materiality in *Agurs* was whether the judge believes that the nondisclosed evidence creates a reasonable doubt that otherwise did not exist. The *Bagley* standard of materiality is whether there is a "reasonable probability that, had the evidence been disclosed to the defense, the result of the proceeding would have been different." Is either test tied exclusively to the judge's own evaluation of the evidence? If a case troubled the jury, could a judge find a reasonable probability of a different outcome, even though a reasonable doubt does not exist in the judge's own mind?

3. *Favorable evidence.* The cases refer to favorable evidence as a method of describing material evidence. What is favorable evidence? Is helpful evidence favorable? For example, knowledge of evidence incriminating to the defendant may be helpful but it is not regarded as favorable. Are negative test results favorable? Are inconclusive test results favorable? The prosecutor's initial responsibility is to ascertain whether any evidence in the government's possession qualifies as favorable. If the evidence qualifies as favorable, the prosecutor must decide if it is material.

4. *Admissibility of favorable evidence.* The lower courts have differed as to whether *Brady* applies to information that may be favorable to the defense, but which is inadmissible at trial, *e.g.*, inadmissible hearsay that the crime was committed by another person. Some courts limit *Brady* to material that would be admissible at trial, while others apply *Brady* to any information that might be useful in preparing a defense strategy.

In *Wood v. Bartholomew*, 516 U.S. 1 (1995), the Supreme Court assessed the materiality of evidence from undisclosed, inadmissible polygraph results. The Court rejected the defendant's argument that more discovery could have been done with knowledge about the test results as "mere speculation," especially when trial counsel stated during a habeas corpus hearing that knowledge about the result would not have changed his approach to cross-examination at trial.

5. *Harmless error analysis.* Less than one year after the Court announced that "*Bagley* error . . . cannot subsequently be found harmless," the Court in *Wood v. Bartholomew, supra*, retreated. After pointing out that it was not " 'reasonably likely' that disclosure of polygraph results . . . would

have resulted in a different outcome at trial," the Court stated that even without the pertinent witness's testimony, the case against the defendant was "overwhelming."

6. *Cumulative effect of all undisclosed evidence. Kyles v. Whitley*, 514 U.S. 419 (1995) defined materiality as undisclosed evidence considered collectively, not item-by-item. Does the cumulative standard of materiality require the prosecutor to inquire in every case what, if any, evidence is undisclosed and to disclose when she believes that the materiality standard is satisfied? Does that duty include a duty to learn about any favorable evidence known to the police or anyone else acting on behalf of the government in connection with the case?

7. *Timely disclosure.* Must the disclosure of favorable, material evidence be timely? What is a timely disclosure? Is disclosure timely if the prosecutor discloses material, favorable information during the trial? Should delayed disclosure always be grounds for reversal? The argument often made is that disclosure is so delayed that the defendant is unable to use the information *effectively* at trial, thereby also affecting the court's ability to reach a just result. In *United States v. O'Keefe*, 128 F.3d 885 (5th Cir.1997), following disclosure, the trial court granted a continuance for defense counsel, who conducted a "devastating" cross-examination. The appellate court affirmed the denial of a new trial.

Should a conviction be reversed due to the late revelation of exculpatory material, because the defense trial strategy might have been different if the information had been disclosed earlier? For example, in *United States v. Scarborough*, 128 F.3d 1373 (10th Cir.1997), defense counsel argued that its opening statement to the jury, its cross-examination of witnesses, and any decision about whether the defendant would testify might have been "substantially different." The trial court denied the motion to dismiss the indictment, stating that any harm could be cured by cross-examination of the witness. In addition, the exculpatory material was used in closing argument. Despite its misgivings about what happened at the trial, the appellate court fell back on the materiality standard and found that earlier disclosure would not have created added doubt about the defendant's guilt nor would it have affected the result of the trial. Do you agree?

8. Brady *and guilty pleas.* In *United States v. Ruiz*, 536 U.S. 622 (2002), the Supreme Court held that prosecutors are not required to disclose impeachment information relating to informants or other witnesses before entering into a binding plea agreement with a criminal defendant. Although constitutional fair trial guarantees provide that defendants have the right to receive exculpatory impeachment material for trial, Justice Breyer stated that a defendant who pleads guilty foregoes a fair trial and various other constitutional guarantees.

9. *Disclosure of confidential information.* In *Pennsylvania v. Ritchie*, 480 U.S. 39 (1987), the Court held that a criminal defendant charged with child abuse cannot conduct an unsupervised search of child welfare agency confidential files to find exculpatory evidence. However, the defendant could request material specific information, and the trial court could decide the materiality of the evidence by inspecting it in chambers.

A plurality in *Ritchie* specifically rejected a claim that the Confrontation Clause afforded a criminal defendant the right to pretrial discovery of any and all records containing impeachment evidence. "Generally speaking, the Confrontation Clause guarantees an opportunity for effective cross-examination, not cross-examination that is effective in whatever way, and to whatever extent, the defense might wish." In his concurring opinion in *Ritchie*, Justice Blackmun suggested that the Confrontation Clause is violated when adequate cross-examination is impeded by the denial of access to impeachment evidence: "I do not believe, however, that a State can avoid Confrontation Clause problems simply by deciding to hinder the defendant's right to effective cross-examination, on the basis of a desire to protect the confidentiality interests of a particular class of individuals, at the pretrial, rather than at the trial, stage."

10. *Discovery of informant's identity.* In *Roviaro v. United States*, 353 U.S. 53 (1957) the Court established an exception to the general rule against disclosure, and held that "where the disclosure of an informer's identity . . . is relevant and helpful to the defense of an accused, or is essential to a fair determination of a cause, the privilege [of nondisclosure] must give way." The Court suggested that disclosure turns on "balancing the public interest in protecting the flow of information [to the police] against the individual's right to prepare his defense." The *Roviaro* balancing test is further circumscribed by the distinction between informants who are participants in the criminal offense and those who are mere "tipsters." Where the informant is a tipster who merely supplies information, knowledge of his or her identity would not be essential in preparing the defense of the accused. In contrast, "where the informant is an actual participant, and thus a witness to material and relevant events, fundamental fairness dictates that the accused have access to him as a potential witness." *McLawhorn v. State*, 484 F.2d 1 (4th Cir.1973).

11. *Discovery orders against the victim.* Your client was charged with sodomy and statutory rape. You are aware that the alleged victim has made prior false claims of rape. You are particularly skeptical of the physical findings of the sexual assault nurse examiner. May you move the court for disclosure of the complaining witness' prior medical records and an independent medical examination of the complaining witness? As prosecutor, on what basis would you oppose the motion? The examination was ordered in *Clark v. Commonwealth*, 31 Va.App. 96, 521 S.E.2d 313 (1999).

> A trial court has discretion to require a complaining witness to submit to an independent physical examination, provided the defendant makes a threshold showing of a compelling need or reason. . . . In addition, after a defendant demonstrates a compelling need or reason, the trial court is then required to balance the defendant's due process and Sixth Amendment rights to present evidence in his or her favor against the complaining witness' welfare. . . . When considering the effects that a required examination may have upon the complaining witness, the trial court must be mindful of the due process rights of the complaining witness. Accordingly, the complaining witness should receive notice and have an opportunity to be heard before a decision is rendered involving his or her rights.

Problems

1. How should an appellate court assess the existence and "materiality" of a *Brady* violation in the following situation? The prosecution's key witness, Mr. Brown, testified that he had seen the defendant commit the crime. The prosecution failed to disclose to the defense that in the course of negotiating a "deal" with Brown's attorney, the attorney indicated that Brown had previously stated on multiple occasions that he had not seen the defendant at all on the day of the crime.

(A) Is it relevant that the "prior statement that [the prosecutor] failed to disclose was not that of his witness, Brown, but that of Brown's *lawyer?*" In *Spicer v. Warden*, 194 F.3d 547 (4th Cir.1999) the dissent maintained that "the lack of identity between the speakers is crucial . . . because *Brady* presupposes that the earlier statement must indeed be that of the witness." The majority held, however, that "the impeaching nature of the statements does not depend on whether the state was a direct or indirect audience. For purposes of determining whether evidence is 'favorable' to the defendant, it is the content of the statements, not their mode of communication to the state, that is important."

(B) Can the suppressed inconsistent statement be material under *Brady* in light of the fact that at trial, "Brown had already been impeached with evidence of his prior convictions, as well as the extremely favorable terms of his plea agreement, so that any additional impeachment evidence would be of marginal value." *Spicer v. Warden* found that the suppressed statement was material because "impeachment with a prior inconsistent statement relating to the central issue that the jury was required to decide is a far more serious blow to the prosecution's case than simply pointing out the common situation that Brown's testimony resulted from a plea bargain."

2. Carriger was convicted of murder. In his petition for habeas corpus, he claimed that the state had withheld Dunbar's Department of Corrections file, which would have revealed the latter's history of lying to police and blaming his crimes on others. In this case, in return for immunity, Dunbar had reported to the police that Carriger had confessed to the murder in his presence. The prosecutor claimed that he never actually possessed Dunbar's corrections file. Dunbar was the star witness at trial, although he was known to the prosecutor and the police to be a career burglar and a six-time felon On cross-examination, he stated that he was incapable of committing murder and that he had never used force in any burglary. The prosecutor argued in closing that Dunbar was not a liar, and that if there was any indication of his guilt he would be on trial with Carriger. The corrections file showed that Dunbar (a) had been committed to a state hospital because of violent rages and threats against his family, (b) was dishonorably discharged from the Army for uncontrolled aggressive and physically assaultive behavior, (c) had admitted being involved in a shootout with a policeman, (d) had used a gun in at least one burglary, and (e) had been diagnosed as having a "sociopathic personality." He also committed 92 burglaries in the six months following release from his first burglary sentence.

Was the information about Dunbar material to Carriger's defense? Is the need for disclosure particularly acute when the prosecution presents witnesses who have been granted immunity from prosecution in exchange for their testimony? Assess the credibility of the prosecutor's claim that he never possessed the file. What does Dunbar's record indicate about the thoroughness or good faith of the police investigation?

3.   Is there a distinction between evidence which is favorable, or material, or helpful to the defense. For example, although *Brady* clearly applies to evidence that might impeach a prosecution witness, does *Brady* extend to evidence that might impeach a defense witness, or rehabilitate a defense witness impeached by the prosecution? Consider the following situation: the defense called an expert to testify on the effects of the defendant's heroin addiction. On cross-examination, the following exchange occurred:

Q.   And you have given some of the research that you have conducted in this area, has part of your research included you actually taking certain drugs yourself? It has, hasn't it? Certain of these illegal drugs?

A.   Not as part of my research, no.

Q.   Have you been arrested for using drugs yourself?

A.   Yes, I have.

Q.   And that was during a lunch break while you were testifying as an expert in a case, just like this case, right?

A   Yes

Q.   And in that case you were caught by some plain clothes officers, snorting cocaine in your Porsche, is that correct?

A.   That's correct.

Q.   Have you done any illegal drugs today?

A.   No.

Q.   And you are not under the influence at this time, is that right?

A.   No.

Is there any constitutional basis for objecting to the prosecution's failure to disclose the defense expert's arrest record or the identity of witnesses who observed the alleged use of the cocaine? The government maintained that: "it's cross-examination material. It's not real evidence. It's not evidence of this crime. It's not exculpatory evidence. And if the defense counsel didn't know about it in this case, they should have. But ... we are not required to disclose it." The defense countered: "the ascertainment of truth is obviously enhanced when all parties to litigation are aware of the facts. Surprise witnesses, sandbagging, and trial by ambush generally do little to elicit the truth." The defense maintained that it had been "sandbagged" and the ascertainment of truth had been diverted by the sensational account of the expert witness's arrest. *People v. Tillis*, 956 P.2d 409, 18 Cal.4th 284, 75 Cal.Rptr.2d 447 (1998) held that neither the federal constitution nor California's discovery rules required the prosecution to disclose such information.

Note

A violation of *Brady* is most likely to occur where there was a specific request for designated material. But is there a constitutional distinction between a specific request, a general request, and no request at all? Defense counsel who simply request all "exculpatory evidence," diminish the likelihood of a court finding a violation of *Brady*. Erring on the side of caution, defense counsel are more likely to file the type of lengthy motion reproduced below.

MOTION FOR DISCOVERY

The Defendant moves the Court for an Order permitting discovery and inspection of exculpatory evidence. The prosecution is requested to provide the following information:

1.   Any and all exculpatory information or materials.

2.   The names and addresses of any other suspects in the case.

3.   Any physical evidence, information, statements, or notes which are evidence or may lead to evidence that the accused may have a defense to the crime alleged or may have committed an offense lesser than that with which he is charged, or that someone else may have committed the alleged crime.

4.   Any anonymous notes received by the government or its agents, or tapes made by the Government or its agents of any anonymous telephone calls received with regard to this case.

5.   A complete inspection and option to copy the Government's entire file in the above case.

6.   Written or recorded statements, admissions, or confessions made by the Defendant.

7.   Any relevant statements made by the Defendant to any law enforcement officer of this jurisdiction or his agent, or any copies of the same.

8.   The substance of any oral declarations of the Defendant of which a written or other tangible recording has been made and which were made by the Defendant, whether before or after arrest, in response to interrogatories by any person then known to the Defendant to be a law enforcement officer or his agent, or a prosecuting authority or his agent.

9.   All relevant statements, admissions, confessions, or declarations made by the Defendant, whether written, signed or unsigned, oral or electronically recorded, or obtained by eavesdropping.

10.   When, where, and in whose presence any statements, admissions, confessions, or declarations of the Defendant were made.

11.   Who, if the Defendant made any admission, statement, or confession, advised the Defendant of his constitutional rights at any time, and if so, then where, when, and how was he so advised.

12. Copies of any waivers signed by the Defendant, if any.

13. Copies of the Defendant's prior criminal record, if any, which are within the possession, custody, or control of the Government, the existence of which is known, or by the exercise of due diligence may become known, to the prosecuting authority.

14. A specific listing of the felony and misdemeanor convictions, if any, which the Government intends to introduce against the Defendant.

15. The nature, date, and place of any criminal offenses or acts of misconduct, other than those charged in the present indictment and those offered for impeachment purposes, which the Government will attempt to prove at the trial against the Defendant.

16. Copies of records or reports of physical or mental examinations of the Defendant which are within the possession, custody, or control of any Government agency, the existence of which is known, or by the exercise of due diligence may become known to the Government's Attorney and which are obtainable with the permission of the Defendant.

17. By what means was the Defendant identified as the alleged perpetrator of the crimes charged.

18. (a) If said identification was by real, demonstrative, or tangible evidence such as, but not limited to, blood, hair, fingerprints, clothing, etc., where, when, and by whom was said evidence obtained.

(b) If said identification was by said real, tangible, or demonstrative evidence, then the Defendant hereby respectfully requests the Court to permit him to inspect and/or copy, or photograph said items or objects.

19. If said identification was by means of a photograph, then:

(a) What person or persons identified the Defendant?

(b) Where, when, and under what circumstances was the identification made, and who presented said photographs?

(c) On how many occasions was the person or persons requested to view photographs for purposes of identification, and what were the dates and times?

(d) How many photographs and what photographs were show on each of such occasions?

20. If said identification was by means of a photograph, then the Defendant respectfully requests the Court to order the Government and/or its agents to specify and produce, in the sequence shown, all photographs shown so that the Defendant can inspect and/or copy all Photographs of the Defendant and/or anyone else.

21. The names and addresses of all other persons arrested for the same alleged incident and a report on the status of their cases.

22. The names, ages, and addresses of all witnesses to be called by the Government

23.   The name or names of any person other than informants, who were not informants with knowledge that they were acting as such at the time of the alleged offenses, who participated directly or indirectly in the alleged criminal acts which are the subject of the pending proceeding in the knowledge or possession of the Government, or were present at the time of commission of the acts.

24.   The name or names and addresses of any other informants involved. 25. The criminal, youthful offender, and juvenile records of any informant, including matters pending.

26.   The dates, times, places, and the kinds and amounts involved of any financial or other compensation paid or made to any informant.

27.   The number of, dates of, and statute involved of any convictions which were initiated by information supplied by any informant.

28.   The name or names and addresses of those persons who witnessed the alleged crime, if said information is known to any Government agent

29.   The name or names of any persons who provided the police with information leading to the arrest in the above matters.

30.   The names and addresses of any persons interviewed regarding this case by the Government or its agents or employees whom the Government does not intend to call as a witness.

31.   The list of names and addresses of anyone who might give favorable testimony on behalf of the Defendant if those persons are known to any Government agent.

32.   A list of the names of the arresting police officers.

33.   A list of the names of those officers involved in the investigation of the case.

34.   All police reports in the case.

35.   Any statement, before a grand jury or otherwise, by any witness who is to be called to testify, said statement being within the possession, custody, or control of the Government or any governmental agency.

36.   All relevant oral statements made by the Government's witnesses and which are known to any agent of the Government.

37.   (a) The juvenile record, including any charges pending of all witnesses to be called by the Government.

(b) Any current juvenile probation or parole and any pending juvenile matter of a criminal nature of any Government witness.

38.   All uncharged criminal misconduct of any Government witness, which is known to any agents of the Government.

39.   The criminal record, including any charges pending, of all witnesses to be called by the Government.

40. All information relating to any understanding or agreement between any Government witness and the Government, including the Government's Attorney, any Prosecutor, State Police, or any Police Department, probation officers, or any of their agents regarding prosecutions of said witness for past, present, or future criminal conduct and regarding sentencing or sentencing recommendations as to any such witness.

41. The nature of any other promise or consideration given by any agent of the Government to any person in return for information, assistance, or testimony of that person.

42. The nature of any threat of unfavorable treatment given by any agent of the Government to any person in order to obtain information, assistance, or testimony from that person.

43. Whether any Government witness was taking and/or to any degree under the influence of alcohol and/or any drug at and near the time of the event to which that witness is to testify, and if so, then what was the amount and type of the alcohol and/or drug.

44. Any mental, psychological, or physical problem that any Government witness has, including but not limited to alcoholism or mental illness or defect, and reports of same.

45. The identity and location of buildings, places, or portions thereof, which are in the possession, custody, or control of any governmental agency and which are material to the defense or which the prosecuting authority intends to introduce as evidence in chief at the trial.

46. Books, photographs, papers, documents, or tangible objects obtained from or belonging to the Defendant and/or obtained from others involved in the case by seizure or process.

47. All books, tangible objects, papers, photographs, or documents which are within the possession, custody, or control of any Government agency and which are material to the preparation of the Defendant's defense or are intended for use by the prosecuting authority as evidence in chief at the trial.

48. Whether or not a knife or gun or other dangerous or deadly instrument or dangerous or deadly weapon, or any instrument was used during the commission of the alleged offenses, and if so, the kind and description of such weapon, dangerous instrument, knife, gun, or instrument.

49. An inspection or examination of any weapon or any instrument which is alleged to have been used in the alleged crimes.

50. Any objects, if any, taken in the alleged crime.

51. Clothing worn by the Defendant when arrested and a description of it.

52. Copies of results or reports of scientific tests, experiments, or comparisons made in connection with the particular case which are

known to the prosecuting authority and within the possession, custody or control of any governmental agency and which are material to the preparation of the defense or are intended for use by the prosecuting authority as evidence in chief at the trial.

53.   Copies of results or reports of scientific tests, experiments, or comparisons made in connection with the particular case which are known to the prosecuting authority and within the possession, custody, or control of any governmental agency made in connection with this case and which will not be used by the prosecuting authority as evidence in chief at the trial.

54.   What, if any, fingerprints of the Defendant and/or anyone else were lifted at or near the scene of the alleged offenses, and/or from any other places or objects related to the incident; and the Defendant requests an inspection and examination of said fingerprints and a listing of the names and addresses of those whose fingerprints were lifted.

55.   Copies of the search and arrest warrants issued, if any, and if so, copies of the affidavit in support thereof, the application, and the return of the warrant. 56. The date, time, and place of the initial arrest of the Defendant and any co-defendant or co-conspirator.

WHEREFORE, the Defendant respectfully prays that his Motion for Discovery and Inspection of Exculpatory Evidence be granted.

Note

Despite the motion for extensive disclosure, the right to discover potentially exculpatory evidence is not unlimited, nor will discovery be ordered upon pure speculation as to the possibly exculpatory nature of the requested materials. The defendant is entitled to inspect material only upon a "plausible" showing that the material might have exculpatory relevance. *United States v. Alexander*, 748 F.2d 185 (4th Cir.1984).

Exercise

On December 14, 1998, your client was in the home of Clay Snow drinking moonshine whiskey with Snow, John Knight, James Crawford and Shirley Gallihugh. They sat in a small living room with no more than five feet separating the three men. Around 5 p.m. some petty arguments and disagreements occurred between your client and Crawford. One person called the other a "damn liar," then your client and Crawford stood up and moved toward each other. Snow got between the two men and wrapped his arms around your client's waist to prevent violence. Snow felt Crawford behind him, and all three men started moving sideways toward the bed. Snow then heard gunfire and turned to see Crawford take tree to four steps toward the dining room door before going down to his knees and collapsing on the floor. Your client admits shooting Crawford but claims he did so in self-defense. He maintains that Crawford jumped on top of him and choked him. When he saw Crawford reach for his pocket, he thought Crawford was reaching for a gun.

Before trial, the prosecutor furnished you with all the photographs of the crime scene in the prosecutor's possession. You conclude, however, that the photos do not afford you an adequate means of understanding the crime scene and determining the location and relationship between the objects of furniture in Snow's house. You feel that you need to know the actual size of the room in order to understand the explanation of events given to you by your client because it would be difficult to examine and cross-examine witnesses about the details of events that occurred at a location with which you are unfamiliar. Snow denied your request to view the crime scene and you would like the court to order Snow to permit your inspection of the crime scene. Draft a motion which will give you access to the crime scene.

Precisely what are you requesting from the court, and what is the court's authority to order such an inspection? Will you request:

(a) Discovery from the state?

(b) Some variation on a subpoena duces tecum to Mr. Snow?

(c) A search warrant to inspect the crime scene?

(d) Enforcement of a constitutional guarantee of compulsory process which establishes the defendant's right to call for evidence in his behalf?

B. PRESERVATION OF EVIDENCE

The constitutional right to discovery of exculpatory evidence does not require the government to preserve all potentially exculpatory evidence for possible discovery by defendants. For example, police may be unable to recall all other investigative "leads" they pursued before arresting the suspect. Evidence must be preserved when its exculpatory value was apparent before the evidence was destroyed and when the evidence was of such a nature that the defendant would be unable to obtain comparable evidence by other reasonably available means. But *Arizona v. Youngblood* held that "unless a criminal defendant can show bad faith on the part of the police, failure to preserve potentially useful evidence does not constitute a denial of due process of law."

ARIZONA v. YOUNGBLOOD

488 U.S. 51 (1988).

CHIEF JUSTICE REHNQUIST delivered the opinion of the Court.

Respondent Larry Youngblood was convicted by a Pima County, Arizona, jury of child molestation, sexual assault, and kidnaping. The Arizona Court of Appeals reversed his conviction on the ground that the State had failed to preserve semen samples from the victim's body and clothing. We granted certiorari to consider the extent to which the Due Process Clause of the Fourteenth Amendment requires the State to preserve evidentiary material that might be useful to a criminal defendant.

On October 29, 1983, David L., a 10–year–old boy, attended a church service with his mother. After he left the service at about 9:30 p.m., the boy went to a carnival behind the church, where he was abducted by a middle-aged man of medium height and weight. The assailant drove the boy to a secluded area near a ravine and molested him. He then took the boy to an unidentified, sparsely furnished house where he sodomized the boy four times. Afterwards, the assailant tied the boy up while he went outside to start his car. Once the assailant started the car, albeit with some difficulty, he returned to the house and again sodomized the boy. The assailant then sent the boy to the bathroom to wash up before he returned him to the carnival. He threatened to kill the boy if he told anyone about the attack. The entire ordeal lasted about 1½ hours.

After the boy made his way home, his mother took him to Kino Hospital. At the hospital, a physician treated the boy for rectal injuries. The physician also used a "sexual assault kit" to collect evidence of the attack. The Tucson Police Department provided such kits to all hospitals in Pima County for use in sexual assault cases. Under standard procedure, the victim of a sexual assault was taken to a hospital, where a physician used the kit to collect evidence. The kit included paper to collect saliva samples, a tube for obtaining a blood sample, microscopic slides for making smears, a set of Q–Tip-like swabs, and a medical examination report. Here, the physician used the swab to collect samples from the boy's rectum and mouth. He then made a microscopic slide of the samples. The doctor also obtained samples of the boy's saliva, blood, and hair. The physician did not examine the samples at any time. The police placed the kit in a secure refrigerator at the police station. At the hospital, the police also collected the boy's underwear and T-shirt. This clothing was not refrigerated or frozen.

Nine days after the attack, on November 7, 1983, the police asked the boy to pick out his assailant from a photographic lineup. The boy identified respondent as the assailant. Respondent was not located by the police until four weeks later; he was arrested on December 9, 1983.

On November 8, 1983, Edward Heller, a police criminologist, examined the sexual assault kit. He testified that he followed standard department procedure, which was to examine the slides and determine whether sexual contact had occurred. After he determined that such contact had occurred, the criminologist did not perform any other tests, although he placed the assault kit back in the refrigerator. He testified that tests to identify blood group substances were not routinely conducted during the initial examination of an assault kit and in only about half of all cases in any event. He did not test the clothing at this time.

Respondent was indicted on charges of child molestation, sexual assault, and kidnaping. The State moved to compel respondent to provide blood and saliva samples for comparison with the material gathered through the use of the sexual assault kit, but the trial court denied the motion on the ground that the State had not obtained a sufficiently large semen sample to make a valid comparison. The prosecutor then asked the State's criminologist to perform an ABO blood group test on the rectal swab sample in an attempt to ascertain the blood type of the boy's assailant. This test failed to detect any blood group substances in the sample.

In January 1985, the police criminologist examined the boy's clothing for the first time. He found one semen stain on the boy's underwear and another on the rear of his T-shirt. The criminologist tried to obtain blood group substances from both stains using the ABO technique, but was unsuccessful. He also performed a P–30 protein molecule test on the stains, which indicated that only a small quantity of semen was present on the clothing; it was inconclusive as to the assailant's identity. The Tucson Police Department had just begun using this test, which was then used in slightly more than half of the crime laboratories in the country.

Respondent's principal defense at trial was that the boy had erred in identifying him as the perpetrator of the crime. In this connection, both a criminologist for the State and an expert witness for respondent testified as to what might have been shown by tests performed on the samples shortly after they were gathered, or by later tests performed on the samples from the boy's clothing had the clothing been properly refrigerated. The court instructed the jury that if they found the State had destroyed or lost evidence, they might "infer that the true fact is against the State's interest."

The jury found respondent guilty as charged, but the Arizona Court of Appeals reversed the judgment of conviction. It stated that " 'when identity is an issue at trial and the police permit the destruction of evidence that could eliminate the defendant as the perpetrator, such loss is material to the defense and is a denial of due process.' " The Court of Appeals concluded on the basis of the expert testimony at trial that timely performance of tests with properly preserved semen samples could have produced results that might have completely exonerated respondent. The Court of Appeals reached this conclusion even though it did "not imply any bad faith on the part of the State." The Supreme Court of Arizona denied the State's petition for review, and we granted certiorari. We now reverse.

[Our] most recent decision in this area of the law, *California v. Trombetta*, 467 U.S. 479 (1984), arose out of a drunk-driving prosecution in which the State had introduced test results indicating the concentration of alcohol in the blood of two motorists. The defendants sought to suppress the test results on the ground that the State had failed to preserve the breath samples used in the test. We rejected this argument for several reasons: first, "the officers here were acting in 'good faith and in accord with their normal practice,' second, in the light of the procedures actually used the chances that preserved samples would have exculpated the defendants were slim, and, third, even if the samples might have shown inaccuracy in the tests, the defendants had 'alternative means of demonstrating their innocence.' In the present case, the likelihood that the preserved materials would have enabled the defendant to exonerate himself appears to be greater than it was in *Trombet-*

ta, but here, unlike in *Trombetta*, the State did not attempt to make any use of the materials in its own case in chief."

Our decisions in related areas have stressed the importance for constitutional purposes of good or bad faith on the part of the Government when the claim is based on loss of evidence attributable to the Government. In *United States v. Marion*, 404 U.S. 307 (1971), we said that "[n]o actual prejudice to the conduct of the defense is alleged or proved, and there is no showing that the Government intentionally delayed to gain some tactical advantage over appellees or to harass them." Similarly, in *United States v. Valenzuela–Bernal*, we considered whether the Government's deportation of two witnesses who were illegal aliens violated due process. We held that the prompt deportation of the witnesses was justified "upon the Executive's good-faith determination that they possess no evidence favorable to the defendant in a criminal prosecution."

The Due Process Clause of the Fourteenth Amendment, as interpreted in *Brady*, makes the good or bad faith of the State irrelevant when the State fails to disclose to the defendant material exculpatory evidence. But we think the Due Process Clause requires a different result when we deal with the failure of the State to preserve evidentiary material of which no more can be said than that it could have been subjected to tests, the results of which might have exonerated the defendant. Part of the reason for the difference in treatment is found in the observation made by the Court in *Trombetta*, that "[w]henever potentially exculpatory evidence is permanently lost, courts face the treacherous task of divining the import of materials whose contents are unknown and, very often, disputed." Part of it stems from our unwillingness to read the "fundamental fairness" requirement of the Due Process Clause, as imposing on the police an undifferentiated and absolute duty to retain and to preserve all material that might be of conceivable evidentiary significance in a particular prosecution. We think that requiring a defendant to show bad faith on the part of the police both limits the extent of the police's obligation to preserve evidence to reasonable bounds and confines it to that class of cases where the interests of justice most clearly require it, *i.e.*, those cases in which the police themselves by their conduct indicate that the evidence could form a basis for exonerating the defendant. We therefore hold that unless a criminal defendant can show bad faith on the part of the police, failure to preserve potentially useful evidence does not constitute a denial of due process of law.

In this case, the police collected the rectal swab and clothing on the night of the crime; respondent was not taken into custody until six weeks later. The failure of the police to refrigerate the clothing and to perform tests on the semen samples can at worst be described as negligent. None of this information was concealed from respondent at trial, and the evidence—such as it was—was made available to respondent's expert who declined to perform any tests on the samples. The Arizona Court of Appeals noted in its opinion—and we agree—that there was no suggestion of bad faith on the part of the police. It follows, therefore, from what we have said, that there was no violation of the Due Process Clause.

The Arizona Court of Appeals also referred somewhat obliquely to the State's "inability to quantitatively test" certain semen samples with the newer P–30 test. If the court meant by this statement that the Due Process Clause is violated when the police fail to use a particular investigatory tool, we strongly disagree. The situation here is no different than a prosecution for drunken driving that rests on police observation alone; the defendant is free to argue to the finder of fact that a breathalyzer test might have been exculpatory, but the police do not have a constitutional duty to perform any particular tests.

The judgment of the Arizona Court of Appeals is reversed, and the case is remanded for further proceedings not inconsistent with this opinion.

Reversed.

JUSTICE BLACKMUN, with whom JUSTICE BRENNAN and JUSTICE MARSHALL join, dissenting.

The Constitution requires that criminal defendants be provided with a fair trial, not merely a "good faith" try at a fair trial. Respondent here, by what may have been nothing more than police ineptitude, was denied the opportunity to present a full defense. That ineptitude, however, deprived respondent of his guaranteed right to due process of law. In reversing the judgment of the Arizona Court of Appeals, this Court, in my view, misreads the import of its prior cases and unduly restricts the protections of the Due Process Clause. An understanding of due process demonstrates that the evidence which was allowed to deteriorate was "constitutionally material," and that its absence significantly prejudiced respondent. Accordingly, I dissent. * * *

Notes and Questions

1. Are at least some of the dissent's concerns addressed by one state's modification of *Arizona v. Youngblood*? See *Galbraith v. Commonwealth*, 18 Va.App. 734, 446 S.E.2d 633 (1994):

> Determining the intentions of the police in failing to preserve evidence requires consideration of the nature of the evidence. If it is clear that, had the evidence been properly preserved, it would have formed a basis for exonerating the defendant, then absent a showing to the contrary we must assume that the police were not acting in good faith.

Compare *United States v. Chase Alone Iron Eyes*, 367 F.3d 781 (8th Cir. 2004) (negligence in destroying evidence does not amount to bad faith).

2. While the usual remedy for a *Brady* violation is a new trial for the defendant, what is the proper remedy in lost or destroyed evidence cases? A new trial seems inappropriate because the alleged exculpatory evidence no longer exists. Should the charges be dismissed? Should the results performed

on any destroyed or lost evidence be suppressed? Should an instruction like the court gave the jury in *Youngblood* be sufficient, *i.e.*, that the jury may draw adverse inferences from the loss or destruction of the evidence?

Exercise

Your client informs you that he was arrested for reckless driving. Incident to arrest, the police searched his automobile and seized a number of items including a small bag with a residue of white powder. He admits that he possessed cocaine in the past, but does not believe that the white powder contains any drug residue. You anticipate that the prosecution will send the powder to the State Crime Lab for testing. You would like your own expert to test the powder, but because of its small quantity you fear that the crime lab will use up all the powder during its testing procedures. What action should you take? Is the following motion adequate?

MOTION TO PRESERVE PORTIONS OF SUBSTANCES FOR INDEPENDENT TESTING BY THE DEFENSE

The defendant is charged with possession of narcotics. The government has submitted to the Consolidated Laboratories a substance seized from the defendant's automobile. The quantity of said substance is minute, and a single chemical analysis performed by the Consolidated Laboratories could consume the entire substance, unless the Laboratory sets aside and preserves a portion of the substance.

The defendant desires to have preserved for possible independent testing a portion of the substance seized from the defendant's automobile and submitted to the Consolidated Laboratories.

WHEREFORE, the defendant moves the Court for an order directing the government and the Consolidated Laboratories to preserve an adequate amount of the said seized substance to assure the opportunity for defense counsel to have independent scientific testing of said substance.

C.   DISCOVERY UNDER RULES AND STATUTES

Brady's due process obligation to disclose exculpatory evidence overrides any limitations on discovery provided for by a jurisdiction's discovery statutes or rules. If *Brady* is inapplicable, however, each state is free to set discovery requirements as broadly or narrowly as it pleases. The only constitutional limitation on the state's choice is that the state must be even handed in its treatment of the prosecution and the defense. In *Wardius v. Oregon*, 412 U.S. 470 (1973) the state required the defendant to disclose his intent to present an alibi defense, but the defendant had no right of discovery against the prosecution. The Supreme Court stated:

> Although the Due Process Clause has little to say regarding the amount of discovery which the parties must be afforded, it does speak to the balance of forces between the accused and his accus-

er. . . . In the absence of a strong showing of state interests to the contrary, discovery must be a two-way street. The State may not insist that trials be run as a 'search for truth' so far as defense witnesses are concerned, while maintaining 'poker game' secrecy for its own witnesses. It is fundamentally unfair to require a defendant to divulge the details of his own case while at the same time subjecting him to the hazard of surprise covering refutation of the very pieces of evidence which he disclosed to the State.

Given the limited holding of *Wardius*, it is not surprisingly to find a great deal of variation among the states' discovery provisions. While some jurisdictions provide for broad discovery, others place severe limitations on the government's obligation to disclose portions of its case. Rule 16 of the Federal Rules of Criminal Procedure (in the statutory supplement) serves as a model for discovery rules in many jurisdictions.

Notes

1. *Items within the control or possession of the prosecution.* Discovery generally extends only to those discoverable items within the prosecutor's control or possession. Federal Rule 16(a)(1)(B) refers to material "within the government's control; and the attorney for the government knows or through due diligence could know" that the evidence exists. The due diligence requirement may impose on the prosecution "the responsibility to interview all government personnel involved in a case in order to comply with its discovery obligations." *Harrison v. Commonwealth*, 12 Va.App. 581, 405 S.E.2d 854 (1991). *But compare United States v. Gatto*, 763 F.2d 1040 (9th Cir.1985) holding that federal prosecutors did not "control or possess" evidence seized by state officials in a independently conducted search.

2. *The defendant's written or recorded statements.* Even though statements of co-conspirators are imputed to the defendant for purposes of the hearsay rule, such statements are not discoverable under Federal Rule 16(a)(1)(B). *United States v. Roberts*, 811 F.2d 257 (4th Cir.1987) (en banc). But consider the dissent in *Roberts*: "The practical result is that while an accused may protect himself against the risk of being surprised at trial by his own falsely reported statements, he may not protect himself against the much more treacherous risk of surprise by falsely attributed or reported hearsay statements of a 'co-conspirator' admitted against him by the 'fiction' that they are his own."

3. *The defendant's oral statements.* Federal Rule 16 requires disclosure only when the defendant's oral statement was made "in response to interrogation by a person the defendant knew was a government agent." A confession made to a private citizen who then repeats the confession to the police is a statement of the citizen, not a statement of the defendant for discovery purposes. *See Hackman v. Commonwealth*, 220 Va. 710, 261 S.E.2d 555 (1980). Disclosing the identity of, and statements made by, prosecution witnesses is deemed to increase the chances for harassment or intimidation of the witnesses by the defense. A witness's pretrial statements will be disclosed in the federal system *after* the witness testifies at trial. *See* discussion of the *Jencks* rule, *infra*.

4. *The defendant's criminal record.* Federal Rule 16 and most states provide for disclosure of the defendant's criminal record. On the surface there seems to be little need to disclose to the defendant information of which he is already aware. Aside from the possibility that the client has forgotten or lied to defense counsel about any prior convictions, the prime benefit of such disclosure is the opportunity to resolve *pretrial* any disputes as to the correctness or scope of the prior convictions.

The federal rules and most states do not address disclosure of prior misconduct not resulting in a criminal conviction. Such evidence may be admissible at trial to prove motive, modus operandi, or other recognized exceptions to evidence rules prohibiting the use of the defendant's uncharged misconduct. In the absence of specific discovery provisions, the trial court retains discretion to permit or deny disclosure of uncharged misconduct.

5. *Documents and tangible objects.* Discovery generally applies to items which the prosecution intends to use at trial or which were obtained from the defendant. Other than diminishing the opportunity to surprise the defendant at trial, the prosecution has no substantial interest in objecting to disclosure of documents and objects. The prosecution's desire to shield internal memorandum and other documents deemed to be the prosecutor's "work product is recognized in Rule 16(a)(2)."

6. *Scientific reports.* Scientific evidence is practically impossible for the defense to contest or rebut at trial without an opportunity to examine it pretrial, and allow defense experts an opportunity to prepare a rebuttal of the scientific reports. The most commonly utilized scientific reports are autopsy findings, testing of drugs, blood, urine, and breath, analysis of seaman, fingerprints, ballistics, handwriting or voice, and physical or mental examination of the accused or the alleged victim.

7. *Prosecution witnesses.* Many states require the prosecution to provide the defense with the names and addresses of persons whom the prosecution intends to call as witnesses. Other jurisdictions specifically prohibit pretrial disclosure of the witnesses' identity because of concerns that the defense may harass, intimidate or suborn perjury on the part of the witness. [The defendant has no constitutional right to receive notice that a witness will identify him in court. *United States v. Peoples*, 748 F.2d 934 (4th Cir.1984).]

Exercises

1. Your client was caught up in a major DEA "sting" operation focusing on the manufacture and sale of PCP. Your client allegedly delivered certain controlled chemicals often used in the manufacture of PCP, and was paid for these chemicals with a large quantity of PCP. The exchange was made with Melvin Jones, an undercover agent of the Drug Enforcement Agency. You interviewed Mr. Jones who related that your client was merely one of many persons who had purchased drugs and chemicals during the two month sting.

Your client denies dealing with Mr. Jones, and you question whether Mr. Jones can remember the details of this one alleged "drug-deal" during a lengthy sting operation involving many people. You also are aware that the DEA often uses a hidden video camera to record its sting operations. You would like to discover if there is any record of the alleged exchange between your client and Mr. Jones. On what grounds can you request disclosure of any existing videotape?

(A) Could the videotape, if it exists, contain any exculpatory evidence under *Brady* in light of your client's assertion that the purchase never took place?

(B) Is the videotape a document or tangible object within the meaning of the federal rules?

(C) Is the videotape a recorded statement of the defendant and thus discoverable?

2. In addition to, or in place of the videotape, can you request disclosure of:

(A) The identity of any other DEA agents or law enforcement officials who were present and observed the alleged exchange?

(B) Any summary or memorandum of the exchange prepared by law enforcement officials?

(C) The identity of other defendants who had dealings with the DEA sting operation within a one week period of your client's alleged exchange?

(D) The status of charges against other defendants prosecuted because of the sting operation?

(E) Any plea bargains struck between the prosecution and these other defendants?

3. Your client believes that he was selected for this sting operation and for federal prosecution because he is black. A Drug Enforcement Administration report, published six months before the sting operation, concluded that "[l]arge-scale, interstate trafficking networks controlled by Jamaicans, Haitians and Black street gangs dominate the manufacture and distribution of crack and PCP." A friend in the Office of the Federal Public Defender informed you that in every one of the crack and PCP cases closed by the office in the past year, the defendant was black.

(A) In order to support your claim of selective enforcement you seek information on prosecution policies over the past three years. Draft a motion specifying what type of information you desire from the prosecution's files.

(B) The government opposes your motion on grounds that Federal Rule 16a(1)(C) refers to only government documents which are "material to the preparation of the defendant's defense," and within the meaning of the rule, a defense is limited to rebuttal of the prosecution's case-in-chief. Draft a response.

(C) Are the chemicals alleged delivered by your client discoverable? Are you entitled to all the chemicals or only a representative sample?

(D) If you have the sample tested, is your expert's report discoverable by the prosecution?

(E) Can you discover the report filed by the prosecution's expert?

(F) Can you discover the expert's written summary of what he anticipates his trial testimony would be if called to the witness stand?

(G) Would it matter if the prosecution planned to use the expert's testimony as part of the case-in-chief, or only in rebuttal of any expert witness the defense might offer?

4. Suppose that you are defending a client charged with child abuse that occurred more than 10 years ago. You suspect that the alleged victim "recaptured" this memory of child abuse while under hypnosis. Of course you could inquire into this matter on cross-examination when the victim testifies, but pretrial discovery would allow you to submit a motion *in limine* asking the trial court to bar any hypnotically enhanced memory. *See Rock v. Arkansas*, 483 U.S. 44 (1987) ("a witness other than the defendant, who has been hypnotized prior to trial is, as a matter of law, incompetent to testify as to those facts or circumstances which the witness recalled for the first time during, or subsequent to, hypnosis"). Would your jurisdiction grant the following motion?

MOTION FOR DISCLOSURE OF HYPNOSIS OR DRUG INTERVIEW OF POTENTIAL WITNESSES

The Defendant moves the Court for an order requiring the Government to disclose whether any potential witness in this case has been requested to submit to an interview under hypnosis, has agreed to submit to an interview under hypnosis, has refused to submit to an interview under hypnosis, or has actually submitted to an interview under hypnosis, with regard to this case. In the event of any potential witness who actually submitted to an interview under hypnosis, the order should further require the Government to disclose all details of the interview, including the name of the person who placed the witness under hypnosis, the name of the witness, the content of the questions and answers during said interview, and any other information about the substance or procedure of the interview.

The term "potential witnesses" shall mean any person who has any information which the Government believed might be relevant to this case, which witness was subsequently interviewed by any agent of the Government regarding this case.

Notes and Questions

1. In the federal system the *Jencks* rule strikes an accommodation between protecting witnesses from possible pretrial harassment, and providing the defense with an opportunity to impeach witnesses who have made statements inconsistent with their trial testimony. In *Jencks v. United States*, 353 U.S. 657 (1957) the Court exercised its supervisory power over federal courts to require disclosure of prior statements by witnesses *after* they testify. Congress enacted the Jencks Act, 18 U.S.C. § 3500, and the

essence of the Jencks Act is now contained in Rule 26.2 of the Federal Rules of Criminal Procedure (in the statutory supplement).

2. Why is the discovery of prior statements restricted to trial witnesses? Is there another obligation by the prosecution which would require disclosure of some prior statements it has obtained from potential witnesses? Why does Rule 26.2 require the intervention of the court in every exchange of statements? Counsel seeking the statements must move the court for disclosure. Why not instead require the party holding the statement to turn it over, unless there is information which should not be disclosed, now already covered by Rule 26.2(c)?

3. Despite the provision in Rule 26.2(d) for a recess in order for counsel to "examine the statement and prepare to use it in the proceedings," what is the purpose of postponing the disclosure until *after* the witness has testified? If disclosure occurred on the day before witness is called to testify, short recesses would not be necessary and counsel receiving the statement would have a better opportunity to examine it in a more deliberate manner.

4. Does the definition of a "statement" enable a party to seek a witness's tax return? Corporate records? Computer studies? The case law has rejected discovery of those items under Rule 26.2. *See United States v. Carrillo*, 561 F.2d 1125 (5th Cir.1977) (tax return); *United States v. Page*, 808 F.2d 723 (10th Cir.1987) (corporate records); *United States v. Alexander*, 789 F.2d 1046 (4th Cir.1986) (computer programs and data printouts).

5. Is there any obligation on the prosecutor to disclose prior statements obtained from potential witnesses? What about prior statements by declarants whose hearsay will be introduced at trial? Consider the problem below.

Problem

Suppose the government introduces in evidence the out-of-court statements of the defendant's unindicted co-conspirator, who has fled the country and cannot be called to the witness stand. Could you invoke the Jencks Act to obtain any prior statements by the co-conspirator? Federal Rule of Evidence 806 equates hearsay with live testimony to the extent that if an out-of-court statement is admitted, the opposing party may impeach the statement with "any evidence which would be admissible for those purposes if the declarant had testified as a witness." In light of Rule 806, can you invoke the Jencks Act to obtain other statements made by the co-conspirator after he "testifies" via hearsay? To date, only one federal Court of Appeals has addressed the defendant's right to discover a hearsay declarant's statements under the Jencks Act. *United States v. Williams–Davis*, 90 F.3d 490 (D.C.Cir.1996) held "that a declarant is treated as a witness for purposes of Rule 806 does not mean he becomes one for purposes of the Jencks Act."

If the declarant is not a witness for purposes of the Jencks Act, does that remove the Act's prohibition against pretrial discovery of statements by government witnesses? The Second and Fourth Circuits have held that the underlying "witness safety" purposes of the Jencks Act require that nontestifying declarants be treated like testifying government witnesses, thus their statements are shielded from pretrial discovery. *In re United States*, 834 F.2d

283 (2d Cir.1987); *United States v. Roberts*, 811 F.2d 257 (4th Cir.1987) (en banc). Does this inconsistent judicial interpretation of the Jencks Act allow the government to employ a "Heads I win. Tails you lose" approach? *I.e.*, when defendants seek pretrial discovery, courts shield hearsay from disclosure by ruling that hearsay declarants are "witnesses" under the Jencks Act. But when defendants seek discovery at trial, courts deny disclosure on grounds that declarants are not witnesses within the meaning the Jencks Act.

D.   DISCOVERY BY THE PROSECUTION

Many jurisdictions give the prosecution an unconditional right to be notified prior to trial that the defendant intends to raise the defense of insanity and to present expert testimony to support this claim. Such provisions allow the prosecution the time to prepare its own expert witnesses to rebut the claim of insanity. Federal Rule 12.1 (in the statutory supplement) embodies the approach utilized by a majority of states. The Federal Rules of Criminal Procedure also mandate the disclosure of defendant's intent to raise the defense of alibi, [Federal Rule 12.2 in the statutory supplement], an actual or believed exercise of public authority on behalf of a law enforcement or Federal intelligence agency, [Federal Rule 12.3 in the statutory supplement], or the names of corporate parties with an interest in the case, [Federal Rule 12.4 in the statutory supplement].

Exercise

1.   The defense served notice that it would raise an alibi defense establishing that the defendant was in Chicago at the time the offense allegedly occurred in New York. At trial, however, the defendant testifies that he was in Pittsburgh at the time of the crime. The federal rules speak to the "Inadmissibility of Withdrawn Alibi," but are there any constitutional restrictions on admitting a withdrawn alibi?

(A) Was the notice of alibi a "statement" of the defendant which can now be used to impeach his trial testimony?

(B) Does it matter whether defense counsel or the defendant signed the notice of alibi?

2.   Suppose the alibi changed from Chicago to Pittsburgh because defense counsel uncovered additional information that resolved some confusion over the date of the crime and the date of the defendant's trip. As defense counsel what action could you take to preclude the prosecution from impeaching your client with the prior notice of alibi?

(A) Could you file an amended notice of alibi? Does an amended notice remove the inconsistency between the original notice of alibi and the actual testimony?

(B) Could you obtain a pretrial ruling against use of the original notice of alibi for impeachment, or is the "additional information uncovered" merely an explanation for the inconsistency? [An explanation of the inconsistency could only be used on reexamination of the defendant after the prosecution offers evidence of the inconsistency].

3.   Suppose the same defendant testifies that he did not commit the crime, but he never mentions being in another city at the time of the crime.

(A) As the prosecutor, what would you do when surprised by this shift in defense strategy? Could you request a continuance? Could you raise the now abandoned alibi on cross-examination? Is the notice of an alibi defense inconsistent with the defendant's actual testimony?

(B) As defense counsel, what steps would you take to block the prosecutor from making any use of the notice of alibi? May the prosecution use the discovery process to "lock" the defense into a particular trial strategy, or be forced to pay the consequences for deviating from the announced reliance on an alibi?

Note

Other than notice of an insanity or alibi defense, many states condition the prosecution's right to discovery upon whether the defense has been granted discovery. Thus if the defendant files no motion to discover the prosecution's evidence, the prosecution will have no right to discover defense evidence. If, however, the defendant has been granted discovery, the prosecution may be granted a reciprocal right to discovery. For example, the accused may be ordered to reveal whether he intends to raise self-defense, entrapment, or other affirmative defenses. At least with respect to an alibi defense, *Williams v. Florida* held that such disclosure rules do not violate the Fifth Amendment.

WILLIAMS v. FLORIDA
399 U.S. 78 (1970).

Justice White delivered the opinion of the Court.

Prior to his trial for robbery in the State of Florida, petitioner filed a "Motion for a Protective Order," seeking to be excused from the requirements of Rule 1.200 of the Florida Rules of Criminal Procedure, 33 F.S.A. That rule requires a defendant, on written demand of the prosecuting attorney, to give notice in advance of trial if the defendant intends to claim an alibi, and to furnish the prosecuting attorney with information as to the place where he claims to have been and with the names and addresses of the alibi witnesses he intends to use. In his motion petitioner openly declared his intent to claim an alibi, but objected to the further disclosure requirements on the ground that the rule "compels the Defendant in a criminal case to be a witness against himself" in violation of his Fifth and Fourteenth Amendment rights. The motion was denied.

Florida's notice-of-alibi rule is in essence a requirement that a defendant submit to a limited form of pretrial discovery by the State whenever he intends to rely at trial on the defense of alibi. In exchange for the defendant's disclosure of the witnesses he proposes to use to establish that defense, the State in turn is required to notify the defendant of any witnesses it proposes to offer in rebuttal to that defense. Both sides are under a continuing duty promptly to disclose the names and addresses of additional witnesses bearing on the alibi as they become available. The threatened sanction for failure to comply is the exclusion at trial of the defendant's alibi evidence—except for his own testimony—or, in the case of the State, the exclusion of the State's evidence offered in rebuttal of the alibi.

In this case, following the denial of his Motion for a Protective Order, petitioner complied with the alibi rule and gave the State the name and address of one Mary Scotty. Mrs. Scotty was summoned to the office of the State Attorney on the morning of the trial, where she gave pretrial testimony. At the trial itself, Mrs. Scotty, petitioner, and petitioner's wife all testified that the three of them had been in Mrs. Scotty's apartment during the time of the robbery. On two occasions during cross-examination of Mrs. Scotty, the prosecuting attorney confronted her with her earlier deposition in which she had given dates and times that in some respects did not correspond with the dates and times given at trial. Mrs. Scotty adhered to her trial story, insisting that she had been mistaken in her earlier testimony. The State also offered in rebuttal the testimony of one of the officers investigating the robbery who claimed that Mrs. Scotty had asked him for directions on the afternoon in question during the time when she claimed to have been in her apartment with petitioner and his wife.

We need not linger over the suggestion that the discovery permitted the State against petitioner in this case deprived him of "due process" or a "fair trial." Florida law provides for liberal discovery by the defendant against the State, and the notice-of-alibi rule is itself carefully hedged with reciprocal duties requiring state disclosure to the defendant. Given the ease with which an alibi can be fabricated, the State's interest in protecting itself against an eleventh-hour defense is both obvious and legitimate. Reflecting this interest, notice-of-alibi provisions, dating at least from 1927, are now in existence in a substantial number of States. The adversary system of trial is hardly an end in itself; it is not yet a poker game in which players enjoy an absolute right always to conceal their cards until played. We find ample room in that system, at least as far as "due process" is concerned, for the instant Florida rule, which is designed to enhance the search for truth in the criminal trial by insuring both the defendant and the State ample opportunity to investigate certain facts crucial to the determination of guilt or innocence.

Petitioner's major contention is that he was "compelled to be a witness against himself" contrary to the commands of the Fifth and Fourteenth Amendments because the notice-of-alibi rule required him to give the State the name and address of Mrs. Scotty in advance of trial and thus to furnish the State with information useful in convicting him. No pretrial statement of petitioner was introduced at trial; but armed with Mrs. Scotty's name and address and the knowledge that she was to be petitioner's alibi witness, the State was able to take her deposition in advance of trial and to find rebuttal testimony. Also, requiring him to reveal the elements of his defense is claimed to have interfered with his right to wait until after the State had presented its case to decide how to defend against it. We conclude, however, as has apparently every other court that has considered the issue, that the privilege against self-incrimination is not violated by a requirement that the defendant give notice of an alibi defense and disclose his alibi witnesses.

The defendant in a criminal trial is frequently forced to testify himself and to call other witnesses in an effort to reduce the risk of conviction. When he presents his witnesses, he must reveal their identity and submit them to cross-examination which in itself may prove incriminating or which may furnish the State with leads to incriminating rebuttal evidence. That the defendant faces such a dilemma demanding a choice between complete silence and presenting a defense has never been thought an invasion of the privilege against compelled self-incrimination. The pressures generated by the State's evidence may be severe but they do not vitiate the defendant's choice to present an alibi defense and witnesses to prove it, even though the attempted defense ends in catastrophe for the defendant. However "testimonial" or "incriminating" the alibi defense proves to be, it cannot be considered "compelled" within the meaning of the Fifth and Fourteenth Amendments.

Very similar constraints operate on the defendant when the State requires pretrial notice of alibi and the naming of alibi witnesses. Nothing in such a rule requires the defendant to rely on an alibi or prevents him from abandoning the defense; these matters are left to his unfettered choice. That choice must be made, but the pressures that bear on his pretrial decision are of the same nature as those that would induce him to call alibi witnesses at the trial: the force of historical fact beyond both his and the State's control and the strength of the State's case built on these facts. Response to that kind of pressure by offering evidence or testimony is not compelled self-incrimination transgressing the Fifth and Fourteenth Amendments.

In the case before us, the notice-of-alibi rule by itself in no way affected petitioner's crucial decision to call alibi witnesses or added to the legitimate pressures leading to that course of action. At most, the rule only compelled petitioner to accelerate the timing of his disclosure, forcing him to divulge at an earlier date information that the petitioner from the beginning planned to divulge at trial. Nothing in the Fifth Amendment privilege entitles a defendant as a matter of constitutional right to await the end of the State's case before announcing the nature of his defense, any more than it entitles him to await the jury's verdict on the State's case-in-chief before deciding whether or not to take the stand himself.

Petitioner concedes that absent the notice-of-alibi rule the Constitution would raise no bar to the court's granting the State a continuance at trial on the ground of surprise as soon as the alibi witness is called. Nor would there be self-incrimination problems if, during that continuance, the State was permitted to do precisely what it did here prior to trial: take the deposition of the witness and find rebuttal evidence. But if so utilizing a continuance is permissible under the Fifth and Fourteenth Amendments, then surely the same result may be accomplished through pretrial discovery, as it was here, avoiding the necessity of a disrupted trial. We decline to hold that the privilege against compulsory self-incrimination guarantees the defendant the right to surprise the State with an alibi defense.

JUSTICE BLACK, with whom JUSTICE DOUGLAS joins, concurring in part and dissenting in part.

The Court today holds that a State can require a defendant in a criminal case to disclose in advance of trial the nature of his alibi defense and give the names and addresses of witnesses he will call to support that defense. This requirement, the majority says, does not violate the Fifth Amendment prohibition against compelling a criminal defendant to be a witness against himself. Although this case itself involves only a notice-of-alibi provision, it is clear that the decision means that a State can require a defendant to disclose in advance of trial any and all information he might possibly use to defend himself at trial. This decision, in my view, is a radical and dangerous departure from the historical and constitutionally guaranteed right of a defendant in a criminal case to remain completely silent, requiring the State to prove its case without any assistance of any kind from the defendant himself. * * *

Notes and Questions

Would the rationale of *Williams v. Florida* apply to compulsory disclosure of an intent to raise any affirmative defense, e.g. entrapment? Suppose that the defendant is charged with selling cocaine, and the defendant is required to give pretrial notice that he will raise the defense of entrapment which will be established by witnesses A and B who were eyewitnesses to the transaction. May the government call witnesses A and B (whose identity was previously unknown to the prosecution) to prove its case-in-chief, or is this a form of prohibited self-incrimination? Does it matter if the defendant choose to abandon the entrapment defense and would not have called A and B as defense witnesses?

Problem

The prosecution filed a discovery motion for: (1) All exculpatory evidence in the defendant's or defense counsel's possession. (2) The names of all witnesses the defendant, or defense counsel interviewed in connection with the case. (3) The names of all witnesses the defense intends to call at trial, the nature of the testimony the witnesses would give, and the written or recorded statements of such witnesses. Are any of the requested items outside the scope of the defendant's Fifth Amendment protection? Would the defendant lose any Fifth Amendment protection by planning to introduce the evidence at trial?

E. REGULATION OF DISCOVERY

The criminal defendant's right to pretrial discovery may come in conflict with the privacy rights of victims or other third parties. All jurisdictions empower the court to issue protective orders or limit the scope and terms of discovery, subject of course to constitutional limitations. If either party fails to comply with the court's discovery orders the court generally has a number of options for dealing with the violation.

Other possible sanctions authorized in various states include: instruct the jury to assume the accuracy of certain facts that might have been established through the nondisclosed material; hold the offending party in contempt of court; declare a mistrial; or in the case of a violation by the government, dismiss the prosecution. (Nondisclosure of *Brady* material may be sufficient to invalidate a guilty plea if there is a reasonable probability that, had the evidence been disclosed to the defense, the defendant would not have pleaded guilty and would have insisted on going to trial). *Banks v. United States*, 920 F.Supp. 688 (E.D.Va.1996). The least drastic and preferred remedy for violations of discovery orders is to order immediate disclosure and offer a continuance for the party to examine the material. In appropriate cases, however, *Taylor v. Illinois* recognizes that more drastic remedies are constitutionally permissible.

TAYLOR v. ILLINOIS

484 U.S. 400 (1988).

JUSTICE STEVENS delivered the opinion of the Court.

As a sanction for failing to identify a defense witness in response to a pretrial discovery request, an Illinois trial judge refused to allow the undisclosed witness to testify. The question presented is whether that refusal violated the petitioner's constitutional right to obtain the testimony of favorable witnesses. We hold that such a sanction is not absolutely prohibited by the Compulsory Process Clause of the Sixth Amendment and find no constitutional error on the specific facts of this case.

A jury convicted petitioner in 1984 of attempting to murder Jack Bridges in a street fight on the south side of Chicago on August 6, 1981. The conviction was supported by the testimony of Bridges, his brother, and three other witnesses. They described a twenty-minute argument between Bridges and a young man named Derrick Travis, and a violent encounter that occurred over an hour later between several friends of Travis, including the petitioner, on the one hand, and Bridges, belatedly aided by his brother, on the other. The Incident was witnessed by twenty or thirty bystanders. It is undisputed that at least three members of the group which included Travis and petitioner were carrying pipes and clubs that they used to beat Bridges. Prosecution witnesses also testified that petitioner had a gun, that he shot Bridges in the back as he attempted to flee, and that, after Bridges fell, petitioner pointed the gun at Bridges' head but the weapon misfired.

Two sisters, who are friends of petitioner, testified on his behalf. In many respects their version of the incident was consistent with the prosecution's case, but they testified that it was Bridges' brother, rather than petitioner, who possessed a firearm and that he had fired into the group hitting his brother by mistake. No other witnesses testified for the defense.

Well in advance of trial, the prosecutor filed a discovery motion requesting a list of defense witnesses. In his original response, petitioner's attorney identified the two sisters who later testified and two men who did not testify. On the first day of trial, defense counsel was allowed to amend his answer by adding the names of Derrick Travis and a Chicago Police Officer; neither of them actually testified.

On the second day of trial, after the prosecution's two principal witnesses had completed their testimony, defense counsel made an oral motion to amend his "Answer to Discovery" to include two more witnesses, Alfred Wormley and Pam Berkhalter. In support of the motion, counsel represented that he had just been informed about them and that they had probably seen the "entire incident."

In response to the court's inquiry about the defendant's failure to tell him about the two witnesses earlier, counsel acknowledged that defendant had done so, but then represented that he had been unable to locate Wormley. After noting that the witnesses' names could have been supplied even if their addresses were unknown, the trial judge directed counsel to bring them in the next day, at which time he would decide whether they could testify. The judge indicated that he was concerned about the possibility "that witnesses are being found that really weren't there."

The next morning Wormley appeared in court with defense counsel. After further colloquy about the consequences of a violation of discovery rules, counsel was permitted to make an offer of proof in the form of Wormley's testimony outside the presence of the jury. It developed that Wormley had not been a witness to the incident itself. He testified that prior to the incident he saw Jack Bridges and his brother with two guns in a blanket, that he heard them say "they were after Ray [petitioner] and the other people," and that on his way home he "happened to run into Ray and them" and warned them "to watch out because they got weapons." On cross-examination, Wormley acknowledged that he had first met the defendant "about four months ago" (*i.e.*, over two years after the incident). He also acknowledged that defense counsel had visited him at his home on the Wednesday of the week before the trial began. Thus, his testimony rather dramatically contradicted defense counsel's representations to the trial court.

After hearing Wormley testify, the trial judge concluded that the appropriate sanction for the discovery violation was to exclude his testimony. The judge explained:

"THE COURT: All right, I am going to deny Wormley an opportunity to testify here. He is not going to testify. I find this is a blatant violation of the discovery rules, willful violation of the rules. I also feel that defense attorneys have been violating discovery in this courtroom in the last three or four cases blatantly and I am going to put a stop to it and this is one way to do so."

The Illinois Appellate Court affirmed petitioner's conviction. The court concluded that in this case "the trial court was within its discretion in refusing to allow the additional witnesses to testify." The Illinois Supreme Court denied leave to appeal and we granted the petition for certiorari. * * *

In the State's view, no Compulsory Process Clause concerns are even raised by authorizing preclusion as a discovery sanction, or by the application of the Illinois rule in this case. The State's argument is supported by the plain language of the Clause, by the historical evidence that it was intended to provide defendants with subpoena power that they lacked at common law, by some scholarly comment, and by a brief excerpt from the legislative history of the Clause. We have, however, consistently given the Clause the broader reading reflected in contemporaneous state constitutional provisions.

As we noted just last Term, "[o]ur cases establish, at a minimum, that criminal defendants have the right to the government's assistance in compelling the attendance of favorable witnesses at trial and the right to put before a jury evidence that might influence the determination of guilt." Few rights are more fundamental than that of an accused to present witnesses in his own defense. Indeed, this right is an essential attribute of the adversary system itself. The right to compel a witness' presence in the courtroom could not protect the integrity of the adversary process if it did not embrace the right to have the witness' testimony heard by the trier of fact. The right to offer testimony is thus grounded in the Sixth Amendment even though it is not expressly described in so many words.

Petitioner's claim that the Sixth Amendment creates an absolute bar to the preclusion of the testimony of a surprise witness is just as extreme and just as unacceptable as the State's position that the Amendment is simply irrelevant. The accused does not have an unfettered right to offer testimony that is incompetent, privileged, or otherwise inadmissible under standard rules of evidence. The Compulsory Process Clause provides him with an effective weapon, but it is a weapon that cannot be used irresponsibly. * * *

The principle that undergirds the defendant's right to present exculpatory evidence is also the source of essential limitations on the right. The adversary process could not function effectively without adherence to rules of procedure that govern the orderly presentation of facts and arguments to provide each party with a fair opportunity to assemble and submit evidence to contradict or explain the opponent's case. The trial process would be a shambles if either party had an absolute right to control the time and content of his witnesses' testimony. Neither may insist on the right to interrupt the opposing party's case and obviously there is no absolute right to interrupt the deliberations of the jury to present newly discovered evidence. The State's interest in the orderly conduct of a criminal trial is sufficient to justify the imposition and enforcement of firm, though not always inflexible, rules relating to the identification and presentation of evidence.

The defendant's right to compulsory process is itself designed to vindicate the principle that the "ends of criminal justice would be defeated if judgments were to be founded on a partial or speculative presentation of the facts." Rules that provide for pretrial discovery of an opponent's witnesses serve the same high purpose. Discovery, like cross-examination, minimizes the risk that a judgment will be predicated on incomplete, misleading, or even deliberately fabricated testimony. The "State's interest in protecting itself against an eleventh hour defense" is merely one component of the broader public interest in a full and truthful disclosure of critical facts.

To vindicate that interest we have held that even the defendant may not testify without being subjected to cross-examination. * * *

Petitioner does not question the legitimacy of a rule requiring pretrial disclosure of defense witnesses, but he argues that the sanction of preclusion of the testimony of a previously undisclosed witness is so drastic that it should never be imposed. He argues, correctly, that a less drastic sanction is always available. Prejudice to the prosecution could be minimized by granting a continuance or a mistrial to provide time for further investigation; moreover, further violations can be deterred by disciplinary sanctions against the defendant or defense counsel.

It may well be true that alternative sanctions are adequate and appropriate in most cases, but it is equally clear that they would be less effective than the preclusion sanction and that there are instances in which they would perpetuate rather than limit the prejudice to the State and the harm to the adversary process. One of the purposes of the discovery rule itself is to minimize the risk that fabricated testimony will be believed. Defendants who are willing to fabricate a defense may also be willing to fabricate excuses for failing to comply with a discovery requirement. The risk of a contempt violation may seem trivial to a defendant facing the threat of imprisonment for a term of years. A dishonest client can mislead an honest attorney, and there are occasions when an attorney assumes that the duty of loyalty to the client outweighs elementary obligations to the court.

We presume that evidence that is not discovered until after the trial is over would not have affected the outcome. It is equally reasonable to presume that there is something suspect about a defense witness who is not identified until after the eleventh hour has passed. If a pattern of discovery violations is explicable only on the assumption that the violations were designed to conceal a plan to present fabricated testimony, it would be entirely appropriate to exclude the tainted evidence regardless of whether other sanctions would also be merited. * * *

A trial judge may certainly insist on an explanation for a party's failure to comply with a request to identify his or her witnesses in advance of trial. If that explanation reveals that the omission was willful and motivated by a desire to obtain a tactical advantage that would minimize the effectiveness of cross examination and the ability to adduce rebuttal evidence, it would be entirely consistent with the purposes of the Confrontation Clause simply to exclude the witness' testimony.

The simplicity of compliance with the discovery rule is also relevant. As we have noted, the Compulsory Process Clause cannot be invoked without the prior planning and affirmative conduct of the defendant. Lawyers are accustomed to meeting deadlines. Routine preparation involves location and interrogation of potential witnesses and the serving of subpoenas on those whose testimony will be offered at trial. The burden of identifying them in advance of trial adds little to these routine demands of trial preparation.

It would demean the high purpose of the Compulsory Process Clause to construe it as encompassing an absolute right to an automatic continuance or mistrial to allow presumptively perjured testimony to be presented to a jury. We reject petitioner's argument that a preclusion sanction is never appropriate no matter how serious the defendant's discovery violation may be.

Petitioner argues that the preclusion sanction was unnecessarily harsh in this case because the *voir dire* examination of Wormley adequately protected the prosecution from any possible prejudice resulting from surprise. Petitioner also contends that it is unfair to visit the sins of the lawyer upon his client. Neither argument has merit.

More is at stake than possible prejudice to the prosecution. We are also concerned with the impact of this kind of conduct on the integrity of the judicial process itself The trial judge found that the discovery violation in this case was both willful and blatant. In view of the fact that petitioner's counsel had actually interviewed Wormley during the week before the trial began and the further fact that he amended his Answer to Discovery on the first day of trial without identifying Wormley while he did identify two actual eyewitnesses whom he did not place on the stand, the inference that he was deliberately seeking a tactical advantage is inescapable. Regardless of whether prejudice to the prosecution could have been avoided in this particular case, it is plain that the case fits into the category of willful misconduct in which the severest sanction is appropriate. After all, the court, as well as the prosecutor, has a vital interest in protecting the trial process from the pollution of perjured testimony. Evidentiary rules which apply to categories of inadmissible evidence—ranging from hearsay to the fruits of illegal searches—may properly be enforced even though the particular testimony being offered is not prejudicial. The pretrial conduct revealed by the record in this case gives rise to a sufficiently strong inference "that witnesses are being found that really weren't there," to justify the sanction of preclusion.

The argument that the client should not be held responsible for his lawyer's misconduct strikes at the heart of the attorney-client relationship. Although there are basic rights that the attorney cannot waive without the informed and publicly acknowledged consent of the client, the lawyer has—and must have—full authority to manage the conduct of the trial. The adversary process could not function effectively if every tactical decision required client approval. Moreover, given the protections afforded by the attorney-client privilege and the fact that extreme cases may involve unscrupulous conduct by both the client and the lawyer, it would be highly impracticable to require an investigation into their relative responsibilities before applying the sanction of preclusion. In responding to discovery, the client has a duty to be candid and forthcoming with the lawyer, and when the lawyer responds, he or she speaks for the client. Putting to one side the exceptional cases in which counsel is ineffective, the client must accept the consequences of the lawyer's decision to forgo cross-examination, to decide not to put certain witnesses on the stand, or to decide not to disclose the identity of certain witnesses in advance of trial. In this case, petitioner has no greater right to disavow his lawyer's decision to conceal Wormley's identity until after the trial had commenced than he has to disavow the decision to refrain from adducing testimony from the eyewitnesses who were identified in the Answer to Discovery. Whenever a lawyer makes use of the sword provided by the Compulsory Process Clause, there is some risk that he may wound his own client.

The judgment of the Illinois Appellate Court is affirmed.

JUSTICE BRENNAN, with whom JUSTICE MARSHALL and JUSTICE BLACKMUN join, dissenting.

Of course, discovery sanctions must include more than corrective measures. They must also include punitive measures that can deter future discovery violations from taking place. In light of the availability of direct punitive measures, however, there is no good reason, at least absent evidence of the defendant's complicity, to countenance the arbitrary and disproportionate punishment imposed by the preclusion sanction. The central point to keep in mind is that witness preclusion operates as an effective deterrent only to the extent that it has a possible effect on the outcome of the trial. Indeed, it employs in part the possibility that a distorted record will cause a jury to convict a defendant of a crime he did not commit. Witness preclusion thus punishes discovery violations in a way that is both disproportionate—it might result in a defendant charged with a capital offense being convicted and receiving a death sentence he would not have received but for the discovery violation—and arbitrary—it might, in another case involving an identical discovery violation, result in a defendant suffering no change in verdict or, if charged with a lesser offense, being convicted and receiving a light or suspended sentence. In contrast, direct punitive measures (such as contempt sanctions or, if the attorney is responsible, disciplinary proceedings) can graduate the punishment to correspond to the severity of the discovery violation.

The arbitrary and disproportionate nature of the preclusion sanction is highlighted where the penalty falls on the defendant even though he bore no responsibility for the discovery violation. In this case, although there was ample evidence that the defense attorney willfully violated Rule 413(d), there was no evidence that the defendant played any role in that violation. Nor did the trial court make any effort to determine whether the defendant bore any responsibility for the discovery violation. Indeed, reading the record leaves the distinct impression that the main reason the trial court excluded Wormley's testimony was the belief that the defense counsel had purposefully lied about when he had located Wormley.

In the absence of any evidence that a defendant played any part in an attorney's willful discovery violation, directly sanctioning the attorney is not only fairer but *more* effective in deterring violations than excluding defense evidence. The threat of disciplinary proceedings, fines, or imprisonment will likely influence attorney behavior to a far greater extent than the rather indirect penalty threatened by evidentiary exclusion. Such sanctions were available here.

Deities may be able to visit the sins of the father on the son, but I cannot agree that courts should be permitted to visit the sins of the lawyer on the innocent client. Although we have sometimes held a defendant bound by tactical errors his attorney makes that fall short of ineffective assistance of counsel, we have not previously suggested that a client can be punished for an attorney's *misconduct*. The rationales for binding defendants to attorneys' routine tactical errors do not apply to attorney misconduct. An attorney is never faced with a legitimate choice that includes misconduct as an option. Although it may be that "[t]he adversary process could not function effectively if every tactical decision required client approval," that concern is irrelevant here because a client has no authority to approve misconduct. Further, misconduct is not visible only with hindsight, as are many tactical errors. Consequently, misconduct is amenable to direct punitive sanctions against attorneys as a deterrent that can prevent attorneys from systemically engaging in misconduct that would disrupt the trial process. There is no need to take steps that will inflict the punishment on the defendant.

* * * Accordingly, absent evidence that the defendant was responsible for the discovery violation, the exclusion of criminal defense evidence is arbitrary and disproportionate to the purposes of discovery and criminal justice and should be *per se* unconstitutional. I thus cannot agree with the Court's case-by-case balancing approach or with its conclusion in this case that the exclusion was constitutional.

The Court's balancing approach, moreover, has the unfortunate effect of creating a conflict of interest in every case involving a willful discovery violation because the defense counsel is placed in a position where the best argument he can make on behalf of his client is, "Don't preclude the defense witness—punish me personally." In this very case, for example, the defense attorney became noticeably timid once the judge threatened to report his actions to the disciplinary commission. He did not argue, "Sure, bring me before the disciplinary commission; that's a much more appropriate sanction than excluding a witness who might get my client acquitted." I cannot see how we can expect defense counsel in this or any other case to act as vigorous advocates for the interests of their clients when those interests are adverse to their own.

It seems particularly ironic that the Court should approve the exclusion of evidence in this case at a time when several of its members have expressed serious misgivings about the evidentiary costs of exclusionary rules in other contexts. Surely the deterrence of constitutional violations cannot be less important than the deterrence of discovery violations. Nor can it be said that the evidentiary costs are more significant when they are imposed on the prosecution.

F.   ETHICAL CONSIDERATIONS

In light of the Court's suggestion in *Kyles v. Whitley* that "the prudent prosecutor will resolve doubtful questions in favor of disclosure," should the prosecutor adopt an "open door" policy and submit the entire case file for inspection by the defense? This certainly eases the administrative and ethical burden on the prosecutor to search the case file for potentially exculpatory evidence that should be surrendered to the defense. Many prosecutors, however, regard such an open door policy as an abrogation of their responsibility to zealously advocate the people's case against the defendant.

Appellate courts often suggest that when the exculpatory nature of the material is in doubt, the prosecutor should submit the material to the trial court for an in camera review and ruling on its possible exculpatory value. In practice, however, trial courts discourage counsel from submitting lengthy and detailed case files for inspection by the court. At best, the trial court will rule on disputes involving a specifically identified item, but the trial court will not undertake the prosecutor's burden of searching the government files for exculpatory material. In the end, the prosecutor cannot avoid the ethical and constitutional duty to play dual roles as a advocate for the government and a "fair-minded" official concerned with truth, justice, and the American way. The ABA Standards for Criminal Justice [§ 3–3.11 Prosecution Function] mandate that the prosecutor make reasonably diligent efforts to comply with proper discovery requests. [The same mandate applies to defense counsel under The ABA Standards for Criminal Justice § 4–4.5 governing the Defense Function].

Defense counsel also must reconcile their dual roles as advocates for the defendant and as members of the bar charged with responsibilities to the legal profession. Standards of professional responsibility and statutory prohibitions against concealing evidence require defense counsel to turn over certain items (*i.e.*, the fruits and instrumentalities of the crime) to the police. Defense counsel usually avoid such dilemmas by refusing to accept such evidence from their clients. The rule of thumb for defense counsel is—look don't touch.

Neither defense counsel nor the prosecutor may advise or direct witnesses not to cooperate with opposing counsel. The American Bar Association, Model Rules of Professional Conduct, 3.4(a) provides: "A lawyer shall not unlawfully obstruct another party's access to evidence or unlawfully alter, destroy or conceal a document or other material having potential evidentiary value. A lawyer shall not counsel or assist another person to do any such act." The ABA Standards for Criminal Justice [§ 3–3.1(d) Prosecution] provide that a prosecutor "should not" and "it is unprofessional conduct" for defense counsel [ABA Standards for Criminal Justice § 4–4.3(d) Defense] to advise any person or cause any person other than defense counsel's client to be advised to decline to give to counsel for the other side information which such person has the right to give. Either counsel, however, may inform witnesses of their right to decide whether to grant or refuse an interview.

Problems

1. Suppose you are defense counsel for a defendant charged with purchasing cocaine. What do you do if the defendant brings you a white powder and says, "If you get this stuff tested, I'll bet it isn't cocaine." If you refuse to accept the powder, how do you respond when the client asks, "Well what am I supposed to do with this stuff?"

2. Suppose you send the powder to a testing laboratory which reports that the substance is cocaine. What action do you take now?

3. Suppose the prosecutor files a discovery motion requesting that you produce "any and all monies, weapons, or narcotics paid or delivered into your care, custody, or control by the defendant." What result?

4. As a prosecutor, how would you respond to a call from the victim asking you whether he should/must talk to defense counsel? What if the victim indicates that he won't talk to defense counsel unless you are present?

Chapter 18

GUILTY PLEAS

A. PLEA ALTERNATIVES & FREQUENCY OF GUILTY PLEAS

After an indictment or criminal information has been filed, the defendant is typically arraigned on that charging document and is asked to enter a plea in open court. At that time, the defendant may plead guilty, not guilty, or, in many jurisdictions—if permitted by the court in the interests of justice—enter a plea of nolo contendere, i.e. indicating that he or she is simply not contesting the charges. See, e.g., Fed. R.Crim.P. 11(b) (in the statutory supplement). Generally a "nolo plea" (as they are commonly called) is identical to a guilty plea except that, unlike a guilty plea (that has not been withdrawn), a nolo plea cannot be used as an admission of guilt against the defendant in a subsequent civil proceeding. In addition, in most jurisdictions, instead of pleading guilty or not guilty (or entering a nolo plea), the defendant can invoke a psychological condition by pleading not guilty by reason of insanity or, in some jurisdictions, guilty but mentally ill.

In many states, a defendant may enter a conditional guilty plea, reserving in writing the right to appeal specified pretrial motions without having to proceed to a complete trial in order to preserve the issues for appeal. See, e.g., Fed.R.Crim.P. 11(a)(2) (in the statutory supplement). Conditional pleas require that the court and the prosecutor approve the conditional guilty plea, and any defendant who prevails on appeal may later withdraw the conditional plea.

It is literally true that most cases in which criminal charges are filed by a prosecutor in the United States end in a guilty plea being offered by the defendant. A 1990 study undertaken for the Bureau of Justice Statistics of the U.S. Department of Justice ("BJS") which focused on the prosecution of adult felony arrests in thirty-five American jurisdictions deemed to be "nationally representative of the largest 200 prosecutors' offices" revealed that guilty pleas were proffered by defendants in 68% of the cases brought in these jurisdictions, ranging from a rate of 86% disposition by guilty plea in Littleton, Colorado, to a 56% rate in

Manhattan, New York. U.S. Dept. of Justice, The Prosecution of Felony Arrests, 1987 1, 6 (1990).

As pointed out in another BJS report, "[s]ometimes guilty pleas are traded explicitly for a less severe charge or sentence, but they also result from a defendant's straightforward admission of guilt. This may stem from a hope or impression that such a plea will be rewarded by a lighter sentence or from a concern that a trial will reveal damaging evidence." U.S. Dept. of Justice, Report to the Nation on Crime and Justice 83 (2d ed. 1988). Moreover, "[t]he predominance of guilty pleas is not new in the criminal justice system. A study in Connecticut covering 75 years (1880 to 1954) concludes that between 1880 and 1910 10% of all convictions were obtained by trial." Id.

Exercise

Check your jurisdiction's statutes, court rules and judicial decisions about the following:

1. What are the types of pleas which a defendant may enter at the time of the arraignment?

2. At the arraignment following the return of an indictment or information, what happens if a defendant refuses to enter a plea? For example, in that situation does the court enter a plea on behalf of the defendant?

3. If your jurisdiction uses a conditional guilty plea, what is the procedure for preserving an issue for later appeal?

4. If your jurisdiction uses a guilty but mentally ill plea, what is the difference between it and a plea of not guilty by reason of mental disease or defect (also known as an insanity plea), in terms of the relative burdens of proof, as well as the relative treatment consequences of a verdict returned on each plea?

5. If your jurisdiction recognizes the use of a nolo contendere plea, what is the strategic advantage of that plea? If your jurisdiction recognizes an Alford plea, what is the strategic advantage for that plea?

B. PLEA NEGOTIATION

Although more commonly called "plea bargaining," the unseemly sound and implications of the term "bargaining" have resulted in the increasingly common use of the rather more genteel phrase "plea negotiations" in some of the more recent scholarly literature and decisional law.

Fed.R.Crim.P. 11(c)(1) (in the statutory supplement) illustrate the different types of "plea agreements" which may be reached between a defendant and the government, and the procedure used to implement and safeguard such agreements.

Notes and Questions

1. A defendant has no constitutional right to plea bargain with the prosecutor. *Weatherford v. Bursey*, 429 U.S. 545 (1977). Accordingly, a prosecutor has the discretion to plea bargain with some defendants but not with others. Similarly, the prosecutor has the discretion to offer "package deals" to all defendants or no deal at all. See *United States v. Crain*, 33 F.3d 480 (5th Cir.1994). Prosecutors nevertheless cannot base the decision to plea bargain upon unjustifiable standards such as race, religion or other arbitrary classification. *Bordenkircher v. Hayes*, 434 U.S. 357 (1978).

2. In *United States v. Hyde*, 520 U.S. 670 (1997), the Court observed that the Federal Rules:

> explicitly envision a situation in which the defendant performs his side of the bargain (the guilty plea) before the Government is required to perform its side (here, the motion to dismiss four counts). If the court accepts the agreement and thus the Government's promised performance, then the contemplated agreement is complete and the defendant gets the benefit of his bargain. But if the court rejects the Government's promised performance, then the agreement is terminated and the defendant has the right to back out of his promised performance (the guilty plea), just as a binding contractual duty may be extinguished by the nonoccurrence of a condition subsequent. See J. Calamari & J. Perillo, Law of Contracts § 11–7, p. 441 (3d ed.1987); 3A A. Corbin, Corbin on Contracts § 628, p. 17 (1960).

3. Fed.R.Crim.P. 11(c)(1) prohibits the judge from participating in plea negotiations. What constitutes impermissible judicial participation? Conditioning acceptance of a plea on the outcome of a suppression hearing? Advising a defendant about the obvious risks of pleading guilty? Suggesting a stronger penalty during plea negotiations following rejection of an earlier agreement? Threatening to reject a plea to fewer than all of the crimes charged? Describing to defendant the differences in the potential sentences after a trial and pursuant to a proposed plea bargain? What is the remedy for improper judicial participation in plea bargaining? Plea withdrawal? Resentencing on the guilty plea? Judicial disqualification?

4. What is the purpose of Fed.R.Crim.P. 11(b)(3)'s requirement that there be a factual basis for a guilty plea? In *McCarthy v. United States*, 394 U.S. 459 (1969), the Court noted that the requirement protects a defendant from pleading voluntarily without realizing that her conduct is not actually within the charge. Most courts recognize that the evidence for the factual basis, whether from the prosecutor or from the defendant, need only be enough from which a court can reasonably find that the defendant is guilty of the particular offense.

5. Notwithstanding Fed.R.Crim.P. 11(f)'s general prohibition on the admissibility of plea-statements, the Court in *United States v. Mezzanatto*, 513 U.S. 196 (1995) held that a defendant could agree prior to plea discussions that any statement he made during those discussions could be used to impeach any contradictory statement if the case was tried. The Court found that waiver was not inconsistent with the rule's goal of encouraging

voluntary settlement, because it "makes no sense to conclude that mutual settlement will be encouraged by precluding negotiation over an issue that may be particularly important to one of the parties to the transaction."

6. When a defendant fails to make a contemporaneous objection to a violation of Federal Rule 11, the standard of review is under the plain error rule of Federal Rule 52(b), even though Rule 11(h) contains a harmless error provision. Analysis of the allegation may include the entire record and is not limited the plea proceedings. United States v. Vonn, 535 U.S. 55 (2002).

1. *Policy Concerns*

ROBERT E. SCOTT & WILLIAM J. STUNTZ— PLEA BARGAINING AS CONTRACT[1]

101 Yale L.J. 1909–10, 1911–12, 1913–15, 1966–68 (1992).

Most criminal prosecutions are settled without a trial. The parties to these settlements trade various risks and entitlements: the defendant relinquishes the right to go to trial (along with any chance of acquittal), while the prosecutor gives up the entitlement to seek the highest sentence or pursue the most serious charges possible. The resulting bargains differ predictably from what would have happened had the same cases been taken to trial. Defendants who bargain for a plea serve lower sentences than those who do not. On the other hand, everyone who pleads guilty is, by definition, convicted, while a substantial minority of those who go to trial are acquitted.

There is something puzzling about the polarity of contemporary reactions to this practice. Most legal scholars oppose plea bargaining, finding it both inefficient and unjust. Nevertheless, most participants in the plea bargaining process, including (perhaps especially) the courts, seem remarkably untroubled by it. Not only is the practice widespread, but participants generally approve of it. Why is plea bargaining at once so widely condemned and so widely tolerated?

One place to look for an answer is in the law and literature of plea bargaining as contract. Plea bargains are, as the name suggests, bargains; it seems natural to argue that they should be regulated and evaluated accordingly. But while that argument is common, there is little agreement on where it leads. Two of the harshest and most influential critics of plea bargaining, Albert Alschuler and Stephen Schulhofer, maintain that contract theory supports prohibiting any bargained-for allocation of criminal punishment. The courts, on the other hand, have proceeded to construct a body of contract-based law to regulate the plea bargaining process, taking for granted the efficiency and decency of the process being regulated. The many academic arguments for abolishing (or at least severely restricting) plea bargaining have thus been largely ignored. It is tempting to explain this reaction as a product of the chasm between an overly fastidious academic world and the unpleasant realities

1. Reprinted by permission of the Yale Law Journal Company and Fred B. Roth- man & Company from *The Yale Law Journal* Vol. 101, pages 1909–1968.

of modern criminal processes. But the intuition that plea bargaining is fundamentally flawed is too strong and too widespread to be so casually dismissed.

[T]he criminal process that law students study and television shows celebrate is formal, elaborate, and expensive. It involves detailed examination of witnesses and physical evidence, tough adversarial argument from attorneys for the government and defense, and fair-minded decisionmaking from an impartial judge and jury. For the vast majority of cases in the real world, the criminal process includes none of these things. Trials occur only occasionally—in some jurisdictions, they amount to only one-fiftieth of total dispositions. Most cases are disposed of by means that seem scandalously casual: a quick conversation in a prosecutor's office or a courthouse hallway between attorneys familiar with only the basics of the case, with no witnesses present, leading to a proposed resolution that is then "sold" to both the defendant and the judge. To a large extent, this kind of horse trading determines who goes to jail and for how long. That is what plea bargaining is. It is not some adjunct to the criminal justice system; it is the criminal justice system.

The idea of allocating criminal punishment through what looks like a street bazaar has proved unappealing to most outside observers. Critics point to the seeming hypocrisy of using an elaborate trial process as window dressing, while doing all the real business of the system through the most unelaborate process imaginable. They emphasize the unfairness (and inaccuracy) of determining defendants' fate without full investigation, without testimony and evidence and impartial factfinding; they emphasize too how this unfairness disproportionately harms the poor and unsophisticated. Perhaps especially, they note the seeming pervasiveness of coercion and fraud in the system. Defendants accept bargains because of the threat of much harsher penalties after trial; they are thus forced to give up the protections that the trial system's many formalities provide. And judges often give bargained-for sentences because of what prosecutors and defense lawyers do not say at sentencing; the sentencing hearing seems rigged to support the deal that the two attorneys have already struck.

[B]efore marshaling arguments from contract that support limitations on contractual autonomy, we must first ask why plea bargains deserve a presumption of enforceability in the first place. The answer is simple: the freedom to exchange entitlements subsumes a freedom to contract for such an exchange. Either freedom is supported by norms of efficiency and autonomy. Parties who are denied either freedom to contract or freedom to exchange entitlements suffer unnecessary constraints on their choices, constraints that undermine the value of the entitlements themselves. This norm of expanded choice is so powerful in ordinary contracts that it justifies not only state subsidization of an enforcement mechanism, but also an array of default rules that delineate the terms of typical bargains, terms that define the contractual relationship unless the parties design their own alternatives.

If the freedom to exchange entitlements were denied altogether in the allocation of criminal punishment, defendants would not have the option of pleading guilty in exchange for foregoing the burden and expense of a full trial. That is, not only plea bargains, but unbargained-for guilty pleas would be forbidden. Virtually no one argues that such a result would be socially desirable; the academic critics are not opposed to pleas, but only to plea bargains. But the line between granting defendants the option to plead guilty to forgo a trial and denying them the option to plead guilty to forgo the risk of a more severe punishment is far from clear. If the right to select a plea is an entitlement that can be traded for some purposes, why not for others? And if defendants may unilaterally exchange this entitlement for certain benefits under certain circumstances, then what justifies a prohibition on a party's freedom to contract for such an exchange?

The affirmative case for the enforceability of plea bargains is, then, fairly straightforward. The defendant has the right to plead not guilty and force the prosecutor to prove the case at trial. The prosecutor has the right to seek the maximum sentence for the maximum offense that can be proven. It is easy to imagine some circumstances where each party values the other's entitlement more than his own. If so, the conditions exist for an exchange that benefits both parties and harms neither. The defendant will trade the right to plead not guilty and force a trial for the prosecutor's right to seek the maximum sentence.

As with the typical executory contract, the parties to plea bargains do not actually trade the entitlements per se; instead they exchange the risks that future contingencies may materialize ex post that will lead one or the other to regret the ex ante bargain. Before contracting, the defendant bears the risk of conviction with the maximum sentence while the prosecutor bears the reciprocal risk of a costly trial followed by acquittal. An enforceable plea bargain reassigns these risks. Thereafter, the defendant bears the risk that a trial would have resulted in acquittal or a lighter sentence, while the prosecutor bears the risk that she could have obtained the maximum (or at least a greater) sentence if the case had gone to trial. Since it is difficult to know a priori which party enjoys the comparative advantage in risk reduction, a policy of contractual autonomy is the only way that parties can reduce the social losses that result from uncertainty and frustrated expectations.

Moreover, the gains the participants realize from the exchange presumably have social value, not just value to the bargaining parties. Plea bargaining provides a means by which prosecutors can obtain a larger net return from criminal convictions, holding resources constant. Criminal defendants, as a group, are able to reduce the risk of the imposition of maximum sanctions. Assuming that these social gains are not achieved at the expense of individual defendants, the system appears normatively acceptable in principle. In short, the existence of entitlements implies the right to exploit those entitlements fully, which in turn implies the right to trade the entitlement or any of its associated risks.

[T]he central problem with both sides of the plea bargaining debate is the same: they do not take contract seriously enough. Both at the level of broad abstraction—is plea bargaining defensible in principle?—and at the level of doctrinal detail—how and when should prosecutorial promises be enforced?—contract law and theory have a great many useful insights for this pervasive, and pervasively criticized, practice. At the broadest level, contract provides a framework for thinking about when consensual allocation ought to be permitted. That framework offers a fairly clear answer to the most basic questions policymakers (legislative or judicial) might want answered. In contract terms, plea bargains do not amount to duress; they are not, in general, unconscionable; they do not have the key characteristics of slavery contracts; and they are distributionally fairer than the likely alternative. Given the range of areas where our legal system tolerates (indeed, subsidizes) consensual allocation, it is hard to argue that contract is impermissible here. Seeing plea bargaining as contract thus helps one understand why the lawyers and judges who engage in and regulate the practice seem so comfortable with it.

But while consensual allocation has the same virtues here as elsewhere, it has an important flaw, one that infects not only plea bargaining but many other features of the criminal justice system. Innocent defendants have a hard time signaling their innocence in ways that guilty defendants cannot copy. This is not true of all stages in the process—police interrogation, for example—but it is true of plea negotiations. The upshot is that prosecutors have good reason to underestimate the odds that any given defendant might be innocent. This might not be a problem if trials were perfect, but of course they are not. And the consequences of this structural difficulty are likely to be substantial because of innocent defendants' risk aversion, a characteristic that may lead them to accept deals that do not discount for the possibility of acquittal. Understanding the bargaining dynamic of plea negotiations thus helps explain the discomfort so many outside observers feel about them.

Current legal doctrine not only fails to solve that structural problem (solutions may not exist); it makes the problem worse. By failing to enforce prosecutors' sentencing promises, the law encourages courts to raise sentences in precisely those cases where the defendant is most likely to be innocent. By underprotecting against defense attorney error, the law increases the chances of risk averse innocent defendants accepting deals that treat them as certain convictions. And by permitting prosecutorial manipulation of broad mandatory sentencing statutes, the doctrine reduces prosecutors' incentives to separate innocent from guilty defendants at the charging stage. All these effects are unnecessary. By following appropriate contract models, one can devise different rules that reduce the harm to innocent defendants and meanwhile reduce transaction costs and inefficiency for everyone else.

The puzzle is that these systemic doctrinal problems have persisted so long, with so little attention. The reason, we think, has to do with the nature of the plea bargaining debate. Though it has long been under-

stood that plea bargaining is a species of contract, the debate about it has been framed not in the language of bargains, but chiefly in the language of rights. That may have something to do with its either-or character: either the defendant's rights trump the bargain or the rights do not apply; either plea bargaining is wholly impermissible or it raises no constitutional (read: important) issue. Rights rhetoric has led to a great deal of discussion of whether plea bargaining is a good thing, but little attention to what the law that surrounds it ought to look like.

The time has come to put rights talk to one side and view plea bargaining through the lens of contract. Contract makes the positive reactions of plea bargaining participants seem sensible, for plea bargains are indeed paradigmatically value-enhancing bargains. Contract makes the disquiet of the critics seem sensible too, since the bargaining dynamic shortchanges the innocent. And contract offers a range of second-best solutions, doctrinal reforms that can help prosecutors and defendants alike. These kinds of solutions may be less interesting than grand constitutional theory. In this context, they may also be more useful.

Note

One of the few grounds upon which a guilty plea may be set aside is if a court determines that it is involuntary. In *Brady v. United States*, 397 U.S. 742 (1970), the Court held that defendant must prove that the fear of the possible consequences of not pleading guilty destroyed the ability to balance the risks and benefits of going to trial. The Court found that Brady's plea was voluntary even though it was motivated by his desire to avoid the death penalty. Should the plea in the next case be characterized as involuntary?

BORDENKIRCHER v. HAYES

434 U.S. 357 (1978).

Mr. Justice Stewart delivered the opinion of the Court.

The question in this case is whether the Due Process Clause of the Fourteenth Amendment is violated when a state prosecutor carries out a threat made during plea negotiations to reindict the accused on more serious charges if he does not plead guilty to the offense with which he was originally charged.

The respondent, Paul Lewis Hayes, was indicted by a Fayette County, Ky., grand jury on a charge of uttering a forged instrument in the amount of $88.30, an offense then punishable by a term of 2 to 10 years in prison. After arraignment, Hayes, his retained counsel, and the Commonwealth's Attorney met in the presence of the Clerk of the Court to discuss a possible plea agreement. During these conferences the prosecutor offered to recommend a sentence of five years in prison if Hayes would plead guilty to the indictment. He also said that if Hayes did not plead guilty and "save[d] the court the inconvenience and necessity of a trial," he would return to the grand jury to seek an indictment under the Kentucky Habitual Criminal Act which would subject Hayes to a mandatory sentence of life imprisonment by reason of his two prior felony convictions. Hayes chose not to plead guilty, and the prosecutor did obtain an indictment charging him under the Habitual Criminal Act. It is not disputed that the recidivist charge was fully justified by the evidence, that the prosecutor was in possession of this evidence at the time of the original indictment, and that Hayes' refusal to plead guilty to the original charge was what led to his indictment under the habitual criminal statute.

A jury found Hayes guilty on the principal charge of uttering a forged instrument and, in a separate proceeding, further found that he had twice before been convicted of felonies. As required by the habitual offender statute, he was sentenced to a life term in the penitentiary. The Kentucky Court of Appeals rejected Hayes' constitutional objections to the enhanced sentence, holding in an unpublished opinion that imprisonment for life with the possibility of parole was constitutionally permissible in light of the previous felonies of which Hayes had been convicted, and that the prosecutor's decision to indict him as a habitual offender was a legitimate use of available leverage in the plea-bargaining process.

On Hayes' petition for a federal writ of habeas corpus, the United States District Court for the Eastern District of Kentucky agreed that there had been no constitutional violation in the sentence or the indictment procedure, and denied the writ. The Court of Appeals for the Sixth Circuit reversed the District Court's judgment. While recognizing "that plea bargaining now plays an important role in our criminal justice system," the appellate court thought that the prosecutor's conduct during the bargaining negotiations had violated the principles of *Blackledge v. Perry*, 417 U.S. 21, which "protect[ed] defendants from the vindictive exercise of a prosecutor's discretion." Accordingly, the court ordered that Hayes be discharged "except for his confinement under a lawful sentence imposed solely for the crime of uttering a forged instrument." We granted certiorari to consider a constitutional question of importance in the administration of criminal justice.

It may be helpful to clarify at the outset the nature of the issue in this case. While the prosecutor did not actually obtain the recidivist indictment until after the plea conferences had ended, his intention to do so was clearly expressed at the outset of the plea negotiations. Hayes was thus fully informed of the true terms of the offer when he made his decision to plead not guilty. This is not a situation, therefore, where the prosecutor without notice brought an additional and more serious charge after plea negotiations relating only to the original indictment had ended with the defendant's insistence on pleading not guilty. As a practical matter, in short, this case would be no different if the grand jury had indicted Hayes as a recidivist from the outset, and the prosecutor had offered to drop that charge as part of the plea bargain.

The Court of Appeals nonetheless drew a distinction between "concessions relating to prosecution under an existing indictment," and threats to bring more severe charges not contained in the original

indictment—a line it thought necessary in order to establish a prophylactic rule to guard against the evil of prosecutorial vindictiveness. Quite
apart from this chronological distinction, however, the Court of Appeals
found that the prosecutor had acted vindictively in the present case since
he had conceded that the indictment was influenced by his desire to
induce a guilty plea. The ultimate conclusion of the Court of Appeals
thus seems to have been that a prosecutor acts vindictively and in
violation of due process of law whenever his charging decision is influenced by what he hopes to gain in the course of plea bargaining
negotiations.

We have recently had occasion to observe: "[W]hatever might be the
situation in an ideal world, the fact is that the guilty plea and the often
concomitant plea bargain are important components of this country's
criminal justice system. Properly administered, they can benefit all
concerned." *Blackledge v. Allison*, 431 U.S. 63, 71. The open acknowledgment of this previously clandestine practice has led this Court to
recognize the importance of counsel during plea negotiations, the need
for a public record indicating that a plea was knowingly and voluntarily
made, and the requirement that a prosecutor's plea-bargaining promise
must be kept. The decision of the Court of Appeals in the present case,
however, did not deal with considerations such as these, but held that
the substance of the plea offer itself violated the limitations imposed by
the Due Process Clause of the Fourteenth Amendment. For the reasons
that follow, we have concluded that the Court of Appeals was mistaken
in so ruling.

This Court held in *North Carolina v. Pearce*, 395 U.S. 711, 725, that
the Due Process Clause of the Fourteenth Amendment "requires that
vindictiveness against a defendant for having successfully attacked his
first conviction must play no part in the sentence he receives after a new
trial." The same principle was later applied to prohibit a prosecutor from
reindicting a convicted misdemeanant on a felony charge after the
defendant had invoked an appellate remedy, since in this situation there
was also a "realistic likelihood of 'vindictiveness.' "

In those cases the Court was dealing with the State's unilateral
imposition of a penalty upon a defendant who had chosen to exercise a
legal right to attack his original conviction—a situation "very different
from the give-and-take negotiation common in plea bargaining between
the prosecution and defense, which arguably possess relatively equal
bargaining power." The Court has emphasized that the due process
violation in cases such as *Pearce* and *Perry* lay not in the possibility that
a defendant might be deterred from the exercise of a legal right, but
rather in the danger that the State might be retaliating against the
accused for lawfully attacking his conviction.

To punish a person because he has done what the law plainly allows
him to do is a due process violation of the most basic sort, and for an
agent of the State to pursue a course of action whose objective is to
penalize a person's reliance on his legal rights is "patently unconstitu-

tional." But in the "give-and-take" of plea bargaining, there is no such element of punishment or retaliation so long as the accused is free to accept or reject the prosecution's offer.

Plea bargaining flows from "the mutuality of advantage" to defendants and prosecutors, each with his own reasons for wanting to avoid trial. Defendants advised by competent counsel and protected by other procedural safeguards are presumptively capable of intelligent choice in response to prosecutorial persuasion, and unlikely to be driven to false self-condemnation. Indeed, acceptance of the basic legitimacy of plea bargaining necessarily implies rejection of any notion that a guilty plea is involuntary in a constitutional sense simply because it is the end result of the bargaining process. By hypothesis, the plea may have been induced by promises of a recommendation of a lenient sentence or a reduction of charges, and thus by fear of the possibility of a greater penalty upon conviction after a trial.

While confronting a defendant with the risk of more severe punishment clearly may have a "discouraging effect on the defendant's assertion of his trial rights, the imposition of these difficult choices [is] an inevitable"—and permissible—"attribute of any legitimate system which tolerates and encourages the negotiation of pleas." It follows that, by tolerating and encouraging the negotiation of pleas, this Court has necessarily accepted as constitutionally legitimate the simple reality that the prosecutor's interest at the bargaining table is to persuade the defendant to forgo his right to plead not guilty.

It is not disputed here that Hayes was properly chargeable under the recidivist statute, since he had in fact been convicted of two previous felonies. In our system, so long as the prosecutor has probable cause to believe that the accused committed an offense defined by statute, the decision whether or not to prosecute, and what charge to file or bring before a grand jury, generally rests entirely in his discretion. Within the limits set by the legislature's constitutionally valid definition of chargeable offenses, "the conscious exercise of some selectivity in enforcement is not in itself a federal constitutional violation" so long as "the selection was [not] deliberately based upon an unjustifiable standard such as race, religion, or other arbitrary classification." To hold that the prosecutor's desire to induce a guilty plea is an "unjustifiable standard," which, like race or religion, may play no part in his charging decision, would contradict the very premises that underlie the concept of plea bargaining itself. Moreover, a rigid constitutional rule that would prohibit a prosecutor from acting forthrightly in his dealings with the defense could only invite unhealthy subterfuge that would drive the practice of plea bargaining back into the shadows from which it has so recently emerged.

There is no doubt that the breadth of discretion that our country's legal system vests in prosecuting attorneys carries with it the potential for both individual and institutional abuse. And broad though that discretion may be, there are undoubtedly constitutional limits upon its exercise. We hold only that the course of conduct engaged in by the prosecutor in this case, which no more than openly presented the defendant with the unpleasant alternatives of forgoing trial or facing charges on which he was plainly subject to prosecution, did not violate the Due Process Clause of the Fourteenth Amendment.

Accordingly, the judgment of the Court of Appeals is reversed.

MR. JUSTICE BLACKMUN, with whom MR. JUSTICE BRENNAN and MR. JUSTICE MARSHALL join, dissenting.

[Prosecutorial] vindictiveness, it seems to me, in the present narrow context, is the fact against which the Due Process Clause ought to protect. I perceive little difference between vindictiveness after what the Court describes as the exercise of a "legal right to attack his original conviction," and vindictiveness in the "Give-and-take negotiation common in plea bargaining." "Prosecutorial vindictiveness in any context is still prosecutorial vindictiveness." The Due Process Clause should protect an accused against it, however it asserts itself. The Court of Appeals rightly so held, and I would affirm the judgment.

It might be argued that it really makes little difference how this case, now that it is here, is decided. The Court's holding gives plea bargaining full sway despite vindictiveness. A contrary result, however, merely would prompt the aggressive prosecutor to bring the greater charge initially in every case, and only thereafter to bargain. The consequences to the accused would still be adverse, for then he would bargain against a greater charge, face the likelihood of increased bail, and run the risk that the court would be less inclined to accept a bargained plea. Nonetheless, it is far preferable to hold the prosecution to the charge it was originally content to bring and to justify in the eyes of its public.

MR. JUSTICE POWELL, dissenting. * * *

No explanation appears in the record for the prosecutor's decision to escalate the charge against respondent other than respondent's refusal to plead guilty. The prosecutor has conceded that his purpose was to discourage respondent's assertion of constitutional rights, and the majority accepts this characterization of events.

It seems to me that the question to be asked under the circumstances is whether the prosecutor reasonably might have charged respondent under the Habitual Criminal Act in the first place. The deference that courts properly accord the exercise of a prosecutor's discretion perhaps would foreclose judicial criticism if the prosecutor originally had sought an indictment under that Act, as unreasonable as it would have seemed. But here the prosecutor evidently made a reasonable, responsible judgment not to subject an individual to a mandatory life sentence when his only new offense had societal implications as limited as those accompanying the uttering of a single $88 forged check and when the circumstances of his prior convictions confirmed the inappropriateness of applying the habitual criminal statute. I think it may be inferred that the prosecutor himself deemed it unreasonable and not in the public interest to put this defendant in jeopardy of a sentence of life imprisonment.

There may be situations in which a prosecutor would be fully justified in seeking a fresh indictment for a more serious offense. The most plausible justification might be that it would have been reasonable and in the public interest initially to have charged the defendant with the greater offense. In most cases a court could not know why the harsher indictment was sought, and an inquiry into the prosecutor's motive would neither be indicated nor likely to be fruitful. In those cases, I would agree with the majority that the situation would not differ materially from one in which the higher charge was brought at the outset.

But this is not such a case. Here, any inquiry into the prosecutor's purpose is made unnecessary by his candid acknowledgment that he threatened to procure and in fact procured the habitual criminal indictment because of respondent's insistence on exercising his constitutional rights. * * *

The plea-bargaining process, as recognized by this Court, is essential to the functioning of the criminal-justice system. It normally affords genuine benefits to defendants as well as to society. And if the system is to work effectively, prosecutors must be accorded the widest discretion, within constitutional limits, in conducting bargaining. This is especially true when a defendant is represented by counsel and presumably is fully advised of his rights. Only in the most exceptional case should a court conclude that the scales of the bargaining are so unevenly balanced as to arouse suspicion. In this case, the prosecutor's actions denied respondent due process because their admitted purpose was to discourage and then to penalize with unique severity his exercise of constitutional rights. Implementation of a strategy calculated solely to deter the exercise of constitutional rights is not a constitutionally permissible exercise of discretion. I would affirm the opinion of the Court of Appeals on the facts of this case.

CHESTER MIRSKY—PLEA REFORM IS NO BARGAIN[2]

Newsday p.70 (City edition, March 4, 1994).

Since 1860, the history of criminal justice in New York City has been that of the "vanishing jury." Criminal courts have relied, instead, on guilty pleas, using a method commonly described as "plea bargaining." Earlier on, those denied their right to a jury trial were immigrants and members of ethnic minorities; today, they are mostly people of color. District attorneys, Legal Aid lawyers and judges claimed that their professional skills enable them to negotiate the outcome of these people's cases so that the guilty will not go free and the innocent will not be wrongfully convicted. Under this professional view, jury trials are essen-

2. Reprinted by permission.

tially unnecessary and wasteful of the public till. The result, in New York City, as in most cities in the United States, is that over 90 percent of all criminal cases are disposed of without trial, with guilty pleas accounting for roughly 80 percent of all dispositions in felony indictments.

Handling criminal cases summarily through guilty pleas has enabled the police to routinely "sweep" neighborhoods for people who engage in criminal activity or simply look suspicious. These cases pass through the court gates with minimal screening by prosecutors, and in the certain knowledge that however many cases the police choose to dump into the courts, they will be disposed of quickly and without much fuss. In New York City, more than a quarter-of-a-million cases are disposed of annually in Criminal Court, while in Supreme Court more than 30,000 indictments are often filed.

Several structural features enable New York City's courts to operate without trials. First, courts often attribute guilt to defendants based on their socioeconomic status alone, without regard to the sufficiency of the prosecution's evidence; second, the police are not required to provide evidence to support their allegations; third, lawyers and judges use stereotypes to pigeonhole defendants and charges in pursuit of cost-efficient docket management.

Ironically, the most vocal critics of the plea-bargaining system have not been the doyens of the defense bar, but prosecutors and judges who have complained that the quality of justice has suffered and the city has wasted its time and money. Such criticisms surfaced again last year, when Bronx District

Attorney Robert Johnson initiated a "plea bargaining ban," and Kings County D.A Charles Hynes imposed a "74–day time limitation" (from arraignment) on plea bargaining.

Under the Bronx plea ban, defendants are now convicted of the top count of the indictment, eliminating opportunities for defendants to obtain a lesser sentence on a reduced charge in exchange for the time saved by avoiding a jury trial. The ban ostensibly increases the severity of prison sentences for violent felons and drug dealers.

For his part, the Kings County district attorney contends that his time-limitation on plea bargaining will expedite case processing and thereby reduce pre-trial detention and court appearances, saving the city millions of dollars in jail expenses as cases no longer spin from one adjourned date to another. Hynes, however, unlike Johnson, encourages plea bargaining during the 74 days between arraignment and the final plea offer.

The Bronx plea-bargaining ban has proven a disaster from a quality-of-justice as well as a cost-benefit perspective. The ban has caused cases to age dramatically, increasing significantly the cost to the city in pre-trial detention. By the end of last September, almost half of all pre-trial detainees held in New York City's correctional facilities for more than

365 days were from the Bronx, one of the least populous boroughs. The defendant's right to a speedy trial is all but forgotten, along with the state's interest in a speedy prosecution. Defendants languish in jail so long that their cases often disintegrate, resulting in a substantial increase in dismissals of serious felony indictments. Average sentences are actually less severe than before the ban because Bronx judges are doing everything they can to induce violent felons and drug dealers to plead guilty to the top charge, and thus avoid even greater case backlog.

The time limitation on plea bargaining in Kings County, on the other hand, has accelerated guilty pleas and also saved money, although this has occurred only in cases where the district attorney has not been required to provide the defendant full disclosure of the police case. Where disclosure has been mandated, the number of guilty pleas has increased, but without any time-savings. Thus, while Hynes' program has succeeded in getting more defendants to plead "in the dark," it also raises serious questions about the quality of justice and the coercive nature of the process itself.

Unless we close the floodgates and reduce the number of cases brought to court, reform efforts will ultimately fail. It makes little sense to ban plea bargaining in the Bronx without requiring the police and district attorney to decline to prosecute in superior court the substantial number of cases—such as small drug sales by addicts, and nonviolent thefts of insubstantial sums—that don't belong there in the first place. Similarly, it is perverse to reduce the cost of pre-trial detention and the number of court appearances in Kings County at the expense of the rights of the innocent who may be forced to plead guilty to avoid a greater penalty later—without ever knowing whether the prosecution could sustain its burden of proof at trial.

Nevertheless, the ring of desperation in both district attorneys' attempts at reform should not go unheard. Both are testimony that business as usual is breaking down in criminal justice.

Problem

An English newspaper, The Guardian, carried the following story on June 1, 1993:

A formal plea bargaining system would lead to innocent people pleading guilty and to unfair sentences, the law reform group Justice concludes in a report today.

The group, the British section of the International Commission of Jurists, echoes doubts voiced last Friday by Lord Taylor, the Lord Chief Justice and the senior judge in England and Wales. He said he had "misgivings" about such a system, under which judges would tell defendants in advance what sentence they would receive if they pleaded guilty.

The warning comes as the Royal Commission on Criminal Justice finalises its report, due out at the end of this month. It is thought to favour a formal plea bargaining system. the move is also supported by Barbara Mills, Director of Public Prosecutions, 90 per cent of barristers and two-thirds of judges.

At present, defendants in most courts can expect a lesser sentence in return for a guilty plea, but judges may not indicate the sentence in advance.

A year ago, the Bar Council said judges should be able to indicate the sentence to the defendant in open court, but without the jury or the public present. It described this as "the single most effective form of judicial intervention" to save court time and money, arguing it would slash the numbers of "cracked trials"—those aborted at the last minute, often through late guilty pleas.

The Justice report, Negotiated Justice, blames inefficiency as the major factor in cracked trials. it cites as two critical factors the lack of liaison between prosecution and defence and the fact that more than half of defendants only meet their barristers for the first time on the day of trial.

Justice claims plea bargaining would lead to inaccurate and sometimes unfair sentences, as judges would have to indicate them at an early stage without full information. The defence would not be able to present information on mitigation or degree of culpability when the defendant was still claiming to be innocent.

It says: "The risk of a defendant being unduly pressurised, intimidated, misled or badly advised into wrongly or unwisely pleading guilty are too great."

Instead it calls for formalisation of the informal system of plea discounts and for a Sentencing Commission to draft and update sentencing guidelines.

Clare Dyer, "Jurists Add to Doubt Over Plea Bargaining," The Guardian p. 4 (June 1, 1993).3

How is this proposed plea bargaining system different from the system found commonly in the United States? Do you think it is more or less desirable than the American system? Would you be in favor of adopting this British proposal in this country? Why or why not?

2. *Legality and Enforcement*

SANTOBELLO v. NEW YORK

404 U.S. 257 (1971).

MR. CHIEF JUSTICE BURGER delivered the opinion of the Court.

We granted certiorari in this case to determine whether the State's failure to keep a commitment concerning the sentence recommendation on a guilty plea required a new trial.

The facts are not in dispute. The State of New York indicted petitioner in 1969 on two felony counts, Promoting Gambling in the

First Degree, and Possession of Gambling Records in the First Degree. Petitioner first entered a plea of not guilty to both counts. After negotiations, the Assistant District Attorney in charge of the case agreed to permit petitioner to plead guilty to a lesser-included offense, Possession of Gambling Records in the Second Degree, conviction of which would carry a maximum prison sentence of one year. The prosecutor agreed to make no recommendation as to the sentence.

On June 16, 1969, petitioner accordingly withdrew his plea of not guilty and entered a plea of guilty to the lesser charge. Petitioner represented to the sentencing judge that the plea was voluntary and that the facts of the case, as described by the Assistant District Attorney, were true. The court accepted the plea and set a date for sentencing. A series of delays followed, owing primarily to the absence of a presentence report, so that by September 23, 1969, petitioner had still not been sentenced. By that date petitioner acquired new defense counsel.

Petitioner's new counsel moved immediately to withdraw the guilty plea. In an accompanying affidavit, petitioner alleged that he did not know at the time of his plea that crucial evidence against him had been obtained as a result of an illegal search. The accuracy of this affidavit is subject to challenge since petitioner had filed and withdrawn a motion to suppress, before pleading guilty. In addition to his motion to withdraw his guilty plea, petitioner renewed the motion to suppress and filed a motion to inspect the grand jury minutes.

These three motions in turn caused further delay until November 26, 1969, when the court denied all three and set January 9, 1970, as the date for sentencing. On January 9 petitioner appeared before a different judge, the judge who had presided over the case to this juncture having retired.

Petitioner renewed his motions, and the court again rejected them. The court then turned to consideration of the sentence. At this appearance, another prosecutor had replaced the prosecutor who had negotiated the plea. The new prosecutor recommended the maximum one-year sentence. In making this recommendation, he cited petitioner's criminal record and alleged links with organized crime. Defense counsel immediately objected on the ground that the State had promised petitioner before the plea was entered that there would be no sentence recommendation by the prosecution. He sought to adjourn the sentence hearing in order to have time to prepare proof of the first prosecutor's promise. The second prosecutor, apparently ignorant of his colleague's commitment, argued that there was nothing in the record to support petitioner's claim of a promise, but the State, in subsequent proceedings, has not contested that such a promise was made.

The sentencing judge ended discussion, with the following statement, quoting extensively from the pre-sentence report:

"Mr. Aronstein [Defense Counsel], I am not at all influenced by what the District Attorney says, so that there is no need to adjourn the sentence, and there is no need to have any testimony. It doesn't make a particle of difference what the District Attorney says he will do, or what he doesn't do.

"I have here, Mr. Aronstein, a probation report. I have here a history of a long, long serious criminal record. I have here a picture of the life history of this man. He is unamenable to supervision in the community. He is a professional criminal." This is in quotes. "And a recidivist. Institutionalization—"; that means, in plain language, just putting him away, "is the only means of halting his anti-social activities," and protecting you, your family, me, my family, protecting society. "Institutionalization." Plain language, put him behind bars.

"Under the plea, I can only send him to the New York City Correctional Institution for men for one year, which I am hereby doing."

The judge then imposed the maximum sentence of one year.

[T]his record represents another example of an unfortunate lapse in orderly prosecutorial procedures, in part, no doubt, because of the enormous increase in the workload of the often understaffed prosecutor's offices. The heavy workload may well explain these episodes, but it does not excuse them. The disposition of criminal charges by agreement between the prosecutor and the accused, sometimes loosely called "plea bargaining," is an essential component of the administration of justice. Properly administered, it is to be encouraged. If every criminal charge were subjected to a full-scale trial, the States and the Federal Government would need to multiply by many times the number of judges and court facilities.

Disposition of charges after plea discussions is not only an essential part of the process but a highly desirable part for many reasons. It leads to prompt and largely final disposition of most criminal cases; it avoids much of the corrosive impact of enforced idleness during pre-trial confinement for those who are denied release pending trial; it protects the public from those accused persons who are prone to continue criminal conduct even while on pretrial release; and, by shortening the time between charge and disposition, it enhances whatever may be the rehabilitative prospects of the guilty when they are ultimately imprisoned. * * *

However, all of these considerations presuppose fairness in securing agreement between an accused and a prosecutor. It is now clear, for example, that the accused pleading guilty must be counseled, absent a waiver. [T]he plea must, of course, be voluntary and knowing and if it was induced by promises, the essence of those promises must in some way be made known. There is, of course, no absolute right to have a guilty plea accepted. A court may reject a plea in exercise of sound judicial discretion.

This phase of the process of criminal justice, and the adjudicative element inherent in accepting a plea of guilty, must be attended by safeguards to insure the defendant what is reasonably due in the circumstances. Those circumstances will vary, but a constant factor is that when a plea rests in any significant degree on a promise or agreement of the prosecutor, so that it can be said to be part of the inducement or consideration, such promise must be fulfilled.

On this record, petitioner "bargained" and negotiated for a particular plea in order to secure dismissal of more serious charges, but also on condition that no sentence recommendation would be made by the prosecutor. It is now conceded that the promise to abstain from a recommendation was made, and at this stage the prosecution is not in a good position to argue that its inadvertent breach of agreement is immaterial. The staff lawyers in a prosecutor's office have the burden of "letting the left hand know what the right hand is doing" or has done. That the breach of agreement was inadvertent does not lessen its impact.

We need not reach the question whether the sentencing judge would or would not have been influenced had he known all the details of the negotiations for the plea. He stated that the prosecutor's recommendation did not influence him and we have no reason to doubt that. Nevertheless, we conclude that the interests of justice and appropriate recognition of the duties of the prosecution in relation to promises made in the negotiation of pleas of guilty will be best served by remanding the case to the state courts for further consideration. The ultimate relief to which petitioner is entitled we leave to the discretion of the state court, which is in a better position to decide whether the circumstances of this case require only that there be specific performance of the agreement on the plea, in which case petitioner should be resentenced by a different judge, or whether, in the view of the state court, the circumstances require granting the relief sought by petitioner, i.e., the opportunity to withdraw his plea of guilty. * * *

MR. JUSTICE DOUGLAS, concurring.

[I] join the opinion of the Court and favor a constitutional rule for this as well as for other pending or oncoming cases. Where the "plea bargain" is not kept by the prosecutor, the sentence must be vacated and the state court will decide in light of the circumstances of each case whether due process requires (a) that there be specific performance of the plea bargain or (b) that the defendant be given the option to go to trial on the original charges. One alternative may do justice in one case, and the other in a different case. In choosing a remedy, however, a court ought to accord a defendant's preference considerable, if not controlling, weight inasmuch as the fundamental rights flouted by a prosecutor's breach of a plea bargain are those of the defendant, not of the State.

MR. JUSTICE MARSHALL, with whom MR. JUSTICE BRENNAN and MR. JUSTICE STEWART join, concurring in part and dissenting in part.

* * * When a prosecutor breaks the bargain, he undercuts the basis for the waiver of constitutional rights implicit in the plea. This, it seems to me, provides the defendant ample justification for rescinding the plea.

Where a promise is "unfulfilled," specifically denies that the plea 'must stand.' Of course, where the prosecutor has broken the plea agreement, it may be appropriate to permit the defendant to enforce the plea bargain. But that is not the remedy sought here.4 Rather, it seems to me that a breach of the plea bargain provides ample reason to permit the plea to be vacated.

It is worth noting that in the ordinary case where a motion to vacate is made prior to sentencing, the government has taken no action in reliance on the previously entered guilty plea and would suffer no harm from the plea's withdrawal. More pointedly, here the State claims no such harm beyond disappointed expectations about the plea itself. At least where the government itself has broken the plea bargain, this disappointment cannot bar petitioner from withdrawing his guilty plea and reclaiming his right to a trial.

I would remand the case with instructions that the plea be vacated and petitioner given an opportunity to replead to the original charges in the indictment.

Notes and Questions

1. In *Blackledge v. Allison*, 431 U.S. 63 (1977), the Court made the following observations about the plea bargaining process:

Whatever might be the situation in an ideal world, the fact is that the guilty plea and the often concomitant plea bargain are important components of this country's criminal justice system. Properly administered, they can benefit all concerned. The defendant avoids extended pretrial incarceration and the anxieties and uncertainties of a trial; he gains a speedy disposition of his case, the chance to acknowledge his guilt, and a prompt start in realizing whatever potential there may be for rehabilitation. Judges and prosecutors conserve vital and scarce resources. The public is protected from the risks posed by those charged with criminal offenses who are at large on bail while awaiting completion of criminal proceedings.

These advantages can be secured, however, only if dispositions by guilty plea are accorded a great measure of finality. To allow indiscriminate hearings in federal postconviction proceedings [w]ould eliminate the chief virtues of the plea system—speed, economy, and finality. And there is reason for concern about that prospect. More often than not a prisoner has everything to gain and nothing to lose from filing a collateral attack upon his guilty plea. If he succeeds in vacating the judgment of conviction, retrial may be difficult. If he convinces a court that his plea was induced by an advantageous plea agreement that was violated, he may obtain the benefit of its terms. A collateral attack may also be inspired by "a mere desire to be freed temporarily from the confines of the prison."

Yet arrayed against the interest in finality is the very purpose of the writ of habeas corpus—to safeguard a person's freedom from detention in violation of constitutional guarantees. "The writ of habeas corpus has played a great role in the history of human freedom. It has been the judicial method of lifting undue restraints upon personal liberty." And a prisoner in custody after pleading guilty, no less than one tried and convicted by a jury, is entitled to avail himself of the writ in challenging the constitutionality of his custody.

2.   Courts recognize that the law of contracts governs plea agreements. See, e.g., *United States v. Vaval*, 404 F.3d 144 (2d Cir.2005). As such, one or both parties may breach the agreement, although the existence of a breach seems to be fact-specific. Some courts have noted that due process requires that any ambiguity in the terms of an agreement should be construed against the prosecution, consistent with the defendant's reasonable understanding of the agreement. See, e.g., *United States v. Guzman*, 318 F.3d 1191 (10th Cir.2003) (court construes any ambiguities against government as drafter of the agreement); *Peavy v. U.S.*, 31 F.3d 1341, 1346 (6th Cir.1994) (although plea agreements are generally analyzed under contract law, analogy to contract law is not complete because guilty plea involves waiver of fundamental constitutional rights).

3.   Defendant Carlton Legall executed a plea agreement with the government in which both sides agreed to take no appeal if Legall's sentence for the offense of conspiracy to import a controlled substance fell within a range of 120 to 135 months imprisonment. The district court sentenced Legall to 135 months and he appealed, claiming that the federal sentencing guidelines permit an appeal where the sentence is in violation of a statutory provision as this one was since the trial judge imposed this sentence without a proper specification of reasons. The government agrees that an appeal would normally be appropriate in these circumstances except that Legall waived his right to appeal from a sentence in this range in his plea agreement. Who do you think is right? Why? Should it matter that the 135–month sentence may be illegal under the applicable sentencing guidelines? *United States v. Yemitan*, 70 F.3d 746 (2d Cir.1995).

4.   In a federal plea agreement between a defendant and the government under Fed.R.Crim.P. 11(c)(1)(B) (in the statutory supplement), the prosecutor may be responsible for making a nonbinding sentencing recommendation to the court. In *United States v. Benchimol*, 471 U.S. 453 (1985), the Court held that the prosecutor does not have to "enthusiastically" defend its sentencing recommendation.

Is a promise by the government to recommend a sentence at the low end of the sentencing guideline range breached when the government notes the recommendation in the presentence report but does not affirmatively advocate that sentence to the trial court? Yes, said the appellate court in *United States v. Myers*, 32 F.3d 411 (9th Cir.1994). On the other hand, when the government keeps its promise about not making a sentence recommendation, courts usually preclude additional comments as long as a specific sentence is not being recommended. See, e.g., *Colvin v. Taylor*, 324 F.3d 583 (8th Cir.2003) (no breach when prosecutor rebutted factual assertions that supported defendant's request); *United States v. Gerace*, 997 F.2d 1293 (9th Cir.1993) (no breach when prosecutor was silent at sentencing but opposed leniency at later probation revocation hearing).

5. Assuming that a plea agreement exists between a defendant and the prosecution, who is bound by that agreement? In *Santobello*, the successor of the prosecutor who made a promise to the defendant was bound by that promise. Generally, a plea agreement in a state prosecution is not binding on prosecutors in other jurisdictions or on officials in other parts of the same jurisdiction if they are not parties to the agreement. See, e.g., *Montoya v. Johnson*, 226 F.3d 399 (5th Cir.2000) (state plea agreement providing for concurrent state and federal sentences not binding on federal officials); *United States v. Igbonwa*, 120 F.3d 437 (3d Cir.1997) (promise by federal prosecutor regarding deportation not binding on Immigration and Naturalization Service without its explicit consent in plea agreement).

If a law enforcement official lacks the authority to bind even the prosecutorial entity to whom she reports, any "agreement" between the agent and a defendant will be regarded as enforceable only if the defendant can show that he has detrimentally relied on the official's promise.

6. If a defendant is able to prove that the prosecution has breached a plea agreement, what is the appropriate remedy for the defendant? Withdrawal of the plea? Specific performance of the agreement? Alteration of the sentence? In *Santobello*, the issue of the appropriate remedy was left to the discretion of the trial court. Should the defendant who seeks specific performance be required to prove prejudice?

RICKETTS v. ADAMSON

483 U.S. 1 (1987).

JUSTICE WHITE delivered the opinion of the Court.

The question for decision is whether the Double Jeopardy Clause bars the prosecution of respondent for first-degree murder following his breach of a plea agreement under which he had pleaded guilty to a lesser offense, had been sentenced, and had begun serving a term of imprisonment. The Court of Appeals for the Ninth Circuit held that the prosecution of respondent violated double jeopardy principles and directed the issuance of a writ of habeas corpus. We reverse.

In 1976, Donald Bolles, a reporter for the Arizona Republic, was fatally injured when a dynamite bomb exploded underneath his car. Respondent was arrested and charged with first-degree murder in connection with Bolles' death. Shortly after his trial had commenced, while jury selection was underway, respondent and the state prosecutor reached an agreement whereby respondent agreed to plead guilty to a charge of second-degree murder and to testify against two other individuals—Max Dunlap and James Robison—who were allegedly involved in Bolles' murder. Specifically, respondent agreed to "testify fully and completely in any Court, State or Federal, when requested by proper authorities against any and all parties involved in the murder of Don Bolles. . . . " The agreement provided that "[s]hould the defendant refuse to testify or should he at any time testify untruthfully . . . then this entire agreement is null and void and the original charge will be automatically reinstated." The parties agreed that respondent would receive a prison sentence of 48–49 years, with a total incarceration time of 20 years and 2 months. In January 1977, the state trial court accepted the plea agreement and the proposed sentence, but withheld imposition of the sentence. Thereafter, respondent testified as obligated under the agreement, and both Dunlap and Robison were convicted of the first-degree murder of Bolles. While their convictions and sentences were on appeal, the trial court, upon motion of the State, sentenced respondent. In February 1980, the Arizona Supreme Court reversed the convictions of Dunlap and Robison and remanded their cases for retrial. This event sparked the dispute now before us.

The State sought respondent's cooperation and testimony in preparation for the retrial of Dunlap and Robison. On April 3, 1980, however, respondent's counsel informed the prosecutor that respondent believed his obligation to provide testimony under the agreement had terminated when he was sentenced. Respondent would again testify against Dunlap and Robison only if certain conditions were met, including, among others, that the State release him from custody following the retrial. The State then informed respondent's attorney on April 9, 1980, that it deemed respondent to be in breach of the plea agreement. On April 18, 1980, the State called respondent to testify in pretrial proceedings. In response to questions, and upon advice of counsel, respondent invoked his Fifth Amendment privilege against self-incrimination.

[O]n May 8, 1980, the State filed a new information charging respondent with first-degree murder. Respondent's motion to quash the information on double jeopardy grounds was denied. Respondent challenged this decision by a special action in the Arizona Supreme Court. That court, after reviewing the plea agreement, the transcripts of the plea hearing and the sentencing hearing, respondent's April 3 letter to the state prosecutor, and the prosecutor's April 9 response to that letter, held with "no hesitation" that "the plea agreement contemplates availability of [respondent's] testimony whether at trial or retrial after reversal," and that respondent "violated the terms of the plea agreement." The court also rejected respondent's double jeopardy claim, holding that the plea agreement "by its very terms waives the defense of double jeopardy if the agreement is violated." Finally, the court held that under state law and the terms of the plea agreement, the State should not have filed a new information, but should have merely reinstated the initial charge. Accordingly, the court vacated respondent's second-degree murder conviction, reinstated the original charge, and dismissed the new information.

After these rulings, respondent offered to testify at the retrials, but the State declined his offer. [After failing to obtain federal habeas relief, respondent was then convicted of first-degree murder and sentenced to death.] The judgment was affirmed on direct appeal and we denied certiorari. [The federal district court once again dismissed Adamson's petition for habeas corpus and a Ninth Circuit Court of Appeals panel affirmed that dismissal. However, the Court of Appeals subsequently, sitting en banc, reversed, holding that Adamson had not waived his double jeopardy rights by entering into the plea agreement.] We granted the State's petition for a writ of certiorari to review the Court of Appeals' decision that the Double Jeopardy Clause barred prosecution of respondent for first-degree murder.

We may assume that jeopardy attached at least when respondent was sentenced in December 1978, on his plea of guilty to second-degree murder. Assuming also that under Arizona law second-degree murder is a lesser included offense of first-degree murder, the Double Jeopardy Clause, absent special circumstances, would have precluded prosecution of respondent for the greater charge on which he now stands convicted. The State submits, however, that respondent's breach of the plea arrangement to which the parties had agreed removed the double jeopardy bar to prosecution of respondent on the first-degree murder charge. We agree with the State.

[The] terms of the agreement could not be clearer: in the event of respondent's breach occasioned by a refusal to testify, the parties would be returned to the status quo ante, in which case respondent would have no double jeopardy defense to waive. And, an agreement specifying that charges may be reinstated given certain circumstances is, at least under the provisions of this plea agreement, precisely equivalent to an agreement waiving a double jeopardy defense. * * *

We are also unimpressed by the Court of Appeals' holding that there was a good-faith dispute about whether respondent was bound to testify a second time and that until the extent of his obligation was decided, there could be no knowing and intelligent waiver of his double jeopardy defense. But respondent knew that if he breached the agreement he could be retried, and it is incredible to believe that he did not anticipate that the extent of his obligation would be decided by a court. Here he sought a construction of the agreement in the Arizona Supreme Court, and that court found that he had failed to live up to his promise. The result was that respondent was returned to the position he occupied prior to execution of the plea bargain: he stood charged with first-degree murder. Trial on that charge did not violate the Double Jeopardy Clause. * * *

Respondent cannot escape the Arizona Supreme Court's interpretation of his obligations under the agreement. The State did not force the breach; respondent chose, perhaps for strategic reasons or as a gamble, to advance an interpretation of the agreement that proved erroneous. And, there is no indication that respondent did not fully understand the potential seriousness of the position he adopted. In the April 3 letter, respondent's counsel advised the prosecutor that respondent "is fully aware of the fact that your office may feel that he has not completed his obligations under the plea agreement . . . and, further, that your office may attempt to withdraw the plea agreement from him, [and] that he may be prosecuted for the killing of Donald Bolles on a first degree murder charge." This statement of respondent's awareness of the operative terms of the plea agreement only underscores that which respondent's plea hearing made evident: respondent clearly appreciated and understood the consequences were he found to be in breach of the agreement.

Finally, it is of no moment that following the Arizona Supreme Court's decision respondent offered to comply with the terms of the agreement. At this point, respondent's second-degree murder conviction had already been ordered vacated and the original charge reinstated. The parties did not agree that respondent would be relieved from the consequences of his refusal to testify if he were able to advance a colorable argument that a testimonial obligation was not owing. The parties could have struck a different bargain, but permitting the State to enforce the agreement the parties actually made does not violate the Double Jeopardy Clause.

The judgment of the Court of Appeals is reversed.

JUSTICE BRENNAN, with whom JUSTICE MARSHALL, JUSTICE BLACKMUN, and JUSTICE STEVENS join, dissenting.

The critical question in this case is whether Adamson ever breached his plea agreement. Only by demonstrating that such a breach occurred can it plausibly be argued that Adamson waived his rights under the Double Jeopardy Clause. By simply assuming that such a breach occurred, the Court ignores the only important issue in this case.

Without disturbing the conclusions of the Arizona Supreme Court as to the proper construction of the plea agreement, one may make two observations central to the resolution of this case. First, the agreement does not contain an explicit waiver of all double jeopardy protection. Instead, the Arizona Supreme Court found in the language of ¶¶ 5 and 15 of the agreement only an implicit waiver of double jeopardy protection which was conditional on an act by Adamson that breached the agreement, such as refusing to testify as it required. Therefore, any finding that Adamson lost his protection against double jeopardy must be predicated on a finding that Adamson breached his agreement.

Second, Adamson's interpretation of the agreement—that he was not required to testify at the retrials of Max Dunlap and James Robison—was reasonable. Nothing in the plea agreement explicitly stated that Adamson was required to provide testimony should retrials prove necessary.

[I]n sum, Adamson could lose his protection against double jeopardy only by breaching his agreement, and Adamson's interpretation of his responsibilities under the agreement, though erroneous, was reasonable. The next step in the analysis is to determine whether Adamson ever breached his agreement.

[T]he State argues and the Arizona Supreme Court seems to imply that a breach occurred when Adamson sent his letter of April 3, 1980, to the prosecutor in response to the State's demand for his testimony at the retrials of Dunlap and Robison. In this letter, Adamson stated that, under his interpretation of the agreement, he was no longer obligated to testify, and demanded additional consideration for any additional testimony.

Neither the State, the state courts, not this Court has attempted to explain why this letter constituted a breach of this agreement. Of course, it could not plausibly be argued that merely sending such a letter constituted a breach by nonperformance, for nothing in the plea agreement states that Adamson shall not disagree with the State's interpretation of the plea agreement, or that Adamson shall not send the State a letter to that effect.

[T]he determination of Adamson's rights and responsibilities under the plea agreement is controlled by the principles of fundamental fairness imposed by the Due Process Clause. To grant to one party—here, the State—the unilateral and exclusive right to define the meaning of a plea agreement is patently unfair. Moreover, such a grant is at odds with the basic premises that underlie the constitutionality of the plea-bargaining system. Guilty pleas are enforceable only if taken voluntarily and intelligently. It would be flatly inconsistent with these requirements to uphold as intelligently made a plea agreement which provided that, in the future, the agreement would mean whatever the State interpreted it to mean. Yet the Court upholds today the equivalent of such an agreement. The logic of the plea-bargaining system requires acknowledgment and protection of the defendant's right to advance against the State a reasonable interpretation of the plea agreement.

This right requires no exotic apparatus for enforcement. Indeed, it requires nothing more than common civility. If the defendant offers an interpretation of a plea agreement at odds with that of the State, the State should notify the defendant of this fact, particularly if the State is of the view that continued adherence to defendant's view would result in breach of the agreement. If the State and the defendant are then unable to resolve their dispute through further discussion, a ready solution exists—either party may seek to have the agreement construed by the court in which the plea was entered. By following these steps the State would have placed far fewer demands on the judicial process than were in fact imposed here, and would have fulfilled its constitutional obligation to treat all persons with due respect.

[T]he unfairness of the Court's decision does not end here. Even if one assumes, arguendo, that Adamson breached his plea agreement by offering an erroneous interpretation of that agreement, it still does not follow that the State was entitled to retry Adamson on charges of first-degree murder. As the Court acknowledges, immediately following the decision of the Arizona Supreme Court adopting the State's construction of the plea agreement, Adamson sent a letter to the State stating that he was ready and willing to testify. At this point, there was no obstacle to proceeding with the retrials of Dunlap and Robison; each case had been dismissed without prejudice to refiling, and only about one month's delay had resulted from the dispute over the scope of the plea agreement.

Thus, what the State sought from Adamson—testimony in the Dunlap and Robison trials—was available to it.

The State decided instead to abandon the prosecution of Dunlap and Robison, and to capitalize on what it regarded as Adamson's breach by seeking the death penalty against him. No doubt it seemed easier to proceed against Adamson at that point, since the State had the benefit of his exhaustive testimony about his role in the murder of Don Bolles. But even in the world of commercial contracts it has long been settled that the party injured by a breach must nevertheless take all reasonable steps to minimize the consequent damage. [H]ere it is macabre understatement to observe that the State needlessly exacerbated the liability of its contractual partner. The State suffered a 1–month delay in beginning the retrial of Dunlap and Robison, and incurred litigation costs. For these "losses," the State chose to make Adamson pay, not with a longer sentence, but with his life. A comparable result in commercial law, if one could be imagined, would not be enforced. The fundamental unfairness in the State's course of conduct here is even less acceptable under the Constitution.

[T]he Court's decision flouts the law of contract, due process, and double jeopardy. It reflects a world where individuals enter agreements with the State only at their peril, where the Constitution does not demand of the State the minimal good faith and responsibility that the common law imposes on commercial enterprises, and where, in blind deference to state courts and prosecutors, this Court abdicates its duty to uphold the Constitution. I dissent.

Note

On remand to the Ninth Circuit, that court en banc held that the state's decision to seek the death penalty after originally agreeing to a term of years raised a presumption of prosecutorial vindictiveness which required an evidentiary hearing. *Adamson v. Ricketts*, 865 F.2d 1011 (9th Cir.1988). The prosecutor has the burden of showing that she was motivated by a legitimate purpose. The Ninth Circuit also held that the trial judge acted arbitrarily in imposing the death penalty after accepting a plea for a long prison term which reflected a judicial decision that prison was an appropriate sanction.

Problems

1. Jonathan Pollard, an Intelligence Research Specialist with the United States Navy, admitted spying for the Israeli government. Ultimately, he pleaded guilty pursuant to a plea agreement to one count of conspiracy to deliver national defense information to a foreign government. Pollard agreed to assist the government in damage assessment and not to disseminate any information relating to his crimes without the clearance by the Director of Naval Intelligence. The plea agreement itself was reduced to writing; paragraphs 4(a) & (b) read as follows:

(a) When [Pollard] appears before the Court for sentencing for the offense to which he has agreed to plead guilty, the Government will bring to the Court's attention the nature, extent and value of his cooperation and testimony. Because of the classified nature of the information Mr. Pollard has provided to the Government, it is understood that particular representations concerning his cooperation may have to be made to the Court in camera. In general, however, the Government has agreed to represent that the information Mr. Pollard has provided is of considerable value to the Government's damage assessment analysis, its investigation of this criminal case, and the enforcement of the espionage laws.

(b) Notwithstanding Mr. Pollard's cooperation, at the time of sentencing the Government will recommend that the Court impose a sentence of a substantial period of incarceration and a monetary fine. The Government retains full right of allocution at all times concerning the facts and circumstances of the offenses committed by Mr. Pollard, and will be free to correct any misstatements of fact at the time of sentencing, including representations of the defendant and his counsel in regard to the nature and extent of Mr. Pollard's cooperation. Moreover, Mr. Pollard understands that, while the Court may take his cooperation into account in determining whether or not to impose a sentence of life imprisonment, this agreement cannot and does not limit this court's discretion to impose the maximum sentence.

At sentencing, the government acknowledged that Pollard had offered post-plea cooperation that "has proven to be of considerable value [and that he was] candid and informative in describing his wrongdoing," but argued as well that Pollard was unremorseful, a continuing danger to national security, and that he had violated the plea agreement by giving interviews to a journalist, Wolf Blitzer, without clearance. The government also submitted a highly classified declaration to the sentencing judge from the Secretary of Defense opining that "substantial and irrevocable" damage had been done to national security and, indeed, that it was difficult to "conceive of greater harm to national security [than that done by Pollard and that his punishment] should reflect the perfidy of his actions, the magnitude of the treason committed, and the needs of national security." Pollard was sentenced to life in prison.

Pollard subsequently sought to withdraw his guilty plea, arguing, inter alia, that the government broke its promises to him: (1) by implicitly requesting the maximum punishment: a life sentence; (2) by not outlining adequately the extent and value of his cooperation with the government; and (3) by not limiting its allocution to the "facts and circumstances of the offenses committed." What do you think? Did the government live up to its side of the plea agreement? *United States v. Pollard*, 959 F.2d 1011 (D.C.Cir.), cert. denied, 506 U.S. 915 (1992).

2. Barney Canada, pursuant to a plea agreement with the federal government, pleaded guilty to 26 counts of fraud. In exchange, the government promised to recommend to the court a sentence of 36 months incarceration. The sentencing judge pointed out, however, that someone who had a managerial or supervisory role in such a fraud (as Canada did) should have a three-point enhancement under the federal sentencing guidelines, a calculation not anticipated in the plea agreement, and a factor which would take

the guideline sentencing range to 46 to 57 months. The federal prosecutor did not dispute the sentencing judge's analysis, but agreed with the judge that she was "stuck with" the plea agreement, and asked for "a lengthy period of incarceration." The judge subsequently sentenced Canada to incarceration for 48 months. Canada argues on appeal that the government did not live up to its agreement to recommend 36 months, that it implicitly asked for a longer sentence. The government responds that it did, literally at least, stand by the plea agreement. Do you think that Canada has a good claim? Why or why not? If the court finds that he does, what should the remedy be? Withdrawal of the plea? Dismissal of the charges? Resentencing? Imposition of a 36–month sentence? *United States v. Canada*, 960 F.2d 263 (1st Cir.1992).

3.   In the *Pollard* case discussed in Problem #1, Jonathan Pollard made another argument in attempting to withdraw his guilty plea after the fact. Anne Pollard, Jonathan Pollard's wife, was also implicated in this spy affair. Despite the fact that Anne Pollard had a debilitating gastrointestinal disorder prior to her arrest and, seriously ill, lost forty pounds over a period of three months while confined in the District of Columbia jail after her arrest, the government refused to offer her a plea agreement unless Jonathan Pollard also pleaded guilty. Such plea arrangements are commonly called "wired pleas," i.e. each plea is inextricably linked to the other; if one defendant fails to abide by his or her plea agreement terms, both plea deals fail. After Anne Pollard served three years in prison and was paroled and moved to Israel, Jonathan Pollard sought to withdraw his plea arguing, inter alia, that the government overreached by using unconstitutional pressure (his concern about his wife's health) to force him to plead guilty, in effect, coercing an involuntary plea. Do you think this is a good argument? Why or why not? Does it (should it) make any difference in your analysis that Pollard did not contest his actual guilt?

C. PLEA NEGOTIATION ROLES

1. *The Prosecutor's Role*

ALBERT W. ALSCHULER—THE PROSECUTOR'S ROLE IN PLEA BARGAINING[5]

36 U. Chi. L.Rev. 52–53 (1968).

When a prosecutor grants concessions in exchange for a plea of guilty, he may be acting in any—or all—of several different roles. First, the prosecutor may be acting as an administrator. His goal may be to dispose of each case in the fastest, most efficient manner in the interest of getting his and the court's work done.

Second, the prosecutor may be acting as an advocate. His goal may be to maximize both the number of convictions and the severity of the sentences that are imposed after conviction. In this role, the prosecutor must estimate the sentence that seems likely after a conviction at trial,

5.   Reprinted with permission.

discount this sentence by the possibility of an acquittal, and balance the "discounted trial sentence" against the sentence he can insure through a plea agreement. Were a prosecutor to adopt this role to the exclusion of all others, he would accept a plea agreement only when its assurance of conviction outweighed the loss in sentence severity it might entail.

Third, the prosecutor may act as a judge. His goal may be to do the "right thing" for the defendant in view of the defendant's social circumstances or in view of the peculiar circumstances of his crime—with the qualification, of course, that the "right thing" will not be done unless the defendant pleads guilty.

Fourth, the prosecutor may act as a legislator. he may grant concessions because the law is "too harsh," not only for this defendant but for all defendants.

Note

The relevant portions of the ABA Prosecution Function Standards warn prosecutors against misleading criminal defendants in plea discussions. However, law enforcement personnel are entitled under existing Fifth, Sixth and Fourteenth Amendment law to "mislead" accused defendants who have properly received Miranda warnings, e.g. about inculpatory statements supposedly made by co-defendants or the existence of fingerprints supposedly left at the scene of the crime. Do the ethics rules conflict with prevailing constitutional law? If so, which body of law or rules should a prosecutor follow?

2. Defense Counsel's Role

ALBERT W. ALSCHULER—THE DEFENSE ATTORNEY'S ROLE IN PLEA BARGAINING[6]

84 Yale L.J. 1179, 1181–82, 1184–86, 1206, 1313–14 (1975).

The criminal defense attorney is often seen as a romantic figure—a sophisticated master-of-the-system whose only job is to be on the defendant's side. The attorney's presence can, in this view, be an antidote to the fear, ignorance, and bewilderment of the impoverished and uneducated defendant, not only in the courtroom but throughout the criminal process. In accordance with this view, it is common to regard the right to counsel as a primary safeguard of fairness in plea bargaining. Judge J. Skelly Wright has described the defense attorney as the "equalizer" in the bargaining process. Professor Donald J. Newman, the author of a comprehensive American Bar Foundation study of plea negotiation, has reported that the presence of counsel usually assures a court that a guilty plea is truthful, based on consent, and entered with an awareness of the consequences and of the defendant's rights.

6. Reprinted with permission of the Yale Law Journal Company and Fred B. Rothman & Company from *The Yale Law Journal*, Vol. *84*, pages *1179–1310*.

[I. The Retained Attorney]

To understand the role of the private defense attorney, it is necessary to understand something of the economics of criminal defense work. There are two basic ways to achieve financial success in the practice of criminal law. One is to develop, over an extended period of time, a reputation as an outstanding trial lawyer. In that way, one can attract as clients the occasional wealthy people who become enmeshed in the criminal law. If, however, one lacks the ability or the energy to succeed in this way or if one is in a greater hurry, there is a second path to personal wealth—handling a large volume of cases for less-than-spectacular fees. The way to handle a large volume of cases is, of course, not to try them but to plead them.

These two divergent approaches to economic success can, in fact, be combined. Houston defense attorney Percy Foreman observed that the "optimum situation" for an economically motivated lawyer would be to take one highly publicized case to trial each year and then to enter guilty pleas in all the rest. "One never makes much money on the cases one tries," Foreman explained, "but they help to bring in the cases one can settle." As Boston attorney Monroe L. Inker less elegantly described this facet of law-practice economics, "A guilty plea is a quick buck."

To describe how economically motivated lawyers would behave is not, of course, to say that most lawyers care only about their pocketbooks. Some of them do, however, and an evaluation of the guilty-plea system should include frank recognition of this fact. Every city has its share of what Los Angeles attorney George L. Vaughn called "professional writ-runners and pleaders"—lawyers who virtually never try a case.

[I] found no consensus among the attorneys whom I interviewed concerning the portion of the criminal bar who could fairly be characterized as "cop-out lawyers," in the sense that they invariably urged their clients to plead guilty regardless of the circumstances of particular cases. At one extreme was the viewpoint of San Francisco's Nathan Cohn: "So far as I can tell, all lawyers who work full-time in the criminal courts are primarily interested in moving cases as fast as they can. Only a few lawyers who, like me, are not involved in criminal cases on an everyday basis have a genuine sense of the duty of representation." Another San Francisco defense attorney, Gregory S. Stout, was more restrained: "Of the 40 or 50 lawyers who regularly appear in criminal cases in this city, there are perhaps 20 quick-buck artists."

Donald Kahn, as Assistant State Attorney General in Boston, claimed, "Half of the regular defense bar are guys who plead out constantly." Defense attorney Paul T. Smith made a similar estimate and added, "The practice of criminal law is just a little above shop-lifting in this city."

"There are pleaders by the score in Houston," said defense attorney Richard Haynes. "Of the lawyers who sometimes appear in criminal cases here, there are no more than five whom I would hire. There may be 30 others who do a more-or-less conscientious job. And there are probably 50 or 55 cop-out lawyers." However, Percy Foreman took a different view: "Most defense attorneys in Houston—the vast majority— are not deliberately dishonest. There are no more than 10 or 11 who hustle business, never see their clients, and plead all of them guilty. At the same time, however, at least half of all defense attorneys never take a case intending to prepare for trial."

In other cities, assessments of the size of the "cop-out bar" ranged from more than 50 percent of all defense attorneys to 10 percent or— very rarely—even less. Nevertheless, even those observers who set the figure as low as 10 percent commonly estimated that the "pleaders," with their extremely high caseloads, probably appeared in a majority of all criminal cases in which defendants were represented by retained attorneys. Almost everyone agreed that the conduct of these attorneys posed a major problem for the criminal justice system.

[II. The Performance of the Public Defender Compared
With the Performance of the Private Attorney]

The economic interests of private defense attorneys almost invariably favor pleas of guilty. Public defenders, by contrast, are salaried lawyers whose income does not depend upon the amount of time devoted to individual cases or the methods by which cases are resolved. Nevertheless, in most jurisdictions, public defenders enter guilty pleas for their clients as frequently as private attorneys, and in some jurisdictions, more often.

[Conclusion]

The problem of providing effective representation within the framework of the guilty-plea system is a problem that cannot be resolved satisfactorily. Contrary to the assumption of the Supreme Court and other observers that plea negotiation ordinarily occurs in an atmosphere of informed choice, private defense attorneys, public defenders, and appointed attorneys are all subject to bureaucratic pressures and conflicts of interest that seem unavoidable in any regime grounded on the guilty plea. Far from safeguarding the fairness of the plea-negotiation process, the defense attorney is himself a frequent source of abuse, and no mechanism of reform seems adequate to control the dangers.

As dilemmas multiply, it may be desirable to step back and reexamine the assumptions that an apparent "practical necessity" has thrust upon us. The difficulty of providing effective representation within the guilty-plea system may reflect the intolerable nature of the system itself. The assumption that some form of procedural tinkering or some appeal to professional ideals can resolve every difficulty obscures the nature of the system that we have created—a system in which vital consequences turn on a judgment that is irrelevant to any rational goal of the criminal process and in which the defense attorney invariably has personal interests that depart from those of his client.

The burden should rest with the advocates of plea bargaining to propose some mechanism that can achieve the asserted advantages of the guilty-plea process without, at the same time, yielding the abuses that this article has described. If, as I believe, the task is impossible, we must either endure these abuses or else restructure our criminal justice system to eliminate the overwhelming importance of the defendant's choice of plea, a choice that is usually bent to the purposes of defense attorneys and other participants in the criminal justice system rather than to the interests of the defendant or society.

The problem of providing adequate resources for criminal courts, for prosecutor and defender offices, and for other criminal justice agencies is undeniably difficult. Nevertheless, even the poorest and most primitive societies manage to guarantee a right to trial, and it is hard to believe that our nation cannot find the resources to guarantee this right as well. Rather than rationalize the familiar, the cheap, and the easy, it may be time to reassert the judgment of the framers of the Sixth Amendment: the cost of jury trials is worth paying.

Exercise

Your class should be split evenly between those assigned the role of prosecutors and those assigned to be defense counsel. Both groups should consider the following factual scenario:

The Police Department have arrested George Smith, a pharmacist, for the murder of Arlene Adams, who was 62 years old at the time of her death. At the request of Samuel Adams, age 64, who was Arlene's husband of 36 years, Smith gave Samuel Adams poison that Adams had requested to "help put Arlene out of her misery." Arlene was suffering from a virulent and painful form of bone cancer. Sam has admitted that he mixed the narcotics he acquired from Smith into Arlene's orange juice and had her drink the mixture to relieve her suffering. Sam also admits that he received a call from Smith two hours before giving Arlene the poison in which Smith urged him (unsuccessfully) to reconsider his plan. The Coroner's Office has expressed its belief that Arlene's death was not impending. Arlene's private oncologist has indicated that she could have lived for anywhere from another few months to another few years.

The crime of first degree murder is punishable either by life in prison or death and applies to homicides undertaken with the specific intent to kill. Third degree murder is punishable by up to 20 years in prison and applies to malicious killings, i.e. those homicidal acts undertaken with a conscious disregard of a substantial and unjustifiable risk that death might occur. Involuntary manslaughter is punishable by up to 5 years in prison and applies to deaths caused by an actor's criminal negligence.

George Smith has been released on bond pending a preliminary hearing. Formal charges have not yet been filed by the District Attorney's Office. Smith was arraigned on an "open count of murder." The

District Attorney's Office must file its formal charges prior to the preliminary hearing.

At a time to be set by your professor, selected prosecutors and defense counsel should simulate a preliminary meeting between the two sides (a meeting requested by defense counsel) to discuss what—if any—charges should be filed against George Smith. Both sides should come to class having prepared a "pre-negotiation memorandum," referring to, inter alia:

- the considerations (policy, political, ethical, moral, penological, community, etc.) relevant to this charging decision (from the defendant's side and from the Commonwealth's or State's side respectively);

- what additional information about Samuel and/or Arlene Adams and/or George Smith should be acquired by defense counsel or the District Attorney's Office prior to meeting to discuss charging;

- specific charging recommendations (and arguments in support thereof).

Two student observers should monitor each of the plea negotiation sessions. The observers should draft a memorandum analyzing what they observed, e.g. how did the negotiation proceed?; was a fair resolution reached?; how could each of the sides have better maximized their respective positions?

3. The Judge's Role

When a judge explains the nature of the charge to a defendant, should the judge consider the complexity of the charge or the sophistication of the defendant? Should a defendant's entitlement to relief depend upon whether she would have changed her plea with a more specific explanation of the charge? Although the requirement that the defendant be informed about the mandatory minimum and maximum sentences for the charge is constitutional under Boykin v. Alabama, infra, as well as rule-based, a judge's failure to inform a defendant may be harmless error. See, e.g., *United States v. McDonald*, 121 F.3d 7 (1st Cir.1997). Federal courts inconsistently apply this requirement to any explanation about sentencing options under the federal Sentencing Guidelines. Despite Rule 11's requirement that the judge inform the defendant about the constitutional rights waived by the guilty plea, courts refuse to require that the rights waived be specifically recited, as long as there is no doubt that the plea is voluntary and intelligent. See, e.g., *United States v. Henry*, 113 F.3d 37 (5th Cir.1997).

BOYKIN v. ALABAMA

395 U.S. 238 (1969).

MR. JUSTICE DOUGLAS delivered the opinion of the Court.

In the spring of 1966, within the period of a fortnight, a series of armed robberies occurred in Mobile, Alabama. The victims, in each case, were local shopkeepers open at night who were forced by a gunman to hand over money. While robbing one grocery store, the assailant fired his gun once, sending a bullet through a door into the ceiling. A few days earlier in a drugstore, the robber had allowed his gun to discharge in such a way that the bullet, on ricochet from the floor, struck a customer in the leg. Shortly thereafter, a local grand jury returned five indictments against petitioner, a 27–year–old Negro, for commonlaw robbery— an offense punishable in Alabama by death.

Before the matter came to trial, the court determined that petitioner was indigent and appointed counsel to represent him. Three days later, at his arraignment, petitioner pleaded guilty to all five indictments. So far as the record shows, the judge asked no questions of petitioner concerning his plea, and petitioner did not address the court.

Trial strategy may of course make a plea of guilty seem the desirable course. But the record is wholly silent on that point and throws no light on it.

Alabama provides that when a defendant pleads guilty, "the court must cause the punishment to be determined by a jury" (except where it is required to be fixed by the court) and may "cause witnesses to be examined, to ascertain the character of the offense." In the present case a trial of that dimension was held, the prosecution presenting its case largely through eyewitness testimony. Although counsel for petitioner engaged in cursory cross-examination, petitioner neither testified himself nor presented testimony concerning his character and background. There was nothing to indicate that he had a prior criminal record.

In instructing the jury, the judge stressed that petitioner had pleaded guilty in five cases of robbery, defined as "the felonious taking of money [from] another against his will [by] violence or by putting him in fear [carrying] from ten years minimum in the penitentiary to the supreme penalty of death by electrocution." The jury, upon deliberation, found petitioner guilty and sentenced him severally to die on each of the five indictments.

[The Alabama Supreme Court affirmed.]

It was error, plain on the face of the record, for the trial judge to accept petitioner's guilty plea without an affirmative showing that it was intelligent and voluntary.

[A] plea of guilty is more than a confession which admits that the accused did various acts; it is itself a conviction; nothing remains but to give judgment and determine punishment. Admissibility of a confession must be based on a "reliable determination on the voluntariness issue which satisfies the constitutional rights of the defendant." The requirement that the prosecution spread on the record the prerequisites of a valid waiver is no constitutional innovation. In Carnley v. Cochran, 369 U.S. 506, we dealt with a problem of waiver of the right to counsel, a Sixth Amendment right. We held: "Presuming waiver from a silent record is impermissible. The record must show, or there must be an allegation and evidence which show, that an accused was offered counsel but intelligently and understandingly rejected the offer. Anything less is not waiver.''

We think that the same standard must be applied to determining whether a guilty plea is voluntarily made. For, as we have said, a plea of guilty is more than an admission of conduct; it is a conviction. Ignorance, incomprehension, coercion, terror, inducements, subtle or blatant threats might be a perfect cover-up of unconstitutionality. The question of an effective waiver of a federal constitutional right in a proceeding is of course governed by federal standards.

Several federal constitutional rights are involved in a waiver that takes place when a plea of guilty is entered in a state criminal trial. First, is the privilege against compulsory self-incrimination guaranteed by the Fifth Amendment and applicable to the States by reason of the Fourteenth. Second, is the right to trial by jury. Third, is the right to confront one's accusers. We cannot presume a waiver of these three important federal rights from a silent record.

What is at stake for an accused facing death or imprisonment demands the utmost solicitude of which courts are capable in canvassing the matter with the accused to make sure he has a full understanding of what the plea connotes and of its consequence. When the judge discharges that function, he leaves a record adequate for any review that may be later sought and forestalls the spin-off of collateral proceedings that seek to probe murky memories.

[R]eversed.

Notes and Questions

1. The trial judge has an obligation to determine that the defendant understands what he is doing by pleading guilty. In *Godinez v. Moran*, 509 U.S. 389 (1993), the Court held that the competency standard for pleading guilty or waiving the right to counsel is no higher than the competency standard for standing trial.

A criminal defendant may not be tried unless he is competent and he may not waive his right to counsel or plead guilty unless he does so "competently and intelligently." In Dusky v. United States, 362 U.S. 402 (1960) (per curiam), we held that the standard for competence to stand trial is whether the defendant has "sufficient present ability to consult with his lawyer with a reasonable degree of rational understanding" and has "a rational as well as factual understanding of the proceedings against him." [W]hile we have described the standard for competence to stand trial, however, we have never expressly articulated a standard for competence to plead guilty or to waive the right to the assistance of counsel. * * *

[E]ven assuming that there is some meaningful distinction between the capacity for "reasoned choice" and a "rational understanding" of the proceedings, we reject the notion that competence to plead guilty or to waive the right to counsel must be measured by a standard that is higher than (or even different from) the Dusky standard.

We begin with the guilty plea. A defendant who stands trial is likely to be presented with choices that entail relinquishment of the same rights that are relinquished by a defendant who pleads guilty: He will ordinarily have to decide whether to waive his "privilege against compulsory self-incrimination" by taking the witness stand; if the option is available, he may have to decide whether to waive his "right to trial by jury"; and, in consultation with counsel, he may have to decide whether to waive his "right to confront [his] accusers" by declining to cross-examine witnesses for the prosecution. A defendant who pleads not guilty, moreover, faces still other strategic choices: In consultation with his attorney, he may be called upon to decide, among other things, whether (and how) to put on a defense and whether to raise one or more affirmative defenses. In sum, all criminal defendants—not merely those who plead guilty—may be required to make important decisions once criminal proceedings have been initiated. And while the decision to plead guilty is undeniably a profound one, it is no more complicated than the sum total of decisions that a defendant may be called upon to make during the course of a trial. (The decision to plead guilty is also made over a shorter period of time, without the distraction and burden of a trial.) This being so, we can conceive of no basis for demanding a higher level of competence for those defendants who choose to plead guilty. If the Dusky standard is adequate for defendants who plead not guilty, it is necessarily adequate for those who plead guilty. * * *

Requiring that a criminal defendant be competent has a modest aim: It seeks to ensure that he has the capacity to understand the proceedings and to assist counsel. While psychiatrists and scholars may find it useful to classify the various kinds and degrees of competence, and while States are free to adopt competency standards that are more elaborate than the Dusky formulation, the Due Process Clause does not impose these additional requirements.

2. Can a guilty plea be voluntary if the defendant is unaware of the essential elements of the offense to which he is pleading? In *Henderson v. Morgan*, 426 U.S. 637 (1976), the Court held that a plea was involuntary when neither defense counsel nor the trial court explained that intent was an element of second-degree murder.

We assume, as petitioner argues, that the prosecutor had overwhelming evidence of guilt available. We also accept petitioner's characterization of the competence of respondent's counsel and of the wisdom of their advice to plead guilty to a charge of second-degree murder. Nevertheless, such a plea cannot support a judgment of guilt unless it was voluntary in a constitutional sense. And clearly the plea could not be voluntary in the sense that it constituted an intelligent admission that he committed the offense unless the defendant received "real notice of the true nature of the charge against him, the first and most universally recognized requirement of due process." Smith v. O'Grady, 312 U.S. 329, 334. * * *

There is nothing in this record that can serve as a substitute for either a finding after trial, or a voluntary admission, that respondent had the requisite intent. Defense counsel did not purport to stipulate to that fact; they did not explain to him that his plea would be an admission of that fact; and he made no factual statement or admission necessarily implying that he had such intent. In these circumstances it is impossible to conclude that his plea to the unexplained charge of second-degree murder was voluntary.

Should the trial judge be able to rely on defense counsel disclosing the important elements of the offense to the defendant? In *Bradshaw v. Stumpf*, 545 U.S. 175 (2005), the Court held that "[w]here a defendant is represented by competent counsel, the court usually may rely on that counsel's assurance that the defendant has been properly informed of the nature and elements of the charge to which he is pleading guilty."

What else should a trial judge tell the defendant before accepting a guilty plea? In *Iowa v. Tovar*, 541 U.S. 77 (2004), the Court stated that, prior to a guilty plea, a knowing and intelligent waiver of counsel does not constitutionally require warnings that the absence of counsel 1) raises the possibility that a viable defense would be overlooked, or 2) deprives a defendant of the opportunity for an independent opinion about the wisdom of pleading guilty.

3. Fed.R.Crim.P. 11(b)(3) provides that the court should be satisfied that there is a factual basis for the guilty plea. Can the court accept the plea when there is a factual basis but the defendant also asserts his innocence? In *North Carolina v. Alford*, 400 U.S. 25 (1970), Alford was indicted for first-degree murder, a capital offense. His appointed counsel questioned witnesses who Alford said would substantiate his claim of innocence. The witnesses, however, did not support Alford's story but gave statements that strongly indicated his guilt. Faced with strong evidence of guilt and no substantial evidentiary support for the claim of innocence, Alford's attorney recommended that he plead guilty, but left the ultimate decision to Alford himself. The prosecutor agreed to accept a plea of guilty to a charge of second-degree murder, and Alford pleaded guilty to the reduced charge.

> State and lower federal courts are divided upon whether a guilty plea can be accepted when it is accompanied by protestations of innocence and hence contains only a waiver of trial but no admission of guilt. Some courts, giving expression to the principle that "[o]ur law only authorizes a conviction where guilt is shown." But others have concluded that they should not "force any defense on a defendant in a criminal case," particularly when advancement of the defense might "end in disaster [.]" They have argued that, since "guilt, or the degree of guilt, is at times uncertain and elusive," "[a]n accused, though believing in or entertaining doubts respecting his innocence, might reasonably conclude a jury would be convinced of his guilt and that he would fare better in the sentence by pleading guilty [.]" As one state court observed nearly a century ago, "[r]easons other than the fact that he is guilty may induce a defendant to so plead, [and] [h]e must be permitted to judge for himself in this respect." * * *

> [W]e [cannot] perceive any material difference between a plea that refuses to admit commission of the criminal act and a plea containing a protestation of innocence when, as in the instant case, a defendant intelligently concludes that his interests require entry of a guilty plea

and the record before the judge contains strong evidence of actual guilt. Here the State had a strong case of first-degree murder against Alford. Whether he realized or disbelieved his guilt, he insisted on his plea because in his view he had absolutely nothing to gain by a trial and much to gain by pleading. Because of the overwhelming evidence against him, a trial was precisely what neither Alford nor his attorney desired. Confronted with the choice between a trial for first-degree murder, on the one hand, and a plea of guilty to second-degree murder, on the other, Alford quite reasonably chose the latter and thereby limited the maximum penalty to a 30–year term. When his plea is viewed in light of the evidence against him, which substantially negated his claim of innocence and which further provided a means by which the judge could test whether the plea was being intelligently entered, its validity cannot be seriously questioned. In view of the strong factual basis for the plea demonstrated by the State and Alford's clearly expressed desire to enter it despite his professed belief in his innocence, we hold that the trial judge did not commit constitutional error in accepting it. * * *

4. "When someone pleads guilty, the judge does not examine the strength of the case against the defendant but does try to determine if unfair coercion was used to induce a plea. The right to trial by jury is the right most often explained in open court to a defendant pleading guilty. [A 1987 study] reports that about 32% of the time the defendant was asked if promises other than the plea agreement had been made; 55% of the time defendants were asked if any threats or pressures had caused them to plead guilty. Judges rejected 2% of the guilty pleas they considered." U.S. Dept. of Justice, Report to the Nation on Crime and Justice 83 (2d ed. 1988).

5. The Court regards the Fed.R.Crim.P. 11(b)(1)(C)–(E) list of rights as merely a codification of *Boykin*'s requirements regarding the waiver of constitutional rights. *Libretti v. United States*, 516 U.S. 29 (1995). Thus, a defendant in a property forfeiture case was not entitled to be advised of the right to a jury trial.

6. Fed.R.Crim.P. 11(b)(1) lists some consequences of a guilty plea, e.g., mandatory minimum penalty, maximum possible penalty. If these are regarded as the direct consequences of pleading guilty, what are some collateral consequences of a guilty plea? What distinguishes a direct consequence, which must be disclosed to the defendant, and a collateral consequences, which need not be disclosed?

7. When a prior conviction based upon a guilty plea is used to enhance the defendant's sentence for the current offense, in the absence of a transcript of the prior guilty plea proceeding the burden is on the prisoner to show a *Boykin* violation. The *Boykin* "presumption of invalidity" is trumped by the presumption of regularity attaching to final judgments. *Parke v. Raley*, 506 U.S. 20 (1992).

8. Does a guilty plea constitutes a waiver of constitutional guarantees in addition to those addressed in *Boykin*? Does the Constitution requires a defendant to be aware of all the consequences of her plea? In *United States v. Ruiz*, 536 U.S. 622 (2002), the Court held that the Constitution does not require prosecutors, before entering into a binding plea agreement with a

criminal defendant, to disclose "impeachment information relating to any informants or other witnesses.".

> It is particularly difficult to characterize impeachment information as critical information of which the defendant must always be aware prior to pleading guilty given the random way in which such information may, or may not, help a particular defendant. The degree of help that impeachment information can provide will depend upon the defendant's own independent knowledge of the prosecution's potential case—a matter that the Constitution does not require prosecutors to disclose.

> * * * [T]he Constitution, in respect to a defendant's awareness of relevant circumstances, does not require complete knowledge of the relevant circumstances, but permits a court to accept a guilty plea, with its accompanying waiver of various constitutional rights, despite various forms of misapprehension under which a defendant might labor. It is difficult to distinguish, in terms of importance, (1) a defendant's ignorance of grounds for impeachment of potential witnesses at a possible future trial from (2) the varying forms of ignorance at issue in these cases.

Does *Ruiz* apply when a defendant already had made a pre-plea discovery request for any potentially exculpatory evidence in the state's control? Should the court require the prosecutor to provide the defendant with the evidence before accepting the plea? See, e.g., *State v. Harris*, 266 Wis.2d 200, 667 N.W.2d 813 (App.2003) (defendant allowed to withdraw guilty plea when prosecutor failed to disclose exculpatory information prior to entry of plea).

9. Professor Alschuler has made the following argument:

> Apologists for plea bargaining often contend that, when a plea agreement satisfies the parties, no one else can have legitimate reason for complaint. A bargain that a defendant, advised by able counsel, finds advantageous cannot properly be criticized on the ground that it is unfair to him, and if occasional cases of incompetence or corruption are set aside, the prosecutor's acquiescence in the bargain insures that it is fair to the state as well. A jurisprudential assessment of this argument would require consideration of the concept of voluntariness, of the goals of criminal proceedings, of the mechanisms by which those goals can best be achieved, and, perhaps, of the reasons for prohibiting a variety of consensual arrangements in other contexts. It is sufficient for present purposes to note that one who accepts this central argument for plea bargaining cannot consistently oppose judicial participation in the process, for judicial bargaining apparently meets with the approval of most defense attorneys and a great many prosecutors. At the very least, if the consent of the parties is regarded as determinative, a trial judge should be permitted to negotiate with a defense attorney when both the prosecutor and the defendant acquiesce in this procedure. If the opponents of judicial bargaining are unwilling to create this exception to the prohibition that they propose, some of them must apparently reconsider the significance that the consent of the parties should have in criminal proceedings.

Albert Alschuler, "The Trial Judge's Role in Plea Bargaining, Part I," 76 Colum. L.Rev. 1059, 1152 (1976). Do you agree or disagree with this excerpt?

Why or why not? Do you think that there is something "unseemly" or otherwise inappropriate about judges being involved in plea bargaining? If so, is that a commentary upon the judicial role or on plea bargaining itself?

10. The following document must be read and signed by all criminal defendants (and their defense counsel) pleading guilty or nolo contendere in criminal cases in Pittsburgh, Pennsylvania (Allegheny County). Do you think that having defendants sign a document like this is a good idea? Do you think that most defendants would understand a document like this? Can you think of anything that is not—but should be—included in this document?[7]

IN THE COURT OF COMMON PLEAS OF ALLEGHENY COUNTY, PENNSYLVANIA CRIMINAL DIVISION

COMMONWEALTH OF
PENNSYLVANIA

vs.

_____

GUILTY PLEA EXPLANATION OF DEFENDANT'S RIGHTS

You or your attorney have indicated to the officers of this Court that you wish to plead guilty or nolo contendere to certain specific criminal charges which the Commonwealth of Pennsylvania has brought against you.

In order to have your plea accepted by this Court here today, you must waive your right to confront the prosecution witnesses against you and agree to permit an Assistant District Attorney to summarize the Commonwealth's evidence against you. You must agree to stipulate to the authenticity and accuracy of any Crime Laboratory reports presented by the Commonwealth and to the chain of custody of any of the Commonwealth's evidence involved in your case.

You must fully understand that your plea must be voluntary and no clemency is being promised in exchange for your plea, with the exception of any plea bargain or arrangement previously agreed to between your attorney and the Assistant District Attorney assigned to your case.

By pleading guilty to any charge you are admitting that you committed that offense. By pleading nolo contendere you are stating that you do not contest the charges against you. In either case, the Commonwealth would not have to prove each and every element of the crimes with which you are charged as would be required in a jury or non-jury trial.

Please be advised that you must fully understand that the Constitution of the United States of America and the Constitution of the Commonwealth of Pennsylvania give to you an absolute right to have a trial by jury.

If you intend to waive your Constitutional right to a trial by jury, please answer all the questions on this form. Most of the questions are designed to be answered "yes" or "no." Where general information is requested, please answer the question as fully as possible.

7. The authors appreciate the kindness of former President Judge Robert E. Dauer, Allegheny County Common Pleas Court, in providing them with this document.

If you do not understand the question, you should say so in writing on this form. You should also tell your lawyer and the judge who hears your case so they can explain it to you. You must fully understand all of your rights before your plea can be accepted by the judge.

You should initial each page at the bottom after you have read, understood and completed your answers to the questions on that page. When you have finished all of the questions, you must sign the form at the end.

1.   What is your full name? _____

2.   How old are you today? _____

3.   How far did you go in school? _____

4.   Can you read, write and understand the English language? _____

5.   Do you understand that because you have been charged with more than one offense the court may impose a separate, or consecutive, sentence for each offense? _____

6.   Have you discussed with your attorney the elements of each charged offense? _____

7.   Have you discussed with your attorney the factual basis of each charged offense? _____

8.   Have you discussed with your attorney how the facts in your case prove the elements of each charged offense? _____

9.   Do you understand that both the Constitution of the United States of America and the Constitution of the Commonwealth of Pennsylvania give you an absolute right to a trial by jury? _____

10.   Do you understand that if you want a jury trial, you would take part in the selection of the jury along with your attorney and with the Assistant District Attorney assigned to prosecute your case? _____

11.   Do you understand that you and your attorney and the Assistant District Attorney assigned to prosecute your case would select a jury from a panel of jurors randomly picked by computer from the voter registration lists and other legally approved lists of citizens of Allegheny County? _____

12.   Do you understand that both the defense and prosecution would have the right to "challenge" members of the jury panel and that this means you and the prosecution would have the right to keep certain persons on the jury panel from being a member of the jury in your case? _____

13.   Both you and the prosecution would have as many challenges "for cause" as the court would approve. "For cause" means a good reason why the challenged person could not be an impartial juror in your case. Do you fully understand this? _____

14.   Both you and the prosecution would each also have a number of "peremptory challenges." A "peremptory challenge" is one in which no reason has to be given to prevent a prospective juror from being a

member of your jury. If you are charged with felonies, both you and the prosecution each have seven "peremptory challenges." If you are charged only with misdemeanors, both you and the prosecution each have five "peremptory challenges." Do you fully understand this? _____

15. All twelve members of the jury finally selected would have to be satisfied that the Commonwealth had proven your guilt beyond a reasonable doubt on each charge; that is, the vote of all twelve must be guilty before you could be found guilty? Do you fully understand this? _____

16. You also may choose to be tried before a judge without a jury in what is called a "non-jury" trial and that the judge, in addition to ruling on legal questions and defining the law as in jury trials would also sit as a trier of fact, much like a jury does in a jury trial; and it would be the judge who determines from the evidence presented whether the Commonwealth has proven you guilty beyond a reasonable doubt. Do you fully understand this? _____

17. In either the jury trial or non-jury trial before a judge, you enter the courtroom clothed with the presumption of innocence and that presumption remains with you until such time, if ever, that a jury in a jury trial or judge in a non-jury trial, would find you guilty beyond a reasonable doubt. Do you fully understand this? _____

18. In either a jury trial or in a non-jury trial before a judge, it is the burden of the Commonwealth to prove you guilty "beyond a reasonable doubt," and to do this the Commonwealth must prove each and every element of the crime or crimes with which you are charged "beyond a reasonable doubt" to the satisfaction of all twelve jurors in a jury trial or to the satisfaction of the judge in a non-jury trial. Do you fully understand this? _____

19. A reasonable doubt is an honest doubt arising from the evidence presented or from the lack of evidence and it is the kind of doubt that would cause a reasonable, prudent person to pause or to hesitate before acting in a matter of the highest personal importance. Do you fully understand this? _____

20. In either a jury trial or a non-jury trial before a judge, you have the absolute right to remain silent and need not present any evidence in your own behalf and there is no burden placed on you to prove your own innocence or, for that matter to prove anything since the burden is always or the Commonwealth to prove you guilty beyond a reasonable doubt. Do you fully understand this? _____

21. However, in either a jury trial or a non-jury trial before a judge, you have the right, if you so desire, to testify and to have witnesses testify on your behalf and you would have the right to present any relevant evidence which you would tend or help to prove your innocence and to challenge the evidence and testimony presented by the prosecution. You also would have the right either yourself or through your attorney to cross-examine or question any witnesses presented by the

Commonwealth in order to test their credibility and the truthfulness of their testimony. Do you fully understand this? _____

22. By pleading guilty or nolo contendere you are giving up all of these rights described in the previous questions. Do you fully understand this? _____

23. When you plead guilty or nolo contendere, the Commonwealth would not have to prove each and every element of the crime or crimes with which you are charged by the presentation of witnesses and/or other evidence but the Assistant District Attorney could simply present a summary of the evidence against you. Do you fully understand this? _____

24. By pleading guilty, you are admitting you committed the crime or by pleading nolo contendere, you are stating that you do not challenge or dispute the charges against you. Do you fully understand this? _____

25. By pleading guilty or nolo contendere, you give up the right not only to file pretrial motions, but also you abandon or give up any pretrial motions already filed and not yet decided and any pretrial motions in which decisions were already made. Do you fully understand this? _____

26. Do you understand that by pleading guilty or nolo contendere, you also give up the right to present or assert any defenses on your behalf? _____

27. If you were convicted after a jury trial or non-jury trial before a judge, you could appeal the verdict to a higher court and raise any errors that were committed in the trial court and this could result in a new trial or a dismissal. By pleading guilty you are giving up this right. Do you fully understand this? _____

28. Do you fully understand that if you were convicted after a jury trial or a non-jury trial before a judge, you could challenge in this Court and in the appellate courts whether the Commonwealth had presented enough evidence to prove you guilty beyond a reasonable doubt? _____

29. By pleading guilty or nolo contendere, you give up certain rights of appeal; in a jury trial or a non-jury trial before a judge, you would have the right to appeal any errors that might arise in your case to the Superior Court of Pennsylvania. However, when you plead guilty or nolo contendere, you limit the grounds for those appeals to four specific reasons:

1. that this Court did not have jurisdiction in your case. With rare exception, this Court only has jurisdiction where the crime was committed in Allegheny County;

2. that the sentence or probation imposed by this Court is illegal;

3. that your plea was not knowingly, intelligently, and voluntarily made; and

4. the incompetence or ineffectiveness of the attorney who represents you.

All other grounds for appeal are given up. Do you fully understand this? _____

30. Do you understand that you have the right to file a motion seeking to withdraw your guilty plea or your nolo contendere plea at any time prior to the date of sentencing? _____

31. Do you understand that you must be sentenced within sixty (60) days of the date of the entry of your plea of guilty or your plea of nolo contendere? _____

32. Do you understand you have the right within ten (10) days after you have been sentenced to file a motion seeking to withdraw your guilty plea or your plea of nolo contendere? _____

33. If you were to file a motion seeking to withdraw your plea of guilty or plea of nolo contendere, either prior to sentencing or within ten (10) days after sentencing, that motion must be filed in writing. If you would fail to do so within these time periods, you would forever give up those rights. Do you fully understand this? _____

34. In order to appeal your conviction that results for your plea of guilty or nolo contendere, you must file in writing your motion seeking to withdraw your plea, either prior to sentencing or within ten (10) days after sentencing and state one or more or the four (4) grounds listed below as the basis for a motion seeking to withdraw your plea:

   a) Your plea was not knowingly, intelligent and voluntary;

   b) that your crime was not committed within the jurisdiction of this Court, i.e., not committed within Allegheny County;

   c) that the sentence of this Court is illegal; and/or,

   d) that your attorney was ineffective and incompetent.

   If you do not file this motion within the proscribed time limits, you will have given up this right. Do you fully understand this? _____

35. If your motion seeking to withdraw your plea of guilty or nolo contendere, which is filed prior to sentencing is denied you would have ten (10) days from the date of sentencing to file with this Court a post-sentencing motion challenging the denial of your motion to withdraw your plea of guilty or your plea of nolo contendere. Do you fully understand this? _____

36. Following the imposition of sentence upon you for your entry of either a plea of guilty or a plea of nolo contendere, you have the right to file post-sentencing motions with this Court which include:

   a) a motion challenging the validity of a plea of guilty or nolo contendere;

   b) a motion challenging the denial or a motion seeking a plea of guilty or nolo contendere;

   c) a motion to modify sentence.

   Do you fully understand these rights? _____

37. If you would file any post-sentencing motions, those motions must be decided by this Court within one hundred twenty (120) days of the date of the filing or said motions, or within one hundred fifty (150) days of the filing of those motions if you sought and were granted a thirty (30) days extension, which extension only you can request? Do you fully understand this? _____

38. If your post-sentencing motions are not decided within one hundred twenty (120) days of the date of filing, or within one hundred fifty (150) days of the date of filing, if you sought and received a thirty (30) day extension, then said motions are deemed to have been denied by operation of law and cannot be reconsidered by this Court. Do you fully understand this? _____

39. If this Court would deny your post-sentencing motion within either the one hundred twenty (120) or one hundred fifty (150) day time periods, you would have the right to file with this Court a motion to reconsider the denials of your post-sentencing motions; however, any motion to reconsider the denial of post-sentencing motions must be filed by you and decided by this Court within either the one hundred twenty (120) or one hundred fifty (150) day time limits. If such a motion to reconsider the denial of post-sentencing motion is not filed by you or, if filed, not decided by this Court within the one hundred twenty (120) or one hundred fifty (150) day time limits, then any appellate rights that you have begin to run from the last day of either time limit. Do you fully understand this? _____

40. Should your post-sentencing motion be denied by this Court or by operation of law, you will receive, either from this Court or from the Clerk of Courts, an order of court advising you of your appellate rights, the right to assistance of counsel, if indigent, the right to proceed in forma pauperis, and, the qualified right to bail. Any appeal to the Superior Court must be filed within thirty (30) days of the denial of your post-sentencing motion. Do you fully understand? _____

41. If you wish to file any of these motions with this Court or an appeal to the Superior Court of Pennsylvania and cannot afford an attorney to assist you to do so, this Court will appoint an attorney to assist you to do so, this Court will appoint an attorney for you at no cost to you. Do you fully understand this? _____

42. When you plead guilty or nolo contendere, and your plea is accepted by this Court, all that remains is for the judge to sentence you on the charges to which you are pleading; but if your plea is rejected, your case will be sent back for reassignment to another courtroom and another judge for trial. Do you fully understand this? _____

43. If there is a mandatory minimum sentence applicable and this mandatory sentence is sought by the Commonwealth, then this Court has no discretion to impose a lesser sentence and must impose at least the minimum sentence that is required by law. Do you fully understand this? _____

44. Are you aware that if the offenses with which you are charged do not require a mandatory sentence under the statutory law of Pennsylvania, this Court is not bound by the sentencing guidelines and may deviate from the guidelines; however, if the Court does so, both the District Attorney and you would have a right to appeal such deviation?

_____

45. Do you understand that if you are entering a plea of guilty or a plea of nolo contendere to the charge of Violation of the Controlled Substance, Drug, Device and Cosmetic Act, that independent of any sentence this Court might impose, the Department of Transportation has the right, upon receipt of notice of this conviction, to impose an additional penalty upon you, in the form of the suspension of your driver's license for a period of time ranging anywhere from ninety (90) days to two (2) years? _____

46. Do you understand that if you are entering a plea of guilty or a plea of nolo contendere to the charge of Violation Vehicle Code: Driving Under Influence of Alcohol, a controlled Substance or both, that independent of any sentence this Court might impose, the Department of Transportation has the right, upon receipt of notice of this conviction, to impose an additional penalty upon you, in the form of the suspension of your driver's license for a period of one (1) year? _____

47. Do you understand that any term of imprisonment imposed as a result of your plea may be imposed separately, or consecutively, with any other state or federal term of imprisonment you are currently serving?

_____

48. Do you understand that the conviction that will result from your plea may serve as a violation of any term of state or federal probation or parole? _____

49. Do you understand that a violation of your state or federal probation or parole could result in the imposition of a further separate, or consecutive, term of imprisonment? _____

50. Your plea must be voluntary and your rights must be voluntarily, knowingly and intelligently waived. If anyone has promised you anything other than the terms of a plea bargain, your plea will be rejected. If anyone has forced you or attempted to force you in any way to plead guilty or nolo contendere, your plea will be rejected. Do you fully understand this? _____

51. Has anybody forced you to enter this plea? _____

52. Are you doing this of your own free will? _____

53. Have any threats been made to you to enter a plea? _____

54. Do you understand that if there is a plea bargain in this case the terms of the plea bargain will be stated on the record before the judge and that you will be bound by the terms of the plea bargain as they appear of record? _____

55. Do you understand that this Court is not bound by any plea bargain entered into by you and the District Attorney? _____

56. If the Court rejects the plea bargain after hearing a summary of the evidence, you would then have a right to withdraw your plea and your case would be reassigned to another judge before whom you would have the option of entering a straight plea with no plea bargain involved or have your case heard by that judge in a non-jury trial and, of course, you would still have the right to a trial by jury if you so desire. Do you fully understand this? _____

57. Are you satisfied with the legal advice and legal representation of your attorney? _____

58. Have you had ample opportunity to consult with your attorney before entering your plea, and are you satisfied that your attorney knows all of the facts of your case and has had enough time within which to check any questions of fact or law which either you or your attorney may have about the case? _____

59. Has your attorney gone over with you the meaning of the terms of this document? _____

60. Have you ever had any physical or mental illness that would affect your ability to understand these rights or affect the voluntary nature of your plea? _____

61. Are you presently taking any medication which might affect your thinking or your free will? _____

62. Have you had any narcotics or alcohol in the last forty-eight (48) hours? _____

63. A. If you are entering a plea of guilty you admit that you committed the crime(s) with which you are charged and to which you are pleading guilty. Do you fully understand this? _____

   B. If you are entering a plea of nolo contendere, do you admit that you are not challenging the charges against you? _____

64. Do you understand your rights? _____

I AFFIRM THAT I HAVE READ THE ABOVE DOCUMENT IN ITS ENTIRETY, I UNDERSTAND ITS FULL MEANING, AND I AM STILL NEVERTHELESS WILLING TO ENTER A PLEA TO THE OFFENSES SPECIFIED. I FURTHER AFFIRM THAT MY SIGNATURE AND INITIALS ON EACH PAGE OF THIS DOCUMENT ARE TRUE AND CORRECT.

DATE: # _____

Signature of Defendant

CERTIFICATION OF DEFENSE COUNSEL

I certify that:

(1) I am an attorney admitted to the Supreme Court of Pennsylvania.

(2) I represent the defendant herein.

(3) I know no reason why the defendant cannot fully understand everything that is being said and done here today.

(4) The defendant read the above form in my presence and appeared to fully understand it; I have gone over the form completely with the defendant, explained all of the items on the form and answered any questions he or she had.

(5) I see no reason why the defendant cannot and is not knowingly intelligently and voluntarily giving up his or her rights to trial and pleading guilty.

(6) I made no promises to the defendant other than any that appear of record in this case.

DATE: _____

_____ Attorney for Defendant

D. WITHDRAWING A GUILTY PLEA

It is not uncommon for a defendant who has previously tendered a guilty plea to subsequently seek to withdraw that plea, whether it is days, months, or even years later. In "broken" plea agreement cases, i.e. situations where the defendant believes that he or she has not received the "deal" he or she bargained for, courts generally permit such withdrawal if they agree that the deal was in fact broken. However, where the bargained-for deal is simply to be a "recommendation" or where the prosecutor has agreed simply not to oppose a defense recommendation, and where the prosecutor has not reneged on this particular deal, a defendant cannot count on being able to withdraw a guilty plea if he or she is displeased with the ultimate adjudicative or sentencing outcome. See, e.g., Fed.R.Crim.P. 11(c)(1)(B) & (c)(3)(B) [where the plea agreement requires the prosecutor to "recommend, or agree not to oppose the defendant's request, that a particular sentence or sentencing range is appropriate . . . , (such a recommendation or request does not bind the court) the court must advise the defendant that the defendant has no right to withdraw the plea if the court does not follow the recommendation or request"].

Aside from the broken plea agreement cases, there are innumerable reasons why a defendant might later seek to withdraw his or her guilty plea. Such reasons range from mere second thoughts about the strategic thinking (defendant's and/or defense counsel's) that resulted in a guilty plea, to dissatisfaction with or surprise at the severity of the sentence received, to the emergence of new evidence or new witnesses (or the disappearance of evidence or witnesses). However, once properly tendered, a defendant does not generally have the right to withdraw a guilty plea. Nonetheless, prior to the imposition of sentence, most courts can and do permit such withdrawal if the defendant presents "any fair and just" reason to do so. After the imposition of sentence, withdrawal is rarely permitted absent a finding of manifest injustice or a miscarriage of justice. See, e.g., Fed.R.Crim.P. 11(d)(2).

In *United States v. Hyde*, 520 U.S. 670 (1997), the Court reversed a case in which the trial court permitted the defendant to withdraw a guilty plea after acceptance of a plea but before acceptance of the plea agreement by the court, without offering any justification. The Court observed:

> After the defendant has sworn in open court that he actually committed the crimes, after he has stated that he is pleading guilty because he is guilty, after the court has found a factual basis for the plea, and after the court has explicitly announced that it accepts the plea, the Court of Appeals would allow the defendant to withdraw his guilty plea simply on a lark. The Advisory Committee, in adding the "fair and just reason" standard to Rule 32(e) in 1983, explained why this cannot be so: "Given the great care with which pleas are taken under [the] revised Rule 11, there is no reason to view pleas so taken as merely 'tentative,' subject to withdrawal before sentence whenever the government cannot establish prejudice. Were withdrawal automatic in every case where the defendant decided to alter his tactics and present his theory of the case to the jury, the guilty plea would become a mere gesture, a temporary and meaningless formality reversible at the defendant's whim. In fact, however, a guilty plea is no such trifle, but a "grave and solemn act," which is "accepted only with care and discernment." ' " We think the Court of Appeals' holding would degrade the otherwise serious act of pleading guilty into something akin to a move in a game of chess.

In addition, if the reason a defendant pleaded guilty was that he or she relied on the incompetent legal or tactical advice of defense counsel, where he or she can demonstrate that "there is a reasonable probability that, but for counsel's errors, [defendant] would not have pleaded guilty and would have insisted on going to trial," the guilty plea may be withdrawn as a result of ineffective assistance of counsel. *Hill v. Lockhart*, 474 U.S. 52, 59 (1985).

Problems

1. Defendant James Holland pleaded guilty to one count of first-degree murder and, after a penalty hearing, was sentenced to death. He claims on appeal, inter alia, that he should be permitted to withdraw his plea due to the ineffective assistance of his defense counsel, Elliott Levine. While appeal was pending in this case, Levine sought to have Holland testify on behalf of the defendant, Von Taylor, in an unrelated capital case so that the jury could compare Taylor's acts and background with Holland's. When the trial judge in the Taylor case excluded such testimony by Holland, Levine filed an appeal in which he argued that the testimony should have been permitted because a person like Holland "who has committed multiple murders, has been incarcerated for nearly his whole life, comes from an abusive childhood,

and who has little, if any remorse ... is a prime candidate for the death penalty while [Taylor is] not." If you were an appellate judge hearing this argument, would you vote to permit Holland to withdraw his guilty plea? Why or why not? Does it matter, in your opinion, that Levine seemed to have a conflict of interest in his representation of Holland and Taylor in unrelated cases? *State v. Holland*, 921 P.2d 430 (Utah 1996).

2.   Defendant Richard Anderson pleaded "no contest" to four misdemeanor counts relating to his sale of imported "tea balls," which he claimed were used to provide relief from arthritis. The state of Arizona claimed that the tea balls contained librium, a dangerous drug. At the guilty plea colloquy, Anderson stated that he was pleading guilty "on my attorney's advice." Subsequently, Anderson sought to withdraw his plea, claiming that (although he did not say this in the colloquy) his counsel had told him that he could withdraw his plea if the independent laboratory that was analyzing the tea balls found that they contained no librium. Counsel says that he simply said to Anderson that he would have "an opportunity to move to withdraw his plea." The lab results did turn out to be negative, but the state opposed withdrawal of the plea as the plea was voluntary and no plea agreement was broken. Do you think that Anderson is (or should be) entitled to withdraw his plea? Why or why not? *State v. Anderson*, 147 Ariz. 346, 710 P.2d 456 (1985).

Chapter 19

JURY TRIALS

A. RIGHT TO JURY TRIAL

The Sixth Amendment provides in part that in all criminal prosecutions an "accused shall enjoy the right to a public trial, by an impartial jury of the State and district wherein the crime shall have been committed...." Further, Article III of the Constitution states that "[t]he trial of all crimes ... shall be by jury; and such trial shall be held in the state where the said crimes shall have been committed...." Only recently did the Supreme Court make the Sixth Amendment jury trial right applicable to the states through the Fourteenth Amendment Due Process Clause.

In *Duncan v. Louisiana*, 391 U.S. 145 (1968), the defendant was convicted of simple battery, a misdemeanor under Louisiana law, and punishable by a maximum of two years' imprisonment and a $300 fine. Appellant sought trial by jury, but the trial judge denied the request because the state constitution granted jury trials only when capital punishment or imprisonment at hard labor may be imposed. Appellant was convicted and sentenced to serve 60 days in the parish prison and pay a fine of $150. Justice White upheld the defendant's right to a jury trial, and made the following comments.

> The guarantees of jury trial in the Federal and State Constitutions reflect a profound judgment about the way in which law should be enforced and justice administered. A right to jury trial is granted to criminal defendants in order to prevent oppression by the Government. Those who wrote our constitutions knew from history and experience that it was necessary to protect against unfounded criminal charges brought to eliminate enemies and against judges too responsive to the voice of higher authority. The framers of the constitutions strove to create an independent judiciary but insisted upon further protection against arbitrary action. Providing an accused with the right to be tried by a jury of his peers gave him an inestimable safeguard against the corrupt or overzealous prosecutor and against the compliant, biased, or eccentric judge. If the defen-

dant preferred the common-sense judgment of a jury to the more tutored but perhaps less sympathetic reaction of the single judge, he was to have it. Beyond this, the jury trial provisions in the Federal and State Constitutions reflect a fundamental decision about the exercise of official power—a reluctance to entrust plenary powers over the life and liberty of the citizen to one judge or to a group of judges. Fear of unchecked power, so typical of State and Federal Governments in other respects, found expression in the criminal law in this insistence upon community participation in the determination of guilt or innocence. The deep commitment of the Nation to the right of jury trial in serious criminal cases as a defense against arbitrary law enforcement qualifies for protection under the Due Process Clause of the Fourteenth Amendment, and must therefore be respected by the States.

[In] determining whether the length of the authorized prison term or the seriousness of other punishment is enough in itself to require a jury trial, [we] refer to objective criteria, chiefly the existing laws and practices in the Nation. In the federal system, petty offenses are defined as those punishable by no more than six months in prison and a $500 fine. In 49 of the 50 States, crimes subject to trial without a jury (which occasionally include simple battery) are punishable by no more than one year in jail. We need not, however, settle in this case the exact location of the line between petty offenses and serious crimes. It is sufficient for our purposes to hold that a crime punishable by two years in prison is, based on past and contemporary standards in this country, a serious crime and not a petty offense. Consequently, appellant was entitled to a jury trial and it was error to deny it. * * *

BLANTON v. CITY OF NORTH LAS VEGAS

489 U.S. 538 (1989).

Justice Marshall delivered the opinion of the Court.

The issue in this case is whether there is a constitutional right to a trial by jury for persons charged under Nevada law with driving under the influence of alcohol (DUI). Nev.Rev.Stat. § 484.379(1) (1987). We hold that there is not.

DUI is punishable by a minimum term of two days' imprisonment and a maximum term of six months' imprisonment. Alternatively, a trial court may order the defendant "to perform 48 hours of work for the community while dressed in distinctive garb which identifies him" a DUI offender. The defendant also must pay a fine ranging from $200 to $1,000. In addition, the defendant automatically loses his driver's license for 90 days, and he must attend, at his own expense, an alcohol abuse education course. Repeat DUI offenders are subject to increased penalties.

Petitioners Melvin R. Blanton and Mark D. Fraley were charged with DUI in separate incidents. Neither petitioner had a prior DUI conviction. The North Las Vegas, Nevada, Municipal Court denied their respective pretrial demands for a jury trial. On appeal, the Eighth Judicial District Court denied Blanton's request for a jury trial but, a month later, granted Fraley's. Blanton then appealed to the Supreme Court of Nevada, as did respondent city of North Las Vegas with respect to Fraley. After consolidating the two cases along with several others raising the same issue, the Supreme Court concluded, inter alia, that the Federal Constitution does not guarantee a right to a jury trial for a DUI offense because the maximum term of incarceration is only six months and the maximum possible fine is $1,000. We granted certiorari to consider whether petitioners were entitled to a jury trial, and now affirm.

It has long been settled that "there is a category of petty crimes or offenses which is not subject to the Sixth Amendment jury trial provision." *Duncan v. Louisiana*, 391 U.S. 145, 159 (1968). In determining whether a particular offense should be categorized as "petty," our early decisions focused on the nature of the offense and on whether it was triable by a jury at common law. In recent years, however, we have sought more "objective indications of the seriousness with which society regards the offense." *Frank v. United States*, 395 U.S. 147, 148 (1969). "[W]e have found the most relevant such criteria in the severity of the maximum authorized penalty." *Baldwin v. New York*, 399 U.S. 66, 68 (1970) (plurality opinion). In fixing the maximum penalty for a crime, a legislature "include[s] within the definition of the crime itself a judgment about the seriousness of the offense." *Frank*, 395 U.S., at 149.

In using the word "penalty," we do not refer solely to the maximum prison term authorized for a particular offense. A legislature's view of the seriousness of an offense also is reflected in the other penalties that it attaches to the offense. We thus examine "whether the length of the authorized prison term or the seriousness of other punishment is enough in itself to require a jury trial." *Duncan*, 391 U.S., at 161. Primary emphasis, however, must be placed on the maximum authorized period of incarceration. Penalties such as probation or a fine may engender "a significant infringement of personal freedom," but they cannot approximate in severity the loss of liberty that a prison term entails. Indeed, because incarceration is an "intrinsically different" form of punishment, it is the most powerful indication whether an offense is "serious."

Following this approach, our decision in *Baldwin* established that a defendant is entitled to a jury trial whenever the offense for which he is charged carries a maximum authorized prison term of greater than six months. The possibility of a sentence exceeding six months, we determined, is "sufficiently severe by itself" to require the opportunity for a jury trial. As for a prison term of six months or less, we recognized that it will seldom be viewed by the defendant as "trivial or 'petty.' "But we found that the disadvantages of such a sentence, "onerous though they may be, may be outweighed by the benefits that result from speedy and inexpensive nonjury adjudications." *Ibid.*

Although we did not hold in *Baldwin* that an offense carrying a maximum prison term of six months or less automatically qualifies as a "petty" offense, and decline to do so today, we do find it appropriate to presume for purposes of the Sixth Amendment that society views such an offense as "petty." A defendant is entitled to a jury trial in such circumstances only if he can demonstrate that any additional statutory penalties, viewed in conjunction with the maximum authorized period of incarceration, are so severe that they clearly reflect a legislative determination that the offense in question is a "serious" one.

Applying these principles here, it is apparent that petitioners are not entitled to a jury trial. The maximum authorized prison sentence for first-time DUI offenders does not exceed six months. A presumption therefore exists that the Nevada Legislature views DUI as a "petty" offense for purposes of the Sixth Amendment. Considering the additional statutory penalties as well, we do not believe that the Nevada Legislature has clearly indicated that DUI is a "serious" offense.

In the first place, it is immaterial that a first-time DUI offender may face a minimum term of imprisonment. In settling on six months' imprisonment as the constitutional demarcation point, we have assumed that a defendant convicted of the offense in question would receive the maximum authorized prison sentence. It is not constitutionally determinative, therefore, that a particular defendant may be required to serve some amount of jail time less than six months. Likewise, it is of little moment that a defendant may receive the maximum prison term because of the prohibitions on plea bargaining and probation. As for the 90–day license suspension, it, too, will be irrelevant if it runs concurrently with the prison sentence, which we assume for present purposes to be the maximum of six months.[1]

We are also unpersuaded by the fact that, instead of a prison sentence, a DUI offender may be ordered to perform 48 hours of community service dressed in clothing identifying him as a DUI offender. Even assuming the outfit is the source of some embarrassment during the 48–hour period, such a penalty will be less embarrassing and less onerous than six months in jail. As for the possible $1,000 fine, it is well below the $5,000 level set by Congress in its most recent definition of a "petty" offense, and petitioners do not suggest that this congressional figure is out of step with state practice for offenses carrying prison sentences of six months or less. Finally, we ascribe little significance to the fact that a DUI offender faces increased penalties for repeat offenses. Recidivist penalties of the magnitude imposed for DUI are commonplace and, in any event, petitioners do not face such penalties here.

Viewed together, the statutory penalties are not so severe that DUI must be deemed a "serious" offense for purposes of the Sixth Amend-

---

1. It is unclear whether the license suspension and prison sentence in fact run concurrently. * * * Furthermore, the requirement that an offender attend an alcohol abuse education course can only be described as de minimis.

ment. It was not error, therefore, to deny petitioners jury trials. Accordingly, the judgment of the Supreme Court of Nevada is

Affirmed.

Notes and Questions

1. In *United States v. Nachtigal*, 507 U.S. 1 (1993), the Court relied on *Blanton* in holding that a DUI charge with a maximum penalty of six months' imprisonment, a $5,000 fine, a five-year term of probation, and other penalties was not constitutionally serious. The Court reiterated Blanton's presumption that offenses for which the maximum authorized period of incarceration is six months are presumptively "petty." That legislative judgment, plus the possibility of a probationary sentence or a $5,000 fine, were not sufficiently severe to overcome the presumption. Compare Richter v. Fairbanks, 903 F.2d 1202 (8th Cir.1990), where the court found that a possible 15–year driver's license revocation for a third DUI offense justified a jury trial even though the maximum authorized sentence was six months.

2. In *Lewis v. United States*, 518 U.S. 322 (1996), the Supreme Court held that the scope of the federal jury trial right "does not change where a defendant faces a potential aggregate prison term in excess of six months for petty offenses charged." "[B]y setting the maximum authorized prison term at six months, the legislature categorized the offense ... as petty. The fact that [Lewis] was charged with two counts of a petty offense does not revise the legislative judgment as to the gravity of the particular offense, nor does it transform the petty offense into a serious one."

3. Contempt proceedings are at least quasi-criminal in nature, and a jury must be afforded before a sentence of confinement for more than six months may be imposed for a post-verdict finding of contempt. In *Codispoti v. Pennsylvania*, 418 U.S. 506 (1974), the Court held that a contemnor has a right to jury trial if the sentences imposed aggregate more than six months. The *Lewis* Court distinguished *Codispoti* because the legislature usually has not set a specific penalty for criminal contempt, Instead, "courts use the severity of the penalty actually imposed as the measure of the character of the particular offense."

4. Is a jury trial constitutionally required when the authorized statutory punishment is six months or less, but the penalty includes a fine? Does *Blanton* suggest that the magnitude of a fine may take the case out of the "petty offense" category? Many courts apply the federal statutory standard of a fine of $5,000 or less as the petty offense upper limit.

A jury trial is required when a court imposes serious fines for criminal contempt. See *International Union, United Mine Workers of Am. v. Bagwell*, 512 U.S. 821 (1994), where the court held that contempt fines of $52 million for violation of a labor injunction were criminal and were subject to the jury trial right. However, the Court reiterated the long-accepted idea that direct contempts in the presence of the court are subject to immediate summary adjudication without jury trial.

On the other hand, juvenile court proceedings against a youthful offender are not considered to be criminal in nature, and there is no right to a jury trial in such proceedings. *McKeiver v. Pennsylvania*, 403 U.S. 528 (1971).

5. The constitutional right to a jury trial may be waived by the defendant in favor of a bench trial, although a defendant does not have a right to a bench trial. *Patton v. United States*, 281 U.S. 276 (1930). Because a jury trial is the preferable mode of disposing of factual issues in criminal cases and society has an interest in the disposition of criminal cases, the prosecution and the court must concur in a waiver which is unaccompanied by a guilty plea. In *Singer v. United States*, 380 U.S. 24 (1965), the Court left open the possibility that the right to waive could belong to the defendant alone: "We need not determine in this case whether there might be some circumstances where a defendant's reasons for wanting to be tried by a judge alone are so compelling that the Government's insistence on trial by jury would result in the denial to a defendant of an impartial trial."

A determination that the waiver is made voluntarily and with a full understanding of its consequences must precede the acceptance of a waiver by the court. See *Singer v. United States*. By contrast, the state statutory right to a jury trial for petty offenses which are not subject to the constitutional guarantees may be waived by the mere failure to assert it in a timely manner. Assuming that the prosecutor and the court are willing to concur in any decision by the defendant to waive a jury trial, what strategic considerations may affect a defendant's decision to waive a jury trial?

6. *Apprendi v. New Jersey*, 530 U.S. 466 (2000) struck down a sentencing law enabling a judge to lengthen a jury-imposed sentence by two years if a crime was determined to be a hate crime. The Court held that, other than the fact of a prior conviction, any fact increasing the penalty beyond the prescribed statutory maximum, whether the statute calls it an element or a sentencing factor, must be submitted to a jury, and proved beyond a reasonable doubt. See Chapter 22, Sentencing, *infra*.

B. JURY SIZE AND UNANIMITY

WILLIAMS v. FLORIDA
399 U.S. 78 (1970).

Mr. Justice White delivered the opinion of the Court.

[Williams's motion to impanel a 12–person jury, rather than the six-person jury provided by Florida law in noncapital cases, was denied. Thereafter he was convicted of robbery and sentenced to life imprisonment.]

In *Duncan v. Louisiana*, 391 U.S. 145 (1968), we held that the Fourteenth Amendment guarantees a right to trial by jury in all criminal cases that—were they to be tried in a federal court—would come within the Sixth Amendment's guarantee. Petitioner's trial for robbery on July 3, 1968, clearly falls within the scope of that holding. The question in this case then is whether the constitutional guarantee of a trial by "jury" necessarily requires trial by exactly 12 persons, rather than some lesser number—in this case six. We hold that the 12–man panel is not a necessary ingredient of "trial by jury," and that respondent's refusal to impanel more than the six members provided for by Florida law did not violate petitioner's Sixth Amendment rights as applied to the States through the Fourteenth.

We had occasion in *Duncan v. Louisiana* to review briefly the oft-told history of the development of trial by jury in criminal cases. That history revealed a long tradition attaching great importance to the concept of relying on a body of one's peers to determine guilt or innocence as a safeguard against arbitrary law enforcement. That same history, however, affords little insight into the considerations that gradually led the size of that body to be generally fixed at 12. Some have suggested that the number 12 was fixed upon simply because that was the number of the presentment jury from the hundred, from which the petit jury developed. Other, less circular but more fanciful reasons for the number 12 have been given, "but they were all brought forward after the number was fixed," and rest on little more than mystical or superstitious insights into the significance of "12." Lord Coke's explanation that the "number of twelve is much respected in holy writ, as 12 apostles, 12 stones, 12 tribes, etc.," is typical. In short, while sometime in the 14th century the size of the jury at common law came to be fixed generally at 12, that particular feature of the jury system appears to have been a historical accident, unrelated to the great purposes which gave rise to the jury in the first place. The question before us is whether this accidental feature of the jury has been immutably codified into our Constitution. * * *

The relevant inquiry, as we see it, must be the function that the particular feature performs and its relation to the purposes of the jury trial. Measured by this standard, the 12–man requirement cannot be regarded as an indispensable component of the Sixth Amendment.

The purpose of the jury trial, as we noted in Duncan, is to prevent oppression by the Government. [Given] this purpose, the essential feature of a jury obviously lies in the interposition between the accused and his accuser of the commonsense judgment of a group of laymen, and in the community participation and shared responsibility that results from that group's determination of guilt or innocence. The performance of this role is not a function of the particular number of the body that makes up the jury. To be sure, the number should probably be large enough to promote group deliberation, free from outside attempts at intimidation, and to provide a fair possibility for obtaining a representatives cross-section of the community. But we find little reason to think that these goals are in any meaningful sense less likely to be achieved when the jury numbers six, than when it numbers 12—particularly if the requirement of unanimity is retained. And, certainly the reliability of the jury as a factfinder hardly seems likely to be a function of its size.

It might be suggested that the 12–man jury gives a defendant a greater advantage since he has more "chances" of finding a juror who will insist on acquittal and thus prevent conviction. But the advantage might just as easily belong to the State, which also needs only one juror out of twelve insisting on guilt to prevent acquittal. What few experiments have occurred—usually in the civil area—indicate that there is no discernible difference between the results reached by the two different-sized juries. In short, neither currently available evidence nor theory suggests that the 12–man jury is necessarily more advantageous to the defendant than a jury composed of fewer members.

Similarly, while in theory the number of viewpoints represented on a randomly selected jury ought to increase as the size of the jury increases, in practice the difference between the 12–man and the six-man jury in terms of the cross-section of the community represented seems likely to be negligible. Even the 12–man jury cannot insure representation of every distinct voice in the community, particularly given the use of the peremptory challenge. * * *

Notes and Questions

1. In *Ballew v. Georgia*, 435 U.S. 223 (1978), the Court used empirical data to establish a constitutional minimum of six-person juries and to reject a jury of only five persons as violative of the Sixth and Fourteenth Amendments.

First, recent empirical data suggest that progressively smaller juries are less likely to foster effective group deliberation. [At] some point, this decline leads to inaccurate fact-finding and incorrect application of the common sense of the community to the facts. Generally, a positive correlation exists between group size and the quality of both group performance and group productivity. A variety of explanations have been offered for this conclusion. Several are particularly applicable in the jury setting. The smaller the group, the less likely are members to make critical contributions necessary for the solution of a given problem. Because most juries are not permitted to take notes, memory is important for accurate jury deliberations. As juries decrease in size, then, they are less likely to have members who remember each of the important pieces of evidence or argument. Furthermore, the smaller the group, the less likely it is to overcome the biases of its members to obtain an accurate result. * * *

Second, the data now raise doubts about the accuracy of the results achieved by smaller and smaller panels. [Third,] the data suggest that the verdicts of jury deliberation in criminal cases will vary as juries become smaller, and that the variance amounts to an imbalance to the detriment of one side, the defense. [Fourth,] what has just been said about the presence of minority viewpoint as juries decrease in size foretells problems not only for jury decisionmaking, but also for the representation of minority groups in the community. * * *

[We] readily admit that we do not pretend to discern a clear line between six members and five. But the assembled data raise substantial doubt about the reliability and appropriate representation of panels smaller than six. Because of the fundamental importance of the jury trial to the American system of criminal justice, any further reduction that promotes inaccurate and possibly biased decisionmaking, that causes untoward differences in verdicts, and that prevents juries from truly representing their communities, attains constitutional significance.

2. Despite the *Williams* holding that the federal constitution does not require that a jury be composed of twelve members, many state constitutions require a twelve-person jury for all felony prosecutions and a six-person jury for misdemeanor prosecutions.

APODACA v. OREGON

406 U.S. 404 (1972).

MR. JUSTICE WHITE announced the judgment of the Court in an opinion in which The Chief Justice, Mr. Justice Blackmun, and Mr. Justice Rehnquist joined.

[Three men were convicted in separate trials by Oregon juries which returned less than unanimous (11–1 and 10–2) verdicts.]

In *Williams v. Florida*, 399 U.S. 78 (1970), we had occasion to consider a related issue: whether the Sixth Amendment's right to trial by jury requires that all juries consist of 12 men. After considering the history of the 12–man requirement and the functions it performs in contemporary society, we concluded that it was not of constitutional stature. We reach the same conclusion today with regard to the requirement of unanimity.

[As] in *Williams*, we must accordingly consider what is meant by the concept "jury" and determine whether a feature commonly associated with it is constitutionally required. And, as in *Williams*, our inability to divine "the intent of the Framers" when they eliminated references to the "accustomed requisites" requires that in determining what is meant by a jury we must turn to other than purely historical considerations.

Our inquiry must focus upon the function served by the jury in contemporary society. As we said in *Duncan*, the purpose of trial by jury is to prevent oppression by the Government by providing a "safeguard against the corrupt or overzealous prosecutor and against the complaint, biased, or eccentric judge." "Given this purpose, the essential feature of a jury obviously lies in the interposition between the accused and his accuser of the commonsense judgment of a group of laymen ..." A requirement of unanimity, however, does not materially contribute to the exercise of this commonsense judgment. As we said in Williams, a jury will come to such a judgment as long as it consists of a group of laymen representative of a cross section of the community who have the duty and the opportunity to deliberate, free from outside attempts at intimidation, on the question of a defendant's guilt. In terms of this function we perceive no difference between juries required to act unanimously and those permitted to convict or acquit by votes of 10 to two or 11 to one. Requiring unanimity would obviously produce hung juries in some situations where nonunanimous juries will convict or acquit. But in either case, the interest of the defendant in having the judgment of his peers interposed between himself and the officers of the State who prosecute and judge him is equally well served.

Petitioners nevertheless argue that unanimity serves other purposes constitutionally essential to the continued operation of the jury system. Their principal contention is that a Sixth Amendment 'jury trial' made mandatory on the States by virtue of the Due Process Clause of the Fourteenth Amendment, should be held to require a unanimous jury verdict in order to give substance to the reasonable-doubt standard otherwise mandated by the Due Process Clause.

We are quite sure, however, that the Sixth Amendment itself has never been held to require proof beyond a reasonable doubt in criminal cases. The reasonable-doubt standard developed separately from both the jury trial and the unanimous verdict. As the Court noted in the *Winship* case, the rule requiring proof of crime beyond a reasonable doubt did not crystallize in this country until after the Constitution was adopted. And in that case, which held such a burden of proof to be constitutionally required, the Court purported to draw no support from the Sixth Amendment. * * *

Petitioners also cite quite accurately a long line of decisions of this Court upholding the principle that the Fourteenth Amendment requires jury panels to reflect a cross section of the community. They then contend that unanimity is a necessary precondition for effective application of the cross-section requirement, because a rule permitting less than unanimous verdicts will make it possible for convictions to occur without the acquiescence of minority elements within the community.

There are two flaws in this argument. One is petitioners' assumption that every distinct voice in the community has a right to be represented on every jury and a right to prevent conviction of a defendant in any case. All that the Constitution forbids, however, is systematic exclusion of identifiable segments of the community from jury panels * * *.

We also cannot accept petitioners' second assumption—that minority groups, even when they are represented on a jury, will not adequately represent the viewpoint of those groups simply because they may be outvoted in the final result. They will be present during all deliberations, and their views will be heard. We cannot assume that the majority of the jury will refuse to weigh the evidence and reach a decision upon rational grounds, just as it must now do in order to obtain unanimous verdicts, or that a majority will deprive a man of his liberty on the basis of prejudice when a minority is presenting a reasonable argument in favor of acquittal. We simply find no proof for the notion that a majority will disregard its instructions and cast its votes for guilt or innocence based on prejudice rather than the evidence. * * *

Notes

1. Only Louisiana and Oregon allow juries to convict on less than unanimous votes in felony cases. In *Johnson v. Louisiana*, 406 U.S. 356 (1972), the Court upheld a conviction based upon a 9–3 vote. In dissent, Justice Blackmun wondered where the mathematical niceties would end, claiming that under the Court's reasoning, a vote of 8–4 or 7–5 was permissible.

2. While *Apodaca* does not require unanimity in twelve-person state juries, the Court in *Burch v. Louisiana*, 441 U.S. 130 (1979) held that a unanimous verdict is required of a jury consisting of six members. In federal cases unanimous jury verdicts are required by the Federal Rules unless the parties stipulate otherwise. See F.R.Crim.P. 31.

3. In *Schad v. Arizona*, 501 U.S. 624 (1991), the defendant was convicted of first-degree murder and sentenced to death. First-degree murder included both premeditated and felony-murder theories, and the prosecution offered proof on both. With a general verdict, it was uncertain whether the jury had been unanimous about premeditated murder. A plurality of the Court said that the issue "is one of the permissible limits in defining criminal conduct, [not] one of jury unanimity," and held that Schad's due process rights had not been violated when the trial court grouped felony murder and premeditated murder as alternative ways of committing the single crime of first-degree murder.

Compare *Richardson v. United States*, 526 U.S. 813 (1999), in which a federal statute prohibits engaging in a continuing criminal enterprise (CCE), which is defined as a violation of the drug statutes where the "violation is part of a continuing series of violations." 21 U.S.C § 848. The Court had to decide whether the phrase "series of violations" refers to one element—a "series"—or whether it creates several elements, or violations, each of which requires unanimity. If the Court concluded that the former approach applied, the jury would simply have to find that the defendant engaged in a series of violations, without regard to whether there was jury unanimity about which violations constituted the series. The Court opted for the latter formulation, and held that a jury must agree unanimously not only that a defendant committed a "continuing series of violations" but also which specific violations made up that "continuing series of violations."

4. *Deadlocked jury.* In some instances the jury will report that it is "hung" and is unable to reach a unanimous verdict. If this situation continues the judge may declare a mistrial. A mistrial because of a hung jury usually does not bar a retrial of the defendant. See Chapter 23, on double jeopardy.

Where the jury reports that it is unable to reach a verdict and the trial court determines that further deliberations may be useful, the court may deliver a limited number of instructions to the jury. The court may instruct the jury that, in order to return a verdict, each juror must agree to that verdict; jurors must consult with each other and deliberate to achieve an agreement, without harming individual judgment; each juror must decide the case after impartial appraisal of the evidence with other jurors; during deliberations, a juror may reexamine his or her views and change his or her opinion if persuaded that it is erroneous; and no juror should relinquish his or her honest beliefs about the evidence solely due to the opinion of the other jurors, or merely to return a verdict. See *Lowenfield v. Phelps*, 484 U.S. 231 (1988) (a supplemental instruction, which does not speak specifically to minority jurors but does serve the purpose of avoiding a retrial, is permissible after consideration of the context and circumstances in which it is given). When a jury has been kept together until it appears that there is no probability of agreement upon a verdict, the court may discharge the jury without a verdict.

5. *Inconsistent verdicts.* Because of the possibility of trial on multiple charges, the jury may convict on one count and acquit on another. On occasion such an action may seem wholly inconsistent. In some states, inconsistent verdicts as between separate counts are permissible unless there is a logical inconsistency resulting in more severe punishment. For example, it is inconsistent for the jury to return verdicts on two wanton crimes and one reckless crime when all three crimes occurred simultaneously. On the other hand, verdicts on three assault charges are not inconsistent when the injuries occurred as a result of three independent acts which produced the charges. Moreover, conviction of different degrees of a crime like burglary for different defendants are not regarded as inconsistent. By contrast, consistency among verdicts is not necessary when a federal defendant is convicted on one or more counts and acquitted on others. *Dunn v. United States*, 284 U.S. 390 (1932).

C. SELECTING PROSPECTIVE JURORS

In most states, the master list for prospective jurors is drawn from such sources as all voter registration lists for the county or a list of persons over the age of eighteen holding valid drivers' licenses issued in the county. A computer periodically may generate a randomized jury list of prospective jurors. A jury panel in a court which conducts felony trials consists of as many names as deemed necessary for the impaneling of the number of jurors required.

Each person drawn for jury service may be served with a summons directing him or her to report at a specified time and place and to be available for jury service for a period of time. Often, the summons is accompanied by a jury qualification form which must be completed and returned. The form may seek information about the person's address, date of birth, level of education, employer, and members of the immediate family. The form also may seek information about whether the person has ever sued or been sued, as well as information which could disqualify the person under statutes from serving as jurors, e.g., citizenship of the United States, inability to speak and understand English, physical or mental disabilities which may prevent effective jury service, a current indictment or a past felony conviction against the prospective juror, or recent jury service. Unless the court determines in a particular case that the information contained on the form must be kept confidential or its use restricted in the interest of justice, the form is made available to the parties or their attorneys.

1. *The Fair Cross–Section Requirement*

The Sixth Amendment grants to criminal defendants the right to a "jury of the state and district wherein the crime shall have been committed." From this language has evolved the concept that the petit jury in a criminal case must be selected from a fair cross-section of the community where the crime occurred. Note that this requirement applies only to the jury panel from which the petit jury is selected. The jury which actually decides the case does not have to reflect a cross-section of the community. *Holland v. Illinois*, 493 U.S. 474 (1990). Imagine the difficulties in applying a cross-section requirement to the petit jury, as well as its impact on the voir dire process. As discussed, infra, the Equal Protection Clause of the Fourteenth Amendment dictates restrictions on the composition of the petit jury.

The purposes of the cross-section requirement are: (1) avoiding "the possibility that the composition of juries would be arbitrarily skewed in such a way as to deny criminal defendants the benefit of the common-sense judgment of the community;" (2) avoiding an "appearance of unfairness," and (3) ensuring against deprivation of "often historically disadvantaged groups of their right as citizens to serve on juries in criminal cases." *Lockhart v. McCree*, 476 U.S. 162 (1986). Most of the early fair cross-section cases concerned the systematic exclusion of racial or ethnic groups from the jury panel. Later cases recognized violations of the fair cross-section requirement on the basis of gender. The Supreme Court in *Taylor v. Louisiana*, 419 U.S. 522 (1975) held that a male defendant had standing to challenge the constitutionality of a state law excluding women from jury service unless they had filed a written declaration. The Court also found that a petit jury must be selected from a representative cross-section of the community, because it is a fundamental aspect of the jury trial guarantee in the Sixth Amendment. A cross-section of the community is composed of "large, distinctive groups" which play "major roles in the community."

DUREN v. MISSOURI
439 U.S. 357 (1979).

MR. JUSTICE WHITE delivered the opinion of the Court.

In *Taylor v. Louisiana*, 419 U.S. 522 (1975), this Court held that systematic exclusion of women during the jury-selection process, resulting in jury pools not "reasonably representative" of the community, denies a criminal defendant his right, under the Sixth and Fourteenth Amendments, to a petit jury selected from a fair cross section of the community. Under the system invalidated in *Taylor*, a woman could not serve on a jury unless she filed a written declaration of her willingness to do so. As a result, although 53% of the persons eligible for jury service were women, less than 1% of the 1,800 persons whose names were drawn from the jury wheel during the year in which appellant Taylor's jury was chosen were female.

At the time of our decision in *Taylor* no other State provided that women could not serve on a jury unless they volunteered to serve. However, five States, including Missouri, provided an automatic exemption from jury service for any women requesting not to serve. Subsequent to *Taylor*, three of these States eliminated this exemption. Only Missouri and Tennessee continue to exempt women from jury service upon request. Today we hold that such systematic exclusion of women that results in jury venires averaging less than 15% female violates the Constitution's fair-cross-section requirement.

I

Petitioner Duren was indicted in 1975 in the Circuit Court of Jackson County, Mo., for first-degree murder and first-degree robbery. In a pretrial motion to quash his petit jury panel and again in a post-conviction motion for a new trial, he contended that his right to trial by a jury chosen from a fair cross section of his community was denied by provisions of Missouri law granting women who so request an automatic exemption from jury service. Both motions were denied.

At hearings on these motions, petitioner established that the jury-selection process in Jackson County begins with the annual mailing of a questionnaire to persons randomly selected from the Jackson County voter registration list. Approximately 70,000 questionnaires were mailed in 1975. The questionnaire contains a list of occupations and other categories which are the basis under Missouri law for either disqualification[2] or exemption[3] from jury service. Included on the questionnaire is a paragraph prominently addressed "TO WOMEN" that states in part:

> "Any woman who elects not to serve will fill out this paragraph and mail this questionnaire to the jury commissioner at once." * * *

The names of those sent questionnaires are placed in the master jury wheel for Jackson County, except for those returning the questionnaire who indicate disqualification or claim an applicable exemption. Summonses are mailed on a weekly basis to prospective jurors randomly drawn from the jury wheel. The summons, like the questionnaire, contains special directions to men over 65 and to women, this time advising them to return the summons by mail if they desire not to serve. The practice also is that even those women who do not return the summons are treated as having claimed exemption if they fail to appear for jury service on the appointed day. Other persons seeking to claim an exemption at this stage must make written or personal application to the court.

---

2. Felons, illiterates, attorneys, judges, members of the Armed Forces, and certain others are ineligible for jury service.

3. In addition to women, the following are exempted from jury service upon request: persons over age 65, medical doctors, clergy, teachers, persons who performed jury service within the preceding year,

"[a]ny person whose absence from his regular place of employment would, in the judgment of the court, tend materially and adversely to affect the public safety, health, welfare or interest," and "any person upon whom service as a juror would in the judgment of the court impose an undue hardship."

Petitioner established that according to the 1970 census, 54% of the adult inhabitants of Jackson County were women. He also showed that for the periods June–October 1975 and January–March 1976, 11,197 persons were summoned and that 2,992 of these or 26.7%, were women. Of those summoned, 741 women and 4,378 men appeared for service. Thus, 14.5% (741 of 5,119) of the persons on the postsummons weekly venires during the period in which petitioner's jury was chosen were female. In March 1976, when petitioner's trial began, 15.5% of those on the weekly venires were women (110 of 707). Petitioner's jury was selected from a 53-person panel on which there were 5 women; all 12 jurors chosen were men. None of the foregoing statistical evidence was disputed. [The Missouri Supreme Court affirmed.]

II

We think that in certain crucial respects the Missouri Supreme Court misconceived the nature of the fair-cross-section inquiry set forth in *Taylor*. In holding that "petit juries must be drawn from a source fairly representative of the community," 419 U.S., at 538, we explained that

> jury wheels, pools of names, panels, or venires from which juries are drawn must not systematically exclude distinctive groups in the community and thereby fail to be reasonably representative thereof.

In order to establish a prima facie violation of the fair-cross-section requirement, the defendant must show (1) that the group alleged to be excluded is a "distinctive" group in the community; (2) that the representation of this group in venires from which juries are selected is not fair and reasonable in relation to the number of such persons in the community; and (3) that this underrepresentation is due to systematic exclusion of the group in the jury-selection process.

With respect to the first part of the prima facie test, Taylor without doubt established that women "are sufficiently numerous and distinct from men" so that "if they are systematically eliminated from jury panels, the Sixth Amendment's fair-cross-section requirement cannot be satisfied."

The second prong of the prima facie case was established by petitioner's statistical presentation. Initially, the defendant must demonstrate the percentage of the community made up of the group alleged to be underrepresented, for this is the conceptual benchmark for the Sixth Amendment fair-cross-section requirement. In *Taylor*, the State had stipulated that 53% of the population eligible for jury service was female, while petitioner Duren has relied upon a census measurement of the actual percentage of women in the community (54%). In the trial court, the State of Missouri never challenged these data. Although the Missouri Supreme Court speculated that changing population patterns between 1970 and 1976 and unequal voter registration by men and women rendered the census figures a questionable frame of reference, there is no evidence whatsoever in the record to suggest that the 1970 census data significantly distorted the percentage of women in Jackson County at the time of trial. Petitioner's presentation was clearly adequate prima facie evidence of population characteristics for the purpose of making a fair-cross-section violation.

Given petitioner's proof that in the relevant community slightly over half of the adults are women, we must disagree with the conclusion of the court below that jury venires containing approximately 15% women are "reasonably representative" of this community. If the percentage of women appearing on jury pools in Jackson County had precisely mirrored the percentage of women in the population, more than one of every two prospective jurors would have been female. In fact, less than one of every six prospective jurors was female; 85% of the average jury was male. Such a gross discrepancy between the percentage of women in jury venires and the percentage of women in the community requires the conclusion that women were not fairly represented in the source from which petit juries were drawn in Jackson County.

Finally, in order to establish a prima facie case, it was necessary for petitioner to show that the underrepresentation of women, generally and on his venire, was due to their systematic exclusion in the jury-selection process. Petitioner's proof met this requirement. His undisputed demonstration that a large discrepancy occurred not just occasionally but in every weekly venire for a period of nearly a year manifestly indicates that the cause of the underrepresentation was systematic—that is, inherent in the particular jury-selection process utilized.

Petitioner Duren's statistics and other evidence also established when in the selection process the systematic exclusion took place. There was no indication that underrepresentation of women occurred at the first stage of the selection process—the questionnaire canvass of persons randomly selected from the relevant voter registration list. The first sign of a systematic discrepancy is at the next stage—the construction of the jury wheel from which persons are randomly summoned for service. Less than 30% of those summoned were female, demonstrating that a substantially larger number of women answering the questionnaire claimed either ineligibility or exemption from jury service. Moreover, at the summons stage women were not only given another opportunity to claim exemption, but also were presumed to have claimed exemption when they did not respond to the summons. Thus, the percentage of women at the final, venire, stage (14.5%) was much lower than the percentage of women who were summoned for service (26.7%).

The resulting disproportionate and consistent exclusion of women from the jury wheel and at the venire stage was quite obviously due to the system by which juries were selected. Petitioner demonstrated that the underrepresentation of women in the final pool of prospective jurors was due to the operation of Missouri's exemption criteria—whether the automatic exemption for women or other statutory exemptions—as implemented in Jackson County. Women were therefore systematically underrepresented within the meaning of *Taylor*.

III

[O]nce the defendant has made a prima facie showing of an infringement of his constitutional right to a jury drawn from a fair cross section of the community, it is the State that bears the burden of justifying this infringement by showing attainment of a fair cross section to be incompatible with a significant state interest. Assuming, arguendo, that the exemptions mentioned by the court below would justify failure to achieve a fair community cross section on jury venires, the State must demonstrate that these exemptions caused the underrepresentation complained of. The record contains no such proof, and mere suggestions or assertions to that effect are insufficient.

The other possible cause of the disproportionate exclusion of women on Jackson County jury venires is, of course, the automatic exemption for women. Neither the Missouri Supreme Court nor respondent in its brief has offered any substantial justification for this exemption. In response to questioning at oral argument, counsel for respondent ventured that the only state interest advanced by the exemption is safeguarding the important role played by women in home and family life. But exempting all women because of the preclusive domestic responsibilities of some women is insufficient justification for their disproportionate exclusion on jury venires. What we stated in *Taylor* with respect to the system there challenged under which women could "opt in" for jury service is equally applicable to Missouri's "opt out" exemption:

> It is untenable to suggest these days that it would be a special hardship for each and every woman to perform jury service or that society cannot spare any women from their present duties. This may be the case with many, and it may be burdensome to sort out those who should be exempted from those who should serve. But that task is performed in the case of men and the administrative convenience in dealing with women as a class is insufficient justification for diluting the quality of community judgment represented by the jury in criminal trials. * * *

> If it was ever the case that women were unqualified to sit on juries or were so situated that none of them should be required to perform jury service, that time has long since passed. 419 U.S., at 534–535.

We recognize that a State may have an important interest in assuring that those members of the family responsible for the care of children are available to do so. An exemption appropriately tailored to this interest would, we think, survive a fair-cross-section challenge. We stress, however, that the constitutional guarantee to a jury drawn from a fair cross section of the community requires that States exercise proper caution in exempting broad categories of persons from jury service. Although most occupational and other reasonable exemptions may inevitably involve some degree of overinclusiveness or underinclusiveness, any category expressly limited to a group in the community of sufficient magnitude and distinctiveness so as to be within the fair-cross-section requirement—such as women—runs the danger of resulting in underrepresentation sufficient to constitute a prima facie violation of that constitutional requirement. We also repeat the observation made in *Taylor* that it is unlikely that reasonable exemptions, such as those based on special hardship, incapacity, or community needs, "would pose substantial threats that the remaining pool of jurors would not be representative of the community."

Notes and Questions

1. A jury panel from which a cognizable class of citizens has been systematically excluded is not a representative jury. It is difficult to identify all of the classes of citizens whose exclusion will be held to have impermissibly distorted a jury panel. Any identifiable racial minority would constitute such a class. See *Castaneda v. Partida*, 430 U.S. 482 (1977).

On the other hand, the exclusive use of property tax lists has been said not to present a constitutional infirmity in the jury panel. *Brown v. Allen*, 344 U.S. 443 (1953). Young adults and college students are not a distinctive group. Likewise, the exclusion of young people which results from the intermittent recompiling of the jury lists has been justified in the interest of judicial economy. See *Hamling v. United States*, 418 U.S. 87 (1974).

2. What other groups are "distinctive"? Social Security recipients? Military veterans? Members of large religious groups within a community? Are there more specific ways to decide whether a group is "distinctive"?

2. Jury Selection Process

One way in which a jury may be selected begins with the clerk drawing the number of jurors required for a jury trial from a container holding the names of all members of the jury panel remaining after preliminary proceedings affecting its membership. In order to minimize the risk of a mistrial due to the excuse of jurors during the course of the trial, the trial court may direct the clerk to empanel one or two additional jurors. As their names are called, the jurors are tentatively seated in the jury box to be examined under oath concerning their qualifications. If jurors are excused from service following their examination, the clerk draws additional names until they are replaced.

The basis for challenging individual jurors may be contained in information concerning their qualifications which has been made available before trial. Independent investigation may also have disclosed the basis for challenging certain jurors. In most instances, however, individual jurors are not challenged until they have been examined under oath concerning their qualifications.

In most jurisdictions, the court may conduct the voir dire examination of the jurors or may permit counsel to conduct the examination. Ordinarily, it is best for the court to initiate the examination and then to permit counsel for the parties to conduct further examination. Even if the court conducts the examination, the parties are often entitled to submit supplemental inquiries. Moreover, the initial responses of individual jurors to questions propounded to the jury as a whole may require further inquiry. Any attempt by the court to filter each and every supplemental question proposed by the parties would be cumbersome and time-consuming. Therefore, the court normally permits the parties to make supplemental inquiries directly to the jury. Except for capital cases which may require individual voir dire under state rules, the examination of individual jurors may be restricted by the court. However, on matters requiring individual responses, the separate examination of individual jurors has been strongly encouraged. For example, the ABA Standards Relating to Fair Trial and Free Press, §§ 3, 4, recommends the separate examination of jurors concerning pretrial publicity in order to avoid the incidental exposure of other members of the panel to affirmative responses. Other circumstances might similarly dictate separate examination of jurors regarding sensitive matters.

The purpose of voir dire examination is to determine any possible basis for challenging jurors for cause and to develop background information to be considered in the intelligent exercise of peremptory challenges. In many instances, the jurors are reluctant to admit that they have certain attitudes or prejudices. Another function of the voir dire examination is to condition prejudices and attitudes which cannot be drawn out into the open, in order to minimize their impact on the outcome of the case. Having denied their existence under oath on voir dire examination, the jurors must then bend over backwards to overcome the influence of any secret prejudices.

Because of its central role in the selection of a fair and impartial jury, the voir dire examination is one of the most important parts of the trial. Its importance is augmented by the fact that it is the first opportunity afforded to counsel to address the jury in connection with the case. The impressions which the jurors have about the case and about counsel at the conclusion of the examination may last throughout the entire trial.

Voir dire examination may be used to develop the basis for exercising peremptory challenges as well as challenges for cause. *Mu'Min v. Virginia*, 500 U.S. 415 (1991). Therefore, the examiner may properly explore all matters which may relate to the case to be tried. The potential of anything disclosed on voir dire examination to affect the outcome of the case may also be explored. For example, in *Ward v. Commonwealth*, Ky., 695 S.W.2d 404, 407 (1985), the court observed:

> The trial judge has broad discretion in the area of questioning on voir dire. Generally speaking, questions of jurors in criminal cases should be as varied and elaborated as the circumstances require, the purpose being to obtain a fair and impartial jury whose minds are free and clear from all interest, bias or prejudice which might prevent their finding a just and true verdict. Notwithstanding, questions are not competent when their evident purpose is to have jurors indicate in advance or commit themselves to certain ideas and views upon final submission of the case to them.

In determining the scope of voir dire examination, counsel should consider the limited ability of the jury to absorb and react to lengthy voir dire examination. Accordingly, counsel should restrict the inquiries to facts and attitudes which may actually have some bearing on the outcome of the case. A few carefully worded questions are usually better than a rambling, unstructured examination.

If there are reasonable grounds to believe that a juror cannot render a fair and impartial verdict, the juror shall be excused for cause. However, disqualification is not required merely because a juror does not understand or immediately accept every legal concept [such as mitigation of punishment when a defendant is under the influence of drugs or alcohol] presented during voir dire. The test is not whether a juror agrees with the law when it is presented; it is whether, after having heard all of the evidence, the prospective juror can adjust his views to the requirements of the law and render a fair and impartial verdict.

The court may exercise considerable discretion in deciding whether to excuse an individual juror for cause. To show prejudice from this abuse of discretion, the party challenging the juror must use all peremptory challenges. *Ross v. Oklahoma*, 487 U.S. 81 (1988). Even if the parties fail to make a challenge for cause, the court has an affirmative duty to explore undisclosed information of which it is aware affecting the qualification of an individual juror.

Challenge for Cause Exercises

As you read the following examples of voir dire questions, consider the propriety and the strategic purpose for each category of questions as well as for individual inquiries being asked of prospective jurors. The question for voir dire is in italics; queries and case law follow the question.

1. *Knowledge and opinions.* Ordinarily, the court will read or summarize the indictment or information to the prospective jurors and ask them whether they have any prior knowledge or opinions about the case. However, the questions may be too general to elicit accurate responses. If the court rules permit counsel to address prospective jurors directly, counsel may wish to give a capsule summary of the facts to stimulate the memory of the jurors and then to ask the jurors questions about their knowledge about the case or the defendant. Consider the following illustrative comments and voir dire examination. What answers to these questions may form the basis for a successful challenge for cause? If a trial judge denies the challenge for cause, will an appellate court deem the denial to be an abuse of discretion? The judge might make introductory remarks to the jurors preceding the questioning.

JUDGE: This case involves the fatal shooting of John Doe during an argument at the XYZ Club on Main Street last August. Ron Roe has been arrested and charged with murder in the case. Because guilt or innocence must be judged solely on the basis of the evidence from the witness stand, there are several questions which must be asked to find out whether you already have knowledge or opinions about this shooting:

(A) Have you seen or heard anything about this case in the news media? Should exposure to pretrial publicity alone result in the disqualification of jurors for cause? See *Murphy v. Florida*, 421 U.S. 794 (1975); *Irvin v. Dowd*, 366 U.S. 717 (1961); Chapter 20, on pretrial publicity. The interrogation of jurors about pretrial publicity is obviously necessary to determine this basis for disqualification.

(B) Do you have any knowledge or information about the case from any other source? Is it relevant that one or more of the jurors served on previous juries involving the same defendant or facts or served on the grand jury which returned the indictment? Is hearsay information obtained from discussions with persons interested in the case also relevant? For example, is it a valid basis for a challenge for cause if a prospective juror drove to the crime scene on the evening it occurred and talked to bystanders?

(C) Have you ever formed or expressed an opinion of any kind about this incident? Does the formation of an opinion prior to trial create an inference that the juror cannot be fair and impartial?

2. *Relationships and Associations.* Normally, the court will identify the complainant or victim and the defendant and will ask the prospective jurors whether they are related by blood or marriage to either of them. The court ordinarily identifies counsel for the parties at the same time and inquires whether the jurors have had any prior associations with counsel. The court may also ask the jurors whether they are acquainted with the persons identified or know anything about them. A related line of inquiry is identification of potential witnesses and the relationships and associations between the jurors and these witnesses. Consider the propriety of the following questions. Is the connection between a juror and any of the following a proper subject for inquiry?

JUDGE: The law recognizes that previous relationships and associations with various people may naturally influence your judgment about the case. For this reason, all of the people who are connected with the trial will now be identified so that these relationships and associations may be explored:

(1) The deceased in this case is John Doe.

(2) The defendant on trial is Ron Roe.

(3) The witnesses who may testify in this case include Sheriff Paul Poe, Donna Doe, Charlie Coe and Nina Noe.

(4) The attorneys involved in the case are Peter Prosecutor and Donald Defender.

(5) The trial judge is James Justice.

(A) Are you related to any of these people by blood or marriage? Once a close relationship is established, without regard to protestations of lack of bias, should the court sustain a challenge for cause and excuse the juror? How would you respond as the judge if the challenge was based upon a relationship when the prospective juror was

(1) The third cousin of the victim?

(2) The first cousin of the prosecutor?

(3) The first cousin by marriage of a prosecution witness?

(4) The spouse of the victim's second cousin who knew the victim for a long time?

(B) Do you know any of these people personally? Does acquaintance alone constitute grounds for a challenge for cause? Does information about any of them based upon rumor or gossip?

(C) Have you had any business or social dealings with any of them? Should a prospective juror be excused if a key prosecution witness is employed by the same organization? Is the number of persons employed by the organization relevant?

(D) Have any of you ever sat on a grand jury or trial jury involving any of these people before? Should jurors who have served in previous trials of the same defendant or a codefendant arising out of the same transaction be excused for cause? What about jurors who have previously served in cases involving similar testimony from the same prosecuting witness?

(E) As a result of any prior information or dealings of any kind, are you inclined to give more or less weight to what any of these people say or do than you would if you knew nothing about them? This question goes to the heart of implied bias.

(F) Do you or any of your close friends or relatives belong to any organization or group which has any interest in the outcome of this case?

(G) Have you or any of your close friends or relatives ever been a member of a law enforcement agency in military or civilian life? If a juror is connected with a law enforcement official who is actively involved in the case, should the juror be excused for cause?

(H) Do you have any information or opinions about law enforcement from any source which might influence your judgment about the activities or conclusions of the officers involved in the investigation of this case? Does this question explore the background of the jurors relative to law enforcement in the same way as questions concerning their direct connection with law enforcement agencies? Is the question relevant because it casts light on the attitudes of jurors toward the presumption of innocence?

(I) Have you or any of your close friends or relatives ever been employed by a governmental agency?

(J) Would your service for the government or any attitudes which you may have about governmental service affect your opinions about the role of the government in prosecuting this case?

3. *Attitudes and Prejudices.* Jurors who know nothing about the case or the persons involved in it may nevertheless have fixed attitudes or strong prejudices which would seriously affect their ability to render a fair and impartial verdict. Courts generally permit the exploration of attitudes and prejudices which bear some reasonable relationship to the issues to be decided by the jury. Since the parties are in a better position to determine what attitudes and prejudices may prove to be crucial as the issues are joined during the trial, the voir dire examination in this area is best left to them.

To be effective, an examination in this area must expose the jurors to the issues which they will be asked to decide and to the law and facts upon which the issues will be decided. Because questions in this area tend to preview critical aspects of the trial, they are extremely sensitive and must be drawn with great care. Moreover, the jurors have a limited capacity to absorb lengthy voir dire examination. Therefore, a few selective questions which go directly to the theory of the case are much more effective than a laundry list of factors affecting the trial of cases in general. Consider the propriety of the following questions.

JUDGE: The prosecution will attempt to prove that Ron Roe, who is African–American, murdered a white man, John Doe, for no reason. On the other hand, the defense may show that the shooting resulted from a racial incident started by John Doe. Therefore, there are several questions which must be asked about your attitudes in racial matters:

(A) Do any of you have any conscious prejudice for or against African–Americans?

(B) Have you or your close friends or relatives had any experiences with African–Americans which might influence your judgment one way or the other in deciding this case?

(C) Do any of you feel that African–Americans are more likely to commit crime than other people?

(D) Do any of you feel that African–American persons are more prone to violence than other people and are thus more likely to be at fault in a violent incident such as the one involved in this case?

(E) Would the fact that the case for the prosecution will depend largely on the testimony of a white law enforcement official affect your decision one way or the other?

JUDGE: The defense in this case will attempt to show that Ron Roe shot John Doe in order to defend himself from a violent and unprovoked racial attack. There are several questions which must be asked relating to self-defense.

(F) The law gives a person the right to kill another human being if he believes that it is necessary to kill in order to protect himself from death or serious physical injury. Do any of you disagree with that law?

(G) Can you follow the law and judge the decision which Ron Roe made based on what he believed instead of what you feel that you or some other person might have done in that situation? How is this question relevant to jury selection?

(H) Do any of you believe that Ron Roe had a duty to run away or sustain a serious injury before he had a right to kill in self-defense?

(I) Do you understand that Ron Roe does not have to prove self-defense beyond a reasonable doubt and that you must give the benefit of every reasonable doubt to the defendant in deciding whether the killing was justified on the ground of self-defense?

JUDGE: There will be evidence that Ron Roe owned and was armed with a pistol when this incident occurred. There may also be evidence that he was drinking. Because these matters relate to the issues before you, there are several questions which must be asked about your attitudes in this regard.

(J) Do any of you believe that it is wrong to own or carry a firearm for your own protection, or do any of you believe that the consumption of alcohol, even in moderate quantities, is wrong?

(K) Do any of you belong to any group or organization which has taken a position on the ownership and possession of firearms or the sale and consumption of alcohol?

4. Sentencing Questions. The propriety of an inquiry into the ability of the jurors to consider all penalties within the range provided by law is generally upheld. Consider the propriety of the following comments and questions for prospective jurors.

JUDGE: If you convict the defendant but do not impose the death penalty, you will probably be instructed on murder and manslaughter and given a choice of penalties ranging from ten years to life. There are several questions which must be asked about your attitudes toward these penalties.

(A) Do any of you feel that the penalty of life in prison is too severe for the intentional killing of another person during a mutual argument, regardless of the law and the circumstances which may be involved?

(B) Do any of you believe that the penalty of ten years is too low for the intentional killing of another human being under any circumstances?

(C) If you find the defendant guilty, can you consider all of the penalties provided by law and fix a penalty which is fair according to the law and the evidence?

JUDGE: The prosecution intends to seek the death penalty in this case, and there are some questions which must be asked in this regard.

(D) Do you have any religious or conscientious scruples against the death penalty, or do you have a firm and fixed opinion against it? Although an affirmative answer is not sufficient to sustain a challenge for cause, the inquiry appears to be proper. See *Maxwell v. Bishop*, 398 U.S. 262 (1970); *Boulden v. Holman*, 394 U.S. 478 (1969).

(E) Would your views against the death penalty prevent or substantially impair the performance of your duty as a juror? An affirmative answer to this question is grounds to challenge the juror for cause. *Wainwright v. Witt*, 469 U.S. 412 (1985). Even a single misapplication of this standard invalidates a death sentence. *Gray v. Mississippi*, 481 U.S. 648 (1987). Can a prospective juror be asked on voir dire whether he would consider imposing the death penalty in the particular case?

(F) If you determine under the instructions of the court beyond a reasonable doubt that the defendant is guilty of intentional murder, could you consider the entire range of penalties provided by statutes of this state as outlined to you?

(G) Do you favor the automatic imposition of the death penalty in homicide cases? Because the exercise of a reasoned discretion is required to sustain the imposition of the death penalty, the question goes to the ability of the jurors to follow the law.

(H) If you find the defendant is guilty, would you require him to prove why he should be allowed to live in order to escape the death penalty?

5. *The Juror's Background.* In addition to matters specifically related to the case to be tried, the prospective jurors may have various items in their backgrounds which could have some bearing on their decision in the case, such as their attitude towards the presumption of innocence. Although some inquiry into these general matters is undoubtedly proper, the questions frequently appear to the jurors to be prying into their personal lives. Moreover, extensive general questions soon reach the point of diminishing returns, particularly in the area of courtroom procedure and reasonable doubt.

JUDGE: Unfortunately, some of you may have had some previous exposure to crime in some fashion or another. There are several questions which must be asked about your experiences and attitudes in this regard.

(A) Have you or any of your close friends or relatives ever been a victim of a crime?

(B) Have you or any of your close friends or relatives ever been a party or a witness to a crime of violence?

(C) Have you ever testified in court in connection with a criminal charge?

(D) Would any experiences which you may have had or may have heard about with regard to crime and the courts influence your decision in this case?

(E) In light of any experiences which you or any of your close friends or relatives may have had, would you prefer not to serve on a jury in a criminal case?

(F) In light of any experiences which you or your close friends or relatives may have had, would you rather not serve on a jury in this case?

It is relevant to establish whether a juror has tried a similar case. However, should the juror's deliberative processes be explored? Even an inquiry into the verdict in an earlier case may be misleading. A juror who held out for an acquittal in a previous case may have been waiting for years for a second chance to correct that error. By the same token, a juror who convicted a prior defendant may have had second thoughts about the verdict, resulting in reluctance to return another guilty verdict. Consider the following questions.

JUDGE: Some of you may have previous experience as jurors which might affect your decision in this case. There are several questions which must be asked in this regard.

(G) Have any of you ever served on a jury panel in any court?

(H) Have any of you ever actually served on a jury which tried a civil or a criminal case?

(I) Do you feel that any experience which you may have had as a juror would influence you in any way in deciding the issues in this case?

(J) Do you understand the difference between the burden of proof in a civil case and a criminal case? In other words, in a civil case, you may decide in favor of either party if you believe that the evidence is even slightly stronger or better or more believable than the evidence on the other side. In a criminal case, it is your duty to find the defendant not guilty unless the prosecution proves guilt beyond a reasonable doubt. Do you understand and agree with those principles?

The law presumes a defendant to be innocent until he has been proven guilty beyond a reasonable doubt. It affords a number of procedural protections to safeguard this presumption of innocence. Evaluate the propriety of the following questions. Is it necessary to ask them? What purpose(s) do they serve?

(K) Do you believe that an innocent person is not likely to be arrested and charged with a crime?

(L) Do you understand that the charge which brings the defendant to trial is only a charge and is not evidence at all?

(M) Do you realize that a trial is the only opportunity which the law gives the defendant to present the full facts of this case in order to be cleared of the charge?

(N) As he sits here before you, do you agree that the defendant is presumed innocent?

(O) If you were asked to render a verdict right now, how would you vote?

(P) Do you agree that you are upholding the law just as vigorously when you free an innocent man as you are when you convict a guilty one?

(Q) Would any of you require the defendant to prove innocence to you in some way?

(R) Because the defendant is presumed innocent, do you understand that the prosecution has to present its case first, and the defendant does not even have an opportunity to present any evidence until the prosecution has finished?

(S) Do you realize that the prosecution could choose to call every witness except the defendant to the witness stand before the defendant would have any chance to call them?

(T) Do you agree that witnesses belong to no one, and will you consider everything the witnesses say, regardless of who calls them or who is asking questions at the time?

(U) Will you withhold your judgment until you have heard all of the evidence and the case has been submitted to you for a decision?

(V) Do you understand that the law limits the evidence which you may hear, and that it is my duty to object whenever I believe that evidence is being introduced in violation of the law?

(W) Do you promise not to draw any conclusions from my objections and not to hold anything I may do in performing my duty against my client?

(X) At the conclusion of the case, if there is a reasonable doubt about the guilt of the defendant, will you promise me to find my client not guilty?

3. *Exercising Peremptory Challenges*

By rule in most jurisdictions, both parties can challenge a number of jurors without giving any reason whatsoever. Peremptory challenges, though, are not of constitutional dimension. If multiple defendants are being tried, each defendant usually is entitled to at least one additional peremptory challenge to be exercised independently of any other defendant. Trial courts have the discretion to grant additional peremptory challenges when considering the facts of a particular case. A party generally must exercise all peremptory challenges in order to sustain a claim of prejudice due to the failure of the court to grant a requested challenge for cause.

Traditionally, a party could exercise peremptory challenges without offering any justification or explanation. In *Batson v. Kentucky*, 476 U.S. 79 (1986), however, the Supreme Court described basic principles for challenging the exercise of peremptory challenges based on race.

[A] defendant may establish a prima facie case of purposeful discrimination in selection of the petit jury solely on evidence concerning the prosecutor's exercise of peremptory challenges at the defendant's trial. To establish such a case, the defendant first must show that he is a member of a cognizable racial group, and that the prosecutor has exercised peremptory challenges to remove from the venire members of the defendant's race. Second, the defendant is entitled to rely on the fact, as to which there can be no dispute, that peremptory challenges constitute a jury selection practice that permits "those to discriminate who are of a mind to discriminate." Finally, the defendant must show that these facts and any other relevant circumstances raise an inference that the prosecutor used that practice to exclude the veniremen from the petit jury on account of their race. This combination of factors in the empaneling of the petit jury, as in the selection of the venire, raises the necessary inference of purposeful discrimination.

In deciding whether the defendant has made the requisite showing, the trial court should consider all relevant circumstances. For example, a "pattern" of strikes against black jurors included in the particular venire might give rise to an inference of discrimination. Similarly, the prosecutor's questions and statements during voir dire examination and in exercising his challenges may support or refute an inference of discriminatory purpose. These examples are merely illustrative. We have confidence that trial judges, experienced in supervising voir dire, will be able to decide if the circumstances concerning the prosecutor's use of peremptory challenges creates a prima facie case of discrimination against black jurors.

Once the defendant makes a prima facie showing, the burden shifts to the State to come forward with a neutral explanation for challenging black jurors. Though this requirement imposes a limitation in some cases on the full peremptory character of the historic challenge, we emphasize that the prosecutor's explanation need not rise to the level justifying exercise of a challenge for cause. But the prosecutor may not rebut the defendant's prima facie case of discrimination by stating merely that he challenged jurors of the defendant's race on the assumption—or his intuitive judgment—that they would be partial to the defendant because of their shared race. [The] core guarantee of equal protection, ensuring citizens that their State will not discriminate on account of race, would be meaningless were we to approve the exclusion of jurors on the basis of such assumptions, which arise solely from the jurors' race. Nor may the prosecutor rebut the defendant's case merely by denying that he had a discriminatory motive or "affirm[ing] [his] good faith in making individual selections." If these general assertions were accepted as rebutting a defendant's prima facie case, the Equal Protection Clause "would be but a vain and illusory requirement." The prosecutor therefore must articulate a neutral explanation related to the particular case to be tried. The trial court then will have the duty to determine if the defendant has established purposeful discrimination.

After *Batson*, several cases significantly broadened its scope. First, in *Powers v. Ohio*, 499 U.S. 400 (1991), a white defendant alleged that the prosecutor used peremptory challenges to exclude African–American jurors based on their race. Using third-party standing principles, the Court held that the white defendant had standing to assert an equal protection claim on behalf of the excluded African–American jurors. Second, the Court held that a criminal defendant also cannot engage in purposeful discrimination in the exercise of peremptory challenges. *Georgia v. McCollum*, 505 U.S. 42 (1992). The Court relied on *Powers* to find that the prosecution had third-party standing to assert the equal protection rights of excluded jurors. "As the representative of all its citizens, the State is the logical and proper party to assert the invasion of the constitutional rights of the excluded jurors in a criminal trial."

Third, the Court emphasized that *Batson* applied to both race and gender. In *Hernandez v. New York*, 500 U.S. 352 (1991), the Court found that Hispanics have a right to be free from discrimination in jury selection. Then, in *J.E.B. v. Alabama ex rel. T.B.*, 511 U.S. 127 (1994), the Court extended *Batson* and held that the Equal Protection Clause forbids the exercise of a peremptory challenge based upon the gender of a prospective juror.

A generation after *Batson*, the Court continues to offer guidance to lower courts for applying the steps of the constitutional analysis.

MILLER–EL v. DRETKE

545 U.S. 231 (2005).

JUSTICE SOUTER delivered the opinion of the Court.

[The] numbers describing the prosecution's use of peremptories [in defendant's capital murder trial] are remarkable. Out of 20 black members of the 108–person venire panel for Miller–El's trial, only 1 served. Although 9 were excused for cause or by agreement, 10 were peremptorily struck by the prosecution. * * *

More powerful than these bare statistics, however, are side-by-side comparisons of some black venire panelists who were struck and white panelists allowed to serve. If a prosecutor's proffered reason for striking a black panelist applies just as well to an otherwise-similar nonblack who is permitted to serve, that is evidence tending to prove purposeful discrimination to be considered at *Batson*'s third step. * * *

The prosecution used its second peremptory strike to exclude Billy Jean Fields, a black man who expressed unwavering support for the death penalty. On the questionnaire filled out by all panel members before individual examination on the stand, Fields said that he believed in capital punishment, and during questioning he disclosed his belief that the State acts on God's behalf when it imposes the death penalty. "Therefore, if the State exacts death, then that's what it should be." He testified that he had no religious or philosophical reservations about the death penalty and that the death penalty deterred crime. He twice averred, without apparent hesitation, that he could sit on Miller–El's jury and make a decision to impose this penalty.

Although at one point in the questioning, Fields indicated that the possibility of rehabilitation might be relevant to the likelihood that a defendant would commit future acts of violence, he responded to ensuing questions by saying that although he believed anyone could be rehabilitated, this belief would not stand in the way of a decision to impose the death penalty. * * *

Fields was struck peremptorily by the prosecution, with prosecutor James Nelson offering a race-neutral reason:

> [W]e ... have concern with reference to some of his statements as to the death penalty in that he said that he could only give death if he thought a person could not be rehabilitated and he later made the comment that any person could be rehabilitated if they find God or are introduced to God and the fact that we have a concern that his religious feelings may affect his jury service in this case.

Thus, Nelson simply mischaracterized Fields's testimony. He represented that Fields said he would not vote for death if rehabilitation was possible, whereas Fields unequivocally stated that he could impose the death penalty regardless of the possibility of rehabilitation. Perhaps Nelson misunderstood, but unless he had an ulterior reason for keeping

Fields off the jury we think he would have proceeded differently. In light of Fields's outspoken support for the death penalty, we expect the prosecutor would have cleared up any misunderstanding by asking further questions before getting to the point of exercising a strike.

If, indeed, Fields's thoughts on rehabilitation did make the prosecutor uneasy, he should have worried about a number of white panel members he accepted with no evident reservations. Sandra Hearn said that she believed in the death penalty "if a criminal cannot be rehabilitated and continues to commit the same type of crime." Hearn went so far as to express doubt that at the penalty phase of a capital case she could conclude that a convicted murderer "would probably commit some criminal acts of violence in the future." "People change," she said, making it hard to assess the risk of someone's future dangerousness. "[T]he evidence would have to be awful strong." But the prosecution did not respond to Hearn the way it did to Fields, and without delving into her views about rehabilitation with any further question, it raised no objection to her serving on the jury. White panelist Mary Witt said she would take the possibility of rehabilitation into account in deciding at the penalty phase of the trial about a defendant's probability of future dangerousness, but the prosecutors asked her no further question about her views on reformation, and they accepted her as a juror. Latino venireman Fernando Gutierrez, who served on the jury, said that he would consider the death penalty for someone who could not be rehabilitated, but the prosecutors did not question him further about this view. In sum, nonblack jurors whose remarks on rehabilitation could well have signaled a limit on their willingness to impose a death sentence were not questioned further and drew no objection, but the prosecution expressed apprehension about a black juror's belief in the possibility of reformation even though he repeatedly stated his approval of the death penalty and testified that he could impose it according to state legal standards even when the alternative sentence of life imprisonment would give a defendant (like everyone else in the world) the opportunity to reform. * * *

In sum, when we look for nonblack jurors similarly situated to Fields, we find strong similarities as well as some differences. But the differences seem far from significant, particularly when we read Fields's voir dire testimony in its entirety. Upon that reading, Fields should have been an ideal juror in the eyes of a prosecutor seeking a death sentence, and the prosecutors' explanations for the strike cannot reasonably be accepted.

The prosecution's proffered reasons for striking Joe Warren, another black venireman, are comparably unlikely. Warren gave this answer when he was asked what the death penalty accomplished:

> I don't know. It's really hard to say because I know sometimes you feel that it might help to deter crime and then you feel that the person is not really suffering. You're taking the suffering away from him. So it's like I said, sometimes you have mixed feelings about

whether or not this is punishment or, you know, you're relieving personal punishment.

The prosecution said nothing about these remarks when it struck Warren from the panel, but prosecutor Paul Macaluso referred to this answer as the first of his reasons when he testified at the later Batson hearing:

> I thought [Warren's statements on voir dire] were inconsistent responses. At one point he says, you know, on a case-by-case basis and at another point he said, well, I think—I got the impression, at least, that he suggested that the death penalty was an easy way out, that they should be made to suffer more.

On the face of it, the explanation is reasonable from the State's point of view, but its plausibility is severely undercut by the prosecution's failure to object to other panel members who expressed views much like Warren's. * * * Sandra Jenkins, whom the State accepted (but who was then struck by the defense) testified that she thought "a harsher treatment is life imprisonment with no parole." Leta Girard, accepted by the State (but also struck by the defense) gave her opinion that "living sometimes is a worse—is worse to me than dying would be." The fact that Macaluso's reason also applied to these other panel members, most of them white, none of them struck, is evidence of pretext.

The suggestion of pretext is not, moreover, mitigated much by Macaluso's explanation that Warren was struck when the State had 10 peremptory challenges left and could afford to be liberal in using them. If that were the explanation for striking Warren and later accepting panel members who thought death would be too easy, the prosecutors should have struck Sandra Jenkins, whom they examined and accepted before Warren. Indeed, the disparate treatment is the more remarkable for the fact that the prosecutors repeatedly questioned Warren on his capacity and willingness to impose a sentence of death and elicited statements of his ability to do so if the evidence supported that result and the answer to each special question was yes, whereas the record before us discloses no attempt to determine whether Jenkins would be able to vote for death in spite of her view that it was easy on the convict. Yet the prosecutors accepted the white panel member Jenkins and struck the black venireman Warren.

* * * [W]hen illegitimate grounds like race are in issue, a prosecutor simply has got to state his reasons as best he can and stand or fall on the plausibility of the reasons he gives. A *Batson* challenge does not call for a mere exercise in thinking up any rational basis. If the stated reason does not hold up, its pretextual significance does not fade because a trial judge, or an appeals court, can imagine a reason that might not have been shown up as false. * * *

The whole of the voir dire testimony subject to consideration casts the prosecution's reasons for striking Warren in an implausible light. Comparing his strike with the treatment of panel members who expressed similar views supports a conclusion that race was significant in determining who was challenged and who was not. We do not decide whether there were white jurors who expressed ambivalence just as much as these black members of the venire panel. There is no need to go into these instances, for the prosecutors' treatment of Fields and Warren supports stronger arguments that *Batson* was violated.

The case for discrimination goes beyond these comparisons to include broader patterns of practice during the jury selection. The prosecution's shuffling of the venire panel, its enquiry into views on the death penalty, its questioning about minimum acceptable sentences: all indicate decisions probably based on race. Finally, the appearance of discrimination is confirmed by widely known evidence of the general policy of the Dallas County District Attorney's Office to exclude black venire members from juries at the time Miller–El's jury was selected.

The first clue to the prosecutors' intentions, distinct from the peremptory challenges themselves, is their resort during voir dire to a procedure known in Texas as the jury shuffle. In the State's criminal practice, either side may literally reshuffle the cards bearing panel members' names, thus rearranging the order in which members of a venire panel are seated and reached for questioning. Once the order is established, the panel members seated at the back are likely to escape voir dire altogether, for those not questioned by the end of the week are dismissed.

In this case, the prosecution and then the defense shuffled the cards at the beginning of the first week of voir dire; the record does not reflect the changes in order. At the beginning of the second week, when a number of black members were seated at the front of the panel, the prosecution shuffled. At the beginning of the third week, the first four panel members were black. The prosecution shuffled, and these black panel members ended up at the back. Then the defense shuffled, and the black panel members again appeared at the front. The prosecution requested another shuffle, but the trial court refused. Finally, the defense shuffled at the beginning of the fourth and fifth weeks of voir dire; the record does not reflect the panel's racial composition before or after those shuffles.

The State notes in its brief that there might be racially neutral reasons for shuffling the jury, and we suppose there might be. But no racially neutral reason has ever been offered in this case, and nothing stops the suspicion of discriminatory intent from rising to an inference.

The next body of evidence that the State was trying to avoid black jurors is the contrasting voir dire questions posed respectively to black and nonblack panel members, on two different subjects. First, there were the prosecutors' statements preceding questions about a potential juror's thoughts on capital punishment. Some of these prefatory statements were cast in general terms, but some followed the so-called graphic script, describing the method of execution in rhetorical and clinical detail. It is intended, Miller–El contends, to prompt some expression of hesitation to consider the death penalty and thus to elicit plausibly neutral grounds for a peremptory strike of a potential juror subjected to it, if not a strike for cause. If the graphic script is given to a higher proportion of blacks than whites, this is evidence that prosecutors more often wanted blacks off the jury, absent some neutral and extenuating explanation. * * *

Of the 10 nonblacks whose questionnaires expressed ambivalence or opposition, only 30% received the graphic treatment. But of the seven blacks who expressed ambivalence or opposition, 86% heard the graphic script. * * * [T]he reasonable inference is that race was the major consideration when the prosecution chose to follow the graphic script.

The same is true for another kind of disparate questioning, which might fairly be called trickery. The prosecutors asked members of the panel how low a sentence they would consider imposing for murder. Most potential jurors were first told that Texas law provided for a minimum term of five years, but some members of the panel were not, and if a panel member then insisted on a minimum above five years, the prosecutor would suppress his normal preference for tough jurors and claim cause to strike. * * *

It is entirely true, as the State argues, that prosecutors struck a number of nonblack members of the panel (as well as black members) for cause or by agreement before they reached the point in the standard voir dire sequence to question about minimum punishment. But this is no answer; 8 of the 11 nonblack individuals who voiced opposition or ambivalence were asked about the acceptable minimum only after being told what state law required. Hence, only 27% of nonblacks questioned on the subject who expressed these views were subjected to the trick question, as against 100% of black members. Once again, the implication of race in the prosecutors' choice of questioning cannot be explained away. * * *

In the course of drawing a jury to try a black defendant, 10 of the 11 qualified black venire panel members were peremptorily struck. At least two of them, Fields and Warren, were ostensibly acceptable to prosecutors seeking a death verdict, and Fields was ideal. The prosecutors' chosen race-neutral reasons for the strikes do not hold up and are so far at odds with the evidence that pretext is the fair conclusion, indicating the very discrimination the explanations were meant to deny.

The strikes that drew these incredible explanations occurred in a selection process replete with evidence that the prosecutors were selecting and rejecting potential jurors because of race. At least two of the jury shuffles conducted by the State make no sense except as efforts to delay consideration of black jury panelists to the end of the week, when they might not even be reached. The State has in fact never offered any other explanation. Nor has the State denied that disparate lines of questioning were pursued: 53% of black panelists but only 3% of nonblacks were questioned with a graphic script meant to induce qualms about applying the death penalty (and thus explain a strike), and 100% of blacks but only 27% of nonblacks were subjected to a trick question about the minimum acceptable penalty for murder, meant to induce a disqualifying answer. The State's attempts to explain the prosecutors' questioning of particular witnesses on nonracial grounds fit the evidence less well than the racially discriminatory hypothesis.

If anything more is needed for an undeniable explanation of what was going on, history supplies it. The prosecutors took their cues from a 20–year old manual of tips on jury selection, as shown by their notes of the race of each potential juror. By the time a jury was chosen, the State had peremptorily challenged 12% of qualified nonblack panel members, but eliminated 91% of the black ones.

It blinks reality to deny that the State struck Fields and Warren, included in that 91%, because they were black. The strikes correlate with no fact as well as they correlate with race, and they occurred during a selection infected by shuffling and disparate questioning that race explains better than any race-neutral reason advanced by the State. The State's pretextual positions confirm Miller–El's claim, and the prosecutors' own notes proclaim that the Sparling Manual's emphasis on race was on their minds when they considered every potential juror.

The state court's conclusion that the prosecutors' strikes of Fields and Warren were not racially determined is shown up as wrong to a clear and convincing degree; the state court's conclusion was unreasonable as well as erroneous. The judgment of the Court of Appeals is reversed, and the case is remanded for entry of judgment for petitioner together with orders of appropriate relief.

It is so ordered.

Justice Breyer, concurring.

In *Batson v. Kentucky*, 476 U.S. 79 (1986), the Court adopted a burden-shifting rule designed to ferret out the unconstitutional use of race in jury selection. In his separate opinion, Justice Thurgood Marshall predicted that the Court's rule would not achieve its goal. The only way to "end the racial discrimination that peremptories inject into the jury-selection process," he concluded, was to "eliminat[e] peremptory challenges entirely." Today's case reinforces Justice Marshall's concerns.

To begin with, this case illustrates the practical problems of proof that Justice Marshall described. As the Court's opinion makes clear, Miller–El marshaled extensive evidence of racial bias. But despite the strength of his claim, Miller–El's challenge has resulted in 17 years of largely unsuccessful and protracted litigation—including 8 different judicial proceedings and 8 different judicial opinions, and involving 23 judges, of whom 6 found the *Batson* standard violated and 16 the contrary.

The complexity of this process reflects the difficulty of finding a legal test that will objectively measure the inherently subjective reasons that underlie use of a peremptory challenge. *Batson* seeks to square this circle by (1) requiring defendants to establish a prima facie case of discrimination, (2) asking prosecutors then to offer a race-neutral explanation for their use of the peremptory, and then (3) requiring defendants to prove that the neutral reason offered is pretextual. But *Batson* embodies defects intrinsic to the task.

At *Batson*'s first step, litigants remain free to misuse peremptory challenges as long as the strikes fall below the prima facie threshold level. At *Batson*'s second step, prosecutors need only tender a neutral reason, not a "persuasive, or even plausible" one. *Purkett v. Elem*, 514 U.S. 765 (1995) (per curiam). And most importantly, at step three, *Batson* asks judges to engage in the awkward, sometime hopeless, task of second-guessing a prosecutor's instinctive judgment—the underlying basis for which may be invisible even to the prosecutor exercising the challenge.

Given the inevitably clumsy fit between any objectively measurable standard and the subjective decisionmaking at issue, I am not surprised to find studies and anecdotal reports suggesting that, despite *Batson*, the discriminatory use of peremptory challenges remains a problem.

Practical problems of proof to the side, peremptory challenges seem increasingly anomalous in our judicial system. * * *

[T]he use of race-and gender-based stereotypes in the jury-selection process seems better organized and more systematized than ever before. See, e.g., Post, A Loaded Box of Stereotypes: Despite 'Batson,' Race, Gender Play Big Roles in Jury Selection., Nat. L. J., Apr. 25, 2005, pp. 1, 18 (discussing common reliance on race and gender in jury selection). For example, one jury-selection guide counsels attorneys to perform a "demographic analysis" that assigns numerical points to characteristics such as age, occupation, and marital status—in addition to race as well as gender. See V. Starr & A. McCormick, Jury Selection 193–200 (3d ed. 2001). Thus, in a hypothetical dispute between a white landlord and an African–American tenant, the authors suggest awarding two points to an African–American venire member while subtracting one point from her white counterpart. Id., at 197–199. * * *

These examples reflect a professional effort to fulfill the lawyer's obligation to help his or her client. Nevertheless, the outcome in terms of jury selection is the same as it would be were the motive less benign. And as long as that is so, the law's anti-discrimination command and a peremptory jury-selection system that permits or encourages the use of stereotypes work at cross-purposes.

I recognize that peremptory challenges have a long historical pedigree. They may help to reassure a party of the fairness of the jury. But long ago, Blackstone recognized the peremptory challenge as an "arbitrary and capricious species of [a] challenge." 4 W. Blackstone, Commentaries on the Laws of England 346 (1769). If used to express stereotypical judgments about race, gender, religion, or national origin, peremptory challenges betray the jury's democratic origins and undermine its representative function. See 1 A. de Tocqueville, Democracy in America 287 (H. Reeve transl. 1900) ("[T]he institution of the jury raises the people ... to the bench of judicial authority [and] invests [them] with the direction of society"). * * *

In light of the considerations I have mentioned, I believe it necessary to reconsider *Batson*'s test and the peremptory challenge system as a whole. With that qualification, I join the Court's opinion.

[The dissenting opinion of Justice Thomas, which questions whether Miller–El established racial discrimination, is omitted.]

Notes and Questions

1. After *Miller–El*, it seems clear that not all members of a racial group must be excluded from a jury in order for *Batson* to apply. How would you describe to a colleague the basis of the Court's holding? Which step(s) of the three-step *Batson* analysis is (are) addressed by Justice Souter?

2. If you were a judge contemplating whether a jury selection situation complied with *Batson*, how quantitatively (e.g., percentages of disparity between how groups are treated) or qualitatively (e.g., the methods used which raise an inference of discrimination) parallel with Miller–El would the case have to be?

3. Is the elimination of peremptory challenges raised by Justice Breyer's concurrence the best solution to discrimination problems in jury selection? Concurring justices have endorsed the elimination of peremptory challenges. See, e.g., *Commonwealth v. Maldonado*, 439 Mass. 460, 788 N.E.2d 968 (2003); *People v. Brown*, 97 N.Y.2d 500, 743 N.Y.S.2d 374, 769 N.E.2d 1266 (2002). Would the elimination of peremptory challenges lead to attorneys questioning prospective jurors more strenuously and embarrass them?

4. In *Johnson v. California*, 545 U.S. 162 (2005), the Court held that Batson's first step was not satisfied by merely requiring the objecting party to prove that it is "more likely than not" that the other party's peremptory challenges if unexplained were based on impermissible group bias; the California standard for making a prima facie showing was rejected, and the case was remanded because the trial court failed to demand a neutral explanation for the peremptory strikes after the evidence supported an inference of discrimination.

5. Does *Batson* require the neutral explanation for peremptorily striking a potential juror to be derived from voir dire? Does the neutral explanation have to rise to a level sufficient to satisfy a strike for cause? Most decisions have answered in the negative to each question. A prosecutor may use her own personal knowledge concerning a juror and information supplied from outside sources. The test is not whether the information is true or false; it is whether she has a good-faith belief in the information and whether she can articulate the reason to the trial court in a race-neutral or gender-neutral way which does not violate the defendant's constitutional rights. The trial court then decides whether the prosecutor has acted with a prohibited intent.

6. In *Gilchrist v. Maryland*, 340 Md. 606, 667 A.2d 876 (App.1995), before the jury box was full, each side exercised one peremptory challenge.

After twelve jurors were seated, defense counsel then continue to exercise peremptory challenges as each new prospective juror was seated. All of the peremptory challenges had been used by the defense against white prospective jurors. After the seventh prospective juror was peremptorily challenged by defense counsel, the prosecutor objected, arguing that the defense was attempting to remove all white prospective jurors from the jury in violation of Batson. The following colloquy occurred out of the hearing of the jury. As you read the transcript, consider whether there was a Batson violation? Did the prosecutor establish a prima facie case? Did the trial judge find a prima facie case? Were the explanations given by defense counsel racially neutral? Per Elem, did the trial court "determine[ ] whether the opponent of the strike has carried his burden of proving purposeful discrimination"?

THE COURT: Which juror are you questioning or do you want to go through a reason for each one of them?

ASSISTANT STATE'S ATTORNEY: For each one.

THE COURT: All right. That's seven jurors you've struck. They were all white. Let's go through them one by one and give me the reasons you struck them.

Two of the jurors were challenged by the defendant because they were crime victims, and the other juror was challenged because the defendant was uncomfortable with the way the juror stared at him.

The court found that these were acceptable explanations. The conversation moved on to the other strikes.

DEFENSE COUNSEL: Judge, I personally, by looking at her—I see jurors in the box and I look at the way they relate to each other.

THE COURT: Well, how did she look?

DEFENSE COUNSEL: [S]he reminded me of my Catholic School teacher that I didn't particularly like.... Her look ... at the other people who were in the [jury] box.

DEFENSE COUNSEL: Judge, The next juror was young. I didn't think particularly he would be a strong juror for my case by looking at him.

THE COURT: And why was that?

DEFENSE COUNSEL: Because I look at the way he fits into the persons that are on the panel. And what I'm trying to accomplish from the look of him, from the way he sat—

THE COURT: Well, how did he look from the way he was sitting that made you feel he was not good, other than the fact he was white and young?

DEFENSE COUNSEL: Well, he—number one, most of the jurors would look at my client and look over at the table. He was just like sitting there not relating to anything in the room.

THE COURT: Because he wasn't relating to your client?

DEFENSE COUNSEL: Not relating to anything or anyone in the room. Frankly, I don't think [he] even wanted to be here.

THE COURT: For the next juror?

DEFENSE COUNSEL: Why? He was—I don't have anything written on here.

THE COURT: Let the record reflect he was a young white male in a navy blazer and khaki slacks.

DEFENSE COUNSEL: I believe he was—I remember him, Judge, and ... we say he was unacceptable.

THE COURT: And [why] was that?

DEFENSE COUNSEL: His clothing, his manner.

THE COURT: What was wrong with his clothing and his manner?

DEFENSE COUNSEL: Well, his manner and his clothing suggest to me ... that he wouldn't be able to relate to my client because in this particular case there are—there is the police officer's word against my client's word. My client may very well testify. And because of those things—

THE COURT: Well, how do his clothing have anything to do with it? I don't make the connection.

DEFENSE COUNSEL: The clothing, Judge, means when you go to Brooks Brothers and buy a suit, and maybe not the suit—

THE COURT: The people who go to Brooks Brothers are more likely to believe police than defendants; is that what you're saying?

DEFENSE COUNSEL: Not necessarily so. But given the little information I have about them, I must make judgments about these individuals.

THE COURT: Well, what—well, all right. That's right. So what information did you have ... that required you to strike him?

DEFENSE COUNSEL: ... [H]e's a student. We don't know what he's studying—

THE COURT: Well, we could have asked him.

DEFENSE COUNSEL: Well, some courts don't let you bring them up and ask them.

THE COURT: But you didn't ask.

DEFENSE COUNSEL: He seems rather studious.

THE COURT: Well, so what if he's studious? He's 21 years old.

DEFENSE COUNSEL: Right. He has 16 years of education.

THE COURT: Right.

DEFENSE COUNSEL: That means he's done his college.

THE COURT: Right.

DEFENSE COUNSEL: Those are my reasons.

THE COURT: When you say that someone comes in a navy blazer and khaki slacks, and because he's a student and because of his address that's a reason for striking him—

DEFENSE COUNSEL: I said I don't know anything about his address because I don't know the address. But, Judge, that could have been a black man. Are we saying that black men don't wear blazers and khaki pants?

7. In *Gibson v. State*, 117 S.W.3d 567 (Tex.Ct.App.2003), at the close of jury selection, the following colloquy took place between the trial court and defense counsel:

THE COURT: Now, you have a Batson challenge, [Defense Counsel]. Would you tell me the jurors that you challenge or believe the State struck for racial reasons? I'd like the number only, please, and I will take judicial notice that the Defendant is—the Defendant's race.

DEFENSE COUNSEL: Your Honor, that would go to Juror Number 6 and 11.

THE COURT: Thank you, sir. Will the State give me a race neutral reason why you struck Juror Number 6 . . . ?

PROSECUTOR: Judge, I struck [Juror 6] among other reason because he's a substance abuse counselor.

THE COURT: Okay.

PROSECUTOR: And he told us as much during voir dire.

* * *

PROSECUTOR: Judge, I struck Juror 11 because she had spoken up and said that she would require more than one witness to testify.

THE COURT: All right.

DEFENSE COUNSEL: Your Honor, in response to that, [Juror 7] stated the same thing, that he would need more evidence than one witness though he was not struck by the State.

THE COURT: All right. Can you answer that, please?

PROSECUTOR: I can, Judge. He qualified his answer—And we can go back to the record. But he qualified his record at one point and said, but if there is more evidence I would be okay. And, in fact, there is more evidence in this case. I can't state strongly enough, Judge—I don't want to—We want to give Mr. Gibson a fair trial and if there's anything here that's not fair—

THE COURT: Well, that's what I'm trying to find out. You struck Number 11 for the reason you stated and did not strike Number 7 for the reason you stated; is that correct?

PROSECUTOR: That is correct with the caveat I just added.

THE COURT: Okay, I'm going to deny the Batson challenge. . . . He's given race neutral reasons. Yes, sir.

DEFENSE COUNSEL: Just as a request to clarify your ruling. Their reason for striking [Juror 11], that he needed more evidence and the similar and same reason [Juror 7] was not struck, is that—has he given a sufficient race neutral reason to strike [Juror 11]?

THE COURT: In my judgment he has. They're pre-emptory [sic] challenges and he's given a race neutral reason.

Did the trial court properly deny the defense counsel's Batson challenge?

8. *Swearing and admonishing the jury.* Following selection of the jury and before the trial begins, the jury must be sworn to try the case. The court also should admonish the jurors not to have any communications with each

other or anyone else about the case during the trial, to report any attempted communications to the court, and to refrain from forming or expressing an opinion about the case until it is submitted to the jury. The admonition should be given or referred to every time the court adjourns.

9. *Jury sequestration.* During the trial, sequestration of the jurors generally is within the discretion of the trial court. After the case has been submitted to the jury for deliberation, the jurors may be sequestered unless the parties and the court agree to allow them to separate. A jury is sequestered by placing it in the custody of one or more impartial court officers during any recess of the trial. Although the officers in charge of the jurors have a duty to keep them together, a nominal separation of jurors is not ordinarily grounds for relief. Before he may obtain relief from a violation of the law governing sequestration, the defendant must make a particularized showing that there has at least been a substantial opportunity for improper communications. If a substantial opportunity is established, the prosecution may nevertheless preserve the jury by showing that no impropriety has in fact occurred.

Problems

1. Evaluate the "reasonableness" of the explanation offered for the following peremptory challenges in *Woods v. State*, 675 So.2d 50 (Ala.Crim. App.1995):

A. African–American female struck because her son was charged with burglary.

B. African–American male struck because he was charged with carrying a concealed weapon.

C. White female struck because her stepfather was incarcerated for armed robbery and her husband was charged with burglary.

D. White female struck because her father had been murdered and she indicated that she had been dissatisfied with the prosecution in that case.

E. White female struck because she was single. Does the marital status of the other jurors affect the propriety of this strike?

2. What result when the only African–American on the venire is struck by the prosecutor with a peremptory challenge because "because he absolutely failed to establish eye contact with the State during questioning, and in the State's amateur psychological opinion, seemed not to be possessed of a certain degree of assertiveness which the State prefers to have in jurors." The challenge was upheld in *State v. Jones*, 123 N.M. 73, 934 P.2d 267 (1997).

3. Defense counsel raised a *Batson* objection after the prosecutor used all peremptory strikes to remove men from the jury pool. The trial court then asked the prosecutor to explain the challenges. The prosecutor candidly admitted that he considered gender, but claimed that other factors such as age, education and employment motivated the strikes as well. The trial court announced that the fact that the four strikes were all males does not establish a prima facie case of discrimination and that it accepted the prosecutor's explanation that he had used "other rationales" when making

his strikes. On appeal, as an appellate judge, how would you rule? Did defense counsel establish a prima facie case? If so, did the explanations offered by the prosecutor show what factors related to each juror and how these factors made him believe that each of these jurors should not be on the jury? See *State v. Jagodinsky*, 209 Wis.2d 577, 563 N.W.2d 188 (App.1997) (reversible error for violation of second part of *Batson* analysis).

4. The prosecution exercised two of its three peremptory challenges to dismiss an Asian woman and another woman whose racial identity was not conclusively established in the record but who arguably had an Hispanic surname. When the defendant asked that the State justify using the peremptory strikes, the prosecutor claimed first to be concerned about the Asian's "command of English." As for the second juror, he did not think that the second juror was a minority but believed that she was related to a defendant of the same name that he was currently prosecuting. Was the prosecutor's explanation neutral? Consider the applicability of the following.

In *State v. Bowman*, 945 P.2d 153 (Utah Ct.App.1997), the appellate court stated that an explanation must be: (1) neutral, (2) related to the case being tried, (3) clear and reasonably specific, and (4) legitimate. The legitimacy of the explanation depends upon whether: (1) the alleged group bias was not shown to be shared by the juror in question, (2) failure to examine the juror or perfunctory examination, assuming that no one had questioned the juror, (3) singling the juror out for special questioning was designed to evoke a certain response, (4) the prosecutor's reason is unrelated to the facts of the case, and (5) a challenge based on reasons was equally applicable to juror[s] who were not challenged.

5. If the connection between a case and a proffered reason is tenuous, a court should rule that the reason was a pretext for discrimination. What is the nature of the connection required between the reason offered for a strike and the case on trial? Suppose a prosecutor explains that he struck a juror because rehabilitation for the juror was the primary objective of the criminal justice system. The prosecutor believed therefore that the statement tended to indicate whether the juror was lenient on crime or hard on crime. Was the prosecutor's explanation facially neutral? Was it sufficiently connected to the case on trial? If the trial court implicitly finds that the explanation is credible, how should an appellate court view the trial court's decision to deny the *Batson* challenge? See *Umoja v. State*, 965 S.W.2d 3 (Tex.Ct.App. 1997) (trial judge's rejection of Batson challenge not clearly erroneous).

6. In the trial of a 40–year old man charged with trafficking in marijuana, the prosecution used its challenges to remove two young men. The defense exercised all three of its peremptory challenges, and removed three men (ages 47, 65, and 68). The empaneled jury contained three men (ages 34, 37, and 57); the remaining jurors were women, two of whom were 27 and 28. The defendant raised a *Batson* challenge to the prosecution's two peremptory challenges. What *Batson* argument should defense counsel make? How should the prosecutor respond? See *State v. Taylor*, 142 N.H. 6, 694 A.2d 977 (1997) (no violation).

7. On April 13, the Ku Klux Klan held a rally on the steps of the local courthouse. Although the rally itself occurred without incidents leading to arrests, a member of the Klan, Karl Kody, a 25–year–old unemployed

Caucasian, was arrested for wanton endangerment as he left the gathering when he swung his uniform at a crowd of people who were protesting the Klan's presence. At his jury trial, Karl's attorney, Kalvin Cline, used all three of the defense's available peremptory challenges to remove the following African–Americans from the jury. (Cline's reasons for striking each of the three jurors, though undisclosed to anyone other than Kody at this time, are listed.)

A.   Juror A is Gerald Jones, a 72–year–old retired accountant. Cline felt that Mr. Jones would be antagonistic toward Kody because Kody is unemployed.

B.   Juror B is Victoria Chandler, a 35–year–old garment worker. Cline believed that Ms. Chandler would be hostile toward Kody because of the way he dresses.

C.   Juror C is Stokely Jackson, a 41–year–old salesman who is the President of the local chapter of the NAACP. Cline believed that Jackson would be hostile to Kody because of his political views.

After the defense used its peremptory challenges, no African–American jurors remained on the jury. Prior to swearing in the jurors, is there any motion that you as the prosecutor can present to the judge to question Cline's actions?

Chapter 20

FREEDOM OF THE PRESS
AND FAIR TRIALS

Guarantees of expressive freedom and a fair trial are fundamental to our society, but they do not always coexist harmoniously. In the context of the criminal justice process, freedom of the press may promote or undermine significant societal interests. Media coverage of criminal proceedings promotes self-government by exposing judicial or prosecutorial corruption or incompetence. It may catalyze reform by heightening the public's awareness and understanding of the criminal process. The media's presence and influence also may deter practices inimical to fundamental fairness. Although the press may advance important interest, its presence may be disruptive and may undermine the fairness of the trial process.

A. FAILING TO CONTROL THE PRESS

SHEPPARD v. MAXWELL

384 U.S. 333 (1966).

Mr. Justice Clark delivered the opinion of the Court.

[Marilyn] Sheppard, petitioner's pregnant wife, was bludgeoned to death in the upstairs bedroom of their lakeshore home in Bay Village, Ohio, a suburb of Cleveland. On the day of the tragedy, July 4, 1954, Sheppard pieced together for several local officials the following story: [after dinner] Sheppard became drowsy and dozed off to sleep on a couch. [The] next thing he remembered was hearing his wife cry out in the early morning hours. He hurried upstairs and in the dim light from the hall saw a "form" standing next to his wife's bed. As he struggled with the "form" he was struck on the back of the neck and rendered [unconscious].

From the outset officials focused suspicion on Sheppard. After a search of the house and premises on the morning of the tragedy, Dr. Gerber, the Coroner, is reported—and it is undenied—to have told his men, "Well, it is evident the doctor did this, so let's go get the confession out of him." [On July] 20th, the [press] opened fire with a front-page charge that somebody is "getting away with murder." [The] newspapers emphasized evidence that tended to incriminate Sheppard and pointed out discrepancies in his statements to authorities. At the same time, Sheppard made many public statements to the press and wrote feature articles asserting his innocence. * * *

[The] case came on for trial two weeks before the November general election at which the chief prosecutor was a candidate for common pleas judge and the trial judge, Judge Blythin, was a candidate to succeed himself. Twenty-five days before the case was set, 75 veniremen were called as prospective jurors. All three Cleveland newspapers published the names and addresses of the veniremen. As a consequence, anonymous letters and telephone calls, as well as calls from friends, regarding the impending prosecution were received by all of the prospective jurors. The selection of the jury began on October 18, 1954.

The courtroom in which the trial was held measured 26 by 48 feet. A long temporary table was set up inside the bar, in back of the single counsel table. It ran the width of the courtroom, parallel to the bar railing, with one end less than three feet from the jury box. Approximately 20 representatives of newspapers and wire services were assigned seats at this table by the court. Behind the bar railing there were four rows of benches. These seats were likewise assigned by the court for the entire trial. The first row was occupied by representatives of television and radio stations, and the second and third rows by reporters from out-of-town newspapers and magazines. One side of the last row, which accommodated 14 people, was assigned to Sheppard's family and the other to Marilyn's. The public was permitted to fill vacancies in this row on special passes only. Representatives of the news media also used all the rooms on the courtroom floor, including the room where cases were ordinarily called and assigned for trial Private telephone lines and telegraphic equipment were installed in these rooms so that reports from the trial could be speeded to the papers. Station WSRS was permitted to set up broadcasting facilities on the third floor of the courthouse next door to the jury room, where the jury rested during recesses in the trial and deliberated. Newscasts were made from this room throughout the trial, and while the jury reached its verdict.

On the sidewalk and steps in front of the courthouse, television and newsreel cameras were occasionally used to take motion pictures of the participants in the trial, including the jury and the judge. Indeed, one television broadcast carried a staged interview of the judge as he entered the courthouse. In the corridors outside the courtroom there was a host of photographers and television personnel with flash cameras, portable lights and motion picture cameras. This group photographed the prospective jurors during selection of the jury. After the trial opened, the witnesses, counsel, and jurors were photographed and televised whenever they entered or left the courtroom. Sheppard was brought to the courtroom about 10 minutes before each session began; he was surrounded by reporters and extensively photographed for the newspapers and television. A rule of court prohibited picture-taking in the courtroom during the actual sessions of the court, but no restraints were put on photographers during recesses, which were taken once each morning and afternoon, with a longer period for lunch.

All of these arrangements with the news media and their massive coverage of the trial continued during the entire nine weeks of the trial. The courtroom remained crowded to capacity with representatives of news media. Their movement in and out of the courtroom often caused so much confusion that, despite the loud-speaker system installed in the courtroom, it was difficult for the witnesses and counsel to be heard. Furthermore, the reporters clustered within the bar of the small court-room made confidential talk among Sheppard and his counsel almost impossible during the proceedings. They frequently had to leave the courtroom to obtain privacy. And many times when counsel wished to raise a point with the judge out of the hearing of the jury it was necessary to move to the judge's chambers. Even then, news media representatives so packed the judge's anteroom that counsel could hardly return from the chambers to the courtroom. The reporters vied with each other to find out what counsel and the judge had discussed, and often these matters later appeared in newspapers accessible to the jury. * * *

The jurors themselves were constantly exposed to the news media. Every juror, except one, testified at voir dire to reading about the case in the Cleveland papers or to having heard broadcasts about it. Seven of the 12 jurors who rendered the verdict had one or more Cleveland papers delivered in their home; the remaining jurors were not interrogated on the point. Nor were there questions as to radios or television sets in the jurors' homes, but we must assume that most of them owned such conveniences. As the selection of the jury progressed, individual pictures of prospective members appeared daily. During the trial, pictures of the jury appeared over 40 times in the Cleveland papers alone. The court permitted photographers to take pictures of the jury in the box, and individual pictures of the members in the jury room. One newspaper ran pictures of the jurors at the Sheppard home when they went there to view the scene of the murder. Another paper featured the home life of an alternate juror. The day before the verdict was rendered—while the jurors were at lunch and sequestered by two bailiffs—the jury was separated into two groups to pose for photographs which appeared in the newspapers. * * *

While we cannot say that Sheppard was denied due process by the judge's refusal to take precautions against the influence of pretrial publicity alone, the court's later rulings must be considered against the setting in which the trial was held. In light of this background, we believe that the arrangements made by the judge with the news media caused Sheppard to be deprived of that "judicial serenity and calm to which [he] was entitled." The fact is that bedlam reigned at the courthouse during the trial and newsmen took over practically the entire courtroom, hounding most of the participants in the trial, especially Sheppard. At a temporary table within a few feet of the jury box and counsel table sat some 20 reporters staring at Sheppard and taking notes. The erection of a press table for reporters inside the bar is unprecedented. The bar of the court is reserved for counsel, providing them a safe place in which to keep papers and exhibits, and to confer privately with client and co-counsel. It is designed to protect the witness and the jury from any distractions, intrusions or influences, and to permit bench discussions of the judge's rulings away from the hearing of the public and the jury. Having assigned almost all of the available seats in the courtroom to the news media the judge lost his ability to supervise that environment. * * *

The carnival atmosphere at trial could easily have been avoided since the courtroom and courthouse premises are subject to the control of the court. [T]he presence of the press at judicial proceedings must be limited when it is apparent that the accused might otherwise be prejudiced or disadvantaged. Bearing in mind the massive pretrial publicity, the judge should have adopted stricter rules governing the use of the courtroom by newsmen, as Sheppard's counsel requested. The number of reporters in the courtroom itself could have been limited at the first sign that their presence would disrupt the trial. They certainly should not have been placed inside the bar. Furthermore, the judge should have more closely regulated the conduct of newsmen in the courtroom. For instance, the judge belatedly asked them not to handle and photograph trial exhibits lying on the counsel table during recesses.

Secondly, the court should have insulated the witnesses. All of the newspapers and radio stations apparently interviewed prospective witnesses at will, and in many instances disclosed their testimony. A typical example was the publication of numerous statements by Susan Hayes, before her appearance in court, regarding her love affair with Sheppard. Although the witnesses were barred from the courtroom during the trial the full verbatim testimony was available to them in the press. This completely nullified the judge's imposition of the rule.

Thirdly, the court should have made some effort to control the release of leads, information, and gossip to the press by police officers, witnesses, and the counsel for both sides. * * *

More specifically, the trial court might well have proscribed extrajudicial statements by any lawyer, party, witness, or court official which divulged prejudicial matters, such as the refusal of Sheppard to submit to interrogation or take any lie detector tests; any statement made by Sheppard to officials; the identity of prospective witnesses or their probable testimony; any belief in guilt or innocence; or like statements concerning the merits of the case. [Being] advised of the great public interest in the case, the mass coverage of the press, and the potential prejudicial impact of publicity, the court could also have requested the appropriate city and county officials to promulgate a regulation with respect to dissemination of information about the case by their employees. In addition, reporters who wrote or broadcast prejudicial stories, could have been warned as to the impropriety of publishing material not introduced in the proceedings. * * *

From the cases coming here we note that unfair and prejudicial news comment on pending trials has become increasingly prevalent. Due process requires that the accused receive a trial by an impartial jury free from outside influences. Given the pervasiveness of modern communications and the difficulty of effacing prejudicial publicity from the minds of the jurors, the trial courts must take strong measures to ensure that the balance is never weighed against the accused. And appellate tribunals have the duty to make an independent evaluation of the circumstances. Of course, there is nothing that proscribes the press from reporting events that transpire in the courtroom. But where there is a reasonable likelihood that prejudicial news prior to trial will prevent a fair trial, the judge should continue the case until the threat abates, or transfer it to another county not so permeated with publicity. In addition, sequestration of the jury was something the judge should have raised sua sponte with counsel. If publicity during the proceedings threatens the fairness of the trial, a new trial should be ordered. But we must remember that reversals are but palliatives; the cure lies in those remedial measures that will prevent the prejudice at its inception. The courts must take such steps by rule and regulation that will protect their processes from prejudicial outside interferences. Neither prosecutors, counsel for defense, the accused, witnesses, court staff nor enforcement officers coming under the jurisdiction of the court should be permitted to frustrate its function. Collaboration between counsel and the press as to information affecting the fairness of a criminal trial is not only subject to regulation, but is highly censurable and worthy of disciplinary measures. * * *

[Since] the state trial judge did not fulfill his duty to protect Sheppard from the inherently prejudicial publicity which saturated the community and to control disruptive influences in the courtroom, we must reverse the denial of the habeas petition. The case is remanded to the District Court with instructions to issue the writ and order that Sheppard be released from custody unless the State puts him to its charges again within a reasonable time.

It is so ordered.

B. PRETRIAL PUBLICITY AND DEFENDANT'S RIGHT TO A FAIR TRIAL

1. *Change of Venue*

When potential jurors have read or heard prejudicial publicity, a trial judge should inquire into the nature and extent of the exposure. To prove juror partiality, a juror must show that the publicity either actually prejudiced a juror or pervaded the proceedings that it raised a presumption of inherent prejudice. Recall *Sheppard v. Maxwell*, in which the Court noted that "where there is a reasonable likelihood that prejudicial news prior to trial will prevent a fair trial, the judge should continue the case until the threat abates, or transfer it to another county not so permeated with publicity." During trial, a judge also has broad discretion to sequester the jury and caution the jurors to avoid media accounts of the proceedings.

While a defendant has a right to a state criminal trial in the county of the crime, he or she may desire a trial in another county and may file a motion for a change of venue. The right to request a change of venue belongs to either the defendant or the prosecution. Since venue is largely a creature of statute, statutory procedures should be followed before relief may be granted. On the other hand, a change of venue is a federally protected right which may require the court to overlook statutory procedures in some instances. *Groppi v. Wisconsin*, 400 U.S. 505 (1971). Statutes may permit each party only one application for a change of venue. The application for a change of venue must be timely made or it may be waived.

After an application has been made, the court must determine whether the application establishes a prima facie case for granting a change of venue. If it does not, the application may be denied. If a prima facie showing has been made, the opposing party must then controvert the allegations or the change of venue must be granted. In making its determination the trial court has wide discretion which will not be disturbed if it is supported by sufficient evidence. In many instances the trial judge will defer a decision about the motion until voir dire has indicated whether there is a valid prospect of a fair trial for the defendant. Once in a while, however, circumstances suggest the need to grant the change of venue without the necessity of weighing the nature and extent of awareness about the defendant and the charge.

UNITED STATES v. LINDH

212 F.Supp.2d 541 (E.D.Va.2002).

ELLIS, DISTRICT JUDGE.

John Phillip Walker Lindh ("Lindh") is an American citizen who, according to the ten-count Indictment filed against him in February 2002, joined certain foreign terrorist organizations in Afghanistan and served these organizations there in combat against Northern Alliance and American forces until his capture in November 2001. In seven threshold motions, Lindh sought dismissal of certain counts of the Indictment on a variety of grounds, including lawful combatant immunity and selective prosecution. Lindh also sought dismissal, or alternatively, transfer of venue, arguing that he could not receive a fair trial in this district owing to pre-trial publicity. All motions were denied following extensive briefing and oral argument. Recorded here are the reasons underlying those rulings. * * *

Lindh requests dismissal of the Indictment on the ground that the media attention surrounding this case has been so prejudicial as to deprive him of his Sixth Amendment right to a fair trial. He alternatively requests a transfer of venue to the Northern District of California, the district in which he spent his childhood and where he claims the pre-trial publicity has not been as prejudicial as it has been in this district. Lindh also claims that the Northern District of California is more convenient for the parties and witnesses, pursuant to Rule 21(b), Fed.R.Crim.P.

The principles that govern resolution of this motion are clear and well settled. The Sixth Amendment guarantees that in all criminal prosecutions, the defendant shall enjoy the right to trial "by an impartial jury." In certain extraordinary, circumstances, this fundamental right to trial "by an impartial jury" may be compromised by the presence of pervasive and inflammatory pre-trial publicity. * * * To warrant a dismissal of an indictment on this ground, a defendant must establish that he cannot obtain a fair trial anywhere in the country owing to prejudicial pre-trial publicity. See *United States v. Abbott Laboratories*, 505 F.2d 565, 571 (4th Cir.1974). In other words, dismissal is appropriate only where a defendant establishes that prejudicial pre-trial publicity is "so widespread and pervasive that a change of venue would be ineffective to assure a defendant a fair trial." *Id.* In this regard, it is important to note that "[s]heer volume of publicity alone does not deny a defendant a fair trial." *United States v. Bakker*, 925 F.2d 728, 732 (4th Cir.1991) (citing *Dobbert v. Florida*, 432 U.S. 282 (1977)). * * *

Dismissal of an indictment as a remedy for prejudicial pre-trial publicity is severe and rarely warranted, as it is unlikely that fair and impartial jurors cannot be found in any district. The less severe remedy of transfer is also unwarranted unless a defendant can show that the pre-trial publicity in the district "is so inherently prejudicial that trial proceedings must be presumed to be tainted." *Bakker*, 925 F.2d at 732. * * * Moreover, transfers of venue based on pre-trial publicity are not often granted, as "the effects of pre-trial publicity on the pool from which jurors are drawn is [generally] determined by a careful and searching voir dire examination." *United States v. McVeigh*, 918 F.Supp. 1467 (W.D.Okla.1996). Indeed, "[o]nly where voir dire reveals that an impartial jury cannot be impanelled would a change of venue be justified." *Bakker*, 925 F.2d at 732. In this regard, "it is not required ... that jurors be totally ignorant of the facts and issues involved." *Id.* at 734. Rather, "[i]t is sufficient if the juror can lay aside his impression or opinion and render a verdict based on the evidence presented in court." *Id.*

* * * Put another way, all prospective jurors in this case, as in all cases, will be questioned carefully as to what they have seen or read or heard about the case and whether they have formed any opinions or impressions. No juror will be qualified to serve unless the Court is satisfied that the juror (i) is able to put aside any previously formed opinions or impressions, (ii) is prepared to pay careful and close attention to the evidence as it is presented in the case and finally (iii) is able to render a fair and impartial verdict based solely on the evidence adduced at trial and the Court's instructions of law.

Just as the sheer volume of pre-trial publicity in this case does not compel dismissal or transfer, neither does the nature of that publicity. A review of the parties' submissions on pre-trial publicity relating to this case discloses that the bulk of the publicity is factual, rather than inflammatory, and hence less likely to poison the venire pool. No doubt the publicity in this case also includes some expressions of opinions on newspaper editorial pages or the Internet that were specifically designed to inflame or persuade readers. Yet, on the whole, the record does not warrant a conclusion that prejudicial pre-trial publicity has been so "inherently prejudicial that trial proceedings must be presumed to be tainted" or that Lindh cannot receive a fair trial. And, in any event, the proof of this pudding will be the voir dire results; only those prospective jurors found to be capable of fair and impartial jury service after careful voir dire will be declared eligible to serve as jurors. Past experience provides reasonable assurance that more than a sufficient number of qualified, impartial jurors will be identified as a result of the voir dire in this case.

Nor are Lindh's expert reports—one prepared by Neil Vidmar and the other by Steven Penrod—to the contrary; neither persuasively supports dismissal of the Indictment or transfer to another district. Vidmar developed a survey interview questionnaire to assess the impact of pre-trial publicity in this case. He later supervised the Evans McDonough Company in conducting random telephone interviews of 400 individuals in this district and, for comparison purposes, 200 individuals in Chicago, Minneapolis, San Francisco and Seattle.[1] Penrod, on the other hand, conducted a content analysis of the pre-trial newspaper coverage concerning Lindh and other issues, as reported in the two major newspapers circulated in Alexandria (the Washington Post and the Washington Times) and, for comparison purposes, the two major newspapers circulated in Minneapolis (the Minneapolis Star Tribune and the St. Paul Pioneer Press).[2]

Despite Lindh's arguments to the contrary, the Vidmar report actually supports the conclusion that Lindh is just as likely to receive a

---

1. Among the questions asked of the respondents were (i) what information they know about Lindh; (ii) whether they have a strongly favorable, somewhat favorable, somewhat unfavorable or strongly unfavorable opinion of Lindh; (iii) whether they view Lindh as a terrorist, a traitor, a confused young man or a person on a religious journey; (iv) whether they believe Lindh was involved in the death of CIA agent Spann; (v) whether they believe there is a connection between Lindh and the September 11, 2001 terrorist attacks; (vi) whether they knew someone who was killed or injured in the September 11, 2001 terrorist attacks; (vii) whether they believe Lindh is guilty, probably guilty, probably not guilty or definitely not guilty of the charges against him; (viii) whether they would con-

sider a not guilty verdict very acceptable, acceptable, not acceptable or very unacceptable; (ix) what punishment they believe Lindh should receive if found guilty of the charges against him; and (x) whether they could be fair and impartial if seated as a juror at Lindh's trial.

2. Specifically, the newspaper articles were coded as either favorable or unfavorable toward Lindh on a number of issues, including (i) the personal characteristics of Lindh; (ii) Lindh's connections to the Taliban, al Qaeda and bin Laden; (iii) Lindh's connection to the QIJ prison uprising resulting in the death of CIA agent Spann; (iv) the regional economic and emotional impact of the September 11, 2001 attack on the Pentagon; and (v) the instant charges against Lindh.

fair trial in this district as he is elsewhere in the country. Indeed, Vidmar concludes that "the stated attitudes of jury eligible respondents in Virginia toward Mr. Lindh between April 29 and May 2 did not differ from stated attitudes in the rest of the country." Vidmar Report, p. 22, ¶ 156. Moreover, according to the Vidmar data, approximately three quarters (74%) of the Northern Virginia residents who were polled indicated that they could be fair and impartial if seated as a juror at Lindh's trial. Significantly, this percentage exceeds the corresponding percentage reported by Vidmar for California (68.6%), the jurisdiction to which Lindh seeks a transfer. And, contrary to Lindh's assertions, the fact that a number of the individuals polled in both Virginia and elsewhere knew someone injured or killed in the September 11, 2001 terrorist attacks does not warrant dismissal of the Indictment or a change of venue. Rather, such personal connections to the terrorist attacks are matters adequately addressed and dealt with during the voir dire process.

The Penrod report also does not support dismissal or transfer of the case. Indeed, on more than half the subjects covered by the survey, the Minneapolis newspapers were either harsher in their assessment of Lindh or expressed "unfavorable" opinions to the same extent as did the Alexandria newspapers. Additionally, on those subjects where the Alexandria newspapers were found to be less favorable toward Lindh than the Minneapolis newspapers, the percentages were often so close as to be statistically insignificant. * * * Finally, it is worth noting that Lindh is not entitled to a "favorable" jury, as Penrod appears to suggest; nor is he entitled to a jury that has not been privy to any media reports regarding the instant prosecution, favorable or unfavorable. Rather, what the Sixth Amendment guarantees Lindh, and all criminal defendants, is a fair and impartial jury. Nothing in the studies and data Lindh submitted supports a conclusion that Lindh cannot receive a fair and impartial jury trial in this district.

Lindh's motion to transfer the case to the Northern District of California for purposes of convenience, pursuant to Rule 21(b) is equally unpersuasive. Indeed, contrary to Lindh's contentions, there are multiple reasons for concluding that transfer from this district is inappropriate, including the following: (i) the trial will proceed more expeditiously in this district; (ii) this district is equipped and prepared to cope with the significant security concerns associated with this case; (iii) the prosecution team is comprised largely of attorneys from this district; (iv) the relevant documents are located in this district; (v) the defendant is present in this district, subject to security measures already in place; and (vi) a number of potential witnesses are located in or near this district. Moreover, the fact that four of Lindh's attorneys reside in California rather than in this district is an inconvenience of his own choosing. No claim is made, or can be made, that competent and experienced counsel cannot be found in this district. Of course, Lindh has a Sixth Amendment right to select competent and experienced counsel from another district, which he has done, but he is not entitled to rely on the exercise of that right to effect a change of venue.

In conclusion, it is clear that neither a dismissal of the Indictment nor a transfer of venue is warranted in this case. Specifically, Lindh has failed to meet his burden of establishing that the pre-trial publicity generated in this case, by both the government and the defense, "has been so inflammatory and prejudicial that a fair trial is absolutely precluded and [the] indictment should be dismissed without an initial attempt ... to see if an impartial jury can be impanelled." *Abbott*, 505 F.2d at 571. He has also failed to establish that a transfer of venue based on pre-trial publicity is appropriate, as the publicity involved here is not "so inherently prejudicial that trial proceedings [in this district] must be presumed to be tainted." *Bakker*, 925 F.2d at 732.[15] Nor is a transfer of venue for purposes of convenience warranted under Rule 21(b), Fed. R.Crim.P. Rather, the appropriate course of action in the circumstances is to continue the proceedings in this district and to conduct a thorough voir dire of all potential jurors to ensure the selection of a fair and impartial jury that is able to set aside any pre-conceived notions regarding this case and render an impartial verdict based solely on the evidence presented in the case and the Court's instructions of law.

Notes and Questions

1.   Other factors may support a motion for a change of venue.

a.   The peculiar influence which a trial participant may have in the community may also preclude a fair trial, even if a jury with no actual knowledge of the case could be empaneled.

b.   A state of lawlessness which threatens to erupt into mob violence or which might influence the conduct of the trial may also form the basis for a change of venue.

c.   The need to transfer the defendant to another place for safe-keeping pending trial may require a change of venue. Ultimately, the question remains whether an impartial jury might be had in the community, and neither pretrial publicity nor hostility on the part of some members of the community requires a change of venue if a fair and impartial jury may be empaneled and a fair trial held.

Examine the statutes and case law in your state to learn whether there are additional factors which support a motion for change of venue.

15. This case is easily distinguishable from *United States v. McVeigh*, 918 F.Supp. 1467 (W.D.Okla.1996), where a transfer of venue was ultimately granted based on the impact of defendant's conduct—the bombing of the Murrah Federal Office Building in Oklahoma City—on the particular district in which the case was filed. This unique and extraordinary local impact led the district judge to conclude that "there is so great a prejudice against these two de-fendants in the State of Oklahoma that they cannot obtain a fair and impartial trial at any place fixed by law for holding court in that state." Id. at 1474. Indeed, in *McVeigh*, the very courthouse where the case would have been tried had the case not been transferred suffered collateral damage from the bombing. See id. at 1469. None of the features that motivated transfer in *McVeigh* is present to the same degree in the instant case.

2.   Statutes differ about where a case should be sent if the court grants a motion for a change of venue. For example, if a state court determines that a case should be removed due to emergency conditions, it may transfer the case to any other county in which a fair trial may be held. Or, a statute may provide that, if a court decides to grant a change of venue for any other reason, it must transfer the case to an adjoining county if a fair trial can be held there. If the court finds that a fair trial cannot be had in any adjoining county, the case may then be transferred to the most convenient county in which a fair trial may be had. In your state, where is a judge to transfer a case after granting a change of venue? When media exposure is extensive, is there a strong likelihood that no place exists within a state where a defendant can receive a fair trial?

The court to which a case is removed has the same jurisdiction to dispose of the case as the original court which ordered the transfer. If the indictment is dismissed, the grand jury in the county to which the case has been transferred may thereafter be able to prosecute the action as if the offense had been committed in that county originally. The original court making the transfer has no further jurisdiction to prosecute the action as long as the transfer is in effect.

3.   Although a change of venue is frequently thought of as a contested matter because there is a concern about obtaining a fair trial, the parties may agree to a change where the defendant desires to plead guilty. A somewhat different procedure may exist to transfer the venue to another county for purposes of a plea. The purpose of this latter transfer provision is to permit a defendant to plead guilty in one place based on charges pending in another place. Fed.R.Crim.P. 20 and many corresponding state rules allow a defendant physically located in one place to plead guilty to charges pending in another place.

The federal rule deals with avoiding transportation problems, but there is an added benefit in that a defendant can dispose of multiple cases in a single court. For example, defendants are sometimes charged with multiple crimes, such as bad checks, that occur in several adjacent counties. By appropriate plea negotiations with the various prosecutors involved, the defendant may get a "package deal" on all of his pending charges. In this fashion, a single judge may take the plea and impose sentence in consideration of all the charges. Attorneys who have clients with multi-county charges should consider suggesting to the District Attorney that the transfer provision be utilized to consolidate and dispose of the charges.

The transfer provisions only apply where there is going to be a plea of guilty. If the defendant changes his mind and pleads not guilty, the proceedings are transferred back to the county where the prosecution was initially commenced. When transfer has to be terminated, any statement that the defendant may have made expressing his desire to plead guilty cannot be used against him.

Problems

As a judge, how would you exercise your discretion in the following cases when the defendant(s) move for a change of venue?

1.   Three defendants, all from New York City, were charged in a drug conspiracy in a rural area. One defendant previously was convicted of an informer's girlfriend's death in Vermont state court. Pretrial publicity included local newspaper and television coverage of (1) the defendants' drug arrests, (2) the defendant's prior murder conviction, and (3) the effects of the victim's death on the community. Defendants contended that common knowledge of these events within the venue prevented their fair trial. During voir dire, the court excused any jurors who either (1) knew of defendant's guilty verdict in the earlier trial for murder, or (2) had formed an opinion about the case that prevented their impartial deliberation. The court did not excuse jurors reporting exposure to pre-trial publicity who stated that they could try the case fairly. Defendants further argued that as three black men from New York City, they could not obtain an impartial jury from a largely white population in a rural area. The court inquired whether any of the remaining panel members had beliefs about drugs, firearms, defendants' race, or the fact that defendants hailed from New York City, that would prevent their impartial deliberation; no juror so indicated.

2.   Defendants claimed extensive pretrial publicity. Defendants submitted scores of national and local newspaper and magazine reports about drug-related issues. They also presented radio and television news transcripts describing the growing problem of drug availability for young children. Only about one-third of the articles mentioned the defendants, and those articles were primarily factual in nature, only once referring to confessions given by the defendants.

3.   At the time of his arraignment, defendant moved for a change of venue. The public opinion survey/poll which was filed with the motion indicated that in 100 calls, 98 persons had read or heard about the crime. Eighty-nine of the 100 polled were aware of defendant's name; 73 knew that he had been in prison previously, and 60 were aware of that charge. Ninety-three persons had heard both radio and television stories, some up to at least 100 such reports. Eighty-five considered defendant guilty, while 15 did not respond or stated they did not know. Sixty-five thought he would receive a fair trial in the county.

Defendant renewed his motion during the course of voir dire as prospective jurors gave repeated voice to the community's sentiment that was widespread against him. All potential jurors, save one, had knowledge of the case. Of the 153 or more jurors that were voir dired individually, 112 were excused because they had preconceived opinions about defendant's guilt, could not presume him innocent, or admitted to knowledge of his prior manslaughter conviction. Of 38 jurors who were accepted by the court to comprise the pool from which the trial jury would be selected, 19 had an initial opinion that he was guilty.

2.   *Due Process and Pretrial Publicity*

As you read in *Lindh,* despite concerns about pretrial publicity and juror impartiality, jurors need not be completely ignorant of the facts and issues. A trial judge must assess the jurors' opinions to determine whether the jurors can impartially decide the case. In *Irvin v. Dowd,* 366 U.S. 717 (1961), petitioner was convicted of murder following a trial that was "extensively covered" by the news media and aroused "great excitement and indignation." The trial court granted a change of venue to an adjoining county. The court refused an additional request for change of venue on the basis that Indiana law provided for only a single change of venue. The Court reversed:

> Here the "pattern of deep and bitter prejudice" shown to be present throughout the community was clearly reflected in the sum total of the voir dire examination of a majority of the jurors finally placed in the jury box. Eight out of the 12 thought petitioner was guilty. With such an opinion permeating their minds, it would be difficult to say that each could exclude this preconception of guilt from his deliberations. The influence that lurks in an opinion once formed is so persistent that it unconsciously fights detachment from the mental processes of the average man. Where one's life is at stake—and accounting for the frailties of human nature—we can only say that in the light of the circumstances here the finding of impartiality does not meet constitutional standards. Two-thirds of the jurors had an opinion that petitioner was guilty and were familiar with the material facts and circumstances involved, including the fact that other murders were attributed to him, some going so far as to say that it would take evidence to overcome their belief. One said that he "could [not] give the defendant the benefit of the doubt that he is innocent." Another stated that he had a "somewhat" certain fixed opinion as to petitioner's guilt. No doubt each juror was sincere when he said that he would be fair and impartial to petitioner, but psychological impact requiring such a declaration before one's fellows is often its father. Where so many, so many times, admitted prejudice, such a statement of impartiality can be given little weight. As one of the jurors put it, "You can't forget what you hear and see." With his life at stake, it is not requiring too much that petitioner be tried in an atmosphere undisturbed by so huge a wave of public passion and by a jury other than one in which two-thirds of the members admit, before hearing any testimony, to possessing a belief in his guilt.

MURPHY v. FLORIDA
421 U.S. 794 (1975).

MR. JUSTICE MARSHALL delivered the opinion of the Court.

[Petitioner] was convicted in the Dade County, Fla., Criminal Court in 1970 of breaking and entering a home, while armed, with intent to commit robbery and of assault with intent to commit robbery. [The] robbery and petitioner's arrest received extensive press coverage because petitioner had been much in the news before. He had first made himself notorious for his part in the 1964 theft of the Star of India sapphire from a museum in New York. His flamboyant lifestyle made him a continuing subject of press interest; he was generally referred to—at least in the media—as "Murph the Surf."

The [prior] events [had drawn] extensive press coverage. Each new case against petitioner was considered newsworthy, not only in Dade County but elsewhere as well. The record in this case contains scores of articles reporting on petitioner's trials and tribulations during this period; many purportedly relate statements that petitioner or his attorney made to reporters.

Jury selection in the present case began in August 1970. Seventy-eight jurors were questioned. Of these, 30 were excused for miscellaneous personal reasons; 20 were excused peremptorily by the defense or prosecution; 20 were excused by the court as having prejudged petitioner; and the remaining eight served as the jury and two alternates. Petitioner's motions to dismiss the chosen jurors, on the ground that they were aware that he had previously been convicted of either the 1964 Star of India theft or the Broward County murder, were denied, as was his renewed motion for a change of venue based on allegedly prejudicial pretrial publicity.

Petitioner relies principally upon *Irvin v. Dowd*, 366 U.S. 717 (1961), *Rideau v. Louisiana*, 373 U.S. 723 (1963), *Estes v. Texas*, 381 U.S. 532 (1965), and *Sheppard v. Maxwell*. In each of these cases, this Court overturned a state-court conviction obtained in a trial atmosphere that had been utterly corrupted by press coverage.

In *Irvin v. Dowd* the rural community in which the trial was held had been subjected to a barrage of inflammatory publicity immediately prior to trial, including information on the defendant's prior convictions, his confession to 24 burglaries and six murders including the one for which he was tried, and his unaccepted offer to plead guilty in order to avoid the death sentence. As a result, eight of the 12 jurors had formed an opinion that the defendant was guilty before the trial began; some went "so far as to say that it would take evidence to overcome their belief" in his guilt. In these circumstances, the Court readily found actual prejudice against the petitioner to a degree that rendered a fair trial impossible.

Prejudice was presumed in the circumstances under which the trials in *Rideau*, *Estes*, and *Sheppard* were held. In those cases the influence of the news media, either in the community at large or in the courtroom itself, pervaded the proceedings. In *Rideau* the defendant had "confessed" under police interrogation to the murder of which he stood convicted. A 20–minute film of his confession was broadcast three times by a television station in the community where the crime and the trial took place. In reversing, the Court did not examine the voir dire for evidence of actual prejudice because it considered the trial under review "but a hollow formality"—the real trial had occurred when tens of thousands of people, in a community of 150,000, had seen and heard the defendant admit his guilt before the cameras.

The trial in *Estes* had been conducted in a circus atmosphere, due in large part to the intrusions of the press, which was allowed to sit within the bar of the court and to overrun it with television equipment.

Similarly, *Sheppard* arose from a trial infected not only by a background of extremely inflammatory publicity but also by a courthouse given over to accommodate the public appetite for carnival. The proceedings in these cases were entirely lacking in the solemnity and sobriety to which a defendant is entitled in a system that subscribes to any notion of fairness and rejects the verdict of a mob. They cannot be made to stand for the proposition that juror exposure to information about a state defendant's prior convictions or to news accounts of the crime with which he is charged alone presumptively deprives the defendant of due process. To resolve this case, we must turn, therefore, to any indications in the totality of circumstances that petitioner's trial was not fundamentally fair. * * *

The voir dire in this case indicates no such hostility to petitioner by the jurors who served in his trial as to suggest a partiality that could not be laid aside. Some of the jurors had a vague recollection of the robbery with which petitioner was charged and each had some knowledge of petitioner's past crimes, but none betrayed any belief in the relevance of petitioner's past to the present case. Indeed, four of the six jurors volunteered their views of its irrelevance, and one suggested that people who have been in trouble before are too often singled out for suspicion of each new crime—a predisposition that could only operate in petitioner's favor.

In the entire voir dire transcript furnished to us, there is only one colloquy on which petitioner can base even a colorable claim of partiality by a juror. In response to a leading and hypothetical question, presupposing a two- or three-week presentation of evidence against petitioner and his failure to put on any defense, one juror conceded that his prior impression of petitioner would dispose him to convict. We cannot attach great significance to this statement, however, in light of the leading nature of counsel's questions and the juror's other testimony indicating that he had no deep impression of petitioner at all.

The juror testified that he did not keep up with current events and, in fact, had never heard of petitioner until he arrived in the room for prospective jurors where some veniremen were discussing him. He did not know that petitioner was "a convicted jewel thief" even then; it was petitioner's counsel who informed him of this fact. And he volunteered that petitioner's murder conviction, of which he had just heard, would not be relevant to his guilt or innocence in the present case, since "[w]e are not trying him for murder."

Even these indicia of impartiality might be disregarded in a case where the general atmosphere in the community or courtroom is sufficiently inflammatory, but the circumstances surrounding petitioner's trial are not at all of that variety. Petitioner attempts to portray them as inflammatory by reference to the publicity to which the community was exposed. The District Court found, however, that the news articles concerning petitioner had appeared almost entirely during the period between December 1967 and January 1969, the latter date being seven months before the jury in this case was selected. They were, moreover, largely factual in nature.

The length to which the trial court must go in order to select jurors who appear to be impartial is another factor relevant in evaluating those jurors' assurances of impartiality. In a community where most veniremen will admit to a disqualifying prejudice, the reliability of the others' protestations may be drawn into question; for it is then more probable that they are part of a community deeply hostile to the accused, and more likely that they may unwittingly have been influenced by it. In *Irvin v. Dowd*, for example, the Court noted that 90% of those examined on the point were inclined to believe in the accused's guilt, and the court had excused for this cause 268 of the 430 veniremen. In the present case, by contrast, 20 of the 78 persons questioned were excused because they indicated an opinion as to petitioner's guilt. This may indeed be 20 more than would occur in the trial of a totally obscure person, but it by no means suggests a community with sentiment so poisoned against petitioner as to impeach the indifference of jurors who displayed no animus of their own.

In sum, we are unable to conclude, in the circumstances presented in this case, that petitioner did not receive a fair trial. Petitioner has failed to show that the setting of the trial was inherently prejudicial or that the jury-selection process of which he complains permits an inference of actual prejudice. The judgment of the Court of Appeals must therefore be affirmed.

Judgment affirmed.

MR. CHIEF JUSTICE BURGER, concurring in the judgment.

I agree with Mr. Justice Brennan that the trial judge was woefully remiss in failing to insulate prospective jurors from the bizarre media coverage of this case and in not taking steps to prevent pretrial discussion of the case among them. [I] agree with the Court that the circumstances of petitioner's trial did not rise to the level of a violation of the Due Process Clause of the Fourteenth Amendment.

MR. JUSTICE BRENNAN, dissenting.

[P]etitioner here was denied a fair trial. The risk that taint of widespread publicity regarding his criminal background, known to all members of the jury, infected the jury's deliberations is apparent, the trial court made no attempt to prevent discussion of the case or petitioner's previous criminal exploits among the prospective jurors, and one juror freely admitted that he was predisposed to convict petitioner.

[I] cannot agree with the Court that the obvious bias of this juror may be overlooked simply because the juror's response was occasioned by a "leading and hypothetical question." Indeed, the hypothetical became reality when petitioner chose not to take the stand and offered no evidence. Thus petitioner was tried by a juror predisposed, because of his knowledge of petitioner's previous crimes, to find him guilty of this one.

Others who ultimately served as jurors revealed similar prejudice toward petitioner on voir dire. * * *

Moreover, the Court ignores the crucial significance of the fact that at no time before or during this daily buildup of prejudice against Murphy did the trial judge instruct the prospective jurors not to discuss the case among themselves. Indeed the trial judge took no steps to insulate the jurors from media coverage of the case or from the many news articles that discussed petitioner's last criminal exploits.

It is of no moment that several jurors ultimately testified that they would try to exclude from their deliberations their knowledge of petitioner's past misdeeds and of his community reputation. *Irvin* held in like circumstances that little weight could be attached to such selfserving protestations: No doubt each juror was sincere when he said that he would be fair and impartial to petitioner, but the psychological impact requiring such a declaration before one's fellows is often its father. Where so many, so many times, admitted prejudice, such a statement of impartiality can be given little weight. As one of the jurors put it, "You can't forget what you hear and see."

On the record of this voir dire, therefore, the conclusion is to me inescapable that the attitude of the entire venire toward Murphy reflected the "then current community pattern of thought as indicated by the popular news media," and was infected with the taint of the view that he was a "criminal" guilty of notorious offenses, including that for which he was on trial. It is a plain case, from a review of the entire voir dire, where "the extent and nature of the publicity has caused such a buildup of prejudice that excluding the preconception of guilt from the deliberations would be too difficult for the jury to be honestly found impartial." In my view, the denial of a change of venue was therefore prejudicial error, and I would reverse the conviction.

PATTON v. YOUNT

467 U.S. 1025 (1984).

JUSTICE POWELL delivered the opinion of the Court.

[On] April 28, 1966, the body of Pamela Rimer, an 18–year–old high school student, was found in a wooded area near her home in Luthersburg, Clearfield County, Pa. * * * [Yount was convicted of her murder.]

In January 1981, Yount filed a petition for a writ of habeas corpus in United States District Court. He claimed, inter alia, that his conviction had been obtained in violation of his Sixth and Fourteenth Amendment right to a fair trial by an impartial jury. The case was assigned to a Magistrate, who conducted a hearing and recommended that the petition be granted. The District Court rejected the Magistrate's recommendation. It held that the pretrial publicity was not vicious, excessive, nor officially sponsored, and that the jurors were able to set aside any preconceived notions of guilt. It noted that the percentage of jurors excused for cause was "not remarkable to anyone familiar with the difficulty in selecting a homicide jury in Pennsylvania." * * *

The Court of Appeals for the Third Circuit reversed. The court relied primarily on the analysis set out in *Irvin v. Dowd*, and found that pretrial publicity had made a fair trial impossible in Clearfield County. It independently examined the nature of the publicity surrounding the second trial, the testimony at voir dire of the venire as a whole, and the voir dire testimony of the jurors eventually seated. The publicity revealed Yount's prior conviction for murder, his confession, and his prior plea of temporary insanity, information not admitted into evidence at trial. The voir dire showed that all but 2 of 163 veniremen questioned about the case had heard of it, and that, 126, or 77%, admitted they would carry an opinion into the jury box. This was a higher percentage than in *Irvin*, where 62% of the 430 veniremen were dismissed for cause because they had fixed opinions concerning the petitioner's guilt. Finally, the Court of Appeals found that 8 of the 14 jurors and alternates actually seated admitted that at some time they had formed an opinion as to Yount's guilt. The court thought that many of the jurors had given equivocal responses when asked whether they could set aside these opinions, and that one juror, a Mr. Hrin, and both alternates would have required evidence to overcome their beliefs. The court concluded that "despite their assurances of impartiality, the jurors could not set aside their opinions and render a verdict based solely on the evidence presented."

Judge Garth concurred in the judgment [because] in his view juror Hrin stated at voir dire that he would have required evidence to change his mind about Yount's guilt. This stripped the defendant of the presumption of innocence.

We granted certiorari to consider, in the context of this case, the problem of pervasive media publicity that now arises so frequently in the trial of sensational criminal cases. We reverse the judgment of the Court of Appeals.

As noted, the Court of Appeals rested its decision that the jury was not impartial on this Court's decision in *Irvin*. That decision, a leading one at the time, held that adverse pretrial publicity can create such a presumption of prejudice in a community that the jurors' claims that they can be impartial should not be believed. The Court in *Irvin* reviewed a number of factors in determining whether the totality of the circumstances raised such a presumption. [In] *Irvin*, the Court observed that it was during the six or seven months immediately preceding trial that "a barrage of newspaper headlines, articles, cartoons and pictures was unleashed against [the defendant]." In this case, the extensive adverse publicity and the community's sense of outrage were at their height prior to Yount's first trial in 1966. The jury selection for Yount's second trial, at issue here, did not occur until four years later, at a time when prejudicial publicity was greatly diminished and community sentiment had softened. In these circumstances, we hold that the trial court did not commit manifest error in finding that the jury as a whole was impartial.

The record reveals that in the year and a half from the reversal of the first conviction to the start of the second voir dire each of the two Clearfield County daily newspapers published an average of less than one article per month. More important, many of these were extremely brief announcements of the trial dates and scheduling such as are common in rural newspapers. The transcript of the voir dire contains numerous references to the sparse publicity and minimal public interest prior to the second trial. It is true that during the voir dire the newspapers published articles on an almost daily basis, but these too were purely factual articles generally discussing not the crime or prior prosecution, but the prolonged process of jury selection. In short, the record of publicity in the months preceding, and at the time of, the second trial does not reveal the "barrage of inflammatory publicity immediately prior to trial," amounting to a "huge [wave] of public passion," that the Court found in *Irvin*.

The voir dire testimony revealed that this lapse in time had a profound effect on the community and, more important, on the jury, in softening or effacing opinion. Many veniremen, of course, simply had let the details of the case slip from their minds. In addition, while it is true that a number of jurors and veniremen testified that at one time they had held opinions, for many, time had weakened or eliminated any conviction they had had. The same is true of the testimony of the jurors and veniremen who were seated late in the process and therefore were subjected to some of the articles and broadcasts disseminated daily during the voir dire: the record suggests that their passions had not been inflamed nor their thoughts biased by the publicity.

That time soothes and erases is a perfectly natural phenomenon, familiar to all. Not all members of the venire had put aside earlier prejudice, as the voir dire disclosed. They retained their fixed opinions, and were disqualified. But the testimony suggests that the voir dire resulted in selecting those who had forgotten or would need to be persuaded again.

[The] relevant question is not whether the community remembered the case, but whether the jurors at Yount's trial had such fixed opinions that they could not judge impartially the guilt of the defendant. It is not unusual that one's recollection of the fact that a notorious crime was committed lingers long after the feelings of revulsion that create preju-dice have passed. It would be fruitless to attempt to identify any particular lapse of time that in itself would distinguish the situation that existed in *Irvin*. But it is clear that the passage of time between a first and a second trial can be a highly relevant fact. In the circumstances of this case, we hold that it clearly rebuts any presumption of partiality or prejudice that existed at the time of the initial trial. There was fair, even abundant, support for the trial court's findings that between the two trials of this case there had been "practically no publicity given to this matter through the news media," and that there had not been "any great effect created by any publicity."

* * * The testimony of each of the three challenged jurors is ambiguous and at times contradictory. This is not unusual on voir dire examination, particularly in a highly publicized criminal case. It is well to remember that the lay persons on the panel may never have been subjected to the type of leading questions and cross-examination tactics that frequently are employed, and that were evident in this case. Prospective jurors represent a cross section of the community, and their education and experience vary widely. Also, unlike witnesses, prospective jurors have had no briefing by lawyers prior to taking the stand. Jurors thus cannot be expected invariably to express themselves carefully or even consistently. Every trial judge understands this, and under our system it is that judge who is best situated to determine competency to serve impartially. The trial judge properly may choose to believe those statements that were the most fully articulated or that appeared to have been least influenced by leading.

The voir dire examination of juror Hrin was carefully scrutinized by the state courts and the Federal District Court, as he was challenged for cause and was a member of the jury that convicted the defendant. We think that the trial judge's decision to seat Hrin, despite early ambiguity in his testimony, was confirmed after he initially denied the challenge. Defense counsel sought and obtained permission to resume cross-examination. In response to a question whether Hrin could set his opinion aside before entering the jury box or would need evidence to change his mind, the juror clearly and forthrightly stated: "I think I could enter it [the jury box] with a very open mind. I think I could [very] easily. To say this is a requirement for some of the things you have to do every day." After this categorical answer, defense counsel did not renew their challenge for cause. Similarly, in the case of alternate juror Pyott, we cannot fault the trial judge for crediting her earliest testimony, in which she said that she could put her opinion aside "[i]f [she] had to," rather than the later testimony in which defense counsel persuaded her that logically she would need evidence to discard any opinion she might have. Alternate juror Chincharick's testimony is the most ambiguous, as he appears simply to have answered "yes" to almost any question put to him. It is here that the federal court's deference must operate, for while the cold record arouses some concern, only the trial judge could tell which of these answers was said with the greatest comprehension and certainty.

[We] conclude that the voir dire testimony and the record of publicity do not reveal the kind of "wave of public passion" that would have made a fair trial unlikely by the jury that was empaneled as a whole. We also conclude that the ambiguity in the testimony of the cited jurors who were challenged for cause is insufficient to overcome the presumption of correctness owed to the trial court's findings. We therefore reverse.

It is so ordered.

JUSTICE STEVENS, with whom JUSTICE BRENNAN joins, dissenting.

[The] relevant events all occurred in Clearfield County, Pa., where both Yount and the victim lived. It is a rural county, with a population of about 70,000, served by two newspapers with a combined circulation of about 25,000. Not surprisingly, both newspapers gave front-page coverage to the homicide, the pretrial proceedings, and the trial itself. * * *

The totality of these circumstances convinces me that the trial judge committed manifest error in determining that the jury as a whole was impartial. The trial judge's comment that there was little talk in public about the second trial, is plainly inconsistent with the evidence adduced during the voir dire. Similarly, the trial court's statement that "there was practically no publicity given to this matter through the news media [except] to report that a new trial had been granted by the Supreme Court," simply ignores at least 55 front-page articles that are in the record. Further, the trial judge's statement that "almost all, if not all, [of the first 12] jurors [had] no prior or present fixed opinion," is manifestly erroneous; a review of the record reveals that 5 of the 12 had acknowledged either a prior or a present opinion. The trial judge's "practically no publicity" statement also ignores the first-trial details within the news stories. These included Yount's confessions, testimony, and conviction of rape—all of which were outside of the evidence presented at the second trial. Under these circumstances, I do not believe that the jury was capable of deciding the case solely on the evidence before it. * * *

Notes and Questions

1. Consider the following language from *Irwin v. Dowd, supra*:

[Although] this Court has said that the Fourteenth Amendment does not demand the use of jury trials in a State's criminal procedure, every State has constitutionally provided trial by jury. In essence, the right to jury trial guarantees to the criminally accused a fair trial by a panel of impartial, "indifferent" jurors. The failure to accord an accused a fair hearing violates even the minimal standards of due process. [In] the ultimate analysis, only the jury can strip a man of his liberty or his life. In the language of Lord Coke, a juror must be as "indifferent as he stands unsworn." His verdict must be based upon the evidence developed at the trial. This is true, regardless of the heinousness of the crime charged, the apparent guilt of the offender or the station in life which he [occupies]. "The theory of the law is that a juror who has formed an opinion cannot be impartial." *Reynolds v. United States*, 98 U.S. 145, 155.

It is not required, however, that the jurors be totally ignorant of the facts and issues involved. In these days of swift, widespread and diverse methods of communication, an important case can be expected to arouse the interest of the public in the vicinity, and scarcely any of those best qualified to serve as jurors will not have formed some impression or opinion as to the merits of the case. This is particularly true in criminal cases. To hold that the mere existence of any preconceived notion as to the guilt or innocence of an accused, without more, is sufficient to rebut the presumption of a prospective juror's impartiality would be to establish an impossible standard. It is sufficient if the juror can lay aside his impression or opinion and render a verdict based on the evidence presented in court.

2. When pretrial publicity threatens to prejudice a trial, the trial judge has a duty to ensure that prospective jurors have not formed preconceptions of the defendant's guilt. In *Mu'Min v. Virginia*, 500 U.S. 415 (1991), 8 of the 12 persons sworn as jurors answered on voir dire that they had read or heard something about the case. The defendant argued that his Sixth Amendment right to an impartial jury and his right to due process under the Fourteenth Amendment were violated because the trial judge refused to question further prospective jurors about the specific content of the news reports to which they had been exposed. Citing *Patton v. Yount* and *Irwin v. Dowd*, the Court found that it was sufficient for a trial judge to ask a panel of prospective jurors collectively and in groups of four whether they had formed opinions based on publicity.

3. How is it possible to get an unbiased jury in a case that generates extensive national publicity? Numerous examples abound of cases in which there has been excessive press coverage. Examples include the Rodney King case in which news organizations played videos of the beating over and over to a national and international audience. The O.J. Simpson case received obsessive national attention. Does the fact that both trials resulted in not guilty verdicts suggest that jurors can retain their independence despite extensive press coverage? Do those verdicts suggest that the press may have less impact than we anticipate?

4. The National Broadcasting Company (NBC) plans to air a "docudrama" entitled "The Billionaire Boys Club." The docudrama portrays Joe Bobson planning and committing a murder, and suggests a possible motive for the murder. In addition, the docudrama show Bobson's involvement with a social group referred to as the "Billionaire Boys Club," and portrays "Bobson's personality, activities, and business affairs in ways that further connect him to this murder."

Bobson has already been convicted of murdering one person, and is about to stand trial for the murder depicted in the docudrama. Bobson believes that the film will severely prejudice his right to a fair trial in the second case. In addition, since Bobson's conviction in the first case is on appeal, Bobson worries that the airing of the docudrama will prejudice his right to a fair trial in that case should it be retried.

Suppose that you are Bobson's attorney in the criminal trial. What steps might you to take to ensure Bobson's right to a fair trial?

C. GAG ORDERS

NEBRASKA PRESS ASSOCIATION v. STUART
427 U.S. 539 (1976).

MR. CHIEF JUSTICE BURGER delivered the opinion of the Court.

The respondent State District Judge entered an order restraining the petitioners from publishing or broadcasting accounts of confessions or admission made by the accused or facts "strongly implicative" of the accused in a widely reported murder of six persons. We granted certiorari to decide whether the entry of such an order on the showing made before the state court violated the constitutional guarantee of freedom of the press.

On the evening of October 18, 1975, local police found the six members of the Henry Kellie family murdered in their home in Sutherland, Neb., a town of about 850 people. Police released the description of a suspect, Erwin Charles Simants, to the reporters who had hastened to the scene of the crime. Simants was arrested and arraigned in Lincoln County Court the following morning, ending a tense night for this small rural community.

The crime immediately attracted widespread news coverage, by local, regional, and national newspapers, radio and television stations. Three days after the crime, the County Attorney and Simants' attorney joined in asking the County Court to enter a restrictive order relating to "matters that may or may not be publicly reported or disclosed to the public," because of the "mass coverage by news media" and the "reasonable likelihood of prejudicial news which would make difficult, if not impossible, the impaneling of an impartial jury and tend to prevent a fair trial." The County Court heard oral argument but took no evidence; no attorney for members of the press appeared at this stage. The County Court granted the prosecutor's motion for a restrictive order and entered it the next day, October 22. The order prohibited everyone in attendance from "releas[ing] or authoriz(ing) the release for public dissemination in any form or manner whatsoever any testimony given or evidence adduced"; the order also required members of the press to observe the Nebraska Bar–Press Guidelines.

Simants' preliminary hearing was held the same day, open to the public but subject to the order. The County Court bound over the defendant for trial to the State District Court. The charges, as amended to reflect the autopsy findings, were that Simants had committed the murders in the course of a sexual assault.

Petitioners—several press and broadcast associations, publishers, and individual reporters—moved on October 23 for leave to intervene in the District Court, asking that the restrictive order imposed by the County Court be vacated. The District Court conducted a hearing, at which the County Judge testified and newspaper articles about the *Simants* case were admitted in evidence. The District Judge granted petitioners' motion to intervene and, on October 27, entered his own restrictive order. The judge found "because of the nature of the crimes charged in the complaint that there is a clear and present danger that pre-trial publicity could impinge upon the defendant's right to a fair trial." The order applied only until the jury was impaneled, and specifically prohibited petitioners from reporting five subjects: (1) the existence or contents of a confession Simants had made to law enforcement officers, which had been introduced in open court at arraignment; (2) the fact or nature of statements Simants had made to other persons; (3) the contents of a note he had written the night of the crime; (4) certain aspects of the medical testimony at the preliminary hearing; and (5) the identity of the victims of the alleged sexual assault and the nature of the assault. It also prohibited reporting the exact nature of the restrictive order itself. Like the County Court's order, this order incorporated the Nebraska Bar–Press Guidelines. Finally, the order set out a plan for attendance, seating, and courthouse traffic control during the trial. * * *

The thread running through [earlier] cases is that prior restraints on speech and publication are the most serious and the least tolerable infringement on First Amendment rights. A criminal penalty or a judgment in a defamation case is subject to the whole panoply of protections afforded by deferring the impact of the judgment until all avenues of appellate review have been exhausted. Only after judgment has become final, correct or otherwise, does the law's sanction become fully operative.

A prior restraint, by contrast and by definition, has an immediate and irreversible sanction. If it can be said that a threat of criminal or civil sanctions after publication "chills" speech, prior restraint "freezes" it at least for the time.

The damage can be particularly great when the prior restraint falls upon the communication of news and commentary on current events. Truthful reports of public judicial proceedings have been afforded special protection against subsequent punishment. * * *

We turn now to the record in this case to determine whether, as Learned Hand put it, "the gravity of the 'evil,' discounted by its improbability, justifies such invasion of free speech as is necessary to avoid the danger." To do so, we must examine the evidence before the trial judge when the order was entered to determine (a) the nature and extent of pretrial news coverage; (b) whether other measures would be likely to mitigate the effects of unrestrained pretrial publicity; and (c) how effectively a restraining order would operate to prevent the threatened danger. The precise terms of the restraining order are also important. We must then consider whether the record supports the entry of a prior restraint on publication, one of the most extraordinary remedies known to our [jurisprudence].

Our review of the pretrial record persuades us that the trial judge was justified in concluding that there would be intense and pervasive pretrial publicity concerning this case. He could also reasonably conclude, based on common man experience, that publicity might impair the defendant's right to a fair trial. He did not purport to say more, for he found only "a clear and present danger that pre-trial publicity *could* Impinge upon the defendant's right to a fair trial." (Emphasis added.) His conclusion as to the impact of such publicity on prospective jurors was of necessity speculative, dealing as he was with factors unknown and unknowable.

We find little in the record that goes to another aspect of our task, determining whether measures short of an order retraining all publication would have insured the defendant a fair trial. Although the entry of the order might be read as a judicial determination that other measures would not suffice, the trial court made no express findings to that effect; the Nebraska Supreme Court referred to the issue only by implication.

Most of the alternatives to prior restraint of publication in these circumstances were discussed with obvious approval in *Sheppard v. Maxwell*: (a) change of trial venue to a place less exposed to the intense publicity that seemed imminent in Lincoln County; (b) postponement of the trial to allow public attention to subside; (c) searching questioning of prospective jurors, as Mr. Chief Justice Marshall used in the [Aaron] Burr Case, to screen out those with fixed opinions as to guilt or innocence; (d) the use of emphatic and clear instructions on the sworn duty of each juror to decide the issues only on evidence presented in open court. Sequestration of jurors is, of course, always available. Although that measure insulates jurors only after they are sworn, it also enhances the likelihood of dissipating the impact of pretrial publicity and emphasizes the elements of the jurors' [oaths].

We must also assess the probable efficacy of prior restraint on publication as a workable method of protecting Simants' right to a fair trial, and we cannot ignore the reality of the problems of managing and enforcing pretrial restraining orders. The territorial jurisdiction of the issuing court is limited by concepts of sovereignty. The need for *in personam* jurisdiction also presents an obstacle to a restraining order that applies to publication at large as distinguished from restraining publication within a given [jurisdiction].

Finally, we note that the events disclosed by the record took place in a community of 850 people. It is reasonable to assume that, without any news accounts being printed or broadcast, rumors would travel swiftly by word of mouth. One can only speculate on the accuracy of such reports, given the generative propensities of rumors; they could well be more damaging than reasonably accurate news accounts. But plainly a whole community cannot be restrained from discussing a subject intimately affecting life within it.

Given these practical problems, it is far from clear that prior restraint on publication would have protected Simants' [rights].

Mr. Justice Brennan, with whom Mr. Justice Stewart and Mr. Justice Marshall join, concurring in the judgment.

[The] right to a fair trial by a jury of one's peers is unquestionably one of the most precious and sacred safeguards enshrined in the Bill of Rights. I would hold, however, that resort to prior restraints on the freedom of the press is a constitutionally impermissible method for enforcing that right; judges have at their disposal a broad spectrum of devices for ensuring that fundamental fairness is accorded the accused without necessitating so drastic an incursion on the equally fundamental and salutary constitutional mandate that discussion of public affairs in a free society cannot depend on the preliminary grace of judicial [censors].

Notes and Questions

1. Restraining the press from reporting on judicial proceedings is a method for protecting the defendant's right to a fair trial. Gag orders implicate First Amendment interests. As a preemptive restriction upon expression, such methods trigger the "heavy presumption" that exists against the constitutionality of "any system of prior restraint." *New York Times Co. v. United States*, 403 U.S. 713, 714 (1971) (per curiam). They also impose upon government "a heavy burden [of] justification." Given the constitutional interest that is present, when the goal is ensuring a fair trial, compelling regulatory interests are identifiable at least in the abstract. The Court has established standards allowing gag orders not when risks to fair trial are speculative but only when demonstrable. Even then, prior restraint is permissible only after methods less burdensome to First Amendment interests have been found inapt.

Critics of prior restraint analysis fault the Court for exalting form over forthright factoring of substantive values and risks. *See, e.g.*, James Calvin Jeffries, Jr., *Rethinking Prior Restraint*, 92 YALE L.J. 409 (1983). Methods the Court has identified as less speed restrictions may present unintended risks. Questions have been raised with respect to whether sequestration, especially in lengthy trials, breeds a state of mind that is inimical to fairness. *See, e.g.*, Bernard P. Bell, *Closure of Pretrial Suppression Hearings: Resolving the Free Trial/Free Press Conflict*, 51 FORDHAM L. REV. 1297, 1315 (1983) (noting costs and burdens of sequestration and potential for causing "juror resentment"). Even if the formalities of prior restraint were subtracted from the analysis, it is reasonable to assume that review still would be probing. Because profound interests of self-governance vie against fair trial concerns, as they do when access to a criminal proceeding is at issue, logic ordains that review be no less searching than when closure is at stake.

2. Did *Nebraska Press* strike the right balance? In a number of other countries (England and Canada), the courts restrict press coverage of pending criminal matters through the contempt power. *See* GEOFFREY ROBERTSON & ANDREW G.L. NICOL, MEDIA LAW: THE RIGHTS OF JOURNALISTS AND BROADCASTERS 161–85 (3d ed. 1992); *see also* David A. Anderson, *Democracy and the Demistification of Courts: An Essay*, REV. LITIG. 627, 639 (1995). Should U.S. courts be equally free to restrict such coverage?

D. PRESS ACCESS TO JUDICIAL PROCEEDINGS

Even though the courts cannot prohibit the press from reporting on a trial, must the courts give the press access to the proceeding? Trials themselves historically have been open to the press and public, and the Court has established a presumption in favor of access. *Globe Newspaper Co. v. Superior Court*, 457 U.S. 596 (1982). Tradition, however, has not always cut in favor of open preliminary proceedings. In *Gannett, Inc. v. DePasquale*, 443 U.S. 368 (1979), the Court upheld a trial judge's order closing a suppression hearing at the defendant's request. The outcome in *Gannett* reflected an understanding that the Sixth Amendment guarantee of a public trial accrued not to the press or public but to the defendant. The decision's bottom line was that the Sixth Amendment established no constitutional right for the press or public to attend a criminal trial. The determination rested on the premise "that the public interest is fully protected by the participants in the litigation."

One year after *Gannett*, a defendant's motion to close a trial was defeated by First Amendment concerns. In *Richmond Newspapers, Inc. v. Virginia*, 448 U.S. 555 (1980), opinions by eight justices endorsed the notion of an access right for the press and public even over the defendant's objections. Chief Justice Burger, stressing the presumptive openness of criminal trials, observed that the right to attend such proceedings "is implicit in guarantees of the First Amendment; without the freedom to attend such trials, which people have exercised for centuries, important aspects of freedom of speech and of the press could be eviscerated." Consistent with established First Amendment doctrine, access to trials was configured coextensively for the press and public.

GLOBE NEWSPAPER CO. v. SUPERIOR COURT
457 U.S. 596 (1982).

JUSTICE BRENNAN delivered the opinion of the Court.

Section 16A of Chapter 278 of the Massachusetts General Laws, as construed by the Massachusetts Supreme Judicial Court, requires trial judges, at trials for specific sexual offenses involving a victim under the age of 18, to exclude the press and general public from the courtroom during the testimony of that victim. The question presented is whether the statute thus construed violates the First Amendment as applied to the States through the Fourteenth Amendment.

The Court's recent decision in *Richmond Newspapers* firmly established for the first time that the press and general public have a constitutional right of access to criminal [trials].

Of course, this right of access to criminal trials is not explicitly mentioned in terms in the First Amendment. But we have long eschewed any "narrow, literal conception" of the Amendment's terms, for the Framers were concerned with broad principles, and wrote against a background of shared values and practices. The First Amendment is thus broad enough to encompass those rights that, while not unambiguously enumerated in the very terms of the Amendment, are nonetheless necessary to the enjoyment of other First Amendment [rights].

[Thus] to the extent that the First Amendment embraces a right of access to criminal trials, it is to ensure that this constitutionally protected "discussion of governmental affairs" is an informed one.

Two features of the criminal justice system, emphasized in the various opinions in *Richmond Newspapers*, together serve to explain why a right of access to criminal trials in particular is properly afforded protection by the First Amendment. First, the criminal trial historically has been open to the press and general public. "[A]t the time when our organic laws were adopted, criminal trials both here and in England had long been presumptively open." And since that time, the presumption of openness has remained secure. Indeed, at the time of this Court's decision in *In re Oliver*, the presumption was so solidly grounded that the Court was "unable to find a single instance of a criminal trial conducted in camera in any federal, state, or municipal court during the history of this country." This uniform rule of openness has been viewed as significant in constitutional terms not only "because the Constitution carries the gloss of history," but also because "a tradition of accessibility implies the favorable judgment of experience."

Second, the right of access to criminal trials plays a particularly significant role in the functioning of the judicial process and the government as a whole. Public scrutiny of a criminal trial enhances the quality and safeguards the integrity of the factfinding process, with benefits to both the defendant and to society as a whole. Moreover, public access to the criminal trial fosters an appearance of fairness, thereby heightening public respect for the judicial process. And in the broadest terms, public access to criminal trials permits the public to participate in and serve as a check upon the judicial process—an essential component in our structure of self-government. In sum, the institutional value of the open criminal trial is recognized in both logic and experience.

Although the right of access to criminal trials is of constitutional stature, it is not absolute. But the circumstances under which the press and public can be barred from a criminal trial are limited; the State's justification in denying access must be a weighty one. Where, as in the present case, the State attempts to deny the right of access in order to inhibit the disclosure of sensitive information, it must be shown that the denial is necessitated by a compelling governmental interest, and is narrowly tailored to serve that [interest].

The state interests asserted to support § 16A, though articulated in various ways, are reducible to two: the protection of minor victims of sex crimes from further trauma and embarrassment; and the encouragement of such victims to come forward and testify in a truthful and credible manner. We consider these interests in turn.

We agree with appellee that the first interest—safeguarding the physical and psychological well-being of a minor—is a compelling one. But as compelling as that interest is, it does not justify a *mandatory* closure rule, for it is clear that the circumstances of the particular case may affect the significance of the interest. A trial court can determine on a case-by-case basis whether closure is necessary to protect the welfare of a minor victim. Among the factors to be weighed are the minor victim's age, psychological maturity and understanding, the nature of the crime, the desires of the victim, and the interests of parents and relatives. Section 16A, in contrast, requires closure even if the victim does not seek the exclusion of the press and general public and would not suffer injury by their [presence].

Nor can § 16A be justified on the basis of the Commonwealth's second asserted interest—the encouragement of minor victims of sex crimes to come forward and provide accurate testimony. The Commonwealth has offered no empirical support for the claim that the rule of automatic closure contained in § 16A bars the press and general public from the courtroom during the testimony of minor sex victims, the press is not denied access to the transcript, court personnel, or another possible source that could provide an account of the minor victim's testimony. Thus § 16A cannot prevent the press from publicizing the substance of a minor victim's testimony, as well as his or her identity. If the commonwealth's interest in encouraging minor victim's to come forward depends on keeping such matters secret, § 16A hardly advances that interest in an effective manner. And even if § 16A effectively advanced the State's interest, it is doubtful that the interest would be sufficient to overcome the constitutional attack, for that same interest could be relied on to support an array of mandatory closure rules designed to encourage victims to come forward: Surely it cannot be suggested that minor victims of sex crimes are the *only* crime victims who, because of publicity attendant to criminal trials, are reluctant to come forward and testify. The State's argument based on this interest therefore proves too much, and runs contrary to the very foundation of the right of access recognized in *Richmond Newspapers*: namely, "that a presumption of openness inheres in the very nature of a criminal trial under our system of justice." (plurality opinion).

For the foregoing reasons, we hold that § 16A, as construed by the Massachusetts Supreme Judicial Court, violates the First Amendment to the Constitution. Accordingly, the judgment of the Massachusetts Supreme Judicial Court is *Reversed*.

CHIEF JUSTICE BURGER, with whom JUSTICE REHNQUIST joins, dissenting.

Historically our society has gone to great lengths to protect minors *charged* with crime, particularly by prohibiting the release of the names of offenders, barring the press and public from juvenile proceedings, and sealing the records of those proceedings. Yet today the Court holds unconstitutional a state statute designed to protect not the *accused*, but the minor *victims* of sex crimes. In doing so, it advances a disturbing paradox. Although states are permitted, for example, to mandate the closure of all proceedings in order to protect a 17–year–old charged with rape, they are not permitted to require the closing of part of criminal proceedings in order to protect an innocent child who has been raped or otherwise sexually abused.

The Court has tried to make its holding a narrow one by not disturbing the authority of state legislatures to enact more narrowly drawn statutes giving trial judges the discretion to exclude the public and the press from the courtroom during the minor victim's testimony.

I also do not read the Court's opinion as foreclosing a state statute which mandates closure except in cases where the victim agrees to testify in open court. But the Court's decision is nevertheless a gross invasion of state authority and a state's duty to protect its citizens—in this case minor victims of crime. I cannot agree with the Court's expansive interpretation of our decision in *Richmond Newspapers, Inc. v. Virginia*, or its cavalier rejection of the serious interests supporting Massachusetts' mandatory closure rule. Accordingly, I dissent.

PRESS–ENTERPRISE CO. v. SUPERIOR COURT

478 U.S. 1 (1986).

CHIEF JUSTICE BURGER delivered the opinion of the Court.

[The] right to an open public trial is a shared right of the accused and the public, the common concern being the assurance of fairness. Only recently, in *Waller v. Georgia*, for example, we considered whether the defendant's Sixth Amendment right to an open trial prevented the closure of a suppression hearing over the defendant's objection. We noted that the First Amendment right of access would in most instances attach to such proceedings and that "the explicit Sixth Amendment right of the accused is no less protective of a public trial than the implicit First Amendment right of the press and public." When the defendant objects to the closure of a suppression hearing, therefore, the hearing must be open unless the party seeking to close the hearing advances an overriding interest that is likely to be prejudiced.

Here, unlike *Waller*, the right asserted is not the defendant's Sixth Amendment right to a public trial since the defendant requested a *closed* preliminary hearing. Instead, the right asserted here is that of the public under the First Amendment. The California Supreme Court concluded that the First Amendment was not implicated because the proceeding was not a criminal trial, but a preliminary hearing. However, the First Amendment question cannot be resolved solely on the label we give the event, *i.e.*, "trial" or otherwise, particularly where the preliminary hearing functions much like a full-scale [trial]. * * *

In California, to bring a felon to trial, the prosecutor has a choice of securing a grand jury indictment or a finding of probable cause following a preliminary hearing. Even when the accused has been indicted by a grand jury, however, he has an absolute right to an elaborate preliminary hearing before a neutral magistrate. The accused has the right to personally appear at the hearing, to be represented by counsel, to cross-examine hostile witnesses, to present exculpatory evidence, and to exclude illegally obtained evidence. If the magistrate determines that probable cause exists, the accused is bound over for trial; such a finding leads to a guilty plea in the majority of cases.

It is true that unlike a criminal trial, the California preliminary hearing cannot result in the conviction of the accused and the adjudication is before a magistrate or other judicial officer without a jury. But these features, standing alone, do not make public access any less essential to the proper functioning of the proceedings in the overall criminal justice process. Because of its extensive scope, the preliminary hearing is often the final and most important step in the criminal proceeding. As the California Supreme Court [has] stated the preliminary hearing in many cases provides "the sole occasion for public observation of the criminal justice system."

Similarly, the absence of a jury, long recognized as "an inestimable safeguard against the corrupt or overzealous prosecutor and against the complaint, biased, or eccentric judge," makes the importance of public access to a preliminary hearing even more significant. "People in an open society do not demand infallibility from their institutions, but it is difficult for them to accept what they are prohibited from observing."

Denying the transcript of a 41–day preliminary hearing would frustrate what we have characterized as the "community therapeutic value" of openness. Criminal acts, especially certain violent crimes, provoke public concern, outrage, and hostility. "When the public is aware that the law is being enforced and the criminal justice system is functioning, an outlet is provided for these understandable reactions and emotions." In sum:

> The value of openness lies in the fact that people not actually attending trials can have confidence that standards of fairness are being observed; the sure knowledge that anyone is free to attend gives assurance that established procedures are being followed and that deviations will become known. Openness thus enhances both the basic fairness of the criminal trial and the appearance of fairness so essential to public confidence in the system. *Press–Enterprise I, supra,* at 508 (emphasis in original).

We therefore conclude that the qualified First Amendment right of access to criminal proceedings applies to preliminary hearings as they are conducted in California.

Notes

1. Modern First Amendment doctrine has established that media have no special status or priority in accessing proceedings or information. This premise is consistent with determinations that the press has no special privilege, rooted in the First Amendment, against having to disclose sources when asked to identify them in grand jury proceedings. The Court, in *Branzburg v. Hayes,* 408 U.S. 665, 688 (1972) (plurality opinion), not only stressed that the grand jury has the " 'right to everyman's evidence" but

repudiated the notion that the media's role as the public's proxy would be undermined if confidentiality of sources was not protected. Although the newsgathering function may be perceived as essential to effective functioning of the press, insofar as it facilitates enhanced public knowledge and understanding, the Court has been loathe to develop penumbras of press freedom that might be the equivalent of what freedom of association is to freedom of speech.

Consistent with its refusal to protect functions that arguably advance the aims of press freedom in the grand jury context, the Court has resisted arguments for recognizing media access rights in various criminal justice venues and processes. Although acknowledging that freedom of the press is crucial to informed self-government, it has brooked no distinction between press and public when access to facilities or proceedings is at stake. Questions of access have arisen most notably in the context of prisons, pretrial proceedings and trials. The common constitutional denominator in each of those settings is a refusal to set separate standards for the press and public.

2. Nevertheless, *Press–Enterprise* emphasized the tradition of open preliminary hearings and their similarity to trials in the state. The relevance of First Amendment priorities thus was referenced not to national norms, as was the case with trials, but to a particular state's custom. At least when the nature and traditions of a preliminary hearing are congruent with a trial, it is predictable that First Amendment values will be a dominant factor. Justice Stevens criticized the ruling as inconsistent with *Gannett's* determination that the press and public have no First Amendment right to attend pretrial proceedings.

Closure of pretrial hearings under *Press–Enterprise* is justifiable only if "specific findings are made [that] there is a substantial probability that the defendant's right to a fair trial will be prejudiced by publicity that closure would prevent, [and] reasonable alternatives to closure cannot adequately protect the defendant's free trial rights." Even if those standards were satisfied and proceedings were closed, First Amendment interests would not vanish. As the *Gannett* Court itself indicated, the judge must provide a transcript of the proceeding when the risk of prejudice abates. *Gannett Co., Inc. v. DePasquale*, 443 U.S. 368, 393 (1979).

3. Once trumpeted, the values supporting open trials invariably were drawn upon to exert pressure against the logic of *Gannett* in the pretrial context. Several decisions over the course of the 1980s significantly broadened the scope of access in pretrial proceedings. In *Press–Enterprise Co. v. Superior Court (I)*, the Court extended the First Amendment zone of interest to include voir dire. *Press–Enterprise Co. v. Superior Court*, 464 U.S. 501, 505–10 (1984). Finding that jury selection in criminal trials was presumptively open, the Court stressed the public interest in openness referenced in *Globe Newspaper* and *Richmond Newspapers*. Consistent with those decisions, it also noted that the presumption against closure could be overcome only by a higher interest and narrowly tailored method.

E.   BROADCASTING LEGAL PROCEEDINGS

The right of access to trials and pretrial hearings does not incorporate any freedom for the media to use a particular technology to cover such proceedings. To the contrary, even as cameras and other electronic instrumentalities have become increasingly common in state courts, the judiciary still exercises considerable control over the extent (if any) to which they may be used.

Cameras in the courtroom have become a staple in state courts but, except for some experimentation in the civil context, have been disallowed at the federal level. The Judicial Conference, after overseeing an experiment with cameras in six federal districts and two courts of appeals, voted to maintain a policy against their presence. The Conference's report is set forth in M. Johnson, Federal Judicial Center, *Electronic Media Coverage of Federal Civil Proceedings, An Evaluation of the Pilot Program in Six District Courts and Two Courts of Appeals* (1994). In *Estes v. Texas*, 381 U.S. 532, 542 (1965) a plurality of the Court concluded that televised proceedings entail "such a probability that prejudice will result that it is deemed inherently lacking in due process." Justice Harlan in a concurring opinion, stressed the need for adaptability in the event future circumstances warranted it. As he put it

> [Permitting] television in the courtroom undeniably has mischievous potentialities for intruding upon the detached atmosphere which should always surround the judicial process. Forbidding this innovation, however, would doubtless impinge upon one of the valued attributes of our federalism by preventing the States from pursuing a novel course of procedural experimentation. My conclusion is that there is no constitutional requirement that television be allowed in the courtroom, and, at least as to a notorious criminal trial such as this one, the considerations against allowing television in the courtroom so far outweigh the countervailing factors advanced in its support as to require a holding that what was done in this case infringed the fundamental right to a fair trial assured by the Due Process Clause of the Fourteenth Amendment.

> Some preliminary observations are in order: All would agree, I am sure, that at its worst, television is capable of distorting the trial process so as to deprive it of fundamental fairness. Cables, kleig lights, interviews with the principal participants, commentary on their performances, "commercials" at frequent intervals, special wearing apparel and makeup for the trial participants—certainly such things would not conduce to the sound administration of justice by any acceptable [standard].

As technology reinvented the electronic instrumentalities of trial coverage, so that intrusiveness and distraction were diminished, case law veered in the direction of Justice Harlan's concurring opinion. Responding to liberalized provisions for electronic coverage of judicial proceedings, the Court in *Chandler v. Florida* repudiated the notion that camera in the courtroom per se offended due process.

CHANDLER v. FLORIDA

449 U.S. 560 (1981).

CHIEF JUSTICE BURGER delivered the opinion of the Court.

The question presented on this appeal is whether, consistent with constitutional guarantees, a state may provide for radio, television, and still photographic coverage of a criminal trial for public broadcast, notwithstanding the objection of the accused.

[T]he Florida Supreme Court concluded "that on balance there [was] more to be gained than lost by permitting electronic media coverage of judicial proceedings subject to standards for such coverage." The Florida court was of the view that because of the significant effect of the courts on the day-to-day lives of the citizenry, it was essential that the people have confidence in the process. It felt that broadcast coverage of trials would contribute to wider public acceptance and understanding of decisions. Consequently, after revising the 1977 guidelines to reflect its evaluation of the pilot program, the Florida Supreme Court promulgated a revised Canon 3A(7). The Canon provides:

> "Subject at all times to the authority of the presiding judge to (I) control the conduct of proceedings before the court, (ii) ensure decorum and prevent distractions, and (iii) ensure the fair administration of justice in the pending cause, electronic media and still photography coverage of public judicial proceedings in the appellate and trial courts of this state shall be allowed in accordance with standards of conduct and technology promulgated by the Supreme Court of Florida." * * *

The implementing guidelines specify in detail the kind of electronic equipment to be used and the manner of its use. For example, no more than one television camera and only one camera technician are allowed. Existing recording systems used by court reporters are used by broadcasters for audio pickup. Where more than one broadcast news organization seeks to cover a trial, the media must pool coverage. No artificial lighting is allowed. The equipment is positioned in a fixed location, and it may not be moved during trial. Videotaping equipment must be remote from the courtroom. Film, videotape, and lenses may not be changed while the court is in session. No audio recording of conferences between lawyers, between parties and counsel, or at the bench is permitted. The judge has sole and plenary discretion to exclude coverage of certain witnesses, and the jury may not be filmed. The judge has discretionary power to forbid coverage whenever satisfied that coverage may have a deleterious effect on the paramount right of the defendant to a fair trial. The Florida Supreme Court has the right to revise these rules as experience dictates, or indeed to bar all broadcast coverage or photography in courtrooms.

Appellants rely chiefly on *Estes v. Texas*, and Chief Justice Warren's separate concurring opinion in that case. They argue that the televising of criminal trials is inherently a denial of due process, and they read *Estes* as announcing a *per se* constitutional rule to that effect.

Chief Justice Warren's concurring opinion, in which he was joined by Justices Douglas and Goldberg, indeed provides some support for the appellants' position:

> "While I join the Court's opinion and agree that the televising of criminal trials is inherently a denial of due process, I desire to express additional views on why this is so. In doing this, I wish to emphasize that our condemnation of televised criminal trials is not based on generalities or abstract fears. The record in this case presents a vivid illustration of the inherent prejudice of televised criminal trials and supports our conclusion that this is the appropriate time to make a definitive appraisal of television in the courtroom."

If appellants' reading of *Estes* were correct, we would be obliged to apply that holding and reverse the judgment under [review]. * * *

Justice Harlan's [concurring] opinion, upon which analysis of the constitutional holding of *Estes* turns, must be read as defining the scope of that holding; we conclude that *Estes* is not to be read as announcing a constitutional rule barring still photographic, radio, and television coverage in all cases and under all circumstances. It does not stand as an absolute ban on state experimentation with an evolving technology, which, in terms of modes of mass communication, was in its relative infancy in 1964, and is, even now, in a state of continuing change.

Since we are satisfied that *Estes* did not announce a constitutional rule that all photographic or broadcast coverage of criminal trials is inherently a denial of due process, we turn to consideration, as a matter of first impression, of the appellants' suggestion that we now promulgate such a *per se* [rule].

Not unimportant to the position asserted by Florida and other states is the change in television technology since 1962, when Estes was tried. It is urged, and some empirical data are presented, that many of the negative factors found in *Estes*—cumbersome equipment, cables, distracting lighting, numerous camera technicians—are less substantial factors today than they were at that time.

It is also significant that safeguards have been built into the experimental programs in state courts, and into the Florida program, to avoid some of the most egregious problems envisioned by the six opinions in the *Estes* case. Florida admonishes its courts to take special pains to protect certain witnesses—for example, children, victims of sex crimes, some informants, and even the very timid witness or party—from the glare of publicity and the tensions of being "on camera."

[Inherent] in electronic coverage of a trial is a risk that the very awareness by the accused of the coverage and the contemplated broadcast may adversely affect the conduct of the participants and the fairness of the trial, yet leave no evidence of how the conduct or the trial's fairness was affected. Given this danger, it is significant that Florida requires that objections of the accused to coverage be heard and considered on the record by the trial court. In addition to providing a record for appellate review, a pretrial hearing enables a defendant to advance the basis of his objection to broadcast coverage and allows the trial court to define the steps necessary to minimize or eliminate the risks of prejudice to the accused. Experiments such as the one presented here may well increase the number of appeals by adding a new basis for claims to reverse, but this is a risk Florida has chosen to take after preliminary experimentation. Here, the record does not indicate that appellants requested an evidentiary hearing to show adverse impact or injury. Nor does the record reveal anything more than generalized allegations of [prejudice].

To say that the appellants have not demonstrated that broadcast coverage is inherently a denial of due process is not to say that the appellants were in fact accorded all of the protections of due process in their trial. As noted earlier, a defendant has the right on review to show that the media's coverage of his case—printed or broadcast—compromised the ability of the jury to judge him fairly. Alternatively, a defendant might show that broadcast coverage of his particular case had an adverse impact on the trial participants sufficient to constitute a denial of due process. Neither showing was made in this case.

To demonstrate prejudice in a specific case a defendant must show something more than juror awareness that the trial is such as to attract the attention of broadcasters. No doubt the very presence of a camera in the courtroom made the jurors aware that the trial was thought to be of sufficient interest to the public to warrant coverage. Jurors, forbidden to watch all broadcasts, would have had no way of knowing that only fleeting seconds of the proceeding would be reproduced. But the appellants have not attempted to show with any specificity that the presence of cameras impaired the ability of the jurors to decide the case on only the evidence before them or that their trial was affected adversely by the impact on any of the participants of the presence of cameras and the prospect of broadcast.

Although not essential to our holding, we note that at *voir dire*, the jurors were asked if the presence of the camera would in any way compromise their ability to consider the case. Each answered that the camera would not prevent him or her from considering the case solely on the merits. The trial court instructed the jurors not to watch television accounts of the trial, and the appellants do not contend that any juror violated this instruction. The appellants have offered no evidence that any participant in this case was affected by the presence of cameras. In short, there is no showing that the trial was compromised by television coverage, as was the case in *Estes*.

Notes

1. Since *Chandler*, and notwithstanding federal repudiation of cameras following an experimentation period from 1991–94, electronic coverage has

become a common factor in state proceedings. At least 47 states allow cameras in their courtrooms.

2.   Despite upholding broadcast and photographic coverage of criminal proceedings in a state court, Federal Rule of Criminal Procedure 53 states that such activity "shall not be permitted" in federal courtrooms. In *United States v. Moussaoui*, 205 F.R.D. 183 (E.D.Va. 2002), Court TV unsuccessfully sought to intervene in order to record and telecast the pretrial and trial proceedings.

> The words "shall not be permitted" make clear that this rule is mandatory, leaving the Court with no discretion to ignore the categorical ban. Nor can Rule 53 be rewritten or finessed through technical hairsplitting. * * *

> Advances in broadcast technology . . . have . . . created new threats to the integrity of the fact finding process. The traditional public spectator or media representative who attends a federal criminal trial leaves the courtroom with his or her memory of the proceedings and any notes he or she may have taken. These spectators do not leave with a permanent photograph. However, once a witness' testimony has been televised, the witness' face has not just been publicly observed, it has also become eligible for preservation by VCR or DVD recording, digitizing by the new generation of cameras or permanent placement on Internet web sites and chat rooms. Today, it is not so much the small, discrete cameras or microphones in the courtroom that are likely to intimidate witnesses, rather, it is the witness' knowledge that his or her face or voice may be forever publicly known and available to anyone in the world.

> As the United States argues, this intimidation could lead foreign prosecution witnesses, outside the jurisdiction of the Court, to refuse to testify or withhold their full testimony out of reasonable fears for their personal safety. It could similarly lead witnesses favorable to the defense to refrain from coming forward for fear of being ostracized. The permanent preservation of images of law enforcement witnesses could also jeopardize their future careers or personal safety. How could an agent whose face was known throughout the world ever be able to work undercover or interview witnesses on the street effectively?

> Knowledge that the proceedings were being broadcast may also intimidate jurors. Excluding cameras and other recording devices from the courtroom will help preserve the anonymity of the jurors who are selected to serve and minimize the potential for a "popular verdict." * * *

Chapter 21

SENTENCING

Ordinarily it is a relatively simple matter to ascertain a client's potential "exposure" to a given criminal provision. All crimes contain an express or implied penalty. In the vast majority of cases, the actual punishment is contained in the definition of the offense by reference to statutes defining ranges of imprisonment terms and fines. In some instances, a punishment for a violation of one statute is found by reference to the "class" of the crime.

The possible punishment for each particular offense can be ascertained with relative ease. Where certain enhanced punishments are being sought by the government, pretrial notice will afford knowledge of this possibility. Nevertheless, simply because a punishment is set forth in the statute does not mean that a defendant will always be subject to these penalties. There are certain statutory and constitutional limitations on sentencing which may tend to lessen a particular penalty. In general, these include limitations on resentencing, alterations in the punishment, and certain notice rules. While it is seldom successful, counsel may attack a sentence which constitutes cruel and unusual punishment, violates double jeopardy prohibitions, or violates concepts of equal protection. See. e.g., *Hodgson v. Vermont*, 168 U.S. 262 (1897).

A. NONCAPITAL SENTENCING ALTERNATIVES

Fines and Costs. The punishment for a violation of the law may include a fine in addition to or, in some cases, instead of imprisonment. Due to certain constitutional limitations, a person may not usually be confined for failure to pay the fine or costs.

The general authority for the imposition of fines for violations of the criminal statutes is found in the statutes themselves. The procedure for the collection of fines is governed largely by statute. The controlling question is whether the defendant may be incarcerated for failure to pay the fine. Fines cannot be imposed upon any person determined by the court to be statutorily indigent. While incarceration is still a possibility for an intentional refusal to pay, the court must explore alternative means of satisfaction of the fine. *Bearden v. Georgia*, 461 U.S. 660

(1983). In instances where the defendant desires to appeal a fine, the trial judge may grant a stay of the payment and require bail.

In some jurisdictions, the sentencing court may issue a criminal garnishment order for all fines, court costs, restitution, and reimbursement charges, combining them in a single order of garnishment. Any convicted person owing fines, court costs, restitution, or reimbursement before or after his or her release from incarceration is subject to a lien upon his or her interest, present or future, in any real property.

The costs associated with litigation are also governed by statute. It appears that the defendant is responsible for the payment of costs only upon conviction. However, the defendant cannot be incarcerated for failure to pay costs. *Bearden v. Georgia*, 461 U.S. 660 (1983). Moreover, court costs cannot be imposed upon an indigent defendant.

Recently, states have begun to provide that the sentencing court may order a person incarcerated to reimburse the state or local government for the costs of incarceration. The sentencing court determines the amount to be paid based on the actual per diem, per person, cost of incarceration, the cost of medical services provided to a prisoner less any copayment paid by the prisoner, and the prisoner's ability to pay all or part of the incarceration costs.

Restitution. By statute, a person convicted of certain types of crimes such as a crime involving the taking of, injury to, or destruction of property can be ordered to restore the property or its value to the victim. An order of restitution may defer payment until the person is released from custody. However, the decision by a trial judge not to use this remedy does not deprive the victim of a civil action for the injury sustained.

Forfeiture or Confiscation of Property. A person convicted of certain types of crimes such as controlled substances, intoxicating liquors, eavesdropping devices, deadly weapons, gambling devices, and obscene matter can be ordered to forfeit property used in connection with commission of the offense. Forfeitures, as payments in kind, are "fines" if they constitute punishment for an offense. *Austin v. United States*, 509 U.S. 602 (1993). Thus, forfeiture of vehicles and realty used to facilitate commission of drug trafficking is allowed, because it serves as a punishment under the Eighth Amendment's Excessive Fines Clause.

In *Alexander v. United States*, 509 U.S. 544 (1993), as part of his punishment for violating federal obscenity laws and RICO, the trial court ordered the defendant to forfeit his businesses and almost $9 million acquired through racketeering activity. The Court found that the forfeiture was a permissible criminal punishment, not a prior restraint on speech, because it merely prevented him from financing his activities with assets derived from his prior racketeering offenses. RICO is oblivious to the expressive or nonexpressive nature of the assets forfeited. Petitioner's assets were forfeited because they were directly related to past racketeering violations.

Generally, under the Due Process Clause, the Government must provide notice and a meaningful opportunity to be heard before seizing real property subject to civil forfeiture. *United States v. James Daniel Good Real Property*, 510 U.S. 43 (1993). However, due process does not preclude forfeiture of property used for unlawful purposes by a defendant but which belongs to another person. *Bennis v. Michigan*, 516 U.S. 442 (1996).

Probation and Conditional Discharge. Probation is granted when the sentencing court suspends the execution of a sentence of imprisonment conditionally and releases the defendant under the supervision of a probation officer. Some jurisdictions grant "conditional discharge" when a defendant is released without supervision. These forms of release are regarded as "legislative clemencies," not constitutional rights, granted as a matter of grace.

Eligibility for probation or conditional discharge usually prohibit their use after convictions for such offenses as a capital offense, recidivist status, serious felonies involving the use of a firearm or while the defendant was already on probation of conditional discharge from another felony conviction, or a sex-related offense against a minor. Otherwise, many states require that a defendant be considered for probation or conditional discharge unless the court finds imprisonment to be necessary to protect the public.

Conditions of release are usually stated in writing and furnished to the defendant. All defendants are required to refrain from committing another offense, as well as other conditions such as restitution which the court deems to be reasonably necessary to enable the defendant to lead a law-abiding life. In addition to reasonable conditions, a court may require a defendant to submit to a period of imprisonment in the local jail at times to be determined by the court. This is known as a "split sentence." The court may initiate proceedings to determine whether to revoke the release because of a violation of its conditions.

Home Incarceration. Many states now permit defendants convicted of minor offenses to serve all or part of a definite term of imprisonment under conditions of home incarceration. Some provisions prohibit home incarceration for minor offenders with outstanding charges or a recent violent crime conviction. The sentencing judge may have discretion to order home incarceration as another type of "split sentence" for the defendant to serve part of the sentence at home and part of it in the local jail. As with probation and conditional discharge, a defendant under home incarceration signs an agreement listing all of the conditions for confinement.

Continuous Confinement for a Definite Term or Indeterminate Term. An indeterminate sentence is set within statutory limits, with the parole board having responsibility for deciding precisely when the defendant is eligible for early release. About two-thirds of the states use indeterminate sentences. A determinate sentence (also known as "flat time,") is for a fixed period without the possibility of early release, but supervision often accompanies that release.

B. DEATH AS A PUNISHMENT

1. *The Problem of Fairness*

The death penalty is currently in effect in about three fourths of the states and the federal system. Methods of execution include electrocution, firing squad, gas chamber, hanging, and lethal injection. In *Furman v. Georgia*, 408 U.S. 238 (1972), the Court found that Georgia had not applied the death penalty fairly. Statistics on executions showed that black males who committed murder were executed far more frequently than white males, even though black males were not committing most of the crimes. The Court stated that capital punishment cannot be used unless the states can prove that it is being applied fairly.

Since *Furman*, even those supportive of the death penalty as an appropriate punishment have become concerned about the manner in which it is used. Responding to growing criticism about the administration of the death penalty, a dozen states have commissioned studies of their penalty system to examine racial and geographic disparities within states, as well as serious problems with court-appointed lawyers and the appeals process. For example, the Illinois Commission on Capital Punishment in March, 2002 recommended 85 reforms to the capital punishment system in Illinois. The report fueled a nationwide debate on the death penalty. The commission recommendations included:

- Creating a statewide review panel to conduct a pre-trial review of prosecutorial decisions to seek capital punishment. The panel would be comprised of four prosecutors and a retired judge.

- Significantly reducing the current list of death eligibility factors from twenty to five including: murder of a peace officer or firefighter; murder in a correctional facility; the murder of two or more persons; the intentional murder of a person involving torture; and any murder committed by a suspected felon in order to obstruct the justice system.

- No person may be sentenced to death based solely on uncorroborated single eyewitness or accomplice testimony or the uncorroborated testimony of jail house informants.

- Recommending other reforms concerning the use of jail house informants who purport to have information about the case or statements allegedly made by the defendant, including requiring a preliminary hearing to be conducted by the court as to the reliability of such witnesses and their proposed testimony, full-disclosure of benefits conferred for such testimony, early disclosure to the defense about the background of such witnesses and special cautionary instructions to the jury.

- Videotaping the entire interrogation of homicide suspects at a police station, and not merely the confession.

- Allowing trial judges to concur or reverse a jury's death sentence verdict. This will allow the trial judge to take into account potential improper influences such as passion and prejudice that may have influenced a jury's verdict, consider potential residual doubt about the defendant's absolute guilt, consider trial strategies of counsel, credibility of witnesses and the actual presentation of evidence, which may differ from what was anticipated in making pre-trial rulings in either admitting or excluding evidence.

- The Illinois Supreme Court should review all death sentences to determine if the sentence is excessive or disproportionate to the penalty imposed in similar cases, if death was the appropriate sentence given aggravating and mitigating factors and whether the sentence was imposed due to some arbitrary factor.

- Support the Supreme Court's recommendation for a capital case trial bar and requiring judges to be pre-certified before presiding over capital cases. As part of regular training for judges and counsel, as suggested by the Supreme Court and the Commission, improvements must be made in disseminating information and creating manuals and check lists to be used by counsel and the courts. There must also be better reporting of information concerning capital cases so that the fairness and accuracy of the capital punishment system can be adequately assessed.

- To eliminate confusion and improper speculation, juries should be instructed as to all the possible sentencing alternatives before they consider the appropriateness of imposing a death sentence.

- Like defendants in any other criminal case, capital defendants should be afforded the opportunity to make a statement to those who will be deciding whether to impose the ultimate punishment allowed by the state, a sentence of death.

2. *The Typical Capital Case*

The procedure for the trial of capital cases has been fashioned in response to federal precedent on the issue. The government must establish at least one aggravating circumstance beyond a reasonable doubt in order to impose the death penalty. Current capital punishment provisions are the product of a lengthy series of statutes and court opinions. See, e.g., *Gregg v. Georgia*, 428 U.S. 153 (1976).

In *California v. Brown*, 479 U.S. 538 (1987), the Court stated that there are two prerequisites to a valid death sentence. First, "death penalty statutes [must] be structured so as to prevent the penalty from being administered in an arbitrary and unpredictable fashion.... Second, ... the capital defendant generally must be allowed to introduce any relevant mitigating evidence." Later cases have defined the potential for imposition of the death penalty. For example, in *Tison v. Arizona*, 481 U.S. 137 (1987), the Court stated that the death penalty is not disproportionate for a murder committed with wanton indifference. In *Atkins v. Virginia*, 536 U.S. 304 (2002) held that the Eighth Amendment prohibits capital punishment upon a prisoner who is insane or mentally retarded. And in *Roper v. Simmons*, 543 U.S. 551 (2005), the Court held that the Eighth Amendment forbids imposition of the death penalty on persons who were under the age of 18 at the time they committed their crimes.

The prosecution must give defense counsel adequate notice that it will seek the death penalty. The defendant's guilt is initially determined at a "guilt" phase, and if the defendant is found guilty, a second hearing (the "penalty" phase) is conducted to determine the punishment. If the guilt phase of the proceeding is tried without a jury, the judge alone presides over the penalty phase. Likewise, if a jury has found guilt, the penalty phase is conducted as soon as possible before the same jury. When a defendant pleads guilty to a capital offense, the defendant may demand that a jury be impanelled to determine punishment.

At a pretrial conference, the defendant may allege that a sentence of death is being sought on the basis of race. The defendant must state with particularity how the evidence supports a claim that racial considerations played a significant part in the decision to seek a death sentence in his or her case. Relevant evidence may include statistical evidence or other evidence that death sentences were sought significantly more frequently either upon persons of one race than upon persons of another race, or as punishment for capital offenses against persons of one race than as punishment for capital offenses against persons of another race. The defendant has the burden of proving by clear and convincing evidence that race was the basis of the decision to seek the death penalty. The prosecution may offer evidence in rebuttal of the claims or evidence of the defendant. If the court finds that race was the basis of the decision to seek the death sentence, the court orders that a death sentence cannot be sought in that case.

In *Zant v. Stephens*, 462 U.S. 862 (1983), the Court held that all evidence may be introduced in a capital sentencing hearing even beyond factors in aggravation and mitigation as long as it is relevant, reliable and not prejudicial. Evidence is relevant to punishment if it is relevant to a statutory aggravating circumstance or to a statutory mitigating circumstance later raised by the defendant. See *Bell v. Ohio*, 438 U.S. 637 (1978).

Each jurisdiction defines the aggravating circumstances which must be proved before the death penalty can be imposed. A common aggravating circumstance is that the defendant has been previously convicted of a capital offense. *Romano v. Oklahoma*, 512 U.S. 1 (1994). A prior conviction cannot be used as an aggravating circumstance, however, if an appeal of the conviction is pending.

A second typical aggravating circumstance is that the defendant committed murder or kidnaping while engaged in the commission of a serious form of a felony such as arson, robbery, burglary, rape, or sodomy. See *Schiro v. Farley*, 510 U.S. 222 (1994). The focus of this aggravating circumstance is the commission of one of the listed offenses, regardless of whether the defendant actually could be convicted of the offense. For example, suppose the defendant argued that first degree burglary could not be an aggravating circumstance because the defendant was a 16-year-old child and statutorily could not be tried as an adult for that crime. The fact that the person charged is under a legal disability by reason of age which prevents his being convicted of an offense in no way suggests that the offense has not been committed, or that if the child did in fact commit the offense, it cannot be proved as an aggravating circumstance in conviction of another offense for which he can be tried, convicted and punished as an adult.

A third aggravating circumstance is that by committing murder or kidnaping, the defendant knowingly created a great risk of death to two or more persons in a public place by means of a destructive device or weapon normally hazardous to more than one person. This aggravator is not improper merely because it duplicates one of the elements of the homicide. See *Lowenfield v. Phelps*, 484 U.S. 231 (1988). Presumably, this circumstance applies only in multiple murders or threats to several persons at or shortly prior to or shortly after an act of murder or kidnapping.

Another aggravating circumstance may deal with defendants who either pay for or receive remuneration for a murder. This circumstance appears to apply to the purchaser as well as the perpetrator. Moreover, it applies to persons who commit murder and expect to profit from the victim's death. While many statutes contain no minimum level of profit, the proof may permit the jury to infer that it would be substantial thereby adding to the motive for the crime.

A fifth type of aggravating circumstance may apply to the murder of a prison employee by a defendant who was a prisoner at the time of the homicide. The murder must have occurred while the prison employee was engaged in the performance of duties. A sixth aggravating circumstance deals with the intentional murders of more than one person.

Recently added aggravating circumstances by some states include the intentional killing of a state or local public official or police officer, sheriff or deputy sheriff while the official was engaged in the lawful performance of duties, and a defendant who murdered the victim, either when an emergency protective order or a domestic violence order was in effect, or when any other order designed to protect the victim from the defendant (such as an order issued as a condition of a bond, conditional release, probation, parole, or pretrial diversion) was in effect.

Although there is no burden to do so, as a practical matter the defense may introduce proof of any mitigating circumstances for consideration by the jury. *California v. Brown*, 479 U.S. 538 (1987). The purpose of the mitigating factors appears to be avoidance of the death penalty. The listed circumstances relate generally to matters which were insufficiently persuasive for the factfinder on the issue of guilt. Typical statutory mitigating circumstances include: a lack of a significant history of prior criminal activity, the defendant was under extreme mental or emotional disturbance, the victim participated in the act, the defendant believed he had a moral justification for the conduct, the defendant was only an accomplice, the defendant acted under duress, the defendant suffered from some diminished capacity, or the youth of the defendant. Evidence of statutory mitigating circumstances should be admitted, regardless of its cumulative effect and how long the witness has known the defendant. However, exclusion of mitigating testimony may be harmless.

At the conclusion of all the proof the parties have the right of closing argument with the defense usually having the right of the final argument. Other than the order of argument, in general the rules regarding final jury argument are similar to those in the regular trial. Because of the nature of the hearing there are additional areas of defense objection not usually available in a regular trial. Of particular note is the prohibition of minimizing the jury's responsibility in assessing the death penalty. See *Romano v. Oklahoma*, 512 U.S. 1 (1994). For example, a prosecutor cannot argue to the jury that responsibility for determining the appropriateness of a death sentence rests not with the jury but with an appellate court. *Caldwell v. Mississippi*, 472 U.S. 320 (1985).

At the conclusion of the arguments the judge must instruct the jury in a manner similar to instructions in the guilt phase. Most states use the following format for instructions during the penalty phase. First, with regard to the statutory aggravating and mitigating circumstances, the judge must charge only those factors raised by the proof. *Delo v. Lashley*, 507 U.S. 272 (1993). Second, the judge must instruct the jury as to the authorized sentences. Third, the judge must instruct the jury that imposition of the death penalty is permitted only if it finds the existence of at least one aggravating circumstance beyond a reasonable doubt. Fourth, the judge should instruct the jury on the necessity of unanimity and the presumption of innocence. In addition, the court should instruct on the manner in which aggravating and mitigating circumstances are weighed. For example, in *Kansas v. Marsh*, 126 S.Ct. 2516 (2006), the Court approved the Kansas system by which the death penalty is imposed if the jury finds that aggravating circumstances are either in equipoise with or not outweighed by mitigating circumstances. Finally, the court defines the meaning of "mitigating circumstances." See *Penry v. Lynaugh*, 492 U.S. 302 (1989).

If the jury finds at least one aggravating circumstance beyond a reasonable doubt, its recommendation as to punishment of death must include a written designation of the aggravating circumstance. If the jury does not find at least one aggravating circumstance, the judge cannot impose a sentence of death. In this situation, the judge can impose a sentence of life. When a sentence of death is not imposed, any error committed during the proceeding is subject to a harmless error analysis. An appeal usually is automatic in cases in which the death penalty is imposed. If a death sentence is set aside because of an error in the penalty phase only, a new trial shall apply to the issue of punishment only.

Exercise

Check the statutes in your state to learn whether the death penalty is available as a punishment for homicide. If the death penalty is not used, locate a state in which it is permitted and find the following:

1. What is the notice provision for informing the defendant that the prosecution will seek the death penalty? How far in advance of trial must the notice occur? Is there a provision for notifying the defendant that the prosecution has decided not to seek the death penalty?

2. How many aggravating factors can be the basis for seeking the death penalty? How often has the list changed? Have any factors been removed by the legislature or ruled too vague by the courts? Do recent additions reflect increased concerns about the safety or importance of certain occupations, e.g., prison guards?

3. Are specific mitigating factors listed in the statute? How often has the list changed? Have any factors been removed by the legislature? Do recent additions reflect increased concerns about a defendant's background that a jury should be know?

4. If the jury finds the presence of an aggravating factor, is the death penalty the only possible punishment, or can other penalties still be considered? Even if the jury finds the presence of an aggravating factor, can the mitigating evidence offset the aggravating factor so that the death penalty is not imposed?

5. Can you think of additional aggravating or mitigating factors that the legislature should recognize?

C. PROPORTIONALITY OF PUNISHMENT

EWING v. CALIFORNIA
538 U.S. 11 (2003).

Justice O'Connor announced the judgment of the Court and delivered an opinion in which The Chief Justice and Justice Kennedy join.

In this case, we decide whether the Eighth Amendment prohibits the State of California from sentencing a repeat felon to a prison term of 25 years to life under the State's "Three Strikes and You're Out" law.

* * *

If the defendant has one prior "serious" or "violent" felony conviction, he must be sentenced to "twice the term otherwise provided as punishment for the current felony conviction." If the defendant has two or more prior "serious" or "violent" felony convictions, he must receive "an indeterminate term of life imprisonment." Defendants sentenced to life under the three strikes law become eligible for parole on a date calculated by reference to a "minimum term," which is the greater of (a) three times the term otherwise provided for the current conviction, (b) 25 years, or (c) the term determined by the court pursuant to § 1170 for the underlying conviction, including any enhancements. * * *

On parole from a 9–year prison term, petitioner Gary Ewing walked into the pro shop of the El Segundo Golf Course in Los Angeles County on March 12, 2000. He walked out with three golf clubs, priced at $399 apiece, concealed in his pants leg. A shop employee, whose suspicions were aroused when he observed Ewing limp out of the pro shop, telephoned the police. The police apprehended Ewing in the parking lot.

Ewing is no stranger to the criminal justice system. In 1984, at the age of 22, he pleaded guilty to theft. * * * Only 10 months later, Ewing stole the golf clubs at issue in this case. He was charged with, and ultimately convicted of, one count of felony grand theft of personal property in excess of $400. As required by the three strikes law, the prosecutor formally alleged, and the trial court later found, that Ewing had been convicted previously of four serious or violent felonies for the three burglaries and the robbery in the Long Beach apartment complex.

In the end, the trial judge determined that the grand theft should remain a felony. The court also ruled that the four prior strikes for the three burglaries and the robbery in Long Beach should stand. As a newly convicted felon with two or more "serious" or "violent" felony convictions in his past, Ewing was sentenced under the three strikes law to 25 years to life.

The California Court of Appeal affirmed in an unpublished opinion. Relying on our decision in *Rummel v. Estelle*, 445 U.S. 263 (1980), the court rejected Ewing's claim that his sentence was grossly disproportionate under the Eighth Amendment. Enhanced sentences under recidivist statutes like the three strikes law, the court reasoned, serve the "legitimate goal" of deterring and incapacitating repeat offenders. The Supreme Court of California denied Ewing's petition for review, and we granted certiorari. We now affirm.

The Eighth Amendment, which forbids cruel and unusual punishments, contains a "narrow proportionality principle" that "applies to noncapital sentences." We have most recently addressed the proportionality principle as applied to terms of years in a series of cases beginning with *Rummel v. Estelle*.

In *Rummel*, we held that it did not violate the Eighth Amendment for a State to sentence a three-time offender to life in prison with the possibility of parole. Like Ewing, Rummel was sentenced to a lengthy prison term under a recidivism statute. Rummel's two prior offenses were a 1964 felony for "fraudulent use of a credit card to obtain $80 worth of goods or services," and a 1969 felony conviction for "passing a forged check in the amount of $28.36." His triggering offense was a conviction for felony theft—"obtaining $120.75 by false pretenses." * * *

Three years after *Rummel*, in *Solem v. Helm*, 463 U.S. 277, 279 (1983), we held that the Eighth Amendment prohibited "a life sentence without possibility of parole for a seventh nonviolent felony." The triggering offense in Solem was "uttering a 'no account' check for $100." We specifically stated that the Eighth Amendment's ban on cruel and unusual punishments "prohibits ... sentences that are disproportionate to the crime committed," and that the "constitutional principle of proportionality has been recognized explicitly in this Court for almost a century." The Solem Court then explained that three factors may be relevant to a determination of whether a sentence is so disproportionate that it violates the Eighth Amendment: "(i) the gravity of the offense and the harshness of the penalty; (ii) the sentences imposed on other criminals in the same jurisdiction; and (iii) the sentences imposed for commission of the same crime in other jurisdictions."

Applying these factors in *Solem*, we struck down the defendant's sentence of life without parole. We specifically noted the contrast between that sentence and the sentence in Rummel, pursuant to which the defendant was eligible for parole. Indeed, we explicitly declined to overrule *Rummel*: "[O]ur conclusion today is not inconsistent with *Rummel v. Estelle*."

Eight years after *Solem*, we grappled with the proportionality issue again in *Harmelin* [*v. Michigan*, 501 U.S. 957 (1991)]. Harmelin was not a recidivism case, but rather involved a first-time offender convicted of possessing 672 grams of cocaine. He was sentenced to life in prison without possibility of parole. A majority of the Court rejected Harmelin's claim that his sentence was so grossly disproportionate that it violated the Eighth Amendment. The Court, however, could not agree on why his proportionality argument failed. Justice Scalia, joined by The Chief Justice, wrote that the proportionality principle was "an aspect of our death penalty jurisprudence, rather than a generalizable aspect of Eighth Amendment law." He would thus have declined to apply gross disproportionality principles except in reviewing capital sentences.

Justice Kennedy, joined by two other Members of the Court, concurred in part and concurred in the judgment. Justice Kennedy specifically recognized that "[t]he Eighth Amendment proportionality principle also applies to noncapital sentences." He then identified four principles of proportionality review—"the primacy of the legislature, the variety of legitimate penological schemes, the nature of our federal system, and the requirement that proportionality review be guided by objective factors"—that "inform the final one: The Eighth Amendment does not require strict proportionality between crime and sentence. Rather, it forbids only extreme sentences that are 'grossly disproportionate' to the crime." Justice Kennedy's concurrence also stated that *Solem* "did not mandate" comparative analysis "within and between jurisdictions."

The proportionality principles in our cases distilled in Justice Kennedy's concurrence guide our application of the Eighth Amendment in the new context that we are called upon to consider.

* * * Throughout the States, legislatures enacting three strikes laws made a deliberate policy choice that individuals who have repeatedly engaged in serious or violent criminal behavior, and whose conduct has not been deterred by more conventional approaches to punishment, must be isolated from society in order to protect the public safety. Though three strikes laws may be relatively new, our tradition of deferring to state legislatures in making and implementing such important policy decisions is longstanding.

Our traditional deference to legislative policy choices finds a corollary in the principle that the Constitution "does not mandate adoption of any one penological theory." A sentence can have a variety of justifications, such as incapacitation, deterrence, retribution, or rehabilitation. Some or all of these justifications may play a role in a State's sentencing scheme. Selecting the sentencing rationales is generally a policy choice to be made by state legislatures, not federal courts.

When the California Legislature enacted the three strikes law, it made a judgment that protecting the public safety requires incapacitating criminals who have already been convicted of at least one serious or violent crime. * * *

California's justification is no pretext. Recidivism is a serious public safety concern in California and throughout the Nation. According to a recent report, approximately 67 percent of former inmates released from state prisons were charged with at least one "serious" new crime within three years of their release. * * *

The State's interest in deterring crime also lends some support to the three strikes law. We have long viewed both incapacitation and deterrence as rationales for recidivism statutes: "[A] recidivist statute['s] ... primary goals are to deter repeat offenders and, at some point in the life of one who repeatedly commits criminal offenses serious enough to be punished as felonies, to segregate that person from the rest of society for an extended period of time." *Rummel.* Four years after the passage of California's three strikes law, the recidivism rate of parolees returned to prison for the commission of a new crime dropped by nearly 25 percent. * * *

Against this backdrop, we consider Ewing's claim that his three strikes sentence of 25 years to life is unconstitutionally disproportionate to his offense of "shoplifting three golf clubs." We first address the gravity of the offense compared to the harshness of the penalty. At the threshold, we note that Ewing incorrectly frames the issue. The gravity of his offense was not merely "shoplifting three golf clubs." Rather, Ewing was convicted of felony grand theft for stealing nearly $1,200 worth of merchandise after previously having been convicted of at least two "violent" or "serious" felonies. Even standing alone, Ewing's theft should not be taken lightly. His crime was certainly not "one of the most passive felonies a person could commit." To the contrary, the Supreme Court of California has noted the "seriousness" of grand theft in the context of proportionality review. * * *

In weighing the gravity of Ewing's offense, we must place on the scales not only his current felony, but also his long history of felony recidivism. Any other approach would fail to accord proper deference to the policy judgments that find expression in the legislature's choice of sanctions. In imposing a three strikes sentence, the State's interest is not merely punishing the offense of conviction, or the "triggering" offense: "[I]t is in addition the interest ... in dealing in a harsher manner with those who by repeated criminal acts have shown that they are simply incapable of conforming to the norms of society as established by its criminal law." To give full effect to the State's choice of this legitimate penological goal, our proportionality review of Ewing's sentence must take that goal into account.

Ewing's sentence is justified by the State's public-safety interest in incapacitating and deterring recidivist felons, and amply supported by his own long, serious criminal record. Ewing has been convicted of numerous misdemeanor and felony offenses, served nine separate terms of incarceration, and committed most of his crimes while on probation or parole. His prior "strikes" were serious felonies including robbery and three residential burglaries. To be sure, Ewing's sentence is a long one. But it reflects a rational legislative judgment, entitled to deference, that offenders who have committed serious or violent felonies and who continue to commit felonies must be incapacitated. The State of California "was entitled to place upon [Ewing] the onus of one who is simply unable to bring his conduct within the social norms prescribed by the criminal law of the State." Ewing's is not "the rare case in which a threshold comparison of the crime committed and the sentence imposed leads to an inference of gross disproportionality."

We hold that Ewing's sentence of 25 years to life in prison, imposed for the offense of felony grand theft under the three strikes law, is not grossly disproportionate and therefore does not violate the Eighth Amendment's prohibition on cruel and unusual punishments. The judgment of the California Court of Appeal is affirmed.

[The concurring opinion of JUSTICE THOMAS and JUSTICE SCALIA is omitted]

JUSTICE BREYER, with whom JUSTICE STEVENS, JUSTICE SOUTER, and JUSTICE GINSBURG join, dissenting.

The constitutional question is whether the "three strikes" sentence imposed by California upon repeat-offender Gary Ewing is "grossly disproportionate" to his crime. The sentence amounts to a real prison term of at least 25 years. The sentence-triggering criminal conduct consists of the theft of three golf clubs priced at a total of $1,197. The offender has a criminal history that includes four felony convictions arising out of three separate burglaries (one armed). In *Solem v. Helm*, the Court found grossly disproportionate a somewhat longer sentence imposed on a recidivist offender for triggering criminal conduct that was somewhat less severe. In my view, the differences are not determinative, and the Court should reach the same ultimate conclusion here.

I

This Court's precedent sets forth a framework for analyzing Ewing's Eighth Amendment claim. The Eighth Amendment forbids, as "cruel and unusual punishments," prison terms (including terms of years) that are "grossly disproportionate." In applying the "gross disproportionality" principle, courts must keep in mind that "legislative policy" will primarily determine the appropriateness of a punishment's "severity," and hence defer to such legislative policy judgments. * * *

If courts properly respect those judgments, they will find that the sentence fails the test only in rare instances. * * * And they will only " 'rarely' "find it necessary to " 'engage in extended analysis' "before rejecting a claim that a sentence is "grossly disproportionate."

The plurality applies Justice Kennedy's analytical framework in *Harmelin*. And, for present purposes, I will consider Ewing's Eighth Amendment claim on those terms. To implement this approach, courts faced with a "gross disproportionality" claim must first make "a threshold comparison of the crime committed and the sentence imposed." If a claim crosses that threshold—itself a rare occurrence—then the court should compare the sentence at issue to other sentences "imposed on other criminals" in the same, or in other, jurisdictions. The comparative analysis will "validate" or invalidate "an initial judgment that a sentence is grossly disproportionate to a crime."

I recognize the warnings implicit in the Court's frequent repetition of words such as "rare." Nonetheless I believe that the case before us is a "rare" case—one in which a court can say with reasonable confidence that the punishment is "grossly disproportionate" to the crime.

II

Ewing's claim crosses the gross disproportionality "threshold." First, precedent makes clear that Ewing's sentence raises a serious disproportionality question. Ewing is a recidivist. Hence the two cases most directly in point are those in which the Court considered the constitutionality of recidivist sentencing: *Rummel* and *Solem*. Ewing's claim falls between these two cases. It is stronger than the claim presented in *Rummel*, where the Court upheld a recidivist's sentence as constitutional. It is weaker than the claim presented in *Solem*, where the Court struck down a recidivist sentence as unconstitutional.

Three kinds of sentence-related characteristics define the relevant comparative spectrum: (a) the length of the prison term in real time, i.e., the time that the offender is likely actually to spend in prison; (b) the sentence-triggering criminal conduct, i.e., the offender's actual behavior or other offense-related circumstances; and (c) the offender's criminal history.

* * * [T]he length of the real prison term—the factor that explains the *Solem/Rummel* difference in outcome—places Ewing closer to *Solem* than to *Rummel*, though the greater value of the golf clubs that Ewing

stole moves Ewing's case back slightly in *Rummel*'s direction. Overall, the comparison places Ewing's sentence well within the twilight zone between *Solem* and *Rummel*—a zone where the argument for unconstitutionality is substantial, where the cases themselves cannot determine the constitutional outcome.

Second, Ewing's sentence on its face imposes one of the most severe punishments available upon a recidivist who subsequently engaged in one of the less serious forms of criminal conduct. I do not deny the seriousness of shoplifting, which an amicus curiae tells us costs retailers in the range of $30 billion annually. * * *

This case, of course, involves shoplifting engaged in by a recidivist. One might argue that any crime committed by a recidivist is a serious crime potentially warranting a 25–year sentence. But this Court rejected that view in *Solem*, and in *Harmelin*, with the recognition that "no penalty is per se constitutional."

Third, some objective evidence suggests that many experienced judges would consider Ewing's sentence disproportionately harsh. The United States Sentencing Commission (having based the federal Sentencing Guidelines primarily upon its review of how judges had actually sentenced offenders) does not include shoplifting (or similar theft-related offenses) among the crimes that might trigger especially long sentences for recidivists.

III

* * * A comparison of Ewing's sentence with other sentences requires answers to two questions. First, how would other jurisdictions (or California at other times, i.e., without the three strikes penalty) punish the same offense conduct? Second, upon what other conduct would other jurisdictions (or California) impose the same prison term? Moreover, since hypothetical punishment is beside the point, the relevant prison time, for comparative purposes, is real prison time, i.e., the time that an offender must actually serve. * * *

As to California itself, we know the following: First, between the end of World War II and 1994 (when California enacted the three strikes law), no one like Ewing could have served more than 10 years in prison. We know that for certain because the maximum sentence for Ewing's crime of conviction, grand theft, was for most of that period 10 years. We also know that the time that any offender actually served was likely far less than 10 years. This is because statistical data shows that the median time actually served for grand theft (other than auto theft) was about two years, and 90 percent of all those convicted of that crime served less than three or four years.

Second, statistics suggest that recidivists of all sorts convicted during that same time period in California served a small fraction of Ewing's real-time sentence. On average, recidivists served three to four additional (recidivist-related) years in prison, with 90 percent serving less than an additional real seven to eight years.

Third, we know that California has reserved, and still reserves, Ewing-type prison time, i.e., at least 25 real years in prison, for criminals convicted of crimes far worse than was Ewing's. Statistics for the years 1945 to 1981, for example, indicate that typical (nonrecidivist) male first-degree murderers served between 10 and 15 real years in prison, with 90 percent of all such murderers serving less than 20 real years. Moreover, California, which has moved toward a real-time sentencing system (where the statutory punishment approximates the time served), still punishes far less harshly those who have engaged in far more serious conduct. * * *

As to other jurisdictions, we know the following: The United States, bound by the federal Sentencing Guidelines, would impose upon a recidivist, such as Ewing, a sentence that, in any ordinary case, would not exceed 18 months in prison. * * *

With three exceptions, we do not have before us information about actual time served by Ewing-type offenders in other States. We do know, however, that the law would make it legally impossible for a Ewing-type offender to serve more than 10 years in prison in 33 jurisdictions, as well as the federal courts, more than 15 years in 4 other States, and more than 20 years in 4 additional States. In nine other States, the law might make it legally possible to impose a sentence of 25 years or more—though that fact by itself, of course, does not mean that judges have actually done so. * * *

Notes

1. Proportionality limitations may apply to forfeitures as well. In *United States v. Bajakajian*, 524 U.S. 321 (1998), the defendant was arrested while trying to take $357,144 on a flight to Cyprus, because he had failed to report that he possessed or had control of more than $10,000. After a bench trial on a criminal forfeiture charge, the trial court found the entire amount subject to forfeiture under a criminal forfeiture statute. The court, however, ordered only $15,000 forfeited, reasoning that forfeiture of more than that amount would be "grossly disproportional" to Bajakajian's culpability and thus unconstitutional under the Excessive Fines Clause. The court expressly found that all of the money came from a lawful source and was to be used for a lawful purpose. The Supreme Court agreed that the forfeiture of currency permissible under the statute constituted punishment, because the forfeiture only became possible upon conviction of willfully violating the reporting statute. After concluding that the forfeiture qualified as a "fine," the Court turned to the question of excessiveness. Bajakajian's crime was "solely a reporting offense," and the harm Bajakajian's caused was "minimal" in the sense that the government would be deprived only of information that the $357,144 left the country. Thus, the gravity of the crime compared to the amount in forfeiture sought would be "grossly disproportional."

2. *Death Penalty for Juveniles.* In *Roper v. Simmons*, 543 U.S. 551 (2005), the Court in a 5–4 decision held that the Eighth Amendment forbids imposition of the death penalty on persons who were under the age of 18 at the time they committed their crimes. As in *Atkins v. Virginia*, 536 U.S. 304

(2002) regarding the death penalty for the insane or mentally retarded, the majority found a national consensus against the death penalty. A majority of states had legislatively rejected it and the infrequency of its use even where it was authorized provided sufficient evidence that society regards juveniles as "categorically less culpable than the average criminal." In addition, although international opinion against the death penalty was not controlling, the Court noted that it confirmed the majority's view that the death penalty is a disproportionate penalty for criminals under the age of 18.

3. *Enhanced Sentences for Recidivists.* Recidivist offender statutes like the one applied in Ewing are used by about half the states. A defendant may be sentenced to a maximum of life imprisonment upon proof of a requisite number of prior convictions where the defendant is convicted of certain classifications of felonies. A person cannot be convicted as a recidivist unless a term of imprisonment is imposed as punishment for the underlying charge. Recidivist provisions do not create an independent offense but merely serves to enhance the punishment for a crime committed by a person who qualifies as a recidivist. A conviction for a capital offense such as murder is not subject to enhancement.

A defendant is entitled to notice of being charged as a recidivist before the trial of the underlying substantive offense. A separate indictment meets this requirement just as does a separate count in the indictment charging the substantive offense to which it refers. It is common practice for the indictment to specify the nature, time and place of the prior conviction.

Assuming the defendant is properly charged as a recidivist, trial initially takes place on the underlying felony. During this initial trial, no mention is made of the prior convictions, except for impeachment. The determination of whether the defendant is a recidivist must occur in a separate proceeding from the trial on the underlying felony. This penalty phase usually is conducted with the same jury. The defendant is not entitled to separate juries for the guilt and penalty phases. The evidence at the hearing is very narrow. The only function of the jury is to hear proof of prior convictions and to determine if a defendant's record of recidivism warrants punishment. Accordingly, the courts have denied the defendant an opportunity to introduce evidence of mitigation. During the hearing, the prosecution must prove every element of the recidivist charge beyond a reasonable doubt. A defendant charged with being a recidivist may plead guilty to the charge.

In many jurisdictions, there are two degrees of recidivist status, the elements of which are indistinguishable except for the number of previous felony convictions required. For example, a recidivist in the second degree must have been convicted of one previous felony before committing the current felony. A recidivist in the first degree must have been convicted of two or more previous felonies prior to committing the current felony. Naturally the penalties for a recidivist in the first degree are more severe. Except for prior convictions, any fact increasing sentence beyond the statutory maximum for the crime of conviction must be proved beyond a reasonable doubt. *Apprendi v. New Jersey*, infra.

For both degrees, the defendant's prior conviction must have occurred prior to the date of the commission of the current felony. Likewise, for first degree status, the second felony must have been committed after the conviction of the first felony. For example, if a defendant is convicted and paroled, then commits another felony and is again incarcerated and released, upon committing a third felony, he has two prior felony convictions and is a first-degree offender. However, if the defendant's second conviction did not occur until after commission of the third felony, he has one prior felony conviction for offender status. The prior conviction must be for a felony in the sentencing jurisdiction or conviction of a crime in any other jurisdiction. If the defendant has been convicted of a crime in another state which is a felony in the sentencing jurisdiction, the conviction counts as a prior felony conviction for purposes of the recidivist statute. The prior conviction must have included imposition of a sentence of one year or more or of death.

A defendant who is indicted as a recidivist may challenge the validity of any prior conviction. The defendant must file a motion to suppress any evidence of prior convictions before trial, alleging that a prior conviction was obtained by constitutionally impermissible means. At a hearing on the motion to suppress, the burden is on the prosecution to prove the judgments of conviction for each of the prior offenses. This burden is sustained by a duly authenticated record of a judgment and conviction. When a defendant is found to be a recidivist, the sentence for the principal crime is replaced and enhanced by an indeterminate sentence.

Typically, if a defendant is found to be a recidivist in the second degree, the sentence imposed is "for the next highest degree than the offense for which [he was] convicted." For example, if the principal conviction is for a Class B felony, the enhanced sentence may be for a Class A felony. The sentence ranges for a first degree recidivist may range from twenty to fifty years or life imprisonment for the principal conviction of a Class A or Class B felony, and ten to twenty years for a Class C or Class D felony.

Exercise

Check the statutes in your state to learn whether an enhanced sentence is available for recidivists. If the enhanced sentences are is not used, locate a state in which it is permitted and find the following:

1. What is the notice provision for informing the defendant that the prosecution will seek an enhanced sentence? How far in advance of trial must the notice occur? Is there a provision for notifying the defendant that the prosecution has decided not to seek an enhanced sentence?

2. Can a prior felony conviction be used both to create an offense or enhance a punishment of the second crime and again to enhance the punishment as a recidivist? For example, possession of a handgun by a convicted felon requires proof of a prior felony. Can that same prior felony also be used to enhance the penalty for the current possessory offense?

3. Is there a minimum age for the defendant in order to receive an enhanced recidivist sentence? Is there a minimum age for the defendant when he committed the prior crimes for which enhanced sentencing is now sought?

4. Is the prior felony conviction limited to a felony in your state, or can a felony conviction anywhere be considered? Does it matter whether the felony in another jurisdiction is not considered a felony in your state?

5. Is there a limit on the age of the prior felony conviction, e.g., within five years prior to the date of the commission of the current felony?

6. How does the prosecution prove the prior felony conviction?

7. Is there more than one degree or type of enhanced recidivist sentencing?

D. SENTENCING PROCEDURES

If the defendant has been convicted, the case should proceed to sentencing without unreasonable delay. However, it is customary to postpone sentencing for a short period of time to enable the court to obtain a presentence report. Normally, the judge who presided at the trial conducts the sentencing. Following a felony or misdemeanor conviction, the judge must consider the defendant for probation or conditional discharge as an alternative to imprisonment. If the record does not clearly reflect a consideration of sentencing alternatives, the case must be remanded for proper sentencing.

Regardless of whether the defendant is eligible for alternative sentencing, the court cannot impose a sentence for a felony other than a capital offense without the consideration of a presentence report. The report must be prepared and reviewed by the court before sentencing. The report must be prepared by a probation officer, must include an analysis of the defendant's background and may include a victim impact statement under appropriate circumstances. *Payne v. Tennessee*, 501 U.S. 808 (1991). Before imposing sentence, the trial court must advise the defendant or counsel of the contents of any presentence report. If the defendant wishes to controvert the contents of any report, the court must afford a fair opportunity and a reasonable period of time to challenge them. However, the court need not disclose the sources of confidential information contained in the report.

WILLIAMS v. NEW YORK

337 U.S. 241 (1949).

Mr. Justice Black delivered the opinion of the Court.

A jury in a New York state court found appellant guilty of murder in the first degree. The jury recommended life imprisonment, but the trial judge imposed sentence of death. In giving his reasons for imposing the death sentence the judge discussed in open court the evidence upon which the jury had convicted stating that this evidence had been considered in the light of additional information obtained through the court's "Probation Department, and through other sources." [A state statute required that the court "shall cause the defendant's previous criminal record to be submitted to it, * * * and may seek any information that will aid the court in determining the proper treatment of such defendant." Williams argued that his sentence violated due process, because it was provided by witnesses he had not confronted or cross-examined.]

The narrow contention here makes it unnecessary to set out the facts at length. The record shows a carefully conducted trial lasting more than two weeks in which appellant was represented by three appointed lawyers who conducted his defense with fidelity and zeal. The evidence proved a wholly indefensible murder committed by a person engaged in a burglary. * * *

About five weeks after the verdict of guilty with recommendation of life imprisonment, and after a statutory pre-sentence investigation report to the judge, the defendant was brought to court to be sentenced. Asked what he had to say, appellant protested his innocence. After each of his three lawyers had appealed to the court to accept the jury's recommendation of a life sentence, the judge gave reasons why he felt that the death sentence should be imposed. He narrated the shocking details of the crime as shown by the trial evidence, expressing his own complete belief in appellant's guilt. He stated that the pre-sentence investigation revealed many material facts concerning appellant's background which though relevant to the question of punishment could not properly have been brought to the attention of the jury in its consideration of the question of guilt. He referred to the experience appellant 'had had on thirty other burglaries in and about the same vicinity' where the murder had been committed. The appellant had not been convicted of these burglaries although the judge had information that he had confessed to some and had been identified as the perpetrator of some of the others. The judge also referred to certain activities of appellant as shown by the probation report that indicated appellant possessed "a morbid sexuality" and classified him as a "menace to society." The accuracy of the statements made by the judge as to appellant's background and past practices were not challenged by appellant or his counsel, nor was the judge asked to disregard any of them or to afford appellant a chance to refute or discredit any of them by cross-examination or otherwise.

The case presents a serious and difficult question. The question relates to the rules of evidence applicable to the manner in which a judge may obtain information to guide him in the imposition of sentence upon an already convicted defendant. Within limits fixed by statutes, New York judges are given a broad discretion to decide the type and extent of punishment for convicted defendants. Here, for example, the judge's discretion was to sentence to life imprisonment or death. To aid a judge in exercising this discretion intelligently the New York procedural policy encourages him to consider information about the convicted person's past life, health, habits, conduct, and mental and moral propensities. The sentencing judge may consider such information even though obtained outside the courtroom from persons whom a defendant has not been permitted to confront or cross-examine. It is the consideration of information obtained by a sentencing judge in this manner that is the basis for appellant's broad constitutional challenge to the New York statutory policy.

Appellant urges that the New York statutory policy is in irreconcilable conflict with the underlying philosophy of a second procedural policy grounded in the due process of law clause of the Fourteenth

Amendment. That policy as stated in *Re Oliver*, 333 U.S. 257, is in part that no person shall be tried and convicted of an offense unless he is given reasonable notice of the charges against him and is afforded an opportunity to examine adverse witnesses. That the due process clause does provide these salutary and time-tested protections where the question for consideration is the guilt of a defendant seems entirely clear from the genesis and historical evolution of the clause.

Tribunals passing on the guilt of a defendant always have been hedged in by strict evidentiary procedural limitations. But both before and since the American colonies became a nation, courts in this country and in England practiced a policy under which a sentencing judge could exercise a wide discretion in the sources and types of evidence used to assist him in determining the kind the extent of punishment to be imposed within limits fixed by law. Out-of-court affidavits have been used frequently, and of course in the smaller communities sentencing judges naturally have in mind their knowledge of the personalities and backgrounds of convicted offenders. A recent manifestation of the historical latitude allowed sentencing judges appears in Rule 32 of the Federal Rules of Criminal Procedure. That rule provides for consideration by federal judges of reports made by probation officers containing information about a convicted defendant, including such information "as may be helpful in imposing sentence or in granting probation or in the correctional treatment of the defendant. . . ."

In addition to the historical basis for different evidentiary rules governing trial and sentencing procedures there are sound practical reasons for the distinction. In a trial before verdict the issue is whether a defendant is guilty of having engaged in certain criminal conduct of which he has been specifically accused. Rules of evidence have been fashioned for criminal trials which narrowly confine the trial contest to evidence that is strictly relevant to the particular offense charged. These rules rest in part on a necessity to prevent a time consuming and confusing trial of collateral issues. They were also designed to prevent tribunals concerned solely with the issue of guilt of a particular offense from being influenced to convict for that offense by evidence that the defendant had habitually engaged in other misconduct. A sentencing judge, however, is not confined to the narrow issue of guilt. His task within fixed statutory or constitutional limits is to determine the type and extent of punishment after the issue of guilt has been determined. Highly relevant—if not essential—to his selection of an appropriate sentence is the possession of the fullest information possible concerning the defendant's life and characteristics. And modern concepts individualizing punishment have made it all the more necessary that a sentencing judge not be denied an opportunity to obtain pertinent information by a requirement of rigid adherence to restrictive rules of evidence properly applicable to the trial.

Undoubtedly the New York statutes emphasize a prevalent modern philosophy of penology that the punishment should fit the offender and not merely the crime. The belief no longer prevails that every offense in a like legal category calls for an identical punishment without regard to the past life and habits of a particular offender. This whole country has traveled far from the period in which the death sentence was an automatic and commonplace result of convictions—even for offenses today deemed trivial. Today's philosophy of individualizing sentences makes sharp distinctions for example between first and repeated offenders. Indeterminate sentences, the ultimate termination of which are sometimes decided by nonjudicial agencies have to a large extent taken the place of the old rigidly fixed punishments. The practice of probation which relies heavily on non-judicial implementation has been accepted as a wise policy. Execution of the United States parole system rests on the discretion of an administrative parole board. Retribution is no longer the dominant objective of the criminal law. Reformation and rehabilitation of offenders have become important goals of criminal jurisprudence.

Modern changes in the treatment of offenders make it more necessary now than a century ago for observance of the distinctions in the evidential procedure in the trial and sentencing processes. For indeterminate sentences and probation have resulted in an increase in the discretionary powers exercised in fixing punishments. In general, these modern changes have not resulted in making the lot of offenders harder. On the contrary a strong motivating force for the changes has been the belief that by careful study of the lives and personalities of convicted offenders many could be less severely punished and restored sooner to complete freedom and useful citizenship. This belief to a large extent has been justified.

Under the practice of individualizing punishments, investigation techniques have been given an important role. Probation workers making reports of their investigations have not been trained to prosecute but to aid offenders. Their reports have been given a high value by conscientious judges who want to sentence persons on the best available information rather than on guesswork and inadequate information. To deprive sentencing judges of this kind of information would undermine modern penological procedural policies that have been cautiously adopted throughout the nation after careful consideration and experimentation. We must recognize that most of the information now relied upon by judges to guide them in the intelligent imposition of sentences would be unavailable if information were restricted to that given in open court by witnesses subject to cross-examination. And the modern probation report draws on information concerning every aspect of a defendant's life. The type and extent of this information make totally impractical if not impossible open court testimony with cross-examination. Such a procedure could endlessly delay criminal administration in a retrial of collateral issues.

The considerations we have set out admonish us against treating the due-process clause as a uniform command that courts throughout the Nation abandon their age-old practice of seeking information from out-of-court sources to guide their judgment toward a more enlightened and just sentence. New York criminal statutes set wide limits for maximum and minimum sentences. Under New York statutes a state judge cannot escape his grave responsibility of fixing sentence. In determining whether a defendant shall receive a one-year minimum or a twenty-year maximum sentence, we do not think the Federal Constitution restricts the view of the sentencing judge to the information received in open court. The due-process clause should not be treated as a device for freezing the evidential procedure of sentencing in the mold of trial procedure. So to treat the due-process clause would hinder if not preclude all courts—state and federal—from making progressive efforts to improve the administration of criminal justice. * * * *

Affirmed.

MR. JUSTICE MURPHY, dissenting.

* * * The record before us indicates that the judge exercised his discretion to deprive a man of his life, in reliance on material made available to him in a probation report, consisting almost entirely of evidence that would have been inadmissible at the trial. Some, such as allegations of prior crimes, was irrelevant. Much was incompetent as hearsay. All was damaging, and none was subject to scrutiny by the defendant.

Due process of law includes at least the idea that a person accused of crime shall be accorded a fair hearing through all the stages of the proceedings against him. I agree with the Court as to the value and humaneness of liberal use of probation reports as developed by modern penologists, but, in a capital case, against the unanimous recommendation of a jury, where the report would concededly not have been admissible at the trial, and was not subject to examination by the defendant, I am forced to conclude that the high commands of due process were not obeyed.

Notes

1. Formal sentencing consists of pronouncing sentence in accordance with the previous plea or adjudication of guilt. Any pending motions which may affect the need for sentencing should be decided before sentencing is pronounced. The defendant should be given the common law right of allocution, to identify any reason why the sentence should not be pronounced or why a particular sentence is appropriate. It thus affords regularity to the proceedings and reduces the likelihood of a subsequent attack on the judgment. If the sentence is predicated upon a contested adjudication, the defendant must be advised of rights regarding appeal.

2. In making a sentence determination, the judge should consider the presentence report, sentencing alternatives if any, evidence concerning the nature and characteristics of the criminal conduct, and whether to run any multiple sentences concurrently or consecutively. In addition, the judge may consider the defendant's untruthfulness or refusal to cooperate with law enforcement authorities. The judge "must be permitted to consider any and all information that reasonably might bear on the proper sentence for the

particular defendant, given the crime committed." *Wasman v. United States*, 468 U.S. 559 (1984).

APPRENDI v. NEW JERSEY

530 U.S. 466 (2000).

JUSTICE STEVENS delivered the opinion of the Court.

[A New Jersey hate crime statute provided for an "extended term" of imprisonment if the trial judge found, by a preponderance of the evidence, that "[t]he defendant in committing the crime acted with a purpose to intimidate an individual or group of individuals because of race, color, gender, handicap, religion, sexual orientation or ethnicity." The extended term authorized by the hate crime law is imprisonment for "between 10 and 20 years." After his indictment, Apprendi agreed to plead guilty to possession of a firearm for an unlawful purpose, punishable by five to ten years. The plea agreement allowed the prosecution to request that the sentence be enhanced due to a biased purpose. After an adversarial hearing, the trial court concluded that the crime was motivated by racial bias.]

* * * The question presented is whether the Due Process Clause of the Fourteenth Amendment requires that a factual determination authorizing an increase in the maximum prison sentence for an offense from 10 to 20 years be made by a jury on the basis of proof beyond a reasonable doubt. * * *

At stake in this case are constitutional protections of surpassing importance: the proscription of any deprivation of liberty without "due process of law," Amdt. 14, and the guarantee that "[i]n all criminal prosecutions, the accused shall enjoy the right to a speedy and public trial, by an impartial jury," Amdt. 6. * * *

Any possible distinction between an "element" of a felony offense and a "sentencing factor" was unknown to the practice of criminal indictment, trial by jury, and judgment by court as it existed during the years surrounding our Nation's founding. As a general rule, criminal proceedings were submitted to a jury after being initiated by an indictment containing "all the facts and circumstances which constitute the offence, . . . stated with such certainty and precision, that the defendant . . . may be enabled to determine the species of offence they constitute, in order that he may prepare his defence accordingly . . . and that there may be no doubt as to the judgment which should be given, if the defendant be convicted." J. Archbold, Pleading and Evidence in Criminal Cases 44 (15th ed. 1862). The defendant's ability to predict with certainty the judgment from the face of the felony indictment flowed from the invariable linkage of punishment with crime. * * *

Just as the circumstances of the crime and the intent of the defendant at the time of commission were often essential elements to be alleged in the indictment, so too were the circumstances mandating a particular punishment. "Where a statute annexes a higher degree of punishment to a common-law felony, if committed under particular circumstances, an indictment for the offence, in order to bring the defendant within that higher degree of punishment, must expressly charge it to have been committed under those circumstances, and must state the circumstances with certainty and precision. [2 M. Hale, Pleas of the Crown *170]." Archbold, Pleading and Evidence in Criminal Cases, at 51. If, then, "upon an indictment under the statute, the prosecutor prove the felony to have been committed, but fail in proving it to have been committed under the circumstances specified in the statute, the defendant shall be convicted of the common-law felony only." *Id.*, at 188. * * *

We should be clear that nothing in this history suggests that it is impermissible for judges to exercise discretion—taking into consideration various factors relating both to offense and offender—in imposing a judgment within the range prescribed by statute. We have often noted that judges in this country have long exercised discretion of this nature in imposing sentence within statutory limits in the individual case. * * * As in *Williams [v. New York]*, our periodic recognition of judges' broad discretion in sentencing—since the 19th-century shift in this country from statutes providing fixed-term sentences to those providing judges discretion within a permissible range, has been regularly accompanied by the qualification that that discretion was bound by the range of sentencing options prescribed by the legislature. * * *

We do not suggest that trial practices cannot change in the course of centuries and still remain true to the principles that emerged from the Framers' fears "that the jury right could be lost not only by gross denial, but by erosion." But practice must at least adhere to the basic principles undergirding the requirements of trying to a jury all facts necessary to constitute a statutory offense, and proving those facts beyond reasonable doubt. * * *

It was in *McMillan v. Pennsylvania*, 477 U.S. 79 (1986), that this Court, for the first time, coined the term "sentencing factor" to refer to a fact that was not found by a jury but that could affect the sentence imposed by the judge. * * * [W]e concluded that the Pennsylvania statute did not run afoul of our previous admonitions against relieving the State of its burden of proving guilt * * *.

We did not, however, there budge from the position that (1) constitutional limits exist to States' authority to define away facts necessary to constitute a criminal offense, *id.*, at 85–88, 106 S.Ct. 2411, and (2) that a state scheme that keeps from the jury facts that "expos[e] [defendants] to greater or additional punishment," may raise serious constitutional concern. * * *

* * * *Almendarez–Torres v. United States*, 523 U.S. 224 (1998), represents at best an exceptional departure from the historic practice that we have described. * * * Because Almendarez–Torres had admitted the three earlier convictions for aggravated felonies—all of which had been entered pursuant to proceedings with substantial procedural safe-

guards of their own—no question concerning the right to a jury trial or the standard of proof that would apply to a contested issue of fact was before the Court. Although our conclusion in that case was based in part on our application of the criteria we had invoked in *McMillan*, the specific question decided concerned the sufficiency of the indictment. More important, * * * our conclusion in *Almendarez–Torres* turned heavily upon the fact that the additional sentence to which the defendant was subject was "the prior commission of a serious crime." * * * Both the certainty that procedural safeguards attached to any "fact" of prior conviction, and the reality that Almendarez–Torres did not challenge the accuracy of that "fact" in his case, mitigated the due process and Sixth Amendment concerns otherwise implicated in allowing a judge to determine a "fact" increasing punishment beyond the maximum of the statutory range.

Even though it is arguable that *Almendarez–Torres* was incorrectly decided, and that a logical application of our reasoning today should apply if the recidivist issue were contested, Apprendi does not contest the decision's validity and we need not revisit it for purposes of our decision today to treat the case as a narrow exception to the general rule we recalled at the outset. Given its unique facts, it surely does not warrant rejection of the otherwise uniform course of decision during the entire history of our jurisprudence.

In sum, our reexamination of our cases in this area, and of the history upon which they rely, confirms the opinion that we expressed in Jones. Other than the fact of a prior conviction, any fact that increases the penalty for a crime beyond the prescribed statutory maximum must be submitted to a jury, and proved beyond a reasonable doubt. With that exception, we endorse the statement of the rule set forth in the concurring opinions in that case: "[I]t is unconstitutional for a legislature to remove from the jury the assessment of facts that increase the prescribed range of penalties to which a criminal defendant is exposed. It is equally clear that such facts must be established by proof beyond a reasonable doubt." * * *

JUSTICE O'CONNOR, with whom THE CHIEF JUSTICE, JUSTICE KENNEDY, and JUSTICE BREYER join, dissenting.

* * * In one bold stroke the Court today casts aside our traditional cautious approach and instead embraces a universal and seemingly bright-line rule limiting the power of Congress and state legislatures to define criminal offenses and the sentences that follow from convictions thereunder. * * * [T]the Court marshals virtually no authority to support its extraordinary rule. Indeed, it is remarkable that the Court cannot identify a single instance, in the over 200 years since the ratification of the Bill of Rights, that our Court has applied, as a constitutional requirement, the rule it announces today. * * *

[A]pparently New Jersey could cure its sentencing scheme, and achieve virtually the same results, by drafting its weapons possession statute in the following manner: First, New Jersey could prescribe, in the weapons possession statute itself, a range of 5 to 20 years' imprisonment for one who commits that criminal offense. Second, New Jersey could provide that only those defendants convicted under the statute who are found by a judge, by a preponderance of the evidence, to have acted with a purpose to intimidate an individual on the basis of race may receive a sentence greater than 10 years' imprisonment.

Under another reading of the Court's decision, it may mean only that the Constitution requires that a fact be submitted to a jury and proved beyond a reasonable doubt if it, as a formal matter, increases the range of punishment beyond that which could legally be imposed absent that fact. A State could, however, remove from the jury (and subject to a standard of proof below "beyond a reasonable doubt") the assessment of those facts that, as a formal matter, decrease the range of punishment below that which could legally be imposed absent that fact. Thus, consistent with our decision in *Patterson*, New Jersey could cure its sentencing scheme, and achieve virtually the same results, by drafting its weapons possession statute in the following manner: First, New Jersey could prescribe, in the weapons possession statute itself, a range of 5 to 20 years' imprisonment for one who commits that criminal offense. Second, New Jersey could provide that a defendant convicted under the statute whom a judge finds, by a preponderance of the evidence, not to have acted with a purpose to intimidate an individual on the basis of race may receive a sentence no greater than 10 years' imprisonment.

* * * If either of the above readings is all that the Court's decision means, "the Court's principle amounts to nothing more than chastising [the New Jersey Legislature] for failing to use the approved phrasing in expressing its intent as to how [unlawful weapons possession] should be punished." If New Jersey can, consistent with the Constitution, make precisely the same differences in punishment turn on precisely the same facts, and can remove the assessment of those facts from the jury and subject them to a standard of proof below "beyond a reasonable doubt," it is impossible to say that the Fifth, Sixth, and Fourteenth Amendments require the Court's rule. For the same reason, the "structural democratic constraints" that might discourage a legislature from enacting either of the above hypothetical statutes would be no more significant than those that would discourage the enactment of New Jersey's present sentence-enhancement statute. In all three cases, the legislature is able to calibrate punishment perfectly, and subject to a maximum penalty only those defendants whose cases satisfy the sentence-enhancement criterion. * * *

One important purpose of the Sixth Amendment's jury trial guarantee is to protect the criminal defendant against potentially arbitrary judges. It effectuates this promise by preserving, as a constitutional matter, certain fundamental decisions for a jury of one's peers, as opposed to a judge. * * * Clearly, the concerns animating the Sixth Amendment's jury trial guarantee, if they were to extend to the sentencing context at all, would apply with greater strength to a discretionary-sentencing scheme than to determinate sentencing. In the former scheme, the potential for mischief by an arbitrary judge is much greater, given that the judge's decision of where to set the defendant's sentence within the prescribed statutory range is left almost entirely to discretion. In contrast, under a determinate-sentencing system, the discretion the judge wields within the statutory range is tightly constrained. Accordingly, our approval of discretionary-sentencing schemes, in which a defendant is not entitled to have a jury make factual findings relevant to sentencing despite the effect those findings have on the severity of the defendant's sentence, demonstrates that the defendant should have no right to demand that a jury make the equivalent factual determinations under a determinate-sentencing scheme.

The Court appears to hold today, however, that a defendant is entitled to have a jury decide, by proof beyond a reasonable doubt, every fact relevant to the determination of sentence under a determinate-sentencing scheme. If this is an accurate description of the constitutional principle underlying the Court's opinion, its decision will have the effect of invalidating significant sentencing reform accomplished at the federal and state levels over the past three decades. * * *

[The dissenting opinion of JUSTICE BREYER, with whom THE CHIEF JUSTICE joins, is omitted.]

Notes

1. Soon after *Apprendi* was decided, scores of challengers attempted to take advantage of what Justice O'Connor had termed a "watershed change in constitutional law." *Harris v. United States*, 536 U.S. 545 (2002) held that *Apprendi* is inapplicable to mandatory minimum sentences. Under federal law, carrying a firearm in relation to a drug trafficking offense requires a mandatory minimum sentence of five years. The judge, rather than jury, in Harris's case found that he had flourished a gun and sentenced him to seven years. Justice Kennedy's opinion first decided that the mandatory minimum provision was a sentence enhancement provision rather than a separate offense. This view affirmed *McMillan v. Pennsylvania*, 477 U.S. 79 (1986), which permitted a legislature to specify a condition for a mandatory minimum without making the condition an element of the crime. *Apprendi* did not apply to the mandatory minimum concept at issue, because that decision required a jury determination beyond a reasonable doubt for any fact that increased the penalty for a crime above the prescribed statutory maximum sentence. A "judge may impose the minimum, the maximum, or any other sentence within the range without seeking further authorization from" a jury.

2. By contrast, the Court in *Ring v. Arizona*, 536 U.S. 584 (2002) concluded that it violated *Apprendi* for a sentencing judge sitting without a jury to find an aggravating circumstance necessary for imposition of the death penalty. When the judge made that finding, the defendant was exposed to a penalty greater than that authorized by the jury's verdict alone, in violation of *Apprendi*.

3. *Apprendi* violations are subject to harmless error analysis. As with the failure to submit elements of a crime to the jury, the failure to submit a

sentencing factor to the jury is not a "structural" error. *Washington v. Recuenco*, 126 S.Ct. 2546 (2006).

UNITED STATES v. BOOKER

543 U.S. 220 (2005).

JUSTICE STEVENS delivered the opinion of the Court in part [in which Justice SCALIA, JUSTICE SOUTER, JUSTICE THOMAS, and JUSTICE GINSBURG join].

The question presented . . . is whether an application of the Federal Sentencing Guidelines violated the Sixth Amendment. In each case, the courts below held that binding rules set forth in the Guidelines limited the severity of the sentence that the judge could lawfully impose on the defendant based on the facts found by the jury at his trial. In both cases the courts rejected, on the basis of our decision in *Blakely v. Washington*, 542 U.S. 296 (2004), the Government's recommended application of the Sentencing Guidelines because the proposed sentences were based on additional facts that the sentencing judge found by a preponderance of the evidence. We hold that both courts correctly concluded that the Sixth Amendment as construed in Blakely does apply to the Sentencing Guidelines. In a separate opinion authored by Justice Breyer, the Court concludes that in light of this holding, two provisions of the Sentencing Reform Act of 1984(SRA) that have the effect of making the Guidelines mandatory must be invalidated in order to allow the statute to operate in a manner consistent with congressional intent.

I

Respondent Booker was charged with possession with intent to distribute at least 50 grams of cocaine base (crack). Having heard evidence that he had 92.5 grams in his duffel bag, the jury found him guilty of violating 21 U.S.C. § 841(a)(1). That statute prescribes a minimum sentence of 10 years in prison and a maximum sentence of life for that offense. § 841(b)(1)(A)(iii).

Based upon Booker's criminal history and the quantity of drugs found by the jury, the Sentencing Guidelines required the District Court Judge to select a "base" sentence of not less than 210 nor more than 262 months in prison. See United States Sentencing Commission, Guidelines Manual §§ 2D1.1(c)(4), 4A1.1 (Nov.2003) (hereinafter USSG). The judge, however, held a post-trial sentencing proceeding and concluded by a preponderance of the evidence that Booker had possessed an additional 566 grams of crack and that he was guilty of obstructing justice. Those findings mandated that the judge select a sentence between 360 months and life imprisonment; the judge imposed a sentence at the low end of the range. Thus, instead of the sentence of 21 years and 10 months that the judge could have imposed on the basis of the facts proved to the jury beyond a reasonable doubt, Booker received a 30–year sentence.

Over the dissent of Judge Easterbrook, the Court of Appeals for the Seventh Circuit held that this application of the Sentencing Guidelines conflicted with our holding in *Apprendi v. New Jersey*, 530 U.S. 466, 490 (2000), that "[o]ther than the fact of a prior conviction, any fact that increases the penalty for a crime beyond the prescribed statutory maximum must be submitted to a jury, and proved beyond a reasonable doubt." 375 F.3d 508, 510 (2004). The majority relied on our holding in *Blakely v. Washington* that "the 'statutory maximum' for *Apprendi* purposes is the maximum sentence a judge may impose solely on the basis of the facts reflected in the jury verdict or admitted by the defendant." The court held that the sentence violated the Sixth Amendment, and remanded with instructions to the District Court either to sentence respondent within the sentencing range supported by the jury's findings or to hold a separate sentencing hearing before a jury. * * *

II

It has been settled throughout our history that the Constitution protects every criminal defendant "against conviction except upon proof beyond a reasonable doubt of every fact necessary to constitute the crime with which he is charged." *In re Winship*, 397 U.S. 358, 364, (1970). It is equally clear that the "Constitution gives a criminal defendant the right to demand that a jury find him guilty of all the elements of the crime with which he is charged." *United States v. Gaudin*, 515 U.S. 506, 511, (1995). These basic precepts, firmly rooted in the common law, have provided the basis for recent decisions interpreting modern criminal statutes and sentencing procedures. * * *

In *Blakely v. Washington*, 542 U.S. 296 (2004), we dealt with a determinate sentencing scheme similar to the Federal Sentencing Guidelines. There the defendant pleaded guilty to kidnaping, a class B felony punishable by a term of not more than 10 years. Other provisions of Washington law, comparable to the Federal Sentencing Guidelines, mandated a "standard" sentence of 49–to–53 months, unless the judge found aggravating facts justifying an exceptional sentence. Although the prosecutor recommended a sentence in the standard range, the judge found that the defendant had acted with " 'deliberate cruelty' "and sentenced him to 90 months.

* * * The application of Washington's sentencing scheme violated the defendant's right to have the jury find the existence of " 'any particular fact' "that the law makes essential to his punishment. That right is implicated whenever a judge seeks to impose a sentence that is not solely based on "facts reflected in the jury verdict or admitted by the defendant." We rejected the State's argument that the jury verdict was sufficient to authorize a sentence within the general 10–year sentence for Class B felonies, noting that under Washington law, the judge was required to find additional facts in order to impose the greater 90–month sentence. Our precedents, we explained, make clear "that the 'statutory maximum' for Apprendi purposes is the maximum sentence a judge may impose solely on the basis of the facts reflected in the jury verdict or admitted by the defendant." The determination that the defendant acted with deliberate cruelty, like the determination in Apprendi that the defendant acted with racial malice, increased the sentence that the defendant could have otherwise received. Since this fact was found by a judge using a preponderance of the evidence standard, the sentence violated Blakely's Sixth Amendment rights.

As the dissenting opinions in *Blakely* recognized, there is no distinction of constitutional significance between the Federal Sentencing Guidelines and the Washington procedures at issue in that case. This conclusion rests on the premise, common to both systems, that the relevant sentencing rules are mandatory and impose binding requirements on all sentencing judges.

If the Guidelines as currently written could be read as merely advisory provisions that recommended, rather than required, the selection of particular sentences in response to differing sets of facts, their use would not implicate the Sixth Amendment. We have never doubted the authority of a judge to exercise broad discretion in imposing a sentence within a statutory range. See *Apprendi*, 530 U.S., at 481; *Williams v. New York*, 337 U.S. 241 (1949). Indeed, everyone agrees that the constitutional issues presented by these cases would have been avoided entirely if Congress had omitted from the SRA the provisions that make the Guidelines binding on district judges; it is that circumstance that makes the Court's answer to the second question presented possible. For when a trial judge exercises his discretion to select a specific sentence within a defined range, the defendant has no right to a jury determination of the facts that the judge deems relevant.

The Guidelines as written, however, are not advisory; they are mandatory and binding on all judges. While subsection (a) of § 3553 of the sentencing statute lists the Sentencing Guidelines as one factor to be considered in imposing a sentence, subsection (b) directs that the court "shall impose a sentence of the kind, and within the range" established by the Guidelines, subject to departures in specific, limited cases. Because they are binding on judges, we have consistently held that the Guidelines have the force and effect of laws.

* * * The Guidelines permit departures from the prescribed sentencing range in cases in which the judge "finds that there exists an aggravating or mitigating circumstance of a kind, or to a degree, not adequately taken into consideration by the Sentencing Commission in formulating the guidelines that should result in a sentence different from that described." 18 U.S.C.A. § 3553(b)(1) (Supp.2004). At first glance, one might believe that the ability of a district judge to depart from the Guidelines means that she is bound only by the statutory maximum. Were this the case, there would be no *Apprendi* problem. Importantly, however, departures are not available in every case, and in fact are unavailable in most. In most cases, as a matter of law, the Commission will have adequately taken all relevant factors into account, and no departure will be legally permissible. * * *

Booker's case illustrates the mandatory nature of the Guidelines. The jury convicted him of possessing at least 50 grams of crack in violation of 21 U.S.C. § 841(b)(1)(A)(iii) based on evidence that he had 92.5 grams of crack in his duffel bag. Under these facts, the Guidelines specified an offense level of 32, which, given the defendant's criminal history category, authorized a sentence of 210–to–262 months. See USSG § 2D1.1(c)(4). Booker's is a run-of-the-mill drug case, and does not present any factors that were inadequately considered by the Commission. The sentencing judge would therefore have been reversed had he not imposed a sentence within the level 32 Guidelines range. Booker's actual sentence, however, was 360 months, almost 10 years longer than the Guidelines range supported by the jury verdict alone. To reach this sentence, the judge found facts beyond those found by the jury: namely, that Booker possessed 566 grams of crack in addition to the 92.5 grams in his duffel bag. The jury never heard any evidence of the additional drug quantity, and the judge found it true by a preponderance of the evidence. Thus, just as in *Blakely*, "the jury's verdict alone does not authorize the sentence. The judge acquires that authority only upon finding some additional fact." There is no relevant distinction between the sentence imposed pursuant to the Washington statutes in *Blakely* and the sentences imposed pursuant to the Federal Sentencing Guidelines in these cases. * * *

III

The Government advances three arguments in support of its submission that we should not apply our reasoning in *Blakely* to the Federal Sentencing Guidelines. It contends that *Blakely* is distinguishable because the Guidelines were promulgated by a commission rather than the Legislature; that principles of stare decisis require us to follow four earlier decisions that are arguably inconsistent with *Blakely*; and that the application of *Blakely* to the Guidelines would conflict with separation of powers principles reflected in *Mistretta v. United States*, 488 U.S. 361 (1989). These arguments are unpersuasive. * * *

IV

All of the foregoing support our conclusion that our holding in *Blakely* applies to the Sentencing Guidelines. We recognize ... that in some cases jury factfinding may impair the most expedient and efficient sentencing of defendants. But the interest in fairness and reliability protected by the right to a jury trial—a common-law right that defendants enjoyed for centuries and that is now enshrined in the Sixth Amendment—has always outweighed the interest in concluding trials swiftly. * * *

Accordingly, we reaffirm our holding in *Apprendi*: Any fact (other than a prior conviction) which is necessary to support a sentence exceeding the maximum authorized by the facts established by a plea of guilty or a jury verdict must be admitted by the defendant or proved to a jury beyond a reasonable doubt.

JUSTICE BREYER delivered the opinion of the Court in part. [in which THE CHIEF JUSTICE, JUSTICE O'CONNOR, JUSTICE KENNEDY, and JUSTICE GINSBURG join].

* * * We answer the question of remedy by finding the provision of the federal sentencing statute that makes the Guidelines mandatory incompatible with today's constitutional holding. We conclude that this provision must be severed and excised, as must one other statutory section which depends upon the Guidelines' mandatory nature. So modified, the Federal Sentencing Act, see Sentencing Reform Act of 1984 makes the Guidelines effectively advisory. It requires a sentencing court to consider Guidelines ranges, but it permits the court to tailor the sentence in light of other statutory concerns as well.

I

We answer the remedial question by looking to legislative intent. We seek to determine what "Congress would have intended" in light of the Court's constitutional holding. In this instance, we must determine which of the two following remedial approaches is the more compatible with the legislature's intent as embodied in the 1984 Sentencing Act.

One approach, that of Justice Stevens' dissent, would retain the Sentencing Act (and the Guidelines) as written, but would engraft onto the existing system today's Sixth Amendment "jury trial" requirement. The addition would change the Guidelines by preventing the sentencing court from increasing a sentence on the basis of a fact that the jury did not find (or that the offender did not admit).

The other approach, which we now adopt, would (through severance and excision of two provisions) make the Guidelines system advisory while maintaining a strong connection between the sentence imposed and the offender's real conduct—a connection important to the increased uniformity of sentencing that Congress intended its Guidelines system to achieve.

Both approaches would significantly alter the system that Congress designed. But today's constitutional holding means that it is no longer possible to maintain the judicial factfinding that Congress thought would underpin the mandatory Guidelines system that it sought to create and that Congress wrote into the Act in 18 U.S.C.A. §§ 3553(a) and 3661 (main ed. and Supp.2004). Hence we must decide whether we would deviate less radically from Congress' intended system (1) by superimposing the constitutional requirement announced today or (2) through elimination of some provisions of the statute. * * *

II

Several considerations convince us that, were the Court's constitutional requirement added onto the Sentencing Act as currently written, the requirement would so transform the scheme that Congress created that Congress likely would not have intended the Act as so modified to stand. First, the statute's text states that "[t]he court" when sentencing will consider "the nature and circumstances of the offense and the history and characteristics of the defendant." 18 U.S.C.A. § 3553(a)(1). In context, the words "the court" mean "the judge without the jury," not "the judge working together with the jury." * * *

Second, Congress' basic statutory goal—a system that diminishes sentencing disparity—depends for its success upon judicial efforts to determine, and to base punishment upon, the real conduct that underlies the crime of conviction. That determination is particularly important * * * where an act that meets the statutory definition can be committed in a host of different ways. Judges have long looked to real conduct when sentencing. Federal judges have long relied upon a presentence report, prepared by a probation officer, for information (often unavailable until after the trial) relevant to the manner in which the convicted offender committed the crime of conviction. * * *

To engraft the Court's constitutional requirement onto the sentencing statutes, however, would destroy the system. It would prevent a judge from relying upon a presentence report for factual information, relevant to sentencing, uncovered after the trial. In doing so, it would, even compared to pre-Guidelines sentencing, weaken the tie between a sentence and an offender's real conduct. It would thereby undermine the sentencing statute's basic aim of ensuring similar sentences for those who have committed similar crimes in similar ways.

Several examples help illustrate the point. Imagine Smith and Jones, each of whom violates the Hobbs Act in very different ways. See 18 U.S.C. § 1951(a) (forbidding "obstruct[ing], delay[ing], or affect[ing] commerce or the movement of any article or commodity in commerce, by . . . extortion"). Smith threatens to injure a co-worker unless the co-worker advances him a few dollars from the interstate company's till; Jones, after similarly threatening the co-worker, causes far more harm by seeking far more money, by making certain that the co-worker's family is aware of the threat, by arranging for deliveries of dead animals to the co-worker's home to show he is serious, and so forth. The offenders' behavior is very different; the known harmful consequences of their actions are different; their punishments both before, and after, the Guidelines would have been different. But, under the dissenters' approach, unless prosecutors decide to charge more than the elements of the crime, the judge would have to impose similar punishments. * * *

Now imagine two former felons, Johnson and Jackson, each of whom engages in identical criminal behavior: threatening a bank teller with a gun, securing $50,000, and injuring an innocent bystander while fleeing the bank. Suppose prosecutors charge Johnson with one crime (say, illegal gun possession, and Jackson with another (say, bank robbery. Before the Guidelines, a single judge faced with such similar real conduct would have been able (within statutory limits) to impose similar sentences upon the two similar offenders despite the different charges brought against them. The Guidelines themselves would ordinarily have required judges to sentence the two offenders similarly. But under the dissenters' system, in these circumstances the offenders likely would receive different punishments. * * *

Third, the sentencing statutes, read to include the Court's Sixth Amendment requirement, would create a system far more complex than Congress could have intended. How would courts and counsel work with an indictment and a jury trial that involved not just whether a defendant robbed a bank but also how? Would the indictment have to allege, in addition to the elements of robbery, whether the defendant possessed a firearm, whether he brandished or discharged it, whether he threatened death, whether he caused bodily injury, whether any such injury was ordinary, serious, permanent or life threatening, whether he abducted or physically restrained anyone, whether any victim was unusually vulnerable, how much money was taken, and whether he was an organizer, leader, manager, or supervisor in a robbery gang? See USSG §§ 2B3.1, 3B1.1. If so, how could a defendant mount a defense against some or all such specific claims should he also try simultaneously to maintain that the Government's evidence failed to place him at the scene of the crime? * * *

Fourth, plea bargaining would not significantly diminish the consequences of the Court's constitutional holding for the operation of the Guidelines. Rather, plea bargaining would make matters worse. Congress enacted the sentencing statutes in major part to achieve greater uniformity in sentencing, i.e., to increase the likelihood that offenders who engage in similar real conduct would receive similar sentences. The statutes reasonably assume that their efforts to move the trial-based sentencing process in the direction of greater sentencing uniformity would have a similar positive impact upon plea-bargained sentences, for plea bargaining takes place in the shadow of (i.e., with an eye towards the hypothetical result of) a potential trial.

That, too, is why Congress, understanding the realities of plea bargaining, authorized the Commission to promulgate policy statements that would assist sentencing judges in determining whether to reject a plea agreement after reading about the defendant's real conduct in a presentence report (and giving the offender an opportunity to challenge the report). See 28 U.S.C. § 994(a)(2)(E); USSG § 6B1.2(a). This system has not worked perfectly; judges have often simply accepted an agreed-upon account of the conduct at issue. But compared to pre-existing law, the statutes try to move the system in the right direction, i.e., toward greater sentencing uniformity.

The Court's constitutional jury trial requirement, however, if patched onto the present Sentencing Act, would move the system backwards in respect both to tried and to plea-bargained cases. In respect to tried cases, it would effectively deprive the judge of the ability to use post-verdict-acquired real-conduct information; it would prohibit the judge from basing a sentence upon any conduct other than the conduct the prosecutor chose to charge; and it would put a defendant to a set of difficult strategic choices as to which prosecutorial claims he would contest. The sentence that would emerge in a case tried under such a system would likely reflect real conduct less completely, less accurately, and less often than did a pre-Guidelines, as well as a Guidelines, trial.

Because plea bargaining inevitably reflects estimates of what would happen at trial, plea bargaining too under such a system would move in the wrong direction. That is to say, in a sentencing system modified by the Court's constitutional requirement, plea bargaining would likely lead to sentences that gave greater weight, not to real conduct, but rather to the skill of counsel, the policies of the prosecutor, the caseload, and other factors that vary from place to place, defendant to defendant, and crime to crime. Compared to pre-Guidelines plea bargaining, plea bargaining of this kind would necessarily move federal sentencing in the direction of diminished, not increased, uniformity in sentencing. It would tend to defeat, not to further, Congress' basic statutory goal.

Such a system would have particularly troubling consequences with respect to prosecutorial power. Until now, sentencing factors have come before the judge in the presentence report. But in a sentencing system with the Court's constitutional requirement engrafted onto it, any factor that a prosecutor chose not to charge at the plea negotiation would be placed beyond the reach of the judge entirely. Prosecutors would thus exercise a power the Sentencing Act vested in judges: the power to decide, based on relevant information about the offense and the offender, which defendants merit heavier punishment. * * *

For all these reasons, Congress, had it been faced with the constitutional jury trial requirement, likely would not have passed the same Sentencing Act. It likely would have found the requirement incompatible with the Act as written. Hence the Act cannot remain valid in its entirety. Severance and excision are necessary.

III

We now turn to the question of which portions of the sentencing statute we must sever and excise as inconsistent with the Court's constitutional requirement. Although, as we have explained, we believe that Congress would have preferred the total invalidation of the statute to the dissenters' remedial approach, we nevertheless do not believe that the entire statute must be invalidated. Most of the statute is perfectly valid.

* * * [W]e must sever and excise two specific statutory provisions: the provision that requires sentencing courts to impose a sentence within the applicable Guidelines range (in the absence of circumstances that justify a departure), see 18 U.S.C. § 3553(b)(1), and the provision that sets forth standards of review on appeal, including de novo review of departures from the applicable Guidelines range, see § 3742(e). With these two sections excised (and statutory cross-references to the two sections consequently invalidated), the remainder of the Act satisfies the Court's constitutional requirements. As the Court today recognizes in its

first opinion in these cases, the existence of § 3553(b)(1) is a necessary condition of the constitutional violation. * * *

Without the "mandatory" provision, the Act nonetheless requires judges to take account of the Guidelines together with other sentencing goals. The Act nonetheless requires judges to consider the Guidelines "sentencing range established for . . . the applicable category of offense committed by the applicable category of defendant," the pertinent Sentencing Commission policy statements, the need to avoid unwarranted sentencing disparities, and the need to provide restitution to victims. And the Act nonetheless requires judges to impose sentences that reflect the seriousness of the offense, promote respect for the law, provide just punishment, afford adequate deterrence, protect the public, and effectively provide the defendant with needed educational or vocational training and medical care.

[D]espite the absence of § 3553(b)(1), the Act continues to provide for appeals from sentencing decisions (irrespective of whether the trial judge sentences within or outside the Guidelines range in the exercise of his discretionary power under § 3553(a)). We concede that the excision of § 3553(b)(1) requires the excision of a different, appeals-related section, namely § 3742(e), which sets forth standards of review on appeal. That section contains critical cross-references to the (now-excised) § 3553(b)(1) and consequently must be severed and excised for similar reasons.

Excision of § 3742(e), however, does not pose a critical problem for the handling of appeals. That is because, as we have previously held, a statute that does not explicitly set forth a standard of review may nonetheless do so implicitly. See *Pierce v. Underwood*, 487 U.S. 552, 558–560 (1988) (adopting a standard of review, where "neither a clear statutory prescription nor a historical tradition" existed, based on the statutory text and structure, and on practical considerations). We infer appropriate review standards from related statutory language, the structure of the statute, and the "sound administration of justice." *Pierce*, at 559–560. And in this instance those factors, in addition to the past two decades of appellate practice in cases involving departures, imply a practical standard of review already familiar to appellate courts: review for "unreasonable [ness]." 18 U.S.C. § 3742(e)(3). * * *

Ours, of course, is not the last word: The ball now lies in Congress' court. The National Legislature is equipped to devise and install, long-term, the sentencing system, compatible with the Constitution, that Congress judges best for the federal system of justice. * * *

V

In respondent Booker's case, the District Court applied the Guidelines as written and imposed a sentence higher than the maximum authorized solely by the jury's verdict. The Court of Appeals held *Blakely* applicable to the Guidelines, concluded that Booker's sentence violated the Sixth Amendment, vacated the judgment of the District Court, and remanded for resentencing. We affirm the judgment of the Court of Appeals and remand the case. On remand, the District Court should impose a sentence in accordance with today's opinions, and, if the sentence comes before the Court of Appeals for review, the Court of Appeals should apply the review standards set forth in this opinion. * * *

It is so ordered.

[JUSTICE STEVENS also dissented in part, arguing that the prosecution should be permitted to empanel juries to find "sentencing facts" that would increase a sentence above the maximum term of a presumptive range. Justice Scalia's dissenting opinion criticized the severance remedy, preferring a reasonableness standard.]

Notes and Questions

1. How does *Booker* affect a generation of defendants were sentenced under the Sentencing Guidelines? Immediately after *Booker*, officials from the United States Sentencing Commission, the Department of Justice, and the Congress were cautious about whether further legislative action was necessary.

The instant impact of *Booker* was to throw into disarray the appeals of hundreds of federal criminal cases. Defendants sentenced before *Booker* comprised the largest group potentially seeking a new sentencing hearing. Several circuits quickly decided that *Booker* is not retroactive. See, e.g., *McReynolds v. United States*, 397 F.3d 479 (7th Cir.2005); *Humphress v. United States*, 398 F.3d 855 (6th Cir.2005).

2. *Appellate Review of Sentences After* Booker. What about cases that were on appeal at the time *Booker* was decided? *United States v. Crosby*, 397 F.3d 103 (2d Cir.2005) set out a procedure for a limited remand on sentences invalid under *Booker*. As long as the trial court retains jurisdiction of the case, the trial judge may make a finding of whether she would have imposed a materially different sentence and, if she would have, she keeps the case and resentences. If the case is already on appeal, the circuit would review for "plain error" by the sentencing court when the defendant did not raise an objection.

If a defendant raised an objection and the Guidelines calculation was correct, but erroneous because the Guidelines' use was compulsory, the Second Circuit would remand to the trial court for resentencing in conformity with *Booker*.

Not every circuit has agreed with the *Crosby* approach. For example, in *United States v. Rodriguez*, 398 F.3d 1291 (11th Cir.2005), the court required that when the defendant did not raise the *Booker* issue, he must establish a "reasonable probability" that the trial judge would have imposed a different sentence had the Guidelines not been mandatory.

3. *Appellate Advice for Prospective Trial Court Sentencing*. For future cases, the circuits have attempted to prescribe a sentencing method, now that the mandatory nature of the Guidelines is unconstitutional.

[A]t this point, we can identify several essential aspects of Booker that concern the selection of sentences. First, the Guidelines are no longer mandatory. Second, the sentencing judge must consider the Guidelines and all of the other factors listed in section 3553(a). Third, consideration of the Guidelines will normally require determination of the applicable Guidelines range, or at least identification of the arguably applicable ranges, and consideration of applicable policy statements. Fourth, the sentencing judge should decide, after considering the Guidelines and all the other factors set forth in section 3553(a), whether (i) to impose the sentence that would have been imposed under the Guidelines, i.e., a sentence within the applicable Guidelines range or within permissible departure authority, or (ii) to impose a non-Guidelines sentence. Fifth, the sentencing judge is entitled to find all the facts appropriate for determining either a Guidelines sentence or a non-Guidelines sentence.

United States v. Crosby, 397 F.3d 103 (2d Cir.2005).

4. What is a "reasonable" sentence? Justice Breyer's opinion held that the remedy for the constitutional violation was to make the Guidelines advisory and to replace de novo appellate review of sentences with a reasonableness standard of review. Few appellate courts have seized the opportunity to define "reasonableness." One exception is *United States v. Fleming*, 397 F.3d 95 (2d Cir.2005), in which the court described how an appellate court would assess the reasonableness of a federal sentence.

The appellate function in this context should exhibit restraint, not micromanagement. In addition to their familiarity with the record, including the presentence report, district judges have discussed sentencing with a probation officer and gained an impression of a defendant from the entirety of the proceedings, including the defendant's opportunity for sentencing allocution. The appellate court proceeds only with the record. Although the brevity or length of a sentence can exceed the bounds of "reasonableness," we anticipate encountering such circumstances infrequently.

In the pending case, the District Court sentenced a defendant who had served three sentences of imprisonment and was appearing for his third violation of a term of supervised release. Judge Gershon considered the current violations "massive." She noted that the Defendant had been given the benefit of a substantial departure for his cooperation in connection with his sentence on the prisoner assault charge. See U.S.S.G. § 7B1.4, comment. (n.4) ("Where the original sentence was the result of a downward departure (e.g., as a reward for substantial assistance), ... an upward departure may be warranted."). She identified as the "primary purpose" of her sentence "the necessity for both punishment for [Fleming's] behavior and deterrence." The District Court's explanation was sufficient to facilitate appellate review. Under all the circumstances, we cannot say that the two-year sentence was unreasonable.

Chapter 22

DOUBLE JEOPARDY

In Chapter 16, you studied the double jeopardy implications associated with the joinder of offenses. To review the basic principle, a defendant has both federal and state constitutional protections against being placed in jeopardy twice for the same offense. The pertinent part of the Fifth Amendment states: "[N]or shall any person be subject for the same offense to be twice put in jeopardy of life or limb." The Fifth Amendment Double Jeopardy protection applies to the states through the Fourteenth Amendment. *Benton v. Maryland*, 395 U.S. 784 (1969).

Because the debates of the constitutional framers provided little indication of the intended scope of double jeopardy protection, the courts have interpreted the double jeopardy clause in light of their understanding of its underlying purposes. The essence of the prohibition against double jeopardy is not that a defendant may incur a greater risk of being found guilty in a second trial than in a first trial, or that a second trial may be conducted prejudicially, but rather that the defendant would risk conviction for an offense for which the defendant has already been placed on trial and in jeopardy.

A successful claim involving double jeopardy will bar a trial on the indictment or information. The objection may be raised by a motion to dismiss at any time before trial. Although a failure to raise the objection before the second adjudication may operate as a waiver, it may be raised for the first time in a reviewing court if the double jeopardy issue can be decided as a matter of law on the facts established by the record. *Menna v. New York*, 423 U.S. 61 (1975).

Double jeopardy bars a second prosecution only if jeopardy attached in the original proceeding. In a jury trial, jeopardy attaches when the jury is sworn. *Crist v. Bretz*, 437 U.S. 28 (1978). If a case is tried before a judge, after waiver of a jury, jeopardy attaches when the first witness is sworn. Jeopardy also attaches when the trial court accepts a guilty plea. Conversely, withdrawal of a guilty plea is a waiver of the double jeopardy protection against trial on the charge in the indictment or information. If a case is dismissed or terminated prior to the attachment of jeopardy,

jeopardy has not attached and the defendant may have to respond to the same criminal charges in further proceedings.

One of the requirements for the attachment of jeopardy is that the court hearing the case have proper jurisdiction. When the court exceeds its jurisdiction, a conviction is void and there is no bar to a new trial. Absent a facial jurisdictional defect, the prior adjudication is presumed to have been within the court's jurisdiction. Likewise, a prior conviction or acquittal procured by the defendant to defraud the government of an opportunity to attain the proper sentence does not bar a new prosecution.

The doctrine of dual sovereignty does not prohibit multiple prosecutions for the same offense by courts of different sovereignties. *See, e.g., Heath v. Alabama*, 474 U.S. 82 (1985) (successive prosecutions by different states permissible); *Bartkus v. People of State of Illinois*, 359 U.S. 121 (1959) (successive state and federal trials for same offense permissible). On the other hand, the dual sovereignty theory does not apply to state and municipal prosecutions for the same act because the state and the municipality are regarded as the same sovereign, regardless of how the state chooses to classify its governmental subunits: the subunits derive their power to exist from the sovereign. *See, e.g., Waller v. Florida*, 397 U.S. 387 (1970) (successive prosecutions for same offense based upon violations of state statute and local ordinance prohibited by double jeopardy).

A. MISTRIALS AND THE POSSIBILITY OF A RETRIAL

After jeopardy attaches, a case cannot be terminated without an adjudication because the defendant has a right to have the case completed by a particular factfinder. *Wade v. Hunter*, 336 U.S. 684 (1949). A mistrial declaration is the most common exception to this double jeopardy concept. A mistrial is granted whenever an error has occurred in the trial that cannot be cured by any remedial action of the parties or the court. In most jurisdictions, there is an extensive amount of case law dealing with the types of error in the admission of evidence and the conduct of counsel, witnesses, the court, and jury that are "curable" by instructions or continuances, and which errors require a mistrial. As *United States v. Scott, infra*, will discuss, the term "mistrial" must be distinguished from an acquittal or dismissal in terms of its double jeopardy consequences.

When circumstances suggest that the proceedings should be terminated, with the court declaring a mistrial prior to a formal verdict, the judge at that time need not decide whether a subsequent trial on the same charge would be permissible. The only question before the court is whether the first trial should be discontinued. If the trial judge terminates the proceedings by declaring a mistrial, the court's order reflects a belief that retrial on the same charges should be permitted. Although a double jeopardy claim will not arise until the charges are brought again, that later double jeopardy claim constitutes an attack on the propriety of the original mistrial declaration, *i.e.*, there was no manifest necessity for declaring the mistrial.

Mistrials can be broadly characterized in two areas: (1) where the defendant does not consent to the mistrial; and (2) where the defendant consents to the mistrial. In the first situation, any prosecution motion for a mistrial or the court's declaration of a mistrial on its own motion, over the defendant's objection, creates concern about whether there is "manifest necessity" for declaring a mistrial at the first trial. If the termination of the first trial was manifestly necessary, a retrial is permitted. If the termination was not manifestly necessary, double jeopardy prohibits a retrial. The decision to grant a mistrial is within the trial court's discretion.

ILLINOIS v. SOMERVILLE

410 U.S. 458 (1973).

MR. JUSTICE REHNQUIST delivered the opinion of the Court.

We must here decide whether declaration of a mistrial over the defendant's objection, because the trial court concluded that the indictment was insufficient to charge a crime, necessarily prevents a State from subsequently trying the defendant under a valid indictment. We hold that the mistrial met the "manifest necessity" requirement of our cases, since the trial court could reasonably have concluded that the "ends of public justice" would be defeated by having allowed the trial to continue. Therefore, the Double Jeopardy Clause of the Fifth Amendment [did] not bar retrial under a valid indictment.

On March 19, 1964, respondent was indicted by an Illinois grand jury for the crime of theft. The case was called for trial and a jury impaneled and sworn on November 1, 1965. The following day, before any evidence had been presented, the prosecuting attorney realized that the indictment was fatally deficient under Illinois law because it did not allege that respondent intended to permanently deprive the owner of his property. Under the applicable Illinois criminal statute, such intent is a necessary element of the crime of theft, and failure to allege intent renders the indictment insufficient to charge a crime. [But] Illinois further provides that only formal defects, of which this was not one, may be cured by amendment. The combined operation of these rules of Illinois procedure and substantive law meant that the defect in the indictment was "jurisdictional"; it could not be waived by the defendant's failure to object, and could be asserted on appeal or in a post-conviction proceeding to overturn a final judgment of conviction.

Faced with this situation, the Illinois trial court concluded that further proceedings under this defective indictment would be useless and granted the State's motion for a mistrial. On November 3, the grand jury handed down a second indictment alleging the requisite intent. Respondent was arraigned two weeks after the first trial was aborted, raised a claim of double jeopardy which was over-ruled, and the second trial commenced shortly thereafter. The jury returned a verdict of guilty, sentence was imposed, and the Illinois courts upheld the conviction. Respondent then sought federal habeas corpus. The Seventh Circuit affirmed the denial of habeas corpus prior to our decision in *United States v. Jorn*, 400 U.S. 470 (1971). The respondent's petition for certiorari was granted, and the case remanded for reconsideration in light of *Jorn* and *Downum v. United States*, 372 U.S. 734 (1963). On remand, the Seventh Circuit held that respondent's petition for habeas corpus should have been granted [because] jeopardy had attached when the jury was impaneled and sworn, and a declaration of mistrial over respondent's objection precluded a retrial under a valid indictment. For the reasons stated below, we reverse that judgment.

The fountainhead decision construing the Double Jeopardy Clause in the context of a declaration of a mistrial over a defendant's objection is *United States v. Perez*, 9 Wheat. 579 (1824). Mr. Justice Story, writing for a unanimous Court, set forth the standards for determining whether a retrial, following a declaration of a mistrial over a defendant's objection, constitutes double [jeopardy]. In holding that the failure of the jury to agree on a verdict of either acquittal or conviction did not bar retrial of the defendant, Mr. Justice Story wrote:

> We think, that in all cases of this nature, the law has invested Courts of justice with the authority to discharge a jury from giving any verdict, whenever, in their opinion, taking all the circumstances into consideration, there is a manifest necessity for the act, or the ends of public justice would otherwise be defeated. They are to exercise a sound discretion on the subject; and it is impossible to define all the circumstances, which would render it proper to interfere. * * *

This formulation, consistently adhered to by this Court in subsequent decisions, abjures the application of any mechanical formula by which to judge the propriety of declaring a mistrial in the varying and often unique situations arising during the course of a criminal trial. The broad discretion reserved to the trial judge in such circumstances has been consistently reiterated in decisions of this Court. [In] reviewing the propriety of the trial judge's exercise of his discretion, this Court, following the counsel of Mr. Justice Story, has scrutinized the action to determine whether, in the context of that particular trial, the declaration of a mistrial was dictated by "manifest necessity" or the "ends of public justice."

In *Perez*, this Court held that "manifest necessity" justified the discharge of juries unable to reach verdicts, and, therefore, the Double Jeopardy Clause did not bar retrial. In *Simmons v. United States*, 142 U.S. 148 (1891), a trial judge dismissed the jury, over defendant's objection, because one of the jurors had been acquainted with the defendant, and, therefore, was probably prejudiced against the Government; this Court held that the trial judge properly exercised his power "to prevent the defeat of the ends of public justice." In *Thompson v.*

United States, 155 U.S. 271 (1894), a mistrial was declared after the trial judge learned that one of the jurors was disqualified, he having been a member of the grand jury that indicted the defendant. * * *

While virtually all of the cases turn on the particular facts and thus escape meaningful categorization, it is possible to distill from them a general approach, premised on the "public justice" policy enunciated in *Perez*, to situations such as that presented by this case. A trial judge properly exercises his discretion to declare a mistrial if an impartial verdict cannot be reached, or if a verdict of conviction could be reached but would have to be reversed on appeal due to an obvious procedural error in the trial. If an error would make reversal on appeal a certainty, it would not serve "the ends of public justice" to require that the Government proceed with its proof when, if it succeeded before the jury, it would automatically be stripped of that success by an appellate court. [While] the declaration of a mistrial on the basis of a rule or a defective procedure that would lend itself to prosecutorial manipulation would involve an entirely different question, *cf. Downum*, such was not the situation in the above cases or in the instant case.

In *Downum*, the defendant was charged with six counts of mail theft, and forging and uttering stolen checks. A jury was selected and sworn in the morning, and instructed to return that afternoon. When the jury returned, the Government moved for the discharge of the jury on the ground that a key prosecution witness, for two of the six counts against defendant, was not present. The prosecution knew, prior to the selection and swearing of the jury, that this witness could not be found and had not been served with a subpoena. The trial judge discharged the jury over the defendant's motions to dismiss two counts for failure to prosecute and to continue the other four. This Court, in reversing the convictions on the ground of double jeopardy, emphasized that "[e]ach case must turn on its facts," and held that the second prosecution constituted double jeopardy, because the absence of the witness and the reason therefor did not there justify, in terms of "manifest necessity," the declaration of a mistrial.

In *Jorn*, the Government called a taxpayer witness in a prosecution for willfully assisting in the preparation of fraudulent income tax returns. Prior to his testimony, defense counsel suggested he be warned of his constitutional right against compulsory self-incrimination. The trial judge warned him of his rights, and the witness stated that he was willing to testify and that the Internal Revenue Service agent who first contacted him warned him of his rights. The trial judge, however, did not believe the witness' declaration that the IRS had so warned him, and refused to allow him to testify until after he had consulted with an attorney. After learning from the Government that the remaining four witnesses were "similarly situated," and after surmising that they, too, had not been properly informed of their rights, the trial judge declared a mistrial to give the witnesses the opportunity to consult with attorneys. In sustaining a plea in bar of double jeopardy to an attempted second trial of the defendant, the plurality opinion of the Court, emphasizing the importance to the defendant of proceeding before the first jury sworn, concluded:

> It is apparent from the record that no consideration was given to the possibility of a trial continuance; indeed, the trial judge acted so abruptly in discharging the jury that, had the prosecutor been disposed to suggest a continuance, or the defendant to object to the discharge of the jury, there would have been no opportunity to do so. When one examines the circumstances surrounding the discharge of this jury, it seems abundantly apparent that the trial judge made no effort to exercise a sound discretion to assure that, taking all the circumstances into account, there was a manifest necessity for the sua sponte declaration of this mistrial. *United States v. Perez.* Therefore, we must conclude that in the circumstances of this case, appellee's reprosecution would violate the double jeopardy provision of the Fifth Amendment.

[Respondent] argues that our decision in *Jorn*, which respondent interprets as narrowly limiting the circumstances in which a mistrial is manifestly necessary, requires affirmance. Emphasizing the "valued right to have his trial completed by a particular tribunal," *Jorn*, respondent contends that the circumstances did not justify depriving him of that right. [We] believe that in light of the State's established rules of criminal procedure, the trial judge's declaration of a mistrial was not an abuse of discretion. Since this Court's decision in *Benton v. Maryland*, 395 U.S. 784 (1969), federal courts will be confronted with such claims that arise in large measure from the often diverse procedural rules existing in the 50 States. Federal courts should not be quick to conclude that simply because a state procedure does not conform to the corresponding federal statute or rule, it does not serve a legitimate state policy. * * *

In the instant case, the trial judge terminated the proceeding because a defect was found to exist in the indictment that was, as a matter of Illinois law, not curable by amendment. The Illinois courts have held that even after a judgment of conviction has become final, the defendant may be released on habeas corpus, because the defect in the indictment deprives the trial court of "jurisdiction." The rule prohibiting the amendment of all but formal defects in indictments is designed to implement the State's policy of preserving the right of each defendant to insist that a criminal prosecution against him be commenced by the action of a grand jury. The trial judge was faced with a situation [in] which a procedural defect might or would preclude the public from either obtaining an impartial verdict or keeping a verdict of conviction if its evidence persuaded the jury. If a mistrial were constitutionally unavailable in situations such as this, the State's policy could only be implemented by conducting a second trial after verdict and reversal on appeal, thus wasting time, energy, and money for all concerned. Here, the trial judge's action was a rational determination designed to implement a legitimate state policy, with no suggestion that the implementation of that policy in this manner could be manipulated so as to prejudice the defendant. This situation is thus unlike *Downum*, where the mistrial entailed not only a delay for the defendant, but also operated as a post-jeopardy continuance to allow the prosecution an opportunity to strengthen its case. Here, the delay was minimal, and the mistrial was, under Illinois law, the only way in which a defect in the indictment could be corrected. * * *

The determination by the trial court to abort a criminal proceeding where jeopardy has attached is not one to be lightly undertaken, since the interest of the defendant in having his fate determined by the jury first impaneled is itself a weighty one. *Jorn*. Nor will the lack of demonstrable additional prejudice preclude the defendant's invocation of the double jeopardy bar in the absence of some important countervailing interest of proper judicial administration. But where the declaration of a mistrial implements a reasonable state policy and aborts a proceeding that at best would have produced a verdict that could have been upset at will by one of the parties, the defendant's interest in proceeding to verdict is outweighed by the competing and equally legitimate demand for public justice.

Reversed.

Mr. Justice White, with whom Mr. Justice Douglas and Mr. Justice Brennan join, dissenting.

[Despite] the generality of the *Perez* standard, some guidelines have evolved from past cases, as this Court has reviewed the exercise of trial court discretion in a variety of circumstances. *Jorn* and *Downum*, for example, make it abundantly clear that trial courts should have constantly in mind the purposes of the Double Jeopardy Clause to protect the defendant from continued exposure to embarrassment, anxiety, expense, and restrictions on his liberty, as well as to preserve his "valued right to have his trial completed by a particular tribunal." [Although] the exact extent of the emotional and physical harm suffered by Somerville during the period between his first and second trial is open to debate, it cannot be gainsaid that Somerville lost "his option to go to the first jury and, perhaps, end the dispute then and there with an acquittal." *Jorn*. There was not, in this case any more than in *Downum* and *Jorn*, "manifest necessity" for the loss of that right.

The majority recognizes that "the interest of the defendant in having his fate determined by the jury first impaneled is itself a weighty one," but finds that interest outweighed by the State's desire to avoid "conducting a second trial after verdict and reversal on appeal [on the basis of a defective indictment], thus wasting time, energy, and money for all concerned." The majority finds paramount the interest of the State in "keeping a verdict of conviction if its evidence persuaded the jury." Such analysis, however, completely ignores the possibility that the defendant might be acquitted by the initial jury. It is, after all, that possibility—the chance to "end the dispute then and there with an acquittal,"—that makes the right to a trial before a particular tribunal of importance to a defendant. * * *

Apparently the majority finds "manifest necessity" for a mistrial and the retrial of the defendant in "the State's policy of preserving the right of each defendant to insist that a criminal prosecution against him be commenced by the action of a ground jury" and the implementation of that policy in the absence from Illinois procedural rules of any procedure for the amendment of indictments. Conceding the reasonableness of such a policy, it must be remembered that the inability to amend an indictment does not come into play, and a mistrial is not necessitated, unless an error on the part of the State in the framing of the indictment is committed. Only when the indictment is defective—only when the State has failed to properly execute its responsibility to frame a proper indictment—does the State's procedural framework necessitate a mistrial. * * *

MR. JUSTICE MARSHALL, dissenting. * * *

If the only alternative to declaring a mistrial did require the trial judge to ignore the tenor of previous state decisional law though perhaps declaring a mistrial would have been a manifest necessity. But there obviously was another alternative. The trial judge could have continued the trial. The majority suggests that this would have been a useless charade. But to a defendant, forcing the Government to proceed with its proof would almost certainly not be useless. The Government might not persuade the jury of the defendant's guilt. * * *

Once it is shown that alternatives to the declaration of a mistrial existed, as they did here, we must consider whether the reasons which led to the declaration were sufficient, in light of those alternatives, to overcome the defendant's interest in trying the case to the jury. [Here] again the majority mischaracterized the state policy at stake here. What is involved is not, as the majority says, "the right of each defendant to insist that a criminal prosecution against him be commenced by the action of a grand jury." Rather, the interest is in making the defect in the indictment here jurisdictional and not waivable by a defendant. Ordinarily, a defect in jurisdiction means that one institution has invaded the proper province of another. Such defects are not waivable because the State has an interest in preserving the allocation of competence between those institutions. Here, for example, the petit jury would invade the province of the grand jury if it returned a verdict of guilty on an improper indictment. However, allocation of jurisdiction is most important when one continuing body acts in the area of competence reserved to another continuing body. While it may be desirable to keep a single petit jury from invading the province of a single grand jury, surely that interest is not so substantial as to outweigh the "defendant's valued right to have his trial completed by a particular tribunal." * * *

I believe that *Downum* and *Jorn* are controlling. As in those cases, the trial judge here did not pursue an available alternative, and the reason which led him to declare a mistrial was prosecutorial negligence, a reason that this Court found insufficient in *Downum*.

Notes and Questions

1. *Somerville* is indicative of the clash of interests favoring and opposing reprosecution following a mistrial. The prosecution argues that it has a strong interest in obtaining one reasonable opportunity to establish the defendant's guilt. In addition, any error in declaring the mistrial confers on the defendant an immunity from punishment for the crimes charged. This factor explains the reluctance of courts to second-guess the initial mistrial ruling when considering double jeopardy claims. Defense counsel argue that reprosecution is undesirable because it subjects the defendant to serious burdens even if the defendant is acquitted at a retrial. For example, delay in scheduling the retrial may impede the preparation of the defendant's case and increase the personal strain of a retrial. Invariably, the defense arguments return to the defendant's interest in completing the trial before a jury that was favorably disposed to the defendant's case.

2. *Defense counsel misconduct.* In *Arizona v. Washington*, 434 U.S. 497 (1978), the trial court granted defendant a new trial, but during the opening statements of the retrial, the defense attorney referred to the prosecution's prior misdeeds. The trial court granted the prosecution's motion for a mistrial because the evidence of the first trial would have been inadmissible and the judge feared that the jury had been biased by these comments. The trial judge made no explicit finding of manifest necessity for the mistrial and did not expressly consider alternatives to granting a mistrial. Writing for a 6–3 majority, Justice Stevens said that when a mistrial is justified by a "high degree" of necessity, the defendant's right to a particular tribunal is outweighed by society's right to have one complete opportunity to prosecute the accused. When mistrials are declared due to hung juries, trial judges have considerable discretion to gauge firsthand the amount of time a particular jury needs to reach a verdict. Likewise, when defense counsel makes prejudicial comments to the jury, the trial judge can observe the impact of the statements on the jury and select the appropriate remedy. Justice Stevens observed that if the trial judge lacked broad discretion to erase the effects of prejudicial statements, unscrupulous defense attorneys would take unfair advantage of their clients' double jeopardy rights by intentionally biasing the jury. Therefore, appellate courts should defer to a trial judge's decision to grant a mistrial, unless there is an abuse of that discretion.

In upholding the broad discretion of a trial judge to declare a mistrial, *Washington* did not require trial courts to make express findings of manifest necessity, or explicitly to consider alternatives to the mistrial declaration on the record. The Court failed to provide lower courts with guidance in addressing other sorts of mistrials. For example, should a trial judge have broad discretion in every instance of defense counsel misconduct, such as prejudicial statements made during *closing* arguments after a long trial?

3. Professor Amsterdam has observed that the decision to move for a mistrial is a strategic matter. *See* Anthony G. Amsterdam, *Trial Manual 5 for the Defense of Criminal Cases* (1988). Both counsel should keep in mind several factors.

A) How does the case appear to be proceeding with *this* jury, *i.e.*, what is the probability of favorable verdict?

B) Have trial errors already been committed to which counsel has preserved with appropriate objections, and would those errors likely result in a reversal of a conviction?

C) What is the likely cost, in delay and expense, of a new trial following a mistrial declaration?

D) What are the likely strengths of the parties at a new trial which would differ from their relative strengths at this trial because of, *inter alia*, the discovery of the opposing party's case which the trial has provided, the extent to which each party has learned to try his case and will do a better job next time, and the fixing of witness testimony with which impeachment may be made at a new trial?

Problems

The decision to declare a mistrial is within the trial court's discretion. As a trial judge and in light of the Supreme Court cases you have read, would you find manifest necessity in the following situations when a motion for mistrial is made? As you consider your decision, consider any alternatives (e.g., continuance, curative jury instruction, polling jurors, seeking counsel's consent to proceeding with fewer than the statutory number of jurors) to the mistrial declaration.

1.   The prosecutor has made an improper reference to the defendant's exercise of her right to silence at the time of her arrest. Can your admonition to the jury remove any prejudice?

2.   You grant a codefendant's motion to dismiss all charges in open court, but deny defendant's motion. Can you admonish the jury effectively that the dismissal creates no inference about the remaining defendant's guilt or innocence?

3.   A juror asks to be relieved of jury duty after she receives notification during trial that her father has died and her spouse is hospitalized. The prosecutor moves for a mistrial over the defense counsel's objections. Does it matter whether an alternate juror is available to replace this grieving juror?

4.   A juror is arrested between the guilt and penalty phases of defendant's trial, but quickly is released on his own recognizance. Again, as a result of the circumstances, the prosecutor moves for a mistrial over the defense counsel's objections.

5.   The jury reports to you that it is deadlocked and cannot agree on a verdict. Should the judge send the jury back to the jury room to deliberate or grant a *sua sponte* motion for a mistrial?

6.   The defendant is temporarily absent from the trial while the trial proceeds. The prosecutor moves for a mistrial over the defense counsel's objections.

7.   The prosecutor is ill.

8.   You have granted defense counsel's motion to withdraw as counsel in the middle of the trial.

———

Although the manifest necessity concept may provide an unpredictable test, the declaration of a mistrial at the request of anyone other than the defendant sets the stage for a strong double jeopardy claim. A defense objection to preserve the claim should be made when defense counsel does not believe that the client's interests are best served by acquiescence in a mistrial and a new trial. Fed.R.Crim.P. 26.3 requires that the court consider the views of all parties in before ruling on a motion for mistrial: "Before ordering a mistrial, the court shall provide an opportunity for the government and for each defendant to comment on the propriety of the order, including whether each party consents or objects to a mistrial, and to suggest any alternative."

Generally, a retrial is permissible if the defendant actively sought or consented to a premature termination of the earlier proceedings. As the following case shows, however, a defendant who seeks and obtains a mistrial may still use the double jeopardy protection to avoid a retrial.

OREGON v. KENNEDY

456 U.S. 667 (1982).

JUSTICE REHNQUIST delivered the opinion of the Court.

[Respondent] was charged with the theft of an oriental rug. During his first trial, the State called an expert witness on the subject of Middle Eastern rugs to testify as to the value and the identity of the rug in question. On cross-examination, respondent's attorney apparently attempted to establish bias on the part of the expert witness by asking him whether he had filed a criminal complaint against respondent. The witness eventually acknowledged this fact, but explained that no action had been taken on his complaint. On redirect examination, the prosecutor sought to elicit the reasons why the witness had filed a complaint against respondent, but the trial court sustained a series of objections to this line of inquiry. The following colloquy then ensued:

"Prosecutor: Have you ever done business with the Kennedys?

"Witness: No, I have not.

"Prosecutor: Is that because he is a crook?"

The trial court then granted respondent's motion for a mistrial.

When the State later sought to retry respondent, he moved to dismiss the charges because of double jeopardy. After a hearing at which the prosecutor testified, the trial court found as a fact that "it was not the intention of the prosecutor in this case to cause a mistrial." On the basis of this finding, the trial court held that double jeopardy principles did not bar retrial, and respondent was then tried and convicted.

Respondent then successfully appealed to the Oregon Court of Appeals, which sustained his double jeopardy claim. [The] Court of Appeals accepted the trial court's finding that it was not the intent of the prosecutor to cause a mistrial. Nevertheless, the court held that retrial was barred because the prosecutor's conduct in this case constituted what it viewed as "overreaching." Although the prosecutor intended to rehabilitate the witness, the Court of Appeals expressed the view that the question was in fact "a direct personal attack on the general character of the defendant." This personal attack left respondent with a "Hobson's choice—either to accept a necessarily prejudiced jury, or to move for a mistrial and face the process of being retried at a later time." * * *

Where the trial is terminated over the objection of the defendant, the classical test for lifting the double jeopardy bar to a second trial is the "manifest necessity" standard first enunciated in Justice Story's opinion for the Court in *United States v. Perez*. [The] "manifest necessity" standard provides sufficient protection to the defendant's interests in having his case finally decided by the jury first selected while at the same time maintaining "the public's interest in fair trials designed to end in just judgments." But in the case of a mistrial declared at the behest of the defendant, quite different principles come into play. Here the defendant himself has elected to terminate the proceedings against him, and the "manifest necessity" standard has no place in the application of the Double Jeopardy Clause. *United States v. Dinitz*, 424 U.S. 600 (1976). Indeed, the Court stated [in an earlier case]: "If [defendant] had *requested* a [mistrial], there would be no doubt that if he had been successful, the Government would not have been barred from retrying him." [emphasis in original] * * *

Since one of the principal threads making up the protection embodied in the Double Jeopardy Clause is the right of the defendant to have his trial completed before the first jury empaneled to try him, it may be wondered as a matter of original inquiry why the defendant's election to terminate the first trial by his own motion should not be deemed a renunciation of that right for all purposes. We have recognized, however, that there would be great difficulty in applying such a rule where the prosecutor's actions giving rise to the motion for mistrial were done "in order to goad the [defendant] into requesting a mistrial." *Dinitz*. In such a case, the defendant's valued right to complete his trial before the first jury would be a hollow shell if the inevitable motion for mistrial were held to prevent a later invocation of the bar of double jeopardy in all circumstances. But the precise phrasing of the circumstances which will allow a defendant to interpose the defense of double jeopardy to a second prosecution where the first has terminated on his own motion for a mistrial have been stated with less than crystal clarity in our cases which deal with this area of the law. [The] language [of *Dinitz* at points] would seem to broaden the test from one of intent to provoke a motion for a mistrial to a more generalized standard of "bad faith conduct" or "harassment" on the part of the judge or prosecutor. It was upon this language that the Oregon Court of Appeals apparently relied in concluding that the prosecutor's colloquy with the expert witness in this case amount to "overreaching."

The difficulty with the more general standards which would permit a broader exception than one merely based on intent is that they offer virtually no standards for their application. Every act on the part of a rational prosecutor during a trial is designed to "prejudice" the defendant by placing before the judge or jury evidence leading to a finding of his guilt. Given the complexity of the rules of evidence, it will be a rare trial of any complexity in which some proffered evidence by the prosecutor or by the defendant's attorney will not be found objectionable by the trial court. Most such objections are undoubtedly curable by simply refusing to allow the proffered evidence to be admitted, or in the case of a particular line of inquiry taken by counsel with a witness, by an admonition to desist from a particular line of inquiry. * * *

By contrast, a standard that examines the intent of the prosecutor, though certainly not entirely free from practical difficulties, is a manageable standard to apply. It merely calls for the court to make a finding of fact. Inferring the existence or nonexistence of intent from objective facts and circumstances is a familiar process in our criminal justice system. When it is remembered that resolution of double jeopardy questions by state trial courts are reviewable not only within the state court system, but in the federal court system on habeas corpus as well, the desirability of an easily applied principle is apparent.

Prosecutorial conduct that might be viewed as harassment or overreaching, even if sufficient to justify a mistrial on defendant's motion, therefore, does not bar retrial absent intent on the part of the prosecutor to subvert the protections afforded by the Double Jeopardy Clause. A defendant's motion for a mistrial constitutes "a deliberate election on his part to forgo his valued right to have his guilt or innocence determined before the first trier of fact." *United States v. Scott*, 437 U.S. 82 (1978). Where prosecutorial error even of a degree sufficient to warrant a mistrial has occurred, "[t]he important consideration, for purposes of the Double Jeopardy Clause, is that the defendant retain primary control over the course to be followed in the event of such error." *Dinitz*. Only where the governmental conduct in question is intended to "goad" the defendant into moving for a mistrial may a defendant raise the bar of double jeopardy to a second trial after having succeeded in aborting the first on his own motion. * * *

[We] do not by this opinion lay down a flat rule that where a defendant in a criminal trial successfully moves for a mistrial, he may not thereafter invoke the bar of double jeopardy against a second trial. But we do hold that the circumstances under which such a defendant may invoke the bar of double jeopardy in a second effort to try him are limited to those cases in which the conduct giving rise to the successful motion for a mistrial was intended to provoke the defendant into moving for a mistrial. Since the Oregon trial court found, and the Oregon Court of Appeals accepted, that the prosecutorial conduct culminating in the termination of the first trial in this case was not so intended by the prosecutor, that is the end of the matter for purposes of the Double Jeopardy Clause of the Fifth Amendment to the United States Constitution. * * *

Justice Powell, concurring.

I join the Court's opinion holding that the intention of a prosecutor determines whether his conduct, viewed by the defendant and the court as justifying a mistrial, bars a retrial of the defendant under the Double Jeopardy Clause. Because "subjective" intent often may be unknowable, I emphasize that a court—in considering a double jeopardy motion—should rely primarily upon the objective facts and circumstances of the particular case.

In the present case the mistrial arose from the prosecutor's conduct in pursuing a line of redirect examination of a key witness. The Oregon Court of Appeals identified a single question as constituting "overreaching" so serious as to bar a retrial. Yet, there are few vigorously contested lawsuits—whether criminal or civil—in which improper questions are not asked. Our system is adversarial and vigorous advocacy is encouraged.

Nevertheless, this would have been a close case for me if there had been substantial factual evidence of intent beyond the question itself. Here, however, other relevant facts and circumstances strongly support the view that prosecutorial intent to cause a mistrial was absent. First, there was no sequence of overreaching prior to the single prejudicial question. Moreover, it is evident from a colloquy between counsel and the court, out of the presence of the jury, that the prosecutor not only resisted, but also was surprised by, the defendant's motion for a mistrial. Finally, at the hearing on respondent's double jeopardy motion, the prosecutor testified—and the trial found as a fact and the appellate court agreed—that there was no "intention ... to cause a mistrial." In view of these circumstances, the Double Jeopardy Clause provides no bar to retrial.

Note

Lower courts are unlikely to find the intent necessary to satisfy the *Kennedy* standard. *See, e.g., Hawkins v. Alabama*, 318 F.3d 1302 (11th Cir. 2003) (prosecutor's misconduct was done in secret and not intended to persuade defendant to move for mistrial); *United States v. Wharton*, 320 F.3d 526 (5th Cir. 2003) (defendant failed to show that prosecution affirmatively sought mistrial); *United States v. Vallejo*, 297 F.3d 1154, 1163 (11th Cir. 2002) (defendant did not offer sufficient evidence that prosecutor knew government witness would improperly comment on defendant's post-arrest silence).

B. TERMINATION OF THE CASE BY DISMISS OR ACQUITTAL

In the previous section on mistrials, manifest necessity for the mistrial declaration was crucial in order for the prosecution to retry a defendant who did not want a mistrial. The assumption underlying the mistrial was that the reason for terminating the first trial was not a fatal defect to a second trial. By contrast, prior to the attachment of jeopardy, the reason for terminating a criminal proceeding has no double jeopardy significance.

Once jeopardy has attached, the way in which a trial ends is relevant to double jeopardy principles. Whether the cessation of a trial is a dismissal or acquittal is important to resolving whether the government can appeal the adverse termination of the case and whether the defendant can be reprosecuted. All jurisdictions provide statutory authority for the government to appeal from an adverse termination. *See, e.g.,* 18 U.S.C. § 3731. In the absence of a double jeopardy prohibition, the government can appeal under statutory authority and, if successful, can reprosecute the defendant.

UNITED STATES v. SCOTT

437 U.S. 82 (1978).

MR. JUSTICE REHNQUIST delivered the opinion of the Court.

On March 5, 1975, respondent, a member of the police force in Muskegon, Mich., was charged in a three-count indictment with distribution of various narcotics. Both before his trial in the United States District Court for the Western District of Michigan, and twice during the trial, respondent moved to dismiss the two counts of the indictment which concerned transactions that took place during the preceding September, on the ground that his defense had been prejudiced by preindictment delay. At the close of all the evidence, the court granted respondent's motion. Although the court did not explain its reasons for dismissing the second count, it explicitly concluded that respondent had "presented sufficient proof of prejudice with respect to Count I. * * * "

The Government sought to appeal the dismissals of the first two counts to the United States Court of Appeals for the Sixth Circuit. That court, relying on our opinion in *United States v. Jenkins,* 420 U.S. 358 (1975), concluded that any further prosecution of respondent was barred by the Double Jeopardy Clause of the Fifth Amendment, and therefore dismissed the appeal. The Government has sought review in this Court only with regard to the dismissal of the first count. We granted certiorari to give further consideration to the applicability of the Double Jeopardy Clause to Government appeals from orders granting defense motions to terminate a trial before verdict. We now reverse.

The problem presented by this case could not have arisen during the first century of this Court's existence. The Court has long taken the view that the United States has no right of appeal in a criminal case, absent explicit statutory authority. Such authority was not provided until the enactment of the Criminal Appeals Act, Act of Mar. 2, 1907, which permitted the United States to seek a writ of error in this Court from any decision dismissing an indictment on the basis of "the invalidity, or construction of the statute upon which the indictment is founded." Our consideration of Government appeals over the ensuing years ordinarily focused upon the intricacies of the Act and its amendments. In 1971, however, Congress adopted the current language of the Act, permitting Government appeals from any decision dismissing an indictment, "except that no appeal shall lie where the double jeopardy clause of the United States Constitution prohibits further prosecution." 18 U.S.C. § 3731. * * *

In our first encounter with the new statute, we concluded that "Congress intended to remove all statutory barriers to Government appeals and to allow appeals whenever the Constitution would permit." *United States v. Wilson*, 420 U.S. 332, 337 (1975). [A] detailed canvass of the history of the double jeopardy principles in [*Wilson*] led us to conclude that the Double Jeopardy Clause was primarily "directed at the threat of multiple prosecutions," and posed no bar to Government appeals "where those appeals would not require a new trial." We accordingly held in *Jenkins*, that, whether or not a dismissal of an indictment after jeopardy had attached amounted to an acquittal on the merits, the Government had no right to appeal, because "further proceedings of some sort, devoted to the resolution of factual issues going to the elements of the offense charged, would have been required upon reversal and remand."

If *Jenkins* is a correct statement of the law, the judgment of the Court of Appeals relying on that decision, as it was bound to do, would in all likelihood have to be affirmed. Yet, though our assessment of the history and meaning of the Double Jeopardy Clause in *Wilson, Jenkins,* and *Serfass v. United States*, 420 U.S. 377 (1975), occurred only three Terms ago, our vastly increased exposure to the various facets of the Double Jeopardy Clause has now convinced us that *Jenkins* was wrongly decided. It placed an unwarrantedly great emphasis on the defendant's right to have his guilt decided by the first jury empaneled to try him so as to include those cases where the defendant himself seeks to terminate the trial before verdict on grounds unrelated to factual guilt or innocence. We have therefore decided to overrule *Jenkins*, and thus to reverse the judgment of the Court of Appeals in this case.

[At] the time the Fifth Amendment was adopted, its principles were easily applied, since most criminal prosecutions proceeded to final judgment, and neither the United States nor the defendant had any right to appeal an adverse verdict. The verdict in such a case was unquestionably final, and could be raised in bar against any further prosecution for the same offense.

[It] was not until 1889 that Congress permitted criminal defendants to seek a writ of error in this Court, and then only in capital cases. Only then did it become necessary for this Court to deal with the issues presented by the challenge of verdicts on appeal. And, in the very first case presenting the issues, *United States v. Ball*, 163 U.S. 662 (1896), the Court established principles that have been adhered to ever since. Three persons had been tried together for murder; two were convicted, the other acquitted. This Court reversed the convictions, finding the indictment fatally defective, whereupon all three defendants were tried again.

This time all three were convicted and they again sought review here. This Court held that the Double Jeopardy Clause precluded further prosecution of the defendant who had been acquitted at the original trial but that it posed no such bar to the prosecution of those defendants who had been convicted in the earlier proceeding.

[These,] then, at least, are two venerable principles of double jeopardy jurisprudence. The successful appeal of a judgment of conviction, on any ground other than the insufficiency of the evidence to support the verdict, *Burks v. United States*, 437 U.S. 1, poses no bar to further prosecution on the same charge. A judgment of acquittal, whether based on a jury verdict of not guilty or on a ruling by the court that the evidence is insufficient to convict, may not be appealed and terminates the prosecution when a second trial would be necessitated by a reversal. What may seem superficially to be a disparity in the rules governing a defendant's liability to be tried again is explainable by reference to the underlying purposes of the Double Jeopardy Clause. [T]he law attaches particular significance to an acquittal. To permit a second trial after an acquittal, however mistaken the acquittal may have been, would present an unacceptably high risk that the Government, with its vastly superior resources, might wear down the defendant so that "even though innocent, he may be found guilty." *Green*, 355 U.S., at 188. On the other hand, to require a criminal defendant to stand trial again after he has successfully invoked a statutory right of appeal to upset his first conviction is not an act of governmental oppression of the sort against which the Double Jeopardy Clause was intended to protect. * * *

Although the primary purpose of the Double Jeopardy Clause was to protect the integrity of a final judgment, this Court has also developed a body of law guarding the separate but related interest of a defendant in avoiding multiple prosecutions even where no final determination of guilt or innocence has been made. Such interests may be involved in two different situations: the first, in which the trial judge declares a mistrial; the second, in which the trial judge terminates the proceedings favorably to the defendant on a basis not related to factual guilt or innocence.

[*Jenkins*] held that, regardless of the character of the midtrial termination, appeal was barred if "further proceedings of some sort, devoted to the resolution of factual issues going to the elements of the offense charged, would have been required upon reversal and remand." However, only last Term, in *Lee*, the Government was permitted to institute a second prosecution after a midtrial dismissal of an indictment. The Court found the circumstances presented by that case "functionally indistinguishable from a declaration of mistrial." Thus, *Lee* demonstrated that, at least in some cases, the dismissal of an indictment may be treated on the same basis as the declaration of a mistrial. [O]ur growing experience with Government appeals convinces us that we must re-examine the rationale of *Jenkins* in light of *Lee* and other recent expositions of the Double Jeopardy Clause.

Our decision in *Jenkins* was based upon our perceptions of the underlying purposes of the Double Jeopardy Clause:

> "The underlying idea, one that is deeply ingrained in at least the Anglo–American system of jurisprudence, is that the State with all its resources and power should not be allowed to make repeated attempts to convict an individual for an alleged offense, thereby subjecting him to embarrassment, expense and ordeal and compelling him to live in a continuing state of anxiety and insecurity * * *." *Jenkins*, quoting *Green*, 355 U.S., at 187.

Upon fuller consideration, we are now of the view that this language from *Green*, while entirely appropriate in the circumstances of that opinion, is not a principle which can be expanded to include situations in which the defendant is responsible for the second prosecution. It is quite true that the Government with all its resources and power should not be allowed to make repeated attempts to convict an individual for an alleged offense. This truth is expressed in the three common-law pleas of *autrefois acquit, autrefois convict,* and pardon, which lie at the core of the area protected by the Double Jeopardy Clause. As we have recognized in cases from *Ball*, to *Sanabria v. United States*, 437 U.S. 54, a defendant once acquitted may not be again subjected to trial without violating the Double Jeopardy Clause.

But that situation is obviously a far cry from the present case, where the Government was quite willing to continue with its production of evidence to show the defendant guilty before the jury first empaneled to try him, but the defendant elected to seek termination of the trial on grounds unrelated to guilt or innocence. This is scarcely a picture of an all-powerful state relentlessly pursuing a defendant who had either been found not guilty or who had at least insisted on having the issue of guilt submitted to the first trier of fact. It is instead a picture of a defendant who chooses to avoid conviction and imprisonment, not because of his assertion that the Government has failed to make out a case against him, but because of a legal claim that the Government's case against him must fail even though it might satisfy the trier of fact that he was guilty beyond a reasonable doubt.

We have previously noted that "the trial judge's characterization of his own action cannot control the classification of the action." *Jorn* [A] defendant is acquitted only when "the ruling of the judge, whatever its label, actually represents a resolution [in the defendant's favor], correct or not, of some or all of the factual elements of the offense charged," *Martin Linen*. Where the court, before the jury returns a verdict, enters a judgment of acquittal pursuant to Fed.R.Crim.P. 29, appeal will be barred only when "it is plain that the District Court [evaluated] the Government's evidence and determined that it was legally insufficient to sustain a conviction." Id.

Our opinion in *Burks* necessarily holds that there has been a "failure of proof," requiring an acquittal when the Government does not submit sufficient evidence to rebut a defendant's essentially factual defense of insanity, though it may otherwise be entitled to have its case submitted to the jury. The defense of insanity, like the defense of entrapment, arises from "the notion that Congress could not have intended criminal punishment for a defendant who has committed all the elements of a proscribed offense," *United States v. Russell*, 411 U.S. 423 (1973), where other facts established to the satisfaction of the trier of fact provide a legally adequate justification for otherwise criminal acts. Such a factual finding does "necessarily establish the criminal defendant's lack of criminal culpability," (Brennan, J., dissenting), under the existing law; the fact that "the acquittal may result from erroneous evidentiary rulings or erroneous interpretations of governing legal principles," affects the accuracy of that determination, but it does not alter its essential character. By contrast, the dismissal of an indictment for preindictment delay represents a legal judgment that a defendant, although criminally culpable, may not be punished because of a supposed constitutional violation. * * * [I]n the present case, [defendant] successfully avoided such a submission of the first count of the indictment by persuading the trial court to dismiss it on a basis which did not depend on guilt or innocence. He was thus neither acquitted nor convicted, because he himself successfully undertook to persuade the trial court not to submit the issue of guilt or innocence to the jury which had been empaneled to try him. * * * [Defendant] has not been "deprived" of his valued right to go to the first jury; only the public has been deprived of its valued right to "one complete opportunity to convict those who have violated its laws." *Arizona v. Washington*. No interest protected by the Double Jeopardy Clause is invaded when the Government is allowed to appeal and seek reversal of such a midtrial termination of the proceedings in a manner favorable to the defendant.[1]

We, of course, do not suggest that a midtrial dismissal of a prosecution, in response to a defense motion on grounds unrelated to guilt or innocence, is necessarily improper. Such rulings may be necessary to terminate proceedings marred by fundamental error. But where a defendant prevails on such a motion, he takes the risk that an appellate court will reverse the trial court.

It is obvious from what we have said that we believe we pressed too far in *Jenkins*, the concept of the "defendant's valued right to have his trial completed by a particular tribunal." We now conclude that where the defendant himself seeks to have the trial terminated without any submission to either judge or jury as to his guilt or innocence, an appeal by the Government from his successful effort to do so is not barred by 18 U.S.C. § 3731. * * *

---

1. We should point out that it is entirely possible for a trial court to reconcile the public interest in the Government's right to appeal from an erroneous conclusion of law, with the defendant's interest in avoiding a second prosecution. In *Wilson*, the court permitted the case to go to the jury, which returned a verdict of guilty, but it subsequently dismissed the indictment for preindictment delay on the basis of evidence adduced at trial. * * *

MR. JUSTICE BRENNAN, with whom MR. JUSTICE WHITE, MR. JUSTICE MARSHALL, and MR. JUSTICE STEVENS join, dissenting.

[While] the Double Jeopardy Clause often has the effect of protecting the accused's interest in the finality of particular favorable determinations, this is not its objective. For the Clause often permits Government appeals from final judgments favorable to the accused. *See Wilson* (whether or not final judgment was an acquittal, Government may appeal if reversal would not necessitate a retrial). The purpose of the Clause, which the Court today fails sufficiently to appreciate, is to protect the accused against the agony and risks attendant upon undergoing more than one criminal trial for any single offense. [Society's] "willingness to limit the Government to a single criminal proceeding to vindicate its very vital interest in enforcement of criminal laws" bespeaks society's recognition of the gross unfairness of requiring the accused to undergo the strain and agony of more than one trial for any single offense. *Jorn*. Accordingly, the policies of the Double Jeopardy Clause mandate that the Government be afforded but one complete opportunity to convict an accused and that when the first proceeding terminates in a final judgment favorable to the defendant any retrial be barred. The rule as to acquittals can only be understood as simply an application of this larger principle.

Judgments of acquittal normally result from jury or bench verdicts of not guilty. In such cases, the acquittal represents the factfinder's conclusion that, under the controlling legal principles, the evidence does not establish that the defendant can be convicted of the offense charged in the indictment. But the judgment does not necessarily establish the criminal defendant's lack of criminal culpability; the acquittal may result from erroneous evidentiary rulings or erroneous interpretations of governing legal principles induced by the defense. Yet the Double Jeopardy Clause bars a second trial. [The] reason is not that the first trial established the defendant's factual innocence, but rather that the second trial would present all the untoward consequences the Clause was designed to prevent. The Government would be allowed to seek to persuade a second trier of fact of the defendant's guilt, to strengthen any weaknesses in its first presentation, and to subject the defendant to the expense and anxiety of a second trial. * * *

Notes and Questions

1. In the three years between the *Jenkins* and *Scott* cases, the Court's philosophy about Double Jeopardy changed—from shielding a defendant from the burden of multiple prosecutions (*i.e.*, running the gauntlet twice), to preserving determinations only of innocence, via an acquittal, but allowing retrials following dismissals or mistrials.

2. As *Scott* states, an acquittal occurs when the judge's ruling represents a "resolution [in the defendant's favor], correct or not, of some or all of the factual elements of the offense charged." In *Sanabria v. United States*, 437 U.S. 54 (1978), decided the same day as *Scott*, the Court held that when

a defendant is acquitted at trial, he cannot be retried for the same charge, even if the legal rulings underlying the acquittal were erroneous.

3. By contrast, the Court has held that the government may appeal the grant of *pretrial* motions to dismiss. *Serfass v. United States*, 420 U.S. 377 (1975). Even though a successful government appeal can lead to a new prosecution, the Double Jeopardy doctrine does not bar the appeal because jeopardy had not attached at the time the trial court dismissed the charges. The policy supporting this disposition is that the defendant is not running the gauntlet more than once, *i.e.*, a reprosecution does not provide a second chance for the prosecution because it has not yet had a first chance.

4. *Terminations after hung juries.* In *United States v. Sanford*, 429 U.S. 14 (1976), the trial judge declared a mistrial after the jury was unable to agree on a verdict. Four months later, the judge dismissed the charge because the government had consented to the conduct which formed the basis of the allegation. The Court held that the dismissal was appealable and was akin to the pretrial order in *Serfass*. How would you argue that this case was in a pretrial setting when it was dismissed? What is the argument that the disposition in reality was a post-trial motion for acquittal?

Compare Sanford with the Court's holding in *United States v. Martin Linen Supply*, 430 U.S. 564 (1977). Following a declaration of a mistrial due to a hung jury, the trial court granted defense counsel's timely motion under Federal Rule of Criminal Procedure 29(c) for a judgment of acquittal. The Court treated the disposition as an acquittal and therefore not appealable. Does *Martin Linen* reward the client whose attorney knows the procedural rules and how they function? Do the *Sanford* and *Martin Linen* rulings allow the procedural rules to govern the application of constitutional double jeopardy principles?

5. *Compare Martin Linen* with *United States v. Wilson*, 420 U.S. 332 (1975), where there was a judgment of conviction followed by a post-verdict motion for judgment of acquittal which was granted. The Court held that the prosecution can appeal from the grant of this motion, because there would be no running of the gauntlet a second time. A successful appeal would mean that it would be necessary only to reinstate the jury's verdict if the appellate court believed that the judgment of acquittal had been erroneously granted. In other words, the error of law in granting the judgment of acquittal can be corrected without subjecting the defendant to a second trial. If the Court's concern is that there be no retrial, where does that leave the anxiety associated with the appeal? How is *Martin Linen* distinguishable from *Wilson*?

C. TERMINATION OF THE CASE BY CONVICTION

The general rule is that when a defendant appeals a conviction successfully, Double Jeopardy does not preclude a reprosecution. When a defendant chooses to appeal from a conviction, he seeks to nullify the conviction. If successful, the courts treats the conviction as a nullity, *i.e.*, no trial ever occurred. Thus, the slate is wiped clean, the defendant never ran the gauntlet, and he can be tried "again."

LOCKHART v. NELSON

488 U.S. 33 (1988).

CHIEF JUSTICE REHNQUIST delivered the opinion of the Court.

In this case a reviewing court set aside a defendant's conviction of enhanced sentence because certain evidence was erroneously admitted against him, and further held that the Double Jeopardy Clause forbade the State to retry him as a habitual offender because the remaining evidence adduced at trial was legally insufficient to support a conviction. Nothing in the record suggests any misconduct in the prosecutor's submission of the evidence. We conclude that in cases such as this, where the evidence offered by the State and admitted by the trial court—whether erroneously or not—would have been sufficient to sustain a guilty verdict, the Double Jeopardy Clause does not preclude retrial.

Respondent Johnny Lee Nelson pleaded guilty in Arkansas state court to burglary, a class B felony, and misdemeanor theft. He was sentenced under the [Arkansas] habitual criminal statute, which provides that a defendant who is convicted of a class B felony and "who has previously been convicted of ... [or] found guilty of four [4] or more felonies," may be sentenced to an enhanced term of imprisonment of between 20 and 40 years. To have a convicted defendant's sentence enhanced under the statute, the State must prove beyond a reasonable doubt, at a separate sentencing hearing, that the defendant has the requisite number of prior felony convictions. * * *

At respondent's sentencing hearing, the State introduced, without objection from the defense, certified copies of four prior felony convictions. * * * The case was submitted to the jury, which found that the State had met its burden of proving four prior convictions and imposed an enhanced sentence. The State courts upheld the enhanced sentence on both direct and collateral review, despite respondent's protestations that one of the convictions relied upon by the State had been pardoned.

Several years later, respondent sought a writ of habeas corpus in the United States District Court, contending once again that the enhanced sentence was invalid because one of the prior convictions used to support it had been pardoned. When an investigation undertaken by the State at the District Court's request revealed that the conviction in question had in fact been pardoned, the District Court declared the enhanced sentence to be invalid. The State announced its intention to resentence respondent as a habitual offender, using another prior conviction not offered or admitted at the initial sentencing hearing, and respondent interposed a claim of double jeopardy. After hearing arguments from counsel, the District Court decided that the Double Jeopardy Clause prevented the State from attempting to resentence respondent as a habitual offender on the burglary charge. The Court of Appeals for the Eighth Circuit affirmed. The Court of Appeals reasoned that the pardoned conviction was not admissible under state law, and that "[w]ithout [it], the state has failed to provide sufficient evidence" to sustain the enhanced sentence. We granted certiorari to review this interpretation of the Double Jeopardy Clause.[2] * * *

It has long been settled, however, that the Double Jeopardy Clause's general prohibition against successive prosecutions does not prevent the government from retrying a defendant who succeeds in getting his first conviction set aside, through direct appeal or collateral attack, because of some error in the proceedings leading to conviction. *United States v. Ball*, 163 U.S. 662 (1896) (retrial permissible following reversal of conviction on direct appeal); *United States v. Tateo*, 377 U.S. 463 (1964) (retrial permissible when conviction declared invalid on collateral attack). This rule, which is a "well-established part of our constitutional jurisprudence," is necessary in order to ensure the "sound administration of justice":

> Corresponding to the right of an accused to be given a fair trial is the societal interest in punishing one whose guilt is clear after he has obtained such a trial. It would be a high price indeed for society to pay were every accused granted immunity from punishment because of any defect sufficient to constitute reversible error in the proceedings leading to conviction.

Permitting retrial after a conviction has been set aside also serves the interests of defendants, for "it is at least doubtful that appellate courts would be as zealous as they now are in protecting against the effects of improprieties at the trial or pretrial stage if they knew that reversal of a conviction would put the accused irrevocably beyond the reach of further prosecution." *Ibid.*

In *Burks v. United States*, 437 U.S. 1 (1978), we recognized an exception to the general rule that the Double Jeopardy Clause does not bar the retrial of a defendant who has succeeded in getting his conviction set aside for error in the proceedings below. *Burks* held that when a defendant's conviction is reversed by an appellate court on the sole ground that the evidence was insufficient to sustain the jury's verdict, the Double Jeopardy Clause bars a retrial on the same charge.

Burks was based on the view that an appellate court's reversal for insufficiency of the evidence is in effect a determination that the govern-

---

2. The State has attacked the ruling below on a single ground: that the defect in respondent's first sentence enhancement proceeding does not bar retrial. To reach this question, we would ordinarily have to decide two issues which are its logical antecedents: (1) whether the rule that the Double Jeopardy Clause limits the State's power to subject a defendant to successive capital sentencing proceedings, *see Bullington v. Missouri*, 451 U.S. 430 (1981), carries over to noncapital sentencing proceedings, *see North Carolina v. Pearce*, 395 U.S. 711 (1969); and (2) whether the rule that retrial is prohibited after a conviction is set aside by an appellate court for evidentiary insufficiency, *see Burks v. United States*, is applicable when the determination of evidentiary insufficiency is made instead by a federal habeas court in a collateral attack on a state conviction. The courts below answered both questions in the affirmative, and the State has conceded both in its briefs and at oral argument the validity of those rulings. We therefore assume, without deciding, that these two issues present no barrier to reaching the double jeopardy claim raised here.

ment's case against the defendant was so lacking that the trial court should have entered a judgment of acquittal, rather than submitting the case to the jury. Because the Double Jeopardy Clause affords the defendant who obtains a judgment of acquittal at the trial level absolute immunity from further prosecution for the same offense, it ought to do the same for the defendant who obtains an appellate determination that the trial court should have entered a judgment of acquittal. The fact that the determination of entitlement to a judgment of acquittal is made by the appellate court rather than the trial court should not, we thought, affect its double jeopardy consequences; to hold otherwise "would create a purely arbitrary distinction" between defendants based on the hierarchical level at which the determination was made. The question presented by this case—whether the Double Jeopardy Clause allows retrial when a reviewing court determines that a defendant's conviction must be reversed because evidence was erroneously admitted against him, and also concludes that without the inadmissible evidence there was insufficient evidence to support a conviction—was expressly reserved in *Greene v. Massey*, 437 U.S. 19 (1978) at n. 9, decided the same day as *Burks*. We think the logic of *Burks* requires that the question be answered in the affirmative.

Burks was careful to point out that a reversal based solely on evidentiary insufficiency has fundamentally different implications, for double jeopardy purposes, than a reversal based on such ordinary "trial errors" as the "incorrect receipt or rejection of evidence." While the former is in effect a finding "that the government has failed to prove its case" against the defendant, the latter "implies nothing with respect to the guilt or innocence of the defendant," but is simply "a determination that [he] has been convicted through a judicial *process* which is defective in some fundamental respect."

It appears to us to be beyond dispute that this is a situation described in *Burks* as reversal for "trial error"—the trial court erred in admitting a particular piece of evidence, and without it there was insufficient evidence to support a judgment of conviction. But clearly with that evidence, there was enough to support the sentence: the court and jury had before them certified copies of four prior felony convictions, and that is sufficient to support a verdict of enhancement under the statute. The fact that one of the convictions had been later pardoned by the Governor vitiated its legal effect, but it did not deprive the certified copy of that conviction of its probative value under the statute. It is quite clear from our opinion in *Burks* that a reviewing court must consider all of the evidence admitted by the trial court in deciding whether retrial is permissible under the Double Jeopardy Clause—indeed, that was the *ratio decidendi* of *Burks*, and the overwhelming majority of appellate courts considering the question have agreed. The basis for the *Burks* exception to the general rule is that a reversal for insufficiency of the evidence should be treated no differently than a trial court's granting a judgment of acquittal at the close of all the evidence. A trial court in passing on such a motion considers all of the evidence it has admitted, and to make the analogy complete it must be this same quantum of evidence which is considered by the reviewing court.

Permitting retrial in this instance is not the sort of governmental oppression at which the Double Jeopardy Clause is aimed; rather, it serves the interest of the defendant by affording him an opportunity to "obtai[n] a fair readjudication of his guilt free from error." *Burks*. Had the defendant offered evidence at the sentencing hearing to prove that the conviction had become a nullity by reason of the pardon, the trial judge would presumably have allowed the prosecutor an opportunity to offer evidence of another prior conviction to support the habitual offender charge. Our holding today thus merely recreates the situation that would have been obtained if the trial court had excluded the evidence of the conviction because of the showing of a pardon.

The judgment of the Court of Appeals is accordingly reversed.

JUSTICE MARSHALL, with whom JUSTICE BRENNAN and JUSTICE BLACKMUN join, dissenting. * * *

It seems to me that the Court's analysis of this issue should begin with the recognition that, in deciding when the double jeopardy bar should apply, we are balancing two weighty interests: the defendant's interest in repose and society's interest in the orderly administration of justice. *See, e.g., United States v. Tateo.* [I] do not intend in this dissenting opinion to settle what rule best accommodates these competing interests in cases where a reviewing court has determined that a portion of a State's proof was inadmissible. At first blush, it would seem that the defendant's interest is every bit as great in this situation as in the *Burks* situation. Society's interest, however, would appear to turn on a number of variables. The chief one is the likelihood that retrying the defendant will lead to conviction. *See United States v. Tateo*, (noting society's interest "in punishing one whose guilt is clear"). In appraising this likelihood, one might inquire into whether prosecutors tend in close cases to hold back probative evidence of a defendant's guilt; if they do not, there would be scant societal interest in permitting retrial given that the State's remaining evidence is, by definition, insufficient. Alternatively, one might inquire as to why the evidence at issue was deemed inadmissible. Where evidence was stricken for reasons having to do with its unreliability, it would seem curious to include it in the sufficiency calculus. Inadmissible hearsay evidence, for example, or evidence deemed defective or nonprobative as a matter of law thus might not be included. By contrast, evidence stricken in compliance with evidentiary rules grounded in other public policies—the policy of encouraging subsequent remedial measures embodied in Federal Rule of Evidence 407, for example, or the policy of deterring unconstitutional searches and seizures embodied in the exclusionary rule—might more justifiably be included in a double jeopardy sufficiency analysis. * * *

Notes and Questions

1. Should the defense attorney appeal issues of trial error as well as issues relating to evidentiary insufficiency? In reality or in practice, a convicted defendant will seek reversal for any reason regardless of the Double Jeopardy consequences. After *Burks* and *Nelson*, the risk in offering judges multiple grounds for reversal may lead judges to reverse for trial error because of the possibility of a new trial. Of course, there may not be another trial. Instead, a prosecutor may be willing to plea bargain because the witnesses's memories are faded, or public sentiment about the type of offense has changed.

2. *The thirteenth-juror reversal.* Unlike *Burks*, the Court in *Tibbs v. Florida*, 457 U.S. 31 (1982), held that when an appellate court reverses a conviction because the verdict was against the weight of the evidence, there can be a retrial because such a reversal assumes that there was sufficient evidence at the first trial. The appellate judge simply disagreed with the way in which the jury decided the case.

3. *Implicit acquittals.* Suppose that a state has two degrees of murder and the jury is instructed on both degrees. The jury convicts on the less serious murder charge, which is reversed on appeal for trial error. At a retrial what can be the maximum charge against the defendant? The less serious murder charge, because there was an implicit acquittal of the more serious charge at the first trial. Therefore, Double Jeopardy prohibits a retrial on that charge. The same idea of an implicit acquittal applies to the situation where the judge refuses to instruct on the more serious charge but does instruct on the less serious charge, *i.e.*, there is an implicit acquittal on the more serious charge.

In *Morris v. Mathews*, 475 U.S. 237 (1986), the Court held that, if the trial court erred and did retry and convict the defendant on the more serious charge at a second trial, the appellate court can reduce the charge from a jeopardy-barred offense of the more serious charge to the permissible, less serious charge. By contrast, if the second trial for the jeopardy-barred offense results in a conviction for the less serious charge (which was not jeopardy-barred) a retrial must occur. *Price v. Georgia*, 398 U.S. 323 (1970).

D. CONTROLLING PROSECUTORIAL AND JUDICIAL VINDICTIVENESS

NORTH CAROLINA v. PEARCE
395 U.S. 711 (1969).

Mr. Justice Stewart delivered the opinion of the Court.

When at the behest of the defendant a criminal conviction has been set aside and a new trial ordered, to what extent does the Constitution limit the imposition of a harsher sentence after conviction upon retrial?
* * *

Pearce was convicted in a North Carolina court upon a charge of assault with intent to commit rape. The trial judge sentenced him to prison for a term of 12 to 15 years. Several years later he initiated a state post-conviction proceeding which culminated in the reversal of his conviction by the Supreme Court of North Carolina, upon the ground that an involuntary confession had unconstitutionally been admitted in evidence against him. He was retried, convicted, and sentenced by the trial judge to an eight-year prison term, which, when added to the time Pearce had already spent in prison, the parties agree amounted to a longer total sentence than that originally imposed. The conviction and sentence were affirmed on appeal. Pearce then began this habeas corpus proceeding in the United States District Court for the Eastern District of North Carolina. That court held [that] the longer sentence imposed upon retrial was "unconstitutional and void."

[We hold] that neither the double jeopardy provision nor the Equal Protection Clause imposes an absolute bar to a more severe sentence upon reconviction. A trial judge is not constitutionally precluded, in other words, from imposing a new sentence, whether greater or less than the original sentence, in the light of events subsequent to the first trial that may have thrown new light upon the defendant's "life, health, habits, conduct, and mental and moral propensities." *Williams v. New York*, 337 U.S. 241. Such information may come to the judge's attention from evidence adduced at the second trial itself, from a new presentence investigation, from the defendant's prison record, or possibly from other sources. The freedom of a sentencing judge to consider the defendant's conduct subsequent to the first conviction in imposing a new sentence is no more than consonant with the principle, fully approved in *Williams*, that a State may adopt the "prevalent modern philosophy of penology that the punishment should fit the offender and not merely the crime."

To say that there exists no absolute constitutional bar to the imposition of a more severe sentence upon retrial is not, however, to end the inquiry. There remains for consideration the impact of the Due Process Clause of the Fourteenth Amendment.

It can hardly be doubted that it would be a flagrant violation of the Fourteenth Amendment for a state trial court to follow an announced practice of imposing a heavier sentence upon every reconvicted defendant for the explicit purpose of punishing the defendant for his having succeeded in getting his original conviction set aside. Where, as in each of the cases before us, the original conviction has been set aside because of a constitutional error, the imposition of such a punishment, "penalizing those who choose to exercise" constitutional rights, "would be patently unconstitutional." *United States v. Jackson*, 390 U.S. 570, 581. And the very threat inherent in the existence of such a punitive policy would, with respect to those still in prison, serve to "chill the exercise of basic constitutional rights." But even if the first conviction has been set aside for nonconstitutional error, the imposition of a penalty upon the defendant for having successfully pursued a statutory right of appeal or collateral remedy would be no less a violation of due process of law. A court is "without right to [put] a price on an appeal. A defendant's exercise of a right of appeal must be free and unfettered. [I]t is unfair to use the great power given to the court to determine sentence to place a defendant in the dilemma of making an unfree choice." * * *

Due process of law, then, requires that vindictiveness against a defendant for having successfully attacked his first conviction must play no part in the sentence he receives after a new trial. And since the fear of such vindictiveness may unconstitutionally deter a defendant's exercise of the right to appeal or collaterally attack his first conviction, due process also requires that a defendant be freed of apprehension of such a retaliatory motivation on the part of the sentencing judge.

In order to assure the absence of such a motivation, we have concluded that whenever a judge imposes a more severe sentence upon a defendant after a new trial, the reasons for his doing so must affirmatively appear. Those reasons must be based upon objective information concerning identifiable conduct on the part of the defendant occurring after the time of the original sentencing proceeding. And the factual data upon which the increased sentence is based must be made part of the record, so that the constitutional legitimacy of the increased sentence may be fully reviewed on appeal.

[Nonetheless,] the fact remains that neither at the time the increased sentence was imposed upon Pearce, nor at any stage in this habeas corpus proceeding, has the State offered any reason or justification for that sentence beyond the naked power to impose it. We conclude that in each of the cases before us, the judgment should be affirmed.

Notes

1. A court that is sentencing after retrial can consider any event, such as a conviction for an offense committed before the original sentencing. *Texas v. McCullough*, 475 U.S. 134 (1986); *Wasman v. United States*, 468 U.S. 559 (1984). When a jury imposes the second sentence, the jury's independence minimizes the possibility that prosecutorial vindictiveness will influence the sentence. *Chaffin v. Stynchcombe*, 412 U.S. 17 (1973). Where the court imposes sentence, the double jeopardy clause applies, because the judge could retaliate against the defendant for taking an appeal by imposing a higher sentence on retrial. However, the presumption of vindictiveness does not apply when the initial sentence was based on a guilty plea and the higher sentence follows from a trial on the merits. *Alabama v. Smith*, 490 U.S. 794 (1989).

The availability of an appeal by the defendant does not prohibit a higher punishment on a trial de novo on the same charge. *Colten v. Kentucky*, 407 U.S. 104 (1972). However, a higher offense cannot be charged in the de novo appeal. *Thigpen v. Roberts*, 468 U.S. 27 (1984); *Blackledge v. Perry*, 417 U.S. 21 (1974). The prosecution may also appeal a sentence imposed by the judge without violation of double jeopardy. *Pennsylvania v. Goldhammer*, 474 U.S. 28 (1985); *United States v. DiFrancesco*, 449 U.S. 117 (1980).

2. The double jeopardy prohibition of multiple prosecutions for the same offense limits a court's ability to impose or alter sentences. *See Ex parte Lange*, 85 U.S. (18 Wall.) 163, 21 L.Ed. 872 (1873) (defendant cannot

be subjected to another sentence after suffering fully one punishment for the offense). A sentence imposed at a proceeding sufficiently similar to a trial may be sufficiently final to invoke the protection of the Double Jeopardy Clause. For example, if a life sentence is imposed in a bifurcated sentencing proceeding for a capital offense that resembles a trial on guilt or innocence, the double jeopardy clause prohibits imposition of the death penalty following a successful appeal and retrial. *Bullington v. Missouri*, 451 U.S. 430 (1981). The initial life sentence constitutes an acquittal of the death penalty and thus the double jeopardy clause prohibits the subsequent imposition of a death sentence. *Arizona v. Rumsey*, 467 U.S. 203 (1984). Even if the acquittal were the result of an erroneous evidentiary ruling or an erroneous interpretation of legal principles, the life sentence stands. However, if an appellate court corrects a mistaken legal interpretation of an aggravating factor which does not alter the validity of the punishment, a retrial after a reversal of the conviction for a trial error can result again in a death sentence. *Poland v. Arizona*, 476 U.S. 147 (1986). When a jury's verdict in a capital sentencing proceeding is merely advisory, a court may impose the death penalty despite the jury's verdict of life imprisonment. *Spaziano v. Florida*, 468 U.S. 447 (1984).

3. In *Schiro v. Farley*, 510 U.S. 222 (1994), the trial court found the defendant guilty of murder while committing rape but made no finding on a count of intentional murder. It then imposed the death penalty after finding a statutory aggravating circumstance of intentionally killing while committing rape. The Supreme Court rejected the defendant's claim that the jury's failure to convict him on the intentional murder count operated as an acquittal of intentional murder and that double jeopardy prohibited the use of the intentional murder aggravating circumstance for sentencing purposes. The Court distinguished *Bullington* by noting that case referred only to second capital sentencing proceedings.

4. Can a court increase the sentence when an appellate court rules that the first sentence was invalid, illegal or erroneous? *See, e.g., Jones v. Thomas*, 491 U.S. 376 (1989) (yes).

5. May a trial judge increase a valid sentence after the defendant begins to serve the sentence? *Compare United States v. Arrellano–Rios*, 799 F.2d 520 (9th Cir.1986) (no) with *United States v. Lopez*, 706 F.2d 108 (2d Cir.1983) (yes).

6. Does *Bullington* extend to enhancement/recidivist proceedings on the theory that because such proceedings resemble trials, a decision not to enhance acts as an acquittal on the factual findings necessary to enhance? No, said the Court in *Monge v. California*, 524 U.S. 721 (1998). *Bullington* is limited to capital cases due to its unique character which produces a "heightened interest in accuracy."

Chapter 23

APPEALS

There are significant differences between the trial and appellate stages of a criminal proceeding. The purpose of the trial stage from the State's point of view is to convert a criminal defendant from a person presumed innocent to one found guilty beyond a reasonable doubt.... By contrast, it is ordinarily the defendant, rather than the State, who initiates the appellate process, seeking not to fend off the efforts of the States prosecutor but rather to overturn a finding of guilt made by a judge or a jury below. *Ross v. Moffitt*, 417 U.S. 600, 610 (1974).

In recent years there has been increased concern over the appellate process, particularly in death penalty cases. Critics maintain that justice is neither swift nor sure when death row inmates delay their execution for years while the courts consider multiple challenges to the defendant's conviction or sentence. As illustrated in the chart below, there may be some instances (at least in theory) where the defendant petitions for ten separate reviews of a single conviction.

APPELLATE REVIEW

Direct Appeal	State habeas corpus	Federal habeas corpus
U.S. Supreme Court	U.S. Supreme Court	U.S. Supreme Court
State Supreme Court	State Supreme Court	Court of Appeals
State Intermediate Appellate Court	State Intermediate Appellate Court	Federal Dist. Court
Conviction in State court	State trial court	

Although ten instances of review may seem excessive, one commentator pointed out that, "we would not send two astronauts to the moon without providing them with at least three or four backup systems.

1106

Should we send literally thousands of men to prison with even less reserves?" Lay, *Modern Administrative Proposals for Federal Habeas*, 21 DePaul L.Rev. 701, 709 (1972). In *Jones v. Barnes*, 463 U.S. 745 (1983), Justice Brennan noted that "there are few, if any situations in our system of justice in which a single judge is given unreviewable discretion over matters concerning a person's liberty or property, and the reversal rate of criminal convictions on mandatory appeals in the state courts, while not overwhelming, is certainly high enough to suggest that depriving defendants of their right to appeal would expose them to an unacceptable risk of erroneous conviction." Some of the current debate over post-conviction review was addressed in the Antiterrorism and Effective Death Penalty Act discussed in the next chapter.

Following conviction, the defendant has several avenues of relief available and has access to a number of forums where he can obtain review of his conviction. Motions to set aside the verdict and motions for a new trial are addressed to the trial court. Direct appeal lies to the state appellate courts, while habeas corpus petitions can be filed in both state and federal court. This chapter addresses the forms of judicial review in the order in which they normally arise, and highlights substantive differences between the forms of judicial review, as well as distinct procedural requirements relating to time and form. Although post-conviction remedies require close attention to details, two general themes run throughout the review process.

The *harmless error doctrine*. The complexity of courtroom procedure inevitably leads to some errors, even when attorneys and judges are at their best. The defendant is entitled to a fair trial, not a perfect trial free from all minor or technical defects. If the reviewing courts find error in the record, reversal of the conviction is not warranted if the outcome of the trial would have remained the same in the absence of the error. *I.e.*, a harmless error does not affect the defendant's right to a fair trial, nor does it call into question the accuracy of the finding of guilt. As discussed in section III of this chapter, harmless error is assessed differently depending on the nature of the error and the proceeding in which the error is raised.

The *contemporaneous objection rule* provides that no ruling of the trial court will be considered as a basis for reversal unless the objection was stated together with the ground therefor at the time of the ruling, except for good cause shown. This requirement is designed to preclude trial counsel from "sandbagging" the trial court by not calling possible errors to its attention. Objections must be raised at trial in order to afford opposing counsel an opportunity to respond to the objection and to allow the trial court to rule in the first instance as to the propriety of the objection. Appellate courts, however, are authorized to grant relief from this rule, and may conduct a full review of the conviction when necessary to attain the ends of justice. For example, Federal Rule of Criminal Procedure 52(b) provides that "plain errors or defects affecting substantial rights may be noticed although they were not brought to the attention of the court." As discussed in Section III of this chapter, a more stringent standard for reversal is applied when the defendant fails to object at trial, and on appeal cites plain error by the trial court.

Closely related to the contemporaneous objection rule are the concepts of *curative admissibility* and *proffers of proof*. Curative admissibility retroactively corrects a trial court's initial error in admitting evidence, *i.e.*, when a defendant unsuccessfully objects to evidence which he considers improper and then on his own behalf introduces evidence of the same character, he thereby waives his objection and forfeits his right to contest the trial court's ruling on appeal. [Waiver is not made by the mere cross-examination of a witness or the introduction of rebuttal evidence.] A proffer of evidence requires that when the trial court sustains an objection and excludes evidence, counsel offering the evidence must ensure that the record reflects what the evidence would have been. Failure to make a proffer of evidence deprives the appellate court of the information necessary to rule upon the objection. The offer of proof may be in the form of a stipulation of testimony, or the witness may testify for the record in the absence of the jury.

Exercise

Consider how you would accommodate the interplay between the contemporaneous objection rule, the scope of appellate review, and your trial strategy in the following case: Your client was charged with possession of marijuana with the intent to distribute. Before trial, the Government filed motions *in limine* seeking to admit your client's prior felony conviction [possession of methamphetamine] as character evidence under Federal Rule of Evidence 404(B) and as impeachment evidence under Rule 609(a)(1). The trial court denied the motion to admit the conviction as character evidence, but ruled that if your client testified, evidence of her prior conviction would be admissible as impeachment evidence. What are your options, and what consequences flow from each option?

1.   If your client does not testify, can you contend on appeal that the trial court's in limine ruling deprived your client of the right to testify? Must you make a proffer of what that testimony would have been?

2.   If your client does testify, how will you handle her prior conviction:

(a) Make no mention of it on direct examination and attempt rehabilitation if the government impeaches your client with the prior conviction? How will this approach affect the jury's view of your client's credibility? Will your rehabilitation efforts constitute a waiver of your initial objection?

(b) Should you raise the prior conviction on direct examination to lessen the impact of this evidence on the jury? If this is the most effective trial strategy, does it constitute a waiver of your initial objection and preclude appellate review the court's in limine ruling?

A.   REVIEW BY THE TRIAL COURT

1.   *Trial de novo*

In most appeals, a higher court is asked to scrutinize the trial record for errors that would require reversal of the conviction. Many misdemeanor cases, however, are tried in lower courts, such as police courts or magistrate's courts, from which no record or transcript of the proceedings is available for review by a higher court. These lower courts are sometimes referred to as courts-not-of-record and usually operate without a jury and without all of the procedural safeguards provided in the trial of felony cases. A defendant convicted in such a lower court is often granted an absolute right to a trial de novo in a superior court, sometimes called a court-of-record. Although occasionally referred to as an appeal, the granting of a trial de novo is normally automatic upon the defendant's request. Thus no error need be alleged as to the first trial, and a defendant who exercises his right to a trial de novo is not entitled to judicial review of the sufficiency of the evidence presented to the lower court. *Justices of Boston Municipal Court v. Lydon*, 466 U.S. 294 (1984).

The right to a trial de novo generally exists even when the defendant pled guilty in the lower court. Neither the defendant's plea nor the lower court's judgment are admissible evidence at the trial de novo, but the defendant's prior testimony is admissible at the trial in the higher court. In most situations, Due Process prohibits prosecutorial vindictiveness in increasing the charges at the trial de novo. *Blackledge v. Perry*, 417 U.S. 21 (1974); *Thigpen v. Roberts*, 468 U.S. 27 (1984). However, the punishment imposed at the trial de novo may be harsher than that imposed by the lower court. *Colten v. Kentucky*, 407 U.S. 104 (1972).

Problem

Suppose the defendant is charged with the felony of possession of marijuana with intent to distribute, but plea-bargains to reduce the charge to a misdemeanor of simple possession. The defendant pleads guilty in a court-not-of-record and is sentenced to twelve months in jail. When he subsequently exercises his right to a trial de novo in the superior court, the prosecution reinstitutes the original felony charge upon which he is convicted and sentenced to four years in the penitentiary. Has there been a violation of the defendant's due process rights or the prohibition against double jeopardy? *See Peterson v. Commonwealth*, 5 Va.App. 389, 363 S.E.2d 440 (1987):

> Where a defendant pleads guilty pursuant to a plea agreement and receives the agreed upon sentence, an implied term of the agreement is that the defendant will not appeal what he has bargained for and received. If he does, then he has breached the plea agreement and the Commonwealth is free to reinstate the original charges, as it did in the present case. This conduct is not prosecutorial vindictiveness.

2. *Motions to Set Aside the Verdict*

Prior to appeal to an appellate court, the defense may ask the trial court to set aside the guilty verdict. In some jurisdictions a motion to set aside the verdict is referred to as a judgment NOV (judgment not withstanding the verdict). This motion is similar to, but not identical with, a motion to strike the evidence or a motion for a directed verdict of acquittal. A motion for a directed verdict of acquittal must be made prior to the return of a verdict, *i.e.*, either after the prosecution has rested its case or at the conclusion of all the evidence. The only grounds for a directed verdict is that the evidence is insufficient as a matter of law to sustain a conviction. A motion to set aside the verdict, however, can be made after the verdict is returned, and the motion can be based on: (1) the insufficiency or weight of the evidence; (2) error committed during trial; or (3) newly discovered evidence.

Motions to set aside the verdict because of insufficiency of the evidence or error occurring at trial require the trial judge to review the case, the evidence submitted, and any errors in dealing with the introduction of evidence. Regardless of what occurred at the actual trial, however, the defendant also may move to set aside the verdict because of newly discovered evidence.

Motions for new trials because of newly discovered evidence are not looked upon with favor. The courts generally require that defense counsel prove: (1) the evidence was discovered after the trial concluded; (2) the evidence could not, by the exercise of diligence, have been discovered before the trial terminated; (3) the evidence is material and likely to produce a different verdict at the new trial; and (4) the evidence is not merely cumulative, corroborative, or collateral. These four requirements are not as harsh as they might seem because the defense can present newly discovered evidence to the Governor in a petition for a pardon, or to the parole board in an effort to obtain the defendant's immediate release from custody.

Problem

A defendant charged with murder testified that the deceased said "I will kill you," and reached into his right pocket. The defendant maintained that he acted in self-defense because he knew the deceased often carried a razor and a pistol, and the defendant thought the deceased was reaching for a weapon. While the jury was deliberating, a spectator approached defense counsel and related that he had seen a knife in the deceased's hand. Following conviction, defense moves for a new trial based on this newly discovered evidence. What result? *Connell v. Commonwealth*, 144 Va. 553, 131 S.E. 196 (1926) denied the motion because "under these circumstances, the party discovering such testimony should call it to the attention of the trial court, so that the jury may be recalled to the court room to hear it."

Exercise

The government charged the defendant with knowingly purchasing a fully automatic M–16 rifle at a gun show and later selling it to a pawn shop. The defendant, however, claimed that Rogers, his sister's boyfriend, was the one who purchased the M–16, and that the next time that he saw the rifle was when his sister asked him to pawn it on Rogers's behalf. The defendant did not dispute that he possessed and eventually transferred the firearm described in the indictment. Instead, he argued that he was unaware at the time that the internal mechanism of the M–16 had been altered to convert it to a fully automatic weapon. At trial, the central issue was whether the defendant knew that the M–16 was a fully automatic weapon when he sold it to the pawn shop. The jury found the government's evidence convincing and convicted the defendant.

Three weeks later, the defendant's sister informed defense counsel that the M–16 belonged to Rogers, and that she had asked the defendant to pawn it on Rogers's behalf. She further stated that neither she nor the defendant knew that the M–16 had been converted into a machine gun. She said that at the time of her brother's trial, she had told the defendant that she would not testify truthfully on his behalf because she was involved in an intimate relationship with Rogers and did not want to place her boyfriend in jeopardy.

1. As defense counsel, draft a motion for a new trial based on the information supplied by the defendant's sister?

2. As the prosecutor, on what grounds would you oppose the motion?

B. DIRECT APPEAL IN THE STATE COURTS

Most jurisdictions have created a two-tiered appellate structure in which the convicted defendant has a right of appeal to an intermediate appellate court, but any further appeal to a higher court, usually the State Supreme Court, is often discretionary. The distinction between a right of appeal and discretionary review by an appellate court is important because the United States Supreme Court has held that in felony cases, counsel must be provided to indigent persons exercising their right to appeal. *Douglas v. California*, 372 U.S. 353 (1963). However, counsel need not be provided to indigent defendants seeking discretionary review. *Ross v. Moffitt*, 417 U.S. 600 (1974). The right to counsel on appeal stems from the due process and equal protection clauses of the Fourteenth Amendment, not from the Sixth Amendment. Thus although the Sixth Amendment guarantees the defendant's right to self-representation at trial, there is no such right at the appellate stage. *Martinez v. Court of Appeal*, 528 U.S. 152 (2000).

The appellate process begins with the defendant's filing of a notice or petition of appeal. Such notice informs the parties, the trial judge and the appellate court that the case is being appealed. All jurisdictions require that the notice of appeal be filed within a specified period of time. For example, in the federal system the notice of appeal must be filed within ten days of the date of judgment. "Timely notice of appeal in criminal cases is mandatory and jurisdictional." *U.S. v. Kress*, 944 F.2d 155 (3d Cir.1991).

At the time the notice of appeal is filed, or at a subsequent specified date, the parties must designate portions of the trial record that will be sent to the appellate court. The appellate court bases its review of the case on the trial record which commonly includes: (1) jury instructions given or refused by the trial judge; (2) exhibits offered in evidence; (3) any orders entered by the trial court; (4) any opinion or memorandum decision rendered by the trial judge; (5) any pretrial discovery material requested; and (6) portions of the trial transcript in which the judge ruled upon objections to the introduction of evidence. "A criminal defendant has a right to a meaningful appeal based on a complete transcript. . . .[However,] a new trial is required only when the defendant can show that a flawed transcript specifically prejudices his ability to perfect an appeal." *United States v. Huggins*, 191 F.3d 532 (4th Cir.1999).

Counsel also must alert the appellate court to the basis of appeal by filing a statement of issues that the appellate court is asked to resolve. These issues will be expanded upon in counsels' written briefs which summarize the factual background of the case and set forth relevant legal arguments. The appellate court, usually in its discretion, may hear oral arguments on the issues raised.

Many of the issues that arise in the course of a trial are to be resolved according to the broad discretion of the trial court. On appeal, such rulings will not be disturbed in the absence of an abuse of discretion. The trial court's application of defined legal standards [such as probable cause to arrest] is reviewed *de novo*. The appellate court must accept the trial court's factual determinations, so long as there is evidence to support those findings.

As noted earlier, the contemporaneous objection rule requires counsel to clearly state the nature and basis of any objection. Many appellate courts also require opposing counsel to state the basis for opposing the objection, and require the trial judge to "state on the record" the grounds on which his ruling was based. This requirement may conflict with another appellate rule which allows the reviewing court to sustain the trial court's ruling "if there is any reasonable view of the evidence that will support it." *United States v. Williams* offers one resolution of this potential conflict.

UNITED STATES v. WILLIAMS

951 F.2d 1287 (D.C.Cir.1991).

When a district court's ruling on a pretrial motion involves factual issues, Rule 12(e) of the Federal Rules of Criminal Procedure commands the court to "state its essential findings on the record." The rule serves several functions. Findings on the record inform the parties and other interested persons of the grounds of the ruling, add discipline to the process of judicial decision-making and enable appellate courts properly to perform their reviewing function. If the district court not only fails to make "essential findings on the record," but also expresses nothing in the way of legal reasoning, if it simply announces a result, it may frustrate these objectives. We say "may" because there are cases in which the facts are so certain, and the legal consequences so apparent, that little guesswork is needed to determine the grounds for the ruling. This is not such a case.

Before trial, Christopher Williams unsuccessfully moved to suppress evidence that ultimately resulted in his conviction by a jury for possessing, with intent to distribute, cocaine. The only witnesses at the suppression hearing were two officers (Marsh and Wasserman) of the United States Park Police. The district court viewed both of them as "credible"—the full extent of the court's findings on the record. As best as we can make out from their testimony, the events leading to the search and arrest of Williams are as follows.

[The court reviewed the circumstances leading up to the arrest and search of the defendant].

We will sustain factual findings unless they are "clearly erroneous," a standard we imported from the civil rules for cases tried to the court (Fed.R.Civ.P. 52(a)) because the rules of criminal procedure were silent on the matter. Also, we will review de novo "whether the correct rule of law has been applied to the facts found." The problem we have in this case is twofold. We do not know which facts the district court considered "essential" to its ruling and we do not know what principle of Fourth Amendment law the court believed supported its ruling.

The record suggests three possible grounds on which the district court could have ruled. The first is consent. Sergeant Wasserman's reason for searching Williams sounds like he thought he had consent— Williams said check me out. But the government never raised the issue of consent in the district court. Did the district court nevertheless rule on that basis? The district court's "finding" that Sergeant Wasserman was credible may suggest as much, but we do not know. Before us, Williams argues that his consent was not voluntary. The government counters that he waived the argument by failing to raise it, a curious response indeed, one that makes sense only if the district court ruled on a ground—consent—the government itself may have waived by not raising.

The second possibility is that the district court believed the removal of the bag was a search incident to arrest. This would require the initial detention of Williams to be supported by probable cause. Even crediting fully Officer Marsh's testimony, we are inclined to doubt that what he saw from the window of the moving van amounted to probable cause for arrest. While the district court could have concluded that an arrest occurred when Williams was first approached, all of the testimony at the hearing centered on the question whether the arrest took place immediately prior to or just after the field test.

The third possibility begins with the proposition that this was a limited, investigative detention supported by articulable, reasonable suspicion—in short, a *Terry* stop. . . . The problem with any theory based on a *Terry* stop, however, is that there is no indication the government ever argued *Terry* until the case arrived here. At oral argument in the district court, the prosecutor claimed that the police "had probable cause to stop and arrest the defendant"; defense counsel argued "that there was no probable cause to stop [Williams]." "This Court sits as a court of review.

It is only in exceptional cases ... that questions not pressed or passed upon below are reviewed." *Duignan v. United States*, 274 U.S. 195, 200 (1927). Though Justice Stone was writing of the Supreme Court, the considerations underlying the rule have force for the courts of appeals as well, and "the general rule [is] that a federal appellate court does not consider an issue not passed upon below." *Singleton v. Wulff*, 428 U.S. 106, 120 (1976). We know the *Terry* stop argument was "not pressed ... below"; we cannot tell whether it was nevertheless "passed upon." If the district court thought this was a *Terry* stop, and justified as such, presumably the court could have ruled that removing the bag from Williams' pocket was within the scope of an investigative detention. To our knowledge no case in this circuit goes so far; in light of *Sibron v. New York*, 392 U.S. 40, 64–65 (1968), and *United States v. Place*, 462 U.S. 696, 705–06 (1983), there may be no room for such an extension. Or, as we have said, the court could have found that the sight of the bag was enough to turn reasonable suspicion into probable cause—to justify turning a detention into an arrest and a search.

The possibilities outlined above pose several Fourth Amendment questions, which may not be open and shut in light of the evidence we have recited. Perhaps the district court, in its mind, decided all of these questions against the defendant; perhaps it sustained the search and arrest on a narrow basis; perhaps on an erroneous one. The purpose of an appeal is to review the judgment of the district court, a function we cannot properly perform when we are left to guess at what it is we are reviewing. Given this situation, the obvious solution is to send the case back.

Our only hesitation in remanding stems from *United States v. Caballero*, 936 F.2d 1292 (D.C.Cir.), and several earlier decisions, which indicate that we will sustain a district court's denial of a motion to suppress, despite the court's failure to comply with Rule 12(e), "if there is any reasonable view of the evidence that will support it." The stated rationale is that Rule 12(e) confers on the litigants a personal "right" to have factual findings made, and that "failure to object" to a lack of findings "results in waiver." This has the effect of denying defendants (and the government if it should appeal the granting of a suppression motion) a windfall when the trial court omits a finding apparent on the face of the record, or when, under any possible view of the record, the district court could have reached but one result.

One might wonder why, when there has been such a "waiver," it should follow that we will uphold the district court's decision if "any reasonable view of the evidence" supports it. The idea is that the district court, in reaching its legal conclusion, presumably made whatever factual findings were needed to support the conclusion. Denying a remand because of "waiver," then, means we review facts we infer were actually, albeit silently, found. Our practice of using the "any-reasonable-view-of-the-evidence" standard means that we review those implicit findings under what may be, for all practical purposes, the equivalent of the "clearly erroneous" test we apply to "essential findings" explicitly made in compliance with Rule 12(e). *Caballero* and its antecedents thus rest on two assumptions. One, that the district court asked the right legal questions in making its ruling; two, that it actually weighed the evidence bearing on the facts needed to answer them. When, in a particular case, there is reason to doubt the validity of either or both those assumptions, the court may dispense with what *Caballero* seemingly requires, and remand the case to the district court.

If we knew the district court's legal reasoning in this case, we might have little difficulty in ascertaining the pertinent but unstated findings underlying it, as did the *Caballero* court. If we knew what facts the district court considered "essential" to its ruling (Rule 12(e)), we might be able to piece together the unstated legal grounds for its decision. But we have neither essential findings nor legal reasoning. As Chief Justice Hughes wrote, "it is always desirable that an appellate court should be adequately advised of the basis of the determination of the court below...." *Public Service Comm'n v. Wisconsin Tel. Co.*, 289 U.S. 67, 69–70 (1933). Here the "desirable" is the necessary. Accordingly, we will exercise our inherent power to supervise the district courts. The record is remanded for the factual findings required by Rule 12(e) as well as a statement by the district court of the conclusions of law it has reached on those findings. This panel will retain jurisdiction over the case following remand.

It is so ordered.

[When the case returned to the circuit court, the court noted that the question on remand was: "did the district court [decide the *Terry* issue] although without saying so? On remand, the district court answered yes. * * * Accordingly, the judgment of the district court is affirmed"]. 22 F.3d 1123 (D.C.Cir.1994).

C. HARMLESS ERROR AND PLAIN ERROR

A trial error that is not of constitutional dimension (for example, the trial judge erred in admitting some minor item of evidence) is harmless when it plainly appears from the facts and circumstances of the case that the error did not affect the verdict. Reversal is required for a non-constitutional error only if it "had substantial and injurious effect or influence in determining the jury's verdict." *United States v. Lane*, 474 U.S. 438 (1986).

Application of the harmless error doctrine to constitutional error depends upon the nature of the error. Structural errors "are so intrinsically harmful as to require automatic reversal (i.e., "affect substantial rights") without regard to their effect on the outcome." *Neder v. United States*, 527 U.S. 1 (1999). The Supreme Court has recognized a number of structural errors requiring automatic reversal. They include: (1) unlawful exclusion of members of the defendant's race from a grand jury, *Vasquez v. Hillery*, 474 U.S. 254 (1986); (2) exclusion of a juror reluctant to impose the death penalty, *Gray v. Mississippi*, 481 U.S. 648 (1987); (3) violation of the right to a public trial, *Waller v. Georgia*, 467

U.S. 39 (1984); (4) violation of the right of self-representation, *McKaskle v. Wiggins*, 465 U.S. 168 (1984); (5) a trial presided over by a biased judge, *Tumey v. Ohio*, 273 U.S. 510 (1927); (6) violation of the right to counsel, *Gideon v. Wainwright*, 372 U.S. 335 (1963); (7) a constitutionally inadequate jury instruction on reasonable doubt, *Sullivan v. Louisiana*, 508 U.S. 275 (1993).

In contrast to structural errors, "trial errors" occur during the presentation of the case to the jury, and often involve questions of the admissibility of evidence. For example, *Apprendi* violations are subject to harmless error analysis. As with the failure to submit elements of a crime to the jury, the Court does not regard the failure to submit a sentencing factor to the jury as a "structural" error. *Washington v. Recuenco*, 126 S.Ct. 2546 (2006).

Constitutional errors are treated differently depending on whether they are raised on direct appeal or collateral review. On collateral review, (e.g. habeas corpus petitions) trial errors require reversal of the conviction only if the defendant proves "actual prejudice." *I.e.*, the error had a "substantial and injurious effect or influence in determining the jury's verdict." *Brecht v. Abrahamson*, 507 U.S. 619 (1993). On direct review, however, *Chapman v. California* held that trial errors require reversal of the conviction unless the reviewing court finds such errors to be harmless "beyond a reasonable doubt."

CHAPMAN v. CALIFORNIA

386 U.S. 18 (1967).

JUSTICE BLACK delivered the opinion of the Court.

Petitioners, Ruth Elizabeth Chapman and Thomas LeRoy Teale, were convicted in a California state court upon a charge that they robbed, kidnaped, and murdered a bartender. She was sentenced to life imprisonment and he to death. At the time of the trial, Art I, s 13, of the State's Constitution provided that 'in any criminal case, whether the defendant testifies or not, his failure to explain or to deny by his testimony any evidence or facts in the case against him may be commented upon by the court and by counsel, and may be considered by the court or the jury.' Both petitioners in this case chose not to testify at their trial, and the State's attorney prosecuting them took full advantage of his right under the State Constitution to comment upon their failure to testify, filling his argument to the jury from beginning to end with numerous references to their silence and inferences of their guilt resulting therefrom. The trial court also charged the jury that it could draw adverse inferences from petitioners' failure to testify. Shortly after the trial, but before petitioners' cases had been considered on appeal by the California Supreme Court, this Court decided *Griffin v. State of California*, 380 U.S. 609, in which we held California's constitutional provision and practice invalid on the ground that they put a penalty on the exercise of a person's right not to be compelled to be a witness against himself, guaranteed by the Fifth Amendment to the United States Constitution and made applicable to California and the other States by the Fourteenth Amendment. On appeal, the State Supreme Court, 63 Cal.2d 178, 45 Cal.Rptr. 729, 404 P.2d 209, admitting that petitioners had been denied a federal constitutional right by the comments on their silence, nevertheless affirmed, applying the State Constitution's harmless-error provision, which forbids reversal unless 'the court shall be of the opinion that the error complained of has resulted in a miscarriage of justice.'

We are urged by petitioners to hold that all federal constitutional errors, regardless of the facts and circumstances, must always be deemed harmful. Such a holding, as petitioners correctly point out, would require an automatic reversal of their convictions and make further discussion unnecessary. We decline to adopt any such rule. All 50 States have harmless-error statutes or rules, and the United States long ago through its Congress established for its courts the rule that judgments shall not be reversed for 'errors or defects which do not affect the substantial rights of the parties.' None of these rules on its face distinguishes between federal constitutional errors and errors of state law or federal statutes and rules. All of these rules, state or federal, serve a very useful purpose insofar as they block setting aside convictions for small errors or defects that have little, if any, likelihood of having changed the result of the trial. We conclude that there may be some constitutional errors which in the setting of a particular case are so unimportant and insignificant that they may, consistent with the Federal Constitution, be deemed harmless, not requiring the automatic reversal of the conviction.

In fashioning a harmless-constitutional-error rule, we must recognize that harmless-error rules can work very unfair and mischievous results when, for example, highly important and persuasive evidence, or argument, though legally forbidden, finds its way into a trial in which the question of guilt or innocence is a close one. What harmless-error rules all aim at is a rule that will save the good in harmless-error practices while avoiding the bad, so far as possible.

The federal rule emphasizes 'substantial rights' as do most others. The California constitutional rule emphasizes 'a miscarriage of justice,' but the California courts have neutralized this to some extent by emphasis, and perhaps overemphasis, upon the court's view of 'overwhelming evidence.' We prefer the approach of this Court in deciding what was harmless error in our recent case of *Fahy v. State of Connecticut*, 375 U.S. 85. There we said: 'The question is whether there is a reasonable possibility that the evidence complained of might have contributed to the conviction.' Although our prior cases have indicated that there are some constitutional rights so basic to a fair trial that their infraction can never be treated as harmless error, this statement in *Fahy* itself belies any belief that all trial errors which violate the Constitution automatically call for reversal. At the same time, however, like the federal harmless-error statute, it emphasizes an intention not to treat as harmless those constitutional errors that 'affect substantial rights' of a party. An error in admitting plainly relevant evidence which possibly influenced the jury adversely to a litigant cannot, under *Fahy*, be conceived of as harmless. Certainly error, constitutional error, in illegally admitting highly prejudicial evidence or comments, casts on someone other than the person prejudiced by it a burden to show that it was harmless. It is for that reason that the original common-law harmless-error rule put the burden on the beneficiary of the error either to prove that there was no injury or to suffer a reversal of his erroneously obtained judgment. There is little, if any, difference between our statement in *Fahy v. State of Connecticut* about 'whether there is a reasonable possibility that the evidence complained of might have contributed to the conviction' and requiring the beneficiary of a constitutional error to prove beyond a reasonable doubt that the error complained of did not contribute to the verdict obtained. We, therefore, do no more than adhere to the meaning of our *Fahy* case when we hold, as we now do, that before a federal constitutional error can be held harmless, the court must be able to declare a belief that it was harmless beyond a reasonable doubt. While appellate courts do not ordinarily have the original task of applying such a test, it is a familiar standard to all courts, and we believe its adoption will provide a more workable standard, although achieving the same result as that aimed at in our *Fahy*, case.

Applying the foregoing standard, we have no doubt that the error in these cases was not harmless to petitioners. To reach this conclusion one need only glance at the prosecutorial comments compiled from the record by petitioners' counsel and (with minor omissions) set forth in the Appendix. The California Supreme Court fairly summarized the extent of these comments as follows:

> Such comments went to the motives for the procurement and handling of guns purchased by Mrs. Chapman, funds or the lack thereof in Mr. Teale's possession immediately prior to the killing, the amount of intoxicating liquors consumed by defendants at the Spot Club and other taverns, the circumstances of the shooting in the automobile and the removal of the victim's body therefrom, who fired the fatal shots, why defendants used a false registration at a motel shortly after the killing, the meaning of a letter written by Mrs. Chapman several days after the killing, why Teale had a loaded weapon in his possession when apprehended, the meaning of statements made by Teale after his apprehension, why certain clothing and articles of personal property were shipped by defendants to Missouri, what clothing Mrs. Chapman wore at the time of the killing, conflicting statements as to Mrs. Chapman's whereabouts immediately preceding the killing and, generally, the overall commission of the crime.

Thus, the state prosecutor's argument and the trial judge's instruction to the jury continuously and repeatedly impressed the jury that from the failure of petitioners to testify, to all intents and purposes, the inferences from the facts in evidence had to be drawn in favor of the State—in short, that by their silence petitioners had served as irrefutable witnesses against themselves. And though the case in which this occurred presented a reasonably strong 'circumstantial web of evidence' against petitioners, it was also a case in which, absent the constitutionally forbidden comments, honest, fair-minded jurors might very well have brought in not-guilty verdicts. Under these circumstances, it is completely impossible for us to say that the State has demonstrated, beyond a reasonable doubt, that the prosecutor's comments and the trial judge's instruction did not contribute to petitioners' convictions. Such a machine-gun repetition of a denial of constitutional rights, designed and calculated to make petitioners' version of the evidence worthless, can no more be considered harmless than the introduction against a defendant of a coerced confession. Petitioners are entitled to a trial free from the pressure of unconstitutional inferences.

Reversed and remanded.

————

When a defendant fails to object to a trial error at trial, but later calls the error to the attention of the appellate court, the standard of review is for plain error. An appellate court may review the record for plain error and may reverse the conviction to attain the ends of justice.

UNITED STATES v. OLANO

507 U.S. 725 (1993).

Justice O'Connor delivered the opinion of the Court.

The question in this case is whether the presence of alternate jurors during jury deliberations was a "plain error" that the Court of Appeals was authorized to correct under Federal Rule of Criminal Procedure 52(b).

I

Each of the respondents, Guy W. Olano, Jr., and Raymond M. Gray, served on the board of directors of a savings and loan association. In 1986, the two were indicted in the Western District of Washington on multiple federal charges for their participation in an elaborate loan "kickback" scheme. Their joint jury trial with five other codefendants commenced in March 1987. All of the parties agreed that 14 jurors would be selected to hear the case, and that the 2 alternates would be identified before deliberations began.

The matter arose again the next day, in an ambiguous exchange between Gray's counsel and the District Court:

THE COURT: [H]ave you given any more thought as to whether you want the alternates to go in and not participate, or do you want them out?

MR. ROBISON [counsel for Gray]: We would ask they not.

One day later, on May 28, the last day of trial, the District Court for a third time asked the defendants whether they wanted the alternate jurors to retire into the jury room. Counsel for defendant Davy Hilling gave an unequivocal, affirmative answer.

THE COURT: Well, Counsel, I received your alternates. Do I understand that the defendants now—it's hard to keep up with you, Counsel. It's sort of a day by day—but that's all right. You do all agree that all fourteen deliberate?

Okay. Do you want me to instruct the two alternates not to participate in deliberation?

MR. KELLOGG [counsel for Hilling]: That's what I was on my feet to say. It's my understanding that the conversation was the two alternates go back there instructed that they are not to take part in any fashion in the deliberations.

The District Court concluded that Hilling's counsel was speaking for the other defendants as well as his own client. None of the other counsel intervened during the colloquy between the District Court and Hilling's counsel on May 28, nor did anyone object later the same day when the court instructed the jurors that the two alternates would be permitted to attend deliberations. The court instructed:

We have indicated to you that the parties would be selecting alternates at this time. I am going to inform you who those alternates are, but before I do, let me tell you, I think it was a difficult selection for all concerned, and since the law requires that there be a jury of twelve, it is only going to be a jury of twelve. But what we would like to do in this case is have all of you go back so that even the alternates can be there for the deliberations, but according to the law, the alternates must not participate in the deliberations. It's going to be hard, but if you are an alternate, we think you should be there because things do happen in the course of lengthy jury deliberations, and if you need to step in, we want you to be able to step in having heard the deliberations. But we are going to ask that you not participate.

Both respondents were convicted on a number of charges. They appealed to the United States Court of Appeals for the Ninth Circuit. The Court of Appeals reversed certain counts for insufficient evidence and then considered whether the presence of alternate jurors during jury deliberations violated Federal Rule of Criminal Procedure 24(c): An alternate juror who does not replace a regular juror shall be discharged after the jury retires to consider its verdict.

Because respondents had not objected to the alternates' presence, the court applied a "plain error" standard under Rule 52(b). The court relied on the "language of Rule 24(c), Rule 23(b), the Advisory Committee Notes to Rule 23, and related Ninth Circuit precedent" to hold that Rule 24(c) barred alternate jurors from attending jury deliberations unless the defendant, on the record, explicitly consented to their attendance. The court found that Rule 24(c) was violated in the instant case, because "the district court did not obtain individual waivers from each defendant personally, either orally or in writing." It then held that the presence of alternates in violation of Rule 24(c) was "inherently prejudicial" and reversible per se:

> We cannot fairly ascertain whether in a given case the alternate jurors followed the district court's prohibition on participation. However, even if they heeded the letter of the court's instructions and remained orally mute throughout, it is entirely possible that their attitudes, conveyed by facial expressions, gestures or the like, may have had some effect upon the decision of one or more jurors.

Finally, in a footnote, the court decided that "[b]ecause the violation is inherently prejudicial and because it infringes upon a substantial right of the defendants, it falls within the plain error doctrine."

We granted certiorari to clarify the standard for "plain error" review by the courts of appeals under Rule 52(b). 504 U.S. 908 (1992).

II

"No procedural principle is more familiar to this Court than that a constitutional right," or a right of any other sort, "may be forfeited in criminal as well as civil cases by the failure to make timely assertion of the right before a tribunal having jurisdiction to determine it." *Yakus v. United States*, 321 U.S. 414, 444 (1944). Federal Rule of Criminal Procedure 52(b), which governs on appeal from criminal proceedings, provides a court of appeals a limited power to correct errors that were forfeited because not timely raised in district court. The Rule has remained unchanged since the original version of the Criminal Rules, and was intended as "a restatement of existing law." It is paired, appropriately, with Rule 52(a), which governs nonforfeited errors.

Although "[a] rigid and undeviating judicially declared practice under which courts of review would invariably and under all circumstances decline to consider all questions which had not previously been specifically urged would be out of harmony with ... the rules of fundamental justice," There must be an "error" that is "plain" and that "affect[s] substantial rights." Moreover, Rule 52(b) leaves the decision to correct the forfeited error within the sound discretion of the court of appeals, and the court should not exercise that discretion unless the error " 'seriously affect[s] the fairness, integrity or public reputation of judicial proceedings.' " *United States v. Young*, 470 U.S. 1, 15 (1985).

Rule 52(b) defines a single category of forfeited-but-reversible error. Although it is possible to read the Rule in the disjunctive, as creating two separate categories—"plain errors" and "defects affecting substantial rights"—that reading is surely wrong. As we explained in *Young*, the phrase "error or defect" is more simply read as "error." The forfeited error "may be noticed" only if it is "plain" and "affect[s] substantial rights." More precisely, a court of appeals may correct the error (either vacating for a new trial, or reversing outright) only if it meets these criteria. The appellate court must consider the error, putative or real, in deciding whether the judgment below should be overturned, but cannot provide that remedy unless Rule 52(b) applies (or unless some other provision authorizes the error's correction, an issue that respondents do not raise).

The first limitation on appellate authority under Rule 52(b) is that there indeed be an "error." Deviation from a legal rule is "error" unless the rule has been waived. For example, a defendant who knowingly and voluntarily pleads guilty in conformity with the requirements of Rule 11 cannot have his conviction vacated by court of appeals on the grounds that he ought to have had a trial. Because the right to trial is waivable, and because the defendant who enters a valid guilty plea waives that right, his conviction without a trial is not "error."

Waiver is different from forfeiture. Whereas forfeiture is the failure to make the timely assertion of a right, waiver is the "intentional relinquishment or abandonment of a known right." Whether a particular right is waivable; whether the defendant must participate personally in the waiver; whether certain procedures are required for waiver; and whether the defendant's choice must be particularly informed or voluntary, all depend on the right at stake. Mere forfeiture, as opposed to waiver, does not extinguish an "error" under Rule 52(b). Although in theory it could be argued that "[i]f the question was not presented to the trial court no error was committed by the trial court, hence there is nothing to review," this is not the theory that Rule 52(b) adopts. If a legal rule was violated during the district court proceedings, and if the defendant did not waive the rule, then there has been an "error" within the meaning of Rule 52(b) despite the absence of a timely objection.

The second limitation on appellate authority under Rule 52(b) is that the error be "plain." "Plain" is synonymous with "clear" or, equivalently, "obvious." We need not consider the special case where the error was unclear at the time of trial but becomes clear on appeal because the applicable law has been clarified. At a minimum, court of appeals cannot correct an error pursuant to Rule 52(b) unless the error is clear under current law.

The third and final limitation on appellate authority under Rule 52(b) is that the plain error "affec[t] substantial rights." This is the same language employed in Rule 52(a), and in most cases it means that the error must have been prejudicial: It must have affected the outcome of the district court proceedings. When the defendant has made a timely objection to an error and Rule 52(a) applies, a court of appeals normally engages in a specific analysis of the district court record—a so-called "harmless error" inquiry—to determine whether the error was prejudicial. Rule 52(b) normally requires the same kind of inquiry, with one important difference: It is the defendant rather than the Government who bears the burden of persuasion with respect to prejudice. In most cases, a court of appeals cannot correct the forfeited error unless the defendant shows that the error was prejudicial. This burden shifting is dictated by a subtle but important difference in language between the two parts of Rule 52: While Rule 52(a) precludes error correction only if the error "does not affect substantial rights" (emphasis added), Rule 52(b) authorizes no remedy unless the error does "affec[t] substantial rights." * * *

Rule 52(b) is permissive, not mandatory. If the forfeited error is "plain" and "affect[s] substantial rights," the court of appeals has authority to order correction, but is not required to do so. The language of the Rule ("may be noticed"), the nature of forfeiture, and the established appellate practice that Congress intended to continue all point to this conclusion. "[I]n criminal cases, where the life, or as in this case the liberty, of the defendant is at stake, the courts of the United States, in the exercise of a sound discretion, may notice [forfeited error]."

We previously have explained that the discretion conferred by Rule 52(b) should be employed " 'in those circumstances in which a miscarriage of justice would otherwise result.' " In our collateral-review jurisprudence, the term "miscarriage of justice" means that the defendant is actually innocent. The court of appeals should no doubt correct a plain forfeited error that causes the conviction or sentencing of an actually innocent defendant, but we have never held that a Rule 52(b) remedy is only warranted in cases of actual innocence.

Rather, the standard that should guide the exercise of remedial discretion under Rule 52(b) was articulated in *United States v. Atkinson*, 297 U.S. 157 (1936). The Court of Appeals should correct a plain forfeited error affecting substantial rights if the error "seriously affect[s] the fairness, integrity or public reputation of judicial proceedings." As we explained, the "standard laid down in *United States v. Atkinson* [was] codified in Federal Rule of Criminal Procedure 52(b)," and we repeatedly have quoted the *Atkinson* language in describing plain-error review. An error may "seriously affect the fairness, integrity or public reputation of judicial proceedings" independent of the defendant's innocence. Conversely, a plain error affecting substantial rights does not, without more, satisfy the *Atkinson* standard, for otherwise the discretion afforded by Rule 52(b) would be illusory.

With these basic principles in mind, we turn to the instant case.

III

The Government essentially concedes that the "error" was "plain." We therefore focus our attention on whether the error "affect[ed] substantial rights" within the meaning of Rule 52(b), and conclude that it did not. The presence of alternate jurors during jury deliberations is not the kind of error that "affect[s] substantial rights" independent of its prejudicial impact. Nor have respondents made a specific showing of prejudice.

In theory, the presence of alternate jurors during jury deliberations might prejudice a defendant in two different ways: either because the alternates actually participated in the deliberations, verbally or through "body language"; or because the alternates' presence exerted a "chilling" effect on the regular jurors. Conversely, "if the alternate in fact abided by the court's instructions to remain orally silent and not to otherwise indicate his views or attitude . . . and if the presence of the alternate did not operate as a restraint upon the regular jurors' freedom of expression and action, we see little substantive difference between the presence of [the alternate] and the presence in the juryroom of an unexamined book which had not been admitted into evidence."

Respondents have made no specific showing that the alternate jurors in this case either participated in the jury's deliberations or "chilled" deliberation by the regular jurors. Nor will we presume prejudice for purposes of the Rule 52(b) analysis here. The Court of Appeals was incorrect in finding the error "inherently prejudicial." Until the close of trial, the 2 alternate jurors were indistinguishable from the 12 regular jurors. Along with the regular jurors, they commenced their office with an oath, received the normal initial admonishment, heard the same evidence and arguments, and were not identified as alternates until after the District Court gave a final set of instructions. In those instructions, the District Court specifically enjoined the jurors that "according to the law, the alternates must not participate in the deliberations," and reiterated, "we are going to ask that you not participate." The Court of Appeals should not have supposed that this injunction was contravened. "[It is] the almost invariable assumption of the law that jurors follow their instructions." "[We] presum[e] that jurors, conscious of the gravity of their task, attend closely the particular language of the trial court's instructions in a criminal case and strive to understand, make sense of, and follow the instructions given them." Nor do we think that the mere presence of alternate jurors entailed a sufficient risk of "chill" to justify a presumption of prejudice on that score.

In sum, respondents have not met their burden of showing prejudice under Rule 52(b). Because the conceded error in this case did not "affec[t] substantial rights," the Court of Appeals had no authority to correct it. The judgment of the Court of Appeals is reversed, and the case is remanded for further proceedings consistent with this opinion.

Problem

To what extent may a trial judge rely upon appellate decisions that a particular form of error is generally harmless? *I.e.*, may a trial court anticipate and apply the harmless error doctrine during a trial? Consider the circumstances in *Hackney v. Commonwealth*, 28 Va.App. 288, 504 S.E.2d 385 (1998). A grand jury indicted defendant for grand larceny and possession of a firearm by a convicted felon. In light of well settled precedent that justice requires separate trials "where evidence of one crime is not admissible in the trial of the others," the defendant filed a motion to sever the charge of possession of a firearm by a convicted felon from the larceny charge. The trial judge and defense counsel had the following discussion:

THE COURT: [T]he Commonwealth is going to ask [the] question, "Have you ever been convicted of a felony or a misdemeanor involving lying, cheating and stealing?" They're going to ask that … question at some point during the trial as well.

DEFENSE COUNSEL: If he takes the stand.

THE COURT: If he takes the stand.

DEFENSE COUNSEL: If he takes the stand.

THE COURT: And the Court certainly can't rule that out. [Previous cases recognized that if the defendant testifies, prior convictions are admissible for impeachment purposes, thus rendering harmless any error in denying a motion to sever the charges]. I think the Court would have to overrule Counsel's motion here.

During its case-in-chief, the prosecution introduced prior convictions for three grand larceny and burglary offenses committed by defendant in order to prove a required element of the firearm charge, namely, that defendant was a convicted felon. Defendant testified in his defense to the larceny and firearm charges. On cross-examination, the prosecution elicited for impeachment purposes, testimony from the defendant that he had been previously convicted of three felonies. The jury found defendant guilty of grand larceny and possession of a firearm by a convicted felon.

A panel of the appellate court held that in light of the defendant's decision to testify, the trial court's refusal to sever the charges was harmless error. Upon a rehearing en banc, the full court stated:

> We hold that, as a matter of policy, we will not condone a trial court's clear error in refusing to sever the possession of a firearm by a felon charge predicated on the assumption that an accused will testify and render the error harmless. [The] harmless error doctrine is applicable only upon appellate review or in the trial court upon consideration of a motion to set aside a verdict. When applicable, the harmless error doctrine enables an appellate court or a trial court when considering a motion to set aside a verdict to ignore the effect of an erroneous ruling when an error clearly has had no impact upon the verdict or sentence in a case. The harmless error doctrine should not be used prospectively by a trial court as a basis to disregard an established rule of law.

D. THE RIGHT TO APPEAL

There was no right to appeal in criminal cases at common law, and England did not permit appeals from a criminal conviction until 1907. Appeals as of right in federal courts were nonexistent for the first century of our Nation, and appellate review of any sort was rarely allowed. The States, also, did not generally recognize an appeal as of right until 1889.

At least in dicta, the United States Supreme Court has noted that "a review by an appellate court of the final judgment in a criminal case, however grave the offense of which the accused is convicted, was not at common law and is not now a necessary element of due process." *McKane v. Durston*, 153 U.S. 684 (1894). Justice Scalia recently cited

McKane for the proposition that "there is no constitutional right to appeal," and "a State could, as far as the federal Constitution is concerned, subject its trial-court determinations to no review whatever...." *Martinez v. Court of Appeal*, 528 U.S. 152 (2000). A case challenging this dicta is unlikely to arise because by statute or State constitution, a right of appeal is now universal for all significant convictions.

Once a state provides for appellate review, the review process must not violate equal protection or due process rights. For example, *Douglas v. California*, 372 U.S. 353 (1963) held that indigent defendants are constitutionally entitled to assistance of counsel on a first appeal granted as a matter of right. *North Carolina v. Pearce*, 395 U.S. 711 (1969) stated that "it can hardly be doubted that it would be a flagrant violation of the Fourteenth Amendment for a state trial court to follow an announced practice of imposing a heavier sentence upon every reconvicted defendant for the explicit purpose of punishing the defendant for his having succeeded in getting his original conviction set aside."

Whatever the nature and scope of a right to appellate review, *Ortega–Rodriguez* demonstrates that the right can be waived or forfeited.

ORTEGA–RODRIGUEZ v. UNITED STATES

507 U.S. 234 (1993).

JUSTICE STEVENS delivered the opinion of the Court.

Because we have not previously considered whether a defendant may be deemed to forfeit his right to appeal by fleeing while his case is pending in the district court, though he is recaptured before sentencing and appeal, we granted certiorari.

I

Petitioner is one of three defendants arrested, tried, and convicted of possession with intent to distribute, and conspiring to possess with intent to distribute, over five kilograms of cocaine. After the trial, the District Court set June 15, 1989, as the date for sentencing. Petitioner did not appear and was sentenced in absentia to a prison term of 19 years and 7 months, to be followed by 5 years of supervised release. Though petitioner's codefendants appealed their convictions and sentences, no appeal from the judgment was filed on petitioner's behalf.

The District Court issued a warrant for petitioner's arrest, and 11 months later, on May 24, 1990, he was apprehended. Petitioner was indicted and found guilty of contempt of court and failure to appear. The District Court imposed a prison sentence of 21 months, to be served after the completion of the sentence on the cocaine offenses and to be followed by a 3–year term of supervised release.

While petitioner was under indictment after his arrest, the Court of Appeals disposed of his two codefendants' appeals. The court affirmed one conviction, but reversed the other because the evidence was insufficient to establish guilt beyond a reasonable doubt. Also after petitioner was taken into custody, his attorney filed a "motion to vacate sentence and for resentencing," as well as a motion for judgment of acquittal. The District Court denied the latter but granted the former, vacating the judgment previously entered on the cocaine convictions. The District Court then resentenced petitioner to a prison term of 15 years and 8 months, to be followed by a 5–year period of supervised release. Petitioner filed a timely appeal from that final judgment.

On appeal, petitioner argued that the same insufficiency of the evidence rationale underlying reversal of his codefendant's conviction should apply in his case, because precisely the same evidence was admitted against the two defendants. Without addressing the merits of this contention, the Government moved to dismiss the appeal. The Government's motion was based entirely on the fact that petitioner had become a fugitive after his conviction and before his initial sentencing, so that he cannot now challenge his 1989 conviction for conspiracy and possession with intent to distribute cocaine. In a per curiam order, the Court of Appeals granted the motion to dismiss.

II

It has been settled for well over a century that an appellate court may dismiss the appeal of a defendant who is a fugitive from justice during the pendency of his appeal. The Supreme Court applied this rule for the first time in *Smith v. United States*, 94 U.S. 97 (1876), to an escaped defendant who remained at large when his petition arose before the Court. Under these circumstances, the Court explained, there could be no assurance that any judgment it issued would prove enforceable. The Court concluded that it is "clearly within our discretion to refuse to hear a criminal case in error, unless the convicted party, suing out the writ, is where he can be made to respond to any judgment we may render."

Enforceability is not, however, the only explanation we have offered for the fugitive dismissal rule. In *Molinaro v. New Jersey*, 396 U.S. 365, 366 (1970), we identified an additional justification for dismissal of an escaped prisoner's pending appeal:

> No persuasive reason exists why this Court should proceed to adjudicate the merits of a criminal case after the convicted defendant who has sought review escapes from the restraints placed upon him pursuant to the conviction. While such an escape does not strip the case of its character as an adjudicable case or controversy, we believe it disentitles the defendant to call upon the resources of the Court for determination of his claims.

* * *

III

* * * [T]he justifications we have advanced for allowing appellate courts to dismiss pending fugitive appeals all assume some connection between a defendant's fugitive status and the appellate process, sufficient to make an appellate sanction a reasonable response. These justifications are necessarily attenuated when applied to a case in which both flight and recapture occur while the case is pending before the district court, so that a defendant's fugitive status at no time coincides with his appeal. * * *

The problem in this case, of course, is that petitioner, who fled before sentencing and was recaptured before appeal, flouted the authority of the District Court, not the Court of Appeals. The contemptuous disrespect manifested by his flight was directed at the District Court, before which his case was pending during the entirety of his fugitive period. Therefore, under the reasoning of the cases cited above, it is the District Court that has the authority to defend its own dignity, by sanctioning an act of defiance that occurred solely within its domain.

We cannot accept an expansion of this reasoning that would allow an appellate court to sanction by dismissal any conduct that exhibited disrespect for any aspect of the judicial system, even where such conduct has no connection to the course of appellate proceedings. Such a rule would sweep far too broadly, permitting, for instance, this Court to dismiss a petition solely because the petitioner absconded for a day during district court proceedings, or even because the petitioner once violated a condition of parole or probation. None of our cases calls for such a result, and we decline today to adopt such an approach. * * *

Finally, * * * [o]nce jurisdiction has vested in the appellate court, ... then any deterrent to escape must flow from appellate consequences, and dismissal may be an appropriate sanction by which to deter. Until that time, however, the district court is quite capable of defending its own jurisdiction. While a case is pending before the district court, flight can be deterred with the threat of a wide range of penalties available to the district court judge.

Moreover, should this deterrent prove ineffective, and a defendant flee while his case is before a district court, the district court is well situated to impose an appropriate punishment. While an appellate court has access only to the blunderbuss of dismissal, the district court can tailor a more finely calibrated response. Most obviously, because flight is a separate offense punishable under the Criminal Code, the district court can impose a separate sentence that adequately vindicates the public interest in deterring escape and safeguards the dignity of the court. In this case, for instance, the District Court concluded that a term of imprisonment of 21 months, followed by three years of supervised release, would serve these purposes. If we assume that there is merit to petitioner's appeal, then the Eleventh Circuit's dismissal is tantamount to an additional punishment of 15 years for the same offense of flight. Our reasoning in *Molinaro* surely does not compel that result. * * *

In short, when a defendant's flight and recapture occur before appeal, the defendant's former fugitive status may well lack the kind of connection to the appellate process that would justify an appellate sanction of dismissal. In such cases, fugitivity while a case is pending before a district court, like other contempts of court, is best sanctioned by the district court itself. The contempt for the appellate process manifested by flight while a case is pending on appeal remains subject to the rule of *Molinaro*.

The judgment of the Court of Appeals is vacated, and the case is remanded for further proceedings consistent with this opinion.

So ordered.

Notes and Questions

1. Part of the defendant's plea agreement provided: "Understanding that § 3742 of Title 18 of the United States Code provides for appeal by a defendant of a sentence under certain circumstances and that he may give up or waive said right to appeal, I expressly waive any and all rights conferred by Title 18, U.S.C. § 3742 to appeal my sentence. I also expressly waive the right to appeal my sentence on any other ground and waive the right to attack my sentence in any post-conviction proceeding."

The trial judge determined that the defendant freely and voluntarily entered into the plea agreement. Should the judge have specifically inquired as to whether the defendant knowingly and intelligently waived the right to appeal? *United States v. Wenger*, 58 F.3d 280 (7th Cir.1995) stated:

> Defendant has appealed, despite his promise not to do so. Waivers of appeal are enforceable. Defendant asks us to establish a procedural citadel around the right of appeal, so that waiver will be accepted only following elaborate warnings after the fashion of those used for the most vital constitutional rights. *See Johnson v. Zerbst*, 304 U.S. 458, 464 (1938) (sixth amendment right to counsel); Fed.R.Crim.P. 11(c). But other rights may be surrendered without warnings of any kind and with considerably less formality. E.g., *Schneckloth v. Bustamonte*, 412 U.S. 218 (1973) (fourth amendment right to privacy); *United States v. Mezzanatto*, 513 U.S. 196 (1995) (right to exclude from evidence proffer made as part of plea negotiations). The right to appeal is in the latter category—not simply because it depends on a statute rather than the Constitution but because it has long been seen as the kind of right that depends on assertion. A litigant who does not take a timely appeal has forfeited any entitlement to appellate review. Our legal system makes no appeal the default position. A defendant who finds this agreeable need do nothing. All the waiver in a plea agreement does is to make that outcome a part of the parties' bargain, so that a defendant inclined against appeal or willing to forgo it—perhaps to put an unpleasant episode behind him more quickly—may obtain a concession from the prosecutor. In this case the prosecutor agreed to support a downward departure for acceptance of responsibility, a boon that usually would be unavailable to a defendant arrested (as defendant was) for an intervening offense.

Empty promises are worthless promises; if defendants could retract their waivers (the practical effect, if the procedural hurdles to an effective waiver were set too high) then they could not obtain concessions by promising not to appeal. Although any given defendant would like to obtain the concession and exercise the right as well, prosecutors cannot be fooled in the long run. Right holders are better off if they can choose between exercising the right and exchanging that right for something they value more highly. Defendant exchanged the right to appeal for prosecutorial concessions; he cannot have his cake and eat it too.

2.   In *United States v. Han*, 181 F.Supp.2d 1039 (N.D.Cal.2002), the court held that a waiver of the right to appeal a sentence that is made as part of a plea agreement is a waiver of an unknown error, that is, one which has yet to occur. In light of the requirement that a waiver be knowing and voluntary, a sentence limited only by the statutory maximum and constitutional constraints, does not allow the defendant a fair opportunity to contemplate the *actual*, not theoretical, range of sentence that may be imposed. Accordingly, "a plea agreement [containing a waiver of judicial review], should, at the very least, set forth a maximum sentence which the defendant would accept based upon certain assumptions as they relate to sentencing factors, including criminal history." The court offered the following as "standard language of a waiver of appeal" that could be used in plea agreements:

> In exchange for the government's concessions in this plea agreement, defendant waives, to the full extent of the law, any right to appeal or collaterally attack the conviction and sentence, including any restitution order, unless the Court imposes a sentence in excess of ___ months. If the custodial sentence exceeds ___ months, the defendant may appeal, but the government will be free to support on appeal the sentence actually imposed.

3.   Your client was sentenced to death, but now tells you that he wants to be executed, and orders you not to appeal his sentence. The defendant's mother intervenes and asks you to file a petition as defendant's "next friend" asking the appellate court to re-examine the legal and factual issues. Should the court honor the defendant's waiver; allow the next friend to pursue an appeal; conduct its own review of the case regardless of the wishes of the defendant or next friend?

State v. Robbins, 339 Ark. 379, 5 S.W.3d 51 (1999) held that a defendant sentenced to death can choose not to appeal the sentence as long as he has the capacity to understand the difference between life and death and to knowingly and voluntarily waive his right to appeal. A next friend cannot override the defendant's choice to waive appeal. The court distinguished, however, between the defendant's rights and the court's own responsibility to serve as a check on the arbitrary and capricious imposition of a death sentence. State statutes and its own rules convinced the court that it had an affirmative duty to review the record in all death penalty cases for prejudicial error, regardless of the defendant's refusal to pursue an appeal.

Ethical Considerations

In *Smith v. Robbins*, 528 U.S. 259 (2000) Justice Souter observed that "No one has a right to a wholly frivolous appeal, against which the judicial system's first line of defense is its lawyers. Being officers of the court, members of the bar are bound 'not to clog the courts with frivolous motions or appeals.' "

In *Anders v. California*, 386 U.S. 738 (1967), the Court suggested that when an attorney appointed to represent an indigent defendant on direct appeal finds the case wholly frivolous, he should: (1) advise the court and request permission to withdraw; (2) submit a brief referring to anything in the record that might arguably support the appeal; (3) furnish a copy of the brief to the defendant in time to allow him to raise any points that he chooses; and (4) request the court to conduct a full examination and decide whether the case is wholly frivolous. [These requirements do not apply to counsel's withdrawal from collateral attacks upon the conviction. *Pennsylvania v. Finley*, 481 U.S. 551 (1987)].

An *Anders* brief creates tension between counsel's ethical duty as an officer of the court (which requires him not to present frivolous arguments) and counsel's duty to further his client's interests (which might not permit counsel to characterize his client's claims as frivolous). One former public defender bemoaned the fact that a client's desire to pursue a frivolous appeal requires defense counsel "to do something that the Code of Professional Responsibility describes as unethical; the only choice is as to which canon he or she prefers to violate." Pengilly, Never Cry *Anders*: The Ethical Dilemma of Counsel Appointed to Pursue a Frivolous Criminal Appeal, 9 Crim. Justice J. 45, 64 (1986).

California replaced an *Anders* brief with a *Wende* brief which provides that "counsel, upon concluding that an appeal would be frivolous, files a brief with the appellate court that summarizes the procedural and factual history of the case, with citation of the record. He also attests that he has reviewed the record, explained his evaluation of the case to his client, provided the client with a copy of the brief, and informed the client of his right to file a pro se supplemental brief. He further requests that the court independently examine the record for arguable issues."

The majority in *Smith v. Robbins*, approved the California approach because "The procedure we sketched in *Anders v. California*, is a prophylactic one; the States are free to adopt different procedures, so long as those procedures adequately safeguard a defendant's right to appellate counsel" and the State provides a review process that "reasonably ensures that an indigent's appeal will be resolved in a way that is related to the merit of that appeal."

In dissent Justice Souter maintained that:

It is owing to the importance of assuring that an adversarial, not an inquisitorial system is at work that I disagree with the Court's statement today that our cases approve of any state procedure that "reasonably ensures that an indigent's appeal will be resolved in a way that is related to the merit of that appeal." A purely inquisitorial system could satisfy that criterion, and so could one that appoints counsel only if the

appellate court deems it useful. But we have rejected the former and have explicitly held the latter unconstitutional.

[The] rub is that although counsel may properly refuse to brief a frivolous issue and a court may just as properly deny leave to take a frivolous appeal, there needs to be some reasonable assurance that the lawyer has not relaxed his partisan instinct prior to refusing, in which case the court's review could never compensate for the lawyer's failure of advocacy simple statement by counsel that an appeal has no merit, coupled with an appellate court's endorsement of counsel's conclusion, gives no affirmative indication that anyone has sought out the appellant's best arguments or championed his cause to the degree contemplated by the adversary system.

Appeals of Last Resort

A defendant who fails to obtain a reversal on direct appeal may make collateral attacks on the conviction, such as a petition for a writ of habeas corpus discussed in the next chapter.

As a supplement to judicial review, all jurisdictions grant a convicted defendant an opportunity to appeal to executive authority for a pardon or grant of clemency. For example, Article 2, Section 2, Clause 1 of the U. S. Constitution gives the President "Power to grant Reprieves and Pardons for Offences against the United States, except in Cases of Impeachment." President Gerald Ford pardoned, prior to trial, former President Richard Nixon for his role in the Watergate scandal. Former President Nixon was given a "full pardon," but the President has the power to "forgive the convicted person in part or entirely, to reduce a penalty in terms of a specified number of years, or to alter it with conditions which are in themselves constitutionally unobjectionable." *Schick v. Reed*, 419 U.S. 256 (1974). See generally, Michael Heise, "Mercy by the Numbers: an Empirical Analysis of Clemency and its Structure," 80 Va. L. Rev. 239 (2003).

Chapter 24

COLLATERAL REMEDIES

A. INTRODUCTION

A defendant who fails on direct appeal may file a collateral attack on the conviction, the most common form being a *habeas corpus* petition. Most states have habeas corpus-like proceedings that closely follow federal habeas corpus discussed in the remainder of this chapter. Failure to prevail in state habeas proceedings will not bar a subsequent federal habeas action, in fact, the filing of a state petition is often a necessary component of the federal petition. *See* § III Exhaustion of Remedies.

Habeas corpus, a Latin term meaning "you have the body," is a collateral attack because it is not a continuation of the criminal process, but a civil suit brought to challenge the legality of the restraint under which a person is held. The petitioner in this civil suit, having lost the presumption of innocence upon conviction, has the burden to prove by a preponderance of evidence that his confinement is illegal. The respondent in a habeas action is the prisoner's custodian—the warden or other prison official. Habeas corpus has been called "the most celebrated writ in the English law," and the U. S. Supreme Court paid homage to this "Great Writ of Liberty" in *Fay v. Noia*, 372 U.S. 391 (1963):

> We do well to bear in mind the extraordinary prestige of the Great Writ [in] Anglo–American jurisprudence. Received into our own law in the colonial period, given explicit recognition in the Federal Constitution, Art. I, section 9, cl. 2, incorporated in the first grant of federal court jurisdiction, habeas corpus was early confirmed by Chief Justice Marshall to be a "great constitutional privilege."

> Although in form the Great Writ is simply a mode of procedure, its history is inextricably intertwined with the growth of fundamental rights of personal liberty. For its function has been to provide a prompt and efficacious remedy for whatever society deems to be intolerable restraints. Its root principle is that in a civilized society, government must always be accountable to the judiciary for a man's imprisonment: if the imprisonment cannot be shown to conform

with fundamental requirements of law, the individual is entitled to his immediate release. Thus, there is nothing novel in the fact that today habeas corpus in the federal courts provides a mode for the redress of denials of due process of law. Vindication of due process is precisely its historic office.

However great the scope and focus of the writ, merely filing a habeas corpus petition does not insure that a federal court will review the merits of the petitioner's claim. If the habeas corpus petition is patently frivolous, or if the court can determine the merits of the allegations by reference to records of previous state or federal judicial proceedings, the petition may be denied without a full evidentiary hearing.

WILLIAMS v. TAYLOR
529 U.S. 420 (2000).

JUSTICE KENNEDY delivered the opinion of the Court.

Petitioner Michael Wayne Williams received a capital sentence for the murders of Morris Keller, Jr., and Keller's wife, Mary Elizabeth. Petitioner later sought a writ of habeas corpus in federal court. Accompanying his petition was a request for an evidentiary hearing on constitutional claims which, he alleged, he had been unable to develop in state-court proceedings. The question in this case is whether 28 U.S.C. § 2254(e)(2) bars the evidentiary hearing petitioner seeks. If petitioner "has failed to develop the factual basis of [his] claim[s] in State court proceedings," his case is subject to § 2254(e)(2), and he may not receive a hearing because he concedes his inability to satisfy the statute's further stringent conditions for excusing the deficiency.

Petitioner filed a habeas petition in the United States District Court for the Eastern District of Virginia on November 20, 1996. The petition raised three claims relevant to questions now before us. First, petitioner claimed the prosecution had violated *Brady v. Maryland*, 373 U.S. 83 (1963), in failing to disclose a report of a confidential pre-trial psychiatric examination of prosecution witness Cruse. Second, petitioner alleged his trial was rendered unfair by the seating of a juror who at voir dire had not revealed possible sources of bias. Finally, petitioner alleged one of the prosecutors committed misconduct in failing to reveal his knowledge of the juror's possible bias. [The district court dismissed the petition, deciding that petitioner could not satisfy § 2254(e)(2)'s requirements.] The Court of Appeals concluded petitioner could not satisfy the statute's conditions for excusing his failure to develop the facts and held him barred from receiving an evidentiary hearing.

On October 18, 1999, petitioner filed an application for stay of execution and a petition for a writ of certiorari. On October 28, we stayed petitioner's execution and granted certiorari to decide whether § 2254(e)(2) precludes him from receiving an evidentiary hearing on his claims. We now affirm in part and reverse in part.

IIA

[Section] 2254(e)(2), the provision which controls whether petitioner may receive an evidentiary hearing in federal district court on the claims that were not developed in the Virginia courts, becomes the central point of our analysis. It provides as follows:

"If the applicant has failed to develop the factual basis of a claim in State court proceedings, the court shall not hold an evidentiary hearing on the claim unless the applicant shows that—

"(A) the claim relies on—

"(i) a new rule of constitutional law, made retroactive to cases on collateral review by the Supreme Court, that was previously unavailable; or

"(ii) a factual predicate that could not have been previously discovered through the exercise of due diligence; and

"(B) the facts underlying the claim would be sufficient to establish by clear and convincing evidence that but for constitutional error, no reasonable factfinder would have found the applicant guilty of the underlying offense."

By the terms of its opening clause the statute applies only to prisoners who have "failed to develop the factual basis of a claim in State court proceedings." If the prisoner has failed to develop the facts, an evidentiary hearing cannot be granted unless the prisoner's case meets the other conditions of § 2254(e)(2). Here, petitioner concedes his case does not comply with § 2254(e)(2)(B), so he may receive an evidentiary hearing only if his claims fall outside the opening clause.

There was no hearing in state court on any of the claims for which petitioner now seeks an evidentiary hearing. That, says the Commonwealth, is the end of the matter. In its view petitioner, whether or not through his own fault or neglect, still "failed to develop the factual basis of a claim in State court proceedings." Petitioner, on the other hand, says the phrase "failed to develop" means lack of diligence in developing the claims, a defalcation he contends did not occur since he made adequate efforts during state-court proceedings to discover and present the underlying facts. The Court of Appeals agreed with petitioner's interpretation of § 2254(e)(2) but believed petitioner had not exercised enough diligence to avoid the statutory bar. We agree with petitioner and the Court of Appeals that "failed to develop" implies some lack of diligence; but, unlike the Court of Appeals, we find no lack of diligence on petitioner's part with regard to two of his three claims.

B

We start, as always, with the language of the statute. Section 2254(e)(2) begins with a conditional clause, "[i]f the applicant has failed to develop the factual basis of a claim in State court proceedings," which directs attention to the prisoner's efforts in state court. We ask first whether the factual basis was indeed developed in state court, a question susceptible, in the normal course, of a simple yes or no answer. Here the answer is no.

The Commonwealth would have the analysis begin and end there. Under its no-fault reading of the statute, if there is no factual development in the state court, the federal habeas court may not inquire into the reasons for the default when determining whether the opening clause of § 2254(e)(2) applies. We do not agree with the Commonwealth's interpretation of the word "failed."

We do not deny "fail" is sometimes used in a neutral way, not importing fault or want of diligence. So the phrase "We fail to understand his argument" can mean simply "We cannot understand his argument." This is not the sense in which the word "failed" is used here, however.

We give the words of a statute their " 'ordinary, contemporary, common meaning,' " absent an indication Congress intended them to bear some different import. In its customary and preferred sense, "fail" connotes some omission, fault, or negligence on the part of the person who has failed to do something. To say a person has failed in a duty implies he did not take the necessary steps to fulfill it. He is, as a consequence, at fault and bears responsibility for the failure. In this sense, a person is not at fault when his diligent efforts to perform an act are thwarted, for example, by the conduct of another or by happenstance. Fault lies, in those circumstances, either with the person who interfered with the accomplishment of the act or with no one at all. We conclude Congress used the word "failed" in the sense just described. Had Congress intended a no-fault standard, it would have had no difficulty in making its intent plain. It would have had to do no more than use, in lieu of the phrase "has failed to," the phrase "did not."

Under the opening clause of § 2254(e)(2), a failure to develop the factual basis of a claim is not established unless there is lack of diligence, or some greater fault, attributable to the prisoner or the prisoner's counsel. In this we agree with the Court of Appeals and with all other courts of appeals which have addressed the issue.

III

Now we apply the statutory test. If there has been no lack of diligence at the relevant stages in the state proceedings, the prisoner has not "failed to develop" the facts under § 2254(e)(2)'s opening clause, and he will be excused from showing compliance with the balance of the subsection's requirements. We find lack of diligence as to one of the three claims but not as to the other two.

Petitioner did not exercise the diligence required to preserve the claim that nondisclosure of Cruse's psychiatric report was in contravention of *Brady v. Maryland*. The report concluded Cruse "ha[d] little recollection of the [murders of the Kellers], other than vague memories, as he was intoxicated with alcohol and marijuana at the time." The report had been prepared in September 1993, before petitioner was tried;

yet it was not mentioned by petitioner until he filed his federal habeas petition and attached a copy of the report. Petitioner explained that an investigator for his federal habeas counsel discovered the report in Cruse's court file but state habeas counsel had not seen it when he had reviewed the same file. State habeas counsel averred as follows:

"Prior to filing [petitioner's] habeas corpus petition with the Virginia Supreme Court, I reviewed the Cumberland County court files of [petitioner] and of his co-defendant, Jeffrey Cruse. [I] have reviewed the attached psychiatric evaluation of Jeffrey Cruse.... I have no recollection of seeing this report in Mr. Cruse's court file when I examined the file. Given the contents of the report, I am confident that I would remember it."

The trial court was not satisfied with this explanation for the late discovery. Nor are we.

We conclude petitioner has met the burden of showing he was diligent in efforts to develop the facts supporting his juror bias and prosecutorial misconduct claims in collateral proceedings before the Virginia Supreme Court. Petitioner's claims are based on two of the questions posed to the jurors by the trial judge at voir dire. First, the judge asked prospective jurors, "Are any of you related to the following people who may be called as witnesses?" Then he read the jurors a list of names, one of which was "Deputy Sheriff Claude Meinhard." Bonnie Stinnett, who would later become the jury foreperson, had divorced Meinhard in 1979, after a 17–year marriage with four children. Stinnett remained silent, indicating the answer was "no." Meinhard, as the officer who investigated the crime scene and interrogated Cruse, would later become the prosecution's lead-off witness at trial.

After reading the names of the attorneys involved in the case, including one of the prosecutors, Robert Woodson, Jr., the judge asked, "Have you or any member of your immediate family ever been represented by any of the aforementioned attorneys?" Stinnett again said nothing, despite the fact Woodson had represented her during her divorce from Meinhard. In an affidavit she provided in the federal habeas proceedings, Stinnett claimed "[she] did not respond to the judge's [first] question because [she] did not consider [herself] 'related' to Claude Meinhard in 1994 [at voir dire].... Once our marriage ended in 1979, I was no longer related to him." As for Woodson's earlier representation of her, Stinnett explained as follows:

"When Claude and I divorced in 1979, the divorce was uncontested and Mr. Woodson drew up the papers so that the divorce could be completed. Since neither Claude nor I was contesting anything, I didn't think Mr. Woodson 'represented' either one of us."

Woodson provided an affidavit in which he admitted "[he] was aware that Juror Bonnie Stinnett was the ex-wife of then Deputy Sheriff Claude Meinhard and [he] was aware that they had been divorced for some time." Woodson stated, however, "[t]o [his] mind, people who are related only by marriage are no longer 'related' once the marriage ends in divorce." Woodson also "had no recollection of having been involved as a private attorney in the divorce proceedings between Claude Meinhard and Bonnie Stinnett." He explained that "[w]hatever [his] involvement was in the 1979 divorce, by the time of trial in 1994 [he] had completely forgotten about it."

In ordering an evidentiary hearing on the juror bias and prosecutorial misconduct claims, the District Court concluded the factual basis of the claims was not reasonably available to petitioner's counsel during state habeas proceedings. The Court of Appeals held state habeas counsel was not diligent because petitioner's investigator on federal habeas discovered the relationships upon interviewing two jurors who referred in passing to Stinnett as "Bonnie Meinhard." The investigator later confirmed Stinnett's prior marriage to Meinhard by checking Cumberland County's public records. ("The documents supporting [petitioner's] Sixth Amendment claims have been a matter of public record since Stinnett's divorce became final in 1979. Indeed, because [petitioner's] federal habeas counsel located those documents, there is little reason to think that his state habeas counsel could not have done so as well"). We should be surprised, to say the least, if a district court familiar with the standards of trial practice were to hold that in all cases diligent counsel must check public records containing personal information pertaining to each and every juror. Because of Stinnett and Woodson's silence, there was no basis for an investigation into Stinnett's marriage history. Section 2254(e)(2) does not apply to petitioner's related claims of juror bias and prosecutorial misconduct.

The decision of the Court of Appeals is affirmed in part and reversed in part. The case is remanded for further proceedings consistent with this opinion.

Note

If a federal district court grants a hearing on the habeas petition, both the petitioner and the government must be given the opportunity to present evidence. Upon denial of the petition, the petitioner will be remanded to custody. If the court grants the petition, the petitioner shall be discharged from custody, but the court may suspend execution of its order to allow the government to appeal or to institute a new trial within a specified period of time. The court also has authority to admit the petitioner to bail, pending the government's appeal or initiation of a new trial. When deciding whether to grant release pending appeal to a state prisoner who has won habeas relief a federal court may consider: (1) the risk that the prisoner may flee; (2) the danger the prisoner may pose to the public; (3) the state's interest in continuing custody and rehabilitation; and (4) the prisoner's interest in release pending appeal. *Hilton v. Braunskill*, 481 U.S. 770 (1987).

––––––––––

At common law any person illegally detained could use the writ of habeas corpus to make repeated efforts to gain his freedom. "Res judicata did not attach to a court's denial of habeas relief.... [instead] a renewed application could be made to every other judge or court in the realm, and each court or judge was bound to consider the question of the prisoner's right to a discharge independently, and not to be influenced by the previous decisions refusing discharge." *McCleskey v. Zant*, 499 U.S. 467 (1991). The common law courts tolerated multiple petitions and petitions filed years after the initial trial because the writ of habeas corpus originally performed only the narrow function of testing either the jurisdiction of the sentencing court or the legality of Executive detention. The scope of the writ later expanded beyond its original narrow purview to encompass review of constitutional error that had occurred in the proceedings leading to conviction. [*See* Section II of this Chapter]. The expanded coverage of the writ led the Supreme Court to formulate the doctrines of exhaustion and procedural default as means of limiting abusive and repetitive habeas petitions. The Antiterrorism and Effective Death Penalty Act of 1996 (AEDPA) incorporates and expands upon these doctrines. [*See* Sections III and IV of this Chapter].

Prior to enactment of the AEDPA there was no time limitation on the filing of a writ of habeas corpus, although some courts applied the doctrine of laches on a case-by-case basis. *See e.g., Walker v. Mitchell*, 224 Va. 568, 299 S.E.2d 698 (1983) (six-and-a-half-year delay in filing a habeas corpus petition). The doctrine of laches did not operate as an effective statute of limitations because it required that the government prove actual prejudice from the delay, but "prejudice cannot be presumed solely from the passage of time." *Walker v. Mitchell*, 587 F.Supp. 1432 (E.D.Va.1984).

In order to promote speedy punishment and the finality of criminal justice proceedings, the AEDPA created a rigid one-year limitation for filing a petition for habeas corpus relief. The limitation period begins to run on the latest date of the following: 1) when the judgment of conviction becomes final, 2) when the state action impediment to making a motion was removed, 3) when a right asserted was initially recognized by the Supreme Court and made retroactive, or 4) when the facts supporting the claim presented could have been discovered through due diligence. Se 28 U.S.C. § 2244(d)(1).

Because the statute limited the time for seeking habeas relief, case law has focused on the limitations period. For example, *Johnson v. United States*, 544 U.S. 295 (2005) held that the limitations period begins to run when she receives notice of the order vacating the state conviction, provided that she showed due diligence in seeking to vacate the state conviction. An application for state collateral review is "pending," thereby tolling the one-year limitations period, during the interval between a lower state court's decision on collateral review and the filing of a notice of appeal to a higher state court. *Carey v. Saffold*, 536 U.S. 214 (2002). Applying the third exception to the federal statute, the Court has held that any claim is time-barred if more than twelve months pass before the rule is held to be retroactive. *Dodd v. United States*, 545 U.S. 353 (2005).

If the habeas petition is filed in due time, a state prisoner seeking habeas review in a federal court must meet four requirements: (1) custody; (2) a violation of federal law; (3) exhaustion of other remedies; and (4) the absence of procedural default.

B. CUSTODY

A person is in custody when he is presently serving a sentence for the conviction challenged by the writ, or when he has been released from confinement subject to the control of the parole board, probation officer, or a court which imposed a suspended sentence. In the latter case a writ of habeas corpus is available if the conditions of release "significantly restrain" the petitioner's liberty. *Jones v. Cunningham*, 371 U.S. 236 (1963); *Hensley v. Municipal Court*, 411 U.S. 345 (1973). A prisoner serving consecutive sentences is "in custody" for purposes of challenging any of the sentences. *Peyton v. Rowe*, 391 U.S. 54 (1968). The writ may not be used to attack a conviction that merely imposed a fine or collateral civil disability not resulting in incarceration. Nor may the petitioner attack a sentence that has been fully served unless the prisoner is serving another sentence that was enhanced by the challenged sentence.

Garlotte v. Fordice is typical of the cases defining custody in the context of a claim by the state that the habeas petition is moot because the petitioner is no longer in "custody."

GARLOTTE v. FORDICE

515 U.S. 39 (1995).

JUSTICE GINSBURG delivered the opinion of the Court.

To petition a federal court for habeas corpus relief from a state court conviction, the applicant must be "in custody in violation of the Constitution or laws or treaties of the United States." In *Peyton v. Rowe*, 391 U.S. 54 (1968), we held that the governing federal prescription permits prisoners incarcerated under consecutive state court sentences to apply for federal habeas relief from sentences they had not yet begun to serve. We said in *Peyton* that, for purposes of habeas relief, consecutive sentences should be treated as a continuous series; a prisoner is "in custody in violation of the Constitution," we explained, "if any consecutive sentence [the prisoner] is scheduled to serve was imposed as the result of a deprivation of constitutional rights."

The case before us is appropriately described as *Peyton*'s complement, or *Peyton* in reverse. Like the habeas petitioners in *Peyton*, petitioner Harvey Garlotte is incarcerated under consecutive sentences.

Unlike the *Peyton* petitioners, however, Garlotte does not challenge a conviction underlying a sentence yet to be served. Instead, Garlotte seeks to attack a conviction underlying the sentence that ran first in a consecutive series, a sentence already served, but one that nonetheless persists to postpone Garlotte's eligibility for parole. Following *Peyton*, we do not desegregate Garlotte's sentences, but comprehend them as composing a continuous stream. We therefore hold that Garlotte remains "in custody" under all of his sentences until all are served, and now may attack the conviction underlying the sentence scheduled to run first in the series.

I

On September 16, 1985, at a plea hearing held in a Mississippi trial court, Harvey Garlotte entered simultaneous guilty pleas to one count of possession with intent to distribute marijuana and two counts of murder. Pursuant to a plea agreement, the State recommended that Garlotte be sentenced to a prison term of three years on the marijuana count, to run consecutively with two concurrent life sentences on the murder counts. [T]he court imposed the sentences in this order: the three-year sentence first, then, consecutively, the concurrent life sentences.

Garlotte wrote to the trial court seven months after the September 16, 1985 hearing, asking for permission to withdraw his guilty plea on the marijuana count. The court's reply notified Garlotte of the Mississippi statute under which he could pursue post-conviction collateral relief. Garlotte unsuccessfully moved for such relief. Nearly two years after the denial of Garlotte's motion, the Mississippi Supreme Court rejected his appeal. On January 18, 1989, the Mississippi Supreme Court denied further post-conviction motions filed by Garlotte. By this time, Garlotte had completed the period of incarceration set for the marijuana offense, and had commenced serving the life sentences.

On October 6, 1989, Garlotte filed a habeas corpus petition in the United States District Court for the Southern District of Mississippi, naming as respondent Kirk Fordice, the Governor of Mississippi. Adopting the recommendation of a federal magistrate judge, the District Court denied Garlotte's petition on the merits.

Before the United States Court of Appeals for the Fifth Circuit, the State argued for the first time that the District Court lacked jurisdiction over Garlotte's petition. The State asserted that Garlotte, prior to the District Court filing, had already served out the prison time imposed for the marijuana conviction; therefore, the State maintained, Garlotte was no longer "in custody" under that conviction within the meaning of the federal habeas statute. Garlotte countered that he remained "in custody" until all sentences were served, emphasizing that the marijuana conviction continued to postpone the date on which he would be eligible for parole.

Adopting the State's position, the Fifth Circuit dismissed Garlotte's habeas petition for want of jurisdiction. The Courts of Appeals have divided over the question whether a person incarcerated under consecutive sentences remains "in custody" under a sentence that (1) has been completed in terms of prison time served, but (2) continues to postpone the prisoner's date of potential release. We granted certiorari to resolve this conflict, and now reverse.

II

Had the Mississippi trial court ordered that Garlotte's life sentences run before his marijuana sentence—an option about which the prosecutor expressed indifference—*Peyton* unquestionably would have instructed the District Court to entertain Garlotte's present habeas petition. Because the marijuana term came first, and Garlotte filed his habeas petition after prison time had run on the marijuana sentence, Mississippi urges that *Maleng v. Cook*, 490 U.S. 488 (1989) (per curiam), rather than *Peyton*, controls.

The question presented in *Maleng* was "whether a habeas petitioner remains 'in custody' under a conviction after the sentence imposed for it has fully expired, merely because of the possibility that the prior conviction will be used to enhance the sentences imposed for any subsequent crimes of which he is convicted." We held that the potential use of a conviction to enhance a sentence for subsequent offenses did not suffice to render a person "in custody" within the meaning of the habeas statute.

Maleng recognized that we had "very liberally construed the 'in custody' requirement for purposes of federal habeas," but stressed that the Court had "never extended it to the situation where a habeas petitioner suffers no present restraint from a conviction." "[A]lmost all States have habitual offender statutes, and many States provide . . . for specific enhancement of subsequent sentences on the basis of prior convictions,"; hence, the construction of "in custody" urged by the habeas petitioner in *Maleng* would have left nearly all convictions perpetually open to collateral attack. The *Maleng* petitioner's interpretation, we therefore commented, "would read the 'in custody' requirement out of the statute."

Unlike the habeas petitioner in *Maleng*, Garlotte is serving consecutive sentences. In *Peyton*, we held that "a prisoner serving consecutive sentences 'in custody' under any one of them" for purposes of the habeas statute. Having construed the statutory term "in custody" to require that consecutive sentences be viewed in the aggregate, we will not now adopt a different construction simply because the sentence imposed under the challenged conviction lies in the past rather than in the future.

Mississippi urges, as a prime reason for its construction of the 'in custody' requirement, that allowing a habeas attack on a sentence nominally completed would "encourage and reward delay in the assertion of habeas challenges." As Mississippi observes, in *Peyton* we rejected the prematurity rule of McNally in part because of "the harshness of a rule which may delay determination of federal claims for decades." Mississippi argues that Garlotte's reading of the words "in custody" would undermine the expeditious adjudication rationale of *Peyton*.

Our holding today, however, is unlikely to encourage delay. A prisoner naturally prefers release sooner to release later. Further, because the habeas petitioner generally bears the burden of proof, delay is apt to disadvantage the petitioner more than the State. Nothing in this record, we note, suggests that Garlotte has been dilatory in challenging his marijuana conviction. Finally, under Habeas Corpus Rule 9(a), a district court may dismiss a habeas petition if the State "has been prejudiced in its ability to respond to the petition by [inexcusable] delay in its filing." * * *

Under *Peyton*, we view consecutive sentences in the aggregate, not as discrete segments. Invalidation of Garlotte's marijuana conviction would advance the date of his eligibility for release from present incarceration. Garlotte's challenge, which will shorten his term of incarceration if he proves unconstitutionality, implicates the core purpose of habeas review. We therefore hold that Garlotte was "in custody" under his marijuana conviction when he filed his federal habeas petition. Accordingly, the judgment of the Court of Appeals for the Fifth Circuit is reversed, and the case is remanded for proceedings consistent with this opinion.

JUSTICE THOMAS, with whom THE CHIEF JUSTICE joins, dissenting.

In my view, *Peyton* ought to be construed as limited to situations in which a habeas petitioner challenges a yet unexpired sentence. This would satisfy *Peyton*'s policy concerns by permitting challenges to unserved sentences at an earlier time. More importantly, this interpretation would also make sense of *Maleng v. Cook's* proper insistence that the habeas statute does not permit prisoners to challenge expired convictions. The majority, however, relies upon broad language in one opinion to ignore language in another. Given the statute's text and the oddity of asserting that Garlotte is still serving time under the expired marijuana conviction, I would read *Peyton* narrowly. Accordingly, I dissent.

Note

Apart from custody considerations, "criminal convictions do in fact entail adverse collateral legal consequences." *Sibron v. New York*, 392 U.S. 40 (1968). As a remedy of last resort, a convicted person no longer subject to confinement may seek a common law writ of *coram nobis* to challenge his prior conviction. *See United States v. Morgan*, 346 U.S. 502 (1954) (all federal courts may in exceptional cases grant relief in the nature of coram nobis to a person who is not in custody, under the "all-writs provision," [28 U.S.C. § 1651(a)]). For example, in *Korematsu v. United States*, 323 U.S. 214 (1944) the Supreme Court upheld the conviction of an American citizen of Japanese ancestry for being in a location designated as off limits to all persons of Japanese ancestry. Forty years later, *Korematsu v. United States*,

584 F.Supp. 1406 (N.D.Cal.1984) vacated the conviction on grounds that the government had mislead the courts as to the military necessity of wartime relocation and internment of civilians in 1944.

C. VIOLATIONS OF FEDERAL LAW

Only federal issues are cognizable in federal habeas proceedings; state constitutional or statutory violations are not. The most common habeas corpus claims are ineffective assistance of counsel, incriminating statements obtained by illegal police interrogation, improper judicial or prosecutorial conduct, and insufficient evidence. In most cases errors concerning the admissibility of evidence or instructions to the jury do not amount to constitutional violations. The writ of habeas corpus focuses on the legality of the prisoner's detention under the Fourteenth Amendment right to due process, rather than his ultimate guilt or innocence.

Although 28 U.S.C. § 2254 speaks of a "violation of the Constitution or laws or treaties of the United States," almost all federal habeas petitions allege a violation of the Constitution. A conviction obtained in violation of a federal statute does not warrant habeas review unless the statutory violation qualifies as a "fundamental defect which inherently results in a complete miscarriage of justice, or an omission inconsistent with the rudimentary demands of fair procedure." *Reed v. Farley*, 512 U.S. 339 (1994). Most statutory violations are simply not important enough to invoke the extraordinary habeas jurisdiction.

A defining characteristic of the Warren Court in the 1960's was its willingness to increase federal habeas review of state court convictions by "constitutionalizing" many aspects of criminal procedure.

> The writ of habeas corpus known to the Framers was quite different from that which exists today.... [T]he first Congress made the writ of habeas corpus available only to prisoners confined under the authority of the United States, not under state authority.... It was not until 1867 that Congress made the writ generally available in "all cases where any person may be restrained of his or her liberty in violation of the constitution, or of any treaty or law of the United States." And it was not until well into this century that this Court interpreted that provision to allow a final judgment of conviction in a state court to be collaterally attacked on habeas.

Felker v. Turpin, 518 U.S. 651 (1996).

The Warren Court's approach to federal habeas corpus was partially premised on a belief that the state courts could not be trusted to protect the constitutional rights of criminal defendants. In the landmark case of *Gideon v. Wainwright*, 372 U.S. 335, 351 (1963) Justice Harlan expressed dissatisfaction with many state courts' discharge of their "front-line responsibility for the enforcement of constitutional rights." The Burger and Rehnquist Courts, however, embraced the concept of a "new federalism" by resurrecting faith in the state courts as protectors of individual freedom. *Stone v. Powell* altered the judicial availability of federal habeas relief in Fourth Amendment cases, and was the first step in the Supreme Court's efforts to rein in federal judges reared on the Warren Court's "judicial activism" and distrust of state courts. "The battle over habeas is driven, in the main, not by relatively sterile concerns for federalism and congested federal dockets, but by an ideological resistance to the Warren Court's innovative interpretations of substantive federal rights." Larry Yackle, *The Habeas Hagioscope*, 66 S. Cal. L. Rev. 2331 (1993).

STONE v. POWELL

428 U.S. 465 (1976).

Justice Powell delivered the opinion of the Court.

[Respondent Powell was arrested for violating a vagrancy ordinance, but was later charged with murder and convicted on the basis of evidence seized during a search pursuant to the vagrancy arrest. Powell asserted that the vagrancy ordinance was unconstitutional and the subsequent arrest and search were illegal.]

Respondent alleges violations of Fourth Amendment rights guaranteed them through the Fourteenth Amendment. The question is whether state prisoners who have been afforded the opportunity for full and fair consideration of their reliance upon the exclusionary rule with respect to seized evidence by the state courts at trial and on direct review may invoke their claim again on federal habeas corpus review. The answer is to be found by weighing the utility of the exclusionary rule against the costs of extending it to collateral review of Fourth Amendment claims.

The costs of applying the exclusionary rule even at trial and on direct review are well known: the focus of the trial, and the attention of the participants therein, are diverted from the ultimate question of guilt or innocence that should be the central concern in a criminal proceeding. Moreover, the physical evidence sought to be excluded is typically reliable and often the most probative information bearing on the guilt or innocence of the defendant.

Application of the rule thus deflects the truth finding process and often frees the guilty. The disparity in particular cases between the error committed by the police officer and the windfall afforded a guilty defendant by application of the rule is contrary to the idea of proportionality that is essential to the concept of justice. Thus, although the rule is thought to deter unlawful police activity in part through the nurturing of respect for Fourth Amendment values, if applied indiscriminately it may well have the opposite effect of generating disrespect for the law and administration of justice. These long-recognized costs of the rule persist when a criminal conviction is sought to be overturned on collateral review on the ground that a search-and-seizure claim was erroneously rejected by two or more tiers of state courts.

Evidence obtained by police officers in violation of the Fourth Amendment is excluded at trial in the hope that the frequency of future violations will decrease. Despite the absence of supportive empirical evidence, we have assumed that the immediate effect of exclusion will be to discourage law enforcement officials from violating the Fourth Amendment by removing the incentive to disregard it. More importantly, over the long term, this demonstration that our society attaches serious consequences to violation of constitutional rights is thought to encourage those who formulate law enforcement policies, and the officers who implement them, to incorporate Fourth Amendment ideals into their value system.

We adhere to the view that these considerations support the implementation of the exclusionary rule at trial and its enforcement on direct appeal of state-court convictions. But the additional contribution, if any, of the consideration of search-and-seizure claims of state prisoners on collateral review is small in relation to the costs. To be sure, each case in which such claim is considered may add marginally to an awareness of the values protected by the Fourth Amendment. There is no reason to believe, however, that the overall educative effect of the exclusionary rule would be appreciably diminished if search-and-seizure claims could not be raised in federal habeas corpus review of state convictions. Nor is there reason to assume that any specific disincentive already created by the risk of exclusion of evidence at trial or the reversal of convictions on direct review would be enhanced if there were the further risk that a conviction obtained in state court and affirmed on direct review might be overturned in collateral proceedings often occurring years after the incarceration of the defendant. The view that the deterrence of Fourth Amendment violations would be furthered rests on the dubious assumption that law enforcement authorities would fear that federal habeas review might reveal flaws in a search or seizure that went undetected at trial and on appeal. Even if one rationally could assume that some additional incremental deterrent effect would be presented in isolated cases, the resulting advance of the legitimate goal of furthering Fourth Amendment rights would be outweighed by the acknowledged costs to other values vital to a rational system of criminal justice.

In sum, we conclude that where the State has provided an opportunity for full and fair litigation of a Fourth Amendment claim, a state prisoner may not be granted federal habeas corpus relief on the ground that evidence obtained in an unconstitutional search or seizure was introduced at his trial. In this context the contribution of the exclusionary rule, if any, to the effectuation of the Fourth Amendment is minimal, and the substantial societal costs of application of the rule persist with special force.

MR. JUSTICE BRENNAN, with whom MR. JUSTICE MARSHALL concurs, dissenting.

It is simply inconceivable that a constitutional deprivation suddenly vanishes after the appellate process has been exhausted. Federal habeas corpus review of Fourth Amendment claims of state prisoners was merely one manifestation of the principle that "conventional notions of finality in criminal litigation cannot be permitted to defeat the manifest federal policy that federal constitutional rights of personal liberty shall not be denied without the fullest opportunity for plenary federal judicial review." *Fay v. Noia,* 372 U.S. 391, 424 (1963). This Court's precedents have been "premised in large part on a recognition that the availability of collateral remedies is necessary to insure the integrity of proceedings at and before trial where constitutional rights are at stake. Our decisions leave no doubt that the federal habeas remedy extends to state prisoners alleging that unconstitutionally obtained evidence was admitted against them at trial."

The only result of today's holding will be that denials by the state courts of claims by state prisoners of violations of their Fourth Amendment rights will go unreviewed by a federal tribunal. I fear that the same treatment ultimately will be accorded state prisoners' claims of violations of other constitutional rights; thus the potential ramifications of this case for federal habeas jurisdiction generally are ominous. The Court, no longer content just to restrict forthrightly the constitutional rights of the citizenry, has embarked on a campaign to water down even such constitutional rights as it purports to acknowledge by the device of foreclosing resort to the federal habeas remedy for their redress.

Notes

1.   In *Withrow v. Williams,* 507 U.S. 680 (1993), the Court declined an opportunity to apply *Stone v. Powell* to another favorite target of Court opinions—*Miranda v. Arizona,* 384 U.S. 436 (1966). *Miranda*'s exclusionary rule is similar to the Fourth Amendment rule—both are designed to deter police violations, and both arguably are unrelated to accurate fact-finding. Nevertheless, the *Withrow* Court found that a federal court can hear a petition concerning a *Miranda* violation even if the prisoner had an opportunity for a full and fair hearing of the issue in state court. In rejecting an extension of *Stone* v. *Powell,* the Court stated that "prophylactic though it may be," *Miranda* safeguards a fundamental trial right that is not "necessarily divorced from the correct ascertainment of guilt." Justice Souter also noted that eliminating *Miranda* habeas claims simply would result in the substitution of due process voluntariness claims in their place. *See Miller v. Fenton,* 474 U.S. 104 (1985) ("the voluntariness of a confession is a legal question requiring independent federal determination upon a federal writ of habeas corpus").

2.   In *Rose v. Mitchell,* 443 U.S. 545 (1979), the Court held that a claim of racial discrimination in the selection of a state grand jury is cognizable on federal habeas corpus, even though the claimed error did not affect the determination of guilt and had been heard by the state court. The Court distinguished *Stone* on three grounds. First, the Court was unwilling to assume that state judges could fairly consider claims of grand jury discrimination, since those claims required the state courts to review their own procedures rather than those of the police. Second, the right to a indictment by a grand jury free from discrimination in its selection process is a personal constitutional right rather than a judicially created remedy. Third, state

courts could be expected to respond to a determination that their grand jury selection procedures failed to meet constitutional requirements, *i.e.*, deterrence is effective.

3. Although the Court's opinion in *Stone v. Powell* led to speculation that defendants might be denied habeas corpus review of other constitutional claims, the Supreme Court refused to extend that limiting principle to legal issues which are guilt-related. For example, in *Jackson v. Virginia*, 443 U.S. 307 (1979), the Court held that a claim that a prisoner was convicted on insufficient evidence is cognizable on federal habeas corpus review as a violation of due process. Unlike the Fourth Amendment exclusionary rule, the reasonable doubt standard of proof was deemed to relate to the accuracy of fact-finding. A federal court can hear an insufficiency of evidence claim, even if it was already heard by the state court. *Jackson's* holding, however, limited habeas relief to a showing that no rational trier of fact, viewing the evidence in the light most favorable to the prosecution, "could have found the essential elements of the crime beyond a reasonable doubt."

Exercise

Your client was convicted in State court, largely on the basis of the evidence obtained from a warrantless search of his residence. Following direct appeal in the State courts, your client fired his trial counsel and retained you. Your review of the trial transcript convinces you that the State court incorrectly applied Fourth Amendment precedent and that the federal courts would not uphold the warrantless search. Is there any way that you can obtain federal review of the search without running afoul of *Stone v. Powell*? Can the rationale of *Stone* be reconciled with the rationale of *Kimmelman v. Morrison*, 477 U.S. 365 (1986): "The constitutional rights of criminal defendants are granted to the innocent and the guilty alike. Consequently, we decline to hold either that the guarantee of effective assistance of counsel belongs solely to the innocent or that it attaches only to matters affecting the determination of actual guilt."

In *Kimmelman v. Morrison* the Court ruled that *Stone v. Powell* did not preclude Sixth Amendment ineffective assistance of counsel claims based on defense counsel's failure to move to suppress illegally seized evidence. The Court emphasized that, unlike the Fourth Amendment exclusionary rule, Sixth Amendment rights were fundamental trial rights, going to the fairness of the judicial process. Although the Fourth Amendment claim was one element of proof of the Sixth Amendment claim, "the two claims have separate identities and reflect difference constitutional values." Moreover, "[i]n general, no comparable, meaningful opportunity exists for the full and fair litigation of a habeas petitioner's ineffective assistance claims at trial and on direct review."

May you use *Kimmelman* to create "backdoor" access to federal review of Fourth Amendment issues by combining the Fourth Amendment claim with a Sixth Amendment claim that trial counsel was ineffective in raising the Fourth Amendment claim?

Questions

1. Should every convicted defendant have at least one opportunity to litigate federal constitutional claims in federal court? In theory, a defendant convicted in state court could petition the U.S. Supreme Court for certiorari to review the conviction—without having to show that the state denied him a full and fair hearing on the constitutional claim. In practice, the Supreme Court is unlikely to grant certiorari. Should federal habeas be used to allow the lower federal courts to conduct the type of review that the Supreme Court is unable to provide because of its heavy caseload?

On the other hand, if it is a perversion of federalist principles to have federal district courts essentially serve as appellate courts for the states who have "fully and fairly litigated" the federal issue, why shouldn't *Stone* apply to all claims of violation of federal law? What role does factual innocence play in defining habeas jurisdiction? *See* Section V of this Chapter.

2. To what extent has *Stone v. Powell* been extended by the AEDPA provision that habeas relief will not be granted with respect to any claim that was adjudicated on the merits in state court unless the state adjudication "resulted in a decision that was contrary to, or involved an unreasonable application of, clearly established Federal law, as determined by the Supreme Court of the United States." Is there a distinction between the "contrary to" category and the "unreasonable application" category? Consider *Williams v. Taylor*.

WILLIAMS v. TAYLOR

529 U.S. 362 (2000).

Justice Stevens announced the judgement of the Court and delivered the opinion of the Court with respect to Parts, I, III, and IV, and an opinion with respect to Parts II and V. Justice Souter, Justice Ginsburg, and Justice Breyer join this opinion in its entirety. Justice O'Connor and Justice Kennedy join Parts I, III, and IV of this opinion.

The questions presented are whether Terry Williams' constitutional right to the effective assistance of counsel as defined in *Strickland v. Washington*, 466 U.S. 668 (1984), was violated, and whether the judgment of the Virginia Supreme Court refusing to set aside his death sentence "was contrary to, or involved an unreasonable application of, clearly established Federal law, as determined by the Supreme Court of the United States," within the meaning of 28 U.S.C. § 2254(d)(1) (1994 ed., Supp. III). We answer both questions affirmatively.

In September 1986, Williams was convicted of robbery and capital murder. The jury found a probability of future dangerousness and unanimously fixed Williams' punishment at death. The trial judge concluded that such punishment was "proper" and "just" and imposed the death sentence. The Virginia Supreme Court affirmed the conviction and sentence.

In 1988 Williams filed for state collateral relief in the Danville Circuit Court. Judge Ingram (the same judge who had presided over

Williams' trial and sentencing) held an evidentiary hearing on Williams' claim that trial counsel had been ineffective. Based on the evidence adduced after two days of hearings, Judge Ingram found that Williams' conviction was valid, but that his trial attorneys had been ineffective during sentencing. Among the evidence reviewed that had not been presented at trial were documents prepared in connection with Williams' commitment when he was 11 years old that dramatically described mistreatment, abuse, and neglect during his early childhood, as well as testimony that he was "borderline mentally retarded," had suffered repeated head injuries, and might have mental impairments organic in origin. The habeas hearing also revealed that the same experts who had testified on the State's behalf at trial believed that Williams, if kept in a "structured environment," would not pose a future danger to society.

Judge Ingram found that counsel's failure to discover and present this and other significant mitigating evidence was "below the range expected of reasonable, professional competent assistance of counsel." Counsels' performance thus "did not measure up to the standard required under the holding of *Strickland v. Washington*, 466 U.S. 668 (1984), and [if it had,] there is a reasonable probability that the result of the sentencing phase would have been different." Judge Ingram therefore recommended that Williams be granted a rehearing on the sentencing phase of his trial.

The Virginia Supreme Court did not accept that recommendation. Although it assumed, without deciding, that trial counsel had been ineffective, it disagreed with the trial judge's conclusion that Williams had suffered sufficient prejudice to warrant relief. Treating the prejudice inquiry as a mixed question of law and fact, the Virginia Supreme Court accepted the factual determination that available evidence in mitigation had not been presented at the trial, but held that the trial judge had misapplied the law in two respects. First, relying on our decision in *Lockhart v. Fretwell*, 506 U.S. 364 (1993), the court held that it was wrong for the trial judge to rely " 'on mere outcome determination' " when assessing prejudice. Second, it construed the trial judge's opinion as having "adopted a per se approach" that would establish prejudice whenever any mitigating evidence was omitted.

The court then reviewed the prosecution evidence supporting the "future dangerousness" aggravating circumstance, reciting Williams' criminal history, including the several most recent offenses to which he had confessed. In comparison, it found that the excluded mitigating evidence—which it characterized as merely indicating "that numerous people, mostly relatives, thought that defendant was nonviolent and could cope very well in a structured environment,"—"barely would have altered the profile of this defendant that was presented to the jury," On this basis, the court concluded that there was no reasonable possibility that the omitted evidence would have affected the jury's sentencing recommendation, and that Williams had failed to demonstrate that his sentencing proceeding was fundamentally unfair.

Having exhausted his state remedies, Williams sought a federal writ of habeas corpus pursuant to 28 U.S.C. § 2254. After reviewing the state habeas hearing transcript and the state courts' findings of fact and conclusions of law, the federal trial judge agreed with the Virginia trial judge: The death sentence was constitutionally infirm.

After noting that the Virginia Supreme Court had not addressed the question whether trial counsel's performance at the sentencing hearing fell below the range of competence demanded of lawyers in criminal cases, the District judge began by addressing that issue in detail. He identified five categories of mitigating evidence that counsel had failed to introduce, and he rejected the argument that counsel's failure to conduct an adequate investigation had been a strategic decision to rely almost entirely on the fact that Williams had voluntarily confessed.

According to Williams' trial counsel's testimony before the state habeas court, counsel did not fail to seek Williams' juvenile and social services records because he thought they would be counterproductive, but because counsel erroneously believed that " 'state law didn't permit it.' " Counsel also acknowledged in the course of the hearings that information about Williams' childhood would have been important in mitigation. And counsel's failure to contact a potentially persuasive character witness was likewise not a conscious strategic choice, but simply a failure to return that witness' phone call offering his service. Finally, even if counsel neglected to conduct such an investigation at the time as part of a tactical decision, the District Judge found, tactics as a matter of reasonable performance could not justify the omissions.

Turning to the prejudice issue, the judge determined that there was "a reasonable probability that, but for counsel's unprofessional errors, the result of the proceeding would have been different." He found that the Virginia Supreme Court had erroneously assumed that *Lockhart* had modified the *Strickland* standard for determining prejudice, and that it had made an important error of fact in discussing its finding of no prejudice. Having introduced his analysis of Williams' claim with the standard of review applicable on habeas appeals provided by 28 U.S.C. § 2254(d), the judge concluded that those errors established that the Virginia Supreme Court's decision "was contrary to, or involved an unreasonable application of, clearly established Federal law" within the meaning of § 2254(d)(1).

The Federal Court of Appeals reversed. It construed § 2254(d)(1) as prohibiting the grant of habeas corpus relief unless the state court " 'decided the question by interpreting or applying the relevant precedent in a manner that reasonable jurists would all agree is unreasonable.' " Applying that standard, it could not say that the Virginia Supreme Court's decision on the prejudice issue was an unreasonable application of the tests developed in either *Strickland* or Lockhart. It explained that the evidence that Williams presented a future danger to society was "simply overwhelming," it endorsed the Virginia Supreme

Court's interpretation of *Lockhart*, and it characterized the state court's understanding of the facts in this case as "reasonable,"

We granted certiorari, and now reverse.

Over the years, the federal habeas corpus statute has been repeatedly amended, but the scope of that jurisdictional grant remains the same. It is, of course, well settled that the fact that constitutional error occurred in the proceedings that led to a state-court conviction may not alone be sufficient reason for concluding that a prisoner is entitled to the remedy of habeas. *See, e.g., Stone v. Powell.* On the other hand, errors that undermine confidence in the fundamental fairness of the state adjudication certainly justify the issuance of the federal writ. The deprivation of the right to the effective assistance of counsel recognized in *Strickland* is such an error.

The warden here contends that federal habeas corpus relief is prohibited by the amendment to 28 U.S.C. § 2254, enacted as a part of the Antiterrorism and Effective Death Penalty Act of 1996 (AEDPA). The relevant portion of that amendment provides:

> "(d) An application for a writ of habeas corpus on behalf of a person in custody pursuant to the judgment of a State court shall not be granted with respect to any claim that was adjudicated on the merits in State court proceedings unless the adjudication of the claim—
>
> "(1) resulted in a decision that was contrary to, or involved an unreasonable application of, clearly established Federal law, as determined by the Supreme Court of the United States. . . ."

[The] message that Congress intended to convey by using the phrases, "contrary to" and "unreasonable application of" is not entirely clear. The prevailing view in the Circuits is that the former phrase requires de novo review of 'pure' questions of law and the latter requires some sort of "reasonability" review of so-called mixed questions of law and fact.

We are not persuaded that the phrases define two mutually exclusive categories of questions. Most constitutional questions that arise in habeas corpus proceedings—and therefore most "decisions" to be made—require the federal judge to apply a rule of law to a set of facts, some of which may be disputed and some undisputed. For example, an erroneous conclusion that particular circumstances established the voluntariness of a confession, or that there exists a conflict of interest when one attorney represents multiple defendants, may well be described either as "contrary to" or as an "unreasonable application of" the governing rule of law. [AEDPA] plainly sought to ensure a level of "deference to the determinations of state courts," provided those determinations did not conflict with federal law or apply federal law in an unreasonable way. Congress wished to curb delays, to prevent "retrials" on federal habeas, and to give effect to state convictions to the extent possible under law. When federal courts are able to fulfill these goals within the bounds of the law, AEDPA instructs them to do so. * * *

In sum, the statute directs federal courts to attend to every state-court judgment with utmost care, but it does not require them to defer to the opinion of every reasonable state-court judge on the content of federal law. If, after carefully weighing all the reasons for accepting a state court's judgment, a federal court is convinced that a prisoner's custody—or, as in this case, his sentence of death—violates the Constitution, that independent judgment should prevail. Otherwise the federal "law as determined by the Supreme Court of the United States" might be applied by the federal courts one way in Virginia and another way in California. In light of the well-recognized interest in ensuring that federal courts interpret federal law in a uniform way, we are convinced that Congress did not intend the statute to produce such a result.

In this case, Williams contends that he was denied his constitutionally guaranteed right to the effective assistance of counsel when his trial lawyers failed to investigate and to present substantial mitigating evidence to the sentencing jury. The threshold question under AEDPA is whether Williams seeks to apply a rule of law that was clearly established at the time his state-court conviction became final. That question is easily answered because the merits of his claim are squarely governed by our holding in *Strickland v. Washington*.

It is past question that the rule set forth in *Strickland* qualifies as "clearly established Federal law, as determined by the Supreme Court of the United States." That the *Strickland* test "of necessity requires a case-by-case examination of the evidence," obviates neither the clarity of the rule nor the extent to which the rule must be seen as "established" by this Court. This Court's precedent "dictated" that the Virginia Supreme Court apply the *Strickland* test at the time that court entertained Williams' ineffective-assistance claim. And it can hardly be said that recognizing the right to effective counsel "breaks new ground or imposes a new obligation on the States." Williams is therefore entitled to relief if the Virginia Supreme Court's decision rejecting his ineffective-assistance claim was either "contrary to, or involved an unreasonable application of," that established law. It was both.

The Virginia Supreme Court erred in holding that our decision in *Lockhart v. Fretwell*, modified or in some way supplanted the rule set down in *Strickland....* The trial judge analyzed the ineffective-assistance claim under the correct standard; the Virginia Supreme Court did not. We are also persuaded, unlike the Virginia Supreme Court, that counsel's unprofessional service prejudiced Williams within the meaning of *Strickland*.

In our judgment, the state trial judge was correct both in his recognition of the established legal standard for determining counsel's effectiveness, and in his conclusion that the entire postconviction record, viewed as a whole and cumulative of mitigation evidence presented originally, raised "a reasonable probability that the result of the sentencing proceeding would have been different" if competent counsel had presented and explained the significance of all the available evidence. It follows that the Virginia Supreme Court rendered a "decision that was contrary to, or involved an unreasonable application of, clearly established Federal law."

Accordingly, the judgment of the Court of Appeals is reversed, and the case is remanded for further proceedings consistent with this opinion.

JUSTICE O'CONNOR delivered the opinion of the Court with respect to Part II, concurred in part, and concurred in the judgment. JUSTICE KENNEDY joins this opinion in its entirety. THE CHIEF JUSTICE and JUSTICE THOMAS join this opinion with respect to Part II. JUSTICE SCALIA joins this opinion with respect to Part II.

I

Before 1996, this Court held that a federal court entertaining a state prisoner's application for habeas relief must exercise its independent judgment when deciding both questions of constitutional law and mixed constitutional questions (*i.e.*, application of constitutional law to fact). In other words, a federal habeas court owed no deference to a state court's resolution of such questions of law or mixed questions. If today's case were governed by the federal habeas statute prior to Congress' enactment of AEDPA in 1996, I would agree with JUSTICE STEVENS that Williams' petition for habeas relief must be granted if we, in our independent judgment, were to conclude that his Sixth Amendment right to effective assistance of counsel was violated.

II

A

[Section] 2254(d)(1) defines two categories of cases in which a state prisoner may obtain federal habeas relief with respect to a claim adjudicated on the merits in state court. Under the statute, a federal court may grant a writ of habeas corpus if the relevant state-court decision was either (1) "contrary to . . . clearly established Federal law, as determined by the Supreme Court of the United States," or (2) "involved an unreasonable application of . . . clearly established Federal law, as determined by the Supreme Court of the United States."

The Court of Appeals for the Fourth Circuit properly accorded both the "contrary to" and "unreasonable application" clauses independent meaning. * * * With respect to the first of the two statutory clauses, the Fourth Circuit held in Green that a state-court decision can be "contrary to" this Court's clearly established precedent in two ways. First, a state-court decision is contrary to this Court's precedent if the state court arrives at a conclusion opposite to that reached by this Court on a question of law. Second, a state-court decision is also contrary to this Court's precedent if the state court confronts facts that are materially indistinguishable from a relevant Supreme Court precedent and arrives at a result opposite to ours.

The word "contrary" is commonly understood to mean "diametrically different," "opposite in character or nature," or "mutually opposed." The text of § 2254(d)(1) therefore suggests that the state court's decision must be substantially different from the relevant precedent of this Court. The Fourth Circuit's interpretation of the "contrary to" clause accurately reflects this textual meaning. A state-court decision will certainly be contrary to our clearly established precedent if the state court applies a rule that contradicts the governing law set forth in our cases. Take, for example, our decision in *Strickland v. Washington*. If a state court were to reject a prisoner's claim of ineffective assistance of counsel on the grounds that the prisoner had not established by a preponderance of the evidence that the result of his criminal proceeding would have been different, that decision would be "diametrically different," "opposite in character or nature," and "mutually opposed" to our clearly established precedent because we held in Strickland that the prisoner need only demonstrate a "reasonable probability that … the result of the proceeding would have been different." A state-court decision will also be contrary to this Court's clearly established precedent if the state court confronts a set of facts that are materially indistinguishable from a decision of this Court and nevertheless arrives at a result different from our precedent. Accordingly, in either of these two scenarios, a federal court will be unconstrained by § 2254(d)(1) because the state-court decision falls within that provision's "contrary to" clause.

On the other hand, a run-of-the-mill state-court decision applying the correct legal rule from our cases to the facts of a prisoner's case would not fit comfortably within § 2254(d)(1)'s "contrary to" clause. Assume, for example, that a state-court decision on a prisoner's ineffective-assistance claim correctly identifies *Strickland* as the controlling legal authority and, applying that framework, rejects the prisoner's claim. Quite clearly, the state-court decision would be in accord with our decision in *Strickland* as to the legal prerequisites for establishing an ineffective-assistance claim, even assuming the federal court considering the prisoner's habeas application might reach a different result applying the *Strickland* framework itself. It is difficult, however, to describe such a run-of-the-mill state-court decision as "diametrically different" from, "opposite in character or nature" from, or "mutually opposed" to *Strickland*, our clearly established precedent. Although the state-court decision may be contrary to the federal court's conception of how *Strickland* ought to be applied in that particular case, the decision is not "mutually opposed" to *Strickland* itself.

[The] Fourth Circuit's interpretation of the "unreasonable application" clause of § 2254(d)(1) is generally correct. [A] state-court decision can involve an "unreasonable application" of this Court's clearly established precedent in two ways. First, a state-court decision involves an unreasonable application of this Court's precedent if the state court identifies the correct governing legal rule from this Court's cases but unreasonably applies it to the facts of the particular state prisoner's case. Second, a state-court decision also involves an unreasonable application of this Court's precedent if the state court either unreasonably extends a legal principle from our precedent to a new context where it should not apply or unreasonably refuses to extend that principle to a new context where it should apply.

B

There remains the task of defining what exactly qualifies as an "unreasonable application" of law under § 2254(d)(1). The Fourth Circuit held in *Green* that a state-court decision involves an "unreasonable application of . . . clearly established Federal law" only if the state court has applied federal law "in a manner that reasonable jurists would all agree is unreasonable." The placement of this additional overlay on the "unreasonable application" clause was erroneous. It is difficult to fault the Fourth Circuit for using this language given the fact that we have employed nearly identical terminology to describe the related inquiry undertaken by federal courts in applying the nonretroactivity rule of *Teague.*

Defining an "unreasonable application" by reference to a "reasonable jurist," however, is of little assistance to the courts that must apply § 2254(d)(1) and, in fact, may be misleading. Stated simply, a federal habeas court making the "unreasonable application" inquiry should ask whether the state court's application of clearly established federal law was objectively unreasonable. The federal habeas court should not transform the inquiry into a subjective one by resting its determination instead on the simple fact that at least one of the Nation's jurists has applied the relevant federal law in the same manner the state court did in the habeas petitioner's case. * * *

Under § 2254(d)(1)'s "unreasonable application" clause, then, a federal habeas court may not issue the writ simply because that court concludes in its independent judgment that the relevant state-court decision applied clearly established federal law erroneously or incorrectly. Rather, that application must also be unreasonable. * * *

Throughout this discussion the meaning of the phrase "clearly established Federal law, as determined by the Supreme Court of the United States" has been put to the side. That statutory phrase refers to the holdings, as opposed to the dicta, of this Court's decisions as of the time of the relevant state-court decision. In this respect, the "clearly established Federal law" phrase bears only a slight connection to our *Teague* jurisprudence. With one caveat, whatever would qualify as an old rule under our *Teague* jurisprudence will constitute "clearly established Federal law, as determined by the Supreme Court of the United States" under § 2254(d)(1). The one caveat, as the statutory language makes clear, is that § 2254(d)(1) restricts the source of clearly established law to this Court's jurisprudence.

In sum, § 2254(d)(1) places a new constraint on the power of a federal habeas court to grant a state prisoner's application for a writ of habeas corpus with respect to claims adjudicated on the merits in state court. Under § 2254(d)(1), the writ may issue only if one of the following two conditions is satisfied—the state-court adjudication resulted in a decision that (1) "was contrary [to] clearly established Federal law, as determined by the Supreme Court of the United States," or (2) "involved an unreasonable application of . . . clearly established Federal law, as determined by the Supreme Court of the United States." Under the "contrary to" clause, a federal habeas court may grant the writ if the state court arrives at a conclusion opposite to that reached by this Court on a question of law or if the state court decides a case differently than this Court has on a set of materially indistinguishable facts. Under the "unreasonable application" clause, a federal habeas court may grant the writ if the state court identifies the correct governing legal principle from this Court's decisions but unreasonably applies that principle to the facts of the prisoner's case.

III

Although I disagree with JUSTICE STEVENS concerning the standard we must apply under § 2254(d)(1) in evaluating Terry Williams' claims on habeas, I agree with the Court that the Virginia Supreme Court's adjudication of Williams' claim of ineffective assistance of counsel resulted in a decision that was both contrary to and involved an unreasonable application of this Court's clearly established precedent. Specifically, I believe that the Court's discussion in Parts III and IV is correct and that it demonstrates the reasons that the Virginia Supreme Court's decision in Williams' case, even under the interpretation of § 2254(d)(1) I have set forth above, was both contrary to and involved an unreasonable application of our precedent.

Accordingly, although I disagree with the interpretation of § 2254(d)(1) set forth in Part II of Justice Stevens' opinion, I join Parts I, III, and IV of the Court's opinion and concur in the judgment of reversal.

D. EXHAUSTION OF REMEDIES

Habeas corpus relief usually is unavailable unless the petitioner has exhausted the remedies available in the state courts. She must present the substance of her claim to the state courts in order to give them a fair "opportunity to apply controlling legal principles to the facts bearing upon [her] constitutional claim." *Picard v. Connor*, 404 U.S. 270, 276–77 (1971). To satisfy the exhaustion requirement, a petitioner must present her claims to the state's highest court even though its review is discretionary and even though that court does not address her claim in a written opinion, e.g., the court denies discretionary review. *Dye v. Hofbauer*, 546 U.S. 1 (2005). The exhaustion doctrine is rooted in federal-state comity and requires the state prisoner to use all means available in the state system to correct the alleged error. Federalism considerations simply will not permit a state prisoner to bypass the state courts and initiate the first review of his conviction in the federal courts.

If the petitioner fails to exhaust his state remedies, the federal court may dismiss the petition until such time as the petitioner has exhausted the available state remedies. The only exceptions to the exhaustion of remedies doctrine are when there is an absence of available state remedies or special circumstances render such remedies ineffective to protect the rights of the petitioner. Because the exhaustion of state remedies doctrine is based on comity and is not a jurisdictional requirement, the government may waive the requirement. 28 U.S.C. § 2254(b)(1), (3).

Notes and Questions

1. In light of the stringent requirements for exhaustion of remedies, why would any federal district court apply the AEDPA's provision that the "application for a writ of habeas corpus may be denied on the merits, notwithstanding the failure of the applicant to exhaust the remedies available in the courts of the State." The Supreme Court advised that the district court "should determine whether the interests of comity and federalism will be better served by addressing the merits forthwith or by requiring a series of additional state and district court proceedings before reviewing the merits of the petitioner's claim." *Granberry v. Greer*, 481 U.S. 129 (1987).

2. In addition to interests of comity and federalism, federal habeas corpus has traditionally been governed by equitable principles. Consider the situation in *Whittlesey v. Circuit Court*, 897 F.2d 143 (4th Cir.1990). Whittlesey was convicted and sentenced by a Maryland State court in 1978. In 1980 he escaped from prison, committed other crimes in Florida and began serving a 136–year sentence in the Florida State Prison. In 1986, he filed a petition for post-conviction relief in Maryland state court. The state court dismissed Whittlesey's petition without prejudice because his presence could not be secured for a post-conviction hearing. (Whittlesey sought unsuccessfully to invoke the Interstate Agreement on Detainers as a means of transfer to Maryland for a hearing). In 1987, Whittlesey filed a federal petition for habeas corpus, raising the same issues he had raised in his state petitions. The federal district court dismissed the petition without prejudice on the ground that Whittlesey had not exhausted his state post-conviction remedies.

On appeal to the circuit court, Whittlesey argued:

(1) that he had complied with § 2254(b)'s exhaustion requirement. By its own terms § 2254(b) requires only that an applicant for habeas relief have exhausted the state court remedies available to him, and that since Whittlesey is unable to return for the hearing there are no remedies available.

(2) that his petition falls within the futility exception of § 2254(b), which provides that a habeas writ may be granted despite a failure to exhaust state court remedies if "there is either an absence of available State corrective process or the existence of circumstances rendering such process ineffective to protect the rights of the prisoner." Whittlesey

emphasized that since he is serving a 136–year sentence in Florida, it would be futile for him to wait until he has been released from prison in Florida to pursue his Maryland post-conviction remedy.

A majority of the Fourth Circuit panel held that Whittlesey had not exhausted his remedies because, "the doors of the Maryland state courts stand open for him to present his complaints; that he is unable to enter through those doors until completion of his Florida sentence is the price he must pay for having escaped from the Maryland prison and committed offenses in Florida. It is his own criminal misconduct which has denied Maryland courts the opportunity to hold a hearing, develop a record, and thereby address his claims on the merits. We will not command the district court to review his habeas petition when his own unlawful acts have prevented the state courts from reviewing his claims."

The dissent, however, maintained that "this is one of those hard cases that invites the making of bad law—specifically here, bad exhaustion law. A prisoner who escapes from incarceration in state A only to be incarcerated for conviction of another crime in state B while still a fugitive from state A makes an instinctively unattractive petitioner for federal habeas relief from the original incarceration." The fact of the escape, however, has no more legal relevance to the availability of a federal habeas forum than do any other of the usual run of unsavory events and prior conduct that exist in the backgrounds of many federal habeas petitioners. "The obvious question is: 'What else could the petitioner do?' And the answer, 'Nothing,' as obviously satisfies the ultimate concerns of comity underlying the exhaustion requirement. Whittlesey could spend the rest of his life in a Florida prison without the opportunity to litigate his constitutional claims. That is not right. Whittlesey has exhausted the state remedies that are available to him at the present time. He has the right to a federal habeas forum to present his constitutional claims."

E. ABUSE OF THE WRIT AND PROCEDURAL DEFAULT

1. *Successive Petitions as an Abuse of the Writ*

The exhaustion requirement does not preclude habeas review; it merely delays such review. For example, in *Rose v. Lundy*, 455 U.S. 509 (1982) the Court held that a federal district court must dismiss a petition that combines unexhausted and exhausted claims. Following dismissal, the petitioner must either return to state court to present the unexhausted claims or resubmit only the exhausted claims to the federal court.

A problem arises, however, when the petitioner returns to federal court with a second habeas corpus petition raising the previously dismissed claims which have now been exhausted in the State courts. Could such a petition be barred by the "abuse of the writ" doctrine embodied in the Antiterrorism and Effective Death Penalty Act of 1996?

SLACK v. McDANIEL

529 U.S. 473 (2000).

JUSTICE KENNEDY delivered the opinion of the Court.

Petitioner Antonio Slack was convicted of second-degree murder in Nevada state court in 1990. His direct appeal was unsuccessful. On November 27, 1991, Slack filed a petition for writ of habeas corpus in federal court under 28 U.S.C. § 2254. Early in the federal proceeding, Slack decided to litigate claims he had not yet presented to the Nevada courts. He could not raise the claims in federal court because, under the exhaustion of remedies rule, a federal court was required to dismiss a petition presenting claims not yet litigated in state court. Accordingly, Slack filed a motion seeking to hold his federal petition in abeyance while he returned to state court to exhaust the new claims. Without objection by the State, the District Court ordered the habeas petition dismissed "without prejudice." The order, dated February 19, 1992, further stated, "Petitioner is granted leave to file an application to renew upon exhaustion of all State remedies." After an unsuccessful round of state postconviction proceedings, Slack filed a new federal habeas petition on May 30, 1995. The District Court later appointed counsel, directing him to file an amended petition or a notice of intention to proceed with the current petition. On December 24, 1997, counsel filed an amended petition presenting 14 claims for relief. The State moved to dismiss the petition. As its first ground, the State argued that Slack's petition must be dismissed because it was a mixed petition, that is to say a petition raising some claims which had been presented to the state courts and some which had not. As its second ground, the State cited *Farmer v. McDaniel*, 98 F.3d 1548 (C.A.9 1996), and contended that, under the established rule in the Ninth Circuit, claims Slack had not raised in his 1991 federal habeas petition must be dismissed as an abuse of the writ.

The District Court granted the State's motion. First, the court relied on *Farmer* to hold that Slack's 1995 petition was "[a] second or successive petition," even though his 1991 petition had been dismissed without prejudice for a failure to exhaust state remedies. The court then invoked the abuse of the writ doctrine to dismiss with prejudice the claims Slack had not raised in the 1991 petition. This left Slack with four claims, each having been raised in the 1991 petition; but one of these, the court concluded, had not yet been presented to the state courts. The court therefore dismissed Slack's remaining claims because they were in a mixed petition. Here, Slack seeks to challenge the dismissal of claims as abusive; he does not contend that all claims presented in the amended petition were exhausted.

[The] District Court dismissed claims Slack failed to raise in his 1991 petition based on its conclusion that Slack's 1995 petition was a second or successive habeas petition. This conclusion was wrong. A habeas petition filed in the district court after an initial habeas petition was unadjudicated on its merits and dismissed for failure to exhaust state remedies is not a second or successive petition.

The phrase "second or successive petition" is a term of art given substance in our prior habeas corpus cases. The Court's decision in *Rose v. Lundy*, 455 U.S., at 510, instructs us in reaching our understanding of the term. *Rose v. Lundy* held that a federal district court must dismiss habeas corpus petitions containing both exhausted and unexhausted claims. The opinion, however, contemplated that the prisoner could return to federal court after the requisite exhaustion. It was only if a prisoner declined to return to state court and decided to proceed with his exhausted claims in federal court that the possibility arose that a subsequent petition would be considered second or successive and subject to dismissal as an abuse of the writ.

* * * A petition filed after a mixed petition has been dismissed under *Rose v. Lundy* before the district court adjudicated any claims is to be treated as "any other first petition" and is not a second or successive petition.

* * * The State complains that this rule is unfair. The filing of a mixed petition in federal court requires it to appear and to plead failure to exhaust. The petition is then dismissed without prejudice, allowing the prisoner to make a return trip through the state courts to exhaust new claims. The State expresses concern that, upon exhaustion, the prisoner would return to federal court but again file a mixed petition, causing the process to repeat itself. In this manner, the State contends, a vexatious litigant could inject undue delay into the collateral review process. To the extent the tactic would become a problem, however, it can be countered without upsetting the established meaning of a second or successive petition.

First, the State remains free to impose proper procedural bars to restrict repeated returns to state court for postconviction proceedings. Second, provisions of AEDPA may bear upon the question in cases to which the Act applies. AEDPA itself demonstrates that Congress may address matters relating to exhaustion and mixed petitions through means other than rules governing "second or successive" petitions. E.g., 28 U.S.C. § 2254(b)(2). Third, the Rules of Civil Procedure, applicable as a general matter to habeas cases, vest the federal courts with due flexibility to prevent vexatious litigation. * * * We reject the State's argument that refusing to give a new meaning to the established term "second or successive" opens the door to the abuses described.

It is so ordered.

Notes and Questions

1. Does the abuse of the writ doctrine embodied in § 2244 create at least a qualified form of res judicata? In *Calderon v. United States District Court*, 163 F.3d 530 (9th Cir.1998) (en banc) the Ninth Circuit stated:

We reject the panel majority's use of res judicata because it contravenes the longstanding rule that res judicata has no application in habeas corpus. The entire point of a habeas petition that challenges a state conviction is to relitigate issues that were raised in the state case and resolved against the petitioner. Obviously, then, res judicata, in the traditional sense of that doctrine cannot apply in habeas corpus; otherwise, nearly every habeas petition would be barred by the original trial.

Federal courts have created a doctrine known as "abuse of the writ" that serves as a substitute for res judicata by limiting the availability of successive habeas petitions when a prior one has been denied.... The reason why successive petitions are often deemed abusive is that the first petition provided an adequate opportunity for the petitioner to raise all of his claims, and the petitioner simply chose not to take advantage of that opportunity.... Abuse of the writ evolved as a judicially created equitable doctrine, but it is now codified by the AEDPA.

We also reject the State's argument that the traditional rule against applying res judicata in habeas cases has somehow been abrogated by the AEDPA.... Indeed, even after the AEDPA, it is still true that federal habeas relief exists in order to relitigate claims that were previously decided in state court, so it is quite fanciful to suggest that the AEDPA sub silento introduced res judicata into habeas law. Further, the AEDPA includes specific provisions to govern successive habeas petitions, and res judicata would render those provisions largely superfluous. We conclude that even after the AEDPA, the rule is as it has always been: Res judicata does not apply to habeas cases.

2.   The doctrines of exhaustion and abuse of the writ are in the nature of defenses invoked by the State to bar defendant's who file multiple habeas petitions. May a prosecutor take a pro-active stance to bar possible habeas petitions? For example, if State law does not provide for a life-without-parole sentence, may the prosecutor plea bargain for the defendant's waiver of the right to file a habeas petition challenging a life sentence? Is such a waiver accomplished by the following plea agreement:

> Defendant agrees that he will never apply, orally or in writing for parole, commutation of sentence, reprieve, or any other form of relief from life imprisonment. He understands this means he will be sentenced to serve the remainder of his natural like in the penitentiary. In consideration of the State waiving the death penalty, defendant also hereby gives up his right to ask for the Superior Court Sentence Review panel to review any sentence imposed upon him. He hereby states that the sentence of life imprisonment for his participation in the criminal acts is not excessive.

The Eleventh Circuit noted the absence of any published decisions addressing plea-bargained waivers of the right to seek federal habeas review. The court held that if such a waiver is constitutionally permissible, it did not occur in this case because the defendant did not make a knowing and intelligent waiver of the right to seek federal habeas review. The catch-all phrase—"or any other form of relief from life imprisonment"—is far too general to constitute a valid waiver of a specific right. *Allen v. Thomas*, 161

F.3d 667 (11th Cir.1998). *See also United States v. Goodman,* 165 F.3d 169 (2d Cir.1999).

2. *Procedural Default*

The doctrine of exhaustion and the procedural default rule are two different things. Exhaustion generally requires that before a federal court will review a constitutional claim in habeas, the claim must first be fairly presented to the state court system. . . . The procedural default rule requires that if a state court rejects a habeas petitioner's federal constitutional challenge on the adequate and independent state ground that the claim is defaulted under a state procedural rule, a federal habeas court is ordinarily precluded from reviewing that claim unless the petitioner can show cause for the default and prejudice resulting from it.

Justus v. Murray, 897 F.2d 709 (4th Cir.1990).

The most common form of procedural default is the defendant's failure to present a federal constitutional claim to the trial court and thus preserve the issue for appellate review. The consequence of a procedural default is that the petitioner may be barred from judicial review of the forfeited claim in both state and federal courts. Unlike *Stone v. Powell* which bars federal habeas relief only when Fourth Amendment issues are given a full and fair hearing in the state courts, if there is a procedural bar, there is no hearing on the constitutional challenge in *any* state or federal court.

WAINWRIGHT v. SYKES

433 U.S. 72 (1977).

Mr. Justice Rehnquist delivered the opinion of the Court.

Respondent Sykes was convicted of third-degree murder after a jury trial in the Circuit Court of DeSoto County. He testified at trial that on the evening of January 8, 1972, he told his wife to summon the police because he had just shot Willie Gilbert. Other evidence indicated that when the police arrived at respondent's trailer home, they found Gilbert dead of a shotgun wound, lying a few feet from the front porch. Shortly after their arrival, respondent came from across the road and volunteered that he had shot Gilbert, and a few minutes later respondent's wife approached the police and told them the same thing. Sykes was immediately arrested and taken to the police station.

Once there, it is conceded that he was read his *Miranda* rights, and that he declined to seek the aid of counsel and indicated a desire to talk. He then made a statement, which was admitted into evidence at trial through the testimony of the two officers who heard it, to the effect that he had shot Gilbert from the front porch of his trailer home. There were several references during the trial to respondent's consumption of alcohol during the preceding day and to his apparent state of intoxication, facts which were acknowledged by the officers who arrived at the scene. At no time during the trial, however, was the admissibility of any of respondent's statements challenged by his counsel on the ground that respondent had not understood the *Miranda* warnings. Nor did the trial judge question their admissibility on his own motion or hold a factfinding hearing bearing on that issue.

Respondent appealed his conviction, but apparently did not challenge the admissibility of the inculpatory statements. He later filed in the trial court a motion to vacate the conviction and, in the State District Court of Appeals and Supreme Court, petitions for habeas corpus. These filings, apparently for the first time, challenged the statements made to police on grounds of involuntariness. In all of these efforts respondent was unsuccessful.

Having failed in the Florida courts, respondent initiated the present action under 28 U.S.C. § 2254, asserting the inadmissibility of his statements by reason of his lack of understanding of the *Miranda* warnings.

The simple legal question before the Court calls for a construction of the language of 28 U.S.C. § 2254(a), which provides that the federal courts shall entertain an application for a writ of habeas corpus "in behalf of a person in custody pursuant to the judgment of a state court only on the ground that he is in custody in violation of the Constitution or laws or treaties of the United States."

The area of controversy which has developed has concerned the reviewability of federal claims which the state court has declined to pass on because not presented in the manner prescribed by its procedural rules. The adequacy of such an independent state procedural ground to prevent federal habeas review of the underlying federal issue has been treated very differently than where the state-law ground is substantive. The pertinent decisions marking the Court's somewhat tortuous efforts to deal with this problem are: *Ex parte Spencer*, 228 U.S. 652 (1913); *Brown v. Allen*, 344 U.S. 443 (1953); *Fay v. Noia; Davis v. United States*, 411 U.S. 233 (1973); and *Francis v. Henderson*, 425 U.S. 536 (1976).

In *Fay v. Noia*, respondent Noia sought federal habeas to review a claim that his state-court conviction had resulted from the introduction of a coerced confession in violation of the Fifth Amendment to the United States Constitution. While the convictions of his two codefendants were reversed on that ground in collateral proceedings following their appeals, Noia did not appeal and the New York courts ruled that his subsequent coram nobis action was barred on account of that failure. This Court held that petitioner was nonetheless entitled to raise the claim in federal habeas, and thereby overruled its decision 10 years earlier in *Brown v. Allen*: "(T)he doctrine under which state procedural defaults are held to constitute an adequate and independent state law ground barring direct Supreme Court review is not to be extended to omit the power granted the federal courts under the federal habeas statute."

As a matter of comity but not of federal power, the Court acknowledged "a limited discretion in the federal judge to deny relief ... to an applicant who had deliberately by-passed the orderly procedure of the state courts and in so doing has forfeited his state court remedies." In so stating, the Court made clear that the waiver must be knowing and actual " 'an intentional relinquishment or abandonment of a known right or privilege.' " Noting petitioner's "grisly choice" between acceptance of his life sentence and pursuit of an appeal which might culminate in a sentence of death, the Court concluded that there had been no deliberate bypass of the right to have the federal issues reviewed through a state appeal.

Florida procedure did, consistently with the United States Constitution, require that respondents' confession be challenged at trial or not at all, and thus his failure to timely object to its admission amounted to an independent and adequate state procedural ground which would have prevented direct review here. We thus come to the crux of this case. Shall the rule of *Francis v. Henderson*, barring federal habeas review absent a showing of "cause" and "prejudice" attendant to a state procedural waiver, be applied to a waived objection to the admission of a confession at trial? We answer that question in the affirmative.

[S]ince *Brown v. Allen*, it has been the rule that the federal habeas petitioner who claims he is detained pursuant to a final judgment of a state court in violation of the United States Constitution is entitled to have the federal habeas court make its own independent determination of his federal claim, without being bound by the determination on the merits of that claim reached in the state proceedings. This rule of *Brown v. Allen* is in no way changed by our holding today. Rather, we deal only with contentions of federal law which were not resolved on the merits in the state proceeding due to respondent's failure to raise them there as required by state procedure. We leave open for resolution in future decisions the precise definition of the "cause" and "prejudice" standard, and note here only that it is narrower than the standard set forth in dicta in *Fay v. Noia*, which would make federal habeas review generally available to state convicts absent a knowing and deliberate waiver of the federal constitutional contention. It is the sweeping language of *Fay v. Noia*, going far beyond the facts of the case eliciting it, which we today reject.

The reasons for our rejection of it are several. The contemporaneous-objection rule itself is by no means peculiar to Florida, and deserves greater respect than *Fay* gives it, both for the fact that it is employed by a coordinate jurisdiction within the federal system and for the many interests which it serves in its own right. A contemporaneous objection enables the record to be made with respect to the constitutional claim when the recollections of witnesses are freshest, not years later in a federal habeas proceeding. It enables the judge who observed the demeanor of those witnesses to make the factual determinations necessary for properly deciding the federal constitutional question.

A contemporaneous-objection rule may lead to the exclusion of the evidence objected to, thereby making a major contribution to finality in criminal litigation. Without the evidence claimed to be vulnerable on federal constitutional grounds, the jury may acquit the defendant, and that will be the end of the case; or it may nonetheless convict the defendant, and he will have one less federal constitutional claim to assert in his federal habeas petition. If the state trial judge admits the evidence in question after a full hearing, the federal habeas court [will] gain significant guidance from the state ruling in this regard. Subtler considerations as well militate in favor of honoring a state contemporaneous-objection rule. An objection on the spot may force the prosecution to take a hard took at its whole card, and even if the prosecutor thinks that the state trial judge will admit the evidence he must contemplate the possibility of reversal by the state appellate courts or the ultimate issuance of a federal writ of habeas corpus based on the impropriety of the state court's rejection of the federal constitutional claim.

We think that the rule of *Fay v. Noia*, broadly stated, may encourage "sandbagging" on the part of defense lawyers, who may take their chances on a verdict of not guilty in a state trial court with the intent to raise their constitutional claims in a federal habeas court if their initial gamble does not pay off. The refusal of federal habeas courts to honor contemporaneous-objection rules may also make state courts themselves less stringent in their enforcement. Under the rule of *Fay v. Noia*, state appellate courts know that a federal constitutional issue raised for the first time in the proceeding before them may well be decided in any event by a federal habeas tribunal. Thus, their choice is between addressing the issue notwithstanding the petitioner's failure to timely object, or else face the prospect that the federal habeas court will decide the question without the benefit of their views.

The failure of the federal habeas courts generally to require compliance with a contemporaneous-objection rule tends to detract from the perception of the trial of a criminal case in state court as a decisive and portentous event.

We believe the adoption of the *Francis* rule in this situation will have the salutary effect of making the state trial on the merits the "main event," so to speak, rather than a "tryout on the road" for what will later be the determinative federal habeas hearing. There is nothing in the Constitution or in the language of § 2254 which requires that the state trial on the issue of guilt or innocence be devoted largely to the testimony of fact witnesses directed to the elements of the state crime, while only later will there occur in a federal habeas hearing a full airing of the federal constitutional claims which were not raised in the state proceedings. If a criminal defendant thinks that an action of the state trial court is about to deprive him of a federal constitutional right there is every reason for his following state procedure in making known his objection.

The "cause" and "prejudice" exception of the *Francis* rule will afford an adequate guarantee, we think, that the rule will not prevent a federal habeas court from adjudicating for the first time the federal constitutional claim of a defendant who in the absence of such an adjudication will be the victim of a miscarriage of justice. Whatever precise content may be given those terms by later cases, we feel confident in holding without further elaboration that they do not exist here. Respondent has advanced no explanation whatever for his failure to object at trial, and, as the proceeding unfolded, the trial judge is certainly not to be faulted for failing to question the admission of the confession himself. The other evidence of guilt presented at trial, moreover, was substantial to a degree that would negate any possibility of actual prejudice resulting to the respondent from the admission of his inculpatory statement.

MR. JUSTICE BRENNAN, with whom MR. JUSTICE MARSHALL joins, dissenting.

I believe that *Fay*'s commitment to enforcing intentional but not inadvertent procedural defaults offers a realistic measure of protection for the habeas corpus petitioner seeking federal review of federal claims that were not litigated before the State. I remain convinced that when one pierces the surface justifications for a harsher rule posited by the Court, no standard stricter than *Fay*'s deliberate-bypass test is realistically defensible.

Punishing a lawyer's unintentional errors by closing the federal courthouse door to his client is both a senseless and misdirected method of deterring the slighting of state rules. It is senseless because unplanned and unintentional action of any kind generally is not subject to deterrence; and, to the extent that it is hoped that a threatened sanction addressed to the defense will induce greater care and caution on the part of trial lawyers, thereby forestalling negligent conduct or error, the potential loss of all valuable state remedies would be sufficient to this end. And it is a misdirected sanction because even if the penalization of incompetence or carelessness will encourage more thorough legal training and trial preparation, the habeas applicant, as opposed to his lawyer, hardly is the proper recipient of such a penalty. Especially with fundamental constitutional rights at stake, no fictional relationship of principal-agent or the like can justify holding the criminal defendant accountable for the naked errors of his attorney. This is especially true, when so many indigent defendants are without any realistic choice in selecting who ultimately represents them at trial.

Notes and Questions

1. In *Murray v. Carrier*, 477 U.S. 478 (1986), Justice O'Connor explained the cause and prejudice requirement.

> We think that the question of cause for a procedural default does not turn on whether counsel erred or on the kind of error counsel may have made. So long as a defendant is represented by counsel whose performance is not constitutionally ineffective under the standard established in *Strickland v. Washington*, we discern no inequity in requiring

him to bear the risk of attorney error that results in a procedural default. Instead, we think that the existence of cause for a procedural default must ordinarily turn on whether the prisoner can show that some objective factor external to the defense impeded counsel's efforts to comply with the State's procedural rule. Without attempting an exhaustive catalog of such objective impediments to compliance with a procedural rule, we note that a showing that the factual or legal basis for a claim was not reasonably available to, counsel, or that "some interference by officials," made compliance impracticable, would constitute cause under this standard.

Similarly, if the procedural default is the result of ineffective assistance of counsel, the Sixth Amendment itself requires that responsibility for the default be imputed to the State, which may not "conduc[t] trials at which persons who face incarceration must defend themselves without adequate legal assistance." Ineffective assistance of counsel, then, is cause for a procedural default.

Respondent does not dispute, however, that the cause and prejudice test applies to procedural defaults on appeal, as we plainly indicated in *Reed v. Ross. Reed*, which involved a claim that was defaulted on appeal, held that a habeas petitioner could establish cause for a procedural default if his claim is "so novel that its legal basis is not reasonably available to counsel." That holding would have been entirely unnecessary to the disposition of the prisoner's claim if the cause and prejudice test were inapplicable to procedural defaults on appeal.

[W]e see little reason why counsel's failure to detect a colorable constitutional claim should be treated differently from a deliberate but equally prejudicial failure by counsel to raise such a claim. The fact that the latter error can be characterized as a misjudgment, while the former is more easily described as an oversight, is much too tenuous a distinction to justify a regime of evidentiary hearings into counsel's state of mind in failing to raise a claim on appeal.

The real thrust of respondent's arguments appears to be that on appeal it is inappropriate to hold defendants to the errors of their attorneys. Were we to accept that proposition, defaults on appeal would presumably be governed by a rule equivalent to *Fay v. Noia*'s "deliberate bypass" standard, under which only personal waiver by the defendant would require enforcement of a procedural default. We express no opinion as to whether counsel's decision not to take an appeal at all might require treatment under such a standard, but, for the reasons already given, we hold that counsel's failure to raise a particular claim on appeal is to be scrutinized under the cause and prejudice standard when that failure is treated as a procedural default by the state courts. Attorney error short of ineffective assistance of counsel does not constitute cause for a procedural default even when that default occurs on appeal rather than at trial. To the contrary, cause for a procedural default on appeal ordinarily requires a showing of some external impediment preventing counsel from constructing or raising the claim.

The habeas petitioner must show "not merely that the errors at . . . trial created a possibility of prejudice, but that they worked to his actual and substantial disadvantage, infecting his entire trial with error of constitutional dimensions." Such a showing of pervasive actual prejudice can hardly be thought to constitute anything other than a showing that the prisoner was denied "fundamental fairness" at trial.

"In appropriate cases" the principles of comity and finality that inform the concepts of cause and prejudice "must yield to the imperative of correcting a fundamentally unjust incarceration." We remain confident that, for the most part, "victims of a fundamental miscarriage of justice will meet the cause-and-prejudice standard." But we do not pretend that this will always be true. Accordingly, we think that in an extraordinary case, where a constitutional violation has probably resulted in the conviction of one who is actually innocent, a federal habeas court may grant the writ even in the absence of a showing of cause for the procedural default.

2.　In *Edwards v. Carpenter*, 529 U.S. 446 (2000) presented another layer of review by addressing state vs. federal determination of the right to counsel. A claim of ineffective-assistance-of-counsel must itself be presented to the State courts before the claim can serve as cause to excuse the procedural default of another habeas claim. In turn, a procedurally defaulted ineffective-assistance-of-counsel claim can be excused if the petitioner can satisfy the cause and prejudice standard with respect to the ineffective assistance claim itself.

3.　How does the "cause-and-prejudice" standard differ from the "fundamental miscarriage of justice" standard for excusing a procedural default?

Prejudice is a stricter standard than the "plain error" doctrine applicable on direct review because direct appeal is designed to afford a means for the *prompt* redress of miscarriages of justice. This standard "is out of place when a prisoner launches a collateral attack against a criminal conviction after society's legitimate interest in the finality of the judgment has been perfected by the expiration of the time allowed for direct review or by the affirmance of the conviction on appeal." Thus in *United States v. Frady*, 456 U.S. 152 (1982) prejudice did not follow simply from the fact that a jury instruction was erroneous. (The instruction equated intent with malice and stated that the law presumes malice from the use of a weapon). The Court held that the petitioner failed to show that the error "worked to his actual and substantial disadvantage, infecting his entire trial with error of constitutional dimensions." *I.e.* prejudice must be evaluated by the effect of the error in the context of the whole trial, and the petitioner failed to contradict strong evidence in the record that he had acted with malice.

Cause. In *Reed v. Ross*, 468 U.S. 1 (1984) the Court stated that cause existed for the defendant's failure to raise a due process challenge to shifting the burden of proof to the defendant on an issue of malice, because "burden shifting" was not held unconstitutional until several years after the procedural default. "Where a constitutional claim is so novel that its legal basis is not reasonably available to counsel, a defendant has cause for his failure to raise the claim in accordance with applicable state procedures." In contrast, *Murray v. Carrier*, 477 U.S. 478 (1986) found that the type of discovery claim in question "had been percolating in lower courts for years" at the time of the defendant's default. When the claim was actually raised in the defendant's case, it was not so novel as to excuse a procedural default.

4. If the petitioner can show "cause" under *Reed* because the "new rule" of law could not have been reasonably anticipated, does the petitioner then run afoul of *Teague v. Lane*, 489 U.S. 288 (1989) which held that "new rules of law" generally should not be applied retroactively to cases on "collateral review" such as habeas corpus? Professor Arkin characterized the interaction between *Reed* and *Teague* as "The Prisoner's Dilemma:"

> If a petitioner is able to show that his claim is based on a "new" rule of law, the habeas court will excuse his state procedural default, assuming petitioner can show actual prejudice. But, having shown that the rule under which he seeks relief was not available to him at the time he should have raised it in the state courts, the petitioner may well have won the battle under *Wainwright* only to lose the war to *Teague*. Under most circumstances, the petitioner will have just shown that the very rule under which he seeks relief is not retroactive unless he can fit it into one of the two [extremely limited] *Teague* exceptions. Arkin, "The Prisoner's Dilemma: Life in the Lower Federal Courts After *Teague v. Lane,*" 69 N. Car. L. Rev. 371, 408 (1991). [The two exceptions recognized in *Teague* are: (1) where the new rule places certain kinds of private conduct beyond the power of legislatures to proscribe, and (2) where the new rule requires procedures that are "implicit in the concept of ordered liberty" such as the right to counsel].

5. Suppose defense counsel says that she did not raise an issue in the state court proceedings because the state court would have been unsympathetic to the claim. Does the apparent futility of making an objection constitute cause? No, said the Court in *Engle v. Isaac,* 456 U.S. 107 (1982). The Court also rejected adoption of a rule requiring trial counsel to exercise "extraordinary vision" or to object to every aspect of the proceedings in the hope that some aspect might make a latent constitutional claim.

> We have long recognized that the Constitution guarantees criminal defendants only a fair trial and a competent attorney. It does not insure that defense counsel will recognize and raise every conceivable constitutional claim. Where the basis of a constitutional claim is available, and other defense counsel have perceived and litigated that claim, the demands of comity and finality counsel against labeling alleged unawareness of the objection as a cause for a procedural default.

6. *State interference as cause.* In *Strickler v. Greene,* 527 U.S. 263 (1999), the Court explained the definition of "cause" when the failure to pursue a *Brady* claim will excuse the petitioner's default. She must prove that 1) the prosecutor assured her that he had furnished all Brady material, 2) her reliance on the prosecutor's representations was reasonable, and 3) the prosecutor had withheld evidence favorable to the defense. In *Amadeo v. Zant,* 486 U.S. 214 (1988), the Court held that governmental concealment of evidence that women and African Americans were intentionally under represented on jury lists constituted cause for the defendant's failure to raise a timely challenge to the jury panel.

7.   Interests of comity and federalism do not always dictate deferring to a state's decision to invoke or forgo a procedural bar to a federal habeas petition. Judicial efficiency also guides the court's discretion.

> For example, a federal court may find that a petitioner obviously has procedurally defaulted an issue and may avoid a decision on a complex federal question presented by that issue by denying relief on the basis of the adequate and independent state-law ground despite the failure of a state to assert a procedural bar. . . . Conversely, on occasion the determination of whether a petitioner has defaulted his claims will present difficult issues of state law that are not readily susceptible to decision by a federal court, while the claim advanced by the petitioner patently is without merit. In such a situation, a federal habeas court would not be justified in considering the procedural default issue.

Yeatts v. Angelone, 166 F.3d 255 (4th Cir.1999).

Exercise

John Smith was convicted of capital murder and sentenced to death. Dissatisfied with the representation provided by court-appointed trial counsel, Smith hired Jones to appeal the conviction and sentence. Jones raised a number of Fourth, Fifth, and Fourteenth Amendment issues on appeal, but was precluded from addressing the competency of trial counsel because of a State rule providing that claims of ineffective assistance of counsel cannot be raised on direct appeal, they must be raised in a State habeas corpus petition.

When the direct appeal was denied, Jones filed a state habeas corpus petition again focusing on the Fourth, Fifth, and Fourteenth Amendment issues. He neglected to raise the claim of ineffective assistance of trial counsel. When the state habeas petition is denied, Smith hires you to prepare a federal habeas corpus petition. He is particularly upset with the performance of both trial and appellate counsel, and wants you to establish their ineffectiveness. The State, however, contends that the defendant's claim of ineffective assistance of trial counsel was defaulted because it was not raised in the state habeas petition; and federal habeas review does not lie for ineffective assistance of counsel during the State habeas proceedings. Draft an argument to the federal court explaining why your client is entitled to federal habeas review of the effectiveness of trial and/or state habeas counsel.

[As a general rule, there is no constitutional right to effective assistance of counsel when collaterally attacking a conviction, *Coleman v. Thompson*, 501 U.S. 722, 750 (1991), but an indigent defendant does have a right to effective assistance of counsel on the first appeal as of right, *Douglas v. California*, 372 U.S. 353 (1963)]. See generally *Edwards v. Carpenter*, 529 U.S. 446 (2000).

F. CLAIMS OF ACTUAL INNOCENCE AS "GATEWAYS" TO FEDERAL HABEAS CORPUS REVIEW

A common misperception, at least among the lay public, is that federal courts and ultimately the United States Supreme Court, sit as courts of last resort to correct any and all injustice done to American citizens. Justice Scalia, a frequent critic of expansive federal habeas review, recently explained that:

> It would be marvelously inspiring to be able to boast that we have a criminal-justice system in which a claim of "actual innocence" will always be heard, no matter how late it is brought forward, and no matter how much the failure to bring it forward at the proper time is the defendant's own fault. But of course we do not have such a system, and no society unwilling to devote unlimited resources to repetitive criminal litigation ever could.

Bousley v. United States, 523 U.S. 614 (1998).

In *Herrera v. Collins*, 506 U.S. 390 (1993), the Court refused to recognize that a claim of factual innocence constitutes an independent constitutional issue subject to review on federal habeas corpus. Herrera was convicted of capital murder and sentenced to death. Ten years later, he filed a petition for federal habeas corpus relief claiming that newly discovered evidence, *i.e.*, that his dead brother had committed the murders, showed that he was actually innocent of the crimes. The Court stated that after a final judgment the presumption of innocence is no longer applicable. Moreover, a new claim of innocence is factually based, and habeas corpus relief is not a proper remedy for correcting factual errors. Instead a request for executive clemency is a proper remedy for innocence claims based upon new evidence that is discovered after the time for filing a new trial motion. The *Herrera* Court then assumed

> for the sake of argument in deciding this case, that in a capital case a truly persuasive demonstration of 'actual innocence' made after trial would render the execution of a defendant unconstitutional, and justify federal habeas relief if there were no state avenues open to process such a claim. But because of the very disruptive effect that entertaining claims of actual innocence would have on the need for finality in capital cases, and the enormous burden that having to retry cases based on often stale evidence would place on the States, the threshold showing for such an assumed right would necessarily be extraordinarily high. The showing made by petitioner in this case falls far short of any such threshold

Herrera failed to meet the Court's standard, because his affidavits were based mostly on hearsay, were obtained without the benefit of cross-examination, contained inconsistencies, and failed to overcome the strong trial proof of guilt.

Herrera established that, standing alone, a claim of innocence is not sufficient to warrant federal habeas review. Such claims, however, are a vital component (a gateway) of petitioners' attempts to gain habeas review otherwise barred by the procedural default rule. *Schlup v. Delo*, 513 U.S. 298 (1995) characterized petitioner's claim as *procedural*, rather than the *substantive* claim of innocence raised in *Herrera*. The *Schlup* Court noted:

As a preliminary matter, it is important to explain the difference between Schlup's claim of actual innocence and the claim of actual innocence asserted in *Herrera*. In *Herrera*, the petitioner advanced his claim of innocence to support a novel substantive constitutional claim, namely that the execution of an innocent person would violate the Eighth Amendment. Under petitioner's theory in *Herrera*, even if the proceedings that had resulted in his conviction and sentence were entirely fair and error-free, his innocence would render his execution a "constitutionally intolerable event."

Schlup's claim of innocence, on the other hand, is procedural, rather than substantive. His constitutional claims are based not on his innocence, but rather on his contention that the ineffectiveness of his counsel, *see Strickland v. Washington*, 466 U.S. 668 (1984), and the withholding of evidence by the prosecution, *see Brady v. Maryland*, 373 U.S. 83 (1963), denied him the full panoply of protections afforded to criminal defendants by the Constitution. Schlup, however, faces procedural obstacles that he must overcome before a federal court may address the merits of those constitutional claims. Because Schlup has been unable to establish "cause and prejudice" sufficient to excuse his failure to present his evidence in support of his first federal petition, Schlup may obtain review of his constitutional claims only if he falls within the "narrow class of cases . . . implicating a fundamental miscarriage of justice." Schlup's claim of innocence is offered only to bring him within this "narrow class of cases."

Schlup's claim thus differs in at least two important ways from that presented in *Herrera*. First, Schlup's claim of innocence does not by itself provide a basis for relief. Instead, his claim for relief depends critically on the validity of his *Strickland* and *Brady* claims. Schlup's claim of innocence is thus "not itself a constitutional claim, but instead a gateway through which a habeas petitioner must pass to have his otherwise barred constitutional claim considered on the merits."

More importantly, a court's assumptions about the validity of the proceedings that resulted in conviction are fundamentally different in Schlup's case than in Herrera's. In *Herrera*, petitioner's claim was evaluated on the assumption that the trial that resulted in his conviction had been error-free. In such a case, when a petitioner has been "tried before a jury of his peers, with the full panoply of protections that our Constitution affords criminal defendants," it is appropriate to apply an " 'extraordinarily high' " standard of review.

Schlup, in contrast, accompanies his claim of innocence with an assertion of constitutional error at trial. For that reason, Schlup's conviction may not be entitled to the same degree of respect as one, such as Herrera's, that is the product of an error-free trial. Without any new evidence of innocence, even the existence of a concededly meritorious constitutional violation is not in itself sufficient to establish a miscarriage of justice that would allow a habeas court to reach the merits of a barred claim. However, if a petitioner such as Schlup presents evidence of innocence so strong that a court cannot have confidence in the outcome of the trial unless the court is also satisfied that the trial was free of nonharmless constitutional error, the petitioner should be allowed to pass through the gateway and argue the merits of his underlying claims.

Consequently, Schlup's evidence of innocence need carry less of a burden. In *Herrera* (on the assumption that petitioner's claim was, in principle, legally well founded), the evidence of innocence would have had to be strong enough to make his execution "constitutionally intolerable" even if his conviction was the product of a fair trial. For Schlup, the evidence must establish sufficient doubt about his guilt to justify the conclusion that his execution would be a miscarriage of justice unless his conviction was the product of a fair trial.

[I]n an extraordinary case, where a constitutional violation has probably resulted in the conviction of one who is actually innocent, a federal habeas court may grant the writ even in the absence of a showing of cause for the procedural default.

Claims of actual innocence pose less of a threat to scarce judicial resources and to principles of finality and comity than do claims that focus solely on the erroneous imposition of the death penalty. Though challenges to the propriety of imposing a sentence of death are routinely asserted in capital cases, experience has taught us that a substantial claim that constitutional error has caused the conviction of an innocent person is extremely rare. To be credible, such a claim requires petitioner to support his allegations of constitutional error with new reliable evidence—whether it be exculpatory scientific evidence, trustworthy eyewitness accounts, or critical physical evidence—that was not presented at trial. Because such evidence is obviously unavailable in the vast majority of cases, claims of actual innocence are rarely successful.

Of greater importance, the individual interest in avoiding injustice is most compelling in the context of actual innocence. The quintessential miscarriage of justice is the execution of a person who is entirely innocent. Indeed, concern about the injustice that results from the conviction of an innocent person has long been at the core of our criminal justice system. That concern is reflected, for example, in the "fundamental value determination of our society that it is far worse to convict an innocent man than to let a guilty man go free."

The overriding importance of this greater individual interest merits protection by imposing a somewhat less exacting standard of proof on a habeas petitioner alleging a fundamental miscarriage of justice than on one alleging that his sentence is too severe. As this Court has noted, "a standard of proof represents an attempt to instruct the factfinder concerning the degree of confidence our society thinks he should have in the correctness of factual conclusions for a particular type of adjudication.''

Several observations about this standard are in order. The *Carrier* standard is intended to focus the inquiry on actual innocence. In assessing the adequacy of petitioner's showing, therefore, the district court is not bound by the rules of admissibility that would govern at trial. Instead, the emphasis on "actual innocence" allows the reviewing tribunal also to consider the probative force of relevant evidence that was either excluded or unavailable at trial. Indeed, with respect to this aspect of the *Carrier* standard, we believe that Judge Friendly's description of the inquiry is appropriate: the habeas court must make its determination concerning the petitioner's innocence "in light of all the evidence, including that alleged to have been illegally admitted (but with due regard to any unreliability of it) and evidence tenably claimed to have been wrongly excluded or to have become available only after the trial.''

[A] petitioner does not meet the threshold requirement unless he persuades the district court that, in light of the new evidence, no juror, acting reasonably, would have voted to find him guilty beyond a reasonable doubt.

Because both the Court of Appeals and the District Court evaluated the record under an improper standard, further proceedings are necessary. The fact-intensive nature of the inquiry, together with the District Court's ability to take testimony from the few key witnesses if it deems that course advisable, convinces us that the most expeditious procedure is to order that the decision of the Court of Appeals be vacated and that the case be remanded to the Court of Appeals with instructions to remand to the District Court for further proceedings consistent with this opinion. It is so ordered.

Note

What must be shown in support of an argument for actual innocence, thereby warranting relief from the procedural default rule? In *Bousley v. United States*, 523 U.S. 614 (1998), Bousley pleaded guilty to drug and firearm charges, but reserved the right to challenge the quantity of drugs used in calculating his sentence. He unsuccessfully appealed his sentence, but did not challenge the plea's validity. He sought habeas relief, claiming that his guilty plea lacked a factual basis because the evidence did not show a connection between the firearms in the bedroom of the house and the garage where the drug trafficking occurred. The district court dismissed the petition. While Bousley's appeal was pending, the Supreme Court held that a conviction for using a firearm requires the prosecution to show "active employment of the firearm." In affirming the dismissal of the habeas petition, the Eighth Circuit rejected Bousley's argument that the new Supreme Court case should be applied retroactively. Despite the fact that Bousley had procedurally defaulted on his claims, the Supreme Court held that Bousley should be permitted to make an actual innocence showing. The Court stated that actual innocence means factual innocence, not mere legal insufficiency. The prosecution is not limited to the existing record but may present any admissible evidence of petitioner's guilt. The actual innocence showing also must extend to charges that the prosecution had dropped or abandoned in the course of plea bargaining.

Appendix

SELECTED PROVISIONS OF THE UNITED STATES CONSTITUTION

ARTICLE I

Section 9.   * * *

[2] The privilege of the Writ of Habeas Corpus shall not be suspended, unless when in Cases of Rebellion or Invasion the public Safety may require it.

[3] No Bill of Attainder or ex post facto Law shall be passed.

ARTICLE III

Section 1.   The judicial Power of the United States, shall be vested in one supreme Court, and in such inferior Courts as the Congress may from time to time ordain and establish.   The Judges, both of the supreme and inferior Courts, shall hold their Offices during good Behaviour, and shall, at stated Times, receive for their Services a Compensation, which shall not be diminished during their Continuance in Office.

Section 2.   [1] The judicial Power shall extend to all Cases, in Law and Equity, arising under this Constitution, the Laws of the United States, and Treaties made, or which shall be made, under their Authority;—to all Cases affecting Ambassadors, other public Ministers and Consuls;—to all Cases of admiralty and maritime Jurisdiction;—to Controversies to which the United States shall be a Party;—to Controversies between two or more States;—between a State and Citizens of another State;—between Citizens of different States;—between Citizens of the same State claiming Lands under the Grants of different States, and between a State, or the Citizens thereof, and foreign States, Citizens or Subjects.

[3] The trial of all Crimes, except in Cases of Impeachment, shall be by Jury; and such Trial shall be held in the State where the said Crimes shall have been committed; but when not committed within any State, the Trial shall be at such Place or Places as the Congress may by Law have directed.

Section 3.   [1] Treason against the United States, shall consist only in levying War against them, or, in adhering to their Enemies, giving them Aid and Comfort.   No Person shall be convicted of Treason unless on the Testimony of two Witnesses to the same overt Act, or on Confession in open Court.

[2] The Congress shall have Power to declare the Punishment of Treason, but no Attainder of Treason shall work Corruption of Blood, or Forfeiture except during the Life of the Person attainted.

ARTICLE IV

Section 2. [1] The Citizens of each State shall be entitled to all Privileges and Immunities of Citizens in the several States.

[2] A Person charged in any State with Treason, Felony, or other Crime, who shall flee from Justice, and be found in another State, shall on demand of the executive Authority of the State from which he fled, be delivered up, to be removed to the State having Jurisdiction of the Crime.

ARTICLE VI

[2] This Constitution, and the Laws of the United States which shall be made in Pursuance thereof; and all Treaties made, or which shall be made, under the Authority of the United States, shall be the supreme Law.

AMENDMENT I [1791]

Congress shall make no law respecting an establishment of religion, or prohibiting the free exercise thereof; or abridging the freedom of speech, or of the press; or the right of the people peaceably to assemble, and to petition the Government for a redress of grievances.

AMENDMENT II [1791]

A well regulated Militia, being necessary to the security of a free State, the right of the people to keep and bear Arms, shall not be infringed.

AMENDMENT III [1791]

No Soldier shall, in time of peace be quartered in any house, without the consent of the Owner, nor in time of war, but in a manner to be prescribed by law.

AMENDMENT IV [1791]

The right of the people to be secure in their persons, houses, papers, and effects, against unreasonable searches and seizures, shall not be violated, and no Warrants shall issue, but upon probable cause, supported by Oath or affirmation, and particularly describing the place to be searched, and the persons or things to be seized.

AMENDMENT V [1791]

No person shall be held to answer for a capital, or otherwise infamous crime, unless on a presentment or indictment of a Grand Jury, except in cases arising in the land or naval forces, or in the Militia, when in actual service in time of War or public danger; nor shall any person be subject for the same offence to be twice put in jeopardy of life or limb; nor shall be compelled in any criminal case to be a witness against himself, nor be deprived of life, liberty, or property, without due process of law; nor shall private property be taken for public use, without just compensation.

Amendment VI [1791]

In all criminal prosecutions, the accused shall enjoy the right to a speedy and public trial, by an impartial jury of the State and district wherein the crime shall have been committed, which district shall have been previously ascertained by law, and to be informed of the nature and cause of the accusation; to be confronted with the witnesses against him; to have compulsory process for obtaining witnesses in his favor, and to have the Assistance of Counsel for his defence.

Amendment VII [1791]

In Suits at common law, where the value in controversy shall exceed twenty dollars, the right of trial by jury shall be preserved, and no fact tried by jury, shall be otherwise re-examined in any Court of the United States, than according to the rules of the common law.

Amendment VIII [1791]

Excessive bail shall not be required, nor excessive fines imposed, nor cruel and unusual punishments inflicted.

Amendment IX [1791]

The enumeration in the Constitution, of certain rights, shall not be construed to deny or disparage others retained by the people.

Amendment X [1791]

The powers not delegated to the United States by the Constitution, nor prohibited by it to the States, are reserved to the States respectively, or to the people.

Amendment XIII [1865]

Section 1. Neither slavery nor involuntary servitude, except as a punishment for crime whereof the party shall have been duly convicted, shall exist within the United States, or any place subject to their jurisdiction.

Section 2. Congress shall have power to enforce this article by appropriate legislation.

Amendment XIV [1868]

Section 1. All persons born or naturalized in the United States, and subject to the jurisdiction thereof, are citizens of the United States and of the State wherein they reside. No State shall make or enforce any law which shall abridge the privileges or immunities of citizens of the United States; nor shall any State deprive any person of life, liberty, or property, without due process of law; nor deny to any person within its jurisdiction the equal protection of the laws.

Section 5. The Congress shall have power to enforce, by appropriate legislation, the provisions of the article.

Amendment XV [1870]

Section 1.   The right of citizens of the United States to vote shall not be denied or abridged by the United States or by any State on account of race, color, or previous condition of servitude.

Section 2.   The Congress shall have power to enforce this article by appropriate legislation.

Index

References are to Pages

†